THIRD EDITION

AMERICAN DEMOCRACY

Lewis Lipsitz
UNIVERSITY OF NORTH CAROLINA,
CHAPEL HILL

David M. Speak
CALIFORNIA STATE POLYTECHNIC UNIVERSITY,
POMONA

GEORGIA SOUTHERN UNIVERSITY

ST. MARTIN'S PRESS NEW YORK

Senior Editor: Don Reisman
Director of Development: Richard Steins
Production Supervisor: Alan Fischer
Cover Design: Sheree Goodman
Text Design: Patrice Fodero
Photo Editor: Inge King
Cover Photo: Kunio Owaki/The Stock Market, Inc.

Library of Congress Catalog Card Number: 92-50017
Copyright © 1993 by St. Martin's Press, Inc.
All rights reserved. No part of this book may be reproduced, stored in a retrieval system, or transmitted by any form or by any means, electronic, mechanical, photocopying, recording, or otherwise, except as may be expressly permitted by the applicable copyright statutes or in writing by the Publisher.
Manufactured in the United States of America
8 7 6 5 4 3
f e d c b a

For information, write:
St. Martin's Press, Inc.
175 Fifth Avenue
New York, NY 10010

ISBN: 0-312-06663-5

Acknowledgments

Chapter opening photos:

Chapter 1: Daemmrich/The Image Works; **Chapter 2:** AP/Wide World Photos; **Chapter 3:** National Archives; **Chapter 4:** Library of Congress; **Chapter 5:** Susan Lapides/Design Conceptions; **Chapter 6:** Jim Wilson/New York Times Pictures; **Chapter 7:** Taylor/Fabricius/Gamma-Liaison; **Chapter 8:** Shahn Kermani/Gamma-Liaison; **Chapter 9:** AP/Wide World Photos; **Chapter 10:** AP/Wide World Photos; **Chapter 11:** Paul Conklin/Monkmeyer Press Photos; **Chapter 12:** Paul Conklin/Monkmeyer Press Photos; **Chapter 13:** Paul Conklin/Monkmeyer Press Photos; **Chapter 14:** Susan Biddle/The White House; **Chapter 15:** J. P. Lafont/Sygma; **Chapter 16:** Alex Webb/Magnum Photos; **Chapter 17:** Catherine Smith/Impact Visuals; **Chapter 18:** Bill Perry/UPI/Bettmann; **Chapter 19:** New York Times Pictures; **Chapter 20:** Fredrik D. Bodin/Stock, Boston; **Chapter 21:** Reuters/Bettmann; **Chapter 22:** Alfred M. Bailey/National Audubon Society/Photo Researchers.

To John, Annie, Bill, Sadie, and Jake, and in memory of Max Blatt and Lucho Quiros, who loved political debate.

L. L.

To Beverly, Julia, Emily, and Margaret.

To the Monteverde Monthly Meeting of the Religious Society of Friends for preserving a beautiful part of our future in the rain forest.

D. M. S.

PREFACE

The third edition of *American Democracy*, like the previous two, is a comprehensive and up-to-date introduction to American government. Our theme—indeed the theme of government in the United States—is *democracy*. One of our major goals is to engage students in a dialogue about the definition of democracy and the degree to which American government functions democratically. Our intent is to emphasize that politics involves difficult choices and that political decisions can have different consequences for different groups in American society.

Two centuries have brought us a long way toward remedying many obviously undemocratic aspects of our system, but many challenges remain—in the distribution of economic and political power, in foreign policy, in how political influence is exercised, in the workings of our presidency and Congress, in the vast gaps in public information and understanding.

We are not inclined to dampen our concerns about these things by accepting that the real world can never live up to supposedly utopian ideals. Nor do we think that anyone—least of all the young—should simply be satisfied with what they've got, more or less. Such "realism," in our opinion, is a bad compromise with history. It denies how much effort must continuously be activated if democracy—in this or any other nation—is to survive and prosper.

Our book encourages readers to ask difficult and sometimes uncomfortable questions. To achieve this end, we offer a complete survey of the nuts and bolts of U.S. government and politics within a framework that includes several unique features:

- ***American Democracy* consistently looks at how the American political system fulfills the ideals of democratic government.** The book looks at different concepts of democracy and examines how the institutional arrangements of American government contribute to the expression of democracy. In our discussion of foundations, participation, institutions, and policymaking, we make a systematic effort to link the ideal with the real, to examine how democratic principles fare within the U.S. political process.

- ***American Democracy* offers a comparative perspective.** In discussions of American politics in boxes as well as the main text, we offer contrasts to institutions, policies, and political participation in other countries. We compare, for example, the multiparty, proportional system of representation in Great Britain with the more winner-take-all system in the United States. In doing so, we hope to broaden the reader's awareness of how democratic principles have been applied in other nations, and we emphasize that a belief in the virtues of democracy does not yield a single model on which government must be structured.

- ***American Democracy* examines a variety of timely and controversial subjects** in order to involve students in discussion of current issues, including affirmative action and quotas, health-care reform, school funding, voter alienation, ethics in government, and economic equity. In keeping with our theme, we try to demonstrate that decisions about these issues often involve an inherent tension between fundamental—yet sometimes conflicting—democratic principles. We consider, for example, the tension between the free expression of religion and the prohibition on government-established religion, and highlight cases in which the maintenance of equity and fairness may involve a surrender of the autonomy and influence that citizens exercise on schools and local political institutions.

- ***American Democracy* offers a number of chapters not found in most competitors.** For example, Chapter 7, on American political economy, explores connections between liberalism and capitalism. Chapter 12 examines mass politics and protest by a range of ideological and interest groups. Chapter 20, on building the community, highlights government policy on the issues that most affect people in their daily lives—for example, crime, drugs, education, and obscenity regulations. A closing chapter discusses energy and environmental policy.

- ***American Democracy* includes six policy chapters.** Part IV begins with an overview of the policymaking process. The remaining five chapters allow instructors to pick and choose topics according to their own interests and those of their students.

About the New Edition

The revisions in the third edition of *American Democracy* are extensive. As will be outlined later in this Preface, we have made major additions and improvements in the ancillary package. Another change is immediately apparent to anyone familiar with the previous editions of *American Democracy*: We have retained our comprehensive treatment of all the traditional subjects in American government, but, as befits a time when students and faculty have strong concern about economic issues, we have gone to a paperback format, which more readily allows the use of supplemental readers or point-of-view books. The book has also been redesigned in a more accessible, single-column layout, and there has been greater attention paid to the provision of attractive—and functional—illustrations.

Policy examples in the book have been updated. The 1992 presidential election saw improved voter turnout, but anger and alienation toward government remains strong. A book that considers the realities and the potentials of American democracy has to give careful examination to the implications of continued voter disaffection. There is expanded coverage of the media and politics, including the media and its reportage of the Persian Gulf War. There is full coverage of recent Supreme Court decisions, the movement for term limits, the fiscal crisis of state and local government, the challenges of U.S. foreign policy after the Cold War, and a number of other issues that drive political controversy in the 1990s.

The above changes are apparent in the examples of policymaking and political conflict that are present throughout the text. They are apparent in our chapter introductions, most of which have been rewritten to provide students with a more engaging lead into our discussions of the details of governance. The third edition also features the complete results of the 1992 elections, and considers the opportunities and problems that lie ahead for the new presidential administration. A full discussion of the Reagan-Bush record on foreign policy, energy, and the environment is also provided.

Many other significant changes are apparent in a review of the table of contents. For example, Part I now includes two separate chapters on civil liberties and civil rights (Chapters 5 and 6). Chapter 17, on the making of public policy, uses AIDS as an example of how an issue becomes part of the public policy agenda. Finally, a new Chapter 20 examines public policy and community values. Among the issues it considers are public funding of the arts, crime, the death penalty, the "war on drugs," and controversies over fairness and equity in school funding.

Many of these revisions stem from our obligation to keep our book up-to-date. However, for the third edition, we also have tried to provide more complete and useful teaching tools for loyal fans of our book.

The Plan of This Book

This text is built around the questions and problems of democratic theory as outlined in the first chapter. In every subsequent chapter we will take up a different asp[...] U.S. politics and relate it to the elements of democratic theory. In **Part I** we inv[...] the *foundations* of American democracy. For example, Chapter 2 focuses [...] *political culture*. The key questions are: Just how democratic is our political cu[...] And which aspects of that culture point in a democratic direction, and which d[...]

Next, Chapters 3 and 4 examine basic political arrangements in the United S[...]

specifically, *the Constitution* and *the federal system*. Do these arrangements facilitate or thwart democracy? Does the Constitution, for example, frustrate or enhance majority rule? Do the states do enough to protect democratic rights? Is a government that is "closer to the people" (local government) likely to be more democratic than the state or national government?

Chapters 5 and 6 turn to basic questions of *civil liberties* and *civil rights*. How has U.S. society fared in protecting freedom of speech, press, and religion? What about the rights of the accused, and the question of abortion? Since very few public policies actually result in equal treatment for all, what differences of treatment are just and fair? What does equal protection mean for particular segments of American society: African-Americans, women, gay men and lesbians, and the disabled? How well has the U.S. done in advancing basic social rights, such as the right to pure food and drugs?

Chapter 7 investigates the *U.S. political economy*. Here we turn to issues of democracy's relationship to capitalism, socialism, and mixed economic systems. Do the rich exercise excessive influence? How does an unequal distribution of income and wealth affect democratic processes?

In **Part II** we go beyond the foundations of government and dig more deeply into political *processes*. Here we look at political attitudes, voting, and political participation (Chapter 8); *political parties* (Chapter 9); *campaigns and the media* (Chapter 10) and *mass political action* (Chapter 12). All these chapters explore the issues of democratic representation. In each, the fundamental questions are: How are opinions shaped and acted on in our political life? How effective is the democratic process in expressing and responding to citizen desires? For example, are political parties closely related to popular attitudes? Do the media generate enlightenment? Is mass action constructive and sensible?

In **Part III** (Chapters 13 to 16) we turn to the fundamental political *institutions* of American national government—the Congress, the presidency, the federal bureaucracy, and the court system. How well do each of these institutions meet the needs of democratic politics? More specifically, are they responsive to popular sentiment, honest, protective of democratic rights and liberties, concerned in word *and* deed with creating a more decent society? These general questions break down into more particular ones addressed to each institution. For example, we will ask whether presidential power is great enough to allow the chief executive to function effectively. In the case of Congress, we will be especially concerned with the power of "special interests." Is Congress really a democratic body, or is it too strongly influenced by the well-organized few?

Finally, **Part IV** (Chapters 17 to 22) is concerned with examples of public *policy making*—including economic policy, welfare policy, the maintenance of community values, foreign and defense policy, and energy and environmental policy. The part begins with a chapter on the process of policymaking, using the questions below the surface justifications for particular policies. For example, we ask: in whose interest is the economy managed? What should a democrat demand of the welfare state, and how well does our welfare state measure up to these demands? How is a democratic polity defined by its definition and treatment of crime? Are there different standards for what art the public should be willing to fund as opposed to what it should be willing to allow? What forces shape foreign and defense policy, and what role does public opinion play? What trade-offs may be involved among our economic and security interests, our ideal of advancing democracy, and the ideal of respect for the sovereignty and self-determination of other nations and peoples? How are key decisions made in the areas of energy and the environment? Who benefits most from these decisions? How are common citizens affected by the complex trade-offs involved in energy and environmental problems?

In sum *American Democracy* is a book that raises questions, offers opinions, and encourages you to think about the meanings, problems, and possibilities of democratic life. That is as it should be. Democracy is premised on the participation of citizens. The implication of this is that we *all* must learn to grapple with discrepancies between the ideal and the realities of political life. We hope that this textbook—an owner's manual for your democracy—will help you and your students to do just that.

The Teaching Package

American Democracy offers a complete and comprehensive ancillary package for adopters. The package features

— a combined *Instructor's Manual/Test Item File* that includes learning objectives, key terms, lecture outlines, suggested classroom activities and student projects, chapter summaries, and suggested readings and additional resources that can be brought to the classroom. For each chapter in the text, the test file includes some 75 questions that are graded for their levels of difficulty.

— a *Computerized Test Item File* that has complete authoring capability, for use with IBM or Macintosh systems.

— *Computerized Gradebook Software* that helps instructors manage, analyze, and report grades, available for IBM/DOS, IBM/Windows, and Macintosh systems.

— a *Transparency Package* consisting of some 50 illustrations. These illustrations have been selected from the textbook and enlarged for easier use in the classroom.

— a *Study Guide* that offers learning objectives, key terms, chapter outlines, and sample quizzes.

— *Two Custom Videos:* one on women candidates in the 1992 elections, the other an examination of the controversies involved in money and its influence on the democratic process from the founding to the present. Each video is approximately 20 to 25 minutes in length, and is accompanied by a printed guide containing suggestions for using the video and script.

This package includes several resources, such as videos and transparencies, t new to the third edition. Additionally, items such as the instructor's manual, tes file, and study guide have been completely rewritten. They have been prepar

PREFACE

close coordination with the textbook. While they are designed to ensure that students master the basic information that is essential in any American government course, they keep in mind our theme of American democracy and our attempt to encourage critical examination of the political system. For more information about these ancillaries, please write or call St. Martin's Press, College Desk, 175 5th Avenue, New York, NY, 10010 **(phone: 1-800-446-8923)**; or contact your local St. Martin's sales representative.

Acknowledgments

Like American democracy itself, this textbook is a broadly participatory endeavor. Scores of people have contributed to the creation and continued success of *American Democracy*. In response to individual telephone inquiries, dozens of knowledgeable sources—in academies, in government, and in organizations outside government that participate in American democracy—have offered personal and institutional insights on our political process. Library staffs—at the Honnold Library of the Claremont Colleges, the University Library at Cal Poly, Pomona, the Walter R. Davis Library at the University of North Carolina, and the Claremont branch of the Los Angeles County Public Library—have gone out of their way to provide information and support. Academic reviewers have guided and goaded manuscript revisions. Don Reisman, Richard Steins, Frances Jones, Steven Kutz, and Douglas Bell and their colleagues in the College Division of St. Martin's Press have offered the competence and efficiency of a large publishing house in a personalized small-house atmosphere. Inge King supplied sensitive photo research. Students in our American government courses, in addition to supplying a large measure of the satisfaction that makes up an academic life, have been a direct source of user data for this text. This edition builds on the strengths instilled in previous editions by a comparable, though in most cases different, army of sources, reviewers, librarians, publishing professionals, and students. Some university colleagues deserve special mention for their support of this project: Cheryl Sparks and Jim McCorkell, and faculty members Jeff Obler, Peter Filene, and Jurg Steiner, all of the University of North Carolina; Lane Van Tassell and Warren F. Jones of Georgia Southern University; and Barbara Burt Way and James Williams at Cal Poly Pomona. We would also like to express our appreciation for the reviewers who provided suggestions to St. Martin's Press: Christopher J. Bosso, Northeastern University; Barbara C. Burrell, University of Wisconsin—Madison; Donna E. Childers, Denison University; Maria Guido, Texas A & I University; Michael Hoover, Seminole Community College; James M. Lindsay, The University of Iowa; and Daniel J. Palazzolo, University of Richmond.

Many thanks, friends and collaborators.

Lewis Lipsitz

David M. Speak

CONTENTS IN BRIEF

| *Chapter One* | DEMOCRACY: *The Real and the Ideal* | 3 |

PART ONE
FOUNDATIONS — 49

Chapter Two	AMERICAN POLITICAL CULTURE: *Liberty and Its Tensions*	51
Chapter Three	REVOLUTION AND CONSTITUTION: *The American Way*	83
Chapter Four	AMERICAN FEDERALISM: *Can Democracy Be Divided Fifty Ways?*	117
Chapter Five	CIVIL LIBERTIES: *Are Liberties Effectively Protected?*	157
Chapter Six	CIVIL RIGHTS: *The Meanings of Equality*	193
Chapter Seven	THE AMERICAN POLITICAL ECONOMY: *Inequality and Democratic Politics*	237

CONTENTS IN BRIEF

PART TWO
POLITICS — 269

Chapter Eight	POLITICAL SOCIALIZATION, PUBLIC SENTIMENT, AND ELECTORAL TRENDS: *Is There a Real Majority?*	271
Chapter Nine	POLITICAL PARTIES: *Do They Offer a Choice?*	323
Chapter Ten	CAMPAIGNS, MONEY, AND THE MEDIA: *Beyond the Glitter and the Mud*	361
Chapter Eleven	INTEREST GROUP POLITICS: *Democracy to the Highest Bidder?*	403
Chapter Twelve	MASS POLITICS AND PROTEST: *A Threat or a Necessity?*	441

PART THREE
INSTITUTIONS — 469

Chapter Thirteen	CONGRESS: *The Heart of Democracy?*	471
Chapter Fourteen	THE AMERICAN PRESIDENT: *Unique, Necessary, and Dangerous*	519
Chapter Fifteen	THE BUREAUCRACY: *How Much Service and What Kind?*	555
Chapter Sixteen	THE AMERICAN JUDICIARY: *Nonelected Defenders of Democracy?*	587

PART FOUR
PUBLIC POLICY — 617

| Chapter Seventeen | PUBLIC POLICY: *Processes and Outcomes* | 619 |
| Chapter Eighteen | MANAGEMENT OF THE ECONOMY: *Competing Interests* | 641 |

Chapter Nineteen	THE WELFARE STATE: *Benefiting the Poor and the Nonpoor*	677
Chapter Twenty	BUILDING COMMUNITY: *Values and Limits*	713
Chapter Twenty-One	FOREIGN AND DEFENSE POLICIES: *A Place in the World*	745
Chapter Twenty-Two	ENERGY AND THE ENVIRONMENT: *Preserving or Depleting the American Dream?*	783
EPILOGUE	*On Improving American Democracy*	817
APPENDIX A	*The Declaration of Independence*	A-1
APPENDIX B	*The Constitution of the United States*	B-1
APPENDIX C	*U.S. Presidential Elections*	C-1
APPENDIX D	*Glossary*	D-1

CONTENTS

PREFACE   *v*

Chapter One
DEMOCRACY: *The Real and the Ideal*   3

Various Definitions of Democracy   6
Majoritarian Democracy • Liberal Democracy • Egalitarian Democracy •
A Comprehensive View

Ideal and Real Democracies   10

How Should Power Be Distributed in a Democracy?   14

Problems in Democratic Life   16
Unequal Distribution of Power • Failure to Exercise Rights •
The Relationship between Government and Citizen

■ *The Alienation Index*   22

■ *Participation in Elections: Comparing the United States with Twenty-seven other Nations*   23

Is Democracy Always the Best System?   27

Comparative Perspective: The Consociational Model of Democracy — 29

Struggles to Realize Democratic Ideals — 30
Restricting Democracy • Extending Democracy

■ *Plessy v. Ferguson* — 33

■ *Vote Wisely* — 42

Comparative Perspective: The Referendum in Switzerland — 44
Conclusions • Glossary Terms • Notes • Selected Readings

PART ONE
FOUNDATIONS — 49

Chapter Two
AMERICAN POLITICAL CULTURE: *Liberty and Its Tensions* — 51

What Is Political Culture? — 52
Political Culture and Democracy • Cohesiveness in Political Culture

Comparative Perspective: Political Culture, Old and New — 54

The Liberal Tradition — 54
Economic, Social, and Political Values • The Legacy of Liberalism

Comparative Perspective: Equality, Jämlikhet, *and* Hitoshisa — 58

Two Types of Liberalism — 61
Conservatism: Traditional Liberalism • New Deal Liberalism • The Failure of Radicalism

Limits of Liberalism — 65
Intolerance and Discrimination • Violence and the Rule of Law • Making the World Safe for Democracy—or for Us? • Religion and Morality in Politics

CONTENTS　xvii

- *Immigration Law and National Identity* — 66
- *Political Assassination in America* — 72
- *The Most Violent Nation on Earth?* — 74

Conclusions • Glossary Terms • Notes • Selected Readings

Chapter Three
REVOLUTION AND CONSTITUTION: *The American Way* — 83

Background of the Revolution — 84
The Socioeconomic Environment • The Political Environment • Imperial Authority and American Defiance

The Revolutionary War — 89

Comparative Perspective: The French Revolution and Its Aftermath — 92

Independence and Political Ferment in the United States — 93
The Articles of Confederation • Toward a New Government

The New Constitution — 96
A Stronger National Government • Limitation of Power • Indirect Representation • Four Issues Left for Later Resolution • Ratification • Amending the Constitution

- *Jefferson and Slavery* — 103

An Enduring Political Legacy — 109

Comparative Perspective: Americans Write Another Constitution — 110

Conclusions • Glossary Terms • Notes • Selected Readings

Chapter Four
AMERICAN FEDERALISM: *Can Democracy Be Divided Fifty Ways?* — 117

Federalism: An Overview — 118

Comparative Perspective: Nations, States, and Nation-States   *120*
Division of Powers • Power within the States • Limitations on Government Actions • Interstate Obligations • Statehood and the Alternatives

Comparative Perspective: Federalism in a Unified Germany   *126*

■ *The Northwest Ordinance of 1787*   *129*

The Evolution of Federalism   130
Three Crises of State and Nation • The Role of the Courts • "New Federalisms" • Strengthened State Governments

Responsibilities of the States   139

Tensions in the Federal System   143
Regional Rivalries • Interests Shared across State Lines

■ *Fiscal Strains on the States in the 1990s: A Variety of Sources*   *145*

Federal Intervention   146
Reapportionment • The Drinking Age

The Importance of States   148

■ *One State's Prescription for Health*   *150*

Conclusions • Glossary Terms • Notes • Selected Readings

Chapter Five

CIVIL LIBERTIES: *Are Liberties Effectively Protected?*   157

Comparative Perspective: Button Your Wenhua Shan!   *158*

The Bill of Rights and Constitutional Protections   161

Federalism and Civil Liberties   163

Freedom of Speech   165
Setting Limits on Dissent • The Smith Act Cases • Contemporary Trends • Symbolic Speech and "Fighting Words"

CONTENTS xix

■ *The Alien and Sedition Acts of 1798* *169*

Press Freedom *172*

Freedom of Religion *174*
Establishment of Religion • Free Exercise of Religion

The Rights of the Accused *178*

Abortion *181*

The Right to Vote *185*
Black Americans and the Right to Vote
Conclusions • Glossary Terms • Notes • Selected Readings

Chapter Six

CIVIL RIGHTS: *The Meanings of Equality* **193**

Treatment as Equals *196*

Equality and African-Americans *197*
School Desegregation • Affirmative Action, Set-Asides, and Quotas • Black Americans and Economic Progress

Comparative Perspective: Group Rights and the Question of Quebec *208*

Civil Rights and Women *215*
Government Actions on Gender Discrimination

Equal Treatment for Gay Men and Lesbians *218*

Rights of the Disabled *222*

Basic Social Rights *224*
Pure Food and Drugs • Trade Unions and Collective Bargaining

■ *The Ludlow Massacre of 1913* *227*

Government Repression *228*

CONTENTS

■ *The Harassment of Martin Luther King, Jr.*   *230*
Conclusions • Glossary Terms • Notes • Selected Readings

Chapter Seven

THE AMERICAN POLITICAL ECONOMY: *Inequality and Democratic Politics*   *237*

A Nineteenth-Century Duality   *238*
Capitalism • Socialism

Twentieth-Century Economic Variety   *241*
Mixed Systems • The Soviet Bloc and Repressive Collectivism

■ *The TVA: An Experiment in Socialism*   *242*

The U.S. Political Economy   *247*
Distribution of Income • Distribution of Wealth and Ownership • Corporations and the Economy • Poverty

Public Policy and the Political Economy   *259*
Government Spending, Taxation, and Regulation • Government and Inequality

Conclusions • Glossary Terms • Notes • Selected Readings

PART TWO
POLITICS   *269*

Chapter Eight

POLITICAL SOCIALIZATION, PUBLIC SENTIMENT, AND ELECTORAL TRENDS: *Is There a Real Majority?*   *271*

Majority Rule: An Overview   *272*

Political Socialization   *273*
Childhood • The Role of the School • College and Politics

Public Opinion — 281

■ The Perils of Polling — 282
Gauging Public Opinion • Public Opinion and Democracy • Efficacy and Alienation

Understanding Public Sentiment — 293
Liberalism and Conservatism • Contemporary Views on Specific Issues • Influences on Public Sentiment

■ Rallying around the President — 302

Electoral Trends — 305
The New Deal Antecedents to Contemporary Politics • The Contemporary National Electoral Pattern: Crosscutting Attachments and Divided Government

Nonparticipation — 310
Barriers to Voting • Who Votes?

Comparative Perspective: Fewer Voters but More Voting — 312

Opinion and Policy — 316
Conclusions • Glossary Terms • Notes • Selected Readings

Chapter Nine

POLITICAL PARTIES: *Do They Offer a Choice?* — 323

Characteristics of Political Parties — 325
Three Facets of Political Parties • Functions of Political Parties • Two-Party and Multiparty Systems

Comparative Perspective: The Green Party in Germany — 328

The U.S. Party System — 331
Origins of Contemporary Parties • The System of 1896 • The New Deal Coalition • Since the New Deal • Dilemmas and Contributions of Third Parties • Party Organization • Party Reforms after 1968 • Do the Political Parties Differ?

xxii CONTENTS

Comparative Perspective: The Disciplined Parties of Great Britain — *341*

Current Issues — *349*
Decline of the Parties • Realignment: Who Has the Majority? • Party Responsibility and Party Reform

Conclusions • Glossary Terms • Notes • Selected Readings

Chapter Ten
CAMPAIGNS, MONEY, AND THE MEDIA: *Behind the Glitter and the Mud* — 361

Political Campaigns — *364*
Nonpresidential Campaigns • Presidential Campaigns • The Electoral College

Campaign Financing — *374*
Reform Efforts • Further Reforms

Politics and the Media — *383*
Gathering the News • Framing the Issues

■ *The Press and the Persian Gulf* — *385*

Media and Campaigns — *387*
The Media's Impact on Elections • Imagemaking • Televised Presidential Debates • Media and "Horse Races" • The Media and Campaign Negativity

■ *Who Speaks with Authority about Politics?* — *390*

■ *The Lincoln-Douglas Debates* — *392*

Conclusions • Glossary Terms • Notes • Selected Readings

Chapter Eleven
INTEREST GROUP POLITICS: *Democracy to the Highest Bidder?* — 403

Interest Group Dynamics — 406
Functions of Interest Groups • Problems with Interest Groups • Political Subsystems

Major Interest Groups — 410
Business • Labor • The Defense Budget, the Defense Lobby, and the Peace Lobby • Public-Interest Groups • Single-Issue Groups

Comparative Perspective: Guns and Public Policy — 421

How Lobbying Works — 423
Insider Strategies • Outsider Strategies • Lobbying Target Groups

Comparative Perspective: Lobbying the European Community — 428

Regulation and the Public Interest — 431
Regulatory Efforts • Government and Interest Groups

Conclusions • Glossary Terms • Notes • Selected Readings

Chapter Twelve

MASS POLITICS AND PROTEST: *A Threat or a Necessity?* — 441

Extraordinary Politics — 442
The Whys of Protest • Extraordinary Politics and Government Action

■ *The Invisible Empire* — 446

Protest and Disobedience — 449
Law and Disobedience • Civil Disobedience: A Compromise

Comparative Perspective: Gandhi: The Essence of Nonviolence — 455

How Protest Works — 456
Consciousness-raising • Activating Others • Contexts for Effective Protest • Limitations of Protest Tactics

Protesting Politics Itself: The Push for Term Limits for Legislators — 460

Conclusions • Glossary Terms • Notes • Selected Readings

CONTENTS

PART THREE
INSTITUTIONS — 469

Chapter Thirteen
CONGRESS: *The Heart of Democracy?* — 471

Congress: An Overview — 473
The Nature of Representation • Functions of Congress

The Structure of Congress — 478
The Hierarchy of Congress • Legislative Committees • How a Bill Becomes a Law

Comparative Perspective: The British Parliament — 480

■ *Fragmented Responsibilities* — 486

■ *The Rider: A Key Part of the Legislative Process* — 490

Members of Congress — 493
Personal Characteristics • Influences on Voting Patterns • Congressional Ethics

Tradition and the Postreform Congress — 501

Congress and the President — 503
Congress and Secrets • Congress and the War Powers Resolution • Congress and the Budget

■ *The War Powers Resolution at Work* — 508
Conclusions • Glossary Terms • Notes • Selected Readings

Chapter Fourteen
THE AMERICAN PRESIDENT: *Unique, Necessary, and Dangerous* — 519

The Unique President — 520
Pressing against the Limits of Power • Paradoxes of the Presidency

Comparative Perspective: The Head of State in Germany   522

The Necessary President   526
The Executive Office • The Cabinet • Running Mates • The Rest of the Bureaucracy • Relations with Congress

The Dangerous President   539
The Vietnam War • The Watergate Affair • The Iran-Contra Affair • Operation Desert Shield

■ *Congress Manipulated: The Gulf of Tonkin Resolution*   540

Transitions of Power   547

Comparative Perspective: Political Crisis and Transition in France, 1958   549
Conclusions • Glossary Terms • Notes • Selected Readings

Chapter Fifteen

THE BUREAUCRACY: *How Much Service and What Kind?*   555

Defining the Federal Bureaucracy   558

Structure of the National Bureaucracy   560
Cabinet Departments • Independent Agencies • Regulatory Commissions

Bureaucracy and the Political Process   565
Bureaucratic Discretion • Bureaucratic Expertise • Mobilization of Support

Comparative Perspective: British and French Bureaucracies   568

Bureaucracy Evaluated   571
Is the Bureaucracy Too Unresponsive? • Is There Too Much Bureaucracy? • Are There Too Many Rules?

■ *Seven Propositions about Regulation*   572

■ *One Agency Responds: The FDA and Bureaucratic Reform*   578
Conclusions • Glossary Terms • Notes • Selected Readings

CONTENTS

Chapter Sixteen

THE AMERICAN JUDICIARY: *Nonelected Defenders of Democracy?* 587

A Dual Function 588

Courts as Impartial Forums for Dispute Resolution 591
State Court Systems • The Federal Court System • Recruitment of Judges • The Flow of Litigation

The Judiciary and Policymaking 600
The Decision-making Process • Judicial Review • Self-restraints on Power • Legislative Reactions • Noncompliance

Comparative Perspective: Judicial Review in Britain, Switzerland, and Germany 603

Major Periods in Supreme Court History 605
Focus on the Distribution of Power • Concern for Individual Rights • The Recent Past

The Dilemma of an Expanded Legal System 611
Conclusions • Glossary Terms • Notes • Selected Readings

PART FOUR

PUBLIC POLICY 617

Chapter Seventeen

PUBLIC POLICY: *Processes and Outcomes* 619

■ *How Do We Define "Public Policy"?* 620

The Complexities of Public Policy in the United States: AIDS 621
Getting AIDS on the Agenda • AIDS and the Fragmentation of Power • Funding the Response to AIDS • AIDS and Policy Reactions • AIDS Policy: The Contribution of Individuals and Groups

Comparative Perspective: AIDS Policy in Brazil 626

How Issues Reach the Political Agenda   628

Processing Issues   632
Competing Agendas • Dealing with Issues

Policy Formulation and Implementation   634
Proposals for Action • Implementation

Policy Evaluation   636

The Boundaries of Policymaking   637
Conclusions • Glossary Terms • Notes • Selected Readings

Chapter Eighteen

MANAGEMENT OF THE ECONOMY: *Competing Interests*   641

History of Economic Management   642
Mercantilism • Laissez-Faire and the Growth of Regulation • Controlled Capitalism • The Postwar Experience

■   *The Great Depression, City and Country*   646

Tools of Economic Intervention   649
Microeconomics and Regulation • Macroeconomic Policy

The Politics of Economics: The Supply-Side Debate   659
Reaganomics • Evaluating the Supply-Side Experiment

Emerging Problems   662
Tax Equity and Tax Expenditures • Federal Budget Deficits • The Decline in Industrial Power

Comparative Perspective: Industrial Policy   670
Conclusions • Glossary Terms • Notes • Selected Readings

Chapter Nineteen

THE WELFARE STATE: *Benefiting the Poor and the Nonpoor*   677

The U.S. Welfare State   679

Comparative Perspective: Transfer System Effectiveness: The Impact of Taxes and Transfers on Poverty in Several Nations — 682

Income Security Programs — 683
Social Security • AFDC • Job Programs • Other Income Security Programs

■ Tax Expenditures — 684

Comparative Perspective: Child Care Programs: Sweden versus the United States — 688

Health-Care Programs — 691
Medicare • Other Health-Care Programs • Proposals for Reform

Comparative Perspective: Health Care North of the Border — 698

Nutrition and Housing Programs — 700
Food Stamps • Other Nutrition Programs • Housing Programs • Homelessness

Evaluating the Welfare State — 706
The Conservative Approach • The Liberal Critique
Conclusions • Glossary Terms • Notes • Selected Readings

Chapter Twenty

BUILDING COMMUNITY: *Values and Limits* — 713

Democracy and Social Control — 714

Obscenity, Art, and the Arts — 715
Obscenity • Public Funding for the Arts

Democracy, Crime, and Drugs — 722
Making Choices about Crime • The Criminal Justice Process • The Death Penalty and Crime Rates • The War on Drugs

Comparative Perspective: Legal Prohibition and Practical Tolerance: Setting Limits the Dutch Way — 723

CONTENTS xxix

Education: Fairness and Values   735
Equitable School Funding • Education and Values

■ *Mandatory Testing*   738
Conclusions • Glossary Terms • Notes • Selected Readings

Chapter Twenty-One
FOREIGN AND DEFENSE POLICIES: *A Place in the World*   745

The Making of Foreign Policy   746
The President and the Executive Branch • Influences on Foreign Policy

■ *Out of the Cold: A Role for the CIA?*   750

The Tools of Foreign Policy   752
Diplomacy • Propaganda • Economic Rewards and Punishments • Clandestine Operations and Military Intervention

Global Players   757
States • Nonstate Actors

■ *Amnesty International*   759

A Short History of U.S. Foreign Policy   760
Isolation and Expansion • The Cold War • Gorbachev, *Perestroika*, and the End of the USSR

Foreign Policy after the Cold War   765
The U.S. Invasion of Panama • From Desert Shield to Desert Storm

Major Challenges for the Future   772
Economic Competition through Trade • Human Rights and Foreign Policy • An Equitable Distribution of Wealth Worldwide • The Future of Foreign Policy: A "New World Order?"
Conclusions • Glossary Terms • Notes • Selected Readings

Chapter Twenty-Two
ENERGY AND THE ENVIRONMENT: *Preserving or Depleting the American Dream?*   783

CONTENTS

The United States, Energy, and the Environment — 785

From Exploitation to Protection — 785

Environmental Problems and Government Responses — 789
Air Pollution • Water Pollution • Toxic Chemicals

■ *Global Warming* — 791

Comparative Perspective: Environmental Policy in France: Centralized Market-oriented Control — 798

■ *Endangered Species and the Endangered Species Act* — 800

The Politics of Environmental Issues — 802
Group Strategies • The Reagan Record on the Environment • The Bush Administration and the Environment

Energy: Sources, Problems, Policies — 805
Energy: An Overview • U.S. Energy Use • The Politics of Energy Issues

■ *A Summary of Energy Alternatives* — 810
Conclusions • Glossary Terms • Notes • Selected Readings

EPILOGUE: *On Improving American Democracy* — 817

APPENDIX A: *The Declaration of Independence* — A-1

APPENDIX B: *The Constitution of the United States* — B-1

APPENDIX C: *U.S. Presidential Elections* — C-1

APPENDIX D: *Glossary* — D-1

INDEX — I-1

THIRD EDITION

AMERICAN DEMOCRACY

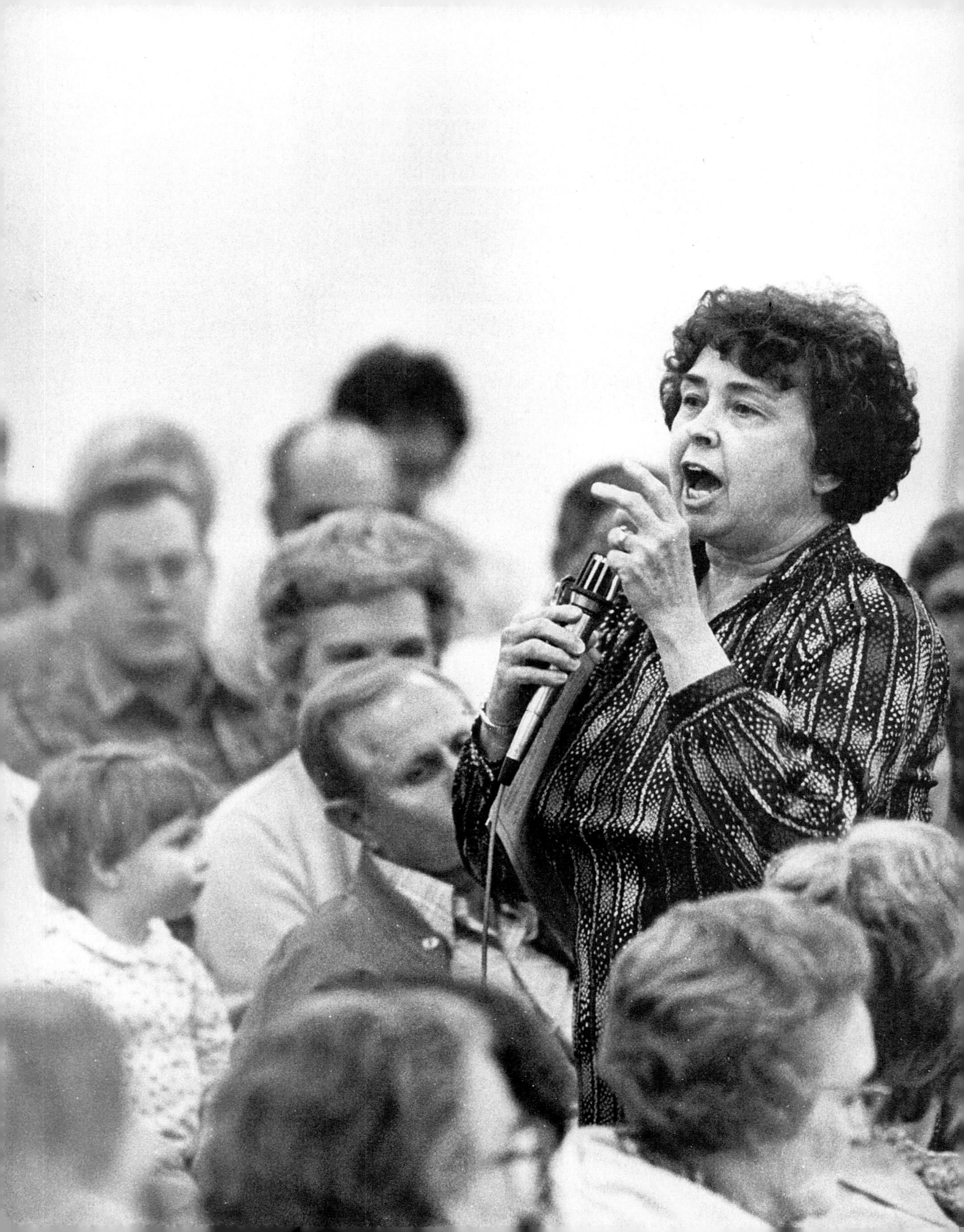

CHAPTER ONE

DEMOCRACY

The Real and the Ideal

CHAPTER OUTLINE

Various Definitions of Democracy

MAJORITARIAN DEMOCRACY
LIBERAL DEMOCRACY
EGALITARIAN DEMOCRACY
A COMPREHENSIVE VIEW

Ideal and Real Democracies

How Should Power Be Distributed in a Democracy?

Problems in Democratic Life

UNEQUAL DISTRIBUTION OF POWER
FAILURE TO EXERCISE RIGHTS
THE RELATIONSHIP BETWEEN GOVERNMENT AND CITIZEN

Is Democracy Always the Best System?

Struggles to Realize Democratic Ideals

RESTRICTING DEMOCRACY
EXTENDING DEMOCRACY

MOST AMERICANS THINK OF THEIR COUNTRY AS A "DEMOCracy." In fact, public opinion research has shown that Americans are particularly proud that they live in a democratic country. There is no point in debating whether or not the United States is a democracy—as if there were only two categories that nations could fit into, the democratic and the undemocratic. In the ordinary sense in which the term is used, the United States clearly is a democratic nation. However, here is a more difficult, more subtle, more interesting question: Just how democratic are we?

To put this question into perspective, imagine a society with a written constitution that grants everyone the right to vote; holds free elections; proclaims its belief in free speech, a free press, and the rights of political parties to organize and advance their views; and so on. Superficially, such a nation might seem democratic. But we would have to look beyond the constitution to find out if, in fact, that was the case. For example, we might, on closer examination, discover that this nation was actually ruled by a small group of wealthy landowners who ignored the constitutional provisions whenever it was convenient to do so. Most of the inhabitants might be relatively poor peasants who depended on the landowners for employment. Anyone voicing serious dissent might be jailed or otherwise intimidated.

3

We draw several conclusions from this hypothetical case. To begin with, the written word is not enough: Democratic provisions in a constitution may or may not be honored in practice. Second, we see that great differences in wealth and power can undermine the drive for democracy. Where very few control most of the wealth and have inordinate access to power, democracy is usually drained of its meaning.

Consider another case: a country that gradually moves toward greater degrees of democracy. Early in this nation's history, only some citizens are granted the right to vote. Over decades, after considerable agitation and struggle, others are permitted to join the vote as well. Finally, after almost two hundred years, suffrage is opened to all. Nonetheless, many citizens remain ignorant about politics, and almost half of those who could vote simply do not bother to do so, even in the most important elections. How democratic would we say such a nation was?

The nation just described, of course, is the United States—in which women and blacks not only were excluded from suffrage for many years but were also denied full legal protections for voting rights until 1920 and 1965, respectively. In our society today, many citizens remain politically uninformed and inactive, with only 50 percent of eligible voters likely to turn out even in presidential elections.

Democracy is a matter of degree and quality. The question of whether or not a country is democratic can be viewed from many perspectives.

- Are the political rights of every citizen effectively protected (and exercised)?
- Is the level of public knowledge high? Is public discussion informed and useful?
- Do most people, and especially most leaders, support the democratic idea?
- Do some people or groups have power and influence in great disproportion to their numbers?
- Does the government honor its stated principles in dealing with the people? Does it violate its own laws?
- Are political institutions honest and leaders trustworthy?
- Does the government often use violence against citizens? Is political life characterized by a high level of coercion?
- Does each citizen have a realistic chance of attaining and maintaining basic security, a reasonable standard of living, and opportunities for education and some amenities?
- Are some groups discriminated against or excluded from full participation in social and political life?
- Do violent confrontations between groups occur outside the political arena?
- Do nongovernmental institutions, such as churches, unions, and social organizations, encourage democratic attitudes and practices?

Some of these questions are fairly easy to answer. For example, it is not hard to see that the degree of democracy in the United States was once sharply diminished by the systematic denial of basic political rights to black Americans. Other questions are tougher to handle. Exactly how much "influence" is too much? Just how great a degree of equality can we reasonably aim for in the power and political leverage exercised by various groups? After all, won't some individuals and some groups always wield greater power than others in even the most democratic polity?

These are the basic issues addressed in this book. Because this is a text on U.S. politics, it covers many topics, from constitutional history to current debate about abortion. But the connecting thread, knitting the chapters loosely together, is the idea of "democracy": We will try to understand the strengths and weaknesses of U.S. politics from a democratic perspective. In each chapter, you will be asked to weigh the democratic issues involved and to decide just how democratic our society is or might be. **Table 1-1** reports a survey of how satisfied Europeans were with the way democracy worked in their countries in the 1980s. Overall, the Danes, West Germans, Greeks, and British expressed the highest levels of satisfaction with democracy, while the Italians, French, Irish, and Belgians reported lower levels of satisfaction. Given a similar sort of question, Americans scored more like the Danes than like the Italians, with 72 percent saying that our political system was "basically sound" despite needing some improvements.

Before discussing specific issues, however, we must decide just what constitutes democracy. To do so, we will now explore the various ways of viewing democracy and then try to come up with an overall definition to serve as a yardstick as we examine the U.S. political system. Along the way we must inevitably make distinctions between democratic ideals and democracy in practice.

TABLE 1-1
SURVEY OF SATISFACTION WITH THE WAY DEMOCRACY WORKS (PERCENT)

Country	Very Satisfied	Fairly Satisfied	Not Very Satisfied	Not at All Satisfied	Don't Know	Index*
Belgium	4	43	33	15	5	2.39
Denmark	20	50	19	5	6	2.89
France	4	34	38	14	10	2.32
Germany (West)	11	61	21	5	2	2.78
Greece	18	39	24	13	6	2.67
Ireland	6	38	30	20	6	2.33
Italy	3	25	45	26	1	2.04
Luxembourg	11	57	24	5	3	2.75
Netherlands	7	51	30	9	3	2.57
United Kingdom	12	48	27	10	3	2.63
European Community (weighted average)	8	43	32	13	4	2.48

*Higher scores reflect relative satisfaction and lower scores relative dissatisfaction. Point system for the index: very satisfied = 4, not at all satisfied = 1.
SOURCE: Jurg Steiner, *European Democracies* (New York: Longman, 1986), chap. 16.

Various Definitions of Democracy

Confusion often arises in discussion about democracy. Frequently this stems from the different premises people have in mind when they use the term. Most people fail to specify their underlying premises, and as a result, we often incorporate into our sense of democracy disparate elements that may or may not relate to it. To avoid such confusion, we must identify the key ideas central to democracy and then clarify precisely how the term will be used in this book.

Majoritarian Democracy

The most basic and straightforward notion of democracy is that of simple majority rule. This means that a majority of the people give their consent to specific policies or leaders. They can do so either directly or through representatives selected to rule in the name of the people. But does **majoritarian democracy** give rise to a reasonably workable, equitable, and fair political system? Will a majority, for example, decide to outlaw certain religions or political factions? Will it take away the property of the few who hold great wealth? Will it be able to run the government in a coherent and sensible fashion? These are questions that a simple definition cannot answer. Yet they are the very questions that have been asked about majoritarian democracy since its beginnings in ancient Greece.

It was in Athens that the issues associated with majority rule first became highly charged. Democracy in ancient Athens took the form of a legislative assembly selected by lot, which meant that any citizen might be called on to serve. In addition, there were popular courts, whose members were also selected by lot. Basic issues of public policy were debated in the assembly, with the citizens listening, participating, and finally voting to decide the issues. Defenders of majority rule in Athens saw this system as a device for allowing the populace to have a voice in political decision making. Any other arrangement, they argued, would tend to place power exclusively in the hands of the rich or the well-born—as had often been the case in Athens before the democratic reforms. For **democrats*** the Athenian political system demonstrated that a random selection of the people could assemble and attend to the public's business in a reasonable fashion. Some also argued that the Athenian experience showed that people who participate in making and enforcing the laws are likely to be more law-abiding. Democracy made for a more committed citizenry.

Critics of majoritarian democracy had no shortage of arguments either. They maintained that democracy could degenerate into sheer mob rule under which no one is safe. Property could be seized by the majority. Unpopular ideas could be suppressed. A popular assembly or jury might be easily swayed by emotion. Worst of all, the critics

---

*The term *democrat*, with a small *d*, refers to people who support democratic ideas and practices. The term *Democrat*, with a capital *D*, refers to supporters of the Democratic party of the United States.

charged, majoritarianism recognized no moral limits to its authority. A majority was empowered to do *anything*. The democrats replied that despite these problems, the majority was likely to rule more wisely than any self-selected group of rich or powerful individuals would.

Many of these same arguments have surfaced again and again throughout Western history. Can the people make decisions? Are experts needed to rule? Will majorities violate the rights of minorities? Or is it more likely that a ruling minority will violate the rights of a majority?

Liberal Democracy

A second, somewhat more complex view of democracy, and the one most familiar to Americans, is what has become known as **liberal democracy**. This concept combined majority rule with respect for civil liberties and protection of individual rights. In general, when people in the Western world today speak of democratic government, this is what they have in mind.

The concept of liberal democracy first came into political thought about three hundred years ago, when a great debate raged in Europe over the powers of kings and the rights of citizens. The monarchs of the seventeenth and eighteenth centuries claimed they ruled by "divine right," but the early liberal democrats envisioned a different kind of political society. Besides arguing for a society based on the consent of those governed, they also began to talk about basic human rights, equality among citizens, and the right to protest and rebel against oppressive governments.

These critics of monarchy were in no sense egalitarians, however. Many of them wanted a government based only on the consent of a small, prosperous middle class; very few were willing to advocate a society based on the consent of *all*. The notion that every person should have a voice in shaping the destiny of political life was so radical that it was barely conceivable. Many of the struggles over democracy in the past two centuries have focused directly on this issue: *Whose* consent is to be sought by a government based on the consent of the governed?

These modern democratic ideas developed in concert with a new socioeconomic system known as **capitalism**. The rising middle classes of the seventeenth and eighteenth centuries wanted to gain full freedom to buy and sell, to accumulate wealth, and generally to conduct business without government interference. Many observers have argued that democracy became possible only because of the rise of capitalism, which emphasized individual rights and individual potential. Capitalists struggled to limit government power, defending the individual's rights to carve out a sphere of private life exempt from government interference. It must be noted, however, that though these efforts contributed to an atmosphere in which democratic ideas could take hold, the simultaneous development of a capitalist economic system and a democratic political system also created problems and tensions that persist to this day (and form the basis of a third view of democracy, to be discussed shortly).

8 DEMOCRACY: THE REAL AND THE IDEAL

Electoral democracy reached Eastern Europe with a stunning suddenness. Here, Hungarians line up at the polling station in 1990 for the first free election in decades. Although elections are a necessary element in democratic politics, they are not necessarily evidence that a thriving democracy is in place. *(AP/Wide World Photos)*

Today the two tenets underlying democracy are majority rule and the protection of basic rights for all citizens. **Majority rule** takes shape mainly through regular elections, though the exact type and timing of elections vary considerably from one nation to another. In the United States the timing of elections is fixed by law—every four years, for example, for the presidency. In Great Britain the prime minister can call an election at any time during a five-year term.

Sometimes majorities are easy to recognize, as when a referendum (a specific issue on the ballot) must be approved or defeated. But in democratic elections, the clarity of majority opinion, and therefore the strength of majority rule, varies according to how clearly the issues are drawn between the competing parties and candidates. On occasion, a numerical majority is actually made up of a collection of minorities, each supporting a particular candidate or party for different reasons. Sometimes parties and candidates deliberately blur the issues to gain more votes. All these factors make it difficult to determine just what majority rule means in any one case. Nonetheless, rule by majorities is a crucial element in democratic life today.

Equally crucial is the protection of **basic rights**. Citizens must have the right to organize groups, to form and join political parties, to acquire information, to protest in various ways, and to express and exchange opinions publicly. Without such rights, public opinion easily could be manipulated, authority abused, and elections made meaningless. And though elections are usually the most significant means of shaping public policy, they are not the only means. U.S. citizens, for instance, can try to influence political parties to nominate candidates holding particular views and also seek change through the courts. They can protest in the streets. They can lobby in Washington. They can peacefully refuse to obey certain laws.

Democracy must protect another set of basic rights as well—the rights fundamental to a decent social and political order. Such protections include prohibitions against the arbitrary exercise of government authority. In the United States, for example, the government is required to follow **due process of law** in dealing with its citizens: People cannot be arrested without reason or confined indefinitely without trial, property cannot be confiscated without cause, and cruel and unusual punishments cannot be imposed. In the struggle against the monarchies of the late eighteenth century, democrats fought to ensure that citizens were not subject to such arbitrary government action.

Finally, the concept of **equal protection of the laws** is critical to democratic life. Equal protection means that no individual or group can be denied the rights and privileges granted to others. The question of who should be given equal protection has been one of the most fiercely contested issues in democratic nations over the past two centuries.

The early adherents of democracy focused most of their attention on curbing the arbitrary exercise of government power and tended to ignore the power wielded by nongovernment institutions such as churches, businesses, and private groups. Also, their conception of rights was relatively limited: They sought primarily to protect rights already in existence. Later proponents of democratic rights took a more far-reaching approach, one in which the government played a much more creative role. For example, many of us would argue that every citizen has the right to an education. Guaranteeing such a right involves positive government action and community decision making, rather than simply the protection of a right already possessed by the citizen. In other words, the views on civil liberties and rights held by our nation's founders were significantly more restricted than those held widely today.

Egalitarian Democracy

A third view of democracy holds that it is not enough to specify and protect liberties and rights; an attempt must also be made to provide for basic social and economic equality. **Egalitarian democracy** finds the spirit of democracy violated in societies in which a few enjoy lives of affluence while many live in poverty. Egalitarian democrats advocate a significant redistribution of wealth and call for the equalization of educational opportunities and vigorous enforcement of laws protecting people from exploitation. For the egalitarian democrat, democracy attains its full meaning only in a society of relative equality.

Such views were first advanced about a century ago by critics of the capitalist system who maintained that real democracy could not work as long as large social and economic inequalities persisted in society. Giving each person a vote would hardly provide for genuine equality of influence, they argued. How could the average worker hope to compete politically with a wealthy and powerful industrialist? It might take an organization of thousands of workers to wield as much real political clout as a single steel company owner. These critics called for radical changes in the patterns of ownership in democratic societies; in their view, greater social and economic equality were preconditions for real rule by the people. Otherwise, they contended, there would be only partial rule by the people and partial rule by those possessing great economic power.

A Comprehensive View

The concept of **democracy** explored in this book incorporates the basic elements of all three interpretations: that democracy (1) must be founded on majority rule as expressed through meaningful, competitive elections; (2) must include effective protections for individual rights and liberties; and (3) must strive to achieve a significant degree of equality among citizens. Beyond these elements, however, the idea of democracy presented here encompasses several other factors: citizen participation that is extensive and informed, government that is honest and does not use unwarranted force to impose order, and foreign policies that serve democratic purposes as much as possible.

Using this rather detailed conception of democracy, we will be examining the government, politics, and policies of the United States today. As a yardstick definition it sets a high standard, and in this text we will be probing democracy to explore the myriad possibilities inherent in it. To be sure, many of them have not been achieved, in the United States or anywhere else; some may not even be within reach. Of course, this definition, like the others just described, is itself controversial and subject to many interpretations—but then, that is what political discourse is all about.

Ideal and Real Democracies

We can construct the ideal circumstances for a democratic society. To begin, imagine a rather small, homogeneous community, with limited and generally acceptable inequalities. The citizens are active, informed participants in the political process. They attend town meetings. They talk and debate, weighing important issues with genuine

DEMOCRACY: THE REAL AND THE IDEAL 11

Our political system provides for one person/one vote, but our economic system leads to a world in which some command far more resources than others. An egalitarian democrat would ask, How much inequality can democracy tolerate and still remain meaningful? (Fredrik D. Bodin/Stock, Boston)

inquisitiveness. They are fiercely committed to the democratic process and to the ideals of democratic life. They are fair-minded and tolerant, accepting and even encouraging dissent. Children are reared in families that stress equality among parents and respect for the young, and they learn early in life that they are personally secure.

No gross differences in wealth, power, and respect separate the citizens. There are no juxtapositions of conspicuous wealth and acute deprivation, no slums located two blocks from expensive homes. There are no color or gender barriers, prejudice and group hatred having long since dissolved in the soothing waters of common citizenship. These democratic citizens take their social and political responsibilities seriously; they inculcate respect for the law, but a respect that is not idolatrous. They recognize that democratic commitments sometimes allow for disobedience to law.

The government of this ideal democracy is highly responsive. Citizens' views are frequently consulted. Political debate, during campaigns, for example, is reasonable and civil. Candidates do not make personal assaults on each other, attempt to obscure the issues, or pander to the baser emotions of the public; an ideal democratic public would reject such tactics quickly and thoroughly. Political leaders are selected from among the most qualified citizens. Leaders and those led relate to each other in an atmosphere of mutual instruction. Leaders attempt to put the difficult issues of political life before the electorate as clearly and fully as they can. The public, for its part, tries to comprehend these matters, and its response helps to inform the directions of future policy. When disputes occasionally go beyond the usual bounds of public discussion and threaten to burst into bitter controversy, the disputants either find ways of compromising or take their disputes before a court system that aids them in reconciling their differences.

Such an ideal democracy was envisioned by early democratic theorists such as the French-Swiss political philosopher Jean-Jacques Rousseau (1712–1778), who felt that political democracy was possible *only* in a small and homogeneous society. This ideal world, of course, has little in common with the reality of contemporary life. However, we now recognize that a minimum level of political democracy can exist under many different conditions, some of them far from the ideal scenario just presented. We know, for example, that most citizens are not very well informed about political matters and that large numbers never participate in political life even in the most minimal way. We know that great disparities in wealth, power, and respect exist in democratic societies and that these differences sharply affect the functioning of democracy. We know that political debate is often deliberately confusing, that leaders sometimes mislead or fail to lead, that politicians can be dishonest, that many of the best potential political leaders never seek or attain office. We also know that many of the people who live in democratic societies are not particularly democratic. Some hold deep-seated prejudices toward certain groups; others would prefer a political system that aided only themselves and groups they support and that even caused harm to others. In other words, many people in democratic societies do not hold democratic attitudes.

What conclusion can we draw from this failure of reality to approximate the ideal? On the one hand, we could be amazed that political democracy exists at all, and even prospers, despite many adverse conditions. On the other hand, we could react with concern, arguing that some contemporary societies have forfeited their claims as democracies.

Many students of politics have adopted the first of these positions, taking what might be characterized as a **minimalist view of democracy**. This view was summed up by Winston Churchill, the British prime minister during World War II and in the 1950s, who stated that democracy was the worst political system, except for all the rest. Churchill, like many others, saw the democratic process as a way of avoiding the greater evils inherent in other political forms. At least in a democracy, minimalists argue, it is possible to get rid of a bad government through periodic competitive elections.

What about the low level of public information in the average electorate? Although this may be unfortunate, they argue, it is probably unrealistic for believers in democracy to think that most people do not take such an interest, for too many citizens participating too actively might cause too much political conflict. In this view, our hopes for democracy must be scaled down. All in all, minimalists tell us, current democracies are doing rather well.

Under the minimalist approach, then, a democracy is any government that has relatively open political debate and competition and also holds periodic elections. From a maximalist perspective, however, democracy can achieve far more. It is the **maximalist view of democracy** that undergirds the organization and approach of this text. We will assume that democracy encompasses much more than open elections,

SUMMARY CHART
DEFINITIONS OF DEMOCRACY

Definition	Characteristics	Example
Majoritarian	Rule by the majority	Ancient Athens is often cited, but its "majority" did not include women, slaves or foreigners. But it did allow and even require participation regardless of property holdings.
Direct Democracy	Decisions made by all citizens (who may discuss and vote in face-to-face meetings)	New England town meeting and other similar arrangements
Representative Democracy	Majority rule *through* elected representatives	Legislatures in contemporary democracies
Liberal Democracy	Rule by the majority, plus protection of minority rights, the right to dissent and form opposition groups	Contemporary democracies, to one degree or another
Egalitarian Democracy	Liberal democracy plus provision of a basic level of social and economic equality for all citizens	Contemporary democracies, to one degree or another
Minimalist Democracy	Regular elections, right to vote, political opposition	Contemporary democracies
Maximalist Democracy	Egalitarian democracy plus a variety of other requirements such as: high levels of citizen knowledge and participation, honest government, relatively equal distribution of power, etc.	None—Maximalist democracy sets a utopian standard to be used as a measure of real world democracies. It is the standard we employ in this book
Consociational Democracy	Liberal democracies which make special provisions to protect certain cultural groups and thereby depart from strict majority rule	Switzerland, The Netherlands, Belgium, Canada

that elections are a necessary but not sufficient condition for democratic life. In examining U.S. democratic institutions we will hold maximalist standards, to see where the problems and tensions lie and what possibilities for improvement can be found.

How Should Power Be Distributed in a Democracy?

Who actually runs the United States? Who calls the important shots? Some observers of American politics argue that a relatively homogeneous group of people—similar in background, lifestyle, and most of all, political outlook—make the key decisions that shape our political and economic life. This elite encompasses the top officials in major corporations and financial institutions, key politicians, the upper stratum of the national bureaucracy, and leading military officials. Of course, the argument goes, these people do not agree on everything, nor do they see or talk to each other constantly. According to theorists of **elitism**, no conspiracy is necessary to maintain elite control. The views and attitudes of this group coincide sufficiently to generate consistent policy goals without conspiratorial collusion. According to this school of thought, the American people, as a whole, are largely excluded from effective political decision making. The people can cast their votes, but that is about all they do—and the range of genuine choice through elections is small. The real power rests in the hands of the members of the elite, who have the information and resources needed to create policy for the nation. It is important to note that the elitist view might be advanced either descriptively (an elite exists in the United States) or prescriptively (elite control is desirable or at least preferable to alternative distributions of power).

An alternative to the elitist view is the more widely held pluralist conception of American politics. Adherents of **pluralism** argue that no one elite group dominates our national life; rather, there are many influential groups, whose degree of influence varies over time and according to the particular policy area involved. In health policy, for example, an array of interest groups exercise influence over decision making—groups of professional health providers like the American Medical Association (AMA), the American Hospital Association (AHA), and the American Public Health Association (APHA); major drug companies, insurance companies, and health service corporations; legislators whose districts or states have large medical establishments; groups like the American Association of Retired Persons (AARP), for whose members health care is a salient issue; and others. In addition, a few groups, including the Heritage Foundation and the American Enterprise Institute, hold strong ideological interests in health policy decisions. Turning to energy policy, we find a different array of groups competing for influence: legislators from energy-producing states such as Texas and Louisiana pitted against legislators from net-energy-consuming regions like the Northeast, major oil companies and automobile manufacturers, environmental groups like the Sierra Club and the Audubon Society, and more.

Thus, the pluralists contend, the patterns of interest group competition vary in different policy areas (sometimes, when distinctively insulated from the general policy debate, these policy areas are called political subsystems). According to one version of the pluralist argument, the U.S. political system is characterized not by majority rule but by "minorities rule," whereby important groups exert controlling influence in the areas of chief concern to them.[1] In the pluralist view, then, the U.S. political process is basically a highly fragmented arena, each portion of which has different participants and different winners and losers.

Theodore Lowi, a prominent political scientist, coined the expression **interest group liberalism** to describe the pattern of political decision making most common in recent U.S. politics.[2] In this form of politics, according to Lowi, each participant in every controversy receives something, and thus each has some impact on the decision-making process. As a result, the government rarely says no to any well-organized interest; instead, it gives some reward, some subsidy, some benefit to each interested party. Although this pluralistic pattern tends to minimize conflict, such a system avoids any thoroughgoing effort to determine what the public interest is in a policy area. Despite Lowi's criticism of interest group liberalism, prescription and description coincide fairly closely for most pluralist theorists. That is to say that these theorists find that pluralist politics are either desirable outright or at least the most attractive democratic arrangement in a large, diverse polity.

So who is right, the pluralists or the elitists? Remember that this question has two parts—whether the actual distribution of power in the United States follows an elitist or pluralist pattern and whether that pattern is the best rendering of democracy for our circumstances. These concerns form much of the substance of this text, so a complete answer must be set aside for now. But a couple of comments are in order right up front.

First, most students of American politics side with the pluralists descriptively. Obviously, different groups do have power in different areas. Moreover, the patterns of group success and failure do change from time to time. For example, the elderly as a group once exercised little influence in U.S. politics, but they have grown into a significant force that cannot easily be ignored in public policymaking. Yet the elitist theory also has descriptive merit. Despite the bewildering array of policy arenas and the proliferation of groups with influence on some aspect of public policy, larger patterns of policymaking do tend to take hold over the long term. Examining these long-term patterns, we discover that some groups benefit much more than others and that certain individuals have disproportionate influence over policymaking. In addition, certain issues simply do not make it on to the policy agenda in American politics.

Second, in addressing the *prescriptive* aspects of theories about who rules America, another concept is useful—that of republican politics. The **republican** position (not to be equated with the Republican party) recalls Plato's argument in *The Republic*. There Plato (Athenian, c. 427–347 B.C.) describes an ideal society in which only the citizens most capable of understanding human affairs (philosophers) would rule on behalf of the whole society. To reflect their role as servants of the city-state, or *polis*,

Plato argued against allowing these rulers any property at all, not even jewelry. And to keep these guardians from mistakenly identifying family interests with the interests of the polis, he advocated keeping them from having families at all—spouses and children would be shared universally. Republicanism in this classical definition is often contrasted with democracy, a contrast based on the extent to which influence in policymaking is concentrated in the hands of a few or spread widely among ordinary citizens.

Contemporary republicans advocate rule by the fittest to rule, often equating that quality with economic success in the private sector. The wisest policy, these contemporary republicans would argue, rarely emerges from throwing policy questions open to the untrained, inexperienced masses. An unequal distribution of influence in policymaking is thus welcomed by republicans. But that preference is not necessarily in conflict with democracy as explained earlier. What distinguishes an elitist distribution of power from a republican one may be a subtle matter of degree and emphasis—the extent to which the influential policymakers become isolated from and unresponsive to the mass of ordinary citizens. Republican theory quite clearly charges policymakers with a duty to care for the common good. When a political elite exercises power for its own good and the public interest takes a back seat, democracy has been subverted. But remember, the most interesting questions concern not whether a particular polity is a democracy but rather how democracy can be fostered and invigorated. Thus we turn next to previewing certain problems in the practice of democracy.

Problems in Democratic Life

To understand more clearly the obstacles to creating a more democratic society, we now turn to some of the most common and fundamental problems in contemporary democracies, including our own. These include the uneven distribution of power, failures to respect democratic rights, and citizen-government conflict that threatens the democratic process.

Unequal Distribution of Power

In *Animal Farm*, the celebrated satirical novel by George Orwell, the farm animals, after revolting and taking control of the farm, proclaim that "all animals are equal." Later, one faction (the pigs) takes increasing control. The rest of the animals wake up one morning to find their slogan, printed on the barnyard wall, altered to "All animals are created equal, but some are more equal than others." That, in fact, is what we find when we look closely at democratic politics: Particular individuals and groups enjoy great advantages in political life. Some of these advantages can pose serious threats to democratic politics. Here we look briefly at three such advantages: those generated by concentrations of wealth and economic power, those accruing from ease of political influence, and those that develop out of oligarchy, when democratic competition for leadership is curtailed.

ECONOMIC POWER Some socialists are fond of saying that economic power more or less equals political power. Though this may not always be true, it is a good approximation. In every democratic society, the financially better off usually have much more political access and influence than their numbers might suggest. For one thing, they can use their money for political purposes. A wealthy campaign contributor is likely to exercise a level of influence hundreds and perhaps thousands of times greater than the average voter. Although money is not everything in politics, it *is* a vital element; the unequal distribution of financial resources tends to skew democracy in the direction of the more affluent.

At another level, many of the major social decisions made in democratic societies fall outside democratic control. Important economic decisions made by corporations affect the lives of tens of thousands and yet are rarely based on democratic consultation. Business decisions made by a few individuals can shut down plants, alter work processes, flood the market with new products. That is, of course, how capitalism is supposed to work, but it also means that a relatively small number of people wield enormous economic power and make significant economic decisions. Yet these individuals are usually far removed from any sort of democratic control. Inevitably, those in politics are highly attentive to the interests and ideas of the business community, since business decisions affect the entire economic climate and may be a major source of trouble or success for political leaders.

In the latter part of the nineteenth century, a groundswell of popular opposition to economically powerful interests erupted in a series of pitched political clashes. Small farmers organized to battle the railroads. Factory workers organized to fight for better wages and decent working conditions. Much of U.S. politics around the turn of the century focused on the issue of economic power, which was then growing more and more concentrated in the hands of a few. Increasingly, government sought to limit and regulate concentrations of private economic power through legislation such as the Sherman Antitrust Act, enacted in 1890 to limit monopolies. Social movements also stirred government reforms on such key social and economic matters as child labor and the purity of food and drugs. In the twentieth century, the government gradually expanded its influence in these areas.

Great inequalities of wealth affect democratic life in yet another way. Often money can help to purchase the sorts of basic rights that should be open to all. For example, in theory the United States guarantees every person a fair trial and decent legal assistance. But in practice we know that money helps a great deal in obtaining the best legal representation. The same holds true in the areas of education and health care. In our society money makes many important options available and may even make the difference between having real choices and having no choices.

To return to the fundamental point: Great inequalities of wealth and great concentrations of economic power both pose serious threats to the relative equality that is one of the basic premises of democratic life. Of course, there are countervailing forces that limit the power of wealth. Sometimes sheer numbers can prevail over the power of money; sometimes powerful organizations such as trade unions can weigh in on the other side of the scale; sometimes the wealthy are divided among themselves. But as long as some have a great deal more than others, democrats have to worry that politics may serve moneyed interests at the expense of majority interests.

SPECIAL INTERESTS   In democratic societies, many groups organize and lobby for favorable policies from the government. Oil companies, for example, hire professional lobbyists to influence Congress, and the American Medical Association makes heavy campaign contributions to candidates the association feels will advance its interests in matters of health policy. The more powerful and better organized such **interest groups** are, the greater the influence they exert on government affairs. Over the years, interest groups often develop very friendly relationships with the legislators and bureaucrats responsible for overseeing their particular interests and as a result seem to be systematically favored by government policy. Once established, such strong alliances are difficult to dislodge. Well-organized segments of society come to enjoy subsidies, protective tariffs, or other benefits. Truckers benefit from one sort of special arrangement, dairy farmers another, tobacco growers another, and sugar producers yet another.

Amid all this special-interest policymaking, who is looking out for the public interest, for the needs and the long-term good of the public at large? When no one is watching out for such interests, democracy suffers, and political life becomes a way of gaining wealth, power, and advantage for the few at the expense of the general public. Just how serious a problem this can be we will see in Chapter 11, which focuses on the role of interest groups in American politics.

OLIGARCHY   We can define **oligarchy** as "rule by the few." By definition, oligarchy and democracy are incompatible. When leadership becomes entrenched and unresponsive, democracy suffers. The problems posed by oligarchies within democracies were first addressed extensively in Robert Michels's 1915 study *Political Parties*. Michels saw a tension between the democratic impulses that prompt the formation of political parties and the pressures toward bureaucratization that seem inevitably to remove initiative from the rank-and-file and place it in the hands of a governing elite better situated to exercise continuous power.

Accusations of oligarchy have been made many times in U.S. history. In the late nineteenth century, for example, popular movements decried economic oligarchy, maintaining that industrialists were able to manipulate the economic and political systems to their advantage at the expense of the ordinary citizen. President Franklin Roosevelt joined in a similar attack on vested economic interests during the 1930s. In 1968 many Democratic party members complained that oligarchy in the party limited the role of popular sentiment in the nominating process. Finally, both trade unions and corporations have been justly accused of oligarchic practices by which leaders are able to perpetuate themselves. (Note that even in a democracy, certain institutions are not usually expected to be organized in a democratic manner. Corporations, for example, are not run by majority rule except in very exceptional circumstances, when stockholders organize to press their interests. Churches, too, are often oligarchic. When are nondemocratic forms of decision making justified and why are provocative questions that can only be touched on peripherally in this book.)

Unresponsive political or economic oligarchies often find themselves locked in bitter and protracted conflicts with the people whom they seek to lead or control. These conflicts are costly for both sides and often fruitless for those challenging the status quo. Democracies must continually strive to reach some balance between effective leadership and mass influence.

Failure to Exercise Rights

According to many theorists, the quality of democratic life in large part depends on the willingness of the polity to embrace democratic attitudes, the degree of alienation among the people, and the level of public awareness and public understanding of the issues before the government. If the masses have undemocratic sentiments, if there is a strong animus against democratic institutions, if many are drawn to authoritarian movements, democracy will be severely tested.

The same holds true if large numbers of people are hostile to the major political institutions, if they feel alienated by politics as it is usually conducted. Finally, if the mass of the population is uninformed, if the average citizen cannot or does not understand what political life and political issues are all about, decisions will be made by the few, without considering the views of the real majority. Let us look more closely at each of these matters.

ANTIDEMOCRATIC ATTITUDES   We cannot be sure exactly what most German citizens were thinking in 1933 when the National Socialist German Workers (Nazi) party received 40 percent of the vote in the last relatively open election held in that country before World War II. No polls were conducted; the opinions of the "average" person were not tapped for posterity. Yet it does not seem too far-fetched to guess that large numbers of Germans no longer had strong ties to democratic politics, if they had ever had such ties. Democratic politics was new in the Germany of that day; only after World War I was a fully democratic political system installed. At a time when German democracy was just beginning to put down roots, many aspects of German society remained resolutely undemocratic. Strong patterns of military tradition and inherited aristocracy persisted. The Nazis represented perhaps the most extreme of the antidemocratic elements: Their ideology was not just critical of democracy but entirely alien to it.

Many factors conspired to give the Nazis their chance at political power in 1933, including a worldwide economic crisis, but there seems little doubt that many Germans had at best a shaky allegiance to democratic institutions and practices. The great majority of them embraced authoritarian leadership and were willing to accept violence and prejudice as integral parts of political and social life.

Josepf Goebbels, Hitler's minister of propoganda, emerges from a polling station in the 1933 German elections. The Nazi Party won a plurality of the vote that year; then, their power secure, they permitted no further political competition in Germany. *(National Archives)*

We cannot afford to be too smug about this, however, or to think that our country could never be like Germany in the early 1930s. Fascist movements in fact arose in almost every European country, as well as in the United States, between the wars. The attitudes we associate with Nazism, such as anti-Semitism and racism, were common throughout the West. After World War II, however, negative attitudes toward Jews declined significantly, as did notions about the inferiority of nonwhites. Perhaps we were simply lucky to have avoided our own version of fascism, or perhaps the strength of our democratic attitudes and institutions have protected us. But even recent data about American attitudes toward freedom of expression are disturbing. In 1954, for example, only 37 percent of the population thought that an atheist should be allowed to make a public speech, and only 6 percent approved of a communist teaching in college (see **Table 1-2**). By 1990 things had improved measurably, but even then fully half of the population objected to atheist teachers, and 37 percent would ban books written by homosexuals from libraries.

Why do such attitudes matter? Why does it matter if millions of Americans are anti-Semitic or racist or have very weak allegiance to democratic ideas? It matters because the sort of equal treatment in social and political life that democracy requires is impossible where prejudice is widespread. And in a time of crisis and conflict, such antidemocratic attitudes may surface and lead to widespread violations of civil liberties or violence against certain groups. This too threatens democratic life, as we will see in Chapter 2.

TABLE 1-2
SUPPORT FOR FREEDOM OF EXPRESSION
IN SPECIFIC SITUATIONS

	Percent Tolerating			
	1954	*1977*	*1987*	*1990*
Allow speech by:				
Atheist	37	62	70	72
Communist	27	56	61	64
Racist	—	59	62	62
Militarist	—	51	58	57
Homosexual	—	62	70	74
Oppose removing from library books written by:				
Atheist	35	59	67	66
Communist	27	55	59	64
Racist	—	61	65	64
Militarist	—	55	60	60
Homosexual	—	55	59	63
Allow to teach in college:				
Atheist	12	39	49	50
Communist	6	39	49	51
Racist	—	41	45	45
Militarist	—	34	41	43
Homosexual	—	49	59	63

SOURCE: Michael Corbett, *Political Tolerance in America* (New York: Longman, 1982), p. 36; NORC General Social Survey, 1987, 1990 (courtesy of the Institute for Social Science Research, University of North Carolina, Chapel Hill).

ALIENATION Experts have offered many definitions of **alienation**. Some authorities have equated it with the sense of being an outsider. Others have associated it with powerlessness, futility, or meaningless. But even though a vast literature in sociology is devoted to exploring and understanding the phenomenon, it is usually not hard to spot alienation when one sees it. Alienated people are turned off; they've given up on something. Alienated people feel that nobody cares, that things have turned against them, that the world is dishonest, that they and people like them are too weak to change things. The extremes of alienation are either total hostility and cynicism or passive withdrawal, complete apathy.

In recent years many Americans have suffered from fairly serious bouts of political alienation. How does this concern democratic politics? If large numbers of people are alienated, politics suffers. First, many people withdraw from political life, reducing the effectiveness and breadth of democracy. Alienation is often expressed in nonvoting, and it comes as something of a shock to many Americans to learn that we have among

(Text continues on page 24)

THE ALIENATION INDEX

The Harris Poll asks respondents whether they agree or disagree with the following statements:

The rich get richer and the poor poorer.
Most people with power try to take advantage of people like yourself.
What you think doesn't count very much anymore.
The people running the country don't really care what happens to you.
You're left out of things going on around you.

The alienation index is calculated by taking an average of the responses to the five statements. The higher the score, the greater the alienation.

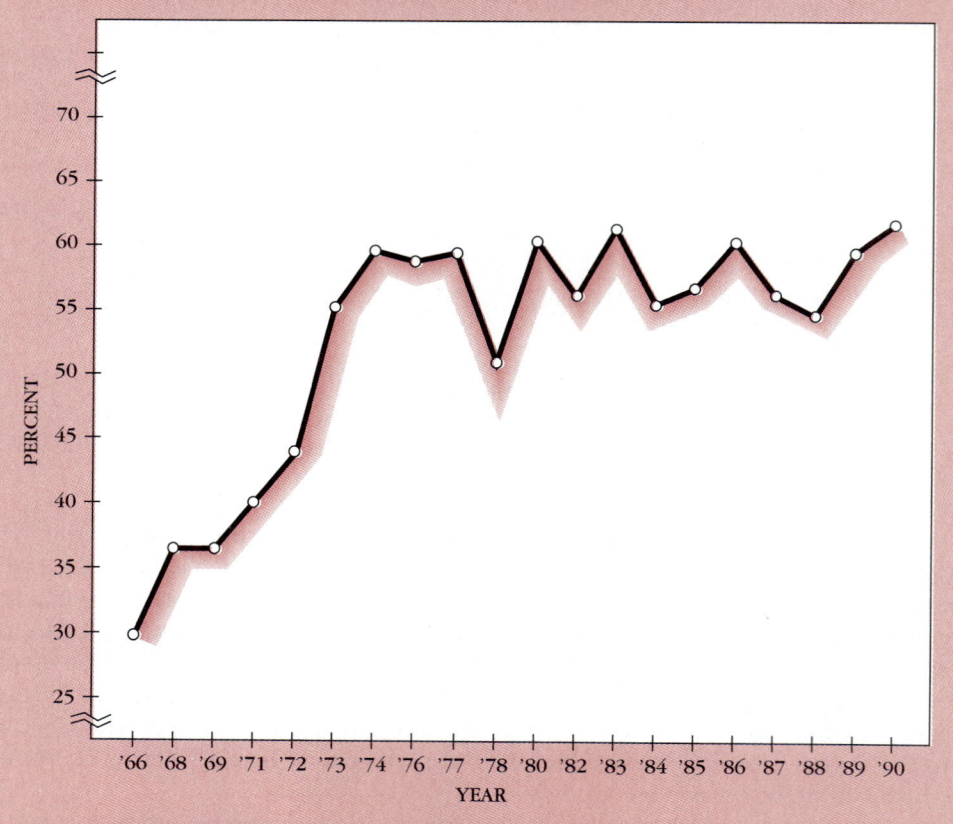

The most alienated voters in the December 1990 poll were those with less than a high school education (69 percent) and those making between $15,000 and $20,000 a year (68 percent). The least alienated were those with a postgraduate education (46 percent) and those making $50,000 and over (47 percent).
Source: Harris Poll, December 9, 1990. Copyright © 1990 Creators Syndicate, Inc. Used with permission.

PARTICIPATION IN ELECTIONS: COMPARING THE UNITED STATES WITH TWENTY-SEVEN OTHER NATIONS

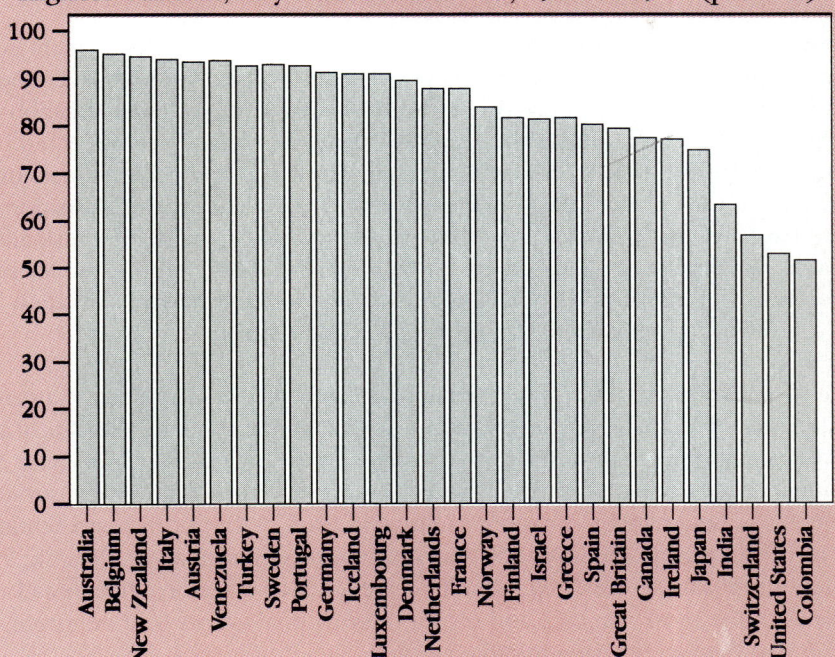

Highest Turnout, Any National Election, 1968 to 1986 (percent)

[Bar chart showing turnout percentages for: Australia, Belgium, New Zealand, Italy, Austria, Venezuela, Turkey, Sweden, Portugal, Germany, Iceland, Luxembourg, Denmark, Netherlands, France, Norway, Finland, Israel, Greece, Spain, Great Britain, Canada, Ireland, Japan, India, Switzerland, United States, Colombia]

Why is turnout in elections in other nations so much higher than in the United States? One reason is that some nations, such as Australia and Belgium, have compulsory voting—laws requiring electoral participation. Another is that other nations commonly hold their elections on nonworkdays, a practice that encourages participation. A third major reason is that other countries automatically register all persons eligible to vote, instead of requiring the individual to take the initiative to register, as in the United States. Registration laws in the American states, on the whole, do little to facilitate voting. (The size of the electorate in all of these countries except the United States is the number of registered voters. In the United States it is the voting-age population as computed by the U.S. Bureau of the Census.)

Source: William J. Keefe, Parties, Politics, and Public Policy *(Washington, D.C.: CQ Press, 1991), p. 196.*

the lowest levels of voter registration and voter turnout among democratic nations. It should be noted that several nations with high turnout rates—Australia, Belgium, and Italy—have laws that make voting compulsory. But this is not true of the others.

Alienated people may also pose a threat to democracy because of the hostility they have built up toward politics. In either case, the circle of meaningful participants in political life is narrowed.

Alienation presents a more complicated problem as well. A skeptic might suggest that some degree of alienation is to be expected in any political process, even the most democratic. Some people will always be put off because the political situation is not going their way. In recent years, for example, many men have been alienated by legislative and corporate initiatives to give women equal pay and professional advancement, making up for years of past discrimination. Perhaps this type of alienation is the price we have to pay for democratic change. The questions we need to ask are who is alienated, why are they alienated, and how widespread and deep is the alienation? The answers to these questions will help us to determine whether alienation is the sign of a defective democracy or the price of needed change.

IGNORANCE In theory, democracy demands an informed and politically aware citizenry. But what kind of information is required? What minimum level of political awareness is necessary to maintain a healthy democracy? Most American citizens have a hard time remembering the names of their national representatives (in a recent survey just over one-third could name their representative in the U.S. House of Representatives). Only a tiny fraction can identify their state and local representatives. Specific knowledge about proposals before Congress or of current policy is scarce. Widespread awareness of all but the most dramatic and recent international events is nonexistent. Does this mean that democracy is impossible here?

Just how much can we expect the public to understand about political life? isn't widespread public ignorance to be expected in any large, complicated modern society? How many of us are prepared to put in the time and energy required to master the intricacies of the General Agreement on Tariffs and Trade (GATT), to explore the scientific basis of alternative energy supplies, to assess the risks of toxic waste dumping, or to learn the particular circumstances of the independent republics that were once the Soviet Union? Clearly many such matters will remain beyond the awareness of ordinary citizens. What, then, can a reasonable democrat hope for?

At a minimum, we should expect the public to grasp, in a general sense, the major alternatives available on important questions of the day. Even if the average person cannot argue at length about the merits of restrictive monetary policy for discouraging inflation, for example, he or she can usually understand the basic economic issues involved in trade-offs between unemployment and inflation. An adequately informed citizenry is possible, provided that plentiful, accurate, and many-sided information about the issues is available and that individuals care enough to seek that information. When one of these factors is missing, widespread public ignorance results, and the quality of democratic life suffers.

DEMOCRACY: THE REAL AND THE IDEAL

The Relationship between Government and Citizen

The democratic ideal requires a relatively open, honest, and responsive relationship between citizens and government. But this relationship is often precarious. The power exercised by the citizenry might not be sufficient to keep the government responsive and under control. The power of political office might lead to corruption or give rise to imperial attitudes more appropriate to a monarchy. Citizens might also abuse the relationship, for example, by evading their responsibilities as voters or by disobeying reasonable and necessary laws.

Every society must also cope with conflict among the citizenry and between citizens and the government. Crime, disorder, and social and political combat challenge every society as well. In a democratic society, citizens expect such conflicts to be dealt with in a manner consistent with democratic norms. Let us now look a bit more closely at the issues of honesty and conflict, assessing how well contemporary societies live up to democratic standards.

HONESTY AND TRUST In our society, citizens and governments relate at many levels. In elections, candidates appeal to citizens for votes. Once in office, legislators and executives make and enforce laws that affect the lives of citizens. Yet the most common

The feelings of powerlessness, of not counting in the political process, can lead to alienation and despair. But people can also rebel against their powerlessness and demand a place in the political system. For African-Americans in the 1960s, the use of the ballot was a key to overcoming decades of powerlessness.
(© Bruce Davidson/Magnum)

way citizens encounter government authority is in the form of the school board official, the social worker, the police officer, the social security bureaucrat, the building inspector—that is, at the local level. Though we are usually taught to trust and respect such authority figures as teachers and police officers, at times encounters with these authorities breed a sense of grievance. In the ghetto, police are frequently feared or hated. Bureaucrats tend to be criticized for their tiresome attention to routine or for their insensitivity. And yet these and other government employees play essential roles in our lives.

The citizen-government encounter, then, is many-sided. Consider, for example, just one of the levels at which citizen and government relate: that of executive leadership. Political executives, such as the U.S. president, play a critical role in modern societies. What presidents say and don't say, what they decide and how they make decisions, and how they communicate their ideas to the public at large have significant conse-

The shootings that shocked the nation. The killing of four antiwar student demonstrators by National Guard troops at Kent State University raised the issue of how government force should be used when dealing with conflict and protest. (John Filo/Valley News Dispatch, Tarentum, PA)

quences for democratic life. At this level, democratic ideals furnish us with rather straightforward standards for judgment. Most obviously, we should expect a high level of integrity in a chief executive, as well as a determined effort to be honest and open with the public. Where such honesty and integrity are lacking, democratic practice is jeopardized. For example, while publicly vowing never to deal with terrorists, the Reagan administration in the mid-1980s secretly traded arms to Iran—an acknowledged instigator of terrorism—in exchange for American hostages being held in Lebanon by Iranian-sponsored terrorists. When this plan became known, the president's approval rating in the polls plunged.

HANDLING CONFLICTS   In May 1970, at the height of political protest over the Vietnam War, four students were shot to death and many others wounded by National Guard troops at Kent State University in Ohio. This tragedy underlined a key issue for democracies: how government authority should be used to deal with conflict and protest.

Throughout much of our history, in fact, deadly force has been used by both citizens and governments to settle disputes. But ours is no longer a frontier society; we are a long way from the Wild West.

Again, the sense of democratic norms is quite clear: We cannot use force, especially deadly force, easily and often if our society truly values individual life. A democrat wants to see such coercion reduced to a minimum. Widespread use of police power inevitably indicates a failure for democratic life. And if force is absolutely necessary, it should be used with considerable care. The painstaking care taken by Federal District Court Judge Patrick Kelly and by U.S. marshals and local law enforcement officers in dealing with massive confrontational abortion clinic protests in Wichita in 1991 is an encouraging example of the restrained use of force. A troubled conscience over the use of police power is a good sign in a democratic society. Whenever democratic leaders find the killing or coercing of some citizens easily acceptable, that nation's democratic ideals are in deep trouble.

Is Democracy Always the Best System?

For most of recorded history, democracy was not regarded very highly by most thinkers. Yet democratic practices have proved themselves rather effective over the past two centuries; the concept of government by consent of the governed has shown its staying power. Few people would now argue for absolute monarchy or for the rule of a hereditary landed aristocracy—political practices that once were extremely common and widely accepted. A remarkable tribute to the democratic ideal's current attractiveness was seen in 1989–1991 in the rush by the former Soviet satellites in Eastern Europe to embrace democratic forms despite substantial social uncertainties and economic costs.

Still, throughout the world, and even in democratic nations, arguments about the limitations of democracy persist. Advocates of authoritarian regimes argue that a par-

SUMMARY CHART
PROBLEMS IN CONTEMPORARY DEMOCRATIC LIFE: A SUMMARY

1. **Unequal Distribution of Power**

Example	*Possible Consequence*
Very unequal distribution of wealth	Excessive influence of the rich
Well-organized special interests	Political influence favoring such groups
Oligarchy—"rule by the few"	Lack of democratic procedure in organizations such as unions and corporations

2. **Failures to Accept Democratic Norms or to Exercise Democratic Rights**

Example	*Possible Consequence*
Existence of undemocratic attitudes in elites or public	Anti-democratic political leaders and movements; attempted coups; episodes of intolerance
Alienation	Apathy, lack of participation
Political ignorance	Manipulation by political leaders

3. **Problems in Relations between Citizens and Government**

Example	*Possible Consequence*
Lack of honesty on part of leaders	Political manipulation; abuses of power
Repression; excessive use of force	Intimidation; violations of rights and of political civility

ticular ruler or group of rulers is best suited to make decisions for the nation as a whole and that strong leadership is required to prevent chaos. Often we hear this argument made to justify military or other dictatorships; Deng Xiaoping and other leaders of the People's Republic of China made such arguments in brutally suppressing a democratic movement in 1989.

Communists often advance a different argument. They defend their rule by maintaining that only their political party with its particular theories truly understands how history works and which policies should be adopted. The communists' arguments often have a strongly moral tinge; dissenters are not only incorrect but immoral. This does not encourage a friendly attitude toward criticism and dissent: You are either with us or against us. As Fidel Castro put it in describing his views on the right to criticize: "Within the Revolution, everything; outside it, nothing." Of course, it was Castro and his supporters who defined what "within the Revolution" meant!

Others assert that democracy is a good idea but should not be pushed too far. In this view, similar to the position held by many of the American Founders, government needs to be "of the people" and "for the people" but not necessarily "by the people." Since the people as a whole will never be very well informed, intelligent, farsighted, or morally enlightened, the more astute, thoughtful, and experienced members of the community must assume a dominant role in political leadership. The people need good, enlightened leaders—individuals who are in many ways "better" than the average citizen. Democracy will work, then, when a dose of elitism infuses the system with

(Text continues on page 30)

COMPARATIVE PERSPECTIVE

THE CONSOCIATIONAL MODEL OF DEMOCRACY

In recent years, some political scientists have concluded that many democratic nations in Western Europe do not really operate according to the norms of majoritarian democracy but have evolved into a somewhat different system. Austria, Belgium, the Netherlands, and Switzerland all seem to have systems based on compromise and coalition rather than on the majoritarian winner-take-all pattern followed in the United States. Known as *consociational democracy*, this system follows certain unwritten rules to preserve stability and avoid conflict.

Each of these nations has clearly identifiable subgroups. Austria has long been divided politically and culturally between socialists and Catholics, Belgium has the French-speaking Walloons and the Dutch-speaking Flemings, the Netherlands has several religious and social-class subcultures, and Switzerland is made up of French, German, and Italian speakers.

In each nation, political patterns have developed to accommodate the interests of subgroups. Leaders of the various groups engage in extensive negotiations to avoid disagreements and splits that might lead to social conflict. Rather than settling issues by majority rule, they seek compromise.

The Swiss, for example, created the Federal Council, a seven-member executive office equivalent to our presidency. Elected by the parliament, the council allows all major political parties a share in government: Each of the three major parties is allocated two seats, and an important smaller party has one. The three linguistic groups are also guaranteed representation. Naturally, such a spirit of compromise extends into public policy.

To take another example, the Netherlands has institutionalized its form of coalition government. Rather than seeking a narrow majority of votes to win power, each party seeks to be a member of one large governing coalition. This pattern has been characterized as "accommodationist" for its effort to allocate a reasonable share of resources to each important group.

Of course, all democratic politics involves some compromise and accommodation. The significant point about consociational systems is that they have established norms of accommodation as part of their political processes, thus depending less on majority rule than America does today.

Sources: Arend Lijphart, The Politics of Accommodation: Pluralism and Democracy in the Netherlands *(Berkeley: University of California, 1968); Val R. Lorwin, "Segmented Pluralism: Ideological Cleavages and Political Cohesion in the Smaller European Democracies,"* Comparative Politics, *January 1971, pp. 141–75; Jeffrey Obler, "Assimilation and the Moderation of Linguistic Conflict in Brussels,"* Administration, *Winter 1974, pp. 400–432; Jeffrey Obler, Jurg Steiner, and Guido Diereckx, "Decision-making in Smaller Democracies: The Consociational Burden,"* Comparative Politics Series, *vol. 6 (Beverly Hills, Calif.: Sage, 1977), pp. 13–14, 21–33.*

the leadership and intelligence it needs. Oddly enough, political elites and activists often do show more respect for the norms of democracy than average citizens do, at least concerning many basic questions of civil liberties.

Another version of the argument for limited democracy was heard in the aftermath of the agitated 1960s and was articulated by Samuel Huntington, who quoted John Adams: "Democracy never lasts long. It soon wastes, exhausts and murders itself. There was never a democracy yet that did not commit suicide." The point is that the dynamics of democracy itself may run counter to other values, such as stability, efficiency, or effective government.

Although this text takes an opposing view, the argument is an important one and should be taken into account. We will return to these issues later. For now, consider that democracy in America, as well as elsewhere, has a good deal to say for itself after more than two centuries. Democratic practices, once widely imagined to be impractical and utopian, have shown that they can work and have yielded substantial measures of popular enlightenment, respect for individual rights, and concern for the common good. Though far from perfect, democratic systems can claim numerous accomplishments. Keep this at the forefront as we examine and attempt to appraise our American version of the democratic idea.

Struggles to Realize Democratic Ideals

Our discussion of democratic ideals and practices may have seemed somewhat abstract. We turn now to a few exemplary cases of the struggle to realize democratic ideals in the highly imperfect real world. These cases are brief, but their significance ought to be clear. From them we can draw many lessons useful in examining the operation of American government today.

Restricting Democracy

We look now at two cases where democracy was curtailed: the failure of Reconstruction after the Civil War, leading to the growth of segregation in the American South, and the phenomenon of McCarthyism, which severely limited expression rights and distorted political debate in this country in the early 1950s.

SEGREGATION IN THE UNITED STATES   Most of us were taught at a young age that the Civil War was fought to free the slaves and to realize the democratic ideal of equality for all. Perhaps a bit later we learned that the situation was more complicated, that democratic ideals were only a part of the story. In any event, the North won, and in the Thirteenth, Fourteenth, and Fifteenth amendments to the Constitution (the Civil War amendments), slavery was abolished and all U.S. citizens were guaranteed equal rights and equal protection under the law.

Oklahoma City, 1939. Segregated drinking fountains were but one part of an elaborate system of racial separation imposed and maintained by law and custom throughout the American South. The races were supposedly accorded separate but equal treatment, but in fact black facilities were generally far inferior to those provided for whites.
(The Bettmann Archive)

For more than a decade after the Civil War, northern troops occupied the South, and lengthy and intense political struggles were waged over how government in the South was to be reconstructed. Some people favored radical measures to secure full equality for freed slaves, and for a time in the 1870s there was some progress toward racial equality. Many blacks were elected to state and local offices, and whites and blacks mixed together on public transportation, in schools, and on juries. But others wished to turn back the clock and return as far as possible to a situation in which whites held the upper hand. In the end, the latter view prevailed. A bloody and terrible war had been fought at least in part to gain some measure of equality for blacks; these gains were substantially wiped out and a new system of white supremacy was restored by the 1880s.

A series of U.S. Supreme Court decisions also helped to restrict the meaning of the constitutional amendments passed after the Civil War. In 1877 the Court found that a state could not prohibit segregation in transportation, and in 1883 it sharply limited the application of the clause in the Fourteenth Amendment mandating equal protection of the laws for all citizens. In 1890 it upheld a Mississippi state law that *required* segregation in transportation.

Then, in the famous case of **Plessy v. Ferguson** in 1896, the Court established a constitutional standard for segregation—not overturned until 1954—declaring that "separate but equal" treatment of the races was legitimate under the Constitution.[3] Being treated as a separate group, the Court majority argued, did not imply inferiority.

> SUMMARY CHART
> ## COMMON ARGUMENTS AGAINST DEMOCRACY
>
> The common person is too ignorant to judge political issues
>
> Political leaders will pander to the lowest common denominator—popular fears and hatreds
>
> Political parties and interest groups will always be run by the few
>
> The wealthy will always have excessive influence
>
> Democracy leads to excessive demands on government creating overload and cynicism
>
> Democratic processes are often inefficient, time consuming, and corrupt
>
> Elections lead to short-run calculations and ignore long-term considerations
>
> The majority will often violate the rights of minorities

In the broadest sense this is true: The law must treat some cases differently and can do so with equal respect for the persons involved. But in the case of racial segregation on public transportation, the facilities spoke for themselves: The differences in comfort, security, and respect offered black passengers blatantly and deliberately violated the spirit of the law. Separate did, in fact, mean "inferior."[4]

As the rest of the country acquiesced, one southern state after another established remarkably comprehensive systems of separation of the races. First, blacks were gradually denied the right to vote through various subterfuges, including the white primary (nominating elections restricted to white voters), literacy tests, poll taxes, and the "grandfather" test (one could not vote unless one's grandfather had voted, which effectively excluded all blacks). Social segregation followed—on streetcars, in theaters, at water fountains, in boardinghouses, restrooms, and waiting rooms, at sporting and other recreational events, in mental institutions, orphanages, prisons, and hospitals, on jobs, in housing, in churches, and finally in funeral homes, morgues, and cemeteries. The breadth of the new system of segregation can be judged by the extremes to which it sometimes was carried: A 1909 curfew law in Mobile, Alabama, required blacks to be off the streets by 10:00 P.M.; a 1915 Oklahoma law required segregated telephone booths; laws in North Carolina and Florida required the separate storage of school textbooks.

A racist ideology elaborated on the new system. Many psychologists and biologists at the turn of the twentieth century held that the black race was inherently inferior to the white race in intelligence and morals. In the meantime, white violence against

(Text continues on page 34)

Plessy v. Ferguson

In 1890 the Louisiana legislature passed a law for the "comfort of passengers" that "all railway companies . . . carrying passengers in their coaches in this State, shall provide equal but separate accommodations for the white and colored races." Until this time the races had traveled together in second-class railway cars, though it was generally "whites only" in first-class cars.

The law evoked a strong protest from the large and vocal black community in New Orleans, leading to a deliberate test of its constitutionality. On June 7, 1892, Homer Adolph Plessy, a man seven-eighths white and one-eighth black, boarded an East Louisiana Railway train in New Orleans and took a seat in a car reserved for whites. When he refused to move to the colored car, he was arrested and brought before Judge John H. Ferguson of the Criminal District Court of the Parish in New Orleans, who ruled against him. The case was appealed to the State Supreme Court and then to the U.S. Supreme Court, which handed down its decision in 1896.

The issue was whether Plessy had been denied his privileges, immunities, and equal protection of the law under the Fourteenth Amendment. Writing for the Court majority, Justice Henry Brown declared that the Louisiana statute did *not* deprive blacks of equal protection of the laws, provided that they were given accommodations equal to whites, thus establishing the precedent for "separate but equal" facilities. He also stated that the Fourteenth Amendment was not intended to abolish distinctions based on color or to enforce social equality, citing many examples of already established segregation in support of his argument. In a complicated, convoluted, and subsequently much denigrated opinion, Brown declared: "If the civil and political rights of both races be equal one cannot be inferior to the other civilly or politically. If one race be inferior to the other socially, the Constitution of the United States cannot put them upon the same plane."

In his famous and eloquent dissent, Justice John Marshall Harlan spoke for the deeper conscience and ideals of the country, writing: "In view of the Constitution, in the eye of the law, there is in this country no superior, dominant, ruling class of citizens. There is no caste here. Our Constitution is color-blind, and neither knows nor tolerates classes among its citizens. In respect of civil rights, all citizens are equal before the law."

blacks increased, with the Ku Klux Klan growing more active. What evolved out of the Civil War and Reconstruction periods turned out to be, from the standpoint of the democratic spirit, about the worst possible outcome short of a return to slavery. This despite the many voices raised in favor of other options, even among southern whites. Many southern conservatives, though taking a paternalistic view of race relations, did not intend to create a system of total separation of the races. Unfortunately, over the final twenty years of the nineteenth century, the South systematically eliminated many legal rights for black people. Formal segregation became the law of the land and, once installed, lasted a long time. This testifies to the failure of democratic leadership to live up to its own ideals.

McCARTHYISM AND THE LIMITING OF DISSENT   In February 1950, Senator Joseph R. McCarthy, a Republican, who had just been elected U.S. senator from Wisconsin, announced that he had a list of 205 Communists who were employed at the State Department. The charge was spectacular and made headlines. It was just the first of many such charges of Communist subversion in the U.S. government that Senator McCarthy made during his brief but extraordinary career. McCarthy was the most prominent among many people in the late 1940s and early 1950s who alleged that spies and subversives had infiltrated American society and government and were destroying our capacity to defend ourselves against the Soviet Union.

McCarthy's charges targeted the highest levels of the government. He went so far as to list former secretary of state and five-star general George C. Marshall (author of the Marshall Plan for European reconstruction) and even President Eisenhower himself as "disloyal." Yet McCarthy was never able to substantiate his charges in even a single case. Despite this, he commanded public attention for several years, a bully ruling public discussion through dramatic charges, bluff, and intimidation. In the hysteria over fears of Communist subversion, many upstanding Americans lost their jobs, self-respect, and personal honor. Loyalty oaths were instituted, particularly for teachers. Investigations on "un-American" activities spread throughout the land. Federal employees and many in the private sector were subjected to security checks—an estimated 13.5 million in all. Many Americans became afraid to express their political views. It was a time of shame and intimidation in American politics. How did it come about?

First, we have to recall the historic context of the time. World War II had just ended, with the United States and the Soviet Union as allies. There were hopes that the wartime alliance would continue and shape the peace. But this was not to be. Conflicts developed that quickly led to the Cold War. The Soviets created a sphere of control in Eastern Europe that was to last until the great revolutions of 1989. America and its European allies created the North Atlantic Treaty Organization to defend themselves. The brief euphoria of victory quickly gave way to an atmosphere of rivalry and fear. Over a short period of years, the Soviets developed their own nuclear weapons; North Korea invaded South Korea, and the United States became involved in a bitter protracted war there; a revolutionary movement triumphed on the Chinese mainland, bringing the world's most populous nation under Communist rule. It seemed to many that communism was an aggressive, international movement, directed from Moscow, which was attempting to destroy the West.

The idea of internal subversion helped to explain the losses America experienced after its World War II victory. Why had Eastern Europe fallen under Soviet influence? How had the Soviets developed the bomb? How had China been "lost?" Many critics of the Democratic administrations of Franklin Roosevelt and Harry Truman, especially conservatives, alleged that "subversives" inside the government had been the cause. This point of view seemed to be supported by revelations that there had in fact been Soviet spies in the Canadian and British bureaucracies. In March 1947, President Truman established an employee loyalty program in the federal government. In the next four years the Civil Service Commission cleared over 3 million people; 2,000 more resigned, and 212 were dismissed for "doubtful loyalty." But no Soviet spy ring was ever uncovered. In the process, however, a list of "subversive" organizations was established, and any association with such groups, even in the distant past, was sufficient to raise some doubt about a person's current loyalty.

The Truman loyalty program, however, did not slow down the zeal of those who wanted to root out subversives. Several spectacular cases focused public attention on the issue. In 1948, Alger Hiss, who had served in the State Department and been

Senator Joseph McCarthy turned his search for "subversives" against the U.S. Army in 1954. Here, McCarthy attacks while Army counsel Joseph Welch listens, incredulous and troubled. Welch later accused McCarthy of lacking all decency. *(Senate Historical Office)*

involved in shaping the charter of the United Nations, was accused by Whittaker Chambers of being a former Soviet agent. Chambers tried to document his charges before the House Un-American Activities Committee (HUAC). Hiss denied that he had been a spy; he was later convicted of perjury. Officials of the Truman administration, including Secretary of State Dean Acheson, had defended Hiss.

In 1949 leaders of the American Communist party were convicted under provisions of the Smith Act, which made it illegal to form a group that advocated the violent overthrow of the U.S. government. The Supreme Court upheld the convictions in *Dennis et al.* v. *United States* (1951) despite the fact that there was no evidence that the party leaders had taken any specific steps toward overthrowing the government.[5] In 1950 a U.S.-British spy ring surfaced involving Julius and Ethel Rosenberg in the United States. The Rosenbergs were convicted of espionage involving information related to the building of nuclear weapons and executed in 1953. Many people believed that one or both of them may have been innocent. Recent information from Soviet archives seems to indicate that they were spies but that the secrets they transmitted were of questionable importance.

In this atmosphere of fear and mistrust, a "witch hunt" developed, focused on exposing individuals regarded as disloyal or unpatriotic. The HUAC held hearings around the country, again and again asking people, "Are you now or have you ever been a member of the Communist party?" It investigated Communist influence in the movie industry, asking witnesses to "name names" of others they had met at Communist party meetings as much as fifteen years before. Even to be called to testify meant public embarrassment and often led to loss of employment and worse. The distinguished playwright Arthur Miller refused to name names and was cited for contempt by the committee, though a court later set aside his conviction. Miller wrote a scathing play, *The Crucible*, set in Salem, Massachusetts, during the time of witch hangings, to express his opposition to what was happening in American society. Miller argued, like many others, that the hysteria of the times was forcing people to hand over their conscience to bullying public officials who preyed on popular fears. Many state legislatures started their own investigations of un-American activities, and thousands of Americans were forced to prove that they were in fact loyal citizens. Critics maintained that these practices were an effort at thought control more appropriate in the sorts of totalitarian societies we were opposed to. Any views even vaguely sympathetic to the USSR, critical of American foreign policy, or seeming to have a socialistic bent became a source of suspicion. The insulting term *pinko* was coined to refer to someone who might not be a "Red" but was sufficiently close to have some of the color rub off. In this atmosphere, self-censorship prevailed, and there was a general suppression of critical voices.

The McCarthy era was not the first "Red scare"—there had been an earlier one after the Bolshevik Revolution of 1917. In both cases, fear and mistrust overrode concerns for civil liberties. During the McCarthy era it was all too easy for politicians to employ the "subversives in government" issue to gain public attention. Richard Nixon, for example, early on established his reputation on this basis. Many average Americans simply did not comprehend the nature of the threat to civil liberties at the time, and many among the political elites were uncertain and anxious to protect themselves from attack as being "soft on communism."

Of course, communism was a real threat, but the fear of domestic subversion created a profound constriction of free thought. It was not until the tragedy of the Vietnam War that it again became possible to question openly the basics of U.S. foreign policy. The hangover of the McCarthy era lasted far beyond the life of its namesake, who was censured by the U.S. Senate in 1954, rapidly lost power, and died in 1958.

Extending Democracy

After reviewing examples of democracy in retreat from storms of public passion, we now turn to two efforts to extend democracy: the fight for women's suffrage and the Progressive legacy of referendum and initiative. As these examples show, even in a democratic system, reform is not always easy.

THE FIGHT FOR WOMEN'S SUFFRAGE   The Grimké sisters of Charleston, South Carolina, were a formidable pair. Long before the issues of women's suffrage and women's rights gained significant support on the public agenda in the United States, the Grimkés were

The power of an idea whose time has come! The demand for women's suffrage had been around for more than half a century in American politics, but it required painstaking work over generations to make reality happen. Woodrow Wilson helped push the necessary constitutional amendment. (The Bettmann Archive)

articulating concepts very close to those we have become familiar with in recent decades:

> Human beings have *rights*, because they are *moral* beings: the rights of all men grow out of the moral nature, and as all men have the same moral nature, they have essentially the same rights.... Now, if rights are founded in the nature of our moral being, then the mere circumstance of sex does not give to man higher rights and responsibilities, than to a woman.
> Angelina Grimké, 1836

> In most families it is considered a matter of far more consequence to call a girl off from making a pie, or a pudding, than to interrupt her whilst engaged in her studies.
> Sarah Grimké, 1838

The Grimkés were among the more radical and forward-looking of the early advocates of women's rights. Like many other campaigners for women's equality, they participated in the antislavery movement. To many women the position of black slaves paralleled the position of women. Both were excluded from full participation in democratic society because of physical attributes.

The Grimkés began their campaign against slavery and for women's suffrage in the 1830s. More than eighty years of prolonged political and social struggle were to pass before the basic democratic right to vote was granted to American women. The story of the battle for suffrage testifies to the tenacity of opposition to democratic rights and, even more, to the tenacity required to overcome such opposition. Looking back, it seems remarkable that the issue was controversial at all. Why, after all, shouldn't women have the right to vote? But in asking the question this way, we fail to understand how deeply rooted were the sentiments that stood in the way of female equality.

Until the late nineteenth century, most men—and most women as well—believed that women had a proper "place" in society, and that place did not include full-fledged participation as citizens. Former president Grover Cleveland voiced this position in 1905: "Sensible and responsible women do not want the vote. The relative positions assumed by men and women in the working out of our civilization were assigned long ago by a higher intelligence than ours." Political life was not entirely out of bounds to women—for example, some women participated in political campaigns in the early part of the nineteenth century—but equal participation was regarded as a violation of the natural order of things. Women were to play a domestic role, maintaining the home and rearing children.

In 1848 the first feminist convention was held in Seneca Falls, New York, and many authorities date the struggle for suffrage from that meeting. The convention issued the so-called Declaration of Sentiments, one of the most significant documents in the history of feminism, which not only called for suffrage but also set forth an entire women's rights ideology of the sort that emerged fully only in the twentieth century. It was clear to some women even then that the struggle for equality between the sexes went far beyond the right to vote.

But that right itself proved difficult to obtain. The passage of the Civil War amendments raised some hopes. When Susan B. Anthony was arrested for casting a ballot in the federal election of 1872, her defense was that the Fourteenth Amendment's privileges and immunities clause gave constitutional status to her claim to the right to vote. A lower federal court did not agree.[6] As mentioned earlier, the Supreme Court thereafter consistently narrowed the scope of the Civil War amendments.

In 1878, a constitutional amendment to give women the right to vote was introduced for the first time in the Senate. Eleven years later, it reached the floor of the Senate but was voted down. Meanwhile, the suffrage movement split into moderate and radical branches, and for a time the movement fell into decline. Yet as social attitudes began to change, some states moved to grant women the vote. The first to do so were in the West—Wyoming, Utah, Colorado, and Idaho. And by the turn of the century, more women had the time and energy necessary to join the movement. Families had grown smaller, and child rearing took up less time. Women were graduating from universities in larger numbers, considerably swelling the pool of leadership for a women's movement.

Women began to organize on a state-by-state basis and to campaign for suffrage reform within the states. Between 1910 and 1913, they succeeded in Washington and California. Then Illinois granted women the right to vote in presidential elections. At the same time, however, the opposition to women's suffrage was also growing. A formal association was created in 1911 to defeat the suffrage effort. This opposition drew support from many sources: textile manufacturers, who feared that women would favor stricter child labor legislation and thus limit the use of children in their factories; brewers and distillers, who feared that women would help to pass laws prohibiting the sale of alcohol; and many southerners, who felt that women's suffrage would endanger white supremacy. And the traditional arguments continued about the appropriate "place" for women. For a long time political leaders played almost no role in the voting rights struggle. In 1912 the Progressive party became the first major political party to endorse the vote for women, but the opposition was still strong enough to bring about the overwhelming defeat of a constitutional amendment in the Senate in 1914.

Women's organizations kept the pressure on at both state and national levels. In 1916 both the Democratic and Republican parties endorsed the idea of the individual states granting suffrage to women. Two years later, women's votes contributed significantly to President Woodrow Wilson's reelection in states in which they could vote for president. Wilson then advised a delegation of Democrats to support the constitutional amendment. In January 1918 the House did so, 274–136, but the Senate rejected the measure by two votes. A new Congress passed the amendment in June 1919, and after fierce battles in state legislatures, the necessary three-fourths of the states ratified it by August 1920. It had been seventy-two years since the Seneca Falls convention and eighty-four since Angelina Grimké had spoken of rights growing out of men's and women's status as equal moral beings.

The ideals on which U.S. political life was founded pointed toward women's suffrage from the start. But cultural assumptions pointed in the other direction—toward a subordinate and unequal role for women in politics and society. To extend democratic rights to half the population required decades of gradual social change plus the determined efforts of women's rights advocates. And the struggles over women's rights continue, as more recent political battles over the equal rights amendment, abortion, parental leave, and many other issues indicate. How equal are women in our society? Should equality extend to every area of life? If so, how should it be extended? It is instructive to keep in mind how long it took to provide the most basic democratic right to 50 percent of the people.

PROGRESSIVE REFORM: LIMITED DIRECT DEMOCRACY

> [He] is a creature who is vile, infamous, degraded and putrescent. Here he sits in senile dementia, with gangrened heart and rotting brain, grimacing at every reform and chattering in impotent rage against decency and morality, while he is going to his grave in snarling infamy.[7]

Hiram Johnson didn't mince words, but political reform isn't for the faint of heart. In case you thought negative campaigning was a recent invention, this was 1910. The object of this tirade was the patrician publisher of the *Los Angeles Times*, Harrison Gray Otis. Johnson was a candidate for governor of California and a Progressive reformer; Otis was not.

The people "came to the government which they had made, intending to use it, and they found that it was already in use," wrote Benjamin Dewitt, Progressive ideologue, in 1915. The **Progressive** heirs of populist democratic enthusiasms believed that the remedy for democratic ills was more democracy. Reforms designed to take back the government from the politicians and special interests included nonpartisan local elections and boards and commissions of appointed "experts" to manage government functions previously run by party pols. One of the most promising reforms was the inauguration of limited direct democracy through the referendum, the initiative, and the recall ("the bastard triplets," according to a Santa Barbara lawyer who declared that of all political evils, "these fads are the worst").

Whereas James Madison had mistrusted the mob, the Progressives mistrusted the mob's chosen representatives. The **referendum** allows ordinary voters a chance to approve or disapprove legislation already passed by the legislature. The **initiative** allows a petition drive go around the legislature to place new legislation—even constitutional amendments—on the ballot for voter approval. The **recall** allows government officials to be removed from office by petition and popular vote. Governor Hiram Johnson persuaded the California legislature to approve all three in 1911.

Referendums in this country date back to the American Revolution, when several states submitted their new constitutions to citizens for approval. But to allow legislation

DEMOCRACY: THE REAL AND THE IDEAL

Danes celebrate the defeat of the referendum on European union in 1992. The narrow defeat of the treaty was a serious setback to plans for European integration, and it was a considerable surprise. Referenda provide an opportunity for citizens to express their opinions very directly on matters of public policy. The outcome is not always what leaders expect. (Nordfoto/Gamma-Liaison)

to be created by ordinary balloting wasn't an accepted notion until the late nineteenth century. California wasn't the first American state to institute the referendum and the initiative—that honor belongs to South Dakota in 1898. By 1918 twenty-three states and many more local governments had adopted this means of letting citizens take lawmaking into their own hands. Voters in Oregon put the initiative to extensive use at the beginning of the twentieth century, rapidly passing a series of reforms that provided for the direct election of U.S. senators, the establishment of the country's first presidential primary, the abolition of the poll tax, and suffrage for women. For a time initiative and referendum (I&R) were known as the "Oregon system."

Use of I&R declined in the 1920s, but there was a surge of popular legislation in the 1930s as people sought solutions to the economic problems of the Great Depression. Voters passed measures to protect the family farm and to provide pensions for the elderly; Nebraskans cut costs by eliminating one house of their state legislature.

What are the advantages of referendum and initiative? Some are a more accountable government; better-informed, more engaged citizens; and a check against a concentration of power in the legislature itself or in cozy relationships between the legislature and certain "client" groups. What are the disadvantages? Legislation or initiatives may be poorly written or may simply be too complicated for ordinary voters to consider carefully. Especially in a large state like California, the process will be available only to organized interests with substantial resources, and the prize may go to the biggest spender—with contributions coming from interests outside the state. Initiatives may

(Text continues on page 43)

Vote Wisely

Proposition 128 ("Big Green"), an initiative on the ballot in California in 1990, contained the following section:

SECTION 15.   Part 8 is added to Division 26 of the Health and Safety Code, to read:

PART 8.   STRATOSPHERIC OZONE LAYER PROTECTION

44450.   For purposes of this Part:

(a) "Group I chemical" means chlorofluorocarbon-11, chlorofluorocarbon-12, chlorofluorocarbon-113, chlorofluorocarbon-114, chlorofluorocarbon-115, halon-1211, halon-1301, halon-2402, carbon tetrachloride, methyl chloroform, and any mixture containing one or more such chemical.

(b) "Group II chemical" means any hydrochlorofluorocarbon (HCFC) and any other chemical determined by the Air Resources Board to have the potential to deplete stratospheric ozone, and any mixture containing one or more such chemical.

44451.   (a) No later than January 1, 1993:

(1) The maximum feasible recovery and recycling of Group I chemicals shall be conducted during the servicing or disposal of any air conditioning and refrigeration systems and appliances, including vehicular air conditioners, and during the disposal of building and appliance insulation;

(2) Any person shall be prohibited from manufacturing, selling, or offering for sale or use any Group I chemical in a container which contains less than 15 pounds of such chemical (except for specific pharmaceutical applications and fire extinguishing applications for which the Board, after a public hearing, has determined there is no commercially available adequate alternative);

(3) Any person shall be prohibited from manufacturing, selling, or offering for sale or use any packaging material which contains or was manufactured with a Group I chemical; and

(4) The Board shall adopt regulations to ensure that any substitute or replacement for a Group I chemical does not endanger human health.

Chlorofluorocarbon-115? Methyl chloroform? Sure, it sounds nasty, but don't you need a degree in organic chemistry just to understand the arguments about whether it is eating a hole in the ozone layer? And look again at 44451 (a) (1): "The maximum feasible recovery and recycling . . ."? Whose standard of feasibility will be used here? Does this mean what's feasible given the laws of physics or the laws of economics? Is this the right stuff to be determined through balloting by ordinary citizens?

encourage shortsighted, selfish policies since the decision is made by private individuals voting secretly; they may also encourage tyrannous majorities.

Since the acid debates surrounding its approval in 1911, the initiative has been an active tool of California politics. National attention focused on the California initiative in 1978 with the passage of Proposition 13, a property tax measure seen as the first shot in a national taxpayers' revolt. The California initiative was back in the news in 1990 with a contest with national implications: a battle between competing environmental initiatives. This battle points up both the strengths and weaknesses of the initiative as a tool for extending democracy.

Six "ecoprops" appeared on the ballot in November 1990. The largest was a sprawling amalgam of environmental protection measures that had failed in the legislature. It was called "Big Green." Big Green had the backing of the Sierra Club, the National Wildlife Federation, the California League of Conservation Voters, and the National Resources Defense Council. It would have established programs to regulate pesticide use to protect food and agricultural workers, phase out the use of certain pesticides (carcinogens or ozone depleters) on food, require reduced emissions of gases contributing to global warming, limit oil and gas extraction in coastal waters, require oil spill prevention and contingency plans, create an oil spill prevention and response fund from fees paid by oil deliverers, establish new water quality criteria and monitoring plans, create an elective office of "environmental advocate," appropriate $40 million for environmental research, and authorize $300 million in bonds for ancient redwood acquisition and forestry projects. Whew! The language of the proposition itself (eleven pages, double-columns, of printing much smaller than what you see on this page) was often highly technical. To complicate matters further, there was a competing initiative on the ballot ("Big Brown," derided the environmentalists) that offered a timber industry alternative to the Big Green forest provisions. This is an example of the Doppelgänger* effect that haunts initiatives—a competing but relatively weak proposition is offered by the opposition in the hope of drawing support away from the initial more rigorous proposition or at least muddying the electoral waters. Supporters of Big Green raised $5 million; opponents, according to the Sierra Club, spent $11 million to defeat it. On election day the distribution of votes looked about like the distribution of dollars—36 percent in favor, 64 percent opposed. Only one environmental proposition out of six passed—a constitutional amendment banning the use of gill nets off the California coast. (Is this a matter for the state *constitution*? See Chapter 2.)

A variety of factors defeated Big Green. Voters were nervous. The United States had begun a massive buildup of troops in the Persian Gulf in response to Iraq's invasion of Kuwait, and the economy was mired in recession. The ballot was long (twenty-eight measures), and voters were cranky as a result of some highly publicized scandals. The opposition had a simple slogan: "It does too much. It costs too much." Environmental measures also lost in Missouri, Oregon, and New York. Monday morning quarterbacks had a heyday explaining the loss. (Text continues on page 45.)

---

*A Doppelgänger is a ghostly counterpart to a living person—especially one that haunts the living double.

COMPARATIVE PERSPECTIVE

THE REFERENDUM IN SWITZERLAND

In Switzerland, final decisions about law and constitutional issues do not rest with a national supreme court or with the people's legislative representatives; they are left firmly in the hands of the people. Based on their own democratic traditions, dating back to the Middle Ages, the Swiss incorporated the popular referendum in their constitution in 1848. At first the referendum could be used only to pass on constitutional amendments proposed by parliament. It was later expanded so that the people could propose constitutional amendments and rule on legislative bills.

How does this work in practice? If fifty thousand signatures are gathered, voters can hold a referendum on any legislative bill. With one hundred thousand signatures, voters can submit a constitutional amendment, which is first debated in parliament and then voted on by the public. There is no limit to the sort of issue that can be proposed as a constitutional amendment in this manner. For example, in recent years a constitutional amendment was passed requiring a system of hiking trails throughout the nation.

When it was first introduced, many observers expected that the referendum would chiefly allow for new initiatives to arise directly from popular sentiments. This has sometimes happened, but more often the effect has been to delay passage of legislation that would otherwise have been enacted by parliament. For example, because of repeated defeats in referendums, Swiss women did not obtain the right to vote until 1971; the Swiss parliament would have agreed to women's suffrage decades earlier. A similar situation delayed laws exempting conscientious objectors from military service.

Sometimes the referendum has tyrannized weak minorities. Some anti-Semitic rules were approved early in the twentieth century, prohibiting Jews from slaughtering animals in a manner required by their religious code. Yet efforts to penalize minorities, such as foreign workers living in Switzerland, have failed. Sometimes referendums have been used merely to educate the public about particular issues; approval was beside the point.

One can raise many questions about the dangers and strengths of the Swiss arrangement. Turnout is often low for referendums, ranging from 30 to 50 percent, and propaganda campaigns can be intense. In the Swiss system we see the danger of delaying useful changes and of failing to respect the rights of less powerful groups. However, the referendum has increased the legitimacy of political decisions: Responsibility shifts from courts, politicians, and bureaucrats directly to the people, who must then accept the praise or the blame for the outcomes.

Source: Jurg Steiner, European Democracies *(New York: Longman, 1986), chaps. 8 and 9.*

But the real question is, should Big Green have come before the voters in the first place? Is this an appropriate way of extending democracy? Proponents say the initiative is valuable as a means of getting around the special interests' hold on the legislature. Particularly in environmental matters, where certain concentrated economic interests on one side compete with large but diffuse interests on the other, the initiative provides democracy's best chance. Opponents say that the initiative process itself merely exaggerates economic advantages, that it encourages shortsighted, selfish voting on pocketbook and social welfare issues, and that many questions are simply too technical to be placed before ordinary voters.

The long-term record of statewide initiatives in America shows no consistent ideological or economic turn. A forty-year study done in 1984 showed a fifty-fifty split between conservative and liberal victories.[8] And voters don't always simply vote their pocketbook. For example, only three out of nineteen major tax cut initiatives were successful on state ballots from 1978 (the year of the Proposition 13 success) to 1984 (when tax cut fever had waned).[9] Oddly enough, political leaders as different in their views as Ronald Reagan and Ralph Nader have strongly advocated the use of I&R. As Nader put it: "We have to exercise that democratic muscle . . . Without it, democracy isn't an accountable mechanism. The [ordinary] legislative option . . . has shown again and again that it is very subject to being bought . . . or rented."[10]

Conclusions

Democracy is easy to love but harder to define. It is harder still to know how to encourage democracy in the rough-and-tumble of ordinary politics and amid the distractions of everyday life. Democracy isn't a place you get to. It isn't a state to be achieved, celebrated, and then frozen in parchment, parades, and the apotheosis of patriots. Democracy is a *process*, a way of political life committed to principles respecting human dignity and the ability of humans to direct their own affairs. Are there cutoff points or plateaus that tell us whether or not a nation is democratic? Although we can specify various criteria for determining whether a country is democratic, no one has devised a universal formula for going about this. In the end, democracy is always a matter of degree, and judgments about the degree of democracy are inherently controversial. Is the United States democratic? Certainly. But as the United States changes, and as the world changes around us, the real question is, what shall we do now to maintain and extend our democratic life together? This text is intended to help to address that question more ably. Is the United States more democratic than it was twenty or fifty or a hundred years ago? In many ways, it undoubtedly is. Are there still issues, suggested by democratic ideals, that the American polity needs to address? Every citizen must answer that question individually. For the authors, this textbook is a partial answer to that question.

Glossary Terms

alienation
basic rights
capitalism
democracy
democrat
due process of law
egalitarian democracy
elitism
equal protection of the laws
initiative
interest group
interest group liberalism

liberal democracy
majoritarian democracy
majority rule
maximalist view of democracy
minimalist view of democracy
oligarchy
Plessy v. *Ferguson*
pluralism
Progressive
recall
referendum
republican

Notes

[1] Robert Dahl, *A Preface to Democratic Theory* (Chicago: University of Chicago Press, 1963), chap. 5.
[2] Theodore S. Lowi, *The End of Liberalism* (New York: Norton, 1979), chap. 3.
[3] 163 U.S. 537.
[4] See Charles Lofgren, *The Plessy Case* (New York: Oxford University Press, 1987).
[5] 341 U.S. 494.
[6] David M. O'Brien, *Constitutional Law and Politics*, vol. 1 (New York: Norton, 1991), pp. 655–656.
[7] *Initiative and Referendum in California: A Legacy Lost?* (Sacramento: League of Women Voters of California, 1984), p. 9.
[8] Austin Ranney, "Referendums and Initiatives, 1984," *Public Opinion*, December 1984–January 1985, pp. 15–17.
[9] David D. Schmidt, "Government by the People," *Public Citizen*, June 1986, p. 39.
[10] Ibid., p. 12.

Selected Readings

VARIOUS DEFINITIONS OF DEMOCRACY

Democratic theory has a long history, starting with the Athenians in the fifth century B.C. Consult Walter Agard, *What Democracy Meant to the Greeks* (Madison: University of Wisconsin Press, 1960); T. R. Glover, *Democracy in the Ancient World* (New York: Cooper Square, 1966). I. F. Stone, after a long career as an insurgent journalist, wrote *The Trial of Socrates* (Boston: Little, Brown, 1988) to argue that the Athenians put Socrates to death for his basic antidemocratic ideals.

Egalitarian democracy is the subject of Ronald M. Glassman, *Democracy and Equality: Theories and Programs for the Modern World* (New York: Praeger, 1989); and of Vernon Van Dyke, *Equality and Public Policy* (Chicago: Nelson-Hall, 1990). **Liberal democracy** is examined in Charles R. Beitz, *Political Equality: An Essay in Democratic Theory* (Princeton, N.J.: Princeton University Press, 1989).

Much has been written about the **elitist theories of government**. For broad comparative studies, see Eva Etzioni-Halevy, *Fragile Democracy: The Use and Abuse of Power in Western Societies* (New Brunswick, N.J.: Transaction Books, 1989); and Samuel James Eldersveld, *Political Elites in Modern Societies: Empirical Research and Democratic Theory* (Ann Arbor: University of Michigan Press, 1989).

For recent studies of elites in the United States, see G. William Domhoff, *The Power Elite and the State: How Policy Is Made in America* (New York: de Gruyter, 1990); William G. Scott and David K. Hart, *Organizational Values in America* (New Brunswick, N.J.: Transaction Books, 1989); Daniel Hellinger, *The Democratic Façade* (Pacific Grove, Calif.: Brooks/Cole, 1991); Thomas R. Dye, *Who's Running America? The Bush Era* (Englewood Cliffs, N.J.: Prentice Hall, 1990).

For treatments of **pluralism**, see a classic, Robert Dahl, *Polyarchy: Participation and Opposition* (New Haven, Conn.: Yale University Press, 1971); as well as these more recent works of narrower focus: Iris M. Young, *Justice and the Politics of Difference* (Princeton, N.J.: Princeton University Press, 1990).

On the controversies of **multiculturalism**, see Arthur M. Schlesinger, *The Disuniting of America: Reflections on a Multicultural Society* (Knoxville, Tenn.: Whittle Direct Books, 1991); and James D. Hunter, *Culture Wars: The Struggle to Define America* (New York: Basic Books, 1991).

STRUGGLES TO REALIZE DEMOCRATIC IDEALS

An enormous amount of material is available on the struggle to achieve **racial equality** in the United States, so we offer only three recent examples: Rhoda Lois Blumberg, *Civil Rights: The 1960s Freedom Struggle*, rev. ed. (Boston: Twayne, 1991); Fred Powledge, *Free at Last? The Civil Rights Movement and the People Who Made It* (Boston: Little, Brown, 1991); and Sean Dennis Cashman, *African-Americans and the Quest for Civil Rights, 1900–1990* (New York: New York University Press, 1991).

A recent treatment of **Joseph McCarthy** and midcentury Red scare in the United States is Richard M. Fried, *Nightmare in Red: The McCarthy Era in Perspective* (New York: Oxford University Press, 1990).

Two distinct historical phases of the fight for **women's suffrage** are treated, respectively, in Israel Kugler, *From Ladis to Women: The Organized Struggle for Women's Rights in the Reconstruction Era* (Westport, Conn.: Greenwood Press, 1987); and Donald L. Haggerty, ed., *The National Woman's Party Papers: The Suffrage Years, 1913–1920* (Sanford, N.C.: Microfilming Corp. of America, 1981).

For an extended consideration of the **initiative**, see Thomas E. Cronin, *Direct Democracy: The Politics of Initiative, Referendum, and Recall* (Cambridge, Mass.: Harvard University Press, 1989). The best comparative work on referendums is David Butler and Austin Ranney, *Referendums: A Comparative Study of Practice and Theory* (Washington, D.C.: American Enterprise Institute, 1978).

PART ONE

FOUNDATIONS

2
AMERICAN POLITICAL CULTURE:
LIBERTY AND ITS TENSIONS

3
REVOLUTION AND CONSTITUTION:
THE AMERICAN WAY

4
AMERICAN FEDERALISM: CAN
DEMOCRACY BE DIVIDED FIFTY WAYS?

5
CIVIL LIBERTIES: ARE LIBERTIES
EFFECTIVELY PROTECTED?

6
CIVIL RIGHTS: THE MEANINGS
OF EQUALITY

7
THE AMERICAN POLITICAL ECONOMY:
INEQUALITY AND DEMOCRATIC
POLITICS

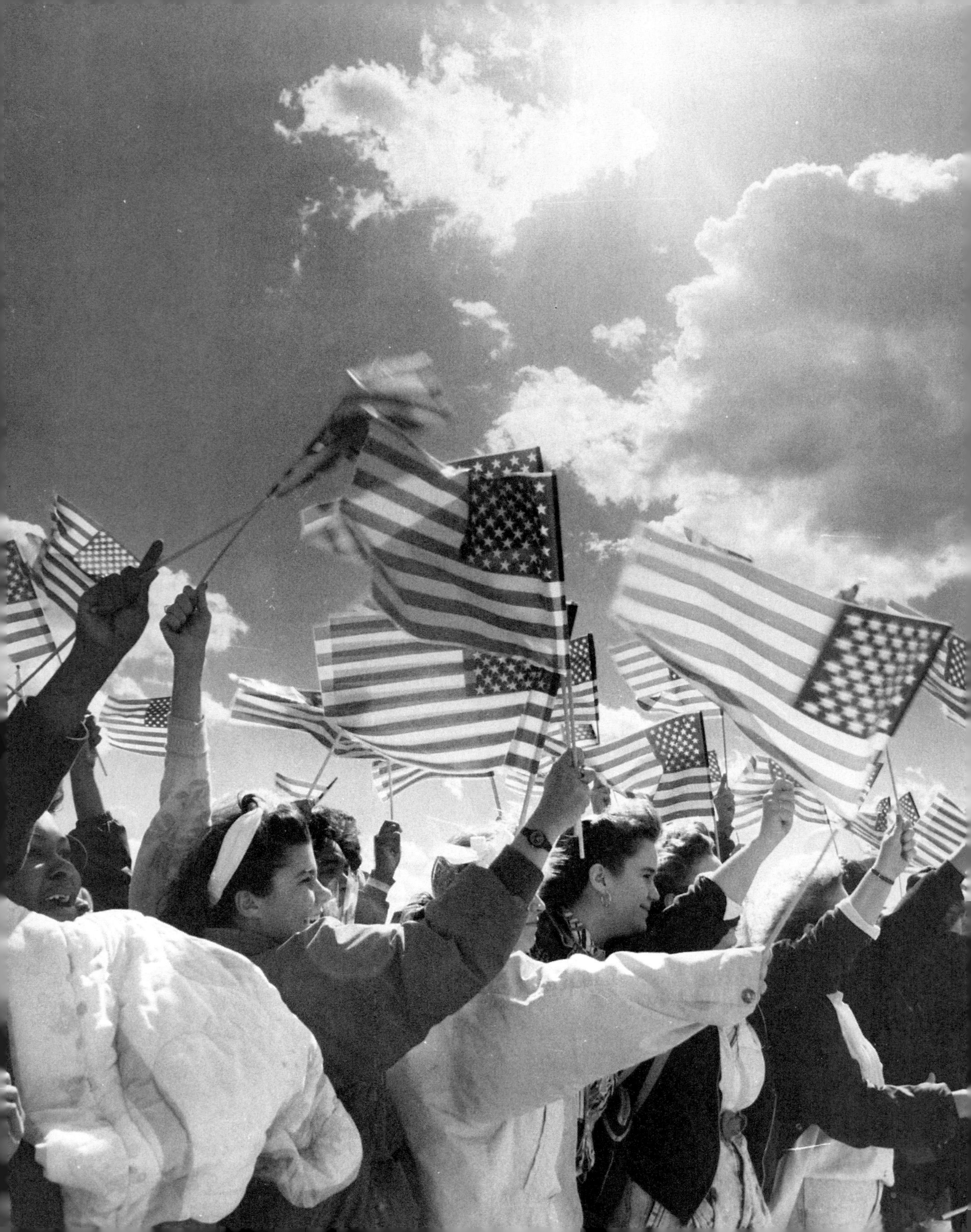

CHAPTER TWO

AMERICAN POLITICAL CULTURE

Liberty and Its Tensions

CHAPTER OUTLINE

What Is Political Culture?
POLITICAL CULTURE AND DEMOCRACY
COHESIVENESS IN POLITICAL CULTURE

The Liberal Tradition
ECONOMIC, SOCIAL AND POLITICAL VALUES
THE LEGACY OF LIBERALISM

Two Types of Liberalism
CONSERVATISM: TRADITION LIBERALISM
NEW DEAL LIBERALISM
THE FAILURE OF RADICALISM

Limits of Liberalism
INTOLERANCE AND DISCRIMINATION
VIOLENCE AND THE RULE OF LAW
MAKING THE WORLD SAFE FOR DEMOCRACY—OR FOR US?
RELIGION AND MORALITY IN POLITICS

THE AMERICAN POLITICAL EXPERIENCE SEEMS AT FIRST GLANCE simple and straightforward enough. In the traditional view of grammar school textbooks, the United States was created as a full-fledged democracy, born in a revolution that rallied around the call for liberty and equality. Since that time, according to this version of history, the nation has gone on to greater and greater heights as a democratic society and as a defender of democracy elsewhere in the world. A closer look at our political history, however, reveals a far more ambiguous and troubling picture. The American experiment with government by the people was certainly innovative and has had worldwide significance. But there have been many rough moments in the evolution of U.S. democracy, from its beginnings to the present day. The very meaning of democracy has sometimes been called into question, and many battles have been waged over the concept of making democracy more meaningful.

One key factor in determining how democracy evolves is the character of a society's political culture. Let us now turn to that issue in connection with democracy in America.

What Is Political Culture?

In this text the phrase *political culture* is given a very broad meaning, befitting the roots of its component words. The ancient Greek *polis* is the basis for our word *political*. The polis was a city-state, like Athens in the Golden Age—a country the size of a city in which life was not so easily divided into such categories as politics, economics, religion, and social life. The polis was the center of an interwoven fabric of relationships that included all of these. In the United States, *political* has come to have a very narrow, decidedly negative meaning. It is often used to refer to the manipulative, underhanded behavior of candidates and elected officials. In this text we use the word much more broadly and positively to refer to everything that binds us together as a people.

Culture grew from its Latin root, *cultura*, which referred to cultivating the soil. *Culture* came to mean cultivating the mind and then to mean the products of such cultivation—the whole way of life (material, intellectual, and spiritual) of a given society.

Political culture, then, means the collection of beliefs, institutions, and artifacts that have to do with our shared life as Americans. What should we as a society and as citizens strive for? What is the proper role of government? what institutions allow for the expression of political opinions? What obligations and rights belong to citizens? In the following sections we will examine the interplay between political culture and democratic values and the role of consensus in political culture.

Political Culture and Democracy

Is it possible to characterize the kind of culture that is compatible with democracy? It is easy, after all, to cite attitudes hostile to democratic government. If, for example, citizens feel that they play no legitimate role in their nation's politics, if a nation's leaders distrust its citizens and one another, if force is accepted as a necessary means of political action, if dissent and opposition are considered unacceptable—such feelings are unlikely to spawn a democratic form of government. But even though it may be easy to point out undemocratic aspects of political culture, it is not so simple to describe the sort of political milieu likely to support democracy. We can, however, specify certain elements that any democratic society would have to include in its cultural repertoire: for example, belief in citizen participation, in the legitimacy of dissent and opposition, and in the meaningfulness of public debate and elections; reasonable respect for law and democratic principles; and tolerance toward other social groups.[1]

In describing the kind of society likely to develop and maintain a democratic political culture, some political scientists have cited high levels of education, affluence, and a large middle class as crucial elements.[2] Yet it is difficult to argue that any or all of these factors actually promote democracy. Democracies have developed under many conditions, and the vagaries of history sometimes help to shape political life in ways that could never be anticipated. At the end of World War II, for example, democracy was actually imposed on West Germany and Japan, two rabidly antidemocratic, fascist societies. Many authorities argued, not surprisingly, that the cultures of these nations were inherently inhospitable to democratic practices. Yet democracy has not only survived but actually thrived in both nations.

Cohesiveness in Political Culture

Consensus, more than any other element, distinguishes stable political cultures. Where political culture lacks consensus, political life is likely to be conflict-ridden, marked by disagreement over fundamentals.[3] In U.S. society, certain basic elements of the political culture, such as the near-sacred status of the Constitution, are virtually unchallengeable. Other facets of U.S. political culture, such as the interplay between religion and politics, have long sparked intense controversy. Our political culture, like most others, encompasses contradictory values, as well as conflicts between the values people proclaim and the values reflected in how they actually behave.

But if conflicts and contradictions characterize much of the style and dynamics of U.S. politics, some key areas of basic agreement, or consensus, mark U.S. political culture as well. Many observers of U.S. history have remarked on the strong consensus on political attitudes achieved in a society made up of so many disparate ethnic and racial groups. Ethnic diversity alone, obviously, does not rule out the development of a cohesive political culture. British colonists, who comprised 60 percent of the original colonial population, established the political processes, dominant language, and social and economic norms of interaction to which subsequent immigrant groups adjusted.

On one occasion in U.S. history the political consensus broke down and the issue had to be settled by war. This was, of course, the Civil War, which erupted out of the clash of differing concepts of citizenship and basic rights, as well as disagreements over how political power should be exercised. The legacy of that conflict still shapes our political life today.

Overall, U.S. political culture has remained sufficiently cohesive to permit orderly government to carry on in spite of the many conflicts and contradictions in our society and our political life. In fact, looking back over the years since the Kennedy administration, it may seem remarkable that our political processes have been able to survive, relatively unchanged, in the face of assassinations, domestic violence, a bitterly opposed and costly war in Asia, and the resignation of a president. Whether this is a testimony to the resilience of our political culture or to its irrelevance is a question we will consider at the conclusion of this text.

COMPARATIVE PERSPECTIVE

POLITICAL CULTURE, OLD AND NEW

America, you are luckier
Than this old continent of ours;
You have no ruined castles
And no volcanic earth.
You do not suffer
In hours of intensity
From futile memories
And pointless battles.
Concentrate on the present joyfully!
And when your children write books
May a good destiny keep them
From knight, robber, and ghost-stories.
   Johann Wolfgang von Goethe (1749–1832), trans. Robert Bly

Early in the nineteenth century, the German poet Goethe expressed this poignant hope for the newly created United States. Unlike Europe, Goethe proclaims, America will not have to live under the shadow of a long and painful history. Note that Goethe's characterization of European history draws on the imagery of feudalism (knights and castles). Like many other observers before and since, he believed that it was the absence of a feudal history that made America different.

We will now look at the pattern of our political culture, exploring the many ways it has supported and strengthened our democratic behavior. We will examine the fundamental values that have shaped U.S. political life, beginning with the liberal democratic tradition that informs much of our political culture. Then we will turn to the limitations of that same political culture, to analyze some cultural and political patterns that have thwarted the evolution of democracy in the United States.

The Liberal Tradition

The United States was conceived in the tradition of eighteenth-century **liberalism**, a social and political set of values that decisively shaped our democratic politics.[4] The cornerstones of this political value system were a belief in government based on the consent of the governed and a belief that certain rights are guaranteed to all persons simply because they are human beings. These rights, as enunciated so eloquently by Thomas Jefferson in the Declaration of Independence, included "life, liberty and the pursuit of happiness." Government, according to eighteenth-century liberals, gains legitimacy by protecting these rights. And when a government violates the rights of its citizens, those citizens have a right to rebel—which is exactly what some of the colonists did.

Liberals placed great emphasis on the liberty of the individual. The concept of the free individual actually evolved over the course of several centuries. In the Renaissance era (roughly 1350–1600), as the tenets of classical humanism were revived and reinterpreted, intellectuals and artists celebrated what they saw as the uniqueness of human potential and the virtually unlimited possibilities of human creativity.[5] To the Renaissance celebration of humanism was added, beginning in the early 1500s, the Protestant Reformation's emphasis on the primacy of the individual conscience and the solitary relation of the individual to God.[6] Paralleling those developments, an economic movement called capitalism—based on private property and individual initiative—advocated freedom for every individual to buy and sell, to invest and gamble, to work and to relocate, as that person saw fit. Finally, seventeenth-century political philosophers

The Fourth of July is a classic American celebration of the nation's origins and reinforces the sense of sharing a common heritage. *(F. W. Binzen/Photo Researchers)*

such as John Locke applied the concept of the free individual to the political realm, arguing that government existed only to safeguard the **natural rights** of individuals.[7] These rights are considered essential human guarantees (such as freedom) that a government cannot curtail or eliminate arbitrarily and remain just.

The ideal society of free individuals envisioned by the liberal thinkers of the seventeenth and eighteenth centuries was a society based entirely on merit and open to all, in which each person was free to pursue any course of action, so long as it did not impinge on the freedom or rights of others. In such an open society, you had only yourself to blame if you failed to take advantage of life's opportunities. In the fledgling United States, a nation consisting primarily of small, individually owned farms and located on the edge of a vast, unexplored continent, these liberal ideas set down particularly tenacious roots.

Economic, Social, and Political Values

Given the tenets of the liberal creed, it is easy to see why the United States acted as a magnet for immigrants. Although some immigrants were refugees from political or religious persecution, most came to the United States to find a better life, lured by the liberal promise that even the lowest born person could, through hard work, climb the ladder of success. The United States, with no hereditary nobility and seemingly no social or political restrictions on individual initiative, drew great waves of immigrants looking for a chance to better themselves.[8]

Along with Americans' faith in individual responsibility went a belief in the small business or individually owned farm as the appropriate vehicle for economic success. Throughout the nation's history, Americans have generally believed that although bigger may be better in some matters, too much bigness was a dangerous thing. Recurrently in U.S. political history, **populist**, or grass-roots, movements have arisen to defend the interests of the common citizen against institutions or power elites perceived as too big and oppressive. In the 1890s the Populist party attacked the big corporations and the railroads. More recently, populist movements have focused their attacks on so-called big government.[9]

Populist agitation, however, has rarely been directed against the capitalist system itself—only against perceived abuses of it. True to their liberal democratic heritage, most Americans continue to believe that capitalism is the best economic system. Private ownership has remained popular, although most people now accept the idea that sometimes big business must be regulated for the public good.

Together with these economic values, eighteenth-century liberalism encompassed political and social values predicated on a considerable degree of equality among citizens. Because all individuals are born with certain rights, all are entitled to have those rights protected by society and government. Each person should be equal before the law—a person cannot claim superiority before a judge, for example, simply by virtue of belonging to a richer or more privileged class. In addition, each person is

"Well, it all depends. Where are these huddled masses coming from?"

High-tech Statue of Liberty with her cellular phone is getting pretty picky when it comes to new immigrants. Although openness to vast numbers of immigrants is a distinctive feature of American social and political life, the doors have often been more open to some than others. Immigration policy is one area where conflicts between American ideals, practical considerations, and nationalistic restrictiveness are fought out. *(Drawing by Handelsman; © 1992 The New Yorker Magazine, Inc.)*

entitled to basic political rights, starting with the right to participate meaningfully in political life.

Eighteenth-century liberals were also suspicious of the power of governments in general. Government power, they felt, could be abused all too easily, subverting the rights of the individual—through excessive taxation, for example. As a safeguard, liberals argued for a contractual arrangement between government and the governed. Government, they said, should be limited to specific functions, and the governed should be guaranteed certain rights; if any of those rights are violated, moreover, individuals have cause for disobedience or even rebellion.

(Text continues on page 60)

COMPARATIVE PERSPECTIVE

EQUALITY, *JÄMLIKHET*, AND *HITOSHISA*

Does "equality" mean the same thing in different political cultures? A group of political scientists led by Sidney Verba not long ago made a cross-cultural study of the idea of equality among the leaders of various groups in the United States, Sweden, and Japan. A study of this sort raises interesting questions about political culture and democracy. What ideas tend to be shared across national boundaries? How do opinions reflect social and economic reality? How wide is the range of opinions in one country compared to others? How are ideas represented in institutional structures? When will agreement in one area be counterbalanced by disagreement in another?

The study identified some common ground. Leaders tended to be male, well-educated, and middle-aged or older in all three countries. Leadership groups in each country were well positioned to exercise political influence. Certain group positions are predictable: In all three countries labor and left groups tend to favor the welfare state and redistribution of income; business and right groups tend to oppose these policies. Groups on the political right in each country tend to place the blame for poverty on individuals; groups on the left tend to cite social factors.

The Verba study discovered significant differences in the *range* of opinion in these political cultures. In Japan and Sweden all groups accepted basic welfare state policies but disagreed on income redistribution. In the United States leaders disagreed about the welfare state but tended to be of one mind about substantial income redistribution (there was uniform opposition to it). As an indication of the range of difference, consider the following: In Sweden support for the welfare state was found even in those groups we would expect most likely to oppose it—business groups and the Conservative party. Yet in the United States the idea of substantial income redistribution was rejected where we would most expect support—among leaders on the left and in labor groups. Look at the diagram from the study, showing the range of opinion on another issue, whether capitalism is basically fair and without major conflict. Not only is the range of opinion in the United States narrower than that in Sweden, but it is located on a different part of the spectrum from either the Swedish or the Japanese range.

(Box continues on page 59)

	Conflict/fairness of capital		
Japan	Conflict exists/ cap. unfair	(left bloc — right bloc)	No conflict/ cap. fair
Sweden	Conflict exists/ cap. unfair	(left bloc ———— right bloc)	No conflict/ cap. fair
United States	Conflict exists/ cap. unfair	(left bloc — right bloc)	No conflict/ cap. fair

This diagram shows the range of opinion along one issue: whether capitalism is basically fair and without major conflicts. Notice that the range of opinion in the United States is much narrower than in either of the other two countries and that the left end of the U.S. range falls *to the right of center* of the ranges in both Japan and Sweden.

Leaders in all three nations tend to accept less of a gap between the top and bottom in political influence than they do in income. This represents a greater preference for political equality than for income equality (a preference for liberal democracy over egalitarian democracy). But this agreement is counterbalanced by substantial disagreement among leaders within each nation about who actually exercises how much influence. Thus the study authors do not predict that these egalitarian political norms will necessarily lead to greater actual political equality.

This study assumes that ideas do matter—that political beliefs are more than rationalizations of selfish calculations and that they do have an impact on politics. Differences in ideas about equality are naturally intertwined with historical differences and different institutional structures. It is difficult to say that one set of differences causes others. But clearly there are different political cultures in these three nations, and those different cultures do have significant implications for democratic politics.

Source: Sidney Verba, Steven Kelman, Gary R. Orren, Ichiro Miyake, Joji Watanuki, Ikuo Kabashima, and G. Donald Ferree, Jr., Elites and the Idea of Equality: A Comparison of Japan, Sweden, and the United States *(Cambridge, Mass.: Harvard University Press, 1987).*

Let us summarize the values that eighteenth-century liberalism contributed to the U.S. democratic tradition:

Individualism: A belief in the central value of the individual, whose rights government is created to defend. Each individual is responsible for his or her own fate.

Liberty: Each person should have the maximum freedom possible, compatible with equal freedom for others.

Equality: All are entitled to equal legal and political rights.

An open society: Each person should be judged on individual merits and be free to enter various occupations and pursuits.

Rule of law: Government must be nonarbitrary, exercising power through equitable laws that are fairly administered.

Limits on government: Since power can easily corrupt, governments must be watched closely and hedged with restrictions lest they infringe on citizens' rights. A written constitution helps to set such limits.

As noble as these tenets of eighteenth-century liberalism surrounded in theory, however, applying them to concrete situations proved extremely difficult. For example, early liberals had grave doubts about whether everyone ought to have the right to vote. In both England and America many liberals were wary of the potential power of "the many" that political equality might create. They feared what was sometimes called the **tyranny of the majority**, or, less politely, mob rule. The U.S. Constitution, significantly, left the issue of voting rights up to the individual states, many of which stipulated that only male citizens who owned a certain amount of property could vote. Still, for white males the right to vote was achieved earlier in the United States (by 1830) than it was anywhere else in the world.

Interestingly, the liberal values on which the United States was founded actually made it a purer liberal society than the European societies that gave birth to liberalism. In Europe liberals were forced to do combat with the defenders of monarchy, of which there were few in the new United States. Of course, there was (and remains) tremendous disagreement over what "democratic liberalism" actually means, but the United States has never experienced the struggles over the very *form* of government that have been fairly commonplace in European history.[10] Compared with Europe, then, the United States was from the start more egalitarian, despite the vast differences in wealth that have always existed here.

Of course, many Americans throughout history have neither supported nor acted on these core liberal values, preferring beliefs and practices often at great variance with the liberal tradition. Nevertheless, liberalism is the American creed. We may not honor it, but it haunts our conscience. It represents our collective ideal, even if it is not always reflected in our collective practice.

AMERICAN POLITICAL CULTURE　　61

The Legacy of Liberalism

The strength of the liberal tradition in the United States has helped democratic government to survive here for more than two centuries. In our political history, apart from the Civil War, there has been no serious challenge to the legitimacy of democratic government and constitutional authority. As the nation's conscience, the liberal tradition has kept alive the hope of equal treatment and basic civil rights for all. Despite long periods of religious, racial, and political intolerance, respect for civil liberties has gradually increased throughout our history. Legal equality for American blacks, long believed to be a virtual impossibility, was achieved after a long struggle. The fundamental liberal commitment to political equality served as a goad in that struggle.[11]

Liberalism has also sustained a considerable distrust of government, which continues to show itself in grass-roots resistance to government intrusions, in tax revolts, and in attacks on the growth of government budgets at all levels. The liberal belief in equality before the law also served as the basis of the Watergate investigations of the early 1970s, leading to the first resignation of a president in U.S. history.

Finally, Americans embrace liberalism's deep commitment to the individual. The capitalist economic system, the central premise of which is private ownership of the means of production, mirrors this emphasis on individual accomplishment. Despite many modifications in this economic system and much greater government involvement in economic life, most Americans still consider capitalism essential to the American way of life.

Two Types of Liberalism

U.S. political debate today revolves around two seemingly opposing viewpoints, usually labeled "liberalism" and "conservatism." But ironically, eighteenth-century liberal ideas and assumptions stand at the core of both views. Regardless of the labels, U.S. political life basically operates within the framework and norms established at the founding of the nation. We will now examine how the beliefs of today's conservatives and liberals both derive from the same liberal tradition and how that tradition has hampered the growth of radical groups in the U.S. political arena.

Conservatism: Traditional Liberalism

By and large, most U.S. **conservatives** are traditional liberals who have kept faith with liberalism as it was propounded more than two hundred years ago.[12] Conservative politicians such as President Ronald Reagan and Senator Jesse Helms of North Carolina reflect the individualist, antigovernment tenets of the liberal tradition. They believe in the strength of U.S. capitalism, as represented by **free enterprise**—allowing supply and demand to regulate the marketplace with minimal government interference. Out of a belief in individual responsibility, they generally disapprove of government programs to aid the disadvantaged. Because of their commitment to capitalism, they prefer to leave dollars in private hands, rather than redistributing wealth through social programs. They want less economic regulation by government and see virtue in what Reagan called the "magic of the marketplace"—the creation of wealth through individual initiative and free enterprise in business and finance, unfettered by government restrictions.

Occasionally, powerful forces on the political right (the Ku Klux Klan, for instance) have championed ideals contrary to the liberal creed, but such fringe elements have never entered the mainstream of conservatism. Today's conservatives usually think of themselves as upholding the truest traditions of the nation, and they are fond of citing the words of the Founders on such issues as the danger of too much government power and the importance of the individual. Unlike most conservatives in Europe, U.S. conservatives are not usually confortable with paternalistic government—with using the power of the state to protect or assist individuals.

New Deal Liberalism

The Great Depression of the 1930s prompted a major shift in U.S. politics. At that time millions of Americans were out of work, banks were failing, many stocks were practically worthless, and much of the population was afraid and in want. President Franklin D. Roosevelt said he saw "one third of the nation ill-housed, ill-clothed and ill-fed." The U.S. economic system had failed, and there was widespread agreement on the need for a restructuring of the economy, in which government would gain far more power over economic affairs and make a firm commitment to the well-being of the common citizen. President Roosevelt's solution was a wide range of social and economic initiatives called the **New Deal**, which involved government regulations and subsidies in the economic sphere and welfare programs in the social sector.

FDR's New Deal was the crystallization of the "new" liberalism, an activist creed committed to the improvement of the average person's conditions of life and particularly to elimination of the worst forms of poverty and deprivation.[13] Politicians committed to the new liberalism, such as Senators Edward Kennedy of Massachusetts and Tom Harkin of Iowa, are not satisfied with letting the economy run according to its own laws, preferring to direct economic activity toward larger social interests. In general, this means initiating social programs aimed at aiding the unemployed, improving health care and housing for low-income people, raising educational opportunities for all, and so on.

The new liberals, like the conservatives, are not entirely consistent in their views and policies. Despite their commitment to social change, liberals often favor balanced budgets and reduced government spending. Conservatives, for their part, frequently defend government subsidies to groups such as farmers while maintaining a general opposition to government spending. Conservatives also are the chief champions of

People either loved or hated Franklin Roosevelt, but no one could ignore him. His politics probably had more enduring influence on our political system than any other 20th-century figure. Here, Roosevelt campaigns with John Nance Garner, his vice-presidential running mate, in 1932, when the nation was in the grip of the Great Depression. *(The Bettmann Archive)*

government involvement in matters of personal morality such as abortion, pornography, and sexuality.

When it comes to an activist government, then, conservatives usually prefer action in the realm of personal life while opposing regulation of business. Liberals tend to take the opposite view—that morals are a matter of personal choice, whereas economic matters have general social significance and therefore legitimately fall within the areas that government may regulate.

The Failure of Radicalism

One consequence of the strength of the U.S. liberal tradition has been the relative failure of radical movements to gain national power. The United States is, in fact, the only industrial democracy without a significant **socialist** political party. The socialist ideology usually favors collective and government ownership over individual or private ownership (see further discussion in Chapter 7). In comparison with the United States, socialists have played a key part in the national politics of European democracies since the nineteenth century, and in recent years democratic socialist parties have held power in France, Spain, Great Britain, Germany, Sweden, Denmark, Norway, Finland, Austria, Greece, the Netherlands, and Portugal. Even in Canada, where the political left has not been a major force nationally until recently, the socialist New Democratic party has elected provincial governments in British Columbia, Saskatchewan, and Manitoba. In the 1990 provincial elections, the New Democratic party won an absolute majority (74 seats of 130) in Ontario, the most populous Canadian province. A socialist state government in the United States is just about unimaginable, as is any significant socialist presence in the federal government.

Many arguments have been advanced to explain the weakness of the American left.[14] Some observers argue that the United States is simply too rich a country: General affluence has made socialism less appealing to the masses. Others contend that the country's many ethnic, racial, religious, and regional divisions have made organizing a party based on social class very difficult. Most observers believe, however, that one of the central factors has been the strength of the liberal tradition. The American emphasis on individualism, with its ideology of opportunity and success, together with this nation's relative equality and lack of feudal heritage, has prevented radical ideas from catching on. European socialists, by contrast, have benefited from the greater class consciousness and solidarity of the working class, as well as a more closed social system than in the United States. It has even proved more difficult to organize trade unions here, and union membership today is much lower in the United States than in most other democratic nations.

This is not to say, however, that socialists have seen no success at all in the United States. Many socialist mayors and legislators were elected around World War I, for example, and California came close to electing a socialist governor during the Depression. We saw something of a left-wing revival in the 1960s. It is also important to note that many programs advocated by socialists have, in fact, become accepted U.S. policies, from social security and unemployment insurance to the many efforts to protect consumers or the very idea of government responsibility for the performance of the economy. Nonetheless, socialist Bernie Sanders's election to Congress from Vermont in 1990 was a political novelty (he chose to caucus with the Democrats so as not to be entirely isolated). The failure of a socialist party to play a significant role in America has had many important political consequences, among them the relative weakness of the American welfare state (to which topic we return in later chapters).

Looking to the other side of the American political spectrum, we see that the far right, including such antidemocratic groups as the Ku Klux Klan, has also failed to gain national power. Outright racist groups have had much greater success at the state and local levels. The Klan, for example, exerted some influence in several states during the 1920s but never succeeded on a national level at anything more than a march in the nation's capital. The Klan had a minor effect on national politics in 1992 when its former Grand Dragon, David Duke, mounted a bid for the Republican presidential nomination. Despite early media attention, Duke encountered difficulty getting on state primary ballots and failed to win much support in states where his name did appear. He suspended his campaign well before the Republican convention.

Clearly on the margin of American politics but harder to characterize in left-right terms is **libertarianism**, an extreme form of the least-government position. While opposing government regulation of the economy (a right-wing position), libertarians also oppose government intervention in personal, moral matters and do not favor a large military establishment (positions from the left). Like most parties out of the center, the Libertarian party in the United States has never fared well in elections.

Both the far left and the far right, then, have played a less significant role in our history than they have in many other democratic nations. Shaped by our own brand of liberalism, the American political spectrum has remained narrower than that of most other democratic nations.

Limits of Liberalism

As we have seen, our nation's liberal heritage has in many ways supported democratic values and practices. Yet we have often failed to live up to the standards of this heritage. Americans are proud to recite the tenets of the liberal faith, but we sometimes find it difficult to put our beliefs into practice. Too often the doors of the "open society" have been shut to some citizens. Respect for law has not prevented bouts of violence. Our attempts to spread democracy to the world have become ensnared in national self-interest. Religious beliefs, supposedly matters of individual concern, have occasionally been thrust into the political arena.

This is not to imply that liberal values are not upheld much of the time. The United States justly deserves its reputation as the "land of opportunity," and many Americans are respectful of the rights of others and generous in sharing their resources. This section focuses on our lapses—areas where contradictions and problems persist in our culture.

Intolerance and Discrimination

"Fellow immigrants," President Franklin Roosevelt once began an address to the Daughters of the American Revolution, a group sometimes noted for its snobbish celebration of special hereditary connections. Roosevelt's irony was well placed. Except for the American Indians, whose journey here came centuries earlier, we are *all* immigrants. Social and economic distinctions often boil down to who got here first and made the most of it.

Despite assimilation by the various immigrants who settled here, however, enough lumps have remained in the so-called melting pot that politicians frequently find it advantageous to pitch their campaigns to specific ethnic groups.[15] Particular ethnic groups have even taken firm hold on local politics in certain areas. Still, only in the latter half of the twentieth century have the members of some ethnic groups been able to attain high elective office. The first Catholic president, John F. Kennedy, was elected in 1960, and it will probably be quite some time before an African-American or a Hispanic-American is elected president.

(Text continues on page 68)

IMMIGRATION LAW AND NATIONAL IDENTITY

Many forces operate to change a nation's **demographics**, the characteristics of its population, including size, distribution, density, age, ethnic or cultural background. Public policy can have an impact on most of these. Health programs can lower death rates; housing programs can encourage relocation from one area to another. Immigration policy represents a nation's official decisions about allowing new members into the society from outside. The United States has long thought of itself as an open society, welcoming new members from abroad. American immigration policy has not always matched that perception. Should immigration policy be driven exclusively by humanitarian concerns? How much should the economic well-being of current Americans affect policy about admitting new ones? Should our egalitarian concerns extend to the world at large, where enormous differences exist in the wealth of nations? Should we use immigration to try to mold ourselves in ethnic and cultural terms (either to maintain current patterns or to create new ones)? As the following brief review indicates, immigration policy grows out of economic and foreign policy concerns at least as much as it results from our identity as a democratic nation.

Michael C. Lemay claims that whereas an "open door" accurately represents U.S. immigration policy up to 1880 (a period when immigration was virtually unlimited), other portal images better represent U.S. policy since. The Chinese Exclusion Act of 1882 ushered in the "Door-Ajar Era," during which immigration was still largely open, but with some significant exceptions. The "Pet-Door Era" lasted from 1920 to 1952, marked by an attempt to control the ethnic and cultural makeup of immigration through a national quota system that allowed a specified maximum number of entrants from chosen nations. The "Dutch Door Era" began in 1950 marked by policies that, while still based on quotas, allowed greater access to people "at the top" (who met special provisions or got favored treatment).* The national quota system and the special provisions added to it gave a decided preference to European immigrants, reinforcing the ethnic and cultural patterns of the first century and a half of U.S. history.

The Immigration Act of 1965 ended the quota system and paved the way for a large increase in the *proportion* of immigration from the Third World but set an annual limit of 270,000 immigrants in all, with no more than 20,000 from any one country. Family reunification was a major priority of these policies.

The Refugee Act of 1980 entangled immigration policy more directly with foreign policy. Refugees from political persecution were allowed entry, but refugees from economic hardship were not. Thus if the United States opposed a particular country's ruling regime, refugee status was more readily obtained. But if the United States supported the regime, it would be unlikely to recognize political refugees from that country—the plight of Salvadorans, for example, in the 1980s and early 1990s.

(Box continues on page 67)

The United States shares a two-thousand-mile border with a Third World nation, Mexico. The problems of illegal immigration across that border led to the Immigration Reform and Control Act (IRCA) of 1986. This act was designed to reduce the number of illegal aliens in the United States by granting amnesty and legal status to some illegal aliens who had been in the country prior to 1982, imposing legal penalties on employers who hired illegal aliens, and creating a "guest worker program" to ensure enough agricultural laborers for western growers who had relied on illegal immigrants in the past.

The law's effects were mixed. The Immigration and Naturalization Service (INS) claimed a 34 percent drop in apprehensions along the border with Mexico, and there were signs that many employers were careful to stay within the new federal law. But some employers, determined to continue using the cheap labor of illegal immigrants, accepted false proof of legal residence, reasoning that penalties were relatively minor and detection was unlikely.

As for the important amnesty provisions, almost 2 million illegal immigrants applied (of whom 92 percent were accepted) before the opportunity ran out in May 1988. This number fell somewhat short of expectations, and there were many complications in connection with amnesty. For example, how would the INS treat members of the same family who had arrived in the United States at different times? The agency initially refused to establish a uniform policy, stating that it would keep spouses together on a humanitarian, case-by-case basis and that it would not deport children of single-parent families. In February 1990 the INS announced that it would stop deportation proceedings against spouses and children of illegal immigrants granted amnesty.

The fears of opponents of the employer sanctions of the IRCA were apparently validated by a 1990 General Accounting Office study, which found that the sanctions cause "widespread discrimination" against people "with a foreign accent or appearance."

The Immigration Act of 1990 did not disturb those sanctions, nor did it alter the general pattern of immigration. It did raise immigration levels to 700,000 per year for 1992 through 1994 and set a minimum of 675,000 after that. And it did increase the emphasis on access to people at the top, tripling the number of visas based on wealth and job skills and establishing a new category of visa strictly for the wealthiest applicants. This new chance to become a permanent resident of the United States became available to persons who would be willing to invest $1 million in a business creating at least ten jobs in the United States. Perhaps the Statue of Liberty should now read, "Give me your tired, your poor, some part of your huddled masses, . . . and toss in a few thousand millionaires to enrich the pot."

Michael C. Lemay, "U.S. Immigration Policy and Politics," in The Gatekeepers: Comparative Immigration Policy, *ed. Michael C. Lemay (New York: Praeger, 1989), pp. 1–21.*

PART ONE • FOUNDATIONS

Throughout U.S. history, foreigners, minority groups, and many people who just seemed different have been subject to both personal intolerance and official discrimination. Discrimination has taken many forms: in employment, in college quotas established to limit the entrance of certain groups, in restrictions on where people can live. Social humiliation, harassment, and even murder have sometimes greeted new Americans. In the middle of the nineteenth century the Nativist party accused newly arrived Catholic immigrants of plotting to take over the nation in the name of the papacy. This was to be the first of many such accusations and efforts to restrict the entry of "foreigners" to the United States. Again and again religious, ethnic, and racial hatreds have flared, necessitating a continuous struggle to keep our society open.[16]

Many immigrant groups have had to contend with blatant discrimination by fellow Americans. In early 1942 close to one hundred thousand U.S. citizens were rounded

After the Japanese attack on Pearl Harbor in December 1941, 100,000 Japanese-Americans were evacuated to remote internment camps in western states for the remainder of the war. The courts upheld the internment as a justifiable wartime measure, but many later concluded that the policy was based more on panic and racism than on a reasoned assessment. In 1988 Congress passed legislation awarding $20,000 to each surviving victim of the internment. *(Clem Albers/National Archives)*

AMERICAN POLITICAL CULTURE

up, forced to leave their homes, and taken to detention camps in remote areas, where they were confined for three years. The only "crime" committed by these people was being of Japanese descent at a time when hatred of the Japanese, who had just attacked Pearl Harbor, was at fever pitch. The government justified its actions on the ground that Japanese-Americans posed a security threat to the country, even though there was no specific evidence that more than a handful had offered or intended to offer aid to the Japanese cause. The vast majority of Japanese-Americans were loyal to U.S. institutions, and yet the U.S. government, with the blessing of the Supreme Court, interned them without trial.[17]

Looking back from the vantage point of more than forty years, we can only be ashamed of what was done. Although the internment camps were not the concentration camps of the Nazis, Japanese-Americans nonetheless were innocent victims of hysteria and prejudice. Recognizing the harm done, Congress in the 1980s moved to compensate victims for their losses. Yet serious tensions over differences in ethnicity, religion, race, and other group characteristics—which periodically flare into the open—remain a problem for democratic politics.

Violence and the Rule of Law

Americans have historically displayed considerable respect for law and legal procedures. Faith in the Constitution, in the Supreme Court, and in the court system in general has helped to keep social and political conflicts within accepted boundaries. In fact, Americans seem overly fond of legal procedures and tend to litigate endlessly about all sorts of matters. Even in the nineteenth century, foreign observers noted that Americans would take each other to court at the drop of a hat. Respect for law and the use of law to settle disputes seem ingrained in our heritage, fitting the liberal tradition's preference for an agreed-on legal framework as the basis of government.

Yet there is also a contrary tradition in the United States—the tradition of the gun. The use of force, by both government and individuals, has played a central role in the nation's growth and in the shaping of our folkways. Settlers fought with Indians, waged a war of independence, feuded over land. The Wild West remains legendary, its heroic figures still popularized in books, on television, and in films.[18] To survive in much of the United States in the nineteenth century, the gun was as necessary as the plow, the ax, or the Bible. The frontier often had no enforceable legal authority, so individuals relied on themselves and their friends to maintain social stability. Americans were also wary of granting to the central government the exclusive right to police. Even today policing remains a predominantly local function in our country. The Constitution expressly provides for the citizen's right to bear arms, which, as the colonists considered it, was necessary for a citizen militia.

Private violence has taken many forms in the United States. Between 1885 and 1916, for example, more than three thousand blacks were lynched and thousands of others brutalized.[19] Throughout the late nineteenth and early twentieth centuries, industrial-

Lynching is a part of U.S. history. Violence and intimidation have been widely used to threaten and punish African-Americans. Thousands were lynched in the decades between the end of Reconstruction and the beginning of the civil rights movement in the 1950s. Violence against other races and ethnic and minority groups is not an American monopoly, as recent events in Germany and other parts of Europe have indicated. *(UPI/Bettmann Newsphotos)*

ists often hired private armies to combat strikes by workers. And there is a long tradition of vigilantes pursuing criminals and others who were thought to threaten communities. Examples of *public* violence are not lacking, either. Police forces, the army, and the National Guard have frequently been used against various perceived threats—Indians, union organizers, protesters, and others.

We do not have to go back very far in history to find striking evidence of the persistence of the violent streak in U.S. society. Five of the last ten presidents have been targets for assassins. The two most prominent black leaders of the 1960s, Martin Luther King, Jr., and Malcolm X, were assassinated. Senator Robert Kennedy was killed and Governor George Wallace crippled by assailants.

A disturbing reminder of the violence in our polity occurred in 1991, when an unarmed motorist named Rodney King, an African-American, was stopped after a high-speed chase, then severely kicked and beaten by several members of the Los Angeles Police Department. Unbeknown to the officers, the incident was recorded on videotape, which was later shown on news broadcasts across the country. Four of the officers directly involved were later tried on state criminal charges. When, in April 1992, the state trial jury acquitted all four of all charges but one, the cycle of violence took another turn. South central Los Angeles erupted into the worst rioting that city had ever seen. Thirty-five persons were killed and hundreds injured. Six thousand National Guard troops were mobilized to help local law enforcement combat anarchy. The smoke from over thirteen hundred arson fires blackened the sky, as looters cleaned out hundreds of businesses.

Compared with contemporary Europe, the United States is a particularly violent country. Police are far more likely to kill citizens in this country, both in normal times and in times of disorder, than they are in the European democracies.[20] Perhaps because Europeans have experienced the violence of which totalitarian governments are capable, they are more sensitive about government use of force. A more important factor, however, may be that far more Americans are armed. Because tens of millions of guns circulate freely in the United States, the police here constantly face the possibility of deadly threat—something that European police rarely have to confront. The large number of guns available has helped to make U.S. homocide rates the highest among democratic countries. Yet various European nations have bred their own brands of violence. Organized terrorism has become all too common in Italy, France, and Germany, as has violence among soccer fans in England.

Many issues related to violence have not been solved in our society. Gun ownership is one: Who should be permitted to own guns? And what kinds of guns should be allowed? Relations between police and citizens have also been controversial in some communities: How can such relations be made cooperative rather than confrontational? Finally, a penchant for violence has often found its way into foreign and military policymaking.[21] Critics of U.S. involvement in the 1991 Persian Gulf War, for example, argued that economic sanctions were not given enough time to operate before the U.S.-led air war against Iraq was launched, resulting in tens of thousands of Iraqi casualties.

Making the World Safe for Democracy—or for Us?

> I have always believed that this anointed land was set apart in an uncommon way, that a divine plan placed this great continent here between the oceans to be found by people from every corner of the earth who had a special love of faith and freedom.
>
> *Ronald Reagan, 1982*

> ## POLITICAL ASSASSINATION IN AMERICA
>
> Four of the eight attempts to assassinate American presidents have succeeded, and there have been four attacks on presidential hopefuls. Abraham Lincoln, of course, was the first victim, shot by John Wilkes Booth in 1865. James Garfield, the twentieth president, was shot by Charles Guiteau at a railroad station in July 1881, only four months after taking office. William McKinley was standing in a receiving line at the Pan American Exposition in Buffalo, New York, when he was shot by Leon Czolgosz, a millworker, in 1901. More than forty years passed before the next attempt, in 1950, when Puerto Rican nationalists Oscar Collazo and Griselio Torresola attempted to storm Blair House and kill Harry Truman, who was residing there while the White House was being renovated. Thirteen years later, in November 1963, John Kennedy was killed in Dallas, Texas, and Lee Harvey Oswald was charged with the assassination. Next there were two attempts on the life of Gerald Ford, both in California in 1975, and both by women, Lynette Fromme and Sara Jane Moore. Finally, John Hinckley attempted to assassinate Ronald Reagan outside a hotel in Washington in 1981.
>
> Among presidential contenders, Theodore Roosevelt was shot during the 1912 campaign but survived. In 1933 an Italian immigrant construction worker, Giuseppe Zangara, fired at the new president-elect, Franklin Roosevelt, missing him but killing Anton Cermak, the mayor of Chicago. In June 1968, Robert Kennedy was shot by Sirhan Sirhan immediately after winning the California presidential primary, and George Wallace was shot and left paralyzed by Arthur Bremer while campaigning in a shopping center in Maryland in 1972.
>
> Most American assassination attempts have been the work of lone assassins,

(Box continues on page 73)

It would be hard to find a more extreme statement of the allegedly special place in the world occupied by the United States. Although many U.S. leaders have been hard-headed, practical people who understood that the United States is very much like other nations, throughout its history there has also been a strong missionary element in U.S. government policy.

Every country occasionally demonstrates a well-developed self-appreciation, but Americans early on displayed an especially lofty view of their role in the world and of the purity of their motives. From the founding of the nation to the present day, Americans have tended to decry other nations for seeking power or imperial domination while asserting that their country was seeking only to spread democracy throughout the world. According to the Founders, we were to act as an example for humankind. As George Washington put it in his first inaugural address, "The preservation of the

AMERICAN POLITICAL CULTURE

not larger political conspiracies. But there are hints of exceptions to this rule—particularly in the case of John Kennedy. Conspiracy theories were rampant after Kennedy's death, especially since the accused assassin was himself killed just days later while in police custody. To investigate matters and calm the public mind, President Lyndon Johnson formed a commission, chaired by Chief Justice Earl Warren and including future president Gerald Ford (then House minority leader). The Warren Commission's report, issued ten months later, upheld the theory that Oswald acted alone. That was what many people had hoped to hear, but the inquiry failed to quiet all doubts.

After a lull in attention, the Kennedy assassination was again the center of national debate in 1991 with the release of film director Oliver Stone's movie *JFK*. Although Stone denied that the film argued for any particular theory of culpability, many viewers inferred a major government conspiracy from the film's action. Some critics attacked the film (which used some real footage of the assassination) as a reckless muddling of fact and fiction, needlessly opening national wounds. Rejoinders to these criticisms hinted at a *continuing* conspiracy to cover up the truth. The public debate increased pressure to open the secret files of the original and subsequent investigations of Kennedy's death. Whatever final conclusion is reached about the events in Dallas in 1963, the *history* of the assassination certainly reveals two facets of the American character: a fascination with violence and a willingness to suspect the worst of our own government.

In a bizarre footnote to this treatment of political assassination, we can report that President Zachary Taylor, who died in office on July 9, 1850, was apparently *not* assassinated. But a suspicion that he had been done in with arsenic by political enemies actually incited historian Clara Rising to have Taylor's body dug up 141 years later and analyzed for traces of poison. None was found.

---

sacred fire of liberty and the destiny of the republican model of government are justly considered . . . staked on the experiment intrusted to the hands of the American people."

And the American example did spread. One Latin American country after another modeled its constitution after our own. And as recently as 1946, a radical nationalist quoted Thomas Jefferson when making a plea for his country's independence. That leader was Ho Chi Minh, the Vietnamese Communist.

The United States has also been famous for its altruism and its generosity toward others. We opened our doors to the refugees of the world. Magazine ads ask us to "save the children" in faraway lands or to send food to drought-stricken countries. When disaster strikes, U.S. aid is often the first to be sent. We train Peace Corps volunteers to assist development around the globe. We like to think of ourselves as an

> ### THE MOST VIOLENT NATION ON EARTH?
>
> WASHINGTON—The United States is "the most violent and self-destructive nation on earth," the Senate Judiciary Committee said in a report released Tuesday.
>
> The report depicted U.S. citizens killing, raping and robbing one another at a furious rate, surpassing every other country that keeps crime statistics.
>
> The nation's citizens committed a record number of killings in 1990—at least 23,300, or nearly three an hour—and a record number of rapes, robberies and assaults, the committee said.
>
> "In 1990 the United States led the world with its murder, rape and robbery rates," the report said. "When viewed from the national perspective, these rates are sobering. When viewed from the international perspective, they are truly embarrassing."
>
> The report noted that the murder rate in the United States was more than twice that of Northern Ireland, which is torn by civil war; four times that of Italy; nine times that of England and 11 times that of Japan.
>
> Violence against women in the United States was even more pervasive, the committee said.
>
> The rape rate in the United States was eight times higher than in France, 15 times higher than in England, 23 times higher than in Italy and 26 times higher than in Japan, according to the report.
>
> Robbery rates followed much the same pattern: six times higher than in England, seven times higher than in Italy—and nearly 150 times higher than in Japan.
>
> The committee's report, based on raw FBI data and preliminary statistics for [1990], based its comparisons on Justice Department statistics for industrialized nations. Crime reporting standards vary in those countries, and crime rates for less-developed Third World nations generally are either unavailable or unreliable.
>
> However, the report made clear that violence in the United States had no equal among the world's developed nations. Nor did 1990 have a modern equal for violence in the United States.
>
> *Source: Tim Weiner (Knight-Ridder News Service), Raleigh (N.C.)* News and Observer, *March 13, 1991, p. 1A.*

idealistic people trying to spread the gospel of democracy and capitalism to the rest of the world. Like Washington and Jefferson, we want the United States to light the way for others, to help to make the world, in President Woodrow Wilson's phrase, "safe for democracy."[22]

But there is another side to U.S. relations with the world—that of a powerful player. Throughout most of the nineteenth century the United States steered clear of entanglements abroad, largely because there was more than enough to do at home. The nation expanded internally, spreading across the continent, fighting constant battles against Indian peoples, as well as waging a war with Mexico. Our treatment of the Indian nations certainly provided no model of democratic (or ethical) practice. The American Indians, by and large, were mistreated, betrayed, and often virtually exterminated.[23] Some U.S. leaders of the time proclaimed that it was our "manifest destiny," our God-given task, to expand across the continent, to put to use the vast resources available in North America. In their view, Native Americans stood in the way of this grand design.

By the end of the nineteenth century the United States was ready to emerge as a world power. After intervening in Cuba and in the Philippines during the Spanish-American War (1898), purportedly to help to end unjust Spanish rule, U.S. military

Operation Just Cause involved an American invasion of Panama and the capture of the Panamanian leader, Manuel Noriega, who was brought to the United States and put on trial and convicted on drug charges. Although many Panamanians supported the U.S. operation, heavy costs were inflicted on civilians and the Panamanian economy. U.S. intervention in Latin America has a long history and has often been extremely controversial in terms of whose interests were being served. (Reuters/Bettmann Newsphotos)

forces actually helped to suppress the independence movements they were supposedly assisting.[24] And throughout the twentieth century our government repeatedly intervened in Latin America to support U.S. interests and to stop radical social movements regarded as threats to our security.

After fighting World War II against the antidemocratic forces of Nazism and fascism, many Americans expected the postwar world to be one in which democratic forces would generally prevail. But the onset of the global rivalry between the United States and the Soviet Union known as the **Cold War** divided the world into communist and Western spheres of influence. From 1945 until very recently, U.S. foreign policy was torn between adopting a primary stance as either an anticommunist or a prodemocratic power. As anticommunists, our policymakers could justify supporting many undemocratic regimes, such as those of Francisco Franco in Spain, Anastasio Somoza in Nicaragua, Ferdinand Marcos in the Philippines, and the shah of Iran. Under a foreign policy oriented more toward democratic values, we would have kept our distance from such dictators.

Debate over the direction of our foreign policy was radically altered by the collapse of the Soviet Union. Some observers predicted that economic competition would replace the arms race of the Cold War era, with Japan and the European Community providing most of the competition. Although battles for market share are fundamentally different from a nuclear standoff, some basic questions remain: What role should our commitment to democratic values play in shaping U.S. foreign policy? Should the United States concentrate on protecting its own security and power or on protecting democratic values? If the latter, how are those values best protected?

Religion and Morality in Politics

In recent years many influential political leaders, including President Ronald Reagan, have advocated a vigorous injection of religion into public life. The most prominent example of this trend has been the widespread support for a constitutional amendment allowing prayer in public schools. To supporters of this amendment and similar measures, religious values can help to define and shape public policies.

Controversy over the proper place of religion in political life is not new to U.S. politics. From the founding of the nation, many people have argued that a democratic society must be based on strong religious values. Proponents of various secular crusades—such as drives to outlaw the sale of alcohol and to regulate matters of personal morality, including forms of marriage and sexual orientation and conduct—have frequently solicited the support of religious groups. And religious values have been invoked by our leaders in support of U.S. foreign policies. Some students of U.S. political life argue that we have fashioned a **civic religion** in which church-related values are combined with a reverence for secular political forms and practices.[25]

Of course, the United States is not the only nation to mix religion and politics in sometimes volatile ways. Battles have been waged over the appropriate political role

The TV character Murphy Brown, played by Candice Bergen, is shown here holding her TV baby. The fact that she, a single woman (in the TV show), decided to have a baby without a father became a focus of controversy during the 1992 presidential campaign. Republican Vice-President Dan Quayle criticized the TV show for undermining respect for intact families where fathers were present. The ensuing discussion about "family values" did not clarify much, but it did highlight questions about exactly what constituted a "family." (Sygma)

of organized religion in most democratic nations for at least two centuries. In modern-day France and Italy, the Roman Catholic church has repeatedly thrust itself into political controversy, especially on such issues as divorce, abortion, and aid to church-sponsored schools. Pope John Paul II has attempted to influence governments worldwide by publicly voicing strong views on new reproductive technologies, among other things.

From time to time, religious groups have also taken action in the sphere of American foreign policy, striving to impose particular religious or humanitarian values in geopolitically sensitive areas. During the 1980s, for example, many American churches carried on active campaigns in Central America—some to gain converts, some to assist various social and political movements or communities. Some conservative Protestant churches, for example, provided and campaigned for aid to the Contras, rebels who were attempting to destabilize the Sandinista government of Nicaragua. But church people from a variety of faiths attempted to assist development projects within Nicaragua as well. In addition, religious ideas, such as the concept of **liberation theology**—a policy developed by Catholic clerics in Latin America whereby parish priests actively promote the cause of political liberation rather than endorsing the status quo—have often had important political significance. In the United States itself, some churches protected exiles from Central America, hiding them and moving them from

> **SUMMARY CHART**
> **SOME IMPORTANT TENSIONS IN U.S. POLITICAL CULTURE**
>
> Between the norm of the "open society" and the realities of discrimination and intolerance
>
> Between respect for the rule of law and the common resort to violence
>
> Between the desire to make the world "safe for democracy" and the pursuit of our interests as a great power
>
> Between tolerance for different lifestyles and values and the wish to enforce certain moral norms on all

one part of the country to another. This struggle to provide sanctuary was sometimes prosecuted by the federal government on the ground that the exiles were in the country illegally. The churches spearheading the sanctuary movement maintained that the lives of these refugees would be in danger if they were forced to return home—to El Salvador, for instance.

Throughout U.S. history, Americans have argued over whether religion should be part of politics. Although the nation has tended to move in a more secular direction, Americans have remained overwhelmingly proreligion in attitude. This apparent contradiction leaves many significant conflicts and questions unresolved. Where should religious values end and public policy begin? Our liberal tradition calls for tolerance and acceptance of a diversity of values and approaches. Yet some people contend that morality can and should be enforced, that public authorities ought to legislate what is good and right for us all. As a predominantly religious people and, at the same time, a liberal society, how do we decide?

CONCLUSIONS

Many of our core political values support democratic practices. As a predominantly liberal society, we officially and unequivocally favor individual rights, tolerance, equal opportunity, the rule of law, and democratic political institutions. Yet Americans have experienced great difficulties in living up to the high standards of democracy. Many groups have been the objects of discrimination and exploitation. We have often reached for the gun to settle disputes, abandoning the rule of law. In foreign relations, the United States has acted both as a defender of democracy and as an imperial world power. Playing both these roles has often left Americans and their leaders confused about just what the nation is supposed to stand for. Finally, some Americans wish to impose their ideas of morality on others, in the name of preserving values essential to democracy. Others maintain that imposing one person's morality on another violates the basic spirit of liberalism.

In short, U.S. political culture is a mix; some elements tend to support democratic practices, and others are hostile to them. The conflicts in U.S. history over equal treatment, tolerance, rule of law, and the direction of foreign policy reveal a dynamic tension that resonates to this day.

Glossary Terms

civic religion
Cold War
conservatives
demographics
free enterprise
liberalism
liberation theology

libertarianism
natural rights
New Deal
political culture
populist
socialist
tyranny of the majority

Notes

[1] William F. Stone, *The Psychology of Politics* (New York: Free Press, 1974), chap. 7; Seymour Martin Lipset, "Values, Social Character and the Democratic Polity," in *The First New Nation: The United States in Comparative and Historical Perspective* (New York: Basic Books, 1963), pp. 274–285.

[2] Seymour Martin Lipset, *Political Man* (Garden City, N.Y.: Doubleday, 1970), chap. 2.

[3] Jarol B. Mannheim, *The Politics Within: A Primer in Attitudes and Behavior*, 2nd ed. (New York: Longman, 1982), pp. 61–64.

[4] Louis Hartz, *The Liberal Tradition in America* (New York: Harcourt, 1964); Alexis de Tocqueville, *Democracy in America* (New York: Harper & Row, 1966).

[5] Erich Fromm, *Escape from Freedom* (New York: Avon, 1965), chap. 2.

[6] Ibid., chap. 3; Erik H. Erikson, *Young Man Luther* (New York: Norton, 1958).

[7] John Locke, *Second Treatise on Civil Government* (New York: Appleton, 1937), chaps. 1–7; Harry K. Girvetz, *The Evolution of Liberalism* (New York: Collier, 1963), chaps. 4 and 5.

[8] Thomas Archdeacon, *Becoming American: An Ethnic History* (New York: Macmillan, 1983).

[9] Lawrence Goodwyn, *The Populist Movement: A Short History of the Agrarian Revolt in America* (New York: Oxford University Press, 1978).

[10] Seymour Martin Lipset, "Values and Democratic Stability," in *The First New Nation*, pp. 207–247.

[11] Gunnar Myrdal, *An American Dilemma* (New York: Harper & Row, 1962).

[12] Girvetz, *Evolution of Liberalism*, chap. 15.

[13] John Dewey, *Liberalism and Social Action* (New York: Capricorn Books, 1963).

[14] John H. M. Laslett and Seymour Martin Lipset, eds., *Failure of a Dream: Essays on the History of American Socialism* (Garden City, N.Y.: Doubleday, 1974).

[15] Daniel P. Moynihan and Nathan Glazer, *Beyond the Melting Pot* (Cambridge, Mass.: MIT Press, 1963).

[16] Terry Eastland and William J. Bennett, *Counting by Race: Equality from the Founding Fathers to Baake and Weber* (New York: Basic Books, 1979); Stanley Feldstein, *The Poisoned Tongue: A Documentary History of American Racism and Prejudice* (New York: Morrow, 1972).

[17] Peter Irons, *Justice at War* (New York: Oxford University Press, 1983).

[18] Joe B. Frantz, "The Frontier Tradition: An Invitation to Violence," in *The History of Violence in America* ed. Hugh David Graham and Ted Robert Gurr (New York: Praeger, 1969), pp. 127–153.

[19] J. F. Kirkham, S. Levy, and W. J. Crotty, eds., *Assassination and Political Violence: Staff Report to the National Commission on the Causes and Prevention of Violence* (Washington, D.C.: U.S. Government Printing Office, 1969), pp. 171–177.

[20] George E. Berkley, *The Democratic Policeman* (New York: Ballantine, 1976).

[21] Theodore Draper, *Abuse of Power* (New York: Viking, 1967), chap. 8.

[22] Reinhold Niebuhr and Alan Heimert, *A Nation So Conceived* (New York: Scribner, 1963).

[23] Richard Drinnon, *Facing West: The Metaphysics of Indian-hating and Empire-building* (New York: New American Library, 1980).

[24] Frederick Merk, *Manifest Destiny and Mission in American History* (New York: Vintage, 1966); Albert K. Weinberg, *Manifest Destiny* (Baltimore: Johns Hopkins, 1970).

[25] Robert N. Bellah, *The Broken Covenant: American Civil Religion in a Time of Trial* (New York: Harper & Row, 1976); Ernest Tuveson, *Redeemer Nation: The Idea of America's Millennial Role* (Chicago: University of Chicago Press, 1980); Robert N. Bellah and Frederick E. Greenspahn, eds., *Uncivil Religion: Interreligious Hostility in America* (New York: Crossroad, 1987).

SELECTED READINGS

POLITICAL CULTURE

For recent work on **political culture**, see William S. Stewart, *Understanding Politics: The Cultures of Societies and the Structures of Governments* (Novato, Calif.: Chandler & Sharp, 1988); Keith Hoggart, *People, Power, and Place: Perspectives on Anglo-American Politics* (Boston: Routledge, 1991).

THE LIBERAL TRADITION

Classic treatments of the **liberal tradition** can be found in Louis Hartz, *The Founding of New Societies* (New York: Harcourt, 1969) and *The Liberal Tradition in America* (New York: Harcourt, 1955), and in Vernon Parrington, *Main Currents in American Thought* (Norman: University of Oklahoma Press, 1987). More recent work in liberal theory can be found in William A. Galston, *Liberal Purposes: Goods, Virtues, and Diversity in the Liberal State* (New York: Cambridge University Press, 1991).

Alonzo L. Hamby provides a recent look at **liberalism** in the twentieth century in *Liberalism and Its Challengers: From FDR to Bush*, 2nd ed. (New York: Oxford University Press, 1992).

U.S. **conservatism** has been a notoriously difficult subject to pin down. For a classic statement, see Friedrich A. von Hayek, *The Road to Serfdom* (Chicago: University of Chicago Press, 1944, 1976). For an assortment of approaches, see Russell Kirk, ed., *The Portable Conservative Reader* (New York: Penguin, 1982); and George Will, *The Pursuit of Happiness and Other Sobering Thoughts* (New York: Harper & Row, 1979).

E. J. Dionne, Jr., has written an engaging history of liberalism and conservatism in *Why American Hate Politics* (New York: Simon & Schuster, 1991).

THE LIMITS OF LIBERALISM

A classic account of **intolerance** in America is Richard Hofstadter, *The Paranoid Style in American Politics and Other Essays* (Chicago: University of Chicago Press, 1979). More recent works include Andrew R. Cecil, *Equality, Tolerance, and Loyalty: Virtues Serving the Common Purpose of Democracy* (Dallas: University of Texas Press, 1990).

For historical treatments of **violence** in America, see Hugh David Graham and Ted Robert Gurr, eds., *Violence in America: Historical and Comparative Perspectives* (Beverly Hills, Calif.: Sage, 1979); and Richard M. Brown, *Strains of Violence: Historical Studies of American Violence and Vigilantism* (New York: Oxford University Press, 1975).

On **gender issues** and liberalism, see Anne Phillips, *Engendering Democracy* (University Park: Pennsylvania State University Press, 1991); and Alison Assiter, *Pornography, Feminism, and the Individual* (Winchester, Mass.: Pluto Press, 1989). **Foreign policy**, American political culture, and liberalism are discussed in Larry May, ed., *Recasting America: Culture and Politics in the Age of the Cold War* (Chicago: University of Chicago Press, 1989); David B. Davis, *Revolutions: Reflections on American Equality and Foreign Liberations* (Cambridge, Mass.: Harvard University Press, 1980); and Gregory A. Fossedal, *The Democratic Imperative: Exporting the American Revolution* (New York: Basic Books, 1989).

COMPARATIVE PERSPECTIVES ON LIBERALISM

A classic study, updated, is Gabriel A. Almond and Sidney Verba, eds., *The Civic Culture Revisited* (Boston: Little, Brown, 1980). For further reading on **Sweden**, see Barry P. Bosworth and Alice M. Rivlin, eds., *The Swedish Economy* (Washington: Brookings Institution, 1987), and Hugh Heclo and Henrik Madsen, *Policy and Politics in Sweden* (Philadelphia: Temple University Press, 1987).

IMMIGRATION LAW AND NATIONAL IDENTITY

For two sides of the **immigration** debate, see William Dudley, ed., *Immigration: Opposing Viewpoints* (San Diego, Calif.: Greenhaven Press, 1990); and Frank D. Bean, Barry Edmonston, and Jeffery S. Passel, eds., *Undocumented Migration to the United States: IRCA and the Experience of the 1980s* (Washington D.C.: Urban Institute, 1990). For a comparative look at immigration policy in the United States, Australia, Britain, Germany, Israel, and Venezuela, see Michael C. Lemay, ed., *The Gatekeepers: Comparative Immigration Policy* (New York: Praeger, 1989).

RELIGION AND POLITICS

For a better understanding of the interplay of religion and politics in American democracy, see Robert Booth Fowler, *Unconventional Partners: Religion and Liberal Culture in the United States* (Grand Rapids, Mich.: Eerdmans, 1989); and F. Forrester Church, *God and Other Famous Liberals: Reclaiming the Politics of America* (New York: Simon and Schuster, 1991).

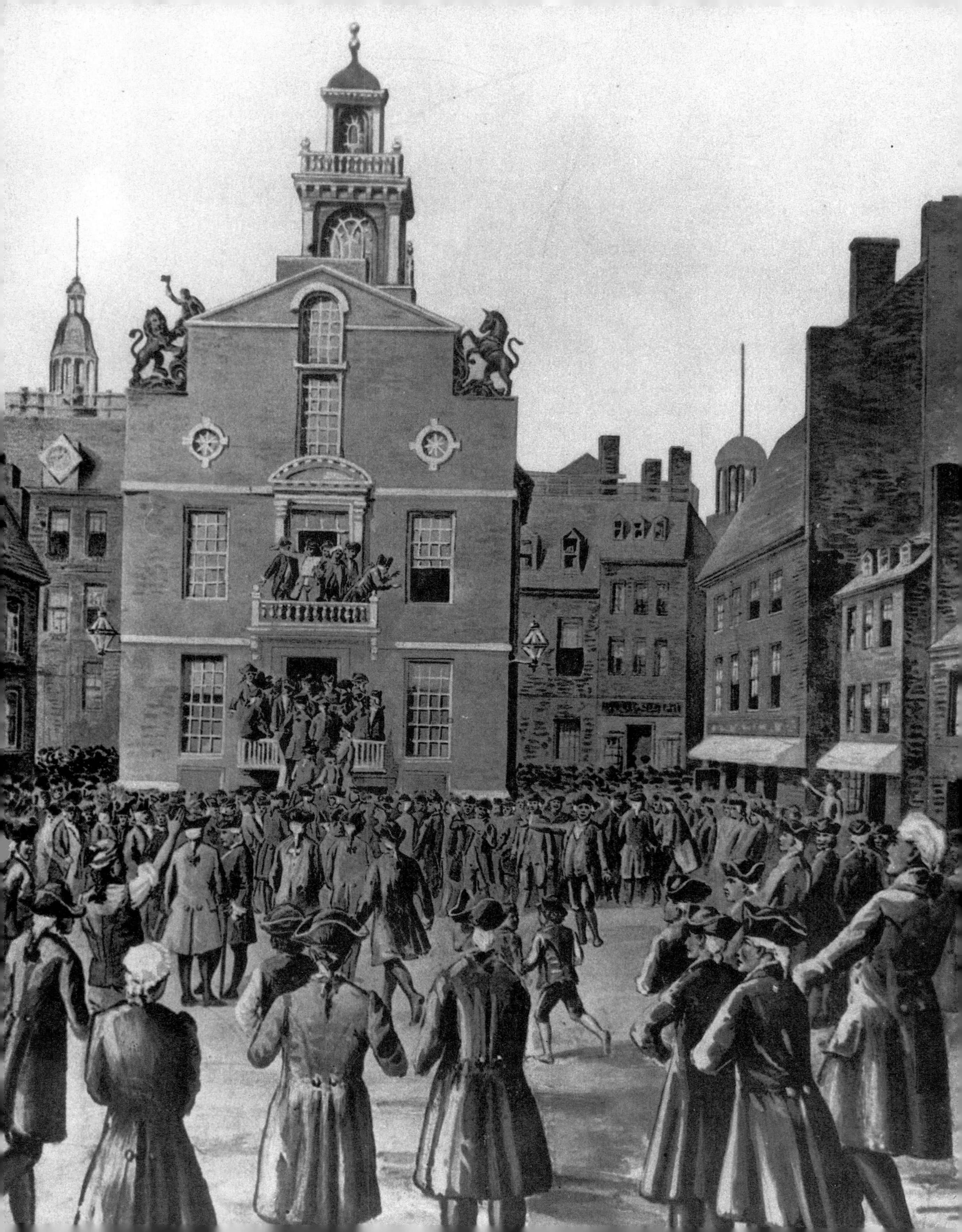

CHAPTER THREE

REVOLUTION AND CONSTITUTION

The American Way

CHAPTER OUTLINE

Background of the Revolution
THE SOCIOECONOMIC ENVIRONMENT
THE POLITICAL ENVIRONMENT
IMPERIAL AUTHORITY AND AMERICAN DEFIANCE

The Revolutionary War

Independence and Political Ferment in the United States
THE ARTICLES OF CONFEDERATION
TOWARD A NEW GOVERNMENT

The New Constitution
A STRONGER NATIONAL GOVERNMENT
LIMITATION OF POWER
INDIRECT REPRESENTATION
FOUR ISSUES LEFT FOR LATER RESOLUTION
RATIFICATION
AMENDING THE CONSTITUTION

An Enduring Political Legacy

THE UNITED STATES GOVERNMENT WAS NOT CREATED IN A single stroke of direct divine intervention. Though perhaps divinely inspired, this decidedly human effort took some time to accomplish. A full eleven years after the Declaration of Independence, and as a result of struggles and compromises that followed the end of the Revolutionary War, our first national charter, the Articles of Confederation, was replaced by the Constitution. Hindsight may make the Articles of Confederation seem fatally flawed. Through twentieth-century eyes, the Articles government seems too weak, destined to be replaced by a strong central government with an energetic executive. But in the late 1780s the replacement was extremely controversial. Alternatives were vigorously debated. It may be useful to ask, then, just how inevitable was the outcome of the Constitutional Convention? Different choices could have been made. Many of the central figures in the American Revolution were not very happy with the results of the Constitutional Convention. The ratification battles were bitter and closely contested. It might seem odd to us that any reasonable person could oppose the Constitution, but it did not seem so at the time. To understand this, it helps to remember

83

that the Revolution itself was more than a simple struggle for democratic ideals and less than an all-out effort based on broad national consensus.

Throughout the revolutionary period the focus of national debate was, naturally, Great Britain's treatment of the colonies. In the postrevolutionary period, different political battles seized the spotlight. The new nation's attention shifted to the problems of managing an independent (and war-ravaged) economy. The framing of the Constitution is characterized by some observers as a "second founding," tempering the more radical democratic impulses of the postrevolutionary period. This second founding drew its inspiration more from an older republican tradition than from the revolutionary themes of the Declaration of Independence and the fraternal themes of the Articles of Confederation. The new Constitution shifted the balance of power toward the central government and away from the states, toward the financially secure and away from the small farmers and merchants whose demands for cheap money and debt relief were often indulged by state legislatures.

The men who gathered at the Constitutional Convention in Philadelphia in 1787 may have shared a general outlook on politics, but not much else. Sharp disagreements divided even the participants whose ideas ultimately prevailed. Central figures changed their minds; most remained dissatisfied with one or another of the compromises resulting from their work. Some prominent members of the Constitutional Convention, including Edmund Randolph, who introduced the famous Virginia Plan, eventually refused to sign. James Madison, called the "father of the Constitution," vigorously opposed ideas that became major features of the final document, including equal representation for states in the Senate. From the beginning our governmental structure was a pieced-together response to specific conditions of the times. The real strength of the Constitution—its ability to survive and prosper—springs from a healthy balance between narrow self-interest and grand idealism. Distinctions between these motives are often difficult to discern, but both were part of the great debate that forged the organic law that has guided our nation for more than two centuries.

How did the American Revolution and the Constitution measure up to the expectations of democracy? This chapter will look at the Revolution itself and the circumstances leading to it; the disputes that followed, engulfing the Articles of Confederation and the new state governments in conflict; and the framing of the Constitution and the mechanisms by which it can be changed. We will examine major revolutionary and constitutional choices—and nonchoices—and their implications. We will then be in a better position to address the question of whether the Constitution still responds to the demands of modern democratic life.

Background of the Revolution

What kind of society was colonial America? How was its economy structured, its wealth distributed? What political ideals were widely shared, and what role did those ideals play in conflicts between the colonies and Great Britain? We shall explore the socioeconomic environment that fostered the revolutionary spirit, the political environment that gave the Revolution momentum, and the exercise of British imperial authority that provoked ever-greater American defiance.

The Socioeconomic Environment

In the 1770s the thirteen American colonies comprised a rapidly growing society of some 2.5 million inhabitants, 60 percent of whom were of English origin. The principal ethnic minorities were Scots, Irish, Welsh, and Germans, plus a significant number of black slaves (28 percent of the southern population). Americans were a young people: Half the population was under sixteen, much of the rest under forty. The population was doubling every twenty years.

Trading was a vital component of the colonial economy. The southern colonies carried on a large volume of direct trade with England, exporting tobacco, rice, and indigo—despite British taxes on American tobacco that consumed an estimated 75 percent of all profits. The middle, or "bread," colonies, consisting of New York, New Jersey, Pennsylvania, and Delaware, traded principally in grain and flour. Pennsylvania was the fastest-growing colony, and Philadelphia, with a population of forty thousand, was America's largest municipality. Only four urban centers other than Philadelphia could properly be called cities: New York; Charleston, South Carolina; Boston; and Newport, Rhode Island. All five cities were Atlantic ports, where news and traffic from abroad arrived first. Apart from these few urban centers, the colonies were overwhelmingly rural. Only 10 percent of the population lived in towns of more than two thousand inhabitants. And despite the importance of trading activities, America was primarily a society of farmers and farmworkers.

Colonial society was not fundamentally egalitarian. In many colonies a small number of aristocratic families exercised great political and social power. Throughout America property ownership had grown increasingly concentrated in the hands of a few. In 1771 a mere 5 percent of Boston families held almost half the total taxable wealth, and in Philadelphia 10 percent of the population held 46 percent of the total.[1]

In contrast, an estimated 20 to 30 percent of the colonial population, excluding slaves, was impoverished. In major cities, food shortages occasionally sparked riots; in rural areas, discontent with the working conditions of tenant farmers led to popular upheavals. Some of the poverty-stricken formed the core of urban mobs that helped to foment revolutionary agitation, and many served in the Continental Army.

Between these extremes of wealth and poverty, however, was a fairly prosperous middle class encompassing 50 to 70 percent of the population. The presence of so large a middle class, combined with the "leveling" tendencies at work in colonial society, gave the colonies a degree of equality unknown in Europe. Social and class distinctions did not carry the weight they did across the Atlantic, and as a result, the colonists displayed a spirit of independent-mindedness, a defiance of authority, and a desire for economic self-betterment unheard of in Europe.

Considerable religious diversity also marked the colonies, and in some areas religious intolerance took hold: In Rhode Island, for example, only Trinitarian Protestants could become full citizens. Yet tolerance of religious differences became the rule rather than the exception, and lively religious dialogues formed a staple of intellectual life.

The Political Environment

By the 1770s most of the colonial governments had been functioning for over a century. Eight of the thirteen were royal colonies, whose governors were appointed by the British king. Connecticut and Rhode Island had charters granted in the seventeenth century allowing for self-government and hence elected their own governors. Maryland, Pennsylvania, and Delaware were so-called proprietary colonies, owned by families—the Penns in Pennsylvania and Delaware, the Calverts in Maryland. All colonial governors had broad powers, including an absolute veto over acts of the legislatures and the power to appoint all judges and militia officers. In most colonies the governor also appointed the members of the upper house of the legislature.

Every colony except Pennsylvania had a legislature with an upper and a lower house. The upper houses, which generally acted only as advisory bodies, were made up of the wealthier and more conservative citizens. In contrast, elections for the lower houses of colonial legislatures were remarkably democratic by the standards of the day. Although the franchise was limited in many areas by property qualifications, in practice most white males were permitted to vote for legislators. It was in the lower houses that opposition to British taxation was most vociferous in the 1770s.

The colonies shared the British political tradition, based to a significant degree on the rule of law and the principle of constitutionalism. Accordingly, the powers exercised by colonial governments were generally limited by written charters. Because more colonists could participate more fully in local politics, they may actually have enjoyed greater political and civil rights than most English citizens.

As heirs to the liberal tradition, most colonial political leaders believed that underlying constitutions and laws were fundamental rights, violations of which entitled citizens to seek redress from the government. If the government did not honor these rights, liberal theory held, citizens could legitimately overthrow that government. Governments, in other words, could and should be held accountable for their actions and the ways in which they upheld the basic interests of citizens.

Imperial Authority and American Defiance

In the early 1760s the British Empire was growing prodigiously. Having defeated France and Spain in the **Seven Years' War** (1756–1763; known in the colonies as the French and Indian War), the British had removed the threats formerly posed to their possessions in the New World by the French in Canada and the Spanish in Florida. As a result, the American colonists were feeling less dependent on the mother country than ever before. At the same time, however, the costs of empire had begun to weigh more and

REVOLUTION AND CONSTITUTION

Many historians have remarked about the political folly of George III and the British government, whose high-handedness provoked the Revolutionary War that led to the loss of the American colonies. In fact, many in England opposed the government's policies from the start. *(National Archives)*

more heavily on the British treasury. Rather than going along with the colonists' desire for more autonomy, especially in economic matters, the British crown sought greater authority over colonial affairs—in particular, the authority to impose direct taxes to defray the costs of defending and expanding the empire.

In both financial and military terms, American participation in the Seven Years' War had fallen far short of expectations by the mother country, which considered that defeating the French and the Spanish directly benefited the colonies. As one measure of the colonies' indifference to British concerns, only three of the thirteen contributed full quotas of troops to the war. In several ways, moreover, disobedience to the crown and nonenforcement of British rules had become common in America. Various acts of Parliament imposing duties on American goods were largely circumvented or ignored by the colonists. In addition, a thriving trade between the French West Indies and American merchants was carried on in violation of British law.

Disobedience turned into defiance when the British Parliament in March 1765 passed the **Stamp Act**, which required "that Americans pay their own protection and defense out of revenues from the sale of stamped paper to be used on some fifty items, including newspapers, pamphlets, playing cards, wills, land deeds, marriage licenses, college diplomas, bills of sale, port clearance papers, and so on." Those who violated the act could be tried and penalized without benefit of jury. The Stamp Act had been conceived by George Grenville, First Lord of the Treasury under King George III. Grenville argued that the act was needed not merely to increase revenues but also to assert Parliament's absolute sovereignty over the colonies. When the Americans argued that because they were not represented in Parliament, Parliament did not have the right to levy taxes on them, Grenville invoked the doctrine of virtual representation. According to this doctrine, a favorite argument of the day, each member of Parliament had a responsibility to the entire empire, and therefore even the American colonists were in some sense represented in Parliament.

The Stamp Act was one in a series of serious miscalculations by British authorities. Intent on asserting control over the colonies, they underestimated the growing colonial spirit of independence and failed to recognize that each new attempt to exert control only aggravated the situation. Without the Stamp Act and similar actions that followed, the British might have been able to capitalize on the relative calm that followed the Seven Years' War. Instead, many colonists came to view the crown with increasing suspicion and to decry London's alleged exploitation of the colonies.

Colonial reaction to the Stamp Act was harsh—and very effective. Several months after the act was passed, the first organized resistance took place in Boston. The so-called Sons of Liberty, a radical group composed of artisans, apprentices, day laborers, and merchant seamen, hanged effigies of Andrew Oliver, the king's agent for stamp distribution in Massachusetts, and Lord Bute, a close friend of the king's. The effigies were hanged from what came to be known as the Liberty Tree. To make their points, the Sons of Liberty never shied away from using force. One group of defiant colonists, carrying the effigies, destroyed a warehouse belonging to Oliver and then burned the effigies in a huge bonfire on a hillside near his home. Several protesters even ransacked Oliver's home, making off with his extensive wine collection. The following day Oliver resigned, and no one would take his place. None of the Sons of Liberty was ever brought to trial.

A year after passing the Stamp Act, Parliament repealed it, only to enact the so-called Townshend duties, which taxed colonial imports of paint, tea, lead, and paper. Again the colonists protested, and eventually all the duties except one—on tea—were repealed. After a few years of relative calm between British authorities and American colonials, Parliament in 1773 granted the East India Company the exclusive right to sell tea to American local dealers. The mandate, which shut out American merchants from the tea trade, prompted the famous Boston Tea Party, in which protesters disguised as Indians dumped tea from British ships into Boston harbor. In response, the British closed the port of Boston—a drastic economic penalty for a city that depended so heavily on trading. In addition, the charter of the colony of Massachusetts was virtually withdrawn, and elections and town meetings were forbidden.

These actions provoked even wider defiance of British authority. Groups of concerned citizens met in several colonies and sent delegates to the First Continental Congress. Convened in Philadelphia in 1774, the Congress promptly called for a boycott of British goods. Armed conflict broke out in Massachusetts the following year, when the British commander in Boston sent troops to seize weapons stored by the colonists in Concord. In 1775 the Second Continental Congress, though hesitating to

REVOLUTION AND CONSTITUTION

Disguised as Indians, rebellious colonists tossed heavily taxed British tea into Boston harbor. (National Archives)

make a final break with Britain, decided to raise an army and began making overtures to France for assistance. Shortly thereafter, the more radical American political leaders finally persuaded the moderates that the colonies needed full independence, and Congress commissioned Thomas Jefferson to write a formal declaration of independence. The radicals won over their more cautious peers with the help of a slim pamphlet, Tom Paine's *Common Sense*, which electrified colonial America when it appeared in January 1776. In *Common Sense*, Paine placed America's struggle in a larger perspective, viewing it as part of all humanity's drive for free government. For Paine the American cause exemplified the universal struggle between liberty and tyranny; the patriots' cause embodied much more than specific grievances against the British crown.

When the Second Continental Congress reconvened in June 1776, Thomas Jefferson presented a draft of the Declaration of Independence. It was amended and approved by the Congress on July 4, 1776, two days after an official resolution of independence from Great Britain had been passed. Jefferson's declaration had been called the single most influential piece of American political writing. Its complete text appears in Appendix A at the end of this book.

The Revolutionary War

The war itself was an unexpectedly protracted and, in military terms, oddly inconclusive affair. The British had every reason to believe that they could subdue the colonials easily. Their army was highly experienced and well trained, and their navy was the

"The first blow for liberty": the battle of Lexington. There was no reason for the great British empire to doubt its ability to subdue the unruly colonists. Yet it has often proved very difficult to wage successful wars against resistant populations—as the French discovered in Indochina in the 1950s and the Soviets learned in Afghanistan in the 1980s. *(National Archives)*

world's largest. By 1778 there were almost fifty thousand British troops in North America, along with thirty thousand German mercenaries. The Americans, starting from scratch, eventually put together the Continental Army of five thousand, supplemented by state militia units. Their officers were inexperienced, although George Washington had gained some actual combat experience in the Seven Years' War.

The British, however, suffered from serious disadvantages: The war had to be waged three thousand miles from the British Isles, the vast and mostly wild American terrain was difficult to conquer in any sense, and there was no single nerve center of revolutionary activity whose destruction would ensure a decisive British military victory. Moreover, even if the British had won the war militarily, they would have had to face the daunting task of restoring imperial domination over the defiant colonials. Finally, many observers criticized the British for waging the war indecisively, vacillating between ill-thought-out attempts to gain a pivotal military victory and efforts to achieve a reconciliation with the revolutionaries.

The American war for independence also became an international contest. France supplied large quantities of munitions to the Americans, and both France and Spain eventually declared war on Great Britain. Other nations, including Sweden, Russia, and Prussia, moved to protect their shipping from British blockades of the colonies. In the end, French support was crucial to the success of the revolutionary effort, with elements of the French fleet and army helping to make the decisive American victory at Yorktown (1781) possible.

The revolutionaries also had to overcome formidable difficulties. Keeping an army in the field was a constant problem for the new nation. Not only was labor in short supply, but popular support often flagged. Desertions from the Continental Army were numerous, and many farmers who did serve refused to extend their tours of duty when planting or harvest season arrived. Cash incentives were required to maintain more than a token force in the field. In January 1777, Congress offered $20, new clothing, and one hundred acres of land in exchange for a pledge to serve for the duration of the war. Nevertheless, there was no rush to enlist. States were given quotas to fill before each new campaign, and often slaves, indentured servants, and propertyless day laborers were paid to take the place of the middle-class farmers who would otherwise have had to serve. The revolutionary ideal was a militia based on a universal obligation to serve; the reality was an army made up largely of the poor and others who responded principally to financial incentives.

Of even greater concern to the revolutionaries, however, was active or passive opposition to the war within the colonies. It has been estimated that up to 20 percent of the white population remained actively loyal to the crown and that close to 50 percent remained neutral in the struggle.[2] More and more colonials became less and less enthusiastic as the war dragged on.

In the end, however, British public opinion deserted the war faster than American public opinion. After the French-American victory at Yorktown, the British abandoned their attempt to crush the rebellion, even though they still had the dominant position militarily. The Americans defeated the British not by gaining a clear-cut military victory but simply by persevering and refusing to lose the war. In the **Treaty of Paris**, signed September 3, 1783, the British government formally recognized the independence of its former colonies. Few treaties have had such far-reaching political ramifications. Around the world, political life was irrevocably changed. The newly won American independence prompted a spurt of political activity.

In Europe the American Revolution had a profound impact. The very idea that a people could declare independence and base it on the ideal of equal rights for all seemed to show that liberty was not just an abstract concept. As each new American state wrote its own constitution and these were translated into French, the American example prompted French revolutionaries to draw up a declaration of human rights and draft a new constitution of their own. Latin American nations too looked to this example in the early nineteenth century, when they fought to free themselves from Spanish domination.

Finally, the new United States was widely seen abroad as the place where ordinary people could enjoy legal rights and could participate fully in political life. This perception, as well as the young nation's reputation as a land of limitless economic opportunity, made the United States attractive to immigrants and provided a model for change.

(Text continues on page 93)

COMPARATIVE PERSPECTIVE

THE FRENCH REVOLUTION AND ITS AFTERMATH

The French and American revolutions seem to have had much in common. Both originated in rebellions against monarchical governments; and both sought constitutional rule, government by consent, and the affirmation of the basic rights of citizens. There the similarities end, however. In comparison with events in France, the American Revolution and its aftermath were mild and orderly indeed.

The French Revolution began in 1789 in a rebellion within the Estates-General, an assembly summoned by King Louis XVI. The Estates-General comprised three estates, or classes, based on the status system of feudal society: the clergy, the nobles, and everyone else (the Third Estate). Once in session, the Estates-General quickly became a forum for reformist and even revolutionary sentiment, and a struggle for control developed between the nobles and the Third Estate. Violence broke out in many parts of the country. A mob in Paris stormed the Bastille (a state prison), murdered its governor after ninety-eight of the insurgents had been killed, and went on to murder the mayor. In the countryside, too, peasants began to rebel against the landed aristocracy.

The Third Estate separated from the Estates-General and declared itself the National Assembly. In effect, through the reform measures it enacted, the Third Estate abolished the feudal system. In August 1789 it issued the Declaration of the Rights of Man and Citizen. A new government, in which the king would have only the power to suspend legislation by veto, was formed in 1791, but the king refused to participate in it. Counterrevolutionary forces, both foreign and domestic, began to threaten the Revolution, and war broke out in 1792 between France and its monarchist neighbors.

While fighting foreign foes, the revolutionary regime began a domestic reign of terror against real and suspected opponents of the government. During this period (1793–1794), an estimated forty thousand people (including the king) were executed, and thousands of others were driven into exile.

From 1795 to 1799 France was a constitutional republic in which all literate citizens had the right to vote. But war pressures and a lack of popular support weakened the republican government, and Napoleon Bonaparte seized power in 1799. He ruled under a form of benevolent despotism until his armies were defeated by foreign powers in 1815. Napoleon suppressed the democratic impulses of the original revolution, establishing, in effect, a new monarchy. For several decades the government alternated between more democratic and more royalist regimes. Not until 1870 was a genuine republic established that was destined to last for a substantial period.

Independence and Political Ferment in the United States

In the United States new political enthusiasms—some noble in vision, some narrow in scope—emerged following the war. Demands for equality, even when it came to slavery, marked much of the political discourse. In 1774 the Continental Congress had urged the abolition of the slave trade, and in 1775 the world's first antislavery society was formed by Quakers in Philadelphia. After the war some northern states granted freedom to slaves who had served in the Continental Army, and most northern states moved to end slavery within their borders.

The new state governments, endowed with sovereign authority, soon demonstrated the trade-offs inherent in the ideals of majoritarian democracy and republican protection for valued principles and individual rights. Just how majoritarian were these new governments to be? Economically, a majoritarian government is liable to be more sensitive to debtors than creditors and more attuned to short-term economic fixes than long-term economic security. Independence left economic control in the hands of the state governments, allowing those governments to pursue local self-interest at the expense of broader national interests.

Another aspect of the revolutionary frame of mind was to deny executive officers the kind of power that might lead to despotism. The legislatures in the several state governments were clearly dominant, the executives subordinate. How little executive power could we afford? Again trade-offs were apparent: A powerful legislature is a safeguard against despotism but also a fertile field for the operation of special interests. As James Madison was to warn in the *Federalist Papers* (No. 10), the tendency to favor particular narrow interests with the division of power into smaller political units—state governments as opposed to a strong national government.

And indeed, parochialism was becoming evident in state legislatures—what Madison described as a "spirit of locality." During and after the Revolution, legislatures became increasingly embroiled in conflicts between various narrow interests. Few legislators were looking out for the interests of the community as a whole. Critics of the actions of the Vermont legislature, for example, complained that laws were altered, altered again, made better, made worse—but were always in flux. Many of the new laws favored particular individuals or groups. Pressure group politics was already a force in U.S. political life.

Before the Revolution, many Americans had seen the legislature as the basis for the people's sovereignty, the bulwark against executive excess. In the war's aftermath, however, fear of legislative excesses grew. As Jefferson put it, "173 despots would surely be as oppressive as one." Many people began to worry about how to ensure that fundamental law would not be tampered with and liberty would thus be kept safe.

On the national level, leaders struggled to consolidate the thirteen states into one nation without creating a strong central authority. At all costs they did not want to risk the abuses of power possible in a centralized system like the British monarchy.

The Articles of Confederation

Soon after declaring independence, American political leaders turned to the task of establishing a new government. In 1781, shortly before the war ended, the last of the thirteen states ratified the nation's first written constitution, the **Articles of Confederation**. The principal political impulse behind the Articles was fear of a strong central authority; its authors wanted to ensure that the new national government was not endowed with the excessive power possessed by the British monarch. In doing so, they created a government that could function effectively only with the unanimous consent of the states. The only national political body under the Articles was the one-house Continental Congress, in which each state had one vote. There was no independent chief executive and no national court system. The Congress had the power to create executive departments and to approve treaties, but it could not print money, levy taxes on the citizens of the states, or regulate interstate commerce.

Political realities soon exposed the weaknesses of this government. Controversies raging among the states simply could not be settled without a national court system and a stronger national government. Many Americans feared that Great Britain would foment and take advantage of interstate rivalries. Further, the central government had so few powers that the focus of blame for social and political problems shifted to state governments. For instance, because only the states could print money, people who felt the squeeze of tight money in the postwar depression looked to the states for help. In Massachusetts, debt-ridden farmers who were facing foreclosure demanded that the

The rebellion of debtor farmers led by Daniel Shays stirred intense passions in New England. Conflicts between debtors and creditors were among the factors leading to the Constitutional Convention in Philadelphia. (Culver Pictures)

A Scene in Shays's Rebellion.

state legislature issue more paper money. When the legislature refused, the farmers led by Daniel Shays, took up arms in August 1786. Their first protests were directed against local courts, which they prevented from conducting business. Later the rebels also forced the state supreme court to adjourn. Only after both state militia and federal troops were called out against Shays and his supporters was the rebellion crushed in early 1787. However, most participants, including Shays, were pardoned by the state legislature.

Shays's Rebellion succeeded, at least in part. Largely because of this uprising, the Massachusetts legislature in 1787 decided not to impose new taxes, lowered court fees, and exempted household goods, clothing, and the tools of one's trade from the debt process (preventing them from being seized to pay off debts). But even of greater importance, Shays's Rebellion spotlighted the need for a strong national government. And it convinced many political leaders, particularly those sensitive to traditional republican values, that a new constitution had to be written with power lodged more fully in the national government, including the power to issue currency.

Toward a New Government

The movement toward what was to become known as the Constitutional Convention was anything but swift and unanimous. Alexander Hamilton, a young New York lawyer and former delegate to the Continental Congress, took the lead in efforts to strengthen the national government. At the Annapolis Convention (1786), in which the states met to discuss interstate trade, he called for a national convention to amend the Articles of Confederation. After Shays's Rebellion, five state legislatures appointed delegates to the proposed convention. The Continental Congress issued a tentative call for a convention as well, but carefully insisted that any revisions of the Articles would require both its approval and the approval of *all* state legislatures. When the convention finally did convene in Philadelphia in 1787, some delegates arrived with instructions to go no further than amendment of the Articles.

On May 14, 1787, the day appointed for the convention to begin, only the delegates of Virginia and Pennsylvania were present. By May 25 nine state delegations had arrived, and work on "revision" of the Articles began. State legislatures in twelve states named a total of seventy-three delegates, of whom fifty-five actually attended the convention and thirty-nine eventually signed the new Constitution. The thirteenth state, Rhode Island, decided not to participate.

Of the fifty-five delegates who met at Philadelphia, thirty-three were lawyers, forty-four had been members of the Continental Congress, twenty-seven had been officers in the Revolutionary War, twenty-five had been to college, twenty-one were rich (and another thirteen were relatively affluent), and nineteen were slave owners.[3] Among the many relatively young delegates were the very influential Alexander Hamilton, who was thirty-two, and James Madison, who was thirty-six. The patriarch of the group was Benjamin Franklin, eighty-one.

The New Constitution

In the summer of 1787 the Constitutional Convention in Philadelphia proposed a dramatic change in government in the United States. Three characteristics of that proposal are so fundamental to our system of government that they deserve special mention here. You will see their ramifications throughout the rest of this book. First, the new government was to be a genuine *national* government able to reach citizens directly, not a confederation government dependent on sovereign states to carry out its will. Second, this was to be a government of *limited powers*. Though the new government was to be much stronger than the old, several mechanisms were established to limit the exercise of the new government's power. The new government was to be given delegated powers that would be shared by three branches in a system of checks and balances. The new government would be part of a **federal system** in which sovereignty was divided between the national government and the state governments. Third, the new government reinforced a republican pattern of *indirect representation* as opposed to direct democracy. A complex and fragmented system was proposed for selecting the officers of the new government. We will examine each of these features.

A Stronger National Government

From the start, the Constitutional Convention sought to broaden its mandate to revise the Articles of Confederation. New proposals presented to the convention called for a thoroughly altered national government, one with greatly strengthened powers. The delegates to the convention readily accepted the idea of a national judiciary and a stronger executive branch. But considerable debate over the shape of the new legislature demonstrated the difficulty of creating a new, strong, national government. Benjamin Franklin favored a **unicameral** (one-house) arrangement. But most delegates supported the idea of a **bicameral** (two-house) legislature, an arrangement adopted by most state governments.

The earliest comprehensive proposal submitted for consideration at the convention was the **Virginia Plan**, set forth by the delegation from that state. Under this plan, a strong national government would include a bicameral legislature: a lower house, elected by the voters, and an upper house, chosen by the members of the lower house. Either tax contributions or population would serve as the basis for proportional represention in both houses. Most of the larger states supported the Virginia Plan.

The smaller states responded with the **New Jersey Plan**, submitted by William Paterson of that state. Paterson's plan called for a national government empowered to levy taxes and to regulate interstate commerce and, significantly, a national supreme court with the power to review state court rulings. On the key question of legislative structure, this plan established a one-house legislature in which each state would have one vote, as had been the case under the Articles.

Debate over the relative merits of the Virginia and New Jersey plans deadlocked the convention for weeks. The problem was finally resolved through the **Connecticut**

REVOLUTION AND CONSTITUTION

Benjamin Franklin, the patriarch of his country. Had he had his way, the wild turkey would be our national symbol, and our legislature would have only one house, as many parliamentary systems today.
(National Archives)

Compromise, proposed by a special committee in which the Connecticut delegation played a pivotal role. The key element of the compromise was the concept of a two-house legislature consisting of an upper house in which the states would be represented equally and a lower house in which representation would be based on population and from which all fiscal measures would originate. Although delegates from the larger states initially opposed the compromise, they soon realized that it was the price they would have to pay for a strengthened national government. In any case, with the struggle for ratification by the states still to come, it was simply good politics to assuage the smaller states' fear that their interests would be neglected in a powerful national government based on proportional representation.

Limitation of Power

The Constitutional Convention, though committed to creating a strong national government, still feared centralized power. Furthermore, many delegates at the convention were concerned about the popular majority's potential abuse of any substantial power. Was it possible to create a government based on the will of the people but not susceptible to the tyranny of the majority? Doubts about relying on the wisdom of "the people" were raised by many delegates, including Alexander Hamilton, who said, "The voice of the people has been said to be the voice of God; and however generally this maxim has been quoted and believed, it is not true in fact. The people are turbulent and changing; they seldom judge or determine right." Fearing mass democracy on the one hand and tyrannical monarchy or oligarchy on the other, the framers created a complex system of government designed to ensure the fragmentation and dispersal of power.

The first major limitation on the new national government was that it was a government of **delegated powers**. Written constitutions empower governments, but they also restrict the exercise of power. One constitution allots certain powers to the national government but insists (implicitly in the main body, explicitly in the Tenth Amendment) that **reserve powers** belong to the state governments. The difference between these categories of powers is important: Delegated powers are theoretically limited to a more or less well-defined group. Reserve powers are all those left over, theoretically unlimited. According to the notion of delegated powers, if the national government wants to act, it needs to find a justification for its action in some positive grant of power in the Constitution. By contrast, a state government is free to do whatever it will *except for* powers granted by the Constitution exclusively to the national government or specifically denied to the states.

The constitutional division of powers creates a federal system of government in which **sovereignty** (a government's ability to control its own choices) is divided between the national government and the several state governments. In certain matters (for example, foreign policy and interstate commerce) the federal government has sovereign power. In other matters (most family law, for example) the states are sovereign. So theoretically at least, most places in the United States have *two* sovereign governments at the same time, each keeping within its own area of control. As you can imagine, life is not as simple as this tidy picture suggests. We will talk later in this chapter and again throughout Chapter 4 about the complications of power in a federal system of government. But initially, the important fact is that the new, stronger, national government created by the Constitution was to be limited by being granted only delegated powers within a federal system.

Having provided for the division of power between the national government and the state governments, the convention delegates also feared concentrations of power within the new national government itself. Their deliberations on this issue reflected the ideas and influence of James Madison, whose views were set forth in 1787 and 1788 in an impressive series of essays, written together with Alexander Hamilton and John Jay and known collectively as the ***Federalist Papers***. As a student of history and political philosophy, Madison was aware that republican government—government based on the will of the people—was most likely to succeed in small societies whose members shared common values and in which wealth was distributed relatively equally. But the United States was a sprawling society in which different interests abounded and wealth was distributed unevenly. For republican government to succeed

Alexander Hamilton saw the nation's vast potential as a manufacturer and argued for a strong central government to create the conditions for prosperity. As one author of *The Federalist Papers*, he helped lay the groundwork for national development. *(National Archives)*

in such a society, Madison argued, the political system must be fragmented so that power could be exercised effectively without encouraging excessive concentrations of it. In this way, he felt, rash or tyrannical actions by powerful interests could be blocked and the necessary measure of political unity preserved.

In *Federalist* No. 51, Madison contended that "you must first enable the government to control the governed; and in the next place, oblige it to control itself." He went on to point out that if the responsibility for decision making could be sufficiently fragmented, the rights of minorities could be protected while minority factions could be prevented from thwarting the properly expressed sentiments of the majority. Madison's ideas were implemented in the constitutional system of **separation of powers** and **checks and balances** (see **Figure 3-1**).

Under the system of checks and balances, governing power within the new national government was to be shared among the legislative, executive, and judicial branches. Since each branch shared its primary function in some fashion with the other branches, a sharing of powers rather than a strict separation of powers was created. For example, the president, through the veto power, could intervene in the legislative process; the Senate was granted power to confirm or reject the president's nominations to the

FIGURE 3-1
THE SEPARATION OF POWERS IN U.S. GOVERNMENT

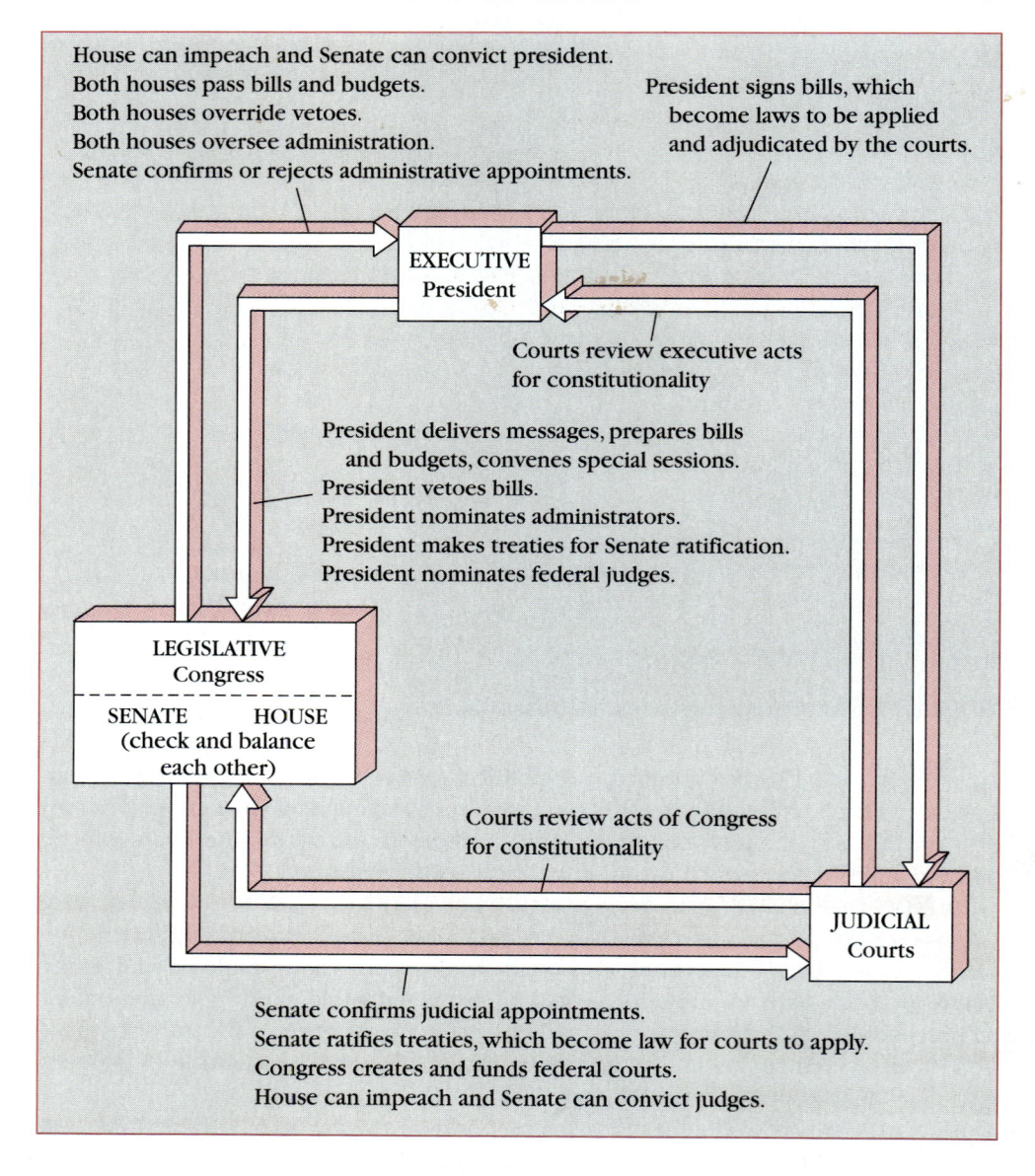

House can impeach and Senate can convict president.
Both houses pass bills and budgets.
Both houses override vetoes.
Both houses oversee administration.
Senate confirms or rejects administrative appointments.

President signs bills, which become laws to be applied and adjudicated by the courts.

EXECUTIVE
President

Courts review executive acts for constitutionality

President delivers messages, prepares bills and budgets, convenes special sessions.
President vetoes bills.
President nominates administrators.
President makes treaties for Senate ratification.
President nominates federal judges.

LEGISLATIVE
Congress
SENATE   HOUSE
(check and balance each other)

Courts review acts of Congress for constitutionality

JUDICIAL
Courts

Senate confirms judicial appointments.
Senate ratifies treaties, which become law for courts to apply.
Congress creates and funds federal courts.
House can impeach and Senate can convict judges.

Supreme Court and the cabinet; Congress was given the power to impeach and remove the president, vice-president, and members of the federal judiciary. Three strictly independent branches working in isolation could result in chaos. The arrangement chosen by the Constitutional Convention—three branches, each of which must gain the cooperation, or at least the acquiescence, of the others—was a system designed to thwart the despotic or careless use of power while encouraging stable and coherent policy. Within the legislature, power was further divided between two houses based on different principles of representation (the House on population, the Senate on statehood).

To the original checks and balances laid out in the Constitution have been added many other refinements in a kind of unwritten constitution—traditions, laws, and procedures that have evolved through political necessity. Consider, for example, the wide range of government officials and agencies and nongovernmental organizations that shape economic policy today. In addition to Congress, the president, and the courts, independent agencies like the Federal Reserve Board, bureaucratic divisions of the executive branch like the Department of Defense (its enormous budget has a significant influence on the economy), state and city governments, and many private organizations all have an important impact on economic policy. In every policy area, a similar army of forces interacts in constantly shifting arrangements.

Madison could not possibly have anticipated the extent to which the constitutional system of checks and balances would evolve and change. Nor could he have anticipated

Some historians regard James Madison as one of this nation's most original political thinkers. His defense of the U.S. Constitution in The Federalist Papers *ranks as one of the most significant discussions ever of power, rights, and consent in a democratic context. Madison recognized how easily power could be abused and suggested ways of counteracting such abuse. (National Archives)*

the development of certain elements of modern politics that have skewed some constitutional checks on power. Whereas in Madison's time political parties were not a significant force, today parties link officials of the various branches of government. Soon after the Constitution was written, the Supreme Court claimed the right to declare legislative acts unconstitutional (a power not explicitly stated in the Constitution) and thus vastly increased the powers of the federal judiciary. Presidents have gained the power to issue executive orders in some matters, bypassing congressional approval on particular pieces of legislation. Within Congress, legislative programs must move through an elaborate thicket of decision points, subject to potential ambushes by any number of interest groups. As political scientist Robert Dahl has observed, "The making of government decisions is not a majestic march of great majorities united upon certain matters of basic policy. It is the steady appeasement of relatively small groups."[4]

Indirect Representation

Following a basically republican pattern of government, the Constitution maintains a system of **indirect representation** in which policy choices are made by representatives at one or more removes from ordinary citizens. The closest link between the public at large and the new government was in the House of Representatives, in which voters chose members directly. Senators, by contrast, were to be chosen by state legislatures. (This system remained in effect until the ratification in 1913 of the Seventeenth Amendment, which mandated direct popular election of senators.) The framers also sought to insulate the presidency from the popular vote. As a result of various political compromises at the convention, the **electoral college**—a somewhat peculiar and complex mechanism—became the method for choosing the U.S. president. State electors make up the electoral college, and each state has a number of electors equal to its total number of senators and representatives. Thus the only truly national political figures are elected by a mechanism rooted in the states. The electoral college has had vast implications for political strategy because presidential candidates must win electoral rather than popular votes (see Chapter 10). The Constitution's selection mechanism for the national judiciary represents an additional layer of insulation between judicial officers and voters, since this power is given to the president and the Senate (each in turn originally selected by representatives of voters, not voters themselves). In all, the pattern of the new Constitution was clear: The government would be protected from the vicissitudes of popular opinion by a complex, multifaceted scheme for choosing policymaking officials.

Four Issues Left for Later Resolution

Four major compromises of the Constitutional Convention are reflected in what is *not* in the Constitution. These issues, which for a variety of reasons were not resolved by the convention, defined battles to be fought another day: (1) what to do about slavery, (2) how to decide contested power claims between the federal government and the

(Text continues on page 104)

JEFFERSON AND SLAVERY

It comes as a shock to many people to learn that the eloquent author of the Declaration of Independence—who spoke of all men being created equal and being endowed with certain unalienable rights—was himself a slaveholder for his entire adult life. Yet the contradictions in Jefferson's attitudes and actions concerning slavery reflect the difficulties that the issue posed at the time the Constitution was written and beyond.

As may have been true for many colonial Americans, Jefferson's first memory was that of being carried on a pillow by a slave. He remained intimately associated with slavery until his death, and the work of slaves helped make possible his architectural and cultural achievements. Yet Jefferson resolved early in life that slavery was abominable and that its eradication would be a prime achievement of the Revolution. In 1774 he delivered his first attack on slavery in print. His pamphlet *A Summary View of the Rights of British America* indicted the slave trade and declared that King George III was guilty of preventing the colonists from abolishing it. Jefferson expanded this attack on the king's role in maintaining slavery when he wrote the original draft of the Declaration of Independence. By blaming the British for slavery, he was able to escape the charge that the colonists themselves—though espousing equality and rights—did not really mean to include everyone in their new political community. Unfortunately for Jefferson, the Continental Congress removed his passage about slavery from the Declaration! Though Jefferson blamed northern slave traders for this excision, it was clear that very few southerners were willing to commit themselves to abolishing slavery if independence were achieved. Thus the Declaration asserts the right of white Americans not to be enslaved by the crown, but it implicitly refuses to apply the same principles to black slaves who might rebel against masters.

Jefferson did not free the slaves at Monticello until his death in 1826. Although he opposed slavery all his life—and philosophized about its evils—he never actively combated it. An optimist about the eventual eradication of slavery, Jefferson believed that the slaves would be emancipated and that they might return to Africa or perhaps go to Haiti.

One student of Jefferson's life argues that although our third president abhorred slavery, he unconsciously shared the racial prejudice on which it was based. In his autobiography Jefferson wrote: "The two races, equally free, cannot live in the same government. Nature, habit, opinion have drawn indelible lines of distinction between them." Even as he articulated the great revolutionary ideas of liberty and equality, Jefferson was a pragmatist—and a product of his own time and place.

Source: John Chester Miller, The Wolf by the Ears: Thomas Jefferson and Slavery *(New York: New American Library, 1977).*

states, (3) just how strong the national government would be, and (4) how to protect civil rights. In each case the convention decided not to decide or left the decision to others.

SLAVERY Although not mentioned explicitly, slavery is clearly implicated in certain passages of the original Constitution. The southern (slaveholding) states sought to include slaves in the population counts used to determine representation in the House of Representatives—without, of course, giving them the right to vote. The South feared that without such additional representation, a northern majority might dominate the new Union. Southern recalcitrance on this matter led to the infamous compromise that each slave would be counted as three-fifths of a person. This was perhaps a pragmatic solution in the context of the time, since outlawing slavery was not yet practical. Yet the compromise starkly revealed the vulnerability of the new nation. In the end, only a war could settle the slavery issue.

The framers of the Constitution also had to deal with the question of the slave trade. In another compromise, the slave trade was allowed to continue until at least 1808, at which time Congress would be permitted to legislate against it. Commerce in human beings was subsequently prohibited by Congress as of January 1, 1808, although for many years thereafter a thriving smuggling business persisted.

THE ARBITER OF POWER A major issue left unresolved by the Constitutional Convention concerned the division of sovereignty between the federal government and the states. The supremacy clause clearly stated that conflicts between federal law and state law in the exercise of concurrent powers would be decided in favor of the federal government. But since each government was to act as sovereign (without review) within its own area of competence, who would decide disputes about the division of power itself? The Constitution's silence on this issue allowed both the federal government and each state government to claim this power. In *Martin* v. *Hunter's Lessee* (1816), for example, Virginia's highest court resisted an order from the U.S. Supreme Court, refusing to recognize any federal authority to review decisions Virginia deemed matters of state law.[5] In *McCulloch* v. *Maryland* (1819), Maryland chose to tax the U.S. Bank in Baltimore, asserting that the Constitution was an act of sovereign states and must be exercised in subordination to the will of the states.[6] These two disputes were resolved in favor of the federal government by the U.S. Supreme Court under ardent nationalist Chief Justice John Marshall, but similar disputes continued to arise. The southern states' secession was just such a claim for state prerogative—that one resolved on the battlefields of the Civil War. Though skirmishes within the federal system continue to this day, the general pattern established by Marshall's Court predominates: The federal government, through the U.S. Supreme Court, decides such matters finally. Since the Civil War at least, state governments have been unwilling to resort to arms to contest that federal dominance.

STRENGTH OF THE NATIONAL GOVERNMENT Although the Constitutional Convention clearly favored a strengthened national government, the full extent of the increase in federal power was left open by a number of provisions that allowed for dramatic increases to be effected later. The clearest example of such open-ended provisions is the so-called elastic clause at the end of Article I, Section 8. In addition to the expansive list of powers in that section, the **elastic clause** gives Congress the power "to make all Laws which shall be necessary and proper for carrying into Execution the foregoing Powers." Beginning with *McCulloch*, in which Marshall uses the clause to justify the creation of a federal bank, this clause has been interpreted broadly by the Supreme Court, giving the federal government significant **implied powers** to supplement those explicitly delegated.

Other provisions allow for an increase in federal power. Although the Constitution establishes only one federal court (the Supreme Court), leaving state courts jurisdiction in federal matters, Articles I and III give Congress the power to establish "inferior courts"—the basis for the powerful federal court system with courts of original jurisdiction in each state. As mentioned, the interstate commerce clause has been the source of a significant expansion of federal power. The power to tax and spend for the general welfare dramatically increased the federal government's power in the twentieth century with the New Deal, the War on Poverty, and a host of other federally financed programs. The ability of Congress to set maximum speed limits on the nation's highways comes from its ability to spend—with strings attached. The delegates to the Constitutional Convention would probably be surprised by the vast power wielded by the federal government today. But some at least would recognize the seeds of this expansion in their own work.

THE PROTECTION OF CIVIL RIGHTS The Constitutional Convention decided that no Bill of Rights was needed in the Constitution, that a responsive government would by its nature protect the rights of the people to whom it owed its continuance in power. Delegates like Madison believed that a proper *process* was the surest guarantee against violations of rights. (Jefferson, who was serving as the American minister to France at the time of the convention, disagreed.) The hotly contested ratification debates persuaded Madison to work for the speedy passage of a Bill of Rights under the amendment process after the new government was in place. When that was accomplished, the Bill of Rights (the first ten amendments) guaranteed civil rights against federal government infringement but not against state governments' actions—that was left up to each state individually. Civil rights advocates were thus confronted with the lengthy and complicated process of persuading the Supreme Court to "incorporate" protections against state actions one by one or the even more complicated process of securing rights state by state. The original Constitution also left the definition of suffrage and the establishment of voting rights up to the states. The framers thus sidestepped the thorny issues of property qualifications and the voting rights of nonwhites. The expansion of suffrage came first through state action and only much later through constitutional amendments.

Drafting and then securing approval for the new Constitution, with its fundamental changes in the shape and scope of government, was a remarkable political feat, perhaps made possible only by deferring resolution of these four issues. Whether or not resolution of one or more of these could have been achieved by the convention, the failure to do so destined the country to years of acrimonious and often violent conflict and, in some cases at least, deferred justice as well.

Ratification

The struggle over ratification of the proposed Constitution was bitter and the outcome very close. The delegates to the Constitutional Convention opted to entrust the ratification process to conventions elected by the people in each state. In this way they circumvented the state legislatures, where opposition to the Constitution was strong, and gained direct access to widespread popular support for the new Constitution. The delegates also specified that once two-thirds of the states had voted for ratification, the Constitution would be in force.

Supporters of the Constitution called themselves **Federalists**, and opponents became known as **Antifederalists**. Rural areas of the nation, populated by farmers and poorer people who feared the groth of centralized power, tended to oppose the new Constitution. Those living in cities and coastal areas generally supported it. Many crosscurrents affected the political struggle, however, and no one factor can explain the outcome.

Critics of the new Constitution immediately scored two powerful points against it. First, they cited the omission of a **Bill of Rights**. If some state constitutions included protections against government infringements on liberty, opponents argued, why shouldn't the national constitution incorporate such protections? The Federalists were forced to yield on this point, and it was agreed that a Bill of Rights would be added once the Constitution was ratified. The Antifederalists also decried what they viewed as an ill-considered rush toward ratification. New political arrangements of such import, they contended, demanded lengthy and thorough deliberation. Though they recognized the merit in this argument, the Federalists knew that quick action was necessary to prevent their opponents from becoming fully organized. The Federalists also carried out a brilliant public relations campaign centered on the *Federalist Papers*.

The strategy adopted by the Federalists worked well. Within a year, nine states had ratified the Constitution, making it legal. But the votes for ratification were close in several states, and two crucial states, Virginia and New York, gave their approval only after the Constitution had been adopted. Rhode Island was the thirteenth state to ratify (1790), after refusing seven times even to call a ratification convention. (See **Figure 3-2**.)

Amending the Constitution

Thomas Jefferson was one of several Founders who worried about the tendency of governments to break down or lose touch with the people over time. Therefore, he proposed that a new constitutional convention be called in each succeeding generation, noting, "We might as well require a man to wear still the coat which fitted him

FIGURE 3-2
RATIFICATION OF THE U.S. CONSTITUTION

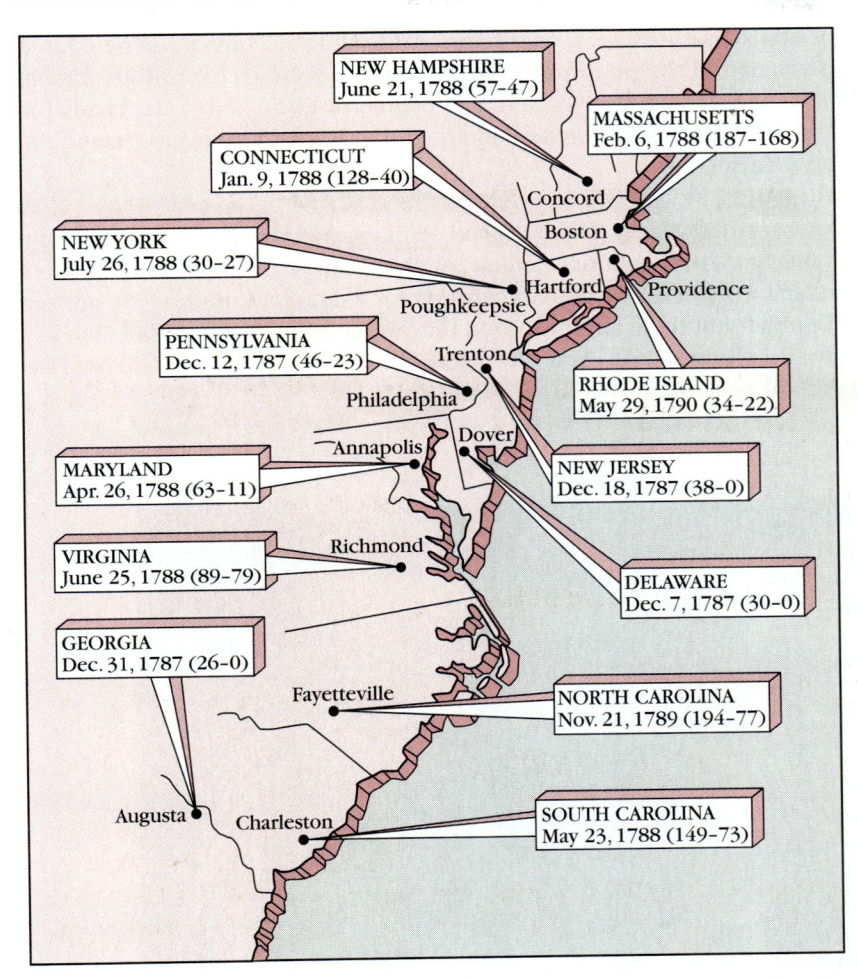

State	Date	Vote
NEW HAMPSHIRE	June 21, 1788	(57–47)
MASSACHUSETTS	Feb. 6, 1788	(187–168)
CONNECTICUT	Jan. 9, 1788	(128–40)
NEW YORK	July 26, 1788	(30–27)
PENNSYLVANIA	Dec. 12, 1787	(46–23)
RHODE ISLAND	May 29, 1790	(34–22)
MARYLAND	Apr. 26, 1788	(63–11)
NEW JERSEY	Dec. 18, 1787	(38–0)
VIRGINIA	June 25, 1788	(89–79)
DELAWARE	Dec. 7, 1787	(30–0)
GEORGIA	Dec. 31, 1787	(26–0)
NORTH CAROLINA	Nov. 21, 1789	(194–77)
SOUTH CAROLINA	May 23, 1788	(149–73)

as a boy, as a civilized society to remain ever under the regimen of their barbarous ancestors." Although the framers did not incorporate this idea into the Constitution, they did provide for a means of amending the Constitution as the need arose.

To be adopted, an **amendment** must be first proposed and then ratified. Each step can be accomplished in either of two ways. For proposal, either two-thirds of the members of each house of Congress must approve the amendment, or two-thirds of the state legislatures must petition Congress to call a national constitutional convention. Only the first of these methods has ever been employed. In the 1960s, however, opponents of the Supreme Court's rulings on reapportionment came within one state legislature of petitioning Congress to call a national constitutional convention, and in the 1980s more than half the state legislatures had petitioned for a constitutional convention to consider an amendment requiring a balanced federal budget. To call such a convention, unprecedented complications would have to be dealt with.[7] Who would determine if the states has presented valid petitions? Could the convention be limited to the one issue named in the petition? If the convention were to exceed its original mandate (as the Constitutional Convention did), would political and social chaos follow? Opponents of the proposed convention argue that it might radically change the structure of our government.

Congress can deflect the threat of petition by the states by passing its own version of the proposed constitutional amendment and sending that version to the state legislatures for approval. When petitions calling for the direct election of U.S. senators began accumulating early in the twentieth century, for example, Congress recognized the strength of public sentiment and proposed the Seventeenth Amendment. One key unanswered question looms large, however: When two-thirds of the states have petitioned Congress for a national convention, must Congress comply? Article V of the Constitution states that Congress *shall* call a convention—not that it *must*.

Much did not run smoothly in the new republic. This print shows a brawl in Congress between Federalist Roger Griswold and Republican Matthew Lyon. Early disputes revolved around U.S. policy toward revolutionary France and laws dealing with freedom of speech. Still, the fledgling nation held together for seventy-three years before being torn apart by the Civil War. *(The Bettmann Archive)*

A constitutional amendment is ratified either by approval by three-fourths of the state legislatures or by approval by three-fourths of ratifying conventions called by the states. Congress determines which method is to be used in each case. Ratifying conventions have been called only once—to approve the Twenty-first Amendment repealing Prohibition (which had been mandated by the Eighteenth Amendment). Congress chose that method because state legislatures were expected to be less likely to vote for repeal.

Ratification by state legislatures hs its own complications. Congress has stipulated that the ratification process be limited to a period of seven years. In 1978, however, the ratification period was extended for the Equal Rights Amendment, amid considerable debate. Several state legislatures then rescinded prior ratifications of the ERA, but such actions were never put to a legal test, and the ERA ultimately failed to be ratified despite the extension. The dominant legal interpretation is that states cannot rescind their approval, although they can always ratify an amendment they had previously rejected.

Democratic theory and practice in this country demand that the amending procedures be both sufficiently flexible and sufficiently representative of majority sentiment. In more than two hundred years, only twenty-seven amendments have been added to the Constitution, ten of which were adopted together as the Bill of Rights. Of course, the *meaning* of the Constitution depends on the elaboration and interpretation of its words. A large part of the Constitution's growth and change over the past two centuries has come not from formal amendments but rather from decisions by courts (particularly the U.S. Supreme Court) interpreting the general and often vague language of the supreme law of the land. Nonjudicial officials engage in constitutional elaboration as well.

Sometimes the amending process has been used in an effort to have the last word in the constitutional system—to overrule even the Supreme Court. At other times it has been employed in attempts to hold back social change. In yet other cases, like the proposed Equal Rights Amendment, it has been the last resort when changes could not be obtained other ways. Though it is difficult to judge the overall impact of amending initiatives on our government system, it is probably fortunate that the Constitution has not been amended more frequently and thus became laden with prohibitions and complications that would make governing extremely difficult. Still, democratic commitments do require that a polity based on a written constitution have some method of amendment that responds to majority impulses.

An Enduring Political Legacy

The world is strewn with scraps of paper called constitutions. Many are subterfuges for coups, caudillos, and corruption. But the U.S. Constitution is rare in its continuing capacity to prescribe rules of governance two centuries after its formulation.

PART ONE • FOUNDATIONS

COMPARATIVE PERSPECTIVE

AMERICANS WRITE ANOTHER CONSTITUTION

Americans have been directly responsible for formulating at least one constitution other than their own. In 1946 the Government Section of the Supreme Commander for the Allied Powers in Japan wrote a new constitution for that nation in six days. Adopted shortly thereafter by the parliament, that constitution has remained Japan's governing document and has never been amended.

This highly unusual procedure arose out of a singular set of circumstances. Following World War II, Japan was occupied by the United States, which was determined to prevent the return of Japan's fascist policies. General Douglas MacArthur was charged, in effect, with the democratization of Japanese society—a task that required drastic alterations in the so-called Meiji constitution, under which Japan had been governed since 1889.

The most elemental difference between the old and new Japanese constitutions lay in the status of the emperor. Under the old constitution the emperor, as sovereign, was the acknowledged source of all authority. Although he could act only through cabinet ministers, the concept that power resided in the person of the emperor symbolically denied the people's sovereignty. The new constitution transformed the emperor from sovereign to figurehead, a "symbol of the state" whose position derives "from the will of the people."

A second revolutionary feature of the new constitution was an extensive listing of unalienable, God-given rights that may not be abridged. The rights spelled out in the 1946 constitution cover not only the areas of speech, religion, and due

(Box continues on page 111)

All constitutions are essentially political documents conceived in power politics and shaped by compromises. Like the U.S. Constitution, however, every successful constitution eventually becomes as much symbol as document. Written interpretations of it resemble analysis of scripture; it comes to prescribe civic virtue and to legitimize good behavior, and an elaborate code of laws and customs builds up around it, presumably shaped by the needs of the day. It is easy to forget that a constitution originally arises as a political document.

For many years the U.S. Constitution was considered an act of divine intervention in human affairs.[8] Americans who (like the Founders) doubted that God acted so directly accepted the slightly different view that the Constitution represented a victory for "straight thinking" over "narrow-mindedness," for visionaries over parochials, for

process of law but also such matters as employment (the right to choose an occupation), emigration, academic freedom, complete equality of the sexes, collective bargaining, and the right of each person to "minimum standards of wholesome and cultured living." In practice, many of these rights have not yet been realized fully, but it is interesting that so many social and political rights that are not included in the U.S. Constitution were incorporated into a modern constitution written by Americans.

The political structure created by the 1946 constitution is a parliamentary system much closer to Great Britain's than to ours. As in the U.S. Constitution, however, there is provision for an independent federal judiciary with the power to review legislation.

The most unusual and controversial element in the 1946 constitution is the "renunciation of war" clause, by which Japan formally eschewed the use or threat of force in international relations. In fact, the constitution seems to rule out the maintenance of *any* armed forces. Contemporary Japan, however, has developed extensive "security forces."

One student of Japanese politics has summarized the 1946 constitution as follows: "It introduces rights, institutions and practices into Japanese politics that undoubtedly go far beyond anything the Japanese themselves might realistically have been expected to establish. In fact, on the basis of the text alone, it is a considerably more democratic document than is the Constitution of the United States."*

---

*Robert E. Ward, Japan's Political System, 2nd ed. (Englewood Cliffs, N.J.: Prentice Hall, 1978), p. 145.

---

the interest of the public over that of the individual.[9] According to this view, the framers discerned the weaknesses of the Articles of Confederation and made thoroughly rational and nonpolitical judgments about the best ways to change our political system. For generations, this interpretation of the Constitution's genesis was almost universally accepted.

In 1913, the historian Charles Beard, in *An Economic Interpretation of the Constitution*, made the shocking argument that the Constitution was a *political* document that had been constructed with political interests in mind.[10] Beard pointed out that the framers were for the most part rich and well-born, that most of them considered the preservation of property as the principal object of government, and that many of them shared John Jay's view that "the people who own the country ought to govern

The Constitutional Convention of 1787. The men who attended the Philadelphia convention knew that only some political arrangements stood the test of time, and that however necessary their efforts were, they were unquestionably experimental. *(The Bettmann Archive)*

it." According to Beard, the wealthy framers, following the dictates of self-interest, developed the Constitution's checks and balances to prevent the unpropertied majority from making unpalatable demands on the propertied minority.

Although historical evidence does not fully support Beard's conclusions, most historians acknowledge that economic interests were very much at issue in the framing and ratification of the Constitution. Among James Madison's fundamental assumptions, in fact, were the notions that economic factors motivated human behavior to a great degree and that political conflict grew out of economic differences between classes of people.

However one judges the framers, it is remarkable that the institutional framework they created has endured. Although the U.S. political system has gradually shifted in a more democratic direction over the years — through the direct election of senators, the expansion of the right to vote, the emergence of mass-based political parties, and the

> **SUMMARY CHART**
>
> **IS THE CONSTITUTION OUTDATED?**
> **SOME ARGUMENTS**
>
> The electoral college prevents direct popular election of the president.
>
> Checks and balances and the separation of powers divide government to prevent concentrations of power thereby making united government and effective policy-making very difficult.
>
> Most contemporary democracies are parliamentary systems where the legislative and executive branches are fused, not separated.
>
> A system of proportional representation in Congress would be more democratic and might encourage the growth of new political parties.

transformation of the electoral college from a group with real power to little more than a rubber stamp—the constitutional system still reflects the framer's fears of majority tyranny and the excesses of popular control.

CONCLUSIONS

Since at least the beginning of the twentieth century, political observers have been calling the constitutional system outdated. Most critics have charged that the system's built-in tensions between the various branches and levels of government thwart government effectiveness. In our form of government, unlike parliamentary democracies, one branch of government is pitted against another: Instead of unity, we seek division. But division of power, however laudable as a check on excessive concentration of power, can also lead to a government of stalemate. In this scenario, nothing can be accomplished except in crisis conditions, and Congress and the executive are locked in a perpetual standoff that makes for irresponsible policymaking or none at all.

The economic and political crises of the twentieth century have greatly strained the constitutional structure. Presidents, in particular, have been forced into many political innovations to keep the ship of state afloat. Many observers argue that presidential power in this century has grown enormously to avoid the stalemate built into the system.

Ultimately, we cannot help but see the Constitution as impressive and enduring but also deeply flawed. It marked a giant step forward for democratic ideas in its own time, but it also left many basic questions of democracy unanswered and incorporated some blatantly undemocratic concepts. We will take up the implications of these crosscurrents more fully in Chapters 5 and 6 when we address civil rights and civil liberties and in Part III, which focuses on government institutions.

GLOSSARY TERMS

amendment
Antifederalists
Articles of Confederation
bicameral
Bill of Rights
checks and balances
Connecticut Compromise
delegated powers
elastic clause
electoral college
Federalist Papers
Federalists
federal system

implied powers
indirect representation
New Jersey Plan
reserve powers
separation of powers
Seven Years' War
Shays's Rebellion
sovereignty
Stamp Act
Treaty of Paris
unicameral
Virginia Plan

NOTES

[1] James Kirby Martin, *In the Course of Human Events* (Arlington Heights, Ill.: AHM Publishing, 1979), pp. 9–11.
[2] George B. Tindall, *America: A Narrative History* (New York: Norton, 1984), pp. 209–210.
[3] Ibid., pp. 262–263; Charles Warren, *The Making of the Constitution* (New York: Barnes & Noble, 1967), pp. 55–60.
[4] Robert Dahl, *A Preface to Democratic Theory* (Chicago: University of Chicago Press, 1956), p. 146.
[5] 1 Wheaton 304.
[6] 4 Wheaton 316.
[7] See Daniel H. Pollitt and Frank Thompson, "Could a Convention Become a Runaway?" *Christianity and Crisis*, Apr. 16, 1979.
[8] See George Bancroft, *History of the United States*, ed. R. B. Nye (Chicago: University of Chicago Press, 1966).
[9] See John Fiske, *The Critical Period of American History, 1783–1789* (Boston: Houghton Mifflin, 1888).
[10] Charles Beard, *An Economic Interpretation of the Constitution* (New York: Macmillan, 1913).

SELECTED READINGS

THE AMERICAN REVOLUTION

For various **perspectives** on the American Revolution, see Seymour Martin Lipset, *The First New Nation: The United States in Historical and Comparative Perspective* (New York: Norton,

1979); Ellen Chase, *Beginnings of the American Revolution*, vol. 3 (Port Washington, N.Y.: Kennikat Press, 1970); James Kirby Martin, *In the Course of Human Events* (Arlington Heights, Ill.: AHM Publishing, 1979); Neil R. Stout, *The Perfect Crisis: The Beginning of the Revolutionary War* (New York: NYU Press, 1976); and Gordon S. Wood, *The Radicalism of the American Revolution* (New York: Knopf, 1992).

THE REVOLUTIONARY WAR

For more extensive discussions on the effects of the Revolutionary War on American **social and political development**, see Charles Royster, *A Revolutionary People at War: The Continental Army and American Character, 1775–1783* (Chapel Hill: University of North Carolina Press, 1980); and J. Franklin Jameson, *The American Revolution Considered as a Social Movement* (Boston: Beacon Press, 1963).

THE CONSTITUTIONAL CONVENTION

There is no shortage of **commentaries** on the Constitutional Convention. See particularly Vernon L. Parrington, *Main Currents in American Political Thought*, vol. 6 (New York: Harcourt, 1927); Gary Wills, *Inventing America* (Garden City, N.Y.: Doubleday, 1978), chap. 27; David G. Smith, *The Convention and the Constitution: The Political Ideas of the Founding Fathers* (Washington, D. C.: University Press of America, 1987).

The best discussion of the **political issues** involved in the writing of the Constitution is still James Madison's *Notes of the Debates in the Federal Convention of 1787*, ed. Adrienne Koch (Athens: Ohio University Press, 1966). The **philosophical underpinnings** of the Constitution can be found in Alexander Hamilton, John Jay, and James Madison, *The Federalist Papers* (Cambridge, Mass.: Belnap Press, 1966); and Paul Conklin, *Self-evident Truths* (Bloomington: Indiana University Press, 1974).

THE RATIFICATION DEBATES AND THE ANTIFEDERALISTS

By some accounts, the **Antifederalist opposition** to the Constitution maintained the spirit of the Declaration of Independence better than the Constitution did. See Cecilia M. Kenyon, ed., *The Antifederalists* (Indianapolis: Bobbs-Merrill, 1966; Jackson Turner Main, *The Antifederalists: Critics of the Constitution, 1787–1788* (New York: Norton, 1974); and W. B. Allen and Gordon Lloyd, eds., *The Essential Antifederalist* (Lanham, Md.: University Press of America, 1985). On the **ratification debates**, see Michael Allen Gillespie and Michael Lienesch, eds., *Ratifying the Constitution* (Lawrence: University Press of Kansas, 1989).

THE CONSTITUTION

There has been a host of new writing on the **Constitution** in connection with the two-hundredth anniversary of its creation. For a sample, see John J. Sexton and Nat Brandt, *How Free Are We? What the Constitution Says We Can and Cannot Do* (New York: Evans, 1986); Richard B. Morris, *Witnesses at the Creation: Hamilton, Madison, Jay and the Constitution* (New York: New American Library, 1986); Harvey Mansfield, *America's Constitutional Soul* (Baltimore: Johns Hopkins University Press, 1991); and Hadley Arkes, *Beyond the Constitution* (Princeton, N.J.: Princeton University Press, 1990).

We the People of the United States, in order to form a more perfect Union, establish Justice, insure domestic Tranquility, provide for the common defence, promote the general Welfare, and secure the Blessings of Liberty to ourselves and our Posterity, do ordain and establish this Constitution for the United States of America.

Article. I.

Section. 1. All legislative Powers herein granted shall be vested in a Congress of the United States, which shall consist of a Senate and House of Representatives.

Section. 2. The House of Representatives shall be composed of Members chosen every second Year by the People of the several States, and the Electors in each State shall have the Qualifications requisite for Electors of the most numerous Branch of the State Legislature.

No Person shall be a Representative who shall not have attained to the Age of twenty five Years, and been seven Years a Citizen of the United States, and who shall not, when elected, be an Inhabitant of that State in which he shall be chosen.

Representatives and direct Taxes shall be apportioned among the several States which may be included within this Union, according to their respective Numbers, which shall be determined by adding to the whole Number of free Persons, including those bound to Service for a Term of Years, and excluding Indians not taxed, three fifths of all other Persons. The actual Enumeration shall be made within three Years after the first Meeting of the Congress of the United States, and within every subsequent Term of ten Years, in such Manner as they shall by Law direct. The Number of Representatives shall not exceed one for every thirty Thousand, but each State shall have at Least one Representative; and until such enumeration shall be made, the State of New Hampshire shall be entitled to chuse three, Massachusetts eight, Rhode-Island and Providence Plantations one, Connecticut five, New-York six, New Jersey four, Pennsylvania eight, Delaware one, Maryland six, Virginia ten, North Carolina five, South Carolina five, and Georgia three.

When vacancies happen in the Representation from any State, the Executive Authority thereof shall issue Writs of Election to fill such Vacancies.

The House of Representatives shall chuse their Speaker and other Officers; and shall have the sole Power of Impeachment.

Section. 3. The Senate of the United States shall be composed of two Senators from each State, chosen by the Legislature thereof, for six Years; and each Senator shall have one Vote.

Immediately after they shall be assembled in Consequence of the first Election, they shall be divided as equally as may be into three Classes. The Seats of the Senators of the first Class shall be vacated at the Expiration of the second Year, of the second Class at the Expiration of the fourth Year, and of the third Class at the Expiration of the sixth Year, so that one third may be chosen every second Year; and if Vacancies happen by Resignation, or otherwise, during the Recess of the Legislature of any State, the Executive thereof may make temporary Appointments until the next Meeting of the Legislature, which shall then fill such Vacancies.

No Person shall be a Senator who shall not have attained to the Age of thirty Years, and been nine Years a Citizen of the United States, and who shall not, when elected, be an Inhabitant of that State for which he shall be chosen.

The Vice President of the United States shall be President of the Senate, but shall have no Vote, unless they be equally divided.

The Senate shall chuse their other Officers, and also a President pro tempore, in the Absence of the Vice President, or when he shall exercise the Office of President of the United States.

The Senate shall have the sole Power to try all Impeachments. When sitting for that Purpose, they shall be on Oath or Affirmation. When the President of the United States is tried, the Chief Justice shall preside: And no Person shall be convicted without the Concurrence of two thirds of the Members present.

Judgment in Cases of Impeachment shall not extend further than to removal from Office, and disqualification to hold and enjoy any Office of honor, Trust or Profit under the United States: but the Party convicted shall nevertheless be liable and subject to Indictment, Trial, Judgment and Punishment, according to Law.

Section. 4. The Times, Places and Manner of holding Elections for Senators and Representatives, shall be prescribed in each State by the Legislature thereof; but the Congress may at any time by Law make or alter such Regulations, except as to the Places of chusing Senators.

The Congress shall assemble at least once in every Year, and such Meeting shall be on the first Monday in December, unless they shall by Law appoint a different Day.

Section. 5. Each House shall be the Judge of the Elections, Returns and Qualifications of its own Members, and a Majority of each shall constitute a Quorum to do Business; but a smaller Number may adjourn from day to day, and may be authorized to compel the Attendance of absent Members, in such Manner, and under such Penalties as each House may provide.

Each House may determine the Rules of its Proceedings, punish its Members for disorderly Behaviour, and, with the Concurrence of two thirds, expel a Member.

Each House shall keep a Journal of its Proceedings, and from time to time publish the same, excepting such Parts as may in their Judgment require Secrecy; and the Yeas and Nays of the Members of either House on any question shall, at the Desire of one fifth of those Present, be entered on the Journal.

Neither House, during the Session of Congress, shall, without the Consent of the other, adjourn for more than three days, nor to any other Place than that in which the two Houses shall be sitting.

Section. 6. The Senators and Representatives shall receive a Compensation for their Services, to be ascertained by Law, and paid out of the Treasury of the United States. They shall in all Cases, except Treason, Felony and Breach of the Peace, be privileged from Arrest during their Attendance at the Session of their respective Houses, and in going to and returning from the same; and for any Speech or Debate in either House, they shall not be questioned in any other Place.

No Senator or Representative shall, during the Time for which he was elected, be appointed to any civil Office under the Authority of the United States, which shall have been created, or the Emoluments whereof shall have been encreased during such time; and no Person holding any Office under the United States, shall be a Member of either House during his Continuance in Office.

Section. 7. All Bills for raising Revenue shall originate in the House of Representatives; but the Senate may propose or concur with Amendments as on other Bills.

Every Bill which shall have passed the House of Representatives and the Senate, shall, before it become a Law, be presented to the President of the United States;

CHAPTER FOUR

AMERICAN FEDERALISM

Can Democracy Be Divided Fifty Ways?

CHAPTER OUTLINE

Federalism: An Overview
DIVISION OF POWERS
POWER WITHIN THE STATES
LIMITATIONS ON GOVERNMENT ACTIONS
INTERSTATE OBLIGATIONS
STATEHOOD AND THE ALTERNATIVES

The Evolution of Federalism
THREE CRISES OF STATE AND NATION
THE ROLE OF THE COURTS
"NEW FEDERALISMS"
STRENGTHENED STATE GOVERNMENTS

Responsibilities of the States

Tensions in the Federal System
REGIONAL RIVALRIES
INTERESTS SHARED ACROSS STATE LINES

Federal Intervention
REAPPORTIONMENT
THE DRINKING AGE

The Importance of States

LET'S ENGAGE IN A LITTLE RAMPANT PARANOIA FOR A MOMENT. Right now you are sitting somewhere reading this text. If you're inside, take a moment to examine the ceiling. What makes you think that the building (house, apartment, library, dorm) around you won't crash in on you any minute? Is that crack significant? If you're outside, *watch out!*—that mosquito may carry yellow fever! Speaking of fevers, recall the last time you saw a physician or other health professional. How do you know that person wasn't just a quack? Maybe your symptoms *really are* serious and you ought to be doing something about them! Speaking of doing something, how about going out for a pizza after you've finished this chapter? Naw, better not. You're liable to get killed on the road by some incompetent driver—or worse, you might get stopped by a sadistic cop with a hangover and overdue child support payments. Just call out for home delivery, assuming that the phone works. But what if the tomato sauce is tainted with ptomaine or the sausage habors salmonella? Poison pizza. Back to that quack? You're not that hungry after all.

Most of us live without such fears, thanks almost exclusively to state and local governments, which provide for

117

building codes, public health projects, professional certification, drivers' licenses, competent police and fire protection, utilities regulation, restaurant inspections, and lots of other things as well. Although the federal government ordinarily dominates the news and casual conversations of politics, our everyday lives are primarily and systematically dependent on functions carried out by the other partners in the federal system—state governments and their political subdivisions at the local level.

In Chapter 3 we talked about how our nation's English colonial background was transformed by a revolution and then a new constitution. This chapter examines the American federal system and the choices our nation has made about which level of government does what. Choices about centralizing, decentralizing, or sharing power across levels of government have a definite impact on political participation and policy. We'll also look at the tensions created by the division of responsibility in our system and various attempts to rectify its shortcomings. When do fairness and justice demand uniform national policies? What issues are best left to state or local control? In 1973, for example, the Supreme Court took abortion largely out of the states' hands by asserting a constitutionally based national policy. Starting in 1989 the Court began to return that issue to the states by allowing greater state regulation of abortion. Which was right? Or again, when should resources be pooled and redistributed across state lines? Building an interstate highway system with federal funds meant that large, sparsely populated states in the West were net gainers, while more densely populated states were net losers. Is that fair? These are questions of democracy, important questions for this book.

Federalism: An Overview

Most Americans hold dual citizenship of a kind: citizenship in the United States and citizenship in a particular state. This duality stems from our federal system, in which power is shared by the national (federal) government and the fifty state governments. The national government and the several state governments claim sovereignty; each of these governments has authority over the persons and resources within its jurisdiction that cannot be taken away by another government. If you are in a state of the United States while reading this page, you are, according to constitutional theory, within the jurisdiction of both a sovereign state and the sovereign United States. Because there are two governments over the same space at the same time, authority is divided between the two along conceptual lines. The state government has authority in matters like those identified at the beginning of this chapter. The national government has authority in matters like interstate commerce and foreign affairs. Thus your driver's license comes from the state; your social security card comes from the national government. The Constitution creates this conceptual division of authority. You are also within a county (or a parish) and may be in a city as well (not to mention school districts and other special districts), but these governments are creatures of the state and cannot claim the autonomy of sovereignty. Their power derives from the state and can be taken away at the state's will.

This dual citizenship has many important consequences, most of which we take entirely for granted. In many states, citizens must pay state income tax as well as federal income tax. And because there are fifty separate state jurisdictions, whenever citizens move from one state to another, they must register to vote in the new state, get a new driver's license, learn different traffic regulations, and so on. Some states make it more difficult than others to get married or divorced. Certain crimes, such as driving while intoxicated, carry rather lenient penalties in some states and severe penalties in others.

From the beginning of our political history the federal system has made for tension between the states and the national government. The major domestic crisis in U.S. history, the Civil War, erupted when several states attempted to secede from the Union. Moreover, the racial issues underlying the secession crisis have resurfaced recurrently in U.S. history, often in struggles pitting state against nation. In the 1960s, for example, the federal government had to intervene forcefully in southern states to protect and extend the civil rights and voting rights of black citizens.

Other nations have suffered similar crises, and many have federal arrangements similar to ours: Canada has provincial governments; Australia, Brazil, Germany, and

A group of big-city mayors leads a parade in Washington seeking federal assistance to hard-pressed urban areas. The needs of big cities are often not high on the list of concerns at the state level. States may contain many complex and conflicting political and economic interests. (Stephen Crowley/The New York Times)

COMPARATIVE PERSPECTIVE

NATIONS, STATES, AND NATION-STATES

One of the challenges of studying politics is to describe political reality—starkly and subtly diverse, constantly changing—in tidy, readily understood language. Often a discipline like political science will develop special terminology to allow more precise descriptions, borrowing words from common parlance for more rigorous definition. A textbook has to walk the line between common usage and academic precision. In this chapter, for example, and throughout this text, *nation* refers to the single overarching sovereign political entity—for us, the United States. We use *state* to mean one of the primary constituent political elements of the United States: California, Illinois, and Minnesota are states. Thus we distinguish between the state governments (in Sacramento, Springfield, St. Paul, etc.) and the national government (in Washington, D.C.). This matches ordinary usage.

Students of international politics use these same words rather differently. A *state* internationally is a sovereign political unit, accorded equal standing in the international community. A *nation* is a group of people living in the same territory and sharing culture, heritage, and sometimes ethnic identity. When a nation in this sense has its own sovereign political structure, it is a *nation-state*. The Treaty of Westphalia (ending the Thirty Years' War in 1648) is usually identified as marking the end of feudal political structures and the beginning of the modern nation-state system. But political lines do not always respect history, culture, and territory. Sometimes several nations are gathered together in a single state—Yugoslavia was created after the First World War as a state composed primarily of Servia, Croatia, Slovenia, Bosnia and Herzegovina, and Montenegro. Sometimes, a nation is split up under two or more states, as in the Kurdish nation under Turkey, Iraq, and Syria. When national distinctions exist within a state, they often

(Box continues on page 121)

India have state governments. Some federal systems allow the regional governments greater responsibility and latitude for action than others. Whatever the particular arrangements, however, all federal systems must cope with one key problem: coordinating the actions of the two levels.

The opposite of a federal system in political structure is a **unitary system**, in which the national government's authority is more or less uniformly enforced throughout the country. Administrative subdivisions are required for the efficient discharge of political

coincide with political subdivisions. Then the tensions of federalism combine with nationalism in a volatile mix. When the sentiments and affections of citizens are more strongly attached to the nation than to the state, these tensions may lead to civil strife and even the breakup of governments, as evidenced by the violent end of Yugoslavia in 1992.

The late 1980s and early 1990s saw high levels of nationalistic fervor in different circumstances around the globe: French-speaking Québecois seeking independence from Canada; Palestinians dispersed across Lebanon, Israel, Syria, and Jordan seeking a Palestinian state; Northern Irish Catholics seeking independence from Great Britain; in southern India, Tamils seeking to join dissatisfied Tamil compatriots from Sri Lanka in a new Tamil state. The patchwork of Eastern Europe, sliced up and sewn together dozens of times since 1648, entered the 1990s a hotbed of nationalistic zeal (in contrast to the European Community's success in moving Western European states into a single economy). Each of these instances (and many more) presented unique circumstances. But the resurgence of nationalism to challenge existing state boundaries has become an inescapable feature of global politics as we move toward the twenty-first century.

The United States has been called a "nation of nations," a reference to the enormous ethnic and national diversity among our largely immigrant population. But with the exception of Native American tribes, nations do not exist within the United States. Most major metropolitan areas can boast ethnic neighborhoods, but these are fragments, assembled family by family from the nation "back home." Regional cultures do exist in the United States, and citizens do identify with their home states. More important ethnic and class identities often divide central cities from suburbs or, for example, African-Americans from their Korean-American neighbors as in the 1992 Los Angeles riots. These differences, however, fall short of defining separate nations within our country. One of the great unfinished tasks of American democracy has been to establish a shared identity that by and large supersedes other national ties.

---

activities, but these subdivisions derive their authority (as in a city's charter) from the central government rather than from the people directly. Although these local units are not self-governing, they often have considered autonomy, and political power may be decentralized to a certain extent. Modern examples of unitary systems include the governments of Great Britain, France, and Sweden.

Before addressing the current status of our federal system, let us examine the legal mechanisms on which the system is based, particularly as they relate to the division of powers, limitations on government actions, and interstate obligations.

Division of Powers

The Constitution establishes the political powers to be exercised by the national government, some of which are granted exclusively. In addition, the Constitution explicitly forbids the national government certain powers, forbids the state governments certain powers, and allows the state governments the residual ("reserve") powers. Because certain powers granted to the national government are not granted exclusively, they can be exercised concurrently by the national government and the state governments. These concurrent powers—exercised independently by two separate governments—should not be confused with "shared powers," which is the phrase we have used to describe the division of powers among three branches of the same government.

As explained in Chapter 3, **delegated powers** are the powers that the Constitution gives to the national government. Most of these are **enumerated powers** (they are named explicitly in the Constitution). Many of the most important of these appear in a list of congressional powers in Article I, Section 8, including the power to control interstate commerce, the power to maintain a single national currency, and the power to declare war (see **Table 4-1**). All of the foregoing are exclusive powers of the national government. Some enumerated powers granted to the national government—such as the power to tax and spend for the general welfare—are not exclusive and can be exercised concurrently by state governments.

In addition to and as a result of the enumerated powers, the national government exercises **implied powers**. For example, if the national government is granted the power to coin money and maintain a currency, does that not imply that the national government also has the power to create a national bank to carry out these functions? In the early days of our government, Alexander Hamilton, along with others of a "nationalist" orientation, argued for such implied powers, whereas Thomas Jefferson and others of a more democratic (state-oriented) bent supported a narrower interpretation of delegated powers. In an 1819 ruling in the case of ***McCulloch* v. *Maryland***, the Supreme Court upheld the federal government's right to create a national bank, legitimizing the concept of implied powers.[1]

This concept has played a major role in the gradual expansion of the powers of the federal government. Many activities of the federal government that now seem fundamental—such as the regulation of key aspects of economic life—are not spelled out anywhere in the Constitution. This is hardly surprising: The Founders could never have anticipated the complexities and problems of modern industrial life. So the Constitution has expanded to meet changing national imperatives, and the doctrine of implied powers has proved valuable in extending the Constitution's reach.

The Tenth Amendment speaks specifically of **reserve powers**, a concept implicit in the original Constitution. Powers not granted to the federal government or prohibited to the states "are reserved to the states . . . or to the people." A large area of law

TABLE 4-1
THE FEDERAL DIVISION OF POWERS

Major Powers of the Federal Government
To tax for federal purposes
To borrow on the nation's credit
To regulate foreign and interstate commerce
To provide currency and coinage
To conduct foreign relations and make treaties
To provide an army and a navy
To establish and maintain a postal service
To protect patents and copyrights
To regulate weights and measures
To admit new states
To "make all laws which shall be necessary and proper" for the execution of all powers vested in the U.S. government

Major Powers of the States
To tax for state purposes
To borrow on the state's credit
To regulate trade within the state
To make and enforce civil and criminal law
To maintain police forces
To furnish public education
To control local government
To regulate charities
To establish voting and election laws
To exercise all "powers not delegated to the United States by the Constitution, nor prohibited by it to the States," except for those "reserved to . . . the people"

SOURCE: Nicholas Henry, *Governing at the Grassroots* (Englewood Cliffs, N.J.: Prentice Hall, 1984), p. 233.

called **police powers** encompasses the authority to care for the health, safety, and welfare of persons within the government's jurisdiction. Since few enumerated powers fell within this area, and given the federal government's very limited original scope of activities, a general assumption was made during the first century of the new government that the police powers belonged among the reserved powers. In the twentieth century, however, the federal government has expanded its activities, using broad interpretations of other enumerated powers to involve itself more directly with the health and welfare of individual citizens. Programs such as social security and Aid to Families with Dependent Children from Franklin Roosevelt's New Deal and Medicare and Head Start from Lyndon Johnson's Great Society demonstrate the federal government exercising its police powers. Powers like these that are exercised both by the federal government and the state governments are called **concurrent powers**. The power to tax and spend is the most obvious specific example of a concurrent power.

Power within the States

All states in the U.S. have **unitary governments**. The political subdivisions of the states—cities, counties, and special districts—do not enjoy political autonomy in the exercise of their power. As creatures of the state, these subunits are wholly dependent on the state and its authority, which comes from the people of the state through the state constitution. But this formal explanation of the difference between the U.S. government and the state governments does little justice to the subtle ways of power.

In fact, in the federal system, the "sovereign" state governments are often docile or only mildly complaining followers of federal direction in matters well within the states' authority—lowering speed limits, for example. Alternatively, the formally subordinate units of state governments may exercise a significant influence on state policy and may sometimes resist state policy directives with impunity. Most states allow some form of "home rule," whereby the state allows the city broad freedom to operate under a city charter. An interesting power reversal sometimes occurs in states with a major metropolitan center. For example, the mayor of New York City may well be a more influential politician (both within the state and in the country at large) than the governor of New York. Albany, the state capital, can sometimes seem a long way from the center of power.

Even more complex is the question of state influence on national policy. The mayors of the nation's largest cities often have a very different political agenda from the governors'. Urban needs, it is argued, require more redistributive fiscal policy and greater federal regulatory intervention. Mayors rarely worry about farm policy, but governors must. Mayors will lobby Congress directly to achieve their own political objectives in competition with their states' chief executives. The remainder of this chapter shows that no simple model adequately describes the complex, surprising, and fascinating American federal system.

Limitations on Government Actions

In the U.S. Constitution, the primary means of limiting government power are, as we have seen, structural: dividing power in a federal system, sharing power with checks and balances among branches of the national government, and—most important—creating a responsive system of representation through frequent, regular elections. In addition to these structural arrangements, the Constitution contains specific substantive limitations on government action. Article I sets certain limits on the actions of states, among other things forbidding them to grant titles of nobility and to pass bills of attainder or ex post facto (retroactive) laws. The Fourteenth Amendment requires that states must observe "**due process of law**"—a guarantee of fair legal procedure that entails many specific obligations. Similar restrictions are applied to the national government in Article I, in the Bill of Rights (Amendments 1 through 10), and in subsequent amendments. In principle, all of these limitations are antimajoritarian, since they are designed to prevent the government from simply following the majority's will—a reflection of the tensions in a democratic system committed to respecting individual rights. Practically speaking, substantive limitations in the Constitution remind us of those tensions and occasionally allow the Supreme Court to block the actions of Congress or the president by invoking constitutional principle.

Interstate Obligations

Article IV requires that states grant "**full faith and credit**" to the acts of other states, return fugitives fleeing from criminal proceedings in other states, and grant all "privileges and immunities" to citizens of other states. Under the full faith and credit provision, the most far-reaching of these requirements, every state must accept as valid the legal proceedings and records of other states, including mortgages, contracts, and birth certificates. As interpreted by the Supreme Court, this provision does not include the obligation to enforce the *criminal* laws of another state; a person wanted for a crime in one state must be extradited to that state for trial. In general, however, state civil laws must be enforced by all other states. Hence whenever a person leaves one state to avoid complying with a contract made there, the state to which he flees must ordinarily enforce that contract in a court of law.

The full faith and credit provision has not been uniformly followed by the states or enforced by the courts, however. In particular, the requirement that states extradite fugitives to other states has often been ignored, with the acquiescence of the Supreme Court. In several famous cases, state governors have refused to extradite fugitives on the grounds that prison conditions were unsafe or that a fair trial could not be obtained in the state seeking the fugitive's return. A major roadblock to extradition was lifted with recent legislation making it a federal crime to cross state lines to avoid prosecution. As a result, extradition has become more common.

Among the most significant privileges and immunities that the states must extend to all U.S. citizens are the right to vote and the right to travel freely. Until relatively recently, many states sought to circumvent this constitutional provision by attaching lengthy residency requirements to the right to vote, even in national elections. The Supreme Court largely ended this practice by ruling that a state must demonstrate the legitimacy of requirements. That right to travel across state lines has generally been accepted by the states. The only significant exception to this rule occurred when

(Text continues on page 128)

COMPARATIVE PERSPECTIVE

FEDERALISM IN A UNIFIED GERMANY

Germany has a federal structure in which fifteen states (*Länder*) are represented in the *Bundesrat*, where they "participate . . . in the legislation and administration of the Federation." Each state (*Land*) maintains important powers in education, law enforcement, and cultural affairs. At the same time, states are limited by federal law (the death penalty is outlawed throughout the country, for example). The state and federal governments jointly exercise certain powers, including those having to do with transportation, energy development, and criminal justice. In most cases the administration of federal legislation is left to the *Länder*; the federal government plays an advisory role rather than a directly administrative one. As a result, the Federal Republic of Germany has a relatively small central bureaucracy.

When the two halves of Germany, separated following the Second World War, reunited in 1990, there was little question that the resulting government would retain a federal structure. The mechanism for achieving unity was the Basic Law, promulgated in 1949 by representatives of the three powers occupying the western sector (the United States, France, and Great Britain) and various German leaders. The Basic Law was designed to be a temporary arrangement, a stand-in for a constitution until reunification occurred—an event delayed forty years by the Cold War. The experiences of the Nazi period made the occupying authorities suspicious of centralized power in the new West German state, so the Basic Law provided for a federal system.

Reunification under the Basic Law could occur in one of two ways: East Germany could "accede" to West Germany, simply coming under the authority of the Basic Law, or the two countries could agree on a voluntary merger with the adoption of a new, common constitution. The Social Democratic and Green political parties favored a new constitution as more democratic, treating East Germany as an equal partner. The Christian Democrats and the Free Democrats argued that accession would be more practical and less time-consuming. That last argument proved decisive, because the East German government was eager to achieve reunification quickly.

(Box continues on page 127)

Whether or not reunification had produced a new constitution, a federal structure was favored both in the east and in the west, though for different reasons. In the east, 1952 reforms under the Communist government had rendered the boundaries of the five *Länder* that made up the eastern territory irrelevant. Upon reunification, the east favored federalism primarily as a means to protect individual liberties and to promote ethnic minorities. (Ethnic diversity is greater in the east than in the west.) In the west, where ten *Länder* had made up the Federal Republic during the division, federalism was seen as an important check on central government power (as it was designed to be). Differences among the western *Länder* had decreased between 1949 and 1990, in part due to constitutional provisions that required "a reasonable equalization" between financially strong and financially weak *Länder*. There had been much voluntary coordination among the ten western *Land* governments as well, producing a trend toward a unitary federal state. In anticipation of the coming reunification, the East German government created five *Länder*, approximating those effaced in 1952.

Reunification was seen as a time to reapportion representation in the *Bundesrat*, where each *Land* is allotted a certain number of votes (from three to eight) that must be cast as a bloc. But the possibility of redrawing the boundaries in the western *Länder* for greater bureaucratic efficiency was rejected by the smaller *Länder*.

Because the former Eastern German *Länder* needed substantial capital development, constitutional provisions for distributing federal revenue from shared taxes were suspended until 1995, as were the equalization statutes. West Germany established a substantial "German unity" fund to ease the accession of the much poorer East German *Länder*.

Reunification reaffirmed federalism in Germany. The future of this system of government, though, is bound to be affected by the continuing process of Germany's integration within the European Community—a process that will take power from both the *Länder* and the federal government. Perhaps the basic features of German federalism will persist—or perhaps they will be replaced by a continental federalism. For now, at least, the *Länder* remain a significant part of political life in Germany.

Source: Wolfgang Welz, "Federalism and German Reunification," in Intergovernmental Perspective, *Summer 1990, pp. 25–28.*

thousands of migrants fleeing the Dust Bowl conditions of the Midwest in the 1930s were prevented from entering California under a state law excluding indigent immigrants. In *Edwards* v. *California* (1941), the Supreme Court struck down the California law as an unconstitutional barrier to interstate commerce.[2]

Statehood and the Alternatives

The Constitution grants Congress the right to admit new states but does not establish any fixed procedures for admission. More than half the present states were once "territories" governed by congressional appointees. One by one, these territories petitioned Congress for statehood, and each eventually was the beneficiary of a congressional **enabling act** allowing its citizens to draft a state constitution. Next came congressional and presidential approval of the draft state constitution and, after any differences had been ironed out, admission to the Union. Sometimes additional requirements have to be fulfilled: The citizens of Hawaii and Alaska, for example, were required to approve admission to statehood at special elections. Once admitted, a state stands in complete legal equality with all other states; none has unique privileges or obligations.

In addition to states, the United States includes one district, one commonwealth, and several territories. The District of Columbia, the seat of our national government, was specified in the Constitution as a *district* granted to the national government by the states of Maryland and Virginia. This arrangement ensured that the national government would not be dependent on the government of any particular state in which it might be located. Despite intense resistance from some members of Congress, in 1961 Washingtonians were given the right to participate in presidential elections through the Twenty-third Amendment. (Southern segregationists and conservatives had sought to exclude from the franchise Washington's predominantly black population, which votes heavily liberal and Democratic.) Home rule by a local mayor and city council was also granted. But the District of Columbia remains without U.S. representatives and senators.

Puerto Rico enjoys the unique status of a *commonwealth*. Puerto Rican citizens can freely emigrate to the United States, and more than 1 million have done so. Though relatively well-off compared with most Caribbean people, Puerto Ricans earn, on average, only about half what citizens of our poorest state earn. They receive many welfare benefits, including social security, food stamps, and Medicare, but they pay no U.S. taxes. Puerto Ricans serve in the U.S. armed forces, but they are not represented in Congress, nor can they vote in presidential elections. Puerto Rico was taken from Spain by the United States in 1898, and it voted to accept commonwealth status in 1950.

U.S. *territories* include the U.S. Virgin Islands, Samoa, Guam, and, until 1978, the Canal Zone. The "Zone," in which the Panama Canal is located, was ceded to Panama in 1978 by treaty. Highly controversial in the United States, the treaty was viewed by

(Text continues on page 130)

The Northwest Ordinance of 1787

The Northwest Ordinance of 1787 has been called the most far-reaching piece of legislation ever enacted in the United States. In mandating that new states were to be created in the area north of the Ohio River, the ordinance stipulated that the new states would enjoy the same legal status as existing states and that slavery would be excluded in this area. By decreeing that newly settled territories would be incorporated into the Union as full-fledged states, the ordinance defused the threat of rivalry between the older states, many of which had sought to expand into the Northwest Territories. It also precluded any move toward colonial subordination of newly settled areas to established states. The system of "elastic federalism" instituted by the Northwest Ordinance, under which statehood was to be granted to those who actually settled and developed new territories, offered perhaps the most sensible method for opening the continent and expanding the Union.

This 1783 map shows the geographic divisions of that time, including the American states, Florida, Canada, Quebec, and Nova Scotia. The land that would be covered by the Northwest Ordinance is situated northwest of the Ohio River. *(The Bettmann Archive)*

some Americans as a giveaway of American rights. In fact, the United States acquired the Canal Zone by fomenting a 1903 rebellion against the government of Colombia that led to the secession of the state of Panama. As Senator S. I. Hayakawa of California put it at one point, the Canal Zone was ours because "we stole it fair and square."

The Evolution of Federalism

President Abraham Lincoln once asserted that "the Union is older than any of the states, and, in fact, it created them as states." President Ronald Reagan took precisely the opposite view, that "the federal government did not create the states; the states created the federal government." Both claims fall short. Realistically, the delegates at the Constitutional Convention had no chance of displacing state power altogether. State power was both the means and the cost of getting a new constitution at all. How has the system changed since 1789, and how can federal arrangements best serve our democratic goals today? We shall answer these questions by examining three crises that decisively changed the shape of U.S. federalism, how the courts have influenced our federal system, and drives by the executive branch to remake federalism—the so-called "new federalisms."

Three Crises of State and Nation

THE CIVIL WAR The crisis with the greatest impact on federalism culminated in the Civil War. In the verbal and ideological battle preceding the war, the renowned South Carolina politician John C. Calhoun raised basic questions about exactly what "nationhood" meant in the United States. "The very idea of an American People, as constituting a single community, is a mere chimera," he argued. "Such a community never for a single moment existed—neither before nor since the Declaration of Independence."[3] For Calhoun, as for Ronald Reagan, the states created the nation: Each state was a sovereign community that voluntarily entered into a compact with the other states to form the national society. A more or less logical deduction from this view was that the states, having agreed to form the Union, could also dissolve it.

Calhoun's concept of federalism was vigorously opposed by Daniel Webster, the eloquent senator from Massachusetts. Webster, whom Lincoln would echo, argued that the United States was created not by a compact between the states but "by the people of the United States in the aggregate." The Constitution, he said, was "the people's Constitution, the people's government, made for the people, made by the people, and answerable to the people." He concluded this argument with the famous line, "Liberty and union, one and inseparable, now and forever."[4]

Webster not only defended a union based directly on the people, but he also pointed out that many common interests of U.S. society as a whole could not be handled by the states. For Webster, as for Alexander Hamilton, national action was abso-

In this painting, Daniel Webster and Henry Clay (seated) listen to John Calhoun. These three men represented distinct positions on the question of national versus state power in pre-Civil War America. Calhoun believed that any large subgroup of the nation should have the power to veto efforts to force change upon it. Webster was a staunch defender of a strong federal government required for national unity. Clay, known as the Great Compromiser, tried to steer a course that would avoid secession and civil war. (Culver Pictures, Inc.)

lutely necessary to secure many worthwhile goals that the individual states were not likely to pursue. Only the national government, Webster contended, had the power and the mandate to address the problems of land use, waterway development, and transportation—all increasingly important as the United States grew into an industrial society.

The North's triumph in the Civil War not only resulted in the abolition of slavery and the permanent demise of the concept of secession, but it also led to a major expansion of the powers of the federal government. During and after the war, federal involvement in banking, transportation, higher education, and land management broadened considerably, as Webster and Lincoln had argued it must.

INDUSTRIAL EXPANSION / The second major crisis of federalism grew out of the vast expansion of industry throughout the nation in the second half of the nineteenth century. With the emergence of giant corporations whose interests stretched across state lines, state governments found it nearly impossible to regulate commerce and industry. Monopolistic and predatory business practices, such as price fixing, flourished despite widespread agitation by farmers, workers, and consumers for legislation restricting the power of business. Attempts by state governments to control large business interests were often struck down as unconstitutional by the Supreme Court. During this period the Court frequently (though with some notable exceptions) used its power to protect economic interests from both the state governments and the federal government. Action by the federal government, principally in the administrations of Theodore Roosevelt (1901–1909) and Woodrow Wilson (1913–1921), was necessary to bring the disruptive forces of industrial power under a modest degree of social control. Congress established new regulations for the conduct of trade, encouraging competition and limiting monopolistic practices, and passed a series of statutes regulating the banking, food and drug, meatpacking, and other industries. The Justice Department, with the acquiescence of the Supreme Court, vigorously enforced antitrust laws. Throughout this era (roughly 1890–1916), then, all branches of the federal government became involved to an unprecedented degree in the regulation of business.

THE GREAT DEPRESSION   The third crisis of federalism developed out of the Great Depression of the 1930s, when the magnitude of the national economic collapse far exceeded the remedial powers of the states. With millions of Americans unemployed, local and state welfare efforts were stretched beyond the breaking point. In his 1933 inaugural address, President Franklin D. Roosevelt argued that since the crisis was national, the solutions also had to be national. He called for extensive planning to be carried out by the federal government. Roosevelt's New Deal inaugurated a new phase of federalism. The earliest New Deal efforts consisted of emergency steps toward national planning for economic recovery. However, as the New Deal took shape, federal efforts were extended into new areas, some previously within the province of the states—welfare and income-maintenance programs, jobs programs, the regulation of wages and prices, and a host of other functions.

The Role of the Courts

The federal courts, particularly the Supreme Court, have played a crucial role in resolving disputes between the federal government and the states. Many key court decisions have shaped the evolution of the U.S. federal system. Historically, the Supreme Court's view of federalism has undergone major shifts. In early U.S. history, the Court promoted the growth of national power. Beginning with the appointment of Roger Taney as Chief Justice in 1836, the Court became more protective of state governments—particularly during Reconstruction and its aftermath. Between the 1870s and the 1930s the Court more frequently extended its protection to commercial interests, to the disadvantage of both state and federal governments. In 1937 the Court bowed to the political reality of the New Deal and allowed expanded federal power in economic regulation joined with more active intervention in matters of civil liberties and civil rights. The Court has generally maintained that pattern though moving toward allowing greater state discretion in rights questions and more careful scrutiny of economic regulations. To get a better sense of the Court's role in the evolution federalism, let us look briefly at some cases that reflect these historical trends.

EXPANDING NATIONAL POWER   In *Gibbons* v. *Ogden* (1824), the Supreme Court reviewed a challenge to the steamboat monopoly granted by the New York legislature to Robert Livingston and Robert Fulton (which they licensed to Aaron Ogden, who operated a ferry between New York City and New Jersey).[5] Chief Justice John Marshall, writing for the Court, rejected the argument that enumerated powers (in this case the commerce clause) ought to be construed strictly. "Why ought they to be so construed?" he asked. "Is there one sentence in the constitution which gives countenance to this rule?" Describing commerce as all branches of commercial intercourse and remarking that the Constitution allows for regulation *among* and not just *between* the states, Marshall found the New York monopoly an intrusion on the federal government's plenary (complete) interstate commerce power and thus null and void. This case advanced national power in two ways: generally, by arguing for a broad reading of enumerated powers, and specifically, by fashioning the commerce clause into a powerful tool for regulation. Like the notion of implied powers asserted in *McCulloch v. Maryland*, this broad reading of national powers at the expense of the states reflects the Court's early efforts to strengthen the national government. In democratic terms, the Court's efforts generally favored more centralized, republican control—a natural extension of the Constitution's replacing the Articles of Confederation.

DUAL FEDERALISM   The doctrine of **dual federalism**, already apparent in Court decisions prior to the Civil War (and central to the Court's splintered finding in *Dred Scott v. Sanford* in 1857),[6] explained federalism as a system in which two naturally distinct sets of functions were assigned to the two levels of government in the federal system. Since the national government and the state governments were assigned identifiably different—and not interchangeable—tasks, the privileges of national citizenship, too, were naturally different from those of state citizenship. When the Fourteenth Amendment was ratified in 1868, requiring the states to protect the privileges and immunities of citizens of the United States, the doctrine of dual federalism was ready at hand to block any national imposition on state power. In the so-called *Slaughterhouse Cases* (1873), another state-sanctioned monopoly was being challenged, this time a slaughterhouse monopoly granted by Louisiana.[7] The excluded slaughterhouse operators challenged the monopoly as, among other things, a denial of their newly protected constitutional privileges and immunities the privilege of carrying on a trade of their choice). The Court wrote, "It is quite clear . . . that there is a citizenship of the United States, and a citizenship of a State, which are distinct from each other, and which depend upon different characteristics or circumstances in the individual." Unfortunately for the excluded slaughterhouse operators, "the privileges and immunities relied on in the argument are those which belong to citizens of the States as such, and . . . they are left to the State governments for security and protection." This interpretation of citizenship ensured that at least this clause of the Fourteenth Amendment would not produce enlarged national supervision of citizens' rights—after all, the rights of *national* citizens were already protected by the national government and did not depend on the newly ratified amendment. And although this case concerned white slaughterhouse operators, the obvious result of the reasoning was to leave newly freed blacks without federal protection of their privileges of citizenship as well. In democratic terms, dual federalism meant that regional differences reflected in different state treatments of citizens would not be replaced by a national standard.

PART ONE • FOUNDATIONS

THE PROTECTION OF COMMERCIAL INTERESTS   The tensions of the federal system were turned to the advantage of commercial interests in the United States in a series of decisions by the Supreme Court that thwarted both federal and state attempts at regulation. In *Lochner* v. *New York* (1905), a New York statute setting maximum working hours for bakers was challenged.[8] The Court declared:

> The act is not within any fair meaning of the term, a health law, but is an illegal interference with the rights of individuals, both employers and employees, to make contracts regarding labor upon such terms as they think best. . . . Statues of the nature of that under review . . . are mere meddlesome interferences with the rights of the individual.

By this reasoning, states were incapacitated from enacting workplace regulations. But the Court also incapacitated the federal government in this area. In *Hammer* v. *Dagenhart* (1918), congressional legislation aimed at child labor was struck down because manufacturing was a local concern, under the jurisdiction of the state and not the federal government through its interstate commerce power: "The maintenance of the authority of the States over matters purely local is as essential to the preservation of our institutions as is the conservation of the supremacy of the federal power in all matters entrusted to the Nation by the Federal Constitution."[9] The Court was not just playing both sides against the middle; it did, however, use the tensions of the federal system to protect what it perceived to be a constitutional value—an unregulated economy. In democratic terms, the Court's action in defending commercial interests was an example of an antimajoritarian assertion of prerogative on behalf of certain protected principles (elite values destined to be replaced in the turmoil of the Great Depression).

A CONCERN WITH RIGHTS   In 1833, in *Barron* v. *Baltimore*, the Supreme court ruled that the restrictions of the Bill of Rights applied only to the national government and not to the state governments.[10] Protection from state violation of these rights, if it was to be had at all, was to come from the states. The Fourteenth Amendment, ratified in 1868 following the Civil War, contained language that could justify national protection of these rights (indeed, at least two members of Congress argued that it did so in debates during its proposal). But the Court steadfastly resisted such an interpretation, as we saw in the *Slaughterhouse Cases*. Starting in the 1920s the Court began to incorporate some of the guarantees of the Bill of Rights into the Fourteenth Amendment, a process that today encompasses most but not all of the specifics of the first eight amendments. The Court's newfound concern with the Bill of Rights was heightened when in 1937 the Court more or less abandoned the business of reviewing economic regulation. The Court-generated tensions in the federal system became rights-centered. As we will see, from 1937 until very recently, economic issues of importance within the federal system were addressed almost exclusively by Congress and the executive branch and not the Supreme Court. (A fuller explanation of the Court's heightened concern with civil rights and liberties will be given in Chapters 5 and 6.)

"New Federalisms"

Changes in the federal system have become commonplace in recent decades. The twentieth century experienced massive shifts in expenditure—and corresponding responsibilities—in American government. In terms of expenditures, the relative importance of both state and federal government has grown, while local spending has declined proportionately (though not absolutely). Underlying these changes is a long-term trend toward more active and complex government intervention in economic and social affairs.

Since 1933 there have been four distinct efforts, led by the president and facilitated by Congress, to create a "new federalism." Let us look at each one to assess its key elements and significance.

FDR'S NEW DEAL The first new federalism was President Franklin D. Roosevelt's New Deal, under which the balance of power tilted toward Washington in an effort to deal with serious problems of national scope. Programs initiated in the New Deal period were often referred to as products of **cooperative federalism**, in which the national government worked directly with local as well as state governments. The key element in cooperative federalism was federal funding for programs administered by state and local governments, including Aid to Families with Dependent Children, construction projects (hospitals, highways, airports, etc.), public health programs, and unemployment compensation.

JOHNSON'S GREAT SOCIETY The second new federalism of modern times emerged in President Lyndon Johnson's Great Society program of the 1960s. Johnson called his program "creative federalism." This translated into a greatly increased level of federal intervention in community affairs. In developing more than two hundred new social and economic programs, President Johnson and his supporters in Congress triggered a vast increase in federal involvement in the day-to-day affairs of U.S. citizens. These programs had a strong urban emphasis; in fact, federal funds often went directly to cities, bypassing state governments entirely. Great Society legislation also channeled large amounts of aid to the disadvantaged. Federal money flowed into such previously sacrosanct preserves of state and local authority as education and law enforcement. Between 1960 and 1970, federal aid to the states increased from $7 billion to $24 billion, and the percentage of federal funds going to urban areas increased from 55 percent to 70 percent of the total.

NIXON'S REVENUE SHARING The Johnsonian concept of federalism was at least partly discarded during the administration of President Richard Nixon. The Nixon administration advocated federal financial assistance for the states but urged that the policy-making and administrative functions of the federal government be reduced. To this end, federal grants to the states were restructured in two principal ways: through the introduction of **revenue sharing** programs, under which a certain portion of federal revenues was disbursed among the states, and through the consolidation of many federal funding programs into block grants, which gave states and localities greater flexibility in putting the funds to use. Prior to these initiatives, federal funding to state and local governments was available primarily in **categorical grants**, which defined acceptable expenditures quite specifically. A **block grant** defines a broad area, such as "community development," within which the state or local grant recipient can choose how to spend the money. Under the State and Local Assistance Act of 1972, state and local governments received $5 to $6 billion a year for five years in large noncategorical grants, to use as they saw fit. One-third of the funds was earmarked for the states and two-thirds for local governments, apportioned according to a formula that took into account population, per capita income, and other factors.

Revenue sharing set the tone for intergovernmental relations in the 1970s, and it was enthusiastically supported by most state and local authorities. The concept also drew criticism, however. Many observers charged that under revenue sharing, less money found its way to poorer citizens and poorer communities, while more money wound up in well-to-do suburbs. Overall, revenue sharing suffered from the excessively complex system of local governments in the United States. Of the eighty thousand or so local governments of various sorts in the United States, one quarter do not even employ one full-time employee, and half of these virtually inactive local entities received revenue sharing funds. As a consequence, money was often distributed in futile, foolish, and wasteful ways.

For these and other reasons, federal efforts to provide direct aid to cities and localities through revenue sharing were not as beneficial as had been expected. With more aid coming from Washington, many states simply allowed the federal government to supply what state legislatures had once furnished. As a result, local governments as well as the states themselves became increasingly dependent on federal aid. In many cases cities received more from Washington than they raised in taxes. Many observers feared that federal controls would follow this aid, impinging on state and local functions such as education, transportation, and welfare. Government, they argued, was getting away from the people. Critics continued to maintain that revenue sharing involved too little federal control.

REAGAN'S NEW FEDERALISM Responding to these concerns, President Ronald Reagan's administration devised the so-called New Federalism program. The Reagan strategy was based on three key elements: devolution, decrementalism, and deregulation. *Devolution* involved an increased delegation of authority to state and local governments. Under *decrementalism*, federal aid was cut from $95 billion in 1981 (accounting for 25 percent of state and local expenditures) to $88 billion in 1982 (22 percent of such expenditures). *Deregulation* involved efforts to reduce federal regulation of business and social activities. The centerpiece of the New Federalism was to be a significant reordering of programs between state and federal levels, under which the federal government was to assume responsibility for certain state and local programs (such as Medicaid) and the states were to assume responsibility for certain predominantly fed-

The Reagan administration sharply cut federal funding to states and localities, contributing to a fiscal crisis in many parts of the nation. Here a steel worker complains about the impact of Reaganomics, though these policies are described by a less friendly term.
(Allan Tannenbaum/Sygma)

eral programs (such as Aid to Families with Dependent Children). In addition, several dozen federal aid programs were to be turned back to the states.

The proposal had one major appeal to the states: It allowed for increased state control over many major programs. At the same time, however, many states and localities saw no way to finance these programs at the funding levels established by the federal government. As a result, the New Federalism proposals garnered mixed reviews, and significant opposition in Congress, as well as at the state and local levels, prevented much of the New Federalism program from being enacted.

Nonetheless, under President Reagan there was a clear shift in federal-state relationships. Most important, federal budget cuts in the early 1980s put considerable financial pressure on state and local governments. In most cases, states were able to replace the lost federal money and maintain social programs at levels higher than had been generally anticipated. The one program that suffered most was the extension of welfare benefits to the working poor. After a Reagan administration initiative removed the working poor from welfare rolls, most states did nothing to restore them.[11]

Yet quite a few states actually increased their support of environmental, educational, and health programs cut back at the national level. Furthermore, many local governments joined civil rights groups in defending the very quotas and affirmative action programs the Reagan administration was attacking.

In addition, revenue sharing programs were eliminated as an economy measure, a move sharply resisted by many local officials. Clearly, the administration had won part of its battle to reverse the patterns of federal-state relationships. But the human and social costs of these adjustments were high. Shifting taxes from federal to state and local levels resulted in greater economic inequality.

From the 1950s through 1978 the federal government supplied state and local governments with an increasing proportion of their annual revenues; these outlays also grew into an ever-greater share of the federal budget. As a consequence, federal aid to states and localities played a larger role in shaping programs at the state and local levels. The uninterrupted expansion of federal aid to state and local governments ended with the Carter and Reagan administrations. Increasingly, states were left to raise more of their own revenues. Federal grants-in-aid as a percentage of state and local outlays dropped from 25 percent in 1980 to an estimated 18.2 percent in 1988. The ball was being tossed increasingly into the states' court. And the states were increasingly ready to respond.

Strengthened State Governments

One of the most important developments in the American federal system has come not from national government but from the states. Remember that our federal system allows each state to remain a separate political entity, and considerable variation exists from state to state. But one trend was clear in the decades following the Second World War: Politically and administratively, the state governments generally became more sophisticated and competent. Increased ability in state governments resulted from a variety of factors. Traditional state activities were given a new emphasis: Education, social services, physical planning, and construction required state and local governments to hire thousands of new employees. The average annual increase in state and local government employees between 1951 and 1960 was two hundred thousand. Between 1960 and 1980, spurred by new federal initiatives, employment in state and local governments increased by more than three hundred thousand a year.[12] These increases were combined with the increasing professionalization of state and local government employment—the new employees were health professionals, planners, educators, and managers. During the 1950s and 1960s many states revised their constitutions, implemented administrative and budgetary reforms, provided important staff support to state legislatures, and increased legislative pay and legislating calendars to encourage legislation as a vocation, not an avocation. When shifting patterns within the federal system in the 1980s and early 1990s confronted the states with new challenges, the states were in much better shape to respond effectively and creatively than they had been thirty years before.

Despite the increased competence of state and local governments, the challenges of the 1990s were formidable. Trying to juggle inadequate revenues and citizens' refusals to accept reduced services and entitlements, states found budgeting an impossible task. Eight states began fiscal year 1992 without budgets in place; two actually shut down nonessential government functions for short periods. California, an economic bellwether state, confronted a $14.4 billion deficit in 1992—the largest state deficit in the history of the country. In 1993 California's governor and legislature failed to agree on a budget sixty days into the new fiscal year. State employees were issued IOUs instead of payroll checks. The crisis was precipitated by a worsening of the same budget crunch that has been prevailing for years. The huge national debt generated during the 1980s and continuing federal budget deficits guaranteed that there would be no general federal bailout for fiscally strapped states. Although the 1990s began with a severe recession, the hardships confronting state governments were rooted in earlier policy choices and were not primarily the result of economic cycles. Were the states, as many state and local politicians charged, the victims of an unfair shift of the burden from the federal government? Were the state budget crises a result of a maladjusted federal system? Just whose chickens were these that were coming home to roost so painfully? To address that question, we need a second look at the distribution of responsibility within our federal system.

Responsibilities of the States

Most of the nation's public business is conducted on the state and local levels; there most political conflicts are settled and most public policy decisions are made and carried out. States and localities handle most of the workaday business of government—schooling, policing, licensing. When the Constitution was written, governments at all levels were not very big, very busy, or very complex. As stated earlier, the police powers were generally thought to have been reserved to the states, but they did not amount to much. Following that pattern, dual federalism assumed that certain *kinds* of powers belonged to the states, that state legislation naturally covered certain areas associated with health, safety, morals, and welfare. National legislation focused on other distinct areas—primarily maintaining foreign relations and discouraging harmful state economic competition. Such a clear division of the areas of government concern—one layer of federal activity and a separate layer of state activity—has been called **layer cake federalism**. As time passed, the federal government responded to crises and took up an expanded executive and legislative agenda until this clear division of responsibility no longer matched reality.

Political scientist Morton Grodzins suggested **marble cake federalism** to describe the new reality, the intervention of the national government in most topical areas traditionally left to the states. In American marble cake federalism in the twentieth century, no matter how you slice the cake, you come up with bits of federal activity intermingled with state activity. Thus, for example, state and local governments maintain substantial latitude when it comes to education—they supply most of the funding

Education is one of the primary responsibilities of state and local governments. In recent years, controversies have swirled around a host of educational issues, including inequalities of funding in different localities, teacher pay and certification, allegations of declining test scores, and plans for school "choice." (Daemmrich/The Image Works)

for public schools, determine the content of the curriculum, set teacher qualifications, and require school attendance or alternative education. The governmental regulation and provision of higher education is also primarily a state responsibility. But the federal government encourages educational reform, the strengthening of national educational standards, and the elimination of discrimination in education. A partnership between the federal government and state and local governments now exists in education, as in most areas of governmental concern.

In transportation, such matters as highway location; construction policies; funding for highways, waterways, airports, railroads, and shipping; gasoline and motor vehicle taxation; and regulation of traffic are among the many responsibilities of state and local governments. Expenditures for transportation is the second-largest category in most state budgets. Nevertheless, although the states and localities carry the primary burden, a substantial minority of funding for transportation comes from the federal government, which plays a leading role in the construction and maintenance of the interstate highway network and all major airports. In fact, the interstate highway system—the largest single public works program undertaken in this century—was a federal initiative begun in 1956 under the Eisenhower administration.

The intermingling of state, local, and national authority is clear in health and welfare policy as well. Health and welfare are areas where the federal role has been to establish national goals, design broad structures to meet these goals, provide substantial funding, and then leave to state and local control decisions about how much is to be spent, rules of eligibility, and methods of administration. The states administer the largest programs in the fields of health and welfare—Aid to Families with Dependent Children, Medicare, Medicaid, food stamps, workers' compensation, and unemployment compensation. Federal participation is such that social service *delivery* is almost exclusively a state and local matter. States and localities also maintain facilities for people who cannot care for themselves, such as orphans, the elderly, and the mentally or physically debilitated.

Administering criminal justice is left primarily to the states. Federal enforcement agencies such as the Alcohol, Tobacco, and Firearms Bureau of the Treasury Department have specialized jurisdiction or, in the case of the Federal Bureau of Investigation (FBI), operate against a relatively small number of federal crimes. State and local governments employ more than 250,000 police officers, who bear the brunt of law enforcement in the United States. Given the disproportion of state to federal criminal sanctions, prosecution and maintenance of courts are largely state and local matters. States and counties maintain extensive jail facilities; more than 90 percent of all convicts are incarcerated in nonfederal prisons.

There is an important federal role in enforcing constitutional guarantees in criminal justice. The U.S. Supreme Court determines the specifics of constitutional standards of due process and equal protection, unreasonable searches and seizures, and cruel and unusual punishments. Federal District Court judges played a major role in reforming state prison systems in the 1960s and 1970s.

Protection of the physical environment has become an increasingly important responsibility at all levels. The federal government performs an important goal-setting function, (as in the Clean Air Act) and has provided funding for specific projects (the Superfund for toxic waste cleanup, for example, and funding for municipal wastewater treatment facilities). But most environmental matters are handled by states and localities. Maintenance of streets and parks, zoning regulations, provision of basic public utilities, rubbish collection, sewage and water systems, and monitoring of air and water pollution—all these tasks must be handled by state and local governments. The federal government plays an important role in reducing negative competition among states (a state may maintain less stringent requirements as an incentive for businesses to relocate there) and in distributing spillover costs (acid rain, produced in one state, may kill forests and pollute lakes in another).

In civil rights matters the federal-state-local interaction resembles that in criminal justice. Since the 1920s, federal courts have been establishing constitutional standards for the protection of civil liberties and civil rights. The Civil Rights Act of 1964 and subsequent congressional legislation have provided significant statutory protection for civil rights. But the enforcement of both state and federal civil rights laws—especially in the areas of employment, schools, and housing—is generally handled by states and communities. Experience has shown how complicated and frustrating it can be to try

Law enforcement is also largely a state and local responsibility. America has a larger percentage of its population in prison than any other democracy. Overcrowding of prisons has, in some states, forced early release of certain offenders. The vast increase in prison, however, has not had any noticeable affect on the crime rate. (Steve Hansen/Stock, Boston)

to make civil rights meaningful over the nation when local and state governments pit themselves against federal power.

The complicated interaction of federal, state, and local governments is evident in each of these policy areas. The complications arise from at least three factors: (1) There are a great many governments in the United States. The last count of municipalities, special districts, and counties (in addition to the fifty states and one national government) come to more than eighty-two thousand. (2) These governments operate within a patchwork of overlapping jurisdictions. As the examples made clear, no topical division of responsibility describes the reality of the system. Almost every issue concerns multiple governments. (3) The Constitution itself, and its subsequent interpretation by various players in the federal system, is ambiguous about allocating responsibility. Responsibilities change as the federal system evolves. These complexities naturally give rise to tensions within the system.

Deil Wright, a noted student of the working of the federal system, advocates the use of the expression **intergovernmental relations** (*IGR*) instead of *federalism*, which Wright claims has become hopelessly imprecise through overuse. He cites a researcher who found "497 literal as well as figurative representations of various models, metaphors, conceptions, and types of federalism."[13] *Intergovernmental relations* more accurately reflects contemporary circumstances in the federal system: the absence of a clear hierarchy, the presence of a variety of players (not just state and federal officials), and the importance of policy considerations over cold legalisms.

Tensions in the Federal System

The politics and structure of the American federal system have changed over the years. Population has shifted, economic and technological advances have been made, investment patterns have favored different areas at different times, and public works have deteriorated. All these factors have shaped the current federal system. Yet in evolving to its present form, the system has sometimes developed inequities, inconsistencies, and inefficiencies. Let us now examine the regional rivalries that create tension in the federal system and the types of issues that strain federal arrangements.

Regional Rivalries

Under a federal system, the federal government can shift resources from wealthier to poorer areas; specific states can be earmarked to receive more federal funds than they contribute in tax dollars. During the Depression, the South, which was particularly impoverished, received an economic boost in the form of increased federal spending. Today the southern states, along with the other so-called Sun Belt states in the Southwest and West, still get back more than they contribute. Meanwhile, states in the so-called Frost Belt, the industrial Northeast and Midwest, generally pay out more to the federal government than they receive.

In recent years, Frost Belt mayors and governors have complained loudly about this inequity in federal disbursements and have called for increased federal assistance to their region. Once an area starts to depend on government assistance, however, it is difficult for either the president or Congress to cut those funds. Any politician running for office in a state threatened with a significant reduction in federal funding would be hard pressed not to denounce it.

Tensions result as well from shifts in political strength. The apportionment of congressional seats (every ten years, after the census) is a convenient measure of political clout. Since reapportionment (discussed later in this chapter) occurs only when a state grows at a rate substantially faster or slower than the national average, shifts in seats represent *relative* growth rates. Moreover, additional seats in the House of Representatives are one of the primary political benefits of rapid growth. Between the 1970 census and the 1980 census, seventeen seats changed hands. Every one of the winners was in the West or the South—Sun Belt states—and every one of the losers was in the Northeast or the Midwest—Frost Belt states. Similarly, between the 1980 census and the 1990 census, the West and South gained 19 seats while the Northeast and Midwest lost 17. Over the entire twenty-year period, New York and Illinois, traditional centers of political strength, lost 12 seats, and California and Florida gained 17.

This trend could have important implications for U.S. political life. Sun Belt voters generally have a more conservative political outlook, so liberal federal legislation and liberal presidential candidates may encounter increasing difficulties. A large question-mark, however, hangs over these calculations—California, a Sun Belt state that has been growing especially fast. Although its citizens spearheaded nationwide efforts to cut state and local taxes in the late 1970s and early 1980s, California is not a clearly conservative state. In fact, it has been an innovator in environmental and energy legislation, and its large and growing Hispanic and Asian-American populations will have a growing—and possibly liberal—impact on national politics.

Economic pressures have also strained interstate relations. As the states compete with one another for industry, they commonly grant special tax breaks to corporations, attempt to keep union activity low, reduce corporate income taxes, and alter state economic policies to suit large businesses. States now take pride in enticing industries away from neighboring states, even when those neighboring states desperately need the jobs and tax revenues. In 1991, for example, Minnesota put together an $838 million financial aid package just to hang onto the state's largest private employer, Northwest Airlines. Northwest let it be known that some forty other cities were competing with Duluth and Hibbing, Minnesota, to play host to two new airplane maintenance facilities that would employ about two thousand people. Minnesota's package, which included a $320 million low-interest loan to allow Northwest to reduce its indebtedness, was derided as foolishly expensive by some observers ($838 million for two thousand jobs?) and an unwarranted assumption of risk for Minnesotan taxpayers; Price Waterhouse, the accounting firm, perceived a "significant risk" that Northwest would not even survive future airline mergers. But the package was adopted with the enthusiastic support of Representative James Oberstar, chair of the House aviation subcommittee, and Northwest's current eighteen thousand employees in the state. Proponents argued that Northwest's existing jobs in the state might be moved to a lower-wage state if concessions were not offered.

Destructive state-versus-state rivalries could be remedied by national action—establishing a uniform federal tax rate for corporations, national health coverage, uniform levels of workers' compensation, and a uniform policy on trade unions. However, at this point, no consensus has emerged to press for such wide-ranging federal action, and the only beneficiaries of the intense interstate competition are the corporations, which win huge concessions from states and cities.

Interests Shared across State Lines

Tensions develop within the federal system from another source as well—the interests that are shared across state lines but not well represented within states. Not surpris-

(Text continues on page 146)

FISCAL STRAINS ON THE STATES IN THE 1990s: A VARIETY OF SOURCES

Since the start of the 1990s it has been clear that nearly all fifty states are likely to experience serious budget problems during the decade, but, reflecting our federal structure, the nature of those problems will vary from state to state. Stephen D. Gold, director of the Center for the Study of the States at the Nelson A. Rockefeller Institute of Government in Albany, New York, begins a discussion of the states' fiscal problems with this riddle: "Why were there so many heroes at the Alamo? Because there was no back door." He cites the following categories of problems confronting the states in different combinations:

The Economy
A strong economy is a big help in avoiding fiscal stress, but the outlook for economic growth is uneven. According to projections by DRI/McGraw-Hill, annual employment growth between 1991 and 1996 will vary from a high of 3.3 percent in Nevada to a low of 0.9 percent in Missouri.

Demographics
States with burgeoning populations of school-age children and low-income people are at a major disadvantage. California is an example of a state with both conditions.

Tax Systems
States that rely little on income taxes or that have tax rates that are not very progressive can boost revenue growth by changing their tax structure. Income taxes in 22 states have a top rate starting at $30,000 or less, implying that they are not very progressive. Higher taxes are no panacea for state budget woes, but they can help.

Spending Policies
States that refuse to touch "sacred cows" will suffer most. Sacred cows vary from state to state, but big state hospitals, prisons and college campuses (that help local economies by creating jobs), formula-driven school aid programs, and earmarked revenues for highways and other programs are examples.

Source: Stephen D. Gold, "The Budget Shootout," State Government News, *February 1992, pp. 6-9.*

ingly, our historical, often arbitrarily determined state boundaries are rarely appropriate perimeters within which to address social, political, and economic problems.

For example, pollution problems in heavily urban areas, including groundwater contamination by toxic chemicals, differ significantly from pollution concerns in the Great Lakes and major river systems. The problems faced by Detroit have much more in common with those of Boston, Houston, and Atlanta than they do with issues significant in other parts of Michigan. So how can state governments dominated by rural, small-town, and suburban votes be expected to respond vigorously to big-city problems like street crime, industrial unemployment, welfare, and housing?

Cities often experience jurisdictional problems of their own. Most metropolitan areas contain dozens or even hundreds of separate government jurisdictions, and power is often fragmented among many different boards and authorities. As a result, big-city finance is a chronic challenge in the United States. Providing regular city services—water and sewer service, solid waste disposal, police protection, and road maintenance—is more expensive in densely populated areas. Yet for central cities, many of the persons using those services during the day drive home to separate municipal suburbs where they pay taxes.

The Reagan and Bush administrations' goal of reducing the size of the federal government and returning power to the states was seen by some observers as involving the abandonment of the cities. Reflecting the administration's position on the extent of federal responsibility, one Reagan domestic policy adviser stated flatly, "It's our view that the cities are not mentioned in the Constitution."[14] Attempts by big-city mayors to put urban problems back on the national agenda in the 1988 presidential campaign were largely unsuccessful. For the next presidential election, two events in the spring of 1992 did raise the visibility of urban decay and despair—the disastrous flooding of the Chicago Loop, caused by damage to aging tunnels beneath the city, and the Los Angeles riots, the most destructive in the twentieth century, in which fire destroyed thousands of buildings and more than fifty people died. Concerned politicians meeting in Washington following the riots endorsed the Conference of Mayors' call for $15 billion in new federal aid to cities. Their concern was that with the rioting quelled, the nation would return to business as usual. "The flames that rose in Los Angeles have died," said New York City Mayor David N. Dinkins, "but dust from the city's ashes remains on each of us. We all know that there, but for the grace of God, goes our city."[15] Despite these events, urban aid did not figure prominently in the 1992 presidential contest.

Federal Intervention

On several occasions the federal government has concluded that states were failing to serve democratic principles or protect citizens' health and welfare. In such cases the national government has intervened (however reluctantly) to set state governments on a more democratic or appropriate path. We shall consider two examples of federal intervention: reapportionment of legislative seats, and raising the drinking age.

Reapportionment

In 1900 three-fifths of the population of the United States lived in rural areas; by 1960 over two-thirds of Americans lived in cities or suburbs. State legislatures, however, did not change to reflect this trend toward urbanization. In 1962, for example, the twenty-four inhabitants of Stratton, Vermont, enjoyed the same level of representation in the state's house of representatives as the entire city of Burlington, with a population of 35,531. At the same time, Los Angeles County's 6,038,771 residents received the same state senate representation as the 14,196 inhabitants of three northern California counties. Such disparities left urban dwellers throughout the country in a far weaker political position than rural constituents.

In *Reynolds* v. *Sims* (1964), the Supreme Court ruled that state legislative districts must be apportioned strictly according to population.[16] In the words of Chief Justice Earl Warren, "Legislators represent people, not trees or acres." Basic to a representative form of government, the opinion continued, was the citizen's right to cast a vote that counts in full. Accordingly, any substantial disparity in the population of legislative districts would have the same effect as allotting a different number of votes to different individuals. This principle of "one man, one vote" was later extended by the Court to cover both houses of state legislatures.

Political scientists still argue over the political consequences of the widespread **reapportionment** of legislative districts that followed the Court's rulings. Some contend that well-apportioned states are scarcely distinguishable in policymaking from malapportioned ones. Perhaps reapportionment has simply shifted power from rural anti-city interests to suburban anti-city interests. In the late 1960s, for example, the New York State legislature declined to provide significant help to the New York City subway system, which carries 2 million riders a day, but did underwrite the losses of the Long Island Railroad, which carries one hundred thousand suburban commuters daily. Perhaps, too, the effects of reapportionment have been more subtle and less dramatic than its proponents had expected.

The Drinking Age

Each state has its own laws regulating the age when men and women are permitted to drink alcoholic beverages. But Congress, through its budgetary powers, has sharply influenced those state laws. Because of this congressional pressure, the nation now has, with only a few exceptions, a uniform drinking age—twenty-one. The story of how this came about illustrates an emerging direction for contemporary federalism.

In the early 1970s many states lowered the drinking age to eighteen. But within a decade, a movement developed to raise it again. Fueling this drive was an increasing concern about the effects of drunk driving among teenagers. By 1984 roughly half the states had raised the drinking age to twenty-one, while others set it at nineteen or twenty. Mothers Against Drunk Drivers (MADD), a powerful grass-roots organization, together with other public-interest groups, pressured state legislatures, arguing that drunk driving was the leading cause of death among teenagers. Indeed, national statistics showed that teens *were* more likely to be involved in drunk-driving accidents. Opponents of federal intervention maintained, however, that teenagers suffered no more casualties than drivers aged twenty-one to twenty-five.

Congress was called on to act. Some members of Congress asserted that national regulation of the drinking age violated the principle of federalism because this was a matter traditionally under state jurisdiction. But the congressional legislation that finally emerged did not create a uniform drinking age directly. Instead, it required that 10 percent of federal highway funds be withheld from any state that failed to raise the drinking age to twenty-one. States could choose to ignore this rule and thereby forfeit some of their highway money.

The Importance of States

> It is one of the happy accidents of the federal system that a single courageous state may . . . serve as a laboratory and try novel social and economic experiments without risk to the rest of the century.[17]
>
> Associate Justice Louis Brandeis (1931)

> The states are prisoners of their own freedom.[18]
>
> Massachusetts state legislator (later Congressman) Barney Frank (1979)

The role of the states in meeting regional demands and in providing opportunities for experimentation on a small scale is a counterweight to these examples of the imposition of national standards on the states through federal intervention. For example, individual states were the first to eliminate the death penalty, provide old-age pensions, and regulate railroads. States also pioneered in developing the income tax, child labor laws, and the vote for women and eighteen-year-olds. State governments can occasionally act more swiftly than the federal government in response to popular sentiment, through processes such as the initiative and the referendum (see Chapter 1).

In health policy, states have been innovators as well. Oregon tried in 1992 to establish a novel system of prioritizing state health expenditures on a traditional utilitarian model ("The greatest good for the greatest number"). The Bush administration reflected the plan as not meeting federal requirements. In 1974, while the rest of the nation watched health care financing fall into disarray, Hawaii instituted a program of comprehensive health insurance. Whether states experience partial success or total

The freedom to drink! Some Americans view it as an essential in the "pursuit of happiness." Should public safety on highways be more important than the liberty of younger citizens to have access to alcohol? For the moment, the nation has decided to rank safety higher. (Arthur Grace/Stock, Boston)

failure in their innovative efforts, their experience is valuable to other states and to the nation—as long as people are paying attention. Oddly, in the American system, even successful experiments at the state level can go unnoticed. The national debate on health care has taken almost no notice at all of two decades of successful Hawaiian experience. At the National Governors' Conference in the summer of 1991, the primary item on the agenda was health care, yet news accounts made no mention of the island state's system.

States and their local subdivisions also keep government closer to the people and provide more opportunities for participation by citizens. "Federalism contains a built-in bias in favor of participation," says one scholar of American federalism.[19] By giving autonomous control over policy and resources to the state, which in turn gives wide discretion to local units, our federal system guarantees the interest of a large number of individuals and groups in units of government that are small enough to be approachable. Ironically, voter turnout for local elections is very low, even by U.S. standards. In a strictly local election, turnout may be as low as 10 percent of eligible voters. It is fair to say that the opportunities for participation afforded by federalism are often underused.

In addition to opportunities to participate, state and local governments provide us with *images of participation* that are an important component of civic education in a democracy. Town meetings, an example of direct democracy at the local level, are still used by more than thirteen hundred towns in six New England states.

(Text continues on page 151)

One State's Prescription for Health

Vigorous efforts to establish a national health insurance program faltered in the early 1970s and again twenty years later. Discussions of various plans failed to create a national consensus on issues of cost control and quality of care. Various models of service provision were advanced, none a clear favorite. These seem favorable conditions for experimentation on the state level—if such experimentation could be carried out in moderate isolation. Enter Hawaii.

Hawaii's solution to the health care problem was enacted in 1974 and entailed requiring businesses to offer health care insurance to all employees. Special state subsidies would cover those exempt from coverage, such as seasonal and part-time workers, and students. Those without health care coverage fell from 17 percent of the population to less than 5 percent. Contrary to some predictions, health care costs did not soar out of control. According to Hawaii's chief health planner, the law created a single, vast pool for spreading insurance risks among the whole population, reducing adminsitrative costs to insurers and reducing the cost to small employers. Most important, the health of the population has improved. Infant mortality fell 50 percent from 1974 to 1991. Life expectancy increased. Hospitals do not refuse to treat uninsured persons (as often happens on the mainland) because the number of such cases is negligible.

So what are we waiting for here on the mainland? Why not hop on the bandwagon? As with all experiments, the big question is whether the results can be reproduced. Will a plan like Hawaii's produce similar benefits in another state or in the nation at large? That's not clear. A state on the mainland would have to be more concerned with migration—outbound businesses and inbound citizens seeking state benefits. But a national program could alleviate most of those problems. Not everyone is happy with Hawaii's health care system. Some small businesses, forced to provide health insurance, have dropped other benefits. Some business owners worry about discouraging new businesses from locating in Hawaii (though Hawaii is the third-fastest-growing state for small business). Hawaii's plantation tradition played a part in reducing opposition to the plan originally—the state has always provided generous minimum-wage protection, workers' compensation, unemployment insurance, and disability income. Those conditions are unusual nationally. So transplanting this tropical flower is problematic.

But whether Hawaii's plan can be transferred directly or not, it certainly provides health care planners in other states and at the national level with a useful example of a system that works. California's state health director, Dr. Molly Joel Coye, calls Hawaii "our most important laboratory" on health care systems.

Source: Edwin Chen, "States Look at Hawaii's Rx for Health Insurance Costs," Los Angeles Times, August 18, 1991, p. A1.

The Constitution and the political system that has developed from it strike a sensitive balance between the federal government and the states, sometimes favoring and sometimes frustrating national intervention. Ratifying constitutional amendments, for instance (see Chapter 3), is a process based on equal representation of states and requiring an extraordinary majority (thirty-eight of fifty states). The result of this arrangement is that the representatives of a relatively small minority can prevent constitutional changes that might impose additional strictures on states. The failure of the proposed Equal Rights Amendment (ERA) is a good example.

In 1972 both houses of Congress passed the Equal Rights Amendment by votes considerably larger than the two-thirds required for a constitutional amendment. Most national political leaders of both parties, including President Nixon (and later Presidents Ford and Carter), endorsed the amendment, which read simply, "Equal rights under law shall not be denied or abridged by the United States or by any State on account of sex."

State approval of the amendment stalled at thirty-five. Then ERA supporters appealed to Congress for more time to win its ratification—beyond the seven-year period originally granted. In the meantime, five states that had passed the ERA voted to rescind approval. Both these developments carried intriguing political implications. Could a state rescind approval? The Constitution is silent on that point. Could Congress legitimately extend the time limit? Opponents argued that the rules were being changed in the middle of the game. Nonetheless, Congress did vote for a three-year extension, until 1982. Close battles ensued in several states, but the necessary three-fourths approval was never obtained. The states that voted against the ERA held only 123 seats out of 435 in the House of Representatives. A survey of the general population taken in the midst of the ratification debate found that 72 percent of respondents supported its passage, including 70 percent of women and 75 percent of men.[20] The ratification process had clearly frustrated the wishes of the majority—as it was designed to do.

Conclusions

Half of all Americans now live in states other than the ones they were born in. Twenty percent of the country's population moves every year. Problems no longer come in state-sized packages—if they ever did. As we have noted, major cities often face issues of national scope, and many environmental, health, energy, and economic problems cannot be confined conveniently within state boundaries. Given these facts, does it make sense to remain tied to the concept of state government?

In practical terms, maintaining states in our governmental scheme is as little a matter for choice now as it was at the Constitutional Convention in 1787. Many persons and groups have a very definite stake in the continued existence of state governments and their subdivisions at the local level. No very radical transformation of American federalism is likely in the near future. Nonetheless, it is important that we continue to understand and evaluate the role of the states in our democratic system.

> **SUMMARY CHART**
> ## FEDERALISM AND DEMOCRACY: PROS AND CONS
>
> **Pros**
> State government is "closer" to the people and therefore more responsive to popular sentiment.
> States can experiment with alternative policies and thereby serve as "laboratories" for improvement.
> State governments are less powerful and therefore less likely to harm citizens.
>
> **Cons**
> Historically, states have been more likely to oppress minorities than the federal government.
> Many interests are more effectively represented at the national than at the state level.
> National government shows a higher level of competence.
> Maintaining 50 different sets of laws leads to confusion and inequity.

People who argue for the continued significance of the states can draw on traditional arguments for decentralization as we have already seen. Yet we must also question the worth of providing fifty separate jurisdictions with fifty kinds of marriage and divorce laws, criminal courts, prison systems, alcoholic beverage controls, tax systems, educational and welfare arrangements, and so on. Is this an indication of a healthy localism or of a confusing lack of national standards?

In toting up the balance sheet of democracy in relation to U.S. federalism, we must note that the denial of basic rights to black citizens was probably made easier by the division of powers between the state and national governments. It can be argued, of course, that had the nation not been divided into states, a form of national segregation might have resulted. In such a case, however, a clear confrontation with the reality of racism might have come earlier, and the issues might have been resolved more thoroughly in a democratic direction. On balance, federalism sheltered racism and blocked solutions to racial problems.

Another negative aspect of our federal system was the long-standing malapportionment of state legislative districts. In this instance, too, democracy was damaged, and that damage clearly grew out of the politics that federal arrangements made possible.

A third negative factor has been the common tendency of many states to neglect minorities, the poor, and other relatively powerless groups. Even more than the federal government, state governments are vulnerable to domination by well-organized and financially powerful groups.

Understanding the parts played by state and local governments, counting up their strengths and their weaknesses in democratic terms, is an important task of citizens and officials alike. Though it is true that no radical transformation of American federalism is likely very soon, the system *has* changed significantly over time. What will our federal system be like in 2020? Would we be better off with a unitary United States divided into administrative regions? How much will the federal system frustrate the development of useful and necessary national uniform standards? Will democracy be stronger for the participation of states and local governments? With history as our guide, we expect the answer to this last question to be mixed.

Glossary Terms

block grant
categorical grant
concurrent powers
cooperative federalism
delegated powers
dual federalism
due process of law
enabling act
enumerated powers
full faith and credit
implied powers

intergovernmental relations
layer cake federalism
marble cake federalism
McCulloch v. *Maryland*
police powers
reapportionment
reserve powers
revenue sharing
unitary government
unitary system

Notes

[1] 4 Wheaton 316.
[2] 314 U.S. 160.
[3] Samuel H. Beer, "The Idea of the Nation," *New Republic*, July 1982, pp. 19–26.
[4] Ibid. p. 19.
[5] 9 Wheaton 1.
[6] 19 Howard 393.
[7] 16 Wallace 36.
[8] 198 U.S. 45.
[9] 247 U.S. 251.
[10] 7 Peters 243.
[11] John Herbers, "State Finance Aid Programs Reduced by U.S., Study Finds," *New York Times*, June 10, 1984, p. 12.
[12] Thomas J. Anton, *American Federalism and Public Policy* (New York: Random House, 1989), p. 42.
[13] Deil Wright, *Understanding Intergovernmental Relations*, 3rd ed. (Belmont, Calif.: Wadsworth, 1988), p. 17.
[14] Unnamed presidential adviser in William K. Stevens, "Cities Press Their Case on Candidates," *New York Times*, December 14, 1987, p. B.10.
[15] Stanley Meisler, "Mayors Demand Urban Aid," *Los Angeles Times*, May 17, 1992, p. A1.
[16] 377 U.S. 533.
[17] Louis Brandeis, *New York State Ice Co.* v. *Liebmann* (dissent), 285 U.S. 262, 311 (1931).
[18] Barney Frank, "Sorry States," *New Republic*, December 29, 1979, p. 22.

[19] Anton, *American Federalism*, p. 4.
[20] J. R. Kluegel and E. R. Smith, *Beliefs about Inequality* (Hawthorne, N.Y.: Aldine, 1986), pp. 218, 222.

Selected Readings

A good place to start in learning more about **federalism** would be Thomas R. Dye, *American Federalism: Competition among Governments* (Lexington, Mass.: Lexington Books, 1990); and Thomas J. Anton, *American Federalism and Public Policy: How the System Works* (New York: Random House, 1989).

To find out more about recent **changes** in the federal system, see Janice C. Griffith, ed., *Federalism: The Shifting Balance* (Chicago: American Bar Association, 1989); Marshall Kaplan and Sue O'Brien, *The Governors and the New Federalism* (Bounder, Colo.: Westview Press, 1991).

For more detail on particular **programs** in our federal system, see Robert Jay Dilger, *National Intergovernmental Programs* (Englewood Cliffs, N.J.: Prentice Hall, 1989); Joseph Francis Zimmerman, *Federal Preemption: The Silent Revolution* (Ames: Iowa State University Press, 1991); and R. Allen Hayes, *The Federal Government and Urban Housing* (Albany: State University of New York Press, 1985).

COMPARATIVE PERSPECTIVES ON FEDERALISM

For a general **theoretical treatment** of federalism, see Jonathan Lemco, *Political Stability in Federal Governments* (New York: Praeger, 1991).

For useful **case studies** of federal systems in Canada and Germany, see Ronald L. Watts and Douglas M. Brown, eds., *Options for a New Canada* (Toronto: University of Toronto Press, 1991); Robert C. Vipond, *Liberty and Community: Canadian Federalism and the Failure of the Constitution* (Albany: State University of New York Press, 1991); and Charlie Jeffery and Peter Savigear, *German Federalism Today* (New York: St. Martin's Press, 1991).

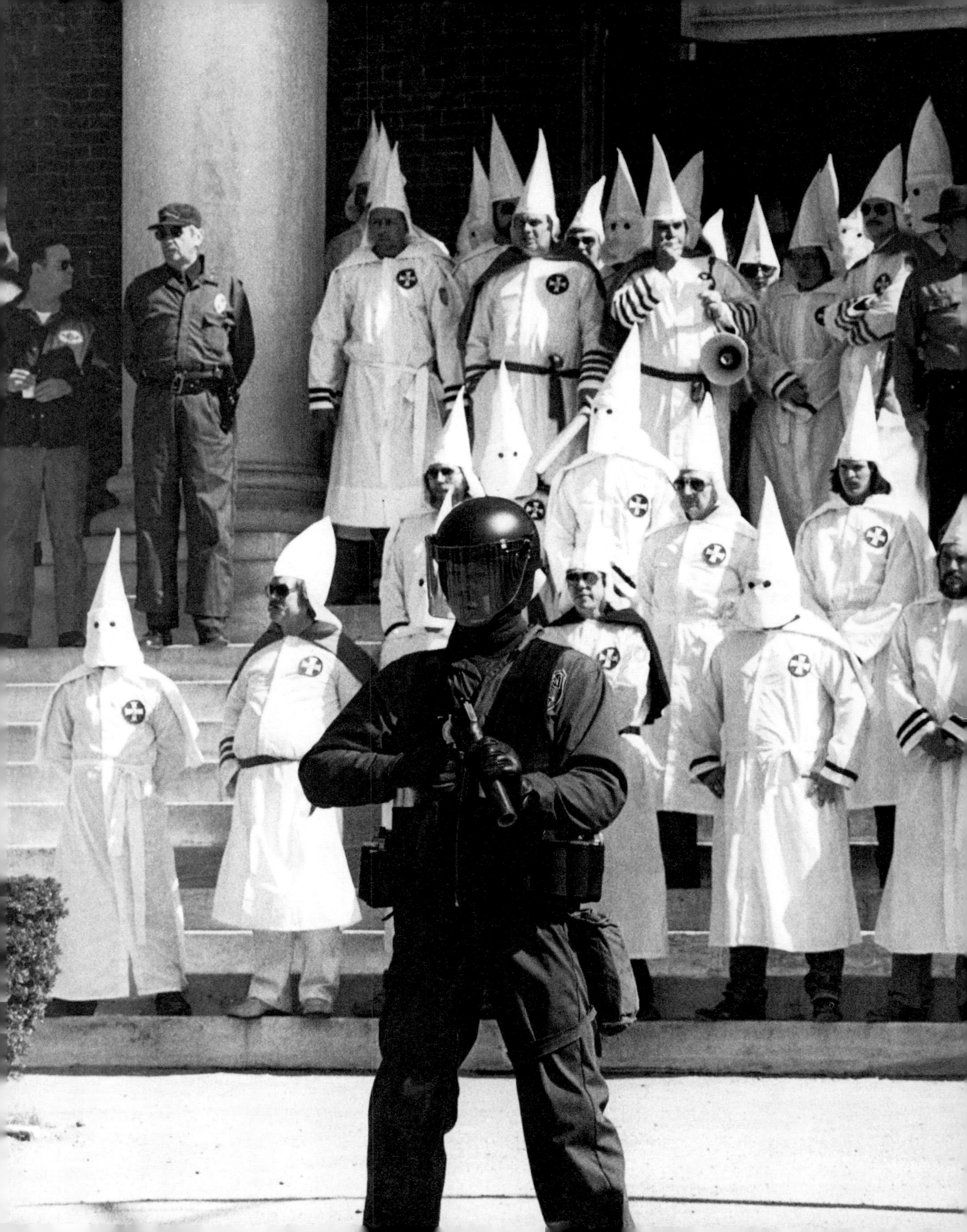

CHAPTER FIVE

CHAPTER OUTLINE

The Bill of Rights and Constitutional Protections

Federalism and Civil Liberties

Freedom of Speech
SETTING LIMITS ON DISSENT
THE SMITH ACT CASES
CONTEMPORARY TRENDS
SYMBOLIC SPEECH AND "FIGHTING WORDS"

Press Freedom

Freedom of Religion
ESTABLISHMENT OF RELIGION
FREE EXERCISE OF RELIGION

The Rights of the Accused

Abortion

The Right to Vote
BLACK AMERICANS AND THE RIGHT TO VOTE

CIVIL LIBERTIES

Are Liberties Effectively Protected?

OCTOBER 1964. A RIGHT-WING COUP STRIKES THE SOVIET UNION. Premier Nikita Khrushchev, author of a mild liberalization in Soviet domestic politics, including an attempt to erase the cult of Stalin, is deposed and placed under house arrest. Leonid Brezhnev eventually assumes control as general secretary of the Communist party and rules until his death in 1979.

August 1991. A right-wing coup strikes the Soviet Union. Soviet President Mikhail Gorbachev is placed under house arrest at his Crimean dacha. Columns of army tanks move into Moscow as a state of emergency is declared and Vice-President Gennady Yanayev assumes command. Over the next three days the coup unravels. Boris Yeltsin, popularly elected president of the Russian Republic, faces down the coup plotters from the Russian Parliament building behind a barricade of Russian citizens. He emerges from the crisis as the most powerful politician in the ensuing period of rapid, radical transformation of the old Soviet Union. The world hails the events as a triumph of democracy—a popularly elected official toughing it out for constitutional forms with the help of thousands of loyal citizens in the streets.

Why did one coup succeed and the other fail? Many things had changed in the USSR between 1964 and 1991. Cellular phones, photocopiers, and fax machines made it impossible for the coup leaders to gain control of communication. The exchange of information among resistance groups reinforced morale and facilitated coordinated efforts. But some of the most important changes were not technological but political, instigated by Gorbachev, who (like the coup plotters themselves) ironically emerged from the 1991 coup most reduced in power—indeed, soon to be out of a job as the Soviet Union itself disintegrated into its constituent republics. Six years earlier Gorbachev had began a process of change in the Soviet Union, based on *perestroika* (restructuring) and *glasnost* (freedom of expression and communication). Open criticism of the party line was tolerated. News-

COMPARATIVE PERSPECTIVE

BUTTON YOUR *WENHUA SHAN*!

In the United States, T-shirts are a standard medium of communication—for commercial messages ("Button Your Fly" advertises a popular brand of blue jeans), political slogans, environmental concerns, and expressions of personality ("UNbutton Your Fly" T-shirts provided a slightly risqué rejoinder to the original commercial message). In the Soviet Union as well, in the days of glasnost, T-shirts were a popular form of personal message board. But in the People's Republic of China, where all forms of expression are tightly controlled by the government, printed T-shirts (called *wenhua shan*, or "cultural shirts") were banned by the government in 1991.

The ban on the manufacture or sale of *wenhua shan* shows, according to one observer, two important strands of contemporary Chinese life: "a deepening sense of alienation among urban young people, and the increasingly frenetic efforts by the authorities to keep a happy face glued on Chinese Communism." The T-shirts in question do not carry messages directly aimed at the government or the ruling Communist party. Instead, the theme is social disaffection: "I'm fed up! Leave me alone!" is a popular item. Others include "Really exhausted" and "I don't know how to please people." A more direct jab at communist doctrine is "Getting rich is all there is." One sly T-shirt had a straightforward slogan, "Be an honest man," written so as to include the characters for *old* and *men*. These characters seemed to be collapsing—perhaps suggesting that the old men who run China are themselves sagging a bit.

"Cultural shirts are not a Chinese invention," reminded the *Chinese Youth Daily*, an official newspaper. "They are only a foreign trick borrowed from the West, where they have existed for decades. If we make a little study, we find that Westerners wear such shirts as an expression of decadent feelings." Not much

(Box continues on page 159)

papers and magazines took advantage of this freedom. Competitive elections were held for a new Congress of Peoples' Deputies and in several republic governments. Bureaucrats not used to reform were directed to take the first steps away from centralized economic planning. Set loose against a background of brutal social control, these changes upset old balances, in part fostering the coup and at the same time making its success unlikely.

For many observers, the failure of the coup was a demonstration of the empowerment and liberation that can result from even a modest attempt to recognize civil liberties and create responsive political bodies. For others, the coup was another re-

---

study was required on that score. The shirts were deemed "unhealthy" in the *Beijing Legal Daily*'s report on the formal ban. The coordinated official media attack on *wenhua shan* included the opinion by the *Beijing Daily* that appropriate messages would be acceptable. The paper suggested "Study hard and make daily progress' and "I train myself for the construction of the motherland." Don't hold your breath, guys.

The old men in the leadership of the People's Republic have a reformist agenda that includes a gradual move toward a limited market economy. As the brutal suppression of mass demonstrations in 1989 showed, however, they are convinced that a tight rein from the top must guide the Chinese people toward reform. Civil liberties are deemed less important than economic progress and even counterproductive.

Mikhail Gorbachev's experience with expanding civil liberties in the Soviet Union cuts both ways here. On the one hand, allowing free expression may let reform get out of control—at least out of the control of the old oligarchy. *Glasnost* in the Soviet Union preceded the unraveling of the empire altogether. But on the other hand, market-oriented reforms may be simply incompatible with the maintenance of centralized control. Following the ban, *wenhua shan* were still available in free markets in Beijing—but not over the counter. One merchant confided: "We're not allowed to sell these, so we don't display them, but we certainly have them. If you want a large order, we can even have them printed for you." One of the samples she pulled out said in large characters, "I can't do a thing." In smaller characters it added: "I'd like to be an entrepreneur, but I don't have the guts. I'd like to be an official, but I don't have the right attitude. I'd like to sell things, but I don't have a license. To hell with earning a living." Judging from the high levels of disaffection among young people in China, she will probably sell lots.

Source: Nicholas D. Kristof, *"Even Gloomy T-Shirts Fall under Censorship,"* New York Times*, July 29, 1991, p. B1.*

minder of the yawning gulf between socialist ideals and Soviet practice and a reminder of the strength of nationalistic zeal. Were Gorbachev's reforms the undoing of this vast empire, or was the Soviet Union simply done in by the times? The neighboring People's Republic of China demonstrated that even in the 1990s, a cadre of old men could keep political power by maintaining tight social control and severely limiting civil liberties.

After the Soviet coup, watching the new republics in the painful process of trying to create—from scratch in some cases—political institutions responsive to ordinary citizens and making fresh judgments about the proper role of government control in everyday life provided the opportunity for Americans to examine our own traditions, reaffirm our own commitment to civil liberties and responsive government and to ask of ourselves what remained to be done.

The ideas of responsive government and civil liberties are simple enough. Government policy should reflect the will of the people and offer protection to citizens from the abuse of government power. Yet even though these concepts sound straightforward, they have been exceedingly difficult to implement. Classical liberalism dominated the American Founders' thinking. This encompassed support for freedom of expression, freedom of religion, protection against arbitrary exercise of government power, and protection of property rights through the enforcement of contracts and the maintenance of a stable currency. As we saw in Chapter 3, keeping government responsive was primarily a matter of regular elections and proper institutional structure (delegated power, checks and balances). In terms of civil liberties, the main task was simply to keep government off people's backs by keeping it small. The dominance of the republican tradition (which feared mob rule and happily entrusted public affairs to the care of a small group of educated, experienced statesmen) meant that the franchise was restricted to white males.

The realities of twentieth-century life have enlarged our conceptions of responsive government and individual liberty. Recognizing that government inevitably plays an active part in modern life, concern for freedom now encompasses the proper limits of social control and the role of government in producing conditions conducive to freedom. The *absence* of government regulation may do more to limit freedom than its judicious exercise. This larger concern for liberty takes in more forms of economic intervention, equal protection concerns (that persons are not arbitrarily held back on the basis of gender, national origin, or ethnic identity), and privacy. It also includes expectations of positive government action to ensure safe, healthy surroundings, education, and the opportunity to work. (If a commitment to universal employment is not part of the national consensus, at least managing the economy to encourage it is.) Our increasing concern for democracy has meant universal suffrage—and guarantees of access and responsiveness that extend to the drawing of district lines. Many of these expanded concerns (they might be called civil and social rights) are controversial, just as the implementation of the earlier notions of civil liberties remain controversial in some respects.

In this chapter we will examine traditional civil liberties as they have been defined and implemented in the United States. After looking at the Bill of Rights and the impact

People-power helped to defeat the coup attempt by Soviet hard-liners. The quest for civil liberties and political freedoms played a key role in the revolutions that swept Eastern Europe and the Soviet Union. *(AP/World Wide Photos)*

of federalism on civil liberties, we will examine freedom of speech, the press, and religion; the rights of the accused; and the issue of abortion. We conclude this chapter with a look at the fundamental mechanism for maintaining a responsive government—the right to vote. Civil rights and social rights are the focus of Chapter 6. In Part IV, which is concerned with contemporary policy debates, we will return to civil liberties and civil rights by exploring, in Chapter 20, the legitimate limits of social control.

If the United States has fallen short of the mark in granting liberties and rights for all, it is to our credit that we have fought over them and incorporated them to a substantial degree in our political life. The ordinary Russian citizens who stood guard around the Russian Parliament building in August 1991 would understand that.

The Bill of Rights and Constitutional Protections

What we call the **Bill of Rights** was not included in the original Constitution. As noted in Chapter 3, the first ten amendments were added in 1791 to mollify the Antifederalists, who agreed to back the Constitution only after assurances that a specific list of liberties would be appended to the new document following ratification.

At the time they were drafted, the protections included in the Bill of Rights were considered sufficient to ensure the opportunity for a decent life for each citizen, to guard against arbitrary government interference, and to protect dissent. The rights most central to the preservation of democratic politics are those cited in the First and Fifth Amendments.

First Amendment: Freedom of speech, press, and assembly; the right to petition for a redress of grievances; freedom of religion, along with prohibition of an "establishment of religion."

Fifth Amendment: Protection from loss of life, liberty, and property without due process of law.

Other significant protections in the Bill of Rights include these:

Fourth Amendment: Prohibition of unreasonable searches and seizures.

Fifth Amendment: Protection from being tried twice for the same crime and from being forced to testify against oneself.

Sixth Amendment: Rights to a speedy trial, to counsel, to confront hostile witnesses, and to know the charges against oneself.

Seventh Amendment: Right to a jury trial.

Eighth Amendment: Prohibition of excessive bail and fines and of cruel and unusual punishments.

The Third Amendment deals with an issue of little importance today, the quartering of soldiers in private homes. Until recently, the Second Amendment's guarantee of the right to bear arms for the purpose of maintaining a militia seemed equally irrelevant to modern life; gun control opponents, however, now cite it as a constitutional bar to government regulation of gun ownership. The Ninth and Tenth Amendments offer vague cautions that the enumeration of rights and powers in the Constitution does not disparage or deny other rights held by the people or the states.

U.S. legal history is replete with controversies over the interpretation of these rights. Does free speech mean that citizens may criticize the government in time of war? May they advocate resistance to the draft? Does the right to assemble mean that groups may gather to advocate violence against other groups? Does prohibition of an "establishment" of religion mean that even nonsectarian prayers in schools are unconstitutional? Does free exercise of religion mean that polygamy is permissible if one's religion permits it? Just when does a search become "unreasonable"? Is the death penalty a "cruel and unusual punishment"?

The issues raised by these questions have formed the constitutional backdrop for significant struggles over the meaning of civil liberties and rights in U.S. political history. Of course, many of the issues we confront today in attempting to give meaning to democratic ideals are rather different from those faced by the framers of the Constitution. The framers did not have to take into account such central elements of modern-day life as the mass media, a powerful and activist government, mass public education, and huge corporations. We can see in the Bill of Rights both issues fundamental to democratic politics at any time and place and issues that reflect more precisely the time and place in which the document originated.

At various times in U.S. history, arguments have raged over one or another of these issues. We shall examine the effect of federalism on civil liberties, evolving notions of freedom of speech, issues surrounding freedom of the press and freedom of religion, due process and the rights of the accused, abortion, and the right to vote.

Federalism and Civil Liberties

For much of U.S. history the protections spelled out in the Bill of Rights were not applied to state governments. As noted in Chapter 4, the Supreme Court held in *Barron v. Baltimore* (1833) that the Bill of Rights was meant to apply solely to the national government.[1] According to the Court, the Bill of Rights placed no restrictions on the actions of state and local governments, which were free to develop their own policies on civil liberties.

This view remained largely unchallenged until the ratification, following the Civil War, of the Thirteenth, Fourteenth, and Fifteenth amendments, which abolished slavery and extended the rights of citizenship (including the vote) to former slaves. The **Fourteenth Amendment**, in particular, raised the question of state versus federal responsibility for the enforcement of civil rights and liberties. That amendment states, in part, that "no State shall make or enforce any law which shall abridge the privileges or immunities of citizens of the United States." If the "privileges and immunities" on which the states were forbidden to encroach were interpreted as those mentioned in the Bill of Rights, the amendment could form the basis for a unitary national civil liberties policy, applicable to every state.

But advocates of a national civil liberties policy suffered a severe setback when the Supreme Court, in the *Slaughterhouse Cases* of 1873, ruled that the Fourteenth Amendment's "privileges and immunities" clause did not extend responsibility for enforcing the Bill of Rights to the states.[2] The Court held that national citizenship must be distinguished from state citizenship.

The Court maintained this stance well into the twentieth century, when it began to apply national standards to state actions under two other clauses of the Fourteenth Amendment: the **due process clause**, which stipulates that no state may deprive a person of life, liberty, or property without due process of law, and the **equal protection clause**, which mandates that no state may deny any person equal protection of the laws. In *Gitlow* v. *New York* (1925), the Supreme Court argued that "freedom of speech and of the press, which are protected by the First Amendment from abridgement by Congress, are among the fundamental personal rights and liberties protected by the due process clause of the Fourteenth Amendment from impairment by the states."[3] Note that the Court did not automatically apply the entire Bill of Rights to the states; rather, it designated certain freedoms guaranteed in the **First Amendment** as so fundamental that they must be universally protected.

Following the *Gitlow* decision, the Supreme Court gradually shifted direction, stipulating more and more provisions of the Bill of Rights that the states were prohibited from violating. Some twentieth-century justices—most notably Hugo Black and William O. Douglas—have argued that the entire Bill of Rights should pertain to the states—the doctrine that was specifically rejected in the *Slaughterhouse Cases*. Although this view has never been explicitly accepted by a majority of the Court, over the years the justices have applied almost the entire Bill of Rights to the states by means of the Fourteenth Amendment's due process and equal protection clauses (see **Table 5-1**). As a result, proponents of a uniform, national civil liberties policy have achieved incrementally what they were unable to achieve in one blow.

TABLE 5-1

CASE-BY-CASE INCORPORATION OF BILL OF RIGHTS PROVISIONS INTO THE FOURTEENTH AMENDMENT

Provision	*Amendment*	*Year*	*Case*
"Public use" and "just compensation" conditions in the taking of private property by government	V	1896 and 1897	*Missouri Pacific Railway Co.* v. *Nebraska*; *Chicago, Burlington & Quincy Railway Co.* v. *Chicago*
Freedom of speech	I	1927	*Fiske* v. *Kansas*; *Gitlow* v. *New York*; *Gilbert* v. *Minnesota*
Freedom of the press	I	1931	*Near* v. *Minnesota*
Fair trial and right to counsel in capital cases	VI	1932	*Powell* v. *Alabama*
Freedom of religion	I	1934	*Hamilton* v. *Regents of University of California*
Freedom of assembly and, by implication, freedom to petition for redress of grievances	I	1937	*De Jonge* v. *Oregon*
Free exercise of religious belief	I	1940	*Cantwell* v. *Connecticut*
Separation of church and state; prohibition of the establishment of religion	I	1947	*Everson* v. *Board of Education*
Right to public trial	VI	1948	*In re Oliver*
Right against unreasonable searches and seizures	IV	1949	*Wolf* v. *Colorado*

TABLE 5-1 *continued*
CASE-BY-CASE INCORPORATION OF BILL OF RIGHTS PROVISIONS
INTO THE FOURTEENTH AMENDMENT

Provision	Amendment	Year	Case
Freedom of association	I	1958	*NAACP* v. *Alabama*
Exclusionary rule as concomitant of unreasonable searches and seizures	IV	1961	*Mapp* v. *Ohio*
Right against cruel and unusual punishments	VIII	1962	*Robinson* v. *California*
Right to counsel in all felony cases	VI	1963	*Gideon* v. *Wainwright*
Right against self-incrimination	V	1964	*Malloy* v. *Hogan*; *Murphy* v. *Waterfront Commission*
Right to confront witnesses	VI	1965	*Pointer* v. *Texas*
Right to privacy	Various	1965	*Griswold* v. *Connecticut*
Right to impartial jury	VI	1966	*Parker* v. *Gladden*
Right to speedy trial	VI	1967	*Klopfer* v. *North Carolina*
Right to compulsory process for obtaining witnesses	VI	1967	*Washington* v. *Texas*
Right to jury trial in cases of serious crime	VI	1968	*Duncan* v. *Louisiana*
Right against double jeopardy	V	1969	*Benton* v. *Maryland*
Right to counsel in all criminal cases entailing a jail term	VI	1972	*Argersinger* v. *Hamlin*

SOURCE: H. W. Chase and C. Ducat, *1980 Supplement to Constitutional Interpretation: Cases, Essays, Materials* (St. Paul: West, 1980), pp. 888–890.

This excursion into constitutional law illustrates a significant national policy choice. According to some theorists, certain liberties are so basic to democratic life that they must be safeguarded throughout the country. Others contend that in a large, complex nation, standards and policies should be developed at the local level. For example, should the laws banning "pornography" in New York City apply the same standards as laws in rural Arkansas? Or should "pornography" mean one thing in New York and something else in an area with radically different social mores? As a polity, we have moved steadily in the first of these directions over the past half-century.

Freedom of Speech

In the classical liberal credo, freedom of speech (and of the press) is considered essential if humankind is to advance intellectually; the competition of ideas is seen as a necessary condition of progress.[4] According to this rationale, even if an unpopular view turns out to be entirely incorrect, it should still be tolerated because the challenge of the false view forces the holders of truth to examine their position and to flex their intellectual muscles.

Political philosopher Alexander Meiklejohn defended freedom of speech from a different perspective: Free speech, he contended, becomes necessary once people have decided to govern themselves. Free speech, in this view, is mandated by a prior commitment to self-government.[5] For the people to decide how government should function, they need free access to information so that they can make intelligent, informed choices. As a logical corollary to this premise, a distinction can be drawn between political speech (speech that is related to self-government) and nonpolitical speech, and only the former must be protected absolutely. Thus, Meiklejohn could argue, quite consistently, free speech for political radicals must be protected, whereas slander and libel may be outlawed.

In the twentieth century, the Supreme Court has largely followed Meiklejohn's approach. Acknowledging that the basic justification for free speech is its contribution to self-government, the Court has repeatedly ruled that public policy requires greater freedom of expression on political than on other matters. Let us now consider Supreme Court rulings on the limits of dissent; cases involving the controversial Smith Act, which outlawed advocating the violent overthrow of the government; contemporary trends in freedom of speech; and the Court's view of symbolic speech and "fighting words."

Setting Limits on Dissent

After the Sedition Act of 1798, Congress made no attempt to regulate free speech until the passage of the Espionage Act of 1917 and the Sedition Act of 1918. Both acts were designed to curb criticism of the government during World War I. In a significant series of cases in the postwar period, the Supreme Court passed on the constitutionality of these acts in rulings that have largely shaped the legal debate on free speech matters to the present day. Through the three cases we shall examine, we can trace a gradual evolution of the Court's approach to setting limits on dissent. Also note how profoundly the political and social atmosphere of the times influenced these cases, which involved extremely controversial political speech.[6]

The three cases—*Schenck* v. *United States* (1919), *Abrams* v. *United States* (1919), and *Gitlow* v. *New York* (1925)—bear striking similarities.[7]

Schenck v. *United States:* In 1917, Charles T. Schenck, a Socialist party official, mailed out leaflets urging eligible young men to resist the draft. The leaflets described conscription as despotism and urged citizens to defend their rights against the interests of Wall Street. Schenck was convicted under the Espionage Act.

Abrams v. *United States:* In 1919, Jacob Abrams and five associates, all Russian immigrants, distributed leaflets (by throwing them out of a factory window in

New York) criticizing U.S. involvement on the side of anti-Bolshevik forces in the Soviet Union. The leaflets branded President Woodrow Wilson a hypocrite and a tool of Wall Street and called on workers to join a general strike. In 1919, four of the defendants were convicted under the Sedition Act and sentenced to twenty years in prison.

Gitlow v. *New York:* In 1925, Benjamin Gitlow, a radical socialist, was convicted under New York State's Criminal Anarchy Act of 1902 of advocating the violent overthrow of the government. The main evidence against him was a theoretical piece he had written titled *Left Wing Manifesto*.

In none of the cases was evidence presented that the pamphlets, leaflets, or theoretical writings had any noticeable effect on the conduct of people who read them. Accordingly, the issue in each case came down to this: Could the government limit freedom of expression because of *possible* interference with a government function or because it found specific views threatening? How far, in other words, did freedom of speech extend?

In *Schenck* the Court unanimously upheld Schenck's conviction. Justice Oliver Wendell Holmes, in expressing the Court's view, attempted to define the free speech issues involved:

> We admit that in many places and in ordinary times the defendants in saying all that was said in the circular would have been within their constitutional rights. But the character of every act depends upon the circumstances in which it is done. The most stringent protection of free speech would not protect a man in falsely shouting fire in a theatre and causing a panic. It does not even protect a man from an injunction against uttering words that may have all the effect of force. The question in every case is whether the words used are used in such circumstances and are of such a nature as to create a clear and present danger that they will bring about the substantive evils that Congress has a right to prevent.

Critics of this famous opinion have argued that although the government may have had the right to prevent obstruction of the draft, Schenck's pamphlet simply did not represent the **"clear and present danger"** alluded to by Holmes.

The convictions of Jacob Abrams and his associates were also upheld by the Court. In this case, however, Justice Holmes and Louis Brandeis dissented, arguing that

> the best test of truth is the power of thought to get itself accepted in the competition of the market.... That at any rate is the theory of our Constitution. It is an experiment, as all life is an experiment... we should be eternally vigilant against attempts to check the expressions of opinions that we loathe and believe to be fraught with danger, unless they so imminently threaten immediate interference with the lawful and pressing purposes of the law that an immediate check is required to save the country.

To the Court majority, however, the convictions were justified on the grounds that the activities involved had a "dangerous or bad tendency"—that they were meant to instigate riot or revolution. These two positions set the parameters for subsequent debate on the limits of speech and opinion.

In *Gitlow*, Holmes and Brandeis again dissented from the Court's majority ruling. Their minority opinion sets out the implications of their views even more fully:

> Every idea is an incitement. It offers itself for belief and if believed it is acted on. . . . If in the long run the beliefs expressed in proletarian dictatorship are destined to be accepted by the dominant forces of the community, the only meaning of free speech is that they should be given their chance and have their way.

A majority of justices upheld Gitlow's conviction. But as we have seen, the Court did take the important step of acknowledging that the Fourteenth Amendment applied to the freedoms of speech and press in the states.

Not until the 1930s did a majority of the Court begin to accept the Holmes-Brandeis view. In several cases decided in that decade, the right of communists to express their views was upheld by the Court on the ground that their activities did not include plans for action but simply the articulation of opinions.

The Smith Act Cases

In 1940, Congress passed the Smith Act, which made it a crime knowingly to advocate or teach or to organize or knowingly to become a member of a group that advocated the violent overthrow of any unit of the U.S. government. The Smith Act, like most other sedition and criminal anarchy statutes, focused more on speech than on acts against the government.

In 1949, indictments were brought under the act against eleven leaders of the U.S. Communist party. They were charged not with committing overt acts against the government or even with planning such acts but rather with teaching the duty and necessity of revolution from Marxist texts. All eleven were convicted, and the Supreme Court in 1951 upheld the convictions in *Dennis et al.* v. *United States*.[8] Writing for the Court majority, Chief Justice Fred M. Vinson argued:

> If the government is aware that a group aiming at its overthrow is attempting to indoctrinate its members and to commit them to a course whereby they will strike when the leaders feel the circumstances permit, action by the Government is required. . . . The damage which such attempts create both physically and politically to a nation makes it impossible to measure the validity in terms of the probability of success, or the immediacy of a successful attempt. . . . We must therefore reject the contention that success or probability of success is the criterion.

From this perspective, it made no difference whether there was any evidence of contemplated or planned-for future action: If people merely disseminated the idea of revolution, the government was justified in prosecuting them.

> ## THE ALIEN AND SEDITION ACTS OF 1798
>
> The French Revolution stirred intense debate in the new United States. Thomas Jefferson and others of similar views, known as Jeffersonian Republicans, welcomed the revolutionary developments in France. The more conservative Federalists, however, generally decried what they viewed as the increasingly destructive and radical direction the revolution seemed to be taking. Feelings ran so high that when Jefferson went to Philadelphia in March 1797 to take the oath of office as vice-president, he noted that "men who have been intimate all their lives, cross the streets to avoid meeting, and turn their heads another way, lest they should be obliged to touch their hats." This deep-seated fear of the radicalism of the French revolutionaries led to the new republic's first brush with political repression.
>
> In 1798 the Federalist-dominated Congress passed the Naturalization Act and the Alien and Sedition Acts, which were ostensibly aimed at protecting the nation from the alleged threat from France. In reality, however, the acts were directed as much at the Republican opposition as at any supposed foreign danger. The Naturalization Act increased the period of residence required to gain U.S. citizenship from five to fourteen years, and the Alien Act and the Alien Enemies Act gave the president the power to expel foreigners by executive decree. Far more controversial was the Sedition Act, which made it a criminal offense to speak or write against Congress or the president with the "intent to defame" or bring either into contempt. Such vague legislation practically invited abuse. Not surprisingly, every person charged under the act was a Republican or Republican sympathizer, including many newspaper editors; every judge and almost every juror in these cases was a Federalist. Of the twenty-five persons prosecuted under the Sedition Act, ten were convicted and punished with heavy fines or jail sentences.
>
> Despite the Sedition Act, criticism of the government continued, and the election of 1800 put Jefferson into the White House. All four acts were allowed to expire in 1800 and 1801.

Commenting on this position in a dissenting opinion, Justice William O. Douglas wrote:

> If this were a case where those who claimed protection under the First Amendment were teaching the techniques of sabotage, the assassination of the President . . . , the planting of bombs, the art of street warfare . . . I would have no doubts. . . . The case was argued as if

those were the facts. That is easy and it has popular appeal, for the activities of Communists in plotting and scheming against the free world are common knowledge. But the fact is that no such evidence was introduced at the trial. . . . What petitioners did was organize to teach and themselves teach the Marxist-Leninist doctrine contained in four books. . . . The opinion of the Court does not outlaw those texts. . . . But if the books themselves are not outlawed, . . . by what reasoning does their use in a classroom become a crime? The crime then depends not on what is taught, but on who the teacher is. . . . Once we start down that road we enter territory dangerous to the liberties of every citizen.

Six years later, in *Yates* v. *United States* (1957), the Court shifted its ground by returning to the "clear and present danger" test.[9] By a 6–1 vote, the Court overturned the convictions under the Smith Act of five second-rank leaders of the U.S. Communist party and ordered that the nine other party officials involved in the case be remanded for new trials. (None was ever retried.) The Court majority in *Yates* argued that conviction under the Smith Act required proof not just that defendants had advocated a belief in revolution in the abstract but that they had advocated action to bring about revolution. The *Yates* decision effectively nullified the Smith Act.

Contemporary Trends

Since *Yates* the Court has not deviated noticeably from the "clear and present danger" standard in comparable cases—most notably, the so-called Pentagon Papers case in 1971. According to that 6–3 Supreme Court ruling, the Pentagon Papers—classified documents on the U.S. involvement in Vietnam—could be published by the *New York Times* and the *Washington Post* under the protection of the First Amendment. During the Vietnam War, several convictions for draft card burning, flag desecration, and similar activities were upheld by the Court, but there were no free speech convictions on the order of *Schenck* or *Abrams*.

In recent decades the Court has established three basic tests of the constitutionality of laws and regulations designed to limit free expression. Under the concept of "strict scrutiny," the government must prove a compelling interest in its restriction of speech. Also, under the doctrine of "overbreadth," statutes that purport to limit expression must be narrowly and specifically drawn. Finally, the Court has paid careful attention to the "chilling effect" of statutes. This means that a law may be held unconstitutional if its mere existence "chills," or impairs, the exercise of First Amendment rights. In *Shelton* v. *Tucker* (1960), for example, the Court cited the chilling effect in invalidating an Arkansas statute that had required every schoolteacher to file an annual report of all organizations to which he or she belonged or contributed money.[10]

Symbolic Speech and "Fighting Words"

Often, political or social views are expressed through symbolic gestures, such as picketing, the wearing of armbands, or the carrying of signs or placards, rather than in reasoned political speech. Sometimes people express themselves in particularly heated or intense ways—cursing, screaming, haranguing. Or they may utter "fighting words" or carry on symbolic activities in schools, public buildings, or other centers of public activity. Such intense or symbolic expressions of views have raised numerous and complicated First Amendment issues.

Over the years the Supreme Court has applied First Amendment protections to various forms of symbolic speech and heated expression of views and denied those protections to others. In *Amalgamated Food Employees Local 590* v. *Logan Valley Plaza, Inc.* (1968), for example, the Court held that the "speech" aspect of picketing is fully protected under the First Amendment but that the conduct of picketers is not.[11] "Because of this intermingling of protected and unprotected elements," the Court decided, "picketing can be subject to controls that would not be constitutionally permissible in the case of pure speech.

Another limitation on symbolic speech came in *United States* v. *O'Brien* (1968), in which the Court held that the burning of draft cards as a symbolic protest was not a constitutionally protected form of free speech.[12] The justices could not accept the principle that an "apparently limitless variety of conduct can be labeled 'speech' whenever the person engaging in the conduct intends thereby to express an idea."

In *Tinker* v. *Des Moines Independent Community School District* (1969), however, the Court upheld the right of students to make a symbolic protest against the Vietnam War by wearing black armbands to school.[13] Such a practice, the justices found, represented a legitimate form of free speech and so was protected under the First Amendment, except for cases in which it would cause serious disruption of school activities.

As for "fighting words," the Court has shown considerable tolerance toward what might seem to be potentially disruptive forms of expression. In 1942, in *Chaplinsky* v. *New Hampshire*, the Court did uphold the right of the state to punish the utterance of "fighting words."[14] In 1972, in contrast, it refused to permit application of a "fighting words" statute against a black man who shouted, "White son of a bitch, I'll kill you" at a white police officer (*Gooding* v. *Wilson*).[15]

The Court upheld the right of a Nazi group to hold a rally and display the Nazi emblem in a heavily Jewish Chicago suburb (*National Socialist Party* v. *Skokie*, 1977), noting that "anticipation of a hostile audience could not justify . . . prior restraint."[16] In addressing the issue of the "angry audience," the Court has generally ruled that assemblies and parades can be halted by police if a risk of imminent violence has been clearly demonstrated. However, the justices have also made it clear that the police must protect the people participating in a rally or meeting, if at all possible.

Gregory Johnson set fire to the American flag in a protest at the 1984 Republican National Convention in Dallas. He was convicted of violating a Texas statute barring desecration of the flag. In *Texas* v. *Johnson* (1989), a closely divided Supreme Court ruled that the flag burning was protected expression under the First Amendment.[17] Amid calls from President Bush for a constitutional amendment to protect the flag, Congress chose a statutory response: the Federal Flag Protection Act of 1989. Voting "against the flag" is a difficult thing for an elected official to do in America. This act was quickly challenged and suffered the same fate as its Texas predecessor, *United*

Burn the American flag? The Supreme Court upheld the constitutional protection of this form of symbolic "speech." President Bush called for a constitutional amendment to ban it, but his efforts failed. *(UPI/Bettmann Newsphotos)*

States v. *Eichman* (1990).[18] The constitutional amendment failed in both houses to gain the requisite two-thirds majority.

Press Freedom

A free press is closely associated with free speech rights, and in many circumstances the protection of one will extend to the other. Still, the First Amendment provides separate, explicit protection for press freedom, and there are some special reasons why this is important. Under modern conditions a free press does more than simply disseminate information, although that is important enough. News organizations have become essential to the discovery and gathering of information. We will turn our attention directly to the place of news media in our democracy in Chapter 10. The following section will pinpoint the start of the Supreme Court's protection of press freedom and then look at two instances of the important role the press plays in discovering information.

The *Saturday Press* was not a nice newspaper. Jay Near, the editor, was antiblack, anti-Catholic, anti-Semitic, and antilabor, and the paper reflected all of that. But when the *Saturday Press* was closed in 1927 under a Minnesota statute prohibiting a public nuisance by any "malicious, scandalous, and defamatory" publication, the editor of the *Chicago Tribune* came to Near's rescue, paying for an appeal as far as the U.S. Supreme Court.

Chief Justice Charles Evans Hughes wrote for the Court in *Near* v. *Minnesota* (1931), making three points: Press freedom is incorporated in the Fourteenth Amendment and thus gains federal protection against state abuse, the general rule of English (and American) law is that a free press requires no **prior restraint** (preventing publication in the first place), and publishers were nevertheless accountable for what they publish.[19] Libelous publication could be punished—after the fact—under criminal and civil libel laws. Furthermore, publishers could be held in contempt of court if publications obstruct judicial functions. To protect press freedom, we must be willing to let publishers publish first and face the consequences later. The Minnesota statute was an unconstitutional infringement on the First and Fourteenth amendments.

Press freedom is essential to fair government under modern conditions both because news organizations "attract" news and because they ferret news out. The Pentagon Papers case, cited earlier, is a good example of the former: Rebuffed by a Senate committee, former aide Daniel Ellsberg turned to the *New York Times* and the *Washington Post* to trigger public debate about an internal government report quite damaging to the case supporting the Vietnam War. The Watergate scandal is a good example of the productive use of the investigative function of news organizations; *Richmond Newspapers* v. *Virginia* (1980) is another.[20] In this case a Virginia trial court granted a defense motion to close a murder trial to the public and to the press. A defendant has a right to an open trial, but that wasn't being asserted here. Do the public and the press have an independent right to open trials? The Court said yes. The Supreme Court's positive response in this case would not have been secured if Richmond Newspapers had not been willing to pay the costs of pressing the question. It is unlikely that an ordinary citizen would have taken up the challenge.

Press freedom can be threatened in a variety of ways. In the United States, news media must compete in the private sector (or on its margins, as in nonprofit public broadcasting). What if economic circumstances make it difficult to support competing sources of news? Most metropolitan areas have lost the once-common advantage of competing daily newspapers. That loss has been compensated in part by the development of local broadcast sources of news. But both print and broadcast news organizations are part of a larger economic consolidation and concentration of ownership in the American economy. One guarantee of democratic press freedom is the existence of many competing sources of news.

Another threat to press freedom comes from libel suits. (**Libel** is defamation of character by print or visual representation.) What if fear of large awards—or even successful defense in an expensive trial—discourages the press from taking on controversial political figures or their policies? The Supreme Court addressed this issue in *New York Times* v. *Sullivan* in 1964.[21] Confrontations between civil rights activists and police propelled four black Alabama clergymen to place a full-page ad in the *New York Times* that included the following paragraph:

> In Montgomery, Alabama, after students sang "My Country, 'Tis of Thee" on the Capitol steps, their leaders were expelled from school, and truckloads of police armed with shotguns and tear-gas ringed the Alabama State College Campus. When the entire student body protested to state authorities by refusing to re-register, their dining hall was padlocked in an attempt to starve them into submission.

L. B. Sullivan was one of three elected commissioners of the city Montgomery at the time. He sued the four clergymen and the *New York Times*, claiming that since the commissioners supervised the police department, the alleged actions of the police would be imputed to him. A sympathetic Alabama state court jury awarded Sullivan $500,000 damages. The Supreme Court overturned the award and established a two-tier standard for libel actions. "The Constitution delimits a State's power to award damages for libel in actions brought by public officials against critics of their actions." A much higher standard of proof is applied in libel suits brought by public figures, giving greater protection to press freedom in discussions of public affairs while maintaining libel law's general protection against defamation. The higher standard applies not just to elected officials. In the 1988 case of *Hustler Magazine* v. *Falwell*, televangelist Jerry Falwell was denied recovering damages for emotional distress from a bawdy parody in *Hustler*.[22]

Freedom of Religion

The very first issue addressed in the First Amendment is the relationship between government and religion—as sensitive an issue today as it was in the eighteenth century. Under the First Amendment, Congress is commanded to make no law "respecting an establishment of religion" (the **establishment clause**) or "prohibiting the free exercise" of religion (the **free exercise clause**).* On the most basic level, both clauses are clear: Congress may not establish a state religion or prohibit particular religions. These prohibitions were certainly relevant to the forms of religious intolerance and the official state religions found abundantly in eighteenth-century Europe and America. Throughout the nineteenth century, few controversies developed between the national government and religious groups. In the twentieth century, however, many such controversies have arisen—some very subtle and difficult to resolve. Let us now probe the

---

*As we will see later in this chapter, the phrase "establishment of religion" has been subject to many interpretations. Some people have argued that it prohibits only an official state religion; others have maintained that it excludes all favoritism toward any religion or even toward religion in general.

CIVIL LIBERTIES

ramifications of the establishment clause and various interpretations of the free exercise clause.

Establishment of Religion

Was it the intention of the framers of the Bill of Rights merely to prevent the establishment of a national church, such as the Church of England, or to prohibit *any* acts of government that would support certain religions or even religion in general? Authorities who have taken the latter view have spoken of the need for a "wall of separation" between church and state, to keep government entirely out of matters associated with religion. Most recent church-state controversies have revolved around the many ways that government and religion do or could interact.

The best known of these debates centers on prayer in public schools. In a series of decisions in the early 1960s, a divided Supreme Court banned even nonsectarian prayers from public schools. In *Engel* v. *Vitale* (1962), for example, the Court majority declared unconstitutional the saying of a nondenominational prayer written by the New York State Board of Regents for use in state public schools.[23] The Court later outlawed

School prayer. No one can prevent students from contemplating their own thoughts, but the Supreme Court has made it clear that *organized* efforts by the government to encourage religious observance in public schools are unconstitutional. *(Bryce Flynn/Stock, Boston)*

Bible reading in public schools, even in those that permitted children to be excused if their parents objected. Because such practices promoted religion in general, the Court argued, they could not be permitted under the establishment clause. As an alternative, the Court pointed out that religion could be *studied* in an academic context.

These rulings met with immediate and intense opposition. Many school districts simply refused to comply with the Supreme Court guidelines. In addition, proponents of school prayer began working toward passage of a constitutional amendment permitting some religious practices in public schools. According to advocates of the proposed amendment, the Bill of Rights was not intended to prohibit all religious exercises in schools or all government involvement with religion.

In 1985 the Supreme Court struck down, by a 6-3 vote, an Alabama law that permitted a one-minute period of silent meditation or prayer in public schools. In *Wallace* v. *Jaffree*, the Court affirmed its earlier rulings that "government must pursue a course of complete neutrality toward religion" but indicated at the same time that "moment of silence" laws could be held constitutional as as long as they did not have as their primary intention the fostering of religious activity in the classroom.[24] The Alabama law, the majority argued, had intended to characterize prayer "as a favored practice." At the time of the ruling, varying versions of the "moment of silence" law existed in twenty-five states.

Another long-running establishment clause controversy concerns public aid to private schools, most of which are church-affiliated. Generally, the Court has taken the position that the state can assist private-school students or support particular private-school programs that are not related to religion but that it cannot provide funding for religious instruction. Thus, whereas the Court has upheld tax aid to parents to offset the costs of busing to private schools and the costs of nonreligious textbooks and other study aids, it has not permitted the use of public funds for teachers' salaries, tuition aid, or maintenance and repair of school facilities.

One other sensitive subject has been the tax-exempt status of religious institutions. Many observers consider the tax-exempt status of church property to be a violation of the constitutionally mandated separation of church and state. The Court ruled on this matter in *Walz* v. *Tax Commission of the City of New York* (1970).[25] Chief Justice Warren Burger argued for the Court majority in this case that tax exemption was constitutional and represents "neither the advancement nor the inhibition of religion." He distinguished tax exemption, an indirect economic subsidy, from direct subsidies, which violate the establishment clause.

Church-affiliated schools and colleges may not, however, keep their tax exemptions while violating federal civil rights legislation, as the Court's ruling in *Bob Jones University* v. *United States* (1983) made clear.[26]

Since 1971, the so-called **Lemon** test, introduced by Chief Justice Burger in *Lemon* v. *Kurtzman*, has been the Supreme Court's primary tool for sorting out establishment cases.[27] It has three parts: "First, the statute must have a secular legislative purpose; second, its principle or primary effect must be one that neither advances nor inhibits religion . . . ; finally, the statute must not foster 'an excessive government entanglement with religion.' " Failing any one of these will defeat government aid to religion. Having a test like this is one way for the Court to maintain a consistent stance on a particular issue. It also increases public understanding of the Court's position, thus forestalling unnecessary suits. But no test can eliminate controversy or substitute for careful judicial reasoning in each case. There are signs that the *Lemon* test may well be modified or abandoned as the Court continues to find its way through establishment cases one at a time.

Free Exercise of Religion

The right to the free exercise of religion has been consistently upheld by the Supreme Court. As Justice Samuel F. Miller wrote in an 1872 case (*Watson* v. *Jones*) involving a dispute within the Presbyterian church, "In this country the full and free right to entertain any religious doctrine which does not violate the laws of morality and property, and which does not infringe personal rights, is conceded to all."[28] Note how many possible conflicts are contained within those qualifying phrases, however. Many of the legal conflicts associated with the free exercise clause have hinged on differing interpretations of the "laws of morality."

In *Reynolds* v. *United States* (1878), for example, the Supreme Court upheld a federal law prohibiting polygamy in U.S. territories.[29] The law had been challenged by the Mormon church, which encouraged its followers to practice polygamy. In upholding the statute, the Court distinguished between religious *beliefs*, which enjoy the full protection of the Constitution, and *actions* based on those beliefs, which can be regulated by government. To allow a person to engage in illegal behavior because of religious beliefs, the Court noted in *Reynolds*, "would be to make the professed doctrines of religious beliefs superior to the law of the land." But exactly *why* polygamy should be illegal, the Court did not make clear. It could be argued that this was a case of the majority deciding what "appropriate morality" should be.

Following *Reynolds*, very few free exercise questions were addressed by the Supreme Court until the early 1940s, when several cases involving the Jehovah's Witnesses reached the Court. At issue in *Minersville School District* v. *Gobitis* (1940) was the expulsion from school of two Jehovah's Witness children who had refused to participate in the mandatory salute to the flag and recitation of the Pledge of Allegiance on the grounds that such an oath violated their religious beliefs and constituted idolatry.[30] The Supreme Court upheld the expulsions, rejecting the contention that the free exercise clause had been violated. Justice Felix Frankfurter, writing for the majority, noted the importance of symbols in American life and argued that "the flag is a symbol of our national unity, transcending all internal differences, however large, within the framework of the Constitution." There was only one dissenter on the Court.

Then, remarkably, the Court reversed itself only three years later, in *West Virginia State Board of Education* v. *Barnette* (1943).[31] Three new members had joined the Court in the intervening years, and in *Barnette* three other justices admitted that they had been wrong in *Gobitis*. In upholding the right of Jehovah's Witnesses to decline to swear an oath, Justice Robert H. Jackson, writing for the majority, stated, "If there is any fixed star in our constitutional constellation, it is that no official, high or petty, can prescribe what shall be orthodox in politics, nationalism, religion, or other matters of opinion or force citizens to confess by word or act their faith therein."

The Supreme Court has also affirmed the right to object to military service on religious grounds. In *United States* v. *Seeger* (1965), the Court extended this concept to cover "sincere and meaningful" religious beliefs that may not be related to a supreme being.[32] Five years later, in *Welsh* v. *United States*, the justices upheld the rights of a conscientious objector whose refusal to serve in the armed forces was based on "considerations of public policy."[33] However, the Court has consistently refused to sanction so-called selective objection to military service—objection based on opposition to a particular war, as opposed to all wars.

The Rights of the Accused

The rights of people accused of crimes have always posed difficult issues for democratic societies. There are the inevitable tensions between the need to protect the accused, on the one hand, and to prosecute the guilty, on the other; particularly in times of social strain and tension, the balance seems to tip in the direction of increased police powers. Another complicating factor in U.S. society has been the disproportionate presence in the ranks of defendants of members of minority groups and the poor.

Under Chief Justice Earl Warren, the Supreme Court in the 1960s introduced radical changes into the process by which criminal suspects are apprehended and guilt or innocence is determined. Overall, the Warren Court attempted to tighten the requirements for establishing legal guilt, principally by placing constraints on the kinds of evidence that could be introduced and the procedures that could be followed in criminal courts. The touchstone of the Court's approach to defining the rights of the accused was the Fifth Amendment's injunction that no person "be deprived of life, liberty or property, without due process of law." In comparison with its predecessors (as well as its successors), the Warren Court took a decidedly expansive view of the meaing of "due process."

The Court significantly broadened the accused's right to counsel, which is guaranteed in the Sixth Amendment. In a series of cases, the justices ruled that the accused has the right to be represented by an attorney during interrogation by police, at lineups, during preliminary hearings, at trial, and during the appeals process. Moreover, in the landmark case of *Gideon* v. *Wainwright* (1963), the Court held that if a defendant could not afford to hire an attorney, the state must provide one.[34] Only if representation by an attorney were guaranteed even to the most indigent defendant, the Court reasoned, would the rights of that defendant be adequately protected.

The second basic principle advanced by the Warren Court—exclusion of "tainted" evidence—meant that if in obtaining evidence against a defendant, law enforcement officers violated the defendant's constitutional rights (by conducting unauthorized searches or improper interrogations, for example), that evidence must be excluded from the trial. In part the exclusionary rule was grounded in skepticism of the validity of illegally obtained evidence (the result of coercive police techniques, for instance). But the exclusionary rule was primarily designed to regulate the conduct of law enforcement. If evidence obtained in illegal searches and seizures or interrogations could not be used in court, then, presumably, law enforcement officers would be less likely to engage in such practices.

In a further effort to curb police abuses of the rights of suspects, the Court in *Miranda* v. *Arizona* (1963) dictated guidelines to be followed by police in the interrogation of suspects.[35] All persons arrested, the Court declared, must be informed of their right to remain silent and their right to legal representation during questioning and must be warned that anything they say may be used against them in court.

To their proponents, the Warren Court's decisions on due process went to the very heart of civil liberties doctrine—the need to protect the dignity and humanity of citizens. The Court argued that certain police and prosecutorial procedures simply violated the basic human rights that citizens ought to enjoy. Another defense of the Court's approach is the argument that the best way to avoid the conviction of an innocent person is to establish strict procedural rules governing arrest, interrogation, and trial. Finally, some of the procedural protections set up by the Court, such as the principle of exclusion, were designed to prevent too much intrusion by police in the lives of citizens. Random searches, dragnet arrests, and threatening interrogations of suspects may be useful tools in catching lawbreakers, but they cannot be justified in a society of limited government.

The Warren court's decisions on due process continue to spark controversy. As we noted in Chapter 2, U.S. society remains divided between the drive for efficient apprehension and punishment of people who break laws and the desire for restrictions on the powers of the state in its dealings with individuals.

In the 1960s, public opinion held that the Warren Court had gone too far in protecting criminals at the expense of law-abiding citizens. The election of President Richard Nixon in 1968 ushered in a gradual retreat from the positions taken by the Warren Court. In his appointments to the Court, President Nixon selected justices who favored efficient law enforcement, and by the mid-1970s the Court's approach to due process rights had changed significantly. Under Chief Justice Warren Burger the Court, for example, narrowed the application of the "*Miranda* rules." The Burger Court did not explicitly overrule *Miranda*, but it whittled away at the breadth of the Warren Court decisions in that and other due process areas.

Through most of the 1980s the Court vacillated in its approach to the exclusionary rule and the *Miranda* warnings, sometimes upholding them, sometimes amending them, often in closely split votes. The Reagan administration, led by Attorney General Edwin Meese, sought to severely curtail these protections. A 1987 Justice Department staff report stated: "The interesting question is not whether *Miranda* should go, but how we should facilitate its demise and what we should replace it with." The report went on to state that "overturning *Miranda* would . . . be among the most important achievements of this administration."

To a minor extent, the Court acquiesced. For example, in *Colorado* v. *Spring* (1987), it held that police need not inform suspects of the crimes about which they may be questioned in order for them to waive their constitutional right to remain silent.[36] Police, in other words, need not specifically list all crimes that may come up in the questioning. The Court also upheld an oral confession given by a suspect who was told of his or her rights and who refused to make a written statement.

By contrast, the Court ruled unanimously that a suspect's decision to remain silent under questioning could not later be used against him or her as proof of sanity at the time of arrest. The majority stated that the *Miranda* warnings "contained an implicit promise, rooted in the Constitution, that silence will carry no penalty."[37]

A split (5–4) Court also found in *Maine* v. *Moulton* (1985) that once a suspect invokes the right to counsel, the police must not question that suspect without counsel being present.[38] This also excludes the use of an undercover informant to try to solicit information.

By the late 1980s and early 1990s a fairly consistent narrowing tendency was apparent in the Court's rulings concerning criminal procedure. In *Arizona* v. *Mauro* (1987), defendant Mauro was informed of his rights, requested an attorney, and then was taped while making a phone call to his wife; the tape was admissible.[39] In *New York* v. *Harris* (1990), an incriminating statement made after a warrantless and nonconsensual entry into the defendant's home was deemed admissible.[40] In *Illinois* v. *Perkins* (1990), a defendant in jail prior to arraignment made incriminating statements to an undercover agent posing as a fellow inmate. No *Miranda* warnings were given, but the statements were found admissible.

Support for the broad Warren era holdings had been led by William Brennan, who left the Court in 1990, and Thurgood Marshall, who stepped down the following year. Opposition often came from William Rehnquist, who became Chief Justice in 1986 after Warren Burger's retirement. Marshall's departure left only one Warren era justice, Byron White, a centrist on some matters but to the right on criminal procedure (emphasizing efficient criminal prosecution over defendants' rights). The Reagan and Bush appointees to the Court have generally shared that orientation.

One important avenue for narrowing the rights available to criminal defendants is through the restriction of habeas corpus review. The writ of **habeas corpus** allows a person being held prisoner to have another court review the imprisonment's justification. Practically speaking, habeas corpus was a means of allowing federal district courts to review state criminal prosecutions. Because district courts are more accessible than the U.S. Supreme Court, which can consider only a tiny fraction of the cases presented to it (see Chapter 16), habeas corpus review allowed for greater federal oversight of criminal cases in the states. Since the mid-1970s, federal courts have found due process violations in no fewer than 40 percent of the convictions and sentences reviewed.[41] The Rehnquist Court has systematically cut back on habeas corpus review, contending that this writ floods the federal courts with cases that should properly be resolved in the states and that the availability of this "second guess" review improperly and unnecessarily retards the disposition of cases—particularly capital punishment cases, which are notoriously slow in reaching final resolution. In 1991, for example, the Supreme Court ruled that federal courts could not consider an appeal from death row inmate Roger Coleman because five years earlier Coleman's court-appointed lawyer was three days late in filing an appeal in the Virginia Supreme Court. (Coleman was executed in 1992.) Opponents of the Court's recent moves suggest that federal habeas corpus review is the only way to ensure uniform application of due process rules to criminal defendants.

In general, the rights of persons suspected or accused of crimes are not a popular concern. Most of us find it hard to imagine ourselves on the receiving end of a police interrogation or to empathize with people who are. It is easier to conjure up the role of victim and to demand effective protection against potential harm. The strongest defense of these civil liberties is thus liable to come not from the majority or its elected representatives but from the judiciary, particularly the federal judiciary. Ardent judicial protection during times like the Warren era will be balanced against periods like the present, when the rights of the accused must depend on enlightened democratic concern.

Abortion

In recent decades the Supreme Court has elaborated a doctrine of "personal privacy" in cases involving contraception and abortion. In 1965 the Court voided a Connecticut law forbidding the issuance of birth control information, on the ground that the law violated the rights of marital privacy. The Court majority spoke of "zones of privacy" and cited the Ninth Amendment, which states that rights not spelled out in the Bill of Rights are retained by the people. Justice Hugo Black, dissenting, argued that the Court was creating a new right not to be found anywhere in the Constitution.

Eight years later, in a momentous decision on abortion handed down in *Roe* v. *Wade* (1973), the Court majority noted that "the Constitution does not explicitly mention any right of privacy . . . [but] the Court has recognized that a right of personal privacy . . . does exist under the Constitution."[42] The Court ruled that during the first trimester (three months) of pregnancy, the decision to choose an abortion was a private matter between a woman and her physician. In the second trimester, states could impose restrictions to protect the mother's health; in the third trimester, states could ban abortions altogether in recognition of the status of the developing fetus.

Since it was decided in 1973, *Roe* v. *Wade* has been unceasingly controversial. Some people hailed the decision as a decisive step forward for the civil liberties and the civil rights of women. Others regarded it as fundamentally immoral, a license for fetal murder. Opponents argue that the Court's ruling failed to take into account the

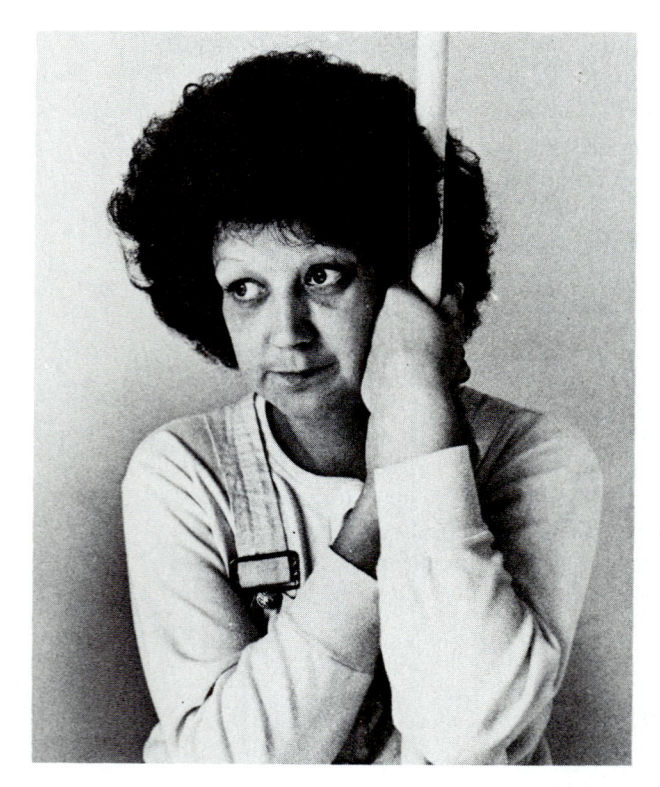

Norma McCorvey, the woman whose desire to have an abortion led to the Supreme Court *Roe* v. *Wade* decision. *(AP/Wide World Photos)*

unborn child's "right to life." Others argue that the trimester scheme was a blatant example of "judicial legislation" that should have been left to the political branches of government.

Challenges to *Roe* fall into three categories: changing the Constitution, cutting funding, and setting up roadblocks at the state level. The effort to pass a constitutional amendment that would allow both the federal government and the state governments the power to restrict abortion has not gotten very far. Efforts to restrict access to abortions by restricting funding have been more successful. Since 1976, Congress has annually passed Hyde amendments (named after the chief sponsor, Representative Henry Hyde of Illinois), which prohibit the use of federal funds for most abortions. The Court upheld the Hyde amendment in *Harris* v. *McRae* (1980).[43] As federally financed abortions dropped from 295,000 in 1976 to 2,400 in 1979, many private abortion clinics lowered fees for women who could not afford to pay. In 1988 the Court upheld the Adolescent Family Life Act, which prohibited federal funding of organizations involved with abortions. That same year Ronald Reagan's secretary of health and human services promulgated regulations that prohibited any agency receiving federal family planning funds from providing counseling concerning the use of abortion or referral to abortion services. Outraged health professionals charged that the regulations amounted to a gag rule, infringing on the obligation to offer the patient complete, professional advice. The regulations were upheld by the Supreme Court in *Rust* v. *Sullivan* (1991).[44] Legislation overturning the restriction was vetoed by President Bush, who later revised the regulations, allowing physicians but not other health care providers to discuss abortion. The administration found this a good compromise, but opponents argued that the revisions would not change much. As far as these critics were concerned, the gag rule was still in place.

Efforts at restricting access to abortion through state laws acceptable to the Supreme Court, after early failures, have been increasingly successful. In 1974, for example, almost immediately after *Roe*, Missouri passed a law requiring a husband's consent to his wife's decision to have an abortion. Two years later, in *Planned Parenthood of Missouri* v. *Danforth* (1976), the Court invalidated this statute, arguing that a husband was entitled to influence but not to a veto over his wife's decision.[45] In that same case the Court invalidated strict rules that parental consent be obtained by a minor seeking an abortion. But in 1985, Ohio passed a consent law designed to meet the Court's objections. The law required a parent's or guardian's consent for a minor's abortion but provided a "judicial bypass" procedure whereby a juvenile court could authorize the young woman to consent to the abortion if parental consent was not in her best interest. The Supreme Court upheld the statute by a 6-3 vote.[46]

In 1986, in *Thornburgh* v. *American College of Obstetricians and Gynecologists*, the Court, voting 5-4, struck down a Pennsylvania law designed to discourage women from opting for abortion.[47] The law set out detailed instructions specifying how a woman must give her "informed consent," and it also spelled out a series of procedures that doctors were obliged to follow. In *Webster* v. *Reproductive Health Services* (1989), the Supreme Court upheld a Missouri statute whose preamble stated that "the life of each human being begins at conception."[48] The law also prohibited the use of public facilities for abortions or the use of public funds for abortion counseling, enjoined public employees from performing abortions, and required physicians to conduct viability tests before performing abortions. This decision was widely perceived as an invitation from the Court to states to pass restrictive abortion laws. Several states acted quickly; a Pennsylvania statute was the first to reach the Court, which it did in 1992, an election year. The Court's decision reaffirmed *Roe* v. *Wade*, acknowledging the importance of maintaining settled law, but it also permitting greater state restrictions on abortion. Neither side in the debate was satisfied, assuring continued attention to *Roe*.

It is important to remember that *Roe* provided *federal* constitutional protection against regulations of abortion. Even in the absence of *Roe*, states may offer their own protection of a woman's right to choose an abortion, either in the state constitution or simply by not restricting abortion through statute. So as the Supreme Court restricts the scope of *Roe* v. *Wade*—or if it chooses to overturn that decision completely in a post-*Webster* challenge—the question of abortion moves to each of the states individ-

FIGURE 5-1

A LOOK AT STATE ABORTION LAWS

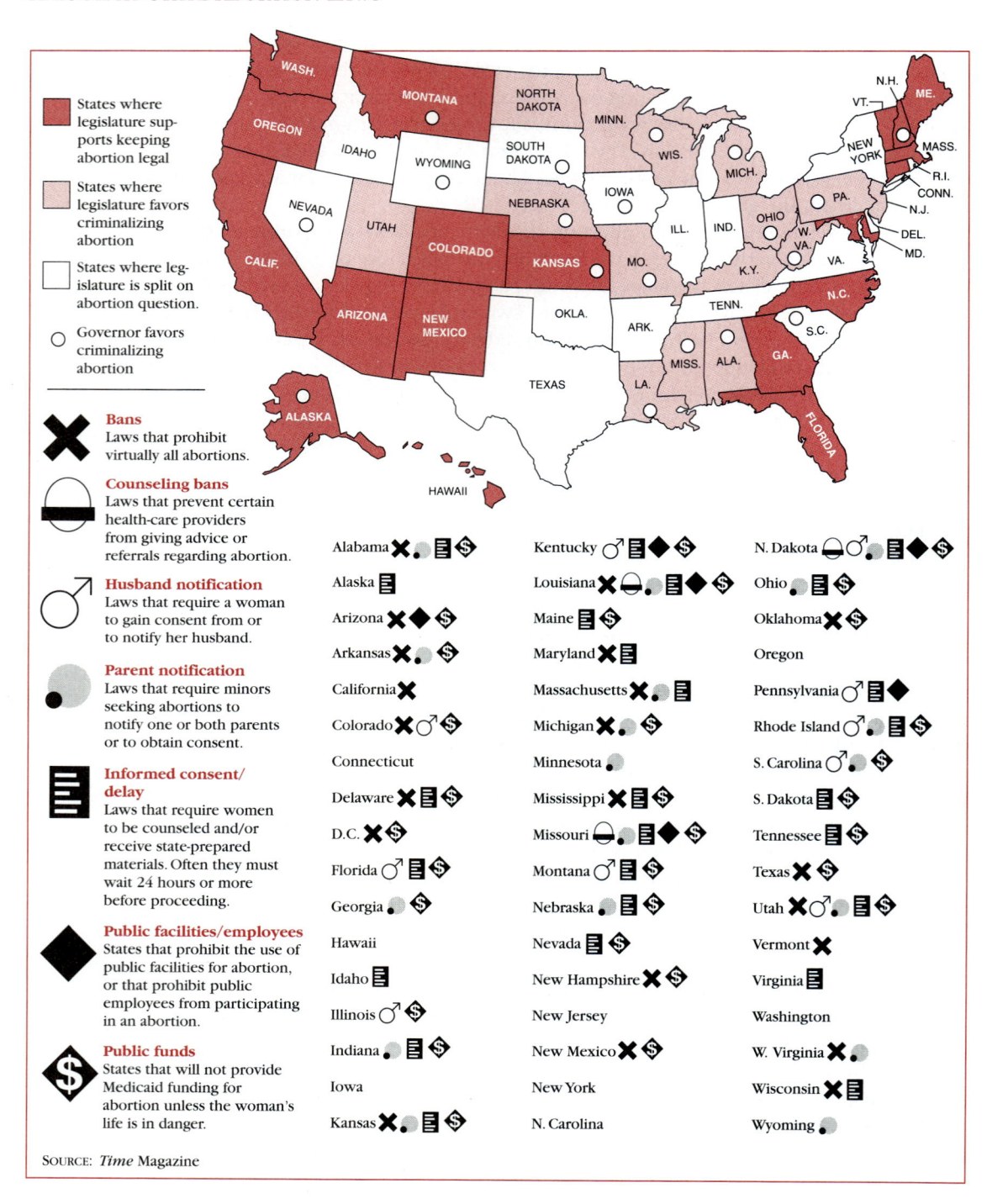

■ States where legislature supports keeping abortion legal

▨ States where legislature favors criminalizing abortion

□ States where legislature is split on abortion question.

○ Governor favors criminalizing abortion

✗ Bans
Laws that prohibit virtually all abortions.

⊖ Counseling bans
Laws that prevent certain health-care providers from giving advice or referrals regarding abortion.

♂ Husband notification
Laws that require a woman to gain consent from or to notify her husband.

● Parent notification
Laws that require minors seeking abortions to notify one or both parents or to obtain consent.

☰ Informed consent/delay
Laws that require women to be counseled and/or receive state-prepared materials. Often they must wait 24 hours or more before proceeding.

◆ Public facilities/employees
States that prohibit the use of public facilities for abortion, or that prohibit public employees from participating in an abortion.

$ Public funds
States that will not provide Medicaid funding for abortion unless the woman's life is in danger.

Source: *Time* Magazine

Alabama ✗ ● ☰ $
Alaska ☰
Arizona ✗ ◆ $
Arkansas ✗ ● $
California ✗
Colorado ✗ ♂ $
Connecticut
Delaware ✗ ☰ $
D.C. ✗ $
Florida ♂ ☰ $
Georgia ● $
Hawaii
Idaho ☰
Illinois ♂ $
Indiana ● ☰ $
Iowa
Kansas ✗ ● ☰ $

Kentucky ♂ ☰ ◆ $
Louisiana ✗ ⊖ ● ☰ ◆ $
Maine ☰ $
Maryland ✗ ☰
Massachusetts ✗ ● ☰
Michigan ✗ ● $
Minnesota ●
Mississippi ✗ ☰ $
Missouri ⊖ ● ☰ ◆ $
Montana ♂ ☰ $
Nebraska ● ☰ $
Nevada ☰ $
New Hampshire ✗ $
New Jersey
New Mexico ✗ $
New York
N. Carolina

N. Dakota ⊖ ♂ ● ☰ ◆ $
Ohio ● ☰ $
Oklahoma ✗ $
Oregon
Pennsylvania ♂ ☰ ◆
Rhode Island ♂ ● ☰ $
S. Carolina ♂ ● $
S. Dakota ☰ $
Tennessee ☰ $
Texas ✗ $
Utah ✗ ♂ ● ☰ $
Vermont ✗
Virginia ☰
Washington
W. Virginia ✗ ●
Wisconsin ✗ ☰
Wyoming ●

184

ually. A ballot initiative that put the prochoice protections of *Roe* into law passed in Washington state in November 1991, for example. But the measure, originally considered a shoo-in, won by a very slim margin. The battle in the states will be heated.

After a period of quiescence, antiabortion activists have renewed picketing of abortion clinics, in part to bring public attention to the issue and in part at least to discourage individual women from entering the clinics. Large, disruptive demonstrations outside clinics in 1991 and 1992 led to court injunctions and arrests. Antiabortion protesters claimed a violation of their speech rights; the judges claimed to be protecting the business interests of the clinic owners (ironically, a stronger legal basis than the women's right to choose).

In the absence of a strong moral consensus in U.S. society on this issue, any effort to ban abortion could well suffer a fate similar to that of Prohibition in the 1920s. The number of abortions performed would decrease, but many women would seek illegal, "back alley" abortions where no public regulation exists to ensure safety. The social and individual costs would be very high if abortion were driven underground by state criminal statutes. In the prochoice-antiabortion debate, it is important to remember that no one is in favor of abortions. The ultimate solution to this crisis is to develop a comprehensive system of social support for families, family life education, and family planning. That would achieve a dramatic reduction in the number of abortions performed in this country, a goal still far away. In the meantime, the controversy about abortion is bound to continue.

The Right to Vote

The franchise—the right to vote—is the most fundamental instrument of responsive government in a democracy. Citizens to whom it is denied are effectively excluded from the most essential element of the democratic process, the chance to register one's political views and to help to shape the mandate of popular sentiment. Like most political issues, this one is not as simple as it first appears. Voting must take place within a meaningful electoral process. Every person's vote must be a meaningful part of that process. Imagine a system in which everyone gets to vote but only one party's candidate appears on the ballot. Imagine one in which a clearly defined majority opposes and overwhelms the vote of an insular minority. Or envision one in which a minority successfully elects representatives only to have them frozen out of legislative deliberations. There is a lot more to the right to vote than simply being handed a ballot—but it starts with that.

In recounting the history of the right to vote in the United States, we see a gradual and often bitterly contested broadening of the franchise. At the time the Constitution was ratified, all states except Vermont still imposed property or taxpaying qualifications on the franchise. Only in Vermont was there *universal manhood suffrage*, the democratic ideal of the day. Women were not seriously considered as potential voters; nor were slaves. By the 1820s most states had dropped property qualifications for voting, and after 1817 universal (free) male suffrage was a prerequisite for admission to the Union. At that point the United States enjoyed far more democratic suffrage than any other nation, despite the exclusion of more than half the adult population (slaves and women).

Black Americans and the Right to Vote

The Declaration of Independence proclaims that "all men are created equal, that they are endowed by their Creator with certain unalienable Rights, that among these are Life, Liberty and the pursuit of Happiness." This revolutionary statement is cited as proof of the fundamental American commitment to equal opportunity. And yet it was written by a slaveowner (Thomas Jefferson) and adopted by a Continental Congress that refused to take action against the slave trade.

When Africans first arrived at Jamestown, Virginia, in the early 1600s, slavery was almost unknown in English society. Initially, blacks were treated as indentured servants who could earn their freedom. However, this approach eventually yielded to an entrenched system of slavery as the need for cheap labor grew and the belief took hold that "savages" of another race were not entitled to the same protections accorded white people. Judges began to recognize sales and wills specifying complete servitude. Intermarriage between whites and blacks, which had been allowed, was forbidden in many colonies. Step by step, the debasement and dehumanization of blacks became crystallized in law, and the law deepened and strengthened prejudice. Finally, the institution of slavery created a web of powerful economic interests that were dependent on it. It took a bloody civil war to force a change in this situation.

Abolition of slavery and full equality for ex-slaves were the primary goals of the Radical Republicans, who dominated Congress in the late 1860s. By 1876, only eleven years after the end of the Civil War, the Constitution had been permanently altered by the addition of the Thirteenth, Fourteenth, and Fifteenth amendments, which outlawed slavery, made equal protection of the laws a fundamental legal principle, and guaranteed voting rights for ex-slaves. Southern states had to ratify the amendments in order to be readmitted to the Union. During this period the broad protections of the new constitutional provisions were supported by eleven major civil rights acts passed by Congress.

This monumental civil rights achievement, however, did not outlast the immediate postwar period. By the 1880s most of the post–Civil War civil rights laws had been rendered inoperative by Court interpretations and by the unwillingness of either Congress or the executive branch to enforce them. It required several generations of constant struggle to alter the patterns of legal segregation established in the late nineteenth and early twentieth centuries.

Black political empowerment in the twentieth century advanced along a deliberate path defined by organizations like the National Association for the Advancement of colored People (NAACP) and depending heavily on the natural organizational strength of black churches and community groups. The NAACP chose a legal strategy, engaging the federal courts to accomplish what was impossible in the majoritarian-sensitive "political branches" of the federal government. Because the Civil War and the legacy of slavery had starkly regionalized the country on issues of race, little help could be expected from state governments—especially those in the South, where black political disfranchisement was most obvious and most severe.

The first efforts were aimed at opening up educational opportunities—a story reserved for Chapter 6. In the late 1950s and early 1960s, having secured a string of educational desegregation decisions from the Supreme Court but not having much real progress to show for it, the civil rights movement began to use the tools of mass protest. The objectives centered directly on political participation, a goal that could unit both integrationists (who sought to join blacks into mainstream society) and nationalists (who sought the empowerment of a distinct black community). Since the collapse of reconstruction, southern states had adopted a variety of mechanisms designed to prevent blacks from registering to vote or to keep black votes from counting. Literacy tests and poll taxes, ostensibly race-neutral, were administered to thwart black voters. Cynical exceptions like the **grandfather clause** were devised to admit illiterate whites to polling booths. In areas where one-party dominance made the party primary the only real election, exclusive **white primaries** were defended by the fiction that political parties were private affairs, not a regular part of the state's electoral machinery.

Some of these mechanisms, like the white primary, were defeated by judicial decision. Others required federal constitutional or statutory correction—and that meant getting past a powerful southern delegation in Congress. Success ultimately depended on the confluence of very disparate factors: the effectiveness (and threat) of mass protests in the streets; the powerful reasoning and charisma of leaders like Malcolm X and Martin Luther King, Jr.; the assassination of John Kennedy and Lyndon Johnson's legislative mastery harnessed to his drive to confound liberal skepticism of a southern politician; and the blood of activists and innocents. In 1965, King led a dramatic march from Selma, Alabama, to the state capitol in Montgomery to challenge the laws that restricted black political participation. Television captured scenes of Alabama state police attacking marchers who tried to cross the E. Petis Bridge in Selma. Such scenes stunned the country. All of this and more motivated a set of legislative acts designed to eliminate the front-line barriers to black political participation.

The most important of these was the Voting Rights Act of 1965, outlawing any voting qualification or prerequisite to voting based on race or color. These provisions applied to all jurisdictions in which fewer than half the persons of voting age were registered to vote or voted in November 1964 (a qualification that applied to Alabama, Georgia, Louisiana, Mississippi, South Carolina, Virginia, Alaska, thirty-four counties in North Carolina, and one county each in Maine, Arizona, and Idaho). In these states, any changes in electoral laws or districting required approval by the federal district court in the District of Columbia or by the U.S. attorney general. More positively, the Voting Rights Act provided for federal voting examiners to register voters where the attorney general deemed it necessary. With this act, the major front-line barriers to black political participation were abolished. Two years after passage of the act, black registration in the South had increased by more than 1,280,000. The percentage of black Americans registered to vote jumped from 33 percent in 1964 to 59 percent in 1972. Black electoral success in local and then in state and congressional elections came in time. But the battle was not over.

The Voting Rights Act had anticipated the possibility that electoral district lines could be drawn to minimize black voting strength and had provided for challenging such "voting dilution" in federal district courts. In at-large voting, for example, where two or more officials are elected from a single district, a cohesive majority (whites voting for whites) can effectively freeze out all black candidates. Alternately, a concentration of black voters can be divided into ineffective fragments in each of several single-member districts. But what standards would judges apply in determining the presence of invidious voting dilution? And what remedies are available? Would the demonstration of discriminatory intent on the part of the people drawing the lines be required? Or would it be enough to show results—that black candidates were consistently defeated?

In 1980 the Supreme Court found that at-large voting was not necessarily discriminatory,[49] and two years later it ruled that intent is necessary to prove invidious vote dilution.[50] Such proof is inevitably much harder to obtain, and thus the Court's decision signaled fewer successful challenges. The intent standard also fails to account for institutional patterns that disadvantage minorities whether or not there is an intent to discriminate. In its 1982 extension of the Voting Rights Act, Congress responded to the intent standard by prescribing that judges should look at "the totality of circumstances"—the process and the results—to determine the presence of a "meaningful vote." Although nudging judicial decision makers away from the intent standard per se, this new statutory language did not provide a clear standard for consistent judicial evaluation of individual voting schemes.

By 1986 the Supreme Court was acknowledging acceptance of a simple standard to judge invidious voting dilution: proportional black electoral success.[51] In a district with a 40 percent black population, a 30 to 50 percent black share of elected officials is sufficient to defeat voting dilution challenges. Proponents argue that electoral success is by definition the best standard to judge elections. Critics charge that this standard is doubly flawed: Electoral schemes may encourage the success of black candidates who are not "authentic representatives" of the black population, and even authentic representatives can be frozen out of the legislative process, in which case black electoral success still becomes a dead end for effective black political participation.[52] The continuing controversy demonstrates one clear fact: Maintaining genuine democracy in a diverse and fragmented population is no simple matter.

CONCLUSIONS

Looking back over U.S. history, we can take pride in this country's increasing protection of civil liberties and its expanding franchise. The basic institutions of government are now more responsive to women than they were seventy-five years ago. Black citizens have much greater access to political participation than they had just forty years ago. Civil liberties rest on a more secure, uniform, national standard than they did when this century began.

Our history shows, however, that progress, tolerance, and civility were accompanied by repression, neglect, and the erosion of liberty in our past. That history should teach us the constant need to reassess civil liberties and the instruments of political participation. Twentieth-century democrats cannot view civil liberties and responsive government in the manner of eighteenth-century liberals. New conceptions of liberty and participation inevitably spark new controversies and disputes.

Overall, the United States of the 1990s is a freer country than it has ever been—a nation more attentive to the civil liberties of its citizens. However, some U.S. citizens still suffer the deprivation of true liberty, out of neglect, harassment, or the inability to put liberty to use. When this happens, true democrats believe that their own liberty has lost some of its meaning.

GLOSSARY TERMS

Bill of Rights
clear and present danger
due process clause
equal protection clause
establishment clause
First Amendment
Fourteenth Amendment
free exercise clause

grandfather clause
habeas corpus
Lemon test
libel
Miranda v. *Arizona*
prior restraint
white primaries

NOTES

[1] Peters 243.
[2] 16 Wallace 36.
[3] 268 U.S. 652.
[4] John Stuart Mill, *On Liberty* (New York: Crofts, 1947); and John Milton, *Aeropagitica*. ed. John Hales (London: Oxford University Press, 1961).
[5] Alexander Meiklejohn, *Free Speech in Relation to Self-government* (New York: Harper & Row, 1948), and *Political Freedom* (New York: Oxford University Press, 1965).
[6] H. Pollack and A. B. Smith, *Civil Liberties and Civil Rights in the United States* (St. Paul, Minn.: West, 1978).
[7] 249 U.S. 47; 250 U.S. 616; 268 U.S. 652.
[8] 341 U.S. 494.
[9] 354 U.S. 298.
[10] 364 U.S. 479.
[11] 391 U.S. 308.
[12] 391 U.S. 367.
[13] 393 U.S. 503.

PART ONE • FOUNDATIONS

[14] 315 U.S. 568.
[15] 405 U.S. 518.
[16] 432 U.S. 43.
[17] 109 S.Ct. 2533.
[18] 110 S.Ct. 2404.
[19] 283 U.S. 697.
[20] 448 U.S. 555.
[21] 376 U.S. 254.
[22] 485 U.S. 46.
[23] 370 U.S. 421.
[24] 472 U.S. 38.
[25] 397 U.S. 664.
[26] 461 U.S. 574.
[27] 403 U.S. 602.
[28] 13 Wall 679.
[29] 98 U.S. 145.
[30] 310 U.S. 586.
[31] 319 U.S. 624.
[32] 380 U.S. 163.
[33] 398 U.S. 333.
[34] 372 U.S. 335.
[35] 384 U.S. 436.
[36] 479 U.S. 564.
[37] *Wainwright* v. *Greenfield*, U.S. (1986).
[38] *Maine* v. *Moulton* 474 U.S. 159 (1985).
[39] 481 U.S. 520.
[40] 110 S.Ct. 1640.
[41] David Bruck and Leslie Harris, "Habeas Corpse," *New Republic*, July 15, 1991, p. 10.
[42] 410 U.S. 113.
[43] 448 U.S. 297.
[44] 111 S.Ct. 1759 (1991).
[45] 428 U.S. 552.
[46] *Ohio* v. *Akron Center for Reproductive Health* (1990), 110 S.Ct. 2972.
[47] 476 U.S. 747.
[48] 492 U.S. 490.
[49] *Mobile* v. *Bolden* (1980), 446 U.S. 55.
[50] *Rogers* v. *Lodge* (1982), 458 U.S. 613.
[51] *Thornburg* v. *Gingles* (1986), 478 U.S. 30.
[52] See Lani Guinier, "The Triumph of Tokenism: The Voting Rights Act and the Theory of Black Electoral Success, *Michigan Law Review*, March 1991, pp. 1077–1154.

SELECTED READINGS

There are many good **introductory texts** on constitutional law that offer a fairly comprehensive treatment of civil liberties issues. Susan M. Leeson and James C. Foster, *Constitutional Law: Cases in Context* (New York: St. Martin's Press, 1992), provides good contextual background.

For recent work on general **civil rights theory**, see Armstead L. Robinson and Patricia Sullivan, eds., *New Directions in Civil Rights Studies* (Charlottesville: University Press of Virginia, 1991); and Ellen Frankel Paul, Fred D. Miller, Jr., and Jeffrey Paul, eds., *Reassessing Civil Rights* (Oxford: Blackwell, 1991).

For **historical essays** on civil rights under the U.S. Constitution, see Robert A. Licht, ed., *The Framers and Fundamental Rights* (Washington, D.C.: American Enterprise Institute, 1991); Helen E. Viet, Kenneth R. Bowling, and Charlene Bangs Bickford, eds., *Creating the Bill of Rights: The Documentary Record from the First Federal Congress* (Baltimore: Johns Hopkins University Press, 1991).

For further reading on **free speech** issues, see R. George Wright, *The Future of Free Speech Law* (New York: Quorum Books, 1990); Donna A. Demac, *Liberty Denied: The Current Rise of Censorship in America*, rev. ed. (New Brunswick, N.J.: Rutgers University Press, 1990).

On **freedom of the press**, consult Lee C. Bollinger, *Images of a Free Press* (Chicago: University of Chicago Press, 1991); and Philip S. Cook, ed., *Liberty of Expression* (Washington, D.C.: Wilson Center Press, 1990).

Freedom of religion is the subject of the essays in James Davison Hunter and Os Guinness, eds., *Articles of Faith, Articles of Peace: The Religious Liberty Clauses and the American Public Philosophy* (Washington, D.C.: Brookings Institution, 1991). See also Derek Davis, *Original Intent: Chief Justice Rehnquist and the Course of American Church-State Relations* (Buffalo: Prometheus Books, 1991).

On the **rights of the accused**, see Leonard W. Levy, Kenneth L. Karst, and Dennis J. Mahoney, eds., *Criminal Justice and the Supreme Court: Selections from the American Constitution* (New York: Macmillan, 1990). For a comparative case study on these issues, see the following books: Robert Y. Thornton, *Preventing Crime in America and Japan: A Comparative Study* (Armonk, N.Y.: Sharpe, 1992); and A. Didrick Castberg, *Japanese Criminal Justice* (New York: Praeger, 1990); and Keith D. Ewing and C. A. Gearty, *Freedom under Thatcher: Civil Liberties in Modern Britain* (New York: Oxford University Press, 1990).

Consider finding out more about some of the **people** involved in civil liberties issues in W. Wat. Hopkins, *Mr. Justice Brennan and the Freedom of Expression* (New York: Praeger, 1991); Martin Luther King, Jr., Papers Project, *A Guide to Research on Martin Luther King, Jr., and the Modern Black Freedom Struggle* (Stanford, Calif.: Stanford University Libraries, 1989).

On **abortion**, see Peter S. Wenz, *Abortion Rights as Religious Freedom* (Philadelphia: Temple University Press, 1992).

FREEDOM WON'T WAIT!!!
NO JUSTICE NO PEACE
The fight continue
freedom won't wai
how long will it ta
before we see the
"NO JUSTICE NO P
TITLE: FREEDOM WON'T
ARTIST: NONI OLABISI
ASSISTANTS: ORONDE S
DELROY SINCLAIR, RENE
ANGELO MICHEAL
ORED BY THE SOCIAL AND P
SOURCE CENTER AND MADE
GH A CONTRACT WITH THE
DEPARTMENT, CITY OF LOS
ALS UNLIMITED· NEIGHBC
392. (310) 822-9560

CHAPTER SIX

CHAPTER OUTLINE

Treatment as Equals

Equality and African-Americans
SCHOOL DESEGREGATION

AFFIRMATIVE ACTION, SET-ASIDES, AND QUOTAS

BLACK AMERICANS AND ECONOMIC PROGRESS

Civil Rights and Women
GOVERNMENT ACTIONS ON GENDER DISCRIMINATION

Equal Treatment for Gay Men and Lesbians

Rights of the Disabled

Basic Social Rights
PURE FOOD AND DRUGS

TRADE UNIONS AND COLLECTIVE BARGAINING

Government Repression

CIVIL RIGHTS

The Meanings of Equality

THE WARE SCHOOL IN AUGUSTA WAS THE ONLY PUBLIC BLACK high school in Georgia during the nineteenth century. The Reconstruction era legislation that allowed Richmond County to establish schools and levy taxes for their support stipulated that the County Board of Education "would provide the same facilities for white and Negro children, the same length of term and the same level of teaching."[1] By 1876 a county-supported high school was available for white girls, another one for white boys. In 1880 a black high school was created, named after Edmund Asa Ware, an officer of the Freedman's Bureau and president of Atlanta University. Richard Wright, valedictorian of the first graduating class from Atlanta University, was persuaded to become the Ware School's first principal. The school was an immediate success. At Ware's fourth graduation the mayor of Augusta presided and the school board president assured Professor Wright that his school had met all expectations.

But the Ware School was just one leaf caught in the changing tide of southern race relations. In 1897, Ware was closed. Three private black high schools (with tuition rates comparable to the public school)* had produced declining enroll-

---

*Reflecting the undeveloped state of public education in the nineteenth century and the opinion of some people that publicly supported high school education (white and black) was frivolous, tuition ($15 for whites, $10 for blacks) replaced tax revenue for the direct operating costs of the three public high schools.

ments at Ware. Richmond County experienced a shortage of primary school space for black children. The school board argued that Ware's building could be used to provide primary education for five times as many children as were currently enrolled in the black high school. The economy was bad; the board promised that when times got better, the school would reopen. The two white high schools were unaffected.

One hundred and fifty citizens filed suit. Since the school board was under no obligation to offer public high school at all, the plaintiffs argued a violation of equal protection under the Fourteenth Amendment. If the board could not afford a black high school, it should not pay for white high schools either. Superior Court Judge Enoch Calloway agreed. The Georgia Supreme Court reversed Calloway and sided with the board. When the U.S. Supreme Court upheld the state supreme court, the Ware School case provided official sanction for the ensuing half-century of segregated public education in the South.[2]

> We cannot say that this action by the state court was, within the meaning of the Fourteenth Amendment, a denial by the state to the plaintiffs . . . of the equal protection of the laws or of any privileges belonging to them as citizens of the United States. We may add that . . . the education of the people in schools maintained by state taxation is a matter belonging to the respective states, and any interference on the part of the Federal authority with the management of such schools cannot be justified except in the case of a clear and unmistakable disregard of rights secured by the supreme law of the land. We have here no such case to be determined.

The Supreme Court's finding of no "clear and unmistakable disregard of rights secured by the supreme law of the land" in the death of the Ware School (it never reopened) left state and local officials free to maintain separate and grossly unequal segregated school systems.

The bitter irony of the Ware School case is that the words quoted were penned by John Marshall Harlan, who only three years earlier in *Plessy* v. *Ferguson*, had written a stinging dissent calling for a "colorblind Constitution."[3] Looking back from the end of the twentieth century, we can declare that blindness did afflict the Richmond County School Board in closing Ware while leaving the white schools open. A signal lack of vision, sprung from common cultural and political assumptions of the time, caused the U.S. Supreme Court to uphold that decision. Prevailing opinion and racial prejudice rendered the Constitution blind not to color but to justice.

But using that kind of hindsight to judge public policies from a century ago is easy. A textbook on American democracy would not be worth its salt if it treated civil rights as matters of straightforward moral choices. It is no easier for us now to see beyond our socialized predilections than it was for John Harlan to see beyond his in 1899. The difficult part is to look at arguments about civil rights *today*, to pierce contemporary clouds of contentiousness, confusion, and hypocrisy to advance human dignity and freedom in our everyday lives.

"We hold these truths to be self-evident, that all men are created equal." The Declaration of Independence boldly asserts a principle at the very heart of our national consciousness. Proper respect for human dignity requires an equal respect for all humans, no matter what their rank or station in life. The gradual but dramatic expansion of the franchise in the United States covered in chapter 5 is based on the notion that on one level at least, all citizens are, by rights, equal participants in American politics. In 1962 and 1964 the Supreme Court produced a set of reapportionment decisions for congressional districts and state legislatures based on the principle of "one person, one vote." A county of four thousand people could not fairly have the same representation in the legislature as a county of forty thousand people. Every citizen's vote in the political process should be equal.[4]

In mathematics, equality is a straightforward concept. In the reapportionment cases, the Supreme Court determined that as far as voting was concerned, political equality was fairly straightforward as well. Representation in legislative districts should be based on equal numbers of voters for each representative. Though the Court did not (and could not realistically) demand mathematical precision in drawing district lines, the standard allowed for only a tiny variance from mathematical equality for district populations. The reapportionment decisions were hugely controversial, for two reasons: They had the potential to upset existing partisan balances in state legislatures and Congress, and the simple, reasonable, attractive principle of one person, one vote had been explicitly *rejected* by the framers when they established a Senate with equal representation for *states*, not people. If unit representation was good enough for states under the U.S. Constitution, why couldn't states apply it to their own subdivisions?

A philosophical principle at least as ancient as Aristotle says that fairness demands that one treat equals equally *and unequals unequally*. Now the question becomes, as citizens, in what ways are we equal and in what ways are we naturally and properly unequal? Let's go back to the Declaration of Independence. "We hold these truths to be self-evident, that all men are created equal, and that they are endowed by their Creator with certain unalienable rights, that among these are Life, Liberty and the pursuit of Happiness." No matter how complete an original state of equality, give people the liberty to pursue their own happiness and before long, *inevitably*, significant inequality will arise. Is this wrong? Not necessarily. But it does point to another core value in the American political culture: achievement. To be free to achieve and to be *rewarded* for achievement is as important to Americans as equality is. In everything from cheerleader tryouts to astute stock portfolio management, we believe that achievement deserves to be recognized and rewarded. The freedom to achieve and to be rewarded *unequally* for achievement is a contradictory, competing value to equality. How do we choose between conflicting values?

A citizen's civil rights are, in effect, guarantees that he or she will be treated *fairly* and *equally* by government and by the segments of society that must meet the same standards. In eighteenth-century America, with limited government and a fairly simple economy, civil rights did not amount to much. The Fifth Amendment guarantees that no person will "be deprived of life, liberty, or property, without due process of law," an old common law notion that covers a broad range of issues of government treatment of individuals. But it wasn't until the Fourteenth Amendment was added in the middle of the nineteenth century that the Constitution even mentioned **equal protection of**

the laws. As the federal government became heavily engaged in providing education and economic opportunity for citizens, questions arose about the proper role of government in ensuring equality and fairness in rewarding achievement. In this chapter we examine education and economic opportunity and the treatment of blacks and women. We will explore the notion of affirmative action and the problem of quotas. We will look at efforts to protect the civil rights of gay and lesbian Americans and the move to provide disabled persons with greater access to participation. The chapter concludes with a look at the notion of social rights and provides two examples of this twentieth-century expansion of our understanding of rights: the provision of pure foods and drugs and the regulation of worker unions. It is impossible to discuss civil rights without probing the government's part in social control. Some of the most prominent controversies in this area are covered in Chapter 20: privacy and expression issues (obscenity, pornography, public arts funding), crime and punishment (especially the problems of drugs), safe workplace protections, and mandatory testing (for drugs and for AIDS).

Treatment as Equals

In considering matters of equality in a democracy, a clear distinction should be drawn between "equal treatment" and "**treatment as equals**." Ronald Dworkin explains this difference in a story about a parent with two children. One child is desperately ill and will die if not given adequate medication. The other child is only slightly ill and will almost certainly recover even without medicine. If the parent has only one dose of medicine, it would be cruelly wrong to treat the children equally, dividing the single dose of medicine between the two. Such treatment would likely result in the death of one child. The parent should treat the children *as equals*, meaning with an equal respect for each child's health, even though that means giving one child all the medicine and the other child none.[5] Similarly, democratic governments should treat people as equals even when that sometimes means (as it inevitably will) treating them differently.

Our government has always recognized distinctions that require different treatment of certain citizens. Those differences in treatment have been more or less controversial, depending on the circumstances and the political climate of the time. Some of the policies that treated persons differently in the past have come to be discredited—slavery and segregation of public facilities are painful examples. Some policies that treat different groups differently are maintained currently, as in the Selective Service system (now conducting registration for a draft but not a draft itself), which applies to young men but not to young women. The Supreme Court has recognized the principle of unequal treatment and has thrown its weight behind specific policies that treat groups differently. In 1981, in the case *Michael M.* v. *Superior Court of Sonoma County*, the Supreme Court upheld a California statutory rape law even though the criminal penalties of that law could only apply to males.[6] Justice William Rehnquist concluded that in this instance, a "criminal sanction imposed solely on males . . . serves to 'equalize' the deterrents" to engage in intercourse. The general principle underlying this ruling is that there are times when treatment as equals requires something other than strictly equal treatment. The fascinating and troubling task is to decide when all persons, given equal respect, should be treated the same and when they should be treated differently.

Equality and African-Americans

Moving from the stultifying legacy of slavery toward equal treatment and full participation for blacks in America has proved to be this country's single largest political challenge. In Chapter 5 we looked at the struggle for black suffrage. Here we will look at the battle to gain full access to public education; at affirmative action, set-asides, and quotas; and at continuing disparities in black economic participation.

School Desegregation

As mentioned earlier, in *Plessy* v. *Ferguson* (1896), the Supreme Court sanctioned as constitutional the establishment of "separate but equal" facilities for whites and blacks. The pernicious effects of this doctrine were especially evident in the creation throughout the South of rigidly separate and decidedly unequal school systems for blacks and whites. After years of determined litigation spearheaded by lawyers for the National Association for the Advancement of Colored People (NAACP), the Supreme Court in the 1930s began to recognize that segregation in education denied blacks basic civil rights. A first step in this direction came in the case of *Missouri ex rel. Gaines* v. *Canada* (1938).[7] Lloyd Gaines, a citizen of Missouri and a black graduate of Lincoln University, had applied for admission to the all-white law school of the University of Missouri. Rather than admit Gaines to the state law school, Missouri offered to pay his tuition at any other law school that would admit blacks. Gaines refused to accept this compromise and took his case to court. The Supreme Court held that Gaines was "entitled to be admitted to the law school of the state university in the absence of other and proper provision for his legal training within the state."

The Court went beyond the *Gaines* decision in *Sweatt* v. *Painter* (1950), in which the justices rejected Texas's contention that its new law school for blacks provided the same educational opportunities as those at the University of Texas.[8] In this decision, the Court argued that by segregating black students from whites, the state was denying blacks the interactions essential to a successful law career. This came close to saying that such segregated education could never in fact be "equal."

The decisions handed down in *Gaines* and *Sweatt* permitted the NAACP to challenge the whole structure of educational segregation. After the Supreme Court accepted school segregation cases for review in 1952, the U.S. Justice Department en-

It took Federal troops dispatched by President Dwight D. Eisenhower to ensure the integration of the schools in Little Rock, Arkansas, in 1957. The Little Rock crisis was one of many as school desegregation was met with intense resistance. *(UPI/Bettmann Newsphotos)*

tered the fray on the side of those arguing that segregated schools were unconstitutional. Then, in 1954, after a long delay and extremely careful consideration, the Supreme Court unanimously ruled that segregated schools were unconstitutional in **Brown v. Board of Education of Topeka**.[9]

The *Brown* case signaled a decisive change in the U.S. legal system's approach to the issue of segregation. In the decades following *Plessy*, the Supreme Court had applied increasingly strict standards to the "separate but equal" doctrine but had not questioned the constitutionality of segregation itself. Blacks were granted relief not because they were segregated but because they were denied equality in a segregated system. In the set of cases from which the landmark *Brown* decision derived, however, the facts showed that in all the school districts involved, "the Negro and white schools . . . have been equalized, or are being equalized." In *Brown*, therefore, the Court chose to face the issue of school segregation itself.

The substance of the Court's unanimous ruling in *Brown* was that segregated education *in itself* deprives black children of equal educational opportunities. In a famous footnote to the *Brown* opinion, the Court cited psychological evidence that black children suffered from a loss of self-esteem and viewed being black as inferior to being white. This sense of inferiority, the Court argued, interfered with the black child's motivation to learn and retarded educational and mental development.

Despite the historic *Brown* decision's call for the desegregation of public schools, only about one in every hundred black children in the South attended a desegregated school a decade later. During most of that period, the president and Congress could not decide how to implement desegregation, leaving the matter to the courts. Using the appealing rhetorical banner of "freedom of choice," the courts developed a legal doctrine that put the full burden of desegregation on black families, who could challenge the racial status quo only by choosing to enroll their children in predominantly white schools, entering into long and difficult litigation, and accepting all the risks their actions entailed. This system clearly inhibited desegregation.

Finally, at the urging of President Lyndon Johnson, Congress passed the **Civil Rights Act of 1964**, which gave the attorney general the power to file desegregation lawsuits and prohibited federal aid to school districts that remained segregated. For the first time, the government placed the full force of the federal bureaucracy behind desegregation. The Department of Health, Education and Welfare (HEW)—since 1979 broken into two cabinet departments, Education and Health and Human Services—was charged with creating a single set of national standards and setting up a procedure for forcing school districts to desegregate *before* they received any federal assistance. School districts that refused to comply would not only lose needed funds but would also face the threat of litigation by the Justice Department or by civil rights groups.

President Johnson and his ranking officials committed themselves to enforcing the law. During the first year of enforcement, more school districts were desegregated than during the entire preceding decade. All but a handful of southern school districts agreed to implement desegregation plans. In the Deep South, where absolute resistance had been the rule, freedom-of-choice plans with token integration became the norm.

The Supreme Court lent the desegregation movement moral force in 1968 in Virginia, in the case of *Green* v. *School Board of New Kent County*.[10] Local authorities, the Court held, must "take whatever steps might be necessary to convert to a unitary system in which racial discrimination would be eliminated root and branch." Unless freedom of choice led to comprehensive integration in a particular community, it was not constitutionally acceptable.

The courts, HEW, and the Justice Department had finally begun to work together. HEW handled most of the massive administrative and political problems involved in desegregation. The courts upheld HEW standards and moved to settle unresolved issues in school desegregation law. The Justice Department threatened districts attempting to defy HEW and prompted the courts to develop new legal principles, which took hold rapidly in the South.

DE FACTO VERSUS DE JURE SEGREGATION   While the schools of the South were undergoing a period of drastic change, however, schools in the rest of the nation were becoming more segregated than ever. In the North, people maintained that segregation in their schools was different from that found in the South—it was not imposed by state or local officials but rather was the unplanned result of having children attend neighborhood schools where intense housing segregation was the rule. Northerners

PART ONE • FOUNDATIONS

distinguished their **de facto** ("in fact") **segregation** from the southern variety of **de jure** ("under law") **segregation**.

Because the constitutional guarantee of equal protection of the laws applies only to officially imposed segregation, it seemed that nothing much could be done about de facto segregation. For a decade and a half the courts accepted this distinction and required no significant urban desegregation outside the South.

BUSING   In *Swann* v. *Charlotte-Mecklenburg Board of Education* (1971), the Supreme Court finally faced the question of busing.[11] As long as whole neighborhoods were segregated, schools could be integrated only by getting students out of their neighborhoods. The most straightforward means was busing children from one neighborhood to another to attend school. Since *Brown* had left implementation up to local federal district courts, a variety of schemes had been tried. Mecklenburg County had a single school district that encompassed both Charlotte—a sizable city—and the suburban and rural areas surrounding it. Under district court orders, the Charlotte-Mecklenburg school system had an extensive busing plan. Did the Constitution as interpreted in *Brown* and *Green* allow the school district to take race into account to

Hostile reactions to busing occurred in many parts of the country in the mid-1970s, and antibusing sentiment was especially strong in Boston. In this frightening and ironic photo, a demonstrator uses the American flag to stab a black businessman in Boston's City Hall Plaza. The wielder of the flagpole, a 17-year-old, pleaded guilty to assault and battery with a dangerous weapon. *(Stanley J. Forman, Pulitzer Prize, 1977—Title: "The Soiling of Old Glory")*

overcome de facto segregation? Or, as Justice Harlan had claimed seventy-five years earlier, did the Constitution demand colorblind policies (which would leave nonofficial segregation untouched)?

In supporting the district court's busing order, the Supreme Court noted that segregated residential patterns were themselves in part the result of federal, state, and local action. The prior existence of de jure segregation contributed to current de facto segregation. The government's responsibility to provide "equal protection of the law" extended far enough to cover a mandated busing plan to desegregate schools within a single school district. The proposition that the Constitution requires colorblind policy has never persuaded a majority of the Supreme Court.

Once the neighborhood school argument fell in the South, the doctrine was rapidly and successfully attacked in northern cities. Civil rights lawyers found that the history of segregation in northern districts almost always entailed some official involvement in racial separation, through such factors as zoning and school site decisions, real estate deals, and residential convenants. Federal judges across the country took the Court's strong action in *Swann* as a mandate for rapid, comprehensive desegregation and soon began handing down decisions requiring extensive transportation of pupils in a number of northern cities.

Local reaction to school busing orders was intense. Angry protesters filling television screens were as likely to speak in the accents of Michigan, Boston, or southern California as Louisiana or Texas. As political criticism grew, President Richard Nixon announced in August 1971 that HEW and the Justice Department would do everything possible to curtail busing and that officials who disobeyed this directive would be summarily dismissed. The Nixon administration then took the extraordinary step of formally asking that its own desegregation proposals be *disregarded* by the courts. Coming just weeks before schools opened, the president's new position provoked further confusion and resistance.

Opposition to school busing by a majority of Americans intensified when several federal district courts ordered that students be transferred across city-suburban lines, if necessary, to achieve integration. The judges felt compelled to prescribe this remedy because the schools in several of the nation's largest cities—including New York, Chicago, Detroit, Atlanta, Baltimore, Cleveland, Houston, and Richmond—already had such large enrollments of minorities that integration within the cities' school systems seemed impossible. Adding to this problem was the growing tendency of white families to move from cities to suburbs to avoid forced busing—a phenomenon known as *white flight*. These families were vehemently opposed to busing their children back into city schools.

Antibusing sentiment had a profound effect on Congress. Unlike many other matters, legislators' votes on racial issues tend to reflect their constituents' attitudes. Race is such an emotional matter in U.S. society that when public attitudes are mobilized at the local level, members of Congress often feel that their political survival depends on going along with the dominant mood.[12] When asked about "busing of Negro and white schoolchildren from one school district to another" in a 1971 Gallup poll, 82 percent of the respondents opposed it or had no opinion, whereas only 18 percent supported it. Surveys taken among educators showed that three-fourths of school superintendents and teachers were opposed to busing.

The busing controversy raised basic questions about government's ability to sustain civil rights law in the face of a hostile majority. The historical evidence strongly suggests that when the hostile majority remains actively opposed and the issue continues to dominate politics, the courts tend to pull back. Restraints on judicial action can come from within the court system, from new members appointed to the courts, from judicial acceptance of some form of congressional restriction, or from a constitutional amendment.

In *Millikan* v. *Bradley* (1974), the Supreme Court established standards that would make mandated integration between separate school systems in city and suburbs quite unlikely.[13] The Court was signaling the limits of judicially enforced integration. At the same time, the prospects for statutory or constitutional action to limit or prevent school busing diminished considerably. Efforts to pass antibusing legislation failed in the House in 1979. Busing fell off the front page.

BEYOND BUSING   Lacking strong leadership from the federal government, school desegregation in most areas of the nation has been put on the back burner since the early 1980s. *Magnet schools* have been used to overcome de facto segregation in some school districts. A school district puts extra resources into special programs (in the arts, for example, or the physical and biological sciences) at particular schools to create a "magnet" so that parents from all over the district will want to send their kids to that school. In 1990 a closely split Supreme Court upheld a federal district court's order requiring the Kansas City, Missouri, school board to raise taxes to pay for an extensive magnet school program.[14] When successful, magnet schools can achieve desegregation even though neighborhoods in the district remain sharply segregated. Such programs have experienced only limited success, sometimes creating an internal segregation between the special courses and the regular curriculum. And of course magnet schools do not break down the segregation between urban and suburban school districts. Furthermore, special programs are expensive and are especially vulnerable to cutbacks when local school districts become financially strapped.

A more systematic challenge to school desegregation has arisen recently in the form of school vouchers and intentionally segregated schools designed to serve black males, for example. **Voucher systems**, in which parents of school children are given credits that can be taken to public *or private* schools to cover tuition, were implemented on the assumption that public education could be forced to improve if placed in direct competition with private alternatives. In some urban areas with voucher systems, specialized "African-American experience" programs have been created to meet the particular educational challenges of black urban youth. The argument for these schools is patterned after arguments in favor of traditionally black colleges and women's colleges: to create a supportive segregated experience sensitive to the special circumstances of a particular subset of society. These segregated programs are chosen by black parents on the basis of perceived advantages for their children.

How are we to evaluate arguments that turn existing debates upside down? In matters like church and state, at least, the federal courts have recognized a distinction between primary and secondary education, on the one hand, and higher education, on the other. Schoolchildren are more vulnerable to negative socialization experiences. So accepting an argument for a traditionally black state college or a women's college does not necessarily justify segregated high schools and grade schools. But the segregated school systems against which *Brown* was directed did not offer parents and children a choice; the new voucher schools ostensibly do. Opponents of vouchers foresee the further weakening of mainstream public schools as resources are drawn away by alternatives. According to these critics, as school offerings splinter, genuine choice disappears—especially for children whose parents do not take an assertive interest in their education. The very terms of the debate about ethnic identity and education are once more open to question. The integration-segregation continuum has been dissolved by fundamental questions about group identity in a democracy.

Affirmative Action, Set-Asides, and Quotas

Again we ask, exactly what does *equality* mean? Does it mean that the door of opportunity be cleared of all legal barriers or that the people who actually pass through that door represent a true ethnic and gender cross section of the population? Does it mean simply that more African-Americans, for example, enter the middle class or become business executives and government officials or that blacks as a group achieve real economic parity with whites? Is equal opportunity a *legal* concept, measured by inputs (laws, policies, etc.), or a *social* concept, measured by outputs (social and economic results)?

Affirmative action entails positive steps taken to increase the number of women, blacks, and other minorities in educational and economic opportunities. Affirmative action covers a spectrum of activity, from taking special steps to recruit participants from underrepresented groups at one end to establishing participation quotas at the other. Lyndon Johnson first required the federal government to take affirmative action in executive order 11246, issued after the passage of the 1964 Civil Rights Act.

We will look first at the case in which Justice Lewis Powell provided a basic framework for considering these issues and at subsequent treatment of affirmative action. The issue of government set-asides (requirements that a certain proportion of government contract expenditures be given to minority groups) comes next. We conclude with a discussion of the use of quotas as a rhetorical political strategy.

THE BAKKE CASE   At age thirty-one, Allan Paul Bakke became interested in pursuing a career in medicine and determinedly set out to receive training as a physician. In his initial attempts to gain admission to medical school, he was rejected by both the University of Southern California and Northwestern University—by the latter chiefly because of his age. The following year he sought entry into eleven medical schools, none of which admitted him. One of these schools was the University of California at Davis, which had a special admissions program for students who were well qualified for medical school but who would not have been admitted through the regular competitive admissions procedures. Almost all special admissions applicants were minority students. Of the one hundred places at the Davis medical school, sixteen were reserved for special admissions. When Bakke applied yet again and was again turned down despite scoring higher on his admission exams than some minority applicants who were accepted, he sought legal redress. In a lawsuit filed in state courts, he charged that he had been the victim of discrimination, in that the affirmative action program of the Davis medical school had unfairly reduced the number of places available for more qualified students. Bakke's main purpose in bringing the suit was not so much to challenge racial quotas in general as to get himself into medical school.

When the California Supreme Court upheld Bakke's position, the state appealed the case to the U.S. Supreme Court. The case involved a serious conflict between two apparently worthy goals: affirmative action to aid disadvantaged groups and equal treatment for all, regardless of race, ethnicity, or gender. At the same time, law and medical schools were facing mounting pressure to admit minorities: In 1970, only 1 percent of American lawyers and only 2 percent of doctors and 6 percent of medical students were black.

The political atmosphere surrounding the Bakke case was notably charged as well. The public was growing increasingly disenchanted with affirmative action programs, on the ground that they led to reverse discrimination. For example, many employers had been required to hire and promote more women and minority group members as a condition for doing business with government agencies. To avoid losing business, employers gave preference in hiring and promotion to applicants on the basis of race and gender—making it correspondingly more difficult for white males, who sometimes raised the claim of reverse discrimination.

The Supreme Court decision in *Regents of the University of California* v. *Bakke*, handed down in the spring of 1978, was marked by a notable lack of unanimity.[15] The Court ruled, 5-4, that Bakke should be admitted to the David medical school. But the Court *really* divided 4-1-4. One block of four justices took the position that the Civil Rights Act of 1964 prohibits racial quotas like those used by the Davis medical school. The other group of four argued that the Davis program was constitutionally valid. The central vote belonged to Justice Lewis Powell, Jr., who spoke for a two-sided majority of five: four colleagues in approving the constitutionality of affirmative action and the other four in rejecting the way in which the medical school had implemented its own affirmative action admissions policy. Bakke was ordered admitted, but affirmtive action was not per se unconstitutional.

In his *Bakke* opinion, Powell finds a legitimate state interest in taking ethnic identity and other personal characteristics into account so that the medical school could attain a "diverse student body" to contribute to "the robust exchange of ideas" (a First Amendment concern). But according to Powell, in reserving "a specified number of seats in each class for the preferred ethnic groups," the medical school misperceived the nature of the state's legitimate interest.

It is not an interest in simple ethnic diversity, in which a specified percentage of the student body is in effect guaranteed to be members of selected ethnic groups, with the remaining percentage of undifferentiated aggregation of students. The diversity that furthers a compelling state interest encompasses a far broader array of qualifications and characteristics of which racial or ethnic origin is but a single though important element. [The medical school's] special admissions program, focused *solely* on ethnic diversity, would hinder rather than further attainment of genuine diversity.

In an appropriate affirmative action program, Powell concluded, "race or ethnic background may be deemed a 'plus' in a particular applicant's file, yet it does not insulate the individual from comparison with all other candidates for the available seats."

Powell's argument in *Bakke* laid the groundwork for constitutional affirmative action without quotas. Ethnic identity and gender, for example, *can* be included in a fair selection process. Fixed percentages for minority representation, however, distort healthy comparisons of competing candidates. Fairness requires flexibility in comparisons. The government's interest in diversity (whether couched in terms of role models, the robust exchange of ideas, or some other principle) always goes beyond numerical quotas. According to this model established by Powell, ethnicity and national origin *can* figure in government policy—they are important features of the social landscape. But the use of such characteristics will engage the courts' "strict scrutiny" to prevent their misuse.

Bakke turned out not to be a legal landmark like *Brown* in 1954. The absence of a clear majority and the subtlety of Powell's argument ensured continued controversy. When is a minority hiring goal flexible enough to meet constitutional standards, and when is it a quota? If affirmative action is being imposed from without—from the federal government to its contractors, for instance—or within any organization from the top down, can compliance be measured without specific expectations? Are those quotas? Assume that a range of acceptable outcomes is defined, say, 30 to 40 percent female participation rate in management positions. What prevents the bottom of the range from becoming a ceiling? Success in reaching the minimum acceptable level triggers reduced response, perhaps even a return to the practices that caused the imbalance originally.

SET-ASIDES   In 1941, Franklin Roosevelt ordered defense contractors to cease discriminatory hiring practices. From that time through the Carter administration, the federal government expanded the use of its own buying power to advance economic opportunity for minority groups and women.* In addition to requiring contractors to implement affirmative action plans (starting in 1965), the federal government began to use **set-asides**. In the 1977 Public Works Employment Act (PWEA), 10 percent of the $4

---

*Women, although a majority in the American population at large, are still a minority (of about 45 percent) in the work force. More important, because of the traditional exclusion of women from political and economic power, women as a group share many of the characteristics of an insular minority (lack of representation, lack of relative mobility, disproportionate exploitation, lack of visibility and representation).

billion in federal funds given to state and local governments would be "set aside" for "minority-controlled businesses." In *Fullilove* v. *Klutznick* (1980), the Supreme Court upheld the PWEA's set-aside.[16] State and local governments followed the federal example, with dramatic results. The city of Atlanta, for instance, increased procurement from minority business enterprises (MBEs) from $42,000 to $43 million. In the decade from 1973 to 1983. By 1989, Atlanta had awarded over $300 million in contracts to minority- and female-owned businesses.[17]

At the federal level, the 1980s were a time of conflicting signals on affirmative action and set-asides. In a ruling that reversed earlier decisions supporting affirmative action arrangements in employment, the Supreme Court found in *Memphis Fire Department* v. *Stotts* (1984) that a court could not order an employer to protect the jobs of recently hired black employees at the expense of whites who had greater seniority.[18] In the majority opinion, Justice Byron White stated that the policy of the Civil Rights Act of 1964 was "to provide make-whole relief only to those who have been actual victims of illegal discrimination." The question is whether an *entire group* is entitled to affirmative action to remedy discrimination without any one member having to prove that he or she was actually discriminated against.

The importance of seniority was reaffirmed by another sharply divided Court in 1986 in *Wygant* v. *Jackson Board of Education*.[19] In this case the Court ruled that laying off more senior white teachers violated the constitutional principle of equal protection. But the Court did agree that carefully constructed affirmative action programs were indeed constitutional.

Back in 1972 a federal district court found that for almost four decades the Alabama Department of Public Safety had systematically excluded blacks from employment as state troopers. The Court imposed a hiring quota and ordered the department to refrain from discriminatory hiring and promotion practices. By 1983 the hiring quota had been frustrated by department actions, and only four blacks had been promoted. Two consent decrees had failed to correct matters. The district court then ordered that one-half of all promotions to the rank of corporal go to blacks if qualified blacks were available. In *United States* v. *Paradise* (1987), the Supreme Court upheld the district court order, in part because the quota was narrowly tailored and operated only as long as qualified blacks were available for promotion.[20] The long history of the Alabama Department of Public Safety's documented discrimination against black applicants and employees no doubt influenced this decision.

In *City of Richmond* v. *Croson* (1989), the Supreme Court struck down a city ordinance with a 30 percent subcontractor set-aside for minority business enterprises.[21] Writing for a plurality, Justice Sandra Day O'Connor was not convinced that the Richmond plan was "narrowly tailored to remedy past discrimination since it is not linked to identified discrimination in any way.... There is no inquiry into whether or not the particular MBE seeking a racial preference has suffered from the effects of past discrimination by the city or prime contractors." *Croson* was seen by some Court observers as the death knell for both set-asides and affirmative action. "Narrow tailoring," requiring each MBE to demonstrate past discrimination against itself, significantly restricts the availability of set-asides. Similarly, requiring proof of specific past discrimination to uphold affirmative action plans would significantly decrease their use.

But a consistent pattern was not yet forthcoming. In *Metro Broadcasting* v. *Federal Communications Commission* (1990), a bare five-person majority upheld the FCC's preferential treatment policies designed to encourage minority ownership of radio and TV stations.[22] Justice William Brennan, writing for the Court, noted that "race-conscious standards adopted by Congress to address racial and ethnic discrimination are subject to a different standard than such classifications prescribed by state and local governments." It was enough that the congressional standards served an important governmental objective ("broadcast diversity") and that they were substantially related to the achievement of that objective.

WHEN IS A QUOTA NOT A QUOTA? Justice Powell's argument against quotas in *Bakke* legitimizes public policy based on significant characteristics like ethnicity by describing obtuse uses of these characteristics that are beyond acceptability. The point is that ethnicity, though sometimes important, is never the sole criterion in deciding policy. A quota short-circuits the consideration of other relevant facts. Sometime during the 1980s the quota issue came to have a life of its own, primarily by standing in for the fundamental disagreement between the legal and social interpretations of equality. Unfortunately, the debate about quotas has also been exploited by some people as an acceptable way to advance a generally discredited racist stance.

The Civil Rights Bill of 1991 offers a good lesson in the complications of civil rights policy in the 1990s. Part of the debate was about the legal versus social definition of equal opportunity. Some of the debate was partisan posturing in anticipation of the 1992 presidential election. To separate the former from the latter, a bit of background is required.

In 1971 the Supreme Court held, in *Griggs* v. *Duke Power Co.*, that job tests that had the effect of screening out blacks violated Title VII of the 1964 Civil Rights Act unless the employer could prove that the test was performance-related.[23] The point of the **disparate impact test** is to get employers to concentrate on results rather than merely procedures in eliminating employment discrimination. Although later qualified, the *Griggs* decision and its disparate impact test produced significant changes in employment practices. According to one commentator, *Griggs* "deserves more credit for integrating America's work place than any other decision."[24] The disparate impact test was turned on its head by the Court in 1989, in *Wards Cove Packing Co.* v. *Antonio*.[25] *Wards Cove* gave the *employee* the burden of proving that employment practices with a disparate impact *did not* have an adequate business justification. Such a shift in the burden of proof, practically speaking, can reduce or even eliminate protection against employment discrimination.

The argument about disparate impact is a variant of the larger argument about society's responsibility in providing equality. Supporters of the disparate impact test

(Text continues on page 210)

COMPARATIVE PERSPECTIVE

GROUP RIGHTS AND THE QUESTION OF *QUEBEC*

According to one mainstream interpretation, the United States Constitution grants rights to *persons*, not groups. Group rights are, from this vantage point, not justified in the language of the Constitution itself, where, for example, the Fourteenth Amendment begins "All *persons* . . . are citizens" and continues, "No state shall . . . abridge the privileges and immunities of *citizens* . . . nor deprive any *person* of life, liberty, or property . . . nor deny to any *person* . . . equal protection of the laws."

But in spite of such provisions, the law *does* treat different groups as groups, as, for instance, when Justice William Rehnquist observed, in upholding California's statutory rape law, "We need not be medical doctors to discern that young men and young women are not similarly situated with respect to the problems and risks of sexual intercourse." That decision, in *Michael M.* v. *Sonoma County Superior Court* (1981), upheld a statute with a strict gender differentiation.* Are cultural and ethnic differences also a legitimate subject for law? On the one hand, there is the difficulty of justifying one group's special treatment over another. On the other hand, ethnic and cultural differences form an important part—in some cases the most important part—of community identity. Our national law has always treated members of Native American tribes differently. Those legal distinctions, however, are historically based on the United States' gradual and imperfect usurpation of the sovereignty of those tribes. Are there other legitimate group rights based on cultural or ethnic differences? Our neighbor to the north has been forced to confront this issue head on, in a challenge to the preservation of the nation itself.

Canada's federal system was designed in 1867 to avoid the "errors" of the United States Constitution, which had recently led to the disastrous Civil War. The Canadian national government was granted "all the great powers of sovereignty," including unqualified power to regulate trade and commerce and to make and enforce criminal law, and (unlike the U.S. national government) broad residual powers over areas not delegated to the provinces. The provincial governments were given "exclusive" power to govern "property and civil rights."

Although the arrangements differed from those at Philadelphia, the Canadian constitution was the result of similar compromises. One side argued that the central government should have power to maintain unity and to protect individual and minority rights within the provinces. The other argued that the provinces should have power to promote collective self-government. This latter was partic-

(Box continues on page 209)

ularly important to Quebec, which was a majority French-speaking province within a majority English-speaking nation. If Quebec is given enough autonomy to protect its distinctive culture from assimilation, has the national government given up its responsibility to protect the English-speaking minority in Quebec? In recent years the century-old compromises have begun to unravel. Serious and increasingly militant talk of Quebec's seceding from the confederation threatens the nation's continued existence.

At the center of current debate, and a stand-in for larger issues, is Quebec's Bill 101, the Charter of the French Language, mandating, among other things, that only French can be used on commercial signs and posters and as company names. In December 1988 the Supreme Court of Canada struck down core sections of the bill as an unacceptable limitation on "commercial expression," which it ruled a "fundamental freedom." According to the court, Bill 101 threatened "an important aspect of individual self-fulfillment and personal autonomy." Quebec responded with a new bill, mandating French-only on outside signs but allowing some use of bilingual signs indoors. To protect this new bill from the Supreme Court, the Quebec National Assembly invoked the "notwithstanding" clause of the Charter of Rights, a clause that "essentially permits provincial legislatures to override certain rights protected by the Charter." This maneuver caused Canadian Prime Minister Brian Mulroney to rail against the constitutional provision, proclaiming that a "constitution that does not protect the inalienable and imprescriptible individual rights of individual Canadians is not worth the paper that it is written on." Although a national crisis was avoided, the underlying issues have not yet been resolved.

In October 1992 constitutional reform designed to preserve the nation while giving Quebec greater autonomy was endorsed by the prime minister and each of the provincial premiers. But voters defeated the measure in six of the ten provinces. Although the current structure is unsatisfactory to many Quebeçois, the shape of acceptable reform has not emerged. What structure of government will best protect the rights of all Canadians? Whatever the outcome, we can only hope that there is more humor than truth to the Canadian quip that Americans are forever looking back to their Civil War, while Canadians are constantly looking ahead to theirs.

*450 U.S. 464.
Sources: Robert C. Vipond, "The Canadian Constitutional Crisis: Who's Right on Rights?" *Intergovernmental Perspectives*, Fall 1991, pp. 49–52; Ronald L. Watts, "Canada's Constitutional Options: An Outline," in *Options for a New Canada*, ed. Ronald L. Watts and Douglas M. Brown (Toronto: University of Toronto Press, 1991).

argue that with an employment screening device that disproportionately excludes blacks, other minorities, or women, the harm is in the exclusion, whether intentional or not. The federal government, they argue, has the authority and the responsibility, under the Fourteenth Amendment and civil rights statutes, to eliminate this harm. Opponents of disparate impact charge that the government's responsibility reaches no further than to eliminate *intentional* discrimination on the basis of ethnic identity or gender. These critics argue that to go further illegitimately interferes with personal and economic freedom and substitutes "group rights" for individual freedom. although based on the Civil Rights Act of 1964, the disparate impact test was a judicial creation, neither endorsed nor repudiated by Congress.

The Civil Rights Bill of 1990 was written in part to overturn *Ward's Cove* and maintain the disparate impact test. The bill returned an increased burden of proof to employers, namely, that any employment screening device must have "a significant relationship to successful performance on the job." President Bush labeled the bill a "quota bill" and vetoed it. The 1991 version of the bill inserted specific language outlawing quotas, but the president's position remained unchanged. Finally a compromise was achieved that allowed the president to sign the Civil Rights Act of 1991 without substantial change. Both sides can be faulted for clouding the issue. Was this a quota bill? No. To avoid litigation and adverse judgments, employers might improperly (and illegally) implement quotas for employment, but as Justice Powell argued in *Bakke*, quotas are not necessary in affirmative action programs. Vulnerability under the disparate impact test can be reduced or eliminated by effective affirmative action. But the 1991 act definitely was an affirmative action bill. The sponsors of the bill, while vociferously repudiating the deadly "quotas" label, seemed reluctant to step out front in support of the bill's affirmative action core. Neither position in the quotas debate advanced public understanding, each preferring short-term political gain to long-term public good.

In spite of the Court's apparent vacillation on affirmative action and set-asides, personnel changes and the distribution of votes on the Court seem to point toward further restriction of race-conscious policies in the future. The quotas debate has made affirmative action a chancy issue in Congress and in presidential politics. Has the time come to move beyond affirmative action and set-asides to colorblind policies where, officially at least, ethnic identity and gender don't matter? Such questions are controversial because they can be answered in two ways. For many opponents of affirmative action, the determination is, "Have we abolished explicit, official policies that discriminate against people on account of their ethnic identity, national origin, or gender?" If so, that is all that the government of a free society can legitimately do. For many supporters of affirmative action, the question is, "Are the residues of racism and sexism in our society so strong as significantly to limit the opportunities available to some people because of their ethnic identity or gender?" If so, further public action is required. These are fundamental questions of politics and policy. To allow you to assess the whole range of issues involved in this debate, we now take a brief look at the economic situation of blacks in America.

Black Americans and Economic Progress

Black Americans have made considerable progress in achieving equal treatment under the law. Yet despite more than two decades of civil rights legislation and despite efforts at affirmative action, millions of blacks continue to lag considerably behind whites, particularly in economic status and in prospects for financial improvement.

Median family income figures demonstrate the gap that still exists between white and black earners. Unemployment figures echo the continuing gaps that separate black workers from their white counterparts. June 1991 figures showed white unemployment about half that of blacks (6.2 percent versus 11.8 percent)—the basic pattern for most of the twentieth century. As for the distribution of jobs across ethnic lines, **Table 6-1** shows that whites are much more likely to hold managerial and professional jobs while blacks are much more likely to be in service occupations (with lower salary and status).

Manufacturing jobs were an important avenue for economic success for African-Americans in the middle years of the twentieth century. But as the century draws to a close, the U.S. economy is changing from a manufacturing base to a service base. That transformation results in the displacement of workers in the declining industries. A Bureau of Labor Statistics study released in 1991 found that blacks faced a higher risk of job displacement because of the types of jobs held; blacks were hit harder by economic downturns than whites:

> the proportion of blacks reemployed was quite low and differences between blacks and whites in the likelihood of reemployment were large; . . . blacks experienced considerably longer periods of joblessness than did whites; and following displacement, the proportion of blacks employed in manufacturing industries and production-related occupations fell by more than did the proportion of whites employed in the same industries and occupations.

TABLE 6-1

Distribution of Employed Civilians in Occupation Categories by Race, June 1991 (Percent)*

Occupation Category	White	Black
Managerial and professional specialty	27.0	16.2
Technical, sales, and administrative support	31.1	28.2
Service occupations	12.6	23.7
Precision production, craft, repair	11.8	8.9
Operators, fabricators, and laborers	13.9	20.6
Farming, forestry, and fishing	3.7	2.4

*Totals do not add to 100 due to rounding.
SOURCE: *Employment and Earnings* (Washington, D.C.: U.S. Department of Labor, Bureau of Labor Statistics, July 1991).

In addition, whites were more likely to regain employment in a similar industrial or occupational group.[26]

This study confirms the relatively tenuous economic status of African-Americans and the vulnerability of the gains they have achieved.

Since 1980 the black population has made gains in high school education—graduation rates increased from 75.4 percent in 1980 to 80.5 percent in 1988. That improvement narrowed the gap between black and white high school graduation rates from 11.6 percent in 1980 to 6.5 percent in 1988. But success in high school graduation rates did not translate into an increased college graduation rate for blacks. The college graduation rate stayed level from 1980 to 1988 (about ten points behind the also flat white rate). For those African-Americans who do graduate from college, economic prospects brighten—within limits. A black man aged twenty-five or older with four years or more of college can expect to earn, on average, only three-quarters as much as a comparably educated white man ($31,380 compared to $41,090 in a Census Bureau study released in 1991).

One of the clearest messages from demographic statistics over the past twenty or thirty years is that it is hard to prosper economically as a single parent. As two-parent households increasingly turn to two incomes to make ends meet, single parents are squeezed into poverty in greater numbers. Children in low-income and poor families find it relatively harder to achieve academic and economic success, reproducing cycles of poverty from one generation to the next. Whereas the proportion of all households headed by women (no husband present) increased from 10.7 percent in 1970 to 16.5 percent in 1990, the proportion of black female householders rose from 28.0 percent to 43.8 percent over the same period (see **Figure 6-1**). The contrast with white households is startling: In 1990 fully 83 percent of all white family households consisted of married couple families, but only 50 percent of black family households. These numbers point to a significant gap across ethnic lines that will reinforce income and education gaps in the future.

As a group, blacks are economically less well off than whites in our society. The economic disparities will inevitably reproduce themselves to some extent in the future. How are we to account for these inequalities? What effect do these disparities have on democracy? Without attempting any apportionment of blame but remembering the history of official as well as unofficial discrimination, what steps, if any, should government policy take to reduce the disparities?

The report of the Kerner Commission, issued in 1968 in the wake of widespread urban rioting, argued that white racism was the primary factor limiting blacks' struggle for equality. The report suggested that a change in "white attitude and behavior" toward blacks was the essential element in moving society toward more genuine and thoroughgoing equality in all areas. In terms of ethnic strife in America, 1968 was a long time ago. In the wake of the 1992 Los Angeles riots (more destructive than that city's Watts riots in 1965, which prompted the creation of the Kerner Commission), many people dusted off their copies of the commission's report and found that not

FIGURE 6-1
TYPE OF FAMILY AS A PERCENTAGE OF ALL FAMILY HOUSEHOLDERS, BY RACE; 1970–1990

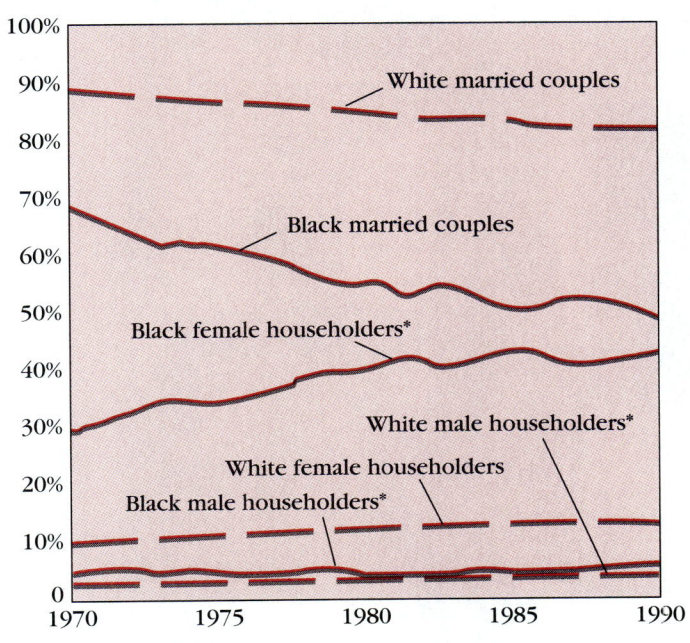

*No spouse present.
SOURCE: U.S. Bureau of the Census, *Current Population Reports, Population Characteristics*, Series P-20, No. 447, "Household and Family Characteristics, March 1990 and 1989" (Washington, D.C.: U.S. Government Printing Office, 1990).

enough had changed. Although definite progress has been made in reducing the amount of overt racism in American society, many people believe that racism is still the primary problem, exercising its poison in the same and more subtle ways. Some observers fault the Reagan and Bush administrations for failing to enforce civil rights laws vigorously. Others decry the notion that racism and discrimination can adequately explain the persistence of inequality for African-Americans. According to these analysts, the problem lies within the black community itself. The breakup of the family is often cited as a major destabilizing force, as well as the ill effects of federal welfare programs. Critics argue that some programs themselves contribute to a reduction of work incentives and induce attitudes of dependence among recipients. These explanations of inequality follow the traditional split between conservatives, who hold individuals responsible for social problems and tend to oppose governmental solutions, and liberals, who tend to emphasize social responsibility for the plight of individuals and seek solutions in interventionist social policy.

The Los Angeles riots of 1992 demonstrated that life had changed little for many African-Americans in that city. Rage, arson, and looting were touched off by the acquittal of four Los Angeles police officers in the beating of Rodney King. There were clear parallels to the Watts riot 27 years earlier, also touched off by tensions between police and area residents and rooted in a sense of deprivation and hopelessness. *(Reuters/Bettmann Newsphotos)*

According to one theory, a new generation of scholars, both black and white, sees the problem of ethnic inequality in different terms. Labeled the "synthesis school of race relations," these scholars make two central assumptions:

The first is that the problems of blacks and other minorities are today more a function of class than race, and thus unlikely to be significantly improved by legal efforts to reduce racial discrimination. The second is that a political coalition capable of advancing a broader social-reform agenda is unlikely to develop as long as liberals stress policies, such as affirmative action, that drive low- and middle-income whites to the GOP [Republican party].[27]

This new point of view is distinguished primarily by the rejection of traditional solutions to current social ills. These scholars tend, like liberals, to identify social roots to poverty, for example, and to support activist policy to reduce it. But preferential treatment along ethnic divisions is seen as counterproductive to the goal of social equality, a conservative stand.

In 1991, George Bush nominated African-American Clarence Thomas to the Supreme Court. His nomination testimony before the Senate Judiciary Committee was designed to avoid association with any particular social philosophy, but his documented hostility to affirmative action highlighted divisions within the community of civil rights activists. The NAACP opposed the nomination. Some traditional conservatives supported it. The debate surrounding the nomination involved many of the issues raised by the synthesis school. On one side, the new opposition to affirmative action met with a good deal of skepticism. It was charged that a black opponent of preferential treatment would find fast advancement within conservative circles as a useful token—a way of reassuring whites that it was acceptable to abandon active programs for racial equality. Racism can readily count on innocence, misunderstanding, and personal ambition to hide its shortcomings, these skeptics charged. On the other side, critics of the "civil rights establishment" parried that the institutionalization of "benign discrimination" has created a group of persons with a large stake in the treatment process itself, rather than the cure. Beyond this level of ad hominem sniping lies a set of questions fundamental to democracy. Even most critics agree that affirmative action works—it does provide greater opportunities for targeted groups. Is it fair? How can society overcome a legacy of exploitation while providing fair and equal treatment to its members? This last question reappears in slightly different circumstances in our next subject: the civil rights of women.

Civil Rights and Women

We saw in Chapter 1 the effort required to extend voting rights to women. The Nineteenth Amendment granting women the vote was, like the Civil War amendments before it, a signal victory but an incomplete one. Full, fair, and equal participation in American democracy would require more than the right to vote. In this section we will look at gender discrimination in the law, economic discrimination against women, and the controversial concept of comparable worth. These are essential questions for American democracy in the 1990s.

Government Actions on Gender Discrimination

Two of the most important pieces of civil rights legislation of the 1960s were to have great effect on the issue of gender discrimination: the Equal Pay Act of 1963, which required that men and women receive equal remuneration for similar jobs, and Title

VII of the Civil Rights Act of 1964, which prohibited sexual discrimination in employment and by state and local governments. In 1972 the Title VII provisions were extended to educational institutions under Title IX. The enactment of Title IX led to a steady stream of litigation brought by women—and occasionally men—who felt they had been discriminated against in admissions procedures, financial aid, extracurricular activities, athletics, health services, sex-stereotyped courses, counseling programs, dormitory rules, and other campus regulations.

Two executive orders lent momentum to the drive to reduce discrimination based on gender. A 1967 executive order forbade discrimination in federal employment and required companies with $50,000 or more in federal contracts to submit affirmative action plans for women in addition to such plans for minorities. Another executive order, promulgated in 1969, called for equal opportunities for women throughout the federal government itself and established a program to implement this commitment.

At the same time, the courts began to play a more significant role in redefining gender discrimination. Until 1971 the courts had largely upheld the government's authority to "classify by gender." Some court decisions prevented women from entering certain professions (such as bartending); other decisions were aimed at "protecting" women (as in certain family issues connected with child custody and alimony). For decades the courts, reflecting the views of society as a whole, found that a woman's place was in the home.

As legislative and social attitudes changed, however, the courts faced many new problems. From 1974 to 1977 the Supreme Court dealt with more cases related to the rights of men and women than it had decided in all its previous history. Since that period, gender discrimination cases have been on the Court's agenda continually.

One significant early case concerned a young man who committed suicide at the age of nineteen. His mother, Sally Reed, applied to be the administrator of his estate; his father applied two weeks later. Both were residents of Idaho, and under Idaho law, "between persons equally entitled to administer a decedent's estate, males must be preferred to females." The American Civil Liberties Union took the case to the Supreme Court, which unanimously ruled that the drawing of a sex line was inconsistent with the equal protection provisions of the Fourteenth Amendment.[28]

Although the Court has struck down sex discrimination in a number of other cases involving both men and women, it has not been willing to exclude gender considerations completely. Most important, in a 6–3 decision handed down in 1981, it upheld the all-male draft registration mandated by Congress.[29] The Court majority argued that Congress had carefully studied the inclusion of women and had decided that for reasons of "military flexibility," women should be excluded. The Court minority argued that the all-male provision violated equal protection guarantees in the Constitution. In 1984 the Supreme Court narrowed some of the protections against gender discrimination in education in the Grove City College case (examined in detail in Chapter 13), in which it found that the government could enforce antidiscrimination requirements in federal law only in the *specific* educational program or activity receiving federal money and not in all programs at the university in question. The *Grove City College* decision was later rendered void when Congress passed the Civil Rights Restoration Act of 1988, over President Reagan's veto.

No clear legal guidance exists for drawing gender-linked lines, in part because the Supreme Court has not been as hard on gender discrimination as on racial discrimination. The Court has argued that certain gender distinctions are legally valid because men and women are not always "similarly situated." In the *Michael M.* case, discussed earlier in this chapter, the Court upheld a California statutory rape law, thus leaving the man but not the woman at risk of criminal prosecution. The Court accepted the state's argument that its law properly addressed a natural asymmetry between the sexes. Gender distinctions were also upheld in a 1974 Court decision upholding a Florida statute giving widows but not widowers a $500 property tax exemption, on the assumption that, upon losing a spouse, women as a class suffered economic disadvantages not shared by men.[30] In *Gedulig* v. *Aiello* in 1974 the Court upheld California's disability insurance program against charges of sexual discrimination because the program did not cover disability resulting from normal pregnancy.[31] The Court said that the state was not obligated to restructure the program. In all cases like those just described, the root consideration is the same: When is it legitimate to treat women as a class differently from men? In sorting out these questions, the Court must cut through the stereotypes and prejudices of the past concerning what gender roles ought to be.

What about "protective" discrimination along gender lines? Exposure to lead is dangerous to your health. It is also dangerous to unborn children—even gametes prior to conception. The Occupational Health and Safety Administration (OSHA) has defined unsafe levels of exposure to lead for, among others, women planning to have a family. Johnson Controls, Inc., made batteries in which lead ws a primary ingredient. Eight of its employees became pregnant while testing in excess of the critical lead levels. Johnson announced a policy barring lead exposure jobs to all women except those who could provide proof of the inability to bear children. Was this merely a wise precaution, benevolent concern for the next generation (tied to a fear of civil litigation), or improper discrimination against women? The Supreme Court had already identified a bona fide occupational qualification (BFOQ) test that allowed discrimination that was tied to job performance. But a unanimous Court found the Johnson policy a violation of the Civil Rights Act of 1964.[32] No BFOQ existed, since fertile women performed job tasks as efficiently as anyone else. That finding leaves the larger question unanswered. How should society balance claims of fetal protection against unfair restrictions on employment? At least one principle is clear: It is unfair to ban women from tasks that might impair their ability to have healthy offspring when such policies do not consider comparable risks for men.

The Supreme Court has accorded affirmative action for women a lower priority than racially based affirmative action. Racial policies receive the "strict scrutiny" of the Court, whereas gender-based policies are reviewed under a less exacting standard. Not until 1987 did the Court specifically uphold an affirmative action program's move to redress gender-based discrimination. In 1979, Diane Joyce was named the road dispatcher for the Santa Clara County (California) Transportation Agency. Paul Johnson was not given the job, even though he received a higher interview score than Joyce. In giving Joyce the job, the agency director took a variety of factors into account, including qualifications, test scores, and affirmative action considerations. No woman had ever held one of the agency's "skilled craft worker" jobs. Justice Brennan, writing for the Court, upheld the agency's actions, finding that "no persons are automatically excluded from consideration; *all* are able to have their qualifications weighed against those of other applicants."[33] The decision clarified the status of affirmative action programs. According to the ruling, a carefully constructed affirmative action program is not unconstitutional when gender or race is taken into account as one of a variety of factors in making hiring or promotion decisions, when affirmative action considerations don't wholly override considerations of seniority, and when a history of discrimination or a clear pattern of current disparity exists. But the Court's willingness to accept affirmative action programs does not guarantee that such programs will be created or that guidelines will be vigorously enforced. Those actions largely depend on other players in the political system.

Equal Treatment for Gay Men and Lesbians

The exact number of gay men and lesbians in the United States is not easy to estimate, but current guesses range from 5 to 10 percent of the population. Kinsey's studies in the 1950s also showed that something like half of all Americans have had some homosexual experience in their lives, most in adolescence. Until recently, homosexual activity between consenting adults was commonly unlawful in many American communities, reflecting deeply held homophobic attitudes.

Gay rights nonetheless became an issue starting in the 1960s, partly because so many gays publicly proclaimed their homosexuality and began to mobilize and exercise their political and economic power. Gay activism stressed a political agenda aimed at eliminating all statutory manifestations of discrimination, in housing, employment, even the tax laws. The gay rights movement was met with significant and impassioned opposition—based on such groundless fears that homosexuality is "contagious" or that gays might be more likely than heterosexuals to lead children astray—and despite the fact that the American Psychological Association had abandoned its position that homosexuality was a mental illness.

The gay rights movement achieved some successes, especially at the local level, in the 1970s, but during the 1980s anti–gay rights activists mounted some striking reversals. Antidiscrimination legislation was repealed in Dade County, Florida, and there were even defeats in liberal communities like Eugene, Oregon, and St. Paul, Minnesota. These events took place, however, in the context of what many observers believed was a growing acceptance of sexual orientation as a protected right or liberty. One element in the debate was the question of a community's right to enforce the viewpoint of the majority in sexual matters ranging from pornography to abortion. It seems unlikely, in any case, that sexual behavior can be effectively discouraged or even controlled by law.

The most obvious official federal discrimination against homosexuals concerns the Defense Department policy that deems gay persons "incompatible with military service." In the ten years from 1982 to 1991 the U.S. military discharged more than thirteen thousand people as homosexuals. The ban on homosexuals in the military seems inconsistent with civil service rules that prohibit discrimination on the basis of sexual orientation. The rationale for the ban seems anachronistic, based on fears of improper sexual advances and affairs corrosive to discipline—which the increased presence of women in the military should have discredited by now. The ban certainly denies the military access to a pool of talent and needlessly restricts career choices. Many homosexuals currently serve in the armed forces but must conceal their sexual orientation to avoid being discharged. A discharge for homosexuality can damage employment prospects. Gallup polls show that about 60 percent of Americans believe that homosexuals should be allowed to serve in the military—up almost ten points from a decade earlier.[34] Perhaps the time has come to reexamine this policy.

Domestic partnership and job benefits regulations are important issues for gay men and lesbians. Although the Supreme Court recognized marriage as "one of the basic civil rights of man" as early as 1942, in *Skinner* v. *Oklahoma*,[35] no state currently knowingly issues marriage licenses to same-sex couples. State laws assume that lawful marriage involves two people of opposite sex. Local governments have been more receptive to gay interests. San Francisco has a domestic partner ordinance that allows unmarried couples to register to qualify for hospital visitation rights, bereavement leave, and any new policy that affects the marital status of heterosexual couples. In 1989, New York's highest court decided that unmarried couples, be they homosexual or heterosexual, are entitled to benefits under New York City's rent control laws. It was the first time that the highest court in any state had given official recognition to gay and lesbian relationships. But these are isolated examples. In most local jurisdictions, gay couples have no legal means of legitimizing their status.

What about job benefits for homosexuals' partners? If an employer provides health insurance to an employee and spouse, should it provide the same benefits to a gay or lesbian employee's long-term partner? Employers faced with skyrocketing health coverage costs may be reluctant to add a whole new category of qualified recipients. Fears of high health costs among gay partners compound the reluctance. But rising costs cannot address the issue of fair access to benefits. Besides, domestic partner plans, when available, are used more by unmarried heterosexuals than by gay couples. And fears that homosexuals are a high-risk group for health insurers seem to be contradicted by the experience of a small number of municipalities (Berkeley, and Santa Cruz, California; Seattle; Madison, Wisconsin), nonprofit organizations (Greenpeace, the National Organization for Women, the American Friends' Service Committee, Planned Parenthood), and corporations (Ben & Jerry's Homemade, Inc.; Lotus Software) that have pioneered in offering domestic partners benefits. "Smoking and exercise are better predictors of who will file claims then are sexual orientation or marital status," said

The U.S. Navy discharged Petty Officer Keith Meinhold after he publicly announced that he was gay. The Navy was ordered to reinstate Meinhold under court order, but the antigay policies of the military remained in effect.
(Paul Sakuma/Wide World Photos)

Lyn S. Thompson, vice president of the Washington-based Consumers United Insurance Company, the only insurer that routinely includes domestic partners in its policies.[36] Since gay couples face legal barriers to marriage, a stronger case could be made for gay domestic partners than for unmarried heterosexual partners.

If fairness suggests that benefits policies should recognize committed gay couples as well as committed heterosexual couples, is this a matter for federal civil rights legislation (perhaps an extension of the ban on sexual orientation discrimination in employment practices)? Should courts recognize common law gay marriages without changes in state marriage laws?

An interesting test of gay rights issues occurred in Georgia in the 1980s. Michael Hardwick, a homosexual living in Atlanta, was arrested in 1982 for engaging in oral sex in the privacy of his home with another consenting man. Under Georgia criminal law, the penalty for conviction could have been as much as twenty years in prison. Although the state prosecutor decided not to submit the charge to the grand jury unless

The increasingly open acknowledgment of their sexual orientation on the part of many gay men and lesbians has created a range of new public issues. Among the foremost are the questions of whether the law should recognize gay marriages and permit couples of the same sex to adopt children. (Hella Hammid/Photo Researchers)

there was additional evidence, Hardwick challenged the Georgia statute in a civil suit in federal court. That suit gave the Supreme Court the chance to weigh in on the issue of gay rights. Although the Georgia sodomy statute applied to *any* oral or anal sex act and thus could be used against heterosexuals as well as homosexuals, Justice Byron White, writing for a five-person majority, chose to frame the question only in terms of the homosexual issue. The question, for White, was "whether the Federal Constitution confers a fundamental right upon homosexuals to engage in sodomy." The Court's answer was no. The Circuit Court's decision that the constitutional right to privacy extended to homosexual sodomy was in error. Justice Harry Blackmun wrote in dissent:

> This case is no more about a "fundamental right to engage in homosexual sodomy," as the Court purports to declare, than *Stanley* v. *Georgia* was about a fundamental right to watch obscene movies, or *Katz* v. *United States* was about a fundamental right to place interstate bets from a telephone booth. Rather, this case is about "the most comprehensive of rights and the right most valued by civilized men," namely, "the right to be left alone" *Olmstead* v. *United States* (1928). . . .
>
> This case involves no real interference with the rights of others, for the mere knowledge that other individuals do not adhere to one's value system cannot be a legally cognizable interest, let alone an interest that can justify invading the houses, hearts, and minds of citizens who choose to live their lives differently. . . .
>
> I can only hope . . . that the Court will soon reconsider its analysis and conclude that depriving individuals of their right to choose for themselves how to conduct their intimate relationships poses a far greater threat to the values most deeply rooted in our nation's history than tolerance of nonconformity could ever do.[37]

The sentiments expressed by Justice Blackmun did not convince the Court in 1986, and the reconsideration he hoped for does not seem likely soon.

Rights of the Disabled

By one estimate, there are 37 million people with some form of disability in the United States.[38] This number includes the deaf, the blind, the physically and mentally handicapped, and those with various learning disabilities. Until the 1970s they were rarely a factor in the minds of the people who shape public policy and were more likely to be objects of pity or aversion than active participants in determining their own fates. But a combination of grass-roots activism and federal legislation has moved the rights of the disabled to a central position on the public agenda at the national, state, and local levels.

The Rehabilitation Act of 1973 and the Education for All Handicapped Children Act of 1975 were crucial steps along the path to equal rights for the disabled. The 1973 legislation had been vetoed twice by President Nixon (on financial grounds) before it finally was passed. Section 504 of this act requires that handicapped people have equal access to all federally financed programs. Though the legislation had been on the books for several years, activists for the disabled argued that it was not being implemented, and in the spring of 1977 they staged a series of sit-ins in the offices of the Department of Health, Education and Welfare. Soon thereafter, regulations implementing the act were issued. The 1975 legislation on education ensured disabled children free public education regardless of the severity of their disability. It established new norms, ending separate education and bringing disabled children into the educational mainstream.

The Americans with Disability Act (ADA), passed in 1991, was a landmark in the recognition of the rights of the disabled. As disabled people became more visible, their particular concerns became better understood. For many, *access* was a high priority. *(Day Williams/Photo Researchers)*

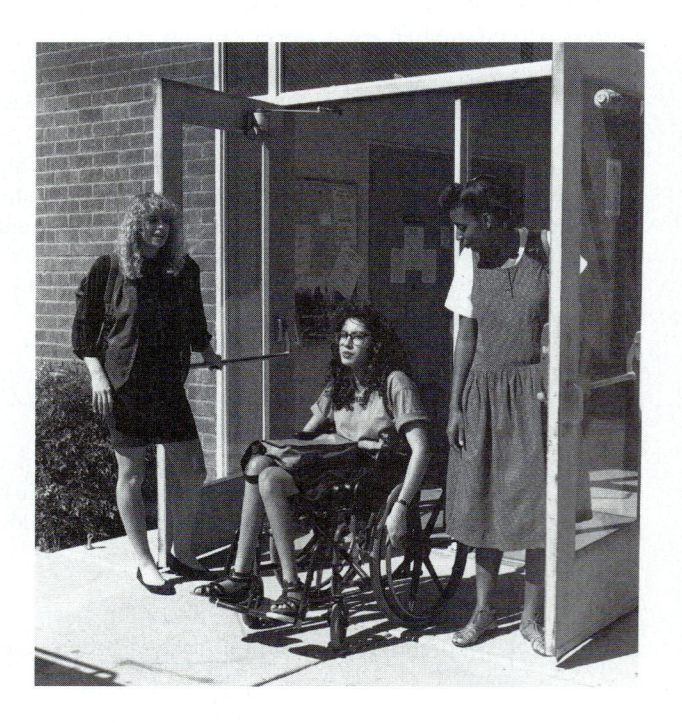

Early intervention is the most effective means of overcoming disabilities that affect learning. For example, a 1985 study of Head Start, the federally subsidized preschool program for poor and disabled children, showed a five-dollar public saving for every dollar invested in Head Start. The 1975 All Handicapped Children Act offered the first federal incentives to states to provide preschool programs for disabled children. With the help of subsequent legislation, by 1991 all but two states had committed themselves to extensive preschool programs aimed at disabled children aged three to five. There may be as many as a million children in the nation eligible for such help. Because of funding shortfalls and a shortage of trained professionals, no state has been able to serve every eligible child. Economic retrenchment at both the state and federal levels threatens to undermine these commitments. But in spite of the distance left to travel, America's disabled children have made dramatic progress in gaining access to public education.

The Americans with Disabilities Act of 1990 similarly represents a dramatic new commitment to providing access to social and economic participation for all Americans. Signing the act on the South Lawn of the White House, President Bush called the law "a declaration of independence" for disabled Americans. The law bans employment discrimination in all businesses with more than fifteen employees and protects recovering drug abusers, alcoholics, and people with AIDS as well as those with more traditionally defined disabilities. Most retail establishments and public transportation systems will be required to provide handicapped access. By 1994, telephone companies must offer equipment for hearing- or speech-impaired persons to communicate over ordinary phones. The public and private cost of these changes will be substantial.

The greatest threat to further progress for disabled Americans lies in the fiscal restraints of government in the 1990s. New initiatives are hard to sell when established programs are being trimmed to reduce deficits. The second impediment to progress comes from a reluctance to enforce federal regulations vigorously. The Americans with Disabilities Act imposes significant costs on private enterprises. The Reagan and Bush administrations, in line with their general market-oriented philosophy of governing, have not been energetic watchdogs in civil rights and workplace safety. The most comprehensive protection in law is worth little without some enforcement muscle behind it. Local initiative is often necessary to spur government compliance with national standards.

Sometimes progress brings its own problems. Many parents of deaf children, for example, prefer education in a school where signing is the primary form of communication. For these parents, mainstreaming their children into the regular public schools is not considered an advantage.[39] The deinstitutionalization of the mentally ill, which began in the late 1960s, was regarded at first as a positive step. The idea, however, has in many ways failed on the practical level because large numbers of the mentally ill have ended up homeless, living uncared for in the streets. The local mental health clinics that were supposed to supply services to such people never received the expected funding and support.

The costs of providing special education, of removing barriers to access, and providing needs-sensitive facilities are not small, but the investment provides a significant return. Fewer than 25 percent of disabled men and 13 percent of disabled women hold full-time jobs. Their earnings average only two-thirds those of all workers.[40] Enlarging the protection of the civil rights of disabled persons pays tangible economic rewards. The democratic rewards are even greater.

Basic Social Rights

Eighteenth-century liberals conceived of rights and liberties primarily as protections against the encroachments of government. It was the arbitrariness of government—its tendency to intrude into the lives of citizens, to become tyrannical—that most concerned the framers of the Constitution.

But in the late nineteenth century the view of government as tyrant began to make way for a more benign attitude. As rapid industrialization swept through the country, reformers pressed for an activist government—one committed to guaranteeing citizens' rights to health, safety, education, and human services in an increasingly mechanized and dehumanizing industrial society. This radical shift was prompted by the Industrial Revolution.

From a relatively small, agrarian society, the United States had been transformed into a booming industrial society powered by a modern capitalist economy and characterized by rapid urbanization and increasing mechanization of transport and industry. Out of these developments arose a series of complex social problems that involved such fundamental issues as the right to basic security in regard to health and safety. Reformers sought to have government intervene to ensure decent housing for all, to limit the hours employees worked in factories, to protect workers from unsafe working conditions, to provide public health services to counteract serious illnesses, to guarantee that all citizens received a basic education, and so on. Unlike eighteenth-century liberals, then, the social activists of the late nineteenth century envisioned an activist government—one that involved itself in the day-to-day affairs of its citizens. In their view, such a government was essential for a just society.

In Part IV, which deals with contemporary issues of public policy, we will look at recent controversies over government intervention to protect the general welfare. Here the new concepts of basic **social rights** are illustrated through two important examples of government action: the creation of the federal Food and Drug Administration and government's role in the drive to form trade unions and to institute collective bargaining.

Pure Food and Drugs

In his novel *The Jungle*, published in 1906, Upton Sinclair drew a graphic sketch of the conditions at the Chicago stockyards. Sinclair had spent seven weeks observing meatpacking workers on the job and studying the meat inspection laws. He wrote *The*

Jungle to expose the abominable conditions of the factory workers, but the novel sparked greater public concern over unsanitary ingredients in food and drugs. The following passage from Sinclair's novel demonstrates why the public reacted with such outrage:

> There would come all the way back from Europe old sausage that had been rejected, and that was moldy and white—and it would be dosed with borax and glycerine and dumped into hoppers, and made over again for home consumption. There would be meat that had tumbled out on the floor, in the dirt and sawdust, where the workers had trampled and spit uncounted billions of consumption [tuberculosis] germs. There would be meat stored in great piles in rooms; and the water from leaky roofs would drop over it, and thousands of rats would race about on it. It was too dark in those storage places to see well, but a man could run his hand over these piles of meat and sweep off handfuls of the dried dung of rats. These rats were nuisances and the packers would put poisoned bread out for them—they would die, and then rats, bread, and meat would go into the hoppers together. . . . The meat would be shoveled into carts, and the man who did the shoveling would not trouble to lift out a rat even if he saw one—there were things that went into the sausage in comparison with which a poisoned rat was a tidbit.[41]

Sinclair's revelations, combined with the efforts of others who had revealed the widespread use of dangerous substances in food and drugs, led to the passage of the Pure Food and Drug Act and the Meat Inspection Act of 1906, under which federal authorities were empowered to ban some forms of adulteration of food and drugs and to stop the use of hazardous preservatives. Over the next two decades, additional legislation broadened the scope of government concern. A 1912 law banned false health claims for patent medicines; a 1913 law required package labels to include the quantity of various contents; a 1919 law required net weight labels on packaged meat.

Not until 1927, however, did Congress create an agency to enforce this legislation. The Food, Drug and Insecticide Administration (which became the Food and Drug Administration in 1931) recognized that technological changes and various court decisions had largely outdated the 1906 law under which it operated. Yet another scandal was required before the agency gained adequate regulatory powers. When a new "wonder drug," elixir sulfanilamide, was marketed without prior safety testing, it caused the deaths of more than one hundred people. Under the existing law, the FDA had been powerless to prevent the drug from reaching the market—it was empowered to take action against a drug only after it had been demonstrated to cause death or illness. Public outrage over the FDA's inability to stop the marketing of elixir sulfanilamide prompted passage of the Food, Drug and Cosmetic Act of 1938, which specified that drugs be tested prior to distribution, set tolerance levels for toxic substances, provided for factory inspection, strengthened truth-in-labeling provisions of existing laws, and extended health coverage to cosmetics.

Even this strengthening of the health and safety laws did not guarantee that all food, drugs, and other consumer products reaching the market were safe, but it did signal a clear recognition of government's responsibility to ensure the safety of food and drugs.

A silicone breast implant. An intense and important controversy raged over the safety of these devices, with the Food and Drug Administration (FDA) at the center of it. The FDA first issued a warning and then banned the implants as unsafe. This controversy highlighted the often difficult issues of health and safety regulation and the central importance of Federal regulatory agencies. *(George Frey/Picture Group)*

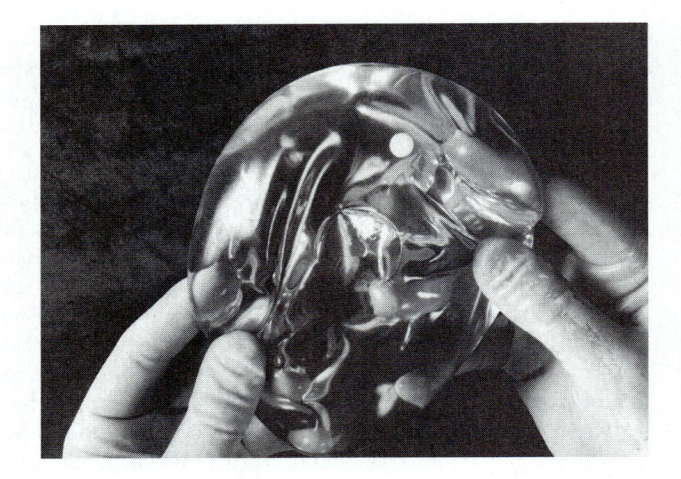

The basic right involved here—one that remains highly controversial in specific applications—is the right to safe, noninjurious products.

Trade Unions and Collective Bargaining

Although the rights of workers to organize and to bargain with management are not thought of as fundamental human rights, they are indispensable to the successful functioning of an industrial society. More important, they are closely connected with the meaning of democracy in modern times. Without the opportunity to form trade unions, workers often have little defense against exploitation by management. In the absence of an effective workers' organization, working conditions and pay can largely be dictated by management—a situation resembling tyranny far more than democracy. The right to form a union, then, is one of the basic democratic rights required for a decent life in a modern society.

The history of the union movement in the United States has been punctuated by many episodes of violence. For decades government forces were brought to bear against workers who attempted to form unions. Until 1842 the courts typically held that union activity per se was illegal. After that date courts were more willing to grant unions the right to exist but generally refused to recognize a union's right to strike or to compel employers to bargain collectively. Beginning in the 1880s, court orders against union activities were widely used to break strikes, and state militia, National Guard, and regular army forces often intervened in labor disputes on the side of employers.

The first piece of federal legislation to provide some protection for labor was the Clayton Act of 1914, which prohibited the issuance of injunctions (court orders) against strikes, boycotts, and picketing except to prevent "irreparable damage." The courts, however, remained generally hostile to unions, and Congress was slow to act on behalf

THE LUDLOW MASSACRE OF 1913

Attempts to unionize the coal and mineral miners of Colorado began in the 1890s. Concerted unionizing efforts early in the twentieth century led to the arrest of union organizers and the firing of union sympathizers. The mines were subsequently worked by nonunion laborers, most of whom were recent immigrants from Europe or Mexico. For a time these workers proved relatively docile, despite the wretched conditions found in the mining camps, where disease was rampant, sanitation poor, and alcoholism common. Water for drinking and washing flowed directly from the mines, without prior treatment. Miners were paid only in scrip, or company money, which could be used only in company-owned stores. Many conditions in the camps violated state law, but because the mining companies exerted great influence over Colorado politics, the state did not intervene to improve conditions.

Eventually the workers organized, and in September 1912 they called for a forty-hour workweek, an eight-hour workday, union recognition, and various other work-related improvements. When the mining companies refused to budge on the unionization issue, the workers went on strike. Both miners and employers expected the strike to be serious and violent. The workers had stockpiled weapons, in the well-founded belief that the companies would resort to violence to break the strike. The companies brought in detectives and deputy sheriffs to protect their property. Finally, the governor called out the state militia. A six-month stalemate ensued, and the companies began to import strikebreakers.

On April 19, 1913, in circumstances that are still disputed, a confrontation between state militia and strikers led to violence. A strikers' camp in Ludlow was burned and thirty-three people were killed, including eleven women and children. After this "Ludlow massacre," the strikers prepared for open warfare, and the governor called on President Woodrow Wilson to send federal troops. Ten days later the U.S. Army occupied the area, and calm was restored. The union failed to gain recognition.

The Ludlow massacre was one of the most dramatic examples of labor-management violence in U.S. history.

---

of unions. The Great Depression forced political leaders to recognize that fundamental changes were necessary in the economic life of the nation.

Two pieces of legislation, in particular, signaled government acceptance of unions as a permanent and legitimate force in U.S. society. The Norris-LaGuardia Act of 1932 prohibited the enforcement of "yellow dog" contracts in federal courts. Such unionization, required that employees sign a pledge not to join a union as a condition of employment. The Norris-LaGuardia Act also prohibited the federal courts from issuing injunctions against strikes. In effect, then, the act neutralized the role of the federal courts in labor disputes.

The Wagner Act, passed in 1935, went further. Under this measure, workers were guaranteed the right to form unions and to bargain with management. The Wagner Act also created the National Labor Relations Board (NLRB), which was empowered to investigate unfair labor practices by employers and to issue cease-and-desist orders enforceable through the federal courts. Not only did this act effectively end violent labor strife in the United States by firmly establishing the right to collective bargaining, but it also helped to create an atmosphere in which unions were more likely to develop. And between 1935 and 1947, union membership increased from 4 million to 15.5 million.

After World War II, federal legislators adopted a more critical stance toward unions. The Taft-Hartley Act of 1947, for example, regulated union activities and prohibited strikes by federal employees. Under Section 14B of the act, states were empowered to pass "right to work" laws, which require that union membership not be a *condition* of employment. Such provisions were adopted by twenty states, despite vigorous opposition by organized labor. The Landrum-Griffin Act of 1959 then mandated more democratic practices *within* unions and established a union membership "bill of rights."

Today debates continue over union power and management practices. Many observers charge that unions have become too powerful and often obstruct more than facilitate labor relations. Others point out that the United States is one of the least unionized nations in the industrialized democratic world and that many U.S. workers still suffer from a lack of basic protections. For our purposes, the foregoing discussion illustrates that political recognition and protection of basic trade union rights came only after a series of painful, costly battles that reflected the social class divisions in U.S. society, in which the many own little property and the few control most of it. The issue of the effects on democratic life of an extremely unequal distribution of property is one we will examine closely in Chapter 7.

Government Repression

Our national history has shown an admirable commitment to defending civil liberties and rights, but the drive to undermine them has run equally strong. Attempts by the federal government to prosecute and harass opponents date back to the Alien and Sedition Acts of the John Adams administration, as we saw in Chapter 5. As a rule, the tempo of repression quickens when some people in government perceive threats to established patterns of social and political life. As a result, throughout U.S. history, groups advocating radical change or appearing to question established norms have often been the targets of government repression.

In the early years of the twentieth century, for example, a concerted campaign of prosecutions was directed against the Industrial Workers of the World (IWW), a militant industrial union. Many of its leaders were eventually imprisoned. Then, in the aftermath of World War I and the Russian Revolution, a near-hysterical fear of communism swept the country. During this "Red scare," the press relentlessly portrayed anarchists and radicals as serious threats to law and order and to the government itself. In January 1920 about four thousand alleged radicals were arrested. Many were deported and many others imprisoned. Most were held without benefit of legal assistance, and some were even prevented from contacting their families.

This pattern of antiradical activity combined with repression or subversion of civil rights was repeated in the 1950s, as we saw in the discussion of McCarthyism in Chapter 1. In the 1960s, civil rights and antiwar activities led to another outburst of repressive activities. Presidents Lyndon Johnson and Richard Nixon, believing that the antiwar movement and the New Left posed a serious threat to American society, felt that drastic action was needed to stop disruptions. The federal government's intelligence-gathering and investigatory agencies kept close track of many activists such as Dr. Martin Luther King, Jr. Informers infiltrated groups considered radical, regardless of whether those groups had broken laws or taken part in violence. Illegal break-ins and wiretaps by law enforcement officials were used to monitor such organizations.

The states also joined in the antiradical campaign. Julian Bond, the first black elected to the Georgia state legislature in one hundred years, was denied his seat because of his association with the Student Nonviolent Coordinating Committee, which had outspokenly opposed the Vietnam War. In this case, however, the federal courts stepped in to uphold Bond's rights to the legislative seat.

To some observers, these outbreaks of government repression represented justifiable responses to real threats to the social order. If groups seek to alter society through violence or to subvert institutions, it is argued, repression is called for—although in this view repression usually is called "maintaining order." It is true that at times the threats have been real and at other times it has been difficult to decide whether threats were real or not. Were anarchists sending bombs through the mail in 1919? Was the U.S. Communist party trying to subvert the government in the 1930s and 1940s? Did antiwar radicals plan to destroy property and disrupt public order during the Democratic Convention in 1968? Were black radicals of the 1960s talking revolution and violence?

The scant elements of truth in these allegations persuaded political leaders and much of the rest of the population that drastic steps had to be taken. Yet repression, not just maintaining order, carried the day in each case. Authorities ignored civil liberties, used excessive force, and intimated people with sympathies for the targets of repression.

In searching for reasons why government has sometimes resorted to repressive tactics, some authorities contend that government repression is directed against the perceived enemies of private property and the capitalist enterprise. Still others cite a decidedly lukewarm commitment to civil liberties among U.S. political elites. According

(Text continues on page 231)

THE HARASSMENT OF MARTIN LUTHER KING, JR.

For more than six years, from 1962 to 1968, the Federal Bureau of Investigation engaged in daily surveillance of civil rights leader Martin Luther King, Jr. Though not publicly revealed until after King's death in 1968, the FBI's campaign against him did much private damage to King's reputation and brought serious emotional turmoil to him and his closest relatives.

The FBI's pursuit of King began six years after he first became a national figure, during the Montgomery, Alabama bus boycott of 1955-1956. In early 1962 the FBI learned that one of King's closest political advisers was a white New York attorney, Stanley D. Levison, who had come to the bureau's attention a decade earlier when he was playing a crucial role in the U.S. Communist party. Wiretaps were placed on Levison's telephones and microphones covertly installed in his office, but no evidence of sinister connections or plotting was forthcoming. Nevertheless, FBI director J. Edgar Hoover sent grim warnings about the Levison-King friendship to President John F. Kennedy and his brother Robert, the attorney general. The Kennedy brothers finally approved Hoover's request that FBI wiretaps be placed on King's home and office phones in Atlanta.

The new electronic surveillance transformed the FBI's interest in King almost overnight. Concern about Levison quickly was replaced by an obsession that King's private life was unacceptable for such a prominent minister and public leader. Agents were assigned to tail King as he traveled from city to city and hotel room to hotel room, and transcribed accounts of his most private moments were sent out to the White House and to dozens of federal agencies. Bureau operatives attempted to interest the news media in the personal material about King, and one FBI executive mailed an anonymous threatening letter to King—enclosing an embarrassing tape and warning of imminent exposure—just days after the black leader had been awarded the 1964 Nobel Peace Prize for his pioneering civil rights efforts. Much to the FBI's disappointment, its attempts to smear or destroy King publicly went for naught; reporter after reporter rebuffed the bureau's approaches on the grounds that King's private life was not news.

Frustrated but not dissuaded, the FBI kept up its close watch on King's activities, becoming particularly agitated when he strongly denounced the Vietnam War policies of President Lyndon Johnson and advocated a massive but nonviolent "poor people's campaign" directed at the nation's Capitol. Thorough and painstaking congressional investigations have shown no FBI complicity in King's 1968 assassination. The full record of the bureau's activities against King, however, reveals that millions of dollars were spent on one of the most appalling violations of personal privacy and civil liberties in U.S. government history.

to this view, many at the top levels of our political establishment are concerned more with maintaining their own power than with respect for the Bill of Rights.

Of course, political elites alone cannot be blamed for repression; it also has a popular base. As we will see in Chapter 8, tolerance for dissent has had a long struggle to become established in the United States. Even reasonable people often disagree about what should be tolerated. For example, should groups preaching racial or religious hatred be permitted to exercise First Amendment rights? Should groups that do not respect civil liberties be entitled to those liberties? Such questions defy simple answers. Yet our constitutional protections play a key role in shoring up defenses against repression.

Conclusions

> We hold these truths to be self-evident, that all men are created equal.
>
> Thomas Jefferson, 1776

> In view of the constitution, in the eye of the law, there is in this country no superior, dominant, ruling class of citizens. There is no caste here. Our constitution is color-blind.
>
> John Marshall Harlan, 1896

Thomas Jefferson owned slaves and lived in a time when suffrage rights belonged almost exclusively to white male property owners. A century later, Justice Harlan, found no denial of equal protection in the closing of the Ware School in Augusta, a decision that became the justification for a half-century of segregated, inferior education for blacks in many parts of this country. Jefferson and Harlan were not hypocrites. Far from being short-sighted, narrow-minded political hacks, they are properly counted among the visionary political actors of their respective times. But like all of us, they were inescapably of their times. They were bound in part by common understandings and prejudices that limited their vision.

The U.S. Constitution guarantees citizens "life, liberty, and the pursuit of happiness." The Canadian constitution promises "peace, order, and good government," a fair contrast with the accentuated individualism of political culture in the United States. For us, the idea of equality is always tempered by the idea that we should be free to achieve according to our talents and desires, and we should be rewarded for achievement, *unequally*. The tension between these two ideals forms a constant backdrop to political debate in the United States. Should the federal government prohibit the use of ethnic identity or gender as factors in employment decisions? Should the city provide wheelchair access to public transportation, even though the costs are high and the number of wheelchair riders is low? Should a truck driver get paid more than a clerk-typist? Should we treat committed homosexual relationships as we do committed heterosexual relationships, and both the same as heterosexual marriages?

In his efforts to gain protection for the domestic auto industry, Chrysler chairman Lee Iaccoca popularized the concept of a "level playing field": Remove artificial handicaps and let natural talent and determination carry the day. We're willing to compete and to accept the results, win or lose, as long as the playing field is level. But that's the catch. Given our immersion in the prejudices of our time, how do we decide which differences are artificial or arbitrary and which are important and natural? Treatment as equals demands respect for differences as well as commonalities. Today the great challenge for civil rights policies—and for all citizens who profess a love of freedom—is to transcend the prejudices of our time to the extent that we can, get a glimpse of a larger vision of democracy than the one we live, and then figure out how that translates into the specifics of everyday life.

GLOSSARY TERMS

affirmative action
Brown v. *Board of Education of Topeka*
Civil Rights Act of 1964
comparable worth
de facto segregation
de jure segregation

disparate impact test
equal protection of the laws
set-asides
social rights
treatment as equals
voucher systems

NOTES

[1] Edward J. Cashin, *The Story of Augusta* (Augusta: Richmond County Board of Education, 1980), p. 158. The story of Ware school is drawn from Cashin's book, with details added from Helen Callahan, *Augusta: A Pictorial History* (Virginia Beach: Donning, 1980).

[2] *Cumming et al.* v. *Richmond County Board of Education* (1899), 175 U.S. 528, 545.

[3] 163 U.S. 567.

[4] The primary "one person, one vote" cases are *Reynolds* v. *Sims* (1964), 377 U.S. 533, and *Wesberry* v. *Sanders* (1964), 376 U.S. 1. These decisions were made possible by an earlier decision, *Baker* v. *Carr* (1962), 369 U.S. 186, which determined that legislative malapportionment did involve a constitutionally protected right that could properly be addressed by the Court.

[5] See Ronald Dworkin, *Taking Rights Seriously* (Cambridge, Mass.: Harvard University Press, 1977).

[6] 450 U.S. 464.

[7] 305 U.S. 337.

[8] 339 U.S. 629.

[9] 347 U.S. 483.

[10] 391 U.S. 430.

[11] 402 U.S. 1.

[12] Warren E. Miller and Donald E. Stokes, "Constituency Influence in Congress," *American Political Science Review*, March 1963, pp. 45–46.

[13] 418 U.S. 717.
[14] *Missouri* v. *Jenkins* (1990), 110 S.Ct. 1651. Two of the justices in this five-person majority (Brennan and Marshall) retired from the Court within a year of this decision, calling its future into question.
[15] 438 U.S. 265.
[16] 448 U.S. 448.
[17] Mitchell F. Rice, "Government Set-asides, Minority Business Enterprises, and the Supreme Court," *Public Administration Review*, March-April 1991, p. 115.
[18] 467 U.S. 561.
[19] 476 U.S. 267.
[20] 480 U.S. 149.
[21] 488 U.S. 469.
[22] 110 S.Ct. 2997.
[23] 401 U.S. 424.
[24] Paul Gewirtz, professor of law at Yale Law School, in "Discrimination Endgame," *New Republic*, August 12, 1991, p. 19.
[25] 109 S.Ct. 2115.
[26] Lori G. Kletzer, "Job Displacement, 1979–86: How Blacks Fared Relative to Whites," *Monthly Labor Review*, July 1991, p. 17.
[27] Ronald Brownstein, "Beyond Quotas," *Los Angeles Times Magazine*, July 28, 1991, p. 38.
[28] *Reed* v. *Reed* (1971), 404 U.S. 71.
[29] *Rostker* v. *Goldberg* (1981), 453 U.S. 57.
[30] *Kahn* v. *Shevin* (1974), 416 U.S. 351.
[31] 417 U.S. 484.
[32] *Autoworkers* v. *Johnson Controls, Inc.* (1991).
[33] *Johnson* v. *Transportation Agency of Santa Clara Cty* (1987), 480 U.S. 616.
[34] "Gay Soldiers, Good Soldiers," *New York Times*, September 1, 1991, p. E10.
[35] 316 U.S. 535.
[36] Claudia H. Deutsch, "Insurance for Domestic Partners," *New York Times*, July 28, 1991, p. F23; also the source for the names of most domestic partner insurers listed.
[37] *Bowers* v. *Hardwick* (1986), 478 U.S. 186.
[38] Catherine Foster, "Disability Rights on the Agenda," *Christian Science Monitor*, July 8, 1988, p. 17.
[39] Catherine Foster, "The Deaf Will Be Heard," *Christian Science Monitor*, July 29, 1988, p. 20.
[40] "A Law for Every American," *New York Times*, July 27, 1990, p. A10.
[41] Upton Sinclair, *The Jungle* (New York: Viking, 1946), p. 135.

SELECTED READINGS

For a good fundamental treatment of the concept of **treatment as equals**, see Ronald Dworkin, *Taking Rights Seriously* (Cambridge, Mass.: Harvard University Press, 1977).

For recent scholarship on **segregation in education**, see Christine H. Rossell, *The Carrot or the Stick for School Desegregation Policy: Magnet Schools or Forced Busing* (Philadelphia: Temple University Press, 1990); Paul R. Dimond, *Beyond Busing: Inside the Challenge to Urban Segregation* (Ann Arbor: University of Michigan Press, 1985).

For historical treatment of **desegregation**, see J. Anthony Lukas, *Common Ground: A Turbulent Decade in the Lives of Three American Families* (New York: Knopf, 1985); Bernard Schwartz, *Swann's Way: The School Busing Case and the Supreme Court* (New York: Oxford University Press, 1986); Jack Peltason, *Fifty-eight Lonely Men: Southern Federal Judges and School Desegregation* (Urbana: University of Illinois Press, 1971); Richard Kluger, *Simple Justice* (New York: Vintage Books, 1977); and Fred Powledge, *Free at Last?* (New York: HarperCollins, 1992).

Michel Rosenfeld provides a good general treatment of **affirmative action** in *Affirmative Action and Justice: A Philosophical and Constitutional Inquiry* (New Haven, Conn.: Yale University Press, 1991). See also Bron Raymond Taylor, *Affirmative Action at Work: Law, Politics, and Ethics* (Pittsburgh: University of Pittsburgh Press, 1991). For **opposing viewpoints**, see Gertrude Ezorsky, *Racism and Justice: The Case for Affirmative Action* (Ithaca, N.Y.: Cornell University Press, 1991); and Stephen L. Carter, *Reflections of an Affirmative Action Baby* (New York: Basic Books, 1991). For **comparative perspectives** on these questions, see Michael L. Wyzan, ed., *The Political Economy of Ethnic Discrimination and Affirmative Action: A Comparative Perspective* (New York: Praeger, 1990).

For information about **African-Americans' economic status**, see James E. Blackwell, *The Black Community: Diversity and Unity*, 3rd ed. (New York: HarperCollins, 1991); Christopher Jencks and Paul E. Peterson, eds., *The Urban Underclass* (Washington, D.C.: Brookings Institution, 1991); and Andrew Hacker, *Two Nations, Black and White, Separate, Hostile, Unequal* (New York: Scribner, 1992).

For more reading on **gender and civil rights**, try Susan Gluck Mezey, *In Pursuit of Equality: Women, Public Policy, and the Federal Courts* (New York: St. Martin's Press, 1992); and Joan Hoff-Wilson, *Law, Gender, and Injustice: A Legal History of U.S. Women* (New York: New York University Press, 1991). The concept of **comparable worth** can be explored in these works: Ellen Frankel Paul, *Equity and Gender: The Comparable Worth Debate* (New Brunswick, N.J.: Transaction Books, 1989); and Linda M. Blum, *Between Feminism and Labor: The Significance of the Comparable Worth Movement* (Berkeley: University of California Press, 1991).

For a history of **gay and lesbian activism**, see Barry D. Adam, *The Rise of a Gay and Lesbian Movement* (Boston: Twayne, 1987). Comparative perspectives can be found in Simon Sheperd and Mick Wallis, eds., *Coming On Strong: Gay Politics and Culture* (Boston: Unwin Hyman, 1989).

On the special challenges of providing civil rights for **disabled persons**, see Stephen L. Percy, *Disability, Civil Rights, and Public Policy: The Politics of Implementation* (Tuscaloosa: University of Alabama Press, 1989).

On **pure food and drugs**, see James Harvey Young, *Pure Food: Securing the Federal Food and Drugs Act of 1906* (Princeton, N.J.: Princeton University Press, 1989).

On **collective bargaining and trade unions**, see Lowell Turner, *Democracy at Work: Changing World Markets and the Future of Labor Unions* (Ithaca, N.Y.: Cornell University Press, 1991); and Neal Q. Herrick, *Joint Management and Employee Participation: Labor and Management at the Crossroads* (San Francisco: Jossey-Bass, 1990). Excellent case studies of the interaction of collective bargaining and civil rights in Poland's Solidarity union are presented in A. Kemp-Welch, trans. and ed., *The Birth of Solidarity*, 2nd ed. (New York: St. Martin's Press, 1991). On the **Ludlow Massacre**, see George S. McGovern and Leonard F. Guttridge, *The Great Coalfield War* (Boston: Houghton Mifflin, 1972).

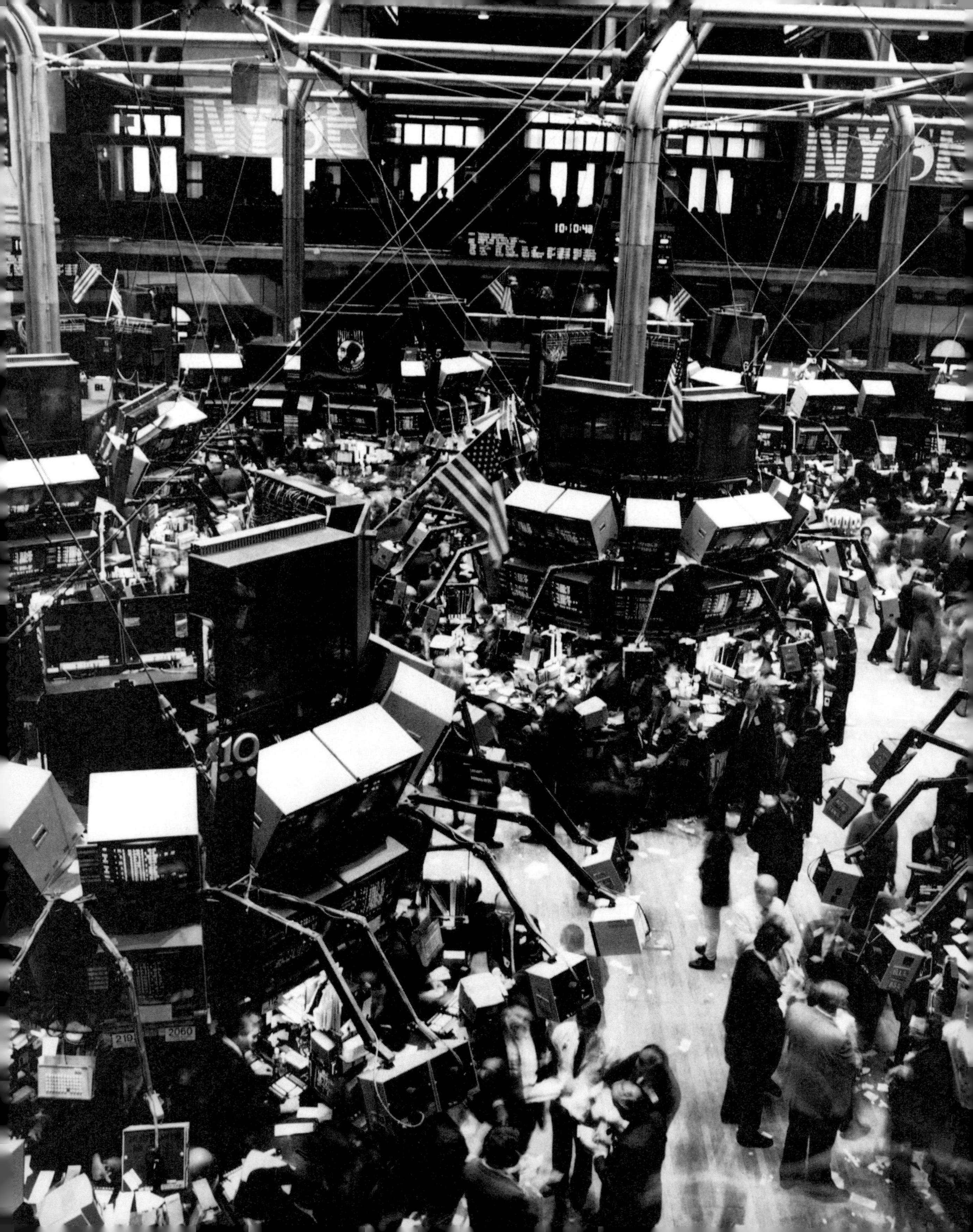
NYSE
10:10:40
10
2060

CHAPTER SEVEN

THE AMERICAN POLITICAL ECONOMY

Inequality and Democratic Politics

CHAPTER OUTLINE

A Nineteenth-Century Duality
CAPITALISM
SOCIALISM

Twentieth-Century Economic Variety
MIXED SYSTEMS
THE SOVIET BLOC AND REPRESSIVE COLLECTIVISM

The U.S. Political Economy
DISTRIBUTION OF INCOME
DISTRIBUTION OF WEALTH AND OWNERSHIP
CORPORATIONS AND THE ECONOMY
POVERTY

Public Policy and the Political Economy
GOVERNMENT SPENDING, TAXATION, AND REGULATION
GOVERNMENT AND INEQUALITY

THE IDOL OF COMMUNISM, WHICH SPREAD EVERYWHERE SOCIAL strife, animosity and unparalleled brutality, which instilled fear in humanity, has collapsed.

On June 17, 1992, Russian President Boris Yeltsin appeared before a joint session of the U.S. Congress, declaring the death of communism and appealing for aid to help his nation reestablish market mechanisms after seventy years of trying to operate a centrally planned economy. Sounding a little like a real estate salesperson, Yeltsin proclaimed: "We are inviting the private sector of the United States to invest in the unique and untapped Russian market—and I am saying: Do not be late."[1] Dozens of Soviet founding fathers must have been spinning in their granite tombs. Conservative commentators in the United States gloated. To be honest, if Karl Marx himself had been in the audience, he might well have cried, "Foul! The Soviet Union was *not* a fair trial of socialist ideals." Nevertheless, across the political spectrum, many people breathed a sigh of relief at the end of the dangerous, expensive all-out competition of the Cold War. A Russian president in Washington hawking investment opportunities would have been absolutely inconceivable only a few years before.

The collapse of the Soviet empire, and the scramble of many of the resultant newly independent nations to acquire market systems, encourages us to look beyond the simplistic economic dualisms of Cold War rhetoric. Like fans at some global football game, popular debate during that time often resembled a shouting match between advocates of "capitalism" on one side and "socialism" or "communism" on the other. In the United States it was difficult (for elected officials, almost impossible) to find a comfortable seat outside the "capitalist" cheering section. In the Soviet Union the reverse was true. Regrettably, little enlightening exchange was possible. Then the Soviet Union disintegrated and the terms of debate changed.

This chapter takes up **political economy**, a term encompassing such specific matters as the day-to-day management of inflation or the regulation of farm prices but also such far-reaching issues as the distribution of wealth and income in society, the ownership and definition of property, and the range of government power. All of these economic issues and questions are affected by the actions of the government—and government, in turn, is shaped by the economic structure of the larger society. We can learn a great deal about what a government accomplishes, and fails to accomplish, by looking at its economic organization. In this chapter we look first at the debate of the past hundred years over how a modern economy should be structured and the implications of that debate for democratic politics. Then we focus on how the U.S. economy is structured. Finally, we explore the connections between U.S. social and economic structures and the ways in which U.S. government policy is made.

A Nineteenth-Century Duality

One hundred years ago, as industrial capitalism was rapidly developing everywhere in the Western world, defenders and opponents of this economic system predicted an intense struggle over its future. Capitalism and socialism were seen as the great alternatives. Socialists believed that their system held out the prospect of genuine economic equality combined with democratic politics. Capitalists contended that only their system would protect individual freedom and promote economic growth and high productivity. Compromise between the two alternatives seemed elusive.[2]

By comparing the theories of socialism and capitalism, we can clarify the debate about the "just society" that has preoccupied Western political thinkers since the eighteenth century. We must recognize, however, that in the United States socialism has not played a prominent role, at least in comparison to Western Europe. In this country, the debate over the political economy has been carried on not so much between socialists and capitalists as between the more liberal reformers of capitalism and the more conservative defenders of it. Generally, U.S. liberals have sought to amend, humanize, or improve the capitalist system rather than to substitute socialism for it. In this section we spotlight capitalism as it evolved and the theory of socialism; in the next section we examine contemporary mixed systems that incorporate elements of both.

Capitalism

The essential elements of **capitalism** are private ownership of the means of production and a competitive market system, driven by the profit motive, through which wealth and resources are distributed. The major capital goods in such a society—factories, machines, land, and money—are owned by individuals or groups who have the right to use this property for private gain. What goods are produced, what they cost, and who will receive them are determined by the competitive operations of the marketplace according to the costs of supply and the demands of consumers.[3]

According to eighteenth-century proponents of capitalism, the ideal capitalist society would be made up of many small enterprises competing for a portion of the market. Government would play a minor role in this society, handling various public functions, such as building and maintaining roads; conducting foreign policy and providing for the national defense; and enforcing the law. In this liberal-capitalist concept of minimum government, espoused by many early leaders of the United States, government was seen as the chief threat to freedom. In this view, freedom to do business as one pleased was linked with freedom of conscience and freedom of speech. The ideal government functioned as a "night watchman"—a guardian of the existing distribution of property.

In the early nineteenth century it was widely believed that **laissez-faire** (unregulated) capitalism would liberate society from the tyrannies of political oppression, bureaucratic control, and stifling traditions. Capitalism, many theorists held, would create a new world of immense wealth, a far more efficient and productive economy—without any conscious direction from governmen. In attempting to profit as much as possible, each person would create wealth, and this would benefit the whole society.[4] Selfishness, in other words, would serve social ends. In this ideal capitalistic world, individuals would be judged on their merits—the value of their skills in the marketplace—not on such noneconomic criteria as social status, color, gender, or religion.

On its own terms, capitalism succeeded almost immediately. The new economic system revolutionized the production and distribution of goods, stimulated worldwide trade, and broke down ancient and often oppressive traditions and social barriers. The economic freedom of capitalism and the political freedom of democracy formed a perfect partnership for great numbers of people.

Yet from the first, the capitalist system prompted strong criticism. Its more conservative critics viewed capitalism as inimical to communal ties and social bonds. Nineteenth-century conservatives were also unhappy with capitalism's antigovernment stance. Government was needed, these conservatives argued, to protect the weak (such as children who worked fourteen-hour days in mines and factories) and to limit the

Coal miners, circa 1908. Child labor was an everyday fact of early capitalism, and one that required government action to correct. These young coal miners worked fourteen-hour days and received little or no schooling. Not until the second decade of the twentieth century was child labor curtailed in the United States. *(The Bettmann Archive)*

ferocity of competition. Certain values, these critics argued, were more important than profit.[5]

More radical opponents of capitalism challenged the system's basic premises. They charged that capitalism extolled the value of equality but actually created inequality. Under nineteenth-century capitalism, wealth was distributed very unequally, and it seemed likely to remain that way. Capitalism not only exploited the workers, but it was also highly inefficient, radicals argued. Cycles of inflation and depression caused great suffering and wasted vast resources.

Radicals also charged that capitalism made real democracy difficult to achieve. As long as wealth was distributed so unequally, the few who were rich would wield excessive political power while the many who were poor would exercise too little. Then, too, in a capitalist economy decisions affecting the lives of millions were made by a handful of powerful capitalists who controlled the means of production; this arrangement was inherently undemocratic. For these reasons, most radicals called for some form of collective ownership of the means of production to democratize economic decision making.

Socialism

Whereas the elements of capitalism are fairly clear-cut, there is less agreement on the meaning of **socialism**. Most socialists, however, would argue that private ownership of the means of production should be replaced by some form of social ownership, that the market system should be replaced by some sort of planned economy, and that the distribution of wealth should be considerably more equal than it is under capitalism.[6]

Some early socialists—including the most famous, Karl Marx and Friedrich Engels—predicted that capitalism would inevitably collapse under the weight of its internal problems and that socialism would automatically take its place. Others favored gradual reform, a slow transition from capitalism to socialism through parliamentary processes. Almost all traditional socialists, however, counted on using the vast productive apparatus created by capitalism to achieve a more just social order. In theory, socialism would work in a more rational, planned fashion than capitalism, avoiding the problems of economic boom and bust often associated with a market economy. Socialism would also promote a more just social order, since wealth would be distributed more equally and large concentrations of wealth would be abolished. In addition, the system would foster a more compassionate and community-minded society, actively concerned about members who were not economically productive. Socialism would encourage individuals to pursue values more worthy than profit and would neutralize the crass commercialism of capitalism.

Critics of socialism predicted disaster.[7] How could any planner manage the complexities of a modern economy? they asked. Government planning, critics argued, would only produce great inefficiency and concentrate power in the hands of government bureaucracy. Overall, the growth of government power under socialism would threaten democracy and freedom itself. And socialism, in attempting to bring life's uncertainties under control and provide security for all, would merely stultify human creativity.

Twentieth-Century Economic Variety

Mixed Systems

The apocalyptic and utopian forecasts of the early proponents of capitalism and socialism fell very wide of the mark. Rather than evolve into strictly socialist or capitalist societies, the Western industrial democracies adopted a mix of capitalist and socialist elements. The exact mix of elements differs from one society to another: The United States, for example, is more capitalist in orientation; Great Britain and Sweden are more socialist.

These mixed systems developed in fits and starts, often spurred by efforts to deal with the crises of capitalism. In many countries, socialist-type reforms, backed by growing trade union movements and socialist political groups, began gathering momentum

> ## THE TVA: AN EXPERIMENT IN SOCIALISM
>
> In the early 1930s fully 98 percent of the farms in the Tennessee River valley had no electricity, and the few that did paid exorbitant rates to private power companies. The entire area, although rich in natural resources, was steeped in a chronic state of poverty. Water power was being wasted, forests were being destroyed by improper cutting and management, thousands of acrs of farmland were being abandoned, and much industry had left the area. With this as a backdrop, Senator George Norris of Nebraska, a Republican, sponsored legislation calling for the creation of a publicly owned Tennessee Valley Authority (TVA) to provide cheap electrical power to residents of the economically deprived Tennessee River valley.
>
> However, in 1931 President Herbert Hoover vetoed Norris's proposed TVA program. To Hoover, state involvement in the economy amounted to "socialism" and was therefore totally abhorrent.
>
> But Norris persisted, and with the backing of President Franklin D. Roosevelt, the TVA was established by Congress in May 1933. The enterprise was gigantic in scope, involving the generation of power, the development of natural resources, and a significant amount of economic planning for an area three-fourths the size of England. It also represented the first essentially socialist project entered into by the U.S. government.
>
> The TVA was an outstanding success by most estimates. Twenty-five dams were built, extensive flood control projects were carried out, nitrate production was established, thousands of miles of electric transmission lines were built, and huge amounts of power were sold at low rates to local communities.
>
> Today the TVA concentrates primarily on its role as a producer of electrical power—the third largest in the country. It sells power to 160 municipal and rural electrification cooperatives, fifty large industrial customers, and the Energy Department. By the middle of the 1980s the TVA seemed to be running out of steam, largely due to its involvement in the nation's largest and most ambitious nuclear

(Box continues on page 243)

in the late nineteenth and early twentieth centuries. The first steps toward what we now call the **welfare state** were taken then, including systematic government aid to the poor and the unemployed, public housing, and government provision of old-age pensions. As government took a more and more active role in regulating the economic marketplace, new government agencies were created to protect consumers and workers. Some measures were also designed to break up large concentrations of industrial power, and a few tentative efforts were made to protect the environment.

power program. Seventeen TVA nuclear generating plants were planned in the 1960s, when nuclear power was widely seen as the future of energy production. But then safety and environmental concerns radically altered the economics of nuclear power (see Chapter 22). The TVA spent $11 billion on ten nuclear plants that were never completed. Of the ones that were finished, five (representing almost one-fifth of the TVA's total production capacity) were shut down in 1985 for safety reasons. To absorb these losses, TVA rates were rising faster than its private competitors', and the government's power company was in danger of pricing itself out of the market.

But then the TVA demonstrated that government agencies as well as private corporations can respond to changes in the market. A new chairman of its three-person board of governors in 1988 instituted effective cost-cutting measures that saved $800 million in two years. Two of the mothballed nuclear units came back on line in 1989, and five more would return to operation in the next few years. The new chairman made a commitment to keep rates steady for three years, improving competitiveness. Most interestingly, since the TVA is limited by statute to operate only within the Tennessee River valley, the new TVA leadership decided that the best long-term plan for remaining competitive in power generation is to encourage the development of the local economy. The TVA's territory forms the heart of Appalachia, chronically one of the most depressed areas of the country. Special rates were implemented to encourage new employment in the region, bringing this government experiment back in line with its original broader mission to serve the economic development of the Tennessee River valley. As a former chair of the board of governors said, "Our mission ought to be activist. We should be the one developing ideas for the electric car, for hammering out practical answers to acid rain. The TVA ought not to be, as President Carter once said, just another utility."

Sources: William E. Schmidt, "The TVA Has Come to a Bend in the River," New York Times, *May 20, 1984, p. E5; James Cook, "Entrepreneurial Power,"* Forbes, *March 19, 1990.*

The Great Depression of the 1930s represented a watershed in the evolution of mixed economies. In grappling with widespread unemployment and social dislocations, governments intervened in the market and created new social programs. This trend toward increasing government intervention firmly took hold during World War II, when governments were forced to do extensive economic and social planning. The Western democracies emerged from the war with new capabilities for dealing with modern economic life.

In the post–World War II period, proponents of socialism gained ground in Western Europe. In Great Britain and Scandinavia, socialist parties held the reins of government in the immediate postwar era, and in West Germany, France, the Netherlands, and other countries they became political forces to be reckoned with. The Labour party of Great Britain nationalized (placed under government ownership) the failing coal mining industry, as well as the steel industry, road transport, and other major industries. The British also created a system of socialized medicine and greatly increased the reach of the welfare state.

Generally speaking, socialist parties in power proved more moderate than many analysts had expected.[8] In Scandinavia, for example, few industries were nationalized. Instead, Scandinavian socialists concentrated on keeping employment and economic growth high while extending the scope of government benefits. The goal was still equality, socialists argued; the exact means didn't matter much. In addition, the results of nationalization were often disappointing. In Britain, most workers found their lives little changed by the shift from private to government ownership.

At the same time, capitalism also prospered. The new mixed economies allowed for extensive government stimulation of economic growth—and growth there was. When no serious depression occurred after World War II, many experts argued that the boom-and-bust cycle characteristic of unregulated capitalist economies had been banished permanently, thanks largely to government stimulation of the economy.[9]

The **mixed economies** of most Western democracies today can be characterized as follows:

- Private ownership of the means of production is predominant, although the government's role in the economy is substantial (see **Table 7-1**).
- Government regulation of economic life has become an accepted state of affairs. Through taxation and spending, regulation of interest rates, and other means, the government seeks to maintain high levels of employment and economic growth and to keep inflation under control.
- The government regulates many important details of economic life, including working conditions, environmental conditions, and matters affecting health and safety.
- The government is deeply involved in promoting the welfare of the citizenry. Basic welfare state programs include old-age insurance, aid to the poor, health insurance or socialized medicine, and other provisions for groups such as unemployed young people, the handicapped, and students.
- Cooperation between government and business is widespread. The government provides aid to failing industries, special tax breaks to businesses, and subsidies to various groups (such as farmers) and enters into joint private-public ventures (as in oil exploration). The relationship between government and business is sometimes cooperative and sometimes antagonistic.
- Considerable inequality in the distribution of wealth and income persists, even where socialists have held power for long periods. Generally, however, wealth is not so unequally distributed as it was fifty years ago.

TABLE 7-1
PUBLIC ENTERPRISES AS A PERCENTAGE OF THEIR INDUSTRY IN VARIOUS COUNTRIES

	Post	Telecom-munications	Elec-tricity	Gas	Oil	Coal	Rail	Air	Motor	Steel	Ship-building
United States	90	0	25	0	0	0	25	0	0	0	0
Japan	100	33	0	0	n.a.	0	25	0	0	0	0
Germany	100	100	75	50	25	50	100	100	25	0	25
France	100	100	100	100	n.a.	100	100	75	50	75	0
Italy	100	100	75	100	n.a.	n.a.	100	100	25	75	75
United Kingdom	100	0	100	25	25	100	100	0	0	75	50
Canada	100	25	100	0	0	0	75	75	0	0	0
Australia	100	100	100	100	0	0	100	75	0	0	n.a.
Austria	100	100	100	100	100	100	100	100	100	100	n.a.
Belgium	100	100	25	25	n.a.	0	100	100	100	50	0
Netherlands	100	100	75	75	n.a.	n.a.	100	75	50	25	0
Spain	100	50	0	75	n.a.	50	100	100	0	50	75
Sweden	100	100	50	100	n.a.	n.a.	100	50	25	75	75
Switzerland	100	100	100	100	n.a.	n.a.	100	25	0	0	n.a.

n.a. = not available.
SOURCE: Howard Oxley, Maria Maher, John P. Martin, Giuseppi Nicoletti, and Patricia Alonso-Gamo, *The Public Sector: Issues for the 1990s*, OECD Department of Economics and Statistics Working Paper No. 90 (Washington, D.C.: Organization for Economic Cooperation and Development, 1990), table 17.

Encompassing such diverse elements, this type of political economy defies easy labels. Some observers call it *neocapitalism*—a name that emphasizs its continuity with the capitalism of the past. Others consider it *conservative socialism*—a paradoxical term that emphasizes how much has changed, both in economic life and in the way socialists now think about economic problems.

The Soviet Bloc and Repressive Collectivism

The Russian Revolution in 1917 was the first page in a different economic story to be written in the Union of Soviet Socialist Republics and the countries it came to dominate. With the ascension to power of V. I. Lenin in November of that year, the USSR became the first modern state committed to communist rule.* Starting in 1939 with a short-

---

*__Communism__ differs from socialism by advocating the elimination of all private property. A true communist system relies exclusively on social incentives rather than material incentives to stimulate individual labor. (The benefits of society would be distributed to each individual according to need and would be created by effort from each individual according to ability.) Marx and Engels saw socialism as a stage in the inevitable progress toward communism, which would be marked by the dissolution of classes and the withering away of the coercive mechanisms of government.

Irony seems the precise word for this juxtaposition of reality and the world of advertising. Flood victims in Louisville, Kentucky, wait in line for assistance in 1937. America was still mired in the Great Depression, but that doesn't seem to have affected the family in the car. Our beliefs count for a lot. If we *believe* that America is the finest country on earth, that, in itself, creates an important political reality. *(Margaret Bourke-White,* Life *Magazine © 1937 Time Inc.)*

lived nonaggression pact with Nazi Germany, the USSR, through negotiation and military action (including brutal invasions of Poland, Hungary, and Czechoslovakia) came to dominate most of Eastern Europe. For nearly half a century the Soviets imposed and maintained Communist party rule in these countries through positive incentives (massive military and economic aid) and military sanctions. Planned economies (usually with flourishing black markets) were linked together by Soviet dominance. In general (although each case was different), the Soviet-dominated countries eliminated the worst social inequities, and industrialization advanced, but inefficiencies abounded, and special privileges for party members belied egalitarian rhetoric. Shortages of consumer goods, even foodstuffs, were the norm. The cost of maintaining a huge military structure was enormous.

Critics of socialism point to the collapse of Communist party domination in Eastern Europe in 1989 and 1990 and the disintegration of the Soviet Union in 1991 as evidence of the inefficiency and ultimate unworkability of centrally planned economies. In response to these charges, Western socialists point to the distortions of both external

Soviet domination and institutionalized internal domination by the party apparatus in qualifying the lesson of the Eastern European and Soviet experience. Plain old nationalism was a major component in the recent transformation of the political map in this part of the world. Political leaders on both sides of the old Cold War seemed to agree that more extensive use of market mechanisms was desirable and necessary in the several nations of the former Soviet bloc as part of integrating into the Western-dominated world economy.

Given the variety of models of development among the emerging nations of the Southern Hemisphere and the economies of the former Soviet empire, touting a single ideal model for national economies may be premature. Unlimited possibilities exist for creative arrangements to meet particular national circumstances. Important differences exist in the way ownership is defined and the limits under which it operates. For example, **employee stock ownership plans (ESOPs)**, whereby the company's stock is held primarily or exclusively by the company's own employees are just one alternative form of ownership that is neither capitalist nor socialist. Forms of worker ownership and worker management have been attempted in various countries, and an extensive system of workers' councils were a feature of socialism in Yugoslavia prior to that nation's disintegration. Until recently, some reformers in communist nations advocated the development of *market socialism*, a system in which markets would be used to replace or supplement central planning in determining which goods would be produced. Some such reforms had already been implemented in Hungary. In Sweden, in another approach, some democratic socialists have advocated reducing the amount of private ownership across the whole economy by having workers own increasing amounts of company stock, but Swedish voters have not supported this approach. The collapse of communist systems has not led to the creation of blends of capitalism and socialism but to the aggressive pursuit of market strategies in Eastern Europe and the former USSR. Many democratic socialists in Western democracies have questioned the relevance of their ideas. And yet vast and serious problems remain, and the social welfare state continues to be popular with many voters. The nineteenth-century debate continues on many issues, including privatization of government functions, national health care, and the structure of the tax system.

The U.S. Political Economy

In one sense, the United States enjoys an embarrassment of riches: Americans comprise only 5 percent of the world's population and yet generate 30 percent of all the goods and services produced annually in the world. The U.S. **gross national product** (the value of all goods and services produced) is more than $5 trillion a year—by far the largest national economy on the planet. Americans also use about 40 percent of the world's output of raw materials and produce about 40 percent of the world's waste products and pollution.

PART ONE • FOUNDATIONS

The United States has dominated international economic life since the end of World War II. Beginning in the 1970s, however, that dominance began to wane. A number of factors figured in the U.S. economic downturn, including the Vietnam War, energy shortages and oil price increases, the effects of a severe recession in the early 1980s followed by huge government budget deficits, and the growing economic power of other nations. With the collapse of the Soviet Union, the United States entered the 1990s with a preeminence of military might it had not enjoyed since just after the Second World War. Economic matters were quite different, though. The Persian Gulf War in 1991 provided clear evidence of altered global circumstances. The United States engineered and led the U.N.-sanctioned military effort to oust Iraq from its occupation of Kuwait, with U.S. armed forces and U.S. military technology dominating the massive operation. But to pay for its participation, the United States depended on its allies for most of the direct costs, securing commitments from Germany, Japan, Saudi Arabia, and others for $35 billion of the original total estimate of $58 billion.

Both cause and sign of the relative weakening of American economic strength are the U.S. **trade deficits** (excesses of imports over exports) that began in 1971 and ballooned in the 1980s (see **Figure 7-1**). In 1985 the United States ceased being a net capital exporter and became a net capital importer (that means that residents of other nations have greater investments in the United States than Americans have abroad). One sign of future economic strength is the development of technology. In 1965, U.S. residents were granted more than 80 percent of U.S. patents; by 1987 only 54 percent of U.S. patents went to U.S. residents. Since 1986 the U.S. has imported more high-technology goods than it has exported.[10] Although in absolute terms the United States is still the largest national economy, its economic *hegemony* (leadership or domination over other nations) has eroded since the 1960s.

We now turn to four key issues affecting the U.S. political economy: the distribution of income, the distribution of wealth and ownership, corporations and the economy, and poverty in the world's richest country.

FIGURE 7-1

U.S. TRADE BALANCE, 1981–1991 (BILLIONS OF DOLLARS)

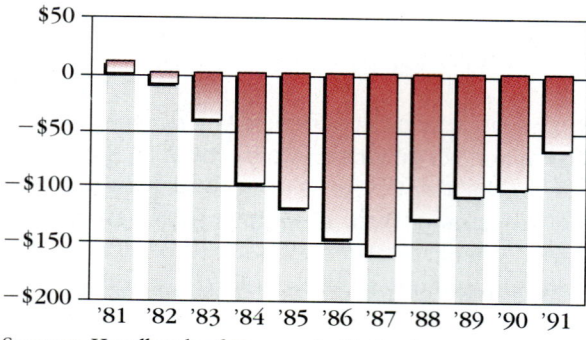

SOURCE: Handbook of Economic Outlook.

Distribution of Income

Americans do not share equally in either the nation's affluence or its economic problems; our society includes many gradations of wealth and poverty. Traditionally, sociologists view societies as divided into **social classes**—fairly distinct groups, differentiated by occupation or income, that usually have different lifestyles and may clash politically. Some sociologists regard the distinction between white-collar and blue-collar jobs as the fundamental division in society. Others emphasize property ownership, dividing society into owners and nonowners. Still others focus on income and lifestyle criteria.

Most Americans classify themselves on the basis of annual income, the amount of money brought into the household in a given year. Although these judgments are highly subjective, people with annual incomes ranging from $20,000 to $100,000 commonly think of themselves as being "middle-class." Such a broad category obviously includes people with radically different lifestyles, political views, occupations, incomes, and degrees of wealth.

The recession of 1991. A thousand job-seekers line up for the few positions available at a New Hampshire company. The problem of unemployment, though far less serious than during the Great Depression, continued to be a feature of market economies and contributed to declining U.S. economic conditions in the early 1990s. *(Rodney Curtis/Impact Visuals)*

A truer picture of the nation's economic classes can be obtained by dividing the population into fifths (*quintiles*) according to income level and determining the percentage of the nation's total income each fifth of the population receives. In 1990 the poorest quintile of the U.S. population received less than 4 percent of the national income, while the richest quintile received over 46 percent. Moreover, the second-poorest fifth received about 10 percent of all income, whereas the next-to-richest fifth received just under 25 percent. These inequalities of income have grown more pronounced since 1970, as **Figure 7-2** shows.

The inequality of income in the United States is not distributed uniformly—a much higher than average percentage of black and Hispanic persons in the United States are poor. Poverty rates are also higher than average for children under eighteen and for residents of central cities, rural areas, and the South. In absolute terms, however, there are more than twice as many poor persons in the United States who are white than black and three times as many poor whites as poor Hispanics (see **Table 7-2**).

Merely reciting such dry statistics tells us little about the quality of life of the poorest of our citizens or about the political consequences of unequal income distribution. As for the latter question, a study of income inequality in fifty-five countries found a strong negative correlation between income inequality and democratic stability.[11] That is, countries with high levels of income inequality were much less likely to have stable democracies. This relationship held even when each country's level of development was controlled for (see **Table 7-3**). Such findings support egalitarian democrats in their

FIGURE 7-2

SHARE OF HOUSEHOLD INCOME, BY QUINTILE; 1970, 1980, AND 1990

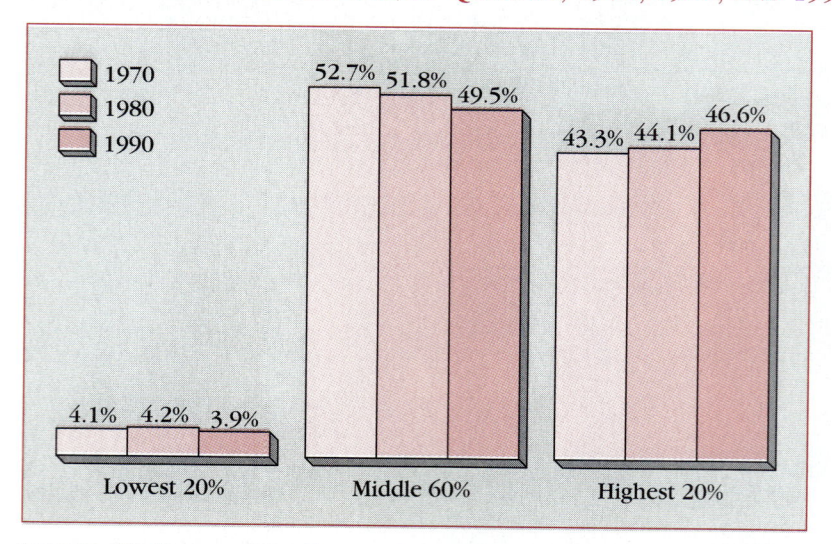

	1970	1980	1990
Lowest 20%	4.1%	4.2%	3.9%
Middle 60%	52.7%	51.8%	49.5%
Highest 20%	43.3%	44.1%	46.6%

SOURCE: U.S. Bureau of the Census, *Current Population Reports*, Series P-60, No. 174 (Washington, D.C.: U.S. Government Printing Office, 1991).

TABLE 7-2

AMERICANS LIVING IN POVERTY, 1990

Group	Persons below Poverty Level (thousands)	Percentage of Group
All Americans	33,585	13.5
White	16,622	8.8
Black	9.837	31.9
Hispanic origin (any race)	6,006	28.1
Other	1,422	15.4

SOURCE: U.S. Bureau of the Census, *Current Population Reports*, Series P-60, No. 175 (Washington, D.C.: U.S. Government Printing Office, 1991).

contention that true democracy can exist only in the absence of large disparities in income and wealth. Income inequality in the United States is not high on a global scale (see **Table 7-4**), but it is higher than in many developed Western democracies and, as we indicated earlier, has been increasing gradually since 1970.*

Social mobility has always been highly valued in the United States. Individual achievement in America is measured in large part by changes in one's relative standing in society. Thus it is important to understand several distinct aspects of mobility.[12] *Structural mobility*, or "forced mobility," occurs because of changes in the overall economy. For example, from the nineteenth century to the twentieth, the proportion of Americans employed in agriculture dropped dramatically while industrial employment increased. This meant that a large number of workers experienced structural mobility from agricultural labor to industrial labor, generally beneficial in wage terms. The U.S. economy is currently shifting from an industrial base to a service base (a larger percentage of employees provide services than produce goods). Although the overall impact of this shift is not yet clear, some observers fear that reverse or downward structural mobility will result (new jobs created have lower wages than the jobs that disappear).

Absolute mobility refers to general improvement or decline in all social strata. From the Second World War through the early 1970s, the United States and most industrialized nations experienced positive absolute mobility. Since then, however, some indicators show a decline in standard of living, or downward absolute mobility. Finally, sociologists define *relative mobility* as movement between social strata—the subject of most popular conversations about mobility. Relative mobility can be affected by

---

*The most commonly used measure of income distribution is an inequality index developed by Italian economist Corrado Gini. The **Gini index** rates perfect equality at 0 and perfect inequality at 1. The higher the index, the greater the inequality of the distribution of incomes. An alternative to simple quintile shares, the Gini index provides a means of calculating the effect of taxes and transfers on income distribution and of comparing income distribution in various nations.

TABLE 7-3
STABILITY OF DEMOCRACY AND INCOME INEQUALITY, 1960–1980

Upper 20 Percent Income Share (%)	Stability of Democracy — Unstable	Stability of Democracy — Stable
69.2	Peru	
62.1	Brazil	
61.8	Panama	
61.0	Lebanon	
58.6	Turkey	
56.6	Malaysia	
54.0	Philippines	
54.0		Venezuela
51.4	Chile	
50.6		Costa Rica
50.0		Trinidad
49.2		India
47.4	Uruguay	
46.5		Italy
46.4		France
45.2		West Germany
44.5		Sri Lanka
44.0		Barbados
43.0		Australia
42.8		United States
41.5		New Zealand
41.0		Canada
41.0		Japan
40.0		Netherlands
39.9		Israel
39.8		Belgium
39.4		Ireland
39.2		United Kingdom
38.0		Switzerland
37.5		Denmark
37.3		Norway
37.0		Sweden
36.8		Finland

SOURCE: Edward N. Muller, "Democracy, Economic Development, and Income Inequality," *American Sociological Review*, February 1988, p. 63.

TABLE 7-4
HOUSEHOLD INCOME DISTRIBUTION IN SELECTED COUNTRIES, 1990

		Percent of Income Going to Households		
Country	Household Gini	Lowest 20 Percent	Top 20 Percent	Top 10 Percent
Netherlands	.2664	8.3	36.2	21.5
Japan	.2773	8.7	37.5	22.4
Switzerland	.3002	6.6	38.0	23.7
West Germany	.3037	7.9	39.5	24.0
Norway	.3118	6.0	38.2	22.8
Sweden	.3205	7.4	41.7	28.1
United Kingdom	.3219	7.0	39.7	23.4
United States	.3359	5.3	39.9	23.3
Canada	.3376	5.3	40.0	23.8
France	.3530	5.5	42.2	26.4
Italy	.3595	6.2	43.9	28.1
Australia	.3975	5.4	47.1	30.5
El Salvador	.3957	5.5	47.3	29.5
Egypt	.3964	5.8	48.0	33.2
India	.4022	7.0	49.4	33.6
Thailand	.4180	5.6	49.8	34.1
Mexico	.5155	2.9	57.7	40.6
Kenya	.5452	2.6	60.4	45.8
Iran	.5489	3.4	62.7	47.4
Peru	.5612	1.9	61.0	42.9
Panama	.5642	2.0	61.8	44.2
Brazil	.5994	2.0	66.6	50.6

SOURCE: Denny Braun, *The Rich Get Richer: The Rise of Income Inequality in the U.S. and the World* (Chicago: Nelson-Hall, 1991), pp. 75–76.

economic conditions (good times may allow many people to rise from one class to another; bad times may precipitate more people downward from one class to a lower one). Government policy can also affect relative mobility, through the elimination of discrimination as a barrier to individual success, for example, or by providing greater access to education.

Distribution of Wealth and Ownership

Wealth is the monetary value of what an individual or a household owns, adjusted for indebtedness. Ordinarily, wealth is divided between durable goods (for example,

PART ONE • FOUNDATIONS

FIGURE 7-3
GETTING RICHER

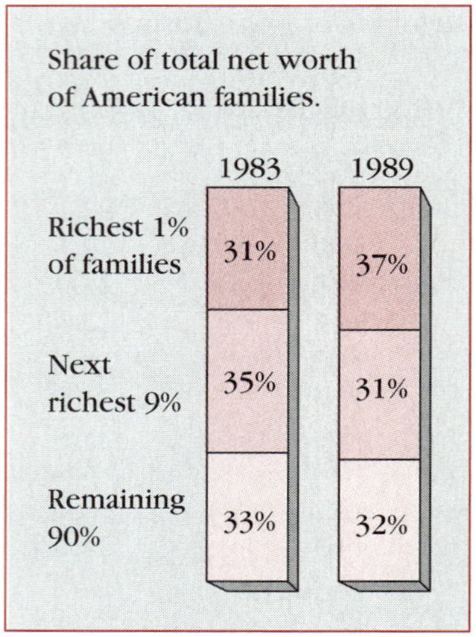

Share of total net worth of American families.

	1983	1989
Richest 1% of families	31%	37%
Next richest 9%	35%	31%
Remaining 90%	33%	32%

Figures may not total 100 because of rounding.
SOURCE: *New York Times*, April 21, 1992, p. A6.

houses, cars, appliances) and financial assets (including stocks, bonds, savings, life insurance). Wealth is distributed far less equally than income in the United States, and while U.S. income inequality grew in the 1980s, wealth inequality grew even faster. Although the share of wealth held by the wealthiest 1 percent of the population hardly changed between 1963 and 1983, it jumped from 31 percent in 1983 to 37 percent in 1989, according to the Federal Reserve Board's Survey of Consumer Finances (see **Figure 7-3**). The concentration of wealth in few hands had reached its highest levels since the 1920s, prior to the Great Depression and the New Deal. The wealthiest 1 percent of the population owned 62 percent of American business assets, while the bottom 90 percent owned less than 10 percent (see **Figure 7-4**). The richest 10 percent of the population owned 90 percent of real estate assets other than principal residences and one-third of the nation's assets in principal residences. The richest 1 percent of the population owned 49 percent of publicly held stock, 78 percent of bonds and trusts, and 45 percent of nonresidential real estate. In 1989 the bottom 90 percent of the population held less than one-third of the total net worth of American families (32 percent). The next 9 percent of the population held almost as much (31 percent). The top 1 percent held the rest—37 percent of the net wealth of American families.[13]*

---

*Since the government does not require the reporting of wealth (as it does income), wealth figures are somewhat less reliable than income figures. But there is general agreement among economists that disparities in wealth are greater than disparities in income and that wealth inequality did increase during the 1980s.

FIGURE 7-4
WHO OWNS WHAT

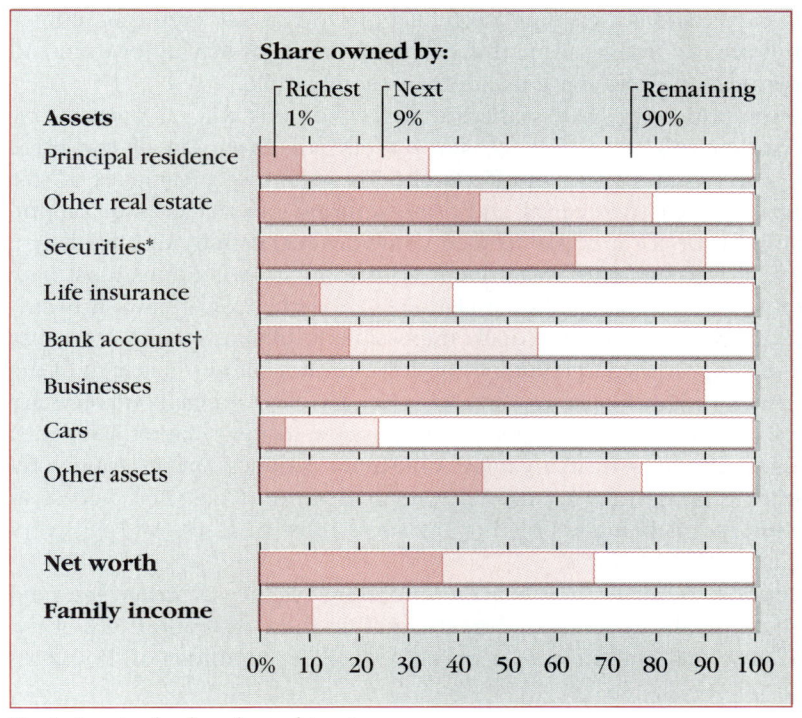

*Includes stocks, bonds, and trusts.
†Includes all deposits in checking, savings and other accounts.
SOURCE: *New York Times*, April 21, 1992, p. A6.

Such differences of economic life not only imply radical differences in lifestyle and opportunities for personal fulfillment, but they also have profound political consequences. Economic power can translate into political power through contributions, advertising, and various sources of influence and assistance. Great concentrations of wealth also place in the hands of a few people decision-making power in economic matters that affect the lives of the multitude—factories can be closed or opened, investments shifted, new products marketed or not developed. Democracy in the political arena, then, faces what is primarily an oligarchy in the economic sphere.

Corporations and the Economy

Today the U.S. economy is largely a corporate economy. Although vast numbers of small businesses are still in operation, much economic activity is controlled or heavily influenced by the decisions of a fairly small number of large corporations and financial institutions. This "corporatist" structure also has an influence on the American political economy, not always of the sort predicted by classical capitalist theory. While on one level it is true that corporations are simply useful fictions to embody aggregate individual interests, critics of corporatism argue that corporate interests may differ from and displace both individual interests and those of the general public.

One of the assumptions of a free market is that conditions will encourage new entries into the market and force unsuccessful players out. In an era of corporate colossi, how can a newcomer break in effectively? The daunting advantages of size reach beyond such complex engineering and manufacturing jobs as cars and computers. How easy would it be for a newly formed company successfully to introduce a new breakfast cereal or deodorant? Since under contemporary conditions most new products (even those backed by established giants) fail, the chances of new-entry success are miniscule, making financing virtually impossible to obtain. A large corporate base is necessary to support the large number of new-product failures in search of the small number of new-product successes. Opportunities for entering many markets are thus limited. Some entrepreneurial success is still possible in new market segments. Apple Computer actually did start in a garage. Consumer products on the fringe (environmentally aware products, for example) sometimes make it big. But success in today's market often means being gobbled up by an established giant. And for every success there are a thousand failures.

What about leaving the market? When a corporation reaches a certain size and diversity, failures can be absorbed, even repeated within the corporation. When the survival of a very large corporation itself is at stake, entailing hundreds of thousands

Neil Bush, son of President George Bush, was touched by the savings and loan scandal. He was fined for unethical practices connected with the misuse of his position at the Silverado Savings and Loan bank in Colorado. Bank deregulation during the Reagan years led to widespread abuses and bank failures and to one of the most costly scandals in American history. (Ron Dirito/Sygma)

of jobs, its well-being is so intertwined with the well-being of the whole economy that the country may be unwilling to allow it to fail. In 1979 a $1.5 billion federal loan guarantee plan was created for the Chrysler Corporation using exactly this argument. The savings and loan crisis of the late 1980s and early 1990s provided dozens of examples of companies that were "too big to fail" (the social and economic costs of going under are large enough to coerce public bailouts). And if loan guarantees or other public bailouts won't work, there's always what Michael Harrington called "lemon socialism." This American innovation consists of leaving profitable ventures in the private sector but absorbing unprofitable ones into the public sector. Thus Santa Fe still profitably carries freight by rail but Amtrak (a subsidized government corporation) carries rail passengers.

Of course, the U.S. economy is by no means entirely "corporatized," and corporations are not the only groups that wield political clout. As politics has penetrated every area of economic life, individuals with common economic interests have formed pressure groups to gain political influence. Doctors, teachers, blue-collar workers, sellers of insurance—all are politically organized. This is inevitable in an economy in which political and economic factors are interwoven so thoroughly. If an industry, a corporation, or some sector of the economy fails to become organized in a politically effective way, it may well find itself vulnerable to political forces outside its control.

Poverty

Any assessment of the political economy in the United States must address the question of poverty. How many Americans suffer severe deprivation? Perhaps more important, what progress is being made toward reducing their number? The issue is not simple. Most of us do not interact with the poor, who populate the margins of our society—the ghettos, barrios, migrant farmworker camps, and Indian reservations. Also subject to dispute are who make up "the poor" and how prevalent poverty is. Let us now turn to these two issues.

DEFINITIONS The federal government's definition of poverty is based on calculations made by Mollie Orshansky for the Social Security Administration in the early 1960s.[14] At the core of her computations was an estimate of the dollar equivalent of the minimum amount of nutrition needed for a person to survive. She then multiplied this economy food budget by three, to reflect the findings of a series of studies in 1955 that low-income families spent two-thirds of their budgets on nonfood essentials such as clothing, shelter, and fuel. The figure then arrived at became the basis for establishing poverty lines for various groups of people—those in urban or rural areas, families of four or single individuals, and so on. A person whose income fell below the poverty line of his or her group was counted as "poor."

As **Table 7-5** demonstrates, progress toward the eradication of poverty has been disappointing. Much headway was made between 1960 and 1970, but since then the percentage of persons below the poverty level has remained fairly constant, with the

TABLE 7-5
POVERTY IN AMERICA, 1960–1990

Year	Persons below Poverty Level (thousands)	Percentage of U.S. Population
1960	39,851	22.2
1965	33,185	17.3
1970	25,420	12.6
1975	25,877	12.3
1980	29,272	13.0
1985	33,064	14.0
1990	33,585	13.5

SOURCE: U.S. Bureau of the Census, *Current Population Reports*, Series P-60, No. 171 (Washington, D.C.: U.S. Government Printing Office, 1991).

actual number of persons in poverty increasing. And if we take issue with the government's statistical definition of poverty, the picture becomes even less encouraging. By the government's own admission, the nutrition provided by the economy food budget is only *minimally* adequate: It's designed for "emergency or temporary" periods, not for the long term.

DISTRIBUTION Although half of all poor people in the United States are non-Hispanic white (less than 9 percent of the non-Hispanic white population), a disproportionate 32 percent of all blacks and 28 percent of Hispanics are poor. Thirty-two percent of all families headed by females with no husband present are poor, compared with only 6 percent of all married-couple families. Social attitudes and policies sharply affect who will become and remain poor; poverty is largely a product of generations of discrimination, sexism, exploitation, and neglect. Being born into a poor family places heavy burdens on even the most enterprising of people—the fight for a good education, a decent job, and other opportunities is steeply uphill.

Government policies have had a marked effect on the distribution of poverty. Over the past decades the percentage of elderly people who are poor has declined sharply (from 28 percent in 1966 to around 11 percent in 1990), largely because of higher social security payments. Children, especially those living with their mothers and not fathers, have not been as well served by government programs designed to keep them from poverty. The highest incidence of poverty is among members of black and Hispanic female-headed households with children under eighteen and no husband present. More than *half* of these households are poor.

Interestingly, Americans' attitudes about the causes of poverty have remained fairly constant. Americans tend to believe that poverty emanates largely from factors within the individual; society or the economy, then, is not to blame. Yet most people do recognize that structural conditions in the society do play some role. A similar pattern emerges in explanations about why people are rich: The three factors listed as most important are personal drive and risk taking, hard work, and inheritance. Luck, dishonesty, exploitation, and "pull" are all ranked considerably lower, as is talent.

Public Policy and the Political Economy

Heading into the twenty-first century, the industrial democracies face two problems. One is that the successful methods of economic management that Western democratic governments pioneered in the 1930s and expanded in the 1950s no longer seem able to respond fully to the complex economic problems of today. The other is that energy and environmental issues—declining energy sources, depletion of land and forest, population pressures, environmental pollution that affects air and oceans—have added new dimensions to the economic equation, especially in a changing international economic system. Neither conservatives nor liberals (nor, in Europe, democratic socialists) have offered very persuasive solutions to these deep-rooted problems. With this in mind, we now turn to the ramifications of government spending, taxation, and regulation and government's impact on inequality.

Government Spending, Taxation, and Regulation

The U.S. government has always affected our economic life. Yet until relatively recently, the government's spending, taxation, and regulatory policies were only marginally significant in terms of the overall economy. In 1929 federal spending represented only 9.8 percent of the U.S. gross national product. Outlays to combat the Depression of the 1930s pushed government spending to 19 percent of the GNP. During World War II government expenditures rose dramatically; to finance military production, the government spent 41 percent of the GNP in both 1943 and 1944. When peace came, government outlays temporarily dropped back to prewar levels, only to rise again in the Cold War era, to 23 percent of the GNP. In 1991 federal outlays were 25 percent of the GNP.

When the government disposes of a quarter of a nation's GNP, it is obvious that the priorities of government spending have great social and political ramifications. There are four basic issues: (1) How large should the overall budget be? (2) Is the national debt a problem? (3) Who should carry the tax burden? (4) How should government expenditures be allocated?

On the first two issues, modern-day liberals and conservatives generally take opposing views. Liberals tend to favor an involved and active government, and they frequently argue that government spending is too low. Conservatives, by contrast, usually consider government spending a major social issue in itself, campaigning vigorously for budget cuts. In addition, conservatives often call for a balanced budget—one in which the outflow of funds is roughly matched by government revenues from taxes and other sources. Liberals tend to argue that deficit spending stimulates economic growth. These positions are not written in stone, of course: Liberals as well as conservatives have opposed bloated budget deficits, and it was the conservative administration of President Ronald Reagan that amassed the largest government debt in U.S. history.

The question of who should carry the tax burden is even more controversial. Should individuals pay most of it, or should corporations? How can we strike a proper balance between the two? Ronald Reagan was fond of saying that corporations can't pay taxes—ultimately only *people* pay taxes. Though in one sense this is true, more practically, the choice between taxing individuals and taxing corporations does spread the tax burden differently among economic strata, and the choice represents different political costs. The majority of the U.S. tax burden currently falls on individuals.

Whatever spending level is decided on, and whoever ultimately foots the bill, there will always be differences of opinion about spending and taxing priorities. After the Second World War, conservatives usually emphasized military preparedness as a top priority, whereas liberals called for increased spending on social programs. More recent developments have blurred these lines, as, for instance, the development of an effective senior citizen lobby has made entitlement programs such as Medicare and social security hard to touch by conservatives and liberals alike. And the end of the Cold War initiated a lively debate about reductions in the defense budget in which members of Congress often seemed to allow narrow constituency concerns (local defense contract

Astronauts on a space shuttle flight wrestle with an errant satellite. The space program, with its spectacular achievements and bitter failures, was not exempt from budget controversies. Was the nation rich enough to support further space exploration while the deficit soared and many called for increased attention to domestic needs? *(NASA)*

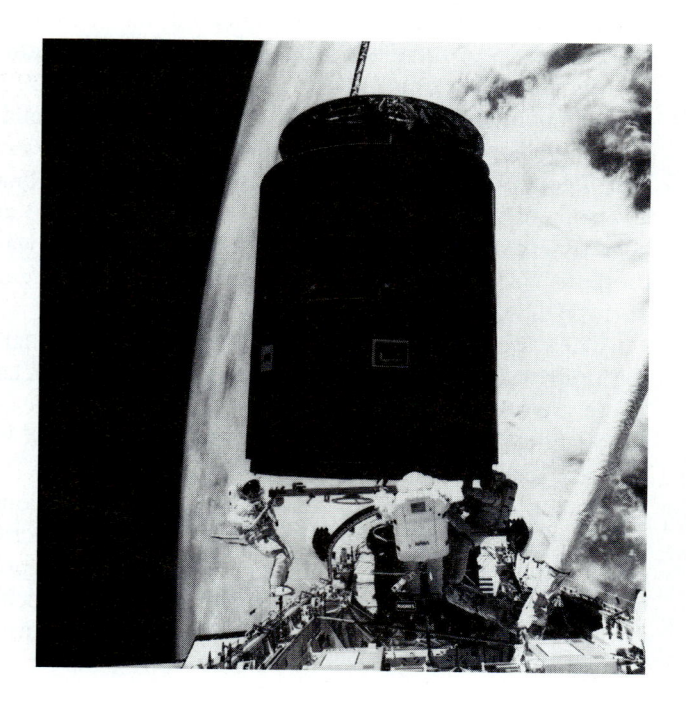

and jobs) to prevail over national policy considerations. Sitting behind every debate about budget priorities in the recent past has been huge federal deficits and the ballooning federal debt, which tripled in size during the 1980s.

Since the 1950s, defense spending as a percentage of the GNP has alternately risen and fallen. Government expenditures on defense declined from a Vietnam War high of 9.5 percent of GNP in 1968 to 5.1 percent in 1979, only to rise and then fall slightly again during the Reagan and Bush administrations. As a rule, U.S. outlays on defense proportionately exceed those of other Western democracies. Federal government spending on social programs has increased significantly since 1965. Currently, expenditures for social programs make up well more than half of all federal expenditures.

Despite increases in social welfare spending, the U.S. government still spends significantly less than its European counterparts on public welfare. Our income tax levels are also significantly lower, and they have increased less since 1960. Most Americans are probably unaware that their taxes are lower than taxes in most other industrialized democratic nations.

Not surprisingly, the European welfare states have gone further than the United States toward eliminating poverty, deprivation, and neglect. In Norway, for example, where the pretax distribution of income is similar to ours, government policy has virtually ended poverty. The Norwegians allot more of their total GNP for use by the government, and a greater percentage of government expenditures goes into **transfer**

People of differing political views usually differ on economic priorities as well. Conservatives have typically emphasized national defense spending, while liberals have championed social programs. *(Mimi Forsyth/Monkmeyer)*

payments (money paid to individuals through social programs). The Norwegian tax structure is also highly progressive (that is, the higher one's income, the higher the rate of taxation).

This example illustrates that even in a predominantly capitalist society like Norway, the government can go to great lengths to combat economic deprivation. It also reflects profound differences in Norwegian and American attitudes toward what government should do and for whom.

But while the U.S. government may not accord the highest priority to alleviating deprivation, it does perform many essential social welfare functions. The government regulates the trade cycle; provides social welfare benefits to individuals, without which many more people would fall below the poverty line; and oversees a wide-ranging system of economic regulation designed, in many respects, to protect individuals.

Government and Inequality

Should government actively promote economic equality? Some theorists argue that government has no business interfering with the distribution of income and wealth in society. Others maintain that the redistribution of income is a legitimate government activity, designed to increase equality and assist those in greatest financial need.[15]

In fact, governments do become deeply enmeshed in economic activity, and their rules and programs do benefit and protect various groups. The question is, how much should government do and for whom? American conservatives contend that since the New Deal, government programs have distorted the workings of the marketplace and sapped individual incentive. Government has tried to produce too much equality, they claim, and has muddled the job. Liberal and socialist critics, by contrast, point out that most reforms undertaken to promote greater equality have been necessitated by the failings of capitalism and have not fundamentally changed U.S. economic patterns.

Both sides can cite evidence to support their views. Since the 1930s, government-administered social programs have clearly led to a certain amount of redistribution of income (not wealth). Similarly, government regulatory activities in the areas of health and safety have helped to protect workers and consumers from serious hazards, and civil rights legislation has helped to improve the economic lot of women and minorities. Still, much government activity has undeniably been designed to bolster big business interests and keep capitalism running as smoothly as possible. Efforts to promote positive social change, critics charge, have had no effect on the majority of the disadvantaged.

Contrary to popular notions, the federal income tax does not redistribute much income. **Figure 7-5** shows the proportions of income quintiles after each of a series of government impacts (taxes and transfers). Accounting for the federal income tax, the Gini index changes by only .021. The highest-income quintile of the population holds 51.1 percent of the income before federal income taxes and retains 48.8 percent after. The lowest-income quintile holds 1.1 percent of all income before the federal income tax and 1.3 percent of it after.

FIGURE 7-5
EFFECT OF TAXES AND TRANSFERS ON INCOME DISTRIBUTION IN THE UNITED STATES, 1990

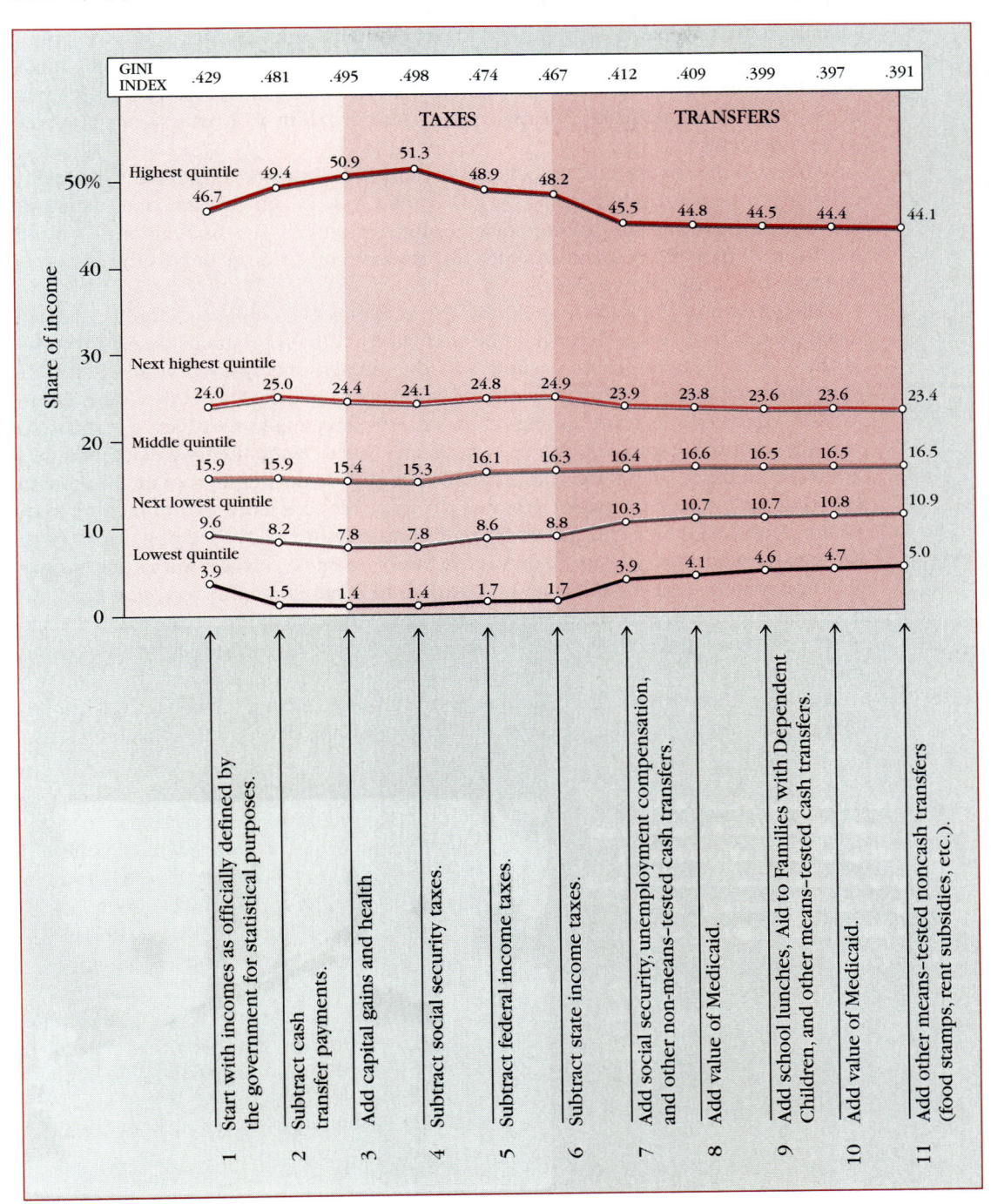

GINI INDEX	.429	.481	.495	.498	.474	.467	.412	.409	.399	.397	.391

TAXES — TRANSFERS

Highest quintile: 46.7, 49.4, 50.9, 51.3, 48.9, 48.2, 45.5, 44.8, 44.5, 44.4, 44.1

Next highest quintile: 24.0, 25.0, 24.4, 24.1, 24.8, 24.9, 23.9, 23.8, 23.6, 23.6, 23.4

Middle quintile: 15.9, 15.9, 15.4, 15.3, 16.1, 16.3, 16.4, 16.6, 16.5, 16.5, 16.5

Next lowest quintile: 9.6, 8.2, 7.8, 7.8, 8.6, 8.8, 10.3, 10.7, 10.7, 10.8, 10.9

Lowest quintile: 3.9, 1.5, 1.4, 1.4, 1.7, 1.7, 3.9, 4.1, 4.6, 4.7, 5.0

1. Start with incomes as officially defined by the government for statistical purposes.
2. Subtract cash transfer payments.
3. Add capital gains and health.
4. Subtract social security taxes.
5. Subtract federal income taxes.
6. Subtract state income taxes.
7. Add social security, unemployment compensation, and other non-means-tested cash transfers.
8. Add value of Medicaid.
9. Add school lunches, Aid to Families with Dependent Children, and other means-tested cash transfers.
10. Add value of Medicaid.
11. Add other means-tested noncash transfers (food stamps, rent subsidies, etc.).

SOURCE: U.S. Bureau of the Census, 1991.

Substantially more redistribution occurs through transfer payments. The Gini index falls .079, from .463 to .384, in the calculation of government transfer payments. This includes transfers that do not depend on income, like social security and unemployment compensation, as well as transfers that are "means-tested" (have income qualifications). The income share of the poorest quintile rises from 1.4 percent to 5.1 percent—a significant increase. The highest quintile goes from 48.1 percent of all income to 43.5 percent.

Although the net effect of all government taxes and transfers is to reduce inequality of incomes in the United States, as you would expect, no fundamental change is wrought in the relationship of one social stratum to another. The distribution of wealth, for the most part affected only indirectly by the current structure of government taxes and transfers, changes even less.

The growth of the welfare state also led to new social conflicts. Should disadvantaged groups be given preference in hiring policies? Which programs deserve priority in the federal budget—those dealing with the elderly, unemployed youth, cities, or environmental matters? What about intergenerational transfers? Effective lobbying efforts by organizations representing senior citizens have made social security benefits virtually impossible to cut during austere budget times. When the budget ax then falls harder on transfers like AFDC and programs like WIC (a nutrition program for women and children), some observers claim that the net effect is a large shift of income from young people to senior citizens, or taking from the future to pay the past. Add this to the constraining effect of current deficits on future budgets (as larger shares of revenues go to pay interest on the debt) and, according to some commentators, you have the potential for intergenerational warfare. In many ways, economic competition, once more or less confined to the marketplace, has now been partly redirected into the political arena.

Critics of the U.S. political economy pose another troubling question: How just are current arrangements in the U.S. political economy? Many critics charge that our system

The Concorde supersonic jetliner was developed under British-French collaboration. Europeans are generally more comfortable with a large government role in economic life, including government ownership of major portions of the economy. *(British Airways Picture)*

merely facilitates each interest group's attempts to bring pressure on the political process to gain special benefits or to protect its position. And even if every organized group enjoys some degree of access, the best organized and the most persistent usually win the greatest benefits.[16]

Overall, then, government has earned a mixed record in promoting equality. Our national governments have shifted emphasis from one administration to another. The social programs of Lyndon Johnson's War on Poverty, for example, significantly improved the lot of the poor, while the policies of the Reagan and Bush administrations did little to decrease poverty and significantly increased inequality.

Conclusions

In the 1990s, governments in the United States confront some commonly acknowledged economic problems: (1) How do we finance the costs of government and its programs? Nearly every observer agrees that huge federal budget deficits need to be reduced. Yet we demand that programs and services be maintained. Who should pay? (2) How can we maintain a competitive position in the world economy? Should the federal government erect trade barriers or define an industrial policy? How should government encourage investment, research, and development? (3) How much and what sort of government economic intervention should there be? (4) How can we achieve the most humane, productive, and just economy for all Americans—indeed, since our global impact is so large, for all citizens of the world?

In light of democratic theory, two further issues stand out: (5) How much economic equality is necessary to make democracy workable and reasonably just, and what are the implications of income distribution for the quality of democratic life? (6) How can government economic policy best encourage and protect political freedom?

None of these questions has a simple answer or one that can adequately be stated in nineteenth-century economic terms or Cold War dualisms. No economic program will satisfy everyone. But the questions are there, nonetheless, whether you favor more government intervention or less, more equality or less. The democratic challenges of political economy are great.

Glossary Terms

capitalism
communism
convergence theories
employee stock ownership plans (ESOPs)
Gini index
gross national product
laissez-faire
mixed economies

political economy
social classes
socialism
trade deficit
transfer payments
wealth
welfare state

NOTES

[1] "Excerpts from Yeltsin's Speech to Lawmakers," *Los Angeles Times*, June 18, 1992, p. A6.

[2] For a provocative discussion of this period and the ideological alternatives, see Karl Polanyi, *The Great Transformation* (Boston: Beacon Press, 1957); Adam Smith, *The Wealth of Nations* (New York: Modern Library, 1937); and George Lichtheim, *A Short History of Socialism* (New York: Praeger, 1971).

[3] Joseph Schumpeter, *Capitalism, Socialism, and Democracy*, 3rd ed. (New York: Harper & Row, 1950); David Ricardo, *Principles of Political Economy and Taxation* (New York: Dutton, 1962); John Maynard Keynes, *The General Theory of Employment, Interest, and Money* (New York: Harcourt Brace Jovanovich, 1965).

[4] An early expression of this novel concept can be found in Bernard Mandeville, *The Fable of the Bees*, published in 1714.

[5] These views can be found in the works of the poet Samuel Taylor Coleridge as well as in the writings of Thomas B. Macaulay, a British historian, essayist, and statesman; and British Prime Minister Benjamin Disraeli.

[6] For two thoughtful discussions on socialism, see George Lichtheim, "What Socialism Is and Is Not," *New York Review of Books*, April 9, 1970; and Robert I. Heilbroner, "Socialism and the Future," *Commentary*, December 1961, pp. 35–45.

[7] See, for example, the apocalyptic fears of one conservative in Friedrich Hayek, *The Road to Serfdom* (Chicago: University of Chicago Press, 1944).

[8] For an example of this moderation, see C. A. R. Crosland, *The Future of Socialism* (New York: Macmillan, 1957).

[9] A good discussion of this argument can be found in Andrew Schonfield, *Modern Capitalism* (New York: Oxford University Press, 1965).

[10] Statistics and characterization of U.S. strength from Barry B. Hughes, *Continuity and Change in World Politics* (Englewood Cliffs, N.J.: Prentice Hall, 1991), p. 22.

[11] Edward N. Muller, "Democracy, Economic Development, and Income Inequality," *American Sociological Review*, February 1988, pp. 50–68.

[12] The definitions in this discussion of mobility are from Daniel W. Rossides, *Social Stratification: The American Class System in Comparative Perspective* (Englewood Cliffs, N.J.: Prentice Hall, 1991), pp. 104–109.

[13] Sylvia Nasar, "Fed Report Gives New Data on Gains by Richest in '80s," *New York Times*, April 21, 1992, p. A1.

[14] Mollie Orshansky, "Counting the Poor," *Social Security Bulletin*, (1963), pp. 2–21.

[15] See Irving Kristol, *Two Cheers for Capitalism* (New York: Basic Books, 1978); and Michael Harrington, *Decade of Decision* (New York: Simon & Schuster, 1980).

[16] Grant McConnell, *Private Power and American Democracy* (New York: Random House, 1970).

SELECTED READINGS

For recent work on **capitalism**, see Patricia Hogue Werhane, *Adam Smith and His Legacy for Modern Capitalism* (New York: Oxford University Press, 1991); and Robert J. S. Ross, *Global Capitalism: The New Leviathan* (Albany: State University of New York Press, 1990).

A good introduction to **socialism** can be found in Michael Harrington, *Socialism, Past and Future* (New York: Arcade, 1989). Other recent scholarship includes the essays in Ota Sik, ed., *Socialism Today: The Changing Meaning of Socialism* (New York: St. Martin's Press, 1991).

Mixed economies and other twentieth-century variations can be explored in John P. Freeman, *Democracy and Markets: The Politics of Mixed Economies* (Ithaca, N.Y.: Cornell University Press, 1989); Branko Milanovic, *Liberalization and Entrepreneurship: Dynamics of Reform in Socialism and Capitalism* (Armonk, N.Y.: Sharpe, 1989); and Robert B. Reich, *The Work of Nations: Preparing Ourselves for 21st-Century Capitalism* (New York: Knopf, 1991).

For recent syntheses of comparative scholarship on the **distribution of wealth and income**, see Daniel W. Rossides, *Social Stratification: The American Class System in Comparative Perspective* (Englewood Cliffs, N.J.: Prentice Hall, 1990); and Denny Braun, *The Rich Get Richer: The Rise of Income Inequality in the United States and the World* (Chicago: Nelson-Hall, 1991).

For domestic analyses of income and wealth distribution, see Michael Sherraden, *Assets and the Poor: A New American Welfare Policy* (Armonk, N.Y.: Sharpe, 1991); and Kevin Phillips, *The Politics of Rich and Poor: Wealth and the American Electorate in the Reagan Aftermath* (New York: Random House, 1990).

PART TWO

POLITICS

8
POLITICAL SOCIALIZATION, PUBLIC SENTIMENT, AND ELECTORAL TRENDS:
IS THERE A REAL MAJORITY?

9
POLITICAL PARTIES:
DO THEY OFFER A CHOICE?

10
CAMPAIGNS, MONEY, AND THE MEDIA:
BEYOND THE GLITTER AND THE MUD

11
INTEREST GROUP POLITICS:
DEMOCRACY TO THE HIGHEST BIDDER?

12
MASS POLITICS AND PROTEST:
A THREAT OR A NECESSITY?

ANTHONY
AZOFF
6-7-1895
Age: 32 yr.
George
Easton
4-6-1906
Age: 25
DØN'T
KILL
in our

CHAPTER OUTLINE

Majority Rule: An Overview

Political Socialization
CHILDHOOD
THE ROLE OF THE SCHOOL
COLLEGE AND POLITICS

Public Opinion
GAUGING PUBLIC OPINION
PUBLIC OPINION AND DEMOCRACY
EFFICACY AND ALIENATION

Understanding Public Sentiment
LIBERALISM AND CONSERVATISM
CONTEMPORARY VIEWS ON SPECIFIC ISSUES
INFLUENCES ON PUBLIC SENTIMENT

Electoral Trends
THE NEW DEAL ANTECEDENTS TO CONTEMPORARY POLITICS
THE CONTEMPORARY NATIONAL ELECTORAL PATTERN: CROSSCUTTING ATTACHMENTS AND DIVIDED GOVERNMENT

Nonparticipation
BARRIERS TO VOTING
WHO VOTES?

Opinion and Policy

CHAPTER EIGHT

POLITICAL SOCIALIZATION, PUBLIC SENTIMENT, AND ELECTORAL TRENDS

Is There a Real Majority?

THE UNDERLYING PREMISE OF DEMOCRATIC POLITICAL LIFE IS that elections actually matter—that the hoopla of campaigns, the political competition, the media blitz, the primaries, the vote, and the various political parties fundamentally influence the course of society. But do they?

In one sense, they certainly do. Throughout modern history, struggles to win the right to vote and to create real political competition have helped citizens of many countries to gain control of government. And in many countries without elections (or without honest elections), citizens can neither register their views on public policy nor retain or remove the people holding political office. Governments can be changed by other means—revolutions, coups d'état, politically directed strikes, and the like. But such methods are costly and uncertain. Elections offer a regular—and safe—means of choosing who will occupy political offices.

The question has more complicated implications, however. In many countries, elections change very little: The same individuals or individuals holding the same views are elected over and over, and they maintain the political status quo. In many Latin American countries, for example, one group of oligarchs succeeds another, and the well-being of the public at large is ignored. As a slogan written on a wall in Ecuador once stated: "One hundred years of elections, one hundred years of misery."

Elections, then, are not magic. They make meaningful change possible, but they do not guarantee it. Under what conditions do elections reflect true majority sentiment and have a significant impact on political processes? Among the key elements underlying meaningful elections are an informed and involved citizenry; competing political parties offering programs that differ from each other, that will be carried out to a significant degree, and that actually address major social issues; and political campaigning that helps to raise public knowledge and clarify issues, rather than to disguise or cloud them. Such, in any case, is the democratic ideal.

In Part II we probe the political workings of our government—how majority sentiment influences electoral trends, the impact of political parties, political campaigns in a media-wise world, the effects of interest group politics on democracy, and the politics of protest. Through various political processes, citizens can voice their views, promote particular public policies, and add a healthy diversity to political life. However, democracies must also guard against threats from political excesses—influence peddling, triumphs of campaign razzle-dazzle over substance, patterns of political compromise that skirt the public interest.

Majority Rule: An Overview

In analyzing majority sentiment—the view on particular issues held by a majority of the public—we first explore two major topics: political socialization and public opinion. Examining the process of socialization reveals how political attitudes are shaped in this country; exploring trends in public opinion reveals what those attitudes actually are. While probing these areas, we will encounter several significant issues related to American democracy. At the broadest level, for example, we will be asking whether the American public can generally be characterized as an informed, thoughtful, and democratic group. We will also examine whether American political values are truly democratic. Do we endorse freedom of speech and freedom of the press? Do we support a reasonable level of tolerance for unpopular views?

After a look at the ways in which Americans acquire their political attitudes and information and the specifics of measuring and assessing public opinion, we will consider the structure of public sentiment in the United States, the patterns of electoral competition, the consequences of nonparticipation for American democracy, and the effect of public opinion on policy decisions. Overall, we will address two key questions: Are American elections meaningful? and How close do we come to satisfying the democratic ideal?

As a logical starting point, let us now delve into the complex of factors that shapes us initially as political and social beings—principally, the family and the school system. Through these agencies we are socialized—inculcated with distinctly American social and political values and attitudes. Of course, a person's values and issue positions may change in response to new experiences and the stream of events. Political education continues throughout life. But because much of the imprint of early socialization is retained, an interest in the workings of democracy naturally leads us back to the shaping of the values of the child.

Political Socialization

The words have a heavy ring, but their meaning is not difficult to comprehend. **Political socialization** refers to the processes through which an individual acquires the political attitudes and behavior common to a particular culture. Every culture must socialize its members—indoctrinate them into its language, customs, mores, and institutions. By the time children are just a few years old, they have been stamped by the formative forces of society.

But which values are inculcated and whose interests do these values serve? Socialization can serve exploitative purposes: American blacks and women, for example, were long socialized to believe in their own inferiority. It is easier for most Americans to acknowledge that this phenomenon takes place in other societies, such as China or South Africa, than to admit that it occurs in the United States as well. It would serve us well to remember, however, that socialization is a two-edged sword in all societies, including our own.

Most Americans take substantial pride in their country and look favorably on its capitalistic economic system. These attitudes, which are inculcated early on, usually form a deeply rooted base or diffuse support for the political and economic structures of U.S. society.[1] A base of *diffuse support* is a set of favorable attitudes toward political and social structures, institutions, and processes that stands firm regardless of day-to-day events. For most citizens, that is, temporary discontent with the government of the day or with the government's approach to specific problems leaves untouched a reservoir of goodwill and tolerance toward government institutions. Drawing on this deeply rooted support, the United States has weathered many crises since the 1950s with relatively little change in its fundamental political structures and practices.

Diffuse support can be distinguished from *specific support*, which refers to approval of particular policies and practices and is therefore more likely to be withdrawn when an unpopular policy is implemented. From the standpoint of democratic politics, the issue is not whether most of us have positive feelings about the main institutions of U.S. society—that seems to be the case in all reasonably stable societies. Rather, the key issue is how diffuse support and specific support are balanced at any given time. If diffuse support is carried too far or prevents citizens from appreciating current realities, it hinders critical inquiry and cripples political debate. Citizens must strike a balance between admiring a system's merits and critically assessing its flaws and deficiencies.

Before we examine three phases of socialization, a caveat is in order. Despite a general recognition that significant socialization happens very early in life, we still don't have a lot of solid knowledge about early political socialization. Data are hard to gather because young children must be interviewed individually (some people argue that even interviews, if conducted by an unfamiliar adult, are unreliable). **Longitudinal studies**, in which data are gathered from the same individuals as they age, are much rarer than **cross-sectional studies**, in which the data are gathered all at one time from children in different age groups. Cross-sectional data must make the unwarranted assumption that two years from now, this year's first graders will look like this year's third graders. Different periods of history may reflect very different political socialization patterns. Finally, it is difficult to identify the relative strength of different agents of socialization. For example, because almost all children go to school in the United States, we can't measure children who go to school against children who don't. Socialization ordinarily involves a lot of *redundancy*—the same message from different sources. Did this bit of political education or social stereotyping come from school, home, peers, or television—or all of these sources? In sum, not enough direct research has been done on early political socialization.[2]

Now we turn to three critical phases in the socialization process: early childhood, grade school experiences, and college and its influence on political attitudes and outlooks.

Childhood

Although much remains to be learned about how children acquire their views of society and politics, we do know that both family and school play key roles in socialization and that socialization is both a direct and an indirect process. In **direct socialization**, children are deliberately taught specific political views, values, and behaviors. **Indirect socialization** involves attitudes and behavior patterns that are acquired through emulation. For example, children may learn through direct socialization that the Constitution guarantees all Americans equal rights. Through indirect socialization, however, they may gain a sense that some are "more equal than others" as they grasp cues subtly conveyed by adults.

Most children recognize the political community—the nation and the symbols associated with it, like the flag—before they have any inkling about the workings of politics itself. By the age of six or seven, children come to realize that they are "Amer-

Two first-graders in New York pledge allegiance to the American flag. Rituals of this sort, begun at an early age and repeated countless times, are frequently effective in developing a strong sense of national identity. But, it is important to note that rituals alone cannot—and from a democratic standpoint, should not—be able to inculcate loyalty. *(Wojnarowicz/The Image Works)*

icans," to associate themselves with the American flag, to believe that theirs is a "free" country, and to develop a sense of national loyalty.

Young children believe that the national government consists mainly of the president and his "helpers." Similarly, they identify local government principally with the mayor or other local executive and, perhaps, the neighborhood police officer. To children, then, authority is highly personalized and idealized. "Government" appears to consist of a series of individuals performing executive functions; legislatures and courts have no significant place in a child's political consciousness.

According to studies conducted in the late 1950s and early 1960s, American grade school pupils tend to view the president as a "benevolent leader," or a "superfriend"— well intentioned, helpful, hardworking, honest, and invariably correct in decisions and actions. Why such a benign and favorable image of the president? For one thing, children tend to transfer feelings from parents (especially fathers) to others in authority; thus presidents and other authority figures are viewed as children wish to view their parents. Also, parents, teachers, and other adults often deliberately advance the "benevolent leader" image. Even adults who are critical of the president in the company of other adults may screen out negative references and introduce children to politics in a positive light.[3]

When these findings about socialization were first published, they were thought to apply to all American children. Later, however, investigators discovered that they applied principally to middle-class white children. Studies of poor white children in Appalachia and Mexican-American children in the Southwest found almost antithetical feelings (see **Table 8-1**). These children were far less likely to see the president as more honest, harder-working, or more knowledgeable than most people—or even as a good person.

These later findings highlight a phenomenon that students of politics have noted in other areas—that social class and ethnicity make for significant differences in attitudes and behavior. Generally, middle-class children are more aware of partisan differences, show a greater sense of political efficacy (a belief that political action will be worthwhile), and are more likely to want to participate in politics than lower-class children.

Figure 8-1 demonstrates the rapid expansion of political knowledge between kindergarten and grade four. (It is interesting to note that 30 percent of the fourth graders in this study—although they had been reciting the Pledge of Allegiance daily for more

TABLE 8-1
CLASS AND ETHNIC DIFFERENCES IN CHILDREN'S VIEWS OF THE PRESIDENT

Question	Response	Mexican-American Children	Appalachian Children	Suburban Chicago Children
1. How hard does the president work compared with most [people]?	Harder	49%	35%	77%
	As hard	27	24	21
	Less hard	24	41	3
2. How honest is the president compared with most [people]?	More honest	*	23	57
	As honest	*	50	42
	Less honest	*	27	1
3. How knowledgeable is the president compared to most men?	Knows more	41	45	82
	Knows about the same	42	33	16
	Knows less	17	22	2
4. What kind of person is the president?	Best in the world	11	6	11
	A good person	63	68	82
	Not a good person	26	26	8

*Data not reported.
SOURCE: Appalachian and Chicago data reported in Dean Jaros, Herbert Hirsch, and Frederic J. Fleron, Jr., "The Malevolent Leader: Political Socialization in an American Subculture," *American Political Science Review* 62 (1968): 568. The Mexican-American data are reported in Herbert Hirsch and Armand Gutiarrez, *The Socialization of Political Aggression and Political Affect: A Subcultural Analysis*, an unpublished paper.

FIGURE 8-1

Growth in Knowledge of Geopolitical Jurisdictions and Corresponding Chief Executives between Kindergarten and Fourth Grade

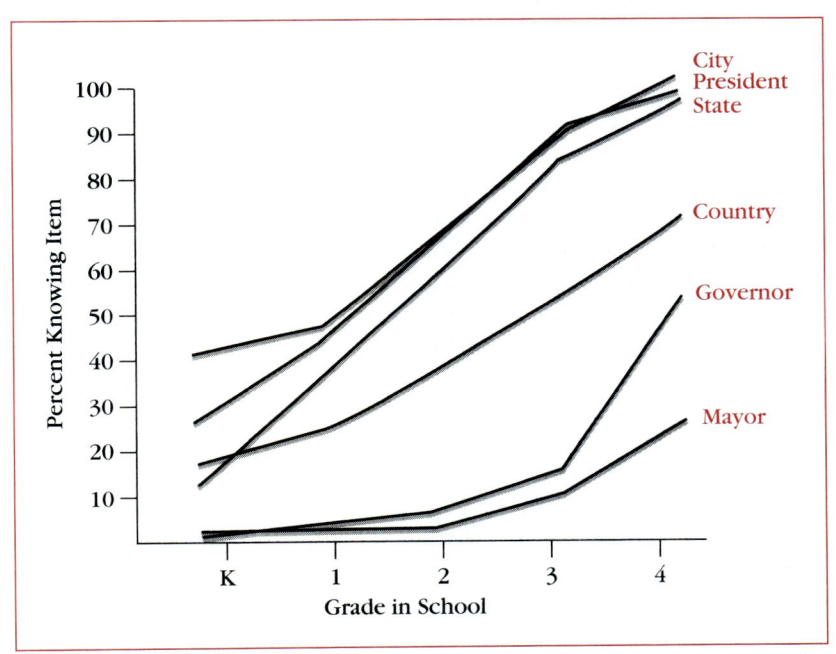

SOURCE: Stanley W. Moore et al., *The Child's Political World: A Longitudinal Perspective* (New York: Praeger, 1985), p. 87.

than four years—could not name their own country.) Political partisanship is also transmitted to children rather early. One study found that by age nine, 60 percent of children were expressing partisan loyalties.[4] This is particularly important in the United States, where party affiliation involves identifying with a party rather than formal membership, dues, and so forth. Yet in spite of the informal way in which we affiliate with parties, research reconfirms the relative stability of party identification and the importance of party identification in predicting presidential voting.[5] Often political loyalties, like religious affiliations, are inculcated through the child's unconscious identification with parental preferences.

Loyalties acquired early in life, however, are subject to later reexamination—socialization does not end at adolescence. A study published in 1991 followed a cohort of high school seniors, noting their party identification and stands on important political issues and measuring differences on these dimensions from their parents' choices at that time and then eight years and seventeen years later.[6] The study authors concluded that the students' initial party identification was not a simple echo of parental choice but included some responsiveness to issue positions. Nevertheless, throughout the seventeen-year period of the study, parental party identification was a greater influence on offspring party identification than any other single factor. As students aged, the influence of parental party identification declined substantially, while issue positions increased in importance. An earlier study had found that young people often—perhaps as much as half the time—do not follow the political lead of their parents.[7] Many declare themselves to be "independents," moving some distance away from the political preferences of their parents. When the parents do not agree on party affiliation, it is even more likely that the children will strike out on their own.

Families influence not only specific political attitudes or behaviors but also general emotional orientations—tolerance, generosity, fear of being different, confidence in oneself—that may later shape political responses. Psychological studies have shown that children who grow up in authoritarian households are more likely to take on authoritarian attitudes and to display prejudice and hostility toward those who challenge authority.[8] Likewise, liberal attitudes and behavior are usually acquired in the family. Of course, many authoritarian or conservative families produce liberal children, and vice versa.

The Role of the School

Although socialization begins in the family, the school also plays a major role in the process. Certainly, American schools have a part in the "melting pot" process. Through education in public schools, various economic, ethnic, and religious groups have come to share a common socialization experience. In this sense, schools can potentially teach tolerance and respect for differences—values essential to democratic life. It is not known, however, how successfully schools perform this function.

Schools also inculcate certain basic cultural values. The textbooks used in elementary schools, for example, usually present preferred cultural norms. *McGuffey Readers*, the nineteenth-century American reading texts, expounded the values of self-reliance, hard work, thrift, free enterprise, and individualism, overlaid with nationalism and religiosity. Through such materials, U.S. public schools indoctrinated and reinforced predominantly middle-class values. Considering the powerful role that textbooks play in the socialization of children, it is not surprising that many controversies have arisen over their content. Textbooks have been the focus of debates over the teaching of evolution (as opposed to biblical views of creation), sex education, sexist and racist biases, and a long list of other topics.

In instilling cultural values, schools traditionally emphasize nationalistic rituals—saluting the flag, reciting the Pledge of Allegiance, singing patriotic songs. Children also are taught early on to respect leading figures in U.S. history, particularly the Founders and various presidents. Many children even seem to view the Pledge of Allegiance as a prayer; in the United States, nationalism and religion often are mutually reinforcing.

Finally, socialization in schools proceeds indirectly, by example. Children learn in school to compete on an individual basis with other students. They learn much about the need to comply with authority (and, sometimes, the need to suppress dissent) and about how and why majorities rule on some matters. Like parents, teachers also serve as role models. Are teachers willing to discuss controversial issues? Do they emphasize the virtues of U.S. political life while deemphasizing its problems? How teachers approach such matters can help to shape the child's growing awareness of how politics works.

Over the last decade, several critiques of U.S. education reached the best-seller lists.[9] A growing consensus held that our teenagers simply were not learning what they needed to know in history, geography, literature, and other areas. A 1986 study found that fewer than half of all U.S. high school students could place the U.S. Civil War in the correct fifty-year time period.[10] Such startling findings have made education an important topic for political discussion. George Bush even promised to be the "education president" in his 1988 presidential campaign. But the enterprise of public education is not susceptible to a quick fix. No consensus has emerged about curriculum reforms or process reforms. What "cultural traditions" should schools teach? Do we improve the quality of instruction by raising teachers' salaries and qualifications? How can we make education more accountable?

In fact, political leaders and the public at large cannot even agree on the precise goals for education: Are schools supposed to make sure that students learn specific facts and information, learn to think for themselves, acquire certain values, score high on standardized tests, gain training for future employment—or a combination of all these?[11] In a democracy, these questions about grade school education can only fully be answered by recognizing the important political implications of socialization in the schools.

College and Politics

In post–World War II America, Republican presidential candidates have usually been favored on college campuses. This choice reflects the social background of most college students: Adolescents from poorer families, who were less likely to be Republican, were also less likely to find themselves on college campuses. Even if a college education tends to exert a liberalizing effect on students of all political persuasions (an argument advanced by many scholars), U.S. college campuses have not historically been scenes of intense political involvement. The one major exception to this pattern was the 1960s (more precisely, the period from 1960 to about 1972).

In February 1960, four black undergraduates at North Carolina Agricultural and Technical State University in Greensboro staged the first "sit-in" protest, refusing to leave the whites-only section of a store lunch counter. Four years later, students at the University of California sat in at an administration building to protest college policies limiting student political activities. From that point on, political protests—prompted by the Vietnam War, the drive for civil rights, and other cultural and social issues—pervaded college campuses.

Student activism sparked bitter debate in the 1960s and early 1970s. Some observers considered activist students humane, conscientious, and committed—individuals who

Student activism, 1988: Students from Gallaudet University in Washington protest the appointment of a non–hearing-impaired president at the world's only liberal arts institution for deaf students. On this, and several other points, they prevailed. *(Rick Reinhard)*

had the courage to act on widely shared ideals. Others saw them as irrational rebels acting out their own troubled emotional lives in the arenas of campus and national politics. Critics of the protest movement called college campuses breeding grounds for political radicalism. By the end of the 1960s, there was widespread speculation that some universities might be torn apart by sustained protest.

But in the 1970s, student activism diminished as the economy worsened and the Vietnam War wound down. By the mid-1970s, disillusionment with politics replaced the earlier activism. Student values also changed; young people were becoming more conservative and pragmatic (see **Figure 8**-2). In the 1984 election, a majority of college students voted for Republican candidate Ronald Reagan.

The high levels of campus activism and strife in the 1960s, contrasted with the relative calm both before and since, indicate that college itself cannot explain the difference. Different cohorts of students will respond differently to the circumstances of college life, prompted by changing experiences and variations in circumstances. Much 1960s activism was linked directly to the Vietnam War and an active draft that disrupted or threatened to disrupt the lives of tens of thousands of college-age students.

Although research has failed to prove the effectiveness of deliberate attempts to teach political values in school, much evidence correlates time spent in school with some civically useful values. Whether the link is direct or indirect, the total number of years spent in school is positively linked to political tolerance, a sense of duty to

FIGURE 8-2

IDEOLOGICAL SELF-IDENTIFICATION OF COLLEGE FRESHMEN, 1970–1990

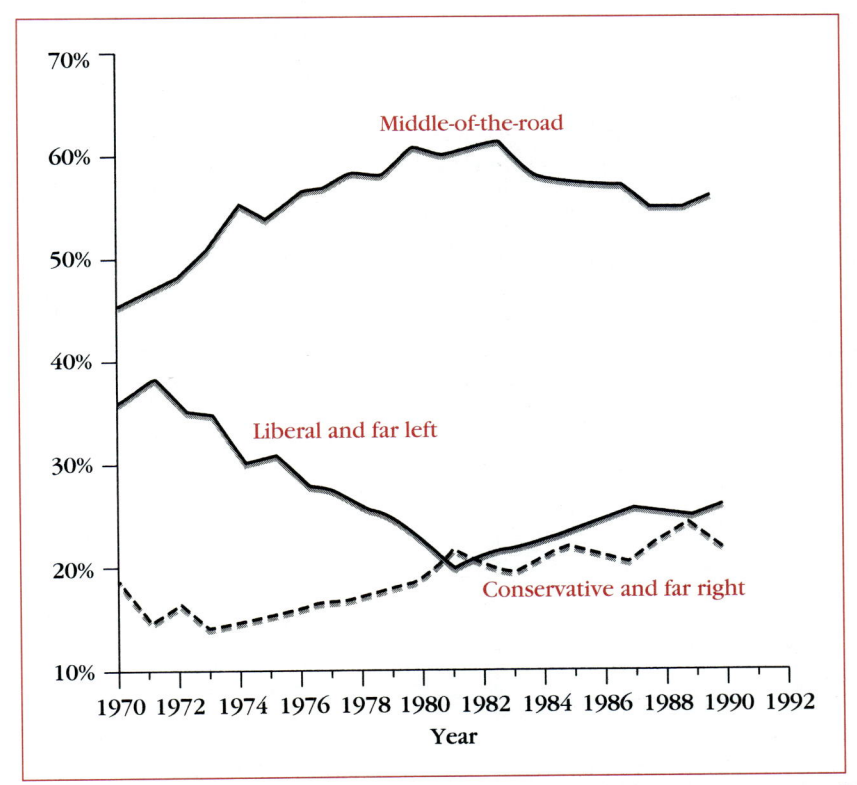

SOURCE: Harold W. Stanley and Richard G. Niemi, *Vital Statistics on American Politics*, 3rd ed. (Washington, D.C.: Congressional Quarterly Press, 1992), p. 163.

participate in politics, political efficacy, political interest, political activity, and political knowledge. Differences are especially distinct between people who have some college and those who have more.[12] The differences noted are partly a result of self-selection. High school seniors bound for college also score higher on these measures than their non-college-bound counterparts. But it is likely that college experience (in the classroom and out) does have some liberalizing effects on noneconomic issue positions.

Public Opinion

Public opinion—the voice of the majority—is one of the basic ingredients in the complex recipe for democracy. For a truly comprehensive understanding of U.S. political life, we need to know not only how politically informed and democratically

(Text continues on page 284)

The Perils of Polling

Varying Distribution of "Opinions" on Abortion

Question	Total	Clearly Prochoice	Qualified	Clearly Prolife
Should a legal abortion be possible if the woman's own health is seriously endangered by the pregnancy?				
Yes	87%	87%		
No	7			7%
It depends	4		4%	
I don't know	2			
Should a legal abortion be possible if there is a strong chance of serious defect in the baby?				
Yes	69	69		
No	21			21
It depends	4		4	
I don't know	6			
If a woman wants to have an abortion and her doctor agrees to it, should she be allowed to have an abortion or not?				
Yes	63	63		
No	24			24
It depends	10		10	
I don't know	3			
Should abortion be legal as it is now or legal only in such cases as rape, incest, or to save the life of the mother, or should it not be permitted at all?				
Legal as now	49	49		
Legal to save mother, rape, or incest	39		39	
Not permitted	9			9
I don't know	3			

(Box continues on page 283)

Varying Distribution of "Opinions" on Abortion

Question	Total	Clearly Prochoice	Qualified	Clearly Prolife
Should a legal abortion be possible if she is not married and does not want to marry the man?				
Yes	42	42		
No	50			50
It depends	5		5	
I don't know	3			
Should a legal abortion be possible if the pregnancy interfered with work or education?				
Yes	26	26		
No	65			65
It depends	5		5	
I don't know	4			

SOURCE: CBS News/New York Times poll, April 13–16, 1989; data from 1,412 telephone interviews.

Public opinion polling is an important source of information for democracy. But poll results must be interpreted carefully. What questions the poll asks may have a big impact on the results. Consider these poll results concerning abortion. From the same group of respondents, certain questions yielded large "prochoice" majorities; other questions, however, yielded "prolife" majorities. If you were a TV news reporter, how would you report these results in a forty-five-second piece? If you were a legislator, how would these results influence your voting? As a citizen, what can you learn from these results?

Source: Albert H. Cantril, The Opinion Connection: Polling, Politics and the Press (Washington, D.C.: Congressional Quarterly Press, 1991), pp. 256–257.

inclined Americans are but also how public opinion affects policymaking and what that means for democratic life. In this section we focus on how public opinion is gauged, its affects on democracy, and political efficacy and alienation—people's feeling that their voice is either heard or ignored by political decision makers.

Gauging Public Opinion

Polls of public opinion have become a fixture of national political life. Hundreds of professional polling organizations operate in the United States. But what is involved in gauging public opinion? What limitations and problems make polling less than totally accurate?

In a democratic polity, the study of public opinion is particularly significant because political life is based on a government responsive to public sentiment. Only since the end of World War II, however, have systematic efforts been made to gauge that sentiment. Contemporary studies of public opinion use *surveys*, in which responses to set questions are elicited from a sample of the population. Survey research is based on two assumptions: that a fairly small sample of people can accurately represent the views of a much larger population and that the answers people give to survey questions are at least reasonably truthful.

The first problem faced by the survey researcher is to define an appropriate *sample* of opinion. The larger the sample selected, the more likely it is to reflect the opinions of the population as a whole.

A key criterion governing sample selection is **randomness**. Ideally, every individual in the population should have an equal chance of being selected. In practical terms, this is difficult to accomplish, since there is no master list of each individual in the United States—and even if there were, the cost of following up on each person randomly selected would be prohibitive. Instead, survey researchers use *cluster sampling*, which involves the selection of a number of geographic units (clusters) within which individuals are sampled. Departures from cluster sampling can lead a surveyor astray. Interviewing people at subway stations or on street corners, for example, can make for highly selective samples and unrepresentative results, as can attempting to judge public sentiment on the basis of letters to the editor or on the number of people who come out to work for a candidate at precinct meetings.

How accurate is public opinion polling? The craft of sampling and polling is highly developed and can produce extremely dependable results. A more useful question for citizens and students of democracy is, When is public opinion polling accurate? Of the hundreds of polling organizations in the United States, most are competent and careful and produce accurate data. But opinion polls are often conducted by nonprofessionals, using unreliable methods (an advertised pay-per-call phone line, the late-night radio DJ asking for call-ins). Some "polls" are actually devices for communicating information to respondents or soliciting funds from them (political party organizations often include opinion questions in solicitation mailings, hoping that recipients will feel more favorably disposed to contribute to an organization that cares about their personal opinions). Even competent, professional poll data can be innocently misinterpreted by news reporters or persons interested in a particular outcome.

Overinterpretation—drawing more information from a particular poll than the data themselves justify—is perhaps the most serious problem with public opinion polling. If large numbers of voters remain undecided close to an election, opinion polls may not be very good at predicting outcomes. The size of Ronald Reagan's 1980 presidential victory, supplemented by many late deciders, surprised even the polltakers. But since the "horse race" aspects of elections have major news value, poll results, even in volatile situations, may receive unwarranted attention. One major polling organization, Yankelovich, Skelly, and White, developed a "mushiness index" to assess the volatility of opinions about particular issues. The mushiness index asks "how much the issue affects the respondent personally, how well informed the respondent feels he or she is on the issue, how much the respondent discusses the issue with family and friends, and the respondent's own assessment of how likely it is that his or her views on the issue will change."[13] Devices like the mushiness index are not widely used in polling because they are time-consuming and expensive to administer and analyze. But they point to important questions about the limits of polling data. Results may show clear, even overwhelming preference for a candidate or position, but how likely is that preference to last? How well informed is the preference?

A poll's accuracy as a gauge of public sentiment also depends in large part on the kinds of questions that are asked. For example, an interviewer who asks only if people approve or disapprove of the president's performance will get one set of results; one who asks respondents to rate the president on a "feeling thermometer"—soliciting how strongly they feel about presidential performance—will get another; and one who attempts to determine people's views on a specific set of presidential actions will get yet another. All these results may or may not match up.

Polls present additional problems as well. For one thing, they can create, rather than reflect, public opinion, usually by fostering the mistaken impression that the public knows or cares more than it really does about particular public issues. Moreover, poll findings don't usually measure to any meaningful extent the depth or sensitivity of public opinion. Polls can also turn people off: Asking people their views has become such a commonplace matter that many people don't believe that the surveyors care much how they *really* feel. Furthermore, probing, open-ended questions might reveal that many of the respondents who routinely answer "Don't know" or "No opinion" care very much about political issues but cannot easily articulate their views.

Then, too, most sample surveys tend to include few members of various minorities, such as Jews, blacks, or Hispanics. As a result, polls often tell us little about the differences of opinion *within* such groups. While black and white opinion is often compared on specific issues, it is much rarer to see a comparison of blacks with other blacks: There simply aren't enough black Americans in a typical sample to allow for any dependable generalizations. Nuances and conflicts within such groups are consequently given short shrift.

AIDS activists demonstrate outside the 6th International Conference on AIDS in San Francisco. In connection with the complexities of AIDS research, political activism played a significant role even at a scientific gathering. The urgency of issues linked to AIDS stirred an unusual intensity. *(Patrick Forden/Sygma)*

Finally, polls can intimidate policymakers, who may shy away from taking necessary action to address difficult social and political problems for fear of going against public opinion. Poll results can also affect the outcomes of elections: On the one hand, supporters may not bother to go out and vote for a candidate who is far behind in the polls; on the other, supporters of a candidate who looks like a sure winner may not bother voting because the outcome seems so certain.

The reservoir of skepticism about polls in the United States draws in part from all of these difficulties. But if they ask the right questions of a carefully chosen sample and stay within the limits of the results, public opinion polls can be an important resource for democracy.

Public Opinion and Democracy

Because public opinion plays so crucial a role in democratic politics, a viable democracy requires a politically informed public. We shall now examine the level of public knowledge in the United States and what it means for democratic norms.

POLITICAL KNOWLEDGE Exactly how much does the public at large know about politics? The answer, perhaps surprisingly, is a matter of considerable debate.[14] Prior to the development of careful survey research, the conventional wisdom, encouraged by rustic images of "sittin' on the front porch talkin' politics," was that Americans knew a good deal about the public affairs of their nation. A series of studies in the 1950s produced evidence that most voters do not know very much about politics.

The classic study, called *The American Voter*, was done by Angus Campbell, Philip Converse, Warren Miller, and Donald Stokes.[15] The typical American voter, according to Campbell and colleagues, knows little about politics, is not very interested in politics, does not organize political ideas coherently, and does not think in a structured, ideological way. By the 1960s the prevailing assumption had swung so far from crediting citizen knowledge that V. O. Key, Jr., felt the need to write a book claiming that voters "are not fools."[16] A study published in 1976 claimed that voter "sophistication" took a dramatic upturn between 1960 and 1964.[17] Debate within political science has centered on two issues: Is the description offered by *The American Voter* mostly accurate over time, or was the voter described there a product of a particular time? And what constitutes knowledge "sophistication," and how important is it to meaningful participation?*

Analysts of the political attitudes and knowledge of Americans sometimes characterize the public as consisting of four groups: chronic know-nothings, the general public, the attentive public, and the opinion leaders and policymakers.[18] Estimates of the sizes of these groups vary. For example, one analyst estimates the chronic know-nothings at 20 percent of the public, whereas another pegs them at only 4 percent. The size of the general public is also hard to gauge; it seems to vary according to the issue involved. Unlike the know-nothings, who never become informed or involved, the general public has some information and can sometimes be stirred to political action. At the next highest level of political involvement is the attentive public, estimated at 15 to 20 percent of the population. The attentive public seeks information, develops opinions, and can have a significant impact on policymaking. The size of the attentive public grows as a particular issue develops and becomes dramatized. Beyond the attentive public are the people who shape opinions and policies the most. This group consists primarily of leaders in politics and the media.

Whatever the size of the attentive public, one thing is clear: Most Americans don't know much about political events and institutions. Look at the level of information

---

*Part of the problem is that gathering information about political knowledge is expensive. Knowledge-level questions tacked onto an opinion survey tend to distract from or distort other items being measured. (Respondents are discomfited by having to admit that they don't know basic facts.) Yet information gathered about the lack of basic facts was so consistent in the early studies that researchers turned to other tasks. The Gallup poll used to ask questions like "How many senators are there from your state?" and "Can you tell me what is meant by the term *electoral college*?" but gave up by 1960. So consistent long-term information about political knowledge is relatively scarce. The debate about how to characterize the American voter now turns on complex questions of epistemology (how we know what we know) and methodology (how to gather and interpret information).

TABLE 8-2
ASSESSING THE U.S. PUBLIC'S POLITICAL KNOWLEDGE

Question	Percentage of Respondents Knowing Correct Answer
Name the current vice-president.	79
How many senators represent each state?	52
How many years does a representative serve in Congress?	30
Name the current secretary of state.	34
Which party has the most members in the House?	69
Name one senator from your state.	59
Name the governor of this state.	78
Name this district's representative in Congress.	37

SOURCE: University of Chicago National Opinion Research Center General Social Surveys, 1978, 1987; ABC/Washington Post Survey, August 1987.

reflected on **Table 8-2**. Whereas most respondents could name the vice-president of the United States and the governor of their state, barely half knew how many senators represented their state, and fewer than 4 in 10 could name their district's representative in Congress. Other polls have revealed that upwards of 20 percent of the American people believe that the Supreme Court is part of Congress and that as few as 1 percent know what congressional committees their representatives serve on or what their representatives' areas of expertise are.[19]

Perhaps even worse, much of the public remains uninformed about pressing public issues of the day. More people seem to have a better idea of what they think the government ought to be doing than of what it is doing. From a democratic point of view this is not a totally dismal state of affairs; after all, it is encouraging that people are willing to say what they want from government. Furthermore, some people would argue that legitimate public judgment need not depend absolutely on specific knowledge of the sort that survey research probes.[20] But it is unsettling to find that so many Americans base their opinions on little more than personal preferences. This leaves the democratic process vulnerable to catchwords, slogans, and simplistic formulas that may become the common coin of public discourse. In addition, a largely ignorant public may respond only to the very broad contours of policy alternatives, and leaders may try to shape public sentiment by playing on prejudice, shallow emotional rhetoric, and the like. The more such demagogic practices prevail, the worse for democracy.

As we have seen, the level of public information, a basic element in the democratic equation, falls short of what it should be in U.S. society. To a certain extent, this degrades the integrity of the democratic process.

DEMOCRATIC NORMS   Democracy also demands popular tolerance and support for democratic norms. This breaks down into two key measures: the level of acceptance of democratic politics and the level of tolerance for dissenting views.

Americans emphatically support the basic rules of democratic politics. According to most surveys, more than 90 percent of the public would agree with the following statements:

Democracy is the best form of government.

Public officials should be chosen by majority vote.

Minorities should be free to criticize majority decisions.

Every citizen should have an equal chance to influence government policy.

However, these are very abstract statements. As more specific elements are introduced into survey questions, the democratic consensus begins to crack. On questions pertaining to demonstrations and protest, undemocratic responses often outnumber democratic ones. Whenever any hint of political extremism appears in a question—such as demonstrations or protests—support for democratic values declines considerably.

How much tolerance is there for unpopular ideas? In 1954, when civil liberties were greatly threatened by anticommunist hysteria, Samuel Stouffer conducted a study of political tolerance in the United States.[21] He discovered that the level of support for the political rights of people who hold controversial views was low indeed. Only 6 percent of respondents said that they would allow a communist to teach, and only 37 percent indicated that they would allow an atheist to make a speech.

It is encouraging to note that public attitudes on these same questions have grown considerably more tolerant in the period since Stouffer's study. By 1990 fully 72 percent of respondents would allow an atheist to speak and 51 percent would allow a communist to teach. Part of this increase can be attributed to the overall increase in education levels in the United States and part to changing socialization patterns in family and school. Although there has been a major shift in the direction of tolerance, it is sobering to note, for example, that more than a third of the respondents in 1990 were *not* willing to let an admitted communist or racist speak, and an even larger proportion—about half the respondents in 1990—were unwilling to allow an atheist or a communist to teach college. Despite significant change, then, there remains a latent reservoir of support for intolerance, perhaps based more on fear and ignorance than on accurate knowledge of the issues involved.

Attitudes toward minorities have also undergone significant changes over the past fifty years. In the early 1940s, for example, antiblack feeling was dominant among the white population of the United States. Over 80 percent of whites favored confining blacks to separate sections of towns; almost 70 percent favored separate restaurants; a similar percentage supported segregated schools; and approximately half favored segregation in public transportation and the armed forces.[22] Since that time, racial attitudes have grown much more tolerant. **Table 8-3** shows that by 1990 fully 93

TABLE 8-3
PUBLIC OPINION OF WHITES ON SCHOOL AND
NEIGHBORHOOD INTEGRATION, 1942–1990 (PERCENT)

| | Blacks and Whites Should Attend | | |
Date	Same Schools	Separate Schools	Don't Know
June 1942	30	66	4
June 1956	49	49	2
Oct. 1964	64	34	2
April 1970	74	24	3
March 1985	92	7	1

If Blacks Lived Next Door

	Would Definitely Move	Might Move	Would Not Move	Don't Know
1963	20	25	55	—
1967	12	23	65	—
1978	4	9	84	3
1990	1	4	93	2

If Many Blacks Lived in Neighborhood

	Would Definitely Move	Might Move	Would Not Move	Don't Know
1963	49	29	22	—
1967	40	31	29	—
1978	20	31	45	4
1990	8	18	68	6

SOURCE: Harold W. Stanley and Richard G. Niemi, *Vital Statistics on Am. Politics*, 3rd ed. (Washington, D.C.: Congressional Quarterly Press 1992), p. 391.

percent of white respondents were willing to have blacks live next door. Support for school integration reached similarly high levels by 1985. These results must be taken with a grain of salt, since other research shows that tolerance is positively affected by distance. Given segregated residential patterns in much of the country, the likelihood that respondents might actually have blacks move in next door is often small. Thus the "correct" answer (the tolerant one) may be an easy one to give. Nevertheless, the trend of the data is clearly in favor of greater tolerance.

Similarly, in 1936 and 1937 only 31 percent of Americans said they would vote for a woman candidate for president, whereas in 1988 about 80 percent indicated a willingness to do so.[23] Over the same time span, willingness to vote for a Jewish candidate rose from 46 to 88 percent. And between 1958 and 1987 the percentage of Americans willing to vote for a black for president rose from 38 percent to 77 percent (see **Figure 8-3**).

FIGURE 8-3
PERCENTAGE OF AMERICANS WILLING TO VOTE FOR A NONTRADITIONAL CANDIDATE FOR PRESIDENT, 1958–1987

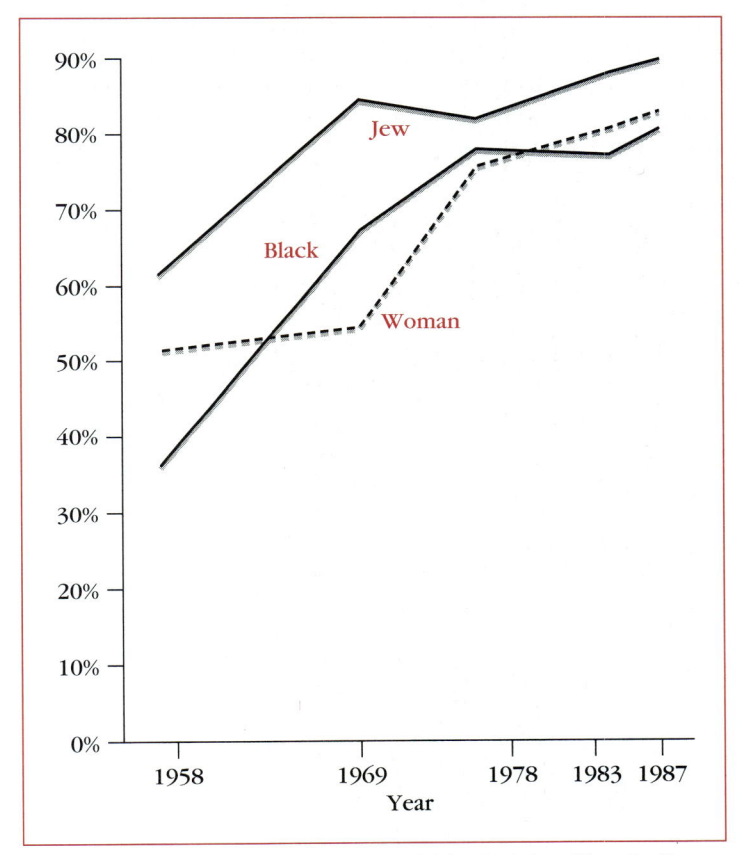

SOURCE: Michael Corbett, *American Public Opinion: Trends, Processes, and Patterns* (White Plains, N.Y.: Longman, 1991), p. 112.

Overall, Americans have indicated only lukewarm support for laws and activities through which racial integration can be achieved. According to many observers, there has been a substantial change in American attitudes toward minorities, but a substantial amount of prejudice remains.

Efficacy and Alienation

Americans display a strong sense of **political efficacy**. This means that they not only are willing to participate in politics but also believe that such participation can be

PART TWO • POLITICS

effective—that their actions will make a difference. Surveys comparing political attitudes in various democratic countries have shown that Americans, to a much greater extent than citizens of other democracies, believe that common citizens should be active in the community, can do something about unjust national regulations, and can successfully challenge harmful local regulations. Such survey results give the impression that the United States is a nation of avid political participants who have a strong sense of their ability to set the political process right, to shape it and make it respond.

Unfortunately, political reality is far more complicated. **Alienation** from government grew sharply from the mid-1960s through the late 1970s and has stayed at high

FIGURE 8-4

INDIVIDUALS' CONFIDENCE IN GOVERNMENT, 1952–1990

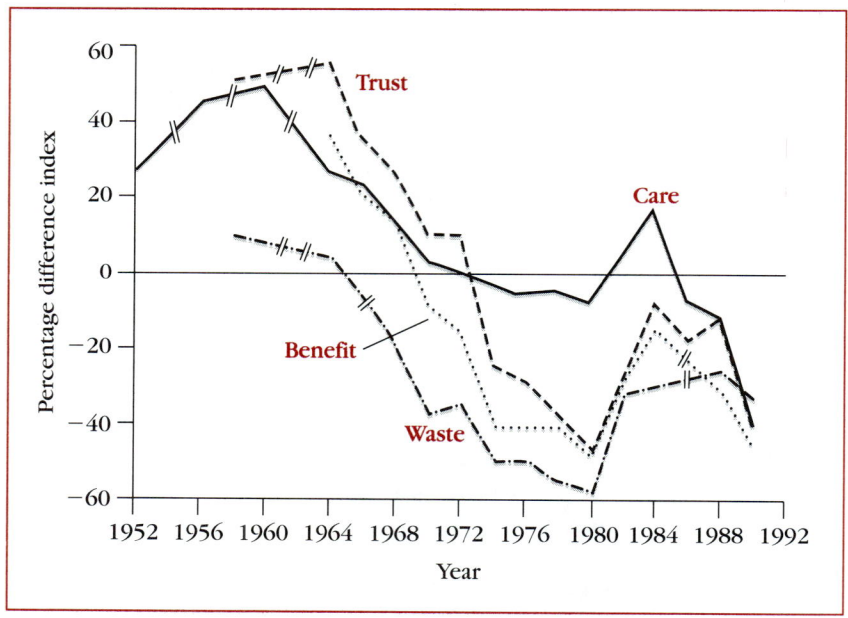

Broken line indicates question not asked that year. National Election Study questions: (Care) "I don't think public officials care much what people like me think." (Trust) "How much of the time do you think you can trust the government in Washington to do what is right—just about always, most of the time, or only some of the time?" (Benefit) "Would you say the government is pretty much run by a few big interests looking out for themselves or that it is run for the benefit of all people?" (Waste) "Do you think that people in the government waste a lot of money we pay in taxes, waste some of it, or don't waste very much of it?" The percentage difference index is calculated by subtracting the percentage of respondents giving a trusting response from the percentage giving a cynical response.

SOURCE: Harold W. Stanley and Richard G. Niemi, *Vital Statistics on American Politics*, 3rd ed. (Washington, D.C.: Congressional Quarterly Press, 1992), p. 169.

levels ever since. The social upheavals of the 1960s and early 1970s—involving civil rights, the Vietnam War, and the Watergate scandals—as well as the growing ranks of homeless people and AIDS patients throughout the 1980s, have all contributed to a far-reaching loss of faith in government.

Alienation from political life has three major components: feelings of distrust, meaninglessness, and powerlessness. *Distrust* means that people lack faith that the government will or can govern effectively; alternatively, they may believe that government is run by and for a few big interests, rather than for the benefit of all people. *Meaninglessness* grows out of a sense that the existing political choices are irrelevant, that it makes no difference who is in power, and that personal goals are unrelated to party politics. *Powerlessness* involves feelings of political impotence—that one is ignored or that the group one identifies with is not taken into account in political decision making.

Naturally, the effect is not always uniform across society. A 1989 study of alienation in the United States charted differences in levels of political alienation and political distrust by socioeconomic class. For example, one class (the "capitalists" between 1976 and 1980) might be experiencing a decrease in political efficacy while others experience an increase.[24] This might be especially true, for example, during a presidential administration that appears to make the concerns of one segment of society a priority. But the high levels of political alienation generated in the 1960s and 1970s reach across classes and have been sustained right into the 1990s (see **Figure 8**-4).

How significant a factor is alienation in political life? It has probably fueled the growth in antigovernment sentiment over the past three or more decades. It may also have played a role in generating political apathy, which remains deep-seated in the United States. Alienation also leads to violence and antisocial behavior, triggered when political frustration boils over and members of the alienated group have little faith that their grievances will receive a fair hearing. At the same time, however, most Americans think highly of the nation and continue to voice satisfaction with life in general.

Understanding Public Sentiment

How structured is the political thinking of most Americans? It seems safe to say that the average American does not espouse an **ideology**—a structured system of ideas applied to political and social issues in a coherent manner. The intense political combat of highly ideological parties, a staple of certain European polities, has largely been absent in the United States. We have something closer to a politics of the center, of pragmatism and moderation. Let us now probe the subtleties of this politics of pragmatism by examining liberalism and conservatism in broad outline, contemporary trends in U.S. politics, views on specific issues, and some key influences on public sentiment.

Liberalism and Conservatism

For much of the twentieth century, "liberal" and "conservative" have been the most common labels in U.S. politics. Like most political labels, these serve as shorthand for two clusters of ideas, each spanning several dimensions. "Conservative" might be applied to a particular position on foreign policy—favoring a strong national defense, for example. It might also be applied to a position favoring the death penalty or opposing abortion. A contrasting "liberal" position could be identified on each of these issues as well. We might identify a liberal and a conservative position on dozens of social, cultural, and political issues, and we speak of a continuum from left (liberal) to right (conservative).

To complicate matters more, these labels are also attached to persons, groups, and texts that combine several conservative or liberal positions. A person can be labeled conservative (Ronald Reagan) or liberal (Edward "Ted" Kennedy). One party can be labeled more conservative than the other (usually the Republican party is considered more conservative than the Democratic party). A single position might be labeled conservative at one time and liberal at another. A "nineteenth-century liberal" position advocating as little government economic regulation as possible has for most of the twentieth century been regarded as a conservative position. Sometimes a false dimension is inferred from these political labels—namely, that conservatives want to keep things the same and liberals want to change things. This is tidy but inaccurate. Some conservative positions advocate maintaining the status quo, but some do not. Many conservative and liberal positions are objectively unrelated to current arrangements. For example, the "conservative" majority on the Rehnquist Supreme Court may want to change many precedents established by the "liberal" Warren Court. Obviously there's more afoot than satisfaction or dissatisfaction with the status quo.

The problem with using labels as linguistic shorthand is apparent: With dozens of possible contexts, there is considerable danger that a message may be distorted by misleading shorthand labels. The ideal solution might be to stop using these terms altogether, but that isn't going to happen. Besides, although some danger of misunderstanding exists, the terms often convey useful information efficiently because they are fairly stable, well recognized, and backed by some rational or historical circumstance.

In the 1960s, for example, there was little danger of being misunderstood if you called yourself a conservative. That meant that you favored a balanced federal budget, a hard line against communists and obscenity, and tough treatment (including capital punishment) of criminals (including "recreational" drug users) and that you probably did not think highly of the United Nations, federal economic intervention, long hair, rock music, or women who burned their bras. In the relative calm from the mid-1970s on, the political spectrum developed some fuzzy edges. A "conservative" president, Nixon, instituted broad economic regulations, including wage and price controls, opened negotiations with "Red" China, and promoted détente with the Soviet Union. In 1976, Democrat Jimmy Carter, who described himself as a born-again Christian, defeated a "more conservative" incumbent, Gerald Ford, and then dramatically increased defense spending in the second half of his term. In the mid-1980s, political lines were more clearly drawn again. A liberal was someone who supported affirmative action, cuts in defense spending, and increased spending on day care; opposed severe obstacles to abortion, aid to the Contra rebels in Nicaragua, and punitive restrictions on persons who had AIDS or carried its virus; and wanted to treat drug abuse as a health problem rather than a problem of criminal justice. Naturally, even when fairly clear understanding exists about "liberal" and "conservative," few persons fit the model exactly. But general agreement makes the shorthand language useful—these terms are then merely imprecise rather than outright confusing.

But by the late 1980s, the clusters were coming unglued again. New patterns of belief and different combinations of issue positions have become common. Such shifts in the social landscape occur in part because of world events. The fragmentation of Eastern Europe and the dissolution of the Soviet Union generated intense shock waves in American politics. One of the most stable elements of conservatism since the Second World War—opposition to communist imperialism—seemed to evaporate almost overnight. The economic muscle of Japan and Europe came to be seen as the greatest external threat to U.S. security. But economic warfare meant trade barriers to some theorists and industrial policy (government coordination of large enterprises) to others. On foreign policy, conservatives and liberals regrouped.

Sometimes the language becomes outdated because of more gradual alterations. A gradual decline in the earning power of all workers that started in the 1970s pushed more and more women into the labor force. This gave women an economic power that irreversibly altered perceptions of a woman's place in the world and simultaneously created new demands for policies to help families (to create more adequate daycare and broaden the availability of parental leave, for example). On these issues too, conservatives and liberals regrouped. A conservative lock on "family values" gave way to a generalized search, on the left and on the right, for relief from the strains on increasingly common two-working-parent and single-parent families.

Policies themselves cause alterations in the political landscape. A decade of huge budget deficits generated in part by a 1981 tax cut has caused both liberals and conservatives to rethink fiscal policy. State and local governments were hit particularly hard by the combination of tax revolt, declining federal transfers, and a ballooning demand for services and benefits. Because larger and larger proportions of government expenditures are in entitlements (see Chapter 7) protected by vigorous interest groups, politicians of all stripes have been forced to abandon traditional economic solutions. The time when only conservatives worried about the national debt was gone.

The result of these changes and others is that "liberal" and "conservative" are now tricky labels to apply. Generalizations about what constitutes a conservative or a liberal are harder to make. The difficulty springs in part from the fact that different strains of thought have always competed for dominance within each camp. Another difficulty springs in part from partisan politics. With two major parties, it is too easy to fall into the trap of equating "Republican" with "conservative" and "Democrat" with "liberal." Even though party activists do display significant differences on political issues, U.S. parties are "umbrella parties," encompassing a wide diversity of political opinion. Thus there are many conservative Democrats (especially in the South) and liberal Republicans (especially in the Northeast and the Northwest). Confusion is heightened by the partisan manipulation of these terms. Democratic wags took Barry Goldwater's 1964 campaign slogan, "You know in your heart he's right," and responded, "Yeah, *far* right." In 1988, George Bush successfully badgered Michael Dukakis for being a liberal yet unwilling to use "the *L* word." Turning a label into an epithet rarely clarifies its meaning.

Perhaps the clusters of ideas behind these labels are most coherent and stable during times when one group identified as conservative or liberal controls one of the two major parties and dominates national politics. Then both the dominant idea cluster and its challenger may be more clearly defined. The early 1990s is not such a period. Within the two major parties, conservative or liberal wings are not clearly in charge. Should a conservative urge government to raise wages to allow more families to survive on one income, thus serving the nuclear family? But that would involve government intervention in the economy usually associated with big-government liberals! One political analyst, E. J. Dionne, Jr., suggests that the disarray in partisan politics is in part caused by the no-longer-relevant content of the idea clusters around "liberal" and "conservative":

> Liberalism and conservatism are framing political issues as a series of false choices. Wracked by contradiction and responsive mainly to the needs of their various constituencies, liberalism and conservatism *prevent* the nation from settling the questions that most trouble it. . . . We are suffering from a false polarization in our politics, in which liberals and conservatives keep arguing about the same things when the country wants to move on. . . .
>
> In fact, many good policy ideas defy ideological classification. Vouchers are thought of as a conservative idea, but one of the most successful voucher programs—food stamps—was a creation of Lyndon Johnson's Great Society [a "liberal" undertaking]. The earned-income tax credit, which essentially subsidizes the wages of poor people who work, is popular among liberals, who like it because it redistributes income, and among conservatives because it is efficient and promotes work.[25]

Whether cause or effect, the current lack of agreement about the terms of American political debate is clearly tied to changes in partisan support and the identities of the two major parties themselves.

The most effective response to the lack of linguistic clarity in political terms is not to throw one's hands up in despair or to stop using political adjectives. Political opinion in America should be approached on a case-by-case basis. To get beyond the labels, it will be helpful for us to examine the distribution of opinion on particular issues that have been and continue to be important politically: social issues, economic issues, and foreign policy.

Contemporary Views on Specific Issues

SOCIAL ISSUES   Many of the most significant social issues in recent American political debates involve aspects of sexuality—abortion, certain issues of women's rights, homosexual rights, and sexual morality itself. On these questions the American public as a whole displays a fundamental ambivalence. The generalization that one large part of the public is "permissive" in these matters and another large part less so misses an important distinction. Many Americans are attached to fairly well defined standards of behavior in these areas but are uncomfortable with governmental action to enforce community standards in matters of personal choice. Though Americans often readily translate community standards, there is an uneasiness about this. So citizens spend a lot of time publicly agonizing over moral issues. To some extent the society's ambivalence arises from separate groups with opposing convictions (fundamentalist Christians and liberal educators squaring off over creation stories in biology class, for example), but sometimes the ambivalence is felt by large numbers of citizens individually.

This personal ambivalence might explain the apparently inconsistent responses to different questions about abortion. Sixty-three percent of the respondents agreed that

Should federally funded family planning clinics discuss abortion as an option? The Bush administration said "No" and prepared to withdraw funding from any clinic that did so. But most Americans disagreed with the "gag order." After his election, President-elect Bill Clinton said he would reverse the Bush administration's stance and allow abortion to be discussed at federally funded clinics. *(Rhoda Sidney/Monkmeyer)*

if a woman wants to have an abortion and her doctor agrees to it, she should be allowed to have it. Sixty-five percent felt that a legal abortion should not be possible if the reason for seeking one was that the pregnancy interfered with work or education. Although the survey data cannot verify this contention, these two positions are consistent with the feeling that an abortion is not justified under the latter circumstances, although the government should not prevent a woman from having one if she chooses. On homosexual rights, about three-quarters of the population consistently supports the contention that homosexual relations are always wrong, but the population splits more evenly over whether homosexual behavior should be illegal. A slight tendency toward less tolerance on the question of legality for homosexuality was noticeable in the 1980s.

Reluctance to support government enforcement of community standards of personal conduct is also apparent in public reaction to the Reagan administration's "gag order" forbidding federally funded family planning clinics to discuss abortion as an option. Two-thirds (66 percent) of the respondents opposed this regulation in Gallup polls taken in 1988 and again in 1991 immediately after the Supreme Court upheld the regulation (in *Rust* v. *Sullivan*). In the 1991 poll, among a "middle-of-the-road group" who support legal abortion only in some circumstances, "concerns about free speech, rather than support for abortion rights, explain their disapproval."[26]

Recent public opinion demonstrates a trend toward increasing sensitivity and compassion toward victims of AIDS: In 1987 more Americans agreed than disagreed with the statement "In general, it's people's own fault if they get AIDS" (51 percent to 44 percent); by the middle of 1991 the public *disagreed* with the statement by almost 2 to 1 (63 percent to 33 percent).[27] Nevertheless, support for AIDS testing, although declining, remains very high. In 1991 fully 87 percent of respondents felt that doctors and dentists should be tested. Around 80 percent also felt that all patients admitted to hospitals, couples applying for marriage licenses, immigrants applying for permanent residence, and inmates in federal prisons should be tested. Nearly half of the respondents (46 percent) felt that all American citizens should be tested.[28]

Race remains an inflammatory political issue in the United States, and significant amounts of racism persist, but there are small signs of increasing racial tolerance. In 1991, for the first time, a plurality of respondents (48 percent) approved of interracial marriage, while 42 percent disapproved; in 1968 only 20 percent approved and 72 percent disapproved. Blacks are significantly more tolerant than whites on this issue. Seventy percent of black respondents in 1991 approved of interracial marriage, compared with 44 percent of white respondents.[29]

There are significant differences in black and white perceptions of civil rights progress. In general, perceptions of progress were less optimistic in 1991 than they were ten years earlier. In 1981 some 77 percent of respondents said that the quality of life for African-Americans had gotten better over the preceding decade; in 1991 only 53 percent agreed to the same statement. Only 40 percent of blacks in the 1991 survey felt that they had as good a chance as whites in terms of job opportunities and promotions, and only 50 percent felt that they had as good an opportunity in terms of education and housing; 70 to 80 percent of whites felt that blacks have as good a chance as whites in those areas. On the question of whether there should be additional federal legislation "aimed at reducing race, religion, and sex discrimination," the black-white proportions are nearly mirror images: 62 percent of blacks felt the need for more legislation and 30 percent did not; 58 percent of whites felt that we did *not* need more legislation, and 34 percent felt that we did.[30] These are significant disparities on issues of vital importance to democratic politics.

There have traditionally been high levels of support in the United States for the death penalty for persons convicted of murder. Support was weakest during the 1960s but climbed during the 1970s and remains high today. Despite the lack of social science data to support such a belief, a bare majority of whites (53 percent) continue to feel that the death penalty acts as a deterrent to crime and lowers the murder rate; a majority of blacks (53 percent) feel that it does not.[31] The increased support for the death penalty is echoed in increased support for generally harsher treatment of criminals.

The Senate confirmation hearings on Clarence Thomas's U.S. Supreme Court nomination ended with extensive testimony on charges that Thomas had sexually harassed an employee, Anita Hill, ten years earlier. Participants and observers (much of the country watched some or all of that portion of the televised hearings) generally agreed that the factual question of harassment was not and probably could never be resolved definitively. But the hearings did raise public consciousness about the issue of sexual harassment. Americans overwhelmingly disapprove of sexual harassment, but there is little agreement about what that consists of. The Thomas hearings sparked debate on the nature of sexual harassment. As with racial discrimination, there is a tendency in public opinion to underestimate the existence and the effects of sexual discrimination.

ECONOMIC ISSUES New Deal–style economic programs remain pouplar with most Americans, a majority of whom continue to support effects to aid the poor, improve housing in urban areas, and provide assistance to people in their old age. For more than three decades, most of the population has favored some national role in health protection. And since the Great Depression, most people have believed that the government ought to guarantee jobs for people who are unemployed. Generally, then, public opinion has remained solidly committed to the liberal **welfare state** programs that originated in the 1930s.[32]

Americans consistently and overwhelmingly express faith in the capitalist system. Yet a large majority of Americans lack confidence in the people running major companies and support the idea of consumer representatives on the boards of corporations.

Antagonism to corporations may stem from a deep-rooted American distrust of bigness per se and the concentration of power that goes with it. That would also explain widespread distrust of big labor in this country.

Americans take a skeptical attitude toward both big business and organized labor but strongly support the capitalist system as a whole.

On environmental matters, high levels of public support that emerged in the 1960s and 1970s have continued. When asked whether we are spending too much or too little on protecting and improving the environment, a majority (recently over 60 percent) responds "too little." Only a small minority—around 5 percent—responds "too much." Even larger majorities support environmental regulations. Over 80 percent in a recent survey responded that environmental regulations had "struck about the right balance" or had gone "not far enough." When asked which of these two statements, "Protection of the environment should be given priority, even at the risk of curbing economic growth" or "Economic growth should be given priority, even if the environment suffers to some extent," came closer to their own point of view, respondents chose the first by more than 2 to 1 (61 percent to 28 percent).[33] Of course comparisons of this sort will fluctuate to some extent with the current health of the economy, but Americans realize that environmental protection will cost money, and they are generally willing to bear that cost.

FOREIGN POLICY As we stated earlier, foreign policy issues are difficult to categorize in liberal and conservative terms. Party differences on foreign policy are also complex and fluid. Most major U.S. foreign policy initiatives have had bipartisan support, and the range of debate about alternatives has been limited. There is an isolationist strain in American politics, often identified as conservative and Republican. This position is associated with strong national defense, protectionist trade policies, and a reluctance to engage in global or regional politics, either positively through aid or negatively through military intervention. Not dominant in either party since World War II, the isolationist strain occasionally resurfaces in electoral appeals such as Patrick Buchanan's 1992 presidential campaign theme, "America first" (Buchanan unsuccessfully challenged George Bush for the Republican nomination). Counterbalancing the isolationist strain in American conservatism is an interventionist strain, advocating global involvement to advance American economic and security interests and to spread the blessings of liberty through democratic institutions and free enterprise capitalism. This strain found expression in the Reagan Doctrine: U.S. support for insurgency or counterinsurgency movements in Third World nations like Nicaragua, where the United States supported the Contra rebels, and El Salvador, where billions of dollars in U.S. aid were used to support the government in a twelve-year civil war.

Internationalism, distinguished from interventionism by its emphasis on international cooperation through multinational organizations, is more associated in recent politics with liberals than conservatives. The concept of human rights is often important to internationalism, which emphasizes reaching agreement rather than simply exercising influence in the world. The United Nations is the most prominent symbol of internationalism today. Sometimes the line between internationalism and interventionism is blurred when, as in the Persian Gulf War in 1991, the United States takes a dominant role in framing issues and leading military forces nominally under UN auspices. A 1988 survey suggests that Americans are overwhelmingly opposed to human rights violations but that they do not usually pay much attention to this issue. The public would rather maintain relations with countries that violate human rights and try to improve things through quiet diplomacy.[34]

POLITICAL SOCIALIZATION, PUBLIC SENTIMENT, & ELECTORAL TRENDS   **301**

International events, such as the Persian Gulf War of 1991, often produce sharp turns in public opinion. George Bush, for example, became a much more popular president after the quick victory over Iraq. But his popularity declined when public attention turned to domestic issues. Twenty months after the dramatic bombing raids against Baghdad, Bush was defeated for re-election. (Reuters/Bettmann Newsphotos)

THE OVERALL PICTURE   One of the most difficult aspects of public opinion analysis is judging how long a trend will last. What appears today to be the wave of the future may be forgotten a few years from now. Superficial disturbances of public sentiment—broad but not very deep—may distort the reading of trends. Public opinion research gives us a series of snapshots. We label periods of public events after the fact or as they wane. And we often revise our evaluations of the past. In 1965, Barry Goldwater's unsuccessful candidacy for the presidency the previous year was being written off as an aberration of Republican politics, but with Ronald Reagan's victories in 1980 and 1984, the 1964 Goldwater campaign was recognized as a harbinger of the future—after the fact.

What will American public opinion be in the year 2000? There will probably be liberals and conservatives, but what mix of ideas will each claim? The range of initial candidates for the presidency in 1992 was much broader than the choice reflected in the two parties' final choices. Which, if any, of the unsuccessful candidates represents the turn of the millennium? An angry populist with a message of racial exclusion? An

> ## RALLYING AROUND THE PRESIDENT
>
> Following certain international crises, the American public tends to rally behind the president, regardless of whether the president's acts are wise or successful. These are known as "rally-around-the-flag events," or simply **rally events**. The president becomes a rallying point for national unity. From the standpoint of democratic theory, this pattern poses some troubling problems. If the public tends to back the president almost instinctively, he will be able to count on support even when it is unwarranted. The president might even be encouraged to "look for trouble" internationally to reverse sagging domestic political fortunes. Excessive and uncritical patriotism could prove dangerous to a democratic society and to the rest of the world.
>
> Richard A. Brody argues against a general patriotic explanation of rally events, noting that sometimes for two apparently similar events, only one will create a rally. On January 23, 1968, a Communist nation (North Korea) seized a U.S. ship, the *Pueblo*, and held its crew as prisoners. President Johnson's approval rating dropped from 48 percent to 41 percent. After a "trial," the captain and crew were released without loss of life. On May 12, 1975, a different Communist nation, Cambodia, seized a U.S. ship, the *Mayaguez*, and its crew of thirty-nine. President Ford authorized a rescue mission in which thirty-eight Marines and airmen were killed and fifty more were wounded. The *Mayaguez* incident boosted Ford's approval rating by eleven points.
>
> Brody suggests that during a rally event the normal partisan distribution of opinion leadership is disrupted. The media's normal sources for opposition opinion (a relatively small number of well-placed persons) are silent because of the quick pace of events, lack of information, and reluctance to oppose the president until the situation has clarified. In most international crises, especially in the early stages, the president retains almost total control of important information and remains the focus of public attention. Most potential opposition is silenced because opponents do not have all the facts or out of a certain deference to presidential leadership. In the absence of media-reported critical opposition, the pub-

(Box continues on page 303)

old-time New Deal liberal? A wealthy maverick from the business world? Whatever the specifics of the next few years, American public opinion will continue to exhibit a dynamic mix of views. The ethic of individualism remains strong, even as welfare state programs enjoy considerable popular support. In American politics, self-reliant individualism, populist appeals to the common folk, and a distrust of "bigness" often coexist in a confusing mélange with more communitarian impulses. This odd mix forms the common ideological underpinning of our nation.

lic gains the general impression that the president's actions are unquestionably correct. By checking for the appearance in the media of elite criticism of presidential action, Brody can distinguish crises that generated a rally effect from those that did not.

A Gallup organization study identified forty-two rally events between 1938 and 1991, at least one for each president. For most of the events, approval boosts were short-term, returning to prior levels within ten weeks. In time more information becomes available, and opposition to the president will be expressed. The events that had the longest-lasting boost effects were Hitler's invasion of Poland (1939), the Japanese bombing of Pearl Harbor (1941), the start of Korean peace talks (1951), Eisenhower's U.N. atom pool speech (1953), the Cuban missile crisis (1962), LBJ's halt to the bombing of North Vietnam (1968), Nixon's Vietnamization speech (1969), the Vietnam peace agreement (1973), the *Mayaguez* incident (1975), the Camp David accords (1978), the start of the Iran hostage crisis (1979), the UN resolution authorizing force against Iraq (1990), congressional approval of using force in the Persian Gulf (1991), and Desert Storm's attack on Iraq (1991). George Bush enjoyed six separate rally events between 1989 and 1991, including five associated with the Gulf War. The combined effect of those events, building on a strong starting point, left Bush with the highest recorded approval rating (89 percent)—but a year later Bush's rating had plummeted lower than any president since Truman.

This phenomenon of rallying around the flag is not unique to the United States. When British Prime Minister Margaret Thatcher dispatched British forces to battle the Argentines in the Falkland Islands, support for her leadership soared. Because the battle for the Falklands, like operation Desert Storm, was brief and successful, Thatcher benefited considerably from a boost that lasted through the next election in 1983.

Sources: Richard A. Brody, Assessing the President: The Media, Elite Opinion, and Public Support *(Stanford, Calif.: Stanford University Press, 1991), pp. 45–78; Larry Hugick and Alec M. Gallup, "'Rally Events' and Presidential Approval,"* Gallup Poll Monthly, *June 1991, pp. 15–27.*

Influences on Public Sentiment

In analyzing public opinion, comparisons among different segments of the population are especially useful. Key factors include education, age gender, religion, and region. Some of the resulting conclusions are elementary—for example, that poor people tend to support the political party that promises the most assistance. Yet even this simple generalization must be qualified. Sometimes race or religion might matter more than poverty in choosing a political party. Other questions are harder to peg: Are women more liberal than men when it comes to divorce? Are younger people more likely than elderly people to support the death penalty?

We will now look at three of the factors that significantly affect people's attitudes: class, education, and gender. By delving into these factors, we can discover some of the driving forces behind American public opinion.

CLASS One of the most enduring divisions in modern politics springs from inequalities in the distribution of wealth and status. Most European political conflict has revolved around such class politics, with workers aligned against the middle class, labor and socialist parties against the bourgeois parties. We can see such patterns clearly in England, Germany, France, Italy, and Scandinavia. Even though Americans are much less class-conscious than Western Europeans, these divisions still play a significant role in U.S. politics. People's occupations are clearly related to their views on many economic questions, and these, in turn, are related to their political party preference.

Comparing lower-status and higher-status people (in terms of income, education, and occupation) over a range of issues, we discover that in general, lower-status people express more liberal views on economic questions, while higher-status people take a more liberal stand on civil rights and liberties. On foreign policy the situation grows more complicated. Higher-status people are more likely to favor internationalist approaches, whereas lower-status people usually support more isolationist policies.

How do such realities affect U.S. politics? We can draw one clear conclusion: that the economic liberalism of the poorer sectors of the population generally translates into support for the Democrats and for trade unions. But qualifications remain. For example, the greater conservatism of less-educated people on civil rights and liberties, as well as on some foreign policy questions, might result in voting for a Republican for president and a Democrat for the House of Representatives. There is also some evidence that economic self-interest is not always the most important factor in attitudes toward spending in particular areas (education and welfare, for example). A more important factor seems to be the "legitimacy of the client or program." Americans approve of spending even when it doesn't benefit them directly, as long as the recipient "deserves" the help.[35]

Income plays a key role in the way people vote. Support for the Democratic party increases steadily as we go down the income scale—a pattern that has persisted in American politics since at least the New Deal. People with higher incomes are far more likely to vote. Going down the income scale, voter turnout drops off steadily.

EDUCATION As we said earlier in this chapter, education is associated with several civically useful values. It is also linked to higher income and higher social status, so the individual effect of education is hard to isolate. Political tolerance is positively related to higher levels of education. The more education people have, the more they support racial equality. People with more education tend to be more conservative on social welfare issues and tend to identify themselves as Republicans. Since party identification is often determined relatively early in life, this link may reflect the fact that Republicans tend to be better off financially and so are better able to send their children to college.

GENDER   On many issues, men do not differ significantly from women. On social welfare issues, men may be slightly more conservative than women, but the difference is not great. Similarly, men may be a bit more socially tolerant than women. Sexual equality scores are essentially the same for men and for women. On certain social issues, however, there are significant differences between men and women. Men are more likely to support capital punishment and less likely to support gun control than women. Women are far less tolerant of pornography than men and less tolerant of marijuana use.[36] A 1991 survey found men much more likely to agree that with the statement "It's people's own fault if they get AIDS" (42 percent of men versus 26 percent of women).[37] The combination of all these positions indicates that overall, liberal or conservative leanings do not differ significantly by gender.

Nevertheless, during the 1980s talk of a "gender gap" became common as certain political differences became more marked. For example, women tended to see Ronald Reagan's economic policies as "unfair" and his foreign policies as "risky," whereas men were more likely to characterize the president as "forceful."[38] This gender gap proved significant in the 1984 presidential election, when the Democrats, to their chagrin, discovered a powerful new minority group: white males. Two-thirds of this group voted for President Reagan, whereas the women's vote was far more evenly divided.[39] While there was a marked decline throughout the 1980s in the percentage of men who identified themselves as Democrats, there was no comparable decline among women.

One study suggests that there are no substantial political differences between men and nonfeminist women but that the gender gap is the reflection of substantial differences between feminist women and nonfeminist women. Feminist women are more egalitarian, more likely to label themselves liberal, and less racist. There is a big gap between men and feminist women on foreign policy but not much difference between men and nonfeminist women. The gap between men and nonfeminist women on domestic issues is not nearly as great as the gap between feminist women and men. Thus the gender gap is not due to male-female differences but rather to the distinctly liberal positions of feminist women.[40] In general, in looking at compositional data, it is useful to remember the variety of persons within each category as well as the differences between categories.

Electoral Trends

Let us now turn to examining how political attitudes affect the political process. We will review the New Deal coalition that dominated American politics for thirty years, contemporary national electoral patterns, and the phenomenon of nonparticipation in politics.

The New Deal Antecedents to Contemporary Politics

The basic outlines of contemporary U.S. politics emerged in the 1960s and were first reflected in the election of 1968. Prior to that time, national politics was dominated by the **New Deal coalition**, a Democratic majority that had twin roots. For nearly a century after the Civil War, the Democratic party enjoyed a monopoly of political power in the South, based in part on the wholesale exclusion of blacks from mainstream political participation. Outside the South, the Democratic majority was born in the Great Depression of the 1930s. The Republican party, discredited by its failure to avert the Depression, lost the allegiance of thousands of voters who became stable Democratic supporters. By combining southern Democrats with new Democratic majorities outside the South, Franklin D. Roosevelt was able to lead an electoral majority in 1932 that encompassed both houses of Congress as well as the national executive.* Thus the New Deal coalition was distinguished by an intertwined set of characteristics including class, religion, and race.

New Deal Democrats tended to be poorer, more urban, and more Catholic than their Republican opposition. Northern blue-collar workers (many with ethnic and immigrant backgrounds) and white southern voters of all classes became the backbone of the Democratic party. Jews and blacks formed part of the Democratic majority, partly because they saw themselves as social and economic underdogs. Most Catholic and Jewish immigrants—Irish, Russians, Italians, Poles, and others—settled in cities already dominated by Democratic party political machines. During the waves of immigration of the nineteenth and early twentieth centuries, many Republicans held strong nativist, antiforeign views, which also drove the newcomers toward the Democrats.

During the dominance of the New Deal coalition, the Republican party was the minority party, the loyal opposition. The core of the Republican party tended to be high socioeconomic status, Protestant, and nonurban. Higher levels of education and income correlated with greater tendency to vote Republican. Protestants (outside the South) have been the most strongly Republican of the three major religious groups

---

*Later, this 1932 electoral change was identified as a **critical (or realigning) election** and compared to similar fundamental electoral shifts that had occurred in the 1890s and the 1830s. According to this typology, in between critical elections there were **maintaining elections**, in which the dominant electoral pattern was extended, and occasional **deviating elections**, temporary breaks from the still-dominant pattern. This categorization, was suggested first by the enormously influential political scientist V. O. Key, Jr., in his article "A Theory of Critical Elections" (*Journal of Politics*, February 1955). Two subsequent books are credited with ensuring the widespread influence of Key's typology: Walter Dean Burnham's *Critical Elections and the Mainsprings of American Politics* (New York: Norton, 1970) and James L. Sundquist's *Dynamics of the Party System: Alignment and Realignment of Political Parties in the United States*, rev. ed. (Washington, D.C.: Brookings Institution, 1983). This typology became the basis for hundreds of analyses of elections in the United States and abroad. Its influence is marked by the fact that it remains the most common means of characterizing U.S. elections, though the typology's explanations have been frustrated for nearly a quarter of a century. See Byron E. Shafer, ed., *The End of Realignment? Interpreting American Electoral Eras* (Madison: University of Wisconsin Press, 1991).

FIGURE 8-5
POLITICAL PARTY PREFERENCE BY RELIGION

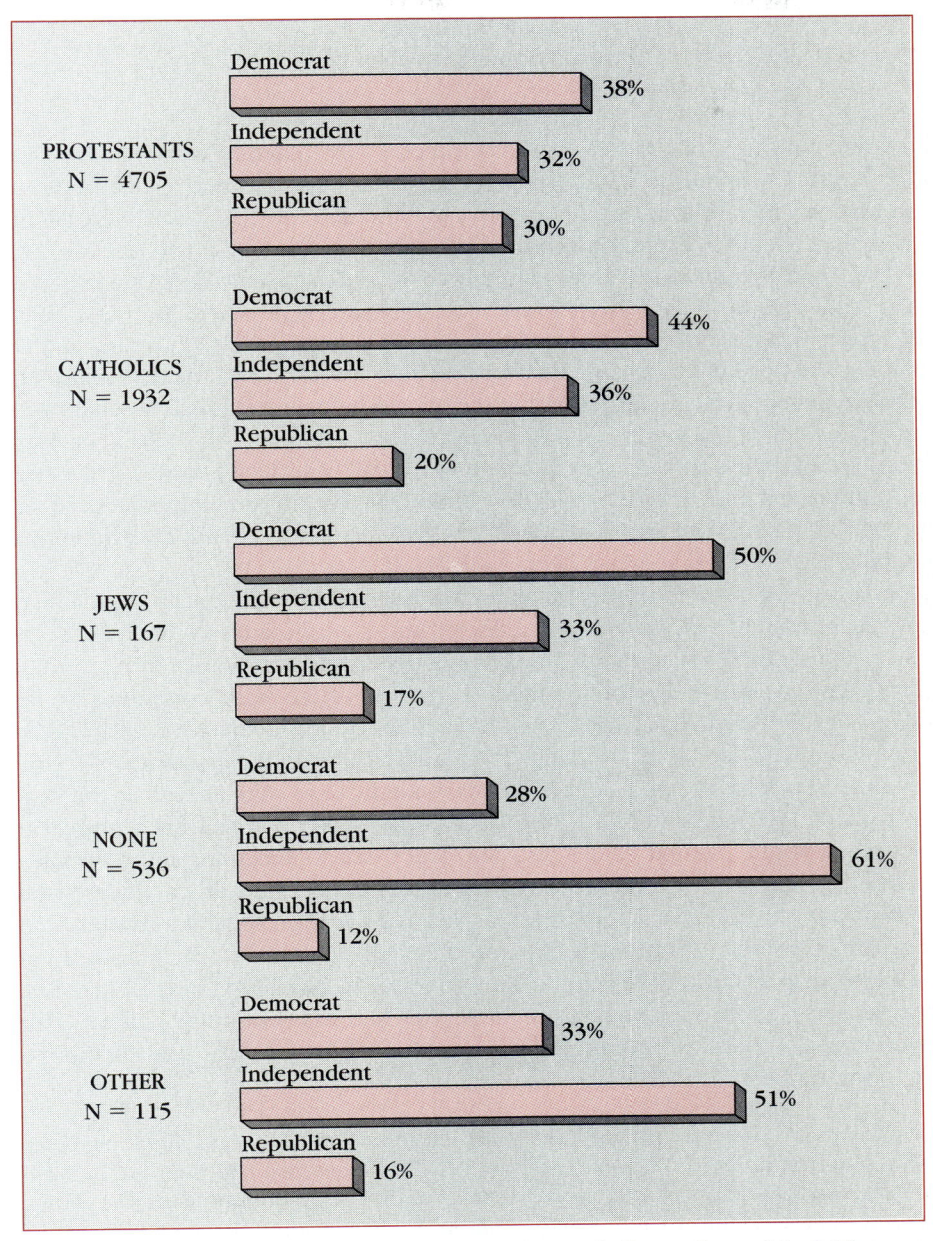

PROTESTANTS
N = 4705
- Democrat 38%
- Independent 32%
- Republican 30%

CATHOLICS
N = 1932
- Democrat 44%
- Independent 36%
- Republican 20%

JEWS
N = 167
- Democrat 50%
- Independent 33%
- Republican 17%

NONE
N = 536
- Democrat 28%
- Independent 61%
- Republican 12%

OTHER
N = 115
- Democrat 33%
- Independent 51%
- Republican 16%

SOURCE: University of Chicago National Opinion Research Center General Social Surveys, 1980–1985.

(see **Figure 8-5**), partly because of heavier representation of Protestants in the business classes in small-town America and also among the wealthier and better-educated.

The Contemporary National Electoral Pattern: Crosscutting Attachments and Divided Government

By the middle of the 1960s a series of developments threatened to tear the New Deal coalition apart. On domestic issues, the civil rights struggle drove a wedge between conservative white southern Democrats on one hand and, on the other, increasingly powerful black Democrats and their liberal allies, both in the South and outside. The 1960s' challenge to traditional values highlighted deep divisions between socially conservative and socially liberal Democrats. The Vietnam War pitted interventionists against internationalists. Most important, the new divisions on foreign policy and on social issues did not match existing divisions on social welfare and the distribution of economic benefits. These pressures within the once-dominant coalition coincided with increasing feelings of distrust and alienation among the population at large. Party identification (see **Figure 8-6**) and voter loyalty fell. Instead of driving a majority of voters to the Republicans in a realigning election, this combination of forces shattered the coalition into segments that expressed themselves electorally by abandoning traditional party voting.

How can we describe the electoral pattern of the past quarter-century? One line of thinking suggests that whereas parties reflected the main boundaries of opinion disagreement during the New Deal era, branches of government now reflect the opinion landscape directly. In foreign policy matters (getting tough with communists), the president became the focus of representative demands. Presidents have a natural advantage in contemporary foreign policy, dominated as it is by the existence of a large military force. Because the president is the symbolic head of state as well as the head of government, presidential politics also became the primary arena for hashing out disagreements about cultural values (law-and-order issues, abortion, and affirmative action, for example). On economic benefits (social security and other welfare state programs, "pork barrel" projects), Congress became the representative institution of choice, with special significance for the House of Representatives. The House is particularly well adapted for protecting specific economic benefits programs, but the Senate, too, knows the business of constituent service and interest group politics. Thus the two elective ("political") branches of our national government lent themselves readily to the new political order.

> The general public, as it turned out, was *liberal* on economic welfare, *nationalist* on foreign policy, and *traditionalist* on cultural values.... When continuing majorities on the major issue divisions of our time were sorted electorally to their relevant institutions, the partisan shape of a new electoral order came into view: the presidency *should* be Republican in such an order; the House *should* be Democratic; and the Senate should be capturable by *either* political party, while retaining an intrinsic Democratic bias.[41]

FIGURE 8-6
PARTY IDENTIFICATION, 1937–1991

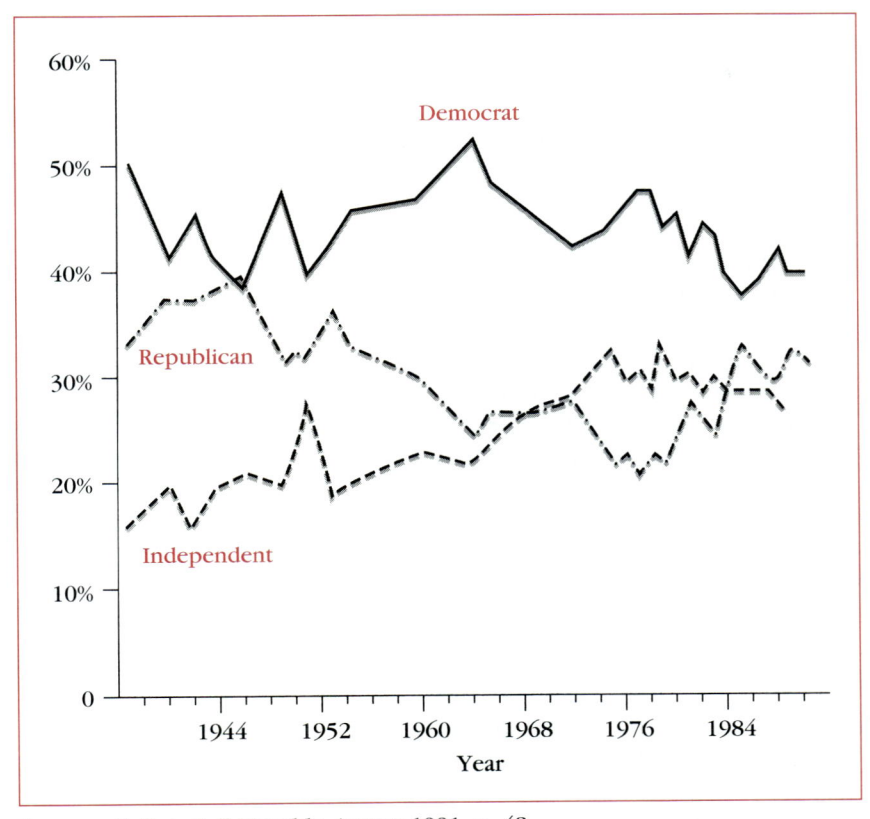

[Figure: Line graph showing party identification percentages from 1937 to 1991 for Democrat, Republican, and Independent, with Democrat generally highest (around 40-55%), Republican and Independent crossing over time between roughly 20-40%.]

SOURCE: *Gallup Poll Monthly*, August 1991, p. 48.

Under this interpretation, the divergent demands of the electorate are appropriately reflected in the separate branches of national government. Deviations from the expected pattern of electoral choice may result from an unusual combination of factors. Jimmy Carter's 1976 election was facilitated by Watergate and its fallout, including Ford's pardon of Nixon and Ford's appointed-incumbent status. Bill Clinton's election in 1992 reflected the destabilization of opinion in foreign policy caused by the collapse of the Soviet Union and a severe recession that tended to overshadow some social concerns.

Another interpretation of the past twenty-five years is that American politics is experiencing an extended period of transition from one party system to another. The decline in party identification is a transitory sign of the current absence of a party that addresses the right issues the right way to please a majority of the population. When the right party appeal appears, stability of party identification will return. Ross Perot's strong showing in the presidential election of 1992 was certainly one sign of dissatisfaction with the two major parties as then constituted.

However we describe it, the current state of American partisan politics raises two concerns. First, divided government makes a governing consensus and government accountability hard to achieve. Second, high levels of nonparticipation ought to be of serious concern to democratic politics. We now turn to the issue of nonparticipation.

Nonparticipation

Every four years, a bit over one quarter of the eligible voting population gets to choose a president; in off years, a smaller proportion of the voting population in each district regularly chooses members of Congress. Such is the current state of the American democracy, where only half of the eligible voters participate in presidential elections and where off-year elections may draw just over one-third of those eligible (see **Table 8-4**). Local elections are worse. A fair proportion of *registered* voters do vote, but in the United States large numbers of eligible persons are not registered to vote. In terms of eligible voters, the United States ranks near the bottom in comparisons of Western-style democracies.[42] From a democratic perspective, there is reason for concern when so many citizens take so little interest in the nation's political life. We now examine barriers to voting and who votes.

Barriers to Voting

The consistently low voter turnouts in U.S. elections can be partly attributed to the law and to elements of the electoral system that make it difficult or even impossible to vote. We can talk about the cost of political participation in time and effort, as well as in real money. Registration is the largest formal barrier to voting. In many countries registration is automatic and therefore cost-free. In the United States elaborate voter registration systems were established around the turn of the twentieth century to combat election fraud. Because even national elections are the states' responsibility, registration requirements vary from state to state. In some parts of the country voter registration systems were used as a means of keeping certain segments of the population from voting (most notoriously, blacks in the South). Until 1972 some states had lengthy residence requirements for registration, but the Supreme Court struck those down as a violation of the right to vote.[43] Many states retain shorter waiting periods (usually a month) that prevent voters from registering on election day. In some states registration requires a personal appearance at the courthouse. Deputy registrars may have tables or booths for limited times at more accessible locations (a mall or a college campus). Many states "purge" voting rolls, eliminating the names of persons who haven't voted in recent elections. Those persons must reregister to be able to vote.

TABLE 8-4
TURNOUT IN PRESIDENTIAL AND CONGRESSIONAL ELECTIONS, 1920–1992

Year	President	U.S. Representative
1920	43.5%	40.8%
1922	—	32.1
1924	43.9	40.6
1926	—	29.8
1928	51.9	47.8
1930	—	33.7
1932	52.4	49.7
1934	—	41.4
1936	56.9	53.5
1938	—	44.0
1940	58.9	55.4
1942	—	32.5
1944	56.0	52.7
1946	—	37.1
1948	51.1	48.1
1950	—	41.1
1952	61.6	57.6
1954	—	41.7
1956	59.3	55.9
1958	—	43.0
1960	62.8	58.5
1962	—	45.4
1964	61.9	57.8
1966	—	45.4
1968	60.9	55.1
1970	—	43.5
1972	55.5	51.1
1974	—	36.3
1976	54.3	49.6
1978	—	37.9
1980	52.6	47.4
1982	—	48.5
1984	52.9	
1986	—	
1988	50.1	44.7
1990	—	36.0
1992	55.2	NA

SOURCE: U.S. Bureau of the Census.

COMPARATIVE PERSPECTIVE

FEWER VOTERS BUT MORE VOTING

Although the United States lags far behind other Western nations in the proportion of its citizens who vote in national elections, it is far ahead of any other Western nation in the *number of votes* cast by one voter in a given four-year period.

The first reason for this phenomenon is federalism. Americans may vote in at least four jurisdictions—federal, state, county, and municipal elections. This four-layer system of government is not usually found in Europe.

The second reason is the separation of powers. Americans are unique in that they are able to vote for both legislative representatives and executive leaders at all levels—from city council members and mayors to members of Congress and president. In a parliamentary system, individuals vote only for legislative representatives.

A third reason is the long ballot. When Americans vote, they may vote for many executive offices, from dogcatcher or coroner to governor and president. By comparison, parliamentary regimes often are not set up so that citizens may vote for lesser executive offices. France is unique in Western Europe in having a powerful, directly elected president. Countries with figurehead presidents (such as Italy) often still choose the president indirectly or without a contest (as in Ireland), and only a few by popular election (for example, Finland and Austria). America is also distinctive in that some of its judges, and in some cases police commissioners or sheriffs, are subject to direct election.

Fourth, the United States has many special-purpose jurisdictions—school boards, sewer districts, and the like—that are directly elected. In Europe such bodies are almost invariably appointed by the central government or do not exist at all.

Fifth, many Americans are able to enact or repudiate legislation through ref-

(Box continues on page 313)

The bottom line is that an American usually has to make a special effort to register to vote; many simply don't bother. A survey of nonvoters following the 1988 presidential election found 17 percent who said they didn't vote because they didn't like the candidates or just didn't care. But the most common reason cited for not voting (37 percent) was that they couldn't vote because they weren't registered.

In 1992, Congress passed the National Voter Registration Bill, called the "motor voter" bill. The bill would have required states to allow registration by mail, to enroll

erendums on legislation and on some taxes affecting current or capital expenditure. The principle of the referendum is not unique to America; in Switzerland, for example, national referendums are pivotal. But state and local governments in the United States use the autonomy of federalism to hold more such ballots collectively in a given year than the whole of Europe put together. The recall of elected officeholders is another distinctive American institution, albeit rarely used.

Sixth, primary elections in the United States allow registered electors the right to cast a ballot and choose among a party's potential candidates. In continental Europe the mechanics of proportional representation allow centralized decision making by party committees that determine the party's candidates. Voters have a limited opportunity to alter party endorsements. Primaries at multiple levels of government in America can double many of the opportunities to vote. In states where a runoff election is prescribed when no candidate secures half the vote in the first primary contest, an individual's opportunity to vote can be trebled.

Such contrasting voting opportunities might first lead an American to ask, Why do Europeans have so few occasions to vote? The answers are several: the heritage of aristocratic rather than populist decision making, the belief in the efficacy and impartiality of civil servants as executive agents of government, and reliance on parties to organize and direct government through parliamentary institutions. A European who inquired about the advantages and disadvantages of the American system of multiple voting would first of all be met with answers emphasizing the principle of direct determination of issues by citizens (such as bond issues or school tax referendums) and the superiority of decision making by elected representatives. A European might wonder whether something was not lost by reducing the standing of experts and civil servants and by the disintegration of parties.

Source: Adapted from Richard Rose, "Citizen Participation in the Presidential Process," Society, *November-December 1978, pp. 43–48.*

voters when they apply for a driver's license, and to register voters at other state agencies such as welfare and unemployment offices. President Bush vetoed the bill, citing concerns about fraud. Why is voter registration still controversial? Elected officials may not see much benefit in expanding the number of voters, since a majority of even a small turnout is all that is needed for reelection. Expanded registration is resisted (implicitly) by some partisan actors because it is perceived as favoring the other party.

Registration represents the major barrier to voting, but other factors could encourage voting, such as election day holidays or weekend elections. Do polls sometimes deter people from voting? The evidence is mixed. A good deal of controversy surrounded the news networks' use of exit polls in 1980 to declare Ronald Reagan the winner by 8:30 Eastern Standard Time—while polls were still open in many states in the West. A few voters deciding not to vote because the game is over won't alter the results in the national election, but in local elections a small effect could change outcomes. There are sound First Amendment reasons not to restrict news coverage, so the solution to this problem probably lies in uniform national voting times—not a very popular suggestion so far.

Who Votes?

Not all groups or classes of Americans are equally likely to vote (see **Table 8-5**). In general, the socially disadvantaged are less likely to vote, and the socially advantaged more likely to show up at the polls regularly. The following factors influence voting habits:

1. *Income.* The more money a person makes, the more likely that person is to vote.
2. *Education.* The higher a person's level of education, the more likely he or she is to vote.
3. *Age.* People between the ages of thirty-five and fifty-five are considerably more likely to vote than younger or older persons. In general, people do not develop regular voting habits until they have established themselves in life. The falloff in voting among the elderly may be due to physical infirmity.
4. *Gender.* Men are more likely to vote than women. In recent elections, however, the voting gap between men and women has been disappearing.
5. *Race.* Whites are more likely to vote than nonwhites. In the past, large differences in turnout between the races stemmed from discrimination against black voters. The difference that remains can be ascribed primarily to education and income differences between whites and nonwhites. Minority voter turnout rises greatly when a member of a minority group is running for office.
6. *Party.* Because Republican voters are more likely to be college-educated and to earn high incomes, Republicans are more likely to vote than Democrats.
7. *Partisanship.* Persons who identify themselves either as Republicans or Democrats are more likely to vote than those who call themselves independents.

It is hardly surprising that the groups most likely to vote—the educated, the well-to-do, the middle-aged, whites, and Republicans—are much more likely to believe in their ability to influence government. One reason for such confidence is that by producing much higher voter turnouts, these groups do indeed have an impact on elec-

TABLE 8-5
VOTER TURNOUT BY CHARACTERISTICS, 1968–1988

	1968	1972	1976	1980	1984	1988
Gender						
Male	69.8%	64.1%	59.6%	59.1%	59.0%	56.4%
Female	66.0	62.0	58.8	59.4	60.8	58.3
Age						
18–20	—	48.3	38.0	35.7	36.7	35.2
21–24	51.0	50.7	45.6	43.1	43.5	38.3
25–34	62.5	59.7	55.4	54.6	54.5	48.0
35–44	70.8	66.3	63.3	64.4	63.5	61.3
45–64	74.9	70.8	68.7	69.3	69.8	67.9
65 and over	65.8	63.5	62.2	65.1	67.7	68.8
Education						
8 years or less	54.5	47.4	44.1	42.6	42.9	36.7
9–11 years	61.3	52.0	47.2	45.6	44.4	41.3
12 years	72.5	65.4	59.4	58.9	58.7	54.7
More than 12 years	81.2	78.8	73.5	73.2	73.3	70.0
Race						
White	69.1	64.5	60.9	60.9	61.4	59.1
Black	57.6	52.1	48.7	50.9	55.8	51.5
Hispanic	N.A.	37.4	31.8	29.9	32.6	28.8

N.A. = not available.
SOURCE: U.S. Bureau of the Census.

tions far out of proportion to their actual numbers. A rich person's vote does not count for any more than a poor person's—unless the rich person votes and the poor person does not.

Since nonvoters are younger, poorer, and less mainstream than voters, wouldn't we expect them to have different political opinions? Do voters differ significantly from nonvoters in their policy preferences? William Crotty, a leading authority on voting participation in the United States, finds that there is a significant difference in political affinity between voters and nonvoters, but "not as marked nor as radical as many might have expected." Nonvoters are slightly more liberal and centrist, more likely to support an increase in welfare state programs, and more tolerant of less conventional lifestyles. But there is little difference between voters and nonvoters on foreign policy issues, federal aid to education, and support for affirmative action. On specific questions about AIDS, abortion, school prayer, the death penalty, homosexuals, the war on drugs, and the role of women in society, little differentiates voters from nonvoters.[44]

Although political scientists tend to concentrate on voting, political participation can take a large number of forms. Much of the volunteerism for which Americans have been known since Tocqueville's visit in the 1830s can properly be considered political participation—from the parent-teacher group at a local elementary school to book review circles to hometown recycling programs. Americans, despite low levels of voter turnout, express relatively high levels of political efficacy (the sense that one can make a difference).

Opinion and Policy

How does public opinion influence government policymaking? Several patterns emerge. For example, when public opinion clearly supports programs already in existence, such as social security, politicians find it very difficult to make changes in them. Such programs usually have wide impact, touching almost everyone to some degree. Popular rebellion forms another recognizable pattern—when public opinion demands action (or the electorate takes action itself, through a referendum, for instance). In recent years popular rebellions have broken out over taxation and environmental issues. Policymakers who ignore broad-based discontent often do so at peril to their careers.

A more complex situation arises when an influential or well-organized minority seizes an issue and propels it to political prominence. Abortion, for example, has stirred such intense feelings among some groups that no other issue matters to them. Examples abound of well-organized minorities and poorly organized majorities in U.S. politics. Usually this occurs because the well-organized have more clearly defined and intensely felt interests at stake. For instance, although the majority of the population supports gun control legislation, the people who oppose it are so committed to their cause that they have effectively blocked such legislation for years. The medical profession has successfully postponed action on national health insurance time and again. In the same way, small numbers of citizens who will benefit greatly from particular tax loopholes press their case on tax reform with great insistence.

A somewhat different pattern emerges when public sentiment and legal edicts conflict. When the courts ordered busing to achieve integration in the public schools, for example, most of the public and much of the political elite opposed those rulings. Efforts to overturn those policies through legislation or constitutional amendment largely failed, but the lack of public and elite support for such policies significantly limited their implementation. Enforcement agencies were deprived of adequate funding; protesting parents kept children out of school or moved from urban areas where integration has been required; and at every level of government, from local school boards to the federal administrative apparatus, attempts were made to slow the implementation of busing. Generally, however, public opposition usually makes itself felt somewhere in the process of turning policies into realities.

In many areas, public opinion is neither well formed nor well organized, even though people may have strongly held views on specific issues. When this is the case—as it often is in matters of foreign policy, for instance—politicians have considerable leeway in policymaking. A good example was Desert Storm, the Bush administration's decision to go to war in January 1991 rather than wait for the economic sanctions to reduce Iraq to submission. Public opinion, although strongly anti-Iraq, was not committed to either strategy for getting Iraq out of Kuwait. The president's own commitments were crucial.

A study of the connections between public opinion and policy shifts in the United States between 1935 and the early 1980s demonstrated that policy is definitely affected when public opinion shifts are sufficiently large.[45] The researchers studied hundreds of national opinion polls and 357 federal, state, and local issues on which public opinion showed a "significant" shift—defined as a change of at least 6 percent. In 153 of these cases (43 percent of the total), government action followed major shifts of opinion fairly quickly. For example, the Civil Rights Act of 1964 was passed after a 12 percent shift of public opinion in favor of greater support for equal rights for black Americans. Not surprisingly, the larger the shift in opinion, the greater the likelihood that policy will shift in the same direction. When the opinion shift was 20 percent or greater, the researchers found, policy shifted 90 percent of the time.

This study illustrates that public opinion does influence policy decisions. It does not tell us, however, what factors cause shifts in public opinion. A whole range of factors come into play here, including mass movements, organized protests, the quality of leadership, media attention, and the general readiness of the public to respond to a particular issue.

Conclusions

Majority rule stands at the core of democratic politics. Through political socialization, children are inculcated with essential democratic beliefs—that ours is a free country, that majority rule serves as the basis of democracy, that individual citizens can make a difference in the political system. These beliefs—and the values of voting and civic participation—are taught and reinforced both at home and at school. In college, young people may adopt political views at odds with those of their parents in an attempt to forge their own political identities.

In theory, democracy is guided by majority rule; in practice, majority sentiment is identified through public opinion polls. Yet even though many Americans hold a deep-rooted belief in their power as individuals to influence the political system, alienation from government—expressed through nonvoting or other forms of nonparticipation—has been a persistent problem in U.S. politics.

Some observers of the U.S. political scene find nothing alarming about the sizable number of American citizens who do not even bother to vote. They note that U.S.

politics has remained remarkably stable, that our constitutional system has endured many tests. In recent times, they point out, one president was assassinated and another resigned from office—and neither of these events, which could have been catastrophic, shook the foundations of U.S. political life. This speaks volumes about the basic stability of our political system. Yet others see trouble for democracy when so many citizens take so little interest in the workings of their society's political system.

Whether or not majorities participate, how much influence does majority sentiment exert on U.S. politics? On this question we must take a cautious view. As we have seen, public sentiment in the United States is not structured along ideological lines. In general, the major shifts in U.S. electoral politics are clearly related to shifts in public sentiment. The New Deal enjoyed strong majority support, much of which remains to this day. Other shifts in law and political practice, especially regarding women's rights, tolerance, and racial equality, also reflect—and in turn influence—the views of emerging majorities. Yet some majority sentiments have not become law: Stricter gun control has not been enacted, national health insurance has not been set up, the federal budget has not been balanced. When majority sentiment does not hold sway, a powerful and well-organized interest group or coalition of groups is usually at work.

You may have noticed a missing link in our discussion. We can discuss the meaningfulness of majority sentiment or the importance of participation only so long before noting the crucial significance of political parties—the institutions that connect mass sentiment to public policy. We will address that dimension of the electoral process in the next chapter.

Glossary Terms

alienation
critical election
cross-sectional study
deviating election
direct socialization
ideology
indirect socialization
longitudinal study
maintaining election

New Deal coalition
political efficacy
political socialization
public opinion
rally events
randomness
realigning election
welfare state

Notes

[1] The expression *diffuse support* is taken from David Easton, *A Systems Analysis of Political Life* (New York: Wiley, 1965), chap. 17.

[2] See Michael Corbett, *American Public Opinion: Trends, Processes, and Patterns* (White Plains, N.Y.: Longman, 1991), pp. 209–219; Stanley W. Moore et al., *The Child's Political World* (New York: Praeger, 1985), chap. 1.

[3] Fred I. Greenstein, "The Benevolent Leader: Children's Image of Political Authority," *American Political Science Review* 54, 1960, pp. 943-945.

[4] Fred I. Greenstein, *Children and Politics* (New Haven, Conn.: Yale University Press, 1965).

[5] Warren E. Miller, "Party Identification, Realignment, and Party Voting: Back to the Basics," *American Political Science Review*, June 1991, pp. 557-568. But see also Jon A. Krosnick, "The Stability of Political Preferences: Comparisons of Symbolic and Nonsymbolic Attitudes," *American Journal of Political Science*, May 1991, pp. 547-576. Krosnick claims that the special importance attributed by research to party identification may be an artifact of the research itself.

[6] Richard G. Niemi and M. Kent Jennings, "Issues and Inheritance in the Formation of Party Identification," *American Journal of Political Science*, November 1991, pp. 970-988.

[7] Bruce A. Campbell, *The American Electorate* (New York: Holt, Rinehart and Winston, 1979), p. 112.

[8] T. W. Adorno et al., *The Authoritarian Personality* (New York: Harper, 1950).

[9] See, for example, Allan Bloom, *The Closing of the American Mind* (New York: Simon & Schuster, 1987); E. D. Hirsch, Jr., *Cultural Literacy* (Boston: Houghton Mifflin, 1987).

[10] Diane Ravitch and Chester E. Finn, Jr., *What Do Your 17-Year-Olds Know?* (New York: Harper & Row, 1987).

[11] Deborah Meier and Florence Miller, "The Book of Lists," *Nation*, January 9, 1988, pp. 25-27.

[12] Corbett, *American Public Opinion*, pp. 215-216.

[13] Herbert Asher, *Polling and the Public: What Every Citizen Should Know*, 2nd ed. (Washington, D.C.: Congressional Quarterly Press, 1992), p. 34.

[14] Discussion drawn from Eric R. A. N. Smith, *The Unchanging American Voter* (Berkeley: University of California Press, 1989).

[15] Angus Campbell, Philip Converse, Warren Miller, and Donald Stokes, *The American Voter* (New York: Wiley, 1960).

[16] V. O. Key, Jr., with Milton C. Cummings, *The Responsible Electorate: Rationality in Presidential Voting, 1936-1960* (Cambridge, Mass.: Harvard University Press, 1966).

[17] Norman H. Nie, Sidney Verba, and John R. Petrocik, *The Changing American Voter* (Cambridge, Mass.: Harvard University Press, 1976).

[18] Much of the material in this section was adapted from Alan D. Monroe, *Public Opinion in America* (New York: Harper & Row, 1975).

[19] R. S. Erikson and N. R. Luttbeg, *American Public Opinion: Its Origins, Content, and Impact* (New York: Wiley, 1973), chap. 2.

[20] See Daniel Yankelovich, *Coming to Public Judgment: Making Democracy Work in a Complex World* (Syracuse, N.Y.: Syracuse University Press, 1991), pp. 44-55.

[21] Samuel Stouffer, *Communism, Conformity, and Civil Liberties* (New York: Doubleday, 1955).

[22] Hadley Cantril, *Public Opinion: 1935-1946* (Princeton: Princeton University Press, 1951).

[23] Michael Corbett, *American Public Opinion: Trends, Processes, and Patterns* (White Plains, N.Y.: Longman, 1991).

[24] Cedric Herring, *Splitting the Middle: Political Alienation, Acquiescence, and Activism among America's Middle Layers* (New York: Praeger, 1989), pp. 49-72.

[25] E. J. Dionne, Jr., *Why Americans Hate Politics* (New York: Simon & Schuster, 1991), pp. 11, 346.

[26] Larry Hugick and Graham Hueber, "Two-Thirds Oppose Supreme Court's Latest Abortion Ruling," *Gallup Poll Monthly*, June 1991, p. 37.

[27] George Gallup, Jr., and Frank Newport, "Large Majorities Continue to Back AIDS Testing," *Gallup Monthly Poll*, May 1991, pp. 25-28.

[28] Ibid.

[29] George Gallup, Jr., and Frank Newport, "For First Time, More Americans Approve of Interracial Marriage than Disapprove," *Gallup Poll Monthly*, August 1991, pp. 60-62.

[30] George Gallup, Jr., and Frank Newport, "Blacks and Whites Differ on Civil Rights Progress," *Gallup Monthly Poll*, August, 1991, pp. 54-59.

[31] Alec Gallup and Frank Newport, "Death Penalty Support Remains Strong," *Gallup Poll Monthly*, June 1991, pp. 40-45.

[32] *Gallup Report*, No. 206, November 1982.

[33] Corbett, *American Public Opinion*, pp. 175-176.

[34] Ibid., p. 180.

[35] Arthur Sanders, "Rationality, Self-interest, and Public Attitudes on Public Spending," *Social Science Quarterly*, June 1988, p. 322.

[36] Corbett, *American Public Opinion*, pp. 237-240.

[37] Gallup and Newport, "Large Majorities," p. 28.

[38] *New York Times*, September 30, 1984, p. 14, and October 21, 1984, p. 15.

[39] Dan Boltz, "Democrats Discover a Power Bloc: White Males," *Washington Post National Weekly Edition*, December 24, 1984, p. 15.

[40] Pamela Johnston Conover, "Feminists and the Gender Gap," *Journal of Politics*, November 1988, pp. 985-1010.

[41] Byron E. Shafer, "The Notion of an Electoral Order: The Structure of Electoral Politics at the Accession of George Bush," in *The End of Realignment? Interpreting American Electoral Eras*, ed. Byron E. Shafer (Madison: University of Wisconsin Press, 1991), p. 51.

[42] See David Glass, Peverill Squire, and Raymond Wolfinger, "Voter Turnout: An International Comparison," *Public Opinion*, December-January, 1984.

[43] *Dunn* v. *Blumstein* (1971), 405 U.S. 330.

[44] William Crotty, "Political Participation: Mapping the Terrain," in *Political Participation and American Democracy*, ed. William Crotty (Westport, Conn.: Greenwood Press, 1991), pp. 4-10.

[45] Benjamin I. Page and R. Y. Shapiro, "Effects of Public Opinion on Policy," *American Political Science Review* 77, 1983, pp. 175-190.

SELECTED READINGS

Among the **classic introductions** to the issues involved in political socialization are R. D. Hess and J. V. Torney, *The Development of Political Attitudes in Children* (Chicago: Aldine, 1967); Bruno Bettelheim, *Children of the Dream* (New York: Avon, 1970); Fred I. Greenstein, *Children and Politics* (New Haven, Conn.: Yale University Press, 1965); and Erik H. Erikson, *Childhood and Society*, 35th anniv. ed. (New York: Norton, 1986).

For recent work on a variety of issues of **political socialization**, see Orit Ichilov, ed., *Political Socialization, Citizenship Education, and Democracy* (New York: Teachers College Press, 1990); Stanley W. Moore et al., *The Child's Political World: A Longitudinal Perspective* (New York: Praeger, 1985); and Richard G. Niemi and M. Kent Jennings, "Issues and Inheritance in the Formation of Party Identification," *American Journal of Political Science*, November 1991, pp. 970-988.

POLITICAL SOCIALIZATION, PUBLIC SENTIMENT, & ELECTORAL TRENDS

For general treatments of **public opinion**, consult one of the following: Albert H. Cantril, *The Opinion Connection: Polling, Politics, and the Press* (Washington, D.C.: Congressional Quarterly Press, 1991); and Herbert Asher, *Polling and the Public: What Every Citizen Should Know*, 2nd ed. (Washington, D.C.: Congressional Quarterly Press, 1992).

For a look at **current public opinions**, consult the *Gallup Poll Monthly*. For good narrative **interpretation of data**, including a good section on how to read survey data, see Michael Corbett, *American Public Opinion: Trends, Processes, and Patterns* (White Plains, N.Y.: Longman, 1991). For lots of useful tables, see Richard G. Niemi, John Mueller, and Tom W. Smith, *Trends in Public Opinion: A Compendium of Survey Data* (Westport, Conn.: Greenwood Press, 1989).

To explore further in public opinion, try Calvin F. Exoo, ed., *Democracy Upside Down: Public Opinion and Cultural Hegemony in the United States* (New York: Praeger, 1987).

For a **Marxist interpretation** of public opinion, see Cedric Herring, *Splitting the Middle: Political Alienation, Acquiescence, and Activism among America's Middle Layers* (New York: Praeger, 1989). James A. Stimson offers evidence of liberal and conservative cycles in *Public Opinion in America: Moods, Cycles, and Swings* (Boulder, Colo.: Westview Press, 1991). Stimson discovers one interesting exception to the finding that public opinion issue positions tend to follow general swings—abortion attitudes change less than other attitudes and according to a pattern all their own.

Arguing against the presence of a general increase in levels of **political knowledge** and political sophistication, Eric R. A. N. Smith, in *The Unchanging American Voter* (Berkeley: University of California Press, 1989), attempts to extend the original work of Angus Campbell, Philip Converse, Warren Miller, and Donald Stokes in *The American Voter* (New York: Wiley, 1960) across time. See also Diane Ravitch and Chester E. Finn, Jr., *What Do Your 17-Year-Olds Know?* (New York: Harper & Row, 1987).

An interesting article that links **cultural intolerance and political freedom** is James L. Gibson, "The Political Consequences of Intolerance: Cultural Conformity and Political Freedom," *American Political Science Review*, June 1992, p. 338.

The classic studies of **voting** in the United States are Bernard R. Berelson et al., *Voting: A Study of Opinion Formation in a Presidential Campaign* (Chicago: University of Chicago Press, 1986); Paul F. Lazarsfeld et al., *The People's Choice: How the Voter Makes Up His Mind in a Presidential Campaign* (New York: Columbia University Press, 1948); Angus Campbell et al., *The American Voter*; and Angus Campbell et al., *The Voter Decides* (New York: Harper & Row, 1954).

For further reading on **electoral trends**, consult Warren E. Miller, "Party Identification, Realignment, and Party Voting: Back to the Basics," *American Political Science Review*, June 1991, pp. 557–568. But see also Jon A. Krosnick, "The Stability of Political Preferences: Comparisons of Symbolic and Nonsymbolic Attitudes," *American Journal of Political Science*, May 1991, pp. 547–576; and Byron E. Shafer, ed., *The End of Realignment? Interpreting American Electoral Eras* (Madison: University of Wisconsin Press, 1991).

Political participation is introduced competently and understandably in William Crotty, ed., *Political Participation and American Democracy* (Westport, Conn.: Greenwood Press, 1991). See also John A. Ferejohn and James H. Kuklinski, eds., *Information and Democratic Processes* (Urbana: University of Illinois Press, 1990); and Daniel Hellinger and Dennis R. Judd, *The Democratic Façade* (Pacific Grove, Calif.: Brooks/Cole, 1991).

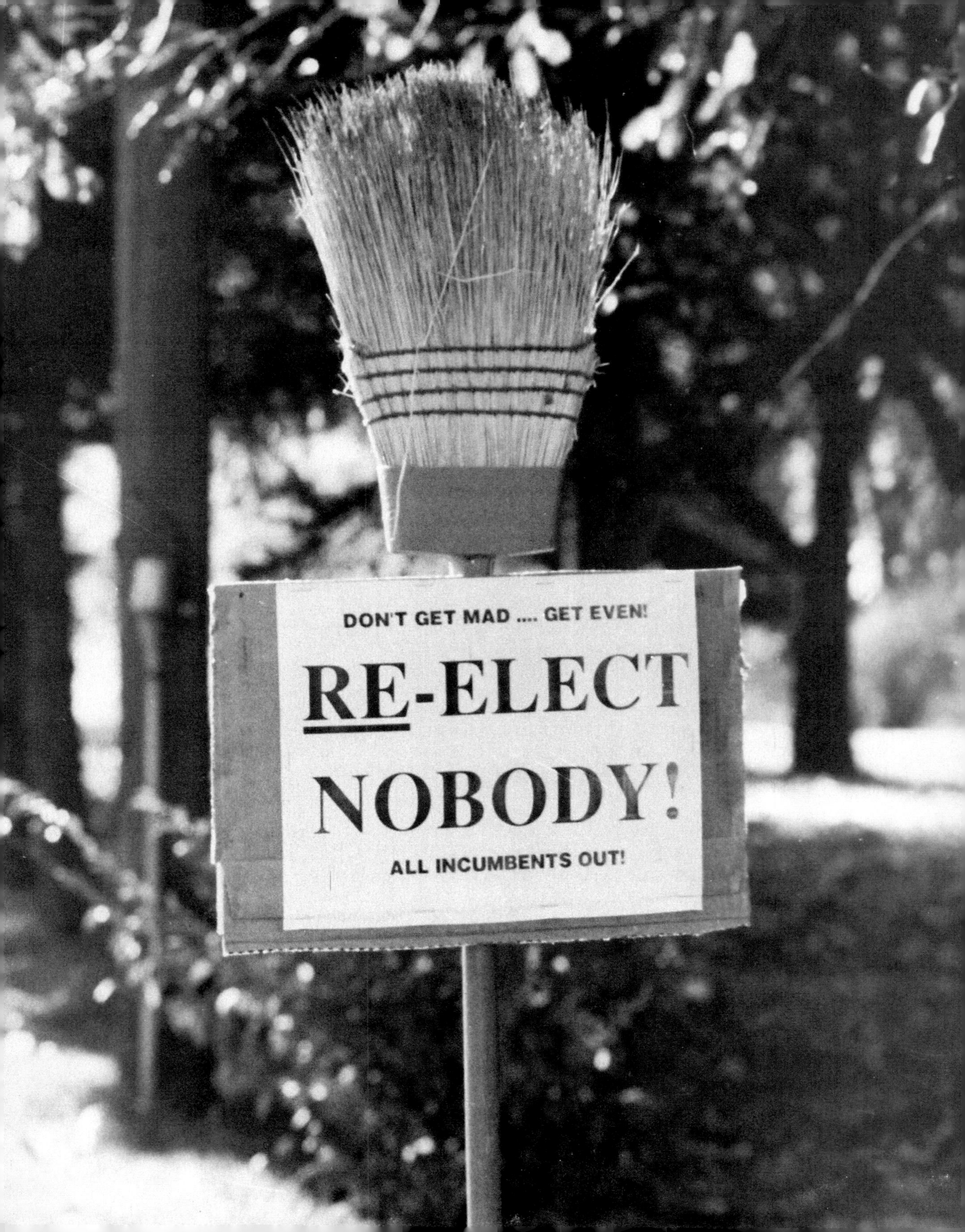
DON'T GET MAD .... GET EVEN!
RE-ELECT
NOBODY!
ALL INCUMBENTS OUT!

CHAPTER NINE

CHAPTER OUTLINE

Characteristics of Political Parties

THREE FACETS OF POLITICAL PARTIES
FUNCTIONS OF POLITICAL PARTIES
TWO-PARTY AND MULTIPARTY SYSTEMS

The U.S. Party System

ORIGINS OF CONTEMPORARY PARTIES
THE SYSTEM OF 1896
THE NEW DEAL COALITION
SINCE THE NEW DEAL
DILEMMAS AND CONTRIBUTIONS OF THIRD PARTIES
PARTY ORGANIZATION
PARTY REFORMS AFTER 1968
DO THE POLITICAL PARTIES DIFFER?

Current Issues

DECLINE OF THE PARTIES
REALIGNMENT: WHO HAS THE MAJORITY?
PARTY RESPONSIBILITY AND PARTY REFORM

POLITICAL PARTIES

Do They Offer a Choice?

CALIFORNIA, THE MOST POPULOUS AMERICAN STATE, HOLDS ITS primary in June, usually too late to be of interest in determining party nominees for the presidency. The year 1992 was no exception in this regard: Republican President George Bush and Governor Bill Clinton were already assured of their parties' presidential nominations before any California ballots were cast. Unremarkably, each gained a majority in his party's California primary. But there was a problem. Exit polls in the Golden State showed that if Ross Perot, a billionaire businessman not associated with either party, had been on the ballot, he'd have beaten both the incumbent president and the presumptive Democratic nominee. A *Newsweek* national poll the same week revealed that if the election were held at that time, Perot would get 35 percent of the vote to Bush's 33 percent and Clinton's 25 percent. Voter dissatisfaction with the status quo was well documented in 1992, fed by a long recession and a series of scandals. One important reason for discounting candidates outside the major parties—the purported difficulty of raising campaign funds—didn't apply to Perot, who was able to fund his own campaign.

Perot had become the most threatening prospect the major parties had seen since 1912, when a disenchanted former Republican president ran on the Bull Moose ticket. That former president, Theodore Roosevelt, drew enough strength

323

away from incumbent William Howard Taft to hand the election to Democrat Woodrow Wilson, ending sixteen years of Republican presidential success.

In party terms the 1992 election may have been the most interesting since that election eighty years earlier. Facing heightened media scrutiny and increasingly sharp criticism of his personal style, Perot dropped out of the presidential race in July but continued behind the scenes to fund efforts to get his name on the ballot in every state. With Perot gone and a successful Democratic national convention, Bill Clinton took a substantial lead in the race. Even when Perot re-entered the contest on October 1 and generated poll support in the high teens, the basic pattern of the election results was already apparent. Nothing that the incumbent president or the independent billionaire did altered that pattern: Clinton was elected with 43 percent of the popular vote and 370 electoral votes to President Bush's 38 percent and 168 electoral votes. Perot's 19 percent of the popular vote did not gain a single electoral vote. But this popular vote total was the best independent candidate showing since Teddy Roosevelt's Bull Moose campaign.

While the two-party system maintained its dominance of the electoral process in 1992, nearly one in five voters had expressed dissatisfaction with the two major parties. Was a new major party being born? Despite Perot's intention to keep his organization alive, its ability to become the foundation of a new major party seemed unlikely on the morning after the election.

But what if a new party did arise to challenge or displace Republicans or Democrats? What would that mean to the American political system? What service do political parties perform in our political system? And what makes a two-party system different from other party systems?

Political parties are generally given short shrift in the classic works on democratic theory, which concentrate on rights, equalities, liberties, and elections. And to many of the Founders of the United States, parties represented a potential threat to decent politics—selfish groups that would seek to exploit government to serve their own interests. James Madison warned of the dangers of "factions" that would use public power to further their own goals. George Washington shuddered at the thought of one faction alternately dominating another—a prospect he characterized as "a frightful despotism."

Even so, U.S. political parties began to develop early on. The beginnings of party disputes were apparent in the controversy over ratification of the Constitution. After George Washington left office, political disputes erupted during the administration of the second president, John Adams. Out of these disputes grew the new republic's first political parties, the Federalists and the Democratic-Republicans.

Why did political parties develop so quickly and so naturally even among people who distrusted the very idea of party? With more than two hundred years of hindsight, we can see that political parties are necessary components of the democratic process. In fact, our perception of democratic politics has shifted 180 degrees from that of the Founders: They could not bear the thought of a political life that included parties; we cannot imagine politics without them.

Why are parties vital to the democratic process? How effectively do contemporary U.S. parties fulfill their roles in democratic politics? With these two questions in mind, we will explore the characteristics of political parties, the U.S. two-party system, and current issues involving American political parties.

Characteristics of Political Parties

Numerous attempts have been made to define the notion of political parties. Some concentrate on shared *ideology*; others on the primary *activity* of parties (contesting elections); and still others on party *organization*. All three of these factors figure significantly in any discussion of parties, and we will touch on all of them in this chapter. A summary description of a political party, developed by contemporary political scientist Hugh Le Blanc, encompasses all three: "An organized effort to win elective office in order to gain political power and control the policies of government."[1]

Let us now consider three facets of political parties, the functions of political parties, and two-party and multiparty systems.

Three Facets of Political Parties

Most political parties have three distinct dimensions: (1) a formal organization, with distinctive internal politics; (2) an active role in the electorate, organizing electoral support; and (3) a visible place in the government, with officeholders on every level (see **Figure 9–1**).

As a formal organization, a party conducts business outside of government. The formal party structure includes the national organization and its leadership, various local organizations, and numerous professionals and activists who are heavily involved in party life.

As part of the electorate, a party relies on long-term voter allegiance to its views. Citizens identify with particular parties, building for those parties a solid base of political support at election time. As we will see, party loyalties in the United States have grown significantly weaker in recent times, and candidates now often establish personal organizations that function outside the party structure.

The party in the government encompasses the many officeholders at all levels who run under the party flag and the numerous officeholders who are appointed by elected officials. Collectively, these elected officials and appointees are responsible for policymaking.

The three aspects of party overlap, of course. Some party professionals may hold office, and strong party identifiers may work for the party organization. The strength of parties is difficult to determine; they function in so many different ways. Generally, however, U.S. parties are considered to be among the weakest political parties in mod-

FIGURE 9-1

THE THREE-PART POLITICAL PARTY

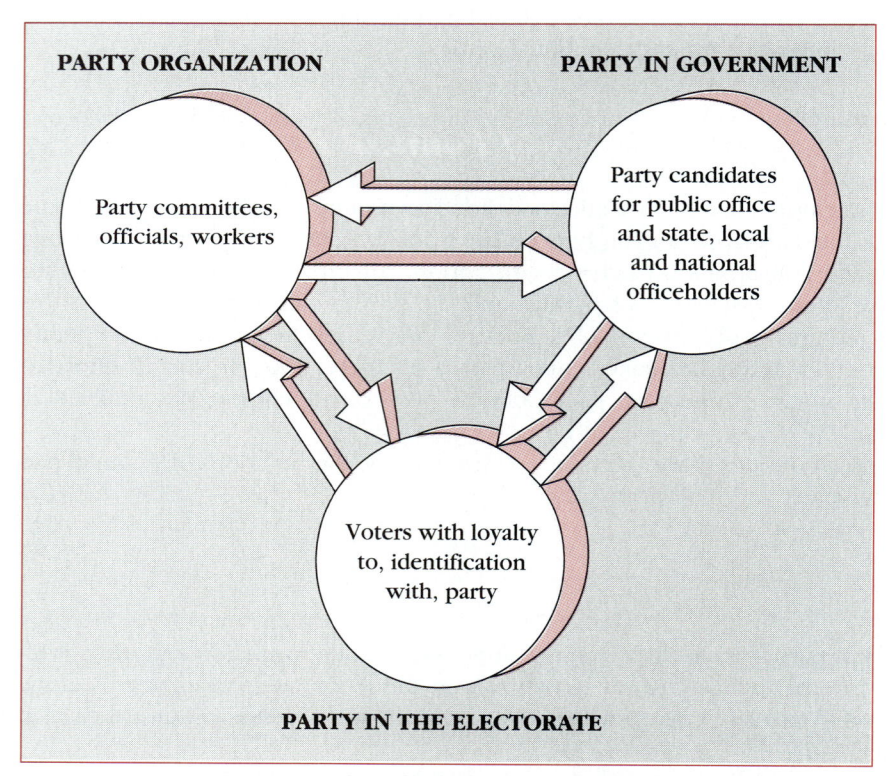

PARTY ORGANIZATION — Party committees, officials, workers

PARTY IN GOVERNMENT — Party candidates for public office and state, local and national officeholders

PARTY IN THE ELECTORATE — Voters with loyalty to, identification with, party

SOURCE: Frank Sorauf and Paul Allen Beck, *Party Politics in America*, 6th ed. (Glenview, Ill.: Scott, Foresman, 1988), p. 10.

ern democracies—they are very loosely organized and relatively undisciplined. Many European political parties have millions of formally enrolled members, whereas U.S. parties usually depend on cadres of full-time staffers.

Functions of Political Parties

Parties provide key links between citizens and government. First, they help to select candidates for office and mobilize the electorate. As parties come to stand for certain policies, voters link themselves with those policies. And some voters simply identify strongly with a party label. In these ways, political parties simplify the often complex choices that voters face.

Parties also organize the government: They are responsible for the functioning of the legislative and executive branches. In the United States, the party with a majority in either house of Congress organizes that house along partisan lines, selecting a majority leader and structuring the committee assignments in its favor. Likewise, the newly elected president generally makes appointments along party lines.

Finally, parties provide for accountability in government. In modern democratic societies, the governing political party ordinarily is held responsible for the conduct of government. Its candidates run on the party record, and voters can pass judgment on the way government is conducted by choosing to reelect those in office or to turn them out.

This overview of the functions of political parties in a democracy leaves many questions unanswered. What if party labels lose their meaning and voters no longer pay much attention to them? What if control of government is so fragmented that no clear lines of responsibility emerge? And what if there are too many political parties—or too few? As the chapter proceeds, we will address all these issues.

Two-Party and Multiparty Systems

"The best system is to have one party govern and the other party watch," asserted Thomas Reed, Speaker of the House, in 1880. The United States, with its two-party system, fits into this category. Most European democracies, however, have multiparty systems: Germany, for example, has two major parties and two minor ones; Italy has eight parties (see **Table 9-1**, page 330).

The U.S. political system has become almost exclusively a two-party system. In recent decades, third parties have had a very difficult time gaining any seats in Congress or state legislatures. In other democracies with predominantly two-party systems, such as Germany, Great Britain, and Canada, third or even fourth parties are often able to gain some seats in the national legislature and may play significant political roles. In Germany, for example, the small Free Democratic party for years played a decisive role in coalition governments. In the 1980s the Green party also had a significant political impact. Even in Great Britain, where the Conservative and Labour parties have alternated in office since the 1930s, the Liberal and Social Democratic parties have at times been able to attract a sizable minority vote.

At several points in U.S. history, third parties have helped to shape the course of national politics. Overall, however, the United States has tended strongly in a two-party direction. Our reliance on the **single-member district** accounts in large part for this two-party emphasis. In a single-member district, whoever gets the most votes in a legislative district represents that district, so votes for a minor party are usually wasted. Countries with multiparty systems, in contrast, commonly use a method of election known as **proportional representation**. Under this system, each party is awarded seats in the legislature in more or less direct proportion to its percentage of the popular vote. Since votes are not wasted in a proportional system, minor parties have an incentive to compete and can build on modest successes.

COMPARATIVE PERSPECTIVE

THE GREEN PARTY IN GERMANY

When an electorate becomes extremely frustrated with the dominant political parties and their policy positions—or lack of positions—one solution is to form a new party. One of the most dramatic new parties to be formed in a democracy in recent years is the **Green party** in Germany. Its policies stress new issues such as environmental degradation and the need for alternative lifestyles. It calls for sharp reductions in nuclear armaments and wants Germany to leave NATO. The Greens have drawn supporters from all groups and age levels in German society, but their core activists are younger, unconventional people who look back to the 1960s, when grass-roots action in West Germany had startling effects on political life. Not all Greens, however, agree on a common agenda.

Begun in 1980, the party's membership by 1983 was estimated at 1.5 to 2 million people. Although they captured only 1.5 percent of the vote in the 1980 national elections in West Germany, far short of the 5 percent necessary to gain representation in the national parliament, the Greens won 5.3 percent of the vote in a state election later that year and entered the state parliament. That victory was followed by showings of 5 percent or better in four other state elections, with the Greens in some cases replacing the Free Democrats as the third parliamentary party. In the March 1983 West German election, the Greens captured 5.6 percent of the vote and entered the 496-member lower house of the federal parliament (the Bundestag) with 27 seats. The high point of Green electoral success occurred in the national election of 1987, in which 8.3 percent of the vote and 44 seats in the Bundestag went to the Greens.

The Green party suffered a major setback with the reunification of East and West Germany in 1990. After actively opposing reunification, the Greens found

(Box continues on page 329)

As our two-party system evolved, strong ties of party identification have been established between the voters and the two major parties: People have come to think of elections in strictly two-party terms. Moreover, electoral laws place minor parties at a distinct disadvantage—for example, new parties must petition to get on the ballot in most states. And since the two major parties are composed of many factions and interests, new groups can usually make their presence felt *within* an established party rather than in a new political group. In multiparty systems, by contrast, governing coalitions are worked out among parties when no party wins a clear electoral majority.

In addition, the way the chief political leader, the president, is selected in the United

themselves shut out in the first elections for the new, unified parliament, gaining only 3.9 percent of the vote. Moreover, with the end of the Cold War, Green opposition to German militarism lost its electoral urgency. Compounding the Green party's difficulties was a phenomenon familiar to third-party activists in the United States: A successful issue for a third party—for the Greens, it was environmental activism—is often picked up by the major parties. The Social Democrats and even the Christian Democrats began to display an environmental sensitivity that the Greens had pioneered a decade earlier.

But the German party system offers minor parties a better chance to maintain themselves than the American two-party system. The electoral setback of 1990 did not signal the end of Green party influence in Germany. In 1991 a coalition of Social Democrats and Greens prevailed over the ruling Christian Democrat—Free Democrat coalition in Hesse state, campaigning for expanded public housing and an end to nuclear power in the state. Even electoral success presents a problem, though. Radical purists within the party are fundamentally opposed to the existing social and political system and thus want the party to serve as a moral conscience in the Bundestag rather than as a partner in administration. Realists, by contrast, favor compromise—making deals and entering into coalitions with other groups. One Green who served as a minister for the environment in a Social democratic state government pointed out: "I don't want just to complain that the rivers are dirty; I want to clean them up." But in contrast, others argue that "the opposition would lose its teeth if it became too legal." Such internal rifts pose the most serious threat to the future of the Green party in Germany.

Sources: Serge Schmemann, "For Germany's Green Movement: Conventional Success Breeds a Schism," New York Times, *October 11, 1987, p. 8; Tamara Jones, "Germany's Green Party Bitter, Divided in Defeat,"* Los Angeles Times, *December 4, 1990, p. A1; Tyler Marshall, "Social Democrats, Greens Lead in German State Election,"* Los Angeles Times, *January 21, 1991, p. A4.*

States lends further support to the two-party arrangement. In many other democratic nations, the executive leader is chosen by the party (or parties, in a coalition government) that controls the parliament, whereas we hold an entirely separate election for president. The national attention focused on this office makes presidential elections the most dramatic political events in the United States. The two established parties, with their loyalists, organizations, and patterns of identification, have a nearly insurmountable advantage in the presidential race.

Finally, most political observers credit the overall moderate nature of American public opinion for pushing us toward two middle-of-the-road political parties. As we

TABLE 9-1
THE POLITICAL SPECTRUM IN SEVERAL DEMOCRATIC NATIONS

	Radical Left	Communist (or former Communist)	Democratic Socialist	Liberal	Christian Democrat	Conservative	Reactionary Right
Great Britain			Labour Party	Liberal Democrats		Conservative Party	
France		French Communist Party (PCF)	Socialist Party	Radical Party	Democratic Center	Independent Republicans (RI); Gaullists (UDR)	National Front (FN)
Germany			Social Democratic Party (SPD); Greens	Free Democratic Party (FDP)	Christian Democratic Union (CDU)	Christian Social Union (SCU)	National Democratic Party (NPD)
Italy	Reform Communist Party	Democratic Party of the Left (PDS)	Italian Socialist Party (PSI); Social Democratic Party (PSDI)	Republican Party (PRI)	Christian Democratic Party (DC)	Liberal Party (PLI)	Italian Social Movement (MSI)
Norway			Left Socialists (VS); Socialist People's Party (SPP)	Labour	Liberals; Liberal People's Party	Christian People's Party (KRF)	Conservatives	Progress Party
United States*				Democratic Party		Republican Party	

*Note that the United States is one of the few democratic countries with only two political parties, although in some other nations (Britain and Germany, for example) two parties predominate.

SOURCE: David M. Wood, *Power and Policy in Western European Democracies*, 3rd ed. (New York: Wiley, 1986); Michael Lauer and Norman Schofield, *Multiparty Government: The Politics of Coalition in Europe* (New York: Oxford, University Press, 1990).

TABLE 9-2
Ideological Awareness among Citizens of Several Democracies

	Actively Use Ideological Thinking	Recognize or Understand Left versus Right	Aware of Nation's Left-Right Placement
Germany	34%	56%	92%
Netherlands	36	48	90
Great Britain	21	23	82
Switzerland	9	39	79
Austria	19	39	75
Italy	55	54	74
United States	21	34	67

SOURCE: Adapted from Russell J. Dalton, *Citizen Politics in Western Democracies* (Chatham, N.J.: Chatham House, 1988), p. 25.

noted in Chapter 2, U.S. political culture draws heavily on a liberal heritage. Both the extreme left and the extreme right have been notably weak in U.S. political life, allowing little room for political success outside the mainstream.

As we can see from **Table 9-2**, Americans hold less ideological views than Europeans. Americans use left-right ideological thinking (left column) less than the Germans, the Italians, or the Dutch but about as much as the British and more than the Swiss. We rank next to the lowest (above Britain) in terms of recognizing or understanding the meaning of the left-right dimension (center column) and in awareness of the nation's left-right placement (right column). These are indications of the lack of self-conscious ideological debate in the United States, which is tied to the lack of self-conscious class orientation.

The U.S. Party System

Over the years the U.S. party system has undergone several basic shifts. Let us now look at how it has evolved and how its evolution has affected democratic politics in the United States.

Origins of Contemporary Parties

In his farewell address, delivered in 1797, President George Washington called on the nation to be wary of the "baneful effects of the spirit of party." This warning resulted from events during his administration that, much to his dismay, clearly signaled the emergence of political party divisions in the new nation.

Two factions had been developing during Washington's eight years in office. Members of one faction, called the **Federalists**, were led by Secretary of the Treasury Alexander Hamilton (and by George Washington himself, despite his disdain for parties in principle). The Federalists were generally wealthy and of high social position. Members of the second group, the so-called **Democratic-Republicans**, were led by Thomas Jefferson and James Madison. Jefferson's party, a coalition of small farmers, small property owners, and local political leaders in the southern and mid-Atlantic states, soon came to dominate U.S. politics. By the mid-1820s the Federalists had lost all political force.

With the election of Andrew Jackson to the presidency in 1828, the party of Jefferson and Madison, renamed the **Democratic party**, was transformed into a mass-membership organization that became the dominant force in U.S. political life. Presidents Jackson and Martin Van Buren reorganized their party to accommodate the new states admitted to the Union and to gain support among the people who became eligible to vote as economic qualifications limiting suffrage were eased.

Between 1828 and 1856 the Jacksonian Democrats faced opposition mainly from the **Whig party**. The Democrats drew their primary political support from the frontier, among farmers in the western states; the Whigs, in contrast, appealed more to New Englanders and especially to people with business interests. Although the Democrats won the presidency and a majority in the House of Representatives in most of those elections, the Whigs attracted a substantial following, electing both William Henry

Andrew Jackson is pictured here on the way to his presidential inauguration in 1829 in Washington. It was during the Jackson era that the idea of a mass-membership political party began to take hold in the United States. Jackson's party, the Democrats, appealed most strongly to those on the expanding western frontier. (Howard Pyle/The Bettmann Archive)

FIGURE 9-2
THE FIVE MAJOR U.S. POLITICAL PARTIES SINCE 1789

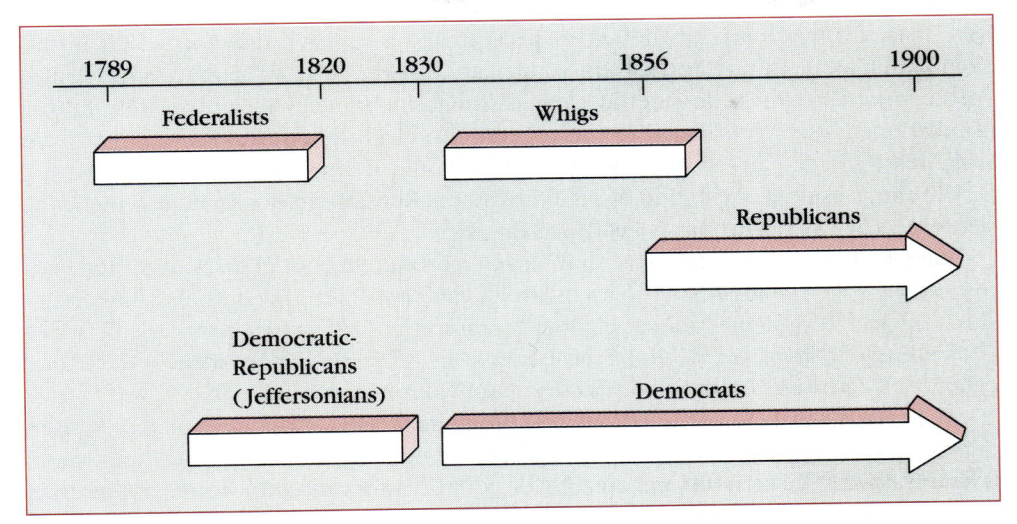

[Timeline chart showing: Federalists (1789–1820), Whigs (1830–1856), Republicans (1856–present), Democratic-Republicans (Jeffersonians) (1789–1830), Democrats (1830–present)]

Harrison and Zachary Taylor to the presidency. The Whig-Democratic rivalry extended beyond the national level to state and local politics.

Both parties were deeply divided by the slavery issue. The Democrats became dominated at that time by their southern wing, which controlled Congress. In the 1850s the Whigs disappeared altogether, many of them merging into the newly formed **Republican party**. In 1860 the Democratic party broke into northern and southern factions that fielded separate presidential candidates, and the Republican presidential candidates, and the Republican presidential nominee, Abraham Lincoln, won election to the White House. The Republicans, originally a small, radical party formed chiefly to oppose the further extension of slavery, quickly forged a coalition of northern industrialists, merchants, workers, farmers, and freed slaves.

Although the Democratic party survived the Civil War, the Republican, or GOP (Grand Old Party), coalition won every presidential election for the next five decades except for those of 1884 and 1892. During this time the Republican base of support slowly shifted to business people and middle-class white Protestants, while the Democrats began to attract the urban, Catholic immigrants and to erode Republican support among workers. (Only five parties have ever achieved sufficient strength to compete nationally; see **Figure 9-2**.)

The System of 1896

Events of the 1890s shaped U.S. politics for generations. At that time, socialist parties were gaining political clout in Europe, and the United States seemed ripe for a parallel development. The **Populist party**, which had arisen in the South and West in the 1880s, demanded many socialist-sounding measures, and a growing trade union movement was pressing its political agenda as well. Workers and Populists together might have forged a new party of the left or precipitated a decisive shift to the left in the Democratic party. But while the Democratic candidate in 1896, William Jennings Bryan, voiced populist views, he steered clear of the labor movement and big-city ethnic populations. Thus Bryan failed to put together an electoral coalition that might have realigned the U.S. party system along left-right political lines. William McKinley's victory in the presidential election of 1896 reinstated Republican dominance, which was reinforced by political reforms instituted in 1896.

Prior to 1896, Americans took an intensely partisan view of politics. Electoral contests were waged as full-scale battles in which each party drummed up partisan enthusiasm through torchlight parades, elaborate campaigns, far-reaching party organization, and extensive patronage. Elections turned on party preference more than on individual candidates. Partisan competition was keen and voter turnout high.

The reforms of 1896 changed political life dramatically. Supporters of the "system of '96," as these reforms came to be known, succeeded in passing new registration laws, reforming the civil service, creating direct primaries (whereby voters, rather than party leaders, chose nominees), and establishing split-ticket balloting. Civil service reforms, in particular, denied parties the patronage that helped to build loyal followings. By these means, reformers hoped to introduce a calmer, less partisan atmosphere in U.S. political life. But new registration complexities kept many people from voting in the first place—a highly significant factor in view of the growing number of foreign-born potential voters. Turnout declined, the parties lost much of their vitality, and the era of modern, candidate-centered politics began. Walter Dean Burnham estimated that after 1896 fully 50 percent of potential U.S. voters remained outside the political process, alienated from parties and politics, and that only about one-third remained firmly attached to the usual electoral systems. The functional result of the system of '96, Burnham stated, "was the conversion of a fairly democratic regime into a rather broadly based oligarchy."[2]

Many experts disagree with this highly critical assessment of the contraction of the active electorate at the turn of the twentieth century, but there is no doubt that a major depoliticization took place at that time. Burnham felt that the system of '96 left a permanent hole in the American political universe, one that in Europe was filled by labor and social democratic parties. In other words, the large-scale politicization of the poor and the working class that might have taken place in the United States in the 1890s simply did not occur.

The New Deal Coalition

Between 1896 and 1932 only the victories of Woodrow Wilson in 1912 and 1916 interrupted the Republican lock on the presidency. And Wilson's election in 1912 was made possible by a split among the Republicans that led to Theodore Roosevelt's candidacy on the third-party Bull Moose ticket.

The Republican party drew its main support in this period from a coalition of middle-class Protestant and native-stock Americans (those whose ancestors came here before the twentieth century, mostly from Britain and Germany). Democratic strength was centered in the South. The border states also leaned toward the Democrats, and pockets of Democratic strength—among immigrant voters and the industrial working class—dotted the larger cities of the Northeast. Overall, the distribution of voter support was decisively in favor of the Republicans.

The collapse of the economy in 1929 and the onset of the Great Depression gave the Democrats a strategic opening. In retrospect it seems odd that during the Depression no third party mounted a serious challenge to the dominance of the two major parties. In any case, Franklin Roosevelt won an overwhelming majority in the 1932 election. As we noted in Chapter 8, Roosevelt's landslide victory ushered in a new era in U.S. politics, one that still shapes the American political landscape today.

The coalition that brought the Democrats to power in 1932 and reelected Roosevelt three times was not entirely new. Some elements of the pre-1932 Democratic strength

The beginning of the New Deal: Franklin Roosevelt addressing the 1932 Democratic Convention. FDR's massive victories in the elections of 1932 and 1936 transformed the shape of party competition. The New Deal coalition was to dominate our politics for at least three decades, and its influence remains even today. *(UPI/Bettmann Newsphotos)*

were still present—the solid South and working-class, Catholic voters. But new groups of voters were largely responsible for the strength of the New Deal coalition. The black population, long loyal to the party of Lincoln, now began to switch to the Democrats in large numbers, attracted by the Roosevelt administration's tentative attack on discriminatory practices and by federal programs for the hungry and the jobless. Labor, heavily concentrated in major cities, also joined the coalition. The experience of the Depression and the economic appeal of New Deal programs redirected U.S. politics along the lines of social class. For the first time since 1896, class factors exerted a decisive influence on election outcomes. The Democrats attracted heavy working-class support and repoliticized many voters who had lost interest in politics, thus overcoming some of the heritage of the system of '96. Still, even during the Depression, class consciousness and voting patterns based on class interests never dominated politics in America as they did in other democratic nations.

Since the New Deal

Since the 1930s the U.S. political party system has evolved greatly; both parties have undergone considerable change without altering their basic identities. The Democrats, for example, have gradually lost their once-solid hold on the South. This process began abruptly in 1948, when the so-called Dixiecrats (southern Democrats who opposed integration) broke from the party after a civil rights plank was passed at the Democrat's national convention. By the elections of 1976 and 1980, Democrat Jimmy Carter, himself a southerner, failed to win the support of a majority of voters in the southern states. Clearly, a portion of the New Deal coalition had shaken loose.

At an ideological level, the shift of some southerners away from the Democratic party reflected the party's increasingly liberal bent. More conservative southerners moved toward the Republicans—a step in line with their true ideological stance. Some southern politicians, like South Carolina Senator Strom Thurmond, actually changed their partisan identities, proclaiming themselves Republicans and running successfully on the Republican ticket. But southern blacks remained firmly committed to the Democrats.

A set of social issues that at times eclipsed economic questions also helped to undermine and reshape the New Deal coalition. In the presidential election of 1952 the issues were communism, corruption, and Korea. In the 1960s public attention focused on violence in the streets, corruption in high office, and the breakdown of traditional values among youth. In 1968 and 1972, Richard Nixon campaigned on a law-and-order platform, focusing on dissenters, crime, and riots in the cities. In 1984 such issues as abortion and school prayer held center stage. These social issues contributed significantly to the gradual disintegration of the New Deal coalition by prompting many white, ethnic, working-class groups once strongly affiliated with the Democrats to throw their support behind Republication candidates, especially in presidential contests.

Both parties have also undergone internal conflicts. Among the Republicans the long-term struggle for control between the more liberal northeastern and western party members and the more conservative Sun Belt group seemed to be decided in 1980 in favor of the conservative Sun Belt Republicans, but conflicts on specific issues remain. As for the Democrats, in the 1960s sharp splits began to appear between the more liberal, affluent, and better-educated McGovern-Kennedy wing of the party and various conservative factions. These rifts remain.

Between the end of World War II and the 1990s, then, the U.S. party system has been in a process of gradual transition. But transition to what? On this matter the experts offer varying predictions. Scenarios for the future shape of our party system range across a broad spectrum—including the prediction that the party system is in such deep trouble that it is likely to disintegrate in the years ahead.

One of our first third parties, the Know-Nothings, is satirized in this 1856 cartoon. Antiforeign sentiment was the party's dominant policy, an issue that was to arise again and again in the country's history. *(The Bettmann Archive)*

In some respects, Ross Perot's 19 percent of the vote in 1992 was the most startling feature of that year's election. The oddity was that Perot was almost a party-of-one, with no organized political group nominating him. His use of the TV talk show and other methods of self-promotion were unique. (Gary Wagner/Picture Group)

Dilemmas and Contributions of Third Parties

Third parties (all parties other than the two major parties) have an unenviable position in the United States, partly because of the many legal and financial barriers they face. Whereas the two major parties are guaranteed columns on the ballot in all states, third parties must go through elaborate, time-consuming, expensive processes to obtain official recognition.

As for financing, major party candidates receive millions of dollars for the presidential contest through the federal election laws. Third-party candidates receive no public funds unless they obtain at least 5 percent of the popular vote. Ross Perot's strength in 1992 was directly related to the insulation that his enormous personal wealth provided from these worries. Without such resources, it would have been unthinkable to mount a credible campaign so late in the electoral season from outside the two major parties.

In U.S. history, only once has a third party (the Republicans) replaced one of the major parties (the Whigs)—and that was well over a century ago, during the crisis that led to the Civil War. But even though third parties have had to struggle to play a significant role in the political process, several have made valuable contributions to U.S. political life.

With the major parties generally staking out the middle ground—thereby merely offering shifts in emphasis on most major issues—third parties often provide an outlet for protest politics focused on "extreme" solutions to controversial issues (see **Table 9-3**). For example, a third party (the Abolitionists) helped to force the issue of slavery onto center stage in U.S. political life, and another one (the Socialist party) was moderately successful in raising important questions about the industrial capitalism in the late nineteenth and early twentieth centuries. Third parties have also pointed the way toward procedural reforms. A third party (the Anti-Masons in 1831) held the first na-

TABLE 9-3
THIRD PARTIES AT THE POLLS SINCE 1832

Election Year	Third Party
1832	**Anti-Masonic party (7 electoral votes)**
	The Anti-Masons, as their name suggests, were opposed to the secret organization known as the Masons, whom they believed wielded undue political influence.
1856	**American party ("Know-Nothings") (8 electoral votes)**
	The American party's major plank was opposition to open immigration.
1892	**People's party ("Populists") (22 electoral votes)**
	The People's party grew out of agrarian protests against the power of big business and the banks.
1912	**Progressive ("Bull Moose") party (88 electoral votes)**
	Founded by dissident Republicans, the Bull Moose party was against monopoly and for conservation and expanded suffrage. Its standard bearer in 1912 was Theodore Roosevelt, seeking a third term as president.
1924	**Progressive party (13 electoral votes)**
	A philosophical continuation of the progressive movement, the party of 1924 ran Senator Robert La Follette as its presidential candidate.
1948	**States Rights Democratic party ("Dixiecrats") (39 electoral votes)**
	The Dixiecrats were segregationist southerners who broke from the Democratic party after the 1948 convention because of the main party's pro-civil rights plank. Strom Thurmond of South Carolina was their presidential candidate.
1968	**American Independent party (46 electoral votes)**
	This was less a party than a movement centering on the presidential candidacy of George C. Wallace, segregationist governor of Alabama.

SOURCE: Adapted from Frank Sorauf and Paul Allen Beck, *Party Politics in America*, 6th ed. (Glenview, Ill.: Scott, Foresman, 1988), pp. 50–51.
NOTE: Ross Perot's campaign for the presidency in 1992 was not based on a third party and failed to get any electoral votes but did win 19% of the popular vote.

tional nominating convention. And a third party (the Progressives) was the first to advocate women's suffrage and to call for a wide range of electoral reforms.

Party Organization

When Will Rogers quipped, "I belong to no organized political party—I am a Democrat," he was poking fun at his own party, but what he said could be applied to either of the major U.S. parties. They are organized in only the loosest sense on the national level, where one might expect them to be most coherent. State party organizations range from the highly active to the virtually moribund. Local party organizations tend to be the most tightly structured. At all three levels U.S. political parties have undergone significant changes in recent decades. This is in sharp contrast to the highly disciplined and centralized parties common in Europe.

LOCAL PARTIES   The most notorious—and frequently the most successful—form of political organization in the United States has been the local **political machine**, a coterie of party professionals who get out the vote and provide constituent services. The most successful of these machines, based on "boss" rule and strong standards of loyalty, reached from the mayor's office through the precincts down to the ward and block levels. Most arose in eastern and midwestern cities after the Civil War, and a few retained power through the 1960s.

The machines were successful partly because they served important political and social functions. They helped to integrate newly arrived immigrant groups into U.S. politics. And in return for votes, rank-and-file members of the machines provided aid to needy families, supplied city jobs, and gave neglected groups recognition that they could not find elsewhere.

For years reformers at both the federal and state levels tried to curtail the power of political machines. The introduction of civil service was intended to limit boss rule by reducing the number of patronage appointments. Sometimes nonpartisan elections limited the influence of machine-controlled voting.

The power and influence of the urban political machine declined slowly. Even before their demise, however, machines represented only one facet of local politics. Local political life in the United States has always been a highly varied affair, ranging from minimally organized and contested elections to highly partisan and sharply fought campaigns for city councils, county governing bodies, even school boards. One of the distinguishing features of U.S. politics is the large number of local officials who are elected rather than appointed.

Local politics has often served as the springboard for people who want to become politically involved. Jimmy Carter, for example, launched his political career by winning election to the Plains, Georgia, board of education. Many studies have focused on the increasing number of "amateurs" who enter local politics and then make their way

(Text continues on page 342)

COMPARATIVE PERSPECTIVE

THE DISCIPLINED PARTIES OF GREAT BRITAIN

Unlike the U.S. Congress, where members often vote against a majority of their own party and oppose party leaders, members of the British Parliament rarely vote against their party on issues of significance. British political parties are highly disciplined organizations; the system provides effective means for keeping legislators in line. In practice this means that Members of Parliament (MPs) who oppose party leaders in any consistent way cannot expect to be endorsed by the national party when they run for reelection. Party nominations in Britain are made by members of the party hierarchy, a process over which the national organization has substantial influence. Thus outspoken opponents who vote against their own party can expect to be denied the chance to run again. In the United States, by contrast, nominations are controlled at the state and local levels; the national party has little say over who runs for office under the party flag.

The British system produces consistent voting patterns in the House of Commons, where party discipline is enforced by the structure of roles and by informal norms and sanctions. Members are expected to attend party meetings in the House and, if possible, to join party committees addressing various policy areas. MPs are also expected to attend important debates and support the party's position; failing to attend to party chores may close off paths to advancement for the offending member.

Responsibility for enforcing discipline rests with the whips. Each party leader in the House of Commons chooses a chief whip, who then appoints assistant, or junior, whips. The whips' authority is real, even though their methods are mostly informal. They use persuasion, if they must, to enforce party discipline. One of the best arguments a majority whip can use is that a vote against the government could help to bring the government down. Whips seldom have to resort to appeals, however. By dispensing favors and accommodating individual MPs, the whips seek to instill reflexive party loyalty in MPs.

Expulsion is an extreme measure, reserved for MPs who have abandoned basic party principles not only in Parliament but also in public speeches and activities.

Party loyalty and discipline are mirrored in parliamentary voting. In practice this means that if the party in power has a solid majority, the opposition has virtually no chance of influencing government policy. It must wait until the next election to try to gain power.

Richard Daley, elected mayor of Chicago six times, was an astute politican to some, a manipulative machine boss to others. The last of the urban political bosses, Daley's efficient vote-getting organizations were able to turn out the faithful time after time. Political machines helped meet the needs of many who otherwise were alienated from the political processes; on the other hand, they fostered corruption, narrow-mindedness, and a wide variety of shady political practices. *(UPI/Bettmann Newsphotos)*

onto the national political scene. Such "purists," as they are often called, see politics as the realm of ideas and principles; the old machine-oriented professionals were far more interested in maintaining party organization and winning elections.[3]

STATE PARTIES   Heading the state party organization is the state committee, ranging from a few dozen to several hundred members. Typically, the county is the basic unit of representation. Members of the state committees are chosen in a variety of ways, including primaries, caucuses, and selection by state convention delegates.

Whatever their theoretical powers, few state committees have any say over state party issues. Usually, the committee meets a few times a year and leaves day-to-day business to the party chairperson, normally the key figure in party matters. In most states the state party chair is closely associated with the governor or other high-ranking state officials. As state politics has grown more competitive—and more expensive—in recent decades, the chairs, and state parties in general, have widened the scope of their functions: They draw on opinion poll data, develop issues for future campaigns, engage in more fund-raising activities, and offer more professional services to candidates. And at almost all levels of politics the pervasive influence of television—through political news coverage, political advertisements, and talk shows—has focused voter attention on candidate personality, significantly diminishing the role of state parties in grooming and selecting candidates for political office.

NATIONAL PARTIES   Originally, the sole function of the national party was to nominate a presidential candidate, who was selected by a **party caucus** composed of party leaders in Congress. By the 1830s, however, **national conventions** had become the accepted means of selecting the party's presidential hopeful. Each state was allowed to decide how to choose its delegates to the convention. The adoption of the national convention system, in turn, made it necessary to create an ongoing organization that would make arrangements for the convention and coordinate the campaign. This function was performed by the **national committee**, created by the Democrats in 1848 and adopted by the Republicans eight years later. In both parties, each state elected a single member to the national committee until the 1920s, when a committee*woman* was added for each state.

For over a century the national committees served only as links from one convention to the next. They did not effectively centralize party control; power still remained primarily in the hands of the state chairpersons. Only a few national chairs had a strong enough influence over party affairs to exercise significant control over the nominating process.

Not until after the tumultuous 1948 convention did the Democratic party take steps to curb the overwhelming influence of state parties in the national convention process. At the 1948 convention several state delegations were allowed to participate even though they were pledged to support the so-called Dixiecrat ticket rather than the Democratic ticket. This capitulation by the national party to Dixiecrat delegations set off a struggle to nationalize party rules. Finally, in 1956 the convention resolved that state parties selecting national convention delegates had to "assure" that the official Democratic party nominee would appear under the party label on the state ballot. (In the 1948 election, Dixiecrat candidate Strom Thurmond, not Democratic candidate Harry Truman, had been listed as the "Democratic" candidate in four states.) In the 1960s the Democrats moved further toward national control of state delegations by stipulating that state delegations be selected on a nondiscriminatory basis. Then, after the strife-ridden 1968 Chicago convention, extensive new rules governing delegate selection were instituted.

Despite these moves toward nationalization of party rules, the Democratic party, like the Republican party, has remained highly decentralized. Formalizing party membership—through requirements that members pay dues and carry party cards—has never taken a high priority. As another indication of the freewheeling approach of U.S. political parties, neither major party requires candidates to adhere to a clearly drawn set of party principles.

The Republican party has pursued nationalization in its own way. Under a series of dynamic national chairpersons, the GOP has expanded the operations of its national office substantially. Beginning in the mid-1960s, the GOP national organization mounted extensive direct-mail fund-raising campaigns. Enough money was raised for the GOP to build its own national headquarters in 1971—the first ever owned by either party. Through the 1970s the GOP also established a highly complex network of services and activities—recruiting and training candidates for state and local races on an unprecedented scale; handling opinion polling, research, media production, and data processing; offering financial assistance to candidates; establishing advisory councils to craft long-term policies; and publishing a party monthly, numerous brochures, and a semiacademic journal. Somewhat belatedly, the Democrats have undertaken similar fund-raising and service efforts, but they still lag behind.

As we can see from **Table 9-4**, Republicans have been far more successful than Democrats in their fund-raising efforts. In general, this has given Republican candidates an edge in financing and campaign services—including polling, direct mail, and candidate training—provided by the party's national committee. Nonetheless, money does not always translate into electoral success, as the Republicans have discovered in recent midterm elections. And the Democrats have begun to learn the ways of effective fund-raising, as the table shows. The Republican cash advantage is being challenged.

Both national party organizations, then, have evolved and taken on new functions. Neither, however, serves as an overall coordinator or arbiter of party policy. Instead,

TABLE 9-4
PARTY COMMITTEE FINANCIAL ACTIVITY IN SEVEN ELECTION CYCLES
(MILLIONS OF DOLLARS)

	1977–1978	1979–1980	1981–1982	1983–1984	1985–1986	1987–1988	1989–1990
Democrats							
Raised	$26.4	$37.2	$39.3	$98.5	$64.8	$127.9	$85.7
Spent	26.9	35.0	40.1	97.4	65.9	121.9	90.9
Contributed	1.8	1.7	1.7	2.6	1.7	1.7	1.5
Coordinated expenses	0.4	4.9	3.3	9.0	9.0	17.9	8.7
Republicans							
Raised	84.5	169.5	215.0	297.9	255.2	263.3	206.3
Spent	85.9	161.8	214.0	300.8	258.9	257.0	213.5
Contributed	4.5	4.5	5.6	4.9	3.4	3.4	2.9
Coordinated expenses	4.3	12.4	14.3	20.1	14.3	22.7	10.7

SOURCE: Federal Election Commission, "Republican Party Spent $123 Million More in '90 than Democrats, Final FEC Report Shows" (press release), December 10, 1991, p. 1.

both follow a course of partial nationalization through party reform, political services, and campaign strategy, reflecting the decentralized nature of U.S. politics.

Party Reforms after 1968

A watershed year in many respects, 1968 marked a turning point for the presidential nominating process. We now turn to the origins and impact of the dramatic Democratic reforms, the more subtle Republican reforms, and the overall effects of these reforms.

DEMOCRATIC REFORMS   Political events in 1968 prompted moves to reform the Democratic party's nominating process. Prior to the 1968 convention, President Lyndon Johnson chose not to seek renomination. While Senators Robert Kennedy and Eugene McCarthy waged a highly visible and intense battle for the presidential nomination in states that had primaries, Vice-President Hubert Humphrey, fearful that widespread opposition to the Vietnam War among rank-and-file Democrats might hurt his candidacy, quietly marshaled support among party regulars in states that did not hold primaries. Humphrey's strategy worked: With little fanfare he garnered enough party support to win the nomination. This outraged many Democrats, largely because they suspected that Humphrey would have lost the nomination in the primary battles.

At the 1968 Democratic convention in Chicago—one of the political low points of the 1960s—control of the proceedings was very tight, and some delegates accused the party bosses of police-style tactics. In the streets of Chicago, protesters of many sorts roamed or paraded through the city, sometimes taunting police, sometimes set upon and beaten by police with little or no provocation. At the deepest level, the legitimacy of the entire U.S. political process was called into question. More specifically, many Democrats became convinced that reform of the nominating process was absolutely essential.

After the 1968 election, the national party chairman appointed a reform commission headed by Senator George McGovern of South Dakota and later chaired by Representative Donald Fraser of Minnesota. The McGovern-Fraser Commission introduced several ambitious reforms, which significantly reduced the power of Democratic party leaders to control or even influence the process of delegate selection.

George McGovern's nomination as the party's 1972 candidate for president signaled a triumph for the reformers. The nomination was achieved at a heavy price to the party, however. Many regular Democrats, most notably labor union leaders, failed to support the party's nominee. After McGovern's decisive defeat in the general election, it appeared that a thorough reform of the reforms might take place. Instead, over the two decades, a series of gradual changes have been made in the delegate selection processes.

Adjustments to the Democrats' delegate selection process have often reflected a split between "party regulars" on one side and "amateurs" or "purists" on the other. The split is sometimes characterized as between "success-minded" and "principle-

Inside the 1968 Democratic National Convention control of the proceedings were so tight that some delegates accused the party bosses of police tactics. Outside, the Chicago police were engaged in actual battles, sometimes with little or no provocation, with anti–Vietnam War and other demonstrators. The nominating process that in 1968 selected Hubert Humphrey, who had not run in a single primary, came in for much criticism and led to vast changes in the ways presidential candidates were selected. *(UPI/Bettmann Newsphotos)*

minded'' Democrats, but other divisions (for intance, between liberals and conservatives) were also involved. The national Democratic party's image of itself encourages openness to outsiders. Yet that openness, according to some analysts, leaves the party vulnerable to defeat by a less fragmented, more professionalized structure on the Republican side. The Democratic party professionals were overshadowed in the 1972 and 1976 conventions. Steps were then taken to include more party regulars in 1980 and again in 1984, when 568 prominent party and elected officials were granted **superdelegate** status based on their positions. Some analysts saw Bill Clinton's nomination in 1992 as a successful accommodation of the party's various factions. Others saw it simply as a sign of the increased strength of moderate-to-conservative Democrats.

What is the best way to choose a presidential candidate? Given the broad, inclusive nature of our political parties, is the goal of choosing a winner incompatible with the attachment to principled policies? What is the optimal mix of ''regular'' and ''purist'' influence on the choice? Because there are no simple answers to these questions, tinkering with convention rules is likely to continue, affected by the success or failure of each succeeding candidate.

REPUBLICAN REFORMS   The resounding defeat of its 1964 presidential candidate, Barry Goldwater, provided the Republican party with impetus to change. But there was never the intense pressure for procedural reform that buffeted the Democratic party. There was no Republican analogue to the traumatic 1968 Democratic convention; no strong minority groups demanded change, and no overriding liberal ideology pressed for it. In response to Democratic reforms, GOP leaders warned against "McGovernizing" the party—weakening the party's role in the presidential nominating process. Republican change, therefore, concentrated on increasing the efficiency and effectiveness of national fund-raising and the provision of candidate support services—at which they soon handily outstripped their Democratic opponents. Nonetheless, the Republicans did institute a more open delegate selection process at the local level. Positive action to end discrimination was discussed, but plans to require action on the issue were dropped, and the 1976 convention refused to endorse any procedures designed to ensure compliance. A party committee in 1981 did recommend that

> political parties should [themselves] determine how their nominees are chosen; state party organizations should have the authority to adjust the delegate selection process to fit their local political traditions; national, time zone or regional primaries should not be imposed; and changes in party rules which require state legislative action should be drafted in a manner which would permit rather than require a party to adopt the change.[4]

Such recommendations were unlikely to disturb any sectors of the party—in striking contrast to the conflict among the Democrats.

EFFECTS OF THE REFORMS   The reforms of the nominating process in both parties sharply increased the number of presidential primaries. Opening up party caucus meetings, meanwhile, led to an influx of new people at the local level. Both these shifts reduced the power of party professionals to control the nominating process. Candidates no longer needed to line up the support of party leaders and officeholders. This was clearly a gain for democratic principles because the reforms encouraged more widespread popular participation and closed off the kind of "back-room" control that had characterized past conventions. The reforms also led to more wide-ranging representation of women, blacks, and younger party members at both national conventions.

In both 1972 and 1976 the Democrats nominated candidates who would have stood little chance under the prereform system. The successes of George McGovern and Jimmy Carter demonstrated that committed political unknowns could seize control of the nominating process, that good showings in the early primaries could propel even an unknown candidate to political prominence, and that the new system placed a premium on the shrewd use of mass media and on the personality and ideas of particular candidates. In both races the Democratic candidate was picked by the voters rather than by party professionals. In addition, the enlarged primary system has opened the door to vigorous campaigns by candidates who would otherwise find it difficult to gain a national forum for their views, such as Pat Robertson and Jesse Jackson.

Who are better equipped to judge a person's presidential caliber, the voters or the party professionals? That is difficult to answer. In primary contests the turnouts are generally far lower than those in general elections, and the better-educated, wealthier, and more issue-oriented voters turn out.[5] Party professionals can no longer ignore new issues and new blood, but they also face increased difficulty in forging a united party.

Many supporters of the enlarged primary process and more open conventions admit that the new system is flawed and that further reforms are necessary. Most maintain, however, that there is no going back to the days of the politician-controlled nominating convention. As one student of the subject put it: "We wouldn't have primaries if the old system had worked. The party machines collapsed in the late 1950s and early 1960s when the electorate changed totally."[6]

Overall, the reforms have created a more competitive and open nominating process. But do they consistently produce candidates competent to govern the nation? And how significantly has this more open process eroded the power of our already weak political parties? We will return to this issue shortly.

Do the Political Parties Differ?

To some observers, the Republicans and the Democrats are like two sides of the same well-worn coin: They may differ, but only on the surface. Others argue that Republicans and Democrats offer the electorate clear choices on many issues. Which view comes closer to the truth?

One way to approach this question is to look at the promises made by each party in election years and to assess how much these promises have differed. Studies of platform pledges over the past half-century show that Democrats and Republicans hold different images of themselves and tend to make different promises to the citizens.[7] Republicans typically place greater emphasis on national defense and on how the government is run, whereas Democrats give greater weight to labor and welfare matters. However, the parties tend to overlap in many areas, particularly foreign policy.

Party differences carry over into Congress as well. There, the parties often divide on many of the issues addressed in their platforms (see **Table 9-5**, page 350).

Can we say, then, that Democrats and Republicans differ enough to offer voters a meaningful choice? We know that the parties do differ in some respects but that they also overlap considerably. And on some important issues both parties fail to present any real alternatives. For example, neither the Democrats nor the Republicans have presented clear alternatives on energy issues or the infrastructure, and many other party positions are confused and even contradictory.

Some observers argue that both U.S. parties lean toward the center, obscuring their disagreements so as to appeal to the widest range of voters. Party leaders moderate their views to avoid alienating voters. The crushing defeats suffered by Goldwater (a staunchly conservative Republican) in 1964 and Dukakis (a perceived liberal Democrat) in 1988, have often been explained in these terms: The candidates voiced views farther either to the right or to the left than those held by the majority of the electorate.

To sum up, research has borne out what common sense indicates: The major parties do differ on many issues and their pledges do make a difference, but parties also ignore some important issues, hedge on others, and often fail to convince the public that the choices they offer are meaningful. This confusing picture of U.S. political life emerges from the internal disarray and lack of overall cohesion of both major parties. We must remember, however, that each party has more liberal and more conservative wings and that coalitions across party lines have been quite common in Congress. Were U.S. parties more tightly disciplined, it would be easier to see and to judge the relationships among party pledges, party differences, and the outcomes of government action. We will look shortly at the issue of party responsibility and the failure of U.S. parties in this regard.

Current Issues

In this final section we consider the current state of the U.S. party system. We examine three related topics: the disaffiliation of voters from the major parties, the prospects for significant shifts in the party system, and the issues of party responsibility and party reform.

Decline of the Parties

Most political scientists agree that the major U.S. political parties are in decline. Some of the signs are obvious. For example, fewer people identified themselves as Democrats in 1990 (39 percent) than in 1937 (50 percent). Those identifying themselves as Republicans declined from a high of 39 percent in 1944 to a low of 24 percent in 1980 before increasing to 35 percent in 1990. Meanwhile, Americans who identify themselves as independents increased from 16 percent in 1937 to 26 percent in 1990.[8] Among younger voters, the trend toward independent status has been marked. It also seems clear that younger voters who identify themselves as independents do not tend to shift toward one of the parties in later years.[9]

As another sign of party erosion, both Democrats and Republicans, in increasing numbers, have broken ranks, voting for candidates of the opposite party. Since the 1960s, large numbers of Democrats, for example, have voted for Republican candidates. The same is true for Republican identifiers. The trend toward ticket-splitting and general defection from party labels is as widespread among older as among younger voters.

(Text continues on page 352)

TABLE 9-5
DIFFERENCES BETWEEN THE PARTIES IN CONGRESS DURING THE BUSH ADMINISTRATION

		Party Conflict	
Legislation	*Bipartisan**	*Moderate[†]*	*Significant[‡]*
Nonmilitary aid to Nicaraguan Contras	R—support (93%) D—support (61%)		
Adoption of 1990 budget resolution	R—support (63%) D—support (62%)		
Allow savings and loans to count "good will" as capital in restructuring	D—oppose (85%) R—oppose (67%)		
Reduce initial construction funds for superconducting supercollider	R—oppose (84%) D—oppose (74%)		
Reduce longer term commitment to produce B-2 ("Stealth") bombers	R—oppose (84%) D—oppose (54%)		
Repeal requirement that employers must prove their health benefit plans are nondiscriminatory, but deny favorable tax treatment to employee benefit plans that discriminate in favor of owners and executives	R—support (99%) D—support (87%)		
Repeal Medicare Catastrophic Coverage Act	D—support (94%) R—support (79%)		
Aid to Poland and Hungary	D—support (94%) R—support (79%)		
Across-the-board cuts in budget authority in all discretionary accounts of the government		R—oppose (95%) D—support (64%)	
Prevent federal law from preempting state laws on oil-spill liability, compensation, and cleanup		D—support (82%) R—oppose (57%)	

TABLE 9-5
DIFFERENCES BETWEEN THE PARTIES IN CONGRESS DURING THE BUSH ADMINISTRATION (*continued*)

Legislation	Bipartisan*	Party Conflict Moderate[†]	Party Conflict Significant[‡]
Phase out honoraria for members and raise salaries		D—support (66%) R—oppose (51%)	
Override President Bush's veto of minimum wage bill			D—support (89%) R—oppose (88%)
Decrease funds for strategic defense initiative (SDI)			D—support (85%) R—oppose (80%)
Restore deductibility for individual retirement accounts (in lieu of capital gains cut) and increase tax rates for the highest incomes			R—oppose (99%) D—support (75%)
Delete child-care provisions and replace with an expanded earned-income tax credit			R—support (91%) D—oppose (86%)
Permit use of federal funds to pay for abortions in cases of "promptly reported" rape or incest			R—oppose (77%) D—support (71%)

R = Republican; D = Democrat. The data in this table show how the parties voted in the House (controlled by the Democrats) on sixteen major issues (designated as "key votes" by *Congressional Quarterly*) during the first session of the 101st Congress (1989–1990). On fully half of these key issues, bipartisanship prevailed. Only five issues produced sharp partisan conflict (minimum wage, SDI, tax rates, child care, and abortion). On key issues, partisanship was less important at the beginning of the Bush administration than during the second term of President Reagan.

*Bipartisan: majorities of both parties in agreement.
[†]Moderate party conflict: party majority against party majority.
[‡]Significant party conflict: at least 70 percent of the voting members of one party aligned against at least 70 percent of the voting members of the other party.
SOURCE: William J. Keefe, *Parties, Politics, and Public Policy in America* (Washington, D.C.: Congressional Quarterly Press, 1991), pp. 256–257.

In addition, voters' perceptions of the parties have grown increasingly negative, indicating a progressive deterioration of party allegiance in the United States. Between 45 and 55 percent of the nation believes that there are no important differences between the parties and see parties as more and more irrelevant to the nation's and the individual voter's primary concerns.[10] Voters focus increasingly on candidates and issues regardless of party. No longer do voters use party labels as the primary measure of a domestic issue's merit ("The Democrats support welfare, so I do, too") or a presidential candidate's fitness for office ("I always vote for the Republican nominee for president"). Other signs of party decline include the rise of single-issue groups (such as the Right to Life movement), the loss of party cohesion in voting in Congress, and candidates' decreasing emphasis on party labels in election and reelection efforts. Some political observers also contend that the rise of television campaigning and the more effective organization of interest groups have undermined the role of parties. We will consider these factors in Chapters 10 and 11.

The decline of the parties is of course linked to the growth of political alienation and mistrust and the decline in voter participation noted in Chapter 8. Taken together, these elements indicate a growing crisis in the U.S. polity that might lead to a basic realignment of voter preferences.

Many reforms have been suggested that might strengthen American political parties. For example, one student of the subject suggests two distinct sets of changes, one to be initiated by the parties themselves, the other requiring assistance from the government.[11] Among the farthest-reaching party-initiated reform proposals are the following:

Building stronger grass-roots party organizations by creating mobile party offices and more daily contact with citizens.

Providing services to party members such as discount credit cards, insurance, cut-rate legal service, and the like—paralleling services offered by labor unions.

Expanding fund-raising activities for and services to political campaigns and recruiting more candidates and volunteers.

Making party institutional advertising (ads emphasizing the party label itself and its meaning) a permanent component of campaigns and airing them during noncampaign periods as well.

Increasing party input in policy formulation by empaneling policy commissions when the party is out of power.

Proposed government-assisted reforms would include these:

Establishing larger federal tax credits for party contributions—up to 100 percent for small contributions.

Channeling money from public financing through the parties, allowing some of it to be used for party-building.

Requiring all TV and radio stations to make available free airtime for major state and national parties.

Raising the current limits on parties' contributions to and coordinated expenses on behalf of federal nominees.

Permitting parties to spend unlimited amounts on volunteer-oriented activities that benefit candidates.

Creating a straight-party voting mechanism in every state, discouraging split-ticket voting.

Reducing the number of nonpartisan elections.

Consolidating elections to strengthen the effects of popular national candidates.

Leaving nominating methods to the parties—holding more caucuses and pre-primary endorsing conventions—thus reducing the significance of presidential primaries.

Taken together, this package of reforms would place parties far closer to the center of our electoral process and help to undo the effects of the party-weakening developments of the past thirty years. Yet no one knows whether the nation as a whole or the parties themselves are sufficiently committed to making these reforms or whether Americans overall favor stronger political parties.

Realignment: Who Has the Majority?

Ronald Reagan's first presidential victory in 1980 and his landslide reelection in 1984 led many observers to speculate that a political realignment of major proportions had finally occurred. The breakdown of the New Deal majority had been predicted for decades, and evidence had been pouring in since the 1950s that FDR's unique coalition of "urban ethnics, Southern Protestants, dirt farmers, Jewish intellectuals, illiterate coal miners, poor blacks and virulent racists"[12] had come apart at the seams.

It was equally unclear how much of a realignment was taking place in the Republican party. Five Republican presidential victories in six outings between 1968 and 1988 added up to an impressive showing, but Republicans failed to come closer to gaining a majority in the House of Representatives during the same period. Democrats held their own in many state races and made a substantial comeback in the Senate in 1986. Some commentators attributed the size of the 1984 Republican landslide to astute management of television by a uniquely telegenic candidate. Others saw the GOP successes in 1980 and 1984 merely as personal triumphs for Ronald Reagan. Finally, there were doubts that a Republican party dominated by its conservative wing could ever constitute an effective national majority. As political observer Kevin Phillips put it: "The Republicans' economic sobriety and commitment to national defense must somehow be . . . broadened and infused with a sense of the common man."[13]

354   PART TWO • POLITICS

The Bush-Quayle ticket in 1992 was hurt by America's economic problems and the absence of an appealing domestic policy agenda. Their defeat may mean a struggle over the future direction of the Republican party. *(Rick Bowmer/AP/Wide World)*

When both parties seek to broaden their bases, and thus to harmonize constituencies that were often at loggerheads, the historic paradox is evident: The broader the party's base, the less clearly defined the issues; the greater the urge to blur differences within the party, the more the danger of overlapping with the opposing party on specific issues. The alternative (to narrow and focus the party appeal, as the 1992 Republican national convention sought to do) offers little chance for electoral success in a two-party race. With this dynamic in place, elections tend to revolve more around public perceptions of the candidates' personalities than around specifically defined issues.

Party Responsibility and Party Reform

Do the two major parties perform the way "responsible" parties should in a democratic society? To many observers the answer is a resounding no. In 1950 a committee of the American Political Science Association published a document, titled "Toward a More

Bill Clinton at the Democratic National Convention in 1992. His selection of Al Gore as a running mate surprised many, but the presence of two young, white Southerners on the ticket may have helped the Democrats win back some of the South. *(Ron Edmonds/AP/ Wide World)*

Responsible Two-Party System,'' that outlined how U.S. parties could become more disciplined and programmatic.[14] In criticizing the existing parties of that period (and such criticisms would apply equally well today), the committee found a number of key deficiencies in the organization and approach of U.S. parties: They did not offer citizens fundamentally distinct policy choices; they were too weak organizationally to carry through their programs; they were not united on any basic principles; they failed to reflect the opinions of the electorate sufficiently. The committee advocated reorganizing the party system along British lines, whereby each party would be highly disciplined, with strong leadership and a large mass membership.

The report did not meet with instant approval. Many political scientists maintained that a weakly organized, somewhat irresponsible pattern of governing had, overall, been a good thing for the United States. Precisely because U.S. parties had not been radically different or grounded in ideological principles, this argument runs, they had helped to keep the political temperature low; to create an atmosphere of compromise and conciliation, rather than one of distrust and fierce ideological battling; to ensure elections that are not highly disruptive; and to maintain considerable continuity as well as a certain measure of change.

Although some of the points made by advocates of such parties clearly make sense, we should also note that democratic theory requires parties that *approach* the "responsible party" model. No one wishes to see parties divide on every issue and fight every battle to the finish. But if party lines are heavily blurred, if lines of responsibility are not clear, the electorate will find it impossible to figure out what parties stand for—if anything.

Perhaps the key to our problems in responsible policymaking lies in the complexity of our federalist system, which pits the federal legislative and executive branches against each other and splits regional policymaking into fifty separate jurisdictions. Here political parties could play a pivotal role, reaching across these jurisdictional lines to create coherent policy. Unfortunately, they frequently fail at this task, leaving citizens bewildered, and policymaking itself becomes fragmented and even contradictory. Despite the increasing talk about party realignment, it appears that in the near future our party system will remain largely "nonresponsible."

Divided government—a consistent Democratic majority in Congress during a period of Republican dominance of the White House—is both a sign of the weakness of the two major parties and an obstacle to renewed party responsibility. Whom were voters to blame for a weak economy as the nation approached the 1992 election? Could the problem be dumped on incumbent Republican President George Bush? It was hard to blame the last Democratic president, Jimmy Carter, who'd left office twelve years earlier. Yet the Democratic majority in both houses of Congress has been at least partly responsible. The last Republican majority in the Senate had disappeared in 1986. And almost no one could remember the last Republican majority in the House of Representatives (the 83rd Congress, elected in 1952). So were the Republicans or the Democrats to blame for the painful recession of 1990–1992?

Even as favorable ratings for George Bush dropped from their record Gulf War highs, public opinion remained skeptical of Bill Clinton. The attention given to party critics Pat Buchanan and Jerry Brown and to nonparty candidate Ross Perot in 1992 was a direct reflection of this skepticism of the main parties. Without being able to hold one party responsible for the status quo, the electorate turns increasingly to personality rather than party in making political choices, or it becomes hostile to *all* incumbents (see Chapter 12 for a discussion of term limits).

In spite of clear signs of voter disenchantment, the 1992 election showed some hope to champions of the two-party system. The Democratic party's success seemed partially the result of the push by the Democratic Leadership Council and others to get the party back toward a moderate center—a classic strategy in a two-party system. The Republican party emerged from 1992 up for grabs. Some Republican strategists spoke of finding a new formula to create the "big tent." Talk of a Republican lock on the Electoral College was muted. Two-party dynamics seemed resilient once again.

CONCLUSIONS

More than two centuries of experience has demonstrated that political parties are an essential part of the democratic process rather than an intrusion into it. Parties provide alternative candidates and policies. They help to shape voter preferences and to educate the electorate. They serve as the key organization link between the citizenry and the operation of government. It is hard to imagine democratic electoral politics without them.

The American party system has been remarkably stable for well over a hundred years. The two major parties now holding sway dominate the political scene and deflect third-party challenges. Our political process makes it difficult for third parties to gain a permanent foothold, though several have influenced national policy and had an impact on elections.

By comparison with European political parties, American parties are relatively decentralized and undisciplined. Our party organizations are built around the fifty states; the national leadership and organization remain fairly weak. Often, therefore, national party leaders have been unable to count on uniform support throughout the party.

By 1992 public satisfaction with the two major American political parties had reached a level where neither held much attraction for many voters. In race after race, outside candidates had demonstrated that party mechanisms could be circumvented, using direct mail and electronic media to reach contributors and voters directly. But it is important to remember the role that parties play in bringing information back up from the grass roots, gathering public sentiment into coherent programs. In the absence of effective two-way communication between voters and candidates for office, democracy is diminished. Campaigns without mediating structures like parties are subject to the manipulation of the already rich and powerful.

Since 1968 the parties have been engaged in a process of change and reform. The presidential nomination process and funding mechanisms for congressional candidates, for example, are significantly different from what they were then. As we have seen, these reforms have been neither consistent nor universally applauded. In the wake of the 1992 elections, one fact remains clear: The two-party system still needs help. Will it disintegrate, to be replaced by something new? Will party realignment reinvigorate current forms? The future of parties in America is unclear.

Glossary Terms

Democratic party
Democratic-Republicans
Federalists
Green party
national committee
national convention
party caucus
political machine
political party

Populist party
proportional representation
Republican party
single-member district
superdelegate
third parties
unit rule
Whig party

Notes

[1] Hugh L. Le Blanc, *American Political Parties* (New York: St. Martin's Press, 1982), p. 3.
[2] Walter Dean Burnham, "The Changing Shape of the American Political Universe," *American Political Science Review*, March 1965, p. 27.
[3] See James Q. Wilson, *The Amateur Democrat: Club Politics in Three Cities* (Chicago: University of Chicago Press, 1962); and Aaron Wildavsky, "The Goldwater Phenomenon: Purists, Politicians, and the Two-Party System," in his *Revolt against the Masses* (New York: Basic Books, 1971).
[4] David E. Price, *Bringing Back the Parties* (Washington, D.C.: Congressional Quarterly Press, 1984), p. 159.
[5] See Le Blanc, *American Political Parties*, chap. 7.
[6] Richard Wade, *New York Times*, April 12, 1984, p. 15.
[7] See Le Blanc, *American Political Parties*, chap. 10; Gerald R. Pomper, *Elections in America: Control and Influence in Democratic Politics* (New York: Dodd, Mead, 1968); and Anthony King, "What Do Polls Decide?" in *Democracy at the Polls*, ed. D. Butter, H. R. Penniman, and A. Ranney (Washington, D.C.: AEI, 1981), pp. 293–324.
[8] These figures come from Gallup poll data.
[9] Price, *Bringing Back the Parties*, p. 51.
[10] Ibid., p. 17.
[11] Larry J. Sabato, *The Party's Just Begun* (Glenview, Ill.: Scott, Foresman, 1988), chaps. 6 and 7.
[12] *Newsweek*, July 16, 1984, p. 15.
[13] *New York Times*, April 19, 1984, p. 25.
[14] Committee on Political Parties, "Toward a More Responsible Two-Party System," *American Political Science Review*, September 1950 (suppl).

Selected Readings

For recent scholarship on various types of **party systems**, see T. J. Pempel, ed., *Uncommon Democracies: The One-Party Dominant Regimes* (Ithaca, N.Y.: Cornell University Press, 1990); and Michael Laver and Norman Schofield, *Multiparty Government: The Politics of Coalition in Europe* (New York: Oxford University Press, 1990).

Two useful reference works on the **history of American political parties** are L. Sandy Maisel, ed., *Political Parties and Elections in the United States: An Encyclopedia* (New York: Garland, 1991); and Kenneth C. Martis, *The Historical Atlas of Political Parties in the United States Congress, 1789-1989* (New York: Macmillan, 1989).

On the **decline of American parties**, see Martin P. Wattenberg, *The Decline of American Political Parties, 1952-1988* (Cambridge, Mass.: Harvard University Press, 1990); and Benjamin Ginsberg and Martin Shefter, *Politics by Other Means: The Declining Importance of Elections in America* (New York: Basic Books, 1990). On the other side of this debate, see L. Sandy Maisel, ed.: *The Parties Respond: Changes in the American Party System* (Boulder, Colo.: Westview Press, 1990). A collection of essays that fall on both sides of this question is gathered together in Benjamin Ginsberg and Alan Stone, eds., *Do Elections Really Matter?* (Armonk, N.Y.: Sharpe, 1991).

Divided government has received much academic attention recently, including the following works: Gary W. Cox and Samuel Kernell, eds., *The Politics of Divided Government* (Boulder, Colo.: Westview Press, 1991); David Mayhew, *Divided We Govern: Party Control, Lawmaking, and Investigations, 1946-1990* (New Haven, Conn.: Yale University Press, 1991); James MacGregor Burns, *Cobblestone Leadership: Majority Rule, Minority Power* (Norman: University of Oklahoma Press, 1990); and Morris P. Florina, *Divided Government* (New York: Macmillan, 1992).

On the **resurgence of a two-party system in the South**, see Alexander P. Lamis, *The Two-Party South*, 2nd ed. (New York: Oxford University Press, 1990); and Earl Black and Merle Black, *The Vital South: How Presidents Are Elected* (Cambridge, Mass.: Harvard University Press, 1992).

Many **comparative studies** of national party systems exist, including Samuel J. Roberts, *Party and Policy in Israel* (Boulder, Colo.: Westview Press, 1990); Anthony M. Messina, *Race and Party Competition in Britain* (New York: Oxford University Press, 1989); and Ronald J. Hrebenar, *The Japanese Party System*, 2nd ed. (Boulder, Colo.: Westview Press, 1992).

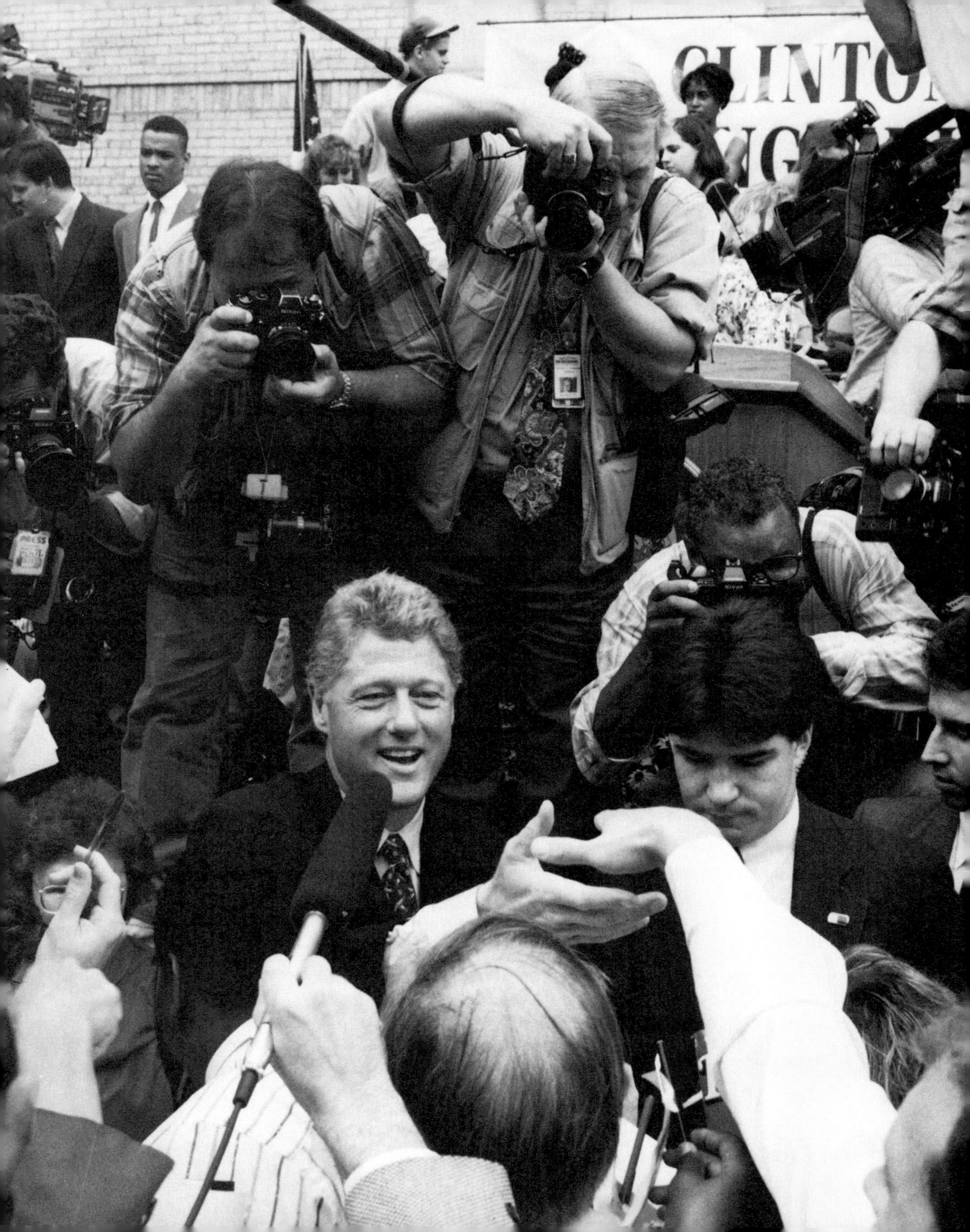

CHAPTER TEN

CAMPAIGNS, MONEY, AND THE MEDIA

Behind the Glitter and the Mud

CHAPTER OUTLINE

Political Campaigns

NONPRESIDENTIAL CAMPAIGNS
PRESIDENTIAL CAMPAIGNS
THE ELECTORAL COLLEGE

Campaign Financing

REFORM EFFORTS
FURTHER REFORMS

Politics and the Media

GATHERING THE NEWS
FRAMING THE ISSUES

Media and Campaigns

THE MEDIA'S IMPACT ON ELECTIONS
IMAGEMAKING
TELEVISED PRESIDENTIAL DEBATES
MEDIA AND "HORSE RACES"
THE MEDIA AND CAMPAIGN NEGATIVITY

GEORGE BUSH: AN AFFABLE INCUMBENT PRESIDENT, ELIGIBLE FOR reelection and enjoying stratospheric approval ratings. Operation Desert Storm: American high-tech weaponry driving a military operation in the Middle East that achieved its stated objectives in a matter of days with strikingly few American casualties. The end of the Cold War: the breakdown of the Soviet empire in Eastern Europe and within the former Soviet Union itself and an end to forty years of icy, death-threatening stares across the border that Churchill dubbed the Iron Curtain at the end of World War II. On top of these three items, throw in an economy that, though bruised, appeared to be recovering from a severe recession in time to look robust for incumbent electioneering.

Eighteen months before the presidential election of 1992, it looked as if the Democrats should pack it in and wait for '96. Some prominent prospective candidates (including the 1988 vice-presidential nominee, Senator Lloyd Bentsen, as well as House Majority Leader Richard Gephardt and Senator

Al Gore, both candidates in 1988) did just that, finding reasons to sit out the race for the Democratic nomination.

Timing is everything in elections, however, and by the end of 1991 the social landscape had taken on a different aspect. The American economy was stuck in a deeper, broader, and longer recession than had been expected in the warm days of the previous summer. With that change, President Bush's identification with foreign policy over domestic policy switched from an asset to a liability.[1] Against the background of a stagnant economy, the savings and loan scandal (a matter of bipartisan responsibility), and a White House chief of staff pilloried in the press as insensitive and too fond of limousines at public expense, Democrats again characterized the Republican party as the party of wealth and privilege, a charge with extra bite during a recession. So the presidential election of 1992 took on new life. Six Democrats had stepped forward as major candidates for their party's nomination. With much improved Democratic prospects, the race for the Democratic presidential nomination heated up. As the incumbent president's approval ratings fell, challenges for the Republican nomination were mounted by unsuccessful Louisiana gubernatorial candidate and former Grand Dragon of the Ku Klux Klan David Duke and speechwriter and political commentator Pat Buchanan.

The party nomination struggles were tame enough. David Duke faded early. Patrick Buchanan demonstrated substantial strength against the incumbent president, gaining almost a third of the votes in several early primaries. His influence was greater than his vote totals, since the president had to move right to fend off Buchanan's conservative challenge to the core Republican constituency. But Buchanan eventually faded as well, once it became clear that even sizable minorities in a two-person contest would not suffice. On the Democratic side, Arkansas Governor Bill Clinton became the early front-runner, in media attention and fund-raising. Clinton's campaign was slowed by concerns about his character, focusing on questions of marital infidelity, avoiding service in Vietnam, and honesty about earlier marijuana use. Dissatisfaction with Clinton's lead was expressed first by support for former Massachusetts Senator Paul Tsongas and then by support for former California Governor Jerry Brown. Each bloodied Clinton's nose in primary contests, though exit polls showed that support for their candidacies was often based on a negative judgment of Clinton. Brown's campaign was particularly noteworthy for its refusal to accept contributions larger than $100 and its successful exploitation of a toll-free phone line to attract large numbers of these small contributions. Brown recited his phone number at every opportunity, sounding like a late-night TV announcer pitching "golden oldies" CDs. Brown was not the first national politician to use a toll-free phone line for fund-raising (Michael Dukakis had one in 1988), but he refined its use and paired it well with his populist ("We the people") campaign message.

Over the long haul, however, Clinton endured. But June 1992 found another candidate with the advantage of momentum—Ross Perot, who was neither Republican nor Democrat. From outside the two major parties he had captured the nation's attention—and the lead in opinion surveys.

Billionaire Perot enlivened the election through a series of ironic contrasts: In spite of his personal fortune he claimed to be the candidate of the little guy, not beholden to special interests. While picturing himself as driven by the wishes of his volunteers, Perot was absolutely free, because of self-financing, to enter and exit the race as he pleased. His advertising portrayed a no-nonsense pragmatist, but his charges of elaborate dirty tricks aimed at himself and his family, and his penchant for having private investigations done of associates and opponents caused some observers to suggest that he was less than stable. As a participant in the presidential debates Perot stuck to effective but simplistic lines about choosing to "continue to slow dance in Washington" or "get the shovel and clean out the barn."

Nevertheless, opinion surveys revealed that Perot earned high marks as the only candidate who "really addressed the issues." As we observed in Chapter 9, his popular success reflected serious disaffection with the two major parties.

Some observers were heartened by the tone of the 1992 presidential campaigns, because the public seemed uninterested and impatient with negative, personal attacks by the candidates on each other. In fact, questions about Bill Clinton's draft record, an extramarital affair, and youthful marijuana use did damage his campaign—particularly during the early primaries. The public considered these issues and accepted Clinton's explanations. An attempt to make something of Clinton's student trip to Moscow and participation in an antiwar demonstration in London in the 1960s may have produced a mild backlash against Bush late in the campaign. In the end, the best efforts of Republican strategists to use the "character issue" to divert attention from a sluggish economy failed. The electorate responded to Clinton's call for a change. His 43 percent popular vote victory was widely interpreted as a mandate to get the country's economy moving again.

The key to Clinton's success, according to most observers, was the poor economy. But the Democrats could easily have forfeited that advantage. Clinton's victory was also a tribute to his ability to portray himself as a "different kind of Democrat." He avoided the "special interest candidate" label and defused the race issue and its subtexts on welfare and crime. Given a three way race, Clinton had to offer a *credible* alternative to the status quo. For at least a plurality of voters, he succeeded.

The ebb and flow of the 1992 presidential contest can tell us a lot about the current state of elections in the United States. Academics and popular commentators have voiced much concern about the reduction of elections (particularly presidential elections) to media shows—an unfortunate mix of glitter, money, and mud with no real substance. The changing tides between the summer of 1991 and November 1992 demonstrate that elections are simultaneously more and less than sound bites and TV spots. The incumbent president's approval rating nose dive and the emergence of a serious nonparty contender for the White House were circumstances beyond the control of the candidates, their handlers, and the studio managers. So the election was still tied to the real world by some link. But what link? On the surface lies a layer of candidate-generated, controlled events: photo opportunities, TV ads, stump speeches, promises, slogans, and proposals. Digging behind the manufactured campaign images, we find campaign strategy and finance and the institutional processes of election in this country. Here, at the level of events involving institutions and processes, we find the substance underlying the images and "news" events that make campaigns such dramatic enterprises.

Democratic theory suggests that elections offer choices—among policies or leaders or at least among visions of a better future. There are disturbing signs that American elections don't offer such choices as effectively as they might. "Who wins?" is obviously an important question to ask about elections. Americans sometimes act as if that is the *only* important electoral fact, as if winning is everything. This goes beyond an unscrupulous "win at any cost" mentality among candidates for elective office. The "winning is everything" mind-set has distorted the way we think about elections and about our political system. No wonder that elections are now directed by marketing experts—the goal of marketing is to elicit a decision to buy. If elections are only about winning, then the measure of success is getting the voter to "buy" the candidate.

In an ideal democracy, elections do more than create winners and losers. Politics is more than a series of horse races. Elections should be an important source of civic education. They should provide a forum for widespread participation in discussions of important events and policies. Elections should provide a symbolic reaffirmation of civic obligation, a strengthening of affective ties to the common good. How well do American elections do these things? Opinions vary. Contemporary concerns about American elections center around three areas: (1) Political campaigns: Do they enlighten? Do they help the nation to identify and elect capable leaders? Or do they simply package candidates and sell them like commercial products? (2) Campaign finance: Have elections become a means for a few large investors to buy negative veto power over public policy? Or do elections provide a fair means of allowing citizens to use their own resources to affect public policy? (3) The media: Do citizens hear critical and constructive commentary in the news media? Or do the media distort and play up the superficial at the expense of the substantial? What role do the media have in politics generally and in electoral politics in particular? This chapter will explore each of these areas in turn, to determine just how well our electoral system serves our democratic goals.

Political Campaigns

In a democracy, the electorate makes choices—that is what elections are all about. How do the choices, as represented by opposing candidates, get onto the ballot? In the United States it is through an often long and tedious process that involves gaining recognition, receiving the endorsement of a party, obtaining funds from supporters, and seeking approval by the voters. Together these activities make up a political campaign.

A campaign can serve democracy well in several ways: by providing a forum for new political leadership, by disseminating information to potential voters, by mobilizing the electorate and thus ensuring that the electoral process reflects popular consent. Sometimes, of course, campaigns do not fulfill all, or any, of these functions. The political leaders presented to the electorate may not be qualified to deal with the pressing problems of the day. Issues may not be clarified; worse, they may be obscured. Finally, when a campaign does not reach many potential voters, the legitimacy of the electoral process may be undermined. Let us examine nonpresidential and presidential campaigns and the electoral college.

Nonpresidential Campaigns

Dividing power among states in a federal system, and then further allotting state power to various local governments, makes it difficult to generalize about political campaigns in the United States. Procedures vary considerably from one jurisdiction to another. In certain states—California, for instance—some elections (city, county, school board, and even some statewide offices) are officially nonpartisan. In such nonpartisan elections, candidate recruitment, selection, and support are less systematic and more idiosyncratic than in partisan elections.

Where election laws do allow for party participation, some means must be used to choose a party's candidates to compete in the general election. Sometimes that choice is made by party leaders; more often the choice is made by ordinary voters in a **primary election**. In a primary, potential candidates vie for nomination as the party's designated candidate in the general election. Primaries may be wide-open affairs or virtual shoo-ins, depending on the circumstances. A popular **incumbent** (the person currently in the office) seeking renomination may go unchallenged in the primary. In congressional races, incumbents run unopposed in primaries more than half the time. Where one

Carol Moseley Braun, an Illinois Democrat, campaigns for the U.S. Senate in 1992. She was one of four new women senators elected. *(Loren Santow/Impact Visuals)*

party is so dominant that it is unlikely that the other party could win, the primary election assumes greater importance than the general election that follows.

Primaries can follow one of three formats, determined at the state level. In a **closed primary**, only voters registered in a particular party may vote in the party's primary. In an **open primary**, voters can choose at the polling place which party primary they wish to vote in, regardless of their registration. A **blanket primary** is one in which voters can choose either party's primary for different offices—for example, the Democratic primary for senator and the Republican primary for governor. Most states use a closed primary.

In the general election campaign, candidates must raise funds, make use of the media, meet voters, gain support from prominent groups and individuals, activate the party faithful, and mobilize campaign workers. In the larger campaigns, armies of professionals work behind the scenes to formulate campaign strategy. Such professionals—including pollsters, computer experts, and media strategists—have become almost indispensable to campaigns for major offices. Small, or even nonexistent, campaign staffs are still common in congressional campaigns—particularly those in which an incumbent faces no substantial opposition.

The time in office between elections—the **interelection stage**—can be seen as part of the election process as well. Once elected, a representative or senator must continue to attend to the political situation in the home district or state. Ties with important groups, individuals, and the party itself must be maintained. Congressional representatives usually try hard to serve constituents to build up a reservoir of goodwill for the future. They generally make every effort to bring as much federal money as possible into their districts. In this connection, conservatives usually do not differ much from liberals. The chance to confer benefits on constituents, along with the higher name recognition that comes with incumbency, can be of great help to a candidate seeking reelection. Incumbency also has its disadvantages, however. An incumbent may offend some constituents by particular votes or actions or may suffer from association with an unpopular administration. Nevertheless, in most circumstances incumbency is one of the strongest advantages that can be brought into an election.

Presidential Campaigns

Although all political races have certain elements in common—stumping for votes, seeking media exposure, fund-raising, taking the pulse of the electorate—the intensity and importance of these activities varies from race to race. In presidential campaigns, *everything* counts. These are the most intense, most expensive, most drawn-out political campaigns in any modern democracy. Let us now examine some of the major events in a presidential race: preconvention moves, the national nominating conventions, and the general election campaign.

PRECONVENTION ACTIVITY   Considering the significance of the presidency in U.S. politics, it is not surprising that some politicians spend years generating the level of support needed to gain the nomination of a major party. For those seeking the office of president, years of public appearances, lectures, and wooing state and local party leaders usually precede the formal opening of the contest.

As we saw in Chapter 9, until relatively recently presidential nominees were generally selected by powerful party leaders at or before party conventions. But in recent decades the process of choosing presidential nominees has become much more open, depending heavily on primaries and caucuses involving ordinary voters. The current means of selecting party nominees—a confusing array of party primaries and caucuses in individual states—satisfies no one entirely. Even though the national parties have been asserting more control over candidate selection, our federal system encourages a fragmented process. And circumstances have been changing so rapidly that many candidates find themselves in the position of army generals—always preparing for the *last* war and unready for tomorrow's battle. This has been particularly true in the case of the Democrats, for whom party reform has been much more pressing and more extensive. But, as we saw in Chapter 9, reforms have significantly changed the process of selecting a presidential candidate in both parties.

The successful campaigns for presidential nominations since 1968 have often been those that avoid making assumptions about the continuity of electoral success. The fact is that in presidential politics, every electoral season is unique, and factors that played one way last time may work quite differently next time. In 1968, Hubert Humphrey followed the traditional Democratic game plan, gaining the support of party regulars (who would make up the majority of convention delegates) while avoiding primaries. But Humphrey's old way of doing things contributed to the sense of powerlessness and alienation that erupted into violence outside the Democratic national convention in Chicago. The sharp contrast between the order of the Republicans in Miami and the chaos in the streets of Chicago undoubtedly worked to Nixon's advantage in his narrow victory over Humphrey. For 1972, George McGovern saw the importance of the new rules for delegate selection (which he had helped to write) and outdistanced other Democratic hopefuls with a four-year-long, grass-roots primary campaign. Four-year-long campaigns subsequently became a standard part of preconvention activity.

In 1976, Jimmy Carter was a former governor of Georgia with little national name recognition. Acknowledging the cumulative effect of early visibility, Carter put unprecedented effort into the Iowa Democratic caucus selection process because it was the first event of the season. The visibility of a surprising success in Iowa parlayed into more contributions for later, more expensive contests. Out of a crowded field, Carter went all the way to the Democratic nomination and the White House. So Iowa became the number one travel destination of candidates and their staffs (from both parties) in the first month of an election year. However, since Carter, Iowa has not given a candidate the same boost. George Bush won in Iowa in 1980 and claimed momentum going into New Hampshire, where he was promptly upstaged and beaten by Ronald Reagan, the eventual nominee. Gary Hart's strong showings in Iowa and New Hampshire nearly derailed preseason favorite Walter Mondale in 1984. In 1988, Democrat Dick Gephardt and Republican Bob Dole did well in Iowa but not after that. George

The field of 1992 Democratic contenders for president. Left to right: Bob Kerrey, Tom Harkin, Jerry Brown, Bill Clinton, and Paul Tsongas. At the time of the New Hampshire primary no one could be certain that Bill Clinton would win the nomination or that he would defeat George Bush in November. *(Reuters/Bettmann Newsphotos)*

Bush came in third in Iowa in 1988 but won the Republican nomination and the general election that year. Iowa Senator Tom Harkin's candidacy in 1992 managed to cool the Iowa frenzy—his natural advantage there encouraged other Democratic candidates to downplay the importance of a strong Iowa showing. But running as if it were last time is a common mistake of presidential campaigns.

Some things change less, or less quickly, of course. These more stable factors in preconvention activity offer qualified verities for campaign observers. If we succumb to the urge to treat presidential campaigns as horse races, asking the following questions may help our handicapping efforts:

1. Who's got the best finances? Money can't guarantee electoral success at any level, but it certainly helps. And its absence usually constitutes an insurmountable obstacle to success. In 1988, with two open presidential party nominations, the two eventual nominees for president were the two with the most substantial monetary support in the period prior to June. Bill Clinton's nomination in 1992 was foreshadowed by his early lead in fund raising. Early con-

tributions have a compounding effect on a campaign's ability to raise money later.

2. Who's leading the dance? Defining the agenda is half the battle, so it is wise to try to figure out whose issues are getting talked about and how those issues are framed for discussion. A candidate always on the defensive—responding to the attacks or suggestions of another candidate—will lose the race.

3. How do a candidate's numbers match expectations? One of the oddities of preconvention activity is that winning and losing may be defined in terms of expectations rather than absolute majorities. A candidate who does much better than expected, though coming in second, "wins" (as Gary Hart did in Iowa in 1984). A candidate who does much less well than expected, though coming in first, "loses." Lyndon Johnson actually dropped out of the 1968 presidential contest because of a poor first-place showing in the New Hampshire primary that year. Expectations are frequently built on notions of a candidate's natural constituencies. When a candidate does not do well at home or does particularly well away from a natural constituency, those are important signs. But remember not to accept simplistic assumptions about constituencies. A liberal senator from Iowa may have a more natural constituency in New York than in Missouri. A news commentator who asserts that a female candidate should naturally do better with female voters is simply wrong.

   After Walter Mondale's defeat by Ronald Reagan in 1984, a group of mostly southern Democrats, concerned about the poor Democratic showing in presidential contests and about what they saw as a "liberal bias" in the selection process, came up with a plan to give the South a greater voice in the nominating process. In an attempt to counteract this liberal bias and choose a more "electable" candidate, several southern states decided to hold their primaries on the same day early in the nominating process. The planners of this megaprimary believed that a contest with a large number of delegates to be gained on a single day in a single region would focus more attention on the South as well as promote the candidacies of more moderate and conservative presidential aspirants (who, it was presumed, would do better in the conservative region). So Super Tuesday was born, as fourteen southern and border states held their primaries on the same day in March 1988. Super Tuesday may have focused more attention on the South in 1988, but in neither party did it advance conservative candidates. Republican moderate George Bush and Democratic liberals Jesse Jackson and Michael Dukakis did very well on Super Tuesday. More conservative southerners Pat Robertson and Al Gore, Jr., did not. In 1992, Super Tuesday can be said to have worked as planned, primarily advancing the moderate southerner Bill Clinton over more liberal opponents.

4. How soon is a candidate successful? An early lead can dissolve quickly—especially in defiance of preseason prognostications about favorites—but a very late start is a heavy burden. With the increase in the number of primaries and

the disappearance of winner-take-all primaries, a substantial margin of convention delegates gained in the first half of the primary season in likely to be unbeatable. The day of multiple ballots in an open convention is probably gone. In both 1988 and 1992 a large field of Democrats with no preseason favorite was pared down to a single presumptive candidate well before the convention.

Asking these four questions should help us play the elections game as it is usually played—simply looking for a winner. But if we want to know how well an election is serving democratic functions, these questions will not provide much help. Some other questions ought to be useful in understanding presidential campaigns in this broader way:

1. Where is the financing coming from? It will be important to look at the source and size of campaign contributions to candidates. Jerry Brown may not have been a messenger with broad appeal in 1992, but his message was an important one: Something must be done to reduce the influence of large campaign contributions. The person who donates $100 to a political campaign does it, without any expectation of return, because he or she feels good about advancing a certain cause. The person who donates thousands of dollars to a political campaign may well have a more self-interested objective in mind. Campaign contributors with an interest in government policy also tend to treat elections as horse races—and to hedge their bets by contributing to more than one candidate and even more than one party.

2. Which candidate is offering realistic assessments of the challenges to be faced? Since Walter Mondale's ill-fated confession of the necessity of raising taxes in 1984, campaign candor has suffered an eclipse (not that it was particularly common before that). Voter disenchantment with the political status quo does not guarantee more substantive policy debate, as demonstrated by Ross Perot's early success in 1992 based on a few pithy epithets about "politics as usual."

3. Which candidate attempts to broaden the campaign's appeal by finding meaningful consensus in society, so as to capture voters from the other party and bring in new voters in the general election? Since party activists in each party tend to be farther from the middle than party identifiers and voters (Democratic activists tend to be more liberal and Republican activists more conservative than their respective voters), both parties have on occasion favored candidates with narrow appeal over broader challengers (the Republicans in 1964 and the Democrats in 1972, for example). As long as campaigns are treated as horse races, there is no advantage for most candidates to engage more people in the process—a majority of a smaller pool is as good as a majority of a larger pool and may be easier to achieve with appeals targeted at particular segments of the voter market.

4. Are campaigns marked by a positive, constructive tone? The effectiveness of negative advertising in recent campaigns may make a positive campaign vul-

nerable. Candidates of all stripes now subtly invoke racial fears and class stereotypes in campaign ads. Since elections do shape our image of ourselves as a nation and the direction of our future, a negative tone may be ultimately self-defeating.

5. Are candidates open and accessible to public scrutiny? In a horse race, success comes not from openness but rather from controlling the candidate's public image, manipulating it in response to market concerns identified in **focus groups** and other marketing techniques. In an ideal democracy, however, part of the public's choice is about the quality of the persons chosen for leadership. Elections should identify *leaders*, not just winners.

These evaluative questions can also be applied to the national party conventions and the general campaigns that follow. These questions will not be as easy to answer as those in the handicapper's list, in part because the media give elections the horse race treatment almost exclusively and because by their nature the questions require evaluation and discussion, not just prediction.

What can be said about candidate selection in presidential races? It is a lengthy, expensive, media-oriented process with limited attention to issues. It involves a variety of individual contests, requiring different appeals (from the personal contact campaigns

Bill Clinton's selection of Al Gore as his running mate surprised many observers because both men were from the same region of the country. Yet, the selection worked and Gore appeared to help the ticket. *(AP/Wide World Photos)*

in Iowa farmhouses to the large-scale media-market campaigns of Super Tuesday). Preconvention debates among candidates offer some chance for airing issue positions, if they are not allowed to degenerate into shouting matches where being heard is as important as being understood. (The preconvention debates of recent campaigns have usually been more interesting and more informative than the later, more formal debates between party nominees.) The fragmented nature of the process as it currently exists is an open invitation to reform. Dissatisfaction with the process is widespread, yet major reforms (which could be imposed on the parties by Congress) are unlikely in the absence of a major election scandal or crisis.

NATIONAL CONVENTIONS   Modern national political conventions retain some superficial flavor of the past. Mass demonstrations, marches, music, and behind-the-scenes negotiations take place now as always, complete with exhausted delegates and smoke-filled rooms. National conventions remain significant undertakings for both major political parties, but they are changing. Today the identity of the nominee, traditionally the most important decision of the convention, is generally known in advance (at every national convention since 1956, one ballot has sufficed to select a nominee). Viewed as a part of a horse race, the convention does not retain much drama. Network news organizations, which used to broadcast large segments of the conventions live during prime time, have been gradually reducing convention coverage.[2] Long speeches by party luminaries are not considered compelling television fare. However, considered as part of more than a horse race, the conventions offer a chance to focus national attention on public issues, to heighten the quality and increase the depth of public debate, and to nurture affective ties to the common good. The parties themselves need to find a substitute for the lost excitement of a roll call vote. Political discussion is worthy of a wide audience, though it will rarely exhibit Hollywood-style drama.

THE RUN FOR GENERAL ELECTION   In the eight weeks between Labor Day (the first Monday in September) and election day (the first Tuesday in November), the candidates and their staffs work ceaselessly to woo voters. During this period, candidates must not only seek to convince voters to vote for them but also broaden their appeal to diverse segments of the electorate and touch base with a variety of special interests.

The candidates work hand in hand with paid political consultants to devise an overall campaign strategy and create a desirable image. Public opinion samples tell consultants what areas of the country the candidate should concentrate on and which issues to emphasize in specific regions. The consultants schedule public appearances, stage "news events" (such as walking tours, rallies, and hospital visits), and make certain that advance work is done properly before a candidate arrives at a destination. Most important, they coordinate a political advertising campaign that culminates in a media blitz during the last two weeks of the campaign. (Image-making through the media will be discussed at length later in the chapter.) The candidate, meanwhile, follows a grueling schedule, flying from one part of the country to another for daily rounds of speechmaking, interviewing, and working the crowds.

In view of the exhausting and drawn-out campaign process, many critics wonder whether the present system offers the most sensible way of selecting a president. Does this system attract the best people to political life? Many observers contend that the most statesmanlike public figures, the potential Jeffersons and Lincolns, are driven away from political life by the intensity and cost of the contemporary campaign process. Why should anyone be expected to spend two or three years running and preparing to run for office? To do so may well imply an uncommon measure of devotion to public service, or it may merely reflect an all-consuming ambition. In other words, have we turned campaigns into huge circuses that favor candidates who are good at performing but not necessarily at governing?

Richard Joslyn, in an effort to judge how closely U.S. campaigns and elections corresponded to the concerns of the electorate, advanced four alternative models of how popular consent works: the "prospective policy choice" approach, the "retrospective policy satisfaction" approach, the "selection of a benevolent leader" approach, and the "election as ritual" approach.[3] In the first of these models, citizens choose candidates on the basis of what they anticipate *future* policies will be. In the second, electoral choices are based on satisfaction with *past* policies. In the third, voters select a reassuring personality as leader. In the fourth, elections serve principally to reinforce deeply held cultural myths.

The model that best fits contemporary U.S. elections is the second, the "retrospective policy satisfaction" approach. It is far easier for the common citizen to assess what has been going on in the world than what directions policy will take. Each presidential election essentially answers one key question: Do you want four more years of this? Although administrations may cover up past policy failures, events frequently confound the pleasing pictures of policy successes that administrations try to cultivate. Voters do, in fact, "punish" administrations when economic conditions take a turn for the worse or foreign policy problems get out of hand.[4] President Bush's defeat in 1992 was a stark example of retrospective voter dissatisfaction with an extended recession.

The Electoral College

The American method of electing a president flies in the face of our modern understanding of democracy. The original 1787 version of the **electoral college** grew out of a series of compromises struck at the Constitutional Convention. As we have already seen, the framers were wary of direct majority rule. The electoral college filtered the choice of the voters in selecting the national leader.

The electoral college works like this: Slates of electors are ordinarily chosen by party conventions in each state, the number of electors being equal to the number of the state's representatives and senators in Congress. Within each state, the popular vote determines which slate of electors is chosen, winner take all. Because slates are pledged to their own party's candidate, their gathering in December in the state capital to vote is a formality (although occasionally an elector will cast a ballot for someone other than his or her pledged candidate). If no candidate were to receive a majority (270) of the electoral college vote from the states, the House of Representatives would choose the president from the top three candidates, with each state casting one vote. The Senate would choose the vice-president.

Critics of the electoral college base their opposition on solid grounds. For one, an electoral college majority need not coincide with a popular vote majority. Three times in U.S. history—in 1824, 1876, and 1888—the majority vote-getter did not win in the electoral college, and America elected a president with a minority of votes. A second argument holds that the electoral college promotes an unwarranted emphasis on the larger states that have more electoral votes. This in turn sways candidates to appeal to critical swing groups in those large states. The shifting of 1 percent of the vote in a state like California, Texas, Illinois, or New York may have much farther-reaching implications under the electoral college system than the shift of a comparable number of votes in Nebraska or New Hampshire.

Several reforms have been proposed, but none has attracted sufficient support to be added to the Constitution. The most minimal change would *require* electors to cast a ballot for the popular vote winner in their state. A more complicated proposal would divide a state's electoral votes in direct proportion to the popular vote in that state, replacing the current winner-take-all system. Finally, some critics favor abolishing the electoral college altogether and electing the president directly by popular vote. What objections are raised to this obviously democratic arrangement? Some analysts argue that the current system has worked well overall and that a national vote would undermine the federal system and create even more distance between voters and candidates. In addition, a very close election in the popular vote (Kennedy's in 1960, for example) can be validated by a more substantial electoral-vote margin. Many strategically placed groups, including urban minorities such as Jews and blacks, also fear that direct election might limit their influence, which is greater under the current system. Jimmy Carter proposed a popular-election amendment in 1977, but it failed to obtain the necessary two-thirds majority in the Senate. So in the absence of a major electoral crisis, the current electoral college system is likely to remain the somewhat awkward and potentially troublesome method of electing our national leader.

Campaign Financing

The cost of winning and holding office in the United States has skyrocketed since 1952. In that year total spending by candidates for public office in this country was $152 million. By 1988 that figure had soared to $2.7 billion (see **Table 10-1** and **Figure 10-1**). Candidates for congressional seats spent $459 million in 1988. In California $73.6 million was spent in the general election on statewide and legislative races in 1990—$29.2 million of that on a single race, between Dianne Feinstein and Pete Wilson for governor. The total for the two-year (1989–1990) election cycle in California was $152.8 million.[5] Although campaign spending is much higher than it ever was, the

TABLE 10-1
TOTAL POLITICAL SPENDING AT FEDERAL, STATE, AND LOCAL LEVELS, 1952–1988

Year	Spending (millions)	Increase
1952	$ 140	—
1956	155	10.7%
1960	175	12.9
1964	200	14.2
1968	300	50.0
1972	425	41.6
1976	540	36.4
1980	1,200	122.0
1984	1,800	50.0
1988	2,700	50.0

SOURCE: Herbert E. Alexander, *Financing Politics: Money, Elections, and Political Reform*, 4th ed. (Washington, D.C.: Congressional Quarterly Press, 1992), p. 83.

rate of increase seems to be slowing. For example, congressional candidates in 1990 spent only $446 million. But a potentially disturbing pattern is developing. The rate of spending by incumbents increased, while challengers spent less. In the 1990 races for U.S. Senate seats, incumbents spent 12 percent more than they did in 1988, although overall spending on Senate seats declined by 10 percent. Spending on House races increased by 3 percent from 1988 to 1990. Spending by House incumbents increased 21 percent. Herbert Alexander, a political scientist and expert on campaign financing, reminds us that these figures must be kept in perspective—$2.7 billion is a lot of money, but it is about the same amount that the nation's two largest advertisers (Procter & Gamble and Philip Morris) spent hawking their wares in 1987.[6] Still, these figures are significantly higher than comparable figures in some other democracies. Great Britain, for example, spent only $10.3 million on its 1983 general election—compared to $83 million spent on a population half the size in the 1982 California elections. Much of the increase in the United States is due to the increased use of television and radio advertising, public opinion polling, and political consultants, as well as the need for ever-larger campaign organizations to coordinate these activities.

High campaign spending poses problems for democracy on several levels. It consumes resources that could be directed to other projects. In addition, when elections require large sums of money, election results may reflect the distribution of wealth more than wisdom. And because officeholders must spend large amounts of time seek-

FIGURE 10-1

THE CAMPAIGN SPENDING DOLLAR IN 1988

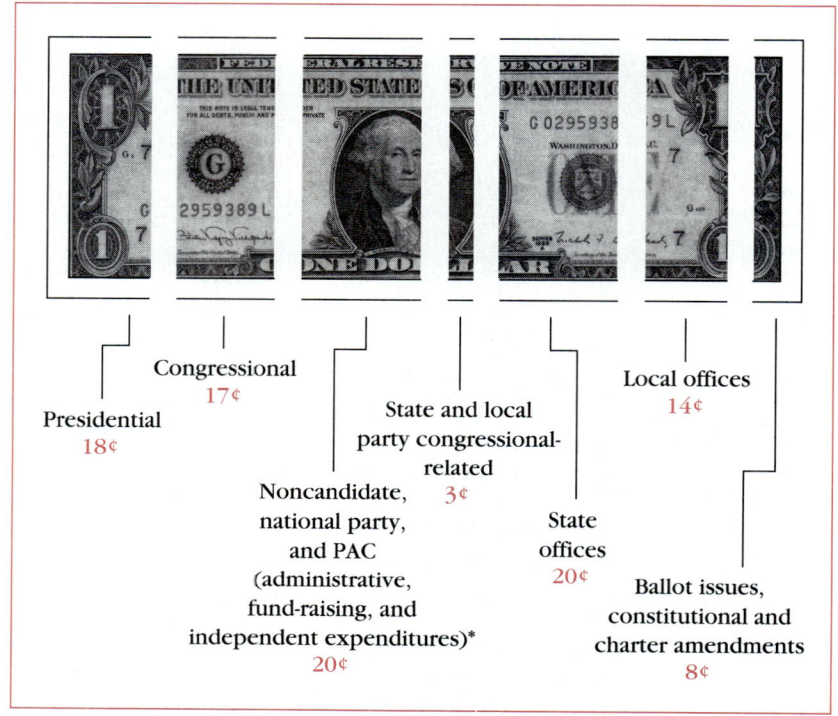

- Presidential 18¢
- Congressional 17¢
- Noncandidate, national party, and PAC (administrative, fund-raising, and independent expenditures)* 20¢
- State and local party congressional-related 3¢
- State offices 20¢
- Local offices 14¢
- Ballot issues, constitutional and charter amendments 8¢

*PAC = political action committee. Not including party and PAC contributions to presidential and congressional candidates; party and PAC contributions to these candidates are included in the presidential and congressional categories.

SOURCE: Herbert E. Alexander, *Financing Politics: Money, Elections, and Political Reform*, 4th ed. (Washington, D.C.: Congressional Quarterly Press, 1992), p. 82.

ing contributions to retain their offices, other matters that should possibly take precedence must be shunted aside.

Financial outlays cannot guarantee victory in an election. No amount of campaign spending could get a Republican elected in some heavily Democratic districts or a Democrat elected in traditional Republican strongholds. Nor could the most lavish expenditures ensure victory for an outspoken opponent of farm subsidies in a rural Iowa district or a committed segregationist in a black ghetto. Moreover, some campaign resources cannot be bought. Scholars, artists, and entertainers do not usually hire themselves out to campaigns; however, if a particular candidate captures their imagination, they may volunteer their time and efforts.

Opportunities exist for free media attention beyond the obvious and often exploited ploy of playing to the evening news. Jesse Jackson mastered the art of free airtime

Jerry Brown emphasized the issue of campaign financing in his effort to win the Democratic presidential nomination. Brown's 800 number for would-be contributors became well known as a symbol of his opposition to money from political action committees (PACS). Here, a very young Brown contributor shows her enthusiasm. *(AP/Wide World Photos)*

during the early primaries of 1988. His campaign had a relatively small budget through Super Tuesday, yet he gained more votes per dollar than any other major candidate. Several candidates learned Jackson's lesson well for the 1992 campaign. Billionaire Ross Perot, for example, first announced his presidential intentions on a televised talk show (you don't get that rich throwing money around). Bill Clinton donned dark glasses and played the saxophone on a late-night variety show, and Jerry Brown seemed to be a constant presence on TV and radio talk shows, touting his toll-free number. In addition to saving campaign funds, appearances in these forums had a desirable populist flavor. When Washington is in disfavor with voters, an appearance on a network TV talk show is worth a good deal more than on a PBS news analysis program.

Having more money than one's opponent cannot guaranee victory, but not having enough money will certainly contribute to defeat. "Enough," as one student of elections writes, "is defined by the distribution of other resources and influences in the campaign."[7] These resources and influences run the gamut from how much name recognition one candidate has relative to the other to incumbency and the characteristics of the district. Most members of Congress find, however, that factors concerning the competition cannot be calculated until relatively close to the campaign itself, whereas substantial fund-raising must start much earlier. Because campaigns cannot accurately determine how much money will be enough, they work toward raising more than enough. And as a former member of Congress confided, it is important to soak up contributions in part so that they won't be out there for some potential competitor to grab.

Who spends the most money? Republicans are usually far better financed than Democrats at all levels of government. Compare the levels of disbursements in the costs of presidential general election campaigns from 1860 to 1988. In nearly every year, the Republican National Committee spent substantially more than its Democratic counterpart. The Republican Senatorial Election Committee outspent the Democratic committee by a factor of nearly 10 to 1. The annual budgets of state political parties reveal the same disproportion.

One recent development in campaign financing in the states mirrors a comparable phenomenon at the national level: the appearance of legislative party campaign committees. Typical large contributors wishing to maximize their influence concentrate their donations on incumbents, particularly those in leadership positions. In terms of campaign financing, this means that money flows where it is least needed. Incumbents in leadership positions soon discovered that an effective way to increase their power was to redistribute this surplus to junior colleagues or hopeful challengers. Even when the money flowing through these channels did not represent a large proportion of all money spent, it was concentrated for maximum effect—directed to close races—based on the leadership's knowledge of the electoral system.[8]

Much of the money raised by the parties and candidates comes from various interest groups. Business and conservative groups, which generally support Republican candidates, tend to outspend labor and liberal groups, which traditionally support Democrats. Lately, the contributions of such groups have been limited by campaign finance reform laws. Let us now examine campaign financing reform efforts and their consequences.

Reform Efforts

The financing of political campaigns—particularly presidential campaigns—has long been a sore point in U.S. politics. In 1962, President John F. Kennedy's Commission on Campaign Costs concluded that the taint of "shoddiness" had to be removed from political campaign financing and that the requirements of the Federal Corrupt Practices Act of 1925 were outdated and useless. It was not until 1971, however, that Congress took any substantial steps to remedy the situation. The Federal Election Campaign Act (FECA), passed that year, limited media spending by candidates in federal elections, required detailed reporting of contributions, and provided for a voluntary $1 checkoff on individual income tax forms to help to pay for presidential elections. To avert a threatened veto by President Nixon, Congress stipulated that the act would apply only after the 1972 elections. Ironically, financing irregularities in the 1972 presidential

CAMPAIGNS, MONEY, AND THE MEDIA

election, culminating in the Watergate scandal, forced Nixon to resign from office and finally triggered large-scale efforts to reform campaign financing.

The 1974 off-year congressional elections swept into office a new wave of representatives and senators bent on changing the way campaigns were conducted. This "Watergate class" was instrumental in passing the far-reaching Federal Election Campaign Act of 1974, which set sharp spending and contribution limits on federal campaigns, beefed up requirements for financial disclosure, and established a scheme for public financing of presidential primaries and presidential general elections. The Federal Election Commission was created to enforce these new rules.

Several developments following the 1974 FECA legislation have resulted in a pattern of campaign financing and regulation quite different from anyone's original expectations. In two decisions the Supreme Court, concerned about the free speech implications of limiting political expenditures, struck down some of the new limitations and upheld others.[9] Individual and group contributions to campaigns could be limited by Congress ($1,000 per candidate, and $5,000 per election), but individual and group expenditures on behalf of candidates but not clearly linked to the campaign or the parties could not. Candidates could not be limited in spending their own money on campaigns, nor could campaigns be limited except when limitations are accepted as a condition of receiving public financing. Presidential candidates who accept spending limits could receive partial funding during the preconvention stage and "full" funding for the general election. (Full funding does not include "soft" money spent by parties or by individuals or groups on behalf of candidates.)

The most visible change in campaign financing since 1974 has been the spectacular increase in **political action committees (PACs)**, which are formed to direct money to certain candidates, causes, or issues. In 1974 there were 608 registered PACs; by 1990 there were 4,677, which spent, altogether, $357,648,557 (see **Table 10-2**). The 1990 figures are down slightly from the preceding electoral cycle (both the number of PACs and dollars spent), reflecting the general leveling off of campaign expenditure

TABLE 10-2

PAC ACTIVITY, 1979–1990

	Number of PACs	Receipts	Disbursements	Contributions to Candidates	Cash on Hand
1989–1990	4677	$372,091,977	$357,648,557	$159,121,496	$103,340,543
1987–1988	4832	$384,617,093	$364,201,275	$159,243,241	$88,963,751
1985–1986	4596	$353,429,266	$339,954,146	$139,839,718	$69,062,430
1983–1984	4347	$288,690,535	$266,822,476	$112,970,044	$55,072,983
1981–1982	3722	$199,452,356	$190,173,539	$87,553,326	$31,526,621
1979–1980	2785	$137,728,528	$131,153,384	$60,189,696	$21,980,251

SOURCE: Federal Election Commission, "1990 PAC Contributions Down Compared to Past Election Cycles, Final FEC Report Finds" (press release), December 10, 1991.

totals. Although the Court upheld restrictions on PAC contributions to candidates, three developments contributed to increasing PAC influence in elections: First, individual candidates could endorse the creation of a PAC that would raise large sums of money to be spent on behalf of the candidate or contributed to other candidates as a means of gaining support and influence. Citizens for the Republic, Ronald Reagan's candidate PAC, raised millions of dollars between 1976 and 1980 to launch Reagan's successful presidential bid. Now nearly all major national politicians form similar "leadership" PACs. Second, "independent" PACs are able to spend unlimited amounts on candidates as long as they avoid direct ties to candidates' campaign organizations. The National Conservative Political Action Committee spent millions both for and against candidates throughout the 1980s to advance a conservative political agenda. Third, state and national parties are allowed to raise unlimited amounts of "soft money" (from PACs and other sources) to be spent on voter registration and other organization-building tasks. The earliest model of such soft-money contributions is the AFL-CIO's Committee on Political Education (COPE) and its contributions to the Democratic party.[10] The result of these developments is that, contrary to reform expectations, American elections are now served by large, widespread, organized mechanisms for pumping huge sums of money into campaigns (see **Figures 10-2** and **10-3**).

FIGURE 10-2

PAC CONTRIBUTIONS BY CANDIDATE STATUS, 1980–1990

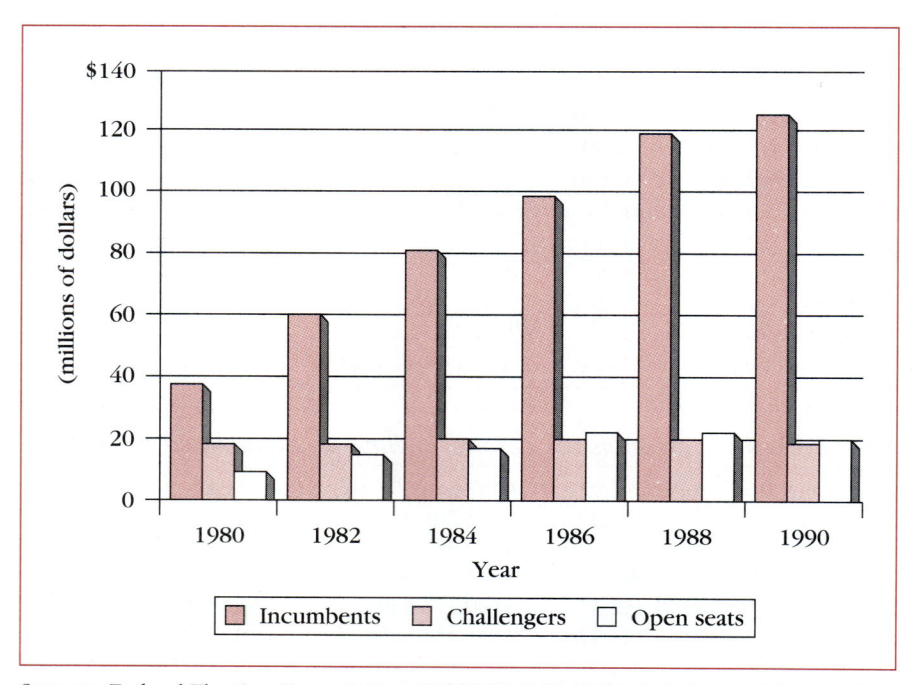

SOURCE: Federal Election Commission, "1990 PAC Contributions Down Compared to Past Election Cycles, Final FEC Report Finds" (press release), December 10, 1991, p. 8.

CAMPAIGNS, MONEY, AND THE MEDIA   381

FIGURE 10-3
PAC CONTRIBUTIONS BY PARTY, 1980–1990

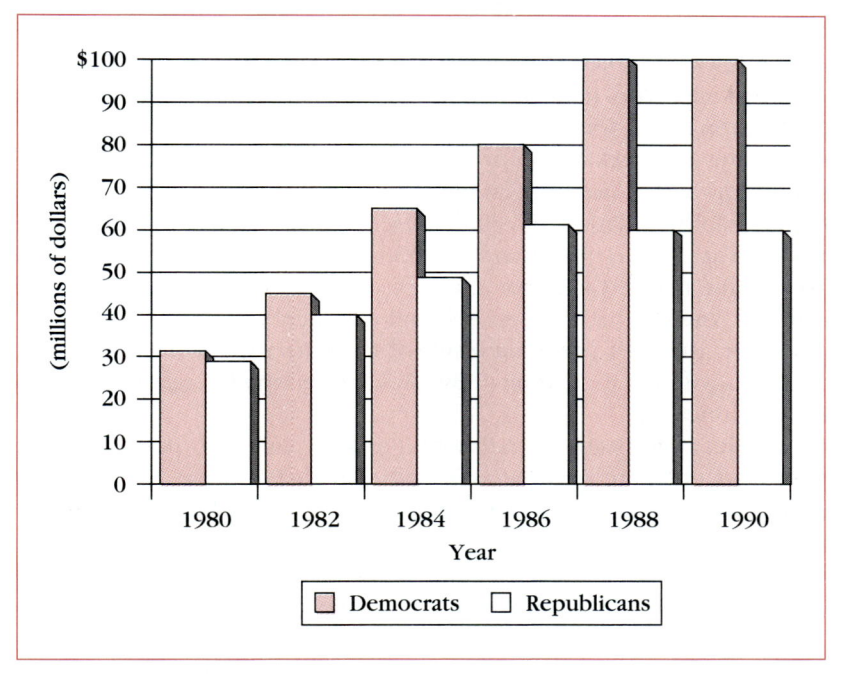

SOURCE: Federal Election Commission, "1990 PAC Contributions Down Compared to Past Election Cycles, Final FEC Report Finds" (press release), December 10, 1991, p. 8.

The current structure of campaign financing in American elections does have consequences for democracy, not strictly in partisan terms. Although the Republican party has traditionally been better financed and although Republicans were quicker to capitalize on campaign reforms, during the 1980s the Democrats in the House of Representatives also learned how to exploit the new rules of the game. By 1988 a majority of corporate PAC money and an even larger proportion of nonbusiness PAC money was going to House Democrats. Given the ideological affinity of corporate capital to the Republican party, such new contribution patterns pointed to deeper consequences for the political system.

First, the current system of campaign financing threatens to freeze elections altogether, by making incumbency an insurmountable advantage. The disproportionate PAC funding of incumbents (as safe bets) means that it becomes even harder for challengers to mount serious campaigns—at a time when one observer noted that if you wanted to design a Congress to maximize the chances for reelection, you couldn't do better than Congress as it is (see Chapter 13). Second, the current system of campaign financing threatens to reduce representation to a collection of vetoes. Consider the comments of two members of Congress: "I take money from labor, and I have to think twice in voting against their interest. I shouldn't have to do that." "We are the only human beings in the world who are expected to take thousands of dollars from perfect strangers on important matters and not be affected by it."[11] For many representatives and senators, PACs come in particularly handy when large campaign debts must be paid off. One longtime senator noted that the problem of financing congressional campaigns "virtually forces members of Congress to go around hat in hand, begging for money from Washington-based special interests, political action committees whose sole purpose for existing is to seek a *quid pro quo*."[12] Though a PAC may not be able to buy legislation, given the nonmajoritarian tendencies of Congress, it may well purchase a veto of unfavorable legislation. As one representative said, "More and more on the floor I hear people say, 'I can't help you. I've gotten $5,000 from this group.' "[13]

Some observers argue that PACs do not exert excessive influence, if only because there are so many in existence that their efforts tend to cancel one another out. Even if this is true, however, the high spending levels of the current campaign financing system, in combination with the increasing political role of nonparty organizations, do raise some legitimate concerns.

For example, consider the heavy spending by PACs on efforts to defeat specific representatives and senators. In recent elections, conservative PACs, like NCPAC, have targeted various liberal candidates, spending large sums in attempts to defeat them. Ideological targeting of this kind contributes to the decline of political parties by supplanting the parties' fund-raising and support functions. It may also jeopardize democratic principles by helping to elect candidates whose views represent only a small—but well-financed—segment of the electorate. (PACs are discussed further in Chapters 11 and 13).

Further Reforms

To many observers, the reforms of the 1970s were too limited in scope. With the weakening of the major parties, the proliferation of PACs, and the increasing importance of the mass media in political campaigns, a drive for more radical reforms has gained momentum.

One of the difficulties of campaign financing reform is that any proposal will affect different candidates differently. Some critics argue that public financing would assist incumbents, who already enjoy many advantages. Others take the opposite view—that it would unfairly aid challengers. Because many Republican members of Congress perceive Democratic proposals as disguised means to enhance Democratic electoral prospects at the expense of Republicans, partisan splits frequently develop over campaign financing legislation.

Additional campaign finance reform moved closer to reality in 1992, when Congress passed a comprehensive reform bill advocated by Common Cause. The bill included absolute spending limits in House and Senate campaigns, aggregate limits on PAC contributions that could be accepted by candidates, and an end to soft-money abuses. President Bush vetoed the legislation.

Politics and the Media

Traditionally, the press has been considered an important check on government power. Ideally, the press should act as a watchdog, subjecting government officials and government policies to careful scrutiny. Without disciplined parties in the United States, the press must often play the role of "loyal opposition," analyzing government proposals and suggesting clear alternatives as well. These key roles for the press assume paramount importance during periods of executive dominance (most of the twentieth century in the United States). Whereas legislatures tend to foster open discussion and regularly give rise to internal debate, executives often do not exhibit these democratic traits.

How well the press fulfills its roles as watchdog and loyal opposition to the presidency has varied considerably in recent years. Several factors account for this. First, presidents tend to shy away from direct contact with the press and rely increasingly on spokespersons whose comments are frequently "off the record." Presidential press conferences, when these are arranged, provide little opportunity for sustained dialogue on any topic. Although President Bush held more press conferences in his first three years in office than his predecessor, Ronald Reagan, did in eight, these sessions were

President John F. Kennedy on television in the early 1960s. Electronic media allowed politics to find its way daily into virtually all American homes. Although large numbers of citizens remained ignorant of the basics of political life, the influence of media in shaping political attitudes in recent decades is undisputed. *(National Archives)*

dominated by issues chosen for attention by the White House, which, anticipating the queries, was ready with carefully prepared responses.

Second, presidents now sidestep the press, reaching the people directly via television addresses. President Reagan was at his best under these controlled circumstances and used them to great advantage. In the 1992 election candidates for the presidency used a variety of techniques—for example, the TV talk show—to get media time without the mediation of news organizations.

Third, from time to time government officials—from presidents on down—attack the credibility or fairness of the press. A memorable confrontation occurred between Vice-President Bush and CBS news anchor Dan Rather during the 1988 presidential primary campaign. For more than ten minutes on live, national TV, Rather and Bush yelled at each other. Rather complained that Bush would not answer his questions about the vice-president's role in the Iran-Contra affair. Bush argued that Rather had "ambushed" him unfairly, simply to create a scene. (It was later asserted that Bush had planned and instigated this confrontation to combat the charge that he was a "wimp.") There is no solid evidence about the extent to which attacks by government officials actually undermine public confidence in the news media, but such attacks do sometimes arouse considerable apprehension among reporters about freedom of the press—especially among broadcast journalists whose medium is subject to federal licensing and thus is potentially vulnerable to retaliation by the executive branch of government.

The Watergate scandal reinforced public acceptance of the press as a watchdog over government activity. Although the *Washington Post* was the only major news source to pay any attention to the Watergate scandal when it first unfolded in 1972 and 1973, the national press eventually gave it wide exposure. By contrast, when the Iran-Contra affair became public in 1986 and 1987, the Reagan administration's covert activities in that undertaking were instantly the lead story in all major news sources, print and broadcast.

Let us now consider how news is gathered and how the news media frame the issues of political debate.

Gathering the News

The American news media enjoy an unusual degree of freedom in exploring political issues. In some other democratic countries, such as Great Britain or France, public discussion of sensitive political issues can run up against serious legal obstacles. The freedom of the American news media was significantly enhanced in the 1970s by the **Freedom of Information Act**, under which common citizens (including reporters) can obtain information that the government might otherwise prefer to keep secret (exceptions are made to protect individual privacy and national security).

Sometimes the press is deliberately manipulated by government officials. On occasion, and for a variety of reasons, officials inside the government "leak" information to the press. The 1971 publication of the **Pentagon Papers**—classified documents on the U.S. involvement in Vietnam—was an example of a massive leak motivated by

CAMPAIGNS, MONEY, AND THE MEDIA   385

> ### THE PRESS AND THE PERSIAN GULF
>
> Military conflicts represent a special challenge to news reporters, since the government necessarily has a large interest in managing events on the battlefield. The Persian Gulf War of 1991 raised a series of questions about the ability of news organizations to gather news independently in active military conflicts.
>
> The United States established severe limitations on press access to the Gulf War. Only 180 reporters were allowed near the front lines, and these traveled in groups of six or more, accompanied by military press officials. "Security review" rules barred reporters from revealing facts that might jeopardize lives or military operations—enforcing field censorship of reports that both restricted content and slowed reporting, sometimes enough to render the reports useless.
>
> How can a government balance the needs of military operations and press freedom? Given instantaneous communication, media reports might have a direct impact on the conduct and outcome of military engagements. What sorts of delays and limitations are defensible for tactical reasons? Moreover, since the Vietnam War, American officials have been acutely aware of the effect that war reporting can have on the civilian population's support for the war effort. If it is a legitimate function of democratic government to encourage support for its own policies, does that function include the management of the news?
>
> War presents an extreme case of a chronic challenge to democracy: What safeguards can be applied to circumstances when the government's interests may potentially diverge from the interests of the commonwealth? A free press is an important component of such safeguards. What limitations of the media, under what circumstances, are justified?

opposition to government policy. Stories in 1987 about a replacement for President Reagan's chief of staff, Donald Regan, were leaked (by Nancy Reagan herself, according to Regan's account) as a tactic to force him out of that position. Sometimes overt government actions are taken to keep news from reaching the public, for example, the U.S. government's strict controls over the press coverage of the Persian Gulf War or the Israeli government's exclusion of reporters from the occupied territories during the first years of the Palestinian uprising in 1987 and 1988.

Framing the Issues

How deeply do reporters probe in researching their stories? As David Halberstam points out in his book *The Best and the Brightest*, many reporters were easily taken in by the

General Norman Schwarzkopf became a familiar figure in American living rooms during the Persian Gulf War. Despite daily war coverage and press briefings by the military, many maintained that military censorship made full coverage of the war impossible. *(AP/Wide World Photos)*

official version of events in Vietnam during much of the time American troops were fighting there. And many critics found press coverage of the Persian Gulf War seriously inadequate. Reporters, confronted with the challenge of probing beneath the self-serving explanations of governments and others, may not have enough background or firsthand knowledge to challenge official judgments.

The American press is sometimes criticized for being too easy on the president. The kid-gloves treatment, to the extent that it exists, may have roots in the American fascination with heroes and in the shared values that reinforce the status quo. But another specific cause may contribute: News organizations are heavily dependent on the government—and particularly the White House—as a source of information. Access can be used to reward sympathetic and punish unsympathetic treatment. Larry Speakes, a Reagan press official, reported that members of the Washington press corps who wrote or broadcast stories unfavorable to the administration had to phone three times before he would accept the call. Such pressure makes it difficult for reporters to secure solid information without getting snared in "cronyism."

Sometimes news media impose their own political agenda on reporting, as in the 1890s, when William Randolph Hearst used his chain of newspapers to arouse American public opinion in favor of war with Spain. At other times, and perhaps more frequently, news reporting becomes the captive of others' political agendas. During the 1950s many newspapers carried banner headlines reporting spectacular (and utterly unsubstantiated) charges of communist subversion in the American government, issued regularly by Senator Joseph McCarthy and others. One of the frustrations of political hostage taking is the issue of press coverage. Do the media play into the hands of the terrorists by covering these events? Extensive media coverage of the American hostages in Iran in 1978–1980 dovetailed with President Jimmy Carter's decision to make the situation a priority for his administration. Whose fault was it that the Carter presidency became a hostage to the hostage crisis?

Recently some researchers have made encouraging conclusions about the ability of citizens in our democracy to deal with the flood of information available to them in the media:

> Average Americans can successfully scrutinize the merits of people and policies from a variety of perspectives. They can recognize their own limits and those of others in information-processing capabilities. They do not make judgments based on a single ideology or the recommendation of a single source. Average people know how to accept and reject information, and they are therefore not likely to be manipulated into large-scale acceptance of schemata that conflict with the basic tenets of American culture.[14]

Other observers might find this account too optimistic.

Important questions remain. Can the press maintain its independence and still gather the information that the citizens of a democracy need? Will reporters dig below the surface to unearth difficult stories? And will editors (and their cost-conscious bosses) give their reporters the time and resources to reach sound conclusions about important issues? Can government officials afford to be open and honest enough to keep in touch with the people through the press?

Media and Campaigns

That the mass media (television, radio, newspapers) play a significant role in U.S. political campaigns is obvious. We now consider four aspects of the media's role in elections: the growing political importance of the mass media, the use of the media for candidate imagemaking; how televised political debates educate the public about the candidates and the issues, and the overall news coverage of elections—the so-called horse races. We then try to assess the relationship between the media and politics in terms of democratic theory.

The Media's Impact on Elections

In democratic elections, candidates and parties always try to communicate with potential voters. Since at least the 1950s, however, the manner in which politicians communicate with the electorate has undergone a fundamental change: The mass media, and especially television, now play the most significant role in that communication process. The new-found potency of the mass media to reshape the political landscape was apparent in the first of the Kennedy-Nixon televised debates in 1960. Many analysts call that single event the decisive factor in Kennedy's victory.

The remarkable emergence onto the national scene of the unknown Jimmy Carter in 1976 and the little-known Ross Perot in 1992 was possible only because of extensive media coverage of their campaigns. Conversely, media attention given to Gary Hart and Joe Biden when they allegedly strayed from acceptable behavior in the 1988 presidential race prompted crises in their campaigns. Compounding the bad press Biden and Hart received for plagiarism and philandering, respectively, was each candidate's response to the crisis while under the intense scrutiny of the press. Eventually, they were forced to withdraw from the race.

The media played a new role in the 1992 presidential campaign. Ross Perot started the trend of appearing on TV talk shows and other candidates joined in. Bill Clinton took to the airwaves and played his saxophone on the Arsenio Hall show one night. *(Reed Saxon/ AP/Wide World Photos)*

These examples illustrate that the media can sometimes make or break a candidate—enhancing a campaign or undermining it. Undeniably, the media have become a singularly powerful force in virtually all major U.S. elections.

How did this happen? Some of the reasons are obvious. Americans spend almost half their leisure time watching TV, listening to the radio, or reading newspapers and magazines. This adds up to seven hours a day of media exposure, with television accounting for 75 percent of the total.[15] Also, because television reaches millions, no candidate can afford to ignore it. Through the media, candidates create images that can decisively influence elections.

Other reasons for the media's growing importance are more subtle. As more and more U.S. voters disaffiliate from the two major parties, for example, candidates increasingly seek to target specific audiences with media messages. Then, too, the enhanced importance of primaries has made the nominating process more visible—and thus more newsworthy. Media organizations, for their part, have also been changing. The major broadcasting networks—CBS, NBC, ABC, and CNN—now cover campaigns in great detail and even commission their own public opinion polls. Media involvement in political campaigns has been aided by several Supreme Court decisions as well. In 1957 the Court ruled that broadcasters could not be held responsible for the content of political spot ads and thereby opened the airways to such ads. Two years later the justices relaxed equal-time requirements for news coverage of candidates. Before that ruling, a network that covered a news event involving one candidate was obligated to provide equal time for coverage of opposing candidates. Then, in 1976, the Court also relaxed the equal-time requirements for political debates, freeing broadcasters from the necessity of including minor party candidates in a debate.[16] Finally, in 1987 the Federal Communications Commission (FCC) abolished the **Fairness Doctrine**, which guaranteed equal airtime to present opposing views. This gave broadcasters even more freedom.

Because of the media's growing impact on political life, heightened tension has characterized some encounters between candidates and the media. Candidates and their organizations (which usually include sophisticated media specialists) seek to use the media to advance their own perspectives. For their part, journalists have to decide which candidates to cover, what activities are newsworthy, and how to treat the themes of a campaign. Are citizens' political perceptions altered by what they read in the papers and see on TV? Is their belief in the electoral process reinforced, legitimizing the way the system works, or are elections a disillusioning experience? We address these issues next.

Imagemaking

Public opinion pollsters and professional political consultants now hold key positions in modern campaigns, often usurping the advisory roles previously filled by party officials. They bring to a campaign the expertise and savvy to use the media and other tools of modern campaigning. Among the services they provide are these:

> ### WHO SPEAKS WITH AUTHORITY ABOUT POLITICS?
>
> Watch and listen to the campaign commercials in the next election cycle. How many female voices do you hear? How many women do you see? What are those women doing? A recent study of more than five hundred campaign ads reveals that very few female voices are used in political commercials and that when women do appear in the ads, they are often in the traditional roles of wife and mother.
>
> Even female candidates, who usually speak for themselves in their ads, will use a male voice-over to say the final words of the commercials, the authoritative words. For example, in her successful campaign for reelection as the governor of Vermont, Democrat Madeleine Kunin's ad used a male voice-over throughout the ad. Though a picture of Governor Kunin appeared at the end of the ad, her voice was never heard.
>
> Political advertisements will frequently use actors to tell little stories about the candidate or an issue. In such ads men dominate the important roles. Women do appear, but often as wives, mothers, or members of an admiring audience. In what are known as testimonial ads, where a "person on the street" will tell the viewer why to vote for the candidate, the person on the street is almost always a man. When a woman appears in this type of ad, she generally speaks on a narrow range of issues, usually social security or crime.
>
> There are, of course, exceptions to these rules. In the 1989 gubernatorial campaign in Virginia, Douglas Wilder, the eventual victor, ran an ad with a male voice-over but with women appearing as scientists and in hard hats. Senator

(Box continues on page 391)

> advertising campaigns for radio, television, and newspapers . . . public relations and press services . . . research and presentations of issues . . . fund-raising solicitations . . . public opinion sampling . . . technical assistance on radio and television production . . . campaign budgeting assistance . . . use of data processing techniques to plan campaign strategy . . . [and] mobilization of support through traditional precinct-level organization, door-to-door campaigns and telephone solicitation of votes.[17]

Fundamentally, modern campaign strategists seek to alter or strengthen images of their candidate. To do so they contrive positive and highly appealing images of their candidates and contrary images of the opposing candidates, and they attempt to persuade the public of the truth of such images. These efforts can both educate and inform, but at their core is **imagemaking**—a process closer to the marketing of products than to public debate and education.

> Warren Rudman, Republican from New Hampshire, used a female voice-over in a commercial for his 1986 reelection bid. The voice discusses the economy and the Gramm-Rudman budget bill. The ad also contained a male character discussing children's issues.
>
> Why are these instances so rare? The consensus among advertising executives is that women's voices are simply not as authoritative as men's. And current research seems to support that view. A recent study by a psychologist revealed that students listening to tapes of a man reading a speech speaking tentatively (using such phrases as "sort of" and "don't you think" and "um") and a woman reading the same speech assertively found the male arguments more persuasive.* In commercial product advertisements, females are increasingly appearing in nontraditional roles, selling nontraditional products (like cars); in political ads things remain as they were in the 1950s. Advertising firms will often tape both male and female voices to run over their ads and then play each for a focus group (a small group of randomly selected voters whose views can be examined in depth during the group session). The firms find that both male and female members of such groups usually rate the ads with the male voice-over as more effective.
>
> Advertisers are unwilling to take chances by presenting women in nontraditional settings or using more female voices in their ads. As one advertising executive said, "I don't know why we don't use more women in our ads. We just do what we've done in the past—we know what works." For the American voter, it is the word of the male that works.
>
> *"Women Who Persuade Men," In Health, May-June 1991, p. 10.*
> Source: June Speakman, Claremont-McKenna College.

This kind of political imagemaking is nothing new, however; it is certainly not unique to the age of mass media. In 1840 the Whigs won a presidential campaign by successfully portraying William Henry Harrison as a man of the people and a successful general. In a campaign legendary for its hoopla and lack of content, the Whigs promised "Tippecanoe and Tyler too," referring to the Battle of Tippecanoe, an insignificant skirmish with the Indians in 1811, and vice-presidential candidate John Tyler. Other candidates also cultivated specific images, from Teddy Roosevelt the "rough rider" to Abe Lincoln the honest "rail-splitter." In each of these cases, as in modern media campaigns, the key issue is to what degree pure imagemaking takes over from a more reasoned and thoughtful assessment of the candidate's character and stands on the issues.

The first presidential candidate to hire an advertising agency was Dwight D. Eisenhower in 1952. His Democratic opponent, Adlai Stevenson, considered advertising beneath the dignity of the political process. Since that time, few politicians competing for major electoral offices have done without media advertising strategies.

In television advertising, the most money is spent on **spot ads**, which usually run thirty seconds or less. The vast majority of spots are candidate-oriented: They ask the electorate to judge the candidate as a person, not as the representative of a party or the champion of a political philosophy. When spots do address political issues, they generally do so in a vague way, only loosely connecting the candidate to a particular position. In 75 percent of all spot ads there is no mention of a political party. Only 20 percent contain enough specific information about a candidate's position on an issue to allow the audience to draw inferences about the candidate's future behavior.

What effect do political ads have on citizen awareness? They can alter, to a modest degree, how the audience views a candidate's character and positions on particular issues, and they can sharpen perceived differences between candidates on the issues. Recent research indicates that political ads may contain more issue content than TV news coverage. This may not mean much, however, since TV news, as we will see, frequently ignores issues. Moreover, issues are always presented with a partisan flavor

---

THE LINCOLN-DOUGLAS DEBATES

Perhaps the most impressive political debates in American history were held during the 1858 Illinois senatorial campaign. The debates pitted one of the nation's most prominent politicians, Stephen A. Douglas, against a rising Illinois Republican who had served two years in the House of Representatives and had two years earlier unsuccessfully sought the Republican vice-presidential nomination—Abraham Lincoln.

By general agreement, conditions at the start of the campaign favored Douglas, by far the better-known candidate. Douglas's plan was to solidify his support in Illinois as his base for a run for the presidency in 1860. In an effort to offset Douglas's well-established reputation, Lincoln challenged him to a series of debates. Douglas reluctantly accepted. Seven three-hour debates were held. In each, the first speaker opened with a one-hour presentation, the other was allowed ninety minutes to reply, and the first had the final thirty minutes.

The debates attracted considerable attention. Large audiences assembled, coming by train and wagon. Newspapers across the country covered the debates, sometimes publishing entire speeches. The contrast between the two candidates was striking: Douglas, less than five feet tall, a shrewd and ingenious debater; Lincoln, tall and awkward, master of the clear moral statement.

The core question of the debates was slavery, a matter that had almost reached a boiling point in the United States.

(Box continues on page 393)

in political ads. A thirty-second spot showing a photo of an aborted fetus and accusing one's opponent of favoring "baby murder" (a euphemism for abortion) ostensibly deals with an issue, but it does little to advance our political understanding. The real danger of political advertising, then, is that it may befuddle or misinform more often than it enlightens the electorate.

Televised Presidential Debates

Presidential debates are not required by law. Given the fact that usually at least one candidate has strong reasons for *not* participating, every presidential debate that occurs is a minor miracle. Vice-President Richard Nixon surprised observers in 1960 by giving his challenger, John Kennedy, the chance to appear with him on national television on an equal footing. Kennedy took advantage of the opportunity, emphasizing his telegenic qualities and giving millions of viewers a more favorable impression of the lesser-known candidate. Analysts generally agree that the debates gave Kennedy a crucial boost toward victory in the election.

Douglas had established a reputation as a pragmatist on the issue, maintaining that the question should be resolved by popular sovereignty, with each state deciding whether to be slave or free. He seemed to accept unquestioningly the conviction of most whites that blacks were inherently inferior and accused Lincoln of being a radical for advocating racial equality. In response, Lincoln admitted there was "a physical difference between the white and black races" but nonetheless favored the containment of slavery within its existing borders and looked toward its gradual extinction. He accused Douglas of being indifferent to the moral dimensions of slavery. "That is the issue which will continue in this country when these poor tongues of Judge Douglas and myself shall be silent. It is the eternal struggle between these two principles—right and wrong—throughout the world."

Douglas spent $80,000 on the campaign, Lincoln $1,000. In the popular vote to elect the state legislature Lincoln's forces won, 126,084 to 121,940. But because Douglas's backers controlled more seats, Lincoln failed to be elected to the Senate. The larger moral and political victory belonged to Lincoln, however, who had established himself as a future national leader able to frame the debate on slavery during the coming crisis.

Sources: A. L. Boulton, ed., The Lincoln and Douglas Debates *(New York: Holt, 1905); Don E. Fehrenbacher,* Prelude to Greatness *(Stanford, Calif.: Stanford University Press, 1962); Harry V. Jaffa,* Crisis of the House Divided *(Garden City, N.Y.: Doubleday, 1959).*

Thereafter, front-runners in presidential campaigns were understandably reluctant to give their opponents a chance to shine on national television. The next debates didn't occur until Jimmy Carter faced President Gerald Ford in 1976. Ford's willingness to appear was tied in part to the fact that as an appointed vice-president who became president when Nixon resigned, he had never run a national campaign before. He needed to reassure voters that he was up to the job (by most accounts the debate didn't help). Since 1976 every presidential election has generated at least one debate. And in 1984 and 1988 there were vice-presidential debates as well. But by 1988 almost everyone recognized that these campaign-controlled media appearances weren't true debates. Even less lively than ordinary press conferences, these debates do little to clarify issue positions or even to provide much sense of the candidates as people. Overprepared and wanting above all to avoid a big mistake, the candidates pitch short bits of their campaign stump speeches, always with an eye out for an opportunity to unleash a devastating one-liner that might dominate subsequent news accounts. These news accounts of the debates can sometimes be as important as the debates themselves in making a winner.

The presidential candidates participated in three debates during the 1992 presidential campaign. The debates were unusual in that Ross Perot, an independent candidate representing no established party, participated. *(Reuters/Bettmann Newsphotos)*

The three 1992 debates proved interesting for a couple of reasons. First, the structure of the debates was new. The two major party campaigns agreed that independent candidate Ross Perot and his vice-presidential running mate James Stockdale should be included in the debates. Then, spurred by the Presidential Debate Commission's recommendations, a variety of formats was used in the debates. The traditional panel of journalists asking alternating questions was supplemented with one debate with a talk show format (with questions from the studio audience).

Second, the dynamics of the debates were unique. President Bush was trailing in the polls and hoped to get a significant boost from the debates. The independent candidate, Ross Perot, hoped to return to a more competitive position following his reentry into the race. Bill Clinton's position in the debates was the most straightforward: He needed to avoid a disastrous mistake and assure voters that he was worthy of their trust. The diverse formats allowed for more give-and-take among the candidates. The vice-presidential debate degenerated into something reminiscent of a playground shouting match. In the end, the four events probably changed very few voters' minds, meaning that only Bill Clinton, the frontrunner, got what he wanted out of the debates.

Is there a future for presidential debates? On the positive side, they attract huge audiences, stimulate interest in the election, and give voters a chance to see the candidates side by side. Presidential debates also help citizens to learn more about the policy positions of the candidates, especially since many of the most *uninformed* citizens are attracted to the debates. As two political observers noted in reference to the 1976 debates, "Watching the debates increased the level of manifest information that all citizens had. . . . Those individuals who watched the debaters exhibited a heightened political awareness at exactly the time when political information is crucial."[18]

On the negative side, debates tend to emphasize the superficial; rarely do debates offer an in-depth discussion of issues. One political scientist characterizes debates as "the political version of the Indianapolis Speedway. What we're all there for . . . is to see somebody crack up in flames."[19] All too often, gaffes, hesitations, sweat on the upper lip, trivial errors, and the like overshadow the crucial discussion of issues and positions. The media usually focus more on the "winner" in each debate than on what was said or not said.

As currently organized, then, TV debates leave much to be desired. Improvements that have been suggested include having the candidates question each other, increasing the number of debates, and removing all format restrictions (a ploy that had limited success when used in preconvention debates among numerous candidates). One observer suggested that it might be revealing to set aside four or five hours during which candidates, alone on the stage, could verbally slug it out. Most of the trite, canned responses would be used up after the first two or three hours. Too grueling? Simply a pretest for the presidency itself. The whimsy of this suggestion at least points to the need to do *something* to increase the usefulness to citizens of debates as a means of evaluating candidates.

Media and "Horse Races"

Jimmy Carter made a telling remark in his 1976 campaign for president: "The only presidents I know who emphasized the issues were Presidents Dewey, Goldwater, and McGovern." Of course, none of these men won election, perhaps because they *were* more concerned with issues than image. The nature of the mass media works against issue-oriented candidates: It takes much time (in broadcasting) or space (in the print media) to explore issues, and time and space are at a premium in the media. Hence the disproportionate emphasis in the media on a candidate's personality, campaign strategy, and relative standing against rivals. These are features of the political "horse race," an inherently more colorful and exciting media subject than discussion of the issues. In a study conducted in 1975 and 1976, Thomas Patterson found that network news programs devoted 24 percent of their presidential campaign coverage to issue-related matters and 62 percent to the "horse race."[20] Studies of the 1984 and 1988 nominating process produced similar findings. Newspaper and television coverage of campaigns do not differ significantly in this respect.

Then, too, the candidates themselves often play down issues. In part this may be due to the centrist thrust of U.S. politics, which encourages the blurring of differences. Some candidates, calculating that an emphasis on issues will cost them votes, turn to personality factors and campaign hoopla to divert the public's attention. Others become personality candidates reluctantly, realizing that the media do not deal well with issues and that personality and television seem made for each other. Of course, issues are not entirely neglected, but in the extraordinarily lengthy U.S. presidential campaigns, they are usually eclipsed by other matters.

The Media and Campaign Negativity

Widespread concern about American elections has focused on the negative factors in recent campaigns. Negativity takes two related forms: exaggerated attention to character, resulting in the almost monomaniacal media search for personal weakness among candidates and the "feeding frenzy" that ensues upon its discovery, and the production of negative personal attacks by the campaigns themselves.

Larry Sabato, a noted observer of parties and elections in the United States, traces the development of the character factor as the central concern of media coverage. Character has always and naturally been a part of politics. But the frenzied search for particular examples of pesonal weakness blossomed in the 1970s and 1980s. "The press has become obsessed with gossip rather than governance; it prefers to employ titillation rather than scrutiny; as a result, its political coverage produces trivialization rather than enlightenment."[21] Besides distracting attention from genuine scandals of governance such as the collapse of the savings and loan industry in the late 1980s due to inadequate regulation and personal greed, and a corrosive effect on journalistic standards of accountability, the concentration on personal character weaknesses also reduces media access to candidates and government officials (why expose oneself unnecessarily?) and increases public cynicism about the press itself as well as encouraging broader cynicism about the political system.

Sabato feels that an earlier gentleman's agreement requiring press silence on personal matters, including such things as FDR's deteriorating health and John Kennedy's womanizing, went too far, leaving the public in the dark on matters of potential significance. He also feels that the "anything goes" rules of recent campaigns go too far in the other direction. Most important for Sabato is that media return to a standard that rejects the publication of unsubstantiated rumor. As *Washington Post* columnist David Broder says, "If you can't make the distinction between rumors and journalism, between gossip and journalism, then you're in the wrong business."[22] Since these issues involve complicated moral choices, we can expect disagreements about specific items to cover or to leave unreported. Some will argue that the distinction between widespread, politically significant conjecture and rumor is sometimes hard to establish. The important point is to engage public discussion of some line to distinguish what is appropriate political news from what is not. Since titillation tends to displace weightier matter, such a discussion is essential to reduce the shallowness and irrelevance of much of what passes for political reporting these days.

The second negative factor that haunts contemporary electoral campaigns is the widespread use of negative, personal attacks on opponents. Ad hominem attacks on electoral opponents are as old as the republic. In 1800, for example, Thomas Jefferson was characterized by the Federalists as "a mean-spirited, low-lived fellow, the son of a half-breed Indian squaw, squired by a Virginia mulatto father." The Jeffersonians responded with suggestions that John Adams wished to "become a King instead of a president" and spread rumors that Adams planned to marry his son to the daughter of King George III, thus bringing the United States back into the British fold. In 1864, *Harper's Weekly* published a list of "terms applied by the friends of General M'Clellan to the President: Filthy Story-Teller, Despot, Liar, Thief, Braggart, Buffoon, Usurper, Monster, Ignoramus Abe, Old Scoundrel, Perjurer, Robber, Swindler, Tyrant, Fiend, Butcher."[23] Lincoln did not respond.

But in spite of a long, lively tradition of opponent bashing, many observers notice a qualitative difference in the past quarter century. Negative appeals have assumed a larger role, displacing other sorts of campaign statements. In 1988, George Bush's handlers, for example, are reported to have sought a fifty-fifty split between the vice-president's positive statements and those meant to undermine support for his opponent.

Negative appeals themselves are a symptom, not a cause, of the electoral changes noted earlier in this chapter and in Chapter 9. With the transition to direct primaries, the reduced influence of political parties, and the resulting decreasing influence of party insiders in candidate selection, mass media have assumed a central role in electoral politics. The assumption became widespread that mass broadcast appeals could not engage in the serious exploration of ideas. Correspondingly, campaigns have become battles of images rather than ideas. Ideas require argumentation, which takes time. But images are the projection of a moment, aurally or visually. To make a point, the repetition of an image replaces the development of an idea. From this vantage point, six thirty-second spot ads are more effective than one five-minute speech.[24] In a battle of images, however, hanging a negative image on the opponent contributes as much to success as the creation of a positive image for oneself. Thus the negative campaign appeal achieves central importance both to the campaign itself and to the news coverage of the campaign. As a symptom of the larger transformation of American political campaigns, negative campaign appeals are not likely to disappear very soon. Recent, modest press efforts to hold candidates accountable for campaign statements may reduce outright falsification in negative spot ads but will not reduce the incentive to produce such ads. Opinion polls indicate high levels of citizen disgust at the negativity of recent campaigns. But until that disgust translates into electoral penalties for the sponsors of attack ads, the American public risks drowning in a flood of campaign mud.

Conclusions

American electoral politics leaves something to be desired as a spectator sport. The players appear and disappear. Contests drag on for months, even years. Elections have their moments, of course. Great amounts of cash are raised and spent; the news media do their share to give elections the excitement of horse races. But what do citizens gain from the extraordinary spectacle of political campaigning and from the ongoing media coverage of political life? Certainly less than they could.

From a democratic perspective, political campaigning in the United States has several serious shortcomings. Money plays far too substantial a role in the electoral process—and will continue to do so in the absence of fundamental reforms. Also, much of the campaign process drains meaning out of elections rather than instilling in the electorate a clear sense of the issues involved. Compared with most other democratic nations, the American way of selecting and electing candidates is very open, very long, and very complicated.

The media could enhance the democratic process considerably by striving for greater depth, placing more emphasis on issues than on aspects of the horse race, and seeking to educate rather than merely to entertain. If the media did a thorough job of fact-gathering and presented stories dramatically enough, presidential candidates would be forced to explain and defend their views on issues of concern to the electorate. And the public itself has an obligation to learn more about political life, to understand issues more clearly, and to demand more of both the media and the campaign process.

Most citizens have a sufficiently good idea of what is happening in political life to make reasoned retrospective judgments on an administration and its policies. Nevertheless, public ignorance abounds, much of it cultivated by candidates and not dispelled by the media. On balance, we can assert that even though our democratic electoral processes—and the media's role in campaigns—are less than satisfactory, they are not disastrously flawed.

GLOSSARY TERMS

blanket primary
closed primary
electoral college
Fairness Doctrine
focus group
Freedom of Information Act
imagemaking
incumbent

interelection stage
open primary
political action committee (PAC)
Pentagon Papers
primary election
sound bite
spot ad

NOTES

[1] See David E. Rosenbaum, "Recession and Reelection Don't Mix," *New York Times*, October 9, 1991, p. C1.

[2] Harold W. Stanley and Richard Niemi, *Vital Statistics on American Politics*, 3rd ed. (Washington, D.C.: Congressional Quarterly Press, p. 76).

[3] Richard Joslyn, *Mass Media and Elections* (Reading, Mass.: Addison-Wesley, 1984), pp. 273-296.

[4] See, for example, Benjamin I. Page, *Choices and Echoes in Presidential Elections* (Chicago: University of Chicago Press, 1978), pp. 223-227.

[5] California Fair Political Practices Commission.

[6] Herbert E. Alexander, *Financing Politics: Money, Elections, and Political Reform*, 4th ed. (Washington, D.C.: Congressional Quarterly Press, 1992), chap. 5.

[7] Frank J. Sorauf, *Money in American Elections* (Glenview, Ill.: Scott, Foresman, 1988), p. 301.

[8] For a careful study of the impact of state legislative party campaign committees, see Anthony Gierzynski, *Legislative Party Campaign Committees in the American States* (Lexington: University Press of Kentucky, 1992).

[9] *Buckley* v. *Valeo* (1976), 424 U.S. 1, and *Federal Election Commission* v. *National Conservative Political Action Committee* (1985), 470 U.S. 480.

[10] W. Lance Bennett, *The Governing Crisis: Media, Money, and Marketing in American Elections* (New York: St. Martin's Press, 1992), p. 53.

[11] Larry J. Sabato, *PAC Power: Inside the World of Political Action Committees* (New York: Norton, 1985), p. 126.

[12] Senator Thomas Eagleton, *New York Times*, February 3, 1983, p. B6.

[13] Bennett, *Governing Crisis*, p. 55.

[14] Doris A. Graber, *Processing the News: How People Tame the Information Tide* (White Plains, N.Y.: Longman, 1988), p. 266.

[15] Doris A. Graber, *Mass Media and American Politics* (Washington, D.C.: Congressional Quarterly Press, 1984), chap. 1; and Joslyn, *Mass Media and Elections*, chap. 1.

[16] Joslyn, *Mass Media and Elections*, intro.

[17]*Congressional Quarterly Weekly Report*, April 5, 1968. Reprinted by permission of Congressional Quarterly, Inc.

[18]Arthur H. Miller and Michael MacKuen, "Learning about the Candidates: The 1976 Presidential Debates," *Public Opinion Quarterly*, Fall 1979, p. 344.

[19]Nelson Polsby, *Time*, October 29, 1984, p. 31.

[20]*Washington Post*, December 5, 1976.

[21]Larry J. Sabato, *Feeding Frenzy: How Attack Journalism Has Transformed American Politics* (New York: Free Press, 1991), p. 6.

[22]Ibid., p. 222.

[23]"A History of Negative Campaigning," *Wigwag*, February 1991, p. 18–21.

[24]Kiku Adatto, "The Incredible Shrinking Sound Bite," *New Republic*, May 28, 1990.

SELECTED READINGS

Theodore H. White started a tradition of behind-the-scenes accounts of **presidential election campaigns** with *The Making of the President 1960*. That book, and each of the subsequent books White wrote covering elections through 1980, provides fast-paced, engaging reading about the American national election process and the important personalities in it. Every election now spawns accounts on the White model. They are usually heavily journalistic in approach, and although they provide a good introduction to the problems of elections, they can be supplemented by more academically oriented items such as Herbert B. Asher, *Presidential Elections and American Politics*, 5th ed. (Pacific Grove, Calif.: Brooks/Cole, 1992); and Stephen J. Wayne, *The Road to the White House, 1992* (New York: St. Martin's Press, 1992). For a good postmortem on the 1988 elections (both presidential and congressional campaigns), try Gerald Pomper et al., *The Elections of 1988: Reports and Interpretations* (Chatham, N.J.: Chatham House, 1989). For a good collection of essays on a range of issues surrounding campaigns, see Benjamin Ginsberg and Alan Stone, eds., *Do Elections Matter?* 2nd ed. (Armonk, N.Y.: Sharpe, 1991). A very thorough look at one small part of presidential campaigns, the **national convention**, can be found in Larry David Smith and Dan Nimmo, *Cordial Concurrence: Orchestrating National Party Conventions in the Telepolitical Age* (New York: Praeger, 1991). For a comparative perspective on presidential campaigns, see John Gaffney, ed., *The French Presidential Elections of 1988: Ideology and Leadership in Contemporary France* (Brookfield, Vt.: Gower, 1989).

Presidential debates, though not academic themselves, have gotten a lot of academic attention. See Susan A. Hellweg et al., *Televised Presidential Debates: Advocacy in Contemporary America* (New York: Praeger, 1992); Kathleen Hall Jamieson and David S. Birdsell, *Presidential Debates: The Challenge of Creating an Informed Electorate* (New York: Oxford University Press, 1988); and James B. Lemert et al., *News Verdicts, the Debates, and Presidential Campaigns* (New York: Praeger, 1991).

On **national campaign financing**, start with Herbert E. Alexander, *Financing Politics: Money, Elections, and Political Reform*, 4th ed. (Washington, D.C.: Congressional Quarterly Press, 1992). A couple of very rich reference sources on campaign contributions and expenditures are Larry Makinson, *Open Secrets: The Encyclopedia of Congressional Money and Politics* (Washington, D.C.: Congressional Quarterly Press, 1992); and Sara Fritz and Dwight Morris, *Handbook of Campaign Spending: Money in the 1990 Congressional Races* (Washington, D.C.: Congressional Quarterly Press, 1992). For a careful empirical analysis of congressional campaign funding, see John Theilmann and Al Wilhite, *Discrimination and Congressional Campaign*

Contributions (New York: Praeger, 1991). For a comparative perspective on campaign financing, see K. D. Ewing, *The Funding of Political Parties in Britain* (New York: Cambridge University Press, 1987).

To understand the complexity of **campaign finance reform**, consult David B. Magleby and Candice J. Nelson, *The Money Chase: Congressional Campaign Finance Reform* (Washington, D.C.: Brookings Institution, 1990); and Margaret Latus Nugent and John R. Johannes, eds., *Money, Elections, and Democracy: Reforming Congressional Campaign Finance* (Boulder, Colo.: Westview Press, 1990).

A good treatment of **media and politics** is Michael Parenti, *Inventing Reality: The Politics of the Mass Media* (New York: St. Martin's Press, 1986). On politics and the explicitly fictional, see Parenti's *Make-Believe Media: The Politics of Entertainment* (New York: St. Martin's Press, 1992). Other treatments of media and politics are Edwin Diamond, *The Media Show: The Changing Face of the News* (Cambridge, Mass.: MIT Press, 1991); Philip M. Seib, *Who's in Charge? How the Media Shape News and Politicians Win Votes*, Dallas: Taylor, 1987); and Doris A. Graber, *Mass Media and American Politics*, 3rd ed. (Washington, D.C.: Congressional Quarterly Press, 1989).

For more information on **political advertising**, see Montague Kern, *30-Second Politics: Political Advertising in the Eighties* (New York: Praeger, 1989); and Diane L. Barthel, *Putting On Appearances: Gender and Advertising* (Philadelphia: Temple University Press, 1988).

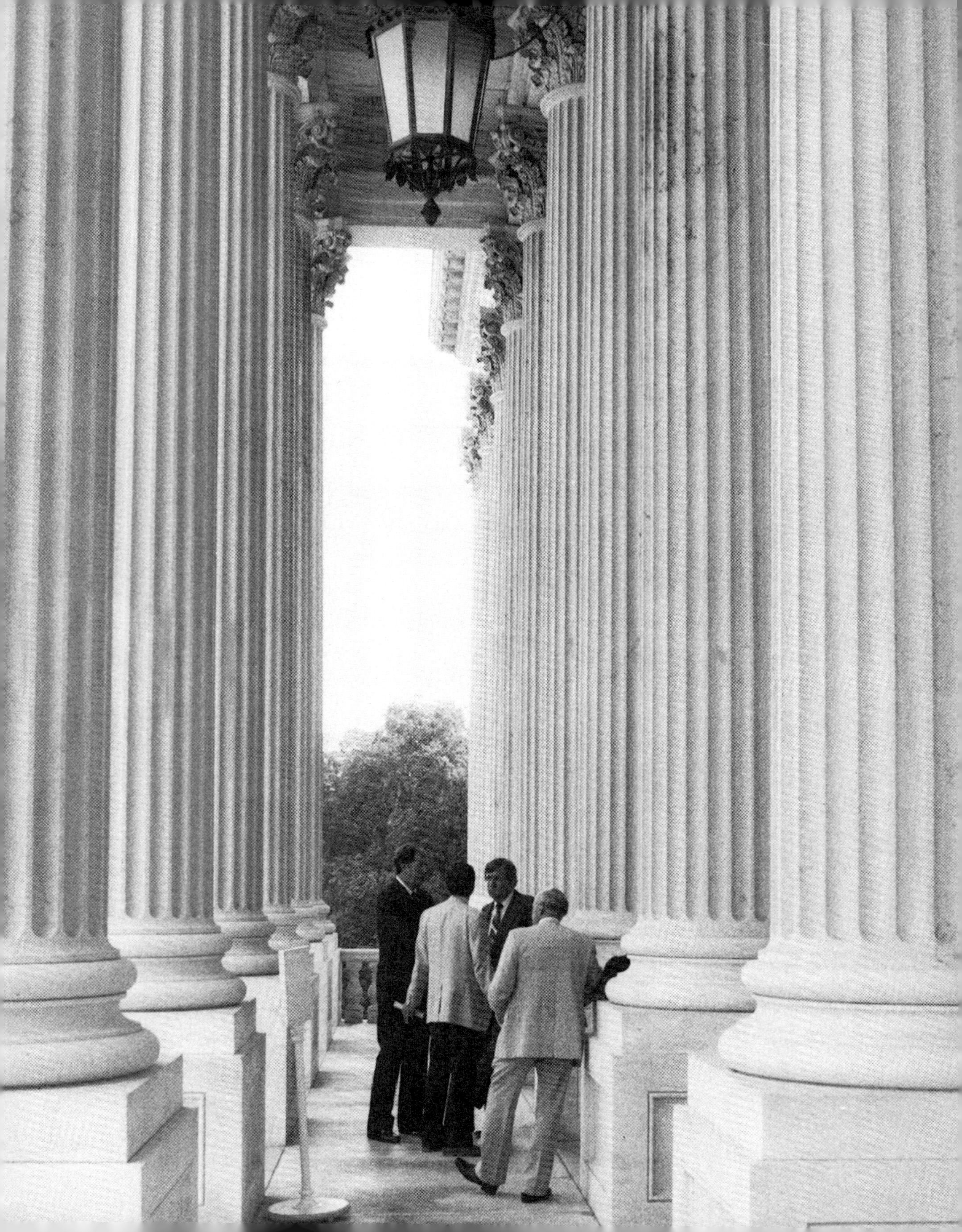

CHAPTER ELEVEN

INTEREST GROUP POLITICS

Democracy to the Highest Bidder?

CHAPTER OUTLINE

Interest Group Dynamics

FUNCTIONS OF INTEREST GROUPS
PROBLEMS WITH INTEREST GROUPS
POLITICAL SUBSYSTEMS

Major Interest Groups

BUSINESS
LABOR
THE DEFENSE BUDGET, THE DEFENSE LOBBY, AND THE PEACE LOBBY
PUBLIC-INTEREST GROUPS
SINGLE-ISSUE GROUPS

How Lobbying Works

INSIDER STRATEGIES
OUTSIDER STRATEGIES
LOBBYING TARGET GROUPS

Regulation and the Public Interest

REGULATORY EFFORTS
GOVERNMENT AND INTEREST GROUPS

FOR SAVINGS AND LOAN INSTITUTIONS—THE SO-CALLED THRIFT industry—the 1980s were the best of times and the worst of times. For the first part of the decade the industry was riding high, with individual players scoring huge profits as many institutions experienced vast expansion. By the third quarter, however, the industry's fortunes had changed so much for the worse that references to the "S&L crisis" gave way to ubiquitous talk of the "S&L scandal." Rapid expansion had been achieved at the expense of prudent investment policy. Many S&Ls failed outright. Federal and state criminal charges were lodged against S&L officers. Even the president's son, Neil M. Bush, was served a cease-and-desist order by the Office of Thrift Supervision for ethical improprieties as a director of a Denver-based savings and loan. The federal agency responsible for insuring depositors' investments, the FSLIC, itself went broke. Taxpayers were left footing a cleanup bill that by some estimates would run to $500 billion. What happened?

The most generous characterization of the thrift industry's problems was that spurred by the bullish business optimism and deregulatory fervor of the Reagan era, thrifts moved improvidently into high-risk, high-yield investments ("junk bonds") and also failed to foresee a major contraction in real estate. Less generous characterizations portray an industry driven by short-term calculations of personal gain propped up by questionable and even illegal links between the thrifts themselves, the industry's regulators, and elected officials willing to exert influence for anyone able to make a generous campaign contribution. By one tally, the thrift industry donated more than $10 million to members of Congress during the 1980s.[1] Republican Senator (later Governor) Pete Wilson of California received the largest amount from S&L sources, a total of $243,334. But California's other senator, Democrat Alan Cranston, did even better, with $143,700 in direct contributions and $850,000 donated to voter registration programs he backed. This latter sum was donated by the owner of Lincoln Savings and Loan, Charles H. Keating, Jr.

Throughout the period, most savings and loans were managed both competently and honestly. Some were mismanaged, however, and ended up in trouble. And a few spectacular cases of improper and incompetent management provided front-page headlines and a useful reminder of the nature of interest group politics in a democratic system like ours. One case in particular became the symbol of the problems: Charles Keating, Alan Cranston, and Lincoln Savings and Loan.

A bitter feud between Lincoln Savings and Loan and federal thrift regulators began in 1985. Officials' charges that Lincoln's rapid, high-risk, growth had violated federal regulations were characterized as a "vendetta" by Lincoln's owner, Keating. He sought the help of powerful elected officials in return, most notably the senators who would come to be known as the Keating Five (in addition to Cranston, Democrats John Glenn of Ohio; Donald W. Riegle, Jr., of Michigan; and Dennis De Concini of Arizona; and Republican John McCain of Arizona). These five and other elected officials got campaign contributions from Keating and Lincoln. The senators and their staff members contacted and sometimes met with federal regulators to inquire about and express concern about the regulators' actions, urging quick action in matters that had been in process for years. The chairman of the Federal Home Bank Board, Edwin J. Gray, testified before the Senate Ethics Committee that the senators had subjected him to "years of private threats and public vilification" designed to pressure the board to alter its policies to favor Keating and Lincoln Savings.[2] The senators asserted that their inquiries represented normal constituent service—like asking after a lost social security check or recommending a son to a service academy. There was, the senators stated, no link between the inquiries and the contributions. (Keating, a bit imprudently, suggested that *he* thought there was a link.) Was this normal government or blatant corruption?

The Senate Ethics Committee hearings on charges against the Keating Five concluded the following:

> that all of the contributions to the senators were within legal limits and were properly reported, as were contributions solicited by the senators for state party organizations, PACs and voter registration organizations;

> that none of the senators' actions considered alone violated any law or broke any Senate rule;

that four of the Five may have demonstrated "poor judgment" (Glenn); or "aggressive conduct with the regulators [that] was inappropriate" (DeConcini); or "conduct [that] gave the appearance of being improper and was certainly attended with insensitivity and poor judgment" (Riegle); the least damaging finding was that McCain's actions "were not improper nor attended with gross negligence and did not reach the level of requiring institutional action against him";

that none of the activity of these four required institutional action by the Senate;

that, in contrast, Cranston "engaged in an impermissible pattern of conduct in which fund raising and official activities were substantially linked."[3]

In the meantime, Cranston had been diagnosed with cancer and had announced his intention to retire from the Senate. He was formally censured by the Senate but maintained throughout that he had been unfairly singled out—that his action did not deviate from Senate norms. Keating was convicted of criminal charges in the conduct of Lincoln Savings and Loan. The cost to the government of originally postponing action on Lincoln Savings was estimated at $1.2 billion.

The most remarkable part of the Lincoln Savings mess was the defense offered by Cranston (and other elected officials accused of impropriety): not denials or explanations but the assertion that the behavior in question was common practice. Even the Senate Ethics Committee seemed to agree that the difference, if there was one, was a matter of degree. The link between contributions and "service" had gotten too close. The shadings among the Keating Five were too subtle for some observers to see, but the Senate was satisfied. Later, Senator Terry Sanford of North Carolina (chosen chair of the Senate Ethics Committee subsequent to the Keating investigation) reportedly said of the Keating senators: "These people didn't do a damn thing wrong," adding that their accusers were "god-damn little regulators who were just really jerks."[4]

Several top officials of the Reagan administration had become entangled in similar controversies. Michael Deaver, Reagan's appointments secretary and close friend, was found guilty of perjury in testimony about his alleged influence peddling after leaving the White House. Lyn Nofziger, former White House political director, was convicted of violating a law that prohibits senior government officials from lobbying their former colleagues for at least a year after leaving office. After studying charges of influence peddling by Attorney General Edwin Meese, a special prosecutor raised questions about Meese's ethical standards but did not recommend criminal prosecution. Under pressure from Congress and public-interest organizations, Meese resigned.

In 1989 the Speaker of the House, Jim Wright, and the House majority whip, Tony Coelho, each resigned in separate ethics scandals involving gifts and favors. These resignations followed but were unrelated to a wave of negative publicity arising from the too direct involvement of members of Congress and their staffs in Department of Defense weapons procurement contracts. To many Americans, this series of influence-peddling scandals meant that political life at the highest levels was riddled with corruption; powerful groups purchased influence and traded on the contacts of highly placed officials to win favored treatment.

Does corruption underlie all efforts to organize and seek political influence? If so, we would be in deep trouble, because individuals and groups of various stripes work to influence the political process at all levels. In fact, the vast majority of organized efforts to influence the political system are entirely legitimate—and often noble. Consider the National Association for the Advancement of Colored People's (NAACP) decades-long legal battle to end segregation in public education, or the efforts of a local tenants' group to protest the town board to prevent the quick-profit conversion of their apartments to unaffordable condominiums.

If we surveyed the American political process overall, we would find a vast proliferation of groups seeking to influence politics in various ways. As in any democratic nation, these range from highly organized and well-financed groups to various ad hoc coalitions that spring up in response to particular problems and later disappear.

Seeking influence is an everyday part of our political process. Because interest groups come in all shapes and sizes, and their goals and tactics are as varied as their makeup, it is important to ask whose interests are represented most effectively? Which groups get the lion's share of benefits that the political process has to offer, and why? How do these groups make themselves felt in the political process? Is this complicated system of pressure group politics democratic? fair? reasonable? We will now take up these questions as we explore the dynamics of interest groups, the major interest groups, how lobbying works, and regulation, representation, and the public interest.

Interest Group Dynamics

Democratic politics lends itself naturally to group activity. People in all democratic societies tend to coalesce around shared interests and ideas. Concerns about wage scales or job security might lead a person to join a union or some other work-related association. The same person might also contribute to an environmental group because of worries about pollution of a nearby recreational lake. This citizen might also take an interest in better town recreational facilities and hence attend town meetings or sign petitions. Finally, our hypothetical American might join a synagogue or church and thereby affirm his or her religious identity—representing a *potential* interest that might be activated under certain circumstances. In U.S. society, such interests spring naturally from the country's economic, religious, regional, ethnic, and racial diversity.

Traditionally, the United States has been characterized as a nation of joiners. Foreigners often marvel at this aspect of American life. In the early 1800s, Alex de Tocqueville remarked:

> The Americans make associations to give entertainments, to found seminaries, to build inns, to construct churches, to diffuse books, to send missionaries to the antipodes; in this manner they found hospitals, prisons and schools. If it is proposed to inculcate some truth or to foster some feeling by the encouragement of a great example, they form a society. Wherever at the head of some new undertaking you see the government in France, or a man of rank in England, in the United States you will be sure to find an association.[5]

This observation remains pertinent today. According to public opinion polls, about 40 percent of Americans are active in at least one organization, and 40 percent of those are affiliated with more than one group. Group membership is closely related to social class and education, however. Better-educated, middle-class people are much more likely to be joiners, which means that their views are usually better represented in the political process.[6]

Organizations that direct their efforts toward political influence are called **interest groups**. Though this term has fewer negative connotations than *pressure group*, a term popular in the past, interest groups can effectively pressure legislators, bureaucrats, and public officials. We now examine the various functions of interest groups and problems for democracy inherent in interest group politics.

Functions of Interest Groups

Interest groups coalesce for various reasons. Some groups serve mainly *symbolic* functions: Ethnic, religious, or racial associations, for example, generally seek to bolster their members' sense of group identity. Such groups may also seek to affirm the symbolic significance of their members' identity in relation to the rest of society. In lobbying to make Rev. Martin Luther King, Jr.'s birthday a national holiday, black groups were making such a symbolic statement.

Economic functions naturally loom large in the aims of many interest groups. Often interest groups promote the economic well-being of whole classes of people or sets of institutions, such as doctors or hospitals. Trade unions and business associations work almost exclusively to further the economic interests of their members.

Groups may also pursue a whole range of noneconomic policy goals. Such goals range from building a monument to Vietnam War dead or ending the use of the stars-and-bars Confederate flag to the preservation of historic sites. Some groups focus on more *ideological* concerns. This category includes People for the American Way (liberal causes), Americans for Constitutional Action (conservative causes), and Common Cause (honest, open government). Because particular issues and overall ideologies tend to blend together, groups seeking specific economic benefits and those pursuing ideological goals often find themselves working toward common ends.

Finally, groups may serve *informational* functions, disseminating information on matters of interest to members and to policymakers. The environmental group Friends of the Earth, for example, publishes a magazine that keeps members up-to-date on environmental issues and related public policy questions.

Problems with Interest Groups

Though interest groups certainly deserve a place in the political arena, the proliferation of such groups has created serious problems in democratic life. As far back as the Constitutional Convention, James Madison warned of the deleterious effects of "factions" on the political process; in his eyes, factions represented potentially dangerous

Interest groups are ubiquitous. Part of democracy is the right to organize and make one's views effectively heard. But how are different interests to be sensibly balanced? (Paul Conklin/Monkmeyer Press Photos)

social elements that by nature would oppose the public interest. In Madison's view, succinctly argued in *Federalist* No. 10, the only way to counteract the dangers was to pit factions against one another so that no majority faction could tyrannize the larger society. This image of counterbalancing factions reflects a commonly held view of the U.S. political process: Because each group is counterbalanced by other groups, no one interest group possesses enough power to impose its views on a wide range of issues.

It would be comforting to think that the network of interest groups is so well balanced that the "public interest" (however that is defined) is ultimately served. Unfortunately, this is often not the case. The system is heavily biased in favor of groups that have the resources that matter most—money, organizational clout, and political and social legitimacy—skewing power disproportionately. The effectiveness of interest groups, in other words, is not determined by the size of their memberships or the intellectual or social merit of their goals.

The interest group system also fosters the decidedly undemocratic notion that some people's views are more important than others': Throughout U.S. history many potential interests have lacked effective representation. When the U.S. Constitution was drafted, for example, all women, all blacks, and white males with little property were shut out of the political process. Groups lacking effective representation must battle—often violently and at considerable cost—to break into the system of group politics. The barriers facing these groups can be daunting: They must overcome the psychological barrier of being ignored or scorned by the rest of society; they may also need to overcome legal hurdles, such as those that confronted blacks and women in their decades-long battles for equal rights; and new groups, especially, may lack the resources of more experienced and better-financed groups.

Ironically, causes with almost universal appeal—such as drives to promote clean air and safe consumer goods—are often the most difficult to organize. Some observers argue that broadly shared interests rarely capture the imagination of prospective supporters, and organizational success therefore eludes them. For potential members of groups dedicated to such causes, it may be hard to see how joining the group will make much difference; that is, the payoffs for joining an interest group dealing with diffuse public issues are usually exceeded by the costs of joining and acquiring information. Nonetheless, such groups do exist and often prosper.

Narrowly focused interest groups, in contrast, can count on staunch support because the people directly affected by a specific public policy have a strong incentive to organize. Suppose, for example, that regulations allowing competition in the sale of eyeglasses were proposed. Consumers might benefit from such regulations, but most of them would have only a vague idea of how those regulations would affect them. Opticians, however, surely would organize to lobby *against* regulations that would, in effect, force them to lower prices. Here we see a chronic problem of interest group politics: Widely shared interests that affect many people slightly are less likely to prompt an organized response than narrowly shared interests that affect a few people more deeply.

A related problem stems from the subtlety of most interest group activity: The process of influence seeking is often hidden from public scrutiny. Interest group lobbying frequently resembles subtle osmosis much more than pressurized arm-twisting. Critics decry this cozy arrangement, charging that it circumvents the open, public debate so crucial to the exercise of democracy.

Political Subsystems

In talking about interest groups, some observers have found it useful to distinguish **political subsystems** from the overarching political system. **Macropolitics**, or high politics, involves major political figures like presidents and congressional leaders, the mass media, the general public, and whole branches of government. Large areas of policy are hammered out in this system. But the macropolitical system cannot possibly deal with all of the policy matters that must be addressed by government these days. Political subsystems develop to handle the hundreds of issues that never reach the level of macropolitics.

James A. Thurber offers a typology of political subsystems: *Dominant* subsystems are those in which a few actors are better organized and tend to dominate more passive interests. *Competitive* subsystems display genuine competition among major players. These might also be characterized as policy interest networks (players might still interact systematically but compete for different outcomes, or there might be a large number of active players in the subsystem, as is the case with agricultural policy in the United States). And *disintegrated* subsystems result from changed circumstances and shifts of power and are usually not able to produce policy at all. An example of a disintegrated system can be found, according to Thurber, following the 1973 OPEC oil embargo. What had been "a classic closed, dominant policy subsystem over import quotas, oil depletion allowances, pricing and distribution, and other key petroleum public policies" disintegrated with the energy shortage of 1973–1974. The energy crisis disrupted the old subsystem, brought in a variety of new players, and effectively precluded the development of systematic energy policy for over a decade. No competent subsystem existed for making policy; the macropolitical system was equally inadequate. Thurber contends that the old dominant subsystem revived and reassembled itself, reasserting control over energy policy without fanfare during the Reagan administration. Even below political subsystems is the area of micropolitics, in which "narrowly focused decision making [involves] a very small, often-closed group of decision makers."[7]

We now turn to an examination of some of the major clusters of interest groups in the United States and to some of the major players within those clusters.

Major Interest Groups

In U.S. politics, several key interests exert a disproportionate measure of influence on decision making at all levels. We now examine how and why business, labor, the defense and peace lobbies, public-interest groups, and single-issue groups gained such prominence in the American political arena.

Business

The interests of people in business cover a wide spectrum. An executive of a large corporation who comes to Washington to lobby for restrictions on Japanese imports has little in common with a local florist who needs a small business loan. Small businesses seek protection against larger rivals. Businesses in depressed areas lobby for government aid, whereas those that prosper generally oppose such assistance. Import policies often spark business rivalry. Accordingly, the business community does not always speak with one voice, and splits within that community often lead to political conflict. In fact, several major pieces of business legislation, such as the Interstate

Commerce Act and the Sherman Antitrust Act, originated in the efforts of smaller companies to protect themselves against larger competitors.

Nevertheless, a certain degree of unity does mark the business community. Generally, business interests oppose tax increases, support restrictions on the power of organized labor, press for cuts in government regulation of business, favor protection against foreign competition, and encourage government to create a favorable climate in which business and investment can grow.

Major business organizations include the Chamber of Commerce, with a membership of more than 180,000 businesses and individuals and a budget of $65 million in 1991; the National Association of Manufacturers (NAM), representing the interests of "big business"; and the Business Roundtable, which represents 190 large companies through the lobbying efforts of high-level business executives.

Specific industries are represented by a host of other groups, such as the Associated Milk Producers, the National Cotton Council, and the American Meat Institute.

Because government programs affect so many businesses, business interests engage in many forms of influence seeking. They attempt to shape public opinion through advertising. They lobby extensively in Washington, D.C., and the various state capitals. They litigate to delay and defeat regulatory legislation. They seek the appointments to top administration positions of people favorable to business. They fund campaigns and support candidates. We will examine several of these strategies later in this chapter.

The connections between interest groups and legislators sometimes become quite relaxed—even silly and odd. Here Representative Bill Emerson and Senator William Cohen model shoes made in their states. Legislators have to be concerned about local interests, or their constituents may take offense. *(Art Stein/Photo Researchers)*

Labor

Most American workers do not belong to labor unions. At their peak, in the 1950s, unions claimed almost 25 percent of the work force. That figure has now declined to about 16 percent. American unions do wield political clout, but they are weaker than those in any other advanced industrial democratic nation.

For most of U.S. history only a very small sector of the economy was organized by unions. Until the Great Depression and the prolabor New Deal of the 1930s, only the skilled crafts, such as carpentry and other building trades, and railroad workers were organized to any significant extent. The Congress of Industrial Organizations, which organized industrial workers in auto, steel, and other major industries, spearheaded the rapid expansion of unionization in the 1930s. After a period of intense rivalry, the CIO and the much older American Federation of Labor merged in 1955 to form the AFL-CIO. Despite the importance of several large individual unions, the AFL-CIO remains labor's paramount organization and the source of most of its politically directed activity.

The AFL-CIO attempts to influence national politics on a whole array of domestic issues—social welfare, employment, job training, minimum wages, child labor, occupational health and safety, consumer protection, the tax code. Individual unions often lobby separately for their own agendas. Sometimes labor and business find themselves on the same side of an issue, as when both try to get government help to improve the competitive position of an industry.

Since the end of world War II, labor has also played a major role in shaping U.S. foreign policy. The AFL-CIO frequently gave aid to anticommunist organizations in other societies, sometimes with help from the Central Intelligence Agency. Many unions supported the Vietnam War, and in the 1972 presidential election found themselves at odds on this issue with the hierarchy of the Democratic party, with which labor had long been affiliated.

Labor's overriding political strategy has been to work within the Democratic party. Few unions overtly support Republican candidates, although both Richard Nixon and Ronald Reagan were endorsed by some segments of organized labor. The AFL-CIO's Committee on Political Education (COPE) amounted to one of the nation's most powerful political action committees long before such organizations began to proliferate in the 1970s. COPE provides indirect funds and services for Democratic candidates by mailing campaign literature, making phone calls, getting out the vote, and other activities.

As for lobbying, the AFL-CIO carries the most clout among labor interest groups. Its 106 affiliated unions, representing everyone from teachers and plumbers to meat cutters and garment workers, enlist some 14 million dues-paying members; counting the families involved, the organization actually represents close to 50 million Americans. The AFL-CIO also supports three hundred lobbyists who work on behalf of fifty member unions, along with hundreds of local pressure groups in all states and congressional districts. On issues considered crucial to all of labor, such as minimum-wage legislation, leaders mobilize the entire organization. On other issues only particular affiliates take an interest. Sometimes portions of the organization clash on goals or strategies; at other times the leadership and the rank-and-file find themselves at odds.

Other active union lobbies include those fielded by the United Mine Workers, the United Auto workers, and the Teamsters. Overall, though, labor's record since World War II has not been impressive on issues closely related to its immediate interests. For the most part, organized labor has been fighting a defensive battle since 1950.

The Defense Budget, the Defense Lobby, and the Peace Lobby

Even during times of major cutbacks, defense is very big business—$291 billion dollars in 1992. And defense spending, through ripple effects, creates a very large number of jobs—perhaps as many as thirty-five thousand for every $1 billion spent. The end of the Cold War confronted American pluralism with a dramatic challenge, with billions of dollars up for grabs. What part of the money formerly spent on defense ought to be redirected to nonmilitary uses? The $6 trillion spent in the four decades following World War II to confront and contain communism had created a huge "military-industrial complex," in President Eisenhower's phrase—an interdependent network of the military establishment and industries producing military matériel that together exert a powerful influence on foreign and economic policy. Large segments of the U.S. economy are directly or indirectly dependent on defense spending. In California perhaps one job in ten is defense-related. The fight to avoid cutting a particular weapon system may pit the intersts of one state or congressional district against another. As one senator put it:

> I think the pressures on Congress from the [military-industrial] complex are great and often successful when they shouldn't be. . . . Part of the problem is that we have a democratic government and every member of Congress is going to try and get as much for his district or state as he can. That's the price we pay for democratic government.[8]

Procurement and base placement practices have made defense spending a prime target of economic interest group activity. Many defense contractors work exclusively for the Department of Defense, staking their very survival on continued defense spending. The number of top defense contractors, however, is rather small. In the 1980s, ten companies received more than 30 percent of all large defense contracts and almost 50 percent of all research and development contracts given out by the Department of Defense. Under these conditions, the contractors themselves naturally become powerful lobbyists for policies and weapon systems that might sustain their business. The Rockwell Corporation, for example, produced and made one hundred prints of the film *The Threat: What Can One Do?* which dealt with the need to build the B-1 bomber. The film was then shown to the public and members of Congress. Rockwell maintained that this project represented merely a public relations effort and therefore was a deductible business expense. Government tax auditors took a different view: They considered the film part of an extensive lobbying effort to get the government to build the B-1 and to guarantee that Rockwell got the contract.

The defense lobby has strong allies among members of Congress, who want to protect jobs and contracts back home, and among Department of Defense bureaucrats, who want to maintain weapon systems and other military programs. Sometimes this kind of alliance develops into an **iron triangle** (see **Figure 11-1**). Typically, it involves a set of interest groups, a portion of the federal bureaucracy, and a congressional committee or some members of a committee. The three sides of the triangle reinforce one another in a strong, protective framework of mutual influence, all in a political subsystem that makes policy outside the glare of normal publicity. People will move from one part of the triangle to another, strengthening the mutuality of interests. Defense Department employees and members of the armed forces frequently find jobs in the defense industry. Defense industry employees may find themselves in the Defense Department. Unless major controversy lifts a set of issues out of this political subsystem onto the larger stage of national debate, the iron triangle effectively makes policy uncontested within its own area. Political scientist Gordon Adams says, "Once molded, the triangle sets with the rigidity of iron. The three participants exert strenuous efforts to keep isolated and protected from outside points of view." Under these conditions, the defense contractors "not only carry out military policy, but often create it."[9]

In the face of decreasing demand for military hardware at home, the defense industry increasingly seeks to sell its merchandise abroad—and the Pentagon is happy to help. The Defense Department takes its U.S.-made planes and tanks to overseas arms

FIGURE 11-1

THE TRADITIONAL IRON TRIANGLE IN DEFENSE

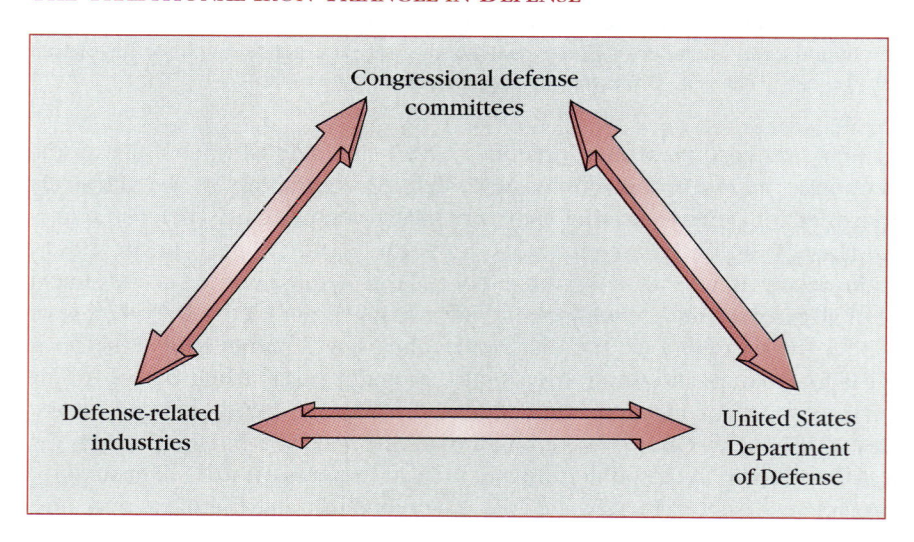

trade fairs—sometimes running up a tab for fuel and maintenance of as much as $1 million per show. American taxpayers foot the bill while the U.S. arms manufacturers take orders and make profits.[10] Meanwhile, the world has become a more volatile place as regional conflicts, fought with equipment designed and manufactured by the major powers, flourish.

The defense budget also becomes the focus of another set of interest groups, sometimes called the peace lobby. These often ideological groups seek to change the role of the United States in the world and to eliminate what are seen as the domestic dislocations of a very large defense establishment. A variety of groups are active in this area, from SANE, a primarily antinuclear weapons group, to Common Cause, which in 1982 branched out from its founding focus on participation and process issues to take up opposition to the MX missile (a land-based intercontinental ballistic missile that was an important part of the Carter and Reagan administrations' plans for "upgrading" America's nuclear arsenal). Although Common Cause did not have subject area expertise in defense issues, its general expertise in mobilizing public opinion and lobbying on Capitol Hill allowed it to play an important coordinating role in the fight against the MX. The anti-MX effort, boosted by the nuclear freeze movement, resulted in a compromise decision in 1985 to cap at fifty the production of this controversial missile, officially (and euphemistically) known as the Peacekeeper.

Times of great change make for hard choices; hard choices make for much interest group attention. The defense lobby and the peace lobby had their work cut out in the early 1990s. How much could the country afford to reduce its military spending? How would the country manage a "build-down" without massive dislocations in areas and industries heavily oriented toward defense? How were we to evaluate new justifications for programs whose old justifications ended with the end of the Cold War? For example, the Strategic Defense Initiative, a huge set of programs designed to counter a large Soviet nuclear threat, was repackaged by the Bush administration to provide GPALS (pronounced "gee, pals"), global protection against limited strikes. Was this offering the best tool for a pressing need or an example of the Big Rationalization? Effective lobbying organizations must sometimes affect the *terms* of the debate and not just its outcome.

Public-Interest Groups

The rise of public-interest lobbies has been one of the most significant developments in recent U.S. political history. One student of the subject defines **public-interest groups** as organizations that seek "a collective good, the achievement of which will not selectively and materially benefit the membership or activists of the organization."[11]

Common Cause and the Ralph Nader consumer protection and investigative organizations are the most prominent of the general-purpose public-interest lobbies. **Common Cause**, founded in 1970 by former Health, Education and Welfare Secretary John

Gardner, attracted 100,000 members in its first six months of existence. In the 1980s its membership stood at about 240,000, down from 300,000 during the Watergate days of 1974. Common Cause has both a paid staff and a volunteer force working out of its Washington office. It frequently focuses on procedural issues, such as open-hearings requirements in Congress, because it believes that better procedures will yield more honest policymaking. Common Cause also supports public campaign financing and reform of the lobbying disclosure laws.

Ralph Nader's career as a consumer activist and the strong network of public-interest organizations he helped to create constitute an extraordinary story in recent U.S. political life. Nader started his career as a champion of the ordinary citizen by taking on some of the biggest targets in U.S. industry—beginning in the mid-1960s with General Motors, whose Corvair he attacked as "unsafe at any speed." In Nader's battle with GM, the consumer activist won a decisive victory: congressional passage of the Motor Vehicle Safety Act of 1966. But that was just the beginning. Nader's efforts have spawned at least fifteen public-interest groups, focused on consumer issues, environmental concerns, health, science, regulatory reform, energy, and other matters.

A middle-aged Ralph Nader speaks in 1992. A crusader for what he regards as the "public interest," Nader has been an important figure on the American political scene and our leading consumer advocate. *(AP/Wide World Photos)*

In the 1960s—the springtime of consumer activism—fourteen major pieces of consumer legislation passed Congress with the help of public-interest-group lobbying. These bills dealt with auto safety, credit bureaus, drugs, flammable fabrics, interstate land sales, natural gas pipeline safety, postal fraud, poultry inspection, product safety, toy safety, truth in lending, truth in packaging, and meat wholesaling.

Not all consumer group efforts, however, have been so successful. The Food and Drug Administration (FDA), for example, has been widely criticized for its allegedly cozy relationship with the industries it regulates. Drives to reform the FDA have had only limited success, and battles continue over issues such as adequate testing of food additives. Controversies over new food labeling requirements reflect the FDA's mixed concern for consumers and food processors. The Consumer Product Safety Commission (CPSC), created in 1972, has also come under fire for its lax enforcement of product safety regulations. In addition, the CPSC has been hampered in its work by two major setbacks, a series of budget reductions and an erosion of its powers.

Despite these reverses, public-interest groups have achieved notable success in U.S. political life. By tapping the resilient capacity for middle-class activism and youthful idealism in the country, they pinpoint weaknesses and problems in politics and social life—particularly problems created by entrenched powers in the economy, Congress, and the government bureaucracy. Public-interest organizations also disseminate information vital to consumers. Had Ralph Nader not researched the Corvair and published a book warning of its design flaws, very few Americans would have realized how unsafe its design was. Public-interest organizations have repeatedly revealed—and thereby shaken up—long-standing relationships among industry interest groups, regulatory agencies, and Congress.

The David-and-Goliath struggles waged by public-interest organizations pit groups whose finances, organizational clout, and recognized legitimacy pale beside those of their adversaries. In addition, since public-interest groups are often critical of the political process itself, they tend to provoke the antagonism of key political players whose support they need in the long run. Yet they carry a few large rocks in their slingshot: They draw support from a deep well of public idealism; they tap the widespread discontent many alienated Americans feel with the political process; and unlike most other interest groups, they are not looking out for their own narrow interests.

In recent years some public-interest activists have joined the political establishment. Cities, states, and the federal government have set up consumer protection agencies, for example, and many former activists now make and enforce policy. As Carol Tucker Foreman, former president of the Consumer Federation of America, stated: "You score your points now by negotiation, by data, not by marching around the White House." Some people in business have also become more attentive to the rights of the consumer; most major corporations now respond to consumer complaints through their own consumer affairs departments. The nature of the issues has changed as well. As Stuart M. Statlee of the U.S. Consumer Product Safety Committee said, "The problems that remain are much more esoteric, much more complicated . . . and in some ways much more costly.[12]

Single-Issue Groups

A **single-issue group** is a well-organized and intensely active organization that focuses exclusively on one issue or set of issues. Among the best known of these groups are the pro- and antiabortion organizations, environmental and consumer groups, and the gun lobby. These groups consider their focus of concern as paramount; for some, support for or opposition to individual legislators rides on lawmakers' views on a single issue. Such groups have enjoyed a measure of success in state and national politics,

James Brady, former press secretary to Ronald Reagan, gives the thumbs-up sign. Brady was wounded and permanently disabled in the assassination attempt on Reagan in 1981. He and his wife Sarah (standing behind him) became active campaigners for gun-control legislation. The "Brady Bill," calling for a seven-day waiting period for purchase of a handgun, was eventually passed by Congress but vetoed by President Bush. Brady called Congress "gutless" on gun control. *(Reuters/Bettmann Newsphotos)*

and they have proliferated. However, political observers are growing increasingly worried about fragmentation and intractability in U.S. politics. Compromise, which stands at the core of democratic politics, becomes elusive in the face of intense, narrow, and well-organized interests.

Moral intensity and a single-issue orientation are nothing new to U.S. politics. But until recently, single-issue groups had been diminishing in intensity and political clout. In the New Deal and the post–World War II period, single-issue economic groups were essentially neutralized as each won a "piece of the pie" through subsidies, tax breaks, favorable legislation, and the like. And moral issues seemed to disappear from political life as Americans apparently grew more tolerant and as older moral concerns, like Prohibition, faded into memory. A bipartisan consensus on foreign policy also muted discontent.

These patterns began to break down in the 1960s as new and intensely felt moral and social issues emerged. People discovered that through concerted action—marching, picketing, signing petitions, and participating in political campaigns—they could make a difference. The single-issue groups of the 1970s put these lessons to work. Let us look more closely at four of these groups: the antiabortion lobby, the gun lobby, environmental groups, and the pro-Israeli lobby.

THE ANTIABORTION LOBBY   Antiabortion groups are considered among the most successful of all single-issue interest groups. They first achieved prominence after the Supreme Court, in *Roe* v. *Wade* (1973), struck down many state laws restricting abortion. Since then, antiabortion organizations have played substantial roles in certain senatorial and congressional races. Many observers credit them with the defeat of several liberal legislators, although some question just how decisively they influenced the outcome of those contests.

High-pitched emotion and occasional violence have characterized antiabortion actions. For example, at the National Right to Life Convention in 1979, speakers compared abortions to the genocidal Nazi extermination of the Jews. In the 1980s several abortion clinics were firebombed, allegedly by antiabortionists. In 1991, a group called Operation Rescue led a six-week blockade of three abortion clinics in Wichita, Kansas, which resulted in over 2,600 arrests.

Besides working to defeat proabortion legislators, antiabortion groups lobbied for legislation prohibiting the use of federal Medicaid funds for abortions except in a few limited circumstances and for administrative regulations prohibiting abortion counseling in federally funded clinics. One successful fight waged by antiabortion groups has been to stop federal funding for research in in vitro fertilization (IVF), a process whereby eggs are surgically removed from the ovaries, fertilized, and then implanted in the womb to develop normally. Right-to-life concerns about destroying fertilized eggs have prevented all federal funding for research since 1974. IVF, successful only about 15 percent of the time, remains extremely expensive. Opponents of the ban argue that IVF is wholly consonant with concern for family values, since it allows infertile couples, using their own genetic material, to bear children. Finally, antiabortion activists have spearheaded the campaign for a constitutional amendment banning abortions. Such an amendment has passed several state legislatures and has been introduced in the House and Senate more than sixty separate times.

THE GUN LOBBY   An overwhelming majority of Americans favor more restrictive regulation of handguns. The political clout and financial resources of the gun lobby, however, have thwarted all gun control efforts at the national level. The National Rifle Association (NRA)—a loose union of hunters, indoor shooting sportsmen, firearms and ammunition manufacturers, conservationists, and sporting goods merchants—stands at the core of that lobby. With the aid of sophisticated computer and direct-mail techniques, the NRA mobilizes its membership around gun control issues. In addition to lobbying Congress directly, the NRA effectively campaigns for or against selected senators and representatives.

NRA supporters are committed, well organized, persistent, and well financed. The organization has run highly graphic and emotional ad campaigns arguing that guns are needed for self-defense. One ad showed a high-heeled shoe with the heel ripped off. The headline read: "He's followed you for two weeks. He'll rape you in two minutes."

By contrast, their opponents, although comprising a numerical majority, are not as well organized and lack the money and intensity of the pro-gun forces. Still, there are signs that the once seemingly invincible power of the NRA may be waning. Organizations such as Handgun Control have been developing organizational clout that sometimes matches the NRA's. In part because of the effective lobbying of Handgun Control and its spokesperson, Sarah Brady, the House of Representatives in 1991 passed the Brady Bill, requiring a seven-day waiting period to buy a handgun. The bill was named after Sarah's husband, James, Ronald Reagan's press secretary, who was wounded and partly paralyzed in the 1981 assassination attempt. The measure died later that year in a Senate filibuster backed by the NRA.

Support for gun control legislation remains high in the country as a whole, particularly among younger Americans. Gun control proposals have been placed on the ballot in various states and localities, and municipalities, such as San Francisco, and one state, Maryland, have banned the sale of certain handguns altogether.

ENVIRONMENTAL GROUPS   Concern about environmental issues such as land use, national parks, and wildlife protection originated in the nineteenth century. Early in the twentieth century President Theodore Roosevelt brought such issues to the forefront of national politics. In many ways, however, environmental activism ebbed for more than half a century thereafter. Amid the rising affluence of post–World War II U.S. society, few Americans considered the hidden and not-so-hidden costs of creating a complex, industrial society.

Since the 1960s, interest groups in the environmental movement have grown enormously (both in numbers and in membership) as concern for the environment has moved to the political mainstream. With this growth the movement encompasses a diversity of organizational goals and styles. The largest, most visible environmental interest groups, called the Big Ten, are the National Audubon Society, the Sierra Club,

(Text continues on page 422)

COMPARATIVE PERSPECTIVE

Guns and Public Policy

Alone among the Western democracies, the United States allows a vast number of guns to circulate in society. According to one estimate, Americans currently possess 200 million guns of all descriptions, of which 60 million are handguns.

In contrast, Western European nations impose tough standards for gun ownership. To obtain a gun in Germany, individuals must undergo physical and mental tests and prove that they have a need to protect themselves. Permission to own a handgun is seldom granted in Great Britain, and rifle ownership is carefully regulated. The penalty for carrying a gun illegally is six months in jail; persons found guilty of using a gun in a crime are sentenced to fourteen years imprisonment. Most British police officers do not carry guns, although they can be specially authorized to use them in certain circumstances.

There is no organization in Europe comparable to the National Rifle Association (NRA), the most powerful and vociferous lobby against any form of gun control. What nurtured the NRA's development in the United States? American defenders of the gun base their arguments on the Second Amendment to the Constitution, which guarantees citizens the right to bear arms (although in the view of most experts, this provision was intended to apply not to individuals but to state militias). The individualistic American tradition has also been an important factor. The right to own a gun has become associated in some people's minds with personal autonomy, freedom, and a certain macho mystique. Advocates of a more permissible gun ownership policy also argue that guns are needed for self-defense.

Why all the fuss about gun control? Advocates of stiffer regulations point to the statistics. According to one estimate, approximately two hundred homicides were committed in self-defense with handguns in 1986, compared with twelve thousand handgun suicides, one thousand accidental deaths, and roughly nine thousand homicides—of which many were crimes of passion that might not have occurred were it not for the presence of a handgun.* Indisputably, more Americans die of gunshot wounds than citizens of countries where tough gun control laws are in place. Most proposals for gun control call for the banning of certain handguns and establishing a waiting period for a gun to be purchased so that dealers can check the background of the purchaser. Some observers draw an analogy between gun ownership and car ownership, seeking mandatory insurance for gun owners, registration with the state, testing, and a tax on guns.

*New Republic, *February 22, 1988, p. 9.*

Environmental issues have jumped to the top of the political agenda, partly because of efforts by groups like Greenpeace. Here, the group joins a flotilla of boats sailing in New York harbor to protest ocean pollution. *(Keith Meyers/New York Times Pictures)*

the Wilderness Society, the Friends of the Earth and the Environmental Policy Institute (now joined), the Environmental Defense Fund, the National Parks and Conservation Association, the Natural Resources Defense Council, the National Wildlife Federation, and the Isaac Walton League.

Whereas much early funding came from foundations, the 1980s saw a vast expansion of direct-mail solicitation. Greatly expanded budgets (the Sierra Club's, for example, grew from $9 million to $30 million during the 1980s) were used to acquire professional scientific, legal, and lobbying talent to monitor, litigate, and persuade, marked by the replacement of flannel-shirted activists with gray-suited professionals. With considerable success in the early objectives—raising public awareness and instigating broad new legislative programs—these groups have moved on to more complex, specialized tasks: monitoring and amending existing programs and trying to identify and demonstrate long-term environmental trends. Much activity is now aimed at state and local governments, the nexus of environmental protection. In terms of interest group politics, the environmental movement has come of age.

PRO-ISRAELI INTERESTS   We often think that foreign policy falls outside the realm of interest groups. After all, during foreign policy crises, urgent decisions are made by the president and presidential advisers, while public ignorance and even apathy hold sway. With this in mind, we might conclude that interest groups simply do not play an important role in the foreign policy arena. But this picture, though accurate up to a point, has sizable gaps. In fact, interest groups attempt to influence foreign policy all the time.

One of the most prominent and effective single-issue foreign policy organizations is the pro-Israeli lobby. Sixty pro-Israeli groups spent $12.7 million on congressional campaigns between 1985 and 1990. Two Arab-American and Muslim-American PACs contributed a total of $85,000 to federal campaigns during the same period. Several PACs lobby for Israel, but the best known is the American Israel Public Affairs Committee (AIPAC). AIPAC has developed an almost legendary reputation. "There's no lobby group that matches it. They're in a class by themselves," says Representative Lee Hamilton, a member of the House Foreign Affairs Committee.[13] In 1991 AIPAC claimed a household membership of 55,000 and a professional staff of over one hundred. Its budget grew from $1.4 million in 1980 to $12 million in 1991.[14]

What makes AIPAC so effective? The lobby gets high marks for presenting a simple, coherent message; providing clear rewards and penalties to its friends and enemies in Congress; supplying timely and reliable information; and perhaps most important, building on an already strong base of support for Israel in Congress and among the American public.[15] Although AIPAC has only six registered lobbyists, its members are urged to become citizen-lobbyists on issues of particular concern. One other key factor in AIPAC's success has been the cohesiveness of the American Jewish community in its support for Israel. There were signs, however, that several factors—the Palestinian uprisings in the occupied territories, known as the *intifada*; the Israeli government's continuation of settlements in the occupied territories; and the media-savvy effectiveness of Palestinian representation at the negotiations before and during the Arab-Israeli peace talks of 1992—were working against the continued dominance of the pro-Israeli forces in U.S. foreign policy.

How Lobbying Works

The major resources available to interest groups are money, the clout that comes with membership size, organizational skills, leadership skills, expertise, knowledge of the political process, motivational commitment, and the intangible but highly significant factor of legitimacy. How are these resources used by groups that seek to influence policymaking?

Money can buy a great deal. It translates into a vast array of potential weapons in the influence-gaining process—campaign contributions, media exposure, the ability to procure the talents of able people. Wealthy organizations can afford to employ large lobbying staffs and offer extensive data-gathering resources to legislators as a means of winning influence.

Size can also translate into power. The AFL-CIO, for example, has organizations in every congressional district. Farm groups wield considerable political clout in certain districts. Even business has become aware of the potential of grass-roots activism. One

Chamber of Commerce lobbyist noted that "lately we've grown aware of the potential impact of the grass-roots membership we have. The Chamber has business proprietors and executives in every congressional district, and we can use them to open a lot of doors for us that were closed before."[16]

Membership unity also matters. Unless a group's members are united around and deeply concerned about an issue, lobbying efforts may fail to make much of an impression. One House member, speaking of agricultural interest groups, put it this way: "If they can't get their own members together, they aren't going to start lobbying."[17]

Lobbyists can parlay political reputation and prestige into influence as well. By developing a solid reputation for honesty and expertise, lobbyists can win the trust and support of legislators. Such a reputation is especially important, of course, for lobbyists with little else to offer by way of political power. A group's overall prestige can also make a difference. For example, because the Business Roundtable is made up of the chief executive officers of the country's largest corporations, it is considered one of the premier business groups.

Striking hospital workers stage a demonstration. Although the AFL-CIO has organizations in every Congressional district, the political clout of labor unions has generally been on the decline in the last twenty-five years, and union membership has dropped sharply.
(Paul Conklin/Monkmeyer Press Photos)

One lobbyist summarized the whole matter of group resources and efforts to obtain influence as follows:

> Different kinds of assets can be effective, but the individual has to, to some extent, decide what are his assets and then use them to the maximum. . . . [B]eing a source of reliable information to congressmen . . . tends to work better and be a more effective tactic if you are a small group or if you're working for a group that doesn't put large amounts of money into campaigns, one that has good contacts with a minimum number of senators and congressmen. . . . The tactics have to vary with the kind of organization.[18]

Most lobbyists attempt to influence government policy either as "insiders" or "outsiders." Insider methods revolve around direct connections between interest groups and the major political players involved—legislators, bureaucrats, or other members of the executive branch. Outsider strategies build on connections between legislators and their home districts.

Insider Strategies

Insider strategies rely on social relationships, friendships, and the political needs of legislators; these elements often come into play while the political process slowly grinds toward a decision. Interest groups that use insider strategies generally try to lighten a legislator's workload by supplying pertinent information, writing speeches, or answering opponents' criticisms. According to one student of the subject:

> The corporate representative is often effective because he is a specialist, trading in information about an industry that may be crucial to the wording and effect of a given piece of legislation. "Every industry has its little quirks," explained one liberal Democrat. . . . "Even if you are against them . . . you need their lobbyist to help you get your head on straight."[19]

This observation illustrates the powerful role of expertise and specialized knowledge possessed by trusted lobbyists. As legislation becomes increasingly intricate and regulation more wide-ranging, the insider's knowledge becomes more and more vital to lawmaking. Hence interest groups possessing knowledge that lawmakers need often gain considerable political leverage.

Insider lobbyists also try to exert influence by pointing out what effects a particular piece of legislation will have on a lawmaker's home district—that it will hurt a certain local hospital, create three thousand more jobs, reduce federal funds now allocated to the area, and so forth. Groups sometimes supply speechmaking materials to overworked legislators and their staffs. As a Senate aide noted:

> My boss demands a speech and a statement for the *Congressional Record* for every bill we introduce or co-sponsor. . . . I can't do it all myself. The better lobbyists, when they have a proposal they are pushing, bring it to me along with a couple of speeches, a *Record* insert, and a fact sheet. They know their clout is tripled that way.[20]

The subtlest insider tactic involves cultivating social relationships with legislators. In this way business contacts and friendships develop between lawmakers and lobbyists. Often these relationships take root at the myriad social gatherings held in the nation's capital. Speaking of such gatherings, one Senate aide explained:

> Let's say the congressman is a liberal. He's suspicious of big business. What does he find? The [corporate] big shot is a darned nice guy. He doesn't have horns and a tail. He charms the wife and he's deferential to the congressmen. They go away feeling a little differently. Maybe it doesn't affect the way he votes, at least not right away. But it's a softening process.[21]

Outsider Strategies

Outsider methods of lobbying mobilize grass-roots sentiments to influence legislators. Lobbyists choose outsider strategies for a variety of reasons: They may represent the most effective way to influence policymaking, they may offer the only alternatives after insider strategies have failed, or they may form one facet in a long-term effort to influence the direction of public opinion. In the last case, the outsider strategy may not be linked to a particular piece of legislation or to any specific outcome.

A number of grass-roots outsider efforts have achieved a measure of prominence and success in recent years. The Chamber of Commerce has generated opposition among businesspeople to labor legislation. In 1983 the American Bankers Association led a highly successful lobbying blitz in which banks encouraged their customers to send letters and postcards to legislators urging the repeal of a withholding tax on interest payments. Thirteen million pieces of mail arrived and the measure was repealed. A less successful outsider effort was mounted in 1992 by the cable television industry in an attempt to stop a bill that would reregulate the cable industry. Despite a storm of broadcast ads and ads included with consumers' monthly cable bills, the effort failed to stop congressional passage of the legislation.

Grass-roots lobbying has grown enormously in recent years as single-issue campaigns and organizations (promoting gun control, abortion, or antitax measures, for example) have broadened their appeals. Moreover, many corporations, taking a longer-range view of political influence, now work to gain public support for their interests through **advocacy advertising**. Advocacy advertising takes the form of well-reasoned essays, appearing in the prominent news media, designed to build a favorable corporate image and to boost public support for the corporation, its products, and its goals. As much as one-third of all corporate advertising is now devoted to advocacy ads. Mobil Oil, for example, uses ads in the news media to offer its views on energy and regulatory issues.

Other outsider strategies seek to influence the general tone of public discourse. A number of corporations contribute to conservative think tanks—centers of research and problem solving—which produce scholarly and popular materials on a range of public issues. Such intellectual leadership helps to shape the political agenda, framing the debate on key issues and even circumscribing the arena in which interest group activity takes place.

One of the most important developments in interest group politics in the past half-century is **direct-mail marketing**. Direct-mail marketing allows interest groups and party organizations "(1) to advertise issues, programs and candidates; (2) to mobilize public pressure on political decision makers; (3) to raise money for electoral campaigns and organizational maintenance; and (4) to recruit new members for citizen action groups."[22] Well over $1 billion is raised each election cycle through direct-mail marketing. High-quality mailing lists are guarded, bought, and sold. "Vulnerable" targets are sent elaborate computer-personalized mailings. This is one area of American politics in which the line between commercial consumerism and political life has vanished completely.

Lobbying Target Groups

To maximize influence, interest group strategies identify different target groups within the government. Some strategies concentrate on the legislative process, others on the executive branch and such regulatory agencies as the Federal Trade Commission or the Securities and Exchange Commission, and still others on the courts. Overall, however, most groups active at the national level seek to influence Congress, either directly (by lobbying for or against legislation) or indirectly (by campaigning for or against congressional candidates). The choice of target for most groups depends on a calculation of political and legal resources. The higher the ratio of political resources (including large membership, lots of cash, and publicly popular cause) to legal resources (statutory or constitutional rights), the more likely the group is to target the legislature or the executive. A higher ratio of legal resources to political resources may direct a group toward the courts or a regulatory agency.

LOBBYING IN CONGRESS   How do lobbyists attempt to influence legislators? They can provide information that bears on important policy decisions, and they can help to plan political strategies. Lobbyists can also supply innovative ideas and approaches, especially when the lobbying organizations have special expertise in important political areas such as health or welfare policy. And, of course, groups can offer campaign support or threaten opposition.

Lobbying groups can also try to influence the internal structure of Congress itself. During the 1950s and 1960s, for example, oil lobbyists succeeded in barring from membership on the House Ways and Means Committee representatives who did not favor the large oil depletion allowance enjoyed by the industry. Having sympathetic members on key committees is crucial to a lobbyist's long-term success.

Finally, lobbyists and legislators often have close personal relationships. Much interaction between them takes place informally—at parties, on vacations, during lunches, at country clubs, and so on. Such friendships spring naturally from the shared

COMPARATIVE PERSPECTIVE

LOBBYING THE EUROPEAN COMMUNITY

As the European Community becomes more integrated and its institutions gain greater legislative authority, lobbying efforts aimed at the EC increase. Lobbying the European Community, in some ways like lobbying Congress, is a complicated business, both institutionally and culturally.

Individuals and groups wishing to lobby the EC must initially address its three major institutions: the European Commission, which has sole authority to initiate legislation; the European Parliament, which offers advisory opinions about proposed legislation; and the European Council, the only community body authorized to adopt legislation (by a "qualified majority" of 54 votes out of 76 if the legislation falls under the 1992 program for integrating Europe, unanimity if it doesn't). After this initial phase, all legislation must go to the twelve member-state parliaments for enabling legislation. Ordinarily, then, lobbying must proceed from EC headquarters to the several member-state capitals. Some issues (such as labor policy) in the American federal system similarly require lobbying state legislatures individually as well as Congress.

The kinds of organizations most active in lobbying the European Community resemble those active in Washington—in some cases, including the U.S. Chamber of Commerce and the National Association of Manufacturers, the very same organizations lobby both. Private-sector players include the Union of Industrial and Employers' Confederations (UNIEC), the official representative of business interests in Europe; the European Trade Union Confederation (ETUC), an umbrella organization representing the interests of workers and labor unions; the European Bureau of Consumer Unions (BEUC), a confederation of consumer groups vigorously advocating legislation to protect the health, safety, and economic interests of consumers; the EC Committee of the American Chamber of Commerce in Belgium, which represents the interests of European companies of American parentage, like IBM, Ford, and Exxon; the Joint European Standards Institute (CEN/CENELEC), to which the EC has delegated a major share of the responsibility for

(Box continues on page 429)

attitudes and backgrounds of many lobbyists and legislators. In addition, former legislators often become lobbyists and maintain ties with ex-colleagues.

LOBBYING IN THE EXECUTIVE BRANCH Lobbying is not confined to Congress; executive branch lobbyists also play a significant political role in shaping proposals before they are sent to Congress. Labor groups, business leaders, and consumer representatives all

developing uniform European technical standards; and the Kangaroo Group, an unusual combination of members of the European Parliament (MEPs) and lobbyists that provides informational and educational services aimed at overcoming barriers to further European integration.

Just as states, counties, and municipalities lobby the federal government in the United States, the European Community has official third-country missions. These missions often work closely with private-sector representatives, as when the official U.S. mission worked with representatives of American banking interests led by American Express to defeat certain reciprocity provisions deemed protectionist by the Americans. Many of the political subdivisions of member states also have a lobbying presence at the EC, including, for example, each of the German Länder, as well as many British municipalities.

Lobbying the EC is, on the whole, much more subdued than lobbying in the United States. As one EC lobbyist said, "You Americans see legislative issues as black and white. We Europeans see shades of grey," Another said, "You Yanks do tend to pound the table a bit harder." One MEP deplored the "gangster style of American lobbyists." The resources for effective lobbying are fairly standard—expertise, information, and credibility rank high. So far, at least, insider strategies are much more common than outsider strategies.

One consultant suggests six themes for lobbying the European Community: "Keep it low-key" (swagger is out); "Keep it short and substantive" (Eurocrats and MEPs are busy); "Keep it long-term" (since Europeans value long-term friendships, "instant" lobbying is definitely out); "Get in early" (it is easier to shape unformed opinions than to change minds that have been made up); "Use the bottoms-up approach" (find and befriend the low-ranking technical specialists, parliament committee staffers, and political group assistants); and "Remain vigilant" (never assume that you have won an issue once and for all). EC lobbying shares a lot with lobbying in other capitals—a lobbyist working the halls of Congress would be well served to keep this list in mind.

Source: James N. Gardner, Effective Lobbying in the European Community *(Deventer, Netherlands: Kluwer, 1991).*

---

seek meetings with the president. Executive branch lobbying also focuses on foreign policy questions—Jewish leaders may work to influence policy toward Israel, or black leaders may lobby for particular policies toward South Africa. Frequently, interest groups and the White House work together.

Just as members of Congress often have close relationships with lobbyists, many executive branch agencies maintain close ties with those they oversee and serve. The

George Bush shakes hands with Prime Minister Kiichi Miyazawa of Japan. On his trip to Japan, Bush served as an advocate of U.S. trade interest and was accompanied by executives from the American automobile industry. *(Reuters/Bettmann Newsphotos)*

Department of Commerce has links with the business community, the Agriculture Department looks toward the interests of farmers, the Veterans Administration presses for veterans' concerns, and so on. Relations between executive agencies and interest groups are frequently cordial. The groups usually seek to perpetuate their friendships by influencing the choice of political appointees to the top positions in these executive hierarchies.

The independent regulatory commissions are also prime targets of lobbyists. Rules made by bodies such as the Federal Communications Commission and the Interstate Commerce Commission have a substantial impact on many of the day-to-day operations of major industries. With that in mind, interest groups often go to great lengths to set forth their views before these agencies. Here, too, relationships between the regulator and the regulated may be cozy.

INTRAGOVERNMENTAL LOBBYING   Lobbying also goes on within the executive branch itself, as well as between the White House and Congress—a phenomenon known as intragovernmental lobbying. The administration of President Dwight Eisenhower was the first to establish a congressional liaison office in the White House to lobby Congress.

Today many executive branch agencies maintain special congressional liaison staffs: Each cabinet department has such an office, as do most regulatory agencies and many federal bureaus. Typically, agency lobbyists coordinate their activities with White House lobbying efforts.

SEEKING INFLUENCE THROUGH THE COURTS Besides influencing legislation, interest groups may pursue specific goals through the courts. Courts are even more likely political targets in the United States than elsewhere because here the courts have the power of judicial review—the power to strike down a law as unconstitutional—as well as the authority to set certain policies by issuing wide-ranging rulings. Interest group activity might involve starting a test case to challenge a statute or regulation outright or to achieve a certain interpretation of the law. Sometimes interest groups add their support to current cases, by providing either counsel or research support through an **amicus curiae** ("friend of the court") **brief**.

A recent case study of the Federal District Court warns against the assumption that interest groups representing the politically disadvantaged are the only ones to target courts.[23] Groups with a powerful electoral advantage use the courts as well—for example, to enforce statutory rights won in the legislature or to advance a narrow range of interests when legislation has favored a broader mix. Various industries have challenged regulations issued by the Environmental Protection Agency or the Occupational Safety and Health Administration, for instance. Although courts do hold out some chance of success to groups whose political resources don't compare to the competition in the legislature (the success of the NAACP's Legal Defense and Educational Fund in fighting for equal protection for African-Americans is a striking example), they are not inherently biased to favor the politically weak. The shift in decision-making patterns from the more liberal Supreme Court under Chief Justice Earl Warren to the more conservative Court under Chief Justice William Rehnquist shows how dramatically court appointments can change the tenor of the judicial system. Interest group activity in the political branches can have an impact on judicial selection by lobbying for certain types of appointments. Even more directly, interest groups can fund judicial electoral campaigns in states where judges are selected by popular election. Some of these elections are enormously expensive. In one rather unusual case, $11.4 million was spent on retention elections for three California Supreme Court justices. When sizable contributions come from lawyers, for example, or anyone else with specific interests, the question of improper influence cannot be ignored.

Regulation and the Public Interest

Since the early 1970s, the absolute volume of interest group endeavors has increased dramatically. The number of lobbyists registered in Washington, D.C., has almost doubled, to fifteen thousand, in recent years (and that figure does not include thousands of unregistered lobbyists). Lobbies now spend an estimated $2 billion a year to influence public policy; about half of that is spent on government lobbying, and the other half goes toward influencing public opinion.

Five hundred corporations now operate their own lobbies, as opposed to only one hundred in the mid-1970s. Why this substantial increase? The growth of lobbying parallels the growing size and complexity of the federal government. The government now regulates an enormous number of areas affecting a wide array of groups. Many seemingly trivial rules or requirements have important ramifications for towns or companies, making the stakes high for the contending interests.

Lobbyists themselves have gained greater sophistication and expertise as well, recognizing more and more how government does or could affect their interests. Most lobbyists now offer guidance and advice to government officials who create the new rules and make the expenditures, as well as informing lawmakers about the possible impact of their work.

Finally, fundamental changes in the power structure in Congress in recent years have given outside influences greater access to legislators. Many members of Congress, especially Democrats, have won election without the benefit of close party ties. As party organizations have declined in power, the nonideological politics of specific issues has replaced party politics to a great extent. For example, business-oriented political action committees support many of the new Democratic members of Congress, who in turn oppose many of the party leadership's prolabor policies.

Concern about the excesses of lobbying data back to the 1830s, when the term *lobbyist* was first coined. Actual or alleged scandals were common in the pre–Civil War period. In the 1850s, Washington was a wide-open city "filled with a variety of gambling houses whose proprietors worked closely with the lobbyists. When a representative or a senator was unlucky enough to fall into debt, as he frequently did, the managers of the gambling halls had him where he would do them the most good."[24] Lobbying scandals continued through the late nineteenth and early twentieth centuries; not until 1946 was legislation regulating lobbying activities actually passed. We now explore efforts to regulate lobbying and the symbiotic relationship between government and interest groups.

Regulatory Efforts

The Federal Regulation of Lobbying Act, part of the Legislative Reorganization Act of 1946, required that persons paid to influence Congress be registered, disclose the source and use of all compensation over $500, and state their general legislative objectives in a report to Congress. The measure, then, did not restrict lobbying; it simply required disclosure, on the theory that publicly available knowledge would create a healthier political climate.

Since its passage, the law has been criticized on legal and constitutional grounds, and critics have deemed it both ineffective and ambiguous. Contentions that it violates the First Amendment protections of free speech and the right to petition were rejected by the Supreme Court in 1954, but the justices interpreted the act very narrowly. In creating the act, Congress showed its ambivalence toward interest group activity. After all, relations between legislators and lobbyists are often mutually beneficial, and Congress has traditionally been uneasy about taking action that would require closer policing of its members.

The 1946 act suffers from some obvious weaknesses. The disclosure rules apply only to lobbying aimed directly at Congress; executive branch, grass-roots, and other forms of lobbying are not addressed. Interest groups are given considerable latitude in interpreting how much of their money is spent on lobbying, and only groups that declare their "principal purpose" to be direct contact with legislators are covered. Then, too, the act does not specify exactly what constitutes a lobbying effort. Finally, because the law designates no clear enforcement agency, the law has been rarely enforced.

To demonstrate the gross inadequacies of federal regulation in this area, let us return to the S&L scandal discussed at the start of this chapter. The huge sums of money that flowed in the early 1980s from the thrift industry to particular candidates and to organizations sponsored by them were perfectly legal. And that encompasses only the most direct efforts to influence policy decisions.

New and tougher regulations for lobbying have been proposed in almost every recent session of Congress, only to be defeated for lack of a consensus. Among the key questions regulators must address are these: Who should have to register? What sorts of lobbying should be covered? Should all contributions to lobbies be made public? Should the overall expenditures of lobbies be limited? How much regulation is constitutional? Some states, notably California, have passed tough regulatory legislation. On the federal level, however, interest group lobbying remains intense, well organized, well funded, and largely beyond the reach of government regulation or control.

Government and Interest Groups

We have already noted that the interests of lobbies frequently coincide with those of both executive agencies and members of Congress. Thus, for example, tobacco growers and manufacturers may find steady allies on the agriculture committees in both houses and in the Department of Agriculture. Such close relationships, like those between regulated industries and regulatory commissions, lead critics to ask who is looking out for the public interest in such situations. Too often the answer is no one.

Public-interest lobbies have attacked this policymaking process, calling for greater independence on the part of government agencies and more open and publicly reported lobbying. Although various political observers may define the public interest in myriad ways, it is easy to see what clearly is *not* in the public interest: policymaking that ignores important affected interests; policymaking carried on out of public view by small, well-organized groups seeking benefits for themselves; policymaking that loses sight of the more permanent and deeper values we supposedly share as a society, such as honesty, equality, and fairness.

Let us consider two specific examples where the public interest might take a back seat to personal concerns. First, is it in the public interest for an expert on the payroll of a private company to serve the government without compensation for an extended period and then return to his private post? He may well have knowledge that is otherwise unavailable to the government, and he may be scrupulously honest, yet he knows that his public service is temporary and that his future lies with the company he will return to. And what if a high government official finds herself in charge of regulating matters that affect a major corporation? She knows that as a government official, she is likely to be replaced when a new administration is voted into office, yet she is acquiring valuable knowledge in the course of government service that she is understandably reluctant to see go to waste. The thought of a subsequent career with the corporation under her jurisdiction may well affect her decisions in office. These cases illustrate that even though particular individuals may not compromise their public trust, a serious problem of persistent and insidious bias exists nonetheless. There may be no conspiracy or corruption, but the public interest may well suffer.

An admiral in charge of procuring great quantities of steel retires and joins a steel company; a general leaves the armed services to head a corporation with important military contracts; a civil aviation administrator resigns to become head of a major airline—such moves have become commonplace. A 1984 study found that more than half of Washington lobbyists had experience within the government, mostly at the federal level (see **Table 11-1**).

In an attempt to curb this disturbing trend, Congress passed an ethics law under which former government officials are permanently prohibited from representing the

TABLE 11-1

PREVIOUS GOVERNMENT EXPERIENCE OF LOBBYISTS

Federal Government	*45.0%*
Congressional	16.9
Executive/commission	22.0
Other (includes field offices, consulting positions, and miscellaneous others)	6.1
State and Local Government	*9.4*
Total with Government Experience	*54.4%*

SOURCE: Robert H. Salisbury, "Washington Lobbyists: A Collective Portrait," in *Interest Group Politics*, 2nd ed., Allan J. Cigler and Burdett A. Loomis (Washington, D.C.: Congressional Quarterly Press, 1986), p. 153.

interests they regulated as civil servants. But "representing interests" is vague, and the law permits "business contacts" between former civil servants and their agencies after one year. In addition, the ethics law does not deal with the past connections of regulators, allowing extensive overlaps between regulators and the domains they regulate which are almost certain to produce a subtle yet important bias in the policymaking process.

Conclusions

Since the 1960s, interest groups in general, and the increasingly numerous single-issue groups in particular, have grown more skillful and more influential. At the same time, Congress has become more vulnerable to interest group pressure. As the power and effectiveness of political parties has ebbed, interest groups have stepped into the political vacuum. Though these developments might have bolstered public-interest groups, by the 1980s, narrowly focused interest group politics was gaining a strong foothold, increasingly fragmenting U.S. political life.

Single-issue groups may coalesce under ideologically based umbrella organizations. Such groups may also play constructive political roles by spotlighting grievances and dramatizing neglected public issues or by counteracting the influence of more powerful but often less visible interest groups. Overall, however, the fragmentation of politics makes compromise difficult and sidesteps the public interest.

The pervasiveness of business influence also poses a serious problem for U.S. politics, as corporate political action organizations have grown dramatically in recent years. Business lobbyists direct their attention to the federal agencies whose regulations affect business life, while corporations mount extensive grass-roots lobbying campaigns, organized by well-financed computer-based operations.

At one time, organized labor matched the lobbying efforts of business groups, but those days are long past. And today public-interest lobbyists spend less than one-thousandth the amount spent by business interests. Especially in recent years, big business has effectively vetoed any legislation it deems sufficiently threatening.

Many groups exert influence on policymaking, but money, persistence, organizational capacities, intensity, and legitimacy determine the degree of influence various groups exercise. Theoretically the system is open to all interest groups. On a practical level, however, only certain groups have substantial input. The direction of decision making is heavily biased toward those who can wield political clout.

Do interest groups, then, enhance democracy or throw a roadblock in the democratic process? Although we might like to believe that in the clash of interest group politics every group's message is accorded equal time, most observers would agree that the unequal distribution of power and influence in our pluralistic system places certain groups at a decided disadvantage. Consider migrant farmworkers or young, unemployed black people—these groups would certainly scoff at the notion that their voices, even raised collectively, carry equal weight with those of multinational corporations or other influential business interests.

The weakness of pluralism lies in its tacit approval of the status quo, reflecting and helping to sustain the undemocratic distribution of power and influence in U.S. political, social, and economic life. This situation is exacerbated when the major political parties do not make the issues sufficiently visible—leaving room for quiet, behind-the-scenes maneuvering by more powerful interests—and when a large segment of the population, disproportionately poor and poorly informed, remains on the sidelines of the political process.

Besides the problem of excluded or relatively powerless groups, what about the public interest? In the battles for group influence, the long-term public interest sometimes falls by the wayside. Are agricultural policies that help to destroy the family farm farsighted? Were oil subsidies that contributed to domestic shortages of the 1970s in the national interest? If welfare policy discourages people from finding work, if the gun lobby keeps millions of new handguns circulating—are those policies desirable in the long run?

Some observers regard the rough-and-tumble politics of the interest group network as the price for open, democratic politics. Robert Samuelson, for example, argues that

> the prejudice against special interests strikes at the heart of the democratic process. One person's special interest is another's crusade. The function of politics is not only to govern in the general interest and to reconcile differences among specific interests; it is also to provide outlets for political and social tensions. . . . No one, of course, should pretend the resulting system is problem-free. . . . The growth of government authority and political activism has led to severe tensions. . . . This is the ongoing drama of government, but it should not be mislabeled. The system is struggling, but it is not corrupt.[25]

But Samuelson also recognizes serious difficulties with interest group activities: "On the one hand, government faces paralysis: a collision of competing interests so severe that nothing happens. . . . On the other hand, there loom the sort of pervasive contradictions that compel government to act in ways that are ultimately self-defeating.[26] These are sobering reflections on the state of the U.S. polity.

GLOSSARY TERMS

advocacy advertising
amicus curiae brief
Common Cause
direct-mail marketing
interest group
iron triangle

macropolitics
political subsystems
public-interest group
Ralph Nader
single-issue group

NOTES

[1]Common Cause, *Facts on File*, July 20, 1990.
[2]*Facts on File Yearbook, 1990*, December 31, 1990, p. 966.

[3] "Excerpts from the Senate Ethics Committee's Statement on the 'Keating Five' Investigation," *Facts on File*, February 28, 1991, p. 140.

[4] "Improper Conduct? No, Just Differently Ethical," *Common Cause Magazine*, January–March 1992, p. 6.

[5] Alexis de Tocqueville, *Democracy in America* (Garden City, N.Y.: Doubleday, 1969), p. 485.

[6] Sidney Verba and Norman H. Nile, *Participation in America* (New York: Harper & Row, 1972).

[7] James A. Thurber, "The Dynamics of Policy Subsystems in American Politics," in *Interest Group Politics*, 3rd ed., ed. Allan J. Cigler and Burdett A. Loomis (Washington D.C.: Congressional Quarterly Press, 1991), pp. 333–335.

[8] Rorie Tempest, "U.S. Defense Establishment Wields a Pervasive Power," *Los Angeles Times*, July 10, 1983, p. 3.

[9] *In Common*, August 1981, p. 7.

[10] Caleb Rossiter, "Arms Dealers Take Taxpayers for a Ride," *Christian Science Monitor*, June 10, 1992, p. 19.

[11] Jeffrey Berry, *Lobbying for the People* (Princeton, N.J.: Princeton University Press, 1977), p. 7.

[12] *New York Times*, April 13, 1985, p. 18.

[13] George D. Moffett III, "Israel Lobby Virtually Unmatched," *Christian Science Monitor*, June 28, 1991, p. 3.

[14] Ibid.

[15] Robert Pear and Richard L. Berke, "Pro-Israel Group Exerts Quiet Might," *New York Times*, July 7, 1987, p. 7.

[16] Norman J. Orenstein and Shirley Elder, *Interest Groups, Lobbying and Policymaking* (Washington, D.C.: Congressional Quarterly Press, 1978), p. 73.

[17] Ibid., p. 75.

[18] Ibid., p. 79.

[19] Ibid., p. 84.

[20] Ibid., p. 85.

[21] Ibid., p. 86.

[22] R. Kenneth Godwin, *One Billion Dollars of Influence: The Direct Marketing of Politics* (Chatham, N.J.: Chatham House, 1988), p. 5.

[23] See Susan M. Olson, "Interest Group Litigation in Federal District Court: Beyond the Political Disadvantage Theory," *Journal of Politics*, August 1990, pp. 854–882.

[24] Ornstein and Elder, *Interest Groups*, p. 97.

[25] Robert J. Samuelson, "The Campaign Reform Failure," *New Republic*, September 5, 1983, p. 35.

[26] Ibid., p. 36.

SELECTED READINGS

For a good standard introduction to **interest groups**, see Allan J. Cigler and Burdett A. Loomis, eds., *Interest Group Politics*, 3rd ed. (Washington, D.C.: Congressional Quarterly Press, 1991); and Mark P. Petracca, ed., *The Politics of Interests: Interest Groups Transformed* (Boulder, Colo.: Westview Press, 1992).

A critical assessment of interest group politics can be found in Kenneth R. Timmerman, *The Death Lobby: How the West Armed Iraq* (Boston: Houghton Mifflin, 1989); see also Theodore

Lowi, *The End of Liberalism* (New York: Norton, 1969); and Michael Parenti, *Democracy for the Few*, 5th ed. (New York: St. Martin's Press, 1988).

To learn about the development of **leadership PACs in Congress** as a significant source of influence and a further erosion of party cohesion, see Ross K. Baker, *The New Fat Cats: Members of Congress as Political Benefactors* (New York: Priority Press, 1989).

For a fascinating **historical study** of influence groups, read William Gamson, *The Strategy of Social Protest*, 2nd ed. (Belmont, Calif.: Wadsworth, 1990). Gamson studied fifty-three "challenging groups," each in a period of particular activity. The groups range from the American Association of University Professors (1914–1922) to the National Female Anti-slavery Society (1832–1840). He concluded that goals, tactics, and organization factors *did* make a difference in success rates for the studied groups.

Comparative perspectives on interest group politics can be pursued in Grant Jordan, ed., *The Commercial Lobbyists: Politics for Profit in Britain* (Aberdeen, Scotland: Aberdeen University Press, 1991); Colin Crouch and Ronald Dove, eds., *Corporatism and Accountability: Organized Interests in British Public Life* (New York: Oxford University Press, 1990); and Michael Rush, ed., *Parliament and Pressure Politics* (New York: Oxford University Press, 1990).

Special types of interest groups are detailed in Lettie McSpadden Wenner, *U.S. Energy and Environmental Interest Groups: Institutional Profiles* (Westport, Conn.: Greenwood Press, 1990); Christine L. Day, *What Older Americans Think: Interest Groups and Aging Policy* (Princeton, N.J.: Princeton University Press, 1990); Gordon Adams, *The Politics of Defense Contracting: The Iron Triangle* (New Brunswick, N.J.: Transaction Books, 1981); and Karen O'Connor and Lee Epstein, *Public Interest Law Groups: Institutional Profiles* (Westport, Conn.: Greenwood Press, 1989). For a **case study** of interest group politics in agriculture, see William P. Browne, *Private Interests, Public Policy, and American Agriculture* (Lawrence: University Press of Kansas, 1988); and John Mark Hansen, *Gaining Access: Congress and the Farm Lobby, 1919–1981* (Chicago: University of Chicago Press, 1991).

Revealing "how-to" books on **lobbying** are Charles S. Mack, *Lobbying and Government Relations: A Guide for Executives* (Westport, Conn.: Quorum Books, 1989), especially Chapter 7 on trade associations and coalitions and Chapter 10 on political action committees; Judith C. Meredith, *Lobbying on a Shoestring*, 2nd ed. (Dover, Mass.: Auburn House, 1989); and Bob Smucker, *The Nonprofit Guide: Advocating Your Cause—and Getting Results* (San Francisco: Jossey-Bass, 1991). See also *American Lobbyists Directory* (Detroit: Gale Research, 1990); and Walter Beecham, ed., *Beecham's Guide to Key Lobbyists* (Washington, D.C.: Beecham, 1989).

Direct-mail marketing is the subject of R. Kenneth Godwin's *One Billion Dollars of Influence: The Direct Marketing of Politics* (Chatham, N.J.: Chatham House, 1988).

ANITA HILL
ROSA PARKS
VOTE
-NO-
IF YOU LIKE YOUR JOB
NOW
NATIONAL ORGANIZATION FOR WOMEN
REJECT
NO
ANITA HILL
American
Heroine
NO BOYS
You
The Women
of this
Say

CHAPTER TWELVE

CHAPTER OUTLINE

Extraordinary Politics

THE WHYS OF PROTEST
EXTRAORDINARY POLITICS
AND GOVERNMENT ACTION

Protest and Disobedience

LAW AND DISOBEDIENCE
CIVIL DISOBEDIENCE: A COMPROMISE

How Protest Works

CONSCIOUSNESS-RAISING
ACTIVATING OTHERS
CONTEXTS FOR EFFECTIVE PROTEST
LIMITATIONS OF PROTEST TACTICS

Protesting Politics Itself: The Push for Term Limits for Legislators

MASS POLITICS AND PROTEST

A Threat or a Necessity?

ON FEBRUARY 1, 1960, FOUR BLACK STUDENTS FROM THE NORTH Carolina Agricultural and Technical University entered Woolworth's in downtown Greensboro, North Carolina. Violating the norms of the segregated society of that day, the four seated themselves at the lunch counter and asked for cups of coffee. The waitress, following southern segregationist tradition, refused them service. But the four did not leave. They remained on their stools until the day ended. It was the first **sit-in** of the 1960s.[1]

The Greensboro **sit-in** proved contagious. The next day twenty students joined the original four. By the end of the week thousands of A&T students and other blacks had violated segregation norms in downtown Greensboro. Some of these protestors were attacked by Ku Klux Klan members and other indignant whites. A few demonstrators were arrested, but all remained nonviolent. With tensions increasing, Woolworth's closed its doors at the end of the week. But the sit-in movement spread, and within a month sit-ins had taken place in more than fifty cities in nine states.

It was a tactic—and an objective—whose time had come. Yet no one had planned the sit-ins. The four students who

441

initiated the sit-in at Woolworth's had decided on that method of protest quite casually. Their action ultimately represented only a small part of a far larger movement involving race relations in the South and, in many ways, the rest of the nation as well. The walls of segregation were about to come tumbling down, but not without the commitment and concerted efforts of tens of thousands and the sympathetic support of millions.

In April 1963 a series of demonstrations and sit-ins took place in Birmingham, Alabama, led by Rev. Martin Luther King, Jr. While black demonstrators remained largely nonviolent, city police used police dogs, fire hoses, and clubs to control them. National television showed scenes of dogs, fangs bared, leaping at black people and other blacks being pinned against storefronts by powerful streams of water. President John Kennedy was said to have been sickened by the picture of the police dog attack.[2] Later that year King led the March on Washington for Jobs and Freedom, at which he made his famous "I Have a Dream" speech. Momentum had gathered for racial change, and the following year Congress enacted legislation prohibiting segregation in public places.

These events—sit-ins, marches, and nonviolent protest campaigns—were not the stuff of ordinary politics. They were extraordinary, unsettling, challenging. They involved dimensions of personal commitment, mass organization and arousal, and conflict that lay outside the day-to-day agenda of political life.

In this chapter we take up some of the issues raised by **extraordinary politics**— the politics of protest and mass involvement. This form of protest can spring from deeply held principles, with protesters pressing for progress toward social justice. Yet protesters can sometimes resort to violence and intimidation as tactics, creating a politics of repression. Do mass politics and protest enlarge democratic options and help to fulfill the promise of democracy? Or do they threaten the civil order and respect for law required in a democracy? In this chapter, we explore the nature and sources of mass protest, as well as government's response to it; how protest and civil disobedience affect democracy; how protest works; and protest expressed through the ballot.

Extraordinary Politics

Extraordinary politics amounts to strategies or actions that heat up the political atmosphere beyond its normal level and seriously raise the stakes in political struggles. Of course, ordinary political actions in one political system can seem extraordinary in another. A protester carrying a sign reading "Down with the Government" would raise few eyebrows in Lafayette Park, across the street from the White House, but a similar protester would prompt a vigorous response in Tienanmen Square in Beijing, where in June 1989 large-scale demonstrations for democracy were brutally squelched, with hundreds or even thousands of casualties. Thousands of protesters were arrested, and thirty-one were executed. Still, even in a society like ours, in which much protest activity is tolerated, public protest represents a step toward extraordinary political action.

The simplicity of the sit-in tactic made it easy to practice in many situations, although sit-ins often brought real danger to the participants, who were sometimes beaten, harassed, and arrested. This sit-in at a lunch counter in Charlotte, North Carolina, occurred in the early 1960s. *(Bruce Roberts/Photo Researchers)*

Extraordinary politics can take a violent or a nonviolent form. It can involve the concerted actions of millions of individuals or the solitary protest of one dedicated person. The most extreme form of extraordinary politics is violent revolution. Even democracies have justified resorting to violence (the American Revolution is a case in point) by arguing that nothing less would have altered an intolerable political situation. Any comprehensive survey of world politics over the past two centuries would reveal that instances of extraordinary politics have been common in virtually all nations.[3]

Protesters and protest movements can draw on many tactics. We saw in Chapter 3 the variety of tactics employed by the American colonists in protests against the British government: They refused to pay certain taxes, they held demonstrations, they intimidated government officials and vandalized property, they banded together in secret and semisecret organizations, they armed themselves, and in the end they made war. New protest tactics are forever being invented.

Between the normal political activities—voting, giving money, lobbying, debating, organizing campaigns—and the extreme politics of revolution, violence, and intimidation lies an extensive repertoire of extraordinary political actions and tactics, including marches, sit-ins, and various acts of civil disobedience.

A democratic political process is designed to allow the preferences of citizens to be expressed through nonviolent political means and established political channels on a regular basis. Yet democratic practices are never perfect—and even if they were, issues that could not be addressed within the context of ordinary politics might arise. The avenues of change may be blocked, or particularly pressing and significant issues may come to the fore. Under such conditions people are likely, sooner or later, to resort to extraordinary politics. In doing so, they raise the political ante and take risks—both for themselves and for the polity as a whole. In U.S. history, several key issues have sparked significant protest movements, including slavery, women's suffrage, the Ku Klux Klan, Prohibition, the antiwar movements of World War I and the Vietnam War, civil rights, the environment, nuclear power, gay rights, and abortion.[4]

It may come as a shock to find civil rights and the Ku Klux Klan in the same category. Though democratic theory does distinguish between violent and nonviolent movements and ones promoting democratic or nondemocratic goals, we must recognize that extraordinary politics can be used by forces of any political or social persuasion; it can be employed to prevent change as well as to make change possible, and it can be used by the powerful as well as by the weak, although we usually consider it a strategy of the weak. And as we will see, government itself sometimes resorts to extraordinary politics in dealing with politically sensitive or explosive situations. We now delve into the nature and sources of mass protest and government response to extraordinary politics.

The Whys of Protest

Protests develop in democratic states for various reasons—usually out of some deep sense of frustration with the status quo. Vital issues may be at stake, and people may feel compelled to take extraordinary action (as in the case of nuclear freeze advocates or contemporary antiabortion demonstrators). Protesters may view governments as unresponsive to moral issues or involved in immoral actions (as did those who opposed slavery or the Vietnam War). Protesters may seek to arouse the conscience of their fellow citizens (the driving force behind the civil rights movement), or they may simply be making a moral statement (as conscientious objectors do). Finally, protest activities may be directed against the private rather than the public sector. Civil rights demonstrators sat in at a Woolworth's store in Greensboro, not at a city office. Auto workers staged dramatic sit-ins at General Motors plants during the 1930s, protesting the company's refusal to recognize their union. Antiabortion demonstrators today gather outside private abortion clinics. In all these examples, protesters felt compelled either to resist a perceived evil or to dramatize a commitment.

Protest may take the form of a riot rather than a concerted political movement. In May 1992, following the acquittal of four police officers accused of using unnecessary force in subduing a black motorist, many parts of Los Angeles erupted into riots coupled

A typical confrontation over the Vietnam War: Protesting young people confront young soldiers at the Pentagon in October, 1967. Although most protesters confined themselves to taunting the military, a few staged nonviolent sit-ins and were dragged off and arrested. *(UPI/Bettmann)*

with widespread looting and arson. At first glance these violent episodes seem to contribute little to the struggle for civil rights; however, riots often have important political consequences, and they almost invariably represent a form of social assertion, albeit often self-destructive.[5] As Emerson once said, "Sometimes a scream is better than a thesis."

One of the most widely argued theories of protest and rebellion (not confined to democratic political contexts) holds that most political protest grows out of a sense of *relative deprivation*, the feeling that one's group is being deprived of the life chances enjoyed by other groups in the society.[6] The precise form that deprivation-caused protest takes depends on how intensely people feel about their deprivation, their views on resorting to protest, how much force is likely to be used against them, how many allies they have, and numerous other factors. Nonetheless, the concept of relative deprivation serves as a useful starting point for exploring the origins of certain forms of protest. Interestingly, people often do not feel deprived until they have entertained

> ### THE INVISIBLE EMPIRE
>
> The Ku Klux Klan, founded in December 1865, was dedicated to using violence and terror to ensure the social and political subordination of blacks in the South. It flourished in the late 1860s, then ceased to exist as an organized group and lay dormant for close to fifty years. Two developments, however, set the stage for a resurgence of Klan activity.
>
> First, between 1878 and 1914 about 23 million people emigrated to the United States; they were not always welcomed by the sons and daughters of earlier immigrants. Second, World War I left many Americans leery of change. To them, modernity signaled the waning of church influence, a breakdown of parental control over children, and the decline of customs and traditions. Distrustful of aliens and threatened by economic dislocation and rapid social change, some Americans developed a siege mentality, which prompted the birth of the Klan.
>
> In 1915 the Klan was reconstituted as the invisible Empire of the Ku Klux Klan, whose stated purpose was to defend the country against "aliens, idlers, strike leaders and immoral women." In 1920 membership stood at only a few thousand, but then Klan founders reorganized the Invisible Empire. The new pitch was "pro-American," and anyone perceived as a threat to "American" interests was considered anti-American. The Klan of 1920 was like a chameleon: anti-Japanese on the West Coast, anti-Mexican in the Southwest, anti-Catholic in the Midwest, antiblack in the South, anti-foreign-born in the big cities, and anti-Jewish on the East Coast. By appealing to people's fears of change, it built a substantial following. As the list of Klan enemies grew to include "bootleggers, dope, graft, nightclubs, violations of the Sabbath, sex and scandalous behavior," by 1921 membership swelled to about one hundred thousand.
>
> In 1922 the Klan helped to elect governors in Georgia, Alabama, California, and Oregon. Texas sent a Klansman to the Senate, and Klan campaigns helped to unseat two Jewish members of Congress. By 1924 nationwide membership

(Box continues on page 447)

increased expectations of a better life in the future. Many revolutions have broken out after people who had experienced some improvement in their situation subsequently lapsed into worsened circumstances.

If one group fears that it is losing power or influence, this can also trigger a move toward extraordinary politics. Threatened groups sometimes reach far beyond the usual range of political action to embrace genuinely violent measures. After the Civil War, for example, southern whites who felt threatened by the new social order founded the **Ku Klux Klan** and attempted, through violence and intimidation, to

was estimated at 2 to 3 million. In August 1925, forty thousand Klan members marched down Pennsylvania Avenue and on to the Washington Monument.

After peaking at 4 to 5 million in the mid-1920s, Klan membership declined precipitously. Klan violence finally backfired, and scandals involving in leadership eroded the organization's base of support. A march in 1926 attracted only half the previous number of participants. Klan-controlled candidates were routed at the polls that fall, and in 1928 the Democratic party nominated Al Smith, a Catholic, as its presidential candidate. By 1930 membership had fallen to a few hundred thousand. It was not until the civil rights struggles of the 1950s and 1960s that a much-reduced Klan was revived yet again.

Klan activity continues today in many parts of the country, although membership is estimated to have fallen to about five thousand nationally. The exclusionary politics of the Klan and similar groups retain a powerful attraction for certain segments of American society. The appeal of exclusionary politics is especially strong in areas where immigration brings distinct ethnic groups into close contact and apparent economic competition near the bottom of the socioeconomic ladder.

A number of white supremacist groups other than the Klan have been active in recent years, including neo-Nazi groups like the Aryan Nation, which calls the U.S. government the "Zionist Occupational Government" ("ZOG"); secret organizations like the Posse Comitatus, which rejects any government above the county level; and the Skinheads, known for their shaved heads and referred to by White Aryan Resistance leader Tom Metzger as "front-line warriors" of white supremacy.* The Klanwatch Project of the Southern Poverty Law Center found a dramatic increase during the 1980s in the number of violent crimes and threats in which there was evidence of bias motivation ("hate crimes"). Such crimes can be directed against minorities of any kind.

*Brad Knickerbocker, "Reports of Racial Violence Grow," Christian Science Monitor, October 5, 1990, p. 6.

---

prevent blacks and their white sympathizers from gaining or maintaining political control in the South.

Extraordinary Politics and Government Action

Protesters do not have a monopoly on extraordinary political activities. Governments, too, often resort to force, intimidation, coercion, and other unconventional tactics to control or keep track of citizens.

The United States has a long and controversial history of the use of government force in social conflicts. For many years government force was employed to protect the property rights of businesses in labor disputes. In 1970 the National Guard shootings at Kent State University in Ohio left four students dead and others injured. Although some people maintained that the troops were protecting themselves from students protesting against the Vietnam War, others argued that the shootings were not necessary.[7]

The government has resorted to other forms of extraordinary political activity as well. In 1919 government agents conducted a nationwide mass arrest of political and labor agitators and deported hundreds of aliens. Similarly, at the outbreak of World War II thousands of Japanese-Americans were rounded up and interned (see Chapter 1). And in more recent times both the FBI and the CIA have engaged in illegal or questionable practices such as infiltrating political groups, wiretapping, bugging, and harassing individuals or organizations suspected of subversive activities.

Government force has also been employed for more positive goals. In the 1950s and 1960s, for example, federal or state forces protected black students seeking to integrate schools and protest marchers in dangerous situations.

In the ideal democratic society, all government officials would recognize the legitimacy of dissent and respect the rights of dissenters. They would be able to tolerate even serious, sustained criticism of their policies without feeling the urge to repress dissent. In the real world, however, even democratic leaders sometimes resort to extreme measures to curb dissent. The tapes of Oval Office conversations during the

South African police arrest a youth following a protest meeting organized by unemployed workers. Protest, political organizing, boycotts, and international pressure all helped to persuade the South African government to turn away from its policy of apartheid.
(Eric Miller/Impact Visuals)

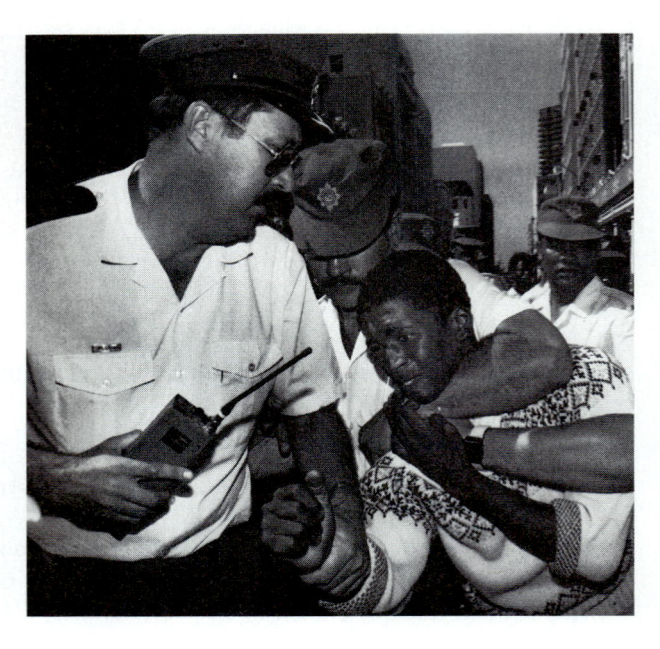

Nixon administration reveal a sense of government under siege by dissenters. President Lyndon Johnson, in a move to brand protesters as traitors, claimed that the protest movement against the Vietnam War was aided by North Vietnam. President Ronald Reagan charged that the Soviet secret police were masterminding the peace movement in the United States and Western Europe.

In dealing with dissent or with alleged threats to national security, the government must carefully judge the amount of force called for in particular situations. Government authorities may simply lose patience and unleash far more force than is warranted. Or they may ignore the rights and dignity of the targets of government force.

Of course, dissenters, to, may interfere with the rights and well-being of various segments of society. During the Vietnam War era, supporters of the war often were not permitted even to state their views on college campuses. And in 1983 United Nations Ambassador Jeane Kirkpatrick was prevented from giving a speech at the University of California at Berkeley by protesting students who shouted her down. Such actions raise basic questions about the limits of protest and the meaning of the First Amendment guarantee of freedom of speech.[8]

Protest and Disobedience

When the normal channels of political expression are closed, citizens with intense grievances must find other ways to express their discontent—through mass demonstrations, sporadic violence, even organized warfare. The period from 1989 through 1992 saw an outpouring of extraordinary politics in the Eastern European nations dominated since the Second World War by the Soviet Union and in the Soviet Union itself. In the face of a reactionary coup d'état in August 1991, the Russian people turned out by the thousands to form a human wall to keep Soviet troops from seizing the Russian parliament building and its occupants, including the most prominent resistor of the coup, Russian President Boris Yeltsin. Ordinary politics failed to prevent a coup; then the coup itself foundered, and the ultimate victory went to the thousands of unarmed citizens in the streets (the natural venue for extraordinary politics). Violence in the collapse of the Soviet Union was minimal. One former Soviet client state, Yugoslavia, was less fortunate. With the disappearance of Soviet domination, Yugoslavia fell into a violent, ghastly civil war in which the dominant republic, Serbia, used massive destructive force in attempting to prevent Bosnia-Herzegovina from seceding.

Extraordinary politics is easier to understand when democratic forms are lacking. What else can people do when they cannot express themselves freely, when there is no First Amendment, when there are no competing political parties or honest elections? Yet many forms of extraordinary politics also take place under more or less democratic regimes.

Next we will explore two complicated issues: why citizens of democracies sometimes feel compelled to engage in extraordinary political activities and when and how such activities can be justified.

An act of civil disobedience may exact a steep price. On September 1, 1987, to protest U.S. intervention in Central America, demonstrators lined the railroad tracks outside the Concord (California) Naval Weapons Station. Authorities had been notified that three demonstrators would sit on the tracks, but for unknown reasons the train was unable to stop in time. Brian Willson's right foot was severed, and surgeons had to amputate his left leg to save his life. He survived and a year later returned to the site with his wife, Holley Rauen (to the right), to renew his protest. *(Marie Felde/Oakland Tribune/Wide World Photos)*

Law and Disobedience

The concept of **civil disobedience** dates back a long way. The ancient Greeks recognized a higher law that prevailed over human law. Christian theologians have long argued over the meaning of Jesus's statement that one should "render unto Caesar that which is Caesar's, and unto God that which is God's" (Matt. 22.21; Mark 12.17). What if the demands of conscience ("render unto God") conflict with the demands of the government ("render unto Caesar")? What if moral justice conflicts with societal laws? In the view of some theologians, a higher law, as expressed in Christian teachings, can *compel* disobedience to human laws in some circumstances. Thus many pacifists argue that their consciences forbid them to kill, even if the state requires military service.[9]

Perhaps the most eloquent and influential advocate of disobedience in American history was Henry David Thoreau (1817–1862). In the 1840s, as a protest against both the Mexican-American War and the institution of slavery, Thoreau refused to pay a portion of his local taxes. For this action he was arrested and jailed. He defended his position in a brief essay titled "On the Duty of Civil Disobedience," in which he re-

FIGURE 12-1
TYPES OF POLITICAL ACTIONS BY CITIZENS AND GOVERNMENTS

CITIZENS' ACTIONS

USUAL POLITICS – – – – – – – – – – – – EXTRAORDINARY POLITICS

Elections	Demonstrations	Civil disobedience	Disruption
Community activity	Protest		Violence
Lobbying	Evasion		Vigilantism
Referenda	Intimidation		Revolution
	Coercion		
	Blacklisting		

GOVERNMENTS' ACTIONS

USUAL POLITICS – – – – – – – – – – – – EXTRAORDINARY POLITICS

Lawmaking			
Executive action		Wiretapping	Use of force
Law enforcement	Threats to prosecute	Surveillance Mass arrest	Armed
Investigation	or intervene		intervention
Regulation		Harassment	

ferred to "a government in which the majority rule in all cases cannot be based on justice." He went on: "I think that we should be men first, and subjects afterward. It is not desirable to cultivate a respect for the law, so much as for the right." And finally: "There will never be a really free and enlightened State, until the State comes to recognize the individual as a higher and independent power."[10]

Thoreau's writings had an enormous impact on modern political and social history. Particularly influenced by Thoreau's defense of civil disobedience were Mohandas Gandhi, India's renowned advocate of nonviolent disobedience to unjust laws, and Rev. Martin Luther King, Jr., the U.S. civil rights activist. We now examine in detail the issues raised by three pointed cases of civil disobedience: King's civil rights campaign in Birmingham, Alabama, the Vietnam War protests, and recent antiabortion protests.

LETTER FROM BIRMINGHAM JAIL In 1963 King led a major civil rights campaign in Birmingham, Alabama. The campaign involved protest marches and deliberate, nonviolent confrontations with city authorities in an effort to break the hold of segregation. Large numbers of protesters were jailed, including King himself. Eight Alabama clergymen published a letter raising questions about King's decision to confront the law rather than negotiate. In a letter written from the Birmingham city jail, King attempted to respond to these questions.[11] Although this letter does not address all the issues involved in civil disobedience, it does offer some compelling arguments for deliberate disobedience of unjust laws.

Excerpts from King's letter appear as a supplement to this chapter (pages 462-466) so that you can consider his position in some detail. Stated briefly, King argues that one can judge whether a law is unjust, and thus may be disobeyed, by means of four criteria: (1) it degrades human personality, (2) it binds one group but not another, (3) it is enacted by an unrepresentative authority, or (4) it is unjustly applied. In King's view, the first three of these criteria applied to Birmingham's segregation ordinances and the fourth applied to otherwise valid laws, such as the need for proper parade permits, that were being unfairly applied to civil rights protesters.

How valid are these criteria? Although they leave room for interpretation, they do serve as reasonable guidelines. The clearest and most easily applicable is the second—that a law should apply equally to all. When majorities make rules that discriminate against minorities, as was the case with segregation statutes, this flagrantly violates democratic norms. Of course, there are also sensible laws that apply to one group and not others, such as those that deny children access to pornography or alcohol. Such laws, however, are based on *reasonable* criteria; they are not arbitrary.

Considering the third criterion (unrepresentative authority), we often recognize when an unrepresentative authority violates democratic norms—particularly when the political process has been deliberately and systematically skewed against one group. Much more problematic is determining instances of degradation of human personality. Different people would certainly apply such a general principle in different ways. Yet most would agree that segregation degraded blacks through the systematic imposition of discriminatory laws and practices.

King's case for direct action against laws perpetuating segregation was, in a way, an easy one to make—although we should remember that it was highly controversial at the time and that King was charged with fomenting anarchy and worse. If we turn to the issues posed by the Vietnam War, however, matters grow more complicated.

VIETNAM AND ILLEGITIMATE AUTHORITY   There has been domestic opposition to most American wars. Abraham Lincoln, as a young congressman, opposed the Mexican War in 1848. During the Civil War, draft riots were common, and opposition to the war was widespread. Many voices were raised against U.S. involvement in World War I and, as we saw in Chapter 5, important civil liberties cases developed out of that dissent. And although World War II was a highly popular war, many conscientious objectors refused to serve in the armed forces. The Vietnam War, however, although supported at first by the American people, eventually became highly unpopular.

In attempting to end the Vietnam War and to change our foreign policy, opponents of U.S. involvement tried many tactics. Individuals refused to serve in the armed forces; some publicly burned their draft cards. Others committed acts of civil disobedience such as blocking the entrances to military facilities with their bodies and sitting in against military recruiters on campuses. In most of these cases the protesters were practicing classic forms of civil disobedience.[12] As the war continued and disenchantment grew more intense, however, radical segments of the antiwar movement advocated an escalation in acts of protest. These radicals envisioned thousands of protesters blocking all the buildings of the federal government, sitting in day after day at the White House, perhaps even bringing to a halt the machinery of government. Some argued that such large-scale protests should be recognized as a legal right.

There was an obvious problem with such proposals: What if people who did not favor antiwar policies reacted by doing their own coercing? Activities of this nature actually did take place, most notably when construction workers attacked student antiwar demonstrators in New York City in 1971. Once the Pandora's box of coercion is opened, things can quickly get out of hand. How should be judge protest activities, then: by the motives or goals of those who commit them or on the basis of how much harm they inflict on society?

ANTIABORTION PROTESTS: RIGHTS IN CONFLICT? For six weeks in the summer of 1991, Operation Rescue, a national right-to-life group, organized a blockade of abortion clinics in Wichita, Kansas. Thousands of antiabortion activists were involved in the blockades and demonstrations. Although a local newspaper poll showed that 78 percent of Wichita residents disapproved of the protesters' tactics, the protests found a warmer reception there than they had in larger cities. The governor of Kansas, Joan Finney, and the local bishop of the Catholic church welcomed the protesters. Televangelist and former presidential candidate Pat Robertson came to town and led a supportive rally attended by twenty-five thousand people.

Federal District Court Judge Patrick Kelly issued an injunction against the blockade and ordered U.S. marshals to keep protesters from blocking the entrance to the clinics. More than 2,600 protesters were arrested, but the clinics were kept closed by the protests. The U.S. Justice Department filed a motion on behalf of Operation Rescue, arguing that the 1871 Civil Rights Act (the basis for Judge Kelly's order) did not protect women seeking to have an abortion. Kelly ordered the founder of Operation Rescue, Joseph Foreman, held on $100,000 bail; Kelly received serious death threats and had to be protected by marshals. After six weeks Operation Rescue moved on.

How can we evaluate the events in Wichita? Antiabortion protesters likened themselves to civil rights activists of the 1960s. A *Washington Post* editorial following the protests countered that 1960s activists were trying to *protect* civil rights, not *deny* people their civil rights. The difference in those two positions grew directly out of two different visions of the dispute itself. Was this a question of fetal right to life or a question of a woman's right to control her own body? (Lunch counter owners across the South thought they had every right to discriminate against blacks in 1960.)

Some guidance can be drawn from Judge Kelly, who supported the protesters' right to demonstrate but drew the line at blocking the entrances to the clinics. Even this distinction may not suffice, though. When does a demonstration get so threatening or coercive that a woman or couple seeking an abortion would find the entrance blocked even though the sidewalk was clear? One editorial writer observed that to succeed, Operation Rescue would have to do more than persuade the courts that it had a right to protest. It would have to persuade the country that its moral position on the issue itself was correct. Consensus on the question of abortion seems far off. In the absence of such consensus, the question of managing protest politics remains a central concern.

Civil Disobedience: A Compromise

Even in a perfect democracy, all the problems of making just, sensible, humane public policy would not disappear. And present-day democracies are far from perfect. Political representatives in democracies can and do act cruelly, unjustly, foolishly. Democratic processes do give citizens relatively effective means by which to change or influence public policies. But these means are limited: Elections occur only occasionally; public opinion may be easily swayed; leaders may deceive or may lack judgment or political courage. As a result, citizens may face difficult moral choices.

In forging an effective strategy of civil disobedience, democratic protesters straddle the line between law and justice. Classic civil disobedience (that espoused by Thoreau, Gandhi, and King) involves a public act committed to arouse the conscience of the society by a person who is fully willing to accept the punishment prescribed by law. Such persons must be morally serious. They must not act secretly or use violence to intimidate or harm. In expressing protest or violating laws, they maintain a respect for others and for the law itself. This strategy offers a sensible compromise that does not threaten democracy and enriches our sense of how individual conscience and social

One of the most influential thinkers and activists of the twentieth century, Mohandas Gandhi led a nonviolent movement to protest British rule of his native India. More than anyone, he elaborated the ideas and tactics of the nonviolent movement.
(Henri Cartier-Bresson/Magnum)

COMPARATIVE PERSPECTIVE

GANDHI: THE ESSENCE OF NONVIOLENCE

Mohandas K. Gandhi (1869–1948), widely regarded as one of the premier political innovators of the twentieth century, pioneered the use of nonviolent direct-action campaigns for political and social justice. Educated as a lawyer in England, Gandhi returned briefly to his native India and then moved to South Africa, where he mobilized the Indian population to combat racial discrimination. After returning to India in 1915, he led nonviolent campaigns to gain independence from British rule and to rectify injustices in Indian society.

Gandhi coined the term *satyagraha*, or "truth force," to describe the essence of a nonviolent mass campaign. Followers of *satyagraha*, Gandhi wrote, believe that it is better to suffer than to inflict suffering on others; that one's opponents are also human and therefore can be persuaded; that nonviolence is a truth-seeking instrument through which a political situation can be opened up; that deep-rooted injustice must be confronted; and that in many cases organized nonviolence offers the only real alternative to violence. In Gandhi's view, a *satyagrahi* (follower of *satyagraha*) must be more than simply a passive sufferer; he or she must confront evil with an intense, disciplined conviction. Yet Gandhi also believed that even a sincere *satyagrahi* could be mistaken, which made nonviolence toward others all the more important.[*]

Gandhi felt that a well-thought-out nonviolent campaign should involve two stages.[†] In preparing for mass action, the campaigners should launch an educational effort to make people aware of the issues involved. Next should come the action phase of the campaign, in which *satyagrahis* commit carefully considered acts of civil disobedience. Communication with opponents should be maintained during this phase; campaigners must be ready to negotiate at all times, as long as basic principles are not sacrificed. Gandhi's own mass campaigns ranged in duration from seven weeks to sixteen months.

Not all of Gandhi's campaigns were entirely successful or entirely nonviolent. But cumulatively they demonstrated the power of organized nonviolence as a method of social struggle. Not only were they crucial in India's evolution toward independence, but they also had a profound impact on the civil rights movement in the United States.

[*]*Mohandas K. Gandhi*, An Autobiography *(Boston: Beacon Press, 1971).*
[†]*Joan V. Bondurant*, Conquest of Violence *(Berkeley, Calif.: University of California Press, 1969).*

norms interact.[13] According to one student of the subject:

> What society needs is a struggle sufficiently equal to compel a process of public reasoning, which is its best protection against error. To prohibit freedom of speech, to forbid strikes and boycotts, and to punish civil disobedience by death would enable governments to overwhelm protest without having to reason. At the other extreme, not only to permit free speech, strikes, and boycotts but also to legalize civil disobedience and disruption . . . would enable the dissenting minority to dictate to the majority. . . . A more equal and fruitful balance might be obtained by permitting boycotts but forbidding disruption and penalizing civil disobedience, but only moderately.[14]

How Protest Works

Effective protest involves more than simply voicing objections to policies or conditions. Many subtle and complex concepts are at work in protest activity. Let us consider the process of consciousness-raising, activating others, the contexts for effective protest, and the limitations of protest tactics.

Consciousness-raising

The first and most difficult step in galvanizing a protest movement involves shaping the consciousness of the protester. The protester—the person who is willing to make the commitment, to take the step of publicly declaring a grievance—stands at the core of all protest. A movement's leaders must make the victims of an unjust social system recognize the injustices perpetrated against them or the needless suffering they endure. For example, when numerous residents along the Love Canal in upstate New York began developing serious illnesses, an active consciousness-raising program was launched by one concerned homemaker to make her neighbors recognize that those illnesses were caused by toxic chemicals contaminating area waterways and groundwater. Once that hurdle was overcome, protest activities could succeed. Because inner change must precede public action, leaders must promote both a new consciousness and a new sense of courage.

Activating Others

Once a new mass consciousness begins to develop, the protest group must forge alliances with other groups in society. The civil rights movement in the United States, for example, needed significant support from outside the African-American community to topple the pillars of segregation. To that end, civil rights leaders sought to activate third parties, to find help both within and outside government institutions. This can

Emotions run high in front of the Supreme Court in 1989. Pastor George Lucas argues with a pro-choice supporter over *Roe* v. *Wade*. One of the dangers of protest and mass politics is that emotions may get out of control on matters of intense concern to all sides. *(UPI/Bettmann)*

be difficult. It is usually accomplished by appeals, by threats, or by a combination of the two.

In making appeals, protesters call attention to the injustice, suffering, or deprivation they face so that outside groups or individuals will be moved to help them. The extent to which appeals generate public concern, which in turn activates government officials, depends on several factors: the actual degree of suffering, the extent to which the public acknowledges this suffering and regards it as unjust, the feeling that the protesting group if worthy of social concern, and the public's belief that the system has the resources to address these concerns.

If appeals fail, threats can be used. The threat of disruption—of making it more difficult for society to carry on its business—is a staple of democratic protest. Gandhi astutely combined appeals and threats in his nonviolent campaigns. He knew that when the streets are filled with demonstrators, the jails filled with protesters, and the court dockets jammed with cases, business grinds to a halt. Governments are then more willing to listen to protesters' grievances.

Traffic congestion as a means of protest—a highly effective, if not infuriating, tactic in urban areas. Here French truckers make their concerns vividly felt to the French public as well as to politicians. *(Alexander Boulat/SIPA Press)*

Threats can also take more sinister forms. For example, protesting groups can threaten or carry out acts of violence. Such tactics, however, often backfire, toughening the resolve of opponents, and creating antagonism instead of support.

Contexts for Effective Protest

Protest is more effective when it takes place in a favorable context. Protesters have a better chance of success when other, more powerful groups in society embrace their objectives or when protest tactics coincide with the objectives of influential politicians or public officials. Antiabortion demonstrators were likely to get a favorable hearing during the Reagan administration, for example.

Protest tactics sometimes force a government to recognize that the protesters deserve to be heard in the political process. But once they gain such a hearing, protesters must rely on influence of a more mundane kind. So although protest activities may place issues on the public agenda, provide a protest group with higher standing in public controversies, or enhance the group's organizational development, protest by itself is not enough to accomplish policy objectives. In fact, it is a somewhat precarious tool on which to rely, as we will see in the next section.

Limitations of Protest Tactics

Effective protest usually lies uneasily on the borderline between legitimacy and illegitimacy. Performing this delicate balancing act, protest demonstrations often run the risk of alienating potentially sympathetic groups and arousing opposing groups to action. As a matter of strategy, leaders must anticipate whether the costs of a given protest tactic will outweigh its benefits (rarely an easy calculation). Decisions involving protest strategy become especially critical once a protest group has begun to gain success, for the wrong choice may jeopardize alliances forged with other groups.

Reluctance to alienate supporters and sympathizers may account in part for the tendencies of protest groups to become more cautious and restrained as they grow in power and status. Protest groups with relatively little power, by contrast, have little to lose. Such groups, however, may lack the resources to organize protest campaigns. In addition, protest success depends on gaining media coverage, which also helps leaders to reach, win over, and mobilize outside groups. Without publicity, protest tactics may be meaningless. The most successful protest leaders in recent years have raised the ability to gain publicity to an art form.

As we saw in Chapter 10, the news media not only report the news can also shape it in significant ways. Protest leaders design tactics based on what editors consider newsworthy. Tactics often escalate in severity or militance because what is news one day will be old hat the following week. Forceful communication dramatizes the goals of a protest movement. Consider the powerful symbolism of the Boston Tea Party in 1773 or the March on Washington in 1963.

Civil disobedience has become far more commonplace than it was thirty years ago, and its political impact is consequently diminished. Protesters may also run up against intense opposition that thwarts the effectiveness of their actions. The targets of protest may command significant resources to limit or undermine protest strategies. For example, established interests may use one or more of the following retaliatory measures:

Delaying tactics: appointing a commission or relegating a problem to study, for instance.

Tokenism: conceding a tiny fraction of what is desired while giving the impression that a significant concession has been made.

Discreditation: attempting to damage a group's credibility or legitimacy in the public arena.

Suppression: using police power against protesters.

Thus even though protest is one of the few resources available to relatively powerless groups, its potential for success is often severely limited.

Protesting Politics Itself: The Push for Term Limits for Legislators

In the late 1980s, rumblings from the heartland, outside state capitals, raising the concern that professional legislators had become too insulated from the people they represent. High rates of incumbent reelection, low rates of turnover, strong ties between financial interests with a stake in favorable legislation and legislators with expensive campaigns, and cozy redistricting schemes that assured incumbent success all led to an active debate about **term limits** as a means of making state legislatures more responsive. In contrast to the image of the professional legislator, the ideal behind the movement for term limits was the citizen legislator, in touch with everyday life because he or she is only temporarily in service to the state.

The concept of term limits is not new in America.[15] The Articles of Confederation specified that members of Congress rotate out after serving three one-year terms within any five-year period. The Virginia Plan, presented to the Constitutional Convention by Edmond Randolph, included a term limitation on members of Congress that was later dropped. The convention's argument against term limits had to do with what properly belonged in a constitution, not the widely accepted notion of short tenure for elected officials. The arguments made in favor of longer Senate terms are clearly based on the assumption that House members would not be returning to office term after term.[16] During the nineteenth century the advantages of limited tenure for legislators in Washington were widely, often implicitly, acknowledged. Abraham Lincoln served a single term in the House of Representatives before returning to Illinois as part of an informal rotation agreement with two Whig adversaries in his district (an unthinkable arrangement today). It didn't serve a candidate or a party well to display an unseemly desire to prolong one's stay in Congress.

Between the middle of the nineteenth century and the middle of the twentieth the pattern of turnover in Congress change significantly. Around 1910, when, as a means of reducing the arbitrary power of the Speaker, seniority was installed as the primary means of distributing power in the House, both individual members and districts discovered an interest in extended tenure. The average tenure of a House member at the turn of the century was five years; now it's ten. The same phenomenon has occurred in state legislatures.

If the American people don't like their representatives enjoying long stays in Washington, why not just clean house more often? Doesn't ordinary politics offer the best solution: simply turning the rascals out at the next election? Several factors militate against this straightforward solution. Since World War II, Congress has discovered constituency service. As the federal bureaucracy has grown and individual benefit programs have proliferated, the opportunity to offer personalized help has grown apace. Every member knows the importance of helping out with a lost social security check or a recommendation to a service academy. That kind of service, added to the representatives' financial advantages of incumbency, the constituent advantage of having a representative with seniority, and the difficulty of holding representatives accountable in circumstances of divided government, has made most incumbents quite secure in their jobs. Ordinary politics reinforces the status quo. As we saw in Chapter 1, direct legislation—bypassing the established legislative mechanisms with the initiative and the referendum—stands between protest and normal electoral politics. Direct-legislation term limits would be enacted by voters, not professional legislators.

Would formal term limits make Congress and the state legislatures more democratic? Some cynical observers suggest that the motivation behind term limits is not to make American legislatures more democratic but to make them less Democratic. After all, since the majority of incumbents in Congress and most state legislatures are Democrats, increased turnover means increased Republican chances for control. But there is more to the push for term limits than partisan maneuvering. A New York Times/CBS poll in 1990 found a 61 percent-to-21 percent majority in favor of "a limit to the number of times a member of the House of Representatives can be elected to a two-year term." Republicans and Democrats demonstrated almost identical levels of support for the idea.[17]

In 1990, three states (Oklahoma, Colorado, and California) used the initiative to adopt some form of term limits for state legislators. Colorado included its congressional delegation in the limits. Reductions in benefits and staff support budgets for legislators were included in the California initiative. Given the current advantages of seniority, a state-by-state limitation of congressional terms would seem to be hard to sell. If every other state is going to reap the relative advantages of seniority, why should one change unilaterally? Speaker of the House Tom Foley made an argument like this in his home state of Washington to help to defeat a term limit measure in 1991. Yet, in November 1992 term limitations for congressional members were approved by voters in fourteen states. If the state-by-state movement should stall, the change to term limits would have to come from an unlikely source: Congress itself, via a proposed constitutional amendment. That would be a little like "expecting the chickens to vote for Colonel Sanders."[18] Nevertheless, some keen observers of national politics believe that congressional term limits may become a reality. Political scientist Walter Dean Burnham said in 1990 that "there really is a term limitation train leaving the station under a growing head of steam. There would seem to be a considerable chance (50-50 or so) that by the end of the decade, a constitutional amendment will be adopted to impose such limitation at the federal level."[19]

Opponents say that term limits will increase the relative weight of organized special interests by decreasing the strength of individual legislators. Lobbyists don't have term limits. Legislative staffs would similarly gain greater relative control. Years of legislative experience would be lost to term limits. And what happens to its internal structure when the House of Representatives must choose a Speaker with only a term or two's experience?

In 1992 term limitation was an idea whose time had come. In Washington State in 1991 term limits were defeated. Are we witnessing the wave of the future, a mass movement of direct legislation to transform legislatures across the land? Or is this rather a disgruntled blip of protest, more likely to remind representatives to stay in touch than to alter the system fundamentally?

Conclusions

If we could devise a system so perfect that government officials never made wrong decisions, we could forget about protest tactics and stick to politics as usual. Of course, such a political process is nowhere to be found. In real democratic politics, some needs are ignored, and others are deliberately neglected. As society changes, some groups and individuals find their values threatened, their status undermined, their expectations dashed.

"A little rebellion now and then is a good thing, and as necessary in the political world as storms are in the physical," declared Thomas Jefferson, in a particularly revolutionary mood. Protest is useful to a democratic society. For people whose consciences are offended by particular actions or policies, it provides a way of expressing discontent or voicing disagreement. Protest also signals that some of our fellow citizens actively oppose particular government policies. It can educate us about the problems that others face. It can arouse the lethargic conscience of the majority. Protest, when successful, helps to focus our attention on matters that might otherwise be ignored.

Nevertheless, protest and extraordinary politics can be a nuisance—or worse, a serious danger to life, liberty, and democratic processes. Protest can be animated by a spirit alien to democracy or carried out such that basic democratic values are put in jeopardy. When the Ku Klux Klan sought to stop blacks from exercising basic political rights—when vigilantism was rampant and intimidation a common occurrence—extraordinary politics posed a serious threat to the democratic process.

Deciding whether protest is justified is no simple task. We can assert, however, that when protest is used as a tool of the weak, when it is carried out in a spirit of moral seriousness, and when its goals are compatible with democratic values (as in the case of the civil rights movement of the 1950s and 1960s), it enriches our political life.

Supplement: Martin Luther King's Letter from Birmingham Jail. (Excerpts)

My Dear Fellow Clergymen:

While confined here in the Birmingham city jail, I came across your recent statement calling my present activities "unwise and untimely." Seldom do I pause to answer criticism of my work and ideas. If I sought to answer all the criticisms that cross my desk, my secretaries would have little time for anything other than such correspondence in the course of the day, and I would have no time for constructive work. But since I feel that you are men of genuine good will and that your criticisms are sincerely set forth, I want to try to answer your statement in what I hope will be patient and reasonable terms.

* * *

Marches were a major dramatic element in the civil rights movement of the 1960s. When Martin Luther King, Jr., led protesters against segregation, their march served as a symbolic affirmation of unity and was a courageous public declaration of their grievances.
(Bruce Davidson/Magnum)

You deplore the demonstrations taking place in Birmingham. But your statement, I am sorry to say, fails to express a similar concern for the conditions that brought about the demonstrations. I am sure that none of you would want to rest content with the superficial kind of social analysis that deals merely with effects and does not grapple with underlying causes. It is unfortunate that demonstrations are taking place in Birmingham, but it is even more unfortunate that the city's white power structure left the Negro community with no alternative.

In any nonviolent campaign there are four basic steps: collection of the facts to determine whether injustices exist; negotiation; self-purification; and direct action. We have gone through all these steps in Birmingham. There can be no gainsaying the fact that racial injustice engulfs this community. Birmingham is probably the most thoroughly segregated city in the United States. Its ugly record of brutality is widely known. Negroes have experienced grossly unjust treatment in courts. There have been more unsolved bombings of Negro homes and churches in Birmingham than in any other city in the nation. These are the hard, brutal facts of the case. On the basis of these conditions, Negro leaders sought to negotiate with the city fathers. But the latter consistently refused to engage in good-faith negotiation.

* * *

You may well ask, "Why direct action? Why sit-ins, marches, and so forth? Isn't negotiation a better path?" You are quite right in calling for negotiation. Indeed, this is the very purpose of direct action. Nonviolent direct action seeks to create such a crisis and foster such a tension that a community which has constantly refused to negotiate is forced to confront the issue. It seeks so to dramatize the issue that it can no longer be ignored. My citing the creation of tension as part of the work of the nonviolent-resister may sound rather shocking. But I must confess that I am not afraid of the word "tension." I have earnestly opposed violent tension, but there is a type of constructive, nonviolent tension which is necessary for growth. Just as Socrates felt that it was necessary to create a tension in the mind so that individuals could rise from the bondage of myths and half-truths to the unfettered realm of creative analysis and objective appraisal, so must we see the need for nonviolent gadflies to create the kind of tension in society that will help men rise from the dark depths of prejudice and racism to the majestic heights of understanding and brotherhood.

The purpose of our direct-action program is to create a situation so crisis-packed that it will inevitably open the door to negotiation. I therefore concur with you in your call for negotiation. Too long has our beloved Southland been bogged down in a tragic effort to live in monologue rather than dialogue. . . .

We know through painful experience that freedom is never voluntarily given by the oppressor; it must be demanded by the oppressed. Frankly, I have yet to engage in a direct-action campaign that was "well timed" in the view of those who have not suffered unduly from the disease of segregation. For years now I have heard the word "Wait!" It rings in the ear of every Negro with piercing familiarity. This "Wait" has almost always meant "Never." We must come to see, with one of our distinguished jurists, that "justice too long delayed is justice denied."

* * *

You express a great deal of anxiety over our willingness to break laws. This is certainly a legitimate concern. Since we so diligently urge people to obey the Supreme Court's decision of 1954 outlawing segregation in the public schools, at first glance it may seem rather paradoxical for us consciously to break laws. One may well ask: "How can you advocate breaking some laws and obeying others?" The answer lies in the fact that there are two types of laws: just and unjust. I would be the first to advocate obeying just laws. One has not only a legal but a moral responsibility to obey just laws. Conversely, one has a moral responsibility to disobey unjust laws. I would agree with St. Augustine that "an unjust law is no law at all."

Now, what is the difference between the two? How does one determine whether a law is just or unjust? A just law is a manmade code that squares with the moral law or the law of God. An unjust law is a code that is out of harmony with the moral law. To put it in the terms of St. Thomas Aquinas: An unjust law is a human law that is not rooted in eternal law and natural law. Any law that uplifts human personality is just.

Any law that degrades human personality is unjust. All segregation statutes are unjust because segregation distorts the soul and damages the personality. It gives the segregator a false sense of superiority and the segregated a false sense of inferiority....

Let us consider a more concrete example of just and unjust laws. An unjust law is a code that a numerical or power majority group compels a minority group to obey but does not make binding on itself. This is *difference* made legal. By the same token, a just law is a code that a majority compels a minority to follow and that it is willing to follow itself. This is *sameness* made legal.

Let me give another explanation. A law is unjust if it is inflicted on a minority that, as a result of being denied the right to vote, had no part in enacting or devising the law. Who can say that the legislature of Alabama which set up that state's segregation laws was democratically elected? Throughout Alabama all sorts of devious methods are used to prevent Negroes from becoming registered voters, and there are some counties in which, even though Negroes constitute a majority of the population, not a single Negro is registered. Can any law enacted under such circumstances be considered democratically structured?

Sometimes a law is just on its face and unjust in its application. For instance, I have been arrested on a charge of parading without a permit for a parade. Now, there is nothing wrong in having an ordinance which requires a permit for a parade. But such an ordinance becomes unjust when it is used to maintain segregation and to deny citizens the First Amendment privilege of peaceful assembly and protest.

I hope you are able to see the distinction I am trying to point out. In no sense do I advocate evading or defying the law, as would the rabid segregationist. That would lead to anarchy. One who breaks an unjust law must do so openly, lovingly, and with a willingness to accept the penalty. I submit that an individual who breaks a law that conscience tells him is unjust, and who willingly accepts the penalty of imprisonment in order to arouse the conscience of the community over its injustice, is in reality expressing the highest respect for law.

* * *

Oppressed people cannot remain oppressed forever. The yearning for freedom eventually manifests itself, and that is what has happened to the American Negro. Something within has reminded him of his birthright of freedom, and something without has reminded him that it can be gained. Consciously or unconsciously, he has been caught up by the *Zeitgeist*, and with his black brothers of Africa and his brown and yellow brothers of Asia, South America, and the Caribbean, the United States Negro is moving with a sense of great urgency toward the promised land of racial justice. If one recognizes this vital urge that has engulfed the Negro community, one should readily understand why public demonstrations are taking place. The Negro has many pent-up resentments and latent frustrations, and he must release them. So let him march; let him make prayer pilgrimages to the city hall; let him go on freedom rides—and try to understand why he must do so. If his repressed emotions are not released in nonviolent ways, they will seek expression through violence; this is not a threat but a fact of history. So I have not said to my people, "Get rid of your discontent." Rather, I have tried to say that this normal and healthy discontent can be channeled into the creative outlet of nonviolent direct action. And now this approach is being termed extremist.

* * *

Before closing I feel impelled to mention one other point in your statement that has troubled me profoundly. You warmly commended the Birmingham police force for keeping "order" and "preventing violence." I doubt that you would have so warmly commended the police force if you had seen its dogs sinking their teeth into unarmed, nonviolent Negroes. I doubt that you would so quickly commend the policemen if you were to observe their ugly and inhuman treatment of Negroes here in the city jail; if you were to watch them push and curse old Negro women and young Negro girls; if you were to see them slap and kick old Negro men and young boys; if you were to observe them, as they did on two occasions, refuse to give us food because we wanted to sing our grace together. I cannot join you in your praise of the Birmingham police department.

* * *

I hope this letter finds you strong in the faith. I also hope that circumstances will soon make it possible for me to meet each of you, not as an integrationist or a civil-rights leader but as a fellow clergyman and a Christian brother. Let us all hope that the dark clouds of racial prejudice will soon pass away and the deep fog of misunderstanding will be lifted from our fear-drenched communities, and in some not too distant tomorrow the radiant stars of love and brotherhood will shine over our great nation with all their scintillating beauty.

Yours for the cause of Peace and Brotherhood,

MARTIN LUTHER KING, JR.

GLOSSARY TERMS

civil disobedience
extraordinary politics
Ku Klux Klan

satyagraha
sit-in
term limits

NOTES

[1] For a detailed description of this incident, see Milton Viorst, *Fire in the Streets* (New York: Simon & Schuster, 1979), chap. 3.

[2] Frederich F. Siegel, *Troubled Journey: From Pearl Harbor to Reagan* (New York: Hill & Wang, 1984), pp. 148–149.

[3] A detailed analysis of civil strife and protest in many nations appears to Ted R. Gurr, "A Comparative Study of Civil Strife," pp. 572–626, and Raymond Tanter, "International War and Domestic Turmoil: Some Contemporary Evidence," pp. 550–569, both in *The History of Violence in America*, ed. Ted R. Gurr and Hugh D. Graham (New York: Praeger, 1969).

[4]See Alec Barbrook and Christine Bolt, *Power and Protest in American Life* (New York: St. Martin's Press, 1980), chap. 9, for a discussion of what issues prompt protest and how group power is exercised in U.S. politics.

[5]David O. Sears and John B. McConahay, *The Politics of Violence: The New Urban Politics and the Watts Riots* (Boston: Houghton Mifflin, 1973).

[6]Ted R. Gurr, *Why Men Rebel* (Princeton, N.J.: Princeton University Press, 1970), chaps. 2, 10.

[7]James Michener, *Kent State: What Happened and Why* (New York: Random House, 1971).

[8]See John Bunzel, *Antipolitics in America* (Westport, Conn.: Greenwood Press, 1979); and Robert Paul Wolff, Barrington Moore, Jr., and Herbert Marcuse, *A Critique of Pure Tolerance* (Boston: Beacon Press, 1965).

[9]See A. J. Muste, "Of Holy Disobedience," in *Civil Disobedience: Theory and Practice*, ed. Hugh Adam Bedau (New York: Pegasus, 1969), pp. 127–134.

[10]Henry David Thoreau, *Walden and Civil Disobedience* (New York: Signet, 1961), p. 223.

[11]For a thoughtful commentary on King's letter, see Curtis Crawford, ed., *Civil Disobedience: A Casebook* (New York: Cromwell, 1973), pp. 226–229.

[12]David Dellinger, *More Power than We Knew* (Garden City, N.Y.: Anchor Press, 1975).

[13]See Elliot Zashin, *Civil Disobedience and Democracy* (New York: Free Press, 1972), chaps. 5–9.

[14]Crawford, *Civil Disobedience*, p. 241.

[15]Much of our discussion is drawn from two works on term limits: Charles R. Kesler, "Bad Housekeeping: The Case against Congressional Term Limitations," *Policy Review*, Summer 1990, pp. 20–25; and John H. Fund, *Term Limitation: An Idea Whose Time Has Come, Policy Analysis* Paper No. 141 (Washington, D.C.: Cato Institute, 1990).

[16]*Federalist* No. 62.

[17]Fund, *Term Limitation*, p. 2.

[18]Colorado State Senator Terry Considine, quoted in Ronald D. Elving "Congress Braces for Fallout from State Measures," *Congressional Quarterly*, September 20, 1990, p. 3144.

[19]Unpublished letter quoted in Fund, *Term Limitation*, p. 24.

SELECTED READINGS

For an introduction to **mass politics**, see William Gamson, *The Strategy of Social Protest*, 2nd ed. (Belmont, Calif.: Wadsworth, 1990), especially Chapter 6, about the use of violence in social protest. Gamson's research shows that users of violence have a higher-than-average success rate in gaining new advantages and even in winning social acceptance. A more general introduction can be had in James De Nardo, *Power in Numbers: The Political Strategy of Protest and Rebellion* (Princeton, N.J.: Princeton University Press, 1985). See also D. K. Gupta, *The Economics of Political Violence: The Effects of Political Instability on Economic Growth* (New York: Praeger, 1990); and Philip Schlesinger, *Media, State, and Nation: Political Violence and Collective Identities* (Newbury Parks, Calif.: Sage, 1991).

On the **philosophical and moral issues** of mass politics, read Michael Walzer, *Obligations* (Cambridge, Mass.: Harvard University Press, 1970); John Rawls, *A Theory of Justice* (Cambridge, Mass.: Harvard University Press, 1972); and J. Ronald Pennock and John W. Chapman, eds., *Nomos XII: Political and Legal Obligation* (New York: Atherton Press, 1970).

For more about **political protest** in the United States, start with Barbara Epstein, *Political Protest and Cultural Revolution: Nonviolent Direct Action in the 1970s and 1980s* (Berkeley:

University of California Press, 1991). Also try Lee E. Williams, *Postwar Riots in America, 1919 and 1946: How the Pressures of War Exacerbated American Urban Tensions to the Breaking Point* (Lewiston, N.Y.: Mellen, 1991).

The richest sources on mass politics and protest are **comparative studies**, including the following representatives of a wide range of work: Jeffrey N. Wasserstrom and Elizabeth J. Perry, eds., *Popular Protest and Political Culture in Modern China: Learning from 1989* (Boulder, Colo.: Westview Press, 1992); Sidney G. Tarrow, *Democracy and Disorder: Protest and Politics in Italy, 1965–1975* (New York: Oxford University Press, 1989); Diane Parness, *The SPD and the Challenge of Mass Politics: The Dilemma of the German Volkspartei* (Boulder, Colo.: Westview Press, 1991); Asghar Ali Engineer, *Communalism and Communal Violence in India: An Analytical Approach to Hindu-Muslim Conflict* (Delhi: Ajanta Publications, 1989); Veena Das, ed., *Mirrors of Violence: Communities, Riots, and Survivors in South Asia* (New York: Oxford University Press, 1990); Washington Office on Latin America, *Colombia Besieged: Political Violence and State Responsibility* (Washington D.C.: Washington Office on Latin America, 1989); Allen Feldman, *Formations of Violence: The Narrative of the Body and Political Terror in Northern Ireland* (Chicago: University of Chicago Press, 1991); and Jeffrey L. Gould, *To Lead as Equals: Rural Protest and Political Consciousness in Chinandega, Nicaragua, 1912–1979* (Chapel Hill: University of North Carolina Press, 1990).

For recent scholarship on **Gandhi** and his pacifist ideals, see John Hick and Lamont C. Hempel, eds., *Gandhi's Significance for Today* (New York: St. Martin's Press, 1989); James K. Mathews, *The Matchless Weapon: Satyagraha* (Bombay: Bharatiya Vidya Bhavan, 1989); Richard Gabriel Fox, *Gandhian Utopia: Experiments with Culture* (Boston: Beacon Press, 1989); and Bhikhu parekh, *Gandhi's Political Philosophy: A Critical Examination* (Notre Dame, Ind.: University of Notre Dame Press, 1989).

For further reading about **Martin Luther King, Jr.**, see Ira G. Zepp, *The Social Vision of Martin Luther King, Jr.* (New York: Carlson, 1989); Lewis V. Baldwin, *To Make the Wounded Whole: The Cultural Legacy of Martin Luther King, Jr.* (Minneapolis: Fortress Press, 1992); and *A Guide to Research on Martin Luther King, Jr.*, compiled by the staff of the Martin Luther King, Jr., Papers Project (Stanford, Calif.: Stanford University Libraries, 1989).

PART THREE

INSTITUTIONS

13
CONGRESS: THE HEART OF DEMOCRACY?

14
THE AMERICAN PRESIDENT: UNIQUE, NECESSARY, AND DANGEROUS

15
THE BUREAUCRACY: HOW MUCH SERVICE AND WHAT KIND?

16
THE AMERICAN JUDICIARY: NONELECTED DEFENDERS OF DEMOCRACY?

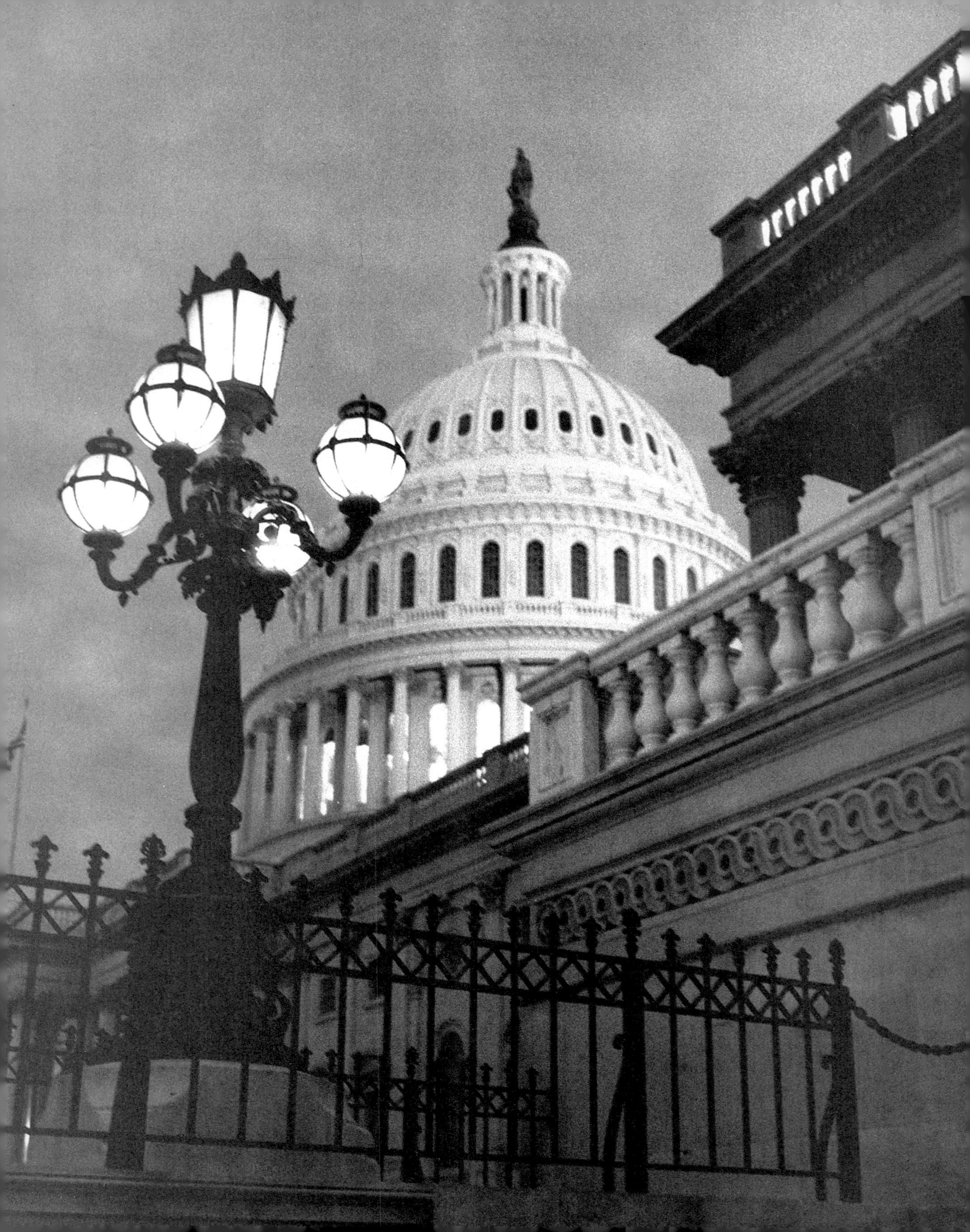

CHAPTER THIRTEEN

CONGRESS

The Heart of Democracy?

CHAPTER OUTLINE

Congress: An Overview
THE NATURE OF REPRESENTATION
FUNCTIONS OF CONGRESS

The Structure of Congress
THE HIERARCHY OF CONGRESS
LEGISLATIVE COMMITTEES
HOW A BILL BECOMES A LAW

Members of Congress
PERSONAL CHARACTERISTICS
INFLUENCES ON VOTING PATTERNS
CONGRESSIONAL ETHICS

Tradition and the Postreform Congress

Congress and the President
CONGRESS AND SECRETS
CONGRESS AND THE WAR POWERS RESOLUTION
CONGRESS AND THE BUDGET

AN ANNUAL SALARY OF $129,500, BLACK-TIE DINNERS, LOTS OF publicity, free trips abroad, fawning sides, a free office and a generous allowance for office furniture, a free gym, free photography, free potted plants from the United States Botanical Garden, and a three-day workweek—sounds like a pretty attractive job. That may be part of the problem. From the outside, the life of a member of the U.S. Congress seems too good to be real. The popular image of life as a member of the national legislature *is* too good to be real, at least for many members of Congress. Consider Leon Panetta, a Democrat, chair of the House Budget Committee. A powerful member of Congress from a heavily Democratic district in California, Panetta should have it made. But a recent account of a week in Panetta's life demonstrated the chasm between image and reality.

The workweek for Panetta began at 6:00 A.M. Tuesday at the end of the red-eye flight from San Francisco. He was met at the airport by a Budget Committee aide and driven to a townhouse he shares with three other members (Panetta pays $400 a month to be able to share sleeping space in the living room with Congressmen Charles Shumer of Brooklyn) for an hour's nap before walking to his office on Capitol Hill. That day he sat for a while in a closet in his office, recording

471

some sound bites concerning a Medicaid reform bill for use on a district radio station. He then participated in a series of meetings—with Budget Committee staff to plan hearings on a balanced-budget amendment, with other Democratic leaders to plan party strategy, and with the president of San Jose State University, who wanted to convert part of Fort Ord, slated to be closed, into a marine biology school. He had lunch with Italian-American business leaders, who mentioned him as a possible vice-presidential candidate and then berated him and his colleagues for being arrogant and inept. After lunch Panetta was driven downtown to address another business group, but since his remarks followed those of President Bush and several newspaper columnists, a third of the audience, weary of talk, walked out as he rose to speak. A stream of constituents came through his office that day bringing small gifts and asking favors. Such meetings are an ethical minefield. The goal is to avoid offending constituents and fund-raisers without creating even the appearance of ethical impropriety. There weren't many votes on the floor that day, but even so, Congressman Panetta's schedule ended around midnight. Two more days like that and anyone would be ready for the weekend.

Panetta arrives home in California on Friday afternoons to deal with whatever has come up in his district. This week a local radio station falsely reports that Panetta was ready to grant extensions on unemployment compensation to the area's agricultural workers. The chair of the House Budget Committee doesn't have that power, but he does have to deal with the flood of inquiries that follows the false report. Most weekend nights are filled with some dinner or benefit, like the Red Cross dinner recently, at which Panetta was asked to wait on tables. Saturdays he meets with constituents; Sundays he answers constituent mail. His wife works unpaid as his local office director. Panetta says, "Anybody who takes this job for the perks is barking up the wrong tree."

But by 1992 a fair proportion of the American population was convinced that members of Congress were overpaid, underproductive, and of suspect moral and ethical stature. In reference to the House banking scandal that was front-page news that year, one of Panetta's constituents, a bellhop at a Monterey hotel, said, "What I want to know is how many checks has Leon bounced lately?" "You get the impression that someone is robbing your integrity for no reason," Congressman Panetta admitted. "And it hurts. I didn't come to Washington to get free office furniture or discounted shoeshines and haircuts. It offends me when this kind of thing comes up."[1]

The act of legislating has long been considered the heart of the democratic political process. Early democratic theorists enshrined "the people" as the ultimate arbiters, the makers of law, who would both limit and extend their own freedom through the legislative acts of their representatives. Lawmaking would be a dignified and solemn process in which the representatives of the people would gather to debate the issues of the day, develop policy for the entire society, compromise differences, and resolve disputes. Democratic politics would remain viable so long as the people were effectively and honestly represented and their representatives were intelligent and committed enough to create workable and democratic laws.

The U.S. Constitution reflects this emphasis on legislation. The legislative article is the first, longest, and most complex of the seven articles in the original body of the

Constitution. The long list of powers granted to the federal government in Section 8 of that article are given to Congress, which, although formally coequal with the other two branches, was clearly the focal point of the new government established in 1789. Yet the descent from the ideal of democratic theory and the framers' expectations for our national legislature to the real world of legislative practice in the 1990s is a steep one. What we see on C-SPAN and read about in the newspapers, though delivered in solemn tones, is often far from the serious, responsible behavior imagined by democratic theory. And in spite of the framers' original vision, the focal point of government has now shifted to the other end of Pennsylvania Avenue, to the White House and the executive branch. There are good reasons for the American public to be disillusioned with Congress. Some of these, like the bartering of influence, are probably endemic to the actual legislative process in any large, complex society. Others, like Congress's inability to enact a responsible budget in a timely fashion, are due to particular contemporary characteristics of our government. Yet despite cause for concern and justification for reform, popular disparagement of Congress tars the whole institution when a selective critique is required. The real Congress is neither the democratic ideal nor the popular caricature. Two main questions need to be asked in looking at the real world of democratic legislative practices: How well do the structure, functioning, and membership of our own national legislature serve the representative tasks we've assigned it? And how many of these representative tasks have been or should be taken over by the president and the executive branch? While we acknowledge that the process can too often be tawdry, imperfect, deceptive, confused, and occasionally corrupt, we must also remember that Congress sometimes surprises us by seizing the initiative in the absence of executive leadership, by providing a healthy counterweight to executive excess, and even by providing individual examples of responsible, intelligent, concerned leadership.

In Part III we take a hard, realistic look at the primary institutions of the U.S. democratic process—Congress, the presidency, the bureaucracy, and the federal judiciary. We will explore how they have evolved, how effectively they work, how responsive they are to the general public, and how they interact—sometimes uneasily—with one another.

In probing the workings of our national legislature, several key questions will be addressed: Is Congress organized so that it can carry out its responsibilities effectively, honestly, democratically? Are the many varied interests in our society, including the public interest, effectively represented? Are our legislators generally honest and competent?

Congress: An Overview

Unlike most national legislatures, the U.S. Congress is an independent legislative body that does not merely pass laws but also initiates and creates them. Congress decides how revenues are to be raised and spent, regulates commerce among the states and with other nations, and has the power to declare war. More generally, the Constitution gives Congress the power "to make Laws which shall be necessary and proper for carrying into execution the foregoing powers, and all other powers vested by this constitution in the government . . . or in any department or officer thereof."[2] This innocuous-sounding statement, which has come to be known as the "elastic clause," has provided the basis for a vast expansion of congressional power. To do what is "necessary and proper" gives Congress a great deal of latitude in deciding when and how to legislate.

These tasks add up to a heavy legislative burden, one that has become more onerous as the world has grown increasingly complex and societal interests have become more diverse and polarized. Does Congress consistently play a creative, constructive role in democratic life? Or does it more often fail to fashion workable policy, to resolve differences sensibly, even to stand for democratic principles?

To answer these questions, we must examine the workings of Congress. But first we need to establish what is meant by the term *representation*. As many a member of Congress has discovered, that is no simple task.

The Nature of Representation

Two classic views define how legislators should represent their constituents. One group of political theorists argues that *representation* should be taken literally—that legislators should vote the way the majority of the people who elected them would vote. This position is known as the *delegate theory*. Adherents of the opposing view, called the *trustee theory*, maintain that representatives have a responsibility to vote their own convictions and to educate and lead their constituents. Constituents who don't like the results can vote the representative out at the next election. In practice, most members of Congress operate at various times under each of these theories.

As an added complication for representative government, none of the members of Congress represents the whole of the country. Each of the 535 national legislators represents a specific segment of the nation, and the interests of that segment often conflict with the interests of the nation as a whole.* To illustrate this fundamental problem, consider the issue of defense spending. When defense spending is cut, many states and districts lose local defense installations that employ thousands of local inhabitants and pump millions of dollars into local economies. Although the national interest might best be served by cutting back on defense, in the calculation of individual representatives that interest is likely to pale in the face of local or regional economic needs. Of course, legislators often do look toward the larger interest, but they tend to be sharply constrained by regional concerns and constituent needs.

Next we probe the diverse functions of Congress. From there we proceed to the structure of Congress, the members of Congress, congressional traditions and reform, and the uneasy interaction between Congress and the president.

---

*In addition to the 100 senators and 435 regular members of the House, there are a resident commissioner from Puerto Rico (since 1900) and nonvoting delegates from the District of Columbia (1971), Guam (1972), the U.S. Virgin Islands (1972), and American Samoa (1980).

Functions of Congress

Congress is more than a machine designed to crank out laws in a mechanical fashion year after year. Among other key functions, it serves as a forum to air public policy issues, crafts and shapes legislative proposals, helps to develop and oversee a national budget, oversees the administration of the laws it enacts, initiates investigations when called for, and serves an ombudsman function for the public by providing constituent service through House members' offices. The senator has the added function of accepting or rejecting executive and judicial appointments made by the president. Each of these functions deserves close examination.

A PUBLIC POLICY FORUM   How are policy issues aired in Congress? Debates on the House or Senate floor occasionally serve this purpose, but most policy issues are thrashed out in committee and subcommittee hearings, in which legislators go over the particulars of public policy, often in considerable detail.[3] As a prime example of the degree of public interest that can be generated by congressional hearings, consider the confirmation hearings for Supreme Court Justice Clarence Thomas. Investigating

The Senate Ethics Committee hears testimony about the "Keating Five"—five senators who, to one degree or another, were linked with failed savings and loan owner Charles Keating. Keating was later sent to prison for illegal transactions. Many felt that he had been able to wield far too much influence on Capitol Hill. *(AP/Wide World Photos)*

allegations that Thomas sexually harassed a female employee, Anita Hill, ten years earlier, the televised hearings got huge audiences and drove other stories off the front page for two weeks. That level of attention to the operation of a congressional committee hadn't been seen since the Iran-Contra hearings in the summer of 1987, when Lt. Col. Oliver North became a folk hero for a portion of the country as he described the Reagan administration's secret maneuvers to thwart stated policy on two fronts: trading arms for hostages in Iran and funding the Contra armed opposition in Nicaragua. In each of these cases, important policy issues penetrated the national awareness more broadly and deeply than is ordinarily the case.

More routinely, the televised coverage of Congress on C-SPAN, which began in the House in 1979 and in the Senate in 1986, provides a regular forum for policy debate. One study found that 27 percent of the public reported having watched televised sessions of Congress.[4] Legislators also use the regular news media and the lecture circuit to address contemporary issues. Senators in particular often speak before national audiences to voice their policy positions. Communication travels the other way, too: Interest groups come to Washington to make their voices heard in the corridors of Congress.

MAKING LAWS   In theory, the legislature makes the laws, but real life is not that simple. Congress contributes to the shaping of laws in many ways. Sometimes Congress initiates legislation, rather than waiting for direction from the president. At other times a president picks up ideas originally voiced by members of Congress. Another crucial element of law-shaping is the detailed consideration of proposed legislation. This process usually takes place in committee and subcommittee hearings and in committee meetings, where legislation is "marked up," or prepared for final consideration. In these discussions, lawmakers delve into the implications of legislative proposals, resolve conflicts, and fine-tune the wording of proposed legislation.

CREATING A BUDGET   Congress is also responsible for legislating a budget. For some time now the budget process has been a chaotic one. Reforms instituted in the past twenty-five years have not solved the problem of finding a role for Congress in generating a budget for a large, administrative government. The budget process will be addressed more fully at the end of this chapter.

OVERSEEING GOVERNMENT PROGRAMS   Through the oversight function, Congress follows up on the implementation of programs that have already been approved. Until relatively recently, Congress usually performed this task in a somewhat haphazard way. Then public concern over excessive taxes and government waste enhanced the political appeal of the oversight function. Methods of oversight range from routine audits and reporting requirements for agencies to more assertive legislative investigations, congressional vetoes, and even impeachment proceedings (by which Congress can remove certain officials from office).

AN INVESTIGATIVE ROLE   In recent years Congress has moved toward a more balanced, serious, and consistent evaluation of federal agencies and programs, principally through studies focused on efficiency and effectiveness in reaching program goals and through investigations. Congressional investigations—focusing on federal programs as well as various controversial aspects of political life—can be wide-ranging and highly publicized affairs. Recent congressional hearings have explored such matters as immigration, influence peddling at the Department of Housing and Urban Development, irregularities in defense procurement, and alleged fraud and racketeering in the savings and loan industry.

AN OMBUDSMAN FUNCTION   For many Americans with a problem involving the federal government, the first step toward a solution is a call to the local district office of a member of Congress. A lost social security check; planning for a family vacation to Washington, D.C.; a desire to get a federal contract; even simple information needs—all these are often initially addressed by congressional staffers rather than employees of the executive bureaucracy. The member's staff then provides an interface between the constituent and the bureaucracy. Members of the House of Representatives, never more than two years away from the next election, are usually happy to provide this kind of service, which partly explains increased staff sizes and contributes to the electoral advantage of incumbency.

ADVICE AND CONSENT: A SENATORIAL PREROGATIVE   The duty of providing advice and consent on presidential appointments is solely a Senate function. Some delegates to the Constitutional Convention of 1787 favored a system whereby the Senate would make all cabinet appointments; other maintained that such appointments should be the prerogative of the president. Under the compromise incorporated in the Constitution, "The President shall nominate, and by and with the Advice and Consent of the Senate shall appoint Ambassadors, other public Ministers and Consuls, Judges of the Supreme Court, and all other Officers of the United States." Although only nine cabinet nominees have been formally rejected by the Senate since 1789, the nominations of hundreds of appointees to cabinet and other offices have been withdrawn when it became clear that they would not gain approval. Many other appointees have had to face tough questioning in Senate committee rooms. Confirmation hearings give the party out of power a chance to retaliate against the "ins" by bringing up potentially damaging issues for the governing administration. They also give legislators a chance to elicit specific policy positions from appointees.

Although most confirmation hearings are mundane affairs, some have been marked by dramatic confrontations. Nominations to the Supreme Court, always highly visible, have often been contentious affairs as well. Clarence Thomas's nomination, mentioned earlier, was one such occasion. Even more fireworks attended President Reagan's 1987 nomination of Robert H. Bork. A range of groups opposed Bork's nomination because of his stand on civil rights and women's issues and his philosophy of narrow constitutional interpretation (he refused to acknowledge the right to privacy, for example, because no such right was specifically spelled out in the Constitution). Reagan would not withdraw Bork's nomination, even after it became clear that supporters could not marshal enough favorable votes in the Senate to confirm. The battle was waged through the Senate Judiciary Committee and onto the floor of the Senate. After Bork's defeat, Reagan's nomination of Douglas H. Ginsburg raised questions about Ginsburg's "judicial temperament." After admitting to using marijuana on several occasions in the past, Ginsburg withdrew his name from consideration. Reagan's next nominee to fill this slot on the Court, Anthony M. Kennedy, sailed through Senate confirmation hearings with little difficulty, gaining unanimous votes both in the committee and in the Senate as a whole.

To reduce the possibility of a rejected nomination, a president may adopt what has been called the "stealth" approach—choosing a nominee without a public record on controversial issues and instructing the nominee to refuse to answer questions on particular matters that might come before the Court. This strategy raises important questions about the nature of the Senate's advice and consent role. Can the Senate legitimately demand to know the issue positions of a particular nominee, or should the Senate's calculation of the nominee's fitness for a judicial position be based entirely on service and character issues?

The Structure of Congress

Democratic legislatures can be either **unicameral** (consisting of a single house) or, like the U.S. Congress, **bicameral** (consisting of two houses). In bicameral legislatures, all laws must run the legislative gauntlet twice—in the case of the U.S. Congress, through the larger House of Representatives and the smaller Senate. The political complexities arising from this situation constitute one facet of the system of **checks and balances** created by the framers of the Constitution: Each house of Congress was meant to "check" the actions of the other. The framers also stipulated that one house be elected on the basis of population and the other be made up of two members from each state. At the time the Constitution was written, it was thought that the House, directly elected every two years by the people, would serve as a populist forum. Senators, by contrast, were to be selected by "the states" (this meant the state legislatures), and only one-third of the Senate body would be chosen every two years. Senators were to be at least thirty years old (House members could be twenty-five) and to have been citizens for at least nine years (as opposed to seven years for House members). Thus, it was thought, shielded from popular pressures, senators would serve as the elder statesmen, checking the more populist imulses of the House.[5]

In 1913 the lofty political status of senators was altered by the Seventeenth Amendment, which required that they be popularly elected. Today senators are subject to many of the same political pressures faced by House members. Often called the most exclusive club in the world, the Senate is still structured to confer substantial political advantages. The one hundred senators serve six-year terms—a lengthy time in office that, in theory at least, allows them to exercise more independence from the immediate concerns of their constituents. Prominent senators can capture wide public attention, counterbalancing to some degree the attention focused on the president. By contrast, the 435 members of the House, who serve two-year terms and usually represent smaller constituencies, rarely gain national recognition; a House member must always keep one eye cocked to constituents' needs and reelection concerns. (**Table 13-1** summarizes some of the major differences between the two houses.)

Congress has developed certain structural or organizational traits in response to its size, workload, and political environment. We look now at the most important of these traits: hierarchy of leadership, specialization of function, and routinization of procedure—in particular, how a bill becomes law.

The Hierarchy of Congress

Congress is inherently less hierarchical than the executive branch. No body of this size could function, however, without some internal structure and hierarchy. Party leaders orchestrate the efforts of various congressional work groups to produce coherent legislative results.[6] In attempting to influence the legislative course of events, party leaders have several resources at their disposal. In many cases they can use parliamentary rules for partisan ends. For example, party leaders—especially those of the majority party—may delay scheduling a controversial bill until they gather enough votes for passage. Another leadership resource involves control or influence over many of the tangible

TABLE 13-1
MAJOR DIFFERENCES BETWEEN THE HOUSE AND THE SENATE

House	*Senate*
Larger (435 members)	Smaller (100 members)
Shorter term of office (two years)	Longer term of office (six years)
Less flexible rules	More flexible rules
Narrower constituency	Broader, more varied constituencies
Policy specialists	Policy generalists
Less press and media coverage	More press and media coverage
Power less evenly distributed	Power more evenly distributed
Less prestige	More prestige
More expeditious in floor debate	Less expeditious in floor debate
Less reliance on staffs	More reliance on staffs
Initiate all money bills	Confirms Supreme Court justices, ambassadors, and heads of executive departments
	Confirms treaties

SOURCE: Walter J. Oleszek, *Congressional Procedures and the Policy Process* (Washington, D.C.: Congressional Quarterly Press, 1978), p. 24.

COMPARATIVE PERSPECTIVE

THE BRITISH PARLIAMENT

The British Parliament, often referred to as the "mother of parliaments" because of its long tradition and wide influence, is made up of the House of Commons and the House of Lords. The functions of the latter are largely ceremonial or advisory; for most purposes, the House of Commons is the equivalent of the U.S. Congress.

In some ways the House of Commons may seem to be a very weak legislative body. The Cabinet (made up of members of Parliament chosen by the governing party or coalition) initiates virtually all legislation. Party control is very tight, so the majority party rarely fails to win a vote when the chips are down. Members of Parliament (MPs) generally follow party instructions, for failure to support the government in a crucial vote could end an MP's political career. The committee system in the House of Commons is also quite weak. There are few standing committees, none of which have anything like the powers and resources enjoyed by congressional committees.

Debate in the House of Commons is informal. Members speak from their own places, rather than from a podium, and are not permitted to read their speeches. Fillbustering is impossible, since all debate must be "germane" to the bill under consideration. Budgets are submitted by the Cabinet, and MPs are permitted only to propose decreases, which then serve as the basis of debate. In general, the opposition parties in the House of Commons have no effective way to obstruct Cabinet policy. For example, the opposition Labour party was able to do little to stop Prime Minister Margaret Thatcher's policies of privatizing the public sector (selling off government agencies to become private enterprises).

By contrast, the U.S. Congress can have a very important influence in such situations, especially through the use of its powers of appropriation.

(Box continues on page 481)

rewards available to individual members, such as choice committee assignments. Leadership PACs also allow party leaders to direct welcome campaign funds to cooperative members. Party leaders also control many psychological rewards; they can often influence the attitude of House colleagues toward a member, with isolation the possible fate of the maverick. Finally, by dominating the legislature's internal communications process, party leaders monopolize vital information: knowledge of the upcoming schedule, the substance of bills, and the intentions of other members of Congress or

> A unique and significant tradition in the House of Commons is the question period, during which Cabinet ministers must answer, on the floor of the Commons, written questions previously submitted to them by MPs. If an MP is not satisfied with the response, he or she can raise further questions orally. Such questioning sometimes develops into a full-fledged debate on important aspects of policy. The prime minister must also submit to such questioning. The U.S. president, in contrast, cannot be questioned directly by Congress, and such questioning of cabinet members as does occur takes place in committee hearings.
>
> One of the most interesting contrasts between the British and U.S. political systems is the official recognition of the opposition's role in the British parliamentary system. The opposition in Britain is an organized countergovernment within Parliament that stands ready to take power. Thus all national political leaders come up through Parliament and have had considerable experience.
>
> The British House of Lords is a seemingly anachronistic institution. Early in the eighteenth century the Lords was the dominant house of Parliament and was made up of the hereditary aristocracy. Over time the House of Commons stripped it of various powers until today it has very little role in legislating. The current House of Lords consists of around eight hundred hereditary peerages and three hundred fifty life peerages (lords temporal), two archbishops, and twenty-four bishops of the Church of England (lords spiritual). Of 1,185 lords in 1987, sixty-seven were women (ineligible prior to 1958). About 30 percent of lords do not attend sessions in the House at all, and fewer than half participate in debate. Average daily attendance is just over three hundred. Membership in the House of Commons is 635.*
>
> Theoretically, the House of Lords has the power to hold bills up for a year, but this power is almost never employed. In general, it does some amending of legislation and conducts unhurried and sometimes useful debate. It also functions as the supreme court of Great Britain.
>
> *Donald Shell, The House of Lords (Oxford: Philip Alan, 1988), chap. 2.

the president. As we will see, the powers wielded by party leaders tend to be greater in the House than in the Senate. Let us now consider these various powers.

LEADERSHIP IN THE HOUSE   The **Speaker of the House**, its presiding officer, is the most influential person on Capitol Hill. Although chosen by the members of the majority party, the Speaker's authority extends over the entire House. The Speaker regulates the flow of legislation by recognizing members on the floor (that is, granting

PART THREE • INSTITUTIONS

Two powerful representatives of the "old Congress"—Sam Rayburn, Speaker of the House, gets a birthday greeting from Senate Majority Leader Lyndon Johnson in 1956. Rayburn's advice to members: "To get along, you have to go along." Both men were extremely skillful players of Capitol politics; each wielded more centralized control over legislation in their respective chambers than is possible today. *(UPI/Bettmann Newsphotos)*

them the right to speak), breaking tie votes, and referring bills to committees. He or she may influence the assignment of members to committees and the activities of the various committee leaders or take the lead in scheduling legislation for floor consideration.

The Speaker is aided by the **majority leader**, the chief floor spokesman for his party and the person charged with mobilizing party voting strength. The majority leader is in turn assisted by the majority **whip**, who notifies members of pending business, polls them on their voting intentions, and works to make sure they are present to vote on key issues. The **minority leader** (who is the opposition party's candidate for Speaker) and minority whip perform similar tasks, although they have fewer rewards to dispense among their colleagues.

LEADERSHIP IN THE SENATE   In the Senate, strong leadership has been much more the exception than the rule. Not until the end of the nineteenth century did coherent leadership patterns appear, and even then Senate leaders were no match for the powerful Speakers presiding on the other side of the Capitol building. This reflects a strong tradition of consensus building and respect for minority viewpoints in the Senate and also its smaller size.

The presiding officer of the Senate has almost no formal power. The vice-president of the United States—the Senate's constitutionally mandated presiding officer—rarely attends sessions. **President pro tempore** of the Senate is an honorific title bestowed on the senior majority-party senator; ordinarily the Senate is presided over by freshman senators taking turns. The most important Senate leader is the majority leader, who helps to steer the party's legislative program through the upper house. The majority leader schedules legislation and influences many of the rewards available to senators, such as committee assignments, travel allowances, and office space. In this century, majority leaders have varied widely in effectiveness.

The opposition party elects the minority leader, who looks after the interests of his or her party members and those of the president, if the chief executive belongs to the same party. Both floor leaders are assisted by whips, who operate much as House whips do, although with noticeably looser reins on the troops.

Legislative Committees

A maxim on Capitol Hill holds that "you can't write a bill on the floor." Complex measures simply cannot be worked out by a large body of legislators. By relying on specialized work groups, or committees, Congress can simultaneously consider a variety of matters, and individual legislators can concentrate on a manageable range of problems.

Committees are the key policymaking bodies in Congress. Of the thousands of bills introduced into Congress each year, only a few are seriously considered by the committees—and only those few have a chance to be enacted into law. As President Woodrow Wilson once observed, "Congress in session is Congress on display, but Congress in committee is Congress at work."

Legislative specialization in Congress has increased as the congressional workload has grown more burdensome and diverse. The Legislative Reorganization Act of 1946 consolidated and reduced the number of **standing** (permanent) **committees** (see **Table 13-2**) but did nothing to halt the proliferation of subcommittees and other work groups, including special and **select committees** (see **Table 13-3**).

Outside the congressional hierarchy, the effective influence of members of Congress is based primarily on committee assignments and positions. In committee, members can give detailed consideration to bills, cultivate close relationships with interest groups and executive agencies affected by legislation, and develop expertise in particular areas. Such expertise is often deferred to by other members, who may not feel they have the specialized knowledge necessary to challenge committee judgments.[7] We now consider the implications of committee assignments, the proliferation of subcommittees, and the consequences of structural fragmentation.

COMMITTEE ASSIGNMENTS Committee assignments are made by the political parties in each house. For the Democrats, the Steering Committee nominates committee members; for the Republicans, the Committee on Committees serves this purpose. Each party caucus (made up of all members of the party in each house) then ratifies the selections. Assignments hinge on several factors: the prestige of a committee, the goals of particular legislators, the seniority of legislators, and whether a committee has in

(Text continues on page 487)

TABLE 13-2
STANDING COMMITTEES OF THE 102ND CONGRESS (1991–1992)

Committee	Number of Members	Number of Subcommittees
House		
Agriculture	43	8
Appropriations	57	13
Armed Services	48	7
Banking, Finance, and Urban Affairs	46	8
Budget	35	6
District of Columbia	12	3
Education and Labor	34	8
Energy and Commerce	42	6
Foreign Affairs	45	9
Government Operations	39	7
House Administration	19	7
Interior and Insular Affairs	41	6
Judiciary	35	6
Merchant Marine and Fisheries	42	5
Post Office and Civil Service	22	7
Public Works and Transportation	52	6
Rules	13	2
Science, Space, and Technology	45	6
Small Business	44	6
Standards of Official Conduct	12	—
Veterans' Affairs	34	5
Ways and Means	36	6
Senate		
Agriculture	18	7
Appropriations	29	13
Armed Services	20	6
Banking, Housing, and Urban Affairs	8	4
Budget	24	—
Commerce, Science, and Transportation	20	8
Energy and Natural Resources	19	5

(continued)

TABLE 13-2 (continued)
STANDING COMMITTEES OF THE 102ND CONGRESS (1991–1992)

Committee	Number of Members	Number of Subcommittees
Senate (continued)		
Environment and Public Works	16	4
Finance	20	8
Foreign Relations	20	7
Governmental Affairs	14	5
Judiciary	14	7
Labor and Human Resources	16	6
Rules and Administration	16	—
Small Business	18	6
Veterans' Affairs	11	—
Joint		
Economic	20	8
Library	10	—
Printing	10	—
Taxation	10	—

TABLE 13-3
SELECT AND SPECIAL COMMITTEES OF THE 102ND CONGRESS (1991–1992)

Committee	Number of Members	Number of Subcommittees
House—Select Committees		
Aging	65	6
Children, Youth, and Families	30	6
Hunger	26	2
Intellience	15	3
Narcotics Abuse and Control	25	—
Senate—Select Committees		
Ethics	6	—
Indian Affairs	8	—
Intelligence	15	—
Senate—Special Committees		
Aging	19	—

NOTE: Select and special committees are given mandates to study and report findings to the whole chamber but cannot report legislation.

FRAGMENTED RESPONSIBILITIES

Many broad subject areas of legislation overlap several committees. For example, a dozen different House committees have environmental responsibilities:

Agriculture: pesticides; soil conservation; some water programs

Appropriations: funding environmental programs and agencies

Banking, Finance, and Urban Affairs: open space acquisition in urban areas

Government Operations: federal executive organizations for the environment

Interior and Insular Affairs: water resources; power resources; land management; wildlife conservation; national parks; nuclear waste

Foreign Affairs: international environmental cooperation

Energy and Commerce: health effects of the environment; environmental regulations; solid waste disposal; clean air; safe drinking water

Merchant Marine and Fisheries: ocean dumping; fisheries; coastal zone management; environmental impact statements

Public Works and Transportation: water pollution; sludge management

Science, Space, and Technology: environmental research and development

Small Business: effects on business of environmental regulations

Ways and Means: environmental tax expenditures

Furthermore, a single piece of legislation can be referred to multiple committees. This overlapping jurisdiction allows members to develop expertise in several areas, provides several access points for interest group influence, and discourages the domination of an issue by any single group. However, such shared responsibility also increases delays and sometimes encourages intercommittee warfare. A House member provides a specific example: "John Dingell feels about his committee [Energy and Commerce] much as Lyndon Johnson felt about his ranch. Johnson didn't want to own the whole world, he just wanted to own all the land surrounding his ranch. Dingell doesn't want his committee to have the whole world, just all the areas surrounding his jurisdiction."

Source: Roger H. Davidson and Walter J. Oleszek, Congress and Its Members, *3rd ed. (Washington, D.C.: Congressional Quarterly Press, 1990), pp. 212–213.*

the past deliberately drawn members from particular states or regions. Although party leaders exercise some influence on all assignments, they generally concentrate on the most prestigious committees—Rules, Appropriations, and Ways and Means in the House; Appropriations, Finance, and Foreign Relations in the Senate. To be appointed to such committees, members must usually demonstrate "responsibility"—the ability to cooperate and accommodate different viewpoints. The most important factors in committee assignments, however, are a member's own desires and the likelihood that the assignment will help his or her reelection. As a result, like-minded legislators usually end up on the same committees, as do members who come from constituencies with similar interests, such as urban areas or farm states.[8]

Obviously, members of Congress want to serve on committees that deal with areas of personal or political interest. The problem with this arrangement is clear, however: A committee made up of such members may pay more attention to the special interests of each local representative than the overall public interest.

Once assigned to a committee, legislators generally have a right to stay there for as long as they serve in Congress. The majority-party member who has served on the committee the longest is usually named chairman. This practice, known as **seniority rule**, once was followed invariably. Today, however, party caucuses can and do pass over the senior member at times to install a more junior member as chair.

SUBCOMMITTEES   Over the past half-century a trend toward "subcommittee government" has emerged. Subcommittees of the standing committees have increasingly taken over the basic responsibility for detailed legislative work, including hearings, debates, and the writing of bills. The sheer number of subcommittees has increased as well. The House had eighty-three in the 84th Congress and 148 in the 102nd. A major committee (such as the Senate or House Appropriations Committee) may have as many as thirteen subcommittees. The growth of subcommittee government has enhanced the effectiveness of lobbying and single-issue groups. By targeting the relatively few legislators sitting on a subcommittee, lobbies can sharply focus their concerns, often at the expense of other groups—or the public interest.

CONSEQUENCES OF STRUCTURAL FRAGMENTATION   As we have seen, Congress has a highly decentralized and fragmented decision-making structure; most of the legislative work is handled by specialized committees and subcommittees. From a democratic point of view, this structure has both positive and negative consequences. On the positive side, the process of specialization helps members to focus their energies and talents on particular areas of policy and thereby develop the expertise that many consider the finest benefit of a legislative career.

But specialization also has many drawbacks. Because policymaking in Congress is fragmented, there is often little coherence in the way the legislature conducts its affairs. Also, since committees usually operate relatively independently, each committee tends to develop a protectionist attitude toward its own area of jurisdiction. Frequently, legislators of a certain ideological persuasion, from a particular geographic area, or representing a specific constituency predominate on a particular committee—those from farm states on agriculture committees, for example. In addition, they develop close relationships with interest groups and agencies in the executive branch that work along similar lines. Congress thus tends to serve many small constituencies rather than to adopt the larger view, the good of the whole nation or the public interest.

How a Bill Becomes a Law

Formal procedures in Congress describe a rigid, prescribed routine, especially when it comes to how a bill becomes a law. As **Figure 13-1** shows, passage of a bill is the final step in a laborious process that involves numerous stages in both the House and the Senate. Substantial variation exists, however, in the actual path that legislation takes within these formal procedures.

Nothing is assured once a bill enters the labyrinth of committee perusal and floor debate; at any stage along the way a proposal can be killed or simply left to die a natural death. In fact, the vast majority of proposals never make it out of committee. Those that do are often so loaded with non-germane amendments (**riders**) that legislators refuse to pass them or the president refuses to sign them. Let us now look at each step of the process of passing a bill to see where these pitfalls lie.

ORIGINATION   Legislation can originate in several ways. Some proposals arise from pressing national problems, as the New Deal legislation of the 1930s did from the Great Depression. Others originate in local problems or constituency demands, such as flood control or the building of a harbor. Still other proposals represent efforts to amend or renew existing legislation.

Bills can originate within either Congress or the administration. When the administration initiates legislation, proposals are prepared, or drafted, either by particular government agencies or by administration officials. When Congress takes the initiative, bills are usually drafted by congressional staff members or by experts placed at the disposal of members of Congress.

About one-third of all bills that are passed are private bills, dealing with the grievances or needs of particular citizens. The other two-thirds are public bills, affecting the general public.

INTRODUCTION   A proposal is introduced into each house by a member who supports it. In the House the member simply hands the bill over to the clerk; in the Senate a member must announce the proposal formally on the Senate floor. Although most bills are introduced simultaneously, or nearly so, in the two houses, a bill may undergo consecutive consideration, first passing through one house, then being considered in the other.

COMMITTEE CONSIDERATION   After the proposal is given an official number, the Speaker (for the House) and the president pro tempore (in the Senate) refer it to the appropriate standing committees. Because most of the substantive work on legislation

(Text continues on page 491)

FIGURE 13-1
HOW A BILL BECOMES A LAW

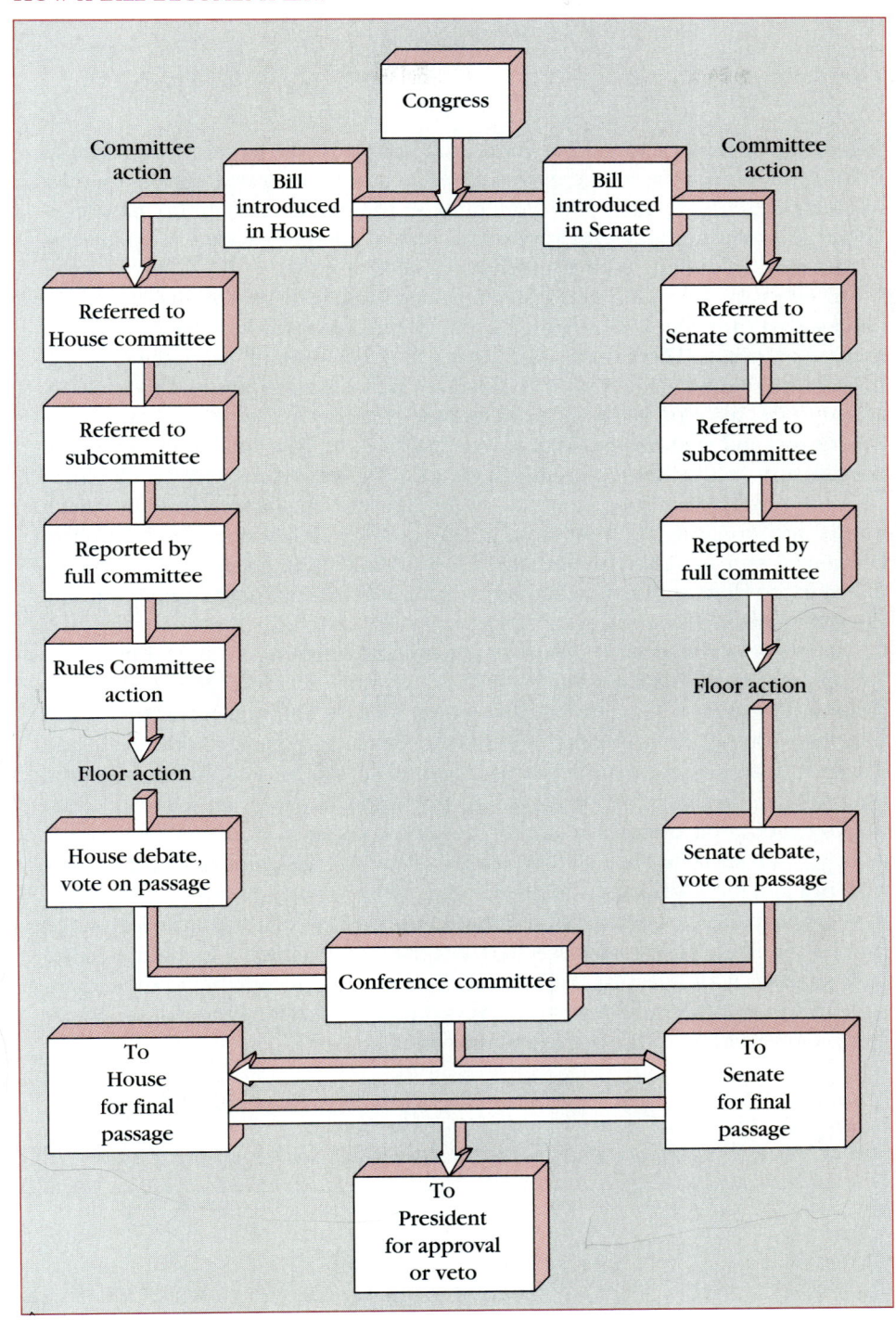

THE RIDER: A KEY PART OF THE LEGISLATIVE PROCESS

Legislators often seek to gain attention for pet proposals by attaching them as riders (nongermane amendments) to important pieces of legislation.* Once a rider has been attached to a bill, it is often difficult to separate it from the main legislation, and the rider may gain approval as part of a larger package. This process occurs most frequently with appropriations bills.

In February 1984, for example, President Reagan made a noncontroversial proposal to provide $90 million in emergency food aid to drought-stricken nations in Africa. The House appropriations subcommittee on agriculture approved the request. Then the full committee raised the amount to $150 million, added to the bill a proposal for $200 million in energy assistance to low-income Americans, and sent the package to the House floor. The full House approved the measure. In the Senate the African aid measure was diverted by the chairman of the appropriations subcommittee on foreign relations, who wanted to attach a rider appropriating $93 million in military aid for El Salvador. The full Senate committee then added to the measure the $200 million in energy assistance contained in the House bill and tacked on a further $21 million for insurgents fighting the government of Nicaragua.

At this point the main sponsors of the original African aid bill, fearing that it would go down to defeat amid battles over Central American policy, shrewdly proposed creating a separate bill that would include $80 million in African aid plus the $200 million in low-income energy assistance. It passed both House and Senate and was signed by the president. Meanwhile, the original bill became laden with even more riders, including money for nutrition programs, summer youth employment, drug interceptor aircraft, dams, and a tunnel. House leaders reacted angrily: "We sent the Senate a $90 million piece of legislation to feed the poor in Africa and it ends up as $1.3 billion."[†]

This example is extreme, but it illustrates how riders can affect the legislative process. In many cases proposals have been killed or derailed by being loaded with so many additions that they ultimately became unacceptable to their sponsors. It is easy to see why many observers criticize the rider system as an unreasonable obstruction to the legislative process.

*Theoretically, only the Senate can add nongermane amendments to a bill, but by twisting the rules, House members can also vote on riders.
[†]Martin Tolchin, "Hitching a Ride on Capitol Hill," *New York Times, May 2, 1984.*

is done in committee, this stage is often crucial in the lawmaking process. Once assigned to a standing committee, most bills are then referred to a specialized subcommittee for detailed discussion. The subcommittees hold hearings, at which interested individuals or groups can voice their views on the proposed legislation. The bill is also referred to committee staff members, who seek expert opinion on its likely effects and costs.

Next, in what is known as the **markup** the subcommittee goes over the bill in detail, often rewriting it on the basis of what the hearings have revealed and what the subcommittee members believe will be acceptable to members of the larger committee. Finally, the marked-up bill goes back to the larger committee with a favorable or unfavorable recommendation. If the committee votes to approve the bill, it goes to the full chamber for consideration. Bills that are not approved in committee are killed.

FLOOR DEBATE   Scheduling a bill for consideration is the result of sometimes extensive negotiation. In the Senate, where the majority leader is in charge, the bargaining often involves the leader of the majority. A majority of the Senate can vote to consider a bill on the floor, or the majority party's Policy Committee can schedule floor action after consultation with the minority leader. In the House the bill must be listed on a particular "calendar" (according to the type of bill it is—private or public, revenue or nonrevenue, controversial or noncontroversial), which determines when the bill will reach the floor. Most bills must also pass through the House Rules Committee, which decides how the bill will be debated—for example, whether or not it can be amended. Once the rules of debate are established, floor consideration is set by the Speaker.

FLOOR ACTION   Every bill that reaches the floor must be considered and voted on by each house. In the House of Representatives the length of debate and the possibility of amendment are dictated by the House Rules Committee. Debate on bills before the whole House are ordinarily allowed an hour or two per side, with party floor managers allocating specific numbers of minutes to each member who wishes to speak. In debates over amendments to a bill, members are allowed only five minutes of speaking time apiece. In the Senate, debate is not limited or subject to specified rules. The smaller size of the Senate permits the luxury of prolonged debate, although in a **filibuster**—the attempt to talk a bill to death—this privilege can be taken to extremes.

After the debate, a vote is taken on the bill. Ordinarily, each house passes its own version of a bill. Those versions may differ in the amounts of money allocated to a particular program, certain specifics of the legislation, or the riders that have been tacked on. When bills differ, either house is free to adopt the other version as a substitute. Alternatively, House and Senate leaders appoint a conference committee to work out a version acceptable to both houses. The size of conference committees increased during the 1980s to the point that a committee of forty members, many drawn from relevant standing committees, is not uncommon. The version of a bill hammered out in conference must then be voted on by each house exactly as it is written; no further amendments are permitted.

PRESIDENTIAL CONSIDERATION   A bill approved by both houses is sent to the president, who may consider it for up to ten days. If the president signs the bill, it becomes law. If the chief executive vetoes (rejects) the bill, it is returned to each house with a message explaining the reasons for the veto. To override a veto, each house must repass the bill by a two-thirds majority; otherwise, the bill is killed for that session of Congress. If Congress adjourns within the ten-day period, allotted for presidential consideration of a bill, the president can exercise what is known as a **pocket veto**: the chief executive kills the bill by refusing to sign it (by "pocketing" it). If the president does not sign the bill within the ten days *and* Congress is in session, the bill automatically becomes law.

IMPLEMENTATION   Once a bill becomes law, the executive branch must put that law into effect. This may mean, for example, issuing new rules in accordance with the bill or establishing a new government agency or independent commission. Implementation may also require allocating funds to a particular project or giving the go-ahead for a study. In implementing a bill, the executive branch must interpret the intentions of Congress, and if Congress does not agree with that interpretation, it may pass further laws to clarify its intentions.

Congressional travels, often described as wasteful, can sometimes serve to educate. Here Senator Nancy Kassebaum of Kansas visits Somalia in the summer of 1992. *(Tim Trenkle/ Courtesy of Senator Kassebaum)*

Members of Congress

The 535 men and women who represent us in Congress have heavy responsibilities and, some would say, an almost impossible task—enacting and overseeing the basic rules by which Americans live and the programs that help to sustain U.S. society.

Would-be legislators face a tough struggle to gain expertise, to master the arts of legislating, and to learn how and when to compromise, reconcile various interests, and withstand pressure. But do they have enough time to acquaint themselves with (much less master) the components of complex legislation? Can our lawmakers vote their clear convictions and still win reelection? Does Congress work in a creative and constructive fashion, or does it merely rubber-stamp the wishes of powerful interests? In short, do our representatives represent only some of the people some of the time?

Before addressing more complex questions, we must first examine the types of people who represent us in Congress—their personal characteristics, their professional concerns, the influences they face in voting, and their ethics.

Personal Characteristics

The typical member of Congress is a well-educated, upper-middle-class fifty-three-year-old white male Protestant, a businessman or lawyer by profession. Of course, many representatives do not fit this prototypical profile, and a few differ on almost every count. Yet the average carries considerable weight. The 103rd Congress, elected in 1992, included only forty African-Americans, nineteen Hispanics, nine Asians or Pacific

Ben Nighthorse Campbell became the first Native American ever selected to the U.S. Senate. A craftsman who makes jewelry, he was elected as a Democrat from Colorado in 1992, a year that saw some growth in the numbers of women and minorities in the Congress. *(Clark Jones/Impact Visuals)*

Islanders, one Native American, and fifty-four women. These numbers are significantly higher than comparable figures for the 102nd Congress, but they do not approach the proportions of any of these groups in the U.S. population. Even more severely underrepresented are blue-collar workers, union members, and housewives. **Table 13-4** profiles the 103rd Congress.

In financial terms, our representatives are considerably better off than the average citizen. Although most legislators live off their $129,500 (in 1992) annual salary, most receive additional income from investments, legal fees, real estate, partnerships, or businesses. There are more than a handful of millionaires in Congress. The substantial financial resources of many of our representatives raise particular ethical challenges. When members retain financial interests in areas that they deal with as legislators, a special effort is required to keep decision making disinterested.

TABLE 13-4
PROFILE OF THE 103RD CONGRESS (1993–1994)

	House	*Senate*		*House*	*Senate*
Party			**Professional Background***		
Democrats	259	56	Acting/Entertainment	1	0
Republicans	175	42	Aeronautics	2	1
Independents	1	0	Agriculture	19	8
			Business/banking	131	24
Average Age			Clergy	2	1
97th Congress	48.4	52.5	Education	66	11
103rd Congress	51.7	58.0	Engineering	5	0
			Homemaking	1	0
Sex			Journalism	24	9
Men	387	92	Labor unions	2	0
Women	48	6	Law	181	88
			Law enforcement	10	0
Religion			Medicine	6	0
Protestants	259	60	Military	0	1
Roman Catholics	118	23	Professional sports	1	1
Jews	32	10	Public service/politics	87	10
Others	26	5			
Minorities					
African-Americans	39	1			
Hispanics	19	0			
Asians/Pacific Islanders	7	2			
Native American	0	1			

*Because some members have more than one occupation, totals are higher than total membership. At the time of publication two Senate seats were yet to be determined.
SOURCE: *Congressional Quarterly Weekly Report* Special Report, November 7, 1992.

Influences on Voting Patterns

What influences a legislator's vote in Congress? If Congress were like practically any other democratic legislature, the answer would be easy: party discipline. But as we have already seen, U.S. political parties are relatively undisciplined organizations. Party identification still exerts a significant influence on the way a legislator votes, but so do ideological commitments (especially along liberal-conservative lines), informal groups in Congress, constituent desires, and interest group pressures. We now examine the influence of political parties, ideology, issue and identity groupings, and other factors on congressional voting patterns.

PARTY Over the years, party identification has been one of the most clear-cut factors in congressional voting. As we might expect in a legislature containing only two parties, many issues are fought out along party lines. But we also know that American parties are umbrella structures, bringing together proponents of many diverse views. Party allegiance, therefore, only partly explains why legislators vote as they do.

Party unity votes (when a majority of one party votes on one side of the issue and a majority of the other party votes on the other side of the issue) are not the norm in Congress. In roll call votes from 1961 to 1990, about 43 percent in each house were party unity votes. As **Table 13-5** demonstrates, party unity scores for Democrats have gone up since the early 1970s, representing in part a dramatic increase in southern Democrats' willingness to vote with their party. This is in part a function of the rise of the Republican party in the South and the flight of some former Democrats to the Republican party. Republican party unity scores were more stable during this period, although northern Republicans, like their southern Democratic counterparts but to a smaller degree, tend to vote less often with their party.

Predictably, party voting has been strongest on organizational issues, such as those voted on at the opening of a session. Party members almost invariably vote for their party's candidates for the chairmanships of committees and for leadership positions. Members also tend to follow the party line if the president or party leaders give a particular policy or issue high priority. For the most part, however, members of Congress understand that pleasing one's constituents, rather than one's party, is most important at election time. Thus party loyalty often takes a back seat to loyalty to the legislator's district or state.

IDEOLOGY Deviations from party unity can be explained in part by ideology. Although American politics has never been formally or self-consciously ideological, like-minded legislators may cluster together on sets of particular questions, confounding party lines altogether. Certain members of Congress may vote together because they share a general approach to public policy and tend to agree on a range of issues.

During the middle years of the twentieth century, for example, a coalition of conservative Democrats (mostly southerners) and Republicans banded together to defeat many liberal initiatives. At first it was primarily a veto group, seeking not so much to

TABLE 13-5
PARTY UNITY SCORES IN CONGRESSIONAL VOTING, 1954–1990 (PERCENT)

	House			Senate		
Year	All Democrats	Southern Democrats	Republicans	All Democrats	Southern Democrats	Republicans
1954	80	n.a.	84	77	n.a.	89
1956	80	79	78	80	75	80
1958	77	67	73	82	76	74
1960	75	62	77	73	60	74
1962	81	n.a.	80	80	n.a.	81
1964	82	n.a.	81	73	n.a.	75
1966	78	55	82	73	52	78
1968	73	48	76	71	57	74
1970	71	52	72	71	49	71
1972	70	44	76	72	43	73
1974	72	51	71	72	41	68
1976	75	52	75	74	46	72
1978	71	53	77	75	54	66
1980	78	64	79	76	64	74
1982	77	62	76	76	62	80
1984	81	68	77	75	61	83
1986	86	76	76	74	59	80
1988	88	81	80	85	78	74
1990	86	78	78	82	75	77

n.a. = not available.

Note: Data show percentage of members voting with a majority of their party on party unity votes. Party unity votes are those roll calls on which a majority of a party votes on one side of the issue and a majority of the other party votes on the other side. The percentages are normalized to eliminate the effects of absences, as follows: party unity = (unity)/(unity + opposition).

SOURCES: *Congressional Quarterly Almanac*, various years; *Congressional Quarterly Weekly Report*, January 9, 1982; January 15, 1983, 188; October 27, 1984, 2804–2805; January 11, 1986, 88; November 15, 1986, 2902–2906; January 16, 1988; November 19, 1988; December 30, 1989; January 6, 1990; December 22, 1990.

initiate its own legislation as to block liberal efforts in the areas of civil rights, social welfare, civil liberties, and foreign policy. Later the conservative coalition took more proactive steps in budget battles and in matters such as school prayer and abortion. One manifestation of the conservative coalition, for example, was the House Boll Weevils, an informal group of southern Democrats who provided strong cross-party support for the major Republican initiatives of the early Reagan years. What bound these members as a group to the Republican minority and distinguished them from their Democratic House colleagues was a sense that government ought to be smaller and taxes ought to be lower. Even though the Democrats held a 243 to 192 majority in the House

After 18 years of service in the House, Representative Stephen Solarz of New York was defeated in a Democratic primary in 1992. Solarz's district had been redrawn because of reapportionment and become predominantly Hispanic. He was defeated by a Hispanic candidate, Nydia Velasquez. Reapportionment and the redrawing of district lines often plays a significant role in the electing of new representatives. *(Vincent Ricardel/New York Times Pictures)*

of Representatives in 1981, the Reagan administration enjoyed a success rate of 82.4 percent on key votes.

Of course, for many members, issue positions may generally match rather than cross-cut party lines, so that ideology and party reinforce one another. The success of a Democratic majority may often represent some considerable commonality of viewpoint, after all. Given the relative weakness of parties to enforce party discipline, it is otherwise hard to explain the level of party unity voting that does occur.

ISSUE AND IDENTITY GROUPINGS   Congress has also spawned informal groups organized around particular interests and identities that influence members' voting patterns. These caucuses, which tend to be bipartisan, focus on specific interest areas. There is a black caucus, a Hispanic caucus, a rural caucus, a Sun Belt caucus, a mushroom caucus, and a textile caucus, among many others. One representative noted: "There's a caucus for just about everything around here and I guess it doesn't hurt. You know, they teach kids in school that this is the United States. But in reality, it is a group of regions and caucuses. It's not the UNITED States."[9]

Whereas the Senate does not officially recognize caucuses, the House of Representatives provides office space to caucuses and allows members to pool funds from their personal office accounts to pay operating expenses and salaries. In the 1980s, concern about the propriety of House caucuses "awash in outside money" led to the adoption of House rules requiring the disclosure of caucus finances and activities and forbidding caucuses from accepting private donations or government grants. In the wake of these restrictions a set of foundations was created, linked to caucuses but free to accept cash

498   PART THREE • INSTITUTIONS

Nine Democratic women who ran for the U.S. Senate in 1992. The 1992 elections saw an increase in the number of female candidates at all levels of government. *(AP/Wide World Photos)*

and spend it in a variety of ways to support the work and interests of House members in a particular area. Although members of Congress are forbidden to accept gifts from foreign governments, the Congressional Human Rights Foundation (tied to the congressional human rights caucus) was able to accept in 1990 a $50,000 gift from Citizens for a Free Kuwait, a group representing the Kuwaiti government. In some instances, such as the congressional Sun Belt caucus and the Congressional Sun Belt Institute, the caucus and the foundation share a single executive director.[10]

The existence of well-funded foundations tied to caucuses not only allows individual members greater independence from political parties but also provides an opportunity to engage in influence-enhancing cash funneling. The strong tendency of Congress to generate single-issue groups reflects and reinforces the particularism that has always characterized our national legislature.

OTHER INFLUENCES   The impact of constituency interests and outside interest groups on the voting patterns of members of Congress is often crucial. Constituency preferences figure prominently in legislators' decisions about how to vote on particular bills. Lawmakers' consideration of these preferences, after all, can sometimes make the difference between victory and defeat at reelection time. Interest groups also carry clout because of the potency of their political action committees. (These topics have been addressed in detail elsewhere in this chapter and in Chapter 11.)

Congressional Ethics

Congress has never enjoyed a reputation for scrupulous ethical behavior. Perhaps the low point in congressional morals was reached in the 1880s and 1890s, when railroads and other big corporations paid cash to advance their interests in Congress. Since then, there have been several periods when a rash of reported incidents of individual impropriety has put Congressional ethics in the spotlight.

Both the House and the Senate rewrote their codes of conduct in 1977, and in 1978 they passed the Ethics in Government Act, which required members of Congress, judges, and top executive officials to file financial disclosure reports. The difficulty with enforcing congressional codes of conduct, however, is that each chamber must police itself. The House Committee on Standards of Official Conduct and the Senate Select Committee on Ethics are responsible for monitoring and responding to ethics violations within each chamber. Critics charge that neither committee has been as aggressive as it should be and that even when one of these committees discovers violations, its response has been remarkably restrained. Senator William Armstrong characterized the difficulty: "When this is all over and after we have voted to denounce him, we will still want him to be our friend. We will still want to go down to the dining room and have lunch with him."[11]

The 101st Congress (1989-1990) was a trying time for the ethics committees. In the first session the House of Representatives lost, in short order, both the majority leader (Tony Coelho of California) and the Speaker (Jim Wright of Texas). Each resigned following ethics investigations. In the second session the Senate denounced Republican Senator Dave Durenburger of Minnesota for financial conduct it labeled "clearly and unequivocally unethical." The House formally reprimanded Barney Frank for improperly using his office to help a male prostitute. The House Committee on Standards of Ethical Conduct concluded that Democrat Gus Savage of Illinois "made improper sexual advances to a young woman while on an official trip to Africa. But the committee did not propose disciplinary action because Savage had apologized to the woman."[12] Republican "Buz" Lukens of Ohio, already defeated in a primary election, resigned from the House after the ethics committee passed a resolution that he made "unwanted and unsolicited sexual advances to a congressional employee." (For a description of the most famous of the ethics cases confronting the 101st Congress, the Keating Five scandal, see Chapter 10.)

While chair of the House ethics committee, Julian Dixon commented:

> I think the committee does a good job of, one, being nonpartisan and, two, investigating facts, evaluating facts, and taking appropriate action. But is the committee on a constant search for improprieties by members of Congress? The answer is no. I think members of Congress have a right to feel the committee is not on a witch hunt.[13]

Warren Rudman, vice-chair of the Senate Select Committee on Ethics, said, "We're not supposed to be the national nanny down here. We're supposed to look for true breaches of ethics by people who have stretched the law for their personal advantage."[14]

One of the biggest congressional stories of 1991, centered around the House bank, provided an example of a public scandal in which there was a good deal more smoke than fire. For over a hundred years, House members' pay had been sent to the House sergeant-at-arms, who held the funds until individual members transferred them to their own accounts at commercial banks. Members were able to write checks on their account at the House "bank." By several accounts the House bank was not very efficiently or professionally run—no sophisticated monthly statements were drawn up, and there were no computerized records to allow members to know when their paychecks were credited or when transfers were debited. For at least half a century the practice was to allow transfers in excess of the monthly paycheck, with the balance to be drawn from the subsequent paycheck when it came. The bank did not consistently notify members of overdrafts. Since members' salaries constituted the only deposits in the bank, the practice of covering overdrafts meant that some members' money was used to cover other members' overdrafts. No public funds were used or lost.

In October 1991 the irregularities of the House banking operation became public, instigating a great public outcry. The House closed its bank. Under pressure it voted to release the names of 247 current and 56 former members of the House who had overdrawn their account at least once. Twenty-two members were singled out for frequent, large overdrafts. In those cases, the appearance of impropriety was strong. But for the vast majority of the members on the list, the overdrafts were apparently a matter of not paying enough attention to detail and accepting without question a long-standing institutional arrangement.

Why the enormous brouhaha? The reason that the House bank drew so much attention was that the scandal played straight into the fears of ordinary persons that people "at the top" operated with disdain for the rules. The political elite, according to this populist reckoning, was living as though its members were not accountable in the ways ordinary persons were. The image of lawmakers overdrawing their accounts without penalty fit this description precisely. One survey found that 78 percent of Americans believed that most members of Congress deliberately kited check after check. The Justice Department appointed a former federal judge as a special prosecutor to look into the scandal. A small number of the worst offenders decided not to seek reelection or were defeated in primary elections; most apologized and tried to carry on with their work. Even if the number of individuals personally culpable of serious ethical lapses in the House banking scandal was small, Congress itself was reminded that the public's willingness to understand and forgive had been worn very thin.

Conflicts of interest pose another subtle but critical problem for congressional ethics. Should a legislator accept campaign contributions from corporations or interest groups and then push legislation that aids them? Members of committees often have financial interests in the very areas covered by their committees, such as real estate and banking. Should they divest themselves of these interests before taking part in votes that would affect their holdings? One important step was taken by the House and the Senate in a recent round of congressional pay increases. Both houses now prohibit their members from accepting personal honoraria for speeches. Prior to these restrictions, members might get very substantial fees for making routine speeches to groups with specific economic interests in legislation. The fees were often little more than thinly veiled contributions skirting campaign regulations. Furthermore, both the House and the Senate have rules governing conflicts of interest, but they are necessarily phrased in general language, and individual members must decide for themselves if a conflict exists. As Senator Tim Wirth of Colorado says, "You can't legislate judgment."[15] But as long as Congress carries out its business without effective strictures on formulating legislation that might yield personal benefits, the *appearance* of impropriety is likely, and impropriety itself is far from impossible. Neither will help Congress improve its reputation.

Tradition and the Postreform Congress

Throughout the middle years of the twentieth century, Congress was popularly characterized by the stereotype of an aging southern senator, a gentleman who had served for many years as a powerful committee chairman.[16] He came from a state with little partisan competition and thus attained seniority by being reelected term after term. He usually determined unilaterally how committee business would be conducted. This powerful senator would vote conservative on most matters; on some, perhaps, he would follow the party line. Above all, he took a decidedly conservative view of the workings of Congress itself—its rules, procedures, traditions, and unspoken understandings. The Congress typified by this stereotypical figure drew the ire of liberals for years. Many liberals argued that marshaling support for significant social change was all but impossible in a Congress dominated by such stodgy conservatives.

From a liberal standpoint several institutional features added to this formula for political stalemate. For many years, conservative senators seeking to delay or kill liberal legislation raised filibustering to a high art. In the other chamber the powerful House Rules Committee, which determines when a bill reaches the floor for debate and under what conditions, gave its chairmen the arbitrary power to block legislation. In both houses of Congress a strong tradition of deference toward senior collegues reinforced the structural bias favoring the status quo. In addition, much of the hands-on legislative work—building consensus, striking compromises, making deals to win support for legislation—was not subject to public scrutiny, giving entrenched power brokers a relatively free hand.

This one-sided portrait does not fairly represent the full spectrum of Congress's operations. Yet the problems and practices it depicts were real, and they troubled all who cared about democratic politics in the United States, including many members of Congress.

In the 1960s and 1970s, reforms were undertaken in congressional rules and structures. In the House of Representatives, the selection of committee chairs became more democratic, and the power of the chairs was reduced. Committee meetings were opened more regularly to public scrutiny. The House Ways and Means Committee was reformed and its influence drastically curtailed. These reforms had significant ramifications. Compared to its immediate predecessor, this reform-era Congress was a far more egalitarian body, one in which junior members could play significant roles. House subcommittees, given greater freedom of action, began delving into new and more controversial areas, such as alleged CIA invasions of privacy and NASA's management of the space shuttle program. In the Senate, filibusters were curtailed somewhat by reducing the size of the majority needed to shut off debate (now three-fifths, down from two-thirds). The reforms achieved their main objective, which was to reduce the overwhelming power of the committee chairs in the old Congress.

Despite these changes, many traditions of the old Congress survive in some form. In the Senate especially, the old, informal rules of the game still govern most interaction. When Barbara Mikulski, once described as "a stocky, 4-foot-11, rough-edged East Baltimore politician" with "the heft of a stevedore and a voice to match" joined the 100th Congress in 1987 as the junior senator from Maryland, observers familiar with her street-fighter style expected fireworks on the Senate floor. It is a tribute to her political skill—but, more important, to the transcendent power of Senate tradition—that there were none. "She understands it's still an all-boys club, and she's going to be a player," said Senator Dennis DeConcini of Arizona. "She already is."[17]

Seniority remains the rule, deference to older members is still expected, and the filibuster stands to this day as a potent obstructionistic tactic. Most observers would agree, however, that liberal-sponsored reforms have made the operations of Congress more democratic. With a sharp reduction in the prerogatives of committee chairs, power remains highly decentralized in some respects.

The new realities and limitations of the 1980s radically altered the environment in which Congress worked and the tools at its disposal:

> Lagging productivity affected not only government tax receipts but also citizens' attitudes toward their economic well-being. . . . A serious recession occurred in the early 1980s and again a decade later. Meanwhile the government's costly and relatively impervious system of entitlements and, after 1981, tax cuts and program reallocations turned the fiscal dividends of the postwar erea into structural deficits. . . .
>
> Disenchantment with the results of government programs, many of which had been shamelessly oversold to glean support for their enactment, led to widespread demands for a statutory cease-fire: disinvestment, deregulation, and privatization. . . —[a] series of tax revolts swept through the states to the nation's capital. The "no new taxes" cry of Presidents Reagan and Bush, however unrealistic and misleading, was politically a long-running hit with politicians and voters.[18]

These pressures (which some analysts termed *cutback politics*) changed Congress once more, affecting internal balances as well as relationships with other institutions and with constituents. The result was the postreform Congress, in which

> (1) fewer bills are sponsored by individual legislators; (2) key policy decisions are packaged into huge "mega-bills," permitting lawmakers to escape adverse reactions to individual provisions; (3) techniques of blame avoidance are employed to protect lawmakers from the adverse effects of cutback politics; (4) noncontroversial, commemorative bills are passed into law—nearly half of all laws produced by recent Congresses; (5) driven by budgetary concerns, party-line voting is at a modern-day high on Capitol Hill; and (6) leadership in the House and Senate is markedly stronger now than at any time since 1910.[19]

Are the postreform changes in Congress conducive to the common good, or do these changes primarily protect and benefit the members and staff of Congress itself?

Although presidential legislative initiatives now receive greater scrutiny and are less likely to be rubber-stamped, it has become more difficult for House members to take initiatives for the public good and easier for interest groups to influence public policy. Much of the real power in Congress has now passed into the hands of those who can exert the most pressure—through direct or indirect lobbying at all stages of the legislative process.

Increasing levels of partisan voting mitigate such generalizations to some degree. Yet this negatively activated partisanship does not signal an end to legislative stalemate. The institutional and social forces within Congress and within the parties, which work against a coherent legislative program, have not been dampened. The legislative process is indeed opening up. But what are the long-term effects on Congress and public policy when individual members become "policy entrepreneurs," who increasingly pursue their own political agendas directly in the media?

Congress and the President

Perhaps the most striking difference between the U.S. Congress and other democratic legislatures is the adversary relationship between the U.S. legislative and executive branches. The two branches both supplement and check each other, as part of the system of checks and balances and **separation of powers** deliberately built into the Constitution. As we have seen, this system was designed to prevent any one institution or group from accumulating too much power. Because the president and Congress are elected separately and have different constituencies, the president may or may not belong to the party that commands a majority in either house of Congress. As a result, presidents frequently have to deal with a hostile majority in at least one house.

Contrast this with the simplified system of a **parliamentary democracy**, in which executive and legislature are one and the same. Elections are held for the parliament, and whichever party wins a majority organizes the government. Rather than a separation of powers between the branches, a parliamentary system features a fusion of power. And because parliaments usually maintain strong party discipline, the majority party is ordinarily able to pass its basic program.

PART THREE • INSTITUTIONS

President Bush greets members of Congress after his State of the Union address. Complaints of "gridlock" developed during Bush's term as he vetoed much legislation. Making a legislative record requires some degree of cooperation between President and Congress, a task made easier when both are controlled by the same party. *(AP/Wide World Photos)*

Of course, parliamentary systems can also be plagued by complications, such as the absence of a clear majority in a multiparty system. And it is true that presidents and Congresses have often worked together harmoniously despite party differences. Nevertheless, the U.S. system of government practically invites muddled lines of legislative responsibility. When legislation is passed or defeated, it may be difficult to sort out which party or branch is responsible for a given result. One observer described the situation as follows:

> A president . . . may have a coherent program to present to Congress. But each house can add to each of his bills, or take things out of them, or reject them outright, and what emerges from the tussle may bear little or no resemblance to what the president wanted. So when an election comes, the president, the senator, the representative, reproached with not having carried out his promises, can always say, "Don't blame me!" . . . It ends up that nobody . . . can be held responsible for anything done or not done. Everybody concerned can legitimately and honestly say it was not his fault.[20]

Despite its status as one of the democratic world's most independent and powerful legislatures, Congress has found its powers gradually diminished in relation to those of the executive branch. Twentieth-century politics, which emphasizes crisis management and organizational sophistication, promoted this trend. The presidency, with its centralized lines of authority and its greater flexibility, has captured center stage whenever national action was called for, sparking and guiding national policy. Congress now largely reacts to presidential initiatives.

This raises one of the most difficult questions about our government: How is the representative function to be divided among separate branches of government? A glance at the Constitution reveals that the framers counted heavily on Congress to express the wishes of the people. Article I, the legislative article, is by far the longest and most complex. It provides for the most direct ties between ordinary citizens and the federal government.

But many people identify the federal government with the president, not Congress. Presidents are glamorous, highly visible individuals, loved by the media. Turnout in presidential elections is always higher than in congressional elections. In an important sense, the president is best able to present certain choices to the people and thus to represent their choices within the government. Where does that leave Congress? The problem is particularly acute in our fast-paced, increasingly complex society. Consider, for instance, the following concerns: How can Congress—a largely decentralized, open body—handle matters requiring secrecy? What role can Congress play in matters of urgent national security that require swift, decisive action? And how can Congress develop a national budget of enormous scope and sophistication, not unduly burdened with **pork barrel projects**—appropriations for political patronage for the home district or state? All these questions reflect the difficulties of sharing power. These thorny issues are addressed next as we take up the role of Congress regarding secrets, the War Powers Resolution, and the budget.

Congress and Secrets

An ongoing problem for Congress involves supervision in areas that require secrecy. Because Congress operates basically as an open institution, executive actors sometimes argue that it can't be trusted with secrets. In fact, the congressional intelligence com-

Senator Bill Bradley of New Jersey (center left) at a fund-raiser in Rhode Island. Many in Congress complain bitterly that a significant portion of their time is occupied by such efforts to raise money, and some have quit Congress in frustration because of it. (Gale Zucker/Stock, Boston)

mittees have an excellent record of maintaining national security secrets—most major leaks in recent history have originated in the executive branch. Nevertheless, there have been instances when executive branch agencies, particularly the intelligence services, have decided to keep members of Congress in the dark. This poses a troublesome problem for democratic government.

In the Iran-Contra affair, which began to unravel in late 1986, members of the Reagan administration sought to make arms-for-hostages deals with Iran while the president categorically rejected such a policy publicly. Members of the executive branch admitted to and defended misleading Congress in these matters. Oliver North was applauded when he said that if he had to choose between "lies and lives," he would rather protect agents in the field and deceive Congress. The controversy and outrage surrounding this affair highlight a fundamental principle of democratic theory: A government may find it necessary to keep *strategies* or *tactics* secret from its people, but if it wants to remain a democracy, it cannot maintain secret *policies*. Whatever the means of representation, the people must be able to ratify—and sometimes reject—the policy choices that are made in their name. Of course, implementation of publicly chosen goals may require secrecy under certain circumstances. The design of military hardware and the specifics of military movements or our precise bargaining positions in direct negotiations may properly be kept from public discussion. But the general questions about what a government should and should not be doing must be matters of open debate. Even in areas where secrecy is justifiable in a democracy, secrets should not be kept from the responsible *representatives* of the people.

The actions undertaken in the Iran-Contra affair violated this principle on two levels: First, the administration pursued a secret policy, in direct opposition to the government's publicly held position; and second, the actual policy was kept secret from the people's representatives in Congress as well as from the public at large. By way of explanation, the administration maintained that the true nature of the negotiations was not made clear to the president either—an explanation that many found unconvincing. There are no simple answers here. When is a strategy broad enough or distinctive enough to require public consideration?

Following the revelations of the Iran-Contra hearings, the White House announced a "philosophy" of secret operations meant to reassure Congress that such operations would not get out of control. Secret operations should be used as a "last resort," should be used only in support of existing policies, and should be of limited duration. But Congress must still make certain that the White House is living by its philosophy. And the executive will continue to fear that some information that should properly be kept secret will be exposed if given to Congress. Accordingly, making and keeping secrets will remain a matter for debate and interbranch conflict.

Congress and the War Powers Resolution

On January 12, 1991, Congress voted to authorize President Bush to go to war against Iraq under United Nations Resolution 678, which in turn authorized member states "to use all necessary means" to force Iraq out of Kuwait if it hadn't ended its occupation by January 15. These two resolutions, one by the American national legislature, the other by the most prominent body of international cooperation in the second half of the twentieth century, can teach a lot about the nature of power and legitimacy in the world today. Was either necessary for President Bush to send U.S. troops against Iraq? Arguably not. Was the legitimacy of the subsequent American military operation, dubbed Operation Desert Storm by the Pentagon, enhanced by these resolutions? Undoubtedly so—that's why the Bush administration had pressed the United Nations for passage of Resolution 678 the preceding November and why President Bush wrote to Congress on January 8 asking for a resolution—the first such request since the Gulf of Tonkin Resolution, which authorized force in Vietnam in 1964. Why did the request come so late, after hundreds of thousands of American forces had been gathered in Saudi Arabia and the UN deadline was only a week away? Both the executive and legislative branches had reasons for avoiding a confrontation over U.S. involvement in the Persian Gulf.

In every discussion from the beginning of the Persian Gulf crisis through the engagement of U.S. air power in Iraq, the president maintained that the decision to commit American troops to battle was his to make in his capacity as commander in chief. Thus the congressional resolution, like the UN resolution, provided helpful affirmation of support but no essential legitimacy to the president's decisions. Yet the Constitution gives the power "to declare war" to Congress—the basis for the argument offered by many members of Congress that in the absence of an attack against American forces, the president could not commit the country to war unilaterally. Which position was correct? Not much enlightenment could be drawn directly from the eighteenth-century notions about declaring war embodied in the framers' distribution of warmaking power between Congress and the president. The recent history of war powers in the United States has been written around the margins of the War Powers Resolution of 1973.

The entire Vietnam War was conducted without a declaration of war by Congress. As that war wore on, many people in Congress concluded that they had allowed the president too much freedom in shaping foreign policy. Presidents Johnson and Nixon had both hidden important developments from Congress. Whereas Johnson usually tried to finesse (or in some cases deceive) Congress, Nixon confronted Congress with direct challenges to its power. He forbade administration representatives from testifying before congressional committees, and he refused to heed Congress's call to halt the bombings in Indochina.

Congress responded with the **War Powers Resolution**, which it passed over Nixon's veto in 1973. This act requires the president to consult with Congress before sending U.S. troops into combat. The resolution states: "The President in every possible instance shall consult with Congress before introducing United States armed forces into hostilities or into situations where imminent involvement in hostilities is clearly indicated by the circumstances." In addition, it requires that in the absence of a declaration of war, the president must report to Congress within forty-eight hours after troops are sent (in cases where it is not possible to consult beforehand). If Congress

PART THREE • INSTITUTIONS

> ## THE WAR POWERS RESOLUTION AT WORK
>
> Since 1973, the War Powers Resolution has been cited to members of Congress every time U.S. military forces are engaged in combat. Experience to date demonstrates the difficulty of reining in executive prerogative. Members of Congress don't want to tie the president's hands in defending the country and usually eschew the political risk of opposing a president in popular "patriotic" adventures.
>
> **Indochina** In the spring of 1975, President Ford conducted a series of rescue missions from Danang, Saigon, and Phnom Penh as U.S. involvement ceased and hostilities increased. Ford maintained that he had authority as commander in chief to use troops to rescue citizens and others. But he "took note" of the resolution by informing Congress in advance of the rescue mission and submitted reports after the operations were completed.
>
> **Mayaguez** In May 1975, Cambodian naval vessels fired on and seized the S.S. *Mayaguez*, a merchant ship in international waters that was en route to Thailand. Ford first attempted to free the ship and crew through diplomatic actions but, when that failed, ordered a military rescue involving U.S. Marines and air attacks on Cambodian vessels. The ship's crew was rescued, but eighteen Marines died. Although Ford clearly complied with the resolution's requirement that a report be submitted promptly, there was considerable debate about whether he consulted members of Congress or merely informed them.
>
> **Iran** When President Carter, in April 1980, ordered an attempted rescue of the forty-nine hostages held in the American embassy in Tehran, he did not consult with members of Congress beforehand or inform them of the mission until after it had been aborted. Administration officials said that consultation would have taken place had the rescue effort proceeded beyond the initial phase. But congressional leaders in both parties said that Carter had not complied with the resolution.
>
> **El Salvador** In early 1981, after the Reagan administration decided to increase the number of U.S. military advisers in El Salvador, House and Senate

(Box continues on page 509)

does not approve the involvement within sixty days, troops must be withdrawn. Every president since Nixon has formally maintained that the War Powers Resolution unconstitutionally infringes on executive prerogative. Most presidents have taken limited steps, however, to appease the congressional desire to be involved.

The history of the War Powers Resolution epitomizes the difficulty of two branches sharing power in responding to threats to national security. The executive tendency

resolutions were introduced asserting that the move required a report under the War Powers Resolution. The controversy led to an agreement between Congress and the administration that the number of advisers would be kept to fifty-five and that they would not be equipped for combat or placed in a hostile situation. The administration also pledged to consult with Congress if it wanted to change the status of the advisers.

Grenada The U.S.-led invasion of Grenada in October 1983 occurred without advance consultation with Congress; briefings for key congressional leaders took place only when the operation was imminent. But the exercise appeared to fit the resolution's definition of an emergency, in which the president was authorized to use troops. The hostilities ceased within several days, and the administration took the position that the resolution did not apply. Nevertheless, the troops were withdrawn before the sixty-day period of emergency presidential authority expired.

Lebanon In 1983, Congress established a timetable for the withdrawal of a U.S. Marine peacekeeping force in Lebanon. However, the troops were unilaterally pulled out by President Reagan in early 1984 after more than 260 servicemen lost their lives in a terrorist attack.

The Iran-Iraq War in the Persian Gulf From May 1987 to August 1988, U.S. naval vessels were sent to the Persian Gulf to protect reflagged Kuwaiti oil tankers. Although Congress did not invoke the resolution, it closely monitored developments.

Panama In December 1989, the United States took military action to oust Manuel Noriega from power in Panama. The operation was short and successful, and Congress was generally supportive.

Desert Storm In early 1991, the United States, in a joint action with other US member nations, launched a massive assault on Iraqi troops in Kuwait and Iraq. One week prior to the US deadline for Iraq's withdrawal, the president asked for and got a resolution from Congress supporting the use of force. The vote was 52–47 in the Senate and 250–183 in the House.

Source: Adapted from Roger H. Davidson and Walter J. Oleszek, Congress and Its Members, *3rd ed. (Washington D.C.: Congressional Quarterly Press, 1990), p. 406.*

is first to refuse to acknowledge conditions under which the War Powers Resolution should be invoked and then to leave Congress out of the decision-making loop prior to taking action. The legislative response to this exclusion is usually cautious to the point of timidity, as no member of Congress wishes to be seen as an obstacle to the president's vigorous defense of the national security.

Most observers believed that the congressional resolution prior to Desert Storm served the constitutional function of a declaration of war.[21] Thus it remains an open question whether President Bush was gaining legal support or only political support for his action. The Persian Gulf War adds to a list of military involvements and intra-branch skirmishes that indicate that the War Powers Resolution is not an effective mechanism for clarifying the distribution of war powers in the United States.

Skirmishes between the president and Congress over foreign policy often cause considerable confusion for foreign governments. They do not understand how the constitutional separation of powers works or that presidential power in foreign affairs is not unlimited. Whom are they to negotiate with, Congress or the president? The world was treated to a clear example of this confusion in 1987 when Speaker of the House Jim Wright, seriously at odds with the White House over Central American policy, met with Nicaraguan President Daniel Ortega in an attempt to further the Central American peace process. In the view of some analysts, Congress approaches foreign policy as if it were another aspect of lawmaking and thus tends "to place a straitjacket of legislation around the manifold complexity of our relations with other nations."[22]

Despite the validity of some of these criticisms, Congress has actually accomplished a great deal through its newly aggressive stance on foreign policy. Admirers of the new Congress point out that it has helped to make future Vietnams less likely, reversed the trend toward unchecked presidential power in foreign affairs, shifted the pattern of American commitments abroad in constructive ways, and broadened the base of foreign policymaking.[23]

Congress and the Budget

Traditionally, the budget process in Congress involved a "war between the parts and the whole." The president's budget was divided up among a large number of committees, each of which dealt with one facet of it. Because little attention was paid to how the various parts affected the whole, Congress, unlike the president, had no overview of the budget. Much of the time congressional committees simply deferred to executive judgment on authorizations and appropriations of funds for programs. The part of the budget subject to congressional consideration usually amounted to less than half of total federal expenditures; the remainder was not subject to annual authorizations. As a result, the executive had a relatively free hand. Moreover, presidents sometimes made their own decisions on how much to spend, unilaterally impounding funds authorized for programs they disapproved of.

The cost of the Vietnam War in combination with LBJ's Great Society programs created what seemed at the time to be very large budget deficits in the late 1960s and early 1970s. Those deficits, and the increased confrontational style of the Nixon administration (including impounding funds—not spending funds that had been authorized), created the impetus for the first of three recent rounds of budget reforms.

Many legislators felt that it was time to reassert Congress's authority as an institution. The Congressional Budget and Impoundment Control Act of 1974, which embodied most sought-after reforms, had several key purposes: to provide Congress with much more information, to streamline committee work on the budget, and to give Congress the power to confront such presidential tactics as impounding federal funds. To these ends, the act established a budget committee in each house and the Congressional Budget Office (CBO) to provide information and technical assistance. The CBO, which acts as a counterweight to the expertise of the executive branch's Office of Management and Budget (OMB), reports to Congress on the economic consequences of both proposed and enacted legislation, develops a yearly report on alternative budget options, and provides expert advice for the congressional committees considering specific fiscal issues. In fact, the CBO is widely thought to be both more accurate in its assessments and more politically neutral than the increasingly politicized OMB.

Congressional committees would now draft two budget resolutions annually for Congress's approval: one to set overall spending and tax goals early in the budget planning process and another to set binding figures before the fiscal year began (July 1). Then, in a step known as *reconciliation*, the House and Senate would agree on a set of matching proposals for each portion of the federal budget. The act also prohibited presidential impoundment of funds appropriated by Congress.

The reformed budget system did not resolve the institutional and partisan pressures at the heart of the budget-making process, however. Conservatives wanted to use the system to place a ceiling on expenditures but were not able to get that ceiling as low as they wished. Liberals, who wanted to use the process to set new priorities, sought open debate about the overall emphasis in each new budget. But these debates fell short of liberals' expectations.

Enhanced congressional control increased the complexity of the budget process. Following the 1974 reforms, the budget process revolved around a "concurrent resolution on the budget," which set ceilings on spending and estimated revenues. But Congress, with a Republican majority in the Senate and a Democratic majority in the House, found itself unable to create a concurrent budget resolution in a timely fashion. It was the genuinely huge budget deficits of the 1980s, however, that created the immediate stimulus to the next set of revisions to the budget process. In 1985, Congress passed the Balanced Budget and Emergency Deficit Control Act, called **Gramm-Rudman-Hollings** after its sponsors. This act moved to centralize the congressional budgeting process further and to set timely deadlines for the completion of legislative tasks. Its most notable features were the establishment of maximum allowable deficits and a provision for the sequestration of funds when deficit limits were exceeded. Sequestration was an automatic, across-the-board cut in funding for all programs (though most entitlement programs, about 43 percent of the budget, and interest payments, about 14 percent of the budget, were exempt from sequestration). The idea was that sequestration would be so painful to the nonexempt programs that Congress would have a serious incentive to stay within the deficit limits.

Even with the subsequent upward revision of the deficit limits, however, Gramm-Rudman-Hollings fell apart. By 1990 various budget policymakers, confronting serious cutbacks to favored programs or failing to win desired concessions, decided that sequestration was better than giving up early. Another problem with the act was that it was very vulnerable to overly optimistic economic projections. By the end of the fiscal year, when projected deficits were far outstripped by the real ones, it was possible to let a current deficit target go unmet and start with a clean slate the following year.

In 1990 the White House and congressional leaders participated in a budget summit at Andrews Air Force Base outside Washington. The closed meetings were scheduled on the assumption that some of the hard choices necessary to achieve a responsibly austere budget could not be made in the glare of publicity. The bipartisan budget compromise agreement reached was then taken back to Congress, where it promptly suffered a dramatic rejection by members who were both dissatisfied with the choices made and testy for having been left out of the process. It was a humiliating defeat for the president and the congressional leadership. In the wake of the budget summit failure, Congress passed the Budget Enforcement Act (BEA) of 1990. The search for a responsible, functional process for creating a national budget continued. The BEA shifted focus away from deficits to spending ceilings, defined in three categories: defense, domestic, and international. Categorical sequestration would occur when spending exceeded established ceilings. The BEA established a five-year package of revenue and expenditure projections and removed some sleight-of-hand options from budget negotiators (like using the social security surplus to reduce current deficits). Under the most recent reforms, all tax and direct-spending legislation must be "deficit-neutral"—that is, each year's legislation increasing spending or reducing revenues must be balanced by corresponding spending cuts or tax increases. A zero-sum game was created, one effect of which was to encourage lobbyists to become familiar with programs beyond their ken so as to be able to make favorable *comparisons* rather than just straightforward claims for their own programs.[24]

Some observers claimed that the net effect of the new reforms was conservative in making new funding within categories difficult. Even the staunchest supporters of defense spending realized that with the collapse of the Soviet Union the defense limits, now isolated in their own category, were too high—that the walls between categories would have to be breached in some fashion. Some members of Congress complained that the new process increased the power of the executive at Congress's expense, bringing the budget reform cycle back full circle to 1974. By 1992, with the country suffering a protracted recession, some members argued that the deficit-neutral provisions hamstrung the nation in responding to economic downturns—an argument for increased spending now, to be made up in later years. In spite of the new rules, much of the debates sounded depressingly familiar.[25]

Because the budget process must bridge the divide created by the sharing of power between branches, it will always be controversial, especially when branches are controlled by different parties. Individual members of Congress will always be particularly sensitive to the needs of their immediate constituents, and this solicitousness, combined with collegial reciprocity, will inevitably threaten budgetary control. Furthermore, the budget process itself is controversial because it affects outcomes. Strengthening one committee at the expense of another or one branch at the expense of another means altering the balance among all the groups whose access to government is greatest at a particular point. Even more, budget choices in times of economic slowdown or reversal are always difficult and are exacerbated by the rising proportion of the budget that is fixed: entitlement programs and interest payments.

The first year after these reforms, Congress managed to produce a budget resolution and 12 of the 13 spending bills by the end of the session. But by 1992 the process was threatening to collapse once more. President Bush pushed hard for a constitutional amendment requiring a balanced budget, but the House measure failed to gain the requisite two-thirds majority. Clearly, the 1990 reforms will not be the last. In American democracy the three branches of government are engaged in a continuous process of defining themselves and their roles in representing the American people. Nothing demonstrates that more clearly than recent efforts to come up with a federal budget.

Conclusions

How should we evaluate Congress from a democratic standpoint? First, we must acknowledge that the U.S. national legislature is unique because the U.S. political process is unique. Unlike parliamentary systems, in which the executive and legislative branches are fused, our system sets these branches at odds. On the one hand, this situation creates unique opportunities for legislative action and power; on the other, it leads to severe and often insoluble problems involving legislative coordination and responsible policymaking. In its role as critic, gadfly, and check on the initiatives of the executive, Congress has shown some improvement in recent decades. That is a definite plus. Regardless of what one thinks of particular presidential policies, it is heartening to see informed and searching debate on those policies on the legislative side. Also on the positive side, Congress has reformed some of the procedures that centralized power too greatly in the hands of an unrepresentative few. Today's Congress may seem at times like a Tower of Babel, but that is preferable to an institution devoted to whispering in the corridors.

On the negative side, it seems unlikely that Congress will ever be able to engage in coherent policymaking under current conditions. Political analysts fault both the internal structure of Congress and, even more, our party system, which does not provide the discipline necessary to keep members attuned to national needs as well as local constituency interests.

There are solutions available for some of Congress's current dilemmas. For instance, increasing the internal coherence of policymaking in Congress may be possible by reducing the immediate external influences that fragment the process so severely now. Public financing of congressional elections might diminish the power of well-oiled interests that use money to purchase legislative access. Also, a strict rule that legislators not serve on committees that could enhance their own financial or personal interests would lessen the likelihood of conflicts of interest. Congress has been strangely lax in not moving in this direction.

Overall, Congress cuts an interesting, exasperating, occasionally commanding presence in U.S. politics. Newly assertive, our national legislature has been challenging presidential authority in the foreign policy arena while deadlocking on many tasks where it traditionally exercises considerable latitude, for example, in the budget process.

GLOSSARY TERMS

bicameral
checks and balances
filibuster
Gramm-Rudman-Hollings
majority leader
markup
minority leader
parliamentary democracy
pocket veto
pork barrel projects
president pro tempore
rider
select committee
seniority rule
separation of powers
sequestration
Speaker of the House
standing committee
unicameral
War Powers Resolution
whip

NOTES

[1] This account of Congressman Panetta's week is drawn from Clifford Kraus, "A Lawmaker's Life: Not So Wonderful," *New York Times*, April 15, 1992, p. A16.

[2] Detailed descriptions of these functions can be found in Malcolm E. Jewell and Samuel C. Patterson, *The Legislative Process in the United States*, 3rd ed. (New York: Random House, 1977); and Randall B. Ripley, *Congress: Process and Policy*, 3rd ed. (New York: Norton, 1983).

[3] For a detailed discussion, see Jewell and Patterson, *The Legislative Process*; Gary Orfield, *Congressional Power; Congress and Social Change* (New York: Harcourt Brace Jovanovich, 1975); and, particularly, Richard Fenno, *Congressmen in Committees* (Boston: Little, Brown, 1973).

[4] Harris poll, 1986.

[5] For a detailed treatment of congressional structures and procedures, see Charles R. Wise, *The Dynamics of Legislation: Leadership and Policy Change in the Congressional Process* (San Francisco: Jossey-Bass, 1991).

[6] For a debate about the effectiveness of party leadership, see Ripley, *Congress*, chap. 6.

[7] On specialization, see David E. Price, "Congressional Committees in the Policy Process," in *Congress Reconsidered*, 2nd ed., eds. Lawrence C. Dodd and Bruce I. Oppenheimer (Washington, D.C.: Congressional Quarterly Press, 1981), pp. 156-185.

[8] Ripley, *Congress*, pp. 168-174.

[9] Roger H. Davidson and Walter J. Oleszek, *Congress and Its Members* (Washington, D.C.: Congressional Quarterly Press, 1981), p. 352.

[10] Carol Matlack, "Off-Campus Cousins," *National Journal*, December 7, 1991, pp. 2959-2962.

[11] *CQ Almanac, 1990* (Washington, D.C.: Congressional Quarterly Press, 1991), p. 103.

[12] Ibid., p. 105.

[13]Jacqueline Calmes, "Ethics Committees: Shield or Sword?" *Congressional Quarterly Weekly Report*, April 4, 1987, p. 592.

[14]Ibid.

[15]"Even without New Guidelines, Senators Tiptoe to the Safe Side," *Congressional Quarterly Weekly Report*, March 2, 1991, p. 527.

[16]Much of the material in this section is drawn from Norman J. Ornstein, "The Democratic Reform Power in the House of Representatives, 1969-75," in *America in the Seventies*, ed. Allan P. Sindler (Boston: Little, Brown, 1977); and Thomas B. Edsall, "Political Reform—Social Retreat," *Dissent*, Summer 1979, pp. 261-265.

[17]Eric Pianin, "The Debut of Senator Mikulski," *Washington Post National Weekly Edition*, July 6, 1987, p. 6.

[18]Roger H. Davidson, "The Emergence of the Postreform Congress," in *The Postreform Congress*, ed. Roger H. Davidson (New York: St. Martin's Press, 1992), p. 13.

[19]Ibid., pp. 14-15.

[20]"TRB," *New Republic*, May 3, 1980, p. 3.

[21]See "Bush Is Given Authorization to Use Force against Iraq," *Congressional Quarterly Weekly Report*, January 12, 1991, pp. 65-71.

[22]Cecil V. Crabb, Jr., and Pat M. Holt, *Invitation to Struggle: Congress, the President, and Foreign Policy* (Washington, D.C.: Congressional Quarterly Press, 1980), p. 205.

[23]Ibid.

[24]See James A. Thurber, "New Rules for an Old Game: Zero-Sum Budgeting in the Postreform Congress," in *The Postreform Congress*, ed. Roger H. Davidson (New York: St. Martin's Press, 1992), pp. 257-278.

[25]See Lawrence J. Haas, "New Rules of the Game," *National Journal*, November 11, 1990, pp. 2793-2797; and George Hager, "Budget Drama, Act II: Scenarios for Chaos," *Congressional Quarterly Weekly Report*, January 25, 1992, pp. 156-159.

SELECTED READINGS

A significant amount of current research published in political science journals concerns Congress, its members and functional subdivisions, and their behavior. Thus this is a good opportunity to explore some of the major general journals in American political science, to get a feel for them and for the kind of work that some political scientists are currently doing. The three journals represented here (and their abbreviations) are the *American Political Science Review (APSR)*, published by the American Political Science Association; the *American Journal of Political Science (AJPS)*, published by the Midwest Political Science Association; and the *Journal of Politics* (JOP), published by the Southern Political Science Association. Each of these journals is published four times a year.

Look for the following **articles**, to start with: John R. Wright, "Contributions, Lobbying, and Committee Voting in the U.S. House of Representatives," *APSR*, June 1990, pp. 417-438; Charles M. Cameron, Albert D. Cover, and Jeffrey A. Segal, "Senate Voting on Supreme Court Nominees: A Neoinstitutional Model," *APSR*, June 1990, pp. 525-534; Richard L. Hall and Frank W. Wayman, "Buying Time: Moneyed Interests and the Mobilization of Bias in Congressional Committees," *APSR*, September 1990, pp. 797-820; Richard L. Hall and Bernard Grofman, "The Committee Assignment Process and the Conditional Nature of Committee Bias," *APSR*, December 1990, pp. 1149-1166; Jeffrey E. Cohen, Michael A. Krassa, and John Hamman, "The Impact of Presidential

Campaigning on Midterm U.S. Senate Elections," *APSR*, March 1991, pp. 165-178; John R. Hibbing, "Contours of the Modern Congressional Career," *APSR*, June 1991, pp. 405-428; Larry M. Bartels, "Constituency Opinion and Congressional Policy Making: The Reagan Defense Buildup," *APSR*, June 1991, pp. 457-474; Keith T. Poole and Howard Rosenthal, "Patterns of Congressional Voting," *AJPS*, February 1991, pp. 229-278; John T. Woolley, "Institutions, the Election Cycle, and the Presidential Veto," *AJPS*, May 1991, pp. 279-304; James M. McCormick and Eugene R. Wittkopf, "Bipartisanship, Partisanship, and Ideology in Congressional-Executive Foreign Policy Relations, 1947-1988," *JOP*, November 1990, pp. 1077-1100; Richard Born, "The Shared Fortunes of Congress and Congressmen: Members May Run from Congress, but They Can't Hide," *JOP*, November 1990, pp. 1223-1241.

For a solid **general introduction** to Congress, start with *How Congress Works*, 2nd ed. (Washington, D.C.: Congressional Quarterly Press, 1991). Then consult Roger H. Davidson and Walter Oleszek, *Congress and Its Members*, 3rd ed. (Washington, D.C.: Congressional Quarterly Press, 1990). To learn about the most recent configuration of congressional power and activity, read David W. Rohde, *Parties and Leaders in the Postreform House* (Chicago: University of Chicago Press, 1991); Allen D. Hertzke and Ronald M. Peters, Jr., eds., *The Atomistic Congress: An Interpretation of Congressional Change* (Armonk, N.Y.: Sharpe, 1992); and Roger H. Davidson, ed., *The Postreform Congress* (New York: St. Martin's Press, 1992). See also David R. Mayhew, *Divided We Govern: Party Control, Lawmaking, and Investigation* (New Haven, Conn.: Yale University Press, 1991).

To find out more about **leadership** in Congress, see Ronald M. Peters, *The American Speakership: The Office in Historical Perspective* (Baltimore: Johns Hopkins University Press, 1990); John J. Kornacki, ed., *Leading Congress: New Styles, New Strategies* (Washington, D.C.: Congressional Quarterly Press, 1990); and C. Lawrence Evans, *Leadership in Committee: A Comparative Analysis of Leadership Behavior in the U.S. Senate* (Ann Arbor: University of Michigan Press, 1991). For a good set of **comparative studies**, see Uwe Thaysen, Roger H. Davidson, and Robert Gerald Livingston, eds., *The U.S. Congress and the German Bundestag: Comparisons of Democratic Processes* (Boulder, Colo.: Westview Press, 1990). For a good look at **constituency service** with comparative data on the British Parliament, see Bruce Cain, John Ferejohn, and Morris Fiorina, *The Personal Vote: Constituent Service and Electoral Independence* (Cambridge, Mass.: Harvard University Press, 1987). For a case study of how a particular bill, the Department of Veteran Affairs bill, became a law, see Paul C. Light, *Forging Legislation* (New York: Norton, 1992).

A recent account of the **day-to-day operations** of Congress can be found in Steven S. Smith, *Call to Order: Floor Politics in the House and Senate* (Washington, D.C.: Brookings Institution, 1989); Walter J. Oleszek, *Congressional Procedures and the Policy Process*, 3rd ed. (Washington, D.C.: Congressional Quarterly Press, 1989); and *How Congress Works*.

A very useful **reference work** on Congress is Norman J. Ornstein, Thomas E. Mann, and Michael J. Malbin, eds., *Vital Statistics on Congress, 1991-1992* (Washington, D.C.: Congressional Quarterly Press, 1992).

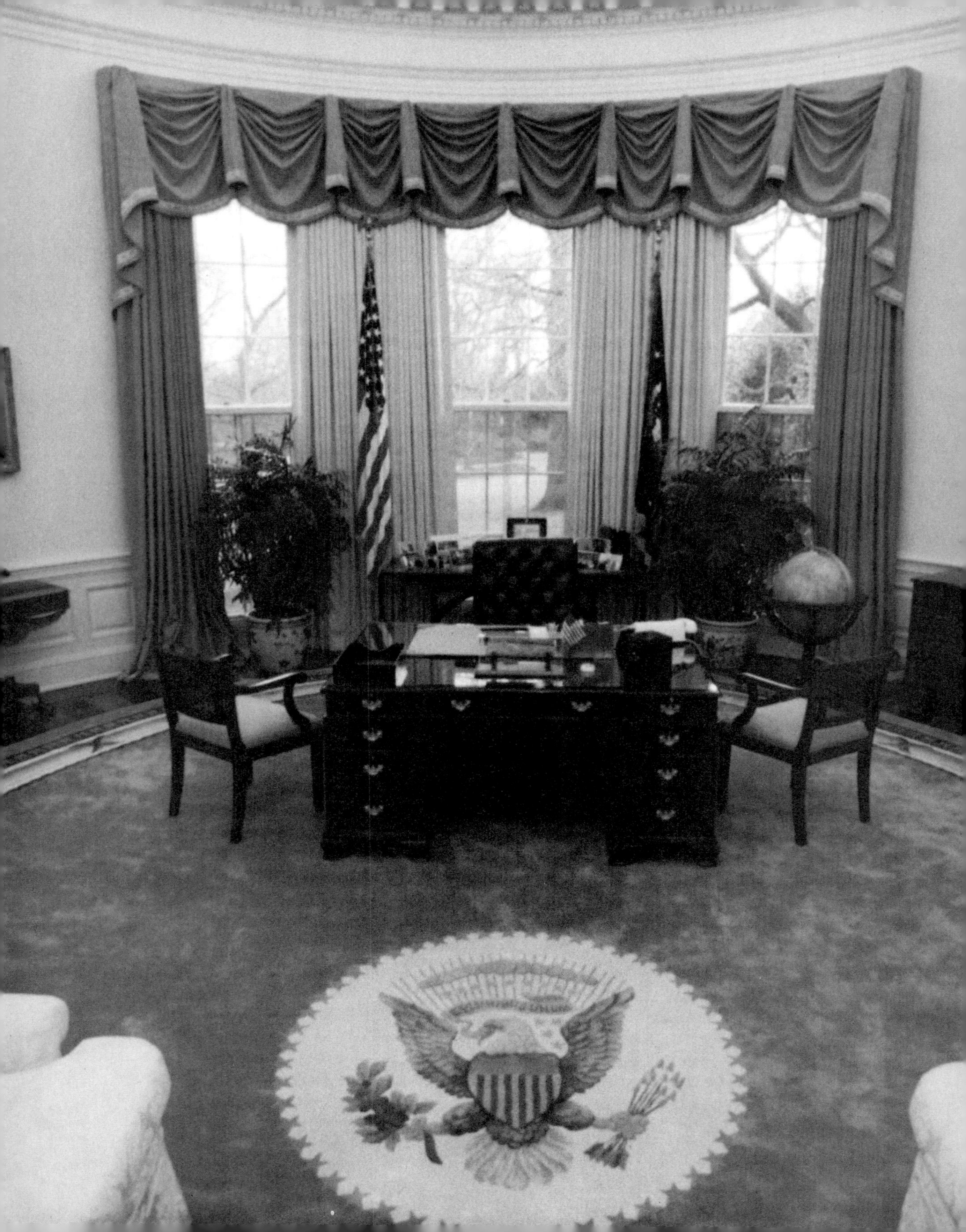

CHAPTER FOURTEEN

THE AMERICAN PRESIDENT

Unique, Necessary, and Dangerous

CHAPTER OUTLINE

The Unique President
PRESSING AGAINST THE LIMITS OF POWER
PARADOXES OF THE PRESIDENCY

The Necessary President
THE EXECUTIVE OFFICE
THE CABINET
RUNNING MATES
THE REST OF THE BUREAUCRACY
RELATIONS WITH CONGRESS

The Dangerous President
THE VIETNAM WAR
THE WATERGATE AFFAIR
THE IRAN-CONTRA AFFAIR
OPERATION DESERT SHIELD

Transitions of Power

THE FRAMERS OF THE CONSTITUTION FACED A DILEMMA WHEN IT came to setting up the executive branch. The political situation under the Articles of Confederation, which had essentially done away with a central executive authority, had clearly been disastrous. Yet few Americans wanted to return to the days of monarchy. Some delegates to the Constitutional Convention suggested a council of states—a plural executive that would administer the departments. At the other extreme, some delegates called for a disguised monarchy in which the president would have monarchical prerogatives but would not be a hereditary ruler. Another option, which the delegates finally settled on, was to establish an effective executive branch whose powers would be limited by checks and balances.

In defining the presidency, the framers needed to accommodate disparate wishes and visions. Political leaders try to reach consensus on different positions as much as possible and to defer choices that cannot be made under current circumstances. Like so many other elements of the Constitution, the provisions of Article II, the executive article, reflect a series of compromises, trade-offs, and deferred choices. A majority of delegates clearly favored a strengthened executive. But how strong? What powers would this office have? And what checks would there be on those powers?

The delegates enumerated certain powers—including the powers to direct all military operations, to grant reprieves and pardons, to see that laws are faithfully executed, and to appoint federal officers—but they were also careful to balance executive power with powers granted to the other branches. The ultimate check on the president was **impeachment**, a procedure by which Congress could remove the chief executive from office. In this two-step process, first the House must vote on whether to impeach (to bring charges against) a president, and then the Senate must try the case.

On many matters relating to the executive, the Constitution remained silent. Out of those silences came some epic battles between presidents and other actors in our political system. For the most part, presidents have been able to expand the power of the office through interpretation of the Constitution. Presidents Woodrow Wilson and Franklin Roosevelt, for example, combined "executive power" with the powers of "commander in chief" to control mobilization of the domestic economy during wartime.

The presidency today—the current product of what the framers concocted and what chief executives over the years have refined and elaborated on—is an office that has a *unique* history, is *necessary* as a source of focus and initiative within our political system, and is *dangerous* because any powerful executive can become a threat to democratic politics. These three characteristics of the presidency will serve as the focal points for this chapter.

The Unique President

The presidency of the United States is unique in part because of its dynamic character. The responsibilities of the office were not well defined at its inception, setting in motion a perpetual competition for power with the other branches of the national government. The presidency has been shaped by presidents, Congresses, and the Supreme Court. The presidency is also what the *current* president, Congress, and Supreme Court (influenced by a lot of other actors) make of it. Every new occupant of the White House can have a significant influence, for good or ill, on the office itself.

In most democratic countries, executive leadership is divided between a symbolic president or monarch and the political leader who actually runs the government—usually the prime minister or premier. In Great Britain, for example, the monarch functions as a symbolic (but powerless) head of state, while the prime minister is the functioning head of government. The prime minister is the leader of the party (or coalition of parties) that holds a majority in Parliament. Typically, the prime minister has been involved in political life and in party affairs for many years. Few prime ministers are newcomers to party politics or to the national political scene.

THE AMERICAN PRESIDENT

Bill Clinton, Hillary Clinton, Al Gore, and Tipper Gore during the 1992 presidential campaign. Bill Clinton was the youngest president since John F. Kennedy. Many expected Hillary Clinton, a lawyer specializing in children's legal rights, to play an active role in the administration. *(Mark Duncan/AP/Wide World Photos)*

The U.S. president, in contrast, serves as both actual political leader *and* symbol of the nation. The president also runs for office separately; a candidate does not become the nation's leader by serving as the head of the majority party or coalition but rather by winning our only genuinely national election. On occasion presidents have emerged from outside the major parties altogether, as war hero Dwight D. Eisenhower did in 1952, or from the periphery of the national political scene, as Jimmy Carter did in 1976. With the increasing importance of primaries and the impact of the news media on the presidential nominating process, the presidential race has been opened to contenders who enjoy scant national recognition at the start. Accordingly, a president may come to office with little, if any, national political experience and few or no connections with other major political figures, even within his or her own party.

The unique political position of the U.S. president also stems from the peculiar strengths and weaknesses of the office. Because the U.S. government is based on a **separation of powers**, with power divided among the three branches, the president must often take an antagonistic stance in relation to both Congress and the federal

(Text continues on page 523)

COMPARATIVE PERSPECTIVE

THE HEAD OF STATE IN GERMANY

Only one other democracy has a presidential system somewhat similar to ours—France under the Fifth Republic, which dates from 1958. In other democracies there is a prime minister or premier, who is head of government, and a separate head of state. The latter may be either a monarch or a civilian, usually known as the president. (Switzerland, the exception, has neither a monarch nor a civilian head of state—showing, as one writer put it, that "a country can survive without any head of state."*

The civilian head of state in the Federal Republic of Germany is the president, who is elected by a special assembly of the federal parliament and deputies from the state parliaments. Since the office was established in 1949, all of its occupants have been leading politicians whose elective political careers had progressed to the point that they no longer had any chance of becoming the actual head of the government (called the chancellor). The president serves for a five-year term and may be reelected once. He must sign all legislation, decrees, and letters of appointment and dismissal—and does not have a choice in doing so.†

The German president has more power than a symbolic monarch, but this power stems largely from personal prestige and respect. He can exercise a certain amount of influence on basic political questions but very little on day-to-day politics. Thus he exercises some degree of political leadership but must avoid becoming excessively political. As one student of the subject put it: "He must earn his prestige through his public statements, which should be neither trivial, abstract, nor too concretely political."‡

It is not entirely clear exactly how far a German president might be able to push his powers to intervene in affairs of state or to influence public opinion. So far the rule has been that a chancellor backed by a solid majority in parliament need not pay much attention to a president's views.

*Jurg Steiner, European Democracies (White Plains, N.Y.: Longman, 1986), p. 161.
†Lewis J. Edinger, Politics in West Europe (Boston: Little, Brown, 1977), p. 19.
‡Steiner, European Democracies, p. 164.

judiciary. And because of the relatively undisciplined nature of U.S. political parties, the president, unlike most European prime ministers, can rarely count on solid support even from his or her own party members.

Compensations abound, however, for these structural weaknesses in the presidency. The president towers over all other figures in U.S. politics. As the head of state as well as the political leader, the president can take a position above the struggles of party. In addition, the average citizen's psychological investment in the president runs very high.[1] Presidents can rally the nation and command support as no other political figure can. Let us now consider how presidents press against the limits of their power and the paradoxes of the office.

Pressing against the Limits of Power

Because of the ambiguity in the nature and range of presidential powers and responsibilities, all presidents from time to time feel the need to press against the limits of their power—either to protect it from encroachment from other political forces or to enhance it to achieve certain policy goals. One student of presidential power argues that presidents who push their powers to the limit exemplify "prerogative government," which strongly resembles monarchy.[2] Typically in such cases, presidential decisions are made without congressional consultation or collaboration and often in secret. Events are managed by the White House rather than by the appropriate executive departments. The president justifies decisions on constitutional grounds—either citing enumerated powers or powers claimed or created by interpreting of the Constitution. When an expansive interpretation is challenged, the president appeals directly to the public for support asserting that the actions taken were prompted by "national security" concerns or the "national interest." Prerogative presidents usually refuse to tailor their actions to party requirements or to majority sentiment in Congress.

We will now explore several historical attempts to expand presidential power, falling generally into three categories: successful expansion, in which other actors in the political system acquiesce in the exercise of presidential power, extending the range of the president's and the presidency's influence; unsuccessful expansion, which involves a successful challenge to the president's use of power and results in some erosion of presidential influence; and attempts that precipitated crises resulting in severe restriction of presidential power.[3]

SUCCESSFUL EXPANSIONS OF PRESIDENTIAL POWER Two historical examples illustrate the successful expansion of presidential influence to foreign policy. In the early 1790s, George Washington decided that the country should remain neutral in the war between Great Britain and France, even though the United States and France were allied by treaty. He issued a proclamation of neutrality and refused to engage the British in naval warfare, as the French has requested. His actions sparked a major constitutional debate over whether the president had the authority to declare the nation neutral. His defenders claimed that such powers were inherent in the Constitution, and those who disagreed did not have the votes to defeat Washington in Congress. Shortly thereafter, Congress actually passed neutrality legislation, and Washington went on to assert other new powers—to recognize foreign governments, to break off relations with other nations, and to negotiate foreign agreements by the executive alone.

In the second case the president and Congress switched roles. After World War II broke out in Europe, President Franklin Roosevelt wanted to help Great Britain in its desperate struggle against Germany, while Congress seemed determined to preserve strict neutrality. Roosevelt therefore engineered a highly controversial military aid deal with Great Britain by using an **executive agreement**, an arrangement between a president and a foreign nation not subject to Senate approval. Under this agreement, known as Lend-Lease, the United States ceded to Britain fifty old destroyers in return for the lease of several bases in the Caribbean. Roosevelt's critics claimed that the transfer violated the 1940 Neutrality Act, but Roosevelt argued that it was an inherent power of the chief executive to dispose of military matériel. Congress, which had been fully informed about the deal, acquiesced. A presumption of legitimacy then took over, and Roosevelt quickly signed a series of war-related executive agreements with other countries. Congress's reluctance to act in the period before the Japanese attack on Pearl Harbor set a pattern of executive initiative that persisted through the 1970s.

UNSUCCESSFUL ATTEMPTS TO EXPAND PRESIDENTIAL POWER Two modern cases spotlight unsuccessful attempts to expand presidential power: President Harry Truman's attempted takeover of strike-bound steel mills and President Ronald Reagan's reinterpretation of a law prohibiting gender discrimination in educational institutions. In 1950, during the Korean War, President Truman ordered the Secretary of Commerce to take over the nation's steel mills, which had been idled during a strike. When the steel companies took the matter to court, Truman argued that constitutional and statutory powers gave him the authority to intervene to preserve the national welfare. There were many precedents for Truman's actions, and the Supreme Court had not ruled against a president's use of prerogative powers since 1866. But Truman misjudged both the temper of the country (public opinion opposed him, 43 percent to 35 percent) and the disposition of the Supreme Court. A majority of the Court held that Congress had already mandated an appropriate government response to strike situations in the Taft-Hartley Act; Truman had chosen not to impose Taft-Hartley sanctions in this case. The majority argued that Truman had taken the power of commander in chief and had "turned inward, not because of rebellion, but because of a lawful economic struggle between industry and labor."[4] Truman's defeat limited how future presidents could deal with labor disputes. After this episode, presidents could not seize factories, even citing national security considerations, unless backed up by special legislation from Congress.

Often political power consists of having one's own interpretation of a law chosen over a conflicting one. Our second case deals with the interpretation of a 1972 law barring gender discrimination by educational institutions. In 1984 the Reagan administration argued before the Supreme Court for a new interpretation of this federal law in the case of *Grove City College* v. *Bell*, suggesting that the law was program-specific in prohibiting discrimination.[5] Under the Reagan administration's interpretation, if a college or university received federal funds for a specific program—the athletic program, for instance—the federal law forbade discrimination *in that program* but not in other programs at the institution. The earlier interpretation of the law held that if an institution accepted federal funds for any of its programs—including federally guaranteed student loans—it was prohibited from gender discrimination in all of them. Depending on one's point of view, the Reagan interpretation would mean much less federal meddling—or much less federal protection against gender discrimination—in higher education. The administration's position prevailed in *Grove City*, setting the stage for four years of legislative attempts to reverse the administration's interpretation. In 1988, Congress passed the Civil Rights Restoration Act, which not only reversed the interpretation in *Grove City* but also *expanded* the coverage of the 1972 law and three others to include gender, age, handicap, and racial discrimination at noneducational institutions as well as educational institutions. President Reagan vetoed the bill, but the House and Senate overrode the veto. Thus an initial victory in an important area of public policy was turned into a major defeat.

ATTEMPTS TO EXPAND PRESIDENTIAL POWER THAT PROVOKED MAJOR CRISES Two attempts to expand presidential power—President Andrew Johnson's approach to Reconstruction and President Richard Nixon's handling of the Watergate affair—backfired, precipitating major crises and resulting in restrictions on presidential power. Since Watergate will be examined later in this chapter, we will focus on the Johnson case here. In this instance, as in Watergate, a president attempted to subvert the law and the basic rules of the political game, destroying his administration in the process.

Soon after inheriting the presidency in 1865 following the assassination of Abraham Lincoln, Johnson became embroiled in a fierce struggle with Congress over Reconstruction, the political rehabilitation of the recently defeated South. Johnson was more conciliatory toward the entrenched, white southern establishment than the majority in Congress, which consistently overrode presidential vetoes of Reconstruction legislation. Matters came to a head when Congress passed the Tenure of Office Act, a measure designed to keep Secretary of War Edwin Stanton, a Johnson opponent, in office. Johnson challenged the constitutionality of the act and fired Stanton. The House then voted to impeach Johnson. Although Johnson's impeachment focused on the Stanton issue, articles of impeachment could have been brought against him on many other grounds, including encouraging violations of law and obstructing Reconstruction.

Johnson survived the Senate trial by a single vote, and Stanton was removed from office. But in the process the presidency suffered a heavy blow. Congress gained a significant measure of control over executive departments, and for the rest of the nineteenth century the presidency was greatly weakened. During this period widespread public sentiment favored a move toward parliamentary government, with the president serving merely as a ceremonial figure. Around the turn of the twentieth century, the nation's successive chief executives began rebuilding the power and prestige of the presidency, seizing on foreign policy issues to recapture center stage.

These examples point up an essential truth about the American presidency: Every president looks for ways to "expand the envelope," to become more effective and more influential than the existing limitations of the office allow. Success and failure in these attempts redefine constitutional relationships.

Paradoxes of the Presidency

An additional factor reinforces the unique, dynamic nature of presidential power in our democracy: ambivalent public sentiment. What does the public expect of the president? The electorate's expectations of the U.S. presidency are not only ambiguous but also often contradictory.[6] Americans generally want a "good person" in the White House—someone honest and trustworthy. Yet they also like tough, forceful, perhaps even ruthless presidents. They admire leaders who can lift the White House above the grubby day-to-day infighting of political life, leaders who can lead *all* the people. Yet the job of president requires preeminently political skills—coalition building, manipulation, partisan dealings. Most Americans want a president who can pull us together, yet one who can also put forward a forceful national agenda, creating a sense of priorities. Finally, we look for a chief executive who will both act as a referee in the political conflict of group interest and take part in that process of interest group conflict, using the powers of the position to serve the public interest.

Winning the office of president—making it through the primaries, the conventions, and the general election—requires ambition, flexibility, and great skill at imagemaking and public relations. But excessive emphasis on these same skills can spell disaster once in office. Some political analysts argue that winning a presidential election requires an *electoral coalition*—a majority of voters, strategically located across the country—whereas actually running the government requires a *governing coalition*, which is something else entirely. As one student of the subject puts it: "What counts then [once in office] is to mobilize support from the leaders of the key institutions in society and government.... This coalition must include key people in Congress, the executive branch, and the private sector 'establishment.' "[7]

No president can fully satisfy popular expectations. Nonetheless, high expectations prompt our chief executives to develop programs and "go to the people" to validate their proposals. This is the "necessary president"—the priority-setter and manager of government.

The Necessary President

The president was a necessary component of the changes the framers introduced in the Constitution of 1787. But in the twentieth century the need for a strong president

More than three decades after his assassination, John F. Kennedy remains an appealing leader to many Americans. Although his administration lasted less than three years, his style struck a responsive chord and created a sense of hopefulness and change. *(Magnum Photos)*

has become compelling. The growth of presidential power has mirrored the evolution of the United States as a superpower. Expanded presidential prerogatives were tied to defense and national security issues. Because of the general fragmentation of power in our political processes, the lack of discipline in U.S. political parties, the size and complexity of the federal government and its agenda, and the profound issues the nation faces, no political figure other than the president can draw together the threads of national policy and provide politically coherent leadership. The president can create national priorities, articulate national needs, and rally national energies. If the president is unwilling ot unable to carry out these functions, they will be carried out, if at all, in a fragmented, haphazard fashion, which is likely to favor private concerns over public ones and short-term, narrow-range fixes over long-term, broad-range solutions.

Of course, presidents, too, are captives of the times in which they come to power—victims of the pressures of the moment. And many presidents have not seized the organizing initiatives available to them. Still, for our political system to work properly, the president must organize power, gather ideas and put them to use, and cope well with crisis.

Presidential campaigns resound with promises. Once in the White House, however, the president must transform those promises into workable policies or programs. This requires the energies and expertise of hundreds of individuals now charged with directing the thousands of individuals who work for or with the federal government.

Since the development of large presidential support staffs in complex structures, presidents have confronted a dilemma: How can they structure their immediate organizational environment to optimize the gathering of vital information and advice and to take necessary action? Two general models are available. One school of thought holds that presidents, like the government itself, should operate within open, nonhierarchical structures, sitting at the center of the "spokes of a wheel." The other argues that efficiency is maximized by a hierarchical system of regulated access. In the open model, leaders in the executive branch should play an important role in the discussion and formulation of policy, and each should have direct access to the president. Limiting access will render the president subject to the undue influence of a few and consequently somewhat out of touch. Franklin Roosevelt, the first president with a large Executive Office, operated as his own chief of staff, gathering information from a web of associations rather than a strict hierarchy. FDR liked to encourage competition among his several sources of advice. His success in managing the executive branch and in changing the course of politics gave a tremendous boost to the open model of presidential administration.

In the hierarchical model, a chief of staff sits at the top of an organized flow of information and advice to the president. This model assumes that to be effective, the president must be protected from an overwhelming flood of demands and information. The champions of the hierarchical model feel that "cabinet government," operating on the open model, becomes unwieldy government by committee. Although most presidents since FDR have chosen a form of the hierarchical model, Richard Nixon's heavy reliance on hierarchy (H. R. Haldeman was the most important among a small group of aides known as the "palace guard") was associated in the public's mind with the Watergate scandal. Presidents Ford and Carter, serving in the wake of Watergate, initially disavowed the hierarchical model. Each tried to operate without a chief of staff but eventually conformed to the post-FDR pattern.

An important determinant in the success of one model or another is personality of the president and of the chief of staff. Acknowledging the importance of the position, one of George Bush's first announcements after being elected president was to name former New Hampshire Governor John Sununu as his chief of staff. Sununu's work was characterized as "effective," and the chief of staff enjoyed the presidential's confidence. As time went on, however, Sununu's control of access and exercise of discretion was increasingly labeled "arrogant" and "self-aggrandizing." In his third year in the position, amid charges of improperly using government and privately provided transportation, Sununu was forced from office. In the end the question is not to choose one approach or the other but rather to achieve a proper balance between openness and controlled access. Furthermore, some complaints about the *process*, however structured, may mask complaints about *outcomes*. For anyone trying to catch the president's ear, how much access is enough?

Although each new president must make choices about how to structure the top echelon of the executive branch, no president starts with a blank slate. Institutional structures have a remarkable resilience, resisting change or elimination; each president inherits a structure that must be molded to suit new leadership styles and goals. We now consider the chief executive's two prime sources of information, advice, and action: the Executive Office and the cabinet, which together comprise the "administration." We then cast an eye on the president's running mates, the rest of the bureaucracy and the president's relations with Congress.

The Executive Office

To deal with the Great Depression, Franklin Roosevelt had to expand the scope of government activity drastically; in doing so, he established the preeminence of the president as the national policymaker. In 1937, Roosevelt appointed a committee to come up with recommendations on administrative management. The committee's recommendations were tersely summed up in one sentence: "The president needs help." In response, Congress established the **Executive Office of the President**, an important departure from the earlier scheme whereby presidents discharged their duties with the aid of a personal secretary and a handful of clerks. The president has direct control over the various components of the Executive Office (see **Figure 14-1**), the most important of which are examined here.

Closest to the president is the **White House Office**, which consists of the president's top personal aides. The titles and corresponding duties change from president to president, but whatever their titles, these assistants are a president's most trusted associates. They are responsible only to the president, who can hire and fire them at will.

The White House Office both advises and acts for the president in the areas of national security, the economy, urban affairs, and other domestic policy matters. Some assistants serve as liaisons with Congress and lobby for the president's legislative programs. Others write speeches, handle press relations, plan trips, work with state and local political leaders, and take care of the ceremonial and social aspects of the office. The key aide in the White House Office is the president's chief of staff, who schedules the president's appointments and filters the information that reaches the Oval Office. In general, the chief of staff has instant access to the chief executive, and the two work closely together. One of the most visible members of the White House Office is the press secretary, who manages daily briefings for the White House press corps.

The largest of the Executive Office components is the **Office of Management and Budget (OMB)**, formerly known as the Bureau of Budget. The OMB has two main functions: to prepare the federal budget and to clear all legislation submitted to Congress by agencies of the executive branch. The OMB also provides the president with summaries and analyses of the budgetary implications of legislation enacted by Congress. As with all agencies in the Executive Office, the impact the OMB has on policymaking depends on both the president and the OMB director. For example, President

FIGURE 14-1

EXECUTIVE OFFICE OF THE PRESIDENT, 1991–1992

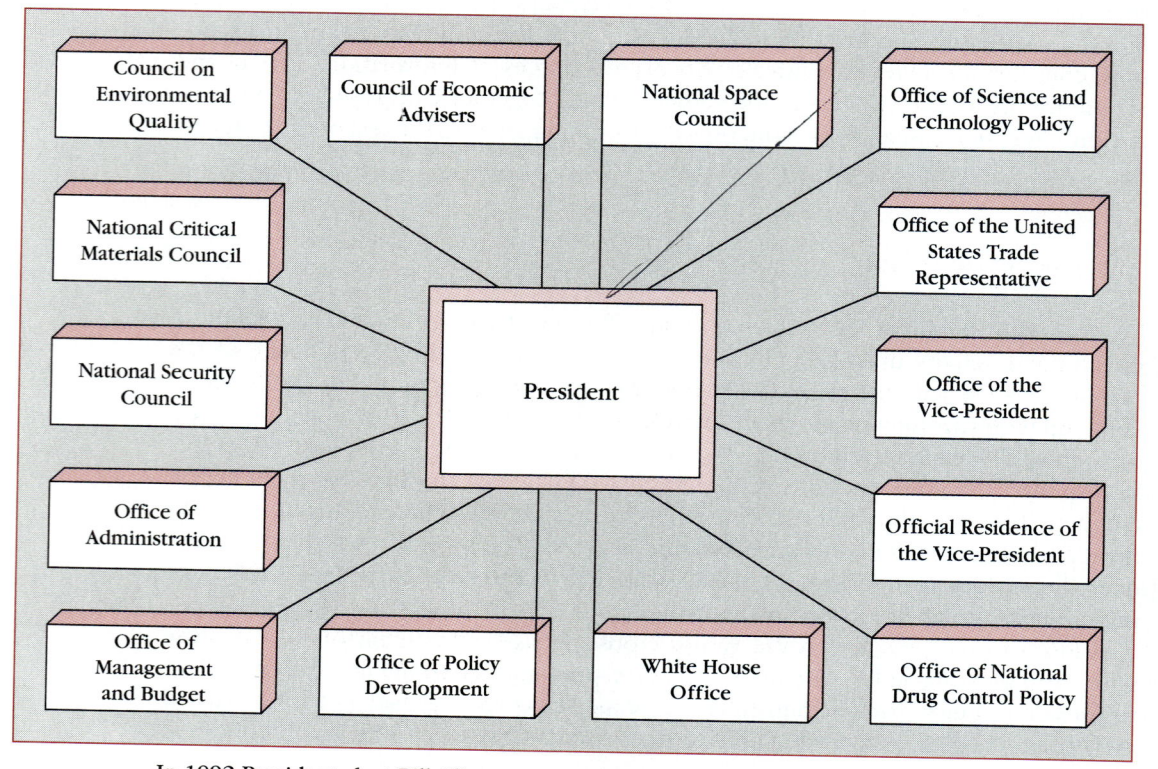

```
Council on              Council of Economic      National Space        Office of Science and
Environmental           Advisers                 Council               Technology Policy
Quality

National Critical                                                      Office of the United
Materials Council                                                      States Trade
                                                                       Representative

National Security                                                      Office of the
Council                            President                           Vice-President

Office of                                                              Official Residence of
Administration                                                         the Vice-President

Office of               Office of Policy         White House           Office of National
Management              Development              Office                Drug Control Policy
and Budget
```

In 1992 President-elect Bill Clinton announced his intention to create an Economic Security Council to coordinate national economic policy.

Reagan gave David Stockman, the administration's first OMB director, a major role in policymaking. George Bush's OMB director, Richard Darman, was similarly influential.

The **National Security Council (NSC)** was created by the National Security Act of 1947 to coordinate domestic, diplomatic, and military policies in matters of national security. The president, vice-president, and secretaries of state and defense sit on the council, with the director of the CIA and the chairman of the Joint Chiefs of Staff serving as statutory advisers. The president may also include in NSC meetings other officials whose knowledge he considers relevant or in whom he has particular confidence. John Kennedy included his brother Robert, the attorney general, in NSC meetings, although the Justice Department is not normally involved in national security affairs. The NSC staff, directed by the assistant to the president for national security affairs, grew to its present size of around two hundred during Henry Kissinger's time as national security adviser. For planning and coordination of U.S. foreign policy ventures, the NSC staff is sometimes used as a substitute for the larger bureaucracies in the State and Defense departments when, as during Kissinger's tenure, the adviser is particularly influential or when the policies in question are to be kept out of public view, as during the events leading to the Iran-Contra scandal.

Other units in the Executive Office of the President include advisory panels like the Council on Environmental Quality, the Council of Economic Advisers, the National Space Council, and the Office of National Drug Control Policy. These units, established by statute or executive order, provide information to the president, monitor implementation of current programs, and formulate policy proposals for consideration. Also included in the Executive Office is the Office of the Vice-President, which serves as the institutional base for whatever policymaking role the vice-president undertakes. The Office of Policy Development demonstrates the dynamic nature of Executive Office units. Originally conceived with great promise (as the Domestic Council) by Nixon to be a counterpart to the National Security Council, the Office of Policy Development under Carter and Reagan was reduced to a minor role supporting cabinet councils. Like the Office of Policy Development, the influence of each Executive Office unit is defined by the president it serves.

The Cabinet

There is no mention of the cabinet in the Constitution. Since George Washington first gathered his principal government officers together in council, presidents have drawn on the cabinet for political advice, guidance on policy and programs, and a variety of other reasons. But chief executives differ in how extensively they call on the cabinet. Andrew Jackson did not even convene his cabinet for two years, whereas James Polk held 350 cabinet meetings.

Today the **cabinet** consists of the heads of the fourteen executive departments—the secretaries of Agriculture, Commerce, Defense, Education, Energy, Health and Human Services, Housing and Urban Development, Interior, Labor, State, Transportation, Treasury, and Veterans Affairs and the attorney general (who heads the Justice Department)—plus other officers granted cabinet rank by the president. (In the Bush administration the Office of Management and Budget and the Office of the U.S. Trade Representative were accorded cabinet rank.) The vice-president also participates in cabinet meetings.

As an institution, the cabinet is difficult for the president to manage, in part because it embodies a set of delicate political balances.[8] The cabinet reflects balances between competing interests—business (Commerce) and labor (Labor), rural (Agriculture) and urban (Housing and Urban Development), diplomacy (State) and military interests (Defense). In addition, fiscal restraint (OMB) is balanced against spending (all departments). "Presidential" departments (State, Defense, Treasury, Justice) face off against "congressional" departments (Agriculture, HHS, HUD). Presidents tamper with these precarious balances at their own risk, as President Johnson discovered when he pro-

President George Bush leads a cabinet meeting. Presidents have varied greatly in their use or nonuse of cabinet deliberations, many turning to a smaller inner circle of advisers rather than to cabinet secretaries for consultation. *(Susan Biddle/The White House)*

posed merging Commerce and Labor and as President Reagan found when he tried to abolish Education and Energy.

The creation of the Executive Office led to an erosion of the cabinet's influence. Once policy formulation (which, with Executive Office support, could happen in the White House itself) was separated from policy implementation (which would continue to be the responsibility of the executive departments), there wasn't much left for the cabinet to do.[9]

Because the cabinet is an unwieldy policymaking body, several proposals have been advanced to reshape it. President Nixon's push to create a "supercabinet" by merging positions fell victim to the storm of Watergate. One scholar has proposed an "executive cabinet," in which positions would be assigned different hierarchical statuses. President Reagan implemented a more modest reform by creating cabinet councils—at first seven of them but then only two (the Economic Policy Council and the Domestic Policy Council). These councils were designed to coordinate policy formulation both among departments and between departments and Executive Office agencies. Despite good intentions, these councils never achieved the power and influence of senior presidential advisers. They became less influential in the latter part of the Reagan administration and in the Bush administration, leaving the cabinet as an institution beyond the margins of power.

In addition to the institutional challenge of the cabinet, presidents confront a challenge in dealing with cabinet members individually. The typical cabinet is rife with political tensions. Often, cabinet secretaries are appointed for political reasons—to appease particular segments of the party or to disarm rivals or critics—yet presidents also demand loyalty and competence from appointees. The question of divided loyalties poses another problem as well: The president invariably expects appointees to be responsive to presidential directives; yet just as inevitably, cabinet members must also respond to the needs and interests of their departmental constituencies if they are to be effective department managers. Presidents then complain that cabinet members are becoming too independent and are being run by the bureaucracy, rather than the other way around. Finally, presidents and cabinet members frequently clash, particularly as national and international crises take up more and more of the president's time and personal contacts with most cabinet members diminish. If the president loses touch, they do as well, and if a cabinet member is not in the president's inner circle, tensions are bound to arise.

Some Washington observers note that cabinet secretries rely heavily on the many assistants who serve under them. While the secretaries deal with the headline issues, the real management of programs often is handled by the so-called subcabinet—undersecretaries, assistant secretries, general counsels, and their staffs. Because these little-known officials exert a profound influence on key policy decisions, finding trustworthy and competent people for these positions can be crucial to the success or failure of administrative programs.

Running Mates

Putting the vice-president and the president's spouse into a single category, "running mates," may seem unusual, but an unusual approach may clear away some cobwebs from two national institutions that have been changing a lot recently. As for vice-presidents, John Nance Garner (Speaker of the House who became FDR's first vice-president) could say that the vice-presidency was "not worth a pitcher of warm spit," but this isn't the 1930s. One Reagan insider said, "Twenty years ago, I wouldn't have advised my worst enemy to take the vice-presidency. It was God's way of punishing bad campaigners, a sort of political purgatory for the also-rans. Now you'd be crazy not to take the job."[10] And about first ladies, Ann Grimes says, "The myth that a first lady doesn't have power is the most enduring and sexist in American politics."[11]

In the last third of the twentieth century, presidents have made more systematic use of these two important support positions to the presidency. Both—one a nationally elected constitutional official and the other related to the presidency by marriage—reflect three truths about American federal executive politics. First of all, the presidency is a personal office, and both the vice-president and the first lady are personal extensions of the president. As we've seen, much of the president's strength comes from the power to persuade, by presenting images of leadership. Presidential power is personal and symbolic. Presidents can use these closely associated figures—their running mates—to supplement their own presentation of leadership. This can be done quite literally, as when the vice-president attends the funeral of a foreign head of state or the first lady stands in for the president at a political rally or fund-raiser. The running mate physically represents the absent president. More imaginatively, presidents can use their spouses and their vice-presidents to expand or complement personal characteristics. Richard Nixon used Spiro Agnew to voice inflammatory rhetoric against intellectuals and ethnic minorities, allowing the administration to make certain appeals without engaging the president personally. Gerald Ford took advantage of the outspoken social tolerance of his wife, Betty, while maintaining a more conservative image for himself. George Bush addressed two vulnerabilities by using Dan Quayle to maintain links with the right wing of the Republican party and using Barbara Bush (a down-to-earth, grandmotherly contrast to her more glittery predecessor, Nancy Reagan) to counteract the image that Bush himself had led a life of privilege.

Second, the presidency is molded by each president in turn, as each reshuffles organizational support patterns. Similarly, each president defines the running mates' role. Although the vice-president does have a formal (mostly ceremonial) role in the Senate and a statutory seat on the National Security Council, each president can choose how much or how little to engage the vice-president in policymaking. Ever since Jimmy Carter gave Vice-President Walter Mondale a voice in presidential decision making, vice-presidents have taken a more active part in the executive branch. Vice-President George Bush was very active behind the scenes in the formulation of foreign policy during the Reagan administration. Vice-President Dan Quayle's Council on Competitiveness, described by a public interest lobbyist as "a power center in the White House," was very effective in blocking regulations that might have a negative impact on business.[12]

The vice-president is given only as much power as the president allows and is further constrained by the need not to break openly with the administration line. But the increasing complexity of the presidency favors a more responsible advising role for vice-presidents. As one Reagan aide said, "We've been through a ten-year evolution in the vice-presidency and there's no turning back. No president can afford to waste an officer who controls that many people and has such a potentially deferent perspective on national issues."[13] The opportunity for greatest vice-presidential influence comes with an outsider president and an insider vice-president. That combination occurred with Eisenhower and Nixon, Carter and Mondale, and Reagan and Bush. Each of those vice-presidents went on to secure a presidential nomination. Most recently, Bill Clinton and Al Gore came to power representing the outsider/insider combination.

Like the vice-president, the role of the president's spouse can be defined anew by each president—and by the spouse in question. Eleanor Roosevelt was the epitome of a strong, active presidential spouse. Rosalyn Carter, who often sat in on White House meetings, was described as her husband's most trusted adviser. Nancy Reagan was identified by friend and foe alike as an influential figure in the Reagan White House, according to some accounts creating a kind of "associate presidency." Political analyst Norman Ornstein cites Rosalyn Carter and Nancy Reagan as important in changing public expectations of presidential spouses. They "sensitized people to the fact that you elect a team, not just a president and a vice-president."[14] Hillary Clinton became the first presidential spouse to come to the White House after establishing a career as an advocacy attorney.

However, acknowledgment of the importance of the "first mate" must also recognize limits. Shortly after her husband became president, Barbara Bush said that assault weapons like the one responsible for the deaths of five children in a California schoolyard should be outlawed "absolutely," a statement that ran counter to the president's stance on gun control. The White House press secretary soon assured reporters that there was no disagreement between the president and his wife on gun control, an assurance that was followed shortly by an announcement that the first lady would thereafter not comment on controversial political issues.[15] The president can still set the limits.

The third truth about electoral politics is that under current traditions, the president has about as much freedom in choosing a vice-president as in choosing a spouse. Although the national convention formally nominates the vice-presidential candidate, the presidential nominee's choice is always accommodated. Though not always true in love, in the matter of choosing a vice-presidential running mate, opposites do attract—that is to say, since such choices are driven more by electoral considerations than by the concerns of governing, one frequent factor in choosing a vice-president is the matter of balance. If the presidential candidate is a liberal from Massachusetts, find a more conservative running mate, from Texas to "balance the ticket" and appeal to a wider audience. Perceived vulnerabilities in a candidate can be addressed by complementary strengths in a running mate, as when Albert Gore brought a record of service in Vietnam and strength on environmental issues to the 1992 Democratic ticket.

In the past quarter-century, three controversies have embroiled the president's vice-presidential choices. In 1972, George McGovern's presidential campaign was barely under way when his vice-presidential pick, Senator Thomas Eagleton of Missouri, was forced to admit that he had undergone psychiatric therapy, including electroshock treatment, but had failed to reveal this to McGovern. The rush of events surrounding the presidential nomination itself were blamed for McGovern's not being more fully informed of the background facts. After an agonizing and electorally costly delay, Eagleton resigned from the ticket, but the damage to McGovern's credibility had been done. The successful vice-presidential candidate that year—Richard Nixon's vice-president, Spiro Agnew—only eleven months later resigned the vice-presidency and pleaded no contest to tax evasion charges stemming from a kickback scheme dating from Agnew's time as governor of Maryland. In 1988, a certain measure of controversy surrounded George Bush's selection of Dan Quayle as his vice-presidential running mate. Concern over Quayle's lack of experience and more generally over his competence caused some observers to suggest again that leaving the vice-presidential choice solely to the presidential candidate, often in the rush of the convention itself, was a disaster-in-waiting. Given the closeness of the vice-president to power, a more regular, institutionalized process for choosing vice-presidential candidates is long overdue.

The Rest of the Bureaucracy

Most presidents experience more frustration than success when they push to make the federal bureaucracy responsive to their own priorities. A president has only a few years to impress a complete set of views on the departments, but the federal bureaucracy encompasses an array of institutions—each with its own routines, priorities, practices—that remain in place as elected administrations come and go. Segments of the bureaucracy with well-established connections with Congress and interest groups have no interest in seeing their programs gutted, curtailed, or radically changed by an incoming administration. According to a former cabinet secretary:

> The longer one examines the awesome burdens and limited resources of those who help the president from within his immediate circle, the more skeptical one becomes of a strategy for overseeing government by "running" it from 1600 Pennsylvania Avenue. The semiheroic, semihopeless posture has been captured many times in several administrations: dedicated men, of great intelligence and energy, working selflessly through weekends and holidays to master an endlessly increasing array of detail on complex subjects beyond their understanding on which decisions must be made "here" because a resolution elsewhere is not to be trusted.... Yet, in the end, the effort to help the president in making government work has not succeeded.[16]

For many members of White House staffs, conflict within the executive branch poses the single most significant problem in contemporary government. Some report more intense and serious conflict between the president and the bureaucracy than between the president and Congress. Although a few staffers believe that bureaucratic noncooperation stems from conspiracies and malevolent designs against the president, the more thoughtful recognize that to some extent conflicts are inevitable. Bureaucrats have many constituents, whereas White House staffers have only one person to please. And many career bureaucrats find White House staffers to be arrogant and bossy, interfering in matters they know little about and politicizing issues needlessly.

Relations with Congress

In Chapter 13 we saw that Congress and the president frequently maintain an adversarial relationship. Although Congress has powerful constitutional tools on its side—control of the purse strings, approval of presidential appointments and treaties, and the veto override—the president can use a wide array of tactics in dealing with Congress. Presidents nowadays have less trouble with entrenched committee chairs and more with independent-minded legislators. Instead of making deals with a few pow-

A political scientist before becoming president, Woodrow Wilson had written about the symbolic role of presidential leadership. In the White House, Wilson used the ceremonial aspects of the presidency, sometimes successfully (as in the U.S. entry into World War I) and sometimes less so (as in seeking support for the League of Nations). Here Wilson tosses out the first baseball of the 1916 season—a presidential action universally applauded. *(UPI/Bettmann)*

erful members of Congress, then, contemporary presidents must persuade and compromise with numerous less powerful ones.

The president, as the most visible actor in national politics, must engage in a variety of generalized goodwill-generating interactions with members of Congress. If the president does not enjoy firm support within the party or if that party does not have majorities in Congress, the president must often woo members of the opposition. Republican presidents since Nixon, facing Democratic majorities in one or both houses of Congress, used wooing tactics to build support wherever it could be found in Congress.

When it comes to specific measures and nominations, the White House can be very direct. The legislative liaison branch of the White House staff is charged with getting the president's point of view across to Congress. Liaison staffers work closely with congressional committees, consult and negotiate with legislators on critical points, and above all try to convey a firm sense of the president's personal commitment to particular policies and programs. If these staffers do not convince Congress that the president is committed to a certain program, White House lobbying for that program will be useless.

In exchanging favors with members of Congress, the president holds a trump card: patronage. Up to five hundred federal district judges, U.S. attorneys, and federal marshals, as well as numerous executive branch officials, are presidential appointees. Presidents often use these positions as bargaining chips in negotiations with opposition-party legislators and independent-minded members of his or her own party.

Such exchanges can backfire, however, especially if members of Congress feel that they are being pressured to trade votes directly for favors. As a result, exchanges are often quite subtle. President Johnson, for example, declared unequivocally that he would not trade patronage for votes in any direct exchange. But a stubborn unwillingness to trade can also spell trouble, as President Carter discovered when, early in his term, he cut nineteen water projects from the budget and called for reviews of another 320. Protests burst from Congress, which rarely faced such blatant presidential interference in its pork barrel traditions. Eventually, Carter decided not to review 307 projects and to restore funding to three of those he had originally dropped from the budget.

When all else fails, a president can resort to outright threats—usually, that federal projects will be eliminated or reduced in the state or district represented by an uncooperative legislator. President Nixon threatened to do so against legislators who were leaning toward opposing his Supreme Court nominees. Nixon also threatened to order IRS audits of particular senators' taxes. In 1985, President Reagan indicated he would have "more time" to campaign for the reelection of Republican senators who voted for his MX missile program. When this strong-arm approach appeared to be backfiring, Reagan quickly backed away publicly from that position. But he gained the votes he needed.

The president has one unparalleled advantage in dealing with a racalcitrant Congress: focusing national attention on selected issues. The president can command a larger audience than an individual legislator, a group of legislators, or even the entire opposition party. Through a major address, a president can raise issues on the national agenda in a fashion that is initially difficult to oppose. Such an address can provoke an immediate surge in support, giving the president more flexibility in bargaining with Congress and other political players. A recent study concluded that the success of presidential speechmaking in building support among various groups does not depend on a president's personal style or oratorical ability: Ford and Carter, neither noted for oratorical skill, were as successful at altering group opinions as the "great communicator," Ronald Reagan.[17] At times the television networks constrain the president's ability to go directly to the people. Early in 1988, for instance, when President Reagan urged the networks to broadcast a speech he was making to urge continued support for the Contras in Nicaragua, only CNN agreed to cover the speech live; ABC, CBS, and NBC turned down the president's request for live coverage. In the judgment of executives at those three networks, the news value of the proposed speech to the nation was negligible because the president had covered the same ground numerous times before.

Televised news conferences offer presidents a forum to appeal to the public as well. President Reagan's unwillingness to hold frequent news conferences gave rise to the unseemly and slightly comical practice of reporters shouting questions at him whenever he appeared in public. Presidents can also give off-the-record news briefings and interviews to get their views across. If the president can create a sense of national crisis by going to the people, the likely increase in presidential popularity can be used to political advantage.

The veto gives the president considerable power with Congress. Even the threat of a veto is a potent political weapon. Knowing that a veto is likely, Congress may modify a bill to meet presidential objections; after a successful veto, it may pass legislation altered to meet presidential demands. Congress rarely musters the two-thirds vote in each house necessary to override a presidential veto—only about 4 percent of vetoes suffer such a fate. George Bush was successful in thirty-five straight vetoes, suffering his first override only weeks before he was beaten by Bill Clinton in the 1992 election. Yet few vetoes of extremely important matters have been overridden. President Nixon's veto of the War Powers Resolution, a measure facilitating congressional participation in decisions to send U.S. military forces into action, for example, was overridden. President Bush's successful veto of the 1990 civil rights bill forced at least superficial modifications in the legislation that allowed the president to sign the 1991 Civil Rights Act while maintaining his opposition to "quotas" (see Chapter 5).

Presidents cannot veto every measure Congress passes. They cannot veto constitutional amendments or bills relating to the internal organization of either house. The president does not have a **line-item veto**, which would allow excising part of a bill but leaving the rest. As one means of forestalling presidential vetoes in recent years, Congress has passed more **omnibus bills**, in which several subjects of legislation are gathered together in a single bill. The president then has to choose whether to accept some undesirable bits or to reject a largely acceptable—perhaps essential—bill. Battles frequently break out in the executive branch (typically between White House staffers and cabinet members or OMB officials) over whether particular bills should be vetoed.

The Dangerous President

Throughout U.S. history, presidents have used the wide latitude available to them in foreign policymaking and their position as symbolic leader to foment crises, go to war, or harass opponents. In the early days of the Republic, Presidents John Adams, Thomas Jefferson, and Andrew Jackson were accused of abusing the powers of the office. During the Civil War, President Lincoln stretched the powers of the office considerably. In the twentieth century, Franklin Roosevelt, John Kennedy, Lyndon Johnson, Richard Nixon, Ronald Reagan and George Bush have all been charged with abuses of power.

Not every accusation is justified, of course; partisanship often plays a role here. For many years, beginning in the 1930s, conservative Republicans attacked the growing power of the presidency, largely out of dislike for particular policies or particular incumbents. The people who attacked the power of the president, who saw it as a threat to the constitutional system, were often the same people who railed against an activist government, preferring to see society remain as it was. During this period, liberals championed the strong presidency because of its potential for making needed changes and responding to urgent national concerns.

In the 1960s this pattern of debate shifted as liberals voiced concern about excessive presidential power and many conservatives found themselves backing the president. The Vietnam War, more than any other factor, accounted for this shift. Liberals came to oppose the war and the mounting—and in their view dangerous—growth of presidential power associated with it. Conservatives, in contrast, tended to support Presidents Johnson and Nixon in their conduct of the war. In 1991 conservatives applauded President Bush's assertion of presidential prerogative to conduct Operations Desert Shield and Desert Storm.

Partisanship aside, there is real cause for concern that the president's constitutional powers and the additional responsibilities of the modern presidency could easily threaten democratic politics. Presidential abuses of power fall into three categories: betraying the public trust, when the president and/or aides deliberately mislead the public or arouse public emotion in a manipulative way; undermining the separation of powers by usurping functions that properly belong to Congress or the courts; and manipulating the political and legal processes.

But particular presidential abuses of power usually fall into more than one of these categories. We now examine three instances of the misuse of presidential power—the Vietnam War, the Watergate affair, the Iran-Contra affair—and a possible fourth, Operation Desert Shield, prior to the Persian Gulf War of 1991.

Congress Manipulated: The Gulf of Tonkin Resolution

In the summer of 1964, President Lyndon Johnson and his advisers were planning to escalate U.S. involvement in the fighting in Vietnam. In early August, North Vietnamese ships allegedly fired on a U.S. destroyer in the Gulf of Tonkin, in what the administration characterized as an unprovoked incident that had taken place in international waters. The next day another incident took place, this one involving two American destroyers; it has never been made clear what (if anything) happened in this incident. President Johnson and his advisers seized on these incidents to press Congress to authorize the president to take any action necessary to deal with North Vietnamese aggression. That way the administration would not have to go through the lengthy and potentially difficult process of obtaining a formal declaration of war.

The president told congressional leaders that he intended to retaliate against North Vietnamese targets and that he wanted a congressional resolution to back him up. Although he emphasized that he wanted only a "limited resolution," the one that reached the floor of Congress authorized him to "take all necessary measures" to repel "any armed attack" on American troops and to prevent "further aggression" in Vietnam. Johnson asked Senator William Fulbright, an Arkansas Democrat and the chairman of the Senate Foreign Relations Committee, to guide the Gulf of Tonkin Resolution through the Senate. Although Fulbright had been critical of the war, he and Johnson enjoyed cordial relations, so he rushed

(Box continues on page 541)

The Vietnam War

The Vietnam War was a "presidential" conflict, fought entirely without a declaration of war from Congress. The war lasted more than a decade, cost this country $165 billion, and claimed 58,000 American lives. Throughout most of the war, Congress more or less passively supported U.S. military involvement, but that support was gained, at least in part, through a series of presidential abuses of power.

According to historian Arthur Schlesinger, we had a taste of the so-called *imperial presidency* under President Johnson and his successor, Richard Nixon.[18] From 1963 to 1974, Schlesinger suggests, presidential power was expanded and abused, and the nation was threatened with a presidential style that ignored reasonable limits on the office.

Schlesinger focuses on two aspects of the expansion and use of presidential powers: *war powers* and the *manipulation of secrecy*. In an era of nearly constant crisis, the president's war powers gradually expanded until they came to include prerogatives

---

the resolution through his committee. His main opposition in the committee was Senator Wayne Morse of Oregon. Morse warned Fulbright that the resolution would give the president all the authority he needed for carrying on an expanded war in Vietnam. Congress, Morse warned, would never be consulted about the war again.

Morse's reservations about the resolution stemmed in part from his awareness of certain falsehoods and distortions in the administration's version of events in the Gulf of Tonkin. (Later congressional investigators discovered that the destroyers had been engaged in disrupting North Vietnamese radar with electronic interference.) Morse pleaded with Fulbright to hold open hearings on the resolution. What was the emergency? Why the need to rush the resolution through? But Fulbright and Johnson had their way: The resolution passed the Senate with two dissenting votes and the House without a single dissent.

Thus the president was given what he claimed was a blank check for conducting the war in Vietnam. But Johnson eventually paid a price for his manipulation of Congress. Fulbright, after learning that he had been lied to and that the administration had deliberately misconstrued the evidence about the Tonkin Gulf incidents, became a determined enemy of the Vietnam War and used his power as Foreign Relations Committee chairman to direct a steady stream of serious criticism at the war. The Gulf of Tonkin Resolution triggered a widespread distrust of the executive branch. This distrust culminated in the passage of the War Powers Resolution of 1973, aimed at limiting presidential warmaking powers.

once associated with monarchs, not elected officials. Both presidents deliberately misled Congress and the public about matters of war and peace. Johnson shrewdly arranged for Congress to pass the Gulf of Tonkin Resolution of 1964, which he claimed gave him virtually a free hand in Vietnam. The information the president gave Congress to justify such sweeping new powers turned out to be at the least misleading and probably deliberately deceptive. Nixon conducted a secret bombing campaign in Cambodia in 1969 and 1970. He then significantly altered the scope and nature of the war—again without consulting Congress or the American people—by ordering an invasion of Cambodia by ground troops in 1970. Every significant expansion of this war was undertaken unilaterally by the president, with Congress entirely excluded or at best given the opportunity to consent meekly after the fact. Even attempts to extricate the United States from the war through international agreements were entirely executive in nature.

In response to these and other perceived abuses of presidential power, Congress passed the War Powers Resolution of 1973, curtailed the president's emergency powers, and imposed some restrictions on future executive agreements (see Chapter 13 for further details). But with increased U.S. involvement as regional conflict heated up in Central America in the 1980s and in the Middle East in the early 1990s, no one could be sure that the lessons of Vietnam—the danger to democracy posed by presidential abuse of power and congressional acquiescence—had been learned.

The Watergate Affair

On the night of June 17, 1972, five burglars were apprehended in the headquarters of the Democratic National Committee, located in the Watergate complex in Washington, D.C. At first, administration spokesmen dismissed the break-in as a "third-rate burglary." But two reporters for the *Washington Post*, Carl Bernstein and Bob Woodward, traced a connection between the break-in and Nixon's reelection campaign committee. Several White House aides in contact with that committee also had a hand in the bungled burglary. A plan to cover up these connections was put into place: Incriminating documents were destroyed, and the Watergate burglars were offered money for their defense and their families in exchange for their silence. Despite efforts by the Democrats to focus attention on the Watergate affair at that point, the administration's coverup muted most calls for further investigation prior to the elections of November 1972. Nixon was returned to office in a landslide.

In January 1973, however, the Watergate burglars were convicted and sentenced to jail, and one of the burglars told Judge John Sirica that they had been pressured into pleading guilty. Sirica reopened the case, and grand jury hearings were held. The Senate Select Committee on Watergate began an investigation in May 1973. Under pressure from Congress and the press, Nixon appointed a special prosecutor to look into the matter, although he and his aides continued to maintain their noninvolvement.

The Senate hearings soon brought some startling facts to light. It became clear that the Nixon administration had violated most of the rules of U.S. political life. White

House personnel and Republican party members illegally wiretapped political opponents' phones, stole documents, lied to grand juries, and engaged in large-scale falsifications about illegal campaign contributions. As the evidence reached closer to the Oval Office, some of Nixon's aides resigned.

Nixon himself might have been able to weather the Watergate storm had it not come to light that he had installed a system that secretly recorded every conversation in the Oval Office. Claiming executive privilege, Nixon refused to release these tapes until the Supreme Court ordered him to supply copies of them to the court hearing the Watergate burglary case.

The tapes doomed Nixon. Some had been suspiciously tampered with. Worse, Nixon and his aides were revealed on the tapes as vindictive schemers bent on settling scores with their enemies and gaining ever more power. With impeachment proceedings imminent, Nixon resigned in August 1974.

Many of the charges against Nixon involved activities that previous presidents had engaged in or condoned. Other chief executives had received illegal campaign contributions, used "dirty tricks" in political campaigns, provided direct or indirect payoffs to people who had helped in election efforts, used government agencies to harass enemies, tried to manage the news, and kept activities secret from the public and Congress. But Nixon's personal involvement in the coverup of crimes and the obstruction of justice distinguished him from other presidents. In the final analysis, the sheer number of violations of law and norms and the range of questionable activities designed to enhance the powers and prerogatives of the president and his cohorts were unique to the Nixon administration. Here was a president and a group of advisers who not only tried to skirt the law but actually believed that the president was above the law.

The Iran-Contra Affair

The Iran-Contra affair exemplifies executive abuse of power.[19] Although President Reagan's specific involvement in the affair remains unclear, the pattern of abuse in this episode closely matches the preceding examples. Leaving the matter of personal presidential culpability aside, this affair demonstrates how power can be abused by members of an administration in the president's name.

The Iran-Contra affair was an odd pairing of operations in two widely separated parts of the globe. In Iran the administration's objective was to win the freedom of American hostages held by terrorist groups in Lebanon that were more or less associated with the revolutionary government of Iran. In Nicaragua the administration sought to support the Contra opposition to the Marxist Sandinista government. Two sets of constraints limited administration action. In its dealings with Iran, the administration was bound by an embargo on arms to Iran and a firmly asserted public policy of refusing to bargain with terrorists for the release of hostages. According to official policy, such bargaining would only encourage terrorists to seize more hostages in the long run. In Nicaragua the administration was contrained by the **Boland Amendment**, signed into

Marine Lt. Col. Oliver North became a folk hero to some and a symbol of the degeneration of democracy to others. North's testimony before Congress about funneling money and arms to the Contras in Nicaragua established him as a well-known member of the Reagan administration. *(Atlan/Sygma)*

law in October 1984 as part of the 1985 omnibus appropriations bills. The Boland Amendment cut off all federal funds for the Contras' military and paramilitary operations, prohibited the American government from soliciting donations for the Contras from third-party countries, and barred the CIA and other U.S. government agencies from participating in covert operations in support of the Contras.

The American government learned of the possibility that sales of U.S. arms to Iran (engaged in a stalemated war with Iraq) might lead to the release of American hostages and a new, more friendly relationship with Iran. Weapon sales were arranged through the Enterprise, a private concern run by a retired U.S. Air Force major general at the direction of Lt. Col. Oliver L. North, a staff member of the National Security Council. Using good old Yankee ingenuity, the Enterprise managed to charge Iran more for the weapons than it had paid the U.S. government for them, generating more than $16 million in "spare cash." North directed that some of this profit be used to support the Contras.

These transactions abused executive power on several counts. Most significantly, the administration was conducting a secret foreign policy in direct contradiction to its publicly stated policy. In addition, active efforts were made to deceive Congress about the nature of these operations. The deception even reached within the executive branch itself; North ordered intelligence agencies not to disseminate information on these operations to the secretaries of state and defense. (Both secretaries claimed to have opposed the plan when they learned about it in broad outline.) The NSC used private individuals and the Enterprise to carry out the government's business, deliberately avoiding accountability for these actions in the political arena. Finally, the NSC itself had been turned from its original mission—to give the president advice on national security matters and foreign policy issues—into a base for covert operations.

The *Executive Summary of the Report of the Congressional Committees Investigating the Iran-Contra Affair* ended with this quotation from Supreme Court Justice Louis Brandeis: "Our Government is the potent, the omnipresent teacher. For good or ill, it teaches the whole people by its example. Crime is contagious. If the Government becomes a law-breaker, it breeds contempt for the law, it invites every man to become a law unto himself, it invites anarchy." The report concluded that the Iran-Contra affair resulted from a failure to heed this message.

Operation Desert Shield

In August 1990 the military forces of Iraq, under the command of President Saddam Hussein, invaded and overwhelmed Kuwait. The United Nations quickly condemned the invasion and imposed an economic boycott to force Iraq's withdrawal. President Bush supported the economic boycott but warned that military action might be necessary to evict Iraq from Kuwait. While Iraqi forces of occupation engaged in gross violations of human rights and stripped Kuwait of wealth, President Bush began Operation Desert Shield, a buildup of U.S. military forces in the Persian Gulf, initially to prevent an invasion of Saudi Arabia and the further disruption of oil supplies from the Middle East. In November, President Bush decided to increase the number of U.S. troops on the ground in the region—eventually to over 400,000. There were two interpretations of this action. The president's supporters argued that the troop buildup was necessary to get Saddam Hussein to back down and withdraw from Kuwait peacefully. The president's critics charged that putting such a huge force in the field meant that the United States could not afford to wait for economic sanctions to work—that we would have to strike soon or back down ourselves. The president went to the United Nations to seek support for evicting Saddam Hussein long before he approached Congress; in fact, he did not ask for a congressional resolution supporting the possible use of force until January 8, 1991—a week before the UN deadline for Iraq's withdrawal. Iraq did not withdraw, and Operation Desert Shield became Operation Desert

Foreign-policy problems have foiled some presidents and increased the popularity of others. Operation Desert Storm seemed to make George Bush an unbeatable candidate in 1992, but this estimate proved to be shortsighted. *(Patrick Durand/Sygma)*

Storm, the U.S.-led attack against Iraqi forces in Kuwait and in Iraq that forced Saddam Hussein to retreat but did not displace him from power in Iraq.

Was Operation Desert Shield another example of the dangerous president in action? By moving without congressional approval to position the United States so that war was likely (if not inevitable), did George Bush go beyond legitimate executive action, as a strict reading of the War Powers Resolution suggests? Or was this no more than the necessary president? Would it be foolish to attempt to tie a president's hands in dealing with international crises like this one? Operation Desert Storm was initially enormously popular in the United States.* A short, dramatic war in which U.S. technology devastated the enemy with only a tiny number of American casualties allowed

---

*The initial popularity of the war was mitigated by later events: Saddam Hussein maintained power after Desert Storm, terrorizing the Kurds in northern Iraq and trying to maintain a secret Iraqi nuclear weapons development program, subsequent accounts revealed the suffering that the war inflicted upon the civilian Iraqi population, initial claims for U.S. technology were revised downward, and official reports came to light revealing that the Bush administration had actively supported Iraq and its leader (as a counterweight to Iran) until very near the time of the invasion of Kuwait.

President Bush to claim that we had finally beaten the Vietnam syndrome—the American public could once more get behind the use of its military might in a just cause.

Whatever judgment is made about Operation Desert Shield, it still raises the outlines of a key dilemma: How can we prevent presidential abuses of power when the president holds such a predominant place in U.S. political life? Most Americans do not favor weakening the presidency in any constitutional manner. And most believe that the United States needs an activist president who leads the nation vigorously. Those views are reinforced by institutional prerogatives: No other political actor can shape and organize the government in a way comparable to the president. Hence we continue to face the ongoing risk of presidential abuse of power.

Transitions of Power

Under normal conditions, presidents leave office because they choose not to run again or are defeated in an election. Only about one-third of U.S. presidents—thirteen in all—have won a second term in office, and only Franklin Roosevelt served more than two terms. (No president can now duplicate Roosevelt's four-term record: Under the Twenty-second Amendment, ratified in 1951, no person may serve as president for more than a total of ten years.) Slightly more than 20 percent of U.S. presidents have died in office, including four who were assassinated: Abraham Lincoln (1865), James Garfield (1881), William McKinley (1901), and John Kennedy (1963). Since 1945, moreover, four out of nine presidents have been attacked by assassins—a record among contemporary Western democracies. So far, no president has been removed from office by impeachment, although Andrew Johnson came close and Richard Nixon resigned before an impeachment trial could be held.

The mechanics of presidential succession are not spelled out in the Constitution. When President William Henry Harrison died one month after taking office in 1841, John Tyler, the vice-president, assumed the presidency. That was the first time a president had died in office, and it sparked a political controversy. Should Tyler simply become president, or should he take office temporarily until a new election could be held? Tyler preferred the first alternative, and Congress acquiesced.

Starting in 1886, statutory provision was made for presidential succession but not presidential disability. Twice in U.S. history, presidents had become seriously disabled—James Garfield after being shot in 1881 and Woodrow Wilson after a stroke in 1919. Others, such as Dwight Eisenhower, had been temporarily incapacitated by illness.

Finally, the Twenty-fifth Amendment, ratified in 1967, addressed the twin issues of succession and presidential disability. It provided that if the president were unable to carry out his duties, the vice-president would serve as acting president. If the president were to decline to step down, he could be removed by a two-thirds vote of each house of Congress. In dealing with succession, the amendment specifies that on assuming

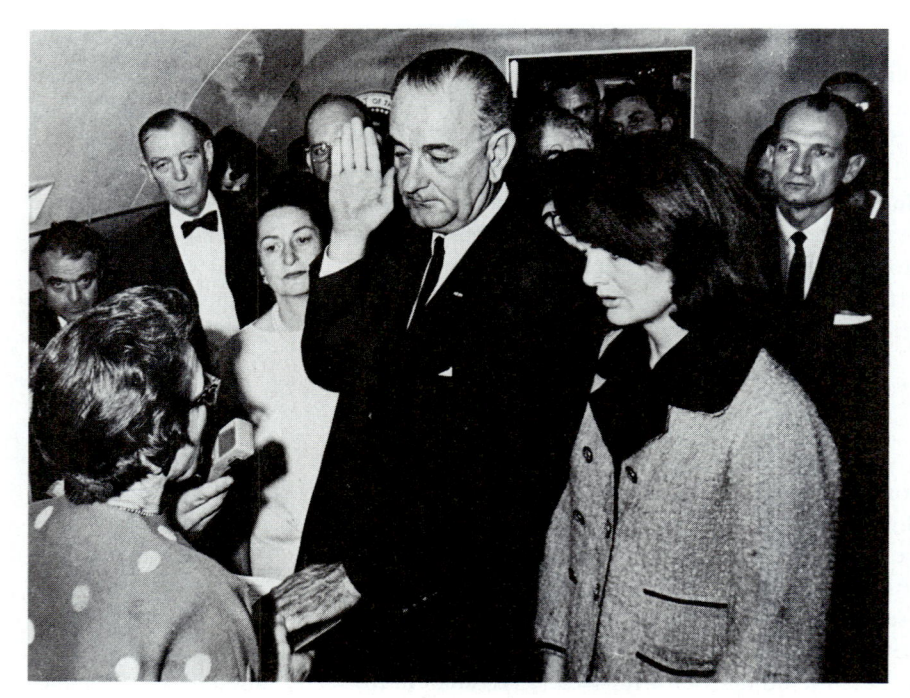

Presidential succession is highly routinized in the United States, whether under traumatic conditions, like the assassination of President Kennedy in 1963, or the calm normalcy of President Bush's succession of Ronald Reagan in 1989. Such a stable transfer of power is a credit to our democracy and the envy of less tranquil political systems. (Dan McCoy/Black Star)

the presidency, the vice-president must nominate a new vice-president, who must then be confirmed by a majority of both houses of Congress. If no new vice-president is selected and the new president must be replaced, an older statutory line of succession starting with the Speaker of the House prevails.

Not long after the Twenty-fifth Amendment was ratified, its provisions were put to use. Nixon's vice-president, Spiro Agnew, resigned from office after pleading no contest to bribery charges. Nixon then nominated Gerald Ford to the vice-presidency. Not long thereafter, Nixon resigned the presidency, and Ford became president. He in turn nominated Nelson Rockefeller as vice-president, and Rockefeller was confirmed by both houses. When he was sworn in as vice-president on December 19, 1974, it marked the first time in U.S. history that neither of the two people holding the highest offices in the nation had been elected to those positions. The procedure worked smoothly, despite the turmoil of Watergate and the novelty of the succession process. The procedures were also engaged in 1985, when Ronald Reagan was briefly unable to serve

(Text continues on page 550)

COMPARATIVE PERSPECTIVE

POLITICAL CRISIS AND TRANSITION IN FRANCE, 1958

During World War II, General Charles de Gaulle was the acknowledged leader of the Free French. After the liberation of France from Nazi occupation, he presided over a provisional government while an assembly wrote a new constitution establishing the Fourth Republic. Disgusted with the weak government he felt had been created, de Gaulle retired to the political sidelines in 1946.

By May 1958, the Fourth Republic had gone through twenty-four governments, and the country was being torn apart over the problem of Algeria—whether to acknowledge the grievances of Algerian rebels opposing French rule or to repress all colonial unrest. The Algerian question proved too much for the successively weaker governments. In 1956, the French army had stood by while French settlers in Algiers attacked their own premier, socialist Guy Mollet, whom they felt had been too weak in dealing with the rebels. The disaffected military coalesced into a powerful and potentially antidemocratic threat to French political stability.

The twenty-third government of the Fourth Republic fell on April 15, 1958, when the hard-line Algerian lobby withdrew its support. Four tense weeks passed before a new government could be formed. Meanwhile, de Gaulle was poised to reclaim political power. As anti-Gaullist politicians scrambled to scrape together enough support to keep him out of power, several prominent military officers planned a coup d'état against the Republic, to be carried out on the orders of the senior military command in Algiers.

What came next has been termed the de Gaulle revolution. Through a process of secret negotiations with members of the government and public pronouncements warning the military to "maintain exemplary behavior," de Gaulle was able to position himself for an official call to establish a new government. Legality was preserved as de Gaulle, like his predecessors, was voted into office by the National Assembly. But his terms for taking the reins of government were stiff: emergency powers and governance by decree, the temporary (six-month) dissolution of the assembly, and the mandate to draw up a new constitution. France had preserved the form, if not the substance, of institutionalized succession.

Sources: Don Cook, Charles de Gaulle *(New York: Putnam, 1983); Bernard Ledwidge,* De Gaulle *(New York: St. Martin's Press, 1982).*

as president during an operation for colon cancer. George Bush became acting president for that short period.

Conclusions

In dealing with the presidency, we tend to reach for extremes. To one generation, presidential leadership holds the key to political soundness, progress, and effective policymaking. To another, the presidency is a source of unbridled hubris. What sort of person should sit in the White House? How much latitude should we give the occupant of the Oval Office? Although presidents sometimes find it necessary to stretch the limits of their power, Congress, the courts, and the electorate may either sanction presidential initiatives or assert their own power to cut the president short.

And how do democracy and the drive for democratic values figure in the scheme of presidential policymaking? Clearly, presidents can enhance their historical standing by championing democratic causes. When Lyndon Johnson introduced the Voting Rights Act of 1965, it marked a turning point in U.S. history. Lending the weight and prestige of the presidency to democratic causes can make the difference between progress and stagnation. But presidents can also work against democratic politics, as Richard Nixon did in his conduct of the Vietnam War and the Watergate affair and as Lyndon Johnson did in deceiving Congress and the American people about his Vietnam policy. In the area of foreign policy, presidents have the most latitude, can do the most damage, and are most likely to play on popular fears. Therefore, it is here that we encounter the most pressing problems for democratic values. Only an informed and vigorous Congress and an attentive public can ensure that presidents do not overreach in foreign affairs.

We expect presidents to lead. But is it possible for presidents to lead without deception and without offering simplistic solutions? The post may be, as Theodore Roosevelt called it, a "bully pulpit" from which to rouse the nation, but by the same token it can be used to exploit public fears, to play on popular stereotypes, and to offer facile solutions to tough problems.

All presidents confront problems and events that they cannot change or wish away. Yet it is clear that the *person* can make a difference. How would President Reagan have responded to the Bay of Pigs crisis or the invasion of Kuwait? How would President Eisenhower have handled Vietnam? Would Michael Dukakis, as president, have dealt with Noriega differently than President Bush? Would President Carter, had he been elected to a second term, have continued the defense buildup as far as Reagan actually did?

In our democratic polity, many critical issues and approaches depend on one person and the people who surround that person. And today an individual can become president of the United States—a global superpower—without the benefit of experience in any comparable office. Therefore, democrats are compelled to keep a watchful eye on the presidency and the president.

Glossary Terms

Boland Amendment
cabinet
delegated powers
executive agreement
Executive Office of the President
impeachment
inherent powers

line-item veto
National Security Council (NSC)
Office of Management and Budget (OMB)
omnibus bill
separation of powers
White House Office

Notes

[1] Richard Pious provides an interesting discussion of American attitudes toward the presidency in *The American Presidency* (New York: Basic Books, 1979), intro. and pt. 1. Fred Greenstein, who studied reactions to the Kennedy assassination, reported that 43 percent of adults suffered loss of appetite; 48 percent, insomnia; 25 percent, headaches; 68 percent, nervousness and tension; 26 percent, rapid heartbeat; and 17 percent perspiration. See his "Popular Images of the President," *American Journal of Psychiatry*, November, 1965, pp. 523-529. Also on this subject consult B. S. Greenberg and E. B. Parker, *The Kennedy Assassination and the American Public* (Stanford, Calif.: Stanford University Press, 1965).

[2] See Pious, *The American Presidency*, chap. 2.

[3] Examples derived from Ibid., pt. 2, secs. 2, 3, and 4.

[4] *Sawyer, Petitioner* v. *Youngstown Sheet & Tube Co. et al.* (1952), 343 U.S. 579.

[5] *Grove City College* v. *Bell* (1984), 465 U.S. 555.

[6] Discussion derived from Thomas E. Cronin, *The State of the Presidency*, 2nd ed. (Boston: Little, Brown, 1980), chap. 1.

[7] Ibid., pp. 19, 22.

[8] Discussion drawn from Nolan Argyle and Ryan Barilleaux, "Past Failures and Future Prescriptions for Presidential Management Reform," *Presidential Studies Quarterly*, Fall 1986, pp. 716-733.

[9] Jeffrey E. Cohen, *The Politics of the U.S. Cabinet* (Pittsburgh: University of Pittsburgh Press, 1988), p. 39.

[10] Paul C. Light, *Vice-presidential Power: Advice and Influence in the White House* (Baltimore: Johns Hopkins University Press, 1984), p. 1.

[11] Ann Grimes, "Nancy & Abigail & Eleanor & Edith," *New York Times*, April 11, 1991, p. A15.

[12] See Kirk Victor, "Quayle's Quiet Coup," *National Journal*, July 6, 1991, pp. 1676-1680; "Dan Quayle, Scourge of Government," *Economist*, November 30, 1991, p. 32; Douglas harbrecht with Peter Hong, "Dan Quayle, Regulation Terminator," *Business Week*, November 4, 1991, p. 31; and Michael Duffy, "Need Friends in High Places?" *Time*, November 4, 1991, p. 25.

[13] Light, *Vice-presidential Power*, p. 2.

[14] Ann Grimes, *Running Mates: The Making of a First Lady* (New York: Morrow, 1990), p. 21.

[15] Donnie Radcliffe, *Simply Barbara Bush: America's Candid First Lady* (New York: Warner Books, 1989), pp. 44-45.

[16] Cronin, *State of the Presidency*, pp. 228-229.

[17] Lyn Ragsdale, "Presidential Speechmaking and the Public Audience: Individual presidents and Group Attitudes," *Journal of Politics*, August 1987, p. 732.

[18] See A. M. Schlesinger, Jr., *The Imperial Presidency* (Boston: Houghton Mifflin, 1973).

[19] Account drawn from Joel Brinkley and Stephen Engelberg, eds., *The Report of the Congressional Committees Investigating the Iran-Contra Affair*, abridged ed. (New York: Times Books/Random House, 1988).

SELECTED READINGS

For **classic treatments** of the American presidency that still have a lot to teach, see Richard Neustadt, *Presidential Power: The Politics of Leadership from FDR to Carter* (New York: Macmillan, 1980); George Reedy, *The Twilight of the Presidency* (New York: New American Library, 1970); and Arthur M. Schlesinger, Jr., *The Imperial Presidency* (Boston: Houghton Mifflin, 1973).

For more recent work, consult Robert E. Di Clerico, *The American President* (Englewood Cliffs, N.J.: Prentice Hall, 1990); and Richard Rose, *The Postmodern President* (Chatham, N.J.: Chatham House, 1991). Useful **reference works** on the presidency include Thomas L. Connelly and Michael D. Senecal, eds., *The Almanac of American Presidents* (New York: Facts on File, 1991); and Leonard W. Levy, *Encyclopedia of the American Presidency* (New York: Simon & Schuster, 1993).

On **presidential spouses**, see Myra G. Gutin, *The President's Partner: The First Lady in the Twentieth Century* (Westport, Conn.: Greenwood Press, 1989); Betty Boyd Caroli, *First Ladies* (New York: Oxford University Press, 1987); and Ann Grimes, *Running Mates: The Making of a First Lady* (New York: Morrow, 1990). The **vice-president** is the subject of Michael Nelson, *A Heartbeat Away: Report of the Twentieth Century Fund Task Force on the Vice-Presidency* (New York: Priority Press Publications, 1988); and two books by Paul C. Light: *Vice-presidential Influence under Rockefeller and Mondale* (Washington, D.C.: Brookings Institution, 1984), and *Vice-presidential Power: Advice and Influence in the White House* (Baltimore: Johns Hopkins University Press, 1984).

To learn more about the interaction between **presidents and the executive branch**, consult Congressional Quarterly's *Cabinets and Counselors: The President and the Executive Branch* (Washington, D.C.: Congressional Quarterly Press, 1989). The **National Security Council** is the subject of John Prado, *Keepers of the Keys: A History of the National Security Council from Truman to Bush* (New York: Morrow, 1991), in which the author concludes that the NSC charter should be updated to prevent ill-conceived foreign policy ventures. On the **structure of the Executive Office**, see Stephen Hess, *Organizing the Presidency*, rev. ed. (Washington, D.C.: Brookings Institution, 1988).

Recent journal articles of interest include Terry Sullivan, "The Bank Account Presidency: A New Measure and Evidence on the Temporal Path of Presidential Influence," *AJPS*, August 1991, pp. 686–723, and the response by George C. Edwards III in the same issue; Daniel E. Ingberman and Dennis A. Yao, "Presidential Commitment and the Veto," *AJPS*, May 1991, pp. 357–389; Jon A. Krosnick and Donald R. Kinder, "Altering the Foundations of Support for the President through Priming," *APSR*, June 1990, pp. 497–512; and Richard Fleisher and Jon R. Bond, "Assessing Presidential Support in the House II: Lessons from George Bush," *AJPS*, May 1992, pp. 525–541.

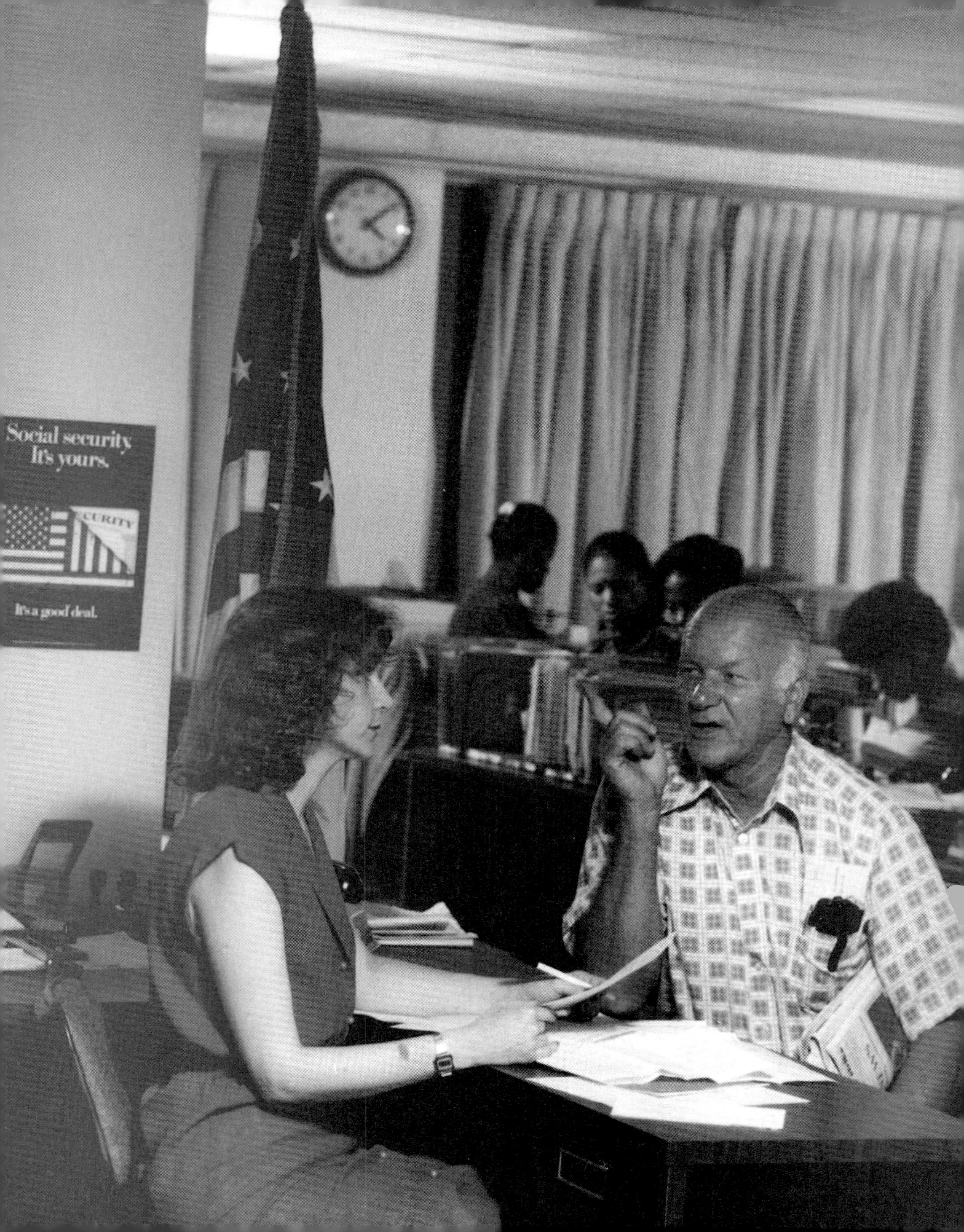
Social security.
It's yours.
CURITY
It's a good deal.

CHAPTER FIFTEEN

CHAPTER OUTLINE

Defining the Federal Bureaucracy

Structure of the National Bureaucracy

CABINET DEPARTMENTS
INDEPENDENT AGENCIES
REGULATORY COMMISSIONS

Bureaucracy and the Political Process

BUREAUCRATIC DISCRETION
BUREAUCRATIC EXPERTISE
MOBILIZATION OF SUPPORT

Bureaucracy Evaluated

IS THE BUREAUCRACY TOO UNRESPONSIVE?
IS THERE TOO MUCH BUREAUCRACY?
ARE THERE TOO MANY RULES?

THE BUREAUCRACY

How Much Service and What Kind?

ON THIS LABOR DAY, WE TAKE SPECIAL PRIDE IN THE RIGHTS AND opportunities that our system of government and innate sense of fairness ensure all American workers. As long as we cherish those rights and opportunities that are uniquely ours, this nation will continue to be blessed with prosperity and progress.
—George Bush, Labor Day, 1990

Presidents always give Labor Day speeches, noble expressions of our national commitment to labor and the worker. Congress embodied one facet of that commitment in the 1970 Occupational Safety and Health Act, establishing the **Occupational Safety and Health Administration (OSHA)**. The act gives OSHA responsibility for developing and promulgating occupational health and safety standards, developing and issuing regulations, conducting investigations, and issuing citations for violations. In most cases the implementation of presidential and legislative policies depends on bureaucratic agencies like OSHA. Without the bureaucracy, policies, from the humblest to the most ambitious, would remain unrealized.

On September 3, 1991, after the long Labor Day weekend, Lillian Wall went to work as usual at the Imperial Food Products chicken plant in Hamlet, North Carolina (population 6,196). Wall's job was to pull prime strips of meat from the center of chilled chicken breasts. She told her best friend, Loretta Goodwin, that she was tired of handling chicken—her hands were always cold. She planned to get a job at a hosiery mill.

The Hamlet chicken plant was inspected every day by a U.S. Department of Agriculture food inspector, whose job was to ensure the safety and wholesomeness of the chicken produced in the plant. Although it had been in operation for more than a decade, and despite two serious fires, Imperial's Hamlet chicken plant had never had a fire safety inspection. Fire safety rules are clearly within OSHA's domain.

How are federal safety inspections carried out? There are two options. One is for OSHA to conduct its own safety inspections. For example, an OSHA safety officer in Pennsylvania found several serious violations of federal safety regulations in an Imperial Food Products plant in February 1987. He also found "a belligerent owner who cursed a lot and accused him of nitpicking." His records from that inspection included the

Health and safety issues arise in many work places. The state and federal agencies in charge of inspection are often understaffed, with the obvious result noted in this cartoon.
(By permission of Mike Luckovich and Creators Syndicate)

note "Two other plants, located in Hamlet, N.C., and Denver, Colorado," but no warning was passed along to inspectors in those states. The alternative is for OSHA to provide federal funding and allow state labor officials to take responsibility for safety inspections—a typical sharing of responsibility in our federal system. In 1991, OSHA allowed twenty-three states to carry out their own workplace safety inspections. Since 1971 the North Carolina Labor Department had had that responsibility for the Tar Heel state.

Since OSHA's domain was the workplace, OHSA inspections were not intended to displace broader state safety programs. In the United States, fire safety has been a state and local responsibility. Local fire departments, county building inspectors, and state safety inspectors frequently share responsibility for fire safety inspections in all categories of buildings, residential as well as commercial. Even for workplaces, the federal OSHA legislation did not disturb that traditional responsibility in states that chose to exercise it, but it did establish uniform federal standards and review procedures. North Carolina's workplace safety and health program had sixteen fully trained inspectors to inspect an estimated 166,000 workplaces—enough to inspect each workplace once every seventy-five years!

Not long after starting work on September 3, Lillian Wall and Loretta Goodwin saw a group of women come out of the room where the chicken cooker was. Another fire had started. Someone said, "We can get out over there." The group went to a door near the garbage bin, but that door had been locked, reportedly to keep out flies and to keep workers from stealing chickens. A fire safety inspection would have ordered that door to be kept unlocked. But there had been no fire safety inspection. Wall, Goodwin, and about forty other people were trying to get out that locked door as smoke filled the plant. Eventually the door was opened, and Goodwin, her stomach distended from inhaled smoke, was pulled to safety on the grass outside the brick building. Months later she still suffered nightmares and obsessive fear of being in enclosed places. Fifty-six workers were injured but survived the fire. Lillian Wall was not so lucky. She died that morning in the chicken plant. So did twenty-four of her co-workers.[1]

Certain terms carry connotations that are hard to escape. *Bureaucracy*, for example, evokes thoughts of endless red tape, inefficiency, and unresponsiveness. To most people the bureaucracy is the faceless entity that forces them to fill out tax forms or to stand in line at post offices or register for a Selective Service system even when there's no draft. But bureaucrats touch people's lives in many other ways as well. OSHA safety inspectors are bureaucrats. The food we eat, the prescription drugs we take, the cars we drive, the sports equipment we play with, even the fire-resistant pajamas we slept in as children—all these fall under regulations established by the federal bureaucracy.

Here, when we speak of **bureaucracy**, we refer to the millions of full-time career employees who do the day-to-day work of government. The bureaucracy's impact on policy is immense. Often bureaucrats must interpret vague and sometimes contradictory directives from the legislature or the political appointees or elected officials of the executive branch. Bureaucrats must often decide how to allocate resources too scarce to complete assigned tasks. Even though on the surface the bureaucracy may appear nonpolitical, bureaucrats often make highly controversial decisions that spark intense political struggle, as this chapter will illustrate. As the primary means of policy implementation, the bureaucracy can help, hinder, or redirect the carrying out of policy.

The tragedy in Hamlet, North Carolina, caused a lot of finger-pointing. Beyond the responsibility of the plant owners, were local officials negligent? Did the state fail in its responsibility to provide enough inspectors and enough inspections? Was OSHA at fault for not coordinating its own efforts more fully or in not paying enough attention to the state-run programs? Should Congress have mandated OSHA to do all inspections (and provided adequate funding for inspectors to do them)? Should the inspectors from the U.S. Department of Agriculture have been trained, in addition to their food wholesomeness concerns, to find workplace safety violations? Without assessing blame, we can use this incident to think about several features of bureaucracy: (1) Bureaucracies carry out a variety of tasks, including policymaking, supervision, and enforcement. In doing so, bureaucracies mix executive, legislative, and judicial functions. (2) The structure of bureaucracy in the United States reflects our federal system, with fractured and overlapping lines of authority. The largest numbers of bureaucrats, and the largest increases in bureaucracies since the Second World War, are to be found in state and local governments. (3) There are no simple answers (all-out centralization or decentralization of responsibility) in optimizing bureaucratic performance. (4) Bureaucracies in action rarely resemble the ideal envisioned by social theorists or described by legislation.

Defining the Federal Bureaucracy

In this chapter we will concentrate on the federal bureaucracy, examining its structure and its role in government and democracy. But as the story of the Imperial chicken plant shows, federal bureaucrats do not work in a vacuum. There are complex interactions between federal, state, and local bureaucracies. Before we go on to describe the federal bureaucracy, however, we should ask what bureaucracy is.

One of the earliest and most important observers of bureaucracy as a distinctive organizational type was the German sociologist Max Weber. He identified the essential characteristics of bureaucracy, including the assignment of clear areas of responsibility within the organization, a specific hierarchy, operation according to established rules, and careful record keeping. Weber distinguished bureaucratic agencies from groups that did not share these characteristics. Although we often complain about bureaucracy, Weber *admired* it as a means of getting beyond the limitations of human individuals (a properly run bureaucracy does not forget or play favorites, it can achieve expertise over a wider area than any human, and it doesn't suffer from human foibles and infirmities). In fact, some of our barbs target the very characteristics that make bureaucracy valuable. Having to fill out forms, for example, feeds the institutional memory. Imagine how you would feel, for example, if you were getting ready to graduate from college and the registrar said, "No one around here remembers your taking freshman English, so you'll have to take it again." A paper trail is a valuable thing. We also complain about the impersonal treatment we receive at the hands of bureaucracies—"I'm just a number." But that same depersonalization means that from a well-run bureaucracy we get the benefits we are entitled to, regardless of party affiliation, religion, or any other personal characteristic that might rub some functionary the wrong way.

Weber's enthusiasm for bureaucracy did not blind him to the dangers of an overly bureaucratic society. There will always be tension between sticking to the rules and making allowances. A tendency to veer too far in *either* direction is dangerous to fairness, effectiveness, and even freedom. The dangers, though, are not in bureaucracy itself. As we've said before, it is important to measure the distance between the ideal and the real. If the intricacies of the federal system and the limitations of political accommodation had been overcome with a single, functional bureaucracy, the story in Hamlet might have had a happier ending. But look back at the introduction to Chapter 4 to be reminded how well government bureaucracy ordinarily functions. Our outrage when "the system" fails to protect is based on our normal expectation of bureaucratic success.

Does real bureaucracy accord with democratic ideals? People who attack bureaucracy claim that through it, big government too often harasses individuals and groups, places too many restrictions on people's actions, and engages in costly and inefficient practices. In this view, bureaucrats have become a power unto themselves, dictating from Washington the way people throughout the country ought to live their lives. In rejoinder, defenders of bureaucracy argue that a modern society could not function without bureaucratic procedures. After all, they say, someone must send out the social security checks and make the appropriate rules for eligibility; someone must police mine safety and check on air pollution; and so on. In addition, they maintain that at times government bureaucracy stands as the sole defender of citizens who would otherwise be powerless against discrimination and other violations of individual rights and threats to health and safety. Rather than abolishing bureaucracy, they conclude, we need to establish a better, more responsive, more efficient bureaucracy. Even if we accept this view, however, we must still answer two fundamental questions: How much bureaucracy is enough? And how well do our current bureaucratic arrangements function?

In the remainder of this chapter we will examine three key issues involving the federal bureaucracy: how it is structured, how bureaucrats interact with the political process, and whether the current proposals for reform of the bureaucracy—civil service reform, third-party government and privatization, and deregulation—address these concerns adequately.

An inspector at a poultry plant in the 1930s. Scandals in the meat-packing industry helped to make the case for government inspection to ensure the safety of food and drugs. *(National Archives)*

Structure of the National Bureaucracy

The Constitution only refers in passing to the structure and role of the federal bureaucracy: It recognizes the president's right to demand periodic reports from the head officials in the executive departments. Undoubtedly, the Founders were aware that the administrative apparatus of government would need to remain flexible, to change with the times. But they also failed to anticipate how much the government would grow. To them, executive departments were small operations aiding the president—hardly a major matter in 1792, when the entire federal government consisted of only 780 employees.

For many years the size and structure of the federal government hardly changed at all (except for temporary expansions during wartime). The permanent bureaucracy grew most dramatically during and after the New Deal (the 1930s and early 1940s), when the federal government pioneered many new social programs. Since 1950 the overall growth of federal government employment has been minimal.

As of November 1991 the federal government had 3,100,036 employees, 2,695,595 of whom were permanent, full-time employees. Only about one in ten of those employees worked in the Washington, D.C., area; the rest worked throughout the United States and abroad.[2] There were approximately 4,236,000 state employees and 10,240,000 employees of local governments. The largest single employer in the country is the Department of Defense, which employs about a third of all federal civilian employees (not counting the uniformed military). General Motors is the country's largest *private* employer, employing around 756,300 persons worldwide, of whom more than 550,000 work in the United States.

About 85 percent of federal civilian employees have made the civil service a career. They are protected by the civil service system, and their salaries, set by Congress, ranged in 1992 from $11,478 (GS 1, step 1) to $83,502 (GS15, step 10). Above the civil service employees is the Senior Executive Service, where job tenure is less secure but salaries range from $90,000 to $112,100. Political appointments, fewer than five hundred persons at the very top of executive agencies, earn "executive-level" salaries of $104,800 to $143,800. Every month the federal payroll is close to $8 billion; state and local payrolls run over $26 billion monthly.

Only about one-sixth of the federal government's civilian jobs are what we ordinarily consider bureaucratic—clerks or administrators. The vast majority of government employees are trained specialists. In 1989, for example, the federal government employed 172,825 engineers and over 10,000 medical officers.[2] In most cases, working for the bureaucracy does not mean being the desk-bound, paper-shuffling bureaucrat of political cartoon fame.

Nonwhites are statistically overrepresented in federal employment, but the disproportion reverses in the upper ranks, where white males predominate beyond their numbers in the general work force. Women are underrepresented in the ranks of federal employees, a disproportion more pronounced at the upper levels. The vast majority of female federal employees occupy traditional "pink-collar ghettos" in secretarial and data entry positions.

Much of the work of government at all levels is done by so-called **contract bureaucracies**—private firms hired by the government. The Department of Defense, for example, hires firms such as Boeing and General Dynamics to design and build military hardware, the Corps of Engineers contracts with private firms to design and construct dams and hydroelectric projects, and most of the personnel involved in the space program are contract bureaucrats. In this way a great many Americans work for the government indirectly—they are not on the federal payroll, and their jobs are not protected by civil service regulations.

The government bureaucracy is not monolithic; it encompasses a huge complex of bureaus, agencies, boards, and commissions, created at different times, with different functions and different mandates. Frequently, one segment of the federal bureaucracy will be at odds with another: A jurisdictional dispute may erupt between two agencies, or policies and clienteles may have conflicting objectives. For example, while the Department of Health and Human Services works to discourage smoking, the Department of Agriculture helps farmers to grow tobacco more efficiently. Similarly, plans by the Corps of Engineers to build a dam may be opposed by the Environmental Protection Agency on the ground that the dam will adversely affect wildlife. The government has grown so large and complex that simply keeping abreast of what other agencies are doing is a monumental task.

Bureaucratic agencies tend to be created according to areas of specialization—one agency handles only law enforcement, another only medical care, and so on. The principle of organization by specialization is illustrated in the structure of the federal executive branch, as outlined in **Figure 15-1**. But don't be fooled by orderly organization charts: The federal bureaucracy encompasses an almost byzantine array of agencies and divisions, set up during the course of more than two centuries in response to specific political pressures. In the twentieth century, as each succeeding administration brought its own political agenda to the executive branch and confronted the established structures of earlier administrations, most found it easier to add a new agency, defining its mission from scratch, than to change the direction of an existing one. Hence inconsistent and overlapping jurisdictions abound. Still, the executive branch frequently attempts to impose order within the bureaucracy. The Environmental Protec-

FIGURE 15-1

THE EXECUTIVE BRANCH: THE PRESIDENT AND THE CABINET

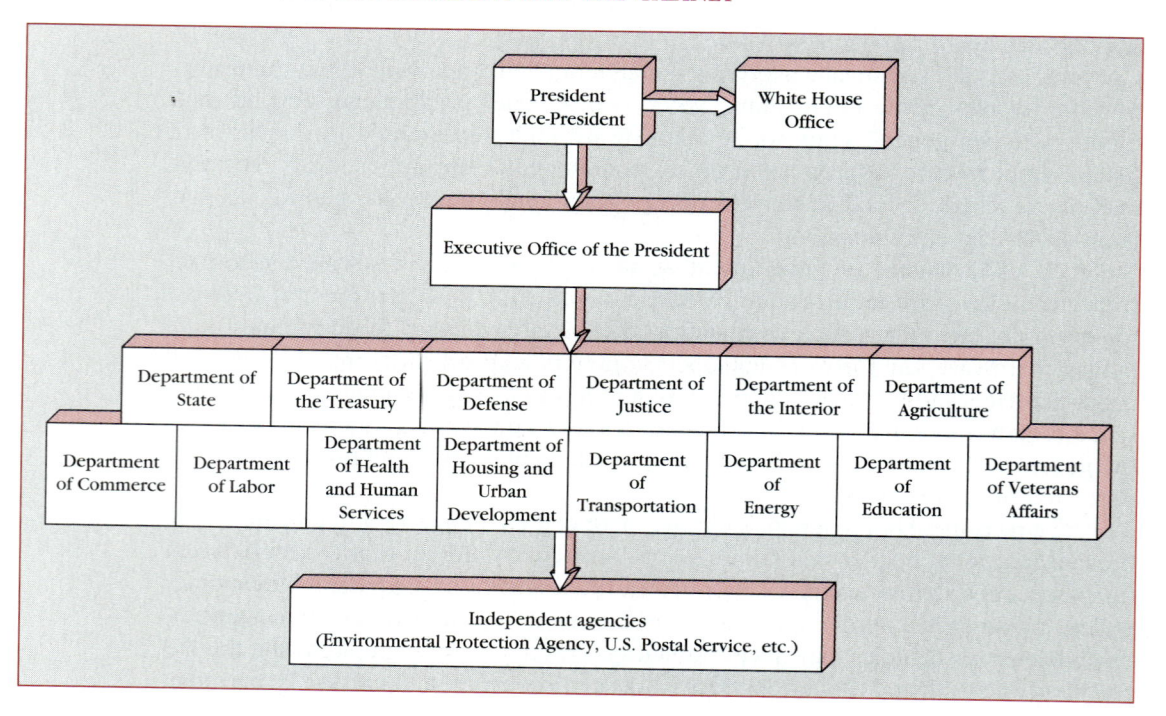

tion Agency, for example, was created by consolidating a group of bodies, each of more limited scope.

Before we consider the problems inherent in bureaucratic specialization, we must examine the primary components of the bureaucracy: the cabinet departments, the independent executive agencies and government corporations, and the regulatory commissions.

Cabinet Departments

In 1789 there were only three **cabinet departments**—State, War, and Treasury. As new needs arose, new departments were created. In 1849 the Department of the Interior was set up to deal with the government's vast landholdings and with the Native American population. The Department of Agriculture was established in 1862, the Justice Department in 1870, and the Departments of Commerce and Labor in 1913. The War and the Navy Departments were merged into the Defense Department in 1947. Health, Education and Welfare, created in 1953, was redesignated Health and Human Services in 1979. Housing and Urban Development appeared in 1965, Transportation in 1966, Energy in 1977, Education in 1979, and Veterans Affairs in 1988.

The fourteen cabinet departments make up the bulk of the federal bureaucracy, employing a majority of federal workers. As we saw in Chapter 14, the head of a department is appointed by the president and serves as the department's representative in the president's cabinet. The other top officials in cabinet departments are also appointed by the president. Many of them have no prior experience in the department, and they rarely remain in office for more than a few years. Just below them, however, are career civil servants who have risen through the ranks and whose experience and skill are vital to the efficient functioning of the departments. These senior civil servants have powers that must be reckoned with when policies are formulated.

Independent Agencies

Independent agencies like the National Aeronautics and Space Administration (NASA), the Environmental Protection Agency (EPA), and the Small Business Administration (SBA), are generally smaller than cabinet departments and tend to have considerably more focused missions. Like cabinet secretaries, the heads of independent agencies serve at the pleasure of the president. These agencies come into being to serve specific functions and are established outside cabinet departments usually to insulate them from partisan or interest group pressure.

The Selective Service system, for example, was created hastily, prior to World War II, as an entity independent of the War Department (now the Department of Defense) to reassure citizens that the draft was a civilian operation with limited scope. The Central Intelligence Agency, another independent organization, fused many competing government intelligence agencies into one organization. The CIA was not placed under

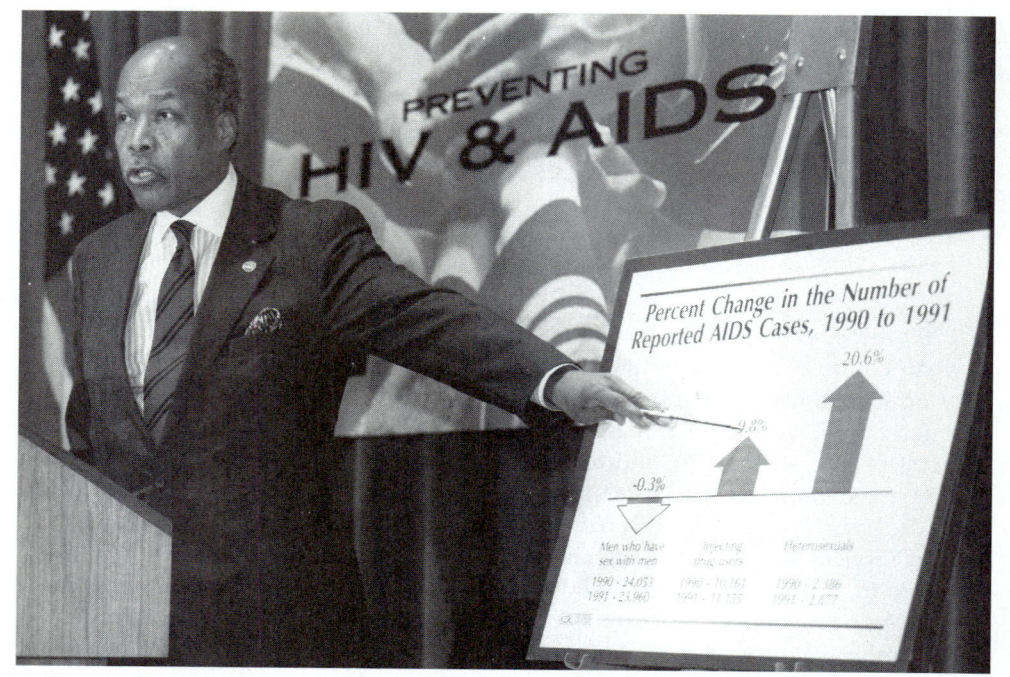

Dr. Louis Sullivan, Secretary of Health and Human Services during the Bush administration, at a press conference launching a new initiative in AIDS education. Cabinet departments like Health and Human Services may encompass a wide variety of programs, some well-established and others on the cutting edge of current problems. *(Reuters/Bettmann)*

a cabinet department because it was designed to resolve interdepartmental power struggles.

Also included among the independent agencies are government corporations—the U.S. Postal Service, the Tennessee Valley Authority (TVA), and the Federal Deposit Insurance Corporation (FDIC). A government corporation, as the name suggests, is intended to operate in a businesslike way in its management practices.

Regulatory Commissions

Another type of independent agency is the **regulatory commission**. These agencies regulate certain kinds of activities, primarily in the economic sphere. They perform a quasi-judicial function: They can bring charges, hold hearings, and impose penalties for violations of rules. The Federal Communications Commission (FCC), for example, may revoke the licenses of television and radio stations for a number of reasons, including a station's failure to provide sufficient community service broadcasting. Regulatory commissions are also quasi-legislative bodies: They make, as well as interpret, rules. For example, the Federal Trade Commission (FTC) imposes a wide variety of regulations on manufacturing and on advertising to protect consumers from unsafe or misrepresented merchandise.

The independent regulatory agencies fall outside the executive branch chain of command, freeing them, to some extent, from politics. Commission members are appointed by the president to relatively long terms, subject to Senate confirmation. Once in office, they are not required to report to the president and may not be removed until the end of their terms, except through impeachment. Unlike cabinet officers and heads of other executive agencies, they do not resign when a new president is elected. A new president can name members to commissions only as terms expire or as vacancies occur because of death or resignation. By law, moreover, members of these agencies must be drawn from both major political parties.

In spite of these precautions, the regulatory commissions become deeply immersed in behind-the-scenes politics. Their activities are of intense concern to interest groups, which, over time, often develop close and sometimes cozy relationships with the agencies. Critics point out that some commission members work harder to protect the interests of drug companies, trucking firms, brokerage houses, and other concerns they are supposed to regulate than to protect the interests of the public.

The history of the Atomic Energy Commission (AEC) illustrates this point. The AEC was originally established with the conflicting goals of encouraging the peaceful uses of nuclear energy and regulating the safety of such uses. In response to well-organized, specific demands, the commission concentrated on helping private energy-producing companies to develop nuclear power-generating facilities. The AEC was "captured" by the power-generating industry and became a primary booster of nuclear power plant construction. According to some accounts, the larger but more diffuse public interest in the safety of nuclear power and the problems of spent fuel disposal were relegated to second place. Congress replaced the AEC with the Nuclear Regulatory Commission in 1974 to redress this imbalance, but only after billions of dollars had been spent planning and constructing nuclear generating units that were never used.

As an additional barrier to effective regulation, these federal commissions typically don't have enough staff members to fulfill their regulatory functions. Hearings to develop new regulations for an industry often pit a handful of civil service accountants and lawyers against battalions of highly paid industry lawyers and accountants.[3]

Bureaucracy and the Political Process

Bureaucracies are embedded firmly in the political process. Consider the example of an automobile safety device, developed in Detroit a quarter-century ago but only recently became the darling of automobile advertising campaigns, the air bag. In 1971, President Richard Nixon's transportation secretary, John Volpe, issued Safety Standard

208, which required the installation of air bags or safety belts in all new cars. The Nixon White House, however, apparently responding to pressure from the automobile industry, postponed implementation of the standard in 1972. Four years later, in 1976, President Gerald Ford's secretary of transportation rescinded 208.

In 1977, with the Carter administration more favorably inclined toward consumer safety, the attempt to get an air bag ruling began again. A revised version of 208, providing automakers with greater time for installation, was promulgated. Either automatic seat belts or air bags would be mandatory on new cars in 1984. But in 1981, the Reagan administration took office with a commitment to deregulate. Shortly thereafter, 208 was completely revoked. In response, a coalition of consumer groups filed suit in federal court. Their litigation was upheld in 1982. The administration and the auto companies appealed the ruling to the Supreme Court, which in 1983 found unanimously against them, saying: "For nearly a decade the automobile industry waged the regulatory equivalent of war against the air bag and lost—the inflatable restraint was proven sufficiently effective."[4]

In late 1983, reacting to the decision, Secretary of Transportation Elizabeth Dole postponed compliance until 1987 and at the same time proposed several other alternatives to air bags. Air bags would be required only if a certain number of states failed to pass mandatory seat belt legislation. Many states did pass seat belt laws in the second half of the 1980s, but the laws were difficult to enforce independently and usually carried nominal penalties. Then the 1987 compliance date was, like earlier deadlines, postponed. While the government backpedaled, the market moved forward. European manufacturers began to offer air bags on expensive models. From the mid-1980s on, Ford and General Motors offered driver-side air bags as an expensive option on a small number of models. In 1988, Chrysler Chairman Lee Iacocca announced that by 1990 all Chrysler cars built in the United States would have driver-side air bags as standard equipment. The market finally caught up with the government's safety experts. As air bags became a selling point, their use spread more quickly throughout automotive offerings.

According to statistics, in the ten years from 1976 to 1985, some 90,000 Americans lost their lives and 600,000 were injured in cars that might have been equipped with air bags.[5] While political struggles overwhelmed the processes of bureaucratic decision making, thousands lost their lives. In this case all three branches of government intervened to change bureaucratic behavior. But where should decisions like this one be made? In Congress? In the courts? Or should bureaucrats look first to their own conception of the public good or the public interest? Under what circumstances are bureaucrats better representatives of the public interest than elected officials subject to direct political pressure?

Further complicating the issue is the need for accountability in government. It can be argued that presidents should be able to put a stamp on an administration—to make policies in line with their political agendas and to have the bureaucracy carry out those policies. As Charles Peters, a bureaucrat turned editor, observes, "The key to democratic politics is accountability. If you don't deliver the goods, the voters can throw you out."[6] Peters goes on to argue in favor of filling administrative positions with qualified politicians and making administrative decisions on a partisan basis, with reelections the compelling motive.

However, this approach creates its own problems: Political considerations can lead to short-term planning and the implementation of splashy programs that actually serve the public less well in the long run. In trying to make government *appear* to be running well, partisan bureaucrats might ignore the reasoned judgments of long-range planners.[7]

Apparently, then, a balance must be worked out between the need for unfettered administrative expertise and the need for responsible and responsive political control. To understand the ramifications of this dichotomy, we must analyze how and to what extent the bureaucracy is involved in the political process. As we will see, the bureaucratic apparatus has evolved into a collection of highly specialized subdivisions, sometimes insulated from the public, sometimes essentially self-governing, often backed by subdivisions of Congress and by powerful interest groups.[8] Bureaucratic discretion, expertise, and support systems strengthen the bureaucracy's political position, while the extensive use of contract bureaucrats weakens it to some extent.

We now turn to bureaucratic discretion—the wide latitude extended to the bureaucracy; bureaucratic expertise; and bureaucratic mobilization of support for or opposition to specific programmatic and policy initiatives.

Bureaucratic Discretion

When bureaucracies are called on to implement legislation—promulgating specific regulations for cleaner air, workplace safety, fireproofing clothing, and the like—bureaucrats have considerable latitude in applying laws to particular cases. This administrative discretion forms the basis for bureaucratic political participation. For example, in 1991 new questions about the safety of silicon gel breast implants arose in connection with allegations that the manufacturer had suppressed negative research findings. The FDA had to decide whether to allow the continued use of breast implants while awaiting further research results or to ban them entirely. (It chose a middle path, limiting their use and issuing warnings.) Similarly, the Justice Department has the power to decide whether or not to prosecute an antitrust case—a decision that may have far-reaching consequences for the national economy. In these and thousands of other cases, government bureaucrats make policy by applying the broad powers granted to them by Congress and the president.

Several factors involved in legislative decision making contribute to bureaucratic discretion. Most fundamentally, the legislature could not possibly establish clear rules covering all contingencies—an exercise for which it has neither the time nor the expertise. Then too, vague rules or guidelines often reflect legislative conflicts that could not be resolved in Congress and so are handed over to the bureaucracy. In this sense bureaucratic administration represents an extension of the legislative process as

(Text continues on page 569)

COMPARATIVE PERSPECTIVE

BRITISH AND FRENCH BUREAUCRACIES

One of the best-known aspects of the British bureaucracy is the "administrative class," made up of approximately 7,500 senior staffers selected through a civil service system. These top civil servants are closely involved in the formulation of public policy. It is their job to screen important information for the ministers of each department, to provide political advice, and to comment on the wisdom and practicality of various policy proposals. What they do *not* do is administer the various departments of the bureaucracy; that task is left to others. British civil servants usually view their jobs as lifetime commitments, not as steppingstones to positions in industry or politics. Most regard themselves as the long-term protectors of the public interest and the upholders of high civil standards. They are sometimes criticized for being too cautious and unimaginative.

France was one of the first European nations to create a modern-style bureaucracy, and the existence of a top administrative class similar to the one in Great Britain has been a distinguishing feature of French bureaucratic organization. At the top of the French administrative hierarchy are several thousand bureaucrats, three hundred to five hundred of whom are highly active in the political decision-making process.

What is most striking about the top French administrators is that they have become almost a hereditary group. The entrance exams for the two schools that train French administrators tend to favor people from upper-class backgrounds. Since the 1960s there has been only a very gradual increase in the number of middle-class students admitted, despite various government efforts to open the schools to all talented individuals. Candidates from working-class and farming backgrounds are almost never accepted. Of the top seven thousand French civil servants in the most prestigious sectors of the bureaucracy, about 75 percent come from the highest levels of Parisian society.

These administrators have long considered themselves not mere civil servants but rather managers for society as a whole and agents of change in the modernization of France. Many top bureaucrats resent French political parties and the French legislature for interfering with plans hatched among the administrative class. A large number of top bureaucrats move into industry if their ambitions are not fulfilled within the bureaucracy. Over 40 percent of the major French business concerns are headed by former bureaucrats.*

When the Socialist government of François Mitterand came to power in 1981, it implemented proposals to decentralize the French bureaucracy. Mitterand's goal was to loosen central bureaucratic control and provide more decision making to local governments in France. It was the first move toward decentralization in a bureaucratic system that had been highly centralized for centuries.

*Henry W. Ehrmann, Politics in France *(Boston: Little, Brown, 1983), pp. 161-174.*

Dr. Mathilde Krim, an AIDS researcher and fund-raiser, represents a major source of bureaucracy's power: expertise. As government's activities become more technical and sophisticated, its general goals and strategies must be implemented by bureaucratic experts. *(Ira Berger)*

particular parties work to advance their interests by lobbying in the offices of the bureaucracy. Indeed, administrative lobbying is as important as legislative lobbying in Washington.[9]

In policymaking matters as well, bureaucracies do not remain neutral. They have interests of their own, and they push those interests vigorously in the political arena. Like most participants in the political system, bureaucrats usually claim that the programs they administer serve the public interest and that expansion of those programs would benefit the nation. Some of these claims are cynical, but most are entirely sincere. Beliving in the value of and the need for their programs, bureaucrats seek to expand—or at least to protect—those programs by lobbying for favorable legislation and increased appropriations.[10] The EPA, for example, actively lobbies for funds to clean up toxic waste sites, and the Department of Agriculture regularly presses for dairy price supports and other farm subsidies.

Bureaucratic Expertise

The power of the bureaucracy also stems from its expertise. Because a bureaucracy is designed to apply specialized competence to an area of policy, bureaucrats frequently have a near-monopoly on expertise in certain political areas. Who, for example, knows more about building a space station or sending a person to Mars than the experts at the National Aeronautics and Space Administration (NASA)? When other policymakers accept such claims of expertise, the bureaucracy gains an important political resource. By the same principle, however, when events like the disastrous in-flight explosion of the space shuttle *Challenger* call an agency's expertise into question, other policymakers are much less likely to let agency decisions go unchallenged.

Economist John Kenneth Galbraith points out that technology has become so complex that it would take a formidable genius to command all of the knowledge and skill required to deal with even a few of the ordinary decisions confronting business or government organizations.[11] Responsibility for decision making has therefore passed to groups of specialists. As Galbraith puts it, modern organizations are composed of a "hierarchy of committees." Decisions tend to flow upward from these committees, and the person at the top usually lacks the special knowledge and skills to challenge those decisions.

Expertise can be used as a political resource in two principal ways: Experts can hold important advisory positions, particularly in relation to the president, or they can make presentations to Congress concerning complex matters about which most legislators know little. The fact that bureaucrats are more knowledgeable in a particular area, however, does not mean that they always get their way. Under the present system, though, they have far greater influence than they would if Congress could turn to an equally knowledgeable alternative source of information.

Mobilization of Support

The bureaucracy also draws political power from its ability to mobilize support among the general public, Congress, and its clientele groups. Government agencies like to demonstrate that they provide useful and beneficial services to the public. These public relations efforts can take the form of public-service television messages, such as the FDA's TV spots on the proper use and storage of hazardous household products, or inexpensive pamphlets, such as the Agriculture Department's extensive series of booklets on cooking, canning, gardening, and other topics. Such efforts, which advertise the agency and enhance its public reputation, fulfill one of the most significant bureaucratic functions: supplying the public with needed information. Sometimes, however, efforts to mobilize public support may cross the line from information dissemination to sheer public relations. The advertising efforts of the Department of Defense, for example, prompted Senator William Proxmire to refer to the "Pentagon propaganda machine." To promote a favorable image of the military, the department aided in the production of war movies, gave tours of military installations to prominent citizens, provided speakers for civic groups, and produced an extensive set of advertisements for military life.

Bureaucratic agencies also try to maintain good relationships with interest groups that are directly affected by their activities. Such groups are commonly referred to as **clientele groups**. The railroads and trucking companies are clientele groups of the Interstate Commerce Commission (ICC), labor unions are the clientele groups of the Labor Department, and so on. As long as these groups benefit from agency programs, they will lobby on the agency's behalf in Congress and the Oval Office. Clientele groups draw much of their strength from their ability to influence Congress. Indeed, as we saw earlier, it is common for a bureaucratic agency, a clientele group, and a congressional subcommittee to be linked in a three-way alliance—the so-called iron triangle (described in Chapter 11). For example, the Pentagon has close ties with large defense contractors, which in turn exert a great deal of influence in Congress.

Bureaucracy Evaluated

The "entrenched bureaucracy" is an easy target for candidates for public office in the United States. U.S. political life is punctuated regularly by attacks on the bureaucracy. Since 1976 every presidential campaign has been marked by a certain level of anti-Washington sentiment. Calls for radical reductions in government waste and a reorganization of government structure are attractive appeals, especially during times of rising constituent expectations and resistance to increased taxation. They tap into what appears to be strong public sentiment against bureaucracy. Polls in 1987 and 1988, for example, found that three-fifths of respondents agreed that "when something is run by the government, it is usually inefficient and wasteful."[12]

Despite negative rhetoric about the bureaucracy, most Americans have decidedly mixed feelings about bureaucratic institutions. In general conversations it is hard to get someone to say anything nice about bureaucrats. When pollsters inquire about bureaucracy in the abstract, negative opinions surface. One study found that only 30 percent of respondents thought that government agencies generally respond well to citizens' concerns. But in the same study fully 71 percent of respondents reported that their own problems had been handled well.[13] When people are asked about actual relationships they have had with various agencies, the report card is generally quite good. And even though vocal concerns about waste are common, polls asking about government spending consistently find majorities (often large majorities) responding that spending is "about right" or "too little" in every area except foreign aid.

We will examine three specific charges against the federal bureaucracy: that it is undemocratic because it is unresponsive to political leadership; that there is, on the whole, too much of it and that it is too distant from the people; and that there are too many rules and regulations governing things that are better left alone. We will also consider the national bureaucracy's responses to those charges: civil service reform, "third-party government" and privatization, and deregulation, respectively.

(Text continues on page 573)

SEVEN PROPOSITIONS ABOUT REGULATION

Economist Lester Thurow spells out seven basic propositions about regulation in his book *The Zero-Sum Society*. His aim is to clarify how regulation works in an industrialized society. Here are the propositions he presents, along with the reasoning behind them:

1. All economies involve rules and regulations; there is no such thing as an unregulated economy. For example, the right to own property is itself a "rule" that requires protection—that is, disputes over property require regulations and enforcement. Normal economic life is unthinkable without such rules of behavior.

2. There are many silly government regulations. For example, it is impossible to write universally applicable rules, for exceptional cases will always turn up. Any attempt to apply a rule uniformly in a large and diverse country is sometimes going to look silly.

3. In many areas, there should be fewer regulations. Many regulations remain in force only because some groups gain from them in terms of income security, while the rest of us pay the cost.

4. In the United States, regulations almost invariably arise from real problems, rather than from ideology. Among these real problems were occupational health and safety, clean air, and private pension failures. It is not, therefore, very useful to be for or against regulations in the abstract.

5. There is no "left" versus "right" when it comes to the virtues of regulation versus deregulation. Liberals do not always support regulation, and conservatives do not always oppose it. On some issues, such as tobacco and alcohol, neither has a clear position.

6. There is no simple correlation between the degree of economic success and the degree of economic regulation. Many successful economies are far more regulated than that of the United States—for example, those of Germany and Japan. In fact, regulation can aid economic growth.

7. Regulations lead to regulations. The drafting of regulations to protect one industry may lead to efforts to protect others. If you protect steel from import competition, for example, you may also have to protect autos in the same way.

Source: Lester Thurow, The Zero-Sum Society: Distribution and the Possibilities for Economic Change *(New York: Basic Books, 1980).*

Is the Bureaucracy Too Unresponsive?

People charge that the bureaucracy is too unresponsive to political initiatives. Bureaucrats, they say, are primarily concerned with keeping their own jobs. A new president finds it almost impossible to make significant changes because the bureaucrats frustrate any drive toward innovation or policy change. To understand these charges we must examine the history of the civil service.

The first federal job appointments were made by George Washington, who declared that his choices were based entirely on "fitness of character." It soon became apparent, however, that most of those found fit were associated with the emerging Federalist party, which Washington and Alexander Hamilton headed. When Thomas Jefferson became president in 1801, he set a precedent by dismissing hundreds of Federalists from government jobs and installing his supporters in their places.

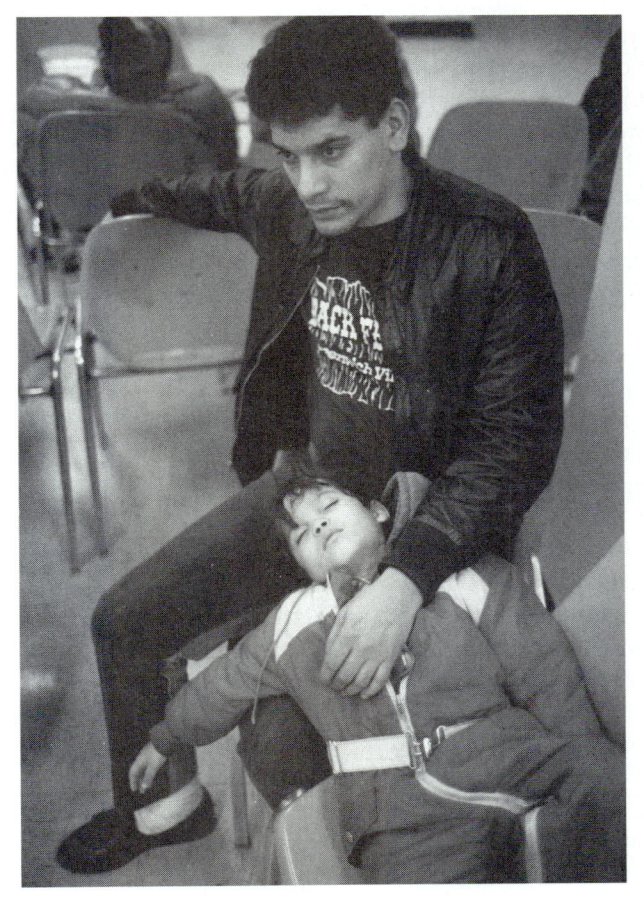

Frustration, anger, and exhaustion can sometimes be a part of the struggle to gain assistance from a complex, confusing, and understaffed system. (Paul Fusco/Magnum Photos)

Thereafter, under what became known as the **spoils system**, elected officials routinely rewarded friends and supporters with government jobs. The spoils system reached its peak under President Andrew Jackson. After his election in 1828, Jackson dismissed more than one-third of the six hundred upper-level officeholders and from 10 to 20 percent of the ten thousand government officials who occupied lower-level positions.

To some extent the spoils system made sense. The political parties needed some form of **patronage** (the power of appointment to government jobs) to reward party workers. During the nineteenth century the government had little need for trained specialists, so a high turnover in personnel usually did not endanger operating efficiency. Furthermore, any president is entitled to fill key positions with people who share his political philosophy. (There is a difference, it should be noted, between a patronage system that rewards political loyalists regardless of competence and a system of partisan appointments that rewards competent loyalists with key policymaking positions. In practice, however, this distinction is sometimes hard to discern.)

Nevertheless, by the 1870s obvious abuses of the spoils system had provoked a clamor for reform. These demands led to action after President James A. Garfield was assassinated by a disappointed office seeker in 1881. With the support of Garfield's successor, Chester A. Arthur, Congress passed a bill establishing the bipartisan Civil Service Commission to administer competitive examinations and make appointments to office based on merit. Under the **civil service system** now in place, the commission sets up formal descriptions of job requirements and classifies civil servants according to job description. Once the various civil service positions are described and classified, examinations are given to determine the candidates best suited for the available positions. After taking examinations, candidates are placed on lists, from which agencies select employees.

The federal civil service system now places college graduates in most bureaus. Very high levels of educational specialization also mark the federal bureaucracy. Chemists employed by the Department of Agriculture, biologists employed by the National Institutes of Health, safety engineers employed by the Federal Aviation Agency—all these professionals typify the high degree of specialization and education found in modern public service.

Yet this emphasis on expertise, to the exclusion of political factors, has its costs. Most civil servants cannot be removed from their jobs except for gross misconduct, and many promotions are based on seniority rather than on merit. The laudable purpose of these procedures—to insulate the bureaucracy from unwarranted political interference—also protects bureaucrats from demands for high performance.

President Jimmy Carter instituted a number of civil service reforms designed to enhance the role of merit in promotions, salary increases, and firings. The Carter administration created a **Senior Executive Service (SES)** apart from the regular civil service. Top managers were given the option of switching to the SES, trading job security for higher pay and rewards for superior performance.

Another of the Carter reforms called for pay raises based on performance, not just longevity, for thousands of middle-level managers and supervisors. The civil service system gained greater flexibility in firing and demotion, but safeguards for employees were provided, but safeguards for employees were provided by an appeal process and union arbitration proceedings. In addition, the Civil Service Commission was split into two bodies: the Office of Personnel Management, charged with managing the federal work force, and the Merit System Protectors Board, designed to protect the rights of employees.

The Carter reforms had several goals: to reward merit more adequately; to keep top civil servants from becoming too deeply entrenched in their positions, unresponsive to changes in policy; and more generally, to produce a British-style senior civil service of capable generalists. Have these reforms made the bureaucracy more responsive? In the first few years of operation the new system seemed to have little impact. Of the six thousand senior civil servants who gave up tenured positions in the late 1970s and early 1980s, only one was dropped for poor performance, and very few were shifted from one part of the bureaucracy to another.[14] But a subsequent study concluded that there was no question that the SES had played a "major role" in President Reagan's ability to obtain the cooperation of the career bureaucracy in implementing his policies. Conversely, a survey of SES careerists found that a "perceived breaking of faith by the larger political system with members of the SES has had a devastating effect on their own perception of the reform," which they came to view as "*punitive* and political." Another study accused the Reagan administration of "blatantly politicizing" the SES.[15] These findings illustrate that responsiveness in the bureaucracy is always subject to trade-offs. We want public servants to do the bidding of the public. Ordinarily that means doing the bidding of elected officials. But we're skeptical enough to assume that sometimes that means *not* doing the bidding of elected officials, whose personal interests may take precedence over the public's. How responsive is responsive enough? That is a question that, like almost all questions in politics, calls for continual reevaluation.

Is There Too Much Bureaucracy?

Other complaints about our national bureaucracy revolve around how much of it there is. Even though federal employment has been relatively stable for more than three decades now, federal programs and expenditures continue to grow. A frequently heard complaint is that the federal government grows by an inner logic that has little to do with the nation's needs. In response to these complaints, two strategies for limiting the size of the federal bureaucracy have been attracting increased attention: "third-party government" and privatization. We turn to these now.

THIRD-PARTY GOVERNMENT **Third-party government** refers to federal programs that are farmed out to states, localities, special districts, nonprofit corporations, hospitals, manufacturers, banks, and other groups outside the bureaucracy. In addition, grants-in-aid, loan guarantees, new forms of contracting and procurement, credit insurance, and a host of other programs are handled through nonfederal organizations. In other words, many federal programs are no longer run by federal bureaucrats.

The federal government's much-criticized social welfare apparatus, for example, is in reality fifty different programs run separately by the fifty states—or, more precisely, about three thousand programs run by the nation's counties. State and local officials have the power to decide the eligibility rules for and the duration and exact amounts of assistance given out under these programs. A welfare recipient in Mississippi, for example, receives substantially less money each month than an individual on welfare in New York. (The difference has as much to do with different levels of political support for welfare in each state as it does with differences in the cost of living.) Likewise, the U.S. Labor Department distributes billions of dollars for employment and training assistance, but the money is actually spent by 450 "prime sponsors" organized by local politicians and community groups.

Such programs create thorny management problems and make for difficulties in coordination. And because the people who operate the programs are not responsible to Congress, which authorizes the programs, little can be done to address even blatant abuses or to make program managers accountable for their actions. In the late 1970s and early 1980s, for example, the federal Comprehensive Employment and Training Act (CETA) program, which was designed to bolster employment opportunities for the chronically unemployed, was found to be riddled with patronage. Local and county officials were placing friends, relatives, and political supporters on the CETA rolls at federal expense. The federal government, under Ronald Reagan, eventually abolished the program entirely. The "bureaucrats in Washington," then, have far less actual control in many areas than the American public believes.

Third-party government programs do offer some advantages. They allow the federal government to draw on the talents and resources of people outside the government, and they give the government greater flexibility in adapting programs to local needs and circumstances.

PRIVATIZATION   The move toward **privatization**, an effort to transfer a wide range of public assets and programs to the private sector, dovetailed with President Ronald Reagan's ideological goal of reducing government's role in society and enhancing the role of private enterprise. The administration argued that private industry would do a better, cheaper job than government bureaucracies in providing many services.

In keeping with this philosophy, the administration placed both Conrail, the government-run freight rail system of the Northeast, and Landsat, the government's land-mapping satellite, on the market. It also housed aliens in detention centers that were privately operated, contracted with private firms to run many airport control towers, and used private consumer credit companies to screen applicants for government loans. Finally, the administration identified eleven thousand commercial activities conducted by government that could be carried on by private contractors, including fire protection, landscaping, protective services, laundry and food services, moviemaking, medical laboratory work, transportation data processing, and geological surveys.

Privatization also encompasses cases such as hiring private credit companies to screen applications for government loans or housing federal detainees in a privately run detention center. In these cases the questions become even more complex. Are there certain tasks that ought to be handled by the government directly, even at higher cost? If private detention centers can replace federal prisons, what about private dispute resolution bodies to ease the load of overworked federal courts? The answers are hardly simple or clear.

Critics charge that the real motivation behind privatization is to get the government out of social policy matters altogether or, more cynically, to provide a little more private pork for favored contractors. Others fear that privatization robs legislatures and executives of effective control over many programs and that the quality of services or the fair treatment of employees would suffer when private firms take over. Finally, some argue that privatization just cannot get the job done in certain areas.

Are There Too Many Rules?

A third set of complaints about the federal bureaucracy focuses on whether there are too many rules, too many forms to fill out, too many strictures on activities that should be unrestricted or at least less restricted. Although these complaints are lodged against all segments of the government, few elements of the bureaucracy spark as much debate as the regulatory agencies.

Federal regulatory agencies affect the health and safety of most individuals, the rules under which most business is carried on, and many other vital matters. Critics of these agencies argue that too much regulating goes on and that the regulators are far from efficient. Complaints estimate that government regulation costs the country tens of billions of dollars each year—although it is rarely estimated how much is saved through regulation. Particular regulations are often singled out as the most burdensome, such as the health and safety rules for the workplace created and enforced by the Occupational Safety and Health Administration. Of course, the regulatory picture is complex: Criticisms applicable to one agency may not apply at all to another. We must also recognize that frequently the participants in the regulatory debate are not disinterested observers.

We turn now to the nature of regulation and several proposed reforms of the regulatory process. In examining these topics, keep in mind two key points: first, that regulation usually costs someone and benefits someone else and that these costs and benefits must be weighed; and second, that proregulation and antiregulation trends follow cycles, and what seems compelling at the moment does not necessarily make sense in the long run.

TYPES OF REGULATION   Both critics and proponents of government regulation commonly make the mistake of lumping together two different types of regulation.[16] One group of regulatory agencies regulates prices, competition, and entry into various industries. Examples of such agencies are the Interstate Commerce Commission and the

(Text continues on page 580)

One Agency Responds: The FDA and Bureaucratic Reform

One-quarter of all American consumer dollars are spent on products that the Food and Drug Administration is charged with regulating—more than $1 trillion a year. In addition to the foods we eat (except meat and poultry, which are the responsibility of the Department of Agriculture), the FDA regulates cosmetics, medicines, and medical devices (from hearing aids to heart valves). The FDA was established by the 1906 Pure Food and Drugs Act and now operates under the 1938 Food, Drug and Cosmetic Act and its several amendments. Not an independent agency, the FDA is formally positioned within the Public Health Service, in the Department of Health and Human Services.

One of the FDA's spectacular successes, due largely to a medical reviewer named Frances O. Kelsey, was in keeping the drug thalidomide off the American market. The drug was sold in Europe, and it resulted in thousands of severely deformed babies. That was in 1960. More recently, the FDA's bill of health has not been so clean. Described by some observers as "comatose," the agency's public image was battered by scandals (one involving falsified drug-company testing and payoffs to FDA employees on generic drug approvals and another involving a faulty heart valve) and by drug company and consumer complaints about costly delays on the approval of new drugs. During the 1980s, given the arrival of marketable biotechnology and the FDA's responsibility for AIDS drug testing and maintaining the purity of the nation's blood supply, the agency's responsibilities were growing while funding (in real dollars) remained flat and its vigor was apparently on the decline. The FDA was under attack from Congress, consumer groups, drug companies, and newspaper editorialists.

Following the release of an independent advisory committee's report in May 1991, Commissioner David Kessler proposed internal reorganization of the FDA, including simplifying the organizational chart and streamlining the review process for enforcement actions (reducing the number of steps in the process from an unwieldy fifteen to a more manageable five). Other reforms desired by Kessler and suggested by the study committee require statutory provision for more enforcement power—the ability to subpoena drug company records, to seize adulterated or misbranded material, and to impose civil penalties on violators. Take the subpoena power, for example: Most federal regulators possess the ability to require the production of certain evidence. The lack of this power at the FDA may have serious consequences. The evidence that caused Commissioner Kessler

(Box continues on page 579)

in 1992 to place a moratorium on the cosmetic use of silicone breast implants had been given to Dow-Corning, the implant maker, by trial lawyers eight years earlier but sealed as a result of a court settlement agreement. Without the subpoena power enjoyed by the Environmental Protection Agency, the Federal Trade Commission, the Department of Agriculture, and others, the FDA had no way of obtaining such information.

No matter how efficient and effective the FDA itself becomes, its mission guarantees continued controversy. Consider drug testing. The traditional method required by the FDA to demonstrate the safety and effectiveness of a drug requires a study group and a control group. The drug being tested is administered to the study group, a placebo is given to the control group, and neither participants nor physicians are told which group they are in. Differences in outcomes are assumed to be the effects of the drug. But in matters like AIDS and cancer treatments, where a drug may mean the difference between prolonged life or quick death, is it ethical to keep the control group on sugar pills? And can we wait for patients in both groups to sicken and die to measure outcomes? Should the FDA accept evidence of "clinical markers" such as an increase in white blood cells as signs of effectiveness?

There will always be a tension between the reduction of risk based on scientific evidence and the possible reduction of suffering based on early intervention. Is dideoxyinosine (ddI) an effective drug for treating the complications of AIDS or a false hope, diverting physicians and patients from other, more effective treatments? In a controversial departure from the requirement of time-consuming clinical tests, the FDA approved the use of ddI in July 1991. Is quicker always better? Congressional action in 1984 to reduce the time in the approval cycle for generic drugs "turned the FDA into a Wild West show," said an economist with a House subcommittee investigating the FDA. The incentives for getting to the FDA first with evidence of safety and effectiveness almost certainly contributed to the payoffs and falsified tests that resulted in scandal. Which drug seeking fast approval is the next thalidomide, a disaster-in-waiting, and which is the next miracle cure? How should the FDA be organized to distinguish one from the other most effectively and speedily, as well as to meet its broader functions? Are the reforms instituted and requested by Commissioner Kessler liable to improve the FDA's image or leave it vulnerable to abuse and scandal?

Sources: Herbert Burkholz, "A Shot in the Arm for the FDA," New York Times Magazine, *June 30, 1991, p. 15;* Philip J. Hilts, "FDA to Get Streamlined Management," New York Times, *June 8, 1991, p. 7;* Erica E. Goode, "Boss of a $1 Trillion World," U.S. News & World Report, *April 27, 1992.*

Federal Communications Commission. Both were created at the request of the regulated industries, whose principal motive was to discourage competition. Generally, regulatory agencies of this type help the regulated industries to maintain artificially high prices and to avoid the rigors of competition.

A new variety of regulatory agency enforces standards of health, safety, and fairness. Agencies of this type include the Environmental Protection Agency (EPA), the Occupational Safety and Health Administration (OSHA), the Consumer Product Safety Commission (CPSC), and the Equal Employment Opportunity Commission (EEOC). These regulators usually come under fire for limiting the freedom of business to do as it wishes and adding to the costs of doing business, despite estimates that this second group of regulatory agencies has been responsible for considerably less than half the costs of all regulation.[17]

The problems targeted by the newer agencies affect many facets of citizens' lives.

> Urban air had become unhealthy as well as unpleasant to breathe. Rivers were catching fire. Many working people were dying from exposure to chemicals on their jobs. Firms were selling products of whose hazards consumers were ignorant. And the nation faced a legacy of racial and sexual discrimination.[18]

Since the establishment of OSHA, the number of accidental workplace deaths has been cut in half, and workers' exposure to harmful substances has been sharply curtailed. Water and air pollution has been reduced, as have pesticide levels in rivers. Racial and sexual discrimination has been diminished.

Of course, the costs of such regulation are usually passed on to consumers, and mistakes, excessive pettiness, and overzealous advocacy have sometimes put regulators on the defensive. But as one observer points out:

> Much of the new social regulation benefits more disadvantaged groups in society. To put it somewhat simply—but not, in my view, unfairly—those who argue, say, that OSHA should "go soft" on its health regulations in order to spare the country the burden of additional costs are saying that some workers should die so that consumers can pay a few bucks less for the products they purchase and stockholders can make a somewhat higher return on their investments.[19]

DEREGULATION Deregulating aspects of the economy gained popularity during the administration of President Jimmy Carter. The first to be deregulated, at least in part, were the railroad and airline industries, followed by the trucking, interstate bus, and banking sectors. Arguments supporting **deregulation**—the drive to eliminate many regulations currently on the books and to cut back on the power of regulatory agencies—center on the premise that government's heavy hand has been suppressing competition and thereby discouraging both innovation and the provision of better service to customers.

What had been a modest movement during the Carter years became a rush of change under President Ronald Reagan. In his first six weeks in office, Reagan lifted price controls on domestic crude oil, abolished the Council on Wage and Price Stability, prevented implementation of dozens of business regulations promulgated in the last days of the Carter administration, dropped energy efficiency standards for appliances and temperature guidelines for office buildings, and urged curbs on the powers of the Federal Trade Commission, Interstate Commerce Commission, Securities and Exchange Commission, and Federal Communications Commission. The effects of deregulation were particularly striking in the automobile industry. The Reagan administration rescinded four major regulations in this area, mandating the installation of automatic seat belts or air bags, the display of crash test results on window price stickers of new cars, the setting of new standards of window visibility for cars and trucks, and the development of new types of speedometers and tamper-resistant odometers.

The Bush administration has been described as the most expansively regulatory since the early 1970s. This characterization, despite Bush's own antiregulatory rhetoric, is explained by a pragmatic approach to politics, coinciding with a primary interest in foreign policy—the same combination that made the Nixon administration a prolific producer of new regulation.[20] But this is regulation by inadvertence, balanced both by the administration's rhetoric and by the efforts of Vice-President Dan Quayle's strongly antiregulatory Competitiveness Council.[21] In 1992, an election year, President Bush installed a well-publicized moratorium on additional regulation, but the forces that create additional regulation remained in place.

The most striking institutional example of deregulation was the abolition of the Civil Aeronautics Board (CAB) in 1984. For a half-century the CAB had set fares and regulated routes and schedules for the air travel industry in the United States. When it was abolished, only a few of its responsibilities were transferred to the Federal Aviation Administration; the rest simply fell by the wayside. The results were mixed. Prices continued a well-established trend downward, and the number of passengers flown continued to rise. The development of "hub and spoke" route systems meant that many small- and medium-sized cities depended almost exclusively on less convenient, smaller commuter planes. But the consumers' major concern about airline deregulation has been safety. A former director of the National Highway and Transportation Safety Board said, "I've felt all along that deregulation has had an adverse effect on safety."[23] Quantitative evidence about air safety itself was far from conclusive: Near-midair collisions increased, but actual accidents did not. How does all this add up? How much does inconvenience cost? And how much does deregulation increase the likelihood of an accident?

Conclusions

Economist Herbert Kaufman points out:

> If there were not such a diversity of interests in our society, if we did not subscribe to such a variety of values, if we were not so intolerant of corruption and insistent on our rights, and if the governmental system were not so responsive, however imperfectly, to so many of these claims on it, we would have a great deal less red tape.[23]

Public bureaucracies spring from the complexity of modern societies. Government agencies often incorporate all the functions of legislatures, executives, and judiciaries: They make rules, enforce them, judge appeals, and adjudicate controversies. How else could we ensure that the disabled receive assistance or that the stock market functions honestly or that food and drugs are not adulterated? How else could we deal with fraud in businesses or monitor the environmental impact of new factories, dams, and housing developments? How else could we educate the young and administer social insurance programs fairly? Or even begin to crack down on price fixing and monopolistic practices in business? Without regulation and careful supervision, society would degenerate into a raw competition that the people with the means and the ambition to exploit others would win hands down.

Public bureaucracy, then, has not been thrust on us by a conspirational group of fools or villains—we all contribute to it. And we certainly could not eliminate it once and for all. The best we can do is try to anticipate major bureaucratic failures before they become tragedies (like Hamlet, North Carolina) and continue to chip away at each individual irritant through the normal processes of politics. As for the magic formulas proposed by some critics of the bureaucracy—wholesale contraction of the federal government, devolution of authority to the states and localities, concentration of authority in administrative "czars" empowered to cut through red tape—on close inspection each turns out to hold little promise, for they all ignore values treasured by many people.

This is not to argue that because bureaucracy is needed, any sort of bureaucracy will do. From the standpoint of democratic theory, bureaucracies should be highly responsive, sensitive to human needs, and respectful of the rights of the common citizen.

Unfortunately, it is difficult to tote up a balance sheet on the U.S. bureaucracy as a whole in light of democratic theory. Some agencies act in a highly autocratic fashion, some diminish freedom rather than protect it, some harass citizens and ignore basic rights. By contrast, many agencies do a creditable job of protecting life and limb, helping to raise the level of public information, and safeguarding democratic rights, equality, and liberty. No sweeping statements, therefore, can be made to characterize the bureaucracy as a whole.

Glossary Terms

bureaucracy	Occupational Safety and Health Administration (OSHA)
cabinet departments	patronage
civil service system	privatization
clientele groups	regulatory commission
contract bureaucracy	Senior Executive Service (SES)
deregulation	spoils system
independent agencies	third-party government

NOTES

[1] The information about the Hamlet tragedy comes from a series of articles in the *Raleigh News and Observer*. "State Called 'Delinquent' in Hamlet Fire," September 12, 1991, p. 10A; Bob Hall, "Hamlet Aftermath: How Could This Happen?" September 15, 1991, p. 1J; Joseph T. Hughes, Jr., "Nowhere to Run," September 15, 1991, p. 1J; and Steve Riley, "A Betrayal of Trust," December 11, 1991, p. 1A; and from Peter T. Kilborn, "In Aftermath of Deadly Fire, a Poor Town Struggles Back," *New York Times*, November 25, 1991, p. A1.

[2] Statistics in this discussion from Andrew Klugh, Statistical Services Branch, Office of Personnel Management; Dudley Ives, General Services Administration; General Motors Public Relations Department; and U.S. Bureau of the Census, *Statistical Abstracts, 1991* (Washington, D.C.: U.S. Government Printing Office, 1991).

[3] Bernard Schwartz, *The Professor and the Commissions* (New York: Knopf, 1959).

[4] *Motor Vehicle Manufacturers Assoc. v. State Farm Mutual Automobile Insurance Co.* (1983), 103 S.C. 2856.

[5] Joan Claybrook et al., *Retreat from Safety* (New York: Pantheon, 1984), pp. 166–185.

[6] Charles Peters, "The Solution: A Rebirth of Patriotism," *Washington Monthly*, October 1978.

[7] Charles Malek, *Washington's Hidden Tragedy: The Failure to Make Government Work* (New York: Free Press, 1978).

[8] Randall B. Ripley and Grace H. Franklin, *Congress, the Bureaucracy and Public Policy* (Homewood, Ill.: Dorsey Press, 1984), chap. 2.

[9] Ibid., chap. 3.

[10] For a discussion of these problems, see Herbert Kaufman, *Red Tape* (Washington, D.C.: Brookings Institution, 1979).

[11] John K. Galbraith, *The New Industrial State*, 2nd ed. (Boston: Houghton Mifflin, 1971), chaps. 2 and 3.

[12] Linda M. Bennett and Stephen Earl Bennett, *Living with Leviathan: Americans Coming to Terms with Big Government* (Lawrence: University Press of Kansas, 1990), p. 80.

[13] Richard E. Cohen, "Regulatory Focus: The Cut-Rate Fares Dilemma," *National Journal*, September 3, 1977, p. 1384.

[14] Leonard Reed, "Bureaucrats 2, Presidents 0," *Harper's*, November 1982, pp. 18–22.

[15] Nolan Argyle and Ryan Barilleaux, "Past Failures and Future Prescriptions for Presidential Management Reform," *Presidential Studies Quarterly*, Fall 1986, pp. 716–733.

[16] This discussion draws on Steven Kelman, "Regulation That Works," *New Republic*, November 25, 1978, pp. 16–20.

[17] Ibid.

[18] Ibid., p. 17.

[19] Ibid., p. 19.

[20] Jonathan Rauch, "The Regulatory President," *National Journal*, November 30, 1991, pp. 2902–2906.

[21] Kirk Victor, "Quayle's Quiet Coup," *National Journal*, July 6, 1991, pp. 1676–1680.

[22] Larry N. Gerston et al., *The Deregulated Society* (Pacific Grove, Calif.: Brooks/Cole, 1988), pp. 232–233.

[23] Kaufman, *Red Tape*, pp. 58–59.

Selected Readings

James Q. Wilson provides a very solid introduction to **contemporary American bureaucracy** in *Bureaucracy: What Government Agencies Do and Why They Do It* (New York: Basic Books, 1989). See also William T. Gormley, Jr., *Taming the Bureaucracy: Muscles, Prayers, and Other Strategies* (Princeton, N.J.: Princeton University Press, 1989). On the level of general theory about **bureaucratic structures**, see Edward S. Greenberg and Thomas F. Mayer, eds., *Changes in the State* (Newbury Park, Calif.: Sage, 1990); and James A. Caporaso, ed., *The Elusive State: International and Comparative Perspectives* (Newbury Park, Calif.: Sage, 1989).

On **expertise**, one of the bureaucracy's primary sources of power, see Frank Fischer, *Technocracy and the Politics of Expertise* (Newbury Park, Calif.: Sage, 1989); and Joseph A. Pechman, ed., *The Role of the Economist in Government: An International Perspective* (New York: New York University Press, 1989).

On **regulation and regulatory reform**, see Michael S. Greve and Fred L. Smith, eds., *Environmental Politics: Public Costs, Private Rewards* (New York: Praeger, 1992); George Hoberg, *Pluralism by Design: Environmental Policy and the American Regulatory State* (New York: Praeger, 1992); and Martha Derthick and Paul J. Quirk, *The Politics of Deregulation* (Washington, D.C.: Brookings Institution, 1985). To learn more about **relations between the bureaucracy and Congress**, read Christopher H. Foreman, Jr., *Signals from the Hill: Congressional Oversight and the Challenge of Social Regulation* (New Haven, Conn.: Yale University Press, 1988).

For recent **comparative studies** of bureaucracy, see Byung C. Koh, *Japan's Administrative Elite* (Berkeley: University of California Press, 1989); James E. Cronin, *The Politics of State Expansion: War, State and Society in Twentieth-Century Britain* (Boston: Routledge, 1991); and Giandomenico Majone, ed., *Deregulation or REregulation? Regulatory Reform in Europe and in the United States* (New York: St. Martin's Press, 1990).

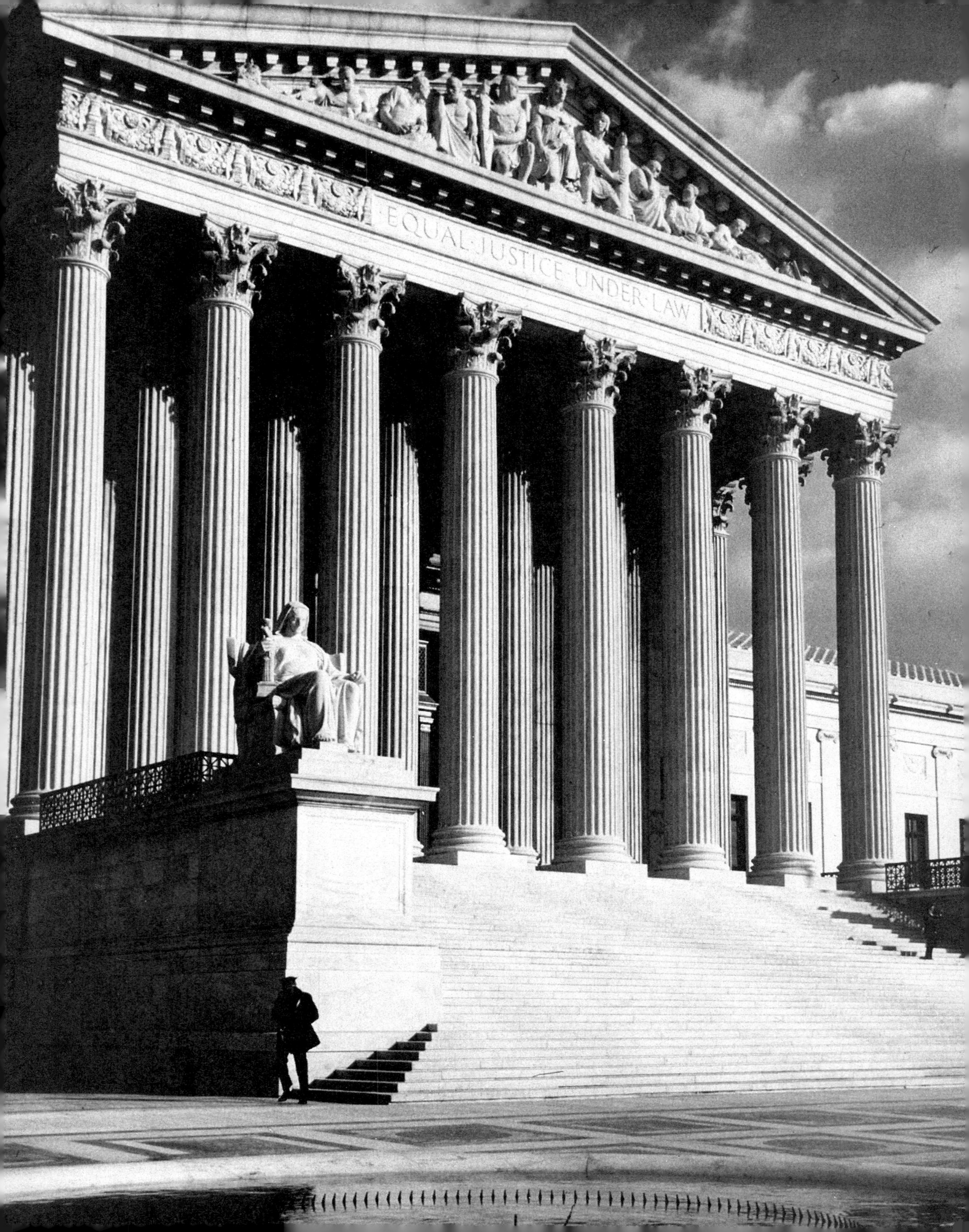
EQUAL·JUSTICE·UNDER·LAW

CHAPTER SIXTEEN

THE AMERICAN JUDICIARY

Nonelected Defenders of Democracy?

CHAPTER OUTLINE

A Dual Function

Courts as Impartial Forums for Dispute Resolution

STATE COURT SYSTEMS
THE FEDERAL COURT SYSTEM
RECRUITMENT OF JUDGES
THE FLOW OF LITIGATION

The Judiciary and Policymaking

THE DECISION-MAKING PROCESS
JUDICIAL REVIEW
SELF-RESTRAINTS ON POWER
LEGISLATIVE REACTIONS
NONCOMPLIANCE

Major Periods in Supreme Court History

FOCUS ON THE DISTRIBUTION OF POWER
CONCERN FOR INDIVIDUAL RIGHTS
THE RECENT PAST

The Dilemma of an Expanded Legal System

"DO YOU WANNA DANCE" WAS A POPULAR TUNE, WRITTEN AND recorded by Bobby Freeman in 1958. Like many songs from that early era of rock-and-roll, this one had staying power. It has been recorded and turned into a hit by at least eight other singers, including Bette Midler, who included it on her 1972 debut album, *The Divine Miss M*. Some years later Young & Rubicam, a major advertising agency, decided that "Do You Wanna Dance" was the right song for a TV commercial the agency was producing for the Lincoln-Mercury Division of the Ford Motor Company. Young & Rubicam obtained copyright permission from Freeman. But when the agency asked the divine Ms. Midler, "Do you wanna sing?" she turned them down, explaining that she does not do commercials. Undeterred, Young & Rubicam hired Ula Hedwig, who had sung backup for Midler for many years. Hedwig was able and willing to sing a convincing imitation of Midler. The car commercial was produced and ran from January to June 1986, when the real Midler filed a lawsuit in a federal district court in Los Angeles. A jury awarded Midler $400,000 in October 1989. On appeal, the U.S. 9th Circuit Court of Appeals decided that "when a distinctive voice of a professional singer is widely known and is deliberately imitated in order to sell a product, the sellers have appropriated what is not theirs and have committed a tort [a legally recognized harm worthy of compensation]." In March 1992 the U.S. Supreme Court upheld the lower courts' decision.[1]

The case of the copycat Midler is not the first of its kind, nor is it liable to become a cornerstone of American jurisprudence. But it does clarify and extend the rights of performers over intangibles such as a distinctive voice or performance. And more to the point, it indicates some interesting features of the operation of law and courts in the United States. In a time of increasingly severe environmental regulations on real property and of novel treatments of intellectual and other intangible property, rulings as in the Midler case are important in resolving how our society will understand and protect property rights in the coming century. And property is just one example of a wide range of issues over which the courts exercise influence.

A Dual Function

Courts in the United States, to a greater extent than in most other countries, have a dual function in government. The most obvious judicial function, in this country as in most, is to provide an official, impartial forum for the resolution of disputes. Legal disputes are divided into two categories: **civil cases** (like Midler's suit against Young & Rubicam), in which a plaintiff seeks justice for an alleged action by the defendant in a dispute about a contract or a tort or some other matter that courts are charged to resolve, and **criminal cases**, in which a prosecutor, representing the people of the city, county, state, or nation, claims that a defendant has broken a criminal law. As a forum for dispute resolution, the courts affect the parties immediately involved in the case.

The second function of courts in the United States is to establish or alter government policy. This function, at least in the degree to which it is carried in the United States, is fairly unique. Our **common law** tradition allows courts to fashion policy in the absence of legislation. Early in the nineteenth century the French statesman Alexis de Tocqueville observed that in America nearly all questions are ultimately brought to courts for resolution. Compounding this national tendency is the tradition of **judicial review**, which allows courts to review and sometimes reverse the decisions of other governmental actors (we will return to the topics of common law and judicial review shortly). Thus courts can respond to and even reverse policy formulated by the "political" branches of government. Judicial power thus addresses the natural tension between majoritarian democracy and individual rights. In our society the Supreme Court, empowered to review the constitutional merits of legislation and executive action, helps to ensure that rights are protected or extended to conform with basic principles of justice. The Court has the power to act as the nation's conscience, upholding its basic commitments, even in the face of reluctant or hostile majorities. So our courts, unlike most, participate directly in making policy.

Two examples demonstrate the profound extent—and the limitations—of the judiciary's power to influence U.S. politics and social life. Consider first the Court's role in the New Deal of the 1930s. Sweeping statutes that substantially expanded federal control over the economy had been passed to address the unprecedented economic crisis of the Great Depression. Enacted hurriedly, some of the legislation was poorly constructed and vague. A majority of Supreme Court justices were convinced that extensive government control of the economy ran counter to democracy. In their view, democratic institutions needed to be saved from democratic representatives. Building from this assumption, and capitalizing on the technical weaknesses of the legislation, the Court's majority declared several key statutes unconstitutional.

In the eyes of many Americans, including President Franklin D. Roosevelt, the Court's actions jeopardized the nation's economic recovery and thus its very existence. The Court came under fire for reading into the Constitution its own conservative, antigovernment economic principles rather than interpreting the document as a flexible set of guidelines to help the nation deal with changing circumstances. Defenders of the Court argued that it was playing an essential role by curtailing the overextension of federal power. Roosevelt's landslide reelection victory in 1936 and his proposal to enlarge the Court (to allow him to appoint more liberal justices) finally persuaded some justices that certain New Deal legislation was legitimate. The Court changed course and began allowing newly reconstructed New Deal statutes to stand. Since this confrontation, the Court has rarely interfered with legislation concerning the federal government's power to regulate economic life. The grave conflict the Court provoked in the 1930s illustrates its power to oppose majoritarian pressures in the short run. However, the ultimate outcome of this conflict demonstrates one key limitation of the Court's power: The Court has little success in opposing a determined majority over an extended period.

A second example, in which the Court played a different sort of role, was the school desegregation decision of 1954, *Brown* v. *Board of Education of Topeka*. In that case (discussed in detail in Chapter 5) the Court held that segregated schools were inherently unequal. This decision involved a moral and legal leap for the Court, overturning a precedent that had stood for fifty-eight years and challenging head-on long-established and deeply rooted local customs. Like the Court's rulings on the New Deal legislation, the *Brown* decision sparked intense anger: Critics charged that the ruling was based on the particular philosophy of the justices rather than on an unbiased reading of the Constitution. Defenders of the Court argued, however, that segregation itself violated the Constitution and that the Court had simply marshaled the courage to acknowledge that. It took nearly twenty years after the *Brown* decision for public schools to undertake serious desegregation efforts. In some controversial cases, then, the Court doesn't always achieve its objectives immediately. But the Supreme Court's stand on this case exemplifies how the Court, because of its insulation from pressing political pressures, can take the lead on important moral issues. In *Brown* the Court made a clear appeal to the conscience of the majority, and this ruling helped to move the country forward in a critical area where leadership lagged in both the executive and the legislative branches.

George Hayes, Thurgood Marshall, and James M. Nabrit, who led the fight against public school segregation in *Brown* v. *Board of Education*. Marshall was appointed an Associate Justice of the Supreme Court in 1967, becoming the first black to sit on the high court. *(AP/Wide World Photos)*

Both functions, dispute resolution and policymaking, are assigned to the American judiciary. Under common law each decision must be based on comparable previous decisions (precedents) and will serve in turn as a guide to future decisions. *Midler* v. *Young & Rubicam* provided a $400,000 judgment for Midler against Young & Rubicam. With the Supreme Court's affirmation of that judgment, the case also clarified policy for all other performers and all other ad agencies in the country. So every case resolves a dispute and also contributes a tiny bit to the establishment or reaffirmation of legal principles. The judiciary's business is composed of a complex mix of specific disputes, procedural concerns, policy questions, partisan politics, and issues of personal power. In terms of effort and impact, dispute resolution is generally the primary concern of lower courts, and policymaking is the primary concern of appellate courts, especially the U.S. Supreme Court.

Courts are different from other political actors in our system insofar as they are bound to make *and justify* their decisions according to the law. In the eyes of the law, judges and justices cannot vote one way or another because their constituents wish them to or even because conscience tells them to. The sole acceptable justification for a judicial decision is that the law directed it. Naturally, these legal norms do not preclude normal human calculations. Justices do follow election returns and do listen to conscience, but whatever the motivation for a decision, it must be justified in terms of the law. This is the foundation of the courts' great power and a primary limitation of that power.

In the remainder of this chapter we will examine the two main judicial functions in the United States, looking first at the structure and operation of court systems and then at the factors surrounding judicial policymaking. How should we organize and operate our courts to provide just decisions effectively and efficiently in millions of disputes? How much power should the courts—especially the U.S. Supreme Court—have in shaping our national life? In a democratic society, should nine nonelected individuals play a decisive role in resolving important national issues?

Courts as Impartial Forums for Dispute Resolution

Many disputes, both civil and criminal, are resolved before they reach the courts at all—the vast majority never come to trial. In civil matters, many grievances are resolved by the parties involved without any court intervention. Lawyers, contrary to popular prejudices, actually spend most of their time keeping clients *out* of court by offering informed but noninstitutional mediation of grievances. Because of the cost and uncertainty involved in turning disputes over to the court, most parties are content to work out agreements prior to trial. These agreements, however, are said to be made "in the shadow of the courthouse" because they reflect each party's estimate of the consequences of going to trial. Using cases that do appear before them to indicate the general shape of acceptable resolutions, courts can indirectly control even disputes that never make it through the courthouse door. The common law principle of **stare decisis** ("let the decision stand") suggests that each case should be decided on the basis of similar cases in the past (precedents), making law stable and predictable. Furthermore, the threat of going to trial, represented by a court date, sets a deadine for dispute resolution.

In criminal matters as well, trials represent a fairly rare occurrence. The first sifting in the criminal justice process happens at the level of law enforcement. The only crimes that enter the criminal justice process are those resulting from a series of important decisions about law enforcement. Should we hire more officers to patrol the streets, looking for pushers and pimps? Should we hire more accountants to ferret out white-collar crime? The net we cast determines the fish we catch. Furthermore, no officer or law enforcement agency could possibly act against every observed infraction of the criminal law. Decisions must be made that reflect agency policy and the judgment of individual law enforcement officers. Stop this car? Audit this return? Once law enforcement has acted against an individual, the prosecutor must decide which cases to carry forward and which to drop (a decision based on the strength of the evidence, the seriousness of the crime, and the likelihood of success in gaining a conviction). In serious federal criminal matters the prosecutor's decision must be validated by a grand jury (which has the power to indict). In other cases a judge or magistrate makes a decision to proceed or not based on an "information hearing." Even among the cases that make it this far through the process, the majority (about 9 out of 10) result in a plea of guilty—usually as a result of a **plea bargain**, in which the prosecutor and defense counsel agree to fewer or reduced charges or a reduced sentence in return for a guilty plea. Such bargains permit the court to process large numbers of defendants quickly, give prosecutors high conviction rates, and allow defendants to reduce the punishment for their actions. All of this assumes, without the benefit of trial, that the defendant, having reached this stage, is actually guilty—an assumption that runs counter to our system's professed ideals but that most participants in the criminal justice system accept as inescapable. Judges must approve of the bargains struck and so have ultimate control over them.

State Court Systems

The American judiciary is actually composed of fifty-one separate court systems: one for the federal government and a separate one in each state. As a member of a federal system of government, each state is free to design a court system according to its own needs, but a common pattern exists. At the bottom, encompassing the largest number of courts and processing the vast majority of all cases, are courts of limited jurisdiction—traffic courts, small-claims courts, juvenile courts, municipal courts, and others—each given responsibility for a narrow range of less serious cases, such as criminal misdemeanors and civil cases involving relatively small amounts of money. The pattern at this level varies considerably from state to state. Above the courts of limited jurisdiction are the trial courts of general jurisdiction, empowered to handle the full range of civil and criminal cases that can be brought to court. This is where most criminal felony trials and major civil trials are held. A trial is what most of us think of when we think of courts—a single judge, perhaps a jury, the examination and cross-examination of witnesses, the presentation of physical evidence, finding the defendant innocent or guilty in criminal cases, responsible or not responsible for damages in a civil case. The jury in this picture is a **petit jury**—one that decides how the case should be resolved—as opposed to a **grand jury**, which has investigative powers and decides whether or not to hold trials in the first place.

Thirty-nine states have an intermediate level, consisting of one or more appellate courts, authorized to hear appeals from trials. Our system provides for a review of trial decisions that is not simply another trial. An **appellate hearing** reviews the decision reached by a trial court, examining questions of law (Did the trial judge interpret the law correctly? Was the trial conducted properly?) but ordinarily accepting the facts as established by the trial court. Thus appellate courts do not take testimony from witnesses and do not use juries. Rather, they base their decisions on the trial record and briefs and oral arguments offered by opposing counsel. An appellate hearing is usually presided over by a panel of judges rather than a judge sitting individually. After the hearing, the judges meet in conference to determine the court's decision. An importance difference in the tasks of trial court and appellate court judges is that the former usually work alone whereas the latter make decisions collegially, working in panels. One or more **opinions** will be written to explain the court's decision or to concur with or dissent from it. Our system of justice assumes that one appeal is adequate for justice. Most cases resolved by trial courts are final; only a tiny handful go on to an appellate hearing.

Above the courts of appeals (or above the courts of general jurisdiction in the states without intermediate courts) are the state supreme courts. These courts represent the last word for matters that start in the state courts. Only about twenty-six state supreme court decisions are heard by the U.S. Supreme Court each year, out of about ten thousand cases decided annually by these state courts of last resort. These courts operate primarily as policymaking courts for their respective states, resolving inconsistent results from lower courts and providing authoritative interpretations of state statutory laws and constitutions.

Starting in the early 1970s several state supreme courts began actively promoting state constitutions as a source of rights over and above those protected by the U.S. Constitution, a movement referred to as the **new judicial federalism**. "State judges are looking around for creative tools to solve problems in new ways," says Utah Supreme Court Justice Christine Durham.[2] State constitutions provide the best opportunity for state courts to carve out new claims within their own jurisdiction. The new judicial federalism was in part a response to the Burger and Rehnquist Courts' refusal to expand or in some cases even preserve advances in civil liberties made by the U.S. Supreme Court under Earl Warren. More fundamentally, it starts from the assumption that the U.S. Constitution sets only *minimum* requirements for rights protection, not maximums. For example, the California Supreme Court, in *Committee to Defend Reproductive Rights* v. *Myers* (1981),[3] determined that the California constitution required the state to pay for abortions for indigents—a requirement that had already been rejected for the federal government by the U.S. Supreme Court in *Maher* v. *Roe* (1977).[4]

The new judicial federalism is only one reason to pay attention to state court decisions. The most important reason for doing so is that in terms of dispute resolution, state court systems are much larger and busier than the federal system. Each year over 300,000 cases are filed in federal courts. But 94 million cases are filed in state courts annually. Contact with a federal court in the United States is thus a much rarer occurrence than contact with a state court.

The Federal Court System

The federal court system, like most state court systems, is structured like a pyramid (see **Figure 16-1**). There are specialized federal courts (Tax Court, the Court of International Trade, and the Court of Claims, for example), but the workhorses of the federal

FIGURE 16-1

The Court System of the United States

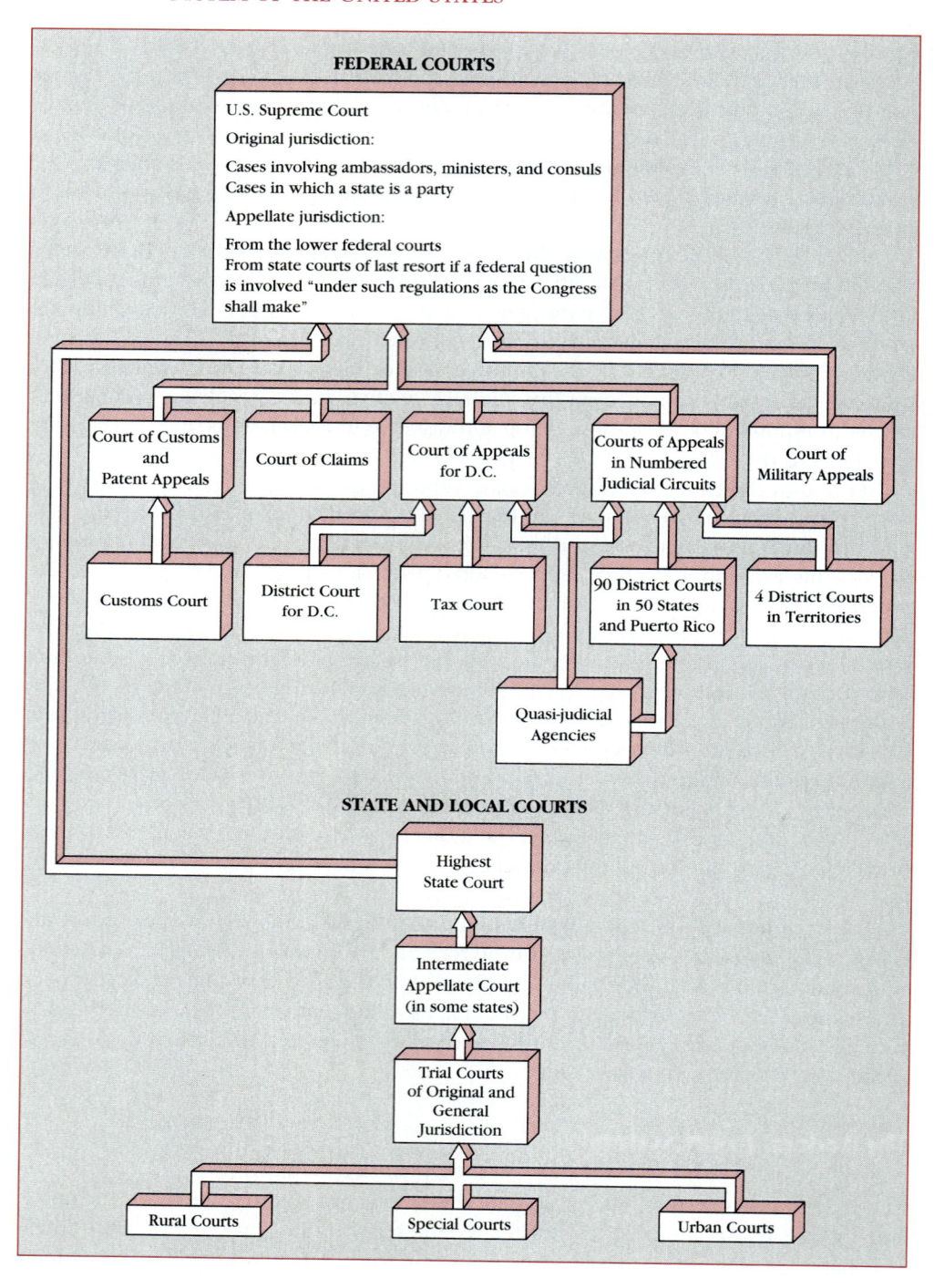

FEDERAL COURTS

U.S. Supreme Court

Original jurisdiction:

Cases involving ambassadors, ministers, and consuls
Cases in which a state is a party

Appellate jurisdiction:

From the lower federal courts
From state courts of last resort if a federal question is involved "under such regulations as the Congress shall make"

- Court of Customs and Patent Appeals
- Court of Claims
- Court of Appeals for D.C.
- Courts of Appeals in Numbered Judicial Circuits
- Court of Military Appeals

- Customs Court
- District Court for D.C.
- Tax Court
- 90 District Courts in 50 States and Puerto Rico
- 4 District Courts in Territories

Quasi-judicial Agencies

STATE AND LOCAL COURTS

Highest State Court

Intermediate Appellate Court (in some states)

Trial Courts of Original and General Jurisdiction

- Rural Courts
- Special Courts
- Urban Courts

594

system are the **federal district courts**. Most cases enter the system through the district courts, and most are resolved without going further. Each state has at least one district, and large states may have as many as four district courts. In 1992 there were ninety-four federal district courts staffed by 575 district court judges. District courts may be divided into administrative divisions. Federal district courts use both grand juries and petit juries. If a criminal defendant or a party to a civil suit loses in the district court, an appeal may be made to the next level of the federal system, the thirteen **U.S. courts of appeals** or *circuit courts*. Of these latter, one is in the District of Columbia and the rest, numbered, take in multistate regions of the country. These courts have no original jurisdiction; all cases they consider have been tried in a lower court. Circuit court judges usually hear cases in rotating panels of three.

The **U.S. Supreme Court** is the highest court in the federal system and the nation. Cases come to the Supreme Court from lower federal courts and from state court systems when a federal question is involved. (A federal case can deal with a federal statute, treaty, or the U.S. Constitution. Federal questions may also arise when the United States is a party to the case, when two states are involved, when a dispute affects citizens of different states, or when official foreign representatives are involved.) The Supreme Court is asked to hear several thousand cases every year, but it is able to hear and decide only between one hundred and two hundred. This means that the Supreme Court has a large measure of control over its own docket; with certain exceptions it can choose which cases it wishes to hear. If it chooses not to hear a case, the lower-court decision is allowed to stand. In deciding which cases to hear, the Court follows the so-called **rule of four**: If four of the nine justices vote to hear a case, the case is placed on the Court's docket. From that point, briefs are filed by the opposing sides, oral arguments are heard, and a decision is rendered.

The chief justice of the United States presides not only over the Supreme Court but also over the **Judicial Conference of the United States**, composed of the chief justice, the chief judge in each circuit court, and a representative district court judge from each circuit. This body, supported by about twenty-five committees of lawyers and judges who meet year round, decides administrative policy for the federal courts and makes recommendations to Congress on issues of judicial administration. Within each circuit a **judicial council**, composed of representative circuit and district court judges, makes administrative policy for the circuit.

Recruitment of Judges

An important influence on judicial decision making is the background of the person appointed to the bench. Various methods of judicial selection exist in the United States, based on different choices on an important issue: Just how politically responsive should judges be? If a judge's only tasks involved impartial dispute resolution according to fixed rules, a great deal of insulation from political pressure might be appropriate. But since judges in the United States also play an important role in the formulation (or

The U.S. Supreme Court in 1992. The Chief Justice always sits in the middle, with the Associate Justices alternating outward to his right and left in descending order of service. Seated (left to right): John Paul Stevens (Ford, 1975); Byron White (Kennedy, 1962); Chief Justice William Rehnquist (Associate Justice, Nixon, 1972); Harry Blackmun (Nixon, 1970); Sandra Day O'Connor (Reagan, 1981). Standing (left to right): David Souter (Bush, 1990); Antonin Scalia (Reagan, 1986); Anthony Kennedy (Reagan, 1988); Clarence Thomas (Bush, 1991). *(Collection of the Supreme Court of the United States)*

reformulation) of policy, some responsiveness to democratic demands also seems called for. Since the judicial responsibility for policy is tied to concern for minority rights against majority pressure, straight majoritarian representation won't do. How to achieve the proper mix of responsiveness to and insulation from popular pressure is an ongoing debate. Compared to the insular federal judiciary, most state systems opt for more direct democratic control over judges, either through the direct election of judges or through some combination of appointment by governor or legislature followed by a periodic vote to decide whether the judge ought to be retained (see **Table 16-1**).

The federal government uses a highly political, nonelectoral judicial selection process. Formally, judges are nominated by the president and confirmed by the Senate. The formal process reveals little of the partisan maneuvering that accompanies the selection of federal judges. In district court appointments, senators of the president's

TABLE 16-1
PRINCIPAL METHODS OF SELECTING JUDGES FOR STATE COURTS

Partisan Election	Nonpartisan Election	Legislative Election	Gubernatorial Appointment	Merit Plan
Alabama*	Georgia*	Connecticut*	California	Alaska*
Arkansas	Idaho	Rhode Island‡	Delaware	Arizona*
Illinois*	Kentucky	South Carolina*	Maine*	Colorado*
Mississippi*	Louisiana	Virginia	Massachusetts	Florida*†
New Mexico	Michigan*		New Hampshire	Hawaii
North Carolina†	Minnesota		New Jersey*	Indiana*
Pennsylvania*	Montana		New York*§	Iowa*
Tennessee*†	Nevada			Kansas*
Texas*	North Dakota			Maryland
West Virginia	Ohio*			Missouri†
	Oregon*			Nebraska
	Washington*			Oklahoma*†
	Wisconsin*			South Dakota*
				Utah
				Vermont
				Wyoming*

*Minor court judges chosen by other methods.
†Most but not all major judicial positions selected this way.
‡Supreme court justices only.
§Appellate judges only.
SOURCE: Council of State Governments, *Book of the States, 1990–1991* (Lexington, Ky.: Council of State Governments, 1990), pp. 210–212.

party from the affected state usually take an important role in suggesting names, since senatorial courtesy ordinarily gives home-state senators in the president's party an effective veto over district court nominations. Before publicly announcing a nomination, the president normally consults with the attorney general and various senators, as appropriate. The American Bar Association's Committee on the Federal Judiciary then prepares a report on the candidate for the Senate Judiciary Committee, which holds a hearing. After the committee votes to recommend the nominee, the full Senate votes. At every stage of this process, participants are intensely lobbied by interest groups, as well as by the nominees and their friends and allies.[5] Because most presidents seek to appoint men or women whose philosophy of government does not radically differ from their own, they tend to pick nominees whose political views have been made known through participation in public life.

Some nominations to the Supreme Court are inherently more controversial than others. Woodrow Wilson's nomination of Louis Brandeis in 1916, for example, caused a heated six-month battle in the Senate, in part because Brandeis was the first Jew nominated to the Court but also because of his ardent activism on behalf of controversial economic reforms. In recent years the process of presidential selection of Supreme Court nominees itself has become more controversial. This conflict began with Ronald Reagan's nomination of Robert Bork to the Supreme Court (described in Chapter 13). In the wake of that failed nomination and the subsequent and also unsuccessful nomination of Douglas Ginsburg, the White House now seems anxious to present in its nominees as small a target for criticism as possible. If the Democrat-controlled Senate could reject a nominee like Bork primarily on the basis of his conservative issue positions, the thinking went, the White House would advance nominees with no record to shoot at. In David Souter, President Bush found a person who had lived wholly outside public scrutiny and who had an almost nonexistent judicial record on controversial federal issues (Souter had served on the New Hampshire Supreme Court). The well-documented record of the next nominee, Clarence Thomas (who had chaired the Equal Employment Opportunity Commission before a brief stint on a federal circuit court), was simply dismissed as irrelevant by supporters wishing to avoid controversy. (The argument was that Thomas in a judicial position would not necessarily decide the same way as he had in an executive branch position.) On the most divisive political issue raised in the hearings, abortion, Thomas steadfastly maintained that he had never formed an opinion or even participated in a serious discussion of the issue. When a former employee charged Thomas with repeated verbal sexual harassment ten years earlier, Thomas flatly denied the charges. Without irrefutable evidence of the harassment charges and given the refusal to take a stand on abortion, senators who might otherwise have opposed the nomination were left without justification for a negative vote. Thomas was confirmed, but on both sides of the fight, participants and observers alike were left wondering how the process could be improved.

Once justices are appointed to the Supreme Court, predictions about their future decisions may be unreliable. Serving on the Supreme Court imposes a unique responsibility; lifetime tenure offers unusual insulation from direct pressure. The combination of these two factors sometimes elicits surprising responses from justices. Eisenhower came to rue his appointment of Earl Warren, who in his earlier career demonstrated a solid conservative record but as chief justice of the United States adopted an activist, liberal posture. Nixon appointees voted to strike down abortion laws and uphold busing—both policies that he did not support. As new appointments moved the whole Court to the right, however, Nixon appointee Harry Blackmun adjusted his own position to the left. In 1992, Reagan appointees Sandra Day O'Connor and Anthony M. Kennedy joined Bush appointee Souter in defying expectations by upholding *Roe* v. *Wade*, the Court's 1973 abortion decision, which both presidents were committed to seeing overturned.

Still, the president's ability to affect the Supreme Court's political orientation cannot be gainsaid, especially if several appointments are made in a short time. Supreme Court vacancies appear, on average, every two or three years. This ongoing recruitment process ties the Supreme Court in to the broad currents of thought that distinguish the political life of the day.

Clarence Thomas at his confirmation hearings before the Senate Judiciary Committee. The hearings had a major impact on public consciousness because of charges of sexual harassment made against Thomas by Anita Hill, a former employee. As the Supreme Court has become a major shaper of national policy, appointments to the Court have stirred increasing political controversy. *(UPI/Bettmann)*

The Flow of Litigation

The flow of litigation through the court system is characterized by a winnowing process. Most cases are decided at the level where they are first heard, either because the losers are satisfied with the outcome or because they do not have the resources to mount an appeal. Appeals can drain litigants of both time and money. The typical Supreme Court case wends it way through the court system for several years. The legal expenses involved—attorneys' fees for legal research, preparation of briefs, time spent in court—can be considerable.

Winnowing occurs not only because litigants give up or run out of resources but also because appellate courts refuse to hear many cases. A case that reaches the Supreme Court must be important enough to the litigants to merit a substantial investment of time and money, but the Court must also deem it important enough to merit consideration on a crowded and limited docket. Cases for which a clear line of precedents establishes an appropriate rule of law rarely reach the Supreme Court (unless, as sometimes happens, members of the Court decide to modify or reverse an existing rule).

Unlike lower courts, the Supreme Court acts as a policy review court; it works toward making decisions that have an impact on the entire legal system. Our legal system assumes that justice can be served under ordinary circumstances by a trial and a single chance for review in an appellate court. This is not to suggest that the work of lower courts is purely technical and unimportant. Lower court decisions dealing with the enforcement of criminal statutes and traffic laws and the application of legal norms in, say, landlord-tenant relations ordinarily have a more direct impact on the daily lives of individual citizens than decisions handed down by the Supreme Court. However, when it comes to developing and modifying legal norms involving important areas of social policy, the appellate courts, and especially the Supreme Court, generally hold sway.

We now turn to the second major function of the American judiciary, participation in policymaking.

The Judiciary and Policymaking

Courts in the United States have enormous power. Many matters that in other nations are considered outside the realm of judicial institutions are treated as legal issues in the United States. To understand the significant policy role played by the courts in this country, we must examine the nature of judicial power, its development, and its limitations. We now spotlight the decision-making process, the concept of judicial review, self-imposed restraints on the power of the courts, legislative reactions to court rulings, and noncompliance with court decisions.

The Decision-making Process

Judges in our system resolve disputes according to the law. In the United States we have four sources of law: the Constitution (written by "the people"), statutes (written by a legislature), case law (precedents decided by the courts), and administrative rules and regulations (established by administrative agencies). Sometimes these sources produce conflicting laws; then the legal hierarchy determines which law should prevail, according to established principles and the dictates of justice and fairness.

The process of applying law to particular cases is often far from straightforward. Precedents may conflict, or there may be no appropriate precedent. Statutes and administrative rules may be poorly written or deliberately vague. The challenge of interpreting the broad provisions of the Constitution is especially difficult. For example, the Court has recognized a constitutional right to privacy though no such right is specifically enumerated. Does a noisy demonstrator who blocks the entrance of an abortion clinic deny a woman seeking treatment her constitutional right to choose an abortion? Can a nineteenth-century Ku Klux Klan law or a federal racketeering statute be used to prosecute the demonstrator? Such questions prompt considerable debate among jurists. Beyond statutes, precedents, and constitutional clauses, personal values and characteristics of judges, their interactions with fellow judges, and the limitations

It took Federal troops dispatched by President Dwight D. Eisenhower to ensure the integration of the schools in Little Rock, Arkansas, in 1957. The Little Rock crisis was one of many as school desegregation was met with intense resistance. (UPI/Bettmann)

placed on them by their positions all influence their decisions and opinions. Judicial decision making, then, cannot be reduced to a mechanical process of applying the relevant law to the facts of a case.

Judicial Review

The extensive powers of the federal courts are rooted in the concept of judicial review. It enables courts to negate the activities of other branches of government by overturning laws and regulations deemed unconstitutional. Critics argue that judicial review is undemocratic because the judges who exercise it serve for long terms or for life and thus are not accountable to the public in the way elected officials are. From the opposite standpoint, judicial review protects the rights of minorities—a vital function in a democratic society. Only the courts, in this view, have the necessary detachment to restrain the volatile and sometimes repressive will of the majority.

The concept of judicial review is not explicitly spelled out in the Constitution. The framers of the Constitution, although certainly aware that judicial review was an issue, did not expressly address the question. Lacking a clear constitutional mandate, the courts simply asserted that they had the power of review, and that power gradually became an integral part of the U.S. legal system.

The Supreme Court first asserted the power to declare federal legislation unconstitutional in **Marbury v. Madison** (1803).[6] In *Marbury* the Court declared that a provision of the Judiciary Act of 1789 violated the Constitution and hence was null and void. This ruling had profound implications. Because many of the provisions of the Constitution are vague, applying them in the context of judicial review gives the courts enormous power. Over the following two decades, the Court built slowly on the provisions of *Marbury*. In *McCulloch v. Maryland* (1819),[7] Chief Justice Marshall cited the supremacy of national law (Article 1) in ruling that Maryland's attempt to tax national banks was unconstitutional. That same year the justices held that states were prohibited from passing legislation impairing contracts.

Since the mid-nineteenth century there has been little dispute over whether the Supreme Court has the power of judicial review. Some Courts have been more active than others in exercising this power, however, and debate continues over how far the Court should go in nullifying the actions of other, more democratic institutions.

Self-restraints on Power

The courts' power of judicial review is circumscribed by a series of self-imposed rules for restraint. For example, courts will consider only cases in which the parties have **standing to sue**, that is, in which the plaintiff (the party that brings suit) can demonstrate actual injury—loss of money, property, freedom, or the like—from the government law or action in question. Standing rules may be relaxed or tightened, depending on the courts' case load burdens and, more important, the likelihood that policy debates that should take place in other arenas will be imposed on the judiciary instead. Without limits on standing rules, any taxpayer could challenge nearly any government policy or action. Many such suits would clog the courts and encourage self-defeating battles between courts and the other branches of the government.

Another rule for self-restraint rests on the **political question doctrine**. Although, as we have noted, the courts are an integral part of the political process and thus must necessarily make decisions with political implications, the courts routinely shun certain types of political disputes. These include matters that would place the Supreme Court in direct conflict with other branches of government, issues involving foreign relations that might embarrass or compromise the government if a multiplicity of voices spoke for the nation in contradictory ways, and matters that have been assigned by the Constitution to other branches for resolution. For instance, federal courts have routinely turned away challenges under the War Powers Resolution, leaving decisions about military deployment directly to Congress and the president.

The Supreme Court can choose to enter public policy disputes and even set an agenda for the development of law. However, too much direct involvement may undermine the Court's legitimacy in the eyes of other political players and the public at large. As Justice Anthony Kennedy said in a speech prior to his nomination to the Supreme Court, "The unrestrained exercise of judicial authority ought to be recognized

(Text continues on page 604)

COMPARATIVE PERSPECTIVE

JUDICIAL REVIEW IN BRITAIN, SWITZERLAND, AND GERMANY

How many words in the British Constitution? That's an old joke, since the British have no constitution—at least not a single document of a particular length, as we do. In Great Britain the absolute ground of government is the expression of the popular will in Parliament—the House of Commons and the House of Lords (see Chapter 13). The fundamental principles of British government are reflected in a series of documents, statutes, and traditions—the *unwritten* constitution. But nothing in this constitution supersedes the popular will, and thus no governmental institution is empowered to check the power of Parliament. If the ruling party in the House of Commons makes a faulty interpretation of the unwritten constitution, that party can be replaced in the next general elections.

Switzerland does have a single document that serves as a constitution. Swiss courts are not empowered to declare a particular law invalid because it is contrary to the constitution, but general voters are. With fifty thousand signatures (not a lot in a nation of 6 million people), any bill passed by the parliament can be submitted to the Swiss electorate in a referendum. Similarly, constitutional amendments proposed by the parliament must be submitted to the general electorate for approval. Furthermore, with one hundred thousand signatures, voters can submit their own constitutional amendment using the constitutional initiative. Such an initiative recently inserted an article establishing a system of hiking trails—an odd provision for a nation's fundamental law. But democracy in action does not always follow the prescriptions of legal theory.

In Germany a fairly substantial power of judicial review does exist—a reaction in part to the lessons of Hitler's Third Reich. Much of Hitler's expanded power was based on newly written laws. Although a weak system of judicial review was in place at the time, it was unable to offer any significant resistance to the Nazis' transformation of law to serve their own ends. When the Federal Republic of Germany was born after World War II, institutional checks on dictatorial power were built into the system, including judicial review, heavily influenced by the U.S. model. The sixteen-member Constitutional Court, elected by the Parliament, has become a moral and political watchdog of the German polity. As in the United States, the German Constitutional Court played an important role in abortion policy, striking down a 1974 liberal abortion law as an unconstitutional violation of the right to life of the unborn child. A less liberal law was subsequently enacted by the parliament.

Source: Jürg Steiner, European Democracies, *2nd ed. (White Plains, N.Y.: Longman, 1991), chap. 4.*

for what it is: the raw exercise of judicial power. If in fact that is the basis of our decisions, then there is no principled justification for our insulation from the political process."[8] Since the Court's power depends entirely on its perceived legitimacy (as Alexander Hamilton reminded us in *Federalist* No. 78, the Supreme Court controls neither the sword nor the purse), self-restraint is critical if the Court is to play a major role in shaping public policy. Individual justices, and the people who evaluate their work, must recognize when the Court is using its political insulation to substitute the choices of a judicial elite for the choices of the people's representatives and, on the contrary, when the Court is properly resisting the unfair demands of an oppressive majority.

Legislative Reactions

An additional limit on the power of the Supreme Court to participate decisively in public policymaking is Congress's ability to overrule unpopular court decisions by passing new laws or proposing constitutional amendments. Even when attempts to overturn Court rulings through the legislative process do not succeed, they give the Court important cues that it may have gone too far and should reconsider the policy it has been pursuing.

In a series of decisions handed down in 1957 and 1958 the Court introduced limits on the power of congressional committees to investigate communists, on the use of criminal sanctions against members of the American Communist party, and on the power of government agencies to dismiss employees whose loyalty was suspect. In Congress and the newspapers, opposition to these decisions grew, and legislation was introduced to overturn them. In addition, Congress threatened to restrict the Court's ability to hear appeals of lower court decisions dealing with such matters as loyalty and security. Although none of this proposed legislation passed, the message to the Court was unmistakable.

During the period from 1959 to 1961 the Court lifted many of the restraints imposed in 1957 and 1958. The congressional and public response prompted the Court to back off a bit in rulings that dealt with the powers of the government to restrict liberty in the name of national security, averting a constitutional crisis.[9]

More recent Court decisions outlawing prayer in public schools and government restrictions on abortion have sparked intense legislative reactions. Efforts to overturn the school prayer decisions have failed to produce the constitutional amendment critics have sought. Critics of the abortion decision have had some success in complicating the process of obtaining an abortion in some states and in restricting funding for Medicaid abortions but not in altering the Court's decision itself. In both these instances the Court has shown little inclination to shift its position, despite the intensity of legislative and popular reactions. In 1992 the Supreme Court ruled that public school officials may not include prayers or invoke the name of God during a grade school or high school ceremony. That same year the Court again upheld *Roe* v. *Wade*, although with what some critics called significant limitations.

Noncompliance

Court decisions are not self-executing: In order for them to take effect, individuals or agencies outside the court must implement them. Some decisions require relatively simple changes in behavior: Let John Smith out of prison or give him a new trial. Other decisions require major changes by large numbers of people and the significant reallocation of resources. Noncompliance and a lack of vigorous enforcement can negate any judicial policy.

Local officials and bureaucracies in both the public and the private spheres frequently assert their braking power on policy emanating from the courts. Local school districts, for example, used a series of evasive schemes to thwart the Supreme Court's goal of school desegregation as mandated in *Brown* v. *Board of Education of Topeka* (1954). A similar record of noncompliance followed the Court's 1966 ruling that all police officers were required to inform criminal suspects about their rights (the Miranda warnings) before interrogating them.[10] Officers were still interrogating suspects without informing them of their rights or were reading them their rights in tones that implied that they were meaningless.[11]

To overcome official noncompliance requires someone willing to assume the costs of challenging official actions that do not conform to established policy. These costs can be high, in personal as well as economic terms. Imagine the costs to an entire family of challenging a school district's popular silent prayer observance or the costs to a person who challenges a chemical plant that employs hundreds of local residents but is polluting the groundwater with toxic chemicals. In addition, complying with the letter of the law sometimes falls far short of the spirit of a particular Court decision. Consider, for example, a police officer who reads a suspect the Miranda warnings in such a way that the suspect knows that invoking these rights will prompt official displeasure and probably some retribution for making the officer's life more difficult. At times even compliance fails to yield the results anticipated by policymakers. Desegregation plans, for instance, often encouraged white flight and helped to create entire school districts segregated along racial lines.

We tend to view instances of noncompliance with Court decisions as signs that something is wrong in the system. But noncompliance can also be viewed as a defining characteristic of the U.S. political system. The court system participates in the political process by deciding cases that sometimes establish broad new policies. At that point these policies reenter the arena of public affairs; other institutions and groups, and society at large, then react to these policies—sometimes through noncompliance—setting the process in motion once again.

Major Periods in Supreme Court History

The Supreme Court's participation in U.S. politics has taken different forms over the past two centuries. During its first 130 years the Court focused primarily on questions involving the distribution of power within and among governments. The Constitution left unanswered important questions about which powers belonged to each branch of the federal government, as well as which powers the federal government could exercise and which were reserved to the states. John Marshall was the first chief justice to lead the Court to consider the great political questions of the day. Let us now consider the Court's rulings on intergovernmental and intragovernmental distribution of power, concern for individual rights, the impact of the Warren Court, and the post-Warren era.

Focus on the Distribution of Power

Under Chief Justice Marshall (whose term ran from 1801 to 1835) the Court established the principle of judicial review of both state and federal laws and activities. During this era the Court also advocated a flexible interpretation of the Constitution to serve changing needs and determined that the national government has implied powers to achieve the ends established in the Constitution. (See the discussion of the *Marbury* and *McCulloch* cases earlier in this chapter.)

Marshall's successor, Chief Justice Roger B. Taney (pronounced "tawny"), whose term extended from 1836 to 1864, took a greater interest in states' rights than Marshall had. The doctrine of dual federalism, developed during this period, reaffirmed the

Perhaps the most important of all Chief Justices, John Marshall, who helped shape the significant power and enduring presence of the Supreme Court as an ultimate arbiter in the American constitutional system.
(UPI/Bettmann)

position of states as sovereign units within the federal system. The most disastrous decision (both for the nation and for the Court) made under Taney was **Dred Scott v. Sandford**.[12] In this 1857 case involving slavery, a badly split Supreme Court declared the Missouri Compromise, which prohibited slavery in certain territories, unconstitutional on the ground that Congress was thereby depriving citizens of their property (slaves) without due process of law. Heavily weighted toward southern interests and based on assumptions that would today be characterized as extremely racist, *Dred Scott* threw the Court's legitimacy into question in the North and propelled the nation toward civil war. The Fourteenth Amendment, adopted in 1866, formally overturned the *Dred Scott* decision.

From the end of the Civil War through the close of the nineteenth century, the Court gradually regained power, bolstered by its close identification with the conservative business interests that dominated this period. As the century waned the Court struck down many state and federal laws designed to aid workers, farmers, and others who had been hurt by rapid industrial development and the evolution of the modern corporation. Interpreting the Fourteenth Amendment narrowly, the Court rendered it useless in extending rights to the newly freed blacks. In addition, the Court supported Jim Crow laws (favoring discrimination and segregation) through decisions like *Plessy v. Ferguson* (1896),[13] establishing the "separate but equal" doctrine that was not overturned until 1954 (see Chapter 5). The Court's conservative, laissez-faire, probusiness stance lasted (with some significant deviations) into the mid-1930s. Then, prompted by the near-crisis brought on by the Court's overturning significant New Deal legislation, the High Court altered its approach, as we saw earlier in this chapter.

Concern for Individual Rights

In the three decades following 1937 the Court moved to guarantee civil rights and civil liberties for all. This was largely achieved by extending the protections of the Fourteenth Amendment to encompass the specific protections of the Bill of Rights (see Chapter 5). There were exceptions to this trend, however: The Court upheld the internment of Japanese-Americans during World War II, and under Chief Justice Fred M. Vinson, who served from 1946 to 1953, the Court upheld prosecutions of American Communist party members.

THE WARREN COURT (1953–1969) The Warren Court established the most controversial record in modern Supreme Court history. Under Chief Justice Earl Warren, the Court decided issues that struck deep into areas of strongly held beliefs about American life. School desegregation, legislative reapportionment, school prayer, pornography, and the rights of the accused—all these issues were tackled head-on by the Warren Court. The Court's rulings frequently sparked vehement public opposition, particularly in the cases of school desegregation, school prayer, and the rights of the accused.

Chief Justice Earl Warren donning his robe and chatting with Associate Justice William O. Douglas. Warren, a Republican appointed by Eisenhower, surprised observers by leading one of the most liberal and controversial courts in history. *(UPI/Bettmann)*

Whereas the Court had been attacked in the 1930s for its conservatism, the Warren Court was criticized for its excessive activism—for making rather than interpreting law. Conservatives called for a return to "strict construction" (literal interpretation) of the Constitution. Supporters of the Court, meanwhile, claimed that the Court's willingness to stretch the Constitution (through "loose construction") made that document useful in the modern era.

The Recent Past

When Earl Warren was succeeded by Warren Burger, joined by three other Nixon appointees, civil libertarians made dire predictions about the course of the Court and the fate of individual rights. Those predictions proved groundless—at least for a long time. First, conservative strict constructionists were, in theory at least, bound to respect established precedents, including those of the Warren era. Second, and more important, the Supreme Court is sometimes misleadingly characterized by reference to the chief justice. An assertive, activist chief justice, with a clear agenda and enough votes on the Court to support it, is well situated to dominate the Court and define an era. But sometimes leadership is shared, is seized by an associate justice, or falters altogether. The Court *has* moved in an increasingly conservative direction in the more than two decades since Warren's departure, echoing the trend of national politics.

But the long march toward conservative lights has been anything but steady and inexorable. In fact, the period following the Warren era also produced a series of individual decisions broadly supportive of the Warren Court precedents and even expanding some of them. Many of these decisions were engineered by William Brennan, an adept player of Court politics. But Burger himself participated in majority decisions

Chief Justice William Rehnquist's tenure continued the pattern of mixed, case-by-case decision making that had been dominant since Earl Warren's retirement in 1969. The six Reagan-Bush appointments moved the Court distinctly to the right, but not in ways that were always predictable. *(Abe Frajndlich/Sygma)*

that must have frustrated his conservative backers. The Court found against the government in the Pentagon Papers case, upheld busing as a constitutional means of addressing de facto segregation, extended the constitutional right to privacy to include the right to secure an abortion, and struck down the death penalty as it was applied prior to 1972.[14] Even after William Rehnquist was elevated to the chief justiceship, the liberal minority on the Court managed some striking victories. Chief Justice Rehnquist himself wrote for the majority in *Hustler Magazine* v. *Falwell* (1988), maintaining that public figures may not recover damages for emotional distress caused by an advertisement parody.[15] In *Texas* v. *Johnson* (1989) the Court upheld the right of a protester to burn a flag outside the 1984 Republican convention in Dallas.[16]

In a 1992 case involving the separation of church and state, a rabbi was invited to give an invocation at a public junior high school graduation. The majority, in a 5-4 decision that might have been handed down by the Warren Court, argued that "what to most believers may seem nothing more than a reasonable request that a nonbeliever respect their religious practices, in a school context may appear to the nonbeliever or dissenter to be an attempt . . . to enforce a religious orthodoxy." The Court ruled that public school officials may not invoke the name of God during school ceremonies.[17] In the same term the Court ruled that cigarette manufacturers can be forced to defend themselves against injury claims in state courts and must pay damages if they conspired to deceive the public about the true dangers of smoking.[18] In a separate case the Court ruled that Mississippi had not done nearly enough to meet its "affirmative duty" to dismantle its formerly segregated system of higher education.[19] Each of these cases was labeled a victory for those who wanted the Court to take an active stand in defending individual rights.

For every activist victory during this period there were two—sometimes several—conservative successes. Busing to achieve integration among central-city and suburban school districts was put largely out of reach in *Millikan* v. *Bradley* (1974).[20] After a series of decisions defending *Roe* from limitations, the Court began to accept significant restrictions on the availability of abortion.[21] States were once more free to use the death penalty after *Gregg* v. *Georgia* (1976),[22] even when statistical evidence showed that it fell disproportionately on African-Americans.[23] The exclusionary rule was not abandoned, but it was significantly limited, in part by the assumption that constitutional errors made by law enforcement officers "in good faith" did not render resultant evidence inadmissible in court.[24] With Brennan's retirement in 1990, it was assumed that the conservative majority on the Court had gained a commanding advantage. Several cases in 1991 and 1992 restricting federal habeas corpus review of state criminal convictions seemed consistent with this reading. But surprises continued as well.

Apart from the uneven recasting of the Warren civil liberties agenda, the most important development in the Supreme Court's decisions since the Warren era involves an increased willingness to consider property questions. When the Court retreated in 1937 from its opposition to the New Deal, it entered a long period of allowing the federal and state governments a free hand in economic regulation. A growing list of cases over the past two decades indicates that property issues are back on the Court's agenda and that a half-century of deference to legislative control of property may be ending.[25]

The Supreme Court is easiest to characterize when it produces a series of decisions that fit some consistent, identifiable pattern. The Warren era was such a period. A fair possibility exists that the Republican-created conservative court of the 1990s will create a comparable period of rulings, though such an outcome is far from assured. The Court's most recent decisions demonstrate divisions within the conservative majority, with states' rights concerns dominant for Rehnquist and O'Connor, for instance, and more hard-line, antigovernment conservative concerns voiced by Scalia and Thomas. Although the Court has come a long way from the liberal Warren era, these divisions may continue the uneven, case-by-case approach that has marked much of its work since.

The Dilemma of an Expanded Legal System

In recent decades Americans have turned more and more to the judiciary to solve their problems. The courts have tackled the complexities of affirmative action, police behavior, environmental pollution, and standards for assistance to the poor.

Judicial responsibility has grown as government has extended the scope of its responsibilities. Yet much of the increase in judicial activity has taken place independent of Congress and the bureaucracy—or even in opposition to their policies. In some cases the courts have seized the initiative, usurping, according to critics, some of the functions of legislatures. In other cases, courts have been forced to fashion broad social policy in order to resolve specific disputes, as the common law tradition requires.

Once considered conservative institutions, the courts were now taking the lead when other institutions, supposedly better designed to grapple with change, were reluctant to act. This happened because federal judges, with life-tenure positions, are protected from waves of popular sentiment. Yet the judicial system's insulation from public opinion has both advantages and drawbacks. On the one hand, judges do not have to account for their actions; this is an obviously undemocratic feature of U.S. politics. On the other hand, only judges can defend the liberties of groups that a majority would rather ignore. And on occasion, courts may be better informed and show a clearer comprehension of complex issues than legislatures or other organs of government.

Along with growth in the powers and activism of the courts has come an epic expansion of the legal profession. The United States has three times as many lawyers per capita as Great Britain, twenty times as many as Japan. Although legal assistance is becoming more important in the United States, it is not uniformly available. The federal government's partial commitment to provide legal services to poor people was, for the most part, withdrawn during the 1980s. The current availability of legal services for poor people is very low. Middle-class people are also being priced out of the legal market by increasing fees.

Some expansion of law is inevitable in a complex society in which economic competition and exploitation are common and individuals seek to protect their rights. As social customs, habits, and traditions break down in a more fragmented and mobile society, law replaces other means of social control. As long ago as the mid-nineteenth century, however, observers like Alexis de Tocqueville were commenting on the tendency of Americans to take all their controversies to court.

How do we deal with our litigious tendencies? Several remedies have been suggested. One is deregulation: If we could eliminate cumbersome government regulations and replace them with greater competition, it is argued, the number of lawsuits could be sharply diminished. However, deregulation can create its own problems, as we saw in Chapter 14.

Another possible remedy is a move toward dejudicialization—keeping issues out of the courts. There are good reasons for doing so. For example, litigants often face a five-year wait to have a case heard in a federal courtroom, and defendants who cannot afford bail may have to wait up to six months in jail before their cases are dealt with. Despite passage of the Speedy Trial Act of 1975, which requires a trial within 125 days after arrest on most charges, delays still pose the most serious problem for the courts. The speedy-trial provisions have also been criticized for not allowing the government sufficient time to prepare a case.

The concept of dejudicialization could be expanded to include the development of neighborhood justice centers, which would resolve disputes through arbitration and mediation. Such centers, which handle family arguments, minor assaults, and disputes between landlords and tenants, bosses and workers, and consumers and stores, already exist in some cities and counties. A Justice Department experiment in Kansas City demonstrated that hearings at such centers commonly take only two hours, and only two weeks elapse before final hearings are held. Eighty-six percent of all cases heard were successfully resolved, with the remainder going into the court system.

Some initiatives must come from Congress as well. For example, the Sherman Antitrust Act, which dates back to the last decade of the nineteenth century, is exceedingly difficult to enforce: It takes an average of eight years before a judgment is reached in an antitrust case. Some cases go on indefinitely. Major corporations are difficult to attack in the courts: some have more lawyers on retainer than the entire Department of Justice has on staff. Only clarification of the Sherman Act by Congress could place less of the burden of proof on the government and thereby make it easier to prosecute antitrust violations.

Conclusions

Over the past half-century the federal courts on the whole have served important democratic purposes in extending equality, strengthening the protection of rights and liberties, and ruling on issues that other branches of government could not or would not resolve. Lacking a legislative consensus, how could reapportionment, school desegregation, and rights of the accused have been settled in any national fashion? Yet the courts, in addressing these issues, entered a political thicket that many legal experts warn against. As a result, the courts have thrust themselves into the center of intense controversy in recent decades.

Policymaking by the courts obviously poses problems. By intruding too far into this area, courts may actively thwart majority rule or weaken legislation designed to protect basic rights. After the Civil War, for example, an interventionist Court undercut the substance of the Fourteenth Amendment and prevented black Americans from achieving legal equality for decades. The same antidemocratic trend characterized the Court's later conservative rulings to thwart unions, delay child labor legislation, and strike down key elements of the New Deal program.

Ideally, the courts can exercise power on behalf of Americans who have little or no political clout. All citizens—be they blacks seeking school desegregation, mental patients whose rights need protection, or unionized workers trying to gain recognition—should be able to turn to the courts when the other components of the political process ignore their interests. Often in recent decades such individuals found an advocate in the courts. From the standpoint of democratic politics, this represents an important development.

However, much depends on the political philosophies of the judges, their concern for democratic life, and their willingness to risk controversy. Given the power of courts in our political process, we are perhaps more dependent than we should be on the instincts and opinions of the people who wear the judicial robes.

Glossary Terms

appellate hearing
civil cases
common law
criminal cases
Dred Scott v. *Sandford*
federal district courts
grand jury
Judicial Conference of the United States
judicial council
judicial review
Marbury v. *Madison*

new judicial federalism
opinions
petit jury
plea bargain
political question doctrine
rule of four
standing to sue
stare decisis
U.S. courts of appeals (circuit courts)
U.S. Supreme Court

Notes

[1] David G. Savage, "Supreme Court Upholds Midler Copycat Ruling," *Los Angeles Times*, March 24, 1992, p. F1.

[2] David W. Neubauer, *Judicial Process: Law, Courts, and Politics in the United States* (Belmont, Calif.: Wadsworth, 1991), p. 353.

[3]625 P.2d 779 (Calif.)
[4]432 U.S. 464.
[5]See Henry R. Glick, *Courts in American Politics* (New York: McGraw-Hill, 1990), chap. 5.
[6]1 Cranch 137.
[7]4 Wheaton 316.
[8]Carl Everett Ladd, *The Ladd Report No. 7* (New York: Norton, 1988), p. 27.
[9]Walter Murphy, *Congress and the Court* (Chicago: University of Chicago Press, 1962).
[10]*Miranda* v. *Arizona* (1966), 384 U.S. 436.
[11]M. Wald et al., "Interrogations in New Haven: The Impact of Miranda," *Yale Law Journal*, July 1967. See especially pp. 1533–1577.
[12]19 Howard 393.
[13]163 U.S. 537.
[14]*New York Times* v. *United States* (1971), 403 U.S. 713; *Swann* v. *Charlotte-Mecklenburg Board of Education* (1971), 402 U.S. 1; *Roe* v. *Wade* (1973), 410 U.S. 113; *Furman* v. *Georgia* (1972), 408 U.S. 234.
[15]435 U.S. 46.
[16]109 S.Ct. 2533.
[17]*Lee* v. *Weisman* (1992), ???? S.Ct. ????.
[18]*Cipollone* v. *Liggett Group* (1992) 112 S.Ct. 2608.
[19]*United States* v. *Fordice* (1992) 112 S.Ct. 2727.
[20]418 U.S. 717.
[21]*Webster* v. *Reproductive Health Services* (1989), 109 S.Ct. 3040; *Rust* v. *Sullivan* (1991), 111 S.Ct. 1759; *Planned Parenthood* v. *Casey* (1992), 112 S.G. 2791.
[22]428 U.S. 153.
[23]*McCleskey* v. *Kemp* (1987), 481 U.S. 278.
[24]*United States* v. *Leon* (1984), 468 U.S. 897; *Oregon* v. *Elstad* (1985), 470 U.S. 298.
[25]For example, *Pennell* v. *City of San Jose* (1988), 485 U.S. 1; *Presault* v. *ICC* (1990), 110 S.Ct. 914; *First Evangelical Lutheran Church* v. *County of Los Angeles* (1987), 482 U.S. 304; and *Nollan* v. *California Coastal Commission* (1987), 483 U.S. 825.

SELECTED READINGS

Start with a good **general introduction** to courts in the United States: David W. Neubauer, *Judicial Process: Law, Courts, and Politics in the United States* (Belmont, Calif.: Wadsworth, 1991). See also John B. Gates and Charles A. Johnson, eds., *The American Courts: A Critical Assessment* (Washington, D.C.: Congressional Quarterly Press, 1991); and Robert A. Carp and Ronald Stidham, *Judicial Process in America* (Washington, D.C.: Congressional Quarterly Press, 1990).

For very different angles on general theory about the **judicial process**, see Gerald N. Rosenberg, *The Hollow Hope: Can Courts Bring About Social Change?* (Chicago: University of Chicago Press, 1991); and Barbara M. Yarnold, *Politics and the Court: Toward a General Theory of Public Law* (New York: Praeger, 1992).

For a narrower **institutional focus**, read Robert A. Carp and Ronald Stidham, *The Federal Courts*, 2nd ed. (Washington, D.C.: Congressional Quarterly Press, 1991); Wolf V. Heydebrand and Carroll Seron, *Rationalizing Justice: The Political Economy of Federal District Courts* (Albany: State University of New York Press, 1990); Christopher E. Smith, *United States Magistrates* in the Federal Courts: Subordinate Judges (New York: Praeger, 1990); and Arthur D. Hellman, ed., *Restructuring Justice: The Innovations of the Ninth Circuit and the Future of Federal Courts* (Ithaca, N.Y.: Cornell University Press, 1990).

The **United States Supreme Court** has been the subject of a very large amount of scholarship. Some good recent examples include Lawrence Baum, *The Supreme Court*, 4th ed. (Washington, D.C.: Congressional Quarterly Press, 1992); David M. O'Brien, *Storm Center: The Supreme Court in American Politics* (New York: Norton, 1990); and *The Supreme Court at Work* (Washington, D.C.: Congressional Quarterly Press, 1990).

Supreme Court nominations are detailed in Henry J. Abraham, *Justices and Presidents: A Political History of Appointments to the Supreme Court*, 3rd ed. (New York: Oxford University Press, 1992); and John Massaro, *Supremely Political: The Role of Ideology and Presidential Management in Unsuccessful Supreme Court Nominations* (Albany: State University of New York Press, 1990).

State court systems are less often the subject of political science research, in part because their variety makes generalization difficult. But a good introduction is available: Harry P. Stumpf and John H. Culver, *The Politics of State Courts* (White Plains, N.Y.: Longman, 1992). N. Gary Holten and Lawson L. Lamar, *The Criminal Courts: Structures, Personnel, and Processes* (New York: McGraw-Hill, 1991) covers the criminal side of both the federal and the state courts.

The **recent past** is the subject of Melvin I. Urofsky, *The Continuity of Change: The Supreme Court and Individual Liberties, 1953–1986* (Belmont, Calif.: Wadsworth, 1991); Charles M. Lamb and Stephen C. Halpern, eds., *The Burger Court: Political and Judicial Profiles* (Champaign: University of Illinois Press, 1991); Bernard Schwartz, *The Ascent of Pragmatism: The Burger Court in Action* (Reading, Mass.: Addison-Wesley, 1990); Nancy Maveety, *Representation Rights and the Burger Years* (Ann Arbor: University of Michigan Press, 1991); and Derek Davis, *Original Intent: Chief Justice Rehnquist and the Course of American Church/State Relations* (Buffalo, N.Y.: Prometheus, 1991).

For recent **comparative perspectives** on judicial systems, see Steven L. Willborn, *A Secretary and a Cook: Changing Women's Wages in the Courts of the United States and Great Britain* (Ithaca, N.Y.: ILR Press, 1989); and Robert M. Hayden, *Social Courts in Theory and Practice: Yugoslav Workers' Courts in Comparative Perspective* (Philadelphia: University of Pennsylvania Press, 1990).

PART FOUR

PUBLIC POLICY

17
PUBLIC POLICY: PROCESSES AND OUTCOMES

18
MANAGEMENT OF THE ECONOMY: COMPETING INTERESTS

19
THE WELFARE STATE: BENEFITING THE POOR AND THE NONPOOR

20
BUILDING COMMUNITY: VALUES AND LIMITS

21
FOREIGN AND DEFENSE POLICIES: A PLACE IN THE WORLD

22
ENERGY AND THE ENVIRONMENT: PRESERVING OR DEPLETING THE AMERICAN DREAM?

DC 37
AFSCME
AFL-CIO
SAYS:
QUALITY HEALTH CARE FOR ALL!
DC 37
GOOD HEALTH CARE FOR ALL NEW YORKERS
GOOD HEALTH CARE FOR ALL NEW YORKERS

CHAPTER SEVENTEEN

PUBLIC POLICY

Processes and Outcomes

CHAPTER OUTLINE

The Complexities of Public Policy in the United States: AIDS

GETTING AIDS ON THE AGENDA

AIDS AND THE FRAGMENTATION OF POWER

FUNDING THE RESPONSE TO AIDS

AIDS AND POLICY REACTIONS

AIDS POLICY: THE CONTRIBUTION OF INDIVIDUALS AND GROUPS

How Issues Reach the Political Agenda

Processing Issues

COMPETING AGENDAS

DEALING WITH ISSUES

Policy Formulation and Implementation

PROPOSALS FOR ACTION

IMPLEMENTATION

Policy Evaluation

The Boundaries of Policymaking

EVERYTHING YOU'VE READ SO FAR IN THIS TEXTBOOK HAS BEEN about public policy in a broad sense. Learning about public policy means knowing something about a nation's political *foundations*—the basic understandings about the proper range and nature of governmental action; the *political processes* by which government choices are made—how officials are chosen and what pressures they respond to; and the *institutions* themselves. Put all of this together and it is clear that in a general way, public policy is what this whole text is about. So why call the final part of this text "Public Policy"? And why have a chapter this late in the game introducing the topic?

Political scientists talk about public policy studies in a more focused way, not encompassing the whole discipline of political science but forming a subfield, supplementing and enriching the discipline with a particular outlook on a narrow range of events. An important part of this outlook is seeing public policy dynamically, as a process rather than as a set of enumerated policies. The phases of the process can be described in different ways but look something like this: agenda setting, policy formulation, legitimation, resource allocation, implementation, evaluation, and response.[1]

Agenda setting is the phase during which a particular situation or problem is identified as appropriate for public

619

> ### How Do We Define "Public Policy"?
>
> Definitions of public policy range from the ultrasimple to the highly complex. Try these two for starters:
>
> *Public policy is whatever governments choose to do or not do.**
>
> *Public policy involves a purposeful course of action (although its effects may not be anticipated) that is based on law and therefore backed up by the police powers of government (although many policies may not actually be enforced), and that government's refusal to act is also a form of public policy.†*
>
> *Thomas R. Dye, Understanding Public Policy (Englewood Cliffs, N.J.: Prentice Hall, 1984), p. 2.
> †James E. Anderson, David W. Brady, Charles S. Bullock III, and Joseph Stewart, Jr., Public Policy and Politics in America (Pacific Grove, Calif.: Brooks/Cole, 1984), p. 4.

action, thus becoming the subject of a public policy debate. Making it onto the *systemic agenda* means gaining a general recognition that some public agency ought to do something about this problem. Getting onto an *institutional agenda* means getting a particular institution—Congress, the state legislature, or the EPA, for example—to consider taking action to address the problem. **Policy formulation** is the phase when possible responses to the problem are spelled out, fought over, and evaluated. One or more action steps (including, possibly, doing nothing) are chosen. **Legitimation** involves taking the formal actions—legislating, making rules, issuing a policy statement—that mark the chosen policy as official. The **resource allocation** phase involves earmarking funds or personnel to address the problem according to the chosen policy. The resources may or may not be adequate to the policy tasks. The policy is put into practice during the **implementation** phase, nearly always involving additional policy choices to be made by the implementers. **Policy evaluation** can be either formal or informal, measuring actual outcomes against the policy's goals and objectives. Following evaluation, a **response** occurs—to maintain, modify, or abandon the policy as implemented. A response might come from any of the various agencies involved in the earlier phases of the policy process or from outside, prompting one agency or another to address the problem once more. This list describes an ideal model. The development of policy in the real world may not include all of these steps in this order. But this is a useful way of thinking about what ought to happen as the policy process moves from initial recognition of a need for policy or policy change through the debate, decision, and detailed application of a policy to the point when the process starts over again. Government agencies may be joined or influenced by private organizations and individuals at every stage of the process.

Even a quick glance at an example of how this process works in the real world will indicate the complexities of policymaking in the United States. The governmental response to AIDS is an instructive example.[2]

The Complexities of Public Policy in the United States: AIDS

The ordinary processes of public policy creation are complicated in the United States by particular characteristics of the American political system discussed in earlier chapters. Most prominent among these are the federal system, the separation of powers, and the pluralist distribution of political power among a variety of governmental and nongovernmental groups. The AIDS crisis demonstrates the special challenges of creating public policy under these conditions.

Getting AIDS on the Agenda

Acquired immune deficiency syndrome (AIDS) could not make it onto the public agenda until it was recognized as a particular problem. Retrospective evidence suggests that AIDS was present in the United States at least as early as 1977, if not earlier. But it was not identified as a specific health problem until 1981–1982. And isolation of the viral cause of AIDS was not recognized in this country until 1984. In the beginning there were only a few young men in Los Angeles and New York with rare cases of cancer or pneumonia. Only after the public reporting of a certain number of cases could the symptoms be identified as a syndrome, indicating a common source. Even at this early stage, the federal bureaucracy was involved. The Centers for Disease Control (CDC) in Atlanta reported in its June 5, 1981, *Morbidity and Mortality Weekly Report (MMWR)* that five young gay men had contracted a rare strain of pneumonia; two had already died. The CDC is a medical detection agency—its task is to collect epidemiological data (incidents of death and disease). But it is not structured to boost something onto the public agenda on its own; it publishes the data and hopes that other agencies will act. The early association of AIDS with homosexual men, then with intravenous drug users and Haitians—all populations on the margins of public awareness—meant that it was difficult to get this budding epidemic on the systemic policy agenda in the United States. Elected politicians, from the president down to local city council members, were slow to acknowledge the seriousness of the threat and reluctant to tie their political fortunes to a scourge that afflicted mainly gay men and drug abusers. Some public figures, like Jerry Falwell of the Moral Majority, even suggested that AIDS was God's way of punishing these forms of "behavior." Such statements by opinion leaders further discouraged positive policy responses.

The institutionalized fragmentation of power in our political system ensures that moving from the general agenda to appropriate institutional agendas is also difficult. In 1981 the newly installed Reagan administration, pushing its "new federalism" was anxious to reduce the absolute size of government and decentralize what was left. In combination with a "family values" theme, this agenda ensured that little initiative on AIDS would originate at the top of the executive branch. The result was inconsistent and sometimes contradictory responses from various agencies in the federal bureaucracy. In 1984, after the **human immunodeficiency virus (HIV)**, the viral cause of AIDS, had been identified, the National Cancer Institute (part of the National Institutes of Health) devoted a large proportion of its resources to developing a test to monitor blood transfusions. At the same time, the Food and Drug Administration was asserting that there was no real threat to the nation's blood supply, in effect denying the need for such a test. It wasn't until 1985 that the federal government first developed a comprehensive plan for its response to AIDS,[3] and the first comprehensive AIDS spending bill did not emerge from Congress until three years later.

AIDS and the Fragmentation of Power

AIDS policy formulation was complicated by the distribution of governing responsibility among three levels of government: federal, state, and local. As the AIDS virus spread, it became clear that a response would involve a variety of agencies across all three levels. Combating a disease like AIDS involves *epidemiological investigation* to keep track of the incidence of the disease; *medical research* to discover causes, cures, and vaccines; *health education* to foster prevention and discourage irrational discrimination against victims; and *treatment* for those already afflicted—with AIDS this means long-term care for increasingly disabled patients.

In the United States traditional issues of public health, such as health education, sanitation, and immunization, are the responsibility of the several states. Much of this work is delegated by the states to local governments, usually county health departments. Some local governments—the city and county of San Francisco, for example— responded relatively early and aggressively to AIDS; most, like Los Angeles County, did not. The difference between the two California metropolises was partly a reflection of different political pressures in each city, but a structural difference was also important. A coordinated response was facilitated by San Francisco's status as a consolidated city and county government. Los Angeles represents the more common pattern, in which the city government is distinct from and often at odds with the county government, making any response more difficult.

At the state level, the states with the largest number of AIDS cases responded sooner and more aggressively, but among these states, different patterns emerged. In California, for example, early AIDS budget allocations emphasized research; in New Jersey

The seriousness of the AIDS epidemic led to efforts to locate potentially vulnerable people rather than waiting for them to turn up at a local hospital. Here outreach workers in Philadelphia distribute condoms and bleach kits (to sterilize needles) to a person they have come to know in their daily work on the streets. *(Harvey Finkle/Impact Visuals)*

efforts focused on prevention and treatment. Such choices reflect a multitude of idiosyncratic details that confront policymakers. (For example, the primary medical research unit of the University of California is in San Francisco—a city hard-hit by AIDS. Much of the California money for AIDS research went to the University of California.)

The policy questions of federalism and AIDS are often constitutional questions as well. During the second half of the 1980s, many state and local governments grappled with proposals to mandate HIV testing for some or all citizens, to mandate the public release of otherwise confidential medical tests in HIV cases, and even to require the isolation of HIV victims. Fortunately, the general legislative response to such proposals has been negative, limiting regulatory activity to "mandatory reporting of AIDS infection, protecting the confidentiality of individuals with AIDS, mandatory HIV antibody testing of all blood donors, general public education, and risk group education."[4] But these policies were developed one by one, as cities, counties, and states made individual policy choices.

Funding the Response to AIDS

In the United States the allocation of resources for public policy is complicated by the traditional American preference for private initiative over government action. This preference means that public agencies sometimes choose not to address certain problems or try to structure public incentives for private initiatives instead of direct public action. The American health-care system is a clear example of this tradition. With a few significant exceptions, health care in the United States is an individual rather than a social responsibility. Most people in the United States pay for their health care through employer or individual health insurance plans. In keeping with this pattern, no federal program has been developed for dealing with the very substantial costs of caring for AIDS patients. Most of these costs are borne by private health insurers, state Medicaid programs, local government-supported public hospitals, and the patients themselves. Thus the choice not to act, not to fund AIDS care separately, has had a dramatic secondary impact on policy choices in other programs.

Furthermore, though again with significant exceptions, medical research is a private rather than a public task in the United States. The development of new medicines, for example, is undertaken almost exclusively by drug companies and nonprofit organizations. The federal government affects those expenditures generally through its policies on drug testing and approval (see Chapter 15) and sometimes specifically, as when Congress passed special legislation in response to a threatened swine flu epidemic in 1976 limiting the liability of vaccine manufacturers. (In that case the vaccine proved more problematic than the disease.) The National Cancer Institute was instrumental in the development of the early AIDS treatment AZT, but Burroughs-Wellcome manufactures it. Two newer AIDS drugs, ddI and ddC, are made by Bristol-Myers Squibb and Hoffman–La Roche, respectively. These private drug companies have the responsibility of gaining FDA approval for their AIDS drugs. Depending on private initiative certainly compounds the complexity of policymaking.

Even when public funding is made available for a policy response in the United States, it is frequently funneled through private organizations. Nonprofit community organizations develop policy proposals according to more or less specific government funding guidelines. In most cases these organizations are not funded exclusively by a single government source but draw on a variety of public and private funds. Some of the earliest, most sustained, and most effective responses to the AIDS crisis have come from this sort of community organization—the Shanti Project in San Francisco, for example, or the Gay Men's Health Crisis in New York.

History also had an impact on federal AIDS funding policy. In 1982, as AIDS was gaining recognition, the U.S. economy was stuck in a severe recession. Back in 1978, Jimmy Carter had begun a buildup of defense forces that was accelerated under Ronald Reagan, taking a larger share of the discretionary budget. In 1981, Congress passed a significant tax cut. The combination of all of these factors meant that funding for new programs, even politically popular ones, was hard to come by. It was a very bad time for a new epidemic.

AIDS and Policy Reactions

Response to public policy is rarely straightforward and predictable. When, as with AIDS, a large set of complex and sometimes contradictory policies is involved, a certain number of side effects are bound to occur. For example, although AIDS could not be transmitted under the normal conditions of a blood donation, the AIDS scare kept some blood donors away. How many? That is hard to say. Survey responses on such questions may be unreliable; trends in numbers of donations have various explanations. More disturbing is the suggestion that once all blood donations were being screened for HIV, a certain number of donors at risk for AIDS were seeking a free, low-visibility HIV test.* Thus the testing might actually have encouraged more infected blood into the blood donation system for a time. The expansion of opportunities for free, anonymous HIV tests should counteract this tendency, but the agencies handling blood donations are often not the agencies in charge of free screening. One agency must develop policy in coordination with another.

Consider two other controversial policy responses to AIDS: publicly provided, free, sterile needles to slow the spread of AIDS resulting from shared needles among intravenous drug users and free condoms at public high schools to slow the transmission of AIDS through casual sex among teens. Intense vocal opposition to such programs has been raised, charging that the government was encouraging and abetting illegal or immoral behavior. Proponents of these programs argue that in both cases the frequency of the behavior (taking drugs and having sex) is not likely to increase because of the availability of safeguards, but for some people the question remains: Is the government sanctioning behaviors that ought to be prohibited outright?

AIDS Policy: The Contribution of Individuals and Groups

The public response to AIDS in the United States, like all public policy, has been the result of a large number of individuals in and out of government who decided to make this issue their own. Some of these, like former U.S. Surgeon General C. Everett Koop, are well known. Others, like newspaper publisher Chuck Ortleb, playwright Larry Kramer, congressional aide and San Francisco activist Bill Kraus, and medical researcher Matilde Krim, are known only among specialized audiences. Many contribute to the creation of policy without even limited recognition. In studying public policy it is easy to fall into the language of institutional action—"the CDC did this," "Congress did that." Vast institutions have that effect, and with justification. Political behavior cannot simply be explained in individual terms. But particular individuals often have a noticeable impact on political outcomes, and the study of public policy must include attention to the *dramatis personae*.

In the struggle to raise the visibility of AIDS issues on the public agenda, group activism also played a very significant role. Groups such as the AIDS Coalition to Unleash Power (ACT-UP), which staged dramatic protests, helped to capture media attention and focus political energy and resources on this complex of issues. It was a particular source of irritation to AIDS activists that for several years President Reagan refused to use the term *AIDS* in public. In a way the president's refusal was a bow in

---

*Reporting on the French experience with AIDS, Michael Pollak writes, "It can be assumed that the introduction of systematic screening of blood products in mid-1985 stimulated many people at risk to donate blood in order to get a free test for HIV." Pollak's speculation is tied to a relatively high percentage of AIDS cases resulting from transfusion.[5]

COMPARATIVE PERSPECTIVE

AIDS Policy in Brazil

Culture and history play an important part in the public policy process. Brazilian AIDS policy is a case in point. Although cases of AIDS were identified in Brazil as early as 1982, the federal government in this South American nation was extremely slow to respond. The common media-reinforced image was that AIDS in Brazil was a problem only for wealthy homosexuals who traveled to New York or Paris and brought cases of the disease back to São Paulo or Rio de Janeiro. In the United States the first well-known person to die of AIDS was Hollywood leading man Rock Hudson, whose death in 1985 caused a major earthquake in public sentiment. The first well-known person to die of AIDS in Brazil was a famous fashion designer whose public lifestyle helped to create the Brazilian version of the myth that AIDS was a gay disease. Epidemiological data demonstrating the falseness of this image did not prevail against popular conceptions. To understand the spread of AIDS in Brazil and the lack of vigorous public response, look first at the two routes of transmission of the disease: sexual contact and blood contact.

Sexual Transmission Until recently, sexual roles in Brazil were defined more in terms of *atividade* (activity) and *passividade* (passivity) than in the categories common in Europe and the United States (homosexual, bisexual, heterosexual). "Passive" or effeminate males were subjected to strongly negative stigma that did not extend to males in active roles in same-sex relations. Hence sexual definition in Brazil was traditionally much more fluid than in the United States. One consequence of this fluidity has been the high rate of heterosexual transmission of AIDS in Brazil. A large number of men move easily into and out of same-sex activity without developing any particular identity as homosexual or bisexual. A related consequence of the fluidity of sexual identity is the relative absence of group activism comparable to gay liberation groups elsewhere. Gay activist groups in the United States (like the Gay Men's Health Crisis in New York) were instrumental in AIDS education efforts, in caring for AIDS patients, and in pressing for local, state, and federal action on AIDS. In the United States cooperation between activist groups increased their effectiveness. In Brazil there were fewer AIDS activist groups, and those that did exist were more diverse and less likely to cooperate. The first major organization of AIDS activists, GAPA (*Grupo de*

(Box continues on page 627)

Apoio à Prevenção à AIDS), got started only in late 1985 in São Paulo. The number and effectiveness of such groups in Brazil have increased over the past several years—a hopeful sign.

Blood Transmission In Brazil, blood donation is valued as a means of earning money rather than as a humanitarian gift. The resultant commercialized blood supply is drawn primarily from the poorest segments of society, where health risks of all sorts are generally higher. On top of this, the Brazilian blood supply has never been subjected to careful regulation. Attempts by the federal government to impose regulations in response to AIDS were initially of limited success, even resulting in the creation of a string of clandestine blood banks run by profiteers in direct defiance of government regulation. Policies to establish mechanisms to screen the Brazilian blood supply for HIV thus had to work against strong currents of history and culture. In contrast, in Great Britain, particularly since the establishment of the National Health system, blood donation has been seen in purely humanitarian terms. The United States presents a mixed case: Some central-city blood banks paid donors cash. Even voluntary donor programs were driven by in-kind inducements (donate now and be taken care of if you need blood later)—a practice abandoned by the American Red Cross and most other blood banks well before the advent of AIDS.

Political Transformations In addition to cultural differences in sexual activity and in motivations for giving blood, the AIDS crisis in Brazil has been played out against a very different political backdrop than in the United States. A twenty-year period of authoritarian military rule and failed demonstrations for a popularly elected president left vast numbers of Brazilians with little sense of political efficacy just as the epidemic was getting under way in the early 1980s. Even when a civilian government was installed in 1985, Brazil's foreign debt and general public health problems were large enough to make a few hundred deaths from AIDS seem relatively insignificant. But that year an executive order did establish an agency to deal with AIDS. The next year mandatory notification of AIDS cases was instituted. In 1987 legislation granted AIDS victims certain social benefits. And in 1988 the new constitution prohibited the commercialization of blood and blood products. After a slow start, Brazil's public policies to combat AIDS were gearing up.

Source: Richard G. Parker, "Responding to AIDS in Brazil," in Action on AIDS, *ed. Barbara A. Misztal and David Moss (Westport, Conn.: Greenwood Press, 1990).*

The Dutch campaign to promote safer sex reached into Amsterdam's well-known "Red Light" district. In 1988 AIDS workers handed out condoms and brochures on preventing the spread of the disease. (Barbara Walton/ AP/Wide World Photos)

the direction of other groups who preferred to keep AIDS lower on the national political agenda. As is usually the case with new public issues, there is conflict about how important the issue is relative to other issues—a question of obvious importance in the case of AIDS since some people feared that spending more money on AIDS research would reduce spending on research linked to other health problems.

The conclusion to be drawn from this brief look at the public policy response to AIDS is that policy in the United States is affected by a variety of complicating factors including federalism, the separation of powers, and the public-private split of our pluralist system. Each of these complications should be borne in mind throughout Part IV. Before turning to specific areas of policy, however, we should examine more generally some key questions about the policy process in the United States: how issues arise and are handled or processed and how policy is formulated, implemented, and evaluated.

How Issues Reach the Political Agenda

Many political scientists assert that the best guide to what government will do next year is what government does this year. In this view, the work of government most often proceeds by tiny steps, or increments: This incremental aspect builds conservatism into policymaking: Budgets go up or down slightly, policies are carried out with greater or lesser vigor—all within a well-established and clearly understood political framework.

Looking back over the development of the U.S. government's policymaking agenda, we can see that government functions arise to meet social needs and to cope with the requirements of coordination, order, stability, and growth. This growth often occurs piecemeal, step by step, over time.

The collapse of the Soviet Union and the end of the Cold War provide a telling example of the influence of past policy over present policymaking. From the end of the Second World War through 1990, the United States spent vast sums on a national defense aimed primarily at the Soviet Union. Despite evidence of serious weakening in the Soviet economy and unrest among the Soviet satellites in Eastern Europe during the 1980s, the Reagan administration pressed for ever-higher defense spending. Then in a thunderclap of international events, the Soviet empire and the Soviet Union itself were gone.

But a $300 billion annual defense expenditure can't just be turned off like the kitchen faucet. Those dollars represent a huge web of jobs, buildings and equipment, and investments, all tied to expectations for the future. Without recognizing any social guarantee of job or investment security, public policymakers must still take into account the damage to the general welfare from large-scale, rapid shifts in the economy. Human nature and the standard operating methods of bureaucracies naturally militate against such shifts. People like to keep their jobs, so they help to keep the agency in business, finding new tasks as necessary and redefining old ones. The Strategic Defense Initiative (SDI), known as "Star Wars," is a good example. Initially conceived as a defensive shield against Soviet nuclear attack, Star Wars had its defenders among academics on research funding; defense contractors, their employees, and investors; members of the military and civilian employees in the Pentagon; members of Congress and their staffs; and business owners and employees whose livelihood was tied to the ripple effect of Star Wars spending.

This vast army of humanity offers a pretty solid defense against the idea that with the disappearance of the Soviet threat, the Star Wars program ought simply to fade away. So new justifications are found for old weapons. SDI adopts "global protection against limited strikes" (GPALS) as its mission. Part of the hoopla over the great accuracy of Patriot missiles in the Persian Gulf War in 1992 was certainly associated with the need to demonstrate the utility of such weapon systems in the post–Cold War world. The Bush administration proposed spending $5.4 billion on SDI in fiscal 1993.

The ability of social and institutional inertia to project the status quo onto the future is not unlimited. Policy does change. Despite efforts to the contrary, the scaling back of the defense industry was already well under way as a contributing factor to the severe recession of 1990–1992. Although the incrementalism engendered by political pressures in a pluralistic system softens the blow, other forces press for change.

History reveals several drastic shifts in the government agenda. The Great Depression, which created massive unemployment and severe economic dislocations, gave rise to one such shift, in the form of the New Deal. And as we noted in Chapter 1, new

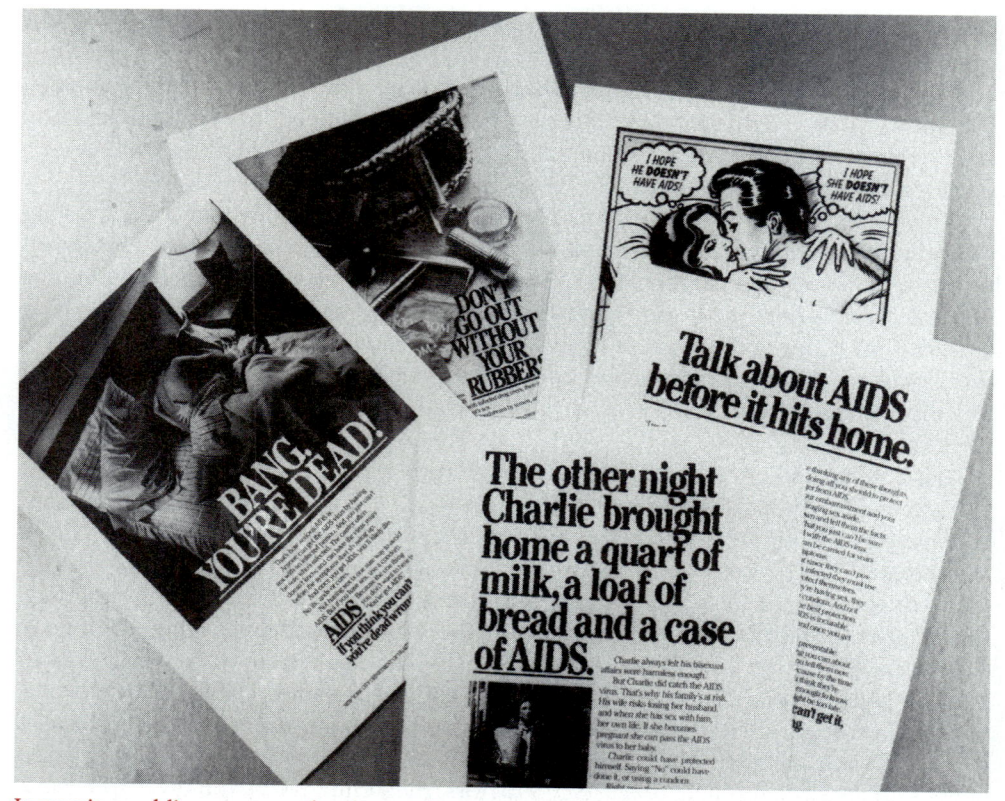

Increasing public awareness has been a key component of AIDS education. Here we see a variety of printed public service ads designed to heighten awareness about how to prevent the disease. *(AP/Wide World Photos)*

groups occasionally break into the arena of policymaking and put their needs on the public agenda. For years women and blacks struggled for the right to participate in setting the political agenda. Yet **incremental politics**—policymaking in steps or increments—describes much of the day-to-day business of government.

Sometimes government acquires new functions because of **spillover effects** in economic and social life. A spillover is an unintended side effect not included in the calculations of the original decision maker. In the absence of government environmental regulation, for instance, a manufacturer will calculate whether to build another factory by assessing the costs and benefits to the manufacturer without taking into account the very real costs (spillovers) that the factory may impose on the people and creatures living near it, such as rising health risks or a reduced quality of life. When water is polluted by industrial waste and people who drink it get sick, there is usually a call for government intervention. Occasionally, spillovers are caused by the government itself. The building of the interstate highway system in the United States stimulated the growth of suburbs and led to the decline of central cities after World War II. The decline of the cities in turn prompted further government action to deal with the new problems of urban areas.

How an issue is defined and its priority in relation to other issues stand at the core of political conflict. The candidate who effectively defines the issues in a campaign usually controls that campaign. Thus opponents battle over whether drug abuse should be treated as a health issue or a criminal justice issue. Is the Clean Air Act to be debated in terms of business regulation and competitiveness or in environmental terms? To cite another example, consider American competitiveness on world markets. Is this an issue of technology, requiring more investment in research and development? Is it a matter

Public policy is often shaped by the need for government to respond to large-scale economic problems. Here new members of the Civilian Conservation Corps (CCC) are about to take up their job of reforestation in the hills of Virginia. The time was the 1930s and the problem was the Great Depression and massive unemployment. *(AP/Wide World Photos)*

of unfair trade practices, requiring hard bargaining and perhaps protectionist legislation? Does it center on the financial markets, which fluctuate with the size of the American budget deficit? The definition of the problem will have an impact on the solutions policymakers pursue.

One of the most controversial public issues focuses on government itself and the types of functions it can legitimately take on. For example, some Americans maintain that government can legitimately set limits to fees that doctors or hospitals charge; others believe that such action goes beyond the appropriate limits for government intervention. In another policy sphere, some people believe that school officials, state legislatures, or Congress can legitimately prescribe that prayers be said in public schools. Others (including a majority of the Supreme Court) contend, however, that prayer in public schools violates constitutional principles and represents wrongful interference by government in the realm of individual conscience. These controversies center not on how government should respond to the issues involved but on whether government can legitimately act at all. For some Americans, government itself—its size, complexity, and power—constitutes one of the major public policy issues.

Processing Issues

Whose agenda becomes the prevailing agenda of politics? And how are issues dealt with once they become part of the national agenda? We now consider how our political system handles competing agendas and deals with issues.

Competing Agendas

We have been spotlighting the larger agenda of political life—the rough ordering of pressing political problems at a particular time. But there are also specific agendas held by interest groups, professional politicians, and the bureaucracy, among others. Conflicts among these various agendas flare up both in and out of government as each group struggles to have its own agenda prevail.

The issues that make up these competing agendas take shape in the measures that Congress acts on, the proposals made by the president, the activities of the federal bureaucracy, and the principal matters before the courts. Sometimes an issue in one political arena is picked up elsewhere: For example, abortion, a matter that Congress refused to address, was finally acted on by the courts. Official agendas may also differ or conflict. Conflicts often generate new issues that must be dealt with. Frequently, battles within the executive branch have clear and important effects on the shape of public policy. For example, competition among the army, air force, and navy for shares of a declining defense budget often stymies budget reductions and may encourage the continued development and acquisition of unnecessary weapon systems.

Dealing with Issues

Once an issue emerges, how is it resolved? Two significant factors come into play here: who participates in dealing with an issue and how much the scope of the issue is enlarged, making new policy options available.[6] New groups may seize on an issue that offers an opportunity to make successful demands for change. For example, the civil rights movement sparked the growth of ethnic consciousness, prompting new groups, such as Hispanics, women, and white ethnics, to make similar demands for attention and equality. The scope of an issue widens as the range of considerations being dealt with expands. In addressing the welfare issue, for example, policymakers might focus narrowly on one problem of the poor, such as adequate housing. Enlarging the scope of this issue might spur decision makers to examine a whole range of related matters—health, employment, even the distribution of wealth. The broader the scope, the wider the range of solutions that policymakers consider—and the more complex the issue.

Many issues reach the public agenda without ever being substantially resolved. Some issues are resolved only at a *symbolic* level. **Symbolic politics** aims at reassurance—giving the public the impression that the issue is being handled or resolved.[7] Consider the health warnings on cigarette packages: For years the federal government's action to counter the hazards of smoking did not go much beyond this symbolic act; in fact, tobacco farmers continue to enjoy generous government subsidies. Local governments, less subject to direct pressure from the tobacco industry and more responsive to the pressures of the antismoking lobby, were the first to enact significant smoking restrictions. Only recently has the balance at the federal level been moving away from the tobacco interests and in favor of more than symbolic government action.

Symbolic political actions can have real consequences, however. Frequently, symbolic policymaking causes public quiescence—people feel reassured and cease to agitate. Commissions established to investigate social problems, such as crime, pornography, or racism, are sometimes designed to buy off activists or at least to buy time for political actors. The recommendations of these commissions, although attended by much publicity, are frequently ignored. In some cases this symbolic demonstration of concern satisfies certain political groups. In other cases, people take the symbols seriously and expect further action to follow.

Issues can also be dealt with by being displaced, deferred, or diverted, rather than being completely resolved.[8] **Displaced issues** are those that flare up and then fade from public view, replaced by other issues or fragments of the original issue. Protection of the U.S. flag was an urgent issue for a short time in 1989 following the Supreme Court's decision upholding a protester's right to burn one. President Bush called for a constitutional amendment to protect Old Glory; Congress passed the Federal Flag Protection Act of 1989 instead. But even though the Court subsequently struck down the new legislation, the issue soon passed from the front pages.

Deferred issues, by contrast, generally return in one form or another. The lack of any comprehensive national energy policy became an issue briefly during the oil shortage of 1973–1974, only to fade from the agenda. Another oil shortage in 1979 returned energy to the headlines, to fade again after oil flowed more freely and Carter administration energy proposals failed in Congress. But debates about energy policy will always come back.

Diverted issues, finally, are handled by calling for a reevaluation of the problems involved. Sometimes the public focus is shifted from the issue itself to a debate over various government-initiated solutions; this has happened in the area of health policy. At other times the issue becomes whether government ought to be involved in a particular area at all: Should there be federal action to deal with abortion, pornography, or inner-city unemployment? Also, particular policies spawned by the original issue may replace that issue as the focus of debate. In the policy debate over school desegregation, for instance, the pros and cons of busing took center stage rather than the drive for desegregation itself.

Policy Formulation and Implementation

When policymakers conceptualize problems and discuss alternative positions, ideological factors enter political debate. One group's solution constitutes a mere gesture to another. Let us now examine how policymakers develop proposals for action and implement those proposals.

Proposals for Action

As we have already seen, proposals for public policy come from many sources. Interest groups concerned with an issue commonly approach their allies in Congress or the administration with specific proposals. Government bureaucracies in the executive branch may also advance policy proposals; in fact, it is part of their job to do so. Privately financed research institutes, or "think tanks," can also originate new policy ideas. Individual legislators and legislative committees or groups develop new policy proposals or refine the proposals offered by others. The courts also lay a powerful role in the process of policy formulation. Only through court decisions were standards established for school desegregation, legislative reapportionment, and criminal justice procedures, for example. Another source of policy proposals—perhaps the most influential one—is the president, who has increasingly become the focus of government leadership.

The alternatives may or may not lead to new policies. Many items have been on the public agenda for years, even decades, without being resolved; they are "nibbled at" rather than dealt with in any thoroughgoing manner. The chaotic state of health policy in the United States exemplifies this political stalemate or nonresolution. Most often issues remain unresolved when interest groups marshal enough power to thwart

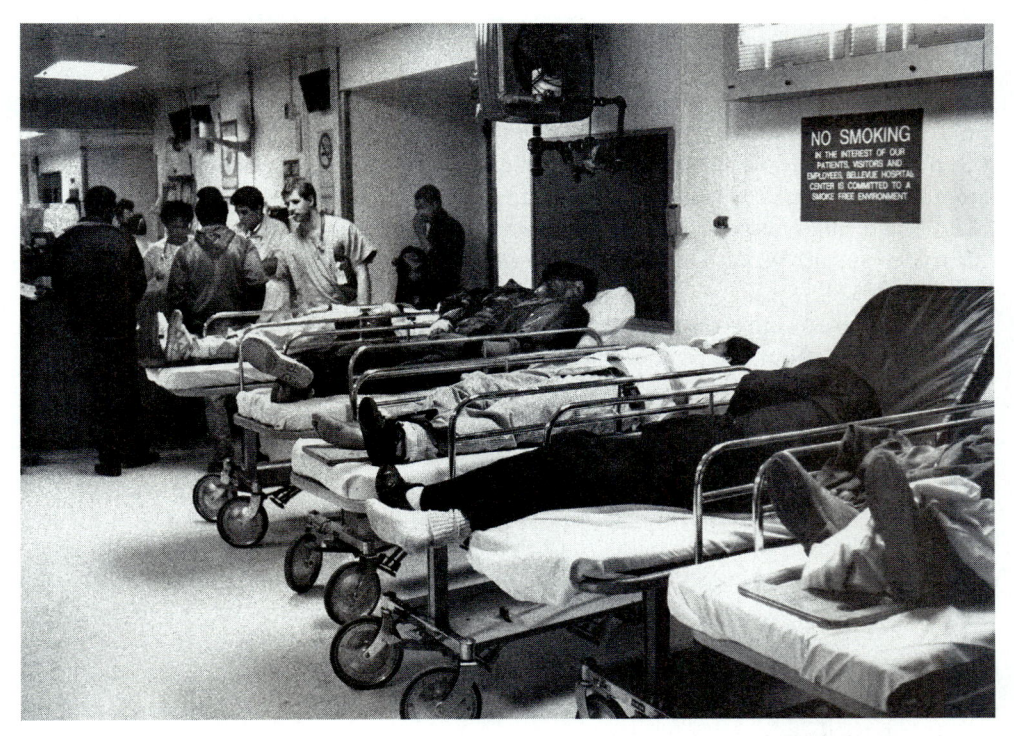

Long-standing problems of public policy do not necessarily get solved. The distribution of health-care resources in the United States has been a chronic problem for decades, and yet many of the difficulties involved have remained resistant to change—and have worsened in recent years. An overcrowded emergency room is testimony to the persistent stalemate in health-care policy. *(George Cohen/Impact Visuals)*

bold action or when confusion or conflict stand in the way of decisive policymaking. The alternatives may be there, but none can be chosen. Instead, incrementalism persists.[9]

In formulating policy, decision makers must balance what needs to be done with what can realistically be accomplished. To enact any wide-ranging piece of legislation, diverse elements must find it acceptable. Here the law of *anticipated reactions* applies.[10] After assessing the expected reactions, policy formulators shape proposals to fit with what is considered possible. This idea of politics as the "art of the possible" is considered a basic, realistic approach to political life. Yet sometimes it is all too easy to argue that nothing is possible at a particular time in a particular branch of the government. The real art in the art of the possible lies in sensing how far current arrangements can be modified by determined action. This can be a hard judgment to make—often only a crisis or large-scale mass action makes possible what was previously beyond the realm of possibility.

Implementation

The process of policy implementation is often overlooked. Most citizens assume that once a bill is passed and a policy has been adopted, the political battles are over and the problems are solved. But implementation presents difficulties of its own. For example, new policies are often phrased in very vague terms. Just what do expressions like "the public interest or convenience," "maximum feasible participation," or "fairness" mean? When a policy is implemented, specifics must be attached to such vague terms.

Implementation also requires information. Very often policymakers simply don't know enough about the conditions in which policies will be carried out. One of the difficulties confronting the Occupational Safety and Health Administration (OSHA), for example, is the huge number of potentially dangerous substances found in workplaces. And governments often look foolish when attempting to carry out ill-conceived policies. When the Kennedy administration tried to overthrow the Cuban government of Fidel Castro by launching the Bay of Pigs invasion in 1961, the result was what one observer called "a perfect fiasco."[11] In this case intelligence estimates turned out to be drastically wrong. Inaccurate information can lead to disaster not only in the foreign policy arena but also in education, housing, welfare, and many other public policy sectors. Often government cannot accurately anticipate the effects of its own actions.

Bear in mind as well that political activity continues during the implementation process. Interest groups lobby actively throughout this stage, trying to shape the decisions of the bureaucrats who implement policy. And sometimes administrative agencies resist new policies. It took a federal circuit court order in 1987 to force OSHA to establish safety and health rules concerning the availability of drinking water and sanitation facilities for migrant workers. There was never any question about the need for such facilities, and evidence showed that fewer than half the farms in America employing eleven or more migrant workers provided drinking water, toilets, and handwashing facilities for these workers. But pressure from agricultural employers kept the rules from being issued in spite of fourteen years of urging by farmworkers' representatives.[12] Even after a final rule was established, the politics of implementation continued. No rule is stronger than the mechanism for enforcing it. The enforcement of workplace safety rules is dependent on effective inspection, for which funding and personnel are routinely inadequate.

Policy Evaluation

In recent years serious attempts have been made to evaluate the effects of public policies. It is important to know, for example, whether efforts to control water pollution are really having any impact or whether occupational health and safety measures are achieving the intended results. Evaluation can give policymakers a sense of the successes and failures of policymaking and thereby help in formulating new guidelines.

Yet systematic evaluations of public policies are often difficult to make and frequently require controversial judgments.

Policies are often carried out haphazardly or, once implemented, grow in an uncontrolled fashion, further complicating the effort to evaluate them. Even when rigorous methods of assessment are conscientiously applied, values and ideologies can cloud the evaluation. For example, to some observers the Great Society programs of the Johnson administration stand as an obvious and almost predetermined failure, whereas others regard them as a reasonable success.[13] In dispute here are not the facts but rather the perspective taken in judging them. Objective methods of evaluation are helpful, but they cannot substitute for political judgment, which figures in ethical factors as well.

Much policy evaluation is still completely unsystematic. Such "seat of the pants" judgments, however, often represent the best we can do in the absence of more objective methods.

The Boundaries of Policymaking

In the United States there are certain limits beyond which policymaking is unlikely to venture. Most fundamentally, there is no real debate over whether the distribution of wealth and economic power is equitable, fair, or democratic. A strong consensus holds that the current capitalistic society, which allows for a large measure of economic inequality, is a "good" society. As we noted in Chapter 2, the absence of a viable political left has kept this issue off the political agenda. In addition, the Constitution sets limits to policy debate. The fundamental structure of the nation, with the fragmentation of power and the preference for private action, is unlikely to come up for debate very soon. Various aspects of our constitutional form of government have come under fire from time to time, as we will see in the following chapters. But the possibility of radical change is effectively kept out of serious political debate.

In spite of these apparent boundaries of policymaking, it is wrong to assume that the nation will not experience profound change, both self-generated and imposed by events beyond our making. A glance at a map shows that the world is a very different place in 1993 from what it was when the previous edition of this textbook appeared in 1989. The unquestioned verities of an entire generation where blown away like so many dried leaves. So suggestions that certain propositions are simply beyond the pale should always be examined skeptically.

CONCLUSIONS

For students of democracy, an important question about public policy is who controls the process over the long term. Where does consensus exist? What questions does this consensus leave out? How is influence exercised in the policy process, and for whose benefit? Do some groups find it impossible to be heard effectively? Are some important interests systematically excluded? If decisions are made by a few, if large numbers of people are excluded or ignorant, if the public interest plays little role in decisions, a democrat has cause for worry.

Democracy does not come easily. In the policy discussions to follow, consider how well most people grasp the main dimensions of the issues. Are most of us reasonably well informed? Do we *want* to know more? Can we trust that the people in authority have a firm grasp of the issues underlying public policy?

It takes more than knowledge, of course, to create a democratic public and to provide an intelligent dialogue in public life. Among policymakers we also hope to find a firm commitment to democratic values, a sense of equality, a good measure of fairness, and a willingness to involve the public in policy debate. In reading the policy chapters, ask yourself how democratic these debates sound. Are our leaders guided by a clear commitment to a democratic ethic?

Glossary Terms

acquired immune deficiency syndrome (AIDS)
agenda setting
deferred issues
displaced issues
diverted issues
human immunodeficiency virus (HIV)
implementation
incremental politics

legitimation
policy evaluation
policy formulation
resource allocation
response (to policy)
spillover effects
symbolic politics

Notes

[1] Charles H. Levine, B. Guy Peters, and Frank J. Thompson, *Public Administration: Challenges, Choices, Consequences* (Glenview, Ill.: Scott, Foresman, 1990), chap. 4.

[2] On the public response to AIDS, see Randy Shilts, *And the Band Played On: Politics, People, and the AIDS Epidemic* (New York: St. Martin's Press, 1987).

[3] James Kinsella, *Covering the Plague: AIDS and the American Media* (New Brunswick, N.J.: Rutgers University Press, 1989), p. 22.

[4] A. E. Benjamin and Philip R. Lee, "Public Policy, Federalism, and AIDS," in *AIDS: Principles, Practices, and Politics*, ref. ed. (Washington, D.C.: Hemisphere, 1989), p. 491.

[5] Michael Pollak, "AIDS Policy in France: Biomedical Leadership and Preventive Impotence," in *Action on AIDS*, ed. Barbara A. Misztal and David Moss (Westport, Conn.: Greenwood Press, 1990), p. 82.

[6] E. E. Schattschneider, *The Semisovereign People* (New York: Holt, 1975).

[7] Murray Edelman, *Politics as Symbolic Action* (New York: Academic Press, 1971).

[8] Robert Eyestone, *From Social Issues to Public Policy* (New York: Wiley, 1978).

[9] On the role of leadership in this process, see R. T. Nakamura and Frank Smallwood, *The Politics of Policy Implementation* (New York: St. Martin's Press, 1980), chap. 4.

[10] See Schattschneider, *The Semi-sovereign People*, chaps. 2, 3.

[11] Irving L. Janis, *Groupthink* (Boston: Houghton Mifflin, 1982), chap. 2.

[12] William Glaberson, "Is OSHA Falling Down on the Job?" *New York Times*, August 2, 1987, sec. 3, p. 1.

[13] On the negative side, see Peter Steinfels, *The Neoconservatives: The Men Who Are Changing America's Politics* (New York: Simon & Schuster, 1979); on the positive side, see John E. Schwartz, *America's Hidden Success* (New York: Norton, 1983).

SELECTED READINGS

For a good general **introduction to public policy**, see Carl E. Van Horn, Donald C. Baumer, and William T. Gormley, Jr., *Politics and Public Policy* (Washington, D.C.: Congressional Quarterly Press, 1989). For more detail, see David B. Robertson and Dennis R. Judd, *The Development of American Public Policy: The Structure of Policy Restraint* (Glenview, Ill.: Scott, Foresman, 1989). More focus on phases of the public policy process marks both Stuart S. Nagel, *Policy Studies: Integration and Evaluation* (Westport, Conn.: Greenwood Press, 1988); and Talib Younis, ed., *Implementation in Public Policy* (Brookfield, Vt.: Gower, 1990).

For **economic analyses** of public policy, see Harvey A. Averch, *Private Markets and Public Intervention: A Primer for Policy Designers* (Pittsburg: University of Pittsburg Press, 1990); and Claude Henry, *Microeconomics for Public Policy: Helping the Invisible Hand* (New York: Oxford University Press, 1989).

To learn more about **public policy and AIDS**, start with Randy Shilts, *And the Band Played On: Politics, People, and the AIDS Epidemic* (New York: St. Martin's Press, 1987); James Kinsella, *Covering the Plague: AIDS and the American Media* (New Brunswick, N.J.: Rutgers University Press, 1989); and Barbara Misztal and David Moss, eds., *Action on AIDS* (Westport, Conn.: Greenwood Press, 1990). See also Sandra Panem, *The AIDS Bureaucracy* (Cambridge, Mass.: Harvard University Press, 1988); *AIDS and the Third World*, 2nd ed. (London: Panos Institute, 1987); and Nancy F. McKenzie, ed. *The AIDS Reader: Social, Political, and Ethical Issues* (Cleveland, Ohio: Meridian Books, 1991). For opposing viewpoints on AIDS and social control issues, see Lynn Hall and Thomas Modi, eds., *AIDS* (San Diego, Calif.: Greenhaven Press, 1988).

For a **comparative perspective** on public policy, see Francis G. Castles, ed., *The Comparative History of Public Policy* (New York: Oxford University Press, 1989). Also useful is the two-volume *International Public Policy Sourcebook* (Westport, Conn.: Greenwood Press, 1989). Volume 1 is edited by Jack Paul DeSario and covers health and social welfare policies. Volume 2 is edited by Fredric N. Bolotin and covers education and environmental policies.

OLD COURT SAVINGS & LOAN

CHAPTER EIGHTEEN

MANAGEMENT OF THE ECONOMY

Competing Interests

CHAPTER OUTLINE

History of Economic Management

MERCANTILISM
LAISSEZ-FAIRE AND THE GROWTH OF REGULATION
CONTROLLED CAPITALISM
THE POSTWAR EXPERIENCE

Tools of Economic Intervention

MICROECONOMICS AND REGULATION
MACROECONOMIC POLICY

The Politics of Economics: The Supply-Side Debate

REAGONOMICS
EVALUATING THE SUPPLY-SIDE EXPERIMENT

Emerging Problems

TAX EQUITY AND TAX EXPENDITURES
FEDERAL BUDGET DEFICITS
THE DECLINE IN INDUSTRIAL POWER

ECONOMICS HAS OFTEN BEEN REFERRED TO AS "THE DISMAL science."* This can actually be taken as a compliment, for most economists like to think of their discipline as a science. The "dismal" part does not please economists, however. One "dismal" aspect of economics is that it deals with scarcity—with alternative ways of allocating resources. It is also filled with numbers and calculations. Economists turn flesh-and-blood human beings and their busy social and commercial lives into dollars and cents and such abstractions as supply and demand. Economists ascend from the real world of people—sweating and working, haggling in the marketplace—to the airy (but usually arid) realm of inflation and recession, money markets and gold standards.

What does economics have to do with democratic concerns? The answer may well be *everything*. Economic matters are intricately intertwined with democratic aspirations. Some students of democratic evolution advance the theory that a certain level of economic development is a prerequisite for the establishment and maintenance of a modern demo-

---

*Expression first used by British writer Thomas Carlyle (1795–1881).

641

cratic society.[1] Historically, they argue, poor and economically primitive societies tend to be authoritarian, intolerant, and politically stagnant. Democratic politics usually evolves only when affluence increases, education is made available to the masses, urbanization helps to widen people's horizons, communications improve, and greater sophistication fosters tolerance and a spirit of compromise.

From another perspective, however, economic crises can sometimes precipitate the decline and destruction of democracies. Consider how the catastrophic economic conditions of the 1920s and 1930s helped to promote fascist movements in many nations. A drastic economic decline in Germany, for example, set the stage for the Nazis' political successes in the 1930s.

History and theory aside, how do economic matters mesh with issues of democratic life in our society today? We must recognize that all public policymaking has economic dimensions. Through the economy, citizens gain rewards and suffer deprivations. In this chapter we focus specifically on the mechanisms of economic management and the ramifications of economic policy for American democracy by spotlighting how the U.S. economy has been and is being managed, the tools of economic intervention, the politics of economics, and emerging problems in the U.S. political economy.

History of Economic Management

By taking a historical perspective we can gain important insights into how the U.S. government currently manages the economy. In the course of U.S. history, the government has adopted three major approaches to economic policy: **mercantilism**, which stressed direct government intervention in the economy; **laissez-faire capitalism**, in which government gave business a relatively free hand; and today's **controlled capitalism**, in which government intervenes to some extent to regulate the economy. By no means, then, is government management of the economy a twentieth-century phenomenon; in the broadest sense, management of the economy is as old as the nation itself.[2] Let us now examine the four stages in the history of U.S. economic management: mercantilism, laissez-faire and the growth of regulation, controlled capitalism, and the years since World War II.

Mercantilism

The economic theory of mercantilism evolved in seventeenth-century Europe. In practice, mercantilism worked this way: The rulers of nation-states such as England and Holland established government-chartered corporations and encouraged their growth through subsidies, or financial support. The corporations were protected from competition through grants of monopoly status, and their output, production, and distribution were extensively controlled. Colonies were formed overseas to provide raw materials for these government-chartered corporations and markets for exports. In

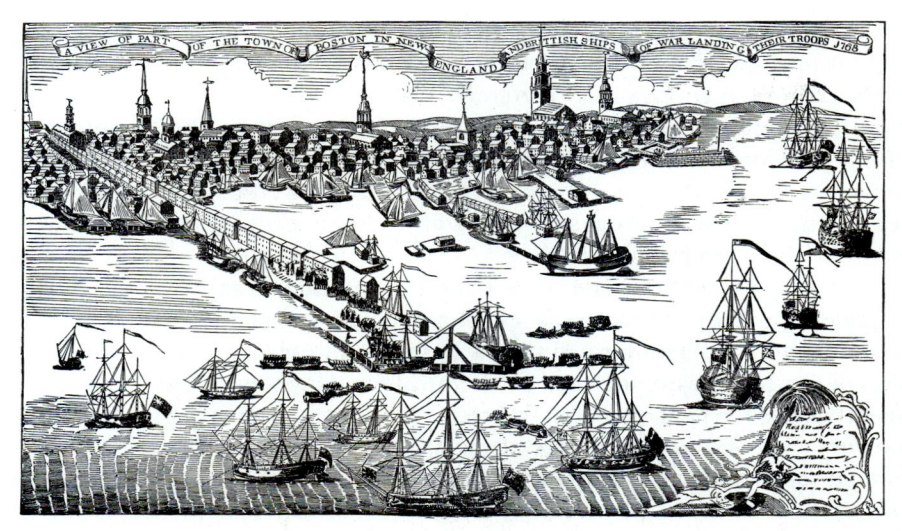

Government control of the economy is at least as old as this print of Boston Harbor. Indeed, mercantilism, a system of economic control through government-chartered corporations, was largely responsible for creating the North American colonies. The British warships depicted here were part of the investment required to keep the outlying economic activities from becoming independent profit centers. *(The Bettmann Archive)*

exchange for these privileges, the semipublic corporations gave the government a share of their profits. Mercantilism benefited both government and business, but profits were often made at the expense of the general public, in nation and colony alike.

The American colonies rebelled against the taxation policies and regulations imposed by the British government. In developing their own political economy, however, Americans eventually adopted many of the same mercantilist policies that aided business growth at the expense of farmers, artisans, and laborers.[3] The U.S. government imposed high taxes on imported goods (protective tariffs), gave subsidies to business, and granted monopoly powers to a national bank. Although the Founders disagreed over how extensive government control of economic affairs should be, consensus held that the protection and promotion of propertied interests was one of the vital functions of government.

Laissez-Faire and the Growth of Regulation

By the mid-nineteenth century, laissez-faire capitalism had replaced mercantilism as the favored economic policy of Western governments. Underlying laissez-faire capitalism was a belief that national wealth would be increased if government restrictions on economic activity were kept to a minimum. In theory this policy called for the abolition of such mercantilist strategies as government-backed corporate monopolies, detailed regulatory laws, and high protective tariffs. In practice the laissez-faire movement "democratized" capitalism by throwing open to all comers sectors of the economy previously restricted to the government-chartered corporations. The new, privately held corporations that emerged under the laissez-faire doctrine wanted to be free of competition from government enterprises and from the detailed regulations imposed on the previously chartered companies. President Andrew Jackson (1829–1837) endorsed the movement and gave it a substantial boost with his successful fight to close down the government-chartered National Bank.

Ironically, however, as the laissez-faire period progressed, competition declined and monopolies returned. The more successful corporations expanded, either buying out their competitors or driving them out of business. In essence, then, the public monopolies of the 1820s were replaced by the private monopolies of the 1880s. This development sparked vehement public protest, particularly from farmers and small business owners, and led to the passage of regulatory legislation. In the 1880s many states, bowing to the demands of western farmers and eastern merchants, imposed restrictions on the rates charged by railroads. Regulatory legislation on the federal level, however, came more slowly because of doubts about its constitutionality. The first federal regulatory commission, the Interstate Commerce Commission, was established in 1887. In 1890, Congress passed the Sherman Antitrust Act, which was designed to prevent monopolies and trusts (the pooling of resources by several companies for the purpose of controlling a market). Only in a few cases, however, was the act vigorously enforced.[4]

Controlled Capitalism

U.S. economic policy changed course again around the turn of the twentieth century as policymakers embraced controlled capitalism, an economic doctrine that is still evolving today. Rather than dismantling large corporations or allowing them to operate unfettered, the government now creates regulatory agencies (see Chapter 15) to oversee and control their activities. Under controlled capitalism, public interests are protected by these regulatory agencies from blatant abuses by business and corporate interests, while private capital is guaranteed a more stable business environment in which to make profits. In addition, the federal government assumes many of the regulatory activities formerly handled by the states. Federal regulatory agencies multiplied first during the Progressive era (1900–1917) and again during the New Deal of the 1930s as the nation tried to cope with the Great Depression. (A **depression** is a severe economic crisis marked by a downward spiral in which investment, hiring, pay, consumption, and savings all plummet at once, leading to further declines. A **recession** is a milder, shorter version of the same tendency.) The Great Depression, an economic catastrophe, marked a turning point in economic management. As such, it is worth examining in greater detail.

There was no single cause for the Great Depression, which swept over all industrialized nations and lasted for close to a decade. Its onset is usually linked to the

Consternation on Wall Street: Black Tuesday, October 29, 1929. The stock market collapse marked the onset of the Great Depression but was merely one factor among a variety of economic imbalances that had developed during the 1920s, including industrial overproduction and marginalized investment. The stock market crash of October 19, 1987, also created consternation, but it was not part of a general economic collapse, partly because of federal regulation of investment. *(UPI/Bettmann)*

collapse of the U.S. stock market in October 1929. But the crash merely brought into sharp relief how severely skewed economic life had become. The 1920s saw a vast expansion of credit buying in the United States and extensive land and stock speculation. Consumers and investors shared a supreme confidence that the high-rolling days of the "Roaring Twenties" would never end. Speculators' "get rich quick" schemes and consumers' overreliance on credit combined with several larger trends to undermine the economy. As the decade progressed, the production of goods increased more rapidly than the incomes required to buy those goods. The distribution of income in the United States also grew increasingly unequal during the 1920s: In 1929 the richest 1 percent of the population received as much income as the poorest 42 percent. These striking economic imbalances propelled the nation into a depression.

Never before had the United States experienced an economic crisis of such scope and proportions. Gross investment fell 35 percent from 1929 to 1930 and 35 percent more from 1930 to 1931. In the next year it fell by 88 percent. From 1929 to 1933 gross national product (the value of all goods and services produced in the nation) dropped by 29 percent, construction declined by 78 percent, and unemployment rose from 3.2 percent to 24.9 percent.[5]

> ## THE GREAT DEPRESSION, CITY AND COUNTRY
>
> ### Ben Isaacs, Owner of a Small Business
>
> I was in business for myself, selling clothing on credit, house to house. . . .
>
> All of a sudden, in the afternoon, October, 1929, . . . I was going on my business and I heard the newspaper boys calling, running all around the streets and giving news and news: stock market crashed, stock market crashed. It came out just like lightning. . . .
>
> We lost everything. It was the time I would collect four, five hundred dollars a week. After that, I couldn't collect fifteen, ten dollars a week. I was going around trying to collect enough money to keep my family going. It was impossible. Very few people could pay you. Maybe a dollar if they would feel sorry for you or what.
>
> We tried to struggle along living day by day. Then I couldn't pay the rent. I had a little car, but I couldn't pay no license for it. I left it parked against the court. I sold it for $15 in order to buy some food for the family. I had three little children. . . .
>
> I didn't want to go on relief. Believe me, when I was forced to go to the office of the relief, the tears were running out of my eyes. I couldn't bear myself to take money from anybody for nothing. If it wasn't for those kids—I tell you the truth—many a time it came to my mind to go commit suicide. Than go ask for relief. But somebody has to take care of those kids. . . .
>
> ### Oscar Heline, a Farmer from Iowa
>
> The farmers became desperate. It got so a neighbor wouldn't buy from a neighbor, because the farmer didn't get any of it. It went to the creditors. And it wasn't enough to satisfy them. . . . First, they'd take your farm, then they took your livestock, then your farm machinery. Even your household goods. And they'd move you off. The

(Box continues on page 647)

Before the Depression, most Americans rejected the idea that government could or should have a hand in shaping the nation's economic life. The New Deal remedies proposed by President Franklin Roosevelt's administration in the 1930s, however, involved large-scale government intervention in the economy. By reducing taxes, starting new programs, and creating new jobs, Roosevelt and his advisers hoped to infuse new life into the economy. The concept of regulating the business cycle by deficit spending—by allowing the government to spend more money than it takes in—was championed by British economist John Maynard Keynes, whose views on economic policy had an enormous impact after 1930. This philosophy of economics, accordingly, is referred to as **Keynesian economics**.

Although it was once thought that there was no way for government to help to end a depression, increased government spending in the late 1930s and during World

farmers were almost united. We had penny auction sales. Some neighbor would bid a penny and give it back to the owner.

Grain was being burned. It was cheaper than coal. Corn was being burned. A county just east of here, they burned corn in their courthouse all winter. '32, '33. You couldn't hardly buy groceries for corn. It couldn't pay the transportation. In South Dakota, the county elevator listed corn as minus three cents. *Minus* three cents a bushel. If you wanted to sell 'em a bushel of corn, you had to bring in three cents. They couldn't afford to handle it. . . .

We had lots of trouble on the highway. People were determined to withhold produce from the market—livestock, cream, butter, eggs, what not. If they would dump the produce, they would force the market to a higher level. The farmers would man the highways, and cream cans were emptied in ditches and eggs dumped out. They burned the trestle bridge, so the trains wouldn't be able to haul grain. Conservatives don't like this kind of rebel attitude and aren't very sympathetic. But something had to be done. . . .

Some of the farmers with teams of horses, sometimes in trucks, tried to get through. He was trying to feed his family, trying to trade a few dozen eggs and a few pounds of cream for some groceries to feed his babies. He was desperate, too. One group tried to sell so they could live and the other group tried to keep you from selling so they could live. . . .

Through a federal program we got a farm loan. A committee of twenty-five of us drafted the first farm legislation of this kind thirty-five years ago. . . . New money was put in the farmers' hands. The Federal Government changed the whole marketing program. . . . People could now see daylight and hope. It was a whole transformation of attitude. You can just imagine. . . . (He weeps.). . . .

Source: Studs Terkel, Hard Times: An Oral History of the Great Depression *(New York: Pantheon, 1970).*

War II did draw the nation out of economic stagnation and bring about a return to high employment levels.

The New Deal experience marked a genuine watershed in U.S. history. Although some observers argued for a reduction in government involvement in and regulation of the economy after World War II, few talked of turning back the clock to the pre–New Deal situation.

The Postwar Experience

After pulling through the rigors of the Depression and World War II, the United States and the Western European nations entered a new phase of economic development.

During the 1950s and much of the 1960s, industrial democracies achieved unprecedented levels of affluence. Economic growth was rapid, but prices remained stable. The capitalist system, previously viewed as predestined to great cycles of boom and bust, was now propelling steady, sustained economic growth. And while the capitalist economies were driven by powerful forces, the system itself was still responsive to government intervention.[6]

The so-called age of affluence began to unravel in the late 1960s. Economic fluctuations became more unpredictable and growth more erratic. Throughout the 1970s both unemployment and inflation increased, a combination of economic ills that, according to accepted understanding, would not occur simultaneously. (Inflation occurs when "too much money chases too few goods," driving the price of goods up and hence the value of money down.) When both appeared in tandem, elected policymakers could not use the traditional remedies to eliminate either one. To decrease unemployment by pumping more money into the economy (by increasing government spending and decreasing taxes) would worsen already high inflation (and further boost interest rates). To decrease inflation by tightening up on money would drive even more people into unemployment. Neither strategy was politically feasible. By the end of the 1970s the combination of a stagnant economy and high inflation ("**stagflation**") presented what many experts considered an insurmountable problem.

The economic policies of the 1980s constituted an odd array of dramatic and in some ways contradictory initiatives. The Federal Reserve Board's aggressive attempt to reduce the money supply was designed to reduce high levels of inflation. Meanwhile, a dramatic tax reduction, engineered by the Reagan administration, was intended to stimulate business expansion by putting more money back into the hands of consumers and investors. However, the tax reduction was not matched by a reduction in overall government spending, so the federal government had to borrow heavily, competing with the private sector for scarce investment dollars.

Interest rates and inflation abated during a severe recession early in the 1980s, solving the problem of stagflation. Starting in 1983 the economy experienced a broad, long-term expansion that lasted through Reagan's second term and into the Bush administration. Supporters claimed success for the Reagan fiscal policies. But according to more skeptical observers, the expansion of the 1980s was fueled by the huge federal deficits—an unparalleled national borrowing binge. Personal and corporate borrowing also increased during the decade, labeled by some observers a "new gilded age." In 1990 the American economy slid into a recession. Although the decline was not as severe as in 1982, the country found it hard to recover from this downturn. A modest recovery in 1991 faltered, perhaps because the Federal Reserve, remembering the rampant inflation of the 1970s, did not act soon enough or forcefully enough to stimulate investment. But timid monetary policy was only part of the explanation. The fiscal response traditionally prescribed to get the economy out of a ditch—lower taxes and increased government spending—was frustrated by record deficits in 1991 and 1992, and the costs of the savings and loan bailout. In spite of the recession, many economic experts advised fiscal restraint. A second modest recovery seemed to be under way as

MANAGEMENT OF THE ECONOMY 649

British economist John Maynard Keynes advocated government intervention to smooth out the peaks and valleys of the business cycle. His prescriptions of deficit spending to stimulate the economy and excess taxation to slow it down could not cure the stagflation of the 1970s. *(UPI/Bettmann Newsphotos)*

the country limped toward the 1992 elections, but economic optimists found the public distrustful.

It is time that we turn to a more careful examination of the tools of governmental intervention in the economy to see why solutions to economic problems are not always clear and not always successful but nearly always controversial.

Tools of Economic Intervention

The United States, along with the Western European democracies, remains a capitalist nation characterized by private control of most of the economy. Yet in every industrial democracy the government now assumes much responsibility for the overall management of economic life. The reasons for this are numerous. For one thing, the public sector has grown so significantly that government itself has become one of the major forces in economic life. In most countries, government is the chief purchaser of goods and services, the largest distributor of income (through income maintenance programs and the jobs it provides), and the largest single borrower of money. Considering these factors, governments can hardly avoid taking a leading role in economic management. Then, too, modern economic theory, as well as political practice, promotes increased government involvement in the economy. The Great Depression convinced many economists and politicians that capitalist economies could not function successfully without government intervention. According to key policymakers, governments could help to stimulate employment and growth and keep prices stable. Finally, governments have become inextricably enmeshed in a set of financial relationships with the private economy—guaranteeing the safety of bank deposits, supporting home loans and payments to farmers, giving tax incentives to certain industries, and bolstering various segments of the economy.

For all these reasons, it would be virtually impossible for any democratic government to detach itself from economic affairs without disastrous consequences. So the real issues today are not whether government should intervene in the economy but rather how government can intervene most effectively, what interventions are most important, and who should gain and lose by this intervention. The tools of economic intervention fall into two large categories: **microeconomics** (issues that involve individual players or sectors in the economic system) and **macroeconomics** (issues that affect the whole economic system, like the supply of money and the cost of credit).

Microeconomics and Regulation

The tools of microeconomics are usually associated with regulatory agencies like the Federal Trade Commission and the Federal Communications Commission. Such regulation is intended to serve the public interest by increasing the effectiveness of the free market (for example, by enforcing truth in advertising so that consumers can make informed choices, or by using antitrust laws to maintain or increase competition in a particular sector of the economy) and sometimes by replacing market forces with a regulated monopoly, as in certain public utilities. Sometimes microeconomic regulation combines these two functions (maintaining a limited number of competitors, as in broadcast television and radio). Let us turn to a specific example.

For forty years the Civil Aeronautics Board (CAB) regulated airline passenger service in the United States. The CAB was abolished in 1984 as part of a general move to deregulate the American economy. As we saw in Chapter 15, concerns about passenger safety and convenience have surfaced from time to time since deregulation. In this chapter we can ask more direct economic questions about deregulation of the airlines. Is this sector of the economy now more efficient? Is the public interest better served? Even a decade after deregulation, the answers were not yet clear. Some facts are clear enough. The industry is increasingly dominated by a few giants while many of the oldest names in the business are now consigned to history. More passengers are flying now than ever, and periodic fare wars have offered substantial bargains to those able to meet certain schedule restrictions. But will the current shakeout leave passengers at the mercy of a handful of remaining carriers? At least one airline analyst—one of the original deregulators who has had the experience of trying to start an new airline in the period of nonregulation—has some fears.

Mark Kahan is still a proponent of deregulation—he's convinced that airline executives are in a better position to know what the public wants than government regulators are. The problem is not deregulation, Kahan says, but the unwillingness of the Reagan and Bush administrations to use antitrust laws to protect competition. He

MANAGEMENT OF THE ECONOMY 651

Headquarters of the European Economic Community (EEC) in Brussels, Belgium. Trade issues involving the United States and the EEC promise to be high on the agenda of future economic policymaking. Disputes in 1992 over French farm subsidies threatened to escalate into a retaliatory trade war when the United States imposed high tariffs on French white wine. *(Rick Gerharter/Impact Visuals)*

suggests addressing the anticompetitive features of reservations systems, the distribution of gates, and frequent-flyer programs without returning to full-fledged regulation.[7] Deregulation was based on false assumptions about the ability of new airlines to challenge established giants. When the industry is reduced to a few large competitors, will broad service and low fares be maintained? Can competition be preserved without re-regulation of the industry?

We now turn to macroeconomics—the factors that affect the entire economy.

Macroeconomic Policy

In the area of economic management, there is widespread agreement that democratic governments should pursue full employment, stable prices, and steady levels of economic growth. But what is the best means of achieving these economic goals? Here political observers have sharp differences of opinion. Should government spend more or reduce taxes? Expand the money supply or contract it? Worry more about inflation or about recession? About rising prices or rising unemployment? In addressing these difficult and complex questions, democratic governments can draw on several tools of macroeconomic management. These fall into the general categories of fiscal policy and monetary policy, which we now examine.

FISCAL POLICY When government decision makers adopt **fiscal policies**, they deliberately manipulate elements of the national budget to change the direction of the economy. Since government at all levels accounts for the expenditure of roughly 35 percent of the GNP in the United States and the federal government alone accounts for more than 20 percent, budgetary manipulations by the government clearly have major economic impacts (see **Figure 18-1**). Government can alter the budget in two ways: through spending policies and tax policies.

When government spends, it pumps money into, and thereby stimulates, the economy. According to Keynesian economics, there are times when government should *deliberately* spend more than it takes in. This produces a budget deficit in the short run, but by stimulating economic growth this so-called deficit spending eventually yields increased tax revenues, thereby eliminating the deficit. In addition, the theory goes, government spending creates employment opportunities and alleviates a good deal of human suffering. Government, then can counteract the worst effects of the business cycle by running a deficit when the economy is sluggish and taking in a surplus when the economy is booming. This approach is known as a countercyclical policy.

FIGURE 18-1

FISCAL 1992: A $1.52 TRILLION BUDGET

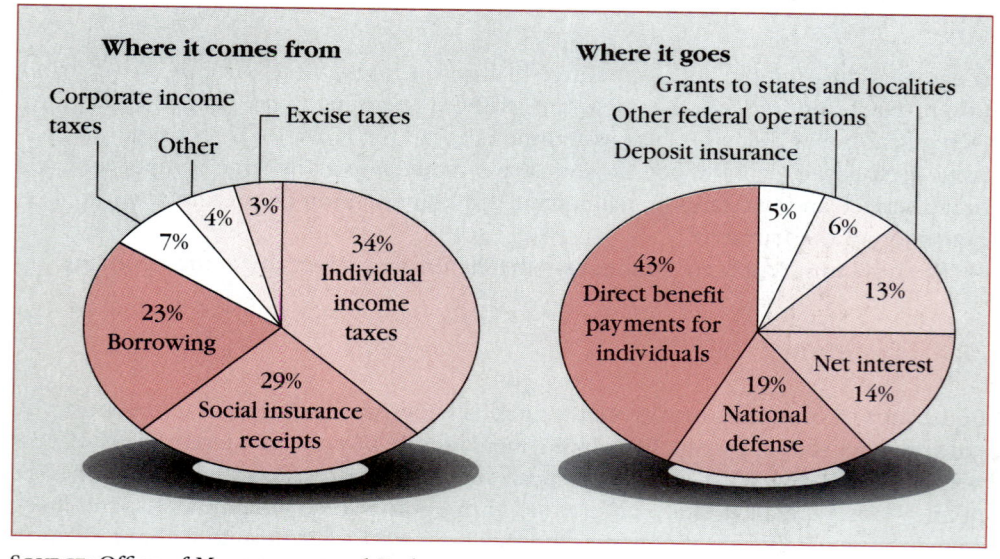

Where it comes from
- Corporate income taxes: 7%
- Other: 4%
- Excise taxes: 3%
- Individual income taxes: 34%
- Social insurance receipts: 29%
- Borrowing: 23%

Where it goes
- Grants to states and localities: 5%
- Other federal operations: 6%
- Deposit insurance: 13%
- Net interest: 14%
- National defense: 19%
- Direct benefit payments for individuals: 43%

SOURCE: Office of Management and Budget.

In practice, however, tinkering with the economy is never so simple. Political considerations play an important part in economic decisions. For example, governments usually avoid raising taxes or cutting back on programs that have substantial political support. Largely as a result, the federal budget has run a surplus only once in the last thirty years. Let us now probe the subtleties of spending policies and the tax system.

Spending Policies. The dictates of fiscal policy demand hard choices. Most basically, governments must set budget priorities. If spending is increased, will that mean more funds for national parks, more for highway construction, more for social security, or more for urban revitalization? Often all pressing priorities simply cannot be addressed at once. In the late 1960s, President Lyndon Johnson attempted to increase spending on the Vietnam War as well as on domestic programs. In doing so, he overstimulated the economy and paved the way for many of the economic problems of the 1970s. President Ronald Reagan sought to curtail federal expenditures overall while increasing spending for defense. These policy decisions forced deep cuts in social programs. Yet fiscal policy does not dictate *where* to expand the budget or to contract it. Such decisions reflect the larger priorities of the administration in office.

In addition, fiscal policymakers must work within substantial constraints. More than half of the national budget is fixed by past commitments, such as those to social security and pensions, interest on the national debt, and contractual obligations. The discretionary portion of the budget is relatively small, and decreasing (see **Figure 18-2**). Cutting the budget becomes more difficult as "fixed" costs (interest on the national debt, social security, and Medicare) increase (see Figure 18-2).

The Tax System. Policymakers also face many difficult decisions in formulating taxation policies. Which taxes should be raised or lowered—the individual income tax, corporate taxes, excise taxes (taxes on commodities)? If taxes are cut, who should receive the chief benefits? If they are raised, how should the burden be spread? Taxes can be used for more than simply raising revenue. A tax code can be used to regulate behavior—to encourage certain kinds of activities and discourage others. Through loopholes and "tax incentives," a tax code sometimes masks real government policy by allowing benefits and transfers of wealth indirectly and unobtrusively. What makes the tax system so complex, and genuine tax reform so difficult, is the large number of specific, diverse, and often conflicting interests that are embedded in the structure itself. Tax breaks, of course, do not necessarily thwart the public interest—many allowances built into the federal tax code serve legitimate public interests. Others do not. The Tax Reform Act of 1986 was originally billed as a means of eliminating from the tax code many special treatments and loopholes. In a process that one political scientist compared to cleaning encrusted barnacles off an old ship's hull, many special-interest tax breaks were removed from the tax code. But barnacles grow back. In the two years following the passage of the Tax Reform Act, more than 840 bills were introduced into either the House or the Senate to modify the act, nearly all of which involved reinstating tax breaks of one sort or another.[8] The process of reencrustation has continued since.

Today Americans pay a host of different taxes, including sales tax, property tax,

FIGURE 18-2

"MANDATORY" PROGRAMS ARE TAKING OVER THE BUDGET

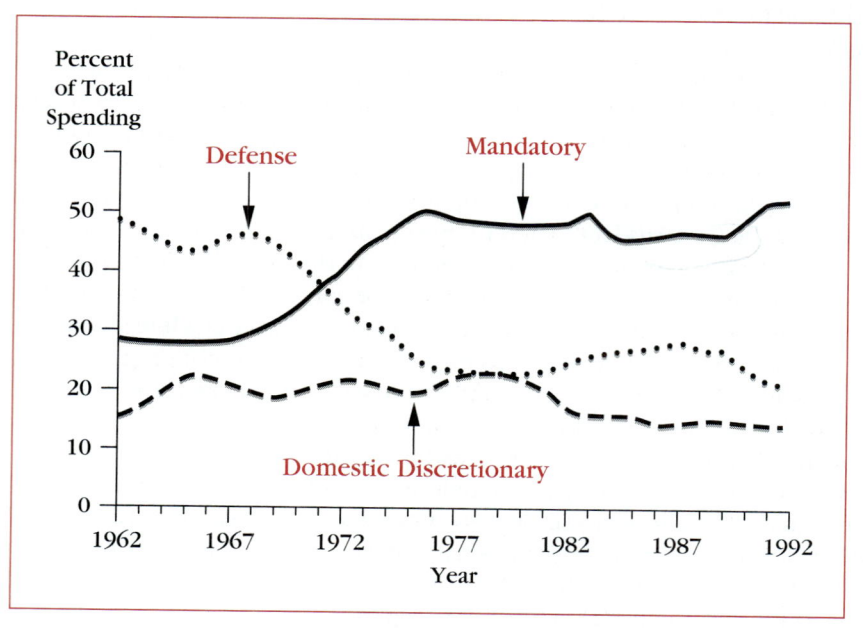

```
Percent
of Total
Spending
```

SOURCE: *The Budget*, 1992 Washington, D.C.: U.S. Government Printing Office, 1991

state and federal income taxes, and social security tax. Some of these are **progressive taxes**—that is, the rate of taxation is related to one's ability to pay. The federal income tax is theoretically a progressive tax, in which progressively higher rates are levied on peole with progressively higher incomes. Actual taxes paid, however, are far less progressive than the rates on paper. This stems from specific tax breaks built into the system. **Regressive taxes** have the opposite effect: They impose a higher-percentage tax on people with lower incomes. A sales tax on food is a regressive tax because lower-income people are likely to spend a higher percentage of their income on food than higher-income people. A **proportional (flat rate) tax** draws the same percentage of income from all income groups. In some ways the social security tax is a proportional levy; however, because it does not tax income beyond a certain point, wealthier taxpayers actually pay a lower percentage than middle-class taxpayers. The overall effect of state and local taxes is clearly regressive—incomes in the lowest 20 percent pay the highest percentage of income among state and local taxpayers. People with the highest 1 percent of incomes pay the smallest percentage of that income in state and local taxes. Although the federal tax burden is generally progressive, only the middle class was paying a higher rate in 1992 than it paid in 1977; both the lowest and the highest income earners were paying at a lower rate than they had twenty-five years earlier[9] (see **Figure 18-3**).

FIGURE 18-3
THE RATES PEOPLE PAY

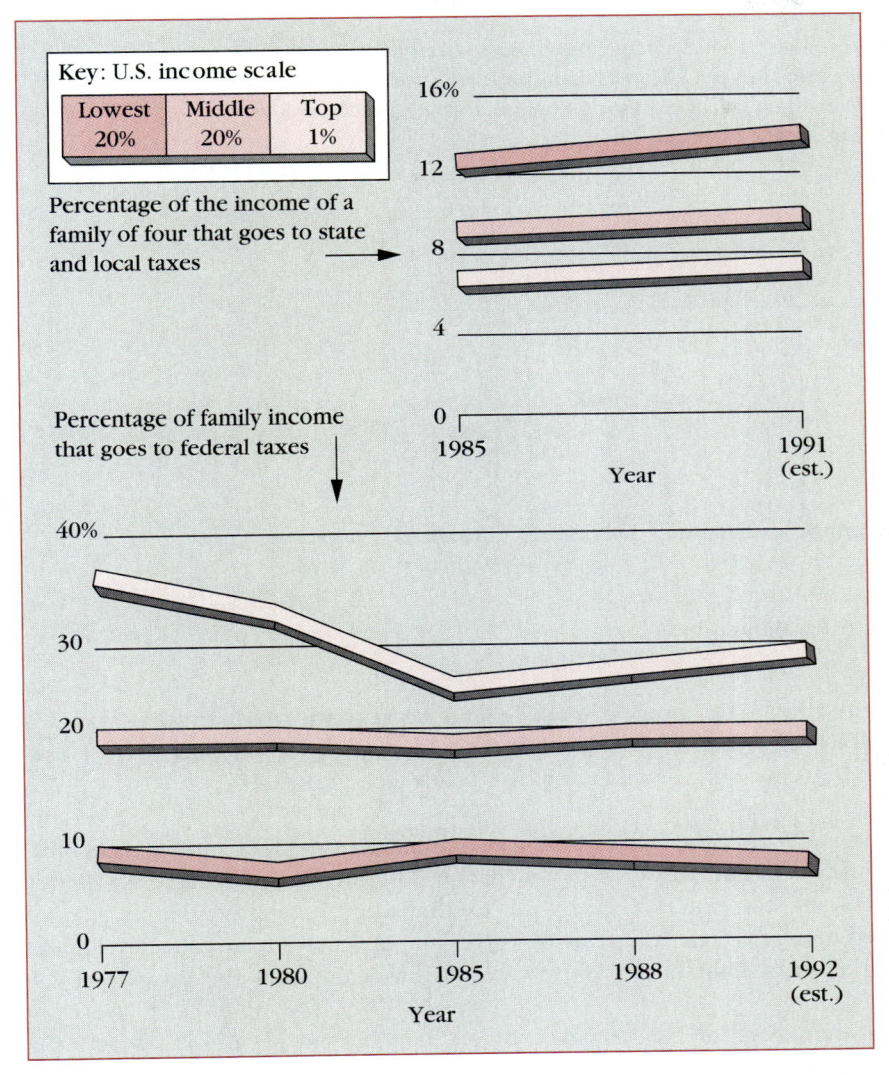

Key: U.S. income scale

| Lowest 20% | Middle 20% | Top 1% |

Percentage of the income of a family of four that goes to state and local taxes →

(Year axis: 1985 to 1991 (est.); values from 0 to 16%)

Percentage of family income that goes to federal taxes ↓

(Year axis: 1977, 1980, 1985, 1988, 1992 (est.); values from 0 to 40%)

SOURCE: *New York Times.*

Despite frequent complaints about taxation in the United States, our overall tax rates are considerably lower than those in many other countries. Also, the increase in tax rates over the past quarter-century has been smaller in the United States than in most other nations. Japan's overall tax rates were substantially lower than U.S. rates in 1965; now they are slightly higher than ours (see **Figure 18-4**). Most federal tax revenue comes from the individual income tax, followed by other payroll taxes (primarily

FIGURE 18-4

TAXES IN OTHER INDUSTRIALIZED COUNTRIES

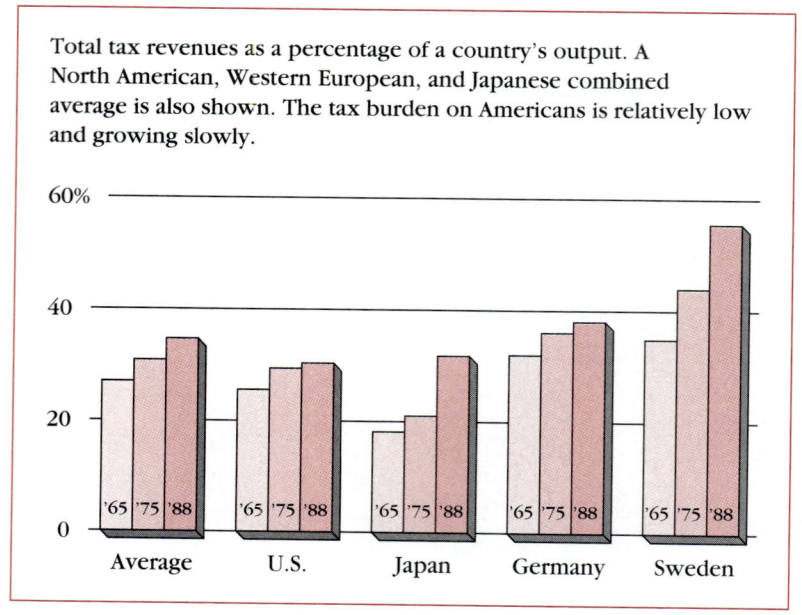

Total tax revenues as a percentage of a country's output. A North American, Western European, and Japanese combined average is also shown. The tax burden on Americans is relatively low and growing slowly.

[Bar chart showing tax revenues as percentage of output for '65, '75, '88 across Average, U.S., Japan, Germany, and Sweden]

SOURCE: *New York Times.*

social security taxes). The proportion of federal tax revenue from corporate taxes is less than half what it was in 1950. Corporate taxes represented 39 percent of the federal total in the 1950s but only 17 percent in the 1980s (see **Figure 18-5**).

MONETARY POLICY   Another major tool of economic management is **monetary policy**, the regulation of the supply of money in the economy. If the demand for money by borrowers and consumers exceeds the existing supply of money, interest rates on borrowed money go up. As a result, people take out fewer loans, and investment declines. In short, a tight money supply could drastically limit the growth of the economy.

The U.S. money supply is controlled by an independent regulatory agency, the **Federal Reserve System (the Fed)**—in essence, the central bank of the United States. The president appoints the members of the Fed's board of governors but has no direct control over them. The Federal Reserve Board oversees twelve regional Federal Reserve banks and approximately 5,200 member banks in the various states. All nationally chartered banks must belong to the Federal Reserve System, and many state banks voluntarily join. The member banks are required to keep a certain percentage of assets in one of the reserve banks. In addition, member banks may borrow money from the reserve banks to finance lending activities.

FIGURE 18-5
BUSINESS VERSUS PERSONAL TAX

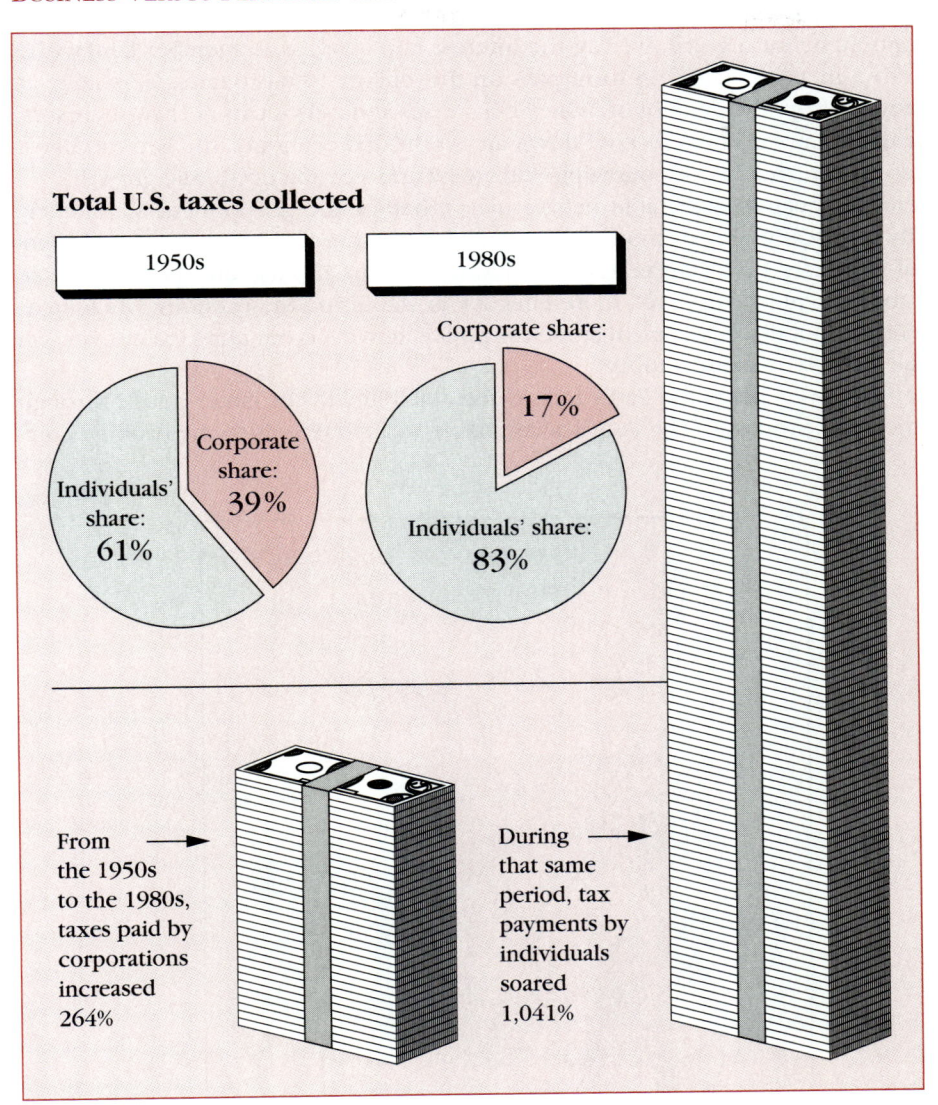

Total U.S. taxes collected

1950s
- Individuals' share: 61%
- Corporate share: 39%

1980s
- Individuals' share: 83%
- Corporate share: 17%

From the 1950s to the 1980s, taxes paid by corporations increased 264%

During that same period, tax payments by individuals soared 1,041%

SOURCE: *Raleigh News and Observer*, December 8, 1991, p. 8J.

The Federal Reserve Board can control the amount of money circulating in the economy by raising or lowering the percentage of money that each member bank must keep in reserve rather than loan out or invest. More frequently, the Fed manipulates the economy by raising or lowering the interest rate charged to member banks (the prime rate); member banks, in turn, pass on this charge to customers. Generally, as interest rates drop, the amount of money businesses and individuals borrow increases, and the economy expands. To cool down an overheated economy, the Fed can boost the interest rate, thereby discouraging borrowing and slowing economic growth.

There has been considerable debate over whether the government should rely primarily on fiscal policy or monetary policy in regulating the business cycle. Proponents of monetary policy argue that it is more direct in application, quicker to take effect, and, if handled properly, more effective in stabilizing the economy. As long as presidents cannot directly control monetary policy, however, our chief executives will continue to prefer the fiscal tools.

Many observers decry the Fed's lack of accountability to the larger public through the democratic process. If the Fed is accountable to anyone, it is to the banking com-

"This should jump-start the economy."

munity. Yet political factors sometimes influence the Fed's decisions as well. In the past the Fed has made sudden shifts linked to the political preferences of its board members and timed to promote the political prospects of a particular administration. George Bush coaxed the Fed to lower interest rates in 1992 to try to stimulate a stalled economy in time for the upcoming elections. At times the Fed has also acted under the assumption that full employment is inflationary—an attitude that some economists label callous because of the human costs involved in unemployment.

Defenders of the current Federal Reserve System contend that bringing it under direct presidential control would signal the intrusion of politics into economic policymaking. However, critics of the Fed argue that such a move would give presidents greater freedom of action when economic crises loom.

The Politics of Economics: The Supply-Side Debate

Economics draws practitioners from every point on the political spectrum. There are liberal economists, conservative economists, radical economists, and many shades in between. When people argue about economics—when they speculate as to why the economy is doing well or badly or dispute exactly what "well" or "badly" means—they are not just talking science or mechanics. Inevitably, they are deeply enmeshed in political debate.

In the real world, economic ideas interact with political realities. Economic theory can be perverted, misused, or skillfully manipulated. Economic ideas can be employed as a form of rhetoric to obscure real problems or twisted to advance political ends. Economic considerations can also be ignored, with either good or bad results. Such interactions between economic theories and the real world of U.S. politics are exemplified in the debate about supply-side economics.

Reaganomics

Ronald Reagan became president at a time marked by high rates of inflation and high unemployment. The Keynesian model offered no politically acceptable solutions to this combination of ills. Further, Reagan was committed to three particular policies that did not, in themselves, promise much hope for recovery within a traditional understanding of economic forces. First, Reagan was determined to reduce the size of the federal government's domestic activities, meaning reductions in both expenditures and regulations. Second, he was committed to a substantial *increase* in defense programs and expenditures. Finally, Reagan sought to reduce the tax burden on individuals and businesses. Spending policies that stimulated the economy were not attractive to a president bent on reducing the size of the federal government domestically. Yet to reduce taxes during a time of high inflation and relatively large budget deficits ran counter to beliefs held strongly by many in the country, including many within the president's own Republican party. From an ideological standpoint, Reagan supported monetary policy, but the early members of the Reagan administration believed that monetary policy was largely beyond their control. What brought together the three policy goals and the hope for economic recovery was **supply-side economics**. This economic theory seemed almost too good to be true—it offered a painless, everybody-wins route to economic recovery. According to supply-side economics, a large, across-the-board, equal cut in income tax rates would not reduce government revenues but rather would raise government revenues (through increased production) and, thereby reducing—rather than increasing—the budget deficits.[11]

In supply-side economics, supply, or production, is the crucial element in economic recovery. Supply-side economists argue that tax cuts encourage more people to invest more money, thereby stimulating vital new productive enterprise. Government taxation, according to the supply-siders, discourages investment and removes incentives to better one's financial state. This in turn leads to a drop-off in government revenue, since there is less income to tax. The supply-side solution to this problem is to slash taxes, thereby increasing incentives and productivity and, in the end, increasing government revenues, since there is more income to tax. Supply-side theorists also call for eliminating various government regulations, such as environmental requirements, that tend to raise the costs of doing business and, in their view, reduce the amount of money available for investment and growth. In their emphasis on the role of the private sector—particularly wealthy investors and corporations—in stimulating economic recovery, the supply-siders took an opposing view from that of the Keynesians. Keynesians rely on government to stimulate demand and create jobs by putting money in the hands of ordinary citizens through deficit spending, government investment, and public works projects.

The Reagan team knew that the large tax cut in 1981 would not be offset immediately by reductions in spending. Reducing expenditures for domestic programs was difficult at best, and reductions in social spending were countered by increases in defense spending. But the economic expansion envisioned by supply-siders would increase revenues enough to allow for a balanced budget before the midterm elections in 1982, according to supply-side theorists, *if* domestic spending could be reduced sufficiently.

In presenting the supply-side package, the administration emphasized that all programs, without exception, would be subjected to careful scrutiny with an eye toward budget trimming. Powerful interest groups, accustomed to receiving large subsidies, would simply have to reconcile themselves to making do with less. The Reagan team also stressed the urgency of immediate action on the package. Congress must act, they claimed, because the health of the whole economy was at stake. Reagan gave assurances that a "safety net" of social programs would be maintained for all truly needy individuals.

Evaluating the Supply-Side Experiment

How well did supply-side economics work? This question has no simple answer. Some supply-siders claim that the theory wasn't given a fair chance. The tax cut in 1981 was followed by modest tax increases in 1982 and again in 1984. And the Fed's extra-tight monetary policy under Paul Volcker certainly tended to restrict economic expansion in 1982 and 1983. The Reagan administration complained that Congress stood in the way of needed reductions in federal expenditures, which prevented balanced federal budgets. Given each of these factors, some supply-siders claim success for the experiment and point to the broad expansion of the economy that lasted through the end of the decade, in contrast to the stagflation that ushered in the 1980s.

But certain factors must be counted against the experiment. First, some observers credit Volcker and the Fed's tight money policy with slaying the stagflation dragon and providing the basis for the subsequent expansion (Volcker was, incidentally, reappointed to the Fed by President Reagan). As for congressional obstruction, critics point out that President Reagan never actually offered a balanced budget to Congress. More important, though, is the critique that supply-side economics as interpreted by the Reagan administration did just what could be expected of a policy that provides big tax cuts to the nation's wealthiest citizens while dramatically increasing defense spending. Huge budget deficits piled up, reducing fiscal flexibility by increasing interest on the national debt. Fueled by large budget deficits each year, the national debt more than doubled, to nearly $3 trillion. By the end of the Reagan administration the national debt was three times the size of all the deficits of the preceding thirty-nine presidents combined.

There was also a disturbing side effect of the Reagan experiment in economics. (Skeptics might argue that far from being a side effect, this was a primary goal of the program.) As we saw in Chapter 7, the inequality of incomes and the disparity of wealth between the nation's richest citizens and everyone else increased significantly during the 1980s. This increased gap between the rich and the rest was accelerated by another item on the Reagan agenda—shifting responsibility for government spending onto the state and local governments, where, as we have seen, tax rates tend to be most regressive.

While the U.S. economy suffered through the long recession that kicked off the 1990s, the popular image of the 1980s as a decade of style and glitter shifted to portray this immediate past as a time of conspicuous consumption to excess. Every economic expansion must end sometime. Was it wrong to blame the economic difficulties of the 1990s on the economic choices of the 1980s? Broad economic policies were chosen in part for their ideological implications. Supply-side economics appealed to people who wished for reduced governmental intervention in economic and personal life. Keynesian economics is more likely to appeal to those who want government to take an active part in ensuring a fair society.

Certain economic strategies are driven by political choices that have little to do with ideology. Tax increases are unpopular and hard to implement; cutting government programs may be more or less difficult, depending on how well organized and well funded the beneficiaries of those programs are. It will always be easier to cut general assistance to poor people than it is to cut farm subsidies or social security. Policymakers must operate with several agendas in mind at once.

Emerging Problems

Not long ago the United States was regarded as the far and away most powerful, most productive, and most successful world economy. That judgment is now debatable. The United States has experienced economic setbacks as well as successes in recent decades. We shall consider an array of problems connected to our political economy: tax equity and tax expenditures, federal budget deficits, the transformation of the work force, and the decline in industrial power.

Tax Equity and Tax Expenditures

In analyzing any tax system, one of the primary issues that arises involves equity—how fairly the tax burden is shared. In a truly equitable system, the people who are better able to pay would be taxed more than those less able to pay. In that way, the tax burden would not fall too heavily on the poorer sectors of the community.

In the United States, however, the less well-off pay a considerable portion of their income in taxes. This anomaly stems in part from the many regressive taxes in the U.S. tax scheme. In addition, the federal income tax structure has always been less progressive than it looked on the surface, primarily because of the large numbers of loopholes available to middle- and upper-income taxpayers. A more dignified name for these loopholes is **tax expenditures**. The term *expenditure* is used because in effect the government is making grants of money to various taxpayers through the tax code rather than through the federal budget. In this sense the various loopholes in the tax code actually constitute a hidden form of government spending (see chapter 19).

The **Tax Reform Act of 1986** was designed to simplify the tax code and make it more equitable. Overall, reformers sought to make the *rate structure* less progressive by dramatically lowering the highest tax rates and reducing the number of tax brackets. (A tax bracket is a range of income within which a particular rate applies. Since 1988 there are only these brackets for the federal income tax: For single individuals with up to $20,350 in taxable income after exemptions and deductions, the tax rate is 15 percent; taxable income between $20,350 and $49,300 is taxed at 28 percent; and income above $49,300 is taxed at 31 percent. The cutoff for the brackets changes with different filing statuses.) At the same time the *actual tax structure* would become more progressive because a large number of loopholes would be closed, ensuring that high-income taxpayers would pay taxes at rates closer to the published ones (because more of their income would be considered taxable). An increase in the personal exemption would reduce or eliminate the tax burden for those with low incomes. No more favorable treatment would be afforded capital gains (investment income), increasing the tax liability of persons with substantial investments.

How effective was tax reform? As for the goal of simplification, the gains were limited and have been seriously eroded. The tax code remains enormously complex, which encourages manipulation by special interests and leaves ordinary taxpayers with the suspicion that the system exploits the little guy to favor the well-connected insider.

Considering fairness, the Tax Reform Act itself sought a barely progressive system of taxation. With the compromises and subsequent changes reinserting favorable tax treatment for particular individuals and groups, the modest progressivity of the original structure is further eroded. According to one calculation, if the tax structure had remained only as progressive as it was prior to the Carter administration's capital gains cut in 1978 and the tax reforms of the Reagan administration, the 1 percent of the population with the highest incomes would have paid an extra $84 billion in taxes in 1992 alone.[12]

Questions of tax equity should include some consideration of tax expenditure items like the deductibility of home mortgage interest, which represent a hidden dimension of budgetary politics. The money not collected in taxes does not appear as a line item in a budget. Such government transfers represent substantial welfare programs for the nonpoor in America, as **Table 18-1** shows. Such programs are not necessarily bad;

TABLE 18-1
ESTIMATES FOR TAX EXPENDITURES (MILLIONS $)

Expenditure	1991	1992	1993
National Defense	2,345	2,400	2,460
International Affairs	8,190	8,740	9,345
General Science, Space, Technology	4,055	2,920	2,220
Energy	1,040	1,460	1,895
Natural Resources and Environment	2,920	2,965	3,030
Agriculture	645	550	420
Commerce and Housing Credit	145,885	152,195	168,085
Transportation	135	145	160
Community and Regional Development	1,905	2,250	2,430
Education, Training, Employment and Social Services	22,180	23,840	24,825
Health	60,065	65,380	71,250
Income Security	83,660	87,960	91,985
Social Security	21,435	22,935	24,490
Veterans Benefits and Services	1,990	2,030	2,085
Interest	945	955	960
Aid to State and Local Government	55,290	58,210	61,590

SOURCE: *The Budget for Fiscal Year 1993* (Washington, D.C.: U.S. Government Printing Office, 1992).

most are defensible. But their relative invisibility gives them an unfair advantage in public debates about economic benefits. For example, a person in the highest tax bracket who buys an expensive house and makes a substantial mortgage interest payment each month receives a larger benefit, in both absolute and proportional terms, than someone with a lower income and a cheaper house. If during tight-budget times when basic services are being cut, large checks from the government continued to go out each month to wealthy homeowners (in place of the low-visibility benefits of tax deductions), people might begin to ask hard questions about this public policy.

Federal Budget Deficits

Despite public commitments to a balanced budget, including vocal support for a balanced-budget amendment to the U.S. Constitution, the Reagan and Bush administrations generated the largest federal deficits in U.S. history (see **Figure 18-6**). How serious a problem is the deficit? Some analysts argue that given a generally healthy economy, the current large deficits are not a serious problem, that sooner or later economic growth will allow the budget to be balanced. However, the increasingly large deficits of the early 1990s (the projected deficit for fiscal 1992 was over $400 billion) during a long, painful recession, clearly demonstrate that large deficits limit the government's flexibility to offer fiscal stimulation to a downward-trending economy and that like all debt, large federal deficits represent borrowing against the future for the present. An increasing percentage of the federal budget must go toward interest payments on the national debt (14 percent in 1992), reducing the resources available to address current and future needs. Some observers warn that intergenerational warfare may result from a set of policies that reduces the opportunities of younger generations to subsidize the comforts of the older.

The problem with large deficits is that they discourage new government investment aimed at making the economy more productive in the long term. Economist Robert Heilbroner has suggested an accounting change to address the problem: the creation of a government capital account. Private corporations in this country (and worldwide) distinguish between receipts and expenditures involving investment projects (capital accounts) from those of ordinary "current" activities. Thus, an investment expenditure that will produce new revenues later but is an expense now is not counted as part of the current account.

Most states and many cities use a capital account; most industrialized countries do as well. Establishing a federal capital account would encounter serious problems, including complex judgments about what constitutes investment and how to calculate depreciation. But, Heilbroner says, these can be overcome. The benefits of separating an unhealthy deficit in the current account from beneficial investment in the capital account is very great. The real problem, as far as Heilbroner is concerned, "lies in America's deep distrust of using government investment as a source of economic growth."[13] That distrust has been overcome in the past, when the government financed the transcontinental railroad and built the Panama Canal, TVA dams, and the interstate highway system. It may be possible again.

The Decline in Industrial Power

As far back as the early 1960s, some observant critics of the American economy noted that the generally rosy picture of U.S. economic achievements had a dark underside. Unemployment always seemed to be higher here than in many European nations. In addition, portions of U.S. industry were not being modernized. Finally, pockets of poverty and deprivation were not sharing in the economic resurgence, and much of the infrastructure (roads, water systems, bridges, and the like) was deteriorating.

Not until the 1970s, however, did the full impact of the nation's industrial decline become clear. At that point the United States ceased to be the world leader in many industrial areas. Even in our own nation, consumers disparaged the quality of American products. Japanese and European cars, TVs, and electrical and electronic appliances

FIGURE 18-6
NOMINAL DEBT AS A PERCENTAGE OF GDP

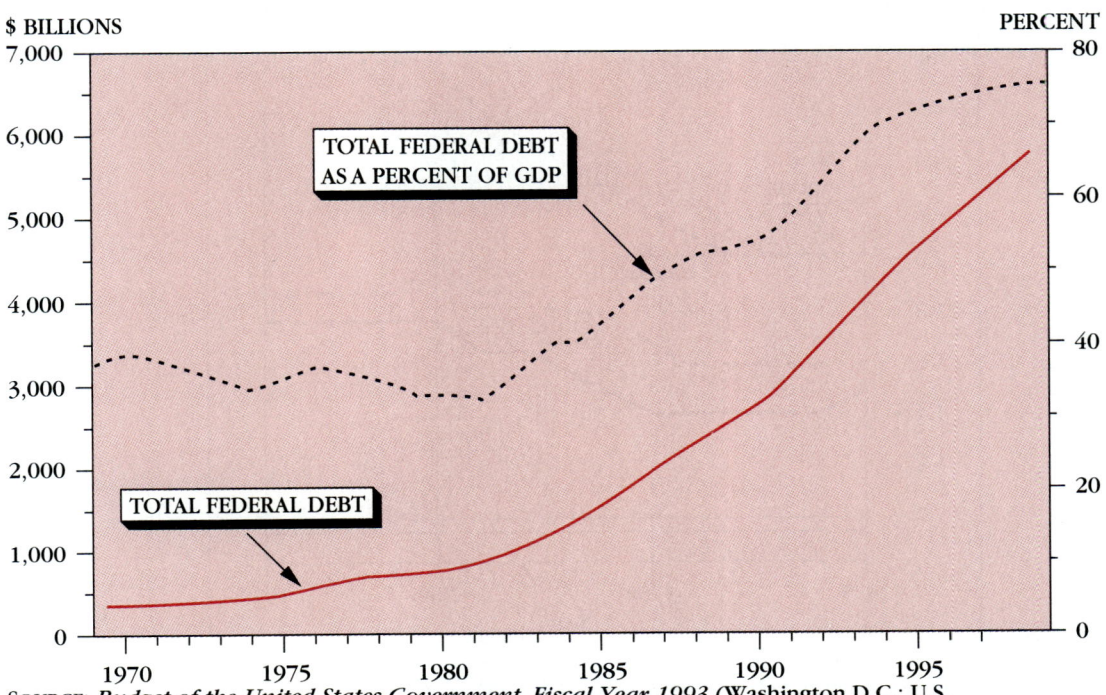

SOURCE: *Budget of the United States Government, Fiscal Year 1993* (Washington D.C.: U.S. Printing Office, 1992), Part I, p. 11.

took over a substantial share of the U.S. market. Some major industries were hit especially hard. Automakers fell on hard times, and the steel industry suffered a steep decline. The industrial heartland of the nation, stretching from Chicago to Boston, became an economically depressed area.

This decline stemmed from several interrelated factors. American industries had failed to innovate. Investment in research and development had flattened out in the United States while climbing dramatically in Japan and Germany. Of the R&D money spent in the United States in the early 1990s, a larger proportion went to defense than to other areas—the reverse had been true in 1980 (see **Figures 18-7 and 18-8**). Capital investments had gone to countries where labor was cheaper and profits higher. The U.S. job market was also undergoing profound changes as more and more of the population moved into service jobs and away from jobs in production industries (see **Figure 18-9**). And through policies that had protected particular industries (such as

FIGURE 18-7

NONDEFENSE RESEARCH AND DEVELOPMENT AS A PERCENTAGE OF GROSS NATIONAL PRODUCT

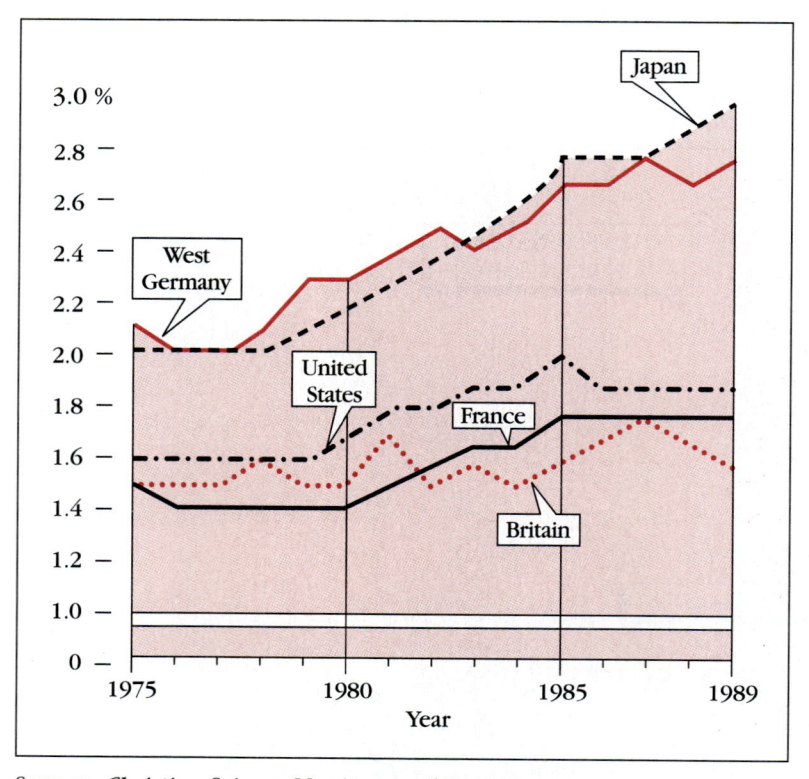

SOURCE: *Christian Science Monitor*, April 7, 1992, p. 7.

FIGURE 18-8
TRENDS IN FEDERAL SPENDING FOR RESEARCH AND DEVELOPMENT

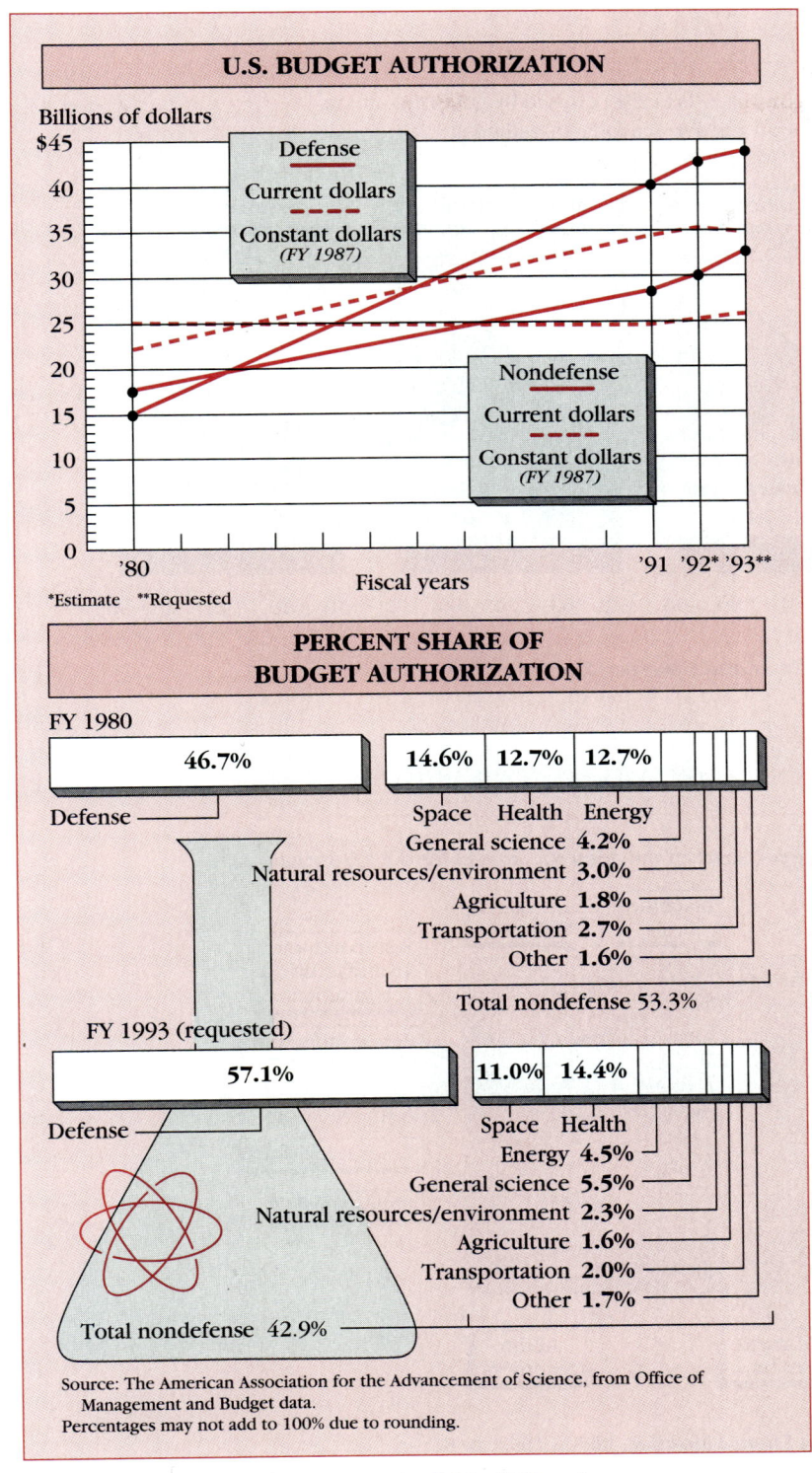

U.S. BUDGET AUTHORIZATION

Billions of dollars

Defense
— Current dollars
--- Constant dollars (FY 1987)

Nondefense
— Current dollars
--- Constant dollars (FY 1987)

Fiscal years '80 ... '91 '92* '93**
*Estimate **Requested

PERCENT SHARE OF BUDGET AUTHORIZATION

FY 1980

Defense 46.7%

Space 14.6% | Health 12.7% | Energy 12.7%
General science 4.2%
Natural resources/environment 3.0%
Agriculture 1.8%
Transportation 2.7%
Other 1.6%

Total nondefense 53.3%

FY 1993 (requested)

Defense 57.1%

Space 11.0% | Health 14.4%
Energy 4.5%
General science 5.5%
Natural resources/environment 2.3%
Agriculture 1.6%
Transportation 2.0%
Other 1.7%

Total nondefense 42.9%

Source: The American Association for the Advancement of Science, from Office of Management and Budget data.
Percentages may not add to 100% due to rounding.

SOURCE: *Christian Science Monitor*, April 29, 1992, p. 1.

FIGURE 18-9
THE DEMISE OF U.S. MANUFACTURING

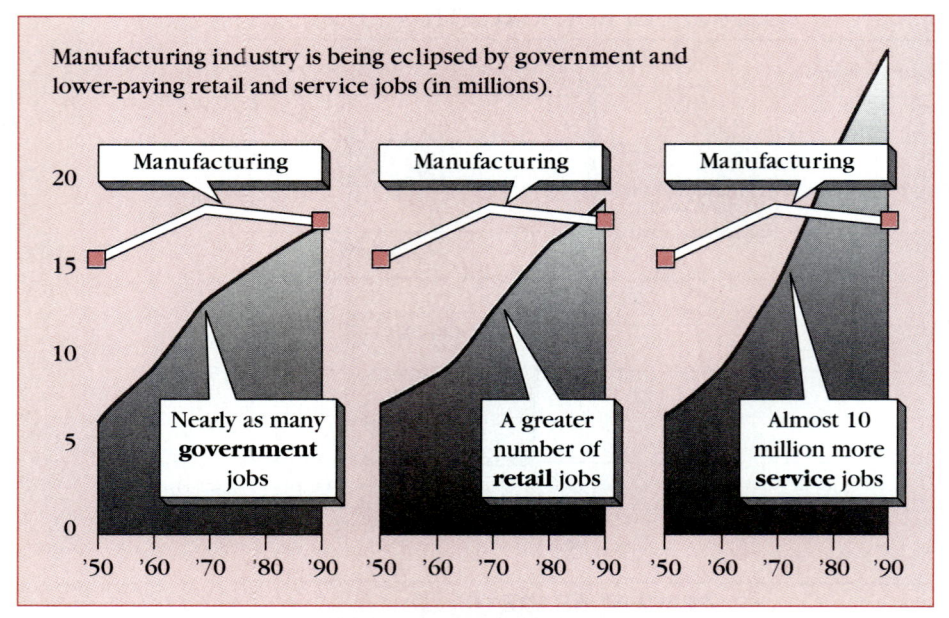

Manufacturing industry is being eclipsed by government and lower-paying retail and service jobs (in millions).

- Manufacturing — Nearly as many **government** jobs
- Manufacturing — A greater number of **retail** jobs
- Manufacturing — Almost 10 million more **service** jobs

(y-axis: 0, 5, 10, 15, 20; x-axis: '50, '60, '70, '80, '90)

SOURCE: *Raleigh News and Observer*, December 8, 1991, p. 8J.

FIGURE 18-10
EROSION OF TECHNOLOGY MARKETS IN THE UNITED STATES

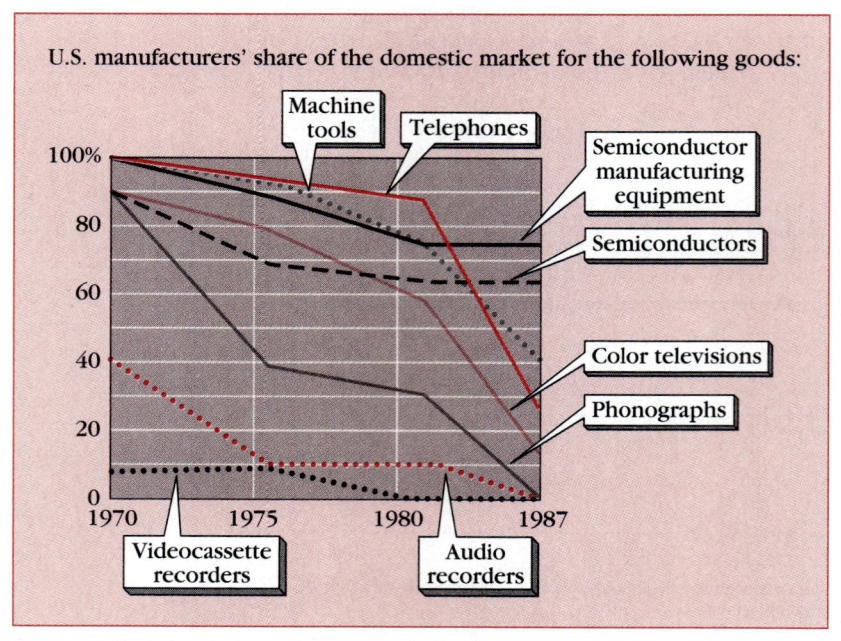

U.S. manufacturers' share of the domestic market for the following goods:

- Machine tools
- Telephones
- Semiconductor manufacturing equipment
- Semiconductors
- Color televisions
- Phonographs
- Videocassette recorders
- Audio recorders

(y-axis: 0 to 100%; x-axis: 1970, 1975, 1980, 1987)

SOURCE: *Christian Science Monitor*, July 1, 1992, p. 8.

MANAGEMENT OF THE ECONOMY 669

steel) against foreign competition, the government had reduced incentives to innovate and compete internationally (see **Figure 18-10**).

The debate about how to revive U.S. industry and its global competitiveness has been lively, centering around two related concepts: (1) free trade versus protectionism and (2) industrial policy. **Protectionism** consists of tariffs and import-export restrictions favoring domestic industries over foreign competitors. Laissez-faire suggests that such restrictions are counterproductive, that the unrestricted market will encourage the most efficient production of goods and services. Support for the North American Free Trade Zone, encompassing Canada, the United States, and Mexico, is grounded in this assertion. By contrast, proponents of protectionist policies contend that certain national interests (maintaining domestic production and control of vital industries, for example, or favoring the welfare of domestic workers over that of foreign workers) outweigh the benefits of a free market. Besides, they contend, because of protectionist policies in other nations, no genuinely free market exists; to act as if it did is to leave one's own interests prey to others' manipulations.

As in all policy areas, these ideal descriptions do not translate directly into the real world. Does the failure of U.S. automakers to sell many cars in Japan indicate the presence of Japanese protectionist policies, or is it a matter of being bested by the

An auto assembly line: a symbol of Japan's ascendance in international trade. What role can and should government play to facilitate the improvement of the U.S. trading position? *(Andy Levin/Photo Researchers)*

COMPARATIVE PERSPECTIVE

INDUSTRIAL POLICY

Democratic governments employ various forms of direct intervention in the economy to promote growth, employment, or economic stability. In many Western European Industrial democracies, as well as in Japan, interventionist policies have become standard and highly sophisticated.* Forms of direct intervention include government ownership of portions of the economy; close collaboration between business and government, including fairly detailed planning of economic goals; and cooperation between government and labor to avoid strikes. These instruments of industrial policy are more highly developed in some nations than in others. France, for example, has emphasized close collaboration between business and government, with extensive use of government loans and credit arrangements to help industry to achieve agreed-on goals. Both France and Great Britain have nationalized certain major industries, although under the Conservative government of Margaret Thatcher in the 1980s many nationalized businesses reverted to private ownership. Both the British and the Swedes are notable for clear, long-term relationships between labor and major political parties. In Germany the banking system plays an important collaborative role with government in the management of the economy. In all these cases there has been a focused, long-term effort to link overall economic goals to specific policies aiding particular industries, though such efforts have not always been successful.

A clear industrial policy has always been lacking in the United States. Except in time of war, the U.S. government has not sought to develop the tools for detailed intervention in particular industries and aspects of the economy. There have been occasional interventions—the government bailout of the failing Lock-

(Box continues on page 671)

domestic competition? Recent tensions between the United States and Japan have often centered on questions of protectionism (theirs) versus lack of productivity (ours).

In a related controversy, some analysts have suggested that the United States needs an **industrial policy**, a governmental effort to coordinate and subsidize sectors of the private economy to maximize global competitiveness. The 1992 presidential election provided a forum for the full range of positions on this debate. Independent candidate Ross Perot advocated a vigorous federal effort to work "industry by industry" to "target the industries of the future." President Bush derided such proposals as a misguided effort to allow the government to pick "winners and losers" in the economy. Democrat Bill Clinton fell somewhere in between, advocating federal funding for cutting-edge technologies and federal efforts to steer defense contractors toward peacetime pro-

heed Corporation during the Nixon administration and the guaranteeing of loans for the near-bankrupt Chrysler Corporation during the Ford and Carter administrations are examples. These instances, however, were not part of an overall plan. Rather, they were simply cases in which particular interest groups were able to plead successfully to have their demands met.

Although some people think that this is as it should be, others believe that the U.S. economy needs precisely the forms of direct intervention that would be part of a coherent industrial policy. Only such a policy, it has been argued, will provide the help needed by many ailing American industries and by those areas of the nation afflicted by chronically high unemployment.

As Robert Solo says, "From [Japan] we learn that the state can play a positive and powerful role in promoting the advance of technology and accelerating the rise in productivity, without diminishing the significance of private enterprise and the market. The communists had to learn that one system cannot undertake to encompass the control of the whole, and survive. The United States, on the other hand, must recognize that there must be some system equipped to act positively on the problem of the whole if it is to stay afloat in the sea of international competition.

This lesson from Japan, in particular, is important to us, for we in the United States have failed to develop any facet of the state as an instrument capable of organizing, coordinating, monitoring, evaluating, supporting, or in any effective way promoting the advance of technology and accelerating the rise of productivity in the critical corporate sector."[†]

*See Arnold J. Heidenheimer, Hugh Heclo, and Carolyn T. Adams, Comparative Public Policy, 2nd ed. (New York: St. Martin's Press, 1983), pp. 141–148.
[†]Robert A. Solo, Opportunity Knocks: American Economic Policy after Gorbachev (Armonk, N.Y.: M.E. Sharpe, 1991), pp. 52–53.

---

duction. Closest to Clinton's position was the suggestion that competitiveness can best be regained by investments in infrastructure and work force. A failure to spend money on education and training and on the means of moving goods, people, and information around the country has reduced our productivity and hence our competitiveness.

Conclusions

According to many students of politics, successful management of the economy, more than any other factor, can determine how history—and the electorate—treats a president. In a reelection campaign or in historical perspective, the president may stand or fall on whether unemployment has been lowered to a reasonable level, inflation has been controlled, or public confidence in the economy has been restored. Of course, administrations are not moved to pay careful attention to economic management by political considerations or historical judgments alone. They are also influenced by ideological factors—by beliefs about how the economy should be run. President Herbert Hoover believed so strongly in not interfering with the free market that he did not take actions that might at least have softened the brunt of the Great Depression. And President Ronald Reagan was sufficiently committed to the free market to push deregulation and tax reductions as top-priority items throughout his administration.

Today every national government comes to power with a specific strategy for economic management as the centerpiece of its political agenda. This holds true not only in the United States but also in all industrialized nations and in most other nations as well. Managing economies has become, in one form or another, a key function of government. Even governments professing that the best way to run the economy is to do *less* managing continue to perform many essential functions: regulating interest rates and the money supply, settling rates of taxation, formulating spending policies, maintaining the extensive network of regulation that affects virtually every form of economic activity, and so on.

In short, economic life has become highly politicized. Many of the battles fought in Congress, between Congress and the executive branch, and in many of our election campaigns now revolve around how the economy should be managed and in whose interest it should be run. How far should government go in reshaping the workings of the marketplace? Should we protect the domestic auto industry? Save failing airlines? And how far should government go in altering the composition of the work force and mending its frayed margins? Is it government's responsibility, for example, to make sure that everyone who wants to work is able to find a job? What part should government play in making sure that people who do work can earn a decent wage?

Consider, as well, how much, if anything, government should do to redistribute income through our tax system. As we have seen, the current tax system is not particularly progressive in impact. Should it be made more so, not just in theory but in practice? From the standpoint of democratic politics, fairness in taxation should stand as a prime goal of our policymakers. Overall, there is good reason to question the fairness of the U.S. system of taxation. From the perspective of democratic theory, a fair method of taxation would seem essential, since this is the way we go about paying for our government.

Another facet of our economic policymaking machinery—the Federal Reserve Board—is accountable to no one, yet the actions of this set of unelected decision makers have far-reaching implications for both the national economy and individual consumers, homeowners, and businesses. Largely insulated from political pressures, the Fed can pursue politically unpopular actions that elected policymakers could not. Yet in light of democratic politics, this arrangement raises serious concerns. If the Fed decides to tighten the money supply for a prolonged period, as it did in the early 1980s, how much individual hardship will we tolerate as the price of economic stability?

Should the Fed, then, be made more responsive to popular pressures, or does the economy benefit from the Fed's independence? At this point, changing the structure of the Federal Reserve Board does not stand high on the political agenda.

A final point, from the perspective of democratic theory, concerns economic planning. Our government does not do very much overall economic planning. Many of us associate the very concept of economic planning with failed communist governments that tried to manage their entire economies. Various sectors of the economy do benefit from planning, however. The government provides farmers with certain price supports, for example, and plans new weapon systems more than a decade in advance. But as a society we are reluctant to engage in the kind of long-term economic planning that might enable us to cope with the most severe problems of dislocation and deprivation that some citizens face. The United States has lived with a considerable level of unemployment for decades. We have also seen central cities deteriorate and whole regions of the nation suffer prolonged economic crises. Yet our distrust of government and our reverence for private property and the workings of the market make it difficult for us to undertake a serious national effort to address these issues.

Glossary Terms

controlled capitalism
depression
Federal Reserve System (the Fed)
fiscal policy
industrial policy
Keynesian economics
laissez-faire capitalism
macroeconomics
mercantilism
microeconomics

monetary policy
progressive taxes
proportional (flat rate) tax
protectionism
recession
regressive taxes
stagflation
supply-side economics
tax expenditure
Tax Reform Act of 1986

Notes

[1] Seymour Martin Lipset, *Political Man* (Garden City, N.Y.: Doubleday, 1960), chap. 2.
[2] W. A. Williams, *The Contours of American History* (Cleveland: World, 1961); Louis Hartz, *Economic Policy and Democratic Thought* (Cambridge, Mass.: Harvard University Press, 1948).
[3] Richard Hofstadter, *The American Political Tradition* (New York: Knopf, 1948).
[4] Clair Wilcox, *Public Policies toward Business* (Homewood, Ill.: Irwin, 1971).
[5] Robert S. McElvaine, *The Great Depression* (New York: Times Books, 1984), chaps. 2, 4.
[6] Arnold J. Heidenheimer, Hugh Heclo, and Carolyn T. Adams, *Comparative Public Policy*, 2nd ed. (New York: St. Martin's Press, 1983), chap. 5.
[7] Mark S. Kahan, "Confessions of an Airline Deregulator," *American Prospect*, Winter 1992, pp. 38–50.

[8]Anne Swardson, "Tax Reform: One Deduction Forward, Two Deductions Back," *Washington Post National Weekly Edition*, April 25, 1988, p. 21.

[9]Peter Passell, "Despite All the Talk of Tax Cuts, People Can Expect to Pay More," *New York Times*, November 17, 1991, p. A1.

[11]Discussion drawn from Herbert Stein, *Presidential Economics*, rev. ed. (New York: Simon & Schuster, 1985), chap. 7.

[12]Robert S. McIntyre, "Borrow 'n' Squander," *New Republic*, September 30, 1991, p. 13.

[13]Robert Heilbroner, "The Deficit: A Way Out," *The New York Review of Books*, November 19, 1992, p. 12.

SELECTED READINGS

For an engaging **history of economics** from Aristotle to Reagan, see John Kenneth Galbraith, *Economics in Perspective: A Critical History* (Boston: Houghton Mifflin, 1987). Galbraith is properly celebrated for his writing about economics. His recent book *The Culture of Contentment* (Boston: Houghton Mifflin, 1992) discusses the 1980s. For **American economic history**, including a good bibliography, check out Teresa L. Amott, *Race, Gender, and Work: A Multicultural Economic History of Women in the United States* (Boston: South End Press, 1991). Also useful is James Stuart Olsen, ed., *Dictionary of United States Economic History* (Westport, Conn.: Greenwood Press, 1992). For early American economic history, we offer two suggestions: Cathy D. Matson and Peter S. Onuf, *A Union of Interests Political and Economic Thought in Revolutionary America* (Lawrence: University Press of Kansas, 1990); and Frank Bourgin, *The Great Challenge: The Myth of Laissez-Faire in the Early Republic* (New York: Braziller, 1989).

For accounts of the **postwar years and the recent past**, Bernard D. Nossiter, *Fat Years and Lean: The American Economy since Roosevelt* (New York: Harper & Row, 1990).

On **tax policy**, read Lawrence Lindsey, *The Growth Experiment: How the New Tax Policy Is Transforming the U.S. Economy* (New York: Basic Books, 1990); on tax policy in developing countries, see Richard Miller Bird, *Tax Policy and Economic Development* (Baltimore: Johns Hopkins University Press, 1992).

For a particular perspective advocating **industrial policy**, try Otis L. Graham, *Losing Time: The Industrial Policy Debate* (Cambridge, Mass.: Harvard University Press, 1992). More technical essays on this topic can be found in Motoshige Itoh et al., eds., *Economic Analysis of Industrial Policy* (Orlando, Fla.: Academic Press, 1991).

For a **comparative perspective**, consult Harold D. Clarke, Marianne C. Stewart, and Gary Zuk, eds., *Economic Decline and Political Change: Canada, Great Britain, and the United States* (Pittsburgh: University of Pittsburgh Press, 1989). To learn more about economic policy in Japan, see Samuel Kernell, *Parallel Politics: Economic Policymaking in Japan and the United States* (Washington, D.C.: Brookings Institution, 1991).

For distinctly different perspectives on the question of **economic decline and the future**, see Henry R. Nau, *The Myth of America's Decline: Leading the World into the 1990s* (New York: Oxford University Press, 1990); Paul R. Krugman, *The Age of Diminished Expectations: U.S. Economic Policy in the 1990s* (Cambridge, Mass.: MIT Press, 1990); and Betty G. Lall and John Tepper Marlin, *Building a Peace Economy: Opportunities and Problems of Post–Cold War Defense Cuts* (Boulder, Colo.: Westview Press, 1992).

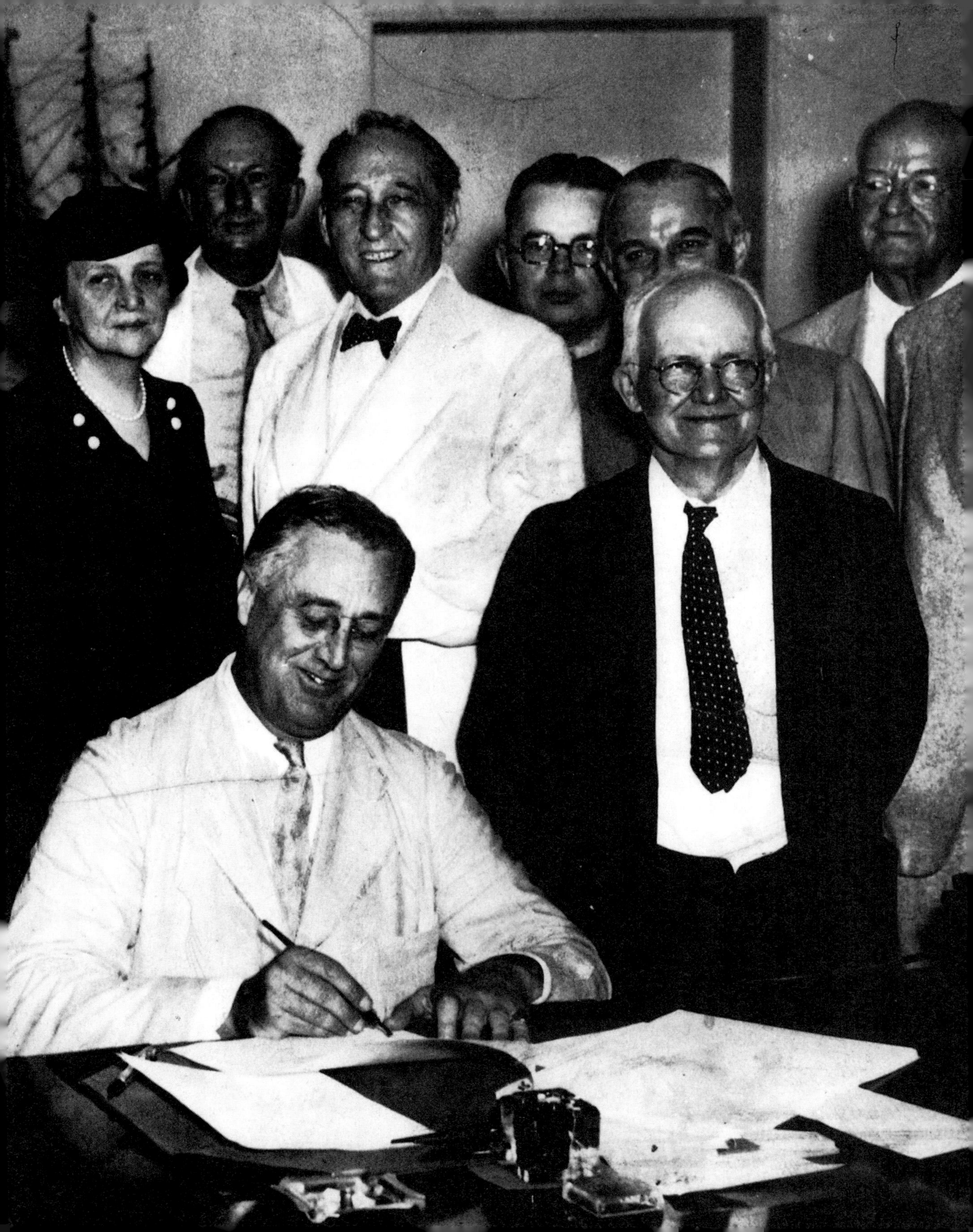

CHAPTER NINETEEN

THE WELFARE STATE

Benefiting the Poor and the Nonpoor

CHAPTER OUTLINE

The U.S. Welfare State

Income Security Programs
SOCIAL SECURITY
AFDC
JOB PROGRAMS
OTHER INCOME SECURITY PROGRAMS

Health-Care Programs
MEDICARE
OTHER HEALTH-CARE PROGRAMS
PROPOSALS FOR REFORM

Nutrition and Housing Programs
FOOD STAMPS
OTHER NUTRITION PROGRAMS
HOUSING PROGRAMS
HOMELESSNESS

Evaluating the Welfare State
THE CONSERVATIVE APPROACH
THE LIBERAL CRITIQUE

IN THE UNITED STATES THE TERM WELFARE IS COMMONLY associated with severe deprivation, prolonged unemployment, lack of incentive to succeed, even lack of "moral fiber" on the part of the recipients. Many Americans think of welfare as a handout, a form of public charity. Similarly, to many people the term *welfare state* conjures up images of needy people receiving food stamps, living in public housing tracts. True, the food stamp program and public housing are part of the welfare state, but only a small part.

As used here, the term **welfare state** refers to the whole complex of benefits, protections, forms of insurance, and services that provide security and a measure of equity for most citizens. Under this definition, the well-dressed retiree depositing a social security check, the suburban couple claiming a mortgage interest deduction on their income tax return, and the farmer taking advantage of price support payments for crops are also images of the welfare state. The government aids many people with housing needs—some through federal housing grants, some through rent supplements, others with the subsidy built into the federal tax code. All of these housing programs are part of the welfare state. The largest single welfare state program, social security, provides benefits almost universal in scope to persons with high incomes as well as those living below the poverty line. The welfare state offers veterans' benefits and education assistance. Taking all welfare state programs together, contrary to popular misconceptions, only one-quarter of the direct benefits payments are **means-tested** (based on ability to pay), including many middle-class favorites such as student loans and Veterans Administration hospital care. Only one dollar out of eight in federal benefits actually goes to Americans in poverty.[1] The popular conception of welfare (isolating only a few welfare programs for the poor) is that it is akin to a general collection to help the least advantaged, but the reality is quite different. In 1991, U.S. households with incomes over $100,000 received, on average, $5,690 worth of federal cash and in-kind benefits. Households with incomes under $10,000 received slightly *less*—$5,560. One recent analysis of the effects of the welfare state yielded the trenchant conclusion that "if the federal government wanted to flatten the nation's income distribution, it would do better to mail all its checks to random addresses."[2] The American welfare state, the result of hundreds of separate policy choices over ninety years, is not a conspiracy to aid the very rich, but it does provide most of its benefits to the nonpoor.

The welfare state is not usually viewed so comprehensively because most of the controversy surrounding the concept of welfare focuses on programs targeted at the needy, such as Aid to Families with Dependent Children (AFDC) and food stamps. In this chapter we spotlight these controversial aspects of the welfare state. But we must recognize that need-related programs are only *aspects* of the welfare state. Therefore, in addressing this segment of public policy, we will explore the underpinnings of *all* welfare state programs.

Fundamentally, the welfare state is designed to ensure a minimum of economic security and a degree of social equality. By the end of World War II, after a century of struggle, most Western societies had arrived at a consensus that individuals should not be allowed to fall below an economic minimum and that opportunities for advancement, principally through the educational system, should be open to all. Beyond this broad agreement, however, lay many areas of controversy, particularly in the United States. To what income level should poor families be supported through public funds— and with what strings attached, if any? How high a level of unemployment can or should society tolerate? Some of these questions deal with practical concerns. For example, how can we best ensure that poor children receive adequate nutrition? But some involve values or beliefs, such as whether a society should foster greater equality in income. Often these practical and ideological issues are intertwined, and when new welfare reform proposals are debated, strongly held convictions surface, generating heated political controversy.

From a democratic standpoint, the welfare state raises three basic issues: security (Do all Americans have the opportunity to live reasonably secure and healthy lives?), equality (Do welfare programs promote economic equality among our citizens, especially in helping to raise the standard of living for the poorest members of society?), and the problem of paternalism (In administering welfare programs, does the government interfere excessively with individual freedom and democratic rights?).

Making judgments on these matters is neither simple nor straightforward. Numerous programs make up the welfare state; their objectives and methods span a wide range, and their scope of achievement varies along a broad spectrum. To assess how—and how well—our welfare state works, we will provide an overview of the U.S. welfare state and then probe income security programs, health care programs, and nutrition and housing programs. Finally, we will evaluate the welfare state and its impact on democracy.

The U.S. Welfare State

Efforts to provide security and various welfare protections were undertaken prior to the 1930s, but the origins of the modern welfare state can be found in New Deal legislation of that decade. New Deal reforms laid the foundation for the "positive state"—one in which the government is an active partner in economic and social life. The New Deal was conceived in response to economic and social problems that had always existed in the United States, but these were greatly exacerbated by the Great Depression. With unemployment idling 25 percent of the work force, millions of people living in abject poverty, and state and local governments running out of resources, national action was imperative. Many other industrialized societies took a similar approach.

Some New Deal programs were designed to undo the economic damage of the Depression and to prevent such a catastrophe from occurring again. Yet even without the crisis of the Depression, some social welfare programs would certainly have evolved in this and other democratic nations. As societies grew more complex and families and communities became more fragmented and less closely knit, political systems were forced to assume some of the responsibilities that had previously been carried out by families, communities, and private groups. And despite vocal criticisms of welfarism and socialism, the basic elements of the welfare state—including social security, a degree of national responsibility for health care, unemployment insurance, and some forms of aid to the poor—now form an integral part of all industrialized democratic societies.

The next significant expansion of the welfare state occurred in the 1960s, during the administration of Lyndon Johnson. Under the heading of the **Great Society**, programs were initiated to help the poor and to provide added security for others in need. Johnson's War on Poverty laid out an enormously ambitious agenda—a greater sharing of wealth and an end to poverty, racial and ethnic equality, equal educational opportunities, employment for everyone seeking a job, and decent housing for all. According to their critics, these programs were overly ambitious, poorly conceived, and either

Children in a Head Start program, along with Medicare, one of the most popular and durable of Lyndon Johnson's Great Society programs. Although many argue that Johnson's "War on Poverty" was lost, these particular programs definitely contributed to improvements in the lives of the people they touched. *(Elizabeth Crews/Stock, Boston)*

ineffectual or actually harmful to the recipients. Rather than helping most Americans to create a better life for themselves, the critics charge, the Great Society left a legacy of dependence and bitterness and gave rise to a self-protective, change-resistent, bloated bureaucracy that continues to dissipate our national resources.

But if the Great Society's ambitions were outsized and unrealistic, its critics too often fail to distinguish the successes and the partial successes from the failures. Poverty rates did decline dramatically in the decade following Johnson's declaration of war. Due significantly to Medicare and expanding social security benefits, poverty among senior citizens showed the largest sustained decreases. The Great Society was less successful in eradicating poverty among children (more difficult to address politically because of their dependent status). But particular Great Society programs like Head Start (which provides economically disadvantaged children with early education, medical screening, and nutrition intervention) are demonstrated successes, limited only by funding constraints (between 1965 and 1992 some 11 million children participated in Head Start programs; during that same period some 50 million more eligible children were left out).[3] Programs like these create substantial savings by reducing the need for later, more costly interventions.

The Johnson administration was the last with a broad set of new welfare state programs to propose. Since that time, few new programs have been created, and support for existing programs has waned. By one estimate inflation reduced real welfare benefits for poor persons by 41 percent between 1971 and 1992.[4] But even with the tightened eligibility requirements and domestic fiscal austerity of the Reagan years, spending on social welfare continued to increase, driven by "indexed" social security payments (that rise automatically with inflation) and surprisingly large increases in the demand for and cost of medical care under Medicare and Medicaid.

Programs aimed at the poor tend to be more controversial than programs created for the overall population or for the nonpoor specifically. Most controversial are public assistance programs. Fierce arguments have raged about welfare payments to mothers in the Aid to Families with Dependent Children program, job training, food stamps, Medicaid, and public housing. All of these programs have been criticized as inadequate and poorly organized, excessively generous, destructive of motivation, and wasteful. In contrast, social insurance programs (like social security) and tax expenditure items (like the deductibility of home mortgage interest and pension funds) are extremely popular.

For at least twenty-five years, then, the public debate has focused on reforming "welfare"—the part of the welfare state that serves poor people. In the meantime, new challenges have arisen to social welfare in the United States, including the enormous costs of AIDS and the appearance of tens of thousands of homeless families and individuals on our streets. Overall levels of poverty in the United States remain high, poverty levels among certain groups (children, for example) are horrendous (one in every five children in the nation is poor), and every economic downturn at least temporarily worsens the figures. Comparative data show that the welfare state in America is much less effective in reducing poverty than its counterparts in other advanced democracies.

We will review specific components of the U.S. welfare state, but first let's look at program types.

There are three types of welfare state programs: **social insurance programs**, such as social security, in which past contributions are related to the benefits received; **public assistance programs**, in which need is the main basis for eligibility; and **tax expenditure items**, in which benefits for particular activities are derived through reductions in tax liability. In the first two categories, benefits are distributed in three ways: through **cash transfers**, such as cash payments for social security or the various types of public assistance to the poor; **services**, like education and job training; and **in-kind transfers**, such as food stamps or Medicaid, which are designated for particular products or services. Most welfare state programs address income security, health nutrition, or housing needs. Each category may encompass several types of programs, some directed at poor people, others targeted for the nonpoor.

COMPARATIVE PERSPECTIVE

TRANSFER SYSTEM EFFECTIVENESS: THE IMPACT OF TAXES AND TRANSFERS ON POVERTY IN SEVERAL NATIONS

A cross-national study using data from 1984 to 1987 showed that taxes and welfare transfers reduce poverty to a much smaller degree in the United States than in any of the other seven countries studied. Particularly discouraging are the data for children aged seventeen or younger: Government efforts in the United States were least effective in reducing poverty among children (from 22.3 percent of all children to 20.4 percent—the worst showing of any of the nations compared). By contrast, government taxes and transfers in the United States reduced poverty among citizens aged sixty-five years and older from 46.5 percent to 10.9 percent (a marked decrease, but still the weakest performance of any of the nations studied).

IMPACT OF TAXES AND TRANSFERS IN SEVERAL NATIONS IN THE MID-1980S

	United States (1986)	Canada (1987)	Austria (1985)	Sweden (1987)	Germany (1984)	Netherlands (1987)	France (1984)	United Kingdom (1986)	Average
All People									
Before*	19.9	17.1	19.1	25.9	21.6	21.5	26.4	27.7	22.4
After†	13.3	7.0	6.7	4.3	2.8	3.4	4.5	5.2	5.9
Change	−6.6	−10.1	−12.4	−21.6	−18.8	−18.1	−21.9	−22.5	−16.5
Aged 65 or Older									
Before	46.5	50.2	54.5	83.2	80.1	56.1	76.2	62.1	63.6
After	10.9	2.2	4.0	0.7	3.8	0.0	0.7	1.0	2.9
Change	−35.6	−48.0	−50.5	−82.5	−76.3	−56.1	−75.5	−61.1	−60.7
Adults (aged 18–64)									
Before	12.8	11.5	12.9	13.4	9.8	17.4	17.6	18.1	14.2
After	10.5	7.0	6.1	6.6	2.6	3.9	5.2	5.3	5.9
Change	−2.3	−4.5	−6.8	−6.8	−7.2	−13.5	−12.4	−12.8	−8.3
Children (aged 17 or younger)									
Before	22.3	15.7	16.4	7.9	8.4	14.1	21.1	27.9	16.7
After	20.4	9.3	9.0	1.6	2.8	3.8	4.6	7.4	7.4
Change	−1.9	−6.4	−7.4	−6.3	−5.6	−10.3	−16.5	−20.5	−9.4

*"Before" figures compare family income based on earnings, property income, and private transfers (such as private pensions, alimony, and child support) to a 40 percent "after tax and transfer income" poverty line.

†"After" figures incorporate the effect of direct taxes, including negative taxes, such as the U.S. earned income tax credit, and public transfers on poverty.

SOURCE: Luxembourg Income Study.

Although many senior citizens face financially precarious circumstances, many more enjoy reasonable security because of New Deal and Great Society programs. "Welfare" is not only for poor people; even older Americans of comfortable financial means participate in entitlement programs like Social Security and Medicare. *(Richard Kalvar/Magnum)*

Income Security Programs

Income security programs are straightforward attempts to raise the level of cash available to beneficiaries. Recipients may be designated by status (for example, disabled people), prior participation (as in social security), or circumstance (AFDC payments are based on low income). Some of these programs are aimed at poor people (AFDC); others benefit nonpoor individuals (the tax expenditure on the deductibility of pension plan contributions). The total cost of federal income security programs, including tax expenditures, was about $616 billion in 1993.

Social Security

The **social security** system has long formed a stable and noncontroversial part of the U.S. welfare state. It encompasses old-age and survivors' insurance (OASI) and disability insurance (DI) programs. The nation's largest income security program, social security, represented about one-fifth of total federal outlays for 1993, providing benefits to one in every six Americans. A prorated share of each employee's wages is collected for social security, and the payments to beneficiaries are prorated in terms of their previous incomes. Benefits are indexed to increase with inflation. About 25 percent of social security recipients have incomes below the poverty line; about 30 percent have an

(Text continues on page 686)

TAX EXPENDITURES

A tax expenditure is a provision in the tax code that produces specific benefits for a target population by relieving it of some part of the tax liability that applies to all other persons. In the United States, tax expenditures began in 1918, a tight-budget year during World War I. Congress wished to increase veterans' benefits but did not want to increase spending directly. The ingenious solution was to make veterans' benefits exempt from the five-year-old federal income tax. The result was the same as if benefits had been increased directly—the veterans got more, and the federal government got a corresponding amount less—but tax expenditures had important political advantages. The amount by which benefits were increased never showed up in the budget itself (it could be found, if at all, in estimating the amount by which the exemption reduced income tax revenues). This was the start of something big. Just the twelve largest tax expenditure items in the 1993 budget totaled an estimated $300 billion dollars—more than the entire budget for national defense.

STEALTH WELFARE: THE TWELVE MOST EXPENSIVE TAX EXPENDITURES IN FISCAL 1993

	Estimated Revenue Loss (billions of dollars)
Net exclusion of employer-provided pension plan contributions and earnings	51.2
Exclusion of employer contributions for medical insurance premiums and medical care	43.1
Deductibility of mortgage interest on owner-occupied homes	42.9
Step-up basis of capital gains at death	28.1
Accelerated depreciation (normal tax method)	26.5
Deductibility of nonbusiness state and local taxes other than on owner-occupied homes	23.8
Exclusion of old-age and survivors' insurance benefits for retired workers	19.4
Deductibility of charitable contributions	18.0
Deferral of capital gains on home sales	13.9
Deductibility of state and local property taxes on owner-occupied homes	12.6
Exclusion of interest on public-purpose state and local debt	11.7
Exclusion of interest on life insurance savings	8.7

SOURCE: Office of Management and Budget.

(Box continues on page 685)

To many people the whole concept of tax expenditures seems a bit strange. They figure, "After all, it's my money in the first place. If the government decides not to take it from me, it's not a public expense, is it?" That logic works with *general* reductions in taxes and tax rates but not when the general tax rates are left in place and specific groups are granted specific exemptions—in that case it's as good as a check in the mail. The goal of tax expenditures, after all, is to deliver specific benefits to particular groups. There may be some reasonable disagreement about whether a charitable contribution, for example, should be counted as income in the first place, but the largest tax expenditure item in the 1993 federal budget, the net exclusion of employer-provided pension plan contributions and earnings, is clearly a federal subsidy of these pensions. The value granted to pension plan holders is exactly the amount by which the general revenue is decreased.

Of course, tax expenditures are not inherently bad—most on the books today are defensible. From an equity standpoint it is important to note that benefits distributed through the tax code tend to be regressive rather than progressive, but that should not disqualify them per se. From a democratic point of view, however, the problem with tax expenditures is that they operate outside the regular budget debate, putting the dispensed benefits at a distinct advantage to benefits lodged in particular line items of the budget. Especially during recessionary times, direct benefits are more subject to scrutiny and more vulnerable to reduction than tax expenditures.

Imagine, for example, a program that passed out checks not to renters or Americans whose finances are simple enough not to itemize deductions but only to people who were fortunate enough to be buying homes or vacation homes or even vacations to the South Seas if these are paid for by refinancing a mortgage. Suppose that this program gave households with incomes over $100,000 checks averaging $3,469 and households in the $20,000 to $30,000 bracket much smaller checks—$516 on average. The cost of passing out these checks would be nearly $43 billion—more than twice what the federal government spends for elementary, secondary, vocational, and higher education. Every member of Congress would cringe at voting for such a program—especially during a recession, when unemployment and poverty rates are high and budget deficits are large. But such a program already exists as a tax expenditure—the deductibility of home mortgage interest. Democracy ought to require that such a program be considered in public budget debates on an equal footing with other benefits programs.

Source: Neil Howe and Phillip Longman, "The Next New Deal," **Atlantic Monthly**, *April 1992, pp. 88–99.*

outside income, such as private pensions or investments, that exceeds their social security income. The average monthly benefit for a retired worker was $603 in December 1990. The 1993 federal outlay for social security was an estimated $302 billion. Since a portion of social security benefits can be excluded from income tax, the tax expenditure associated with social security added $19.4 billion to that figure. For many of the approximately 43 million people who receive monthly social security payments, those checks represent the difference between abject poverty and making do.

Although many people think of social security as a forced savings plan in which the government takes a worker's money now and gives it back later, the program has always worked as a transfer payment from the currently employed to the currently retired. Such a transfer works well as long as the number of active employees expands more rapidly than the number of current beneficiaries—the situation from the beginning of the program in the 1930s through the 1960s. But in the 1980s three key factors caused serious strains in the system: the number of post–World War II baby boomers (people born between 1946 and 1956) entering the work force subsided, workers began to retire earlier, and retirees were living longer. As a result, the ratio between current contributors and current beneficiaries became less favorable. An additional strain came from indexed benefits, which rise substantially in times of high inflation.

In 1983 Congress passed reforms (including more people in the system and raising tax rates) to keep the system in the black. These reforms began to generate large surpluses by 1988. But some observers worry that a crunch might still come when the time to reckon the bill arrives several years hence. Will workers then be willing to pay higher social security taxes to continue the transfer to a large population of retired baby boomers or support higher income taxes to repay loans from the social security trust fund made to cover general federal expenses? Some people question the basic equitability of the system, both in terms of how it distributes income to the elderly and how it shifts income across the generations. As the ratio of workers to beneficiaries declines, the issue of generational equity will certainly become more significant. But the system has worked relatively well for more than half a century and has engendered such widespread support that whatever adjustments are necessary, it should continue functioning successfully into the distant future.

AFDC

In contrast to the widespread acceptance and lack of controversy enjoyed by social security, **Aid to Families with Dependent Children (AFDC)** is the most controversial welfare state program and the one most people cite when they speak pejoratively of "welfare." AFDC, which dates back to the New Deal of the 1930s, provides cash benefits (unusual in programs aimed at the poor) to families with one or more dependent children. Because the program has no national standards, benefits differ from state to state, reflecting not only a differing cost of living but also different levels of political support. State governments determine the level of state participation in this largely federally and state-funded but locally administered program. In 1990 the median monthly benefit was $432—hardly a princely sum even when supplemented by food stamps. The poverty line for a single person in 1990 was $552 per month. AFDC accounted for only .9 percent of federal outlays; and 2.2 percent of state revenues in 1991. Over 40 percent of AFDC families have a single child, and another 30 percent have two children. Only 10 percent of AFDC families have more than three children. Grants usually increase with family size but are usually reduced when the family has earnings or the parent marries.

For many years AFDC ws a noncontroversial program that provided aid mainly to widows and their families not covered by other programs. Dissatisfaction with the program increased due to several factors: The number of recipients rose dramatically in the 1960s and early 1970s, driving up the cost of the program accordingly, and another dramatic increase in recipients occurred in 1990–1992; the original goal of allowing mothers to stay home with their children has been overwhelmed by the common expectation, driven by economic necessity, that most lower- and middle-class mothers now work outside the home; although most recipients use AFDC for short-term support, a substantial minority of recipients remain poor, on welfare, for long periods. All of these developments work against a program that is unfairly identified as the stereotypical welfare program. Reflecting these pressures, median AFDC benefits declined substantially between 1970 and 1990.

Concern that AFDC was promoting welfare dependence led to the Job Opportunities and Basic Skills (JOBS) provisions of the 1988 Family Support Act. Replacing and consolidating earlier welfare-to-work provisions, JOBS requires states to provide education or job training to an increasing number of AFDC recipients. More controversial is the participation requirement for recipients. The goal is to prevent long-term welfare dependence by forcing recipients back into the labor force. Critics of welfare-to-work provisions agree that a job is the best route to dignity and independence but contend that the problem is not lack of motivation that would require coercion; rather the problem is a lack of entry-level jobs that pay enough to stay out of poverty. As we saw in Chapter 18, a single mother working year round at the minimum wage will fall $600 short of the money needed to keep herself and her child above the poverty line.

The problem is not what would have to be counted as an irrational attachment to a life on welfare but rather the creation of genuine rewards for joining the work force. Consider the case of Linda Baldwin, a Chicagoan who, after ten years on welfare, decided to join the work force. She leaves home (a public housing project) at 7:30 every morning to go to her $6.00-an-hour job as a youth counselor in a nonprofit agency and comes back twelve hours later about $7.75 poorer than if she had never left. After working for two years, she is supporting her four children on about $169 less each month than welfare alone would provide. Her $12,480 salary falls nearly $3,000 short of the government poverty line for a family of five. Her health insurance through work provides less coverage than Medicaid does for welfare recipients. She cannot afford dental work for herself or eyeglasses for her son, though these would be covered if she quit work and went back on welfare. Her rent increased when she started to work outside the home. Although her family is larger than 90 percent of the families on AFDC, her wage is also significantly higher than the $4.25 minimum wage. Her situation

COMPARATIVE PERSPECTIVE

CHILD CARE PROGRAMS: SWEDEN VERSUS THE UNITED STATES

The social welfare system of Sweden provides a vast array of services for children and parents. To begin, the nation's compulsory health care system covers all pregnant women and provides contraceptive information, prenatal care and training, and preparation for parenting. Sweden also has an optional parental-leave program. Either parent may choose to stay home with the infant for the first nine months and still draw 90 percent of his or her salary. An additional leave of three months can be taken at a reduced salary, and parents can take up to sixty days leave each year (for each child) in the event of illness.

The Swedish government also provides financial aid to families with children under sixteen. Single parents are given special protection by the system. Child support is required from the absent parent, but if it is not paid, the government advances the money and assumes responsibility for regaining it. National and municipal governments provide a housing allowance to families that meet a means test (in 1983 approximately one-third of Swedish families received some housing supplement). A network of preschool facilities is sponsored and licensed mainly by the national and regional governments; about 37 percent of all preschool children are enrolled in child care programs.

Child care in the United States is less comprehensive, and the delivery of services is more complicated and scattered. People who are financially able can purchase excellent prenatal and infant care, while those who are not must depend on help from various government programs, charities, and voluntary groups. The WIC (Women, Infants and Children) federal program has provided assistance to millions of poor women and children, and help is also available through Medicaid at the state level. Cuts in these programs during the 1980s, however, left large numbers without financial help. The United States is the *only* industrialized Western nation without a statutory maternity leave or parental ben-

(Box continues on page 689)

will improve somewhat when she has paid off a delinquent student loan and gains some advantage from the federal earned-income credit on her taxes. But in the meantime, why does she work? She enjoys her job and hopes that the experience will mean a higher salary in the future. Still, "something is wrong with these laws," she says. "It's like they're telling you to stay home."[5] To change that message, the rewards of working at the bottom of the ladder must change.

efit. In 1978, federal law declared that pregnancy and childbirth must be treated like any illness or disability and therefore could not jeopardize one's job. However, no federal policy yet exists concerning parental leave for childbirth; parents must negotiate leave time with their employers. Americans can claim a tax deduction for dependent children and a means-tested tax credit for child care. Housing subsidies are far less available than in Sweden; although the mortgage interest deduction in the U.S. tax code is a major subsidy to homeowners, it is not targeted for families with children. Child support is also handled differently than in Sweden. When support is not paid, the aggrieved parent must seek relief in the courts. No provision exists yet for the government to supply missing financial support.

Day-care arrangements in the United States are varied. Again, for those who can pay, excellent facilities or caretakers may be found, and over the years, federal programs have provided some day-care facilities. Nonetheless, many parents cannot afford day care and do not qualify for assistance. The Children's Defense Fund estimates that 7 million children under age thirteen now spend part of each day without any adult caretaker.

These different patterns of provision for children reveal differences in each society's philosophy. Sweden is far more committed to a welfare state approach that is comprehensive and emphasizes equality of services. The American approach illustrates a scattered and less comprehensive adoption of welfare measures. The United States more or less provides for those who are worst off but does not extend protections and programs to the degree found in Sweden. The U.S. system reflects our ambivalent attitudes about the welfare state.

Sources: Ruth Sidel, Women and Children Last *(New York: Penguin, 1986); UNICEF,* The State of the World's Children *(New York: Oxford University Press, 1987); R. Berfenstam and I. WilliamOlsson,* Early Child Care in Sweden *(London: Gordon & Breach, 1973); Halbert B. Robinson* et. al., Early Child Care in the United States of America *(London: Gordon & Breach, 1973); Laura Walker, "Early Child Care in Sweden and the United States," unpublished paper. University of North Carolina, Department of Political Science, 1988; Merl C. Hokenstad, "Sweden," in* International Public Policy Sourcebook, *vol. 1 (Westport, Conn.: Greenwood Press, 1989).*

Job Programs

Almost everyone agrees that the best source of income security for poor people is a steady job. Unfortunately, that's as far as consensus reaches. A wide variety of federal programs emphasize one of two general approaches: job placement or job training. The Great Society programs of the 1960s simply focused on placing people in jobs.

One strategy (used, for example, by the Work Incentive Program, aimed at welfare mothers but now discontinued) was to provide federal money to state and local governments to hire poor people to do community service work. But the jobs led nowhere, and when funding for these programs ran out, participants were right back where they started. The Comprehensive Employment and Training Act (CETA), enacted in 1973 to replace several earlier, more diverse programs, tried a different tack. Here the idea was to encourage certain nongovernment employers to hire people for newly created jobs, providing federal funds for a limited time to pay their salaries, with the expectation that the jobs would then be maintained by the employer after program funding ceased. Again, experience showed that these jobs were dead-end positions, frequently dropped when CETA funding ended.

The second approach, job training, took shape in one of the War on Poverty programs called the Job Corps, aimed at young adults aged sixteen to twenty-one. This program is still in existence. Job Corps enrollees go to Job Corps Training Centers to learn a trade, where they are given spending money, which increases over time, as an incentive to stay in the program. Participants spend an average of eight to twelve months at a training center. After graduating from the training center, participants receive placement help and job counseling at local offices in their hometowns. Another training-oriented program, under the Job Training Partnership Act (JTPA), replaced CETA in 1982. Most JTPA participants go through classroom training and then gain help in job placement. Eligibility requirements for JTPA are much stricter than CETA requirements were, substantially reducing the number of participants. Although some on-the-job training is available, most JTPA training takes place in classrooms. To participate, however, a person must have some outside source of income for the period of training, as JTPA does not pay wages or living expenses. This excludes many who might benefit from such training and are eager to receive it. Federal outlays for job training and employment dropped significantly during the 1980s, from $10.8 billion in 1979 to $5.2 billion ten years later. The estimated 1993 spending in this category is $5.8 billion.

Other Income Security Programs

Let us now consider three additional types of income security programs: Supplemental Security Income (SSI), unemployment compensation, and tax expenditures for income security.

SSI In 1974, Congress created the **Supplemental Security Income (SSI)** program to provide added assistance to the aged, blind, and disabled. More like AFDC than social security, SSI pays benefits on the basis of need and is federally funded with state supplements. This program nearly doubled the number of people receiving federal income security assistance (other than through social security). SSI outlays from the federal and state governments totaled $16.6 billion and reached about 4.9 million people in 1990. A recent government study estimated that only about half the people eligible for certain categories of SSI payments were applying for them. One of the major reasons cited by eligible nonparticipants for not seeking benefits was that they "don't like the idea of accepting what some people might call welfare."[6] In this country there is an unfortunate stigma attached to welfare programs aimed primarily at the poor.

UNEMPLOYMENT COMPENSATION Unemployment compensation is a federal program administered by the Labor Department through various state employment agencies. It is predominantly state-funded through a tax on employers.

Benefits differ from state to state, as do eligibility requirements and the length of time benefits can be received. The system covers workers who have a history of regular employment and have lost their jobs but not those who have never held a regular job or who hold jobs not covered by the program, such as domestic work. The federal outlay for unemployment compensation varies with the unemployment rate. It reached $36.6 billion at the height of the recession in 1992. Increasing *underemployment* has reduced the number of persons eligible for unemployment compensation. According to the Federal Reserve Bank of San Francisco, the number of people covered by unemployment insurance declined more than 25 percent during the 1980s.

TAX EXPENDITURES FOR INCOME SECURITY The federal government also provides income security support through tax expenditure items. The largest single item in this category is the exclusion of employer contributions to pension plans, which amounted to a tax expenditure of $51.2 billion in 1993, a very substantial welfare state program for the nonpoor. These benefits are generally regressive; they increase with increased income and are worth more to persons in the highest tax bracket.

Health-Care Programs

Several aspects of the U.S. health-care system are almost universally acknowledged: Many Americans receive excellent health care, American medicine ranks among the most advanced in the world, American health care is the world's costliest, health-care costs are increasing rapidly, many Americans do *not* receive adequate health care, the distribution of care is related to the patient's ability to pay, and the system needs reforming (see **Figure 19–1**). There is no agreement, however, on what sort of reforms should be instituted. Some people argue for a national health insurance scheme that would cover major medical expenses for all; others call for government controls on increasing costs; yet others advocate greater government involvement in the distribution and planning of health care.

In the United States much of the average citizen's health-care bill is paid for out of pocket or through employee benefits. This stands in stark contrast to most other democratic, industrialized nations. The U.S. health-care system has two major elements: a private health-care system, in which costs are paid by consumers or through group

FIGURE 19-1

U.S. LEAD WIDENS IN SPENDING FOR HEALTH CARE

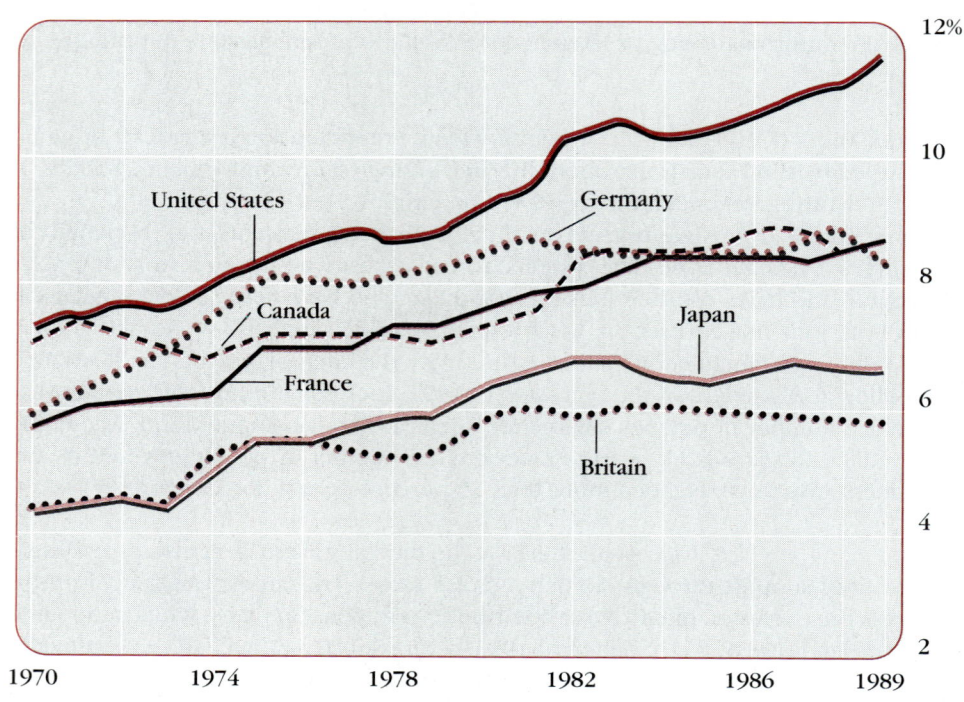

[Line graph showing health care spending as percentage of GDP from 1970 to 1989 for United States, Germany, Canada, France, Japan, and Britain. The U.S. line rises from about 7% in 1970 to nearly 12% in 1989, outpacing all other countries.]

SOURCE: George J. Schieber and Jean-Pierre Poullier, *Health Affairs*, Spring 1991.

insurance plans, and a public system, financed through government programs supplemented by consumer contributions. Americans served only by the various publicly supported health services—the poor—are likely to have the lowest levels of health. Having the money to pay for services or buy insurance makes a significant difference in the quality of health care that individuals receive.

For the average middle-class American covered by some form of private health insurance, basic health care is essentially guaranteed. Still, many insurance plans do not meet important medical needs. Catastrophic illness may boost costs beyond what insurance covers. Preventive measures may not be covered by medical insurance. Thirty-five million Americans have no health insurance coverage at all; they are constantly at risk. The United States is the only country in the industrialized world (except for South Africa) that does not guarantee basic health care for its children. More than one out of five youngsters in America is denied basic preventive care in this system.

Unlike AFDC, which stirs general political controversy, health policy directly engages the interests of powerful groups like the private insurance companies and the American Medical Association. Such groups have traditionally been obstacles to social reform of the health-care system. President Franklin Roosevelt considered adding a national health insurance section to the Social Security Act of 1935 but chose not to because he feared arousing too much political opposition. The issue of a national health-care plan has been politically volatile ever since. One major step toward greater governmental responsibility for health care was taken in 1965 when Congress, under the prodding of President Lyndon Johnson, created the Medicare and Medicaid programs.

Medicare

Since its establishment in 1965, **Medicare** has become one of the mainstays of the U.S. welfare state. Medicare provides payments to everyone eligible for social security, classified as disabled, or suffering from kidney failure. The program has two parts. Part A covers hospital, nursing home, and home health services for a specified period; it is available to all eligible persons and is financed through a payroll tax split between employer and employee. Part B, which covers doctors' bills, outpatient hospital services, home health services, and certain other costs, is a voluntary program based on monthly premiums. Medicare, like private medical insurance, has limited benefits; that

The American health care system is often difficult to figure out, especially for the elderly. One of the most pressing needs is for adequate nursing home care. A portion of that care is provided by government. This photo shows a resident of a Veterans Administration nursing home in Johnson City, Tennessee. *(Kenneth Murray/Photo Researchers)*

is, recipients must pay a portion of the costs out of their own pockets. Despite these limits, Medicare has come to cover an increasing share of the health-care costs of the elderly.

Medicare has expanded rapidly. The steady and sharp increase in Medicare spending since its inception stems from three key factors. First, the establishment of Medicare prompted millions of people to seek medical care they would otherwise have done without. Second, the size of the elderly population covered by Medicare has been growing. Finally, hospital costs have soared, climbing at more than double the inflation rate.

In response to skyrocketing health-care costs and a Medicare budget whose growth had exceeded all expectations, a major change was made in 1983 in the formula for allocating reimbursement for Medicare patients. Instead of reimbursing hospitals on a cost-plus basis (which allowed hospitals to set their own fees), the hospital was now reimbursed according to a predetermined fee, regardless of the actual cost of treatment. The effects of this change were both immediate and far-reaching. Within a year the average hospital stay covered by Medicare had declined 20 percent and hospital occupancy rates had dropped to the lowest point in twenty years. Medical inflation was temporarily cut in half.

Under the old system, hospitals could make internal, hidden transfers of benefits, bringing in a little extra money on Medicare patients to make up for the money lost on indigent patients without insurance. Under the new repayment scheme, such transfers were impossible. In an increasing number of cases, poor patients were turned away from private hospitals and referred to public facilities that became heavily burdened. Many people feared that in the effort to economize, the nation was creating a two-tiered medical system, with separate and unequal care for the poor. Nevertheless, the federal outlay for Medicare continues to climb rapidly. Federal outlays for Medicare were $6.2 billion in 1970, $32.0 billion in 1980, $98.1 billion in 1990, and an estimated $129.3 billion for 1993.

In spite of spiraling expenditures, Medicare still covers only a fraction of the actual health-care costs of participants. For those who can afford it, private "**Medigap**" **insurance** supplements the Medicare coverage. In 1988, Congress passed the Catastrophic Health Care Law to cover enrolees beyond the Medicare limits. But catastrophic health care was funded by a supplemental fee on wealthy seniors. This group rose up in furor over the funding formula, and catastrophic health was quickly repealed, leaving in its wake frustration and a sense of futility among health-care policymakers.

Other Health-Care Programs

We now look at Medicaid, nursing home care, and health research with an eye toward their initial goals, how they are—or are not—reaching those goals, and their overall impact.

MEDICAID **Medicaid**, a state-option program, extends medical assistance to the needy. Each state establishes its own eligibility rules and compensation levels. In many states Medicaid coverage is limited to people receiving public assistance benefits. Other states use broader definitions of the "medically indigent."

Several important differences distinguish Medicaid from Medicare. Medicare is a federal program with its own trust fund (raised from payroll taxes and general revenues); Medicaid is a cooperative federal-state program that depends almost entirely on appropriations from general revenues. Medicare has a strong, politically active constituency (senior citizens); Medicaid, serving 27 million poor people (13 million of whom are children), does not. When the federal government requires states to increase Medicaid eligibility (as in 1991, when all children living at or below the federal poverty level were mandated coverage), the states often compensate by reducing Medicaid payments to doctors. In 1991 the average Medicaid payment to doctors was only 69 percent of the Medicare payment. The result is that fewer physicians are willing to take Medicaid patients, reducing the availability of medical care. A report to Congress in 1991 revealed that forty-four states were having difficulty getting doctors to participate in Medicaid, citing low fees as the most common factor in the problem.[7] Although Medicaid was originally intended to provide health-care protection for the nonelderly poor, 40 percent of Medicaid allocations now cover nursing home care, mostly for the elderly. In 1990, Medicaid benefits payments totaled $68.7 billion for 25.3 million recipients.

NURSING HOME CARE Most people who enter nursing homes are not poor. Most people *in* nursing homes are poor, however, and the nursing home bills are often the reason. Medicare covers only the first twenty days of nursing home care. For the two-thirds of Medicare recipients currently covered by Medigap insurance, some or all of the cost of days 21 to 100 are covered. Very few supplemental insurance policies cover beyond one hundred days. Thus personal resources are quickly called on to cover nursing home costs, which average around $25,000 a year. This burden soon exhausts personal resources, making patients eligible for Medicaid. Although Medicaid benefits vary from state to state, none limit the number of days of nursing home care an enrollee can receive. This has made Medicaid the largest program, public or private, in the United States for financing nursing home care. Medicaid paid for 44 percent of nursing home expenditures in 1990.[8]

HEALTH RESEARCH An important but relatively inconspicuous part of the welfare state involves health research undertaken by or subsidized by the federal government. The advent of AIDS has made federal health research both more visible and more controversial, but federal involvement in health research dates much further back and covers a much broader range than the AIDS crisis suggests. Through the National Institutes of Health (NIH), a group of associated research organizations, and the Centers for Disease Control (CDC), the federal government conducts its own health research. In addition, through a series of grants to universities and private research organizations, the government supports more health-related research. Altogether the federal government spent $10.6 billion on health research and training in 1993. Added to that figure is some significant portion of the $1.8 billion tax expenditure in health-related charitable contributions.

Health research has never been particularly controversial in the United States, yet the heightened visibility of medical research raises important and clearly debatable public policy issues. For example, in 1988 the Reagan administration banned federally funded research using fetal tissue (usually obtained from induced abortions), fearing that such research might encourage or legitimize abortion. Opponents of the ban stressed the potential benefits of such research in finding cures for Parkinson's disease, Alzheimer's disease, diabetes, Huntington's disease, and spinal cord injuries, among others. They argued that fetal tissue research would not encourage abortions and that issues of tissue supplies and handling could easily be addressed through facilitating regulations. In 1992, Congress passed legislation overturning the executive ban, but the legislation was vetoed by President Bush, who then altered federal regulations to allow for research using tissue from spontaneous abortions and ectopic pregnancies. Critics responded that the supply of tissue from such sources would be inadequate and that such tissue would likely be unacceptable for research purposes anyway. Presidential candidate Bill Clinton called the Bush veto "politics pure and simple . . . an ugly bow to the far right."[9]

Choosing the subjects of publicly funded medical research is also controversial. Some very expensive research has resulted in costly procedures that provide great benefits to a very small number of individuals—the development of artificial hearts, for instance. Would a democrat urge that some of those resources should have been directed at research promising more modest gains for much larger numbers of people? And what about health problems that are lifestyle-related—how much public funding should there be to research health problems that result from individual choices? Policy choices have to be made. In a democracy those choices should be the subject of public discussion.

Proposals for Reform

The United States spends more per capita on health care than any other nation. But money for health care doesn't translate directly into good health. Some of the best health care in the world is available in the United States, but medical services are very unevenly distributed and often tied to wealth. Many millions of people, including millions of children, are seriously undeserved. Proposals for universal health care flourished in the early 1970s but were stymied by the complexity of the health-care system and the entrenched forces of the status quo. By the beginning of the 1990s it looked again as if substantial health-care reform was irresistible. Public opinion supported reform of some sort. Among respondents in a 1991 Gallup poll, 91 percent believed that there was a crisis in health care; 85 percent said that the system needed reforming.

Seventy-nine percent of respondents in a 1991 Harris poll favored establishing a system of national health insurance.[10] Increasingly through the 1980s and early 1990s, while wage increases were blocked and wage concessions became more common, organized labor (a traditional supporter of national health plans) placed increased emphasis on job security and health benefits. This time even the American Medical Association, one of the most prestigious and powerful opponents of national health in the past, signed on. But this was the post-Reagan 1990s, and though the symptoms of problems in health care were acute, the prescriptions offered were much more modest than the all-out nationalized health plans floated two decades earlier.

Far from creating a nationalized system of health care as is found in Great Britain, the leading proposals in Congress in 1991 and 1992 were all health-care *insurance* plans, finding one way or another to help Americans to afford care from the existing mix of mostly private health-care providers. They fell into three camps: Canadian-style health care, pay or play, and insurance reform.[11] A *Canadian-style* plan would have taxes pay for government-administered health insurance. The simplest way of achieving this would be to extend Medicare benefits to all legal residents. Government-set fees could be mandatory, or provision for copayment by the patient could allow doctors to charge more. The major stumbling block to this sort of system is the private medical insurers (like Blue Cross), which would be put out of business. Opponents also worried about a huge, unresponsive government insurance bureaucracy that would have enormous control over availability of treatment. *Pay or play* would maintain employment as the primary source of insurance. Employers (even very small ones) would be required to obtain health insurance from private providers or would be required to pay into a government-administered pool that would provide insurance. France and Germany use plans like this, although the insurers there are heavily regulated nonprofit agencies. Pay-or-play plans are opposed by small business owners worried about unbearable increased costs. *Insurance market reform*, the least ambitious of the plans, would force insurers to pool small business insurance policies, creating favorable rates comparable to those negotiated by large firms. Limitations on individual eligibility for insurance (waiting periods, for example, or restrictions on preexisting conditions) could be mandatorily reduced.

Since cost control is essential to any national scheme of health insurance, a variety of mechanisms have been proposed. *Managed care* provides health services through **health maintenance organizations (HMOs)**. Since HMOs contract to provide all needed services for a prearranged fee, the organization has an internal interest in reducing costs by promoting health and avoiding unnecessary services. *Certificates of need* are a means of rationing the providers: Government would decide how many expensive diagnostic centers or cardiac surgery teams a particular locality needs. For example, the United States has two thousand magnetic resonance imaging (MRI) scanners ($2 million apiece); Canada has only fifteen. Proponents of rationing say that this ratio demonstrates the wasteful duplication of services here; opponents say that this ratio reflects Canadian-style impediments to technological innovation there. *Tax reform* would remove health plan tax expenditure incentives from businesses, forcing

COMPARATIVE PERSPECTIVE

HEALTH CARE NORTH OF THE BORDER

Health-care professionals in Canada operate on a fee-for-service basis like that predominant in the United States. Yet unlike the United States, every citizen is guaranteed health care. The difference is universal insurance coverage. Each of the ten provinces and two territories runs its own health insurance plan, with costs shared between the provincial government and the federal government. The universal health insurance pays for all necessary health care—72 percent of all health-care expenditures. Although each province is different, the expenses borne by individuals include drugs, eyeglasses, dental care, cosmetic surgery, and extra fees for private hospital rooms.

Individuals are free to choose their primary physician and to change at any time. When visiting the doctor, making use of the emergency room, or being admitted to the hospital, the patient simply shows a personal health card. Billing is handled by the doctor. Because physicians are reimbursed directly by the government, they are ensured payment with lower overhead costs. One comparison in 1985 determined that Canada spent $21 per person to administer its health system, compared to $95 in administrative costs per person in the United States that year.

Several complaints about the Canadian system are dismissed as myths by proponents like health policy analyst Jane Fulton. She says, for instance, that doctors are not starved in Canada—they earn five times the national average income (up from only twice the national average before universal health care). In some fields

(Box continues on page 699)

each employer into a more realistic evaluation of spending an extra health-care dollar. *Rationing services* could be accomplished by insurers or government. The Oregon state government has implemented a plan that prioritizes procedures, preferring effective, inexpensive treatments for large numbers (prenatal care, for example) over expensive treatments for a few (organ transplants). (The Bush administration vetoed the plan.) Many private insurers currently do not cover most cosmetic surgery or infertility treatment, for example. *Caps on expenditures* would involve an absolute limit on the health-care budget for the country. Proponents say that this would cause the system to weigh the advantages of one service over another; opponents contend that needed care would be denied and medical programs slowed. *Malpractice limitations* would reduce the maximum size of damage awards for malpractice, lowering the cost of malpractice insurance and reducing "defensive medicine"—too many unnecessary

> like urology, Canadian physicians actually make more than their American counterparts. Fulton also reports that waits for services are not long. "In fact, use of the most expensive services in Canada went down when we got our universal health care because people went to see the doctor when they first began to feel sick, and didn't wait to go to the emergency department when they were profoundly ill." She defends the Canadian record on implementing high-tech medicine as one that demonstrates careful choices in contrast to the unregulated proliferation of expensive technology in the United States. Is universal health care too expensive? Overall Canada pays less for health care and, by some indicators like infant mortality, gets superior results. The savings come from lower overhead and negotiated fee schedules.
>
> In spite of widespread support for the Canadian universal health-care system, fiscal restraints are being felt more acutely. There has been increasing talk in recent years about instituting some user fees for health care as a means of raising revenue and cutting costs. Resistance to such an idea is strong, however, in part out of a concern that user fees would drive away the poor and the elderly. Canadians like what their health-care system does for them individually and as a community. One writer explains it like this: "As Canadians perceive it, the United States has patches of superior fabric in its quilt of coverage, fabric that is richer than any part of Canada's blanket. But in Canada the blanket does cover all. Nobody is left out in the cold."
>
> *Sources: Marilyn Dunlop, "Health Care Canadian-Style," and Carla Atkinson, "Fact and Fiction: A View from North of the Border," both in July-August 1992; Mary Williams Walsh, "Canada's Health Care System May Be Catching Virus,"* Los Angeles Times, *November 26, 1991, p. H2.*

medical tests ordered as protection against a suit. Opponents insist that damages should be considered on a case-by-case basis with no arbitrary limit on awards.

In general, the case for health-care reform is compelling. Compared to other advanced democracies, the United States spends a large and ever-increasing amount on a health-care system that is forced to make costly repairs (surgery, hospitalization) or therapeutic compensations for health problems that could have been prevented or treated much less expensively early on. It costs $7,000 to provide hospital care for a child with measles; full vaccination costs only $65. Today a two-year-old in Mexico City is more likely to be fully immunized than a similar child in the United States.[12]

Of all parts of the American welfare state, the health-care system is most obviously in need of change. The compelling arguments for health-care reform and widespread dissatisfaction with the status quo do not ensure that meaningful reform will be accomplished. Not everyone is poorly served at present. Some very large interests are at stake. In a pluralistic democracy in which policy usually changes incrementally, if at all, superficial change—window dressing only—sometimes satisfies the popular appetite without addressing real needs. One of the difficult civic responsibilities of democrats is to distinguish between this sort of diversionary tactic on the one hand and the always incomplete compromises of genuine policy in the public interest on the other.

Nutrition and Housing Programs

Let us now consider the impact of several nutrition and housing programs.

Food Stamps

The **food stamp program**, designed to respond to the problem of hunger in America, actually began as an experiment in 1961. The goal of the food stamp program was to give nutrition-program participants greater choice than was provided by the surplus-commodities program, which passed out a lot of peanut butter and canned chicken that was wasted because recipients didn't like it or want it. From the beginning the food stamp program gained important political support from food producers and marketers, who clearly benefit from the increased purchasing power the program generates for their industry. The linkage between benefits to participants and benefits to producers has always been explicit—food stamp legislation is paired in the House of Representatives with legislation to help farmers. And the food stamp program is administered at the federal level through the Department of Agriculture and not, as we might expect, through the Department of Health and Human Services.

By 1973, food stamps had become the predominent federal program providing nutritional assistance for the poor. The food stamp program provides food coupons for all recipients of public assistance, as well as those whose income falls below specified levels. Administered jointly by the states and the federal government, it is funded entirely by the federal government. Each month the people who qualify receive food coupons redeemable at groceries and supermarkets. Recipients qualify on the basis of need, as determined by income plus other assets. The food stamp program is one of the few government programs open to the working poor; candidates for food stamps need not be utterly destitute to qualify. Most states have established employment and training programs for employable food stamp recipients, as required by the Food Security Act of 1985. The most common feature of these programs is job search assistance.

The food stamp program has dramatically reduced hunger and malnutrition in the United States. Because of food stamps, many poor people at least have food to eat. Along with several other nutrition-oriented assistance programs—particularly those providing school breakfasts and lunches—the food stamp program has been one of the bright spots for the poor in recent times.

Other Nutrition Programs

One major federal program is the Child Nutrition Program, which gives cash subsidies for food to day-care centers and schools. Its largest component is the National School Lunch Program, which provides free or reduced-price lunches to over 24 million children. In addition, the federal government sponsors the Emergency Food Assistance Program, providing commodities to people in urgent, short-term need of food, and the Women, Infants and Children (WIC) program, offering nutrition supplements for one segment of the population.

Altogether the federal outlay for food and nutrition assistance was $34 billion in 1993. In addition, there are indirect nutrition subsidies in the federal agricultural income stabilization programs ($13.3 billion in 1993) and in agriculture-related tax expenditures ($420 million in 1993). Food producers are the direct beneficiaries of these programs, and all citizens theoretically benefit from them indirectly.

But funding does not meet need. Hunger has not disappeared from America. In 1991, WIC served only 57 percent of the poor mothers and young children who qualified for the program. And even though food stamp allotments are at an all-time high, they lag behind the actual cost of a good diet. The Food Research and Action Center estimates that even with WIC, food stamps, and other federal and state nutrition programs, 5.5 million children under age twelve suffer from hunger. Dr. William Bithoney, director of the Malnutrition Clinic at Boston Children's Hospital, says:

> People have trouble believing there's such a thing as a malnutrition clinic in a major American city. In 1983 we did a study that showed [that] 15 percent of poor kids are chronically malnourished. It's probably higher today. Every day we see kids that are so poorly nourished that it directly affects their general health and development.[13]

Housing Programs

Federal programs to provide housing assistance fall into two large categories: (1) tax expenditures and credit programs to lower the cost of buying housing for the nonpoor and (2) programs to provide public housing or housing supplements for the poor. Both categories also benefit the housing industry, an important segment of the economy. Private purchasers of homes in the United States are eligible for the first type of housing assistance, in the form of tax deductions on the amount paid in interest on a home mortgage and the amount paid in home property taxes. These deductions may be used for a principal residence and a second home. The deductibility of mortgage interest and property tax on owner-occupied homes created a tax expenditure of $55.5 billion in 1993. In addition, the federal government provides loans through the Federal Hous-

Former President Jimmy Carter became heavily involved in the privately sponsored Habitat for Humanity program, which builds homes for poor Americans. Such private humanitarian efforts are one way to help remedy the deficit in decent housing for lower-income people. *(UPI/Bettmann)*

ing Administration (FHA) and the Veterans Administration (VA) to qualified purchasers of homes. These loans are offered on more favorable terms than loans from private lenders, thus lowering the cost of borrowing money to buy a home. These housing programs are aimed at a broad spectrum of Americans—everyone able to buy a home.

The second category of federal housing programs is specifically for the poor. Initially, this category was restricted to public housing. Since 1937 the federal government has given funds to local governments to construct or buy inexpensive housing units. Although never glamorous, these housing units were designed to be structurally sound and made available at low rents based on income and family size. Although some small-city public housing projects are very successful, high-density public housing in urban areas is frequently marked by high crime rates and vandalism. Public housing has never been favored by private real estate interests like the National Association of Home Builders and the National Association of Real Estate Boards, which would rather not have the federal government compete with the private sector in building and renting apartments. In 1968, Congress launched a set of subsidy and rent supplement programs to help the working poor to rent or buy a home from designated nongovernment

FIGURE 19-2
THE GROWING SHORTAGE OF LOW-COST HOUSING

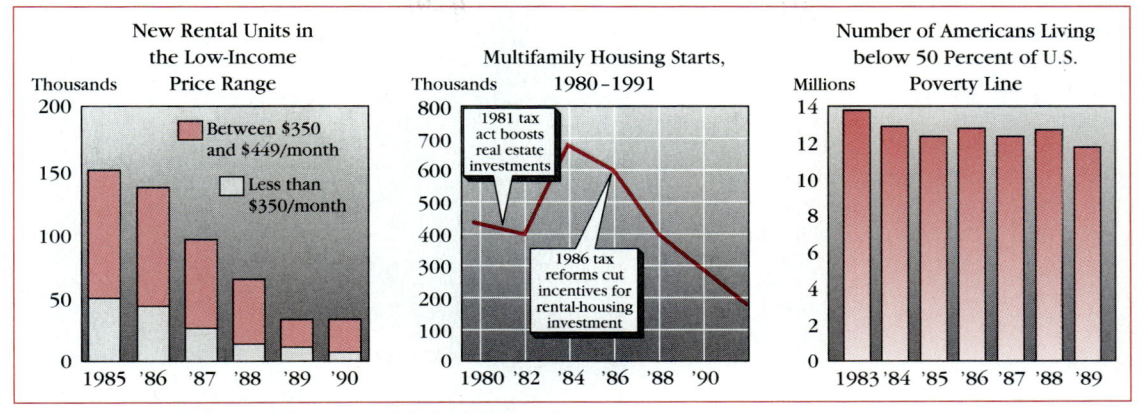

SOURCE: *Christian Science Monitor*, July 3, 1992, p. 8.

sources. Section 8 of 1974 revisions to the legislation provides cash supplements to individuals seeking to buy or rent a home. These supplements are intended to stimulate the construction of private-sector, low-cost housing, always in short supply (see **Figure 19-2**).

More direct stimulus to construction—a tax credit for building multifamily low-income housing—was included in the Tax Reform Act of 1986. By 1992 that credit had been responsible for the construction of 420,000 homes for low-income families—95 percent of all new multifamily low-income housing built during that period. The tax credit (for new construction or the rehabilitation of derelict properties) requires that properties be made available to low-income tenants at restricted rents (currently $450 or less) for fifteen years. A spokesperson for the National Association of Home Builders says, "Without the tax credit, we believe that there would be virtually no rental units being produced right now for under $450 per month. It has become nearly impossible for the private market to produce rental units available to families with low incomes without some kind of compensating tax incentive."[14] Critics point to the significant portion of benefits that end up in the hands of developers and tax accountants and to the built-in reduction of low-rent housing in the fifteen-year limit on rent restrictions.

The Census Bureau has concluded that about 220,000 units of low-income housing are lost each year due to upgrades, abandonment, and demolition; 2.2 million were lost between 1985 and 1989. A Housing and Urban Development study showed that about 5.4 million low-income households in the United States spend more than half their income on rent. In 1993 the total federal direct outlay for housing assistance was $21.8 billion. The total projected cost between 1992 and 1997 of the low-income housing tax credit was estimated at $2.4 billion. The cost in 1993 of the deduction for home mortgage interest was $42.9 billion.

One of the most ignoble disasters in the history of public housing. The Pruitt-Igoe project in St. Louis is destroyed because it became uninhabitable and not worth repairing. Public housing projects have sometimes seemed to intensify the very problems they were supposed to remedy. Although some people have become cynical about government efforts in public housing, others have argued that social problems were simply more difficult to deal with than we had imagined. *(UPI/Bettmann)*

The Bush administration, prompted by HUD Secretary Jack Kemp, pushed Home-ownership Opportunities for People Everywhere (HOPE), a program offering residents grants to modernize and convert their public housing projects into resident-owned cooperatives. HOPE's advocates see ownership as the ultimate American solution to the problems of both the project and the residents, fostering pride and independence. Skeptics see the federal government trying to wash its hand of the projects without addressing the structural economic problems of poor people. Pam Griffin, a job counselor in (and lifetime resident of) a housing project in the Watts section of Los Angeles, found the program condescending. "My American dream is not to own a unit in public housing—come on. A housing project is not the American dream. It's not even the African-American dream.[15]

Homelessness

Housing programs for poor people suffered some of the most severe cutbacks when social spending was reduced during the 1980s. These cutbacks in federal housing programs were coupled with a large increase in homelessness. Current estimates of the number of homeless people in America range from 300,000 to 3 million. Of course there have always been homeless people in this country, as in all countries. But the sheer numbers and variety of individuals living on the streets point to a genuine public policy problem. Whole families, unable to pay rent or meet mortgage obligations, live in dilapidated cars or move from one emergency shelter to another. Studies of homeless children indicate that more than 50 percent display signs of clinical depression and lack of significant developmental progress. Deinstitutionalization—releasing margin-

THE WELFARE STATE 705

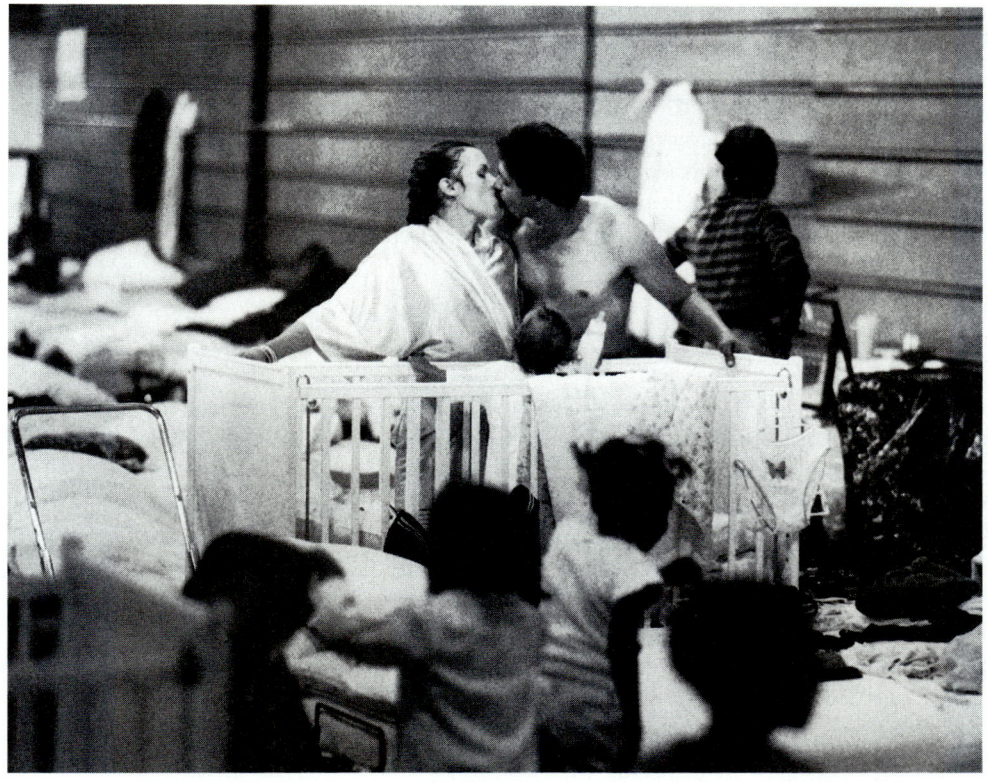

Affection and family life continue even in a public shelter. The problem of homelessness has become an open sore festering all over America. The diagnoses and suggestions for remedies are many, yet the problem has not been effectively dealt with. Why? Many suggest a lack of political will. *(George Cohen/Impact Visuals)*

ally self-sufficient individuals from financially burdened public mental institutions—further swells the ranks of the new street people. In some cities, veterans, most from the Vietnam War, make up close to half of all homeless males.

Traditional conservative explanations of homelessness center on the individuals, picturing them as mental cases, products of pathological families, or people looking to get something for nothing. Traditional liberal explanations center on social causes—structural poverty, alienation, neglect. The most straightforward explanation for the expansion of homelessness in the 1980s is that affordable housing disappeared. Low-rent apartments were upgraded or abandoned, and single-room-occupancy hotels (never great places to live but at least a buffer between better lodging and the streets) were shut down as part of urban renewal campaigns. New low-income housing construction did not keep up with lost units. Add to the general lack of low-income housing the structure of the national job market, in which full-time work at minimum wage cannot keep a single parent with one child out of poverty, and a large part of homelessness is readily explained.

Nevertheless, the homeless are strikingly diverse. Homelessness is a complex problem with many roots. In 1987, Congress passed the Stewart B. McKinney Homeless Assistance Act, offering emergency food and shelter, health services, job training, education, and other support services to the homeless. But funding never approximated need, and as the country slipped into the recession of 1990–1992, the homeless disappeared from the headlines but not from the streets.

Evaluating the Welfare State

How we view the welfare state depends to some extent on our individual political philosophy. The largest obstacle to evaluation is that we are conditioned to consider only certain welfare state programs—those in aid of poor people—as if they were the whole enterprise. This conditioning results from the language we use to describe programs ("assistance" versus "investment credits," for example), the structure of public accounting (direct outlays versus tax expenditure items), and the class- and race-based stereotypes into which we are socialized (such as the "welfare mother"). Any reasoned debate about the welfare state must start more inclusively, considering the whole range of programs by which positive government provides specific benefits to citizens.

The Conservative Approach

Conservatives advocate minimal government involvement in the marketplace—even in the labor market. According to many conservatives, government welfare benefits discourage people from seeking employment, thereby undermining market mechanisms that would deal efficiently with unemployment. When benefits are raised too high, the argument goes, incentives to work are reduced, and the people who do work become discouraged. In areas such as health care and housing, conservatives also contend that the market should do more and the government less. Private enterprise should be looked to as the primary solution.

Conservative critic Charles Murray denounces the Great Society programs of the 1960s. Like many conservatives, he believes that these welfare programs encouraged poverty rather than combated it:

> The first effect of the new [welfare] rules was to make it profitable for the poor to behave in the short term in ways that were destructive in the long term. Their second effect was to mask these long-term losses—to subsidize irretrievable mistakes. We tried to provide more for the poor and produced more poor instead. We tried to remove the barriers to escape from poverty, and inadvertently built a trap.[16]

The Liberal Critique

The U.S. welfare state has been largely a liberal creation, so liberals tend to be defensive about it. But they have also criticized its inadequacies. Liberals cite three key problems with the welfare system, summarized as *too little*, *too complicated*, and *too late*.

To liberals, the system provides less than it should. Many people fall through the cracks, and millions who are eligible for various welfare benefits never apply. As a result, poverty continues to pose a major problem for U.S. society. Many liberals charge that the absence of a comprehensive national health plan constitutes a critical failing of the welfare state. Although liberals differ on how to address the system's shortcomings, they generally acknowledge the need for more comprehensive health coverage.

The criticism that the welfare state has become too complicated centers on the absence of a genuinely national welfare system. Benefits vary considerably from state to state, often with no reasonable basis for the differences. Under the influence of Daniel Patrick Moynihan (later elected as a Democratic senator from New York State),

A day-care center in France. Like some other European democracies, the French provide government-sponsored day care, which is generally judged to be of high quality. In the United States, we have left the provision of these services to the private sector, with mixed results at best. *(Leonard Freed/Magnum)*

President Richard Nixon proposed a nationalization of welfare benefits in 1969 in his Family Assistance Program. Ironically, this initiative was defeated in Congress by a coalition of conservatives who found it too liberal and liberals who found its assistance provisions too stingy.

Finally, many liberals view the current U.S. welfare system as more of a series of Band-Aids than a comprehensive solution to poverty. The various programs, it is argued, patch up the victims of our social and economic systems—those who fail, who fall by the wayside, who can't keep up. But the real problem is that our social and economic systems themselves create so many needy. The proposed solution here is a full-employment economy: With everyone working, the burdens and needs of welfare would be sharply reduced, although not eliminated. At the same time, more people would gain needed skills and self-respect. The Humphrey-Hawkins "full-employment" bill was passed by Congress and signed by President Carter in 1978. Its goal of maintaining unemployment at or below 4 percent is still on the books, but no serious effort to implement this policy has ever been made.

Conclusions

Americans tend to view themselves as an individualistic people, crediting talent and hard work for their successes and blaming personal shortcomings for their failures. But the hard times of the Great Depression demonstrated that poverty and unemployment—the lack of basic security—were not solely personal issues; they were integrally connected with larger social arrangements that no one individual could change. Yet the individualistic ethic persists, intensifying the antigovernment attitudes so common in our nation. Oddly, however, we are quite willing to have government step in to help people during disasters, to bail out major corporations, to aid business through tax loopholes, and to keep farmers solvent.

This ambivalence has stood in the way of solving the pressing problems of need in our midst—problems that affect almost all Americans sooner or later. We have taken some steps, but they have been hesitant, inconsistent, and often inefficient.

When it comes to equality, the U.S. welfare state does effect a modest redistribution of resources, and government programs do aid most of the vulnerable poor. At the same time, some Americans still fall below a minimally decent standard of living. How can we reconcile the increasing numbers of homeless and hungry people in America with the deeply rooted American belief in equality of opportunity?

Finally, consider the paternalism of our welfare state. Various programs demean the people receiving benefits, especially when the recipients must continually prove they are poor enough to qualify. Fortunately, the infamous welfare regulations of the past, which often involved extensive surveillance of poor people, have largely been humanized. But programs designed for poor people still tend to stigmatize recipients rather than empower them.

Moreover, incongruities abound in our system. Whereas elderly millionaires may be entitled to generous pensions and medical care, poor mothers with sick children often go unaided. Programs that serve the large middle-class constituency—social security and Medicare—are difficult to touch politically. The largest elements (in dollar terms) of the welfare state—tax expenditure items—are so inconspicuous as to be absent from most discussions of welfare. The vast majority of Americans who benefit from the welfare state believe in the myth that welfare is for poor people. Programs that are targeted mainly toward the poor—such as food stamps, housing, AFDC, and child nutrition—are far more vulnerable politically because their constituency is smaller, less organized, and generally weaker.

Is there a solution to this complex web of problems? No. There can be no solution because there is no single problem. Are there ways to address individual shortcomings in the welfare state, to shape a bit here and a bit there to mold the whole structure a little closer to our shared goals? Certainly. There are even some hopeful signs that we may identify and implement some of these. Some sort of health-care reform seems more likely now than at any time in two decades. More professionalized state governments are experimenting with various attempts to make welfare work *for* recipients instead of against them. And the strength of federalism is to apply the results of successful experiments in creating uniform policy for the nation.

GLOSSARY TERMS

Aid to Families with Dependent Children (AFDC)
cash transfers
food stamp program
Great Society
health maintenance organization (HMO)
in-kind transfers
means-tested
Medicaid

Medicare
"Medigap" insurance
public assistance programs
services
social insurance programs
social security
Supplemental Security Income (SSI)
tax expenditure items
welfare state

NOTES

[1] The figures in this paragraph are drawn from Neil Howe and Phillip Longman, "The Next New Deal," *Atlantic Monthly*, April 1992, pp. 88–99.

[2] Ibid., p. 90.

[3] Edward Zigler, "Head Start Falls Behind," *New York Times*, June 27, 1992, p. 15.

[4] Marshall Ingwerson, "A Long Way from the New Deal," *Christian Science Monitor*, June 12, 1992, p. 2.

[5] Jason De Parle, "When Giving Up Welfare for a Job Just Doesn't Pay," *New York Times*, July 8, 1992, p. A1.

[6] Martin Tolchin, "Aid Plan Marked by Low Participation Rate," *New York Times*, May 1, 1988, sec. 3, p. 1.

[7] Robert Pear, "Low Medicaid Fees Seen as Depriving the Poor of Care," *New York Times*, April 2, 1991, p. A1.

[8] Alan M. Garber and Thomas E. MaCurdy, *Nursing Home Discharges and Exhaustion of Medicare Benefits* (Cambridge, Mass.: National Bureau of Economic Research, 1991).

[9] Charles Krauthammer, "Bush Stands Steadfast in the Wrong Spot," *Los Angeles Times*, May 24, 1992, p. M5; Marlene Cimons, "Bush Vetoes Repeal of Fetal Tissue Research Ban," *Los Angeles Times*, June 24, 1992, p. A6.

[10] Frank Newport and Jennifer Leonard, "The Crisis in National Health Care," *Gallup Monthly Report*, August 1991, p. 4; Louis Harris, *A 79–19 Percent Majority Favors National Health Insurance for All*, Harris Poll press release, December 22, 1991.

[11] Categories summarized in Donald G. McNeil, Jr., "Washington Tries to Sort Out Health Insurance Proposals," *New York Times*, November 17, 1991, sec. 4, p. 2.

[12] Michael D'Antonio, "Dying Young," *Los Angeles Times Magazine*, July 12, 1992, p. 14.

[13] Ibid., p. 16.

[14] David C. Walters, "Urban-Aid Bill May Restore Housing Credit," *Christian Science Monitor*, July 3, 1992, p. 8.

[15] Marc Lacey, "Watts Residents Go Public on Privatization," *Los Angeles Times*, July 14, 1992, p. B1.

[16] Christopher Jencks, "How Poor Are the Poor?" *New York Review of Books*, May 9, 1985, p. 41.

SELECTED READINGS

The **historical context** of the rise of the welfare state can be found in Neil J. Smelser, *Social Change in the Industrial Revolution* (Chicago: University of Chicago Press, 1959); Karl de Schweinitz, *England's Road to Social Security* (Philadelphia: University of Pennsylvania Press, 1947); and Roy LuBove, *The Struggle for Social Security, 1900–1935* (Cambridge, Mass.: Harvard University Press, 1968). For an interesting historical case study that could be recommended in several chapters of this text but provides a useful vantage point on the nascent American welfare state, read Greg Mitchell, *The Campaign of the Century: Upton Sinclair's Race for Governor of California and the Birth of Media Politics* (New York: Random House, 1992).

For understanding the general contours of the most visible part of the **current American welfare state**, there is a terrific, useful little book, frequently updated: Sar A. Levitan, *Programs in Aid of the Poor*, 6th ed. (Baltimore: Johns Hopkins University Press, 1990). Levitan takes a brief but comprehensive look at major programs and spending patterns. To see a larger share of the welfare state, consult Theodore R. Marmor et al., *America's Misunderstood Welfare State: Persistent Myths, Enduring Realities* (New York: Basic Books, 1990); and Wallace C. Peterson, *Transfer Spending, Taxes, and the American Welfare State* (Boston: Kluwer, 1991).

For useful essays about the relationship of **women and the welfare state**, see Linda Gordon, ed., *Women, the State, and Welfare* (Madison: University of Wisconsin Press, 1990); and Joanne Leslie and Michael Paolisso, eds., *Women, Work, and Child Welfare in the Third World* (Boulder, Colo.: Westview Press, 1989). For a longer treatment, see Dorothy C. Miller, *Women and Social Welfare: A Feminist Analysis* (New York: Praeger, 1990).

On **health-care policy**, see Molla S. Donaldson, Jo Harris-Wehling, and Kathleen N. Lohr, eds., *Medicare: New Directions in Quality Assurance* (Washington D.C.: National Academy Press, 1991); David G. Smith, *Paying for Medicare: The Politics of Reform* (Hawthorne, N.Y.: Aldine, 1992). A practical exposition of alternatives can be found in Elizabeth Vierck, *Paying for Health Care after Age 65* (Santa Barbara, Calif.: ABC-Clio, 1990).

On **job training policy**, try Sharon L. Harlan and Ronnie J. Steinberg, eds., *Job Training for Women: The Promise and the Limits of Public Policies* (Philadelphia: Temple University Press, 1989); and Anthony P. Carnevale et al., *New Developments in Worker Training: A Legacy for the 1990s* (Madison, Wis.: Industrial Relations Research Association, 1990). As we said in Chapter 17, **program evaluation** is an important part of public policy studies. In job training, see the following examples: Charles F. Manski and Irwin Garfinkel, eds., *Evaluating Welfare and Training Programs* (Cambridge, Mass.: Harvard University Press, 1992); and Fred C. Doolittle and Linda Traeger, *Implementing the National JPTA Study* (New York: Manpower Demonstration Research Corp., 1990).

Recent thinking about **homelessness** can be found in Gregg Barak, *Gimme Shelter: A Social History of Homelessness in Contemporary America* (New York: Praeger, 1991), a thoughtfully analytical treatment of recent history; and Joel Blau, *The Visible Poor: Homelessness in the United States* (New York: Oxford University Press, 1992).

For **comparative perspective**, Jack Paul DeSario, ed., *International Public Policy Sourcebook* vol. 1 (Westport, Conn.: Greenwood Press, 1989), is a gold mine of useful case study material. For a more extensive single-country studies, see Inga Persson, ed., *Generating Equality in the Welfare State* (London: Norwegian University Press, 1990); Eric S. Einhorn and John Logue, *Modern Welfare States: Politics and Policies in Social Democratic Scandinavia* (New York: Praeger, 1989); John Hills, ed., *The State of Welfare: The Welfare State in Britain since 1974* (Oxford: Clarendon, 1990).

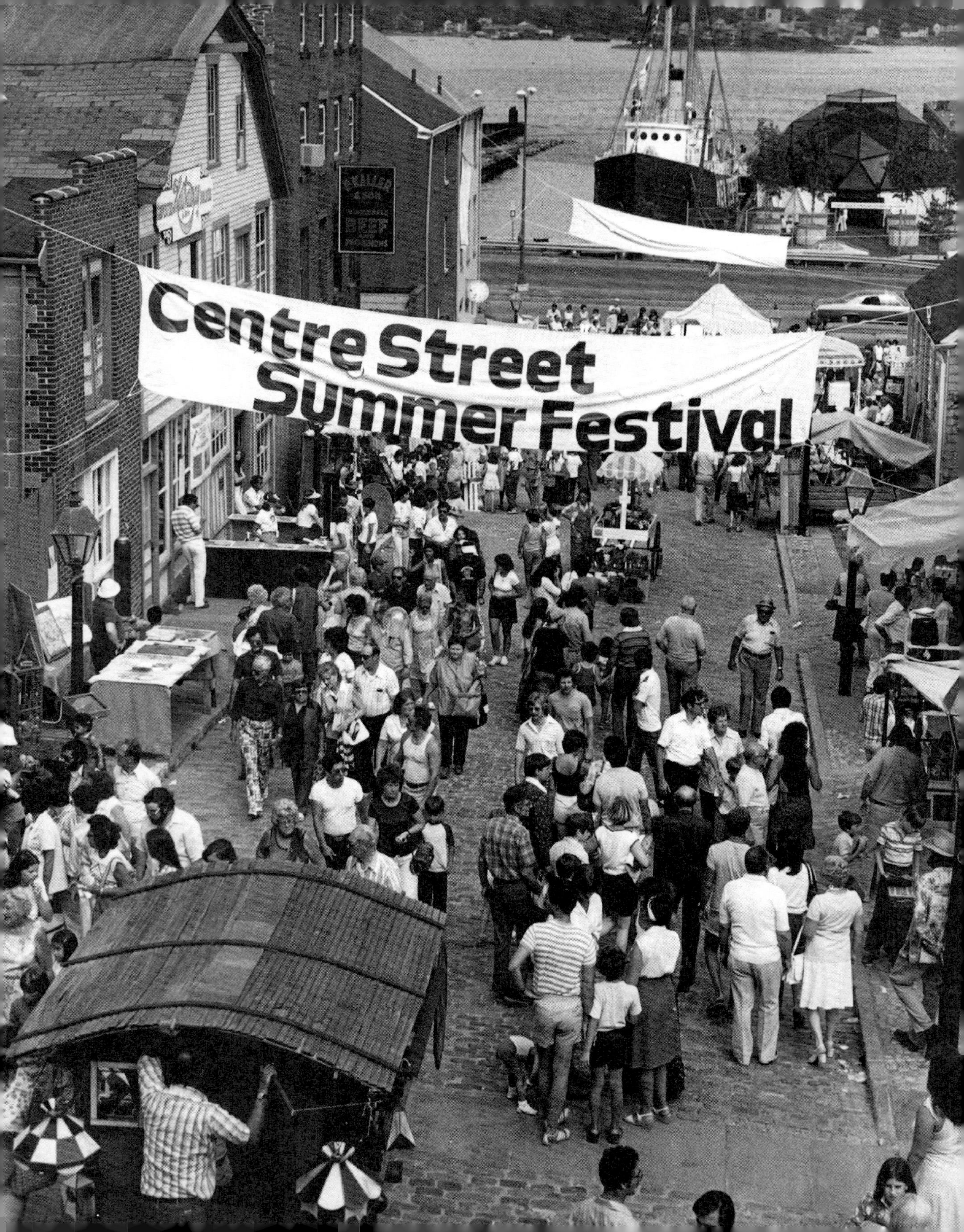
Centre Street
Summer Festival
BEEF

CHAPTER TWENTY

BUILDING COMMUNITY

Values and Limits

CHAPTER OUTLINE

Democracy and Social Control

Obscenity, Art, and the Arts

OBSCENITY
PUBLIC FUNDING FOR THE ARTS

Democracy, Crime, and Drugs

MAKING CHOICES ABOUT CRIME
THE CRIMINAL JUSTICE PROCESS
THE DEATH PENALTY AND CRIME RATES
THE WAR ON DRUGS

Education: Fairness and Values

EQUITABLE SCHOOL FUNDING
EDUCATION AND VALUES

SANTA CRUZ IS A PLACID RESORT ON MONTEREY BAY, SOUTH OF San Francisco. Once known primarily for its boardwalk and its roller coaster, it has become a retirement community and a university town. In recent years Santa Cruz has earned a reputation for being a bastion of 1960s culture, but like lots of small communities, it rarely rises to the attention of the world outside Santa Cruz County. In May 1992 an article about Santa Cruz appeared in the *Los Angeles Times*. It began this way:

> Starting this week, this quiet university beach town promises to give a little extra protection to ugly people. Same for fat people, skinny people, short people, tall people, scarred people, toothless people or anyone else with physical characteristics that might make them a target for discrimination.[1]

Looking past the writer's obvious sarcasm, you should know that the municipal ordinance, forbidding job or housing bias on the basis of height, weight, or "physical characteristic," is taken quite seriously by the townspeople. "It's a basic issue

713

of fairness," says city councilman Neal Coonerty. "People should be judged on the basis of real criteria, their ability to perform the job or pay the rent." Coonerty's interest in sponsoring the law began when he heard about a woman, weighing about three hundred pounds, who applied for a job as a clerk in a natural foods store. The store rejected the woman because of her weight. "It's very much a women's issue," says Coonerty. "Most of the discrimination based on height, weight, and physical characteristics is discrimination against women."

Not everyone is thrilled with the ordinance. The director of the Chamber of Commerce, who supports the law, cites three businesses that decided not to locate in Santa Cruz because of the ordinance. Even the specific case giving rise to the ordinance is ambiguous. The job in the natural foods store entailed stocking shelves on narrow aisles and climbing ladders. It is at least arguable that the obese applicant could not meet bona fide occupational qualifications—the Supreme Court's test for discrimination.

But as the director of the Chamber of Commerce says, "It's not an impediment to doing business," and it just might serve as a good reminder to landlords and employers of the homiletic truth, "You can't judge a book by its cover." In human terms this seems a worthwhile goal.

Democracy and Social Control

In Santa Cruz it's not OK to discriminate against obese people. In Singapore it's not OK to chew gum or smoke. In China it's not OK to have more than one child. In Ireland it's not OK to have an abortion, even if you are a teenage victim of rape. These are public prohibitions, enforced by law.

In Japan the Ministry of Health and Welfare is trying to get more young people to marry and have children. In the Netherlands the Amsterdam city council actually refurbishes abandoned houses for the squatters who occupy them. In the United States the National Endowment for the Arts will support visual artists with grants—as long as no genitals show up in the final product. These are public encouragements, paid for with tax revenue.

Governments preserve and shape the communities they serve in a variety of ways, with regulations and incentives. In Chapters 5 and 6 we talked about civil liberties and civil rights—efforts to ensure for every citizen a part in keeping government democratically responsive and within certain bounds. In Chapters 7 and 18 we looked at economic regulation, and in Chapter 19 we looked at the programs that make up the welfare state—these are all examples of government regulating and distributing economic resources and opportunities. Each of these is a way of defining a political community, preserving and sometimes altering community values. In this chapter we examine other ways of building community by defining the limits and expressing the values that make American democracy unique. The three general areas chosen for inclusion here are but a tiny representation of the many comparable examples that could be explored. We will look at obscenity and art, crime and drugs, and education, asking what players affect policy, what choices have been and might be made, and how a democrat might evaluate policy in each of these areas.

Obscenity, Art, and the Arts

Art—human expression at its most powerful—is one of the defining features of culture. It has also long been an instrument of governing. From the monumental Mayan architecture of Chichén Itzá, the soaring vaults and spires of Salisbury Cathedral, and the massive presence of Napoleon's Arc de Triomphe to the virtues carved on the pediment of the United States Supreme Court Building ("Equal Justice under Law"), public architecture has long been used to inspire and intimidate, to reinforce civic pride and encourage civic duty. In times when government was the prerogative of powerful families, public patronage of the arts was common (from Handel symphonies to Fabergé eggs). Public support for art can advance a particular agenda, as when Adolph Hitler's Third Reich in Germany used art to glorify racial purity and when the Soviet government under Stalin used patriotic art ("Soviet realism") to legitimize individual sacrifice for a collectivist vision of the common good. Or public support for art can advance the general goal of making life richer, more interesting, and more stimulating without overt propagandistic intentions. Whatever the case, art becomes part of public policy.

As a voice of individualism, art can challenge community norms and perhaps weaken support for specific government policies or for the government itself. Sometimes that is the point. So in addition to providing support for art, government has often restricted art, usually labeling it politically or morally unacceptable. The U.S. Supreme Court, for example, has long held that the expression rights of the First Amendment do not apply to obscenity. And although much that has been deemed obscene has little of art in it, genuine art sometimes strikes viewers as obscene, raising important questions about community values and limits. How can we accommodate the legitimate desire to maintain community standards and still protect and foster lively artistic expression?

Art defines life; a community defines itself by its art. Little wonder, then, that public policy sometimes debates art. We will now look at obscenity and public funding for the arts.

Obscenity

For decades the Supreme Court has grappled with the complex problem of defining exactly what is obscene. In case after case the Court has been called on to decide whether a specific magazine, movie, or book is really obscene. And even were society to agree that obscenity should be censored, there would remain the question by what (or whose) standards? Yet a deeper issue is whether there actually is such a thing as obscenity—and if there is, why should it not simply be viewed as a form of speech protected by the First Amendment?

The first significant attempt by a court to define obscenity came in the landmark British case of *Hicklin* v. *Regina* (1868). The case dealt with an antireligious tract called *The Confessional Unmasked*, which described, among other things, the seduction of women during "confessions." The judge in *Hicklin* sought to define obscenity as follows:

> The test of obscenity is this, whether the tendency of the matter charged as obscene is to deprave and corrupt those whose minds are open to such immoral influences, and into whose hands a publication of this sort may fall.

Vague as it was, the *Hicklin* decision became the basic standard for U.S. obscenity cases for almost a century. Under *Hicklin*, even small parts of books or other materials could be taken out of context and declared obscene. In 1934, however, the Supreme Court accepted the argument of the publisher of James Joyce's *Ulysses* that a work should be considered *as a whole*. Finally, in 1957 the Court altogether rejected the *Hicklin* rule in the case of **Roth v. United States**. Although upholding the conviction of Samuel Roth himself, a New York publisher, on the charge of mailing obscene materials, the Court rejected the *Hicklin* rule as unconstitutional and proposed a new standard.

> The test is not whether it would arouse sexual desires or sexually impure thoughts in those comprising a particular segment of the community, the young, the immature or the highly prudish. . . . The test in each case is the effect of the book . . . considered as a whole, not upon any particular classes, but upon all those whom it is likely to reach. . . . You determine its impact upon the average person in the community.[2]

In other words, one class of society should not be singled out in judging the effect of the material. What should count, rather, is how the material, taken as a whole, affects the "average person." This rule was loosened further in 1966 when the Court held that obscene material had to offend national standards, not just those of a small community.[3]

What followed was a liberalization of the application of obscenity laws. As more sexually explicit materials became more easily obtainable, public opposition grew. In **Miller v. California** (1973) the Court shifted ground again, voting 5–4 to uphold a group of obscenity convictions.[4] In the majority opinion, Chief Justice Warren E. Burger argued that there *was* such a thing as obscenity and that it was *not* protected by the First Amendment. To be considered obscene, the Court declared, a work, taken as a whole, must (1) appeal to "prurient interest" in sex, (2) depict or describe in a patently offensive way sexual conduct specifically defined by applicable state law, and (3) lack "serious literary, artistic, political, or scientific value" (the so-called **LAPS test**). The standard for making judgments about the first two points was the "average person, applying contemporary community standards." Thus a stricter definition of "prurient interest" and "patently offensive" was possible in one community than in another—no national standard was necessary. The judgment whether a work has literary, artistic, political, or scientific value was to be made according to a national standard and should not vary from community to community.

While maintaining the *Miller* approach, the Court has made some clarifications in obscenity law. For example, as subjects of and consumers of obscene materials, children can be treated differently from adults. In a rare unanimous obscenity decision, the Court upheld a New York statute providing criminal penalties for knowingly promoting a "sexual performance" by a child under the age of sixteen by distributing material depicting such a performance. Congress passed a statute in 1978, strengthened in 1984, making it a federal crime to use children under the age of eighteen in the production of pornographic material. Cities may use zoning ordinances to limit adult bookstores and theaters to certain parts of town or to prohibit them near schools and churches. For broadcast over public airwaves, the FCC may impose a stricter standard, limiting to late-night hours material that is merely indecent and not obscene. Congress may ban the interstate transmission of obscene (but not merely indecent) commercial messages through "dial-a-porn" services.

The *Miller* standards have not been abandoned, though that may reflect the Court's failure rather than its success in drawing clear lines. Outcomes in particular cases are hard to predict. In many places prosecutors have simply given up enforcing obscenity statutes. Juries have been reluctant to convict, and higher courts have been inclined to overturn convictions. In reviewing a 1983 lower court ruling that an armful of magazines and videos seized in Manhattan were not legally obscene, Judge Thomas J. Meskill concluded that "the community standards in New York are so low [that] nothing is obscene." There has not been an obscenity prosecution in Manhattan since.[5] In all of New York State (population over 18 million), between 1985 and 1990, there were only twenty-three arrests on felony obscenity charges and only one conviction. Paul McGeady, general counsel for Morality in Media, a national antipornography group based in Manhattan, says, "When you have a proper case, you can get a conviction." But, McGeady says, pornographers know where they can operate without interference.

Two highly publicized cases in 1990 reflect the difficulty of obscenity and the law. Both involved material beyond the limits of acceptability for a large part of mainstream America, yet in each the work in question laid claim to artistic sensitivity—one the popular art of rap music, the other the high art of museums and galleries. A jury in Ft. Lauderdale, Florida, acquitted a music store owner of obscenity charges for selling the album *Nasty as They Wanna Be* by the rap group 2 Live Crew. Interviewed later, the jurors said they saw the rappers' lyrics as art. Another jury in Cincinnati acquitted a museum director of obscenity charges for exhibiting homoerotically explicit photographs by Robert Mapplethorpe.

For some people, the failures to convict characterized a community whose moral compass had been subverted by a permissive cultural elite unwilling to set any moral

The controversy surrounding an exhibit of Robert Mapplethorpe's photographs at a Cincinnati museum in 1990 was a reflection of the difficulty of giving a legal definition to obscenity. Although Mapplethorpe's homoerotic photography was clearly beyond the limits of acceptability for much of the population of Cincinnati, a jury acquitted the museum director of obscenity charges. Here a demonstrator protests against the Corcoran Gallery in Washington, D.C., after it withdrew a Mapplethorpe exhibit under pressure from Senator Jesse Helms, a conservative Republican from North Carolina.
(Jerome Friar/Impact Visuals)

limits. For others, these verdicts were vindications of social norms that tolerated without necessarily approving of particular lyrics or images. These latter could claim that the material in question was not forced on an unwilling public—the title *Nasty as They Wanna Be* serves as its own warning, and the gallery exhibit posted ample warning of its nature (for visitors who had somehow missed the national media coverage of the controversy). Since 1990 the recording industry, to fend off state regulations, has applied to certain recordings stickers inscribed "Parental Advisory: Explicit Lyrics." The supporters of a tolerant approach worried that industry's self-censorship might prove little better than government restrictions and that prosecutions like those in Ft. Lauderdale and Cincinnati would also have a chilling effect on free expression. No one seemed satisfied.

Many people question the entire basis for subjecting obscene materials, however defined, to prosecution and censorship. What is wrong, they ask, with appealing to what the Supreme Court has called prurient interest ("having morbid or lascivious longings")? A majority on the President's Commission on Obscenity and Pornography, appointed by Lyndon Johnson, found no connection between exposure to pornography and any sort of crime, sexual or otherwise. If pornography does not demonstrably cause social harm, why should it be subject to legal restraints? Conservatives contend that the widespread availability of obscene materials sooner or later contributes to the destruction of order, civility, and various civic virtues. Is there any evidence supporting such a hypothesis?

Yes, according to an unusual coalition of feminists and conservative and religious groups. Feminist Andrea Dworkin has maintained that "pornography is the theory and rape is the practice" and argues that pornography discriminates against women and hence is a violation of equal protection of the laws. In May 1984, Indianapolis, Indiana, passed an ordinance that declared pornography to be a violation of women's civil rights. According to the ordinance, "Pornography is central in creating and maintaining sex as a basis for discrimination." This statute was later declared unconstitutional by the Supreme Court.

Both sides in the debate take absolutist positions. Some feminists and right-wing crusaders view all pornography as illegitimate, while free speech advocates proclaim a pervasive protection under the First Amendment for virtually all forms of expression. Both arguments seem somewhat inflated. Certain types of pornography appear, at least to common sense, far more pernicious than others—child pornography, for example, or particularly degrading and brutal forms of pornography.

The pattern of laws on the books that are difficult (but not always impossible) to enforce may represent a pluralistic compromise on a difficult issue of community values and limits. Pornography will still be available, but within limits that protect the unwitting and unwilling from exposure. One advocate of this sort of compromise on the pornography issue stated her case as follows:

> To the extent that pornography is symptomatic of, and helps to further, social disintegration, in which the least powerful (especially children) suffer the most, it becomes an appropriate target for action, regulation, and reproof. But with this proviso: the knowledge that we cannot return to a past in which Americans harmoniously shared one set of moral values. Communities must put pornography "in its place" rather than seek to eradicate it altogether.[6]

Public Funding for the Arts

Even if the American democracy could reach a stable consensus on the limits of what it will tolerate in art, a distinct question would remain: What art should public funds pay for? It is one thing to suggest that all kinds of art should be available within a community, as long as people who might be offended can shield themselves from exposure. Should those who are offended nonetheless be made to support that art with their tax dollars? Before we go on to look at specific disputes about public funding for the arts, we should review one of the fundamental features of majoritarian democracy: Even when certain limits are placed on the majority's power, as is true in the United States, setting government policy according to the majority's wishes means that every individual must be willing to support legitimate public policies with which he or she disagrees. Concession to the majority will is necessary to prevent chaos and is purchased by the mutuality of that concession generally. I am willing to support this policy today (though I don't agree with it) because tomorrow, when I'm in the majority and you're opposed to the policy, I want you to cooperate as well. What this means is that in arts funding as with all other positive acts of government, policy is not required to retreat to the lowest common denominator on which total agreement exists.

The highly unconventional memorial to the American dead of the Vietnam War. This public-sponsored monument stirred criticism, particularly from those who felt it did not provide a sufficiently heroic image of our soldiers. But over time, the long, black marble wall with its 58,000 names became a place of deep emotional resonance for most who visited it in Washington, D.C. (Bill Clark/National Park Service)

All governments in the United States, federal, state, and local, have been commissioning art for a long time—mostly commemorative pieces with little controversy. The Works Progress Administration (WPA) hired artists during the Great Depression, primarily as an employment program. That didn't prevent an investigation into the WPA's Federal Theater by the House Un-American Activities Committee in 1938. Partly as a result of that investigation, the Federal Theater ceased to exist on June 30, 1939.[7] Even the business of public monuments can stir controversy. The winning entry in the competition to design the Vietnam War Memorial in Washington, D.C., was a somber, earth-recessed, V-shaped wall inscribed with the names of more than 58,000 Americans killed or missing in the Vietnam War. The wall was too somber for some observers, who saw in it a refusal to glorify the sacrifices of the dead. A large controversy erupted, reopening divisions in the public concerning the war itself. To accommodate the concerns expressed about the original design, a second piece of sculpture—a traditional representation of soldiers in combat gear—was added to the site of the memorial, which was dedicated on November 13, 1982.

If even war memorials can raise a public outcry, what about the public funding of art for art's sake? Founded in 1966, the **National Endowment for the Arts (NEA)** is the primary Federal agency for arts funding. Congress appropriated $152 million to NEA in 1990. A recent round of controversy had its roots in grants to fund two exhibits:

the Robert Mapplethorpe exhibit that later ignited Cincinnati and an exhibit that included a work by Andrés Serrano descriptively titled "Piss Christ." Goaded by conservative Senator Jesse Helms, Congress first banned the endowment from funding projects that were obscene, sadomasochistic, or homoerotic. That ban was later dropped, and the NEA adopted language saying that applicants for grants would be judged on "general standards of decency and respect for the diverse beliefs and values of the American public."[8] The acting chair of NEA, Anne-Imelda Radice, announced her intention to save the endowment by pulling it back from direct confrontations with conservative members of Congress. This goal entailed what some people believed to be a policy of refusing funding for any visual art that showed genitals. Author Wallace Stegner and composer Stephen Sondheim separately refused to accept a National Medal of Arts (administered by the NEA) to protest the new tilt toward political responsiveness. Others accepted Radice at her word when she said, "My objective is to make sure the endowment survives."

Radice quickly vetoed the recommendations of the National Council on the Arts and a professional peer review panel to fund two exhibitions that included sexual themes and images of genitalia. Although Radice claimed that the exhibitions lacked artistic quality, many observers believed that she was toeing the conservative line. One panel of peer reviewers quit to protest the new orthodoxy; another demanded justification for the vetoes and was dismissed.

Within a month a federal district court judge, proclaiming that "artistic expression is at the core of a democratic society," found the NEA's decency standard to be unconstitutionally vague and overbroad. "The right of artists to challenge conventional wisdom and values is a cornerstone of artistic and academic freedom. The fact that the exercise of professional judgment is inescapable in arts funding does not mean that the government has free rein to impose whatever content restrictions it chooses."[9]

Neither the politicians, the arts bureaucrats, the federal judges, nor the artists themselves have had the final word in this battle. What is an ordinary citizen to make of this conflict of values? Are there democratic standards to apply to arts funding?

Can the NEA choose to fund large-scale sculpture but not performance art? Presumably so—even if more performance artists than sculptors are drawn from orientationally and ethnically diverse populations. Can the NEA choose to fund straight art but not gay art, white art but not African-American art? To do so would violate important principles of equal protection, unacceptably limiting positive freedom. Can the NEA fund nonthreatening art and avoid art that challenges established conventions? This may be less a matter of fairness or constitutional values than one of prudence and common sense. To use public funds exclusively to support the social and artistic status quo would miss an important opportunity to grow and to reaffirm values by examining alternatives. In a time when a significant share of funding for the arts is public, a case can be made for at least some art that presses the limits of acceptability. Some risk ought to be undertaken. But to fund only art that the mainstream finds unacceptable is to court a democratic withdrawal of support altogether. This would be a Pyrrhic victory for artistic freedom.

Democracy, Crime, and Drugs

Making Choices about Crime

Crime will always present a challenge to democracy. Although we might like to think of crime as something that happens on the margins of society, many sociologists, from Emile Durkheim (1858–1917) on, have shown that definitions of crime are what *create* the boundaries of society, by marking off behavior that is "beyond the law." A community defines itself in contrast to what it is not. When we are born and then socialized into a particular society, the boundaries that that society has marked off have the appearance of being natural rather than a matter of convention. Persons who violate the boundaries—criminals—seem to us different by nature. There is a long history of looking for the physical traits that set criminals apart from the rest of us—the slope of the forehead, cranial bumps, particular chromosomes. The idea that criminals are different by nature is well reflected in kids' cartoons: the character with close-set, beady eyes and a five o'clock shadow is a real bad guy for sure. But cartoons and phrenology aside, the simple fact is that the only adequate definition of a criminal is "someone who has violated an established criminal law." No other shared characteristic marks this group.

Although establishing a criminal code might seem to us a straightforward matter, many choices reflecting ideology and political power are inscribed in criminal codes. One easy way to think about this is to imagine revolutionary times, when one definition of community is being tossed aside for another. Today the person who strikes the king's officer is a criminal, liable to be hanged. Next week that person will be a hero and patriot. George Washington was a criminal before he was a patriot. If the American Revolution had failed, he would have stayed a criminal.

Even in less extreme circumstances, the choices we make about what is criminal and what is not represent the political triumph of one faction over another or the partial or complete ascendancy of one ideology over another. In some societies it is illegal to charge interest on a loan. In some states it is illegal to drive a motorcycle without a helmet. Should abortion be illegal? Should discrimination against people of color be illegal? What kind of discrimination? When should it be illegal to strike another person? If the other person is threatening you? If the other person is your minor child? Should it be illegal to make large profits at public expense or to hold more than a prescribed amount of capital? Should it be illegal to sleep on the streets? All of these are choices that define criminal activity, making some persons criminals and others not.

Agreeing on basic principles about how to make these choices is not a simple matter. Should society protect individuals from their own unwise choices? Would an ideal democracy use criminal laws to equalize resources and power? **John Stuart Mill**, a nineteenth-century political philosopher, believed that government should allow individuals the greatest liberty possible. Government could not properly force people to act in what it believed to be their own best interests (what one sage has called "the

(Text continues on page 724)

COMPARATIVE PERSPECTIVE

LEGAL PROHIBITION AND PRACTICAL TOLERANCE: SETTING LIMITS THE DUTCH WAY

In the Netherlands social control in a wide range of areas depends on a distinctly Dutch style of mutual concern and tolerance. Typical of this pattern was the official prohibition of Catholicism in the country. The legal prohibition lasted for over two hundred years (well into the nineteenth century), while the clandestine church flourished in attic and barn chapels. The same attitude of legal prohibition and practical tolerance has applied to prostitution at least since the seventeenth century. Prostitutes operate openly and are treated with respect. The minister of justice explained the goal: to "prevent as much as possible a situation in which more harm is caused by criminal proceedings than by the [activity] itself."

Marijuana use may be illegal but is openly tolerated—giving the government much more credibility, some people say, when it sternly opposes crack, heroin, and cocaine use. All Dutch schools teach sex education, and birth control is readily available and cheap. Dutch teenagers are no more sexually active than American teens, though 90 percent of those who are use contraception—a significantly higher rate than among American teens.

This generosity of spirit, a "collective conscience," in handling social problems is traced by historian Simon Schama to the prosperous seventeenth century, when Holland was the wealthiest nation on earth. When squatters (*krakers*) began to occupy abandoned buildings in Amsterdam in the 1960s, they were allowed to stay. In some cases the city council even bought the buildings, renovated them, and then gave them back to the *krakers* at extremely low rents. As a town alderman explained, "If you leave a building empty for five years in a housing shortage, you can't then claim property rights. The squatters had a moral right to do what they did."

Some people complain that the aggressive Dutch tolerance is really a means of absorbing dissidence. That may be, but in its inclusiveness, it is—in some ways at least—an appealing strategy for dealing with problems that in other countries become the basis for division, exclusion, alienation, and strife. A strategy like this one may not be easy to transplant into another national setting, however. When lots of laws are on the books and relatively few prosecutions are undertaken, a lot of discretion is given to the enforcers. Under these conditions enforcement patterns may reflect prejudice, intentional or unconscious. Society's least powerful members and those outside the mainstream are naturally most vulnerable under such conditions.

Source: Richard Reeves, "The Permissive Dutch," New York Times Magazine, *October 20, 1985; David Morris, "Dutch Control Vices with Tolerance, Respect,"* Raleigh News and Observer, *October 11, 1989, p. 11A.*

Aunt Polly state," for its propensity to tell you what's good for you). For Mill the legitimate sphere of governmental authority was simply in keeping the peace and protecting individuals from others, resembling the night watchman state we described in Chapter 1. But even for Mill, some questions remained. If liberty required the freedom to choose a life of prostitution, did it also entail the freedom to be a pimp or a panderer? Mill also recognized that society had a right to protect individuals from unseen harms that they could not reasonably choose to encounter. If no first-time user of hard drugs could reasonably choose to be addicted, has society the right to ban drug use up front? Many people believe that society has positive responsibilities beyond the minimum, though they disagree about what form those responsibilities should take in the criminal law.

Sometimes distinctions are drawn between crimes against persons and crimes against property. While it is true that we should consider breaking another person's arm more serious than breaking his window, it is also true that the quality of our lives is tied to the acquisition and use of property. Property rights are personal rights: the rights of persons to use property. Other distinctions are drawn between violent crime and nonviolent crime. The danger here is that these matters get tied up in socioeconomic differences. A Wall Street account executive with access to hundreds of millions of dollars may cause far more harm to society with illegal trades at a computer terminal than a youth with a gun holding up the convenience store. But viscerally the young offender scares us more and has an identifiable victim. The victims of insider stock trading are diffuse and faceless, though the cumulative pain caused may be enormous. Perhaps unfairly, the youth is likely to be caught sooner and punished more severely.

Advocates of the legalization of drugs or prostitution argue that society should not punish **victimless crimes**—when both parties in an interaction are obtaining what they want (Mill's position). Opponents respond that participants are not always the best judges of harm, that many of these exchanges are not genuinely free choices, and that other people can be victimized by the exchanges (the family of the addict or the spouse now at risk for AIDS). Another controversial argument, used to support motorcycle helmet laws, for example, is that society has a right to protect its investment in individuals and to prevent the costs that spill over from individual choices (three months' care in the county hospital for head injuries).

In making all of these choices, democrats should be sensitive to the tendency for criminal codes to protect the interests of the most powerful in society first. Some fair evaluation of the harm caused (not distorted by class, gender, or ethnic bias) must determine the penalties attached to various crimes. The choices lodged in the criminal codes should always protect the *general* interest—not an easy thing to define.

The Criminal Justice Process

As we said in Chapter 4, criminal justice in the United States is primarily the responsibility of the states, which establish criminal codes and delegate most enforcement

What is a crime? Does it require the presence of a "victim?" If so, how would one characterize prostitution or the use of drugs? Should such "victimless" crimes be decriminalized? *(Robert Eckert/Stock, Boston)*

tasks to county and municipal governments. State and local governments are responsible for about 88 percent of the money spent on criminal justice.

LAW ENFORCEMENT Much discretion lies with law enforcement officers about what crimes will be detected and acted on. Staffing and patrolling decisions will bring certain crimes within view and leave others out. Do you put officers on the street or at computer terminals? Every cop in a car is witness to far more crimes than he or she could possibly respond to. The vast majority are relatively minor. (By a strict accounting, how many traffic laws did you break the last time you drove a car?) Often it is the cop on the beat who decides whether evidence of a particular crime or a suspected criminal is brought into the system or let go. The choices that are made reflect individual and institutional priorities: Is getting prostitutes off the street more important than interdicting drugs? How can society's resources best be used? How can we best help this youngster? They also reflect the realities of later stages in the criminal justice process:

Will the D.A. prosecute this case? Will this battered wife be willing to press charges and testify? Will eighteen months in jail turn this youth into a true criminal? Will the judge dismiss the charges because the prison system is overcrowded?

Once a person has been arrested or evidence of an alleged crime has been formally brought into the system, the prosecutor must decide whether to continue the process or let the matter drop. In serious criminal matters the prosecutor will have to present evidence to a grand jury or a judge to be able to go to trial.

We talked about the courts in Chapter 16; we now skip directly to the system of corrections.

CORRECTIONS   Despite a decline in the number of violent crimes in the United States from 1981 (35.3 per thousand population) to 1991 (31.3 per thousand), prison populations—indeed, all correctional populations (see **Figure 20-1**)—have skyrocketed, due in part to the increased use of fixed sentences and the increased incidence of drug prosecutions. At year-end in 1980 there were 329,000 inmates under the jurisdiction of state and federal prisons; in 1991 there were 804,000 inmates.[10] Women make up less than 6 percent of inmates nationwide. Although we think of prison as a means of

FIGURE 20-1

TREND IN CORRECTIONAL POPULATIONS, 1982–1990

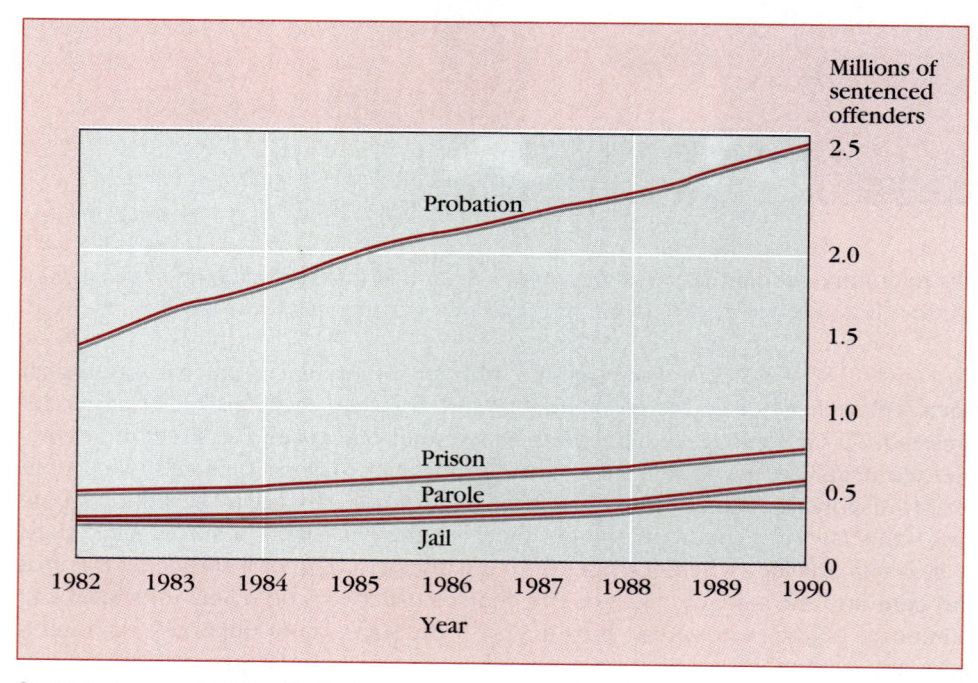

SOURCE: Bureau of Justice Statistics.

segregating (as well as punishing) violent individuals, most prisoners are not in prison for violent crimes. Many people suggest that community-based corrections (alternative service punishments, halfway houses, and probation) is a cheaper, more productive, and more humane response to criminal behavior, one that should be used more extensively. The point is not to coddle criminals but to reduce the costs of corrections and return the perpetrators to productive society sooner and more effectively. In fact the population of convicted persons in community-based corrections has grown even more rapidly than the number of persons in prison. In 1990 there were 2,670,234 adult offenders on probation and 531,407 on parole, together making about 1.7 percent of all U.S. adults.

The Death Penalty and Crime Rates

We now turn briefly to two controversies about crime with particular relevance for democracy in America: the death penalty and crime rates.

THE DEATH PENALTY The death penalty is a mirror in which we see reflected the nation's ambivalence about justice in general. Is the goal to mete out justice through punishment or to rehabilitate wayward members of society? Most people recognize both goals but disagree about the relative weight each should carry. (See **Table 20–1**.) The *penitentiary* was originally conceived as a place of enforced solitude where an errant soul could contemplate mistakes and become penitent, ready to rejoin society. Little of this noble goal remains in contemporary penal institutions. In truth, punishment has always figured prominently in criminal justice systems. The contemporary debate about prison conditions is an echo of this larger division of sentiment. When a federal district court mandates certain minimal conditions, opponents respond, "Why pamper convicts? They deserve what they get." In **capital punishment** the debate is between pure and simple punishment and penalty as deterrent (with rehabilitation left to higher authorities). There is no substantial evidence that capital punishment serves as a deterrent to crime. Supporters of the deterrent position say that this is because the death penalty has not been applied surely and swiftly, prerequisites for effective deterrence. Opponents of this view say that most homicides are crimes of passion in which no thought is given to punishment, and hence no deterrent effect should be expected from capital punishment. The Supreme Court has recognized that capital punishment is different from other punishments and has enforced some (and allowed other) parts of an elaborate series of safeguards making up a lengthy process. There are signs that some members of the Court are now looking for ways to speed the death penalty along.

California's execution of Robert Alton Harris on April 22, 1992, came at the end of a fourteen-year legal battle. During the night that preceded the execution there was a final skirmish between judges of the Ninth Circuit Court of Appeals and the U.S. Supreme Court. That night four separate stays of execution were issued, only to be quashed. Finally, as dawn was breaking, a 7-to-2 ruling from the Supreme Court accompanied by a testy opinion barring any further interference from the circuit allowed the state to execute Harris.

Almost no one is satisfied with capital punishment as it currently exists in the United States. Nearly everyone feels that the process has become hopelessly protracted and convoluted. For some the solution is to simplify the process with fewer appeals to federal courts. For others the solution is to abandon the death penalty altogether. Opponents argue first that mistakes can be made. Federal courts reviewing state death penalty convictions reverse more than 40 percent because the original conviction or death sentence was unlawful.[11] The month before the Harris execution, two Los Angeles men were freed after seventeen years in California prisons for a murder that the district attorney was no longer convinced they committed.[12] Opponents also argue that in spite of judicial safeguards, capital punishment is discriminatorily applied to African-Americans and that it contributes to the brutalization of society. For many proponents of capital punishment the matter is clear: Some crimes are terrible enough that their perpetrators deserve to die.

CRIME RATES Fear is rising in America. More suburban neighborhoods huddle behind gates. Home security system sales are up. Gun sales for personal protection are high. Television is rife with popular shows about "real" crimes and "real" criminals still at large. As we saw in Chapter 2, America has a tradition of violence, well established and deeply rooted. In the 1990s public awareness has been scraped raw by the gritty underside of a tradition that has long been characterized with glamour. But fear is sometimes corrosive to rational public debate, so it is important to look at some facts.

TABLE 20-1
PUBLIC OPINION AND THE DEATH PENALTY

	Favor	*Oppose*
1991	76%	18%
1988	79	16
1985	72	20
1981	66	25
1976	65	28
1972	57	32
1966	42	47
1960	51	36
1953	68	25
1937	65	35
1936	61	39

Gallup Poll Monthly, June 1991

Before we look at actual crime rates in the United States, we should keep two caveats in mind: First, crime rates may not be an accurate reflection of the incidence of crime. The majority of crimes are never reported. We know that some crimes, like rape, are seriously underreported. Victims of sexual crimes often—understandably but irrationally—feel shame, perhaps even guilt, about being the victim of such a crime. Many sexual assaults are perpetrated by friends, raising the daunting possibility that mutual acquaintances may side with the rapist instead of the victim. Add the wholly rational expectation of being tormented in open court by a defense attorney whose task is to impugn the victim's credibility, and saying nothing may seem the best choice. So we know that rape is underreported, but we don't know to what extent. We don't know if certain events (like the Clarence Thomas nomination hearings, in which some members of the Senate Judiciary Committee, playing defense counsel for Thomas, took it upon themselves to impugn Anita Hill's testimony about sexual harassment) tend to increase underreporting or not or by how much if they do. Sexual crimes aren't the only crimes underreported. There are many reasons why victims of crime may not step forward.

Second, overall victimization rates may not tell any particular individual much about the chances of becoming a victim of crime. The news media and entertainment-television hype about violent crime almost certainly makes most Americans fearful out of proportion to their actual risk. If you are a young African-American male living in the District of Columbia, your fears are well grounded: The gun homicide rate for that group is around 225 per hundred thousand—unacceptably high, but still only a bit over 2 percent. If the same young African-American male moves to Miami, Queens, or Philadelphia—still in the top twenty cities for these rates—the risk is halved. Remove any of the other factors—gender, ethnicity, or age—and the risk drops substantially. The message of these statistics is not that violent crime is no problem or that we should be reassured to find some groups at greater risk than others. But an unjustified overreaction to crime rates may exacerbate the problem by encouraging more fear, more guns, and then more violence. Let's look at some statistics.

Personal and household victimization rates are down from the peak levels of the early 1980s (see **Figure 20-2**). There were approximately 34.4 million personal and household crimes in 1990, down from 41.4 million in 1981. More of the crimes that occur are being reported. The National Crime Victimization Survey finds that the percentage of criminal victimizations that were reported to police increased from 32 percent of all crimes to 38 percent of all crimes. As noted, victimization varies with certain characteristics: In 1990 there were 13.9 robberies for every thousand Hispanic Americans and 13.0 robberies for every thousand African Americans but only 4.5 robberies for every thousand whites. The assault rate was 63.5 per thousand people aged sixteen to nineteen but only 1.9 per thousand people aged sixty-five or older. Violent crimes also decreased from peaks in the 1980s, although rape and aggravated assault are both at all-time highs.

Federal drug convictions have risen sharply, from 5,135 in 1980 to 16,077 in 1990 (and remember that most convictions are state, not federal). Helping to explain the

FIGURE 20-2
VICTIMIZATION TRENDS, 1973–1990

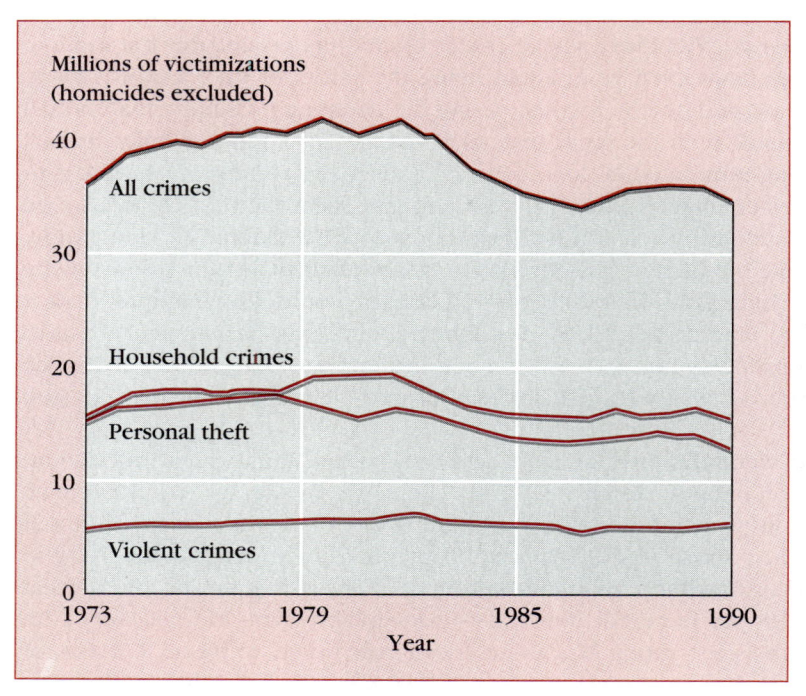

SOURCE: Bureau of Justice Statistics.

increase in prison populations is the fact that more drug offenders are going to prison (see **Figure 20-3**), and for longer sentences. In 1980 some 72 percent of convicted federal drug offenders were sentenced to prison; in 1990 fully 86 percent were sentenced to prison. The average sentence for drug offenders increased from forty-seven months in 1980 to eighty-one months in 1990 (a 72 percent increase). Over that period the percentage of all federal offenders who were convicted of drug offenses rose from 17 percent to 33 percent. Almost half of all federal offenders sentenced to prison in 1990 were convicted of drug offenses. A significant amount of crime that does not end in a drug conviction can also be attributed to drug use. The high cost of a drug habit can quickly exhaust a middle-class income.

"It is bad enough that we have the objective reality of crime to deal with, but when that reaility is exaggerated by the media and by political campaigns, we end up with a perception of victimization that is probably greater than the actual threat," says Professor Richard Evans of the University of Houston.[13] In a democracy it doesn't make sense to spend too much time trying to vindicate or deflate personal perceptions of danger. The feelings of fear are real enough. Constructively addressing the fear of crime

FIGURE 20-3
FEDERAL CRIMINAL CONVICTIONS, 1980–1990

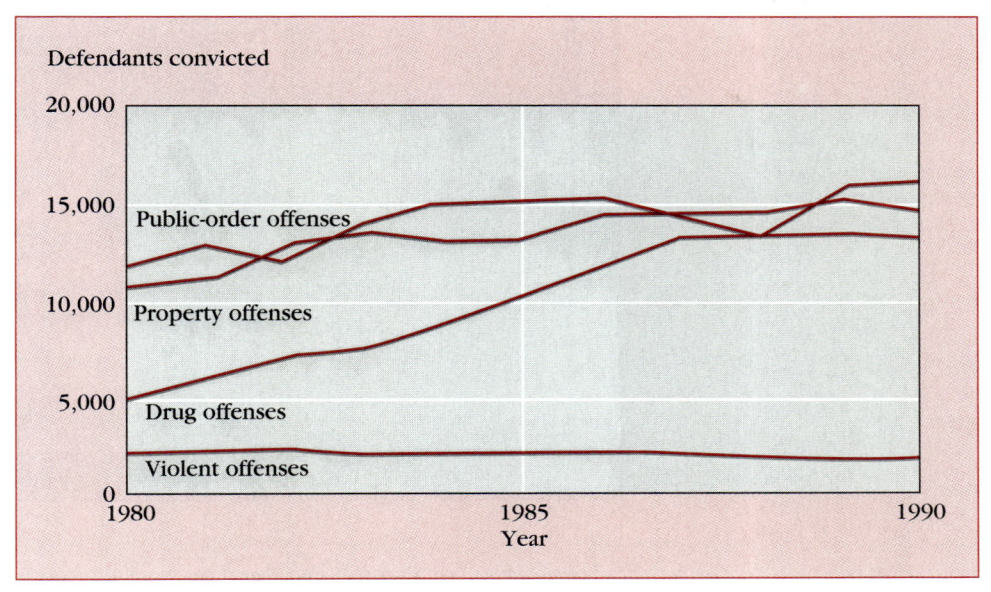

[Line graph showing defendants convicted from 1980 to 1990. Public-order offenses rise from ~12,000 to ~15,000. Property offenses stay around 13,000-14,000. Drug offenses rise from ~5,000 to ~16,000. Violent offenses remain low, around 1,000-2,000.]

SOURCE: Bureau of Justice Statistics.

and violence means doing something about the *roots* of crime. Single-mindedly enlarging enforcement mechanisms without addressing the causes of crime is a self-defeating project. We have already pointed to part of the debate that needs to take place—about poverty—in Chapters 6, 7, and 19. In this chapter we turn next to another factor in the current economy of violence: drugs.

The War on Drugs

Prior to 1875, all drugs were legal in the United States and could be sold over-the-counter without a prescription. This included opium, morphine, cocaine, marijuana, alcohol, and tobacco. Starting with an 1875 San Francisco ordinance banning opium dens, many drugs have been made illegal, with sometimes extreme punishments attached to their sale or use. (In 1970, for example, in Georgia, a first-offense sale of marijuana to a minor was punishable by life imprisonment; a second offense was punishable by death.[14] The federal government first banned the importation of smoking opium in 1909, but the **Harrison Narcotic Act of 1914** was the first major step in the federal government's fight against drugs. Although the act itself was a licensing law, executive enforcement and prosecution turned it into a general prohibition of opium, morphine, heroin, and cocaine, which were then in wide use in wines, colas,

Some European democracies have experimented with a more relaxed attitude toward drug use. For a time, a park in Zürich, Switzerland, became widely used as a place for heroin addicts to inject themselves with drugs. As one addict put it, "This place shocks people. . . . No one starts using drugs, because they see this." Use of the park was later restricted, however, because of the growth of crime. *(Lonny Shavelson/Impact Visuals)*

and patent medicines. The national prohibition of alcohol, instituted by the Eighteenth Amendment to the Constitution in 1919, was a brief experiment, abandoned in 1933. But the restrictions on "hard drugs" begun with the Harrison Act have been maintained and expanded.

The most recent phase in U.S. drug policy began in 1971, when President Richard Nixon declared a "war on drugs." That year the country had an estimated 1.5 million heroin addicts, and legions of long-haired young people were smoking marijuana. Much has changed in the meantime in the federal war on drugs, including consumption patterns. Heroin, although still a problem (the Drug Enforcement Agency estimated 750,000 addicts in 1992),[15] has been surpassed by cocaine as the drug of choice. Since the mid-1980s, "crack" (a form of cocaine that is relatively cheap per dose but appears to be fiercely addictive) has become a severe problem in inner cities. Since 1988, middle-class use of cocaine has declined, but crack use has increased.

Drug-related crime is a much more serious problem now than it was in 1971, which feeds a popular demand for more enforcement. Politicians who need to be "tough on drugs" routinely call for more police, more border searches, and longer prison sentences. Drug-related crime increasingly influences foreign policy debates. The governments of Turkey, Mexico, Thailand, Colombia, Peru, and Bolivia have been threatened with diplomatic isolation or offered bribes for their farmers, herbicides for their drug crops, and helicopters for their police.[16] One observer labeled the 1989 U.S. invasion of Panama the "biggest drug bust of the century." Of the $12 billion the federal government spent in 1992 on drugs, two-thirds of it went to interdiction and enforcement mechanisms.

During the late 1980s there was another flurry of support for legalization as a means of reducing the social harms caused by drugs. The argument for legalization, based on the failure of proscription to stem supply and demand, asserts that the criminalization of drugs itself creates many problems.

> It is not simply that the War on Drugs has failed to work; it has in many respects made things worse. It has spun a spider's web of black-market pathologies, including roughly 25 percent of all urban homicides, widespread corruption of police and other public officials, street crime by addicts, and subversive "narco-terrorist" alliances between Latin American guerrillas and drug traffickers.[17]

Legalization is not an all-or-nothing proposition. Proponents suggest that only the less dangerous drugs could be legalized, or they could be made available through physicians or government outlets. The penalties for use could be reduced. Opponents of legalization predict greater demand and use if legal penalties (and the accompanying social stigma) are removed.

Sometimes spontaneous local action serves as one response to a local crisis. Here citizens protest drug dealing and prostitution in their neighborhood. (Grant LeDuc/Monkmeyer Press Photos)

Even many people who do not favor legalization suggest that enforcement can at best serve as a stopgap, not a solution. Many drug experts feel that the emphasis on enforcement is misguided. They say that although the enforcement money spent may bring increased seizures, arrests, and convictions (all signs of success according to the standards of enforcement), the real war must be waged on a different front: treatment and education. Most of the $3 billion that President Nixon spent on the war on drugs in 1971 was spent in these areas. In federal spending since 1981, enforcement has substantially outstripped treatment and education.

Another question for public policy on drugs involves what some people feel is hypocrisy about the deadliest drugs in America: alcohol (100,000 annual deaths) and tobacco (360,000 annual deaths).[18] These legal drugs are pushed with billions of dollars of advertising each year, and a significant share of their consumption is by children. U.S. Surgeon General Antonia C. Novello has been particularly critical of the tobacco and alcohol industries' implicit efforts to target young people. The cigarette-puffing cartoon character Joe Camel is, according to Novello, an especially egregious example of pandering to children. "In years past, R. J. Reynolds would have us walk a mile for aCamel," she said at a joint press conference with representatives of the American Medical Association. "Today it's time that we invite Old Joe Camel himself to take a hike."[19] The cigarette manufacturer denied that it was targeting youth. Cigarettes are widely available in vending machines, frustrating statutory restrictions on sales to minors.

The federal government did target teenage drinkers with the National Minimum Drinking Age Act of 1984, which gave states large incentives to raise the drinking age to twenty-one. But the legal ban is largely ineffective. According to the surgeon general, at least 8 million American teenagers use alcohol every week, and almost half a million go on a weekly binge (five or more drinks in a row). Junior and senior high school students drink 35 percent of all wine coolers sold in the United States (31 million gallons) and down 1.1 billion cans of beer (102 gallons) each year.[20]

The social costs of this drug use are very high. According to one government study, rape and sexual assault are closely associated with youthful drinking. Among college-age students, 55 percent of the perpetrators and 53 percent of the victims were under the influence of alcohol. Even more disturbing was a survey of high school students: 18 percent of the females—nearly one in five—said it was OK to force sex if the girl was drunk. Among high school males, almost 40 percent—two out of five—said the same thing.[21]

Enforcing alcohol limitations on teenagers is a good example of official policy coming up against the reality of the street. Police point out that enforcing alcohol laws is a no-win situation. Parents do not like having their children arrested for doing what everyone else does. And local police may place a higher priority on stopping illicit drugs, ignoring alcohol. One of the challenges of formulating policy to combat drug use is to square our antidrug rhetoric with the pro-use messages of commercial advertising. It is asking a lot to expect teenagers to be able to distinguish between the two.

The ultimate solution to drug abuse is through education, the next example of policy concerning community values and limits that we will examine.

BUILDING COMMUNITY 735

The clever "Joe Camel" ads stirred controversy because of their potential appeal to children and young people. Although the tobacco company claimed it was not targeting the young, many believed otherwise. Some degree of regulation of cigarette advertising has long been accepted. But how much regulation? *(Irene Bayer/Monkmeyer Press Photos)*

Education: Fairness and Values

Even a brief survey of ways in which our democracy creates and maintains community values should cover education. Within this topic are dozens of controversies that would illuminate an introduction to American politics. We will briefly explore only two: the controversy about equitable school funding and the ongoing debate about enforcing values in school. Most funding for education in this country comes from state and local governments (only about 11 percent comes from the federal government). But the federal government plays an important role in establishing groundrules for education, as the *Brown v. Board of Education* decision outlawing segregation demonstrates. In both cases below policy making is a mix of federal, state and local influences.

Equitable School Funding

In 1968, Edgewood Elementary School in San Antonio, Texas, was in bad shape.[22] The top two floors of the three-story building had been condemned. It lacked basic supplies, books, and air conditioning. Almost half of Edgewood's teachers were not certified. In the United States, primary and secondary education has traditionally been funded through local property taxes. Although Edgewood Independent School District had one of the highest property tax rates in the state, property values were so low that the district tax raised only $37 per pupil. A few miles away on a hill in northern San Antonio, Alamo Heights School District had far lower property tax rates. But because of high property values, Alamo Heights raised $412 per pupil. Even after factoring state supplements into the school districts' budgets, the figures still showed a great discrepancy: $231 per pupil for Edgewood, $543 for Alamo Heights.

Demetrio Rodriguez, a metalworker at Kelly Air Force Base, had two sons at Edgewood Elementary. He decided to do something about the disparities of school funding in San Antonio. After getting nowhere with district administrators and state legislators, Rodriguez turned to the federal courts. On December 23, 1971, a three-judge federal district court gave Edgewood a Christmas present, deciding in *San Antonio Independent School District* v. *Rodriguez* that the Texas school finance system was an unconstitutional violation of the Fourteenth Amendment's equal protection clause. It didn't last. In March 1973 the U.S. Supreme Court ruled 5-4 against Rodriguez. Writing for the majority, Justice Lewis Powell said that education was not a "fundamental right" afforded explicit protection under the U.S. Constitution.

The Texas state legislature promised poor school districts that something would be done, but little was. In the mid-1980s the hundred wealthiest school districts in Texas were spending an average $7,233 per student, while the hundred poorest were spending $2,978. (The range within the state ran from $2,112 to $19,333.) Edgewood went back to court, this time in the state system. In October 1989 the Texas Supreme Court decided *Edgewood* v. *Kirby* in favor of Edgewood, unanimously declaring that the Texas school finance system did not meet the requirements of the Texas state constitution. But the court did not tell the legislature how to equalize school funding. One plan devised by the legislature did not go far enough. In January 1992 a "Robin Hood" plan taking money from the rich districts to give to the poor districts was ruled an unconstitutional statewide property tax. The Texas Supreme Court gave the state until mid-1993 to come up with a better plan. In the meantime, the Robin Hood plan stays in effect, causing much disgruntlement throughout the state. Rich districts are naturally unhappy. Alamo Heights had to give up $5 million of its $19 million annual budget. Even raising property taxes 36 percent left the school district $1 million short, requiring salary freezes and other cutbacks. Meanwhile, Edgewood Independent School District got only $68 more per pupil because the state legislature was unwilling to raise state taxes or move money into education from other categories.

Although there is a lot of talk about school vouchers and other school reforms, few politicians in the United States are willing to take on this explosive issue of equity. What is a fair method of funding education? Uniform rates across every state? What about disparities between states? Opponents of statewide schemes cite the long tradition of local control of education in this country. Can that be tossed aside? Justice Powell aptly wrote in *San Antonio* that to decide for Edgewood would occasion an unprecedented upheaval in public education. . . . The need is apparent for reform in tax systems which have relied too long and too heavily on the local property tax. And certainly innovative new thinking as to public education, its methods and its funding, is necessary to assure both a higher level of quality and a greater uniformity of opportunity. . . . But the ultimate solutions must come from the lawmakers and from the democratic pressures of those who elect them."[23]

Ten state supreme courts have forced their legislatures to remedy disparities between rich and poor districts. Almost half the states are currently being challenged over inequities in public education. Is there room for national policy on this fundamental issue, or should solutions be left to the states?

We now turn to a different sort of issue concerning education, the enforcement of certain values in educational contexts.

Education and Values

As we saw in Chapter 8, schools, from kindergarten through college, are important agents of socialization. Many civically useful values are inculcated in the educational process. Much of this socialization is indirect, reflecting dominant beliefs passed along implicitly. A significant portion of the socialization is direct, managed through decisions about textbooks and curricula. What sorts of values can and should schools teach in our democracy?

Sex education, for example, has proved quite controversial on two counts: Some parents complain that this sort of learning should take place at home and be the responsibility of parents, not schools, and many of these same parents worry that what is taught in sex education at school sends the wrong message—that casual sex among students is acceptable. With the arrival of the AIDS epidemic, the distribution of condoms became the next round of essentially the same debate, but public health concerns seem to have carried the day in large school districts in most major cities at least.

Prayer in school has been another hot issue in education policy. Since the Supreme Court banned prayer and Bible reading in public schools in 1962 and 1963 (see Chapter 5), an outraged segment of the society has argued that nondenominational prayer has an important place in public education. The Supreme Court has not changed its mind on this question, surprising many observers in 1992 with another decision affirming the principle that there should be a wall of separation between church and state. The Court found that a Rhode Island junior high school principal violated the First Amendment when he invited a rabbi to deliver a brief invocation during graduation ceremonies.[24]

Intentional minority segregation in primary education has emerged as a divisive issue about values in education. A small number of cities, including Baltimore and Detroit, have established public all-black all-male schools to address what some people believe are the uniquely pressing problems of young African-Americans today. Proponents say that an "Afrocentric" curriculum is the best way to instill confidence and

> **MANDATORY TESTING**
>
> Even the most ardent civil libertarian recognizes that government's police powers sometimes legitimately encompass the ability to require positive acts from citizens. And even the strongest advocate of government regulation recognize that governments can go too far in their demands on individuals. One civil liberties issue that evokes extreme judgments and yet defies simple solutions is the matter of **mandatory testing**. Testing programs can have a variety of ends—to protect society or individuals from some harm, to produce evidence for a criminal trial, or to ensure fairness. Americans have accommodated themselves to certain mandatory tests under specific circumstances—for example, blood tests to detect traditional sexually transmitted diseases as a requirement for marriage licenses or breath or urine tests to detect alcohol when a person is stopped on suspicion of driving under the influence. These tests raise few eyebrows now (although that was not always the case). But two public health problems—drugs and AIDS—have put mandatory testing back into controversy.
>
> The drug-testing issue came to the fore as a result of two well-publicized Amtrak accidents in the 1980s, in which evidence indicated employee drug use. Should the government as an employer require routine drug tests for government workers? Is the argument for testing more compelling when an employee's use of drugs on the job might endanger the employee or others (consider airline pilots)? If probable cause were used as a standard for imposing tests, what would constitute probable cause to believe that an employee was using drugs? Should the government restrict the ability of private employers to require routine drug tests? Should public educational institutions be permitted to require drug tests of students?

(Box continues on page 739)

self-esteem in students without strong family and community support. Besides, they say, most inner-city schools are effectively segregated anyway, due to white flight and socioeconomic stratification. Opponents say that the move to black-male schools is a false step to address the obvious failure of public education in large cities. They rely on the arguments used to defeat segregation originally: that segregated schools are inherently inferior. And they say that the black-male school doesn't address the underlying problems that leave African-American youngsters at risk in the first place. Are these schools an effective way of reaching a particular population at considerable risk? Or is this an unfortunate Balkanization of education, reinforcing ethnic tensions and inequities?

> Critics of drug-testing programs suggest that uniform testing without probable cause violates the Fourth and Fifth Amendments; that the costs of drug testing are high and the benefits are relatively low; the American society is taking a hypocritical attitude toward hard drugs in the face of its relative indifference about the most commonly abused drug of all, alcohol; and that drug problems are symptoms rather than causes. These critics contend that society would be better served by turning its attention to poverty, the profitability of drug sales, and other social conditions conducive to drug abuse.
>
> AIDS testing as a civil liberties issue has all the complications of drug testing plus more. Some observers suggest that AIDS is a public health problem and not a matter of civil liberties at all. Seeing a serious threat to the public health, these persons would force victims and potential victims to take any action that would reduce the threat, including mandatory tests and even quarantine. Most observers, however, see clear civil liberties implications in any public response to AIDS. In addition to the questions about mandatory testing (Should employers be permitted to require an AIDS test? What about health insurers?), how to handle the results of tests is even more problematic. For example, should doctors be free to warn sexual partners of AIDS patients even if the patients object? Should they be required to do so? Should parents or physicians be required to tell school officials that a child has tested positive for HIV? Should school officials in turn be required to or restricted from informing other parents of the test results?
>
> Various states have struggled with AIDS-testing issues. Some have even instituted tests in particular circumstances—for marriage license applicants and prison inmates, for example—but the general pattern has been not to impose mandatory tests.

In an attempt to eliminate racial and gender discrimination, some colleges and universities have adopted policies that ban the expression of racial or gender slurs. Since academia has long been a bastion of free speech, these policies are very controversial. Shold a student be expelled for yelling racial slurs on campus? Yes, say the advocates of these rules. Otherwise the educational opportunities of ethnic minority students will be necessarily limited. Free expression does have limits, these proponents argue, insofar as it is necessary to maintain a community of civility within which dialogue can take place. "Nonsense," thunders the other side, charging that such rules represent another effort of a liberal cultural elite to impose "politically correct" thinking on campus and on society at large.

In June 1992 the Supreme Court unanimously struck down a St. Paul, Minnesota, ordinance that targeted hate speech and bias crimes. The law barred words that "communicate messages of racial, gender, or religious intolerance." The particular case before the Court concerned a cross-burning incident on the front lawn of an African-American family in St. Paul. A majority of the justices found the defect in the ordinance to be an unconstitutional "content-based discrimination." "Selectivity of this sort creates the possibility that the city is seeking to handicap the expression of particular ideas. The point of the First Amendment is that majority preferences must be expressed in some fashion other than silencing speech on the basis of its content."[25] Four concurring justices found the ordinance only to be overbroad, leaving the possibility that more carefully crafted legislation might have survived. What impact does this decision have on campus regulations? Can civility be institutionally enforced in higher education, or must we hope that socialization has already accomplished that? Do regulations that specifically outlaw certain messages reflect the imposition of a certain ideology? What about language that is deemed to constitute sexual harassment? Is it different from other sorts of derogatory language?

The issues that fall under the topic of maintaining community values in education range widely, touching questions of institutional organization, budget, and content. No single arena—the federal courts, Congress, state legislatures, local school districts—can address these issues definitively.

Conclusions

> Struggles to coerce uniformity of sentiment in support of some end thought essential to their time and country have been waged by many good as well as by evil men.... Ultimate futility of such attempts to compel coherence is the lesson of every such effort from the Roman drive to stamp out Christianity as a disturber of its pagan unity ... down to the fast failing efforts of our totalitarian enemies. Those who begin coercive elimination of dissent soon find themselves exterminating dissenters. Compulsory unification of opinion achieves only the unanimity of the graveyard.[26]

Justice Robert H. Jackson used this stark language during the Second World War to strike down a mandatory flag salute in public schools. The questions of that debate are, in various guises, the questions we have been exploring in this chapter. How does a democratic community maintain itself? What line drawn between art and obscenity will allow for the fullest artistic freedom compatible with important moral values? Where are the limits of the necessary group maintenance functions? Some compulsion is inherent in every public regulation. How much and what kinds of compulsion are necessary? Which items in a criminal code protect a genuine public interest, and which maintain special protection for the well-connected? Which reinforce outmoded stereotypes? One of the problems of a democratic polity is to decide which values are inherent in the notion of democracy itself and which are the intentional or unconscious impositions of a particular faction in society. When is cohesion bought at the cost of undemocratic coercion? How shall we distribute educational opportunity? What values shall we teach our children in public education? These are perennial questions for democracy.

GLOSSARY TERMS

capital punishment
entrapment
Harrison Narcotic Act of 1914
John Stuart Mill
LAPS test
mandatory testing
Miller v. *California*

National Endowment for the Arts (NEA)
pardon
parole
probation
Roth v. *United States*
victimless crime

NOTES

[1] Richard C. Paddock, "Santa Cruz Grants Anti-bias Protection to the Ugly," *Los Angeles Times*, May 25, 1992, p. A3.
[2] 354 U.S. 476.
[3] *Memoirs* v. *Attorney General of Massachusetts* (1966), 383 U.S. 413.
[4] 413 U.S. 15.
[5] Steven Lee Myers, "Obscenity Laws Exist, but What Breaks Them?" *New York Times*, January 19, 1992, p. 1.
[6] Jean B. Elshtain, "The New Porn Wars," *New Republic*, June 25, 1984, pp. 15-20.
[7] James Shearwood, "Congress Has Long Poked Its Nose in the Arts," *New York Times*, February 29, 1992, p. 14.
[8] Diane Haithman, "Judge Voids the NEA's Decency Standard," *Los Angeles Times*, June 10, 1992, p. F1.
[9] Ibid.
[10] All statistics in this section from the Bureau of Justice Statistics.
[11] Malcolm C. Young, "More Punishment Doesn't Decrease Crime," *New York Times*, October 4, 1991, p. A16.
[12] Sheryl Stolberg, "Judge Apologizes, Frees 2 Men in 1973 Murder," *Los Angeles Times*, March 26, 1992, p. A1.
[13] Roberto Suro, "Crime and Its Amplified Echoes Are Rearranging People's Lives," *New York Times*, February 9, 1992, sec. 4, p. 1.
[14] Edward M. Brecher, "Drug Laws and Drug Law Enforcement: A Review and Evaluation Based on 111 Years of Experience," in *Perspectives on Drug Use in the United States* (New York: Haworth Press, 1986), p. 15.
[15] Richard White, "Drugs: The Forgotten Debate," *Christian Science Monitor*, March 20, 1992, p. 19.
[16] Joseph B. Treaster, "20 Years of War on Drugs, and No Victory Yet," *New York Times*, June 14, 1992, sec. 4. p. 7.
[17] Steven Wisotsky, *Beyond the War on Drugs: Overcoming a Failed Public Policy* (Buffalo, N.Y.: Prometheus, 1990), p. xx.

[18]Ibid., p. xxvii.
[19]Stuart Elliott, "Top Health Official Demands Abolition of 'Joe Camel' Ads," *New York Times*, March 9, 1992, p. A1.
[20]Antonia C. Novello, "Alcohol and Kids: It's Time for Candor," *Christian Science Monitor*, June 26, 1992, p. 19.
[21]Ibid.
[22]Account drawn from Barry Siegel, "Parents Get a Lesson in Equality," *Los Angeles Times*, April 13, 1992, p. A1.
[23]411 U.S. 1.
[24]*Lee* v. *Weisman* (1992), 112 S.Ct. 2649.
[25]Linda Greenhouse, "High Court Voids Law Singling Out Crimes of Hatred," *New York Times*, June 23, 1992, p. A1; *RAV* v. *St. Paul* (1992), 112 S.Ct. 2538.
[26]*West Virginia State Board of Education* v. *Barnette* (1943), 319 U.S. 624.

Selected Readings

For an overview on **social control**, see Stanley Cohen and Andrew Scull, eds., *Social Control and the State*, (New York: St. Martin's Press, 1983); Allan V. Horwitz, *The Logic of Social Control* (New York: Plenum, 1990); William G. Staples, *Castles of Our Conscience: Social Control and the American State, 1800–1985* (New Brunswick, N.J.: Rutgers University Press, 1990); and Morris Janowitz, *On Social Organization and Social Control* (Chicago: University of Chicago Press, 1991).

To learn more about **social policy and art**, an eclectic set of essays from the faculty of the University of Iowa can be found in Robert Hobbs and Fredrick Woodward, eds., *Human Rights/Human Wrongs: Art and Social Change* (Iowa City: Museum of Art, University of Iowa, 1988). Another interesting set of essays can be found in Arlene Raven, ed., *Art in the Public Interest* (Ann Arbor: University of Michigan Press, 1989). For a combination of history and social analysis, try Barbara Melosh, *Engendering Culture: Manhood and Womanhood in New Deal Public Art and Theater* (Washington, D.C.: Smithsonian Institution, 1991).

Crime in America is a huge subject, mostly traversed by sociologists, try: Ronald B. Flowers, *Demographics and Criminality: The Characteristics of Crime in America* (Westport, Conn.: Greenwood Press, 1989); Stuart A. Scheingold, *The Politics of Street Crime: Criminal Process and Cultural Obsession* (Philadelphia: Temple University Press, 1991); and Stephen R. Fox, *Blood and Power: Organized Crime in Twentieth-Century America* (New York: Morrow, 1989). For a **comparative perspective**, see Robert Y. Thorton, *Preventing Crime in America and Japan: A Comparative Study* (Armonk, N.Y.: Sharpe, 1992); Roger G. Hood, *The Death Penalty: A World-wide Perspective* (Oxford: Clarendon Press, 1989); and Hans-Gunther Heiland, Louise I. Shelley, and Hisoa Katoh, eds., *Crime and Control in Comparative Perspectives* (Hawthorne, N.Y.: Aldine, 1992).

On **drugs**, read Arnold S. Trebach and Kevin B. Zeese, eds., *Drug Prohibition and the Conscience of Nations* (Washington, D.C.: Drug Policy Foundation, 1990); Lamond Tullis, *Handbook of Research on the Illicit Drug Traffic: Socioeconomic and Political Consequences.* (Westport, Conn.: Greenwood Press, 1991); United Nations Department of Public Information, *The United Nations and Drug Abuse Control* (New York: United Nations, 1989); William O. Walker III, *Drug Control in the Americas*, rev. ed. (Albuquerque: University of New Mexico Press, 1989); Jaime E. Malamud Goti, *Smoke and Mirrors: The Paradox of the Drug Wars* (Boulder, Colo.:

Westview Press, 1992); Mark Kleiman, *Against Excess: Drug Policy for Results* (New York: Basic Books, 1992); and Richard Lawrence Miller, *The Case for Legalizing Drugs* (New York: Praeger, 1991).

On **education and social policy**, start with Joel H. Spring, *American Education: An Introduction to Social and Political Aspects*, 3rd ed. (White Plains, N.Y.: Longman, 1985). Then go on to more daring treatments: Henry A. Giroux, *Teachers as Intellectuals: Toward a Critical Pedagogy of Learning* (Granby, Mass.: Bergin & Garvey, 1988); Henry A. Giroux et al., *Popular Culture, Schooling, and Everyday Life* (Granby, Mass.: Bergin & Garvey, 1989); and Michael W. Apple, *Teachers and Texts: A Political Economy of Class and Gender Relations in Education* (Boston: Routledge & Kegan Paul, 1986). More straightforward treatments include Kathleen P. Bennett and Margaret D. Le Compte, *How Schools Work: A Sociological Analysis of Education* (White Plains, N.Y.: Longman, 1990); and *The Unfinished Agenda: A New Vision for Child Development and Education* (New York: Committee for Economic Development, 1991). For a **comparative perspective** in a revolutionary setting, try Robert F. Arnove, *Education and Revolution in Nicaragua* (New York: Praeger, 1986), but remember that much has changed in Nicaragua since this was written.

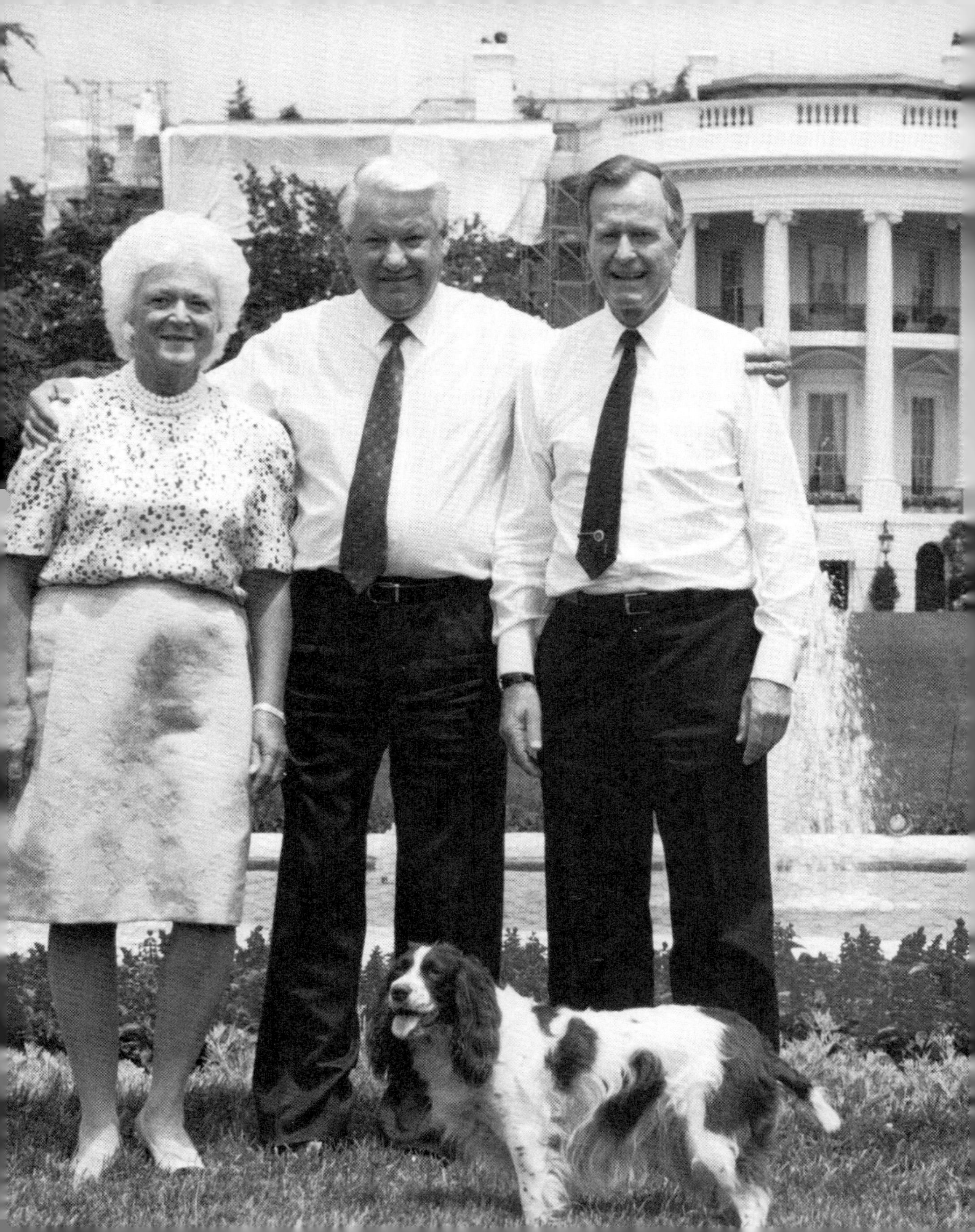

CHAPTER OUTLINE

The Making of Foreign Policy
THE PRESIDENT AND THE EXECUTIVE BRANCH
INFLUENCES ON FOREIGN POLICY

The Tools of Foreign Policy
DIPLOMACY
PROPAGANDA
ECONOMIC REWARDS AND PUNISHMENTS
CLANDESTINE OPERATIONS AND MILITARY INTERVENTION

Global Players
STATES
NONSTATE ACTORS

A Short History of U.S. Foreign Policy
ISOLATION AND EXPANSION
THE COLD WAR
GORBACHEV, *PERESTROIKA*, AND THE END OF THE USSR

Foreign Policy after the Cold War
THE U.S. INVASION OF PANAMA
FROM DESERT SHIELD TO DESERT STORM

Major Challenges for the Future
ECONOMIC COMPETITION THROUGH TRADE
HUMAN RIGHTS AND FOREIGN POLICY
AN EQUITABLE DISTRIBUTION OF WEALTH WORLDWIDE
THE FUTURE OF FOREIGN POLICY: A "NEW WORLD ORDER?"

CHAPTER TWENTY-ONE

FOREIGN AND DEFENSE POLICIES

A Place in the World

THE UNITED STATES EMERGED FROM WORLD WAR II A GREAT power—in fact, the dominant power in the world, both militarily and economically. Forty-six years later, with the collapse of the Soviet Union, the United States emerged from the Cold War as the only military superpower. The U.S. economy was the largest in the world. But many people at home and abroad wondered if the period of American dominance was drawing to a close.

Most observers of the intervening years would count more successes than failures. Most visibly, the Soviet Union, America's primary adversary, collapsed. Those who interpreted the Cold War as an essentially economic competition, in which the Americans and the Soviets pressed to see which nation could survive punishing expenditures on national defense, could declare the United States the unequivocal winner. But the Cold War had brought frustrating and confusing wars in Korea and Vietnam. We had overthrown regimes for dubious reasons, yet stood by while "friendly" governments, like that of the shah of Iran, fell. In Central America the United States continued a long pattern of intervention, pouring billions of dollars into El Salvador to prop up the government while pouring millions into Nicaragua to bring the government down. Both policies were controversial at home, and yet many Americans could not identify which country was which.

During the Cold War against the Soviet Union, Americans often found themselves aiding reputedly undemocratic or even tyrannical governments. But the containment of communism provided at least some overarching justification. Anticommunism was an important factor in nearly all American foreign policy decisions. And then suddenly communism was gone. The collapse of the Soviet Empire and the disintegration of the Soviet Union itself meant that the polestar of U.S. foreign policy had blinked out.

That left a major challenge for the American democracy: to redefine our place in the world. To understand that challenge, this chapter will examine the actors, the influences, and the instruments of foreign policymaking in this country and the global players that foreign policy must consider. We will briefly review the history of American foreign policy, including some major recent events and some challenges for the future. We turn first to the making of foreign policy in this country.

The Making of Foreign Policy

How is American foreign policy made? We shall spotlight the primary policymakers—the president and the executive branch, influences on them, and the instruments available to carry out foreign policy.

The President and the Executive Branch

Presidents are preeminent in U.S. foreign affairs. Traditionally, both the courts and Congress defer to presidential decision making in foreign and military policy. As commander in chief of the armed forces, the president usually enjoys wide latitude in the military and diplomatic arenas. But as we noted in Chapter 14, although the president's powers in foreign affairs are substantial, occasionally presidents simply cannot achieve key foreign policy goals. Woodrow Wilson failed to win Senate approval of U.S. membership in the League of Nations after World War I, Franklin Roosevelt was unable to arouse public support for more vigorous U.S. opposition to Nazism in the late 1930s, Jimmy Carter could not persuade the Senate to approve the SALT II arms control treaty in 1979, and Ronald Reagan had trouble sustaining funding for the Nicaraguan Contras.

The roles played by recent presidents in shaping foreign policy have varied considerably. Dwight D. Eisenhower and Gerald Ford turned most foreign policy matters over to the secretaries of state. John Kennedy, Richard Nixon, and Jimmy Carter were more active participants. Lyndon Johnson and Ronald Reagan were selective about foreign policy, giving certain issues significant personal attention and largely ignoring others. And George Bush was often accused of ignoring domestic politics altogether in order to concentrate on the issues that really mattered to him—foreign policy.

FOREIGN AND DEFENSE POLICIES

Every president is aided by a national security adviser, who coordinates and counsels on foreign policy matters. Another resource presidents rely on is the **National Security Council**, a coordinating and policymaking body consisting of the vice-president, the secretaries of defense and state, and others appointed by the president—usually including the CIA director and the chairman of the Joint Chiefs of Staff.

During recent presidencies, significant disagreements have erupted between secretaries of state and national security advisers. From the president's point of view, policy disagreements and struggles for influence among top advisers can sometimes serve the useful purpose of keeping options out in the open and encouraging the development of new alternatives. However, such policy disagreements can create confusion both at home and abroad, and they can sometimes drive policymaking into unmonitored and even illegitimate channels.

The **State Department**, the key agency in foreign policy, maintains about 3,500 foreign service officers in several hundred posts. State has often been accused of traditionalism, lack of creativity, and organizational diffuseness.

Every president is confronted with the tension between maintaining a professionalized foreign service corps of career diplomats on the one hand and putting personally selected people into embassies around the world on the other. A third consideration is that ambassadorships have long been considered worthy rewards for major campaign contributors or defeated candidates of the president's party. Because of high turnover, these staffing considerations are a constant feature of every presidential administration.

CIA Director Robert Gates, appointed by George Bush, underwent tough scrutiny during his confirmation hearings. In a post–Cold War world, the future role of the CIA was far from clear. *(Ron Edmonds/AP/Wide World Photos)*

Defense policy is officially the province of the secretary of defense, the head of the **Defense Department**. Secretaries of defense often have considerable difficulty coordinating the demands and missions of the various armed services because interservice rivalries are often acute. The Defense Department presides over some four thousand defense installations within the United States and maintains a massive budget; almost three-quarters of the government's purchases of goods and services are defense-related.

The military services are represented by the **Joint Chiefs of Staff (JCS)**, who advise the president as well as the secretary of defense. The chairman of the JCS heads a staff of four hundred and a larger organization of about two thousand. Rifts often develop among the chiefs as each service seeks to maximize its role in defense planning. Logrolling is common in military affairs: Frequently, chiefs endorse the various requests and ideas of other services simply to win support for their own.

The American foreign policy apparatus also gathers intelligence and conducts covert operations. Many government agencies are involved in intelligence work: the FBI, the Defense Intelligence Agency, the State Department's Bureau of Intelligence, the National Security Agency, and, of course, the **Central Intelligence Agency (CIA)**. This patchwork is typical of the American federal bureaucracy and results, especially in an area where secrets are kept, in some duplication of responsibility and interagency rivalry.

Only one office commands a view of all of these agencies involved in the formulation of foreign policy: the president's office. Oversight of foreign policy by Congress is fragmented by the committee structure and tends to be uneven and sporadic. Except in rare times of crisis, the news media in the United States generally spend far more time on domestic news than on foreign news. The public at large is content to stay only vaguely aware of routine foreign policy matters. Consequently, presidential choices and style are extremely important to foreign policy. Furthermore, keeping the vice-president privy to foreign policy consultations (the pattern of presidents since Jimmy Carter) is essential to maintaining continuity in the event of presidential disability or death.

Influences on Foreign Policy

Let us now explore three major influences on foreign policy: political elites, interest groups, and public opinion.

ELITES Political elites play a more central role in foreign policy decisions than in the making of domestic policy. Underlying this phenomenon is the lack of widespread public sophistication about foreign affairs—as well as a frequent lack of interest, although this has changed in recent years. These political elites include top politicians, corporate executives, military brass, people in the media, influential academics, and leaders of groups and institutions especially concerned with foreign policy.

INTEREST GROUPS Many interest groups have a great deal at stake in the way U.S. foreign policy is conducted. Business groups, organized labor, farmers, various ethnic groups, ideological interest groups, and others all attempt to influence the directions of U.S. international relations.

Business interests are pervasive. Some observers argue that U.S. foreign policy since World War II has been largely business-oriented. Others question the extent of corporate power, but none debate that U.S. policies are often shaped by key business leaders and generally reflect business interests. Still, "business" is not a united interest. Businesses frequently oppose one another: Some groups may seek freer trade, for instance, while others try to raise tariffs and protect their market position.

Organized labor also exercises influence over foreign policy. Like business, labor often seeks to protect the interests of workers in industries threatened by foreign imports. The AFL-CIO sometimes attacks government policies that encourage U.S. corporations to invest abroad because such policies usually mean fewer jobs at home. With the decline of certain U.S. industries, such as steel, labor must decide how best to protect its interests: Should the government be asked to aid failing U.S. companies? Should foreign companies be encouraged to invest here? Should U.S. companies be encouraged not to invest elsewhere?

Labor also takes stands on many noneconomic issues. Since the 1950s the AFL-CIO generally maintained a fiercely anticommunist stance. The Vietnam War, however, split labor's ranks. Some labor leaders joined the antiwar movement, whereas others rallied around Presidents Johnson and Nixon and supported escalation of the conflict. At times labor, like business, has launched its own foreign policy initiatives. When Polish workers went on strike in the summer of 1980, the AFL-CIO established a fund to assist the newly formed Polish "free trade unions."

Particular U.S. ethnic groups often take a keen interest in U.S. foreign policies as well. Greek-American views on the struggle between Greeks and Turks on Cyprus have had a marked effect on U.S. actions there. American Jews also maintain a highly visible and well-organized lobby to project their interest in our relations with Israel, the Arab nations, and the Palestinians.

Increasingly, human rights organizations influence foreign policy decisions by doing on-site investigations and other research useful to policymakers and by stimulating public awareness of human rights abuses.

PUBLIC OPINION Some political observers maintain that the public takes a generally passive attitude toward foreign policy. In this view, the public is poorly informed, strongly inclined to patriotic feeling and therefore accepting of direction from above. Within broad limits, political decision makers have a free hand in making foreign policy.

It is difficult to ascertain exactly what constraints public opinion places on policymakers. Clearly, the general structure of popular opinion does influence decision makers to some extent. A president could not unilaterally decide to disarm the nation entirely, for instance, without arousing considerable popular uproar. Still, many poli-

(Text continues on page 752)

Out of the Cold: A Role for the CIA?

With the end of the Cold War, the Central Intelligence Agency, no stranger to controversy, was once again the focus of attention. Was there a mission for the CIA after the USSR was gone? The Persian Gulf War demonstrated the dilemma of intelligence: On the positive side, it was useful to have knowledge of our opponent's secrets; on the negative side, the business of secrets is difficult for a democracy to monitor. At the end of the Gulf War, the CIA told the Senate Intelligence Committee that the CIA had stopped giving intelligence to the Iraqis two years before the invasion of Kuwait. More than half a year later, during hearings on the nomination of a new CIA head, the agency said that it had ceased cooperating with the Iraqis in early 1990—seven or eight months before the invasion. After the nomination was approved, the CIA said that intelligence to the Iraqis continued for three or four months *beyond* early 1990. Further information now indicates that the CIA provided intelligence to Iraq right up until August 1990, the month it invaded Kuwait.* The point is not when the aid did or did not end but rather that the Senate Intelligence Committee was unaware of and then repeatedly misled about the agency's activities.

Thus there are good reasons for democrats to keep a weather eye on the CIA. Because the CIA operates covertly, it is hard to know whether it is doing a good job of carrying out the policy tasks assigned to it or even to know (except in the most general sense) what tasks it has been given. And the specific history of the CIA is enough to give some democrats pause.

The CIA has two basic functions: classic intelligence gathering (from mundane sources like foreign newspapers as well as more exotic ones, such as electronic bugs, spies, and spy planes) and covert action (from disseminating propaganda to economic warfare, sabotage, and subversion).

The history of covert actions by the CIA includes an impressive list of interventions in the affairs of other nations as well as our own. The CIA provided secret subsidies to anticommunist labor unions in Western Europe; overthrew the Mossadegh regime in Iran in 1953 and restored the shah to power; organized a secret army that overthrew the government in Guatemala in 1954; planned the Bay of Pigs invasion of Cuba in 1961; sponsored guerrilla raids against mainland China during the 1950s; supplied support for the French in Indochina; played a key role in installing and later assassinating President Ngo Dinh Diem of South Vietnam; assassinated and attempted to assassinate various foreign leaders, in-

(Box continues on page 751)

cluding Fidel Castro of Cuba, Patrice Lumumba of the Congo, and Rafael Trujillo of the Dominican Republic. By the mid-1960s the CIA was also keeping files on approximately 300,000 Americans regarded as actual or potential subversives, despite a specific ban in its charter against operating within the United States.

In the 1960s and 1970s, controversies over U.S. policy in Cuba and Vietnam, along with fallout from the Watergate scandals, prompted a series of investigations into CIA activities. These probes revealed that the CIA had strayed so far from its original purposes that it was difficult to tell which of the activities linked to it were genuinely independent of agency control and which were being coordinated by the agency. Legislation passed in 1974 required that the president personally approve all major covert actions and that Congress be notified of such actions.

During the Reagan administration, however, the CIA again expanded its range of covert actions, National security adviser, Robert McFarlane, defended such covert operations, arguing that the government needed some space for maneuvering between total war and total peace; covert operations served a useful role in this "gray area." The alternatives, McFarlane maintained, were sending in the Marines or doing nothing. Critics, however, saw danger in this reliance on covert action, as key policy decisions were made outside legislative channels and with no popular input or evaluation.

The question now is what to do with the CIA and other components of the intelligence community. Some experts have suggested abolishing the CIA outright. Others have argued for a shift in emphasis from secrets (snatching the enemy's plans) to mysteries (probing the face of the future).

"With its sophisticated spy satellites, its electronic eavesdropping aircraft and its cable-tapping submarines, America became more adept than any other nation in history at reading the other guy's mail. But it has repeatedly failed to read his mind—in Moscow's Politburo, in Hanoi's war councils, in Tehran's ruling circle of mullahs, in Baghdad's Baath Socialist Party headquarters."[†]

If there is a place out of the Cold War for the American intelligence community, it will almost certainly involve more mysteries—in a broad range of areas—and fewer secrets. But will this new emphasis reduce the threat that covert operations represent to democracy?

[*]Marcus Raskin, "Let's Terminate the C.I.A.," Nation, June 8, 1992, pp. 776–777.
[†]John M. Broder, "Mysteries and Secrets," Los Angeles Times Magazine, April 19, 1992, p. 12.

cies pursued by political leaders in recent years could undoubtedly have been changed without disastrous political consequences for the leaders involved. It seems unlikely, for example, that Ronald Reagan's political career would have suffered much if he had decided *not* to invade Grenada. Nor would George Bush's if he had decided not to invade Panama. One of the clearest examples of the latitude given to presidents in pursuing public policy is the Persian Gulf War in 1991. Although the short, intense war proved to be popular after the fact, there was no significant public pressure to undertake Operation Desert Shield, placing large numbers of troops in Saudi Arabia to prevent Iraq from continuing there after its invasion of Kuwait; to turn Operation Desert Shield into Operation Desert Storm, driving Iraq from Kuwait; or to end the war before Saddam Hussein was ousted. The latitude available to presidents, then, is considerable, though not unlimited.

In recent years the American public has become better educated and better acquainted with the realities of politics in the rest of the world, and a larger and more sophisticated audience for foreign policy issues has therefore developed. As a result, the media occasionally adopt a more critical attitude in this field, and portions of the political elite become disenchanted with U.S. foreign policies. But as the uncritical media treatment of Desert Storm demonstrated, informed, critical response to crisis cannot be built on a foundation of day-to-day disinterest and disengagement.

The Tools of Foreign Policy

The United States government pursues its foreign policy objectives as it does its domestic policy objectives, through a variety of actions, involving words, deeds, and dollars. But the instruments of foreign policy are in some ways unique.

Diplomacy

The finest tool of foreign policy is diplomacy. In the United States, diplomacy is left almost entirely to the president, unfettered, and his subordinates, the secretary of state, and other members of the State Department. Although **diplomatic recognition**, marking the existence of formal relationships between sovereign states, was nearly automatic in the nineteenth century, it has become controversial in the twentieth. Should the United States recognize Bosnia-Herzegovina as a sovereign state despite the wishes of the Serbian-dominated government of Yugoslavia to maintain a national government that includes that state? Granting a breakaway republic legitimacy in the world at large can have life-and-death consequences in a civil war.

Most diplomacy happens after recognition issues are settled. It advances on the strength of reason and eloquence. Two spectacular examples of American diplomacy occurred in the 1970s: First, President Richard Nixon, whose political career was built on a record of anticommunism, reopened diplomatic relations with the stridently communist People's Republic of China. Some observers said that Nixon was the only leader who could risk the domestic political reaction to such a move. Any politician less staunchly opposed to communism would have been accused of caving in or selling out.

The second example of successful diplomacy was the Camp David Peace Accords between Egypt and Israel. The persistence of President Jimmy Carter in using his good offices to facilitate an agreement between mortal enemies and the political courage of President Anwar Sadat of Egypt and Prime Minister Menachem Begin of Israel resulted in the first major step toward accommodation between Israel and its Arab neighbors: face-to-face negotiations held in 1979 at the presidential retreat at Camp David, Maryland.

The unique role of the U.S. president in international policymaking: Jimmy Carter clasps hands with Anwar Sadat of Egypt and Menachem Begin of Israel at the formal signing of the Egyptian-Israeli peace treaty in March, 1979. Carter had put his personal prestige and the prestige of the presidency on the line in his efforts to broker a peace treaty between the historic enemies. *(UPI/Bettmann)*

Propaganda

The use of propaganda as a tool of foreign policy was made possible by the development of mass media—newspapers, radio, films, and television. Like the outsider strategy we talked about in Chapter 11, propaganda attempts to change government action by changing popular perceptions of the actors or issues in question. Common language assumes that the information conveyed in propaganda is false, but it need not be. **Propaganda** is defined as a government's concerted effort to affect public opinion in a particular direction. Propaganda is usually directed at foreign populations, but the porosity of borders to mass media means that effective propaganda must often reach domestic audiences as well.

The **United States Information Agency (USIA)** is in charge of overt propaganda for the United States. One of the showcase instruments of American propaganda is the **Voice of America (VOA)**, which broadcasts about a thousand hours a week of mostly news and information radio in forty-two languages. VOA is not crudely propagandistic: it broadcasts straight news and even policy debates about the United States. But the object of government-sponsored radio beamed abroad is to advance American interests among the foreign masses. The CIA engages in a variety of covert propaganda activities—hiding the source of radio broadcasts encouraging rebels in Soviet-dominated Afghanistan, for example. Americans are also the objects of the propaganda of other nations. Recently a practice has developed of hiring American lobbying or advertising organizations to improve the image of a foreign government among ordinary Americans.

Economic Rewards and Punishments

Even the smallest government can pass out economic rewards and punishments. With a huge national economy like ours behind it, the United States government has extensive power to persuade and coerce through economic means. This comes in a variety of forms. Direct economic aid is a transfer payment from the United States to another country. It is rarely as simple as writing a check, however. Economic aid can come with a variety of stipulations, restricting its use to humanitarian purposes, for example. Unfortunately, such stipulations are easily defeated, since a nation told to spend $1 million of U.S. aid on highways can easily divert the money that it would have spent on highways to some other use—military supplies, for instance. That is why much economic aid takes the form of investment credits (to be spent in the United States) or loan guarantees instead of cash payments. These mechanisms also ensure a return for the American economy on money spent on foreign aid.

Tariffs, boycotts, and quotas are mechanisms by which the government can restrict the access of foreign goods to the American market. Licensing requirements can produce the same effect. These economic instruments can be directed against an entire country or at specific industries across several countries. For over a decade the United

States and Japan have negotiated voluntary import limits on Japanese cars sold in America. Proponents argue that this "levels the playing field" for domestic manufacturers who have not succeeded at marketing American cars in Japan. Advocates of free trade say that such artificial limits are easily subverted by multinational corporations, and even when successful, allow both foreign and domestic producers to raise prices.

An embargo, usually multilaterally imposed (by several nations cooperatively or by an intergovernmental organization like the UN), is used to coerce a country into changing its behavior by cutting it off from outside trade. In extreme cases an embargo may be enforced by a military blockade. Embargoes are favored by some experts as a serious step short of military intervention. The argument against embargoes is that they are not effective (in 1991 and 1992 the UN embargo against Iraq did not dislodge Saddam Hussein either before or after Operation Desert Storm; the embargo against Serbia did not stop its military attacks on Bosnia-Herzegovina in 1992; the 1992 embargo against Haiti did not force the military junta to return the democratically elected government

A flood of Haitian refugees sought asylum in the United States after a military coup in their nation. George Bush, however, ordered that the flow be stopped and many Haitians repatriated. The administration argued that they were economic, not political, refugees. The problem of providing refuge has become a major international issue with often profound and complex repercussions for national politics. (Michael Stravato/AP/Wide World Photos)

to power) and that they tend to hurt the poorest people in the country most. Ruling elites are the last to experience shortages.

Freezing assets and expropriation are means of punishing other states, although expropriation may also be a domestic policy of increasing public ownership of the means of production. In 1979 the United States froze Iranian assets in this country—almost $12 billion worth—to protest the seizure of the U.S. embassy and the taking of hostages in Tehran.

Clandestine Operations and Military Intervention

If diplomacy represents foreign policy of persuasion by reason, clandestine operations and military intervention represent the other extreme: persuasion by force. Clandestine operations may be either subtle (manipulating elections) or direct (supporting or carrying out insurrection). The Reagan administration followed a broad policy of covert operations. The difficulty of covert operations for a democracy is that citizens are not allowed a voice in specific policy—secret policy cannot be subjected to democratic scrutiny. Although there are intelligence oversight committees in both houses of Congress charged with reviewing covert operations, the initiative in this area clearly belongs to the president.

The severest of foreign policy tools is direct military intervention. Since World War II there has been a tendency to seek UN approval of military intervention, as in the Korean and Persian Gulf wars. But the United States has frequently found justification for unilateral military action, as in its invasion of Grenada in 1983, bombing of Libya in 1986, and invasion of Panama in 1989. These recent examples of unilateral U.S. military intervention demonstrate the range of justifications offered. The Grenada invasion was billed as a rescue mission for American medical students studying in Grenada and as a means of displacing a dangerous Marxist regime. The bombing of Tripoli in 1986 was justified by the Reagan administration as a means of warning Libya that it could not sponsor international terrorism with impunity. The pattern of U.S. strikes also indicated that an attempt was made to eliminate Muammar al-Qaddafi, the vocal anti-American Libyan ruler. The invasion of Panama was justified by the Bush administration as a means of cutting off a government-sponsored drug supply operation and to free Panama from a corrupt regime that had subverted democratic elections. In all these instances of direct unilateral military intervention, the president has called the shots. Even though the War Powers Resolution requires advance consultation and congressional ratification of troop commitments to battle after the fact, the fast pace and short length of these operations means that legislators are effectively relegated to the cheerleading section.

The tools available to carry out foreign policy are frequently used in combination, in ongoing operations or one-shot events. As the framers of the Constitution imagined, the president's power is greatest when time is short. Congressional power is designed for long-term operations requiring budget approval. We haven't said anything in this review of the tools of foreign policy about the federal courts. As we saw in Chapter 16, judicial actors are reluctant to intervene in foreign affairs generally, out of fear that the United States will be embarrassed in the world at large by having more than one voice speaking for the government and out of a recognition that judicial expertise may have little to offer on most foreign policy questions.

Next we will review the players on the global stage with whom foreign policy-makers must deal.

Global Players

There was a time, prior to the late-eighteenth-century revolutions in America and France, when sovereignty was exercised personally—kings, queens, and princes were the only actors recognized on the global stage. In 1580, Elizabeth, Queen of England, would carry on relations with Henri III of France or Ivan IV of Russia, for example. With the rise of modern democracies, it became clear that heads of state merely *represented* the states themselves. Individual states (countries) became the focus of an international system that emphasized the pursuit of national interests.

States

To be considered a state, a country must have territory with people, resources, and defined borders; a government; and sovereignty recognized by the global family of states. Recognition is essential to sovereignty. Estonia, for example, is a nation on the Baltic Sea with long traditions. It has territory, people, resources, and a government. After the Soviet takeover in 1940, many Estonians thought of Estonia as a sovereign state occupied by a foreign power. But from 1940 to 1991, Estonia was not a state because the world recognized the USSR as the sovereign entity and Estonia as a political subdivision thereof. In 1991 the world acknowledged Estonia's secession from the Soviet Union and its reassumption of statehood, marked by membership in the United Nations.

There are currently over 180 states in the world, more than twice the number in the 1950s. The increase has come primarily in two waves, the first in the late 1950s and 1960s as former European colonies in Africa and elsewhere became independent, the second in the late 1980s and early 1990s as the Soviet Union disintegrated and nationalism split states like Yugoslavia and Czechoslovakia into smaller sovereign entities.

Nonstate Actors

An understanding that states were the sole international actors persisted until quite recently, when it was recognized that other groups also wielded transnational power.

These nonstate actors fall into two categories: **intergovernmental organizations (IGOs)**, which are voluntary associations of sovereign states, and **nongovernmental organizations (NGOs)**, which are transnational bodies with headquarters in one state and centrally directed operations in two or more other states.[1] Intergovernmental organizations can be global or regional. They can be multipurpose, like the United Nations (UN) and the Organization of African Unity (OAU), or they can have narrowly defined goals, like the Oil Producing and Exporting Countries (OPEC) cartel, which tries to manage oil production and pricing. The largest and most active IGO is the United Nations and its satellite organizations.

THE UNITED NATIONS   The **United Nations** was founded in San Francisco in 1945 as a new and strengthened version of the League of Nations, which had been formed following the First World War. The UN was to be a forum for the peaceful resolution of international disputes (it was forbidden from intervening in domestic affairs) and a mechanism for cooperatively addressing global problems of human health and welfare.

The UN has six major operating units, most prominently the General Assembly, to which all members belong, which serves as the primary forum for international discussions; and the Security Council, composed of fourteen member states (five permanent—the United States, the United Kingdom, France, China, and Russia—and nine rotating Assembly-elected members). The Security Council, which was often hampered during the Cold War by the veto power given each of the five permanent members, allows the major powers to add their particular point of view to debate. Two of the world's most powerful nations, Japan and Germany, do not have permanent seats on the Security Council. The Secretariat facilitates activity undertaken by other units of the UN. The secretary general's position, although formally symbolic, provides a bully pulpit from which a skillful diplomat like Javier Pérez de Cuéllar (1982–1991) can have a major impact on international affairs. The other units of the UN are the International Court of Justice in The Hague, Netherlands; the Trusteeship Council, which oversees territories that were not self-governing when the UN was founded; and the Economic and Social Council, intended to coordinate the satellite organizations, advance human rights, and promote higher living standards. In addition to the UN itself, there are satellite organizations like the World Health Organization (WHO) and the United Nations Educational, Scientific and Cultural Organization (UNESCO), which have proved very effective at addressing specific problems. (In an unprecedented triumph of public health practice, WHO eradicated smallpox worldwide in the 1970s.) The UN budget for 1990–1991 was $1.56 billion, not counting the satellite organizations and special peacekeeping missions, for which members are assessed separately.

The end of the Cold War has dramatically enhanced the role of the UN, in part because superpower rivalry no longer gets in the way of dealing with regional disputes but also because as the 1990s got under way the major powers found themselves in reduced circumstances economically and less willing to act unilaterally. The United Nations, supported by both the United States and the Soviet Union, provided the formal mechanisms for the Persian Gulf War to eject Iraq from Kuwait. In mid-1992 the UN was involved in eleven separate observation and peacekeeping missions around the globe. The UN can provide civilian and military observers, as well as regular troops whose normal task is to separate combatants and supervise cease-fires and demilitarized zones.

OTHER INTERGOVERNMENTAL ORGANIZATIONS   There are many other international governmental organizations, most regional in scope. In the Cold War period following World War II, many of these organizations were formed for mutual security. The North Atlantic Treaty Organization (NATO) in the West and the Warsaw Treaty Organization (Warsaw Pact) in the East were the most prominent mutual-defense organizations of the Cold War. The Warsaw Pact was disbanded in 1991; NATO has maintained a role in post–Cold War Europe. Increasingly, IGOs are based on economic cooperation, such

Amnesty International

Amnesty International was founded in 1961 by a London barrister named Peter Benenson. Benenson had been outraged by a newspaper account of two Portuguese students arrested in a Lisbon restaurant for raising a toast "to freedom." They had been sentenced to seven years in prison. Benenson launched the Appeal for Amnesty, based on the notion that the pressure of public opinion could bring about new protections for "prisoners of conscience." The Appeal grew into Amnesty International. The organization's mandate included these four goals: "to work impartially for those imprisoned for their opinion, to seek for them a fair and public trial, to enlarge the right of asylum and help political refugees to find work, and to urge effective and international machinery to guarantee freedom of opinion." Amnesty's weapons are research and publicity. A paid staff operating out of London researches charges of human rights violations. Local chapters around the world are then notified of and "adopt" particular cases. In addition to generating news coverage of rights abuses (in particular cases or as a result of official policy), chapters sponsor letter-writing campaigns. Can a government ignore thousands of individual letters from around the world? Benenson hoped not. Amnesty International will not adopt prisoners of conscience who advocate violence of any sort. The organization is careful to maintain a nonpartisan stance in the domestic politics of nations where it identifies abuses. Amnesty International sometimes takes controversial stands, as with its decision to oppose the death penalty categorically, but there are few observers of international human rights policies that would deny that Amnesty International and groups like it play an important role in fighting human rights abuse.

as the major free trade organizations. One such economic organization, the European Community, has integrated its member nations to such a significant degree that it begins to display some of the characteristics of statehood. The range of IGOs is great, from the narrow-focus International Lead and Zinc Study Group to the General Agreement on Tariffs and Trade (GATT), which plays a major role in facilitating the global economy.

NONGOVERNMENTAL ORGANIZATIONS   The range of NGOs in the world is much wider than the range of IGOs. A nongovernmental organization might be a **multinational corporation (MNC)**, or it might be an organization like the Palestine Liberation Organization (PLO), which is seeking support for the creation of a sovereign state. Very large MNCs, whose balance sheets make them larger than many states, may actually prescribe state policy or effectively avoid national regulations altogether by being able to transfer assets from one state to another. If national policy choices make wages and taxes high in the United States, the MNC can transfer profits or manufacturing operations to Mexico or the Philippines. If very large personal or environmental damage awards are lodged against an MNC in one country, it can easily empty the coffers of the local subsidiary, leaving little to take.

An important category of NGOs is made up of various international **human rights organizations**, including Helsinki Watch, the Lawyers Committee for Human Rights, and Amnesty International.

A Short History of U.S. Foreign Policy

To understand the present and debate the future, we need to know something about the substance of U.S. foreign policy in the past. The contrapuntal themes of isolationism and expansionism have figured prominently in U.S. national development. Let us now examine these opposing forces and their influence on our national ethos.

Isolation and Expansion

For most of its history, the United States was isolated from the mainstream of international politics. Isolation suited many of our political leaders, who feared, as George Washington put it, "entangling alliances."

Although largely isolated from nineteenth century European power struggles, the United States took a decidedly expansionist approach in the Western Hemisphere. We continually warred with the Native Americans, driving them from their traditional lands. In 1823, President James Monroe enunciated the Monroe Doctrine, warning European powers to keep out of the Western Hemisphere and declaring our right to oversee developments in North and South America. From 1845 to 1848 we fought with Mexico and acquired considerable territory as a result.

By the end of the nineteenth century the United States had begun to intervene farther from home. U.S. forces defeated Spanish troops in both Cuba and the Philippines and then headed off revolutions in both countries. As the United States was becoming a Pacific power, some U.S. leaders advocated an "Open Door" policy—meaning that we stood for free trade with other nations. Nations that preferred a less open door, such as Japan, were coerced into changing their policies.

Between 1900 and 1930, U.S. forces intervened frequently in various Latin American countries, usually to quell revolutions. These interventions were defended as necessary to keep peace in the hemisphere. But critics charged that they were motivated principally by a desire to protect U.S. business interests.

Most Americans did not consider U.S. expansionism a purely selfish endeavor. Interventions, even against Native Americans, were often explained as part of a "mission" to defend the rights of free trade or the rights of self-determination.

THE TWO WORLD WARS   Because of America's isolationist bent, the United States entered both world wars rather late. When we entered World War I in 1917, three years after it had started, President Woodrow Wilson saw U.S. participation as a crusade to free the world from dictatorship and war—to make the world, in his words, "safe for democracy." Wilson struggled to create the League of Nations after World War I, but isolationist sentiment and Wilson's own inflexibility led the Senate to reject U.S. membership in the League. In the aftermath of the war, we settled back into a comfortable isolation from European affairs.

World War II had been raging in Europe for more than two years before we were drawn in in December 1941. President Franklin D. Roosevelt had been anxious to come to the aid of antifascist forces in the late 1930s, but antiwar and isolationist feeling ran high until the Japanese attack on Pearl Harbor and the German declaration of war against the United States a few days later plunged America headlong into the conflict.

The Cold War

From the end of World War II to the disintegration of the Soviet Union in 1991, United States relations abroad—and much of international politics—was dominated by our relationship with the Soviet Union. Although other important developments punctuated international relations—including independence for many former colonies, the emergence of China, and revolution and change in the Third World—the U.S.-Soviet rivalry, with its threat of all-out nuclear war, cast a shadow over global interactions. It is difficult, especially for young Americans who never experienced the tensions of the Cold War, to imagine what an enormous change its end has wrought in global politics. It will be useful here to review some of the features of that period.

The struggle against Nazi Germany in World War II placed the United States and the Soviet Union on the same side of a wartime alliance. As the war was winding down, however, distrust between the two countries began to surface. The Soviets installed

Communist governments in Eastern Europe, and promised free elections were never held. Tensions and suspicions mounted, prompting the West to harden its positions. The division of Europe became permanent, and large armies were stationed at its heart.

Containment was the doctrine that guided U.S. policymakers in the early years of the Cold War. According to this doctrine, the United States had to stand ready to contain the expansionist thrusts of Soviet power until the Soviets learned to accommodate themselves to global realities. The communist world was seen as a monolith, completely unified and directed from the Kremlin. A communist challenge in one part of the world was basically no different from a communist challenge anywhere else. Hence the United States should be ready to intervene wherever communism threatened.

During the 1950s a critical change took place in the Soviet Union: Stalin died in 1953 and was eventually replaced by Nikita Khrushchev. He coined the term **peaceful coexistence** to describe the type of relationship he preferred with the United States—competition by nonmilitary means. Neither side was ready to work out ground rules for peace, however. For example, U.S. policymakers wanted the Soviets to stay out of anticolonial struggles in the Third World, but the Soviet Union viewed anticolonialism as a basic commitment under Marxist-Leninist principles. In many cases the United States responded by forming alliances with any Third World head of state who was sufficiently anticommunist, leading us to befriend dictators in Latin America, Asia, and the Middle East.

Many serious world crises threatened to turn the Cold War into a hot one: the Soviet blockade of Berlin in 1947; the construction of the Berlin Wall in 1961; the 1961 U.S.-sponsored, unsuccessful invasion of Cuba at the Bay of Pigs; and the 1962 Cuban missile crisis, in which President Kennedy blockaded Cuba and demanded that recently-installed Soviet nuclear missiles be removed.

U.S. intervention in Vietnam was predicated on Cold War logic. Vietnamese forces had fought a long war after World War II to win independence from France. When the French withdrew in 1954, they left behind a divided nation in which rival groups vied for control. One group was the Vietminh, made up of Communist nationalists based in the northern part of the country. For the United States the Communist factor in the equation overshadowed the nationalist one, so we took sides with the non-communist forces in the south. Many U.S. leaders reasoned that if the Communist challenge were not met in Vietnam, we would have to meet it again in other parts of Asia. This was known as the domino theory—if one country fell to the Communists, neighboring countries would fall as a consequence, like dominoes.

The U.S. military presence in Vietnam escalated from a few military advisers in the early 1960s to close to half a million combat troops in 1968. More than 50,000 American troops and at least 600,000 North Vietnamese troops died in this prolonged, costly, and destructive war. Much of the Vietnamese countryside was desolated. In the end Congress forced the final withdrawal of U.S. troops by refusing aid to the South Vietnamese during the final North Vietnamese offensive in 1975.

Overall, our position in the world did not suffer greatly as a result of our withdrawal from Vietnam. Our European allies were generally relieved that the war was over, and

The fall of the Berlin Wall and the end of an era. The old shape of international relations was gone, but what would the new one be? No one was entirely sure. *(Reuters/Bettmann)*

normalization of relations with China became possible. Nor did the Soviet Union gain appreciably in world affairs as a result of the war's outcome, although, as many conservatives pointed out, the domino theory seemed to be validated. When South Vietnam fell to the Communists in 1975, neighboring Cambodia and Laos also became Communist.

By the early 1970s, Soviet-U.S. relations seemed to have entered a new stage, which the Soviets called *razriadka* and the West knew as **détente**. Both words connote a form of relaxation or unwinding. Over a period of years, U.S. and Soviet negotiators hammered out a series of agreements that comprised the heart of détente. The agreements covered issues ranging from the control of nuclear weapons to forms of technical cooperation.

Détente progressed, sometimes shakily, until the Soviet Union invaded Afghanistan in December 1979. Calling the invasion an "extremely serious threat to peace," President Carter initiated a series of punitive measures against the Soviet Union, including an embargo on the sale of U.S. grain and high technology. The pattern of U.S.-Soviet relations was suddenly chillier.

With the transition from the Carter to the Reagan administration in 1981, the United States returned to a hard-line policy toward the Soviet Union reminiscent of the harsh anticommunism of the 1950s. This position had substantial public support in the early

1980s. Reagan sharply increased defense spending and strongly supported anticommunist regimes. No one talked of détente anymore, and Reagan did not meet with any of the three Soviet leaders who held office during the first Reagan term.

Gorbachev, *Perestroika*, and the End of the USSR

In March 1985, Mikhail Gorbachev became general secretary of the Soviet Communist party. Realizing that the Soviet economy was in a disastrous condition, he quickly undertook a series of reforms, known popularly by the code words *perestroika* ("restructuring" of the Soviet economy) and *glasnost* (a new "openness" in the Soviet society).

This desire to improve the Soviet economy and standard of living would require a decrease in military spending, and with this reality in mind, the Gorbachev regime became more willing to engage the United States in serious arms reduction negotiations. Even more important than the subsequent summits between Reagan and Gorbachev were the reforms that Gorbachev instituted at home.

Perestroika and *glasnost* involved the extension of modest but important civil liberties in the Soviet Union. Gorbachev's goal was to modify the most repressive and least efficient parts of Soviet communism in order to save the basic structure. But the forces of change became unmanageable. Gorbachev was caught in an increasingly untenable stretch between the self-reinforced clamor for political and economic reform and the demand of the hard-line Communists to maintain control. Adding to Gorbachev's difficulties were the first stirrings of nationalism, most insistent in the Baltic republics of Latvia, Lithuania, and Estonia. The Soviet empire rapidly began to come apart. At the same time, popular discontent toppled Communist regimes in one Eastern European nation after another. In spectacularly swift fashion, even the East German government collapsed, and the infamous Berlin Wall was torn down by euphoric citizens. It was a moment of triumph for democratic ideals, though many tormenting political complications would soon arise in place of the old totalitarian system.

Gorbachev lurched rightward early in 1991, violently suppressing dissent in the Baltics and bringing more hard-liners into top government posts—to no avail. In August a coup attempted to replace Gorbachev with Vice-President Gennady Yanayev, a tractable, hard-drinking pol more acceptable to the old guard. Russian President Boris Yeltsin declared his defiance of the coup. The Russian people took to the streets in support of Yeltsin, and the coup, badly mismanaged, collapsed. Gorbachev was nominally returned to power, but the great, brutal, creaking machinery that had held the Soviet Union together for seventy years was irrevocably damaged. By December, Gorbachev had resigned and the Soviet Union had ceased to exist. The so-called Commonwealth of Independent States, a makeshift mechanism to facilitate cooperation among the now-independent republics that had made up the USSR, was a negligible presence in a landscape dominated by Russia, the largest and most powerful of the descendants of the Soviet Union.

Foreign Policy after the Cold War

Our brief account may have made the end of the Cold War seem abrupt. Indeed, from the vantage point of most people in the United States who lived through World War II or grew up during the Cold War, the end did come swiftly. The increasing cooperation between the United States and the Soviet Union in the period from 1987 to 1991 hinted at what was to come. Yet so many major changes occurred so rapidly that it is difficult to discern the future shape of international relations just yet. The best we can do during this time of transition is analyze the most important recent events and try to pinpoint significant issues for the future.

Let us examine two major American foreign policy initiatives instituted during the final phase of the Cold War. As always, even in the face of momentous change, much stays the same. For example, there was little to distinguish the U.S. invasion of Panama in 1989 from similar episodes stretching back more than a century. Yet our second example, Operation Desert Storm a mere two years later, shows many signs of post–Cold War politics. For one thing, the Soviet Union, largely paralyzed by the worsening economic situation at home, acknowledged its limitations and formally supported the UN sanctions against Iraq. During the Cold War both the Americans and the Soviets would have undertaken elaborate maneuvers to prevent being left out of an important role in the Middle East, and there would have been a lot more hesitation about bringing such a large allied force so close to the Soviet border. Another anomaly was the United States' going to such allies as Germany and Japan to ask for help in bearing the cost of the operation. But aside from these oddities and President Bush's characterization of the operation as the harbinger of a "new world order" based on security for all, the Persian Gulf War was a fairly traditional and familiar event.

The U.S. Invasion of Panama

The U.S. invasion of Panama in December 1989 had more to do with regional politics than it did with the Cold War or its aftermath. The Cold War was certainly a defining influence on our relations with Fidel Castro in Cuba. And the United States used Cold War rhetoric to justify its opposition to the Sandinista government in Nicaragua and the resistance in El Salvador. But in truth our consistently interventionist stance in the region was defined long before, starting with the Monroe Doctrine in 1823, which proclaimed all of the Western Hemisphere to be our back yard. U.S. interest in Central America was particularly acute due to the possibility of ocean-to-ocean transportation there. In fact, the prospect of a canal was the impetus for Panama's very existence. On November 3, 1903, the Colombian province of Panama declared its independence. Colombian forces were deterred from suppressing Panamanian independence by U.S. naval forces. Fifteen days later Panama granted use of the Canal Zone to the United States.

The Panama Canal was constructed, protected, and operated by the United States, which maintained a military presence in the Canal Zone. In 1978 the Carter administration gained ratification for a new treaty (the culmination of efforts by the Nixon and Ford administrations) that called for the gradual return of the Canal Zone and the canal to Panama. But the American interest in the country was still great.

The Panamanian military had long been a decisive influence in Panamanian politics. Manuel Noriega, a child of poverty, rose to power through the military. He climbed through the military intelligence branch and then assumed control of the national guard, which he reorganized into the Panamanian Defense Forces (PDF). Noriega was a powerful figure in Panama in part because of his association with powerful outsiders. He was well connected to a Colombian drug cartel and to the American intelligence community, reportedly on the CIA payroll for twenty years. He was useful to the Reagan administration's covert efforts to aid the Nicaraguan Contras.

From 1985 on, as Noriega consolidated his power in Panama, he became an embarrassment to the Reagan administration. His protection of large-scale drug operations in Panama ran counter to the American administration's drug war rhetoric. As the Iran-Contra scandal played out in congressional hearings on national TV, the usefulness of Panamanian Contra support services diminished. Noriega's manipulation of Panamanian politics became increasingly heavy-handed, and domestic opposition to him grew. By late 1986 the United States had decided that Noriega must go. From 1986 through late 1989 the Reagan and Bush administrations' policy was that Noriega must be removed, but not with U.S. military power. Through a variety of diplomatic moves the United States tried to impress on the PDF that it would be better off without Noriega. Simultaneously, a series of five separate covert operations were authorized, each with the same goal—removing Noriega from power.

In February 1988, Manuel Noriega was indicted on drug charges by a federal grand jury in the United States. President Eric Arturo Delvalle, originally dismissed in the United States as a Noriega lackey, fired Noriega as head of the PDF. A quickly called rump session of the legislature dominated by Noriega loyalists fired Delvalle, who went into hiding. The United States put a series of severe economic measures into effect, including an embargo and a halt to U.S. payments for the canal. Over the next year and a half the Panamanian people were subjected to severe economic hardship.

In May 1989, Panama held elections. Many international observer teams, including one led by former President Jimmy Carter, were on hand to verify that the elections would be free, fair, and open. Polls just before election day indicated that the opposition, led by Guillermo Endara, had a 2-to-1 lead over Noriega's candidate. Following the balloting, the PDF held up release of the election results. Confronted with blatant evidence of irregularities, Carter announced at a news conference, "The government is taking the election by fraud. . . . It's robbing the people of Panama of their legitimate rights."[2] The official results gave the election to the Noriega candidate by a 2-to-1 margin. Demonstrations supporting Endara were brutally attacked by paramilitary groups tied to the PDF. Increasing hostility marked the interactions between the U.S.

military in Panama and the PDF. In October an unsuccessful coup was staged by some military officers under Noriega.

In spite of efforts on a variety of fronts, Noriega remained firmly in control in Panama. Nothing seemed able to dislodge him. By December the United States had determined to use military force to remove what it characterized as a "drug-dealing dictator." When an American soldier was shot and killed at a Panamanian roadblock, the State Department referred to the incident as "Panama's declaration of war on the United States."[3]

At 1:00 A.M. on December 20 the United States launched a massive military invasion of Panama, named, a bit defensively, Operation Just Cause. Some 26,000 American troops were involved (six soldiers for every PDF member and Panamanian police officer); it featured the largest parachute drop since World War II. Twenty-three American military personnel and three American civilians died; 314 Panamanian soldiers died, with estimates of five hundred to one thousand civilian deaths.* The United States justified the invasion formally in terms of defending American lives but characterized the mission as one aimed at ridding both Panama and the United States of a problem. Although one major objective was to snatch Noriega as the invasion began, he escaped to seek refuge in the residence of the Vatican's representative in Panama. From there he eventually surrendered and was taken to the United States, where he was tried and convicted on drug charges.

Was Operation Just Cause justified? Different responses are possible. On the one hand, the United States invaded a sovereign nation and removed its government from power. This extended a long history of U.S. intervention in Central America and was accordingly resented by some Panamanians and other people in the region. The American bully, according to these critics, was at it again, ironically in the position of removing one of its former lackeys. On the other hand, many Panamanians were genuinely relieved to be rid of Noriega. As a result of earlier interventions, the United States did have more extensive treaty rights and obligations within Panama than it had with any of its other neighbors. Although the invasion did allow a friendly government to take power, the United States did not carry out an extended occupation or seek to install a puppet government.

One's response to Operation Just Cause probably has a lot to do with how interventionist one is. Does a large power have the right or obligation to seek justice through military means within another sovereign state? If the use of military force to achieve a just end in another country is off limits, then how about covert operations? How about support (clandestine or open) for an electoral candidate in another state's elections? The concept of democracy must surely be based on mutual respect for the prerogatives of sovereign states. Given the various definitions of democracy, it is no answer to say that support for other democracies (by our definition) is all that is required. To what

---

*These figures have been contested. Later reports indicated that only fifty Panamanian soldiers died and that the number of civilians killed was about three hundred.[4]

extent is it fair to pursue our *own* interests through intervention in another country? Does harboring drug dealers or terrorists leave a country justifiably open to military or other attack?

Next we turn to a different example of forceful U.S. foreign policy. For many people, the case of Iraq's invasion of Kuwait was a much clearer justification of the use of military force.

From Desert Shield to Desert Storm

On August 2, 1990, Saddam Hussein of Iraq invaded Kuwait with 120,000 troops and 850 tanks.[5] The move seems to have caught American foreign policymakers and Middle Eastern diplomats off guard. Not that Saddam Hussein had not signaled his intentions—he had made repeated threats against Kuwait, based on disputed territory, valuable oil fields, and the Iraqi need for direct access to the Persian Gulf.

But surprised or not, within seventy-two hours after the invasion the administration in Washington had decided to resist the Iraqi aggression. This was, according to insider accounts, a decision reached by Bush himself, with the help of a small number of top administration officials. The public justification for American resistance was fluid in the weeks following the invasion. On August 15, Bush said, "Our jobs, our way of life, our own freedom, and the freedom of friendly countries around the world will suffer if control of the world's great oil reserves fell in the hands of that one man, Saddam Hussein." In November the secretary of state offered a one-word summary of the reason to resist the Iraqi takeover: "Jobs." Senate Minority Leader Bob Dole accommodatingly spelled out the justification: "O-I-L." But back in October, President Bush tried to elevate the war to a higher plane: "The fight isn't about oil; the fight is about naked aggression that will not stand."

Having decided to do something to resist Iraq, the president followed Harry Truman's example with the Korean War and went to line up support in the United Nations rather than go to Congress. The precise nature of the continuing threat from Saddam Hussein's troops in Kuwait was described either passively, as a bad example that could not be left unanswered, or actively, as a further threat to Saudi Arabia. Two responses were mounted: Economic sanctions were applied by the United Nations, and troops from a variety of nations, primarily from the United States, were amassed in Saudi Arabia. The American military name of the operation, Desert Shield, capitalized on the perceived need to protect Saudi Arabia from Iraqi invasion, though it became clear fairly soon that the Iraqi troops were not going further and had taken up defensive positions in Kuwait.

The UN resolutions responding to Iraq's aggression gained a pattern of support that would have been impossible during the Cold War. The Soviet Union signed on, prompted by $1 billion in economic aid from the Saudis and U.S. credit guarantees. Syria got $200 million from the European Community and a Japanese loan of $500 million. Other states were persuaded to join the operation, through arm-twisting and economic carrots—or sticks. Yemen was cut off from $70 million in aid for voting the

FOREIGN AND DEFENSE POLICIES

The United Nations Security Council voted to condemn Iraq's invasion of Kuwait in August, 1990. With the United States in the lead, a multinational force was assembled that drove Iraq from Kuwait. Many felt that the UN would have a much higher profile in a post–Cold War world, where peacekeeping actions would often be required. *(UN Photo/John Isaac)*

wrong way. In the end, Operation Desert Shield had an impressive array of support stretching across Cold War divisions. Though several nations had troops in the theater, the military leadership belonged to the United States.

On October 31, with 230,000 American troops already in Saudi Arabia, George Bush made a fateful decision to double that number. That decision meant that the U.S. position was no longer purely defensive. At its most hopeful, the enlargement of troop strength was to present such an overwhelming force as to get Iraq to back down and leave Kuwait. But of course such a threat is based on the willingness to follow through. Although there was considerable sentiment for giving the economic sanctions time to bring Saddam to his knees, the extent of the troop buildup put serious pressure on the Bush administration. Having canceled leaves and extended tours of duty, the Bush administration could not maintain the level indefinitely. The timing was further constrained by a limited window of favorable weather conditions. The result, some said, was that in spite of rhetorical positions, and barring the unlikely event that Saddam would simply turn tail and head home, Operation Desert Shield had been pushed irrevocably into an offensive mode.

Saddam did not back down by the UN-established deadline of January 15, and Operation Desert Shield was transformed into Operation Desert Storm, an attack on Saddam's troops in Kuwait and in Iraq itself. The strategy chosen for the operation was evident in the form the war took. The idea was to use superior (and relatively low-casualty) air power to destroy Iraqi air cover and communications, damage the infrastructure necessary to move and support troops, and then—only once Iraq's forces were battered—move in ground troops to mop up.

The plan worked well. The war consisted of forty-two days of allied air bombardment followed by a mere hundred hours of ground attack. The Iraqi air force offered almost no resistance to allied bombardment, which devastated Baghdad (Saddam actually sent some of his planes to wait out the war in Iran). A UN survey in March characterized the bombing damage as "near apocalyptic" and warned that it threatened to reduce "a rather highly urbanized and mechanized society to a preindustrial age." Resistance to the ground attack was not substantially greater than the air defense. Even before the ground fighting began at 1:00 A.M. on February 24, large numbers of Iraqi soldiers surrendered or turned and fled. By the third day of ground fighting there were fifty thousand Iraqi prisoners. By that same afternoon General H. Norman Schwarzkopf said, "There was nobody between us and Baghdad. If our intention had been to overrun and destroy Iraq, we could have done it unopposed, for all intents and purposes, from this position at that time." But the intention was not to overrun and destroy Iraq—that, according to American planners, would have left a dangerous power vacuum in the region. So President Bush called a halt after one hundred hours of ground action. Though still in power, Saddam Hussein had been driven from Kuwait.

The Gulf War was enormously popular in the United States. Although the administration had braced the public for heavy casualties, the 148 American dead seemed a tiny number to most. Thirty-eight of those were killed by "friendly fire" from allied troops. On the other side, the losses were much higher and were magnified by the disease and deaths suffered after the fact by the civilian population.

What democratic standards govern foreign military involvement in far-flung locations around the globe? How do we make a democratic assessment of policies like Desert Storm, where the costs inflicted on others so radically outweigh the costs to ourselves? By one estimate the ratio of Iraqi to American casualties was 1,000 to 1. There is no easy calculus by which such accounts can be balanced, but we should be aware of the danger that our superior technology and strength may lead us to inflict harm callously in seeking what we consider good.

In the case of Desert Storm, serious questions arose after it came to light that the United States had provided substantial aid (materiél and intelligence) to Iraq in its struggle against Iran, aid that continued right up until the invasion of Kuwait.[6] There is a natural tendency in democracies to seek short-term solutions. It is sometimes hard for elected politicians to see beyond the next election. In foreign policy this may result in a bogyman-of-the-week procession of inconsistent and self-defeating policy swings. Popular reaction to the Iranian hostage crisis drives us into the arms of Iran's enemy, Iraq, until Saddam Hussein attacks Kuwait, which drives us into the arms of Iraq's competitor for power, Syria. Where does it end? How can we best encourage foreign policy that seeks the long-term good of our nation and others?

Many critical voices were raised in 1992 when Yugoslavia descended into civil strife. The United States, along with our European allies, at first carefully avoided any talk of committing troops to stop what rapidly became a ferocious war with heavy civilian casualties. Some observers argued that the conflict was too complex for military intervention to prove useful or efficacious. Others maintained that we did not intervene because no vital resources, like oil, or basic national interests were involved. Yet as the war continued, pressure for intervention mounted. Starvation threatened whole cities, and TV cameras showed the outside world evidence of increasing brutality. Finally, in August 1992, President Bush reluctantly began to argue for some military protection of humanitarian efforts. Many diplomats felt that his proposals were too little and too late. Still, the Yugoslav situation was enormously complicated, and the

Prisoners taken during the fighting between Serbs and Muslims in Sarajevo. The war in the former Yugoslavia raged on despite some degree of outside intervention. Unlike the situation in Iraq, there was a deep reluctance to commit troops to Yugoslavia for fear of becoming trapped in a Vietnam-like situation. Yet could the world stand by while atrocities were being committed and hundreds of thousands made refugees? *(Zoran Petrovic/AP/Wide World Photos)*

exact shape that a useful military intervention might take was not easy to imagine. But could the world sit by and watch such slaughter continue without taking the risks that intervention might bring? Opponents of intervention recalled Vietnam, but was that war the proper analogy for Yugoslavia? At the same time that this debate took place, the UN secretary general made clear his own view that the world had focused too much attention on the Yugoslav civil war while tending to forget massive starvation and equally destructive fighting in a poor African nation, Somalia. Complexities like these seemed to be the sorts of matters that the new post–Cold War American foreign policy would have to weigh. What perspectives would American leadership and the American public bring to them?

Major Challenges for the Future

How long can we go on calling it the post–Cold War era? Sooner or later this time will define itself positively—not by what preceded it but rather by its own events, the successes and failures of the global family of states in the coming decades. We may not yet be in a position to say what, if anything, the Cold War taught us. George Bush hailed the Persian Gulf War for having finally cured the "Vietnam syndrome" (a great power's unwillingness to use its strength for noble ends). Was that the lesson of Vietnam? Are we now subject to the hubris of the Persian Gulf syndrome, in which success in international interventions appears easy and almost costless?

We have space here only to mention some examples of the many choices that the American democracy must make in the coming period. We will look briefly at the challenges of economic competition through trade, foreign policy and human rights, an equitable distribution of wealth worldwide, and the future of U.S. foreign policy. We leave for the next chapter the important international issues of energy and environment.

Economic Competition through Trade

The most important fact for America in terms of global economic competition is that we're no longer the world's biggest marketer of capitalism. "Germany and Europe have gained in economic strength relative to the U.S., hastened by the weakening of the U.S. fiscal situation in the 1980s," says a former chief economist for the World Bank.[7] The integration of the European economies within the European Community increases their weight on the international stage. The other source of competition for the United States is, of course, Japan. The Japanese economy is the wonder story of the Cold War era. Unburdened by the costs of defense, the Japanese flowered. The world's twenty largest financial firms are all Japanese.[8]

With the old capitalist-Marxist debate shoved aside by the former communist world in its haste to institute market reforms, many analysts now see the primary battle among three models: Japanese-style capitalism, with a heavy dose of government planning and coordination; the U.S. model, essentially laissez-faire; and the European model, which emphasizes social welfare. The debate centers on the developing world and the former communist countries, where the choice of economic models is a matter of some urgency.

In order for the United States to be an effective competitor, we will have to play to our strengths. For a long time to come it will be easy to find cheaper labor abroad. Instead of employing protectionist policies that prop up inefficient industries at the cost of long-term competitiveness and higher costs, many experts advocate concentrating on high-tech industries and high-tech production processes. This almost certainly means greater investment in education and training.

The Bush administration pursued a policy of attempting to get trade barriers lowered and the creation of free trade zones. One of its chief efforts was to negotiate a North American free trade zone expanding the U.S.-Canadian agreement, developed in the Reagan years, to include Mexico. Though there was substantial bilateral support in Congress for this policy, much criticism surfaced about the price the nation would have to pay in terms of jobs and potential environmental degradation.

Bush also traveled to Asia with leading U.S. auto executives in an effort to push American exports and particularly to pressure the Japanese to buy American. Though the administration complained about barriers to American exports in the European Community as well as Japan, the United States also continued to erect protectionist barriers to prevent economic harm to its own industries.

The arena of trade and protectionism appeared certain to be one of the most complex and most contentious on the future foreign policy agenda—an arena now far more prominent as the Cold War fades and new rivalries take prominence.

Human Rights and Foreign Policy

Concern for human rights as an explicit element in U.S. foreign policy distinguished the Carter administration. Addressing the United Nations in 1977, President Carter outlined a commitment to basic human rights that included condemnation of all torture and mistreatment of political prisoners. He also established a State Department office for human rights enforcement and endowed it with significant powers. During the Carter years, sanctions were imposed on many alleged human rights violators, including Argentina, the Philippines, South Korea, Ethiopia, Zaire, Guinea, Haiti, Brazil, Guatemala, Chile, Paraguay, and Uruguay. U.S. economic aid, loans, and military sales to these nations were sometimes stopped or limited. Carter's human rights policies also increased concern with human rights internationally.

Were Carter's policies successful or sensible? On the plus side, the United States dissociated itself from some very unsavory regimes and exerted moral pressure, in the view of most Americans. In addition, the policy occasionally had concrete results: Some political prisoners were released, and some regimes did show more respect for human rights. Critics made three chief arguments against the policy. They maintained that little attention had been paid to human rights violations in Communist countries, such as China and the Soviet Union. Further, they attacked Carter for a lack of consistency and for allegedly making enemies needlessly. Finally, critics took the position that the United States should aid its friends, whether those friends were human rights violators or not.

Presidents Reagan and Bush deemphasized human rights in foreign relations as other values gained priority. As vice-president, for example, George Bush spoke of the "wonderful democracy" of the Philippines under Ferdinand Marcos, a virtual dictator whose massive expropriation of wealth from his nation became apparent after he was toppled and fled the country. And we saw earlier in this chapter that the United States under Reagan and Bush maintained ties with Manuel Noriega in Panama and Saddam Hussein in Iraq until they became politically impracticable.

A Human Rights Watch report on the U.S. record in 1991 found that against weak nations and where no U.S. economic or political interests were at stake, the Bush administration boldly defended human rights. But where competing interests were present, as in the case of China or of authoritarian rulers in oil-rich nations like Kuwait, Saudi Arabia, and Indonesia, the United States did little. It is ironic, the human rights monitoring organization said, that when U.S. influence is highest, "rather than use that influence to insist that human rights are a critical element of a new world order, the administration maintains a shortsighted vision of national interest, too ready to sacrifice the pursuit of human rights if it is not cost- and conflict-free."

An Equitable Distribution of Wealth Worldwide

Approximately 1 billion people throughout the world live in desperate poverty—including 750 million in the poorest of conditions. About 10 million die every year of diseases related to malnutrition; half of those are children. Most of the abject poor, who comprise nearly one-fifth of humanity, live in the so-called developing countries of the Third World (see **Figure 21-1**).

The U.S. government has often sounded a strongly humanitarian note in its proclamations about the problems of Third World poverty. President Carter, for example, stated that "we cannot have a peaceful and prosperous world if a large part of the world's people are at or near the edge of hunger." The United States is often in the vanguard of relief efforts when national and human-caused disasters strike. Also, American volunteers and relief agencies play important roles in such crises, and the Peace Corps helps with development projects in many poor nations.

Clearly, such activities serve our own interests. The poor nations are now among our important trading partners. More than 35 percent of U.S. exports go to developing nations.[9] And the developing countries supply us with many critical raw materials and low-cost consumer goods.

FIGURE 21-1
THE 25 POOREST DEMOCRACIES

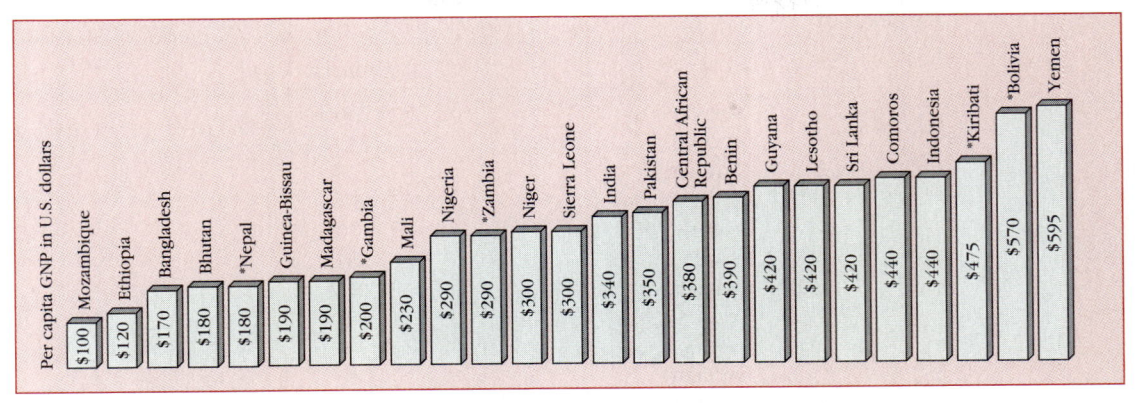

Country	Per capita GNP in U.S. dollars
Mozambique	$100
Ethiopia	$120
Bangladesh	$170
Bhutan	$180
*Nepal	$180
Guinea-Bissau	$190
Madagascar	$190
*Gambia	$200
Mali	$230
Nigeria	$290
*Zambia	$290
Niger	$300
Sierra Leone	$300
India	$340
Pakistan	$350
Central African Republic	$380
Benin	$390
Guyana	$420
Lesotho	$420
Sri Lanka	$420
Comoros	$440
Indonesia	$440
*Kiribati	$475
*Bolivia	$570
Yemen	$595

SOURCES: 1992 Freedom House Survey; U.N. Human Development Report 1991.
*Countries ranked as free, all others partly free.

There are three types of foreign aid agencies: private agencies, like Oxfam and the Save the Children Fund; government agencies, operating bilaterally (from one country to another), such as the United States' Aid for International Development (AID) and Canada's International Development Agency; and agencies formed cooperatively by several governments or international organizations and operating multilaterally. The largest players in foreign aid internationally fall into this last group, including the five **multilateral development banks (MDBs)**. The largest MDB, the World Bank, controls about 70 percent of the money loaned by these MDBs. The World Bank is controlled by the 150 member nations of the bank, according to their share of support for the bank. The United States, which contributes about one-fifth of the bank's assets, has by far the largest vote.[10]

The problem with MDBs as the main source of foreign aid is that loans are not the solution to all the problems of developing countries. In fact, loans become part of the problem when debtor nations must devote large portions of their national economic output to debt service. In addition, development loans tend to exaggerate economic disparities between well-off, comfortable, and abjectly poor nations.

What would the poor nations like from the rich? They want new terms of trade to aid them in selling their goods and worldwide stabilization of prices for the raw materials they export. The many poor nations that are energy-short have called for the creation of an energy affiliate of the World Bank that would provide credits to developing nations.

What policies has the U.S. government followed in dealing with the precarious economic conditions of the Third World? Since the end of World War II, America has

TABLE 21-1
PER CAPITA EXPENDITURES ON FOREIGN AID, 1990

	U.S. Dollars
Norway	$286
Sweden	239
Denmark	228
Netherlands	174
Finland	170
France	167
Switzerland	113
Canada	93
Belgium	90
Germany	80
Japan	73
Italy	59
Australia	57
Britain	46
United States	46
New Zealand	27

SOURCE: *World Monitor*, May 1992, pp. 10-11 (OECD data).

regularly extended economic assistance to poorer nations. But in spite of our generous rhetoric, foreign aid has never been very popular with the American people, many of whom regard it as a kind of international handout. The United States ranks near the bottom of wealthy nations in the percentage of GDP given to nonmilitary foreign aid (see **Table 21-1**).

Why should the United States care about the problems of people in other nations when we have our own problems to deal with? Senator John Danforth, a Missouri Republican, reasons as follows:

> The answer, I think, has to do with who we are and how we perceive ourselves as a country. America is more than a place to hang your hat. It does represent a value system most of us believe in very strongly. That value system has to do with the worth of human beings, whoever they are, wherever they are. We believe that lives are worth saving, that our fellow humans must be fed. But it is not enough to profess this belief. We must act on it.[11]

The Future of Foreign Policy: A "New World Order?"

The Cold War had the handy side effect of providing American citizens and policy-makers alike with a rather simple map of the world and a sense of priorities. The end of the Cold War means that we are in a time of historical transition where priorities are far less clear and America's world role is open to new discussion.

Myriad issues compete for attention. Some analysts feel that one of our highest priorities must be the effort to stabilize and then to assist the development of the states that have emerged from the former communist empire in Europe and Asia, foremost of these being Russia. Secretary of State James Baker argued forcefully that America's long-term national interest is tied to Russia's fate. Russia remains a major nuclear power. The process of dismantling nuclear arsenals has just begun. Economic or political failure in Russia could mean the return of some form of authoritarianism and perhaps a virulent form of Russian nationalism that could threaten the entire region. Yet pleas for increased aid to Russia and the other states found many skeptical listeners in Congress and among the American public. Wasn't it time to keep our resources at home, to pay attention to our own needs? Democratic presidential candidate Bill Clinton said in his acceptance speech: "We've changed the world; now it's time to change America." President Bush protested that Clinton had stolen the line from him. Yet although the world certainly had changed, decisively and irrevocably, those changes had spawned a multitude of new problems that could well come back to haunt us if not attended to effectively now. What would America's stance be in this changed and changing world?

Since the end of the Cold War, the people involved in making our foreign policy have fallen roughly into two camps that represent a jumbling of former patterns of elite opinion. The neoisolationists advocate pulling back, presenting a much lower profile in the world as we concentrate on improving productivity and the quality of life at home. Some theorists have come to this position from the left, with a deep dissatisfaction with what they see as U.S. imperialism abroad. The fewer Vietnam Wars, Nicaraguan Contras, and Panamanian invasions, the better. Others, like 1992 Republican presidential primary candidate Pat Buchanan, come to neoisolationism from the right, with a cry of "America first," saying that we were foolish to think we could help everybody without bankrupting ourselves.

The other thrust of elite opinion in the post–Cold War era maintains that we ought to stay involved in the world, either from an internationalist point of view on the left or an interventionist point of view on the right. For the latter, the issue is pressing the advantage that we have gained by winning the Cold War. Why retreat now, they ask, when our influence can be greatest? From this perspective an American withdrawal from the world might well unleash a host of forces that would threaten the peace in many areas. Without a U.S. military presence, for example, would Europe or Japan begin to rearm? A Pentagon draft document that stirred considerable controversy in early 1992 seemed to argue that it would be wise for the United States to ensure that no superpower rival emerges. This appeared to be a far cry from President Bush's "new world order," which most analysts understood as placing major emphasis on *collective* security, with the United States playing a leading role.

However, theorists who come to the stay-involved position from the political left often cite the responsibility that a major power has to help others still struggling with economic or political hardship. They point out with former President Jimmy Carter that the wealthy nations can hardly hope for a peaceful world when huge disparities of wealth prevail.

Conclusions

After the success of Operation Desert Storm, the United States seemed at the height of its international prestige. The Cold War won, the Vietnam syndrome undone—America seemed in a unique position to influence world events. And yet, within a short time, the increased complexity of world events and issues presented a series of new challenges. How are matters of democratic life related to these new realities of foreign policy? As we noted, questions of human rights, economic equity, and political development are all directly relevant to our future foreign and defense policies. In addition is the question of public opinion and foreign policymaking.

Some practitioners of U.S. politics once argued that foreign affairs were far less important in deciding elections than domestic politics. In 1960, for example, the governor of Illinois told his party's presidential nominee, Richard Nixon, that "what is really important is the price of hogs in Chicago." How ironic this remark now strikes us in light of decades of additional experience! Foreign policy issues have assumed paramount importance in recent presidential elections, and may continue to do so in the near future.

With the end of the Cold War, the old bipartisan foreign policy consensus has broken down, broadening the range of debate on foreign policy. Conflict among opposing views can lead to paralysis or contradictory actions, but it can also help us to clarify our goals as a nation and reassess our policies designed to reach those goals.

Many observers wonder, however, whether it makes sense for a large electorate to debate complex foreign policy issues or the kinds of technical questions that arise, for instance, in negotiations related to nuclear weapons. Yet because foreign policy and defense matters affect us all, policymaking in this area is too important to be left to a few elected officials and their advisers. Certain issues may require a high level of knowledge and expertise, but many others can be understood and assessed by almost any democratic citizen. And because the stakes are high, citizens must voice their views, and policymakers have an obligation to gain informed consent from citizens. If leaders believe that they can simply do whatever they think best in foreign and defense matters, we will all be less safe—and we will lose an essential element of democracy.

As the political philosopher Michael Walzer once commented on the issue of nuclear weapons strategy: "This day-to-day drift is always toward specialized, secret, technically complex, and esoteric doctrine. But real political leaders, *if they can hear the clamor of their constituents*, can stop the drift."[12] We might add that democrats can only hope that constituents care enough to clamor.

Glossary Terms

Amnesty International
Central Intelligence Agency (CIA)
containment
Defense Department
détente
diplomatic recognition
intergovernmental organizations (IGOs)
Joint Chiefs of Staff (JCS)
multilateral development banks (MDBs)
multinational corporation (MNC)
National Security Council
nongovernmental organizations (NGOs)
peaceful coexistence
propaganda
State Department
United Nations
United States Information Agency (USIA)
Voice of America (VOA)

Notes

[1] See John Spanier, "Who are the 'Non-State Actors'?" in *The Theory and Practice of International Relations*, 8th ed., William Clinton Olson (Englewood Cliffs, N.J.: Prentice Hall, 1991).

[2] Margaret E. Scranton, *The Noriega Years: U.S.-Panamanian Relations, 1981–1990* (Boulder, Colo.: Rienner, 1991), p. 162. This discussion of the Panamanian invasion owes much to Scranton's carefully documented account.

[3] Ibid., p. 198.

[4] Douglas Jehl and John M. Broder, "Truth Was Trampled in Panama Invasion," *Raleigh News and Observer*, April 25, 1990, p. 2A.

[5] Details and quotes in this account from Draper, "True History of the Gulf War," *The New York Review of Books*, January 30, 1992, pp. 38–45.

[6] See, for example, the following stories by Douglas Franz and Murray Waas in the *Los Angeles Times*: "Attempted Cover-up of Aid to Iraq to Be Probed," March 8, 1992, p. A1; "Secret Memos Detail U.S. Effort to Aid Iraq," June 5, 1992, p. A4; "Allies' Iraq Arms Sales Unopposed in '89," June 11, 1992, p. A14.

[7] Stanley Fischer, in Steven Greenhouse, "U.S. and World: A New Economist Order Is Ahead," *New York Times*, Apil 29, 1992, p. A7.

[8] Ranked by market capitalization. Jeffrey T. Bergner, *The New Superpowers: Germany, Japan, the U.S., and the New World Order* (New York: St. Martin's Press, 1991), pp. 114–115.

[9] Keith Bradsher, "American Exports to Poor Countries Are Rapidly Rising," *New York Times*, May 10, 1992, p. A1.

[10] Patricia Adams, "All in the Name of Aid," *Sierra*, January–February 1987, pp. 48–49.

[11] John C. Danforth, "Africa: Does Anybody Really Care?" *Washington Post National Weekly Edition*, February 13, 1984, p. 29.

[12] Michael Walzer, "Deterrence and Democracy," *New Republic*, July 2, 1984, p. 21.

Selected Readings

Among **general introductions** to U.S. foreign policy, consider Terry Boswell and Albert Bergesen, eds., *America's Changing Role in the World System* (New York: Praeger, 1987); Henry Kissinger, *American Foreign Policy: A Global View* (Brookfield, Vt.: Gower, 1982); Hans J.

Morgenthau, *In Defense of the National Interest: A Critical Examination of American Foreign Policy* (Lanham, Md.: University Press of America, 1983); Henry T. Nash, *American Foreign Policy: A Search for Security*, 3rd ed. (Homewood, Ill.: Dorsey Press, 1985). For a thorough treatment of the tools of foreign policy, see K. J. Holsti, *International Politics: A Framework for Analysis*, 6th ed. (Englewood Cliffs, N.J.: Prentice Hall, 1992), pt. 3. See also L. Henkin, Michael J. Glennon, and W. D. Rogers, *Foreign Affairs and the U.S. Constitution* (New York: Transnational, 1990); T. E. Mann, ed., *A Question of Balance: The President, Congress, and Foreign Policy* (Washington, D.C.: Brookings Institution, 1990); and Barry Blechman, *The Politics of National Security: Congress and U.S. Defense Policy* (New York: Oxford University Press, 1990).

U.S. relations with **Central America** are covered in Thomas Anderson, *Politics in Central America*, rev. ed. (New York: Praeger, 1988); Richard Nuncio, *What's Wrong, Who's Right in Central America?* (New York: Facts on File, 1986); Martin Needler, *The Problem of Democracy in Latin America* (Lexington, Mass.: Heath, 1987); Walter LeFeber, *Inevitable Revolutions* (New York: Norton, 1984); Karl Bermann, *Under the Big Stick* (Boston: South End, 1986); and Glen Caudill Dealy, *An Honorable Peace in Central America* (Belmont, Calif.: Wadsworth, 1988). See also Thomas W. Walker, *Reagan vs. the Sandinistas* (Boulder, Colo.: Westview Press, 1987); and Peter Dale Scott and Jonathan Marshall, *Cocaine Politics: Drugs, Armies, and the CIA in Central America* (Berkeley: University of California Press, 1990).

For a **comparative perspective**, see Andrew Cox and Stephen Kirby, *Congress, Parliament, and Defense: The Impact of Legislative Reform on Defense Accountability in Britain and America* (New York: St. Martin's Press, 1986); Joel Krieger, *Reagan, Thatcher, and the Politics of Decline* (New York: Oxford University Press, 1986); and, for a British viewpoint, James Piscatori, *Islam in a World of Nation-States* (New York: Cambridge University Press, 1984).

On the **Iran-Contra Affair**, see *The Tower Commission Report*, with an introduction by R. W. Apple, Jr. (New York: Bantam/Times, 1987); *Report of the Congressional Committees Investigating the Iran-Contra Affair*, abr. ed., ed. Joel Brinkley and Stephen Engelberg (New York: Times Books, 1988); Theodore Draper, *A Very Thin Line: The Iran-Contra Affairs* (New York: Touchstone, 1992); Harold H. Koh, *The National Security Constitution: Sharing Power after the Iran-Contra Affair* (New Haven, Conn.: Yale University Press, 1990); and David L. Hall, *The Reagan Wars* (Boulder, Colo.: Westview Press, 1991).

On **warfare**, **weapons**, **and strategic concerns**, see Seyom Brown, *The Causes and Prevention of War* (New York: St. Martin's Press, 1987); Desmond Ball and Jeffrey Richelson, eds., *Strategic Nuclear Targeting* (Ithaca, N.Y.: Cornell University Press, 1986); Joshua M. Epstein, *Strategy and Force Planning: The Case of the Persian Gulf* (Washington: D.C.: Brookings Institution, 1987); Paul Stares, *Space and National Security* (Washington, D.C.: Brookings Institution, 1987); and Wolfram F. Hanreider, *Technology, Strategy, and Arms Control* (Boulder, Colo.: Westview Press, 1986). Deterrence is covered in Robert Jervis, Robert Ned Lebow, and Janice Gross Stein, *Psychology and Deterrence* (Baltimore: Johns Hopkins University Press, 1985); for treatments of particular systems, see Nick Kotz, *Wild Blue Yonder: Money, Politics and the B-1 Bomber* (New York: Pantheon, 1988); and Daniel Ford, *The Button: The Pentagon's Strategic Command and Control System* (New York: Simon & Shuster, 1985).

On new foreign policy challenges, see Ann Markusen and Joel Yudken, *Dismantling the Cold War Economy* (New York: Basic Books, 1992); Miroslav Nincic, *Democracy and Foreign Policy: The Fallacy of Political Realism* (New York: Columbia University Press, 1992); Edward H. Alden and Franz Schurmann, *Why We Need Ideologies in American Foreign Policy* (Berkeley, Calif.: Institute of International Studies, 1990); Jeffrey T. Bergner, *The New Superpowers: Germany,*

Japan, the U.S., and the New World Order (New York: St. Martin's Press, 1991); Greg Schmergel, ed., *U.S. Foreign Policy in the 1990s* (New York: St. Martin's Press, 1991); Graham Allison and Gregory F. Treverton, eds., *Rethinking America's Security: Beyond Cold War to New World Order* (New York: Norton, 1991); and Norman J. Ornstein and Mark Perlman, *Political Power and Social Change: The United States Faces a United Europe* (Washington: AEI Press, 1991).

On Panama an Iraq, see Bruce W. Watson and Peter G. Tsouras, eds., *Operation Just Cause: The U.S. Intervention in Panama* (Boulder, Colo.: Westview Press, 1991); Michael L. Conniff, (Panama and the United States: The Forced Alliance (Athens: University of Georgia Press, 1992); Kevin Buckley, *Panama: The Whole Story* (New York: Simon & Schuster, 1991); Ted. G. Carpenter, *America Entangled: The Persian Gulf Crisis and Its Consequences* (Washington, D.C.: Cato Institute, 1991); Roland Dannreuther, *The Gulf Conflict: A Political and Strategic Analysis* (London: Institute for Strategic Studies, 1992); and Micah L. Sifry and Christopher Cerf, eds., *The Gulf War Reader: History, Documents, Opinions* (New York: Times Books, 1991).

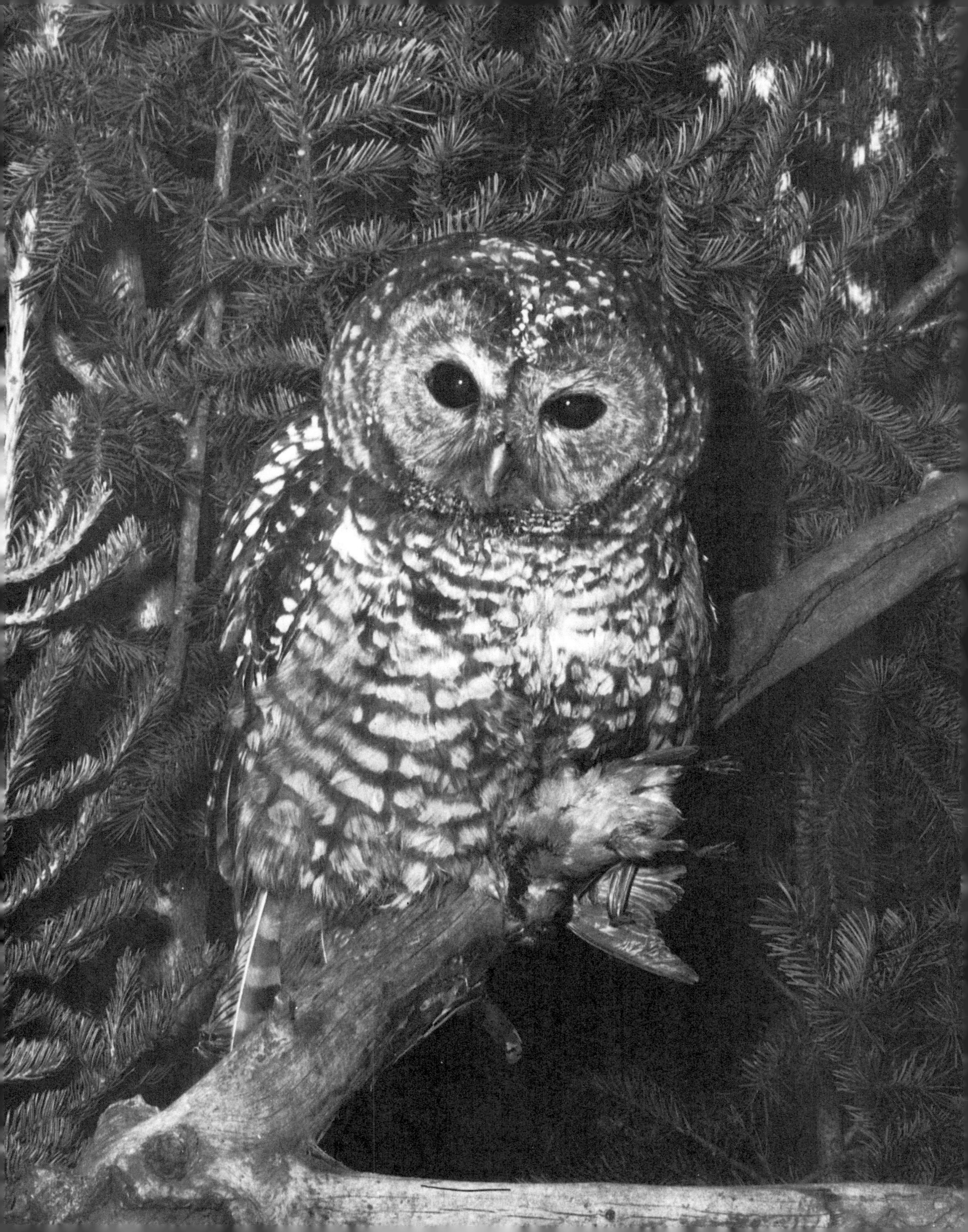

CHAPTER TWENTY-TWO

ENERGY AND THE ENVIRONMENT

Preserving or Depleting the American Dream?

CHAPTER OUTLINE

The United States, Energy, and the Environment

From Exploitation to Protection

Environmental Problems and Government Responses

AIR POLLUTION
WATER POLLUTION
TOXIC CHEMICALS

The Politics of Environmental Issues

GROUP STRATEGIES
THE REAGAN RECORD ON THE ENVIRONMENT
THE BUSH ADMINISTRATION AND THE ENVIRONMENT

Energy: Sources, Problems, Policies

ENERGY: AN OVERVIEW
U.S. ENERGY USE
THE POLITICS OF ENERGY ISSUES

ON WEDNESDAY, JUNE 3, 1992, MORE THAN ONE HUNDRED heads of state joined 30,000 other people gathered in Rio de Janeiro for the United Nations Conference on Environment and Development, the so-called **Earth Summit**, reputedly the biggest international conference ever held. The premise of the meeting was that national solutions were no longer adequate to meet the challenges of protecting the earth while continuing economic development.

If that day was typical, there were *a quarter of a million* more people on earth on that Wednesday than there had been the day before: 140,000 in Asia, 75,000 in Africa, 22,000 in Latin America, and 13,000 throughout the rest of the world.[1] Feeding those newcomers would present a challenge, since more than one in five of the people already here were subsisting on less than $1 a day.

More than 60 million barrels of oil and 17 million tons of coal were consumed that day. During the two weeks that the Earth Summit lasted, global economic activity was about the

783

same as the entire annual output of goods and services in the year 1900. Every day nearly 140,000 new cars, trucks, and buses joined 500 million already on the road.

Of all the people living in cities, seven out of ten were breathing unhealthy air as the Earth Summit got under way. If June 3, 1992, was a typical day for the earth's atmosphere, it was not a good day. Fifty-six million tons of carbon dioxide belched into the air (mostly from fossil fuels and the massive burning of rain forests, some not far from the conference site). The atmosphere was also socked with more than 1,500 metric tons of ozone-depleting chlorofluorocarbons (CFCs) from leaking refrigerators and air conditioners, aerosol cans and manufacturing processes.

The earth is pretty good at fighting back against such assaults, but it is getting harder. Every day during the Rio summit, 180 square miles of forest disappeared. Each morning the conferees got up, there were another 63 square miles of wasteland on earth, due to overgrazing and wind and water erosion. Between sunrise and sunset, more than 400,000 tons of chemical fertilizers would be used to coax more food from the remaining, often degraded farmland.

On the day that the Earth Summit ended, air pollution contributed to the premature death of 800 people. That day at least 15,000 people, most of them children, died from diseases caused by unsafe water.

But there was also good news for the conferees at the Earth Summit. All over the globe efforts were being made to prevent environmental degradation. Recycling aluminum cans, which greatly reduces air pollution, has increased dramatically. In 1972 only 15.4 percent of the cans produced were recycled; by 1991 that proportion had grown to 62.4 percent. In supermarkets around California (which has a mandatory deposit on bottles and cans), machines accept empty cans and bottles, spitting out nickels, dimes, and quarters in return. In Calcutta, a sewage-fed aquaculture system now provides 44,000 pounds of fresh fish each day for sale in the city. In Tokyo, the world's largest city, only 15 percent of commuters drive cars to the office. German auto manufacturers are working to make disassembly and reuse of vehicle components easier and have set up pilot recycling programs. Tunisia has controlled urban land prices and reduced unproductive land ownership by establishing a "rolling land bank" program to buy and sell land. Carbon taxes aimed at cutting greenhouse gases went into effect in Finland and the Netherlands in early 1990 and in Sweden a year later.

Perhaps the best news of all was the Earth Summit itself. The conference achieved agreement on a major climate treaty and a treaty to protect **biodiversity**, signed by almost all of the 178 nations represented. Other achievements included a statement of principles on the protection of forests and a nonbinding agenda for development, which embraces the notion of resource transfer from the industrialized countries to the developing countries to promote sustainable development. Skeptics pointed to the vague rhetoric and incomplete concepts embodied in the agreements at Rio, but the meeting itself was a hopeful sign that a new age of environmentally sensitive diplomacy was at hand.

The United States, Energy, and the Environment

If the Rio summit embodied the idea that individual nations cannot adequately meet environmental and development challenges, it also reflected the current state of international relations. Policies formulated at intergovernmental meetings still need to be implemented by national governments, which establish their own policies. Students of democracy must look to national institutions to understand policy in these areas. For example, the United States lobbied successfully to weaken the Earth Summit climate treaty and refused to sign the biodiversity treaty altogether, asserting that it would "retard biotechnology and undermine the protection of ideas."

Although many Americans were critical of the Bush administration's positions on the summit agreements, the president argued that the United States was constrained to take an unpopular but responsible position. Who was right? The debate involves questions of enormous import: How serious is global warming? How much pollution can we live with? How are the costs of environmentally sound policies apportioned? How much economic growth are we willing to sacrifice for a cleaner environment? What role should national governments and international organizations play in regulating economic growth? How much responsibility do the wealthy countries of the world have to assist the developing countries in protecting resources like the rain forests?

Energy and environmental issues are interrelated. Domestic policies have global consequences, and international policies have domestic consequences. In this chapter, we will set out the major issues involving energy and the environment, examine our choices and government policies, explore the politics of environmental issues, and consider the various sources of energy and issues of energy policy. We begin with a look at the distinctly American context of these issues.

From Exploitation to Protection

Alexis de Tocqueville, a young Frenchman, visited the United States in the 1830s. Like many other foreign observers, he was awed by the bountifulness of the American continent, what he called "Fortune's immense booty to the Americans." Many students of U.S. history have noted the wide-ranging impact of this abundance on the national psychology and political culture of the United States. Abundance influences the way we think about (or fail to think about) our political, social, and economic problems. We long ago accepted a philosophy of growth—of "more" and "bigger"—as our national ethos. Ours was a nation of producers and consumers, enjoying the fruits of our good fortune.

In taking maximum advantage of these vast resources, we have radically transformed this land. Unlike Native Americans, European settlers were not content to live in harmony with nature, using only a small portion of the environment for their purposes. Instead, the settlers sought to make the most of resources, to transform nature and make it serve our needs.

Historically, government has facilitated the process of developing the continent. The U.S. water system and the energy resources related to it, for example, were developed through the federal Bureau of Reclamation and the Army Corps of Engineers. Without a doubt these agencies did a great deal of good; however, critics decry the large numbers of fish killed in the process, the immense tracts of land that were flooded, and the numerous wildlife habitats destroyed as a result. Government policies also promoted land development, the growth of railroads, and the creation of suburbia, a product of the vast network of superhighways. All these developments had deleterious effects on our environment. They also shaped the ways in which we use energy today and the amount of energy we use.

Concern for the environment extends back into the nineteenth century, when nature lovers and sportsmen sought protection for park areas. In 1872, Yellowstone was the first area to be designated a national park. In the first decade of the twentieth century, President Theodore Roosevelt expanded the national forest reserves to 190 million acres.

Pollution had also long been a concern. A few cities began treating their sewage in the nineteenth century. Bot not until 1948 was the first federal water pollution legis-

One of the major symbols of environmentalism, the giant sequoias of California. Some regarded these trees with special reverence; others quipped that if you'd seen one redwood you'd seen them all. But what if it becomes impossible to see even one? (Alexander Lowry/Photo Researchers)

lation passed by Congress. Air pollution, too, had been on the agenda of U.S. municipalities for years. Cincinnati and Chicago passed smoke control ordinances as far back as 1881. California made efforts to control smog and industrial pollution, and it instituted auto emission controls in the 1960s. The first federal air pollution law took effect in 1955.

By the late 1960s, environmental concerns had reached the mainstream of politics. Many Americans had decided that more was not necessarily better, especially if more meant polluted air, fish kills, dying lakes, a landscape strewn with unsightly waste, and crowded, sprawling, and unplanned urban and suburban developments. In May 1970 several environmental groups staged the first Earth Day celebration, designed to heighten public awareness of environmental problems. Later came Sun Day, focusing on solar energy as an alternative to fossil fuels.

Responding to the mounting wave of public concern, Congress passed the National Environmental Policy Act (NEPA) in 1969. The act constituted a pledge by the federal government to protect and renew the environment. The next year an executive order by Richard Nixon established the **Environmental Protection Agency (EPA)**, designed to coordinate environmental policy. The act also laid the groundwork for the President's Council on Environmental Quality (CEQ), which reviews federal programs, recommends legislation, and sponsors independent studies. In addition, the NEPA required that an **environmental impact statement**, spelling out specific effects on the environment, be prepared for any proposal for legislation or other major federal action that might significantly affect the quality of the environment.

The EPA assumed control over the fragmented federal environmental programs and consolidated many of them. For example, it took over water pollution management tasks from the Department of the Interior, air pollution and solid-waste management matters from the Department of Health, Education and Welfare, and the regulation of pesticides from the Department of Agriculture. Soon the EPA became the government's most massive regulatory agency, overseeing the largest budget and staff.

The NEPA was passed by Congress without much controversy, but once it became law it set off sparks. For many federal agencies, there was no more business as usual: Billions of dollars worth of programs had to be reassessed; thousands of hours were spent considering environmental impacts. The law also spawned considerable litigation. Industry and conservative politicians joined forces to resist the EPA's regulatory requirements.

Today most U.S. citizens give environmental issues a high priority. A 1992 poll of Americans revealed that nearly 80 percent believe "we are killing ourselves" by what we're doing to the environment, and 55 percent felt that the problems had gotten worse over the preceding two years. The government "should be doing more," according to 92 percent of the respondents, although only 22 percent said that the government should bear the primary responsibility for a clean environment (41 percent said that it should be the responsibility of the general public, and 34 percent gave that responsibility to industry).

Hoover Dam with Lake Mead behind it, and the power generators below. Built in the 1930s, the dam (and many others like it) provided immense new sources of power. In addition, they created areas for recreation and were useful in flood control. At the time they were built, little attention was paid to the question of any negative effect the dams might have on fish or the natural environment. *(Joe Munroe/Photo Researchers)*

The four issues that respondents named most often, about which they were "very concerned," were the buildup of waste materials (68 percent), the depletion of natural resources (65 percent), industrial pollution associated with acid rain (64 percent), and depletion of the ozone layer (62 percent). When asked if they were doing anything about these problems, 93 percent responded positively: 89 percent recycle rubbish, and 78 percent said they save electricity. Cutting down waste was listed by 69 percent and conserving water by 63 percent. Only 24 percent have boycotted certain products, and just 10 percent said they were members of a conservation or environmental group. Obviously, the low-cost and cost-saving responses are most popular. All of these positive responses reflect a major shift in public opinion in recent years, but it remains to be seen how much the American public is willing to sacrifice to get increased environmental protection.[2]

Let us now look at particular environmental problems and the specific ways in which government has responded to them. Later, we will take a closer look at the political conflicts involved.

Environmental Problems and Government Responses

The environment comprises an extremely complicated, interconnected net of relationships. Poisons poured into the waters can come back to haunt us through the fish we eat or the water we drink. Pollution in the air affects not only our lungs but also rivers, lakes, and trees. The environment also includes other living things—plants, insects, animals, fish—some of which may perish prematurely because of human choices. We are only beginning to understand how we fit into various ecological systems. Whether those systems operate in a healthy fashion has important consequences for us and for nature itself.

Today's environmental problems encompass a range of issues: air pollution, water pollution, toxic waste, solid-waste management, natural resource use, coastal ecology, land use, and noise. In this section we will focus on the first three of these issues, which are considered among the most significant.

Air Pollution

The complications of air quality policy reflect the competing strains of environmental policy generally. The harms from air pollution fall into two categories: direct harm to humans—heart problems, lung cancer, reduced breathing capacity, and so on—and to other creatures from smog and other airborne toxins, and indirect effects such as agricultural devastation from global warming, the death of forests and lakes from acid rain, and further health hazards from ozone depletion. In the United States in 1990 some 4.8 billion pounds of toxic chemicals were released into the air, water, and ground; 46 percent of that total was air pollution.[3]

FEDERAL AIR POLLUTION LEGISLATION   In 1963, Congress passed the **Clean Air Act**, establishing national air quality standards; amendments in 1970 put some teeth into the act. Over the years the EPA has adopted various strategies for achieving cleaner air: imposing standards limiting emissions of pollutants from power plants, for example, and requiring that cars be equipped with emission control devices and that unleaded fuel be used in most new vehicles.

But the agency has relaxed some of its standards in the face of severe political pressures, as well as disagreements among experts. For example, some of the EPA's strategies to reduce pollution from automobiles—such as banning cars from high-pollution areas, raising tolls on access routes, and imposing parking taxes—have encountered fierce opposition. Congress legislated against some of these strategies explicitly in the Clean Air amendments of 1977.

The most recent major piece of federal legislation aimed at cleaning up the atmosphere, the Clean Air Act of 1990, established some worthwhile goals—a 15 percent reduction in smog-producing pollution within six years; a 30 to 60 percent reduction in auto tailpipe emissions by 1998; cleaner gasoline blends for existing autos and new auto-fueling-system canisters to reduce emissions at the gas pump; factory installation of "maximum achievable control technology" to reduce emissions of 189 chemicals, cutting emissions by 90 percent by 2000; and reductions in sulfur dioxide and nitrogen oxide releases to reduce acid rain. But the goals depend heavily on administrative implementation rules. Critics charged that the Bush administration was too slow in promulgating these regulations (even prompting nine states to sue the government to release regulations so that states could meet their mandated responsibilities). The regulations, finally released in 1992, "knocked a hole in the Clean Air Act—and in any claim Mr. Bush might still make to be the environmental president."[4] Supporters of the relaxed regulations, including Vice-President Quayle's Competitiveness Council, argued that stiffer regulations would needlessly delay changes in manufacturing processes aimed at improving efficiency and competitiveness in world markets. That debate indicated that in regulatory matters these days, getting a statute on the books may be just the beginning of the battle.

GLOBAL WARMING   Calling it the **greenhouse effect** makes it sound too cozy for some environmental activists. The debate over **global warming** demonstrates the scientific uncertainty that must be factored into environmental policymaking. Some facts are uncontested: Over the long run, the earth keeps a balanced energy checkbook. The sun supplies the energy income—about 30 percent of the energy that reaches the earth is absorbed, and the rest is reflected away. Thermal (infrared) radiation accounts for the expenditure, keeping everything in balance. If there were no atmosphere to trap some of the infrared radiation on its way out, the earth would be much colder—0 degrees Fahrenheit on average, instead of the balmy 59 degrees at present. This would not be a hospitable place for life as we know it. But naturally occurring carbon dioxide, ozone, and water vapor build up in the atmosphere and capture some of the ongoing radiation, raising surface temperatures to the comfortable level we now enjoy.

Now the controversy starts. If more carbon dioxide is pumped into the air and nothing else counteracts that effect, more energy will be absorbed by the atmosphere, and the surface temperature will rise. The balance is maintained, but the cash on hand (warmth) at the surface is higher. If surface temperatures go up even small amounts, more of the polar ice masses melt, raising sea levels and flooding coastal habitats. Climate patterns would shift, possibly making deserts out of farming regions and changing water supplies for millions of people in densely populated areas. The problem with making such predictions is that climate is the result of a plethora of factors, many not yet well understood. Climatic changes occur naturally, with warming and cooling trends over long periods of time. As for the greenhouse effect, would other factors counterbalance the greenhouse gases? Would slightly warmer temperatures mean little difference to most of the earth? How quickly could humans adapt to what changes did occur?

Most scientists agree that stabilizing greenhouse gases is a worthwhile goal, but there is less agreement over how soon and at what cost this should be done. The Bush

(Text continues on page 792)

GLOBAL WARMING

Carbon dioxide (CO_2) accounts for about half the gases in the atmosphere that trap the sun's heat. The European Community is urging industrialized countries to join it in taking tougher measures to tackle global warming than are laid down in the UN treaty. The effort seems likely to embarrass the United States, the biggest single source of greenhouse gases. Washington opposes binding commitments to limit output of carbon dioxide because of fears of how it could hurt the economy.

Sources of CO_2

About four-fifths of the world's carbon dioxide comes from the burning of fossil fuels. The rest is from destroying vegetation, mainly from the burning of rain forests.

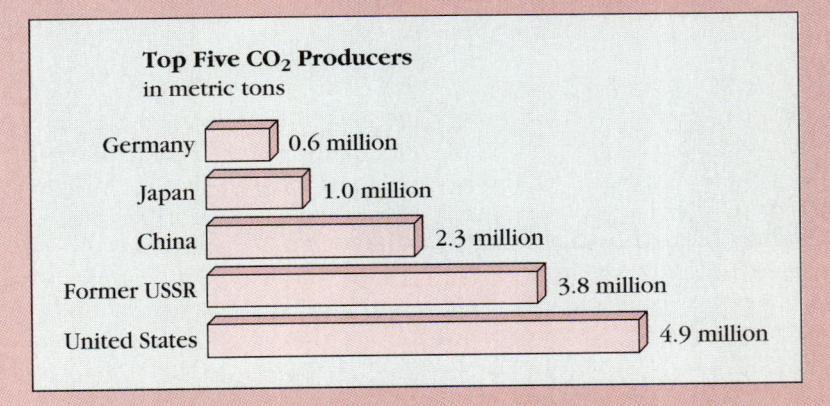

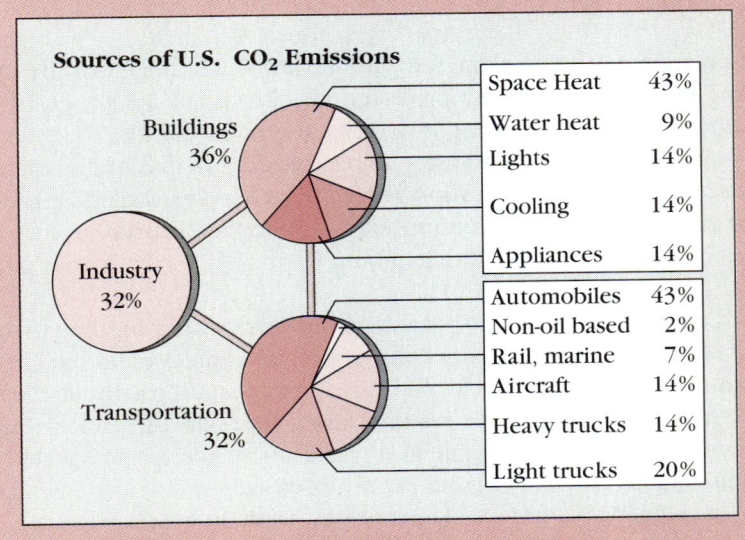

Top Five CO_2 Producers
in metric tons

Germany	0.6 million
Japan	1.0 million
China	2.3 million
Former USSR	3.8 million
United States	4.9 million

Sources of U.S. CO_2 Emissions

Buildings 36%
- Space Heat — 43%
- Water heat — 9%
- Lights — 14%
- Cooling — 14%
- Appliances — 14%

Industry 32%

Transportation 32%
- Automobiles — 43%
- Non-oil based — 2%
- Rail, marine — 7%
- Aircraft — 14%
- Heavy trucks — 14%
- Light trucks — 20%

Source: Los Angeles Times, *June 10, 1992, p. A6.*

Destruction of the world's rainforests has become one of the most pressing issues on the environmental agenda. Besides helping to clear the atmosphere of carbon monoxide, these dense forests provide habitat for a large number of animal and plant species. Yet they are being destroyed (as in this photo of a rainforest in Brazil) at an alarming rate. (Imagens de Terra/Impact Visuals)

administration argued for a cautious wait-and-see approach in light of the uncertainty of the climate models and data and projected jobs losses and higher costs associated with reductions. Proponents of a vigorous response point out that these atmospheric effects are cumulative and not easily reversible, suggesting that big investments now in greenhouse gas reductions will produce even bigger savings later. The Earth Summit treaty aimed at reducing global warming, but the United States prevented the inclusion of timetables for achieving specific reductions.

ACID RAIN One of the subtle environmental hazards created by the combustion of fossil fuels is **acid rain**, a highly acidic form of precipitation. A byproduct of industrial pollutants emitted into the air, acid rain poses problems throughout the industrial world. Some rain now falling on the eastern United States has an acidity roughly equal to that of lemon juice. Although experts disagree about the effects of acid rain, it is known to kill aquatic life and vegetation and to erode stone and steel structures. It may also be introducing dangerous elements into drinking water.

Legislators and administrators have been slow to act on the issue of acid rain. Even when under powerful pressures to reduce industrial emissions, the major source of acid rain, the Reagan administration refused to act, claiming that more research was necessary. For industries that burn high-sulfur coal, the costs of installing the necessary antipollution equipment would raise utility rates 20 to 50 percent, according to industry figures. The United Mine Workers estimated that as many as 80,000 mining jobs might be lost if the use of high-sulfur coal were banned. Environmentalists countered that unless steps were taken to lower the acidity of acid rain, many lakes and forests would be killed entirely, and acid rain's highly corrosive effects on buildings and other structures would cause damage well into the billions of dollars. The 1990 Clean Air Act called for reducing sulfur dioxide release by 10 million tons by 2001. It also instituted a controversial plan to trade pollution release quotas, allowing "clean" plants to sell credits to "dirty" ones.

OZONE DEPLETION   Among the most versatile families of chemicals developed in the past half-century are **chlorofluorocarbons (CFCs)**, which are also among the most destructive and potentially most devastating of chemicals. CFCs are widely used in refrigeration, air conditioning, and the manufacture of plastics and computer chips, as propellants for aerosol cans, and in numerous other products considered vital to contemporary society. Although they enhance our lives, they have also been silently undermining the life support system of the planet. As they rise through the earth's atmosphere, CFCs change character; through various chemical interactions they destroy the ozone layer, which partially screens ultraviolet rays from reaching the earth's surface. It is now understood that ozone (C_3)—which at low altitudes is a pollutant—shrouds the planet in a veil that helps to prevent skin cancer, cataracts, crop and fish damage, and global warming.

The potential dangers of CFCs began to be recognized in 1974, when studies revealed damage to the ozone layer. The EPA recommended a freeze on U.S. production of CFCs in 1980, but the incoming Reagan administration—eager to deregulate and citing a new, more optimistic study—delayed taking action.

In 1987, fifty-three nations signed the Montreal Protocol, agreeing to cut CFC production in half over the next decade. Du Pont then announced plans to phase out CFC production by early in the next century.

Since 1990, activists charge, the federal government has done little to reduce ozone depletion, despite evidence that the ozone hole in the atmosphere is growing faster than predicted. The power exists under the 1990 legislation to speed up CFC reductions, as many observers have urged.

THE COMPLEXITY OF CURES   Some of the trade-offs in environmental protection are fairly straightforward (though still contested): cleaner air will cost more, and, at least in the short run, some jobs may be lost. But the complexities don't end there. Sometimes addressing an air pollution problem of one sort only creates an air pollution problem of another sort—as when regulations force a metal fabricator in Los Angeles to shift from using an ozone-depleting metal degreaser, to a hydrocarbon-based, smog producing degreaser. Sometimes a solution to air pollution will create other sorts of problems altogether—as in the shift from fossil fuel to nuclear generation of electricity. Burning fossil fuels creates a raft of atmospheric problems, but nuclear power creates radioactive waste of a far more durable sort.

Some features of our pluralist system work against effective regulation. The interest in clean air is widely diffuse, shared among virtually all creatures—taken together, a huge interest. But the pollution-producing utilities and factories have very specific interests—the high costs of smokestack clean-up may make business unprofitable. The system will almost always respond first and most vigorously to the insistent voice of the powerful, specifically impacted few over the almost-never-raised voices of the burdened many.

Before laying the blame for air pollution exclusively on a few large enterprises, consider that, according to the EPA, automobiles can be charged with creating 67 percent of the country's carbon monoxide emissions, linked to heart and lung damage; 41 percent of the nitrogen oxide emissions that contribute to acid rain and urban smog; 33 percent of the hydrocarbon emissions (a primary cause of smog), and the same proportion of the carbon dioxide emissions contributing to global warming; and, finally, 18 percent—nearly one-fifth—of the emissions of ozone-destroying CFCs.[5] Automobiles are ecological disasters on wheels, yet millions of Americans choose the convenience of the family car over public transportation. These individual choices are reinforced by policy choices—to fund highway construction over public transport, for example, and to keep gasoline prices low. Barber B. Conable, Jr., former congressman and now head of the World Bank, said:

> The same senators who go and berate the tropical countries for cutting tropical rain forests would abdicate their citizenship before they would vote for a three-cent increase in the gasoline tax [to discourage overconsumption]. The great bulk of the American people believe they have a God-given right to gasoline at its present price. Most of the other countries of the world pay roughly twice as much for gasoline as we do and have very high taxes.[6]

Table 22-1 shows the enormous polluting power of one person per car over public transportation. Clearly, air pollution is a very democratic problem; the responsibility belongs to all of us.

Water Pollution

Many of the nation's rivers, bays, and lakes have become seriously degraded. Industry accounts for approximately 80 percent of the pollutants that deprive water of oxygen. The volume of water used in industrial production is staggering. The steel industry alone uses close to 4 trillion gallons a year, and steel production generates suspended solids, oils, acids, and poisonous gases that mix with the wastewater. Another prime source of water pollution is the waste released by cities into nearby waterways.

TABLE 22-1
POLLUTION EMITTED FROM URBAN TRANSPORT MODES DURING TYPICAL WORK COMMUTES

Mode	Hydrocarbons	Carbon Monoxide	Nitrogen Oxides
	(grams per 100 passenger-miles)		
Rapid rail	0.3	2	49
Light rail	0.4	3	69
Transit bus	20	305	154
Van pool	36	242	38
Car pool	70	502	69
Auto (one occupant)	209	1,506	206

SOURCE: *World Watch*, November-December 1990, p. 22.

Agricultural producers generate over 20 billion tons of waste a year, principally in the form of manure from feedlots. In the Missouri River basin, an area known for cattle production, organic wastes that leach from commercial feedlots into the surrounding water system generate as much pollution as the untreated sewage of 37.5 million people. In addition, agricultural pesticides that find their way into the water supply are responsible for large kills of shellfish, birds, and aquatic animals. Ingested pesticides are also passed up the food chain, further increasing the health risks for animals.

In 1972, Congress passed amendments to the federal **Clean Water Act** that were aimed at restoring and maintaining the "chemical, physical, and biological integrity of the Nation's waters." The new law set a target date of 1983 for achieving fishable, swimmable waters. Subsequent laws extended these protections to oceans and drinking-water supplies.

The 1972 amendments were designed to control **effluent**, the polluted water released by cities and industries. Engineering standards were set, timetables for cleanups were established, and large federal grants were provided to induce cooperation; in particular, Congress appropriated huge sums for wastewater treatment plants. Between 1970 and 1982, the number of people served by municipal wastewater treatment systems almost doubled, to 150 million. The volume of some pollutants entering waterways largely from industrial sources was drastically reduced—oil and grease by 71 percent, dissolved solids by 52 percent, phosphates by 74 percent, and heavy metals by 78 percent.[7]

The 1974 Safe Drinking Water Act, regulated public water supplies to ensure safe, high-quality drinking water, is a natural complement to the 1972 legislation. Though it did not provide federal financing to local governments, it did not impose heavy financial burdens on them until amended in 1986. Unfortunately, this was just as the financing available under the 1972 Clean Water Act was drying up. So the costs of

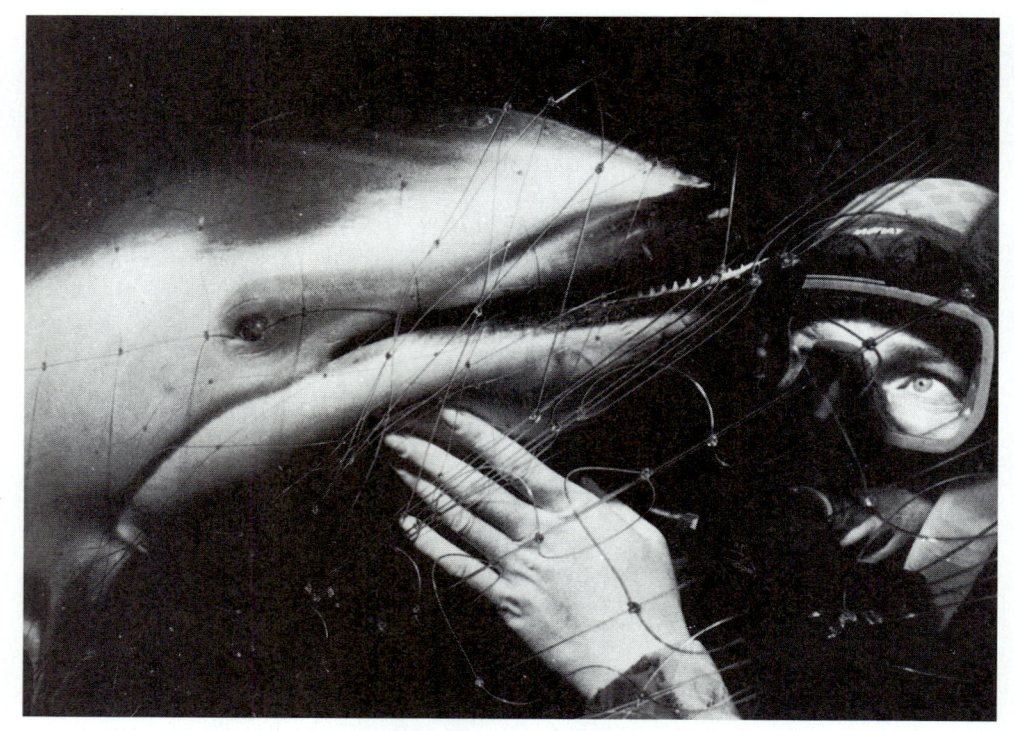

A diver from the environmental group Greenpeace examines a dolphin drowned in a tuna net in the Pacific. On this voyage of the Greenpeace ship *Rainbow Warrior*, at least 30 species of dolphins, birds, and fish were dead or dying in tuna nets. *(AP/Wide World Photos)*

compliance with Safe Drinking Water began to soar as federal money disappeared. Congress deleted construction grants from the Clean Water Act of 1987 after a second Reagan veto, so local governments were left to fend for themselves. Between 1972 and 1989 the federal government had spent $55 to $60 billion on sewage treatment plants and other clean-water projects. The federal share of costs for a particular project might have been as high as 70 percent. When the state picked up another 20 percent, that left the local governments—the water and sewer ratepayers—picking up just 10 percent of the cost. Since local governments, especially in medium and small communities, are unlikely to have the huge resources necessary for major water projects, the federal partnership of the 1972 legislation can be given credit for the substantial progress that was made.

During the 1990s the projected costs of clean water are daunting. The EPA estimates that $83.5 billion will be necessary for sewage treatment plants, and the American Water Works Association estimates that compliance with the Safe Drinking Water Act will cost $120 billion over the same period.[8] There is no consensus about where this money should come from. Since they probably would not qualify, privately owned water companies are not in favor of more federal grants. Surprisingly, some environmental groups also oppose federal grants, arguing that only when water users are made to bear the actual costs of clean water will conservation take hold. Others contend that the real costs of dirty water are not borne directly by users but spill over into the general economy. The water project construction industry is, naturally, much in favor of new federal funding.

The problem in clean water is a typical one for the 1990s, and its roots are mainly in the 1980s. There is a large, identified need for new spending on construction and repair, which has been given special impetus by federal mandates without federal funding. The federal and most state governments face extremely tight budgets. Environmental activists fear that the only to find relief is to abandon or cut back water quality standards, with serious consequences for drinking water and environmental quality in the nations lakes, rivers, and oceans.

Toxic Chemicals

The EPA has classified some 35,000 chemicals as either definitely or potentially hazardous to human health, and a growing body of evidence confirms these hazards. The agency estimates that toxic chemicals have been dumped at 33,800 sites nationwide, at least 1,126 of which pose serious health hazards.[9] Other experts place the figure far higher. The Office of Technology Assessment in 1985 estimated that there were 10,000 priority waste sites and that the cleanup costs would be closer to $100 billion than the $16 to $22 million the EPA had estimated.[10]

Toxic spills became commonplace in the 1980s, and the dangers of leaks and spills were pervasive and worldwide. Several places, including New York City, banned the transport of all toxic chemicals within city limits because a leak would pose a threat to human health and safety. In addition, companies that use and manufacture dangerous substances were made responsible for disposing of them legally. Violations of the new procedures were punishable by stiff penalties, such as $1 million fines and five-year prison terms. Subsequently, however, the EPA moved slowly on setting guidelines for acceptable disposal techniques. Since proper disposal techniques often are costly, many companies simply find cheap and unsafe methods, such as dumping wastes in the ocean or depositing them in unprotected sites.

Beginning in the 1980s, Congress established the **Superfund** to assist state and local governments in cleaning up hazardous toxic dumps. Enforcing the tough new rules about future disposal of toxic material did not prove to be easy, however, despite mandated penalties. Illegal dumping practices were hard to keep track of, much less to stop.

The EPA's approach to the toxic dumping issue took an entirely new turn under the Reagan administration, which moved at a glacial pace on the toxic waste issue. In 1981 and 1982 the EPA allocated less than one-third of the Superfund, and by 1985, only 538 sites were being cleaned up. The EPA's budget for enforcing toxic waste

PART FOUR • PUBLIC POLICY

COMPARATIVE PERSPECTIVE

ENVIRONMENTAL POLICY IN FRANCE: CENTRALIZED MARKET-ORIENTED CONTROL

Government in France is unitary, not federal, and that fact has important consequences for environmental policymaking. French environmental policy is formulated in Paris, with significantly less input from regional or local governments than there is in the United States, where federal mandates must be implemented—and often financed—by state and local governments. Local governments in France have little chance of resisting national environmental policy. The French pattern of policymaking emphasizes centralization, professionalism, and the restriction of interest group influence. French environmental policy was structured during the time of fairly conservative national governments, and this is reflected in the policies themselves. The more recent Socialist governments have not radically altered the original pattern.

French environmental policy has three major objectives: (1) to preserve unique ecological and aesthetic resources, (2) to further economic growth in particular regions, and (3) to ensure a balance between regional and national concerns. Greater consultation with interest groups and local governments does occur when problems are perceived as having "multiple environmental impacts."

In air pollution and hazardous waste disposal the primary engine of policy is the financial incentive offered by the Ministry of the Environment to industries to invest in pollution abatement equipment, usually including cost-sharing measures, low-interest loans, and tax depreciation allowances. Local governments are also entitled to tax transfers from the central government to design their own investment incentives. There is a large and increasing emphasis on cost-benefit analysis in choosing what sorts of incentives to offer.

Water policy was established in 1964, with a national set of charges for consumers and polluters in proportion to the amount of water affected. These

(Box continues on page 799)

control in 1985 was 25 percent below that in 1981, and the agency's director of the Office of Solid Waste admitted that 60 percent of major disposal facilities were not in compliance with new federal laws. The picture improved after 1985 with substantially increased Superfund expenditures.

More recent estimates have placed the costs of toxic cleanup far higher than ever (see **Table 22-2**, page 802). In 1991 one research team cited the figure of $750 billion as the price of dealing with the thousands of hazardous waste sites across the nation,

charges are meant to keep the costs of pollution and use close to the final users. There are national fines and penalties that can be assessed for violations of regulations. The money from the consumption and pollution charges is then allocated from water basin regions for water projects and pollution abatement costs. Each water basin region has an advisory board of appointed citizens to ferret out pollution violations and to legitimize the decisions of the water basin agency.

In France, as opposed to the United States, greater controversy surrounds park and wildlife policy than pollution control. According to one source, this reflects a lack of national consensus on the proper balance between economic development and natural preservation. Modifications to the Urban Code Law in 1958 and 1968 encouraged local governments to acquire adjacent land for "land banks," from which the government could release land according to planned growth strategies. The result of these land banks is visible on the French landscape—greenbelts around Paris and Marseilles and "new town" developments with building height restrictions, population density guidelines, and historic preservation regulations. Since the early 1970s special efforts have been made to preserve important scenic and habitat areas as parkland, but restrictions on tourist developments and urban growth have fallen short of some expectations. France's strong hunting tradition has meant that it lags behind other European nations in wildlife protection measures.

Overall, the French record on environmental policy is as mixed as that of most industrialized nations. (One notable blot on the French record was the charge that it had been involved in the sabotage of a Greenpeace ship, *Rainbow Warrior*; another, related, is the continued nuclear-testing program that Greenpeace was protesting.) The financial investment for environmental programs has ranged from 4.5 to 5.0 percent of national government expenditures (comparable to that in the United States). France has a strong record of cooperation with other European Community members on environmental issues.

Source: David Lewis Feldman, "France," in *International Public Policy Sourcebook,* vol. 2, ed. Fredric N. Bolotin (Westport, Conn.: Greenwood Press, 1989).

---

including many highly toxic dumps used by the military and related to nuclear and chemical weapon development. By 1992, Superfund cleanups had been completed at only sixty-three priority sites. This was clearly going to be a long, slow process. In the meantime, controversies had developed around both questions of priorities and issues of who had the responsibility to pay. Some people have argued that Superfund efforts, though worthwhile in themselves, reflected panicky and distorted priorities. One question is whether cleanups provide sufficient health benefits. Would we not be better

Endangered Species and the Endangered Species Act

Enacted in 1973 with the strong support of President Richard Nixon, the Endangered Species Act has proven to be one of the nation's most powerful and occasionally most controversial environmental laws. The notion behind the law was that human encroachment on natural habitats had become so destructive that specific protections were required to maintain a diversity of plants, insects, and animals.

Since 1973, 727 species have been placed on the list as threatened or endangered. Another 3,000 are potential candidates. Sixteen others have been removed from the list because their situation has improved, while nine have flourished to the point of full recovery. For example, the bald eagle was nearly extinct in the mid-1960s, but now numbers 6,000 and is being considered for removal from the list in some states. Only seven species, plant or animal, have become extinct.

Once on the list, a species is protected from encroachments regardless of the cost. Snail darters delayed construction of a Tennessee dam. Grizzly bears stopped construction of certain Montana roads, and owls curbed logging in the Northwest. This aspect of the law has been highly controversial with developers, logging interests, ranchers, and others arguing that the Act goes too far and should be dismantled. Overall, however, the law has worked with remarkably little conflict. For example, between 1987 and 1991, some 34,000 projects were proposed in areas where there was potential harm to endangered species. In such circumstances, after consultation with the Fish and Wildlife Service, only 367 cases were determined to harm a species and only 18 projects had to be cancelled.

Defenders of the Act point out how well it has worked, allowing projects to

(Box continues on page 801)

off spending some of that Superfund money ($1.75 billion allocated for 1993) for further research into breast cancer, for example? One estimate is that toxic waste sites are the cause of around one thousand cancer cases per year, whereas breast cancer claims 175,000 victims annually.[11] Such comparisons are inherently controversial. Moreover, no one wants to live next door to a waste site and to live in fear that the water one drinks or the air one breathes is dangerous now or might have disastrous consequences twenty years hence.

The good news appeared to be that substantial cleanups might be possible at a fraction of the huge costs being estimated. Such cleanups would not be complete but would eliminate most risks to human health. But will the public be satisfied as long as any risk, however low, remains? In mid-1992 the EPA released information that toxic

be adjusted and compromises worked out without a loss of jobs. Some critics maintain, however, that it will be impossible to prevent extinction of the thousands of threatened species, and that a priority list needs to be established, or that the focus should be on whole ecosystems rather than on individual species. The Bush Administration supported the Act at first, but later took a more negative view. Bush's Secretary of the Interior, Manuel Lujan, called the Act a gross impediment to progress and sought extensive changes.

On a planetary scale, the problem of species extinction is extremely critical. Some estimates are that by 2050 as many as half of current species will be extinct or seriously threatened. Human population growth and the rapid destruction of tropical rainforests are the main reasons. Every eight months, for example, the equivalent of a new Germany is created by current rates of population growth.

Proposed solutions include reduction of population growth through family planning, technical and financial assistance to developing countries to help preserve habitats, scientific research to identify and conserve remaining wildlife and plants. The treaty developed on this topic at the Earth Summit in 1992 encouraged species and habitat preservation as a part of economic and social planning. It also called for the establishment of protected areas and the restoration of degraded ecosystems. The core question is how to balance economic growth in poorer nations with the need to preserve natural diversity. This issue will be one of the most critical of the 21st century.

Sources: William K. Stevens, "Treaty on species may be key turn for ecosystems," Raleigh News & Observer, *May 24, 1992, p. 20A; Timothy Egan, "Strongest U.S. Environmental Law May Become Endangered Species,"* New York Times, *May 26, 1992, p. A1; Edward O. Wilson,* The Diversity of Life, *(Cambridge: Harvard University Press, 1992); Lester R. Brown, et al., "The New World Order," in* State of the World, *1992, (New York: Norton, 1992), pp. 3-20.*

---

emissions into air and water showed clear signs of declining. The Chemical Manufacturers Association claimed that emissions had dropped 35 percent since 1987, but this figure was met with skepticism. Environmental groups claimed that much of this decline had little to do with serious toxic chemicals.

Another pressing environmental hazard comes from pesticides—toxic chemicals widely used in American agriculture. Under the federal Insecticide, Fungicide and Rodenticide Act, a number of common pesticides, including DDT, were banned. However, the law permitted the continued sale of chemicals already on the market, many of which were suspected of causing cancer and birth defects. In the twenty or so years since the act's passage, the EPA has banned 32 of 600 pesticide ingredients, and 47 others have been voluntarily removed from the market. But hundreds of other ingre-

TABLE 22-2
COST OF CLEANING UP POLLUTED SITES

Site Category	Number of Sites (estimated)	Estimated Cost (billions of dollars)
Superfund abandoned sites	4,000	$80–120
Federally owned sites	5,000–10,000	75–250
Corrective action on active private sites	2,000–5,000	12–100
Leaking underground storage (tanks)	350,000–400,000	32
State-law-mandated cleanups	6,000–12,000	3–120+
Inactive uranium tailings	24	1.3
Abandoned mine lands	22,300	55

SOURCE: *New York Times*, September 1, 1991, p. 12.

dients remain to be evaluated, and new ones are introduced every years. This means that before the EPA finishes evaluating them all, we will be well into the twenty-first century. Consider too that pesticides banned in the United States can be marketed abroad, and pesticide manufacturers now aggressively market their products to Third World nations. Critics argue that the use, overuse, and misuse of dangerous pesticides throughout the Third World is poisoning large numbers of people: Estimates range from 500,000 to 1 million people affected to some degree each year. A study in Kenya found high concentrations of DDT in mother's milk. A Philippine study found increased death rates among rice farmers using high levels of pesticides. Germany exports the most pesticides to the Third World, but U.S., Swiss, French, Japanese, and Dutch manufacturers ship substantial quantities of pesticides there as well.[12]

The Politics of Environmental Issues

Environmental issues tend to be highly technical, yet they stir intense political conflict. Groups struggle to define the issues—and resolve them—in accordance with their own views. Let us now examine group strategies and the Reagan and Bush administrations' record on environment.

Group Strategies

In many ways the early environmental movement mirrored the pattern set by the civil rights and peace movements: marches, symbolic protests, and personal commitment.

Later, with the creation of federal and state environmental agencies, political action moved into more traditional channels, such as lawsuits, lobbying, education, and campaign activity. In the area of nuclear power, however, 1960s-style activism remained a major tactic. Some of the new environmental laws encouraged citizen activism: Certain NEPA provisions, for example, give citizens standing to sue, a prerequisite for legal action. Frequently, environmental groups differ over priorities and strategies. Some take a hard line—insisting on the pure preservation of wilderness areas, for example—while others are willing to allow for multiple uses, including recreation and commercial development.

Opposing environmental activists are corporate interests. Business is a major producer, consumer, and polluter. Many businesses are directly affected by the government's decisions on the environment. For example, the lumber industry harvests over one-third of its commercial softwood from federal forests, and tens of millions of federally owned acres are leased for mineral development. Although U.S. business is highly diverse (11 million corporations and three thousand trade associations), the strategies used in combating new environmental standards and attitudes do not vary much from industry to industry.[13] Businesses typically argue that environmental problems are exaggerated, that regulations are too strict and unreasonable, and that these regulations threaten economic growth. When the Oregon legislature passed strict environmental legislation, for example, an Oregon labor lobby argued: "As a result of overzealous, erroneous governmental regulations and actions, that segment which produces jobs and profits has been rendered a serious economic blow."[14] Business interests spend millions of dollars on advertising campaigns to sway the public to their point of view, lobby extensively in Congress and state legislatures, and support political action committees to gain access to candidates.

The Reagan Record on the Environment

Ronald Reagan and his aides strongly favored U.S. economic growth, which in their view meant drastically curtailing environmental rules. Shortly after Reagan took office, administration officials moved to delay the imposition of many new environmental standards; fired the entire staff of the President's Council on Environment Quality, whose views were distinctly proenvironment; made deep cuts in outlays for environmental protection; and dismissed several thousand EPA employees, including attorneys trained in environmental law. Reagan's first secretary of the interior, James Watt, moved to open up coastal areas for oil drilling, proposed the sale of millions of acres of federal land for development, and sought to water down strip-mining laws. In addition, sweeping powers were delegated to the states, which lacked the resources to handle them. In 1983, Reagan appointed as EPA director William Ruckelshaus, a respected figure who had headed the agency under President Nixon. Still, many observers believed that it would take years to repair the damage done to environmental programs.

(By permission of Mike Luckovich and Creators Syndicate)

The Bush Administration and the Environment

During the 1988 presidential campaign, George Bush said he wanted to be known as the "environmental president." The first two years of his administration established a marked contrast with the Reagan years on environmental issues. Bush approved increases for the EPA budget, blocked a Colorado dam that would have flooded a scenic canyon, added more than $100 million for buying land for parks and refuges, put major areas of coastline off limits to oil exploration, promised "no net loss" of wetlands, signed international agreements to ban ivory trading and large-scale drift-net fishing as well as a treaty to protect Antarctica, and—most important of all—strongly supported the 1990 Clean Air Act, a comprehensive and expensive piece of environmental legislation. But then things changed. Over the second two years of the administration there was a marked shift in priorities, even a reversion to the antienvironmental, pro-business approach of the Reagan years.

A series of forces converged to push the administration in this direction. Perhaps most significantly, a coalition of industry groups argued that environmental rules were injuring their economic situation. In a time of general recession, some administration insiders maintained that jobs were being sacrificed to "environmental radicalism." In addition, conservative economists insisted that the costs of complying with the regulations were too high. Some cities complained that new rules would drastically increase the costs to citizens of such services as trash disposal and clean water. Vice-President Quayle and his Council on Competitiveness became a center of resistance to increased regulation, arguing that the environmental movement had exaggerated the threats involved.

The administration dragged its feet on issuing the rules needed to make the Clean Air Act effective. It approved a plan allowing development on 50 percent of the nation's wetlands. It backed rules to make it more difficult for the public to object to new dam projects or to timber cutting or mining on public lands. President Bush tried to open the Arctic National Wildlife Refuge in Alaska to oil exploration, but the plan was defeated in Congress after a furious lobbying effort by environmental groups. The administration waived rules for the automobile, pharmaceutical, and chemical industries, allowing increased pollutants. Finally, the president was the last leader of a major industrial power to announce that he would attend the Earth Summit in Brazil in 1992. Once there, he refused to sign a treaty to protect endangered species and was successful in weakening another treaty on global warming. Interestingly, the Earth Summit issues made it clear that there was substantial conflict within the administration over environmental issues, with the EPA being overruled by the White House.[15]

These many and complex issues became a central focus of the 1992 presidential campaign, particularly in the confrontation between vice-presidential candidates Al Gore and Dan Quayle. Gore, author of a substantial book on world environmental and energy issues, argued that the choice presented between jobs and environment was a false one. He maintained that old, inefficient American industries were costing the nation millions of jobs. He also argued that environmental concerns were serious and pressing and required immediate attention. Quayle argued that many environmental regulations were extreme and unnecessary impediments to vigorous economic growth.

Energy: Sources, Problems, Policies

Energy issues, like environmental issues, are complex, many-sided, and interwoven. Energy choices, moreover, interact with environmental consequences. The most obvious example of this interaction is the greenhouse effect considered earlier. The ways we choose to generate energy and run our transport systems have profound consequences for the entire global environment, not to mention more immediate and local effects on air and water pollution. In addition to these complicated matters, questions of energy policy are also intricately and sometimes dangerously linked to issues of national security—for example, ensuring a steady supply of oil from the Persian Gulf—and matters of trade and general economic well-being.

Until recently, there was really no such thing as an "energy policy" in any conscious, overarching sense.[16] Like environmental issues, energy questions had not perked to the top of the political agenda, either nationally or internationally. In the United States such energy policy as there was tended to be made industry by industry, without a look at the overall picture or much thought to the long-term consequences. There were rules governing the pricing and transport of natural gas, for example, or

A sea otter pup covered with crude oil from the *Exxon Valdez*. The major environmental damage from this single spill vividly illustrated the constant danger presented by the transport of petroleum. *(Tom Walker/Stock, Boston)*

special tax breaks to encourage more drilling for oil. For a long time, coal was a relatively unregulated energy source, while oil and gas were subject to intense local and national political bargaining. Nuclear power development was long subsidized through federal policies but was not much of a focus for national debate.[17]

All of that changed in the late 1960s and early 1970s as a variety of energy issues became the subjects of increasing controversy and as the long-term meaning of energy choices began to be thought about. Let us begin our discussion of energy policies with an overview of how the United States generates and uses energy.

Energy: An Overview

The generation of vast quantities of energy is the lifeblood of modern industrial society. There are a fairly limited number of ways to create that energy. The best-known and so far most common ways of doing so are burning **fossil fuels** (petroleum, natural gas, and coal) or generating electricity in nuclear power or hydroelectric plants. There are important issues of adequate supply and safety connected to each of these alternatives. In the past two decades alternative energy sources have been discussed and, to some extent, developed. These alternatives include **solar power**—using the sun as a passive

TABLE 22-3
TOTAL ENERGY REQUIREMENT IN CONVENTIONAL FUEL EQUIVALENT (SELECT COUNTRIES), 1989

	Total (Terajoules)	Per Capita (Gigajoules)
World	351,375	68
United States	81,490	329
Federal Republic of Germany (West)	11,089	181
France	9,558	171
United Kingdom	9,051	158
Poland	5,138	134
China	28,925	26
Zaire	429	12

SOURCE: *Energy Statistics Yearbook 1989* (New York: United Nations, 1991), Table 4, pp. 90–103.

source of heat or to generate electricity through photovoltaic cells—and other varieties of **renewable energy**, including wind, geothermal, and biomass. Also important is conservation—using energy more efficiently, as by building more fuel-efficient vehicles and appliances, insulating homes better, and shifting to less wasteful modes of transport, such as mass transit and bicycles. In the Netherlands, for example, 30 percent of work trips and 60 percent of school trips are made by bicycle.

As we have already seen, the burning of fossil fuels has helped to cause profound worldwide environmental problems. There are obvious incentives to find alternative ways to run modern industry and transport and to reduce our dependence on oil. Much of the debate about energy policy focuses on whether and how fast to reduce the use of fossil fuels and what alternatives to support for future energy supplies. The Earth Summit commitment of the major industrial powers was part of a realization that the world had to make a rapid transition to energy alternatives before the ecological damage was irreparable. But rapid and far-reaching changes in energy use imply changes in familiar ways of living—and nowhere more so than in the United States, the world's greatest energy user, overall and per capita (see **Table 22-3**).

U.S. Energy Use

Americans are the world champion energy users. At some point in the past that might have been a status to be proud of, befitting our wealth and security. But times have changed. Our profligate use of energy has become a major political debating ground. With 2 percent of the world's population and about 4 percent of known oil reserves, we use 25 percent of the world's oil. Only Canada comes close to us in oil consumption. In 1989, Americans used over twenty-five barrels of oil per person. For Japan the figure

The Germans have taken the lead in recycling. Environmentally safe and recyclable products have gained a significant share of the market in Germany and in some other European democracies. (Ilse Friesem/Monkmeyer Press Photos)

was fifteen barrels. For most European industrial nations it was between ten and fifteen barrels. Overall, Western Europeans use, per person, only about 60 percent of the energy we do. Though the United States is a large country and so inevitably transportation costs account for a larger portion of our energy use, the major reason for higher U.S. consumption is our inefficiency and lack of attention to the problem—undoubtedly a result of our great wealth of resources and our aversion to planning and governmental regulation.

The rate of American oil consumption declined in the 1970s due to deliberate government policy and conservation efforts. Since 1982 the rate has increased again, largely reflecting a return to lower oil prices, a result of increased supplies. As American oil reserves have begun to run out, this has meant importing more and more oil, primarily from the oil-producing nations of the Middle East. At current rates of consumption, American oil reserves will run dry in about ten years, and global oil will last somewhere between fifty and ninety years. The fear of losing our constant supply of oil was undoubtedly one of the factors involved in deciding to go to war to drive Iraq out of oil-rich Kuwait in 1991. Strategic considerations regarding oil have been a focus of presidential policymaking since the Nixon administration. The Strategic Oil Reserve, which now contains 600 million barrels of oil, would be sufficient to replace OPEC (Organization of Petroleum Exporting Countries) oil for a mere ten months. Presidents Nixon, Ford, and Carter called for increased independence from Middle East oil sources. In contrast, Presidents Reagan and Bush focused on increasing supplies of oil through exploration and have paid little attention to shifting away from fossil fuels.

The Politics of Energy Issues

As we have mentioned, there was little debate about enegy policy issues until the 1970s. At that point a major focus was how to ensure greater **energy independence** for the United States in the face of threats to our supply of oil. Other considerations, such as the value of conservation measures, were also part of the picture. Presidents Nixon and Ford both sought to lower oil imports. President Carter pressed for conservation measures and solar energy as well as favoring gradual gas decontrol, an increase in the federal gasoline tax, and a heavy tax on gas-guzzling cars. Toward the end of his administration, Carter also sought large-scale financial subsidies for a synthetic fuels (synfuels) program. In the end, he got much of what he wanted.

All U.S.-produced oil was effectively decontrolled in 1981, but at the same time the oil companies were assessed a special **windfall profits** tax to reduce the financial bonanza accorded them by decontrol. Politically, decontrol of oil could not have been accomplished without this tax: Congress and the public were outraged over the immense profits oil companies were making at the time. Congress mandated that these revenues were to be used for assistance to lower-income persons, to help them cope with increased energy costs; for tax reductions to individuals and businesses; and for energy development and mass transit.

The windfall tax issue illustrates some important points about energy policymaking. In this case, public opinion forced legislators to tax the industry's windfall profits because oil companies were already making enormously high profits, even before decontrol went into effect. Accordingly, the oil companies, once virtually unchallenged in their own domain, had to yield to countervailing political forces. The bureaucracy also had a hand in decontrolling oil: The newly created Department of Energy, a staunch advocate of decontrol, lobbied for it extensively within the government. This gave the process an even stronger push.

Complex in themselves, energy issues also interact with other political concerns: conservation, foreign policy, safety, and the like. In 1987, for example, Congress passed a law setting minimum federal energy efficiency standards for major appliances such as refrigerators, washing machines, and hot-water heaters. Some authorities estimated that the new standards would ensure $28 billion in energy savings by the year 2000, equivalent to the output of twenty-two nuclear power plants. At the same time, after years of debate, speed limits on selected U.S. highways were raised from 55 to 65 miles per hour. Speed limits had been lowered in the 1970s in the wake of the Arab oil embargo of 1973–1974. Originally promoted as a conservation measure (because cars running at lower speeds use less gasoline), the 55-mph limit was not debated in those terms in the 1980s. Instead the debate revolved around safety (the number of lives saved by the lower speed limit) versus convenience. The Reagan administration also moved to reflag Kuwaiti oil tankers in the Persian Gulf, signaling the nation's continued dependence on foreign oil supplies. Then, to boost domestic oil production, the administration advocated oil exploration in the Arctic National Wildlife Refuge in Alaska. Yet many experts maintained that the quantity of oil beneath the refuge (at most one

(Text continues on page 812)

A Summary of Energy Alternatives

Three nonrenewable fossil fuels account for the vast majority of our current energy supplies: crude oil, natural gas, and coal. Nuclear power accounts for less than 2% of overall energy use, but about 15% of electricity supplies. Heating, lighting, air conditioning in residential and commercial buildings uses 37% of energy. Industrial production uses about an equal amount, with the remaining 25% going for transportation. One key question is whether alternative, renewable sources of energy such as solar energy, and conservation can become effective substitutes for fossil fuels, and how quickly this needs to be done.

Oil: Oil is vital, vulnerable, and bound, over the long haul, to grow increasingly expensive. After the squeeze in oil supplies during the 1970s, an oil glut developed in the 1980s and early 1990s. Dire predictions of continual oil shortages turned out to be mistaken. Increased supplies combined with successful conservation measures to bring oil prices down sharply. U.S. dependence on Middle East oil continued to gradually increase as domestic oil reserves ran out. Most experts expected the cheap oil bubble to burst sometime in the near future. But with prices low, there was little additional incentive to conserve energy. Concerned about the greenhouse problem and for a time when gasoline supplies would be less ample, some advocated a stiff increase in gasoline taxes to push automakers and consumers alike in the direction of greater fuel efficiency.

Natural gas: The US has large supplies of natural gas. It has two advantages over other fossil fuels: It burns more cleanly and is easily transportable. It can be substituted for oil in many situations. Currently, industry uses two-thirds of natural gas. Despite large supplies, shortages have occurred, especially in specific regions when needs are greatest. Also, there is sometimes competition among a variety of uses, such as utilities, industries, and domestic households.

Coal: Coal fueled the earlier stages of the industrial revolution. The United States is the Saudi Arabia of coal, with one-third of the world's reserves. Coal accounts for 90% of our remaining domestic fossil fuel resources. Most coal is now used

(Box continues on page 811)

by utilities to produce electricity. Coal poses particularly serious environmental hazards, which include strip mining, acid rain, and other varieties of air pollution.

Nuclear power: Once touted as a solution to the world's energy needs, nuclear power has become less and less attractive in recent decades. Safety issues have become particularly pressing, dramatized by the tragedy of Chernobyl in 1986. Political opposition and increasing costs have led many nations to cancel nuclear projects. France and Japan have embarked on the most extensive use of nuclear power. Presidents Carter, Reagan, and Bush all endorsed expansion of nuclear plant construction.

Alternative sources: Sometimes referred to as the "soft energy" path, solar power includes a variety of energy alternatives. These alternatives have in common the fact that they use renewable energy and not fossil fuels. They are cleaner and environmentally less damaging. But they are presently not being widely employed because of lack of investment and the problems of adjusting to new methods. Among the major solar options are photovoltaic cells, which transform sunlight directly into electricity; biomass, the use of organic waste materials such as manure, rotting plants and trees, garbage and crops specially developed for this purpose as a source of fuel; new high tech windmills that utilize wind energy; passive solar construction methods which utilize sunlight for heating homes; and methane gas as a potential fuel for transport and industry. During the energy crisis of the 1970s many experiments began along these lines, and the Carter administration encouraged alternative energy developments. The Reagan and Bush administrations mostly abandoned these directions.

Conservation: One way to deal with energy needs is to reduce them. Most experts argue that up to half of U.S. energy is simply wasted due to inefficient use. The potential savings through conservation could be enormous. Much has already been accomplished in moving toward greater efficiency. Other measures might include increased use of alternatives to the car such as trains and bikes; stricter building standards; greater fuel efficiency for vehicles; and better designed appliances. Recycling also can contribute significantly to energy conservation. Blessed with large supplies of fossil fuels, Americans have not had to think about such measures in earlier generations.

812 PART FOUR • PUBLIC POLICY

year's supply for the United States) hardly merited the threat to one of the world's most sensitive and rarest ecosystems.

The basically probusiness, market-oriented approach to economics of the Reagan and Bush administrations also pervaded their ideas about energy policy. To put it simply, the energy policy of both administrations consisted of deregulating markets, maintaining the Strategic Oil Reserve to offset supply disruptions, and willingly using military force to protect oil supplies. In the early days of the Bush administration, the Department of Energy proposed a series of far-reaching new approaches to long-term energy issues. These approaches included higher mileage requirements for cars and incentives and requirements for domestic energy conservation. But White House advisers defeated any strong new initiatives. Instead Bush advocated help for more production from coal, oil, and nuclear industries with minimal interest in renewable forms of energy.

Opponents argued that a federal energy policy would have to stress greater conservation efforts along the following lines: federal funding for more public transpor-

Some argue that our government should make major investments in developing alternative sources of energy, such as solar energy. The Carter administration began such investments, but they were virtually wiped out under Reagan and Bush. It seemed likely that the Clinton administration would revive alternative energy initiatives. *(Courtesy of Southern California Edison)*

tation; reduction in the use of cars and highways; switching to alternative fuels such as ethanol, gas, and electricity for transport; energy credits for families and businesses; expansion of the market for renewable energy technologies; and perhaps most controversial, mandating higher auto mileage standards and placing a substantial tax on gasoline along the lines of the Europeans. The future battle lines in the area of energy seemed relatively clear: old energy supplies versus new, autos versus alternative modes of transport, conservation efforts versus increased production. As the number of automobiles mounted worldwide, the issues of air pollution and the burning of fossil fuels were becoming increasingly acute. Yet as oil prices dropped, both Americans and Europeans started to prefer larger cars once again. Would the free market be capable of dealing with problems such as these, and soon enough to fend off permanent damage to the environment? Many people doubted it and called for a stepped-up commitment to conservation and planning for the future.

Conclusions

Can democratic theory shed light on energy and environmental issues? Three issues command our attention here. First, who decides how energy and environmental issues are resolved, and how do they make those decisions? Second, who benefits and who pays for the ways we deal with energy and environmental questions? Are some people being victimized to make life easier for others? Finally, democratic concerns should make us wonder about the long-term significance of our decisions about energy and environmental issues. How will these decisions affect future generations?[18]

Before 1973, most key decisions on energy were made or shaped by the interests most directly involved. Oil interests essentially determined the politics of oil; companies with a strong interest in nuclear power pressed for—and generally obtained—government subsidies for their efforts. In addition, the courts often frustrated citizens' efforts to set limits on degradation of the environment. Air and water pollution and the dumping of toxic wastes had no place on the political agenda.

Now that energy and environmental issues have reached our political agenda, many experts argue that the intricacies of these issues, like the complex problems involved in foreign policy, are simply too difficult for common citizens to comprehend. In some respects, this argument has merit: Few of us have the time or inclination to probe the problems of waste disposal or to master the alternatives to air pollution. But in general, the public has taken a resolutely proenvironment stance. On energy questions, neither policymakers nor the public at large have reached any coherent consensus on how to grapple with our coming energy dilemmas. It seems likely, however, that once such a consensus emerges, popular sentiment will play a constructive role in shaping future energy and environmental policy.

In considering the costs and benefits of energy and environmental policy, basic human rights come into play. If air pollution is taking years off our lives, if toxic dumps increase health risks for millions, if carcinogens in the workplace mean that many people will die prematurely, then core issues of democratic politics are at stake. The basic guideline for democratic policymaking is this: The life and health of some people should not be sacrificed for the ease and convenience of others. An aroused public, concerned about environmental hazards, can demand serious, sustained action by the political leadership.

Democratic commitments should also prompt us to consider the long-term effects of current actions. Should we push for the maximum feasible production now, even if that means polluting the environment further? How vigorously should we press for cleanup of the environment in the immediate future, as opposed to leaving the job to the next generation?

Democratic theory can take us only so far, however. It cannot tell us whether a high-energy, high-consumption lifestyle is preferable to something simpler and more conservation-oriented. It cannot tell us whether the investment in solar options will be worthwhile or not. It cannot tell us how strictly we should enforce laws on toxic dumping. Nevertheless, it does remind us that no one person's life is more important than any other's and that the profits or comforts of a few are not so important as the well-being of the many.

Finally, we must recognize that Americans have always wanted to "develop" their nation. Historically, we have sought more and better, bigger and richer. Now the complex issues of energy and environment cast a shadow over this hallowed American dream. Americans believe in capitalism—but in this area, capitalistic approaches sometimes fall short of the mark. Under capitalism the people who should be paying the real costs of doing business are not forced actually to pay those costs. Therefore, government has a particularly important role to play in energy and environmental issues. What should that role be? Can we preserve the environment and still generate the energy for an "American" lifestyle? And if this proves impossible, who will have the political courage to say so?

Glossary Terms

acid rain
biodiversity
chlorofluorocarbons (CFCs)
Clean Air Act of 1963
Earth Summit
effluent
energy independence
environmental impact statement
Environmental Protection Agency (EPA)

fossil fuels
global warming
greenhouse effect
ozone depletion
renewable energy
solar power
Superfund
windfall profits

Notes

[1] All statistics in this discussion from "A Day in the Life of Mother Earth," *Los Angeles Times*, May 26, 1992, sec. H.
[2] Mark Clements, "How Much Do We Care?" *Parade*, June 14, 1992, pp. 16–17.

[3]Rae Tyson, "EPA: Toxic Emissions Declining," *USA Today*, May 28, 1992, p. 1A.
[4]"Dirty Business on Clean Air," *New York Times*, June 30, 1992, p. A14.
[5]Tom Mather, "Motor Vehicles Are Prime Producers of Pollution," *Raleigh News and Observer*, October 29, 1990, p. 1A.
[6]*Los Angeles Times*, May 26, 1992, p. H11.
[7]Council on Environmental Quality, *Environmental Quality, 1983* (Washington, D.C.: U.S. Government Printing Office, 1983), p. 4.
[8]Jonathan C. Kaledin, "Priming the Pump: Paying for Clean Water in the 1990s," *American Prospect*, Fall 1991, p. 68.
[9]*New York Times*, September 1, 1991, p. A1; *Los Angeles Times*, December 10, 1991, p. A27.
[10]*New York Times*, March 10, 1985, p. 1.
[11]*New York Times*, September 1, 1991, p. A12.
[12]Philip Shabecoff, "Congress Again Confronts Hazards of Killer Chemicals," *New York Times*, October 11, 1987, p. E5; Mort Rosenbaum, "Pesticides Considered Big Threat," *Chapel Hill (N.C.) Newspaper*, October 18, 1987, p. C1.
[13]Walter A. Rosenbaum, *The Politics of Environmental Concern* (New York: Holt, Rinehart and Winston, 1977), pp. 81–87.
[14]Ibid., pp. 83–84.
[15]See Keith Schneider, "Bush on the Environment: A Record of Contradictions," *New York Times*, July 4, 1992, p. A1; see also *New York Times*, August 25, 1991, p. E4.
[16]For background, see David Howard Davis, *Energy Politics* (New York: St. Martin's Press, 1982), chap. 4.
[17]Ibid., chap. 2.
[18]See David Orr and Stuart Hill, "Leviathan, the Open Society and the Crisis of Ecology," December 1978, pp. 457–469; and David Orr, "Perspectives on Energy," *Dissent*, Summer 1979, pp. 280–284.

Selected Readings

For a widely read and influential presentation of an "environmental **ethic**," see E. F. Schumacher, *Small Is Beautiful* (New York: Harper & Row, 1973). A variety of particular **perspectives** are represented in Garrett Hardin and John Baden, eds., *Managing the Commons* (New York: Freeman, 1977); Barry Commoner, *The Closing Circle* (New York: Knopf, 1971); Wendell Berry, *The Unsettling of America* (San Francisco: Sierra Club, 1977); P. Portney et al., *Current Issues in U.S. Environmental Policy* (Baltimore: Johns Hopkins University Press, 1978); S. P. Hays, *Beauty, Health and Permanence* (New York: Cambridge University Press, 1987); Robert Costanza, ed., *Ecological Economics: The Science and Management of Sustainability* (New York: Columbia University Press, 1991); Albert Gore, Jr., *Earth in the Balance: Ecology and the Human Spirit* (Boston: Houghton Mifflin, 1992); Michael J. Lacey, ed., *Government and Environmental Politics: Essays on Historical Developments since World War Two* (Baltimore: Johns Hopkins University Press, 1991).

On **global issues**, see John Firor, *The Changing Atmosphere: A Global Challenge* (New Haven, Conn.: Yale University Press, 1990); Jeremy Rifkin, *Beyond Beef: The Rise and Fall of the Cattle Culture* (New York: Dutton, 1992); Jim MacNeill et al., *Beyond Interdependence* (New York: Oxford University Press, 1991); Hal Kane, *Time for Change: A New Approach to Environment and Development* (Washington, D.C.: Island Press, 1992); Jefferson Tester, David O. Wood, and Nancy A. Ferrari, *Energy and Environment in the 21st Century* (Cambridge, Mass.: MIT

Press, 1991); Frances Cairncross, *Costing the Earth: The Challenge for Governments, the Opportunities for Business* (Cambridge, Mass.: Harvard Business School Press, 1992); R. Dornbusch and J. M. Poterba, eds., *Global Warming: Economic Policy Response* (Cambridge, Mass.: MIT Press, 1991); and Paul R. Ehrlich, *Healing the Planet: Strategies for Resolving the Environmental Crisis* (Reading, Mass.: Addison-Wesley, 1991).

The "not in my back yard" (NIMBY) phenomenon—local residents' resistance to environmentally damaging construction—is explored in Sidney Plotkin, *Keep Out: The Struggle for Land Use Control* (Berkeley: University of California Press, 1987). For an interesting case study of one town's backyard problem, see Anthony F. C. Wallace, *St. Clair: A Nineteenth Century Coal Town's Experience with a Disaster-prone Industry* (New York: Knopf, 1987). See also C. H. Schroeder and R. J. Lazarus, eds., *Assessing the Environmental Protection Agency after 20 Years* (Durham, N.C.: Duke University School of Law, 1991); Peter C. Yeager, *The Limits of Law: The Public Regulation of Private Pollution* (New York: Cambridge University Press, 1991); Dave Foreman, *Confessions of an Eco-Warrior* (New York: Harmony Books, 1991); Terry Lee Anderson, *Free Market Environmentalism* (Boulder, Colo.: Westview Press, 1991); Victor Scheffer, *The Shaping of Environmentalism in America* (Seattle: University of Washington Press, 1991); Robert Glenn Ketchum, *Overlooked in America: The Success and Failure of Federal Land Management* (New York: Aperture Fund, 1991); and John Keeble, *Out of the Channel: The Exxon Valdez Oil Spill in Prince William Sound* (New York: HarperCollins, 1991).

For a **comparative perspective**, see Jeffrey Leonard, *Natural Resources and Economic Development in Central America: A Regional Environmental Profile* (New Brunswick, N.J.: Transaction Books, 1987); Zhores A. Medvedev, *The Legacy of Chernobyl* (New York: Norton, 1990); Michael Colby, *Environmental Management in Development* (Washington, D.C.: World Bank, 1990); W. M. Adams, *Green Development: Environment and Sustainability in the Third World* (London: Routledge & Kegal Paul, 1990); Angus L. Wright, *The Death of Ramón González: The Modern Agricultural Tragedy* (Austin: University of Texas Press, 1990); Murray Feshbach, *Ecocide in the USSR: Health and Nature under Siege* (New York: Basic Books, 1992); and Lester R. Brown, ed., *State of the World, 1992: A WorldWatch Report on Progress toward a Sustainable Society* (New York: Norton, 1992).

On the **energy debate**, see Pietro S. Nivola, *The Politics of Energy Conservation* (Washington, D.C.: Brookings Institution, 1986); D. Kash and R. Rycroft, *U.S. Energy Policy: Crisis and Complacency* (Norman: University of Oklahoma Press, 1984); Amory Lovins, *Brittle Power: Energy Strategy for National Security* (Andover, Mass: Brick House, 1982); J. L. Simon and H. Kahn, *The Resourceful Earth* (London:Blackwell, 1984); and Daniel F. Ford, *Three Mile Island* (New York: Penguin, 1982). On a controversial issue of the late 1980s (who pays when a nuclear power plant is partially or completely built and then canceled?), see Joseph P. Tomain, *Nuclear Power Transformation* (Bloomington: Indiana University Press, 1987). See also *Energy Efficiency and the Environment* (Paris: Organization for Economic Cooperation and Development, 1992); James J. MacKenzie, *Driving Forces: Motor Vehicle Trends and Their Implications* (Washington, D.C.: World Resources Institute, 1990); Erik Arrhenius, *The Greenhouse Effect: Implications for Economic Development* (Washington, D.C.: World Bank, 1990); and David L. McKee, ed., *Energy, the Environment, and Public Policy: Issues for the 1990s* (New York: Praeger, 1991).

EPILOGUE

ON IMPROVING AMERICAN DEMOCRACY

This book has focused on issues of democratic politics. Happily, recent years have been good for democracy. In many nations, democrats have been winning dramatic victories. In what was once the Soviet Empire, in Latin America and elsewhere, elections have replaced coups, and democratically elected leaders have replaced dictators and one-party systems. The process has been exhilarating but it has also made clear that democratic elections are not necessarily a magic cure for all society's ills. Ethnic hatreds, economic collapse, severe deprivations and inequality, struggles for power, corruption, intolerance—all of these and more must be dealt with if democracies are to survive and prosper. And the lessons we can clearly see elsewhere apply to our own older democratic polity as well.

Here in the United States, political alienation and nonparticipation reached new highs in the 1980s. There is considerable doubt about the capacity of our political processes to represent adequately the views of the majority. And there are further doubts about the capacity of the majority to form coherent opinions in the light of the complexity of many issues and with the skillful efforts at political manipulation that have become the norm in political campaigns. America's political processes are in serious need of reform. Among the most significant and immediate we favor are: easing the process of voter registration, public financing of political campaigns, reducing the role of PAC money in political life, making Election Day a holiday, and free TV and radio time for candidates. We also believe that shortening the process of nominating and electing presidents is in order. Only in the United States does this process stretch out over an entire year—and sometimes even longer. These are hardly revolutionary suggestions. In fact most of them have been on the Congressional agenda in recent years, although they have failed either in one house or the other or because of presidential veto.

Political reform alone will not do the trick, however. More pervasive issues are also at stake. For one, we believe that our educational processes are in need of a drastic jolt. Citizens need a clearer sense, not only of the nuts and bolts of government, but of the meanings of civil liberties, civil rights, and social rights, and of the controversies surrounding them. Civics, rather than being the tedious bore it usually is, should become an arena for excited and many-sided debate. Schools will have to risk dealing with contemporary controversies if democratic citizens are to grasp the significance of public issues.

We have also lived through an era of considerable duplicity and violence in American life, an era of division and evasion. In this regard, we think of Lyndon Johnson's refusal to level with the electorate during the 1964 election about his plans to expand the war in Vietnam. We think of Nixon's actions to subvert the democratic processes in 1972. We think of the Iran-Contra efforts to circumvent the democratic process. We think of the efforts—even as late as the 1992 presidential campaign—to brand critics of the Vietnam War as unpatriotic, rather than seeing in their free speech an expression of democracy. We also think of the rioting in American cities, which swept through the summers of the late 1960s and continued again with the Los Angeles riot of 1992. The issues behind those riots continue to plague American life: racism, police brutality, economic deprivation, drugs, educational failure, family disintegration, the loss of hope and of a sense of common humanity. Violence and intolerance, which have been endemic to American life, show themselves in ever new forms and continue to threaten the decency, tolerance, and honesty that a well-functioning democracy requires.

Can politics ever truly be honest? Can the struggle for power really be humanized and contained, or better yet, turned to good purposes? The American theologian Reinhold Niebuhr once wrote: "Man's capacity for justice makes democracy necessary." We hope that our text has helped to make you more sensitive to both capacities as well as more willing to take the risks of involvement, skepticism, and caring that are among the highest political virtues in a polity struggling to come closer to the democratic ideal.

APPENDIXES

A
THE DECLARATION OF INDEPENDENCE

B
THE CONSTITUTION OF THE UNITED STATES

C
U.S. PRESIDENTIAL ELECTIONS

D
GLOSSARY

APPENDIX A

THE DECLARATION OF INDEPENDENCE

When in the Course of human events, it becomes necessary for one people to dissolve the political bands which have connected them with another, and to assume among the Powers of the earth, the separate and equal station to which the Laws of Nature and of Nature's God entitle them, a decent respect to the opinions of mankind requires that they should declare the causes which impel them to the separation.

We hold these truths to be self-evident, that all men are created equal, that they are endowed by their Creator with certain unalienable Rights, that among these are Life, Liberty and the pursuit of Happiness. That to secure these rights, Governments are instituted among Men, deriving their just powers from the consent of the governed. That whenever any Form of Government becomes destructive of these ends, it is the Right of the People to alter or to abolish it, and to institute new Government, laying its foundation on such principles and organizing its powers in such form, as to them shall seem most likely to effect their Safety and Happiness. Prudence, indeed, will dictate that Governments long established should not be changed for light and transient causes; and accordingly all experience hath shown, that mankind are more disposed to suffer, while evils are sufferable, than to right themselves by abolishing the forms to which they are accustomed. But when a long train of abuses and usurpations, pursuing invariably the same Object evinces a design to reduce them under absolute Depotism, it is their right, it is their duty, to throw off such Government, and to provide new Guards for their future security. — Such has been the patient sufferance of these Colonies; and such is now the necessity which constrains them to alter their former Systems of Government. The history of the present King of Great Britain is a history of repeated injuries and usurpations, all having in direct object the establishment of an absolute Tyranny over these States. To prove this, let Facts be submitted to a candid world.

He has refused his Assent to Laws, the most wholesome and necessary for the public good.

He has forbidden his Governors to pass Laws of immediate and pressing importance, unless suspended in their operation till his Assent should be obtained; and when so suspended, he has utterly neglected to attend to them.

He has refused to pass other Laws for the accommodation of large districts of people, unless those people would relinquish the right of Representation in the Legislature, a right inestimable to them and formidable to tyrants only.

He has called together legislative bodies at places unusual, uncomfortable, and distant from the depository of their public Records, for the sole purpose of fatiguing them into compliance with his measures.

He has dissolved Representative Houses repeatedly for opposing with manly firmness his invasions on the rights of the people.

He has refused for a long time, after such dissolutions, to cause others to be elected; whereby the Legislative Powers, incapable of Annihilation, have returned to the People at large for their exercise; the State remaining in the mean time exposed to all the dangers of invasion from without, and convulsions within.

He has endeavoured to prevent the population of these States; for that purpose obstructing the Laws of Naturalization of Foreigners; refusing to pass others to encourage their migration higher, and raising the conditions of new Appropriations of Lands.

He has obstructed the Administration of Justice, by refusing his Assent to Laws for establishing Judiciary powers.

He has made Judges dependent on his Will alone, for the tenure of their offices, and the amount and payment of their salaries.

He has erected a multitude of New Offices, and sent hither swarms of Officers to harass our People, and eat out their substance.

He has kept among us in times of peace, Standing Armies without the Consent of our legislature.

He has affected to render the Military independent of and superior to the Civil power.

He has combined with others to subject us to a jurisdiction foreign to our constitution, and unacknowledged by our laws; giving his Assent to their acts of pretended Legislation.

For quartering large bodies of armed troops among us:

For protecting them, by a mock Trial, from punishment for any Murders which they should commit on the inhabitants of these States:

For cutting off our Trade with all parts of the world.

For imposing taxes on us without our Consent:

For depriving us in many cases, of the benefits of Trial by Jury:

For transporting us beyond Seas to be tried for pretended offences:

For abolishing the free System of English Laws in a neighbouring Province, establishing therein an Arbitrary government, and enlarging its Boundaries so as to render it at once an example and fit instrument for introducing the same absolute rule into these Colonies.

For taking away our Charters, abolishing our most valuable Laws, and altering fundamentally the Forms of our Governments:

For suspending our own Legislature, and declaring themselves invested with Power to legislate for us in all cases whatsoever.

He has abdicated Government here, by declaring us out of his Protection and waging War against us.

He has plundered our seas, ravaged our Coasts, burnt our towns, and destroyed the lives of our people.

He is at this time transporting large Armies of foreign Mercenaries to compleat the works of death, desolation and tyranny, already begun with circumstances of Cruelty & perfidy scarcely paralleled in the most barbarous ages, and totally unworthy the Head of a civilized nation.

He has constrained our fellow Citizens taken Captive on the high Seas to bear Arms against their Country, to become the executioners of their friends and Brethren, or to fall themselves by their Hands.

He has excited domestic insurrections amongst us, and has endeavoured to bring on the inhabitants of our frontiers, the merciless Indian Savages, whose known rule of warfare, is an undistinguished destruction of all ages, sexes and conditions.

In every stage of these Oppressions We have Petitioned for Redress in the most humble terms: Our repeated Petitions have been answered only by repeated injury. A Prince, whose character is thus marked by every act which may define a Tyrant, is unfit to be the ruler of a free People.

Nor have We been wanting in attention to our British brethren. We have warned them from time to time of attempts by their legislature to extend an unwarrantable jurisdiction over us. We have reminded them of the circumstances of our emigration and settlement here. We have appealed to their native justice and magnanimity, and we have conjured them by the ties of our common kindred to disavow these usurpations, which, would inevitably interrupt our connections and correspondence. They too have been deaf to the voice of justice and of consanguinity. We must, therefore, acquiesce in the necessity, which denounces our Separation, and hold them, as we hold the rest of mankind, Enemies in War, in Peace Friends.

We, therefore, the Representatives of the United States of America, in General Congress, Assembled, appealing to the Supreme Judge of the world for the rectitude of our intentions, do, in the Name, and by Authority of the good People of these Colonies, solemnly publish and declare, That these United Colonies are, and of right ought to be Free and Independent States; that they are Absolved from all Allegiance to the British Crown, and that all political connection between them and the State of Great Britain, is and ought to be totally dissolved; and that as Free and Independent States, they have full Power to levy War, conclude Peace, contract Alliances, establish Commerce, and to do all other Acts and Things which Independent States may of right do. And for the support of this Declaration, with a firm reliance on the protection of divine Providence, we mutually pledge to each other our Lives, our Fortunes and our sacred Honor.

APPENDIX B

THE CONSTITUTION OF THE UNITED STATES

Outline of the Constitution

Article I	The Legislative Branch	The three branches of government
Article II	The Executive Branch	
Article III	The Judicial Branch	
Article IV	States and Territories	The other partners in the federal system
Article V	Amendments	A mechanism for changing the Constitution
Article VI	Supremacy Article	Establishes federal supremacy
Article VII	Ratification	Gets the whole thing started

[Italic type indicates passages that were altered by later amendments, which are specified in the notes.]

B-2 APPENDIX B

[1] The *Preamble* "walks before" the Constitution and is used to understand the "intention of the framers." This is a compact among *people*, not *states* (an important distinction when the federal government seeks to limit states' power).

We the People of the United States, in Order to form a more perfect Union, establish Justice, insure domestic Tranquility, provide for the common defence, promote the general Welfare, and secure the Blessings of Liberty to ourselves and our Posterity, do ordain and establish this Constitution for the United States of America.[1]

Article I

Section 1 All legislative Powers herein granted shall be vested in a Congress of the United States, which shall consist of a Senate and House of Representatives.

Section 2 The House of Representatives shall be composed of Members chosen every second Year by the People of the several States, and the Electors in each State shall have the Qualifications requisite for Electors of the most numerous Branch of the State Legislature.[2]

[2] Voting qualifications for national elections are determined by each state, subject to federal limitations (see Amendments 15, 19, 24, 26).

No Person shall be a Representative who shall not have attained to the age of twenty-five Years, and been seven Years a Citizen of the United States, and who shall not, when elected, be an Inhabitant of that State in which he shall be chosen.

[3] "Other persons" means slaves. The word *slavery* does not appear in the Constitution until Amendment 13, which abolishes it. Also see Amendment 14.

Representatives and direct Taxes shall be apportioned among the several States which may be included within this Union, according to their respective Numbers, *which shall be determined by adding to the whole Number of free Persons, including those bound to Service for a Term of Years*, and excluding Indians not taxed, *three fifths of all other persons*.[3] The actual Enumeration shall be made within three Years after the first Meeting of the Congress of the United States, and within every subsequent Term of ten Years, in such Manner as they shall by Law direct. The Number of Representatives shall not exceed one for every thirty Thousand, but each State shall have at Least one Representative; and until such enumeration shall be made, the State of New Hampshire shall be entitled to chuse three, Massachusetts eight, Rhode-Island and Providence Plantations one, Connecticut five, New-York six, New Jersey four, Pennsylvania eight, Delaware one, Maryland six, Virginia ten, North Carolina five, South Carolina five, and Georgia three.[4]

[4] Until 1912, the House of Representatives grew as the country grew, adding members to represent new states and enlarged populations. Since that time the membership has been fixed at 435, resulting in larger districts with every census (currently more than a half million constituents for every member of the House).

When vacancies happen in the Representation from any State, the Executive Authority thereof shall issue Writs of Election to fill such Vacancies.

[5] "Impeachment" is only the formal charge of wrongdoing, like an indictment; removal from office is a separate task—the Senate's.

The House of Representatives shall chuse their Speaker and other Officers; and shall have the sole Power of Impeachment.[5]

Section 3 The Senate of the United States shall be composed of two Senators from each State, *chosen by the Legislature thereof,*[6] for six Years; and each Senator shall have one Vote.

[6]See Amendment 17.

Immediately after they shall be assembled in Consequence of the first Election, they shall be divided as equally as may be into three Classes. The Seats of the Senators of the first Class shall be vacated at the Expiration of the second Year, of the second Class at the Expiration of the fourth Year, and of the third Class at the Expiration of the sixth Year, so that one third may be chosen every second Year; *and if Vacancies happen by Resignation, or otherwise, during the Recess of the Legislature of any State, the Executive thereof may make temporary Appointments until the next Meeting of the Legislature, which shall then fill such Vacancies.*[7]

[7]See Amendment 17.

No Person shall be a Senator who shall not have attained to the Age of thirty Years, and been nine Years a Citizen of the United States, and who shall not, when elected, be an Inhabitant of that State for which he shall be chosen.

The Vice President of the United States shall be President of the Senate, but shall have no Vote, unless they be equally divided.[8]

[8]Today the Senate majority leader (as a *party* official, unanticipated here) "leads" the Senate. The vice-president seldom presides in the Senate, and the position is almost entirely ceremonial.

The Senate shall choose their other Officers, and also a President pro tempore, in the Absence of the Vice President, or when he shall exercise the Office of President of the United States.

The Senate shall have the sole Power to try all Impeachments. When sitting for that Purpose, they shall be on Oath or Affirmation. When the President of the United States is tried, the Chief Justice shall preside: And no Person shall be convicted without the Concurrence of two thirds of the Members present.

Judgment in Cases of Impeachment shall not extend further than to removal from Office, and disqualification to hold and enjoy any Office of honor, Trust or Profit under the United States: but the Party convicted shall nevertheless be liable and subject to Indictment, Trial, Judgment and Punishment, according to Law.[9]

[9]The Watergate special prosecutor decided that Richard Nixon, as a sitting president, could not be indicted (he was termed "an unindicted co-conspirator" by the grand jury); but because he might have been indicted *after* leaving office, Nixon was granted a controversial pardon by his successor, Gerald Ford.

Section 4 The Times, Places and Manner of holding Elections for Senators, and Representatives, shall be prescribed in each State by the Legislature thereof; but the Congress may at any time by Law make or alter such Regulations, except as to the Places of chusing Senators.

The Congress shall assemble at least once in a Year, and such Meeting shall be on the first Monday in December, unless they shall by Law appoint a different Day.[10]

[10]See Amendment 20.

Section 5 Each House shall be the Judge of the Elections, Returns and Qualifications of its own Members, and a Majority of each shall constitute a Quorum to do Business; but a smaller Number may adjourn from day to day, and may be authorized to compel the At-

APPENDIX B

[11] Congress monitors itself. A central assumption of our system is that competing political interests will eventually detect and correct wrongdoing and bad policy. "Eventually" sometimes takes a while.

[12] Regular pay and extensive staff support allow Congress to be "professionalized"—members can devote full time to their legislative tasks. (Increasingly, though, they spend large portions of time raising money for their own elections.)

[13] Immunity from slander and libel charges is extended to speeches on the floor, in committee, or in the *Congressional Record* (which includes vast amounts of text never uttered in either house); the protection does *not* apply to members' newsletters.

[14] Members of Congress cannot simultaneously serve in the executive branch (as they can in parliamentary governments) or in the judiciary. The separation of powers is absolute in terms of personnel. Unfortunately, this separation frees presidents from the often healthy requirement of having to formulate and defend policy in open debate.

[15] Even a *threatened* veto increases the president's ability to persuade Congress on policy issues. But the veto is a blunt, all-or-nothing weapon that does not allow the removal of particular provisions in a bill. A line-item veto would certainly alter this, but would it be an improvement? Does the president already have too much power over legislation? Before deciding, remember that we never know who the *next* president will be.

tendance of absent Members, in such Manner, and under such Penalties as each House may provide.

Each House may determine the Rules of its Proceedings, punish its Members for disorderly Behavior, and, with the Concurrence of two thirds, expel a Member.[11]

Each House shall keep a Journal of its Proceedings, and from time to time publish the same, excepting such Parts as may in their Judgment require Secrecy; and the Yeas and Nays of the Members of either House on any question shall, at the Desire of one fifth of those Present, be entered on the Journal.

Neither House, during the Session of Congress, shall, without the Consent of the other, adjourn for more than three days, nor to any other Place than that in which the two Houses shall be sitting.

Section 6 The Senators and Representatives shall receive a Compensation for their Services, to be ascertained by Law, and paid out of the Treasury of the United States.[12] They shall in all Cases, except Treason, Felony and Breach of the Peace, be privileged from Arrest during their Attendance at the Session of their respective Houses, and in going and returning from the same; and for any Speech or Debate in either House, they shall not be questioned in any other Place.[13]

No Senator or Representative shall, during the Time for which he was elected, be appointed to any civil Office under the Authority of the United States, which shall have been created, or the Emoluments whereof shall have been encreased during such time; and no Person holding any Office under the United States, shall be a Member of either House during his Continuance in Office.[14]

Section 7 All Bills for raising Revenue shall originate in the House of Representatives; but the Senate may propose or concur with Amendments as on other Bills.

Every Bill which shall have passed the House of Representatives and the Senate, shall, before it become a Law, be presented to the President of the United States; if he approve he shall sign it, but if not he shall return it, with his Objections to that House in which it shall have originated, who shall enter the Objections at large on their Journal, and proceed to reconsider it.[15] If after such Reconsideration two thirds of that House shall agree to pass the Bill, it shall be sent, together with the Objections, to the other House, by which it shall likewise be reconsidered, and if approved by two thirds of that House, it shall become a Law. But in all such Cases the Votes of both Houses shall be determined by Yeas and Nays, and the Names of the Persons voting for and against the Bill shall be entered on the Journal of each House respectively. If any Bill shall not be returned by the

President within ten Days (Sundays excepted) after it shall have been presented to him, the Same shall be a Law, in like Manner as if he had signed it, unless Congress by their Adjournment prevent its Return, in which Case it shall not be a Law.

Every Order, Resolution, or Vote to which the Concurrence of the Senate and House of Representatives may be necessary (except on a question of Adjournment) shall be presented to the President of the United States; and before the Same shall take Effect, shall be approved by him, or being disapproved by him, shall be repassed by two thirds of the Senate and House of Representatives, according to the Rules and Limitations prescribed in the Case of a Bill.[16]

Section 8 The Congress shall have Power to lay and collect Taxes, Duties, Imposts, and Excises, to pay the Debts and provide for the common Defence and general Welfare of the United States;[17] but all Duties, Imposts and Excises shall be uniform throughout the United States;

To borrow Money on the credit of the United States;

To regulate Commerce with foreign Nations, and among the several States, and with the Indian Tribes;[18]

To establish an uniform Rule of Naturalization, and uniform Laws on the subject of Bankruptcies throughout the United States;

To coin Money, regulate the Value thereof, and of foreign Coin, and fix the Standard of Weights and Measures;

To provide for the Punishment of counterfeiting the Securities and Current Coin of the United States;

To establish Post Offices and post Roads;

To promote the Progress of Science and useful Arts, by securing for limited Times to Authors and Inventors the exclusive Right to their respective Writings and Discoveries:

To constitute Tribunals inferior to the Supreme Court;[19]

To define and punish Piracies and Felonies committed on the high Seas and Offences against the Law of Nations;

To declare War,[20] grant letters of Marque, and Reprisal, and make Rules concerning Captures on Land and Water;

To raise and support Armies, but no Appropriation of Money to that Use shall be for a longer Term than two Years;

To provide and maintain a Navy;

To make Rules for the Government and Regulation of the land and naval Forces;[21]

To provide for calling forth the Militia to execute the Laws of the Union, suppress Insurrections and repel Invasions:

[16]The "presentment" requirement is one that the Supreme Court, in *INS* v. *Chadha* (462 U.S. 919 [1983]), found missing from the legislative veto; see Chap. 13. Requiring decisions to be shared across branches lets competing interests frame the issues in full, open debate. But it also slows things down and sometimes stymies policymaking.

[17]Section 8 lists the power of Congress, and thus of the federal government, representing, in positive form, complaints about the weaknesses of the Articles of Confederation. The "firm league of friendship" that the Articles created was replaced by a government that did not need the friendship of the states to carry out its will. Then, as now, the economy and national defense were dominant issues, as most of the following clauses demonstrate.

[18]The "interstate commerce clause" has been used to justify much federal activity in the twentieth century. Chief Justice John Marshall pointed out in 1824 (*Gibbons* v. *Ogden*, 9 Wheaton 1) that this clause reads "among" the states—not just between them—allowing the federal government to control commerce *within* states. In *Wickard* v. *Filburn* (317 U.S. 111 [1942]) the Supreme Court agreed that federal interstate commerce power extended even to twelve acres of wheat intended for use on the same small Ohio farm where it was grown.

[19]The vast power of the federal judiciary derives from the ability of Congress to establish a complete system of federal courts to implement federal policy.

[20]In our era of "troop incursions," "insurgency," and "counterinsurgency," declarations of war appear as relics of an ancient time. No war was declared in Korea, Vietnam, or

APPENDIX B

To provide for organizing, arming, and disciplining, the Militia, and for governing such Part of them as may be employed in the Service of the United States, reserving to the States respectively, the Appointment of the Officers, and the Authority of training the Militia according to the discipline prescribed by Congress;[22]

To exercise exclusive Legislation in all Cases whatsoever, over such District (not exceeding ten Miles square) as may, by Cession of particular States, and the Acceptance of Congress, become the Seat of the Government of the United States,[23] and to exercise like Authority over all Places purchased by the Consent of the Legislature of the State in which the Same shall be, for the Erection of Forts, Magazines, Arsenals, dock-Yards, and other needful Buildings;—And

To make all Laws which shall be necessary and proper for carrying into Execution the foregoing Powers, and all other Powers vested by this Constitution in the Government of the United States, or in any Department or Officer thereof.[24]

Section 9 The Migration or Importation of such Persons as any of the States now existing shall think proper to admit, shall not be prohibited by the Congress prior to the Year one thousand eight hundred and eight, but a Tax or duty may be imposed on such Importation, not exceeding ten dollars for each Person.[25]

The Privilege of the Writ of Habeas Corpus shall not be suspended, unless when in Cases of Rebellion or Invasion the public Safety may require it.[26]

No Bill of Attainder or ex post facto Law shall be passed.[27]

No Capitation, or other direct, Tax shall be laid, unless in Proportion to the Census or Enumeration herein before directed to be taken.

No Tax or Duty shall be laid on Articles exported from any State.

No Preference shall be given any Regulation of Commerce or Revenue to the Ports of one State over those of another; nor shall Vessels bound to, or from, one State, be obliged to enter, clear, or pay Duties in another.

No Money shall be drawn from the Treasury, but in Consequence of Appropriations made by Law; and a regular Statement and Account of the Receipts and Expenditures of all public Money shall be published from time to time.[28]

No title of Nobility shall be granted by the United States: And no Person holding any Office of Profit or Trust under them, shall, without the Consent of the Congress, accept of any present, Emolument, Office, or Title, of any kind whatever, from any King, Prince, or foreign State.

Operation Desert Storm in the Persian Gulf. Under modern circumstances is there any way for Congress and the president to share the war power as the framers intended? (See Chapter 13 on the War Powers Resolution.)

[21] Active members of the armed forces are subject to the Uniform Code of Military Justice and do *not* enjoy all the constitutional rights of civilians. Presumably, such rights would make military discipline impossible.

[22] In 1957, when Gov. Orval Faubus used the Arkansas National Guard to help to maintain segregation at Little Rock High School in defiance of a federal court, President Eisenhower called the Guard to national service, thus using the same troops to *integrate* the school.

[23] If one is caught speeding in the District of Columbia or on an army base, it's a federal offense. Despite common usage, then, a "federal offense" is not necessarily more serious than an offense against state law. Most criminal prosecutions are state matters.

[24] This is the "elastic clause," the basis of the federal government's *implied powers*—as in the power to charter a bank in *McCulloch* v. *Maryland* (4 Wheaton 316 [1819]; see Chapter 4).

[25] Section 9 lists what the federal government *cannot* do, including here a shameful provision protecting slavery for the first twenty years of the new government.

[26] *Habeus corpus* is a legal means of having a judge verify grounds for imprisonment, although this clause recognizes exceptions. Courts rarely interfere with military authority during wartime but have overturned military decisions after the conflict (see Ex parte *Milligan*, 4 Wallace 2 [1866]).

[27] Under a *bill of attainder* a legislature functions as a court, convict-

Section 10 No State shall enter into any Treaty, Alliance, or Confederation; grant Letters of Marque and Reprisal; coin Money; emit Bills of Credit; make any Thing but gold and silver Coin a Tender in Payment of Debts; pass any Bill of Attainder, ex post facto Law, or Law impairing the Obligation of Contracts, or Grant any Title of Nobility.[29]

No state shall, without the Consent of the Congress, lay any Imposts or Duties on Imports or Exports, except what may be absolutely necessary for executing its inspection Laws: and the net Produce of all Duties and Imposts, laid by any State on Imports or Exports, shall be for the Use of the Treasury of the United States; and all such Laws be subject to the Revision and Control of the Congress.

No State shall, without the Consent of Congress, lay any Duty of Tonnage, keep Troops, or Ships of War in time of Peace, enter into any Agreement or Compact with another State, or with a foreign Power, or engage in War, unless actually invaded, or in such imminent Danger as will not admit of delay.

Article II

Section 1 The executive Power shall be vested in a President of the United States of America. He shall hold his Office during the Term of four Years, and, together with the Vice President, chosen for the same Term be elected as follows:[30]

Each State shall appoint, in such Manner as the Legislature thereof may direct, a Number of Electors, equal to the whole Number of Senators and Representatives to which the State may be entitled in the Congress; but no Senator or Representative, or Person holding an Office of Trust or Profit under the United States, shall be appointed an Elector.[31]

The Electors shall meet in their respective States, and vote by Ballot for two Persons, of whom one at least shall not be an Inhabitant of the same State with themselves.[32] *And they shall make a List of all Persons voted for, and of the Number of Votes for each; which List they shall sign and certify, and transmit sealed to the Seat of the Government of the United States, directed to the President of the Senate. The President of the Senate shall, in the Presence of the Senate and House of Representatives, open all the Certificates, and the Votes shall then be counted. The Person having the greatest Number of Votes shall be the President, if such Number*

ing and punishing individuals by legislation.

An *ex post facto law* creates criminal liability or increases criminal penalties for actions in the past.

[28]This published "Account of the Receipts and Expenditures of all public Money" does not include the CIA's budget, nor can it practically include large sums of money spent for national security.

[29]Following Section 9 restrictions on the federal government, Section 10 lists what states cannot do. Similar provisions here and in Section 9—such as the prohibition of bills of attainder and ex post facto laws—mean that *no* government in the United States can engage in these activities.

The "Obligation of Contracts" clause reveals the framers' fear that debtors, who naturally far outnumber creditors in our system, would prevail on states to wipe out debts through legislation. The Supreme Court had to stretch a bit to get around this clause in saving the Minnesota Mortgage Moratorium Act during the Great Depression (*Home Building and Loan Association* v. *Blaisdell*, 290 U.S. 398 [1934]).

[30]The short length of Article II and its position *after* the legislative article indicate that the framers viewed Congress as the focus of government. This century has seen a steady shifting of emphasis to the executive branch in the development of national policy (see Chapters 13 and 14).

[31]The electoral college may seem anachronistic today, but it does increase the influence of certain groups and state actors who are unwilling to give it up. It also tends to increase the apparent margin of victory for a successful candidate, which, according to some, makes it easier for the new president to govern. Don't look for any change here soon. (See Chap. 14.)

be a Majority of the whole Number of Electors appointed; and if there be more than one who have such Majority, and have an equal Number of Votes, then the House of Representatives shall immediately chuse by Ballot one of them for President; and if no Person have a Majority, then from the five highest on the List the said House shall in like Manner chuse the President. But in chusing the President, the votes shall be taken by States, the Representation from each State having one Vote; A quorum for this purpose shall consist of a Member or Members from two thirds of the States, and a majority of all the States shall be necessary to a Choice. In every Case, after the Choice of the President, the Person having the Greatest Number of Votes of the Electors shall be the Vice President. But if there should remain two or more who have equal Votes, the Senate shall chuse from them by Ballot the Vice President.[33]

The Congress may determine the time of chusing the Electors, and the Day on which they shall give their Votes; which Day shall be the same throughout the United States.

No Person except a natural born Citizen, or a Citizen of the United States, at the time of the Adoption of this Constitution, shall be eligible to the Office of President; neither shall any Person be eligible to that Office who shall not have attained to the Age of thirty-five Years, and been fourteen Years a Resident within the United States.

The Case of the Removal of the President from Office, or of his Death, Resignation, or Inability to discharge the Powers and Duties of the said Office, the Same shall devolve on the Vice President, and the Congress may by Law provide for the Case of Removal, Death, Resignation, or Inability, both of the President and Vice President, declaring what Officer shall then act as President, and such Officer shall act accordingly, until the Disability be removed, or a President shall be elected.[34]

The President shall, at stated Times, receive for his Services, a Compensation which shall neither be encreased nor diminished during the Period for which he shall have been elected, and he shall not receive within that Period any other Emolument from the United States, or any of them.

Before he enter on the Execution of his Office, he shall take the following Oath or Affirmation:—"I do solemnly swear (or affirm) that I will faithfully execute the Office of President of the United States, and will to the best of my Ability, preserve, protect, and defend the Constitution of the United States."

Section 2 The President shall be Commander in Chief of the Army and Navy of the United States; and of the Militia of the several

---

[32] The bizarre circumstances of the election of 1800 demonstrated the weaknesses of the following provisions and caused the Constitution, indirectly, to acknowledge the existence of political parties. Thomas Jefferson and Aaron Burr, running on the same ticket, tied in electoral college votes, throwing the election into the House of Representatives (which was controlled by the Federalists, whose candidate, incumbent President John Adams, had lost). Although Burr was originally understood to be the vice-presidential candidate, the tie produced much behind-the-scenes maneuvering in the House. This was resolved only when Alexander Hamilton threw his support behind his old rival, Jefferson. Four years later, Hamilton was killed by Burr in a duel.

The fact that the Constitution does not make political parties a formal part of the governing scheme has had some negative consequences. Southern segregationists for years excluded blacks from political participation by barring them from "private" party functions (which were the sole avenue to public office). The Supreme Court originally agreed with that practice, but in 1944 ruled that Amendment 15 prohibits a party's primary from being restricted to white persons (see *Smith* v. *Allwright*, 321 U.S. 649).

[33] See Amendment 12.

[34] Congress has provided for a line of succession that starts with the Speaker of the House of Representatives and the president pro tempore of the Senate before moving to cabinet officers, but Amendment 25 makes the use of this line of succession most unlikely.

States, when called into the actual service of the United States; he may require the Opinion, in writing, of the principal Officer in each of the executive Departments, upon any Subject relating to the Duties of their respective Offices, and he shall have Power to grant Reprieves and Pardons for Offences against the United States, except in Case of Impeachment.[35]

He shall have Power, by and with the Advice and Consent of the Senate, to make Treaties, provided two thirds of the Senators present concur;[36] and he shall nominate, and by and with the Advice and Consent of the Senate, shall appoint Ambassadors, and other public Ministers and Consuls, Judges of the supreme Court, and all other Officers of the United States, whose Appointments are not herein otherwise provided for, and which shall be established by Law;[37] but the Congress may by Law vest the Appointment of such inferior Officers, as they think proper, in the President alone, in the Courts of Law, or in the Heads of Departments.

The President shall have Power to fill up all Vacancies that may happen during the Recess of the Senate, by granting Commissions which shall expire at the End of their next Session.

Section 3 He shall from time to time give to the Congress Information of the State of the Union, and recommend to their Consideration such Measures as he shall judge necessary and expedient;[38] he may, on extraordinary Occasions, convene both Houses, or either of them, and in Case of Disagreement between them, with Respect to the Time of Adjournment, he may adjourn them to such Time as he shall think proper; he shall receive Ambassadors and other public Ministers, he shall take Care that the Laws be faithfully executed, and shall Commission all the Officers of the United States.

Section 4 The President, Vice President, and all civil Officers of the United States, shall be removed from Office on Impeachment for, and Conviction of, Treason, Bribery, or other High Crimes and Misdemeanors.[39]

Article III

Section 1 The judicial Power of the United States, shall be vested in one supreme Court and in such inferior Courts as the Congress may from time to time ordain and establish.[40] The Judges, both of the supreme and inferior Courts, shall hold their Offices during good Behavior, and shall, at stated Times, receive for their Services, a Compensation, which shall not be diminished during their Continuance in Office.

[35] Compare this relatively puny list of presidential powers with those reserved for Congress in Article I, Section 8. The enormous influence that presidents can exercise over U.S. policy comes not from this list but from the opportunities that the presidency offers to inspire, goad, and guide the nation.

[36] Presidents may also sign executive agreements with other governments without Senate ratification, and these may have the legal force of treaties.

[37] The president's appointment power is important—especially for judicial appointments—but it is subject to Senate confirmation. Should the Senate refuse to confirm a nominee based on policy difference or only when the competence of the person is in question? Should presidents seek nominees with no public record on controversial issues, as Bush did with David Souter?

[38] The annual State of the Union address lets the president set before Congress and the nation the outlines of the administration's agenda for the year.

[39] What is a "high crime"? The Constitution doesn't say. In the debate about impeaching Supreme Court Justice William O. Douglas, House Minority Leader Gerald Ford claimed that "high crimes" meant whatever the House decided it meant.

[40] The Constitution establishes only one court, the Supreme Court, on the assumption that at least initially, state courts would be competent to decide matters of federal law. The first major legislation under this Constitution, the Judiciary Act of 1789, took advantage of the power here (and in Article I, Section 8) to create inferior federal courts. Thus every state has two separate court systems, one federal and one state. (See Chapter 16.)

[41] In general, federal jurisdiction exists only when certain *laws* or certain *parties* are involved. The provisions here make sense: Broadly, if federal law (Constitution, statute, or treaty) is involved, if the federal government is a party to the case, or if the parties come from across state boundaries, the case can be heard by a federal court. Amendment 11 returns to the states only part of the prerogative of sovereign entities not to be taken to court without their own permission.

[42] As a practical matter, the Supreme Court does *not* exercise its original jurisdiction—it doesn't have time to conduct trials, so it leaves that to lower federal or state courts.

[43] The right to trial by jury in *civil* (not criminal) cases is guaranteed in Amendment 7.

[44] "Treason" was (and still is, in many places) a convenient charge for governments to use in dispensing with political opponents. The framers took special care here to define treason and to establish specific legal requirements to prove such a charge.

[45] A *corruption of blood* is, literally, visiting the sins of the fathers upon the sons, or imposing penalties on the children and grandchildren of a wrongdoers—a strategy inconsistent with individual responsibility.

[46] Section 1 of Article IV concerns the relations of states to other states; Section 2 concerns the relations of states to *citizens* of other states. Both sections prescribe a sort of golden rule of fair play. Section 2 does not prevent a state from charging out-of-state tuition in its public universities and colleges, for example, but it would prohibit state courts from giving preferential treatment to state residents.

Section 2 The Judicial Power shall extend to all Cases, in Law and Equity, arising under this Constitution, the Laws of the United States, and Treaties made, or which shall be made, under their Authority;—to all Cases affecting Ambassadors, other public Ministers and Consuls;—to all Cases of admiralty and maritime Jurisdiction;—to Controversies to which the United States shall be a Party;—to Controversies between two or more States;—*between a State and Citizens of another State*;—between Citizens of different States;—between Citizens of the same State claiming Lands under Grants of different states, *and between a State, or the Citizens thereof, and foreign States, Citizens, or Subjects.*[41]

In all cases affecting Ambassadors, other public Ministers and Consuls, and those in which a State shall be Party, the supreme Court shall have original Jurisdiction.[42] In all the other Cases before mentioned, the supreme Court shall have appellate Jurisdiction, both as to Law and Fact, with such Exceptions, and under such Regulations as the Congress shall make.

The Trial of all Crimes, except in Cases of Impeachment, shall be by Jury; and such Trial shall be held in the State where the said Crimes shall have been committed; but when not committed within any State, the Trial shall be at such Place or Places as the Congress may by Law have directed.[43]

Section 3 Treason against the United States, shall consist only in levying War against them, or in adhering to their Enemies, giving them Aid and Comfort. No person shall be convicted of Treason unless on the Testimony of two Witnesses to the same overt Act, or on Confession in open Court.[44]

The Congress shall have Power to declare the Punishment of Treason, but no Attainder of Treason shall work Corruption of Blood, or Forfeiture except during the Life of the Person attainted.[45]

Article IV

Section 1 Full Faith and Credit shall be given in each State to the public Acts, Records, and judicial Proceedings of every other State. And the Congress may by general Laws prescribe the Manner in which such Acts, Records, and Proceedings shall be proved, and the Effect thereof.

Section 2 The Citizens of each State shall be entitled to all Privileges and Immunities of Citizens in the several states.[46]

A Person charged in any State with Treason, Felony, or other

Crime, who shall flee from Justice, and be found in another State, shall on Demand of the executive Authority of the State from which he fled, be delivered up, to be removed to the State having Jurisdiction of the Crime.

No Person held to Service or Labour in one State, under the Laws thereof, escaping into another, shall in Consequence of any Law or Regulation therein, be discharged from such Service or Labour, but shall be delivered up on Claim of the Party to whom such Service or Labour may be due.[47]

Section 3 New States may be admitted by the Congress into this Union; but no new State shall be formed or erected within the Jurisdiction of any other State; nor any State be formed by the Junction of two or more States, or Parts of States, without the Consent of the Legislatures of the States concerned as well as of the Congress.[48]

The Congress shall have Power to dispose of and make all needful Rules and Regulations respecting the Territory or other Property belonging to the United States; and nothing in this Constitution shall be so construed as to Prejudice any claims of the United States, or of any particular State.

Section 4 The United States shall guarantee to every State in this Union a Republican Form of Government, and shall protect each of them against Invasion;[49] and on Application of the Legislature, or of the Executive (when the Legislature cannot be convened) against domestic Violence.

Article V

The Congress, whenever two thirds of both Houses shall deem it necessary, shall propose Amendments to this Constitution, or, on the Application of the Legislatures of two thirds of the several States, shall call a Convention for proposing Amendments,[50] which, in either Case, shall be valid to all Intents and Purposes, as Part of this Constitution, when ratified by the Legislatures of three fourths of the several States, or by Conventions in three fourths thereof, as the one or the other Mode of Ratification may be proposed by the Congress;[51] Provided that no Amendment which may be made prior to the Year One thousand eight hundred and eight shall in any Manner affect the first and fourth Clauses in the Ninth Section of the first Article; and that no State, without its Consent, shall be deprived of its equal Suffrage in the Senate.

[47] Another of the constitutional provisions protecting slavery without mentioning it by name. See Amendment 13.

[48] The formation of new states was, for a time, bound up with the issue of slavery. Particularly striking was the case of West Virginia (a mountainous region where slave-based agriculture had never been feasible), which was created from the territory of Virginia at the onset of the Civil War.

[49] What is a "republican form" of government? One that is responsive, but not directly, to the people. But the simplicity of such a definition is often hard to apply (see Chapter 1). The "republican guarantee" clause is now considered a nonjusticiable political question: A complaint under it must be addressed to Congress or the president, not to the courts. See *Luther v. Borden* (7 Howard 1 [1849]), a case arising from claims of two opposed governments to the rightful rule of Rhode Island.

[50] Although a convention to propose amendments has never been called, the *threat* of it, represented by numerous state petitions calling for one, has several times prompted Congress to propose amendments that would not otherwise have been proposed.

[51] With one exception, the task of ratification has always been given to state legislatures. The repeal of Prohibition (see Amendments 18 and 21) was the exception—state legislators were glad to have Congress designate the state convention method for resolving that sticky issue.

Article VI

All Debts contracted and Engagements entered into, before the Adoption of this Constitution, shall be as valid against the United States under this Constitution, as under the Confederation.

This Constitution, and the Laws of the United States which shall be made in Pursuance thereof; and all Treaties made, or which shall be made, under the Authority of the United States, shall be the supreme Law of the Land; and the Judges in every State shall be bound thereby, any Thing in the Constitution or Laws of any State to the Contrary notwithstanding.[52]

The Senators and Representatives before mentioned, and the Members of the several State Legislatures, and all executive and judicial Officers, both of the United States and of the several States, shall be bound by Oath or Affirmation, to support this Constitution;[53] but no religious Test shall ever be required as a Qualification to any Office or public Trust under the United States.[54]

Article VII

The Ratification of the Conventions of nine States, shall be sufficient for the Establishment of this Constitution between the States so ratifying the Same.[55]

Done in Convention by the Unanimous Consent of the States[56] present the Seventeenth Day of September in the Year of our Lord one thousand seven hundred and eighty seven and of the Independence of the United States of America the twelfth. In witness whereof We have hereunto subscribed our Names.

* * *

Articles in addition to, and amendment of, the Constitution of the United States of America, proposed by Congress, and ratified by the several States, pursuant to the fifth Article of the original Constitution.[57]

Amendment 1

Congress shall make no law respecting an establishment of religion, or prohibiting the free exercise thereof; or abridging the freedom of speech, or of the press; or the right of the people peaceably to assemble, and to petition the Government for a redress of grievances.[58]

---

[52] The "supremacy clause" explicitly makes all federal law superior to state law and constitutions. Like the "elastic clause" (Article I, Section 8), this provision justifies certain federal powers. For example, in *Missouri* v. *Holland* (252 U.S. 416 [1920]), the use of federal power to protect migratory birds was justified on the basis of a treaty with Canada.

[53] The difference between an oath (before God) and an affirmation (before fellow citizens) is significant to certain groups like the Society of Friends (Quakers), whose religious beliefs forbid oaths.

[54] Although this passage forbids religious tests for public office, it was 172 years before the first Catholic president (Kennedy, in 1961) and 127 years before the first Jewish member of the Supreme Court (Brandeis, in 1915).

[55] This article, rather like the starter on your car, has no function after the mechanism is set in motion.

[56] Notice the claim to the unanimous consent of the *states*. Actually, fifty-five men attended the convention; nineteen others were chosen but declined. Thirty-nine signed the final document, including Washington, Hamilton, Madison, and Franklin. Thomas Jefferson and John Adams were both in Europe on diplomatic missions.

[57] The first ten amendments form the federal *Bill of Rights*. These (and two never ratified) were proposed by the first Congress, in 1791. Most of these federal restrictions were later "incorporated" under Amendment 14.

[58] The "expression" rights in the First Amendment are central to our

Amendment 2

A well regulated Militia, being necessary to the security of a free State, the right of the people to keep and bear Arms, shall not be infringed.[59]

Amendment 3

No Soldier shall, in time of peace be quartered in any house, without the consent of the Owner, nor in time of war, but in a manner to be prescribed by law.[60]

Amendment 4

The right of the people to be secure in their persons, houses, papers, and effects, against unreasonable searches and seizures, shall not be violated, and no Warrants shall issue, but upon probable cause, supported by Oath or affirmation, and particularly describing the place to be searched, and the persons or things to be seized.[61]

Amendment 5

No person shall be held to answer for a capital, or otherwise infamous crime, unless on a presentment or indictment of a Grand Jury,[62] except in cases arising in the land or naval forces, or in the Militia, when in actual service in time of War or public danger; nor shall any person be subject for the same offence to be twice put in jeopardy of life or limb;[63] nor shall be compelled in any criminal case to be a witness against himself,[64] nor be deprived of life, liberty, or property, without due process of law;[65] nor shall private property be taken for public use, without just compensation.[66]

Amendment 6

In all criminal prosecutions, the accused shall enjoy the right to a speedy and public trial,[67] by an impartial jury of the State and district wherein the crime shall have been committed, which district shall have been previously ascertained by law, and to be informed of the nature and cause of the accusation; to be confronted with the wit-

understanding of democracy. Justice Hugo Black often pointed out the absolute language here ("*no law*"), but hard cases require *some* restriction, if only because these protections bump up against each other.

[59]Is our right to bear arms subordinate to states' rights to have militias? The Supreme Court tends to stay away from hotly contested policy matters, as with gun control.

[60]It's been a long time since "Guess who's coming to dinner?" included the possibility of an army regiment.

[61]Notice that we are protected only from *unreasonable* searches and seizures; most searches can be made "reasonable" through warrants secured from a judge or on the basis of "probable cause."

[62]A grand jury protects us from trumped-up charges, since the jury decides whether the prosecutor has enough evidence for a trial.

[63]The "double jeopardy" clause does not prevent a second trial if the first one was faulty (for example, if illegal evidence was admitted) or if the act constituted two separate offenses (assaulting a president in Atlanta, for example, violates both federal law and Georgia law and can result in two separate prosecutions).

[64]"Taking the Fifth" means refusing to testify against oneself. This provision cannot be used to avoid appearing in a lineup or giving fingerprints. But should it include the right to refuse to give blood, semen, or tissue samples for identification purposes?

[65]"Due process" is a very old con-

cept that has numerous applications. See Amendment 14.

[66] Do land use restrictions that greatly reduce property's value constitute "taking without just compensation"? That argument was used (unsuccessfully) against the first zoning laws and more recently against extensive environmental legislation.

[67] Many trials are not "speedy" in our system, which encourages delays from both sides. A case may take more than a year to come to trial, be many months in trial, and then take years to exhaust appeals. Partly because of this, most criminal proceedings are resolved before a full trial, often through plea bargaining.

[68] The right to counsel originally meant that a defendant's lawyer could not be excluded from the courtroom; now it means that if a defendant cannot afford a lawyer in a criminal trial, the government must provide one (*Gideon* v. *Wainwright*, 372 U.S. 335 [1963].)

[69] This amendment refers to *civil cases*, disputes between two parties in which the court acts as umpire. In *criminal cases* (see Amendment 6) the government prosecutes an individual for violating a criminal statute.

[70] Is capital punishment "cruel and unusual"? A majority of the Supreme Court has never said that it is per se, but the Court has agreed that it is so under certain circumstances. Capital punishment cannot be used against persons who were insane or under sixteen at the time of their crime, *Ford* v. *Wainwright* (477 US 399 [1986]), and *Thompson* v. *Oklahoma*, 487 US 1217 (1988).

ness against him; to have compulsory process for obtaining witness in his favor, and to have the Assistance of Counsel for his defence.[68]

Amendment 7

In Suits at common law, where the value in controversy shall exceed twenty dollars, the right of trial by jury shall be preserved, and no fact tried by a jury, shall be otherwise re-examined in any Court of the United States, than according to the rules of the common law.[69]

Amendment 8

Excessive bail shall not be required, nor excessive fines imposed, nor cruel and unusual punishments inflicted.[70]

Amendment 9

The enumeration in the Constitution, of certain rights, shall not be construed to deny or disparage others retained by the people.[71]

Amendment 10

The powers not delegated to the United States by the Constitution, nor prohibited by it to the States, are reserved to the States respectively, or to the people.[72]

Amendment 11   [January 8, 1798]

The Judicial power of the United States shall not be construed to extend to any suit in law or equity, commenced or prosecuted against one of the United States by Citizens of another State, or by Citizens or Subjects of any Foreign State.[73]

Amendment 12   [September 25, 1804]

The Electors shall meet in their respective states and vote by ballot for President and Vice President, one of whom, at least, shall not be an inhabitant of the same state with themselves;[74] they shall name in their ballots the person voted for as President, and in distinct ballots the person voted for as Vice President, and they shall make distinct lists of all persons voted for as President, and of all persons voted for as Vice President, and of the number of votes for each, which lists they shall sign and certify, and transmit sealed to the seat of the government of the United States, directed to the President of the Senate:—The President of the Senate shall, in the presence of the Senate and House of Representatives, open all the certificates and the votes shall then be counted;—The person having the greatest number of votes for President, shall be the President, if such number be a majority of the whole number of Electors appointed; and if no person have such majority, then from the persons having the highest numbers not exceeding three on the list of those voted for as President, the House of Representatives shall choose immediately, by ballot, the President. But in choosing the President, the votes shall be taken by states, the representation from each state having one vote; a quorum for this purpose shall consist of a member or members from two thirds of the states, and a majority of all the states shall be necessary to a choice. And if the House of Representatives shall not choose a President whenever the right of choice shall devolve upon them, *before the fourth day of March next following*,[75] then the Vice President shall act as President as in the case of the death or other constitutional disability of the President.—The person having the greatest number of votes as Vice President, shall be the Vice President, if such number be a majority of the whole number of Electors appointed, and if no person have a majority, then from the two highest numbers on the list, the Senate shall choose the Vice President; a quorum for the purpose shall consist of two-thirds of the whole number of Senators, and a majority of the whole number shall be necessary to a choice. But no person constitutionally ineligible to the office of President shall be eligible to that of Vice President of the United States.

Amendment 13   [December 18, 1865]

Section 1   Neither slavery nor involuntary servitude, except as a punishment for crime whereof the party shall have been duly convicted, shall exist within the United States, or any place subject to their jurisdiction.[76]

Section 2   Congress shall have power to enforce this article by appropriate legislation.

---

[71] One reason for not including a bill of rights in the original Constitution was that unlisted rights would be prejudiced. But how much protection does this passage give an unnamed right?

[72] A principle of constitutional interpretation is that every provision must have some legal effect. Is this amendment meant to be a barrier to federal action, or does it simply reflect the nature of the federal system? For arguments, see *National League of Cities* v. *Usery* (426 U.S. 833 [1976]) and *Garcia* v. *San Antonio Metropolitan Transit Authority* (469 U.S. 528 [985]).

[73] In *Chisholm* v. *Georgia* (2 Dallas 419 [1793]) a claim to recover a Revolutionary War debt against Georgia was allowed into a federal court. In response to that case, this amendment partly restores the states' sovereign ability to decide when to be sued.

[74] A reflection of the birth of political parties, this amendment separates the elections of the president and the vice-president in the electoral college. (See Article II, Section 1.)

[75] See Amendment 20.

[76] Amendments 13, 14, and 15 are the "Civil War amendments," which, combined, attempt to eliminate the institution of slavery and its effects—a process that remains incomplete well over a century later (see Chapters 5 and 6).

Amendment 14 [July 28, 1868]

Section 1 All persons born or naturalized in the United States, and subject to the jurisdiction thereof, are citizens of the United States and of the State wherein they reside. No state shall make or enforce any law which shall abridge the privileges or immunities of citizens of the United States; nor shall any state deprive any person of life, liberty, or property, without due process of law; nor deny to any person within its jurisdiction the equal protection of the laws.[77]

Section 2 Representatives shall be apportioned among the several States according to their respective numbers, counting the whole number of persons in each State, excluding Indians not taxed. But when the right to vote at any election for the choice of electors for President and Vice President of the United States, Representatives in Congress, the Executive and Judicial officers of a State, or the members of the Legislature thereof, is denied to any of the male inhabitants of such State, being twenty one years of age, and citizens of the United States, or in any way abridged, except for participation in rebellion, or other crime, the basis of representation therein shall be reduced in the proportion which the number of such male citizens shall bear to the whole number of male citizens twenty one years of age in such State.

Section 3 No person shall be a Senator or Representative in Congress, or elector of President and Vice President, or hold any office, civil or military, under the United States, or under any State who having previously taken an oath, as a member of Congress, or as an officer of the United States, or as a member of any State legislature, or as an executive or judicial officer of any State, to support the Constitution of the United States, shall have engaged in insurrection or rebellion against the same, or given aid or comfort to the enemies thereof. But Congress may by a vote of two thirds of each House remove such disability.[78]

Section 4 The validity of the public debt of the United States authorized by law, including debts incurred for payment of pensions and bounties for services in suppressing insurrection or rebellion shall not be questioned. But neither the United States nor any State shall assume or pay any debt or obligation incurred in aid of insurrection or rebellion against the United States, or any claim for the loss or emancipation of any slave; but all such debts, obligations, and claims shall be held illegal and void.[79]

Section 5 The Congress shall have power to enforce, by appropriate legislation, the provisions of this article.

---

[77] Amendment 14 is the most frequently litigated of all amendments, since it is the source of "incorporating" the Bill of Rights as protections against state action. It has three important clauses: (1) "privileges and immunities" (which was gutted by the *Slaughterhouse Cases* in 1873 and never recovered), (2) "due process" (an ancient notion applied to actions as diverse as the right of a baker to contract freely for his own labor without regard for maximum-working-hour laws [see *Lochner* v. *New York*, 198 U.S. 45 (1905)] and the right to view pornographic material in the privacy of one's home [see *Stanley* v. *Georgia*, 394 U.S. 557 (1969)]), and (3) "equal protection," which is the focus for affirmative action and discrimination debates. Notice that "equal protection of the laws" does not mean equal treatment but rather *treatment as an equal*. See Chapters 5 and 6.

[78] This section was meant to exclude, with few exceptions, the entire leadership of the southern states during the Civil War from holding public office. Was Reconstruction a noble but ill-fated attempt to move the nation radically toward a more egalitarian democracy? Or was it simply the victor grinding a heel on the vanquished?

[79] Lincoln had, at one time, advocated compensating former slaveholders for emancipation, but the bitterness of the war and Lincoln's assassination led to this less compromising position.

Amendment 15 [March 30, 1870]

Section 1 The right of citizens of the United States to vote shall not be denied or abridged by the United States or by any State on account of race, color, or previous condition of servitude.

Section 2 The Congress shall have power to enforce this article by appropriate legislation.

Amendment 16 [February 25, 1913]

The Congress shall have power to lay and collect taxes on incomes, from whatever source derived, without apportionment among the several States, and without regard to any census or enumeration.[80]

Amendment 17 [May 31, 1913]

The Senate of the United States shall be composed of two Senators from each State, elected by the people thereof, for six years; and each September shall have one vote. The electors in each State shall have the qualifications requisite for electors of the most numerous branch of the State legislatures.[81]

When vacancies happen in the representation of any State in the Senate, the executive authority of such State shall issue writs of election to fill such vacancies: *Provided*, That the legislature of any State may empower the executive thereof to make temporary appointments until the people fill the vacancies by election as the legislature may direct.

This amendment shall not be so construed as to affect the election or term of any Senator chosen before it becomes valid as part of the Constitution.

Amendment 18 [January 29, 1919]

Section 1 *After one year from the ratification of this article the manufacture, sale, or transportation of intoxicating liquors within, the importation thereof into, or the exportation thereof from the United States and all territory subject to the jurisdiction thereof for beverage purposes is hereby prohibited.*[82]

Section 2 *The Congress and the several States shall have concurrent power to enforce this article by appropriate legislation.*

---

[80] Although a small, short-term, Court-approved income tax had helped to finance the Civil War, when Congress tried to reinstitute it in 1894, the Court found it unconstitutional as a "direct tax" (*Pollock* v. *Farmers' Loan and Trust Co.*, 158 U.S. 601 [1895]). This amendment cleared the way for the one part of the federal government that everyone loves to hate—the Internal Revenue Service.

[81] The Senate, with appointments from state legislatures, had become a club of millionaires. This amendment helped to democratize American government, but the economically well-to-do are still over-represented in Congress.

[82] Should hard drugs be legalized? Serious advocates of such a policy cite the failure of Amendment 18 as evidence that legal attempts to deter consumption fail in their primary goal while encouraging lawlessness and organized crime. The "noble experiment" of Prohibition was ended, after nearly fifteen years, by Amendment 21.

Section 3 *This article shall be inoperative unless it shall have been ratified as an amendment to the Constitution by the legislatures of the several States, as provided in the Constitution, within seven years from the date of submission hereof to the States by the Congress.*

Amendment 19   [August 26, 1920]

The right of citizens of the United States to vote shall not be denied or abridged by the United States or by any State on account of sex.[83]

Congress shall have power to enforce this article by appropriate legislation.

Amendment 20   [February 6, 1933]

Section 1   The terms of the President and Vice President shall end at noon on the 20th day of January, and the terms of Senators and Representatives at noon on the 3rd day of January, of the years in which such terms would have ended if this article had not been ratified; and the terms of their successors shall then begin.[84]

Section 2   The Congress shall assemble at least once in every year, and such meeting shall begin at noon on the 3rd day of January unless they shall by law appoint a different day.

Section 3   If, at the time fixed for the beginning of the term of the President, the President elect shall have died, the Vice President elect shall become President. If a President shall not have been chosen before the time fixed for the beginning of his term, or if the President elect shall have failed to qualify, then the Vice President elect shall act as President until a President shall have qualified; and the Congress may by law provide for the case wherein neither a President elect nor a Vice President elect shall have qualified, declaring who shall then act as President, or the manner in which one who is to act shall be selected, and such person shall act accordingly until a President or Vice President shall have qualified.

Section 4   The Congress may by law provide for the case of death of any of the persons from whom the House of Representatives may choose a President whenever the right of choice shall have developed upon them, and for the case of the death of any of the persons from whom the Senate may choose a Vice President whenever the right of choice shall have devolved upon them.

Section 5   Sections 1 and 2 shall take effect on the 15th day of October following the ratification of this article.

---

[83] Except for the Bill of Rights, the largest cluster of amendments concerns expanding suffrage (15, 19, 23, 24, and 26) or altering electoral procedures (12, 17, 20, and 22). The central importance of elections to democracy is well reflected in our Constitution.

[84] When the Constitution was written, winter travel was difficult, and the pace of public events was much slower. By the 1930s the long gap between the presidential election early in November and the inauguration late in March seemed to allow too much time for mischief by "lame ducks."

Section 6 This article shall be inoperative unless it shall have been ratified as an amendment to the Constitution by the legislatures of three fourths of the several States within seven years from the date of its submission.[85]

Amendment 21   [December 5, 1933]

Section 1 The eighteenth article of amendment to the Constitution of the United States is hereby repealed.

Section 2 The transportation or importation into any State, Territory, or possession of the United States for delivery or use therein of intoxicating liquors, in violation of the laws thereof, is hereby prohibited.

Section 3 This article shall be inoperative unless it shall have been ratified as an amendment to the Constitution by conventions in the several States, as provided in the Constitution, within seven years from the date of the submission hereof to the States by the Congress.[86]

Amendment 22   [February 26, 1951]

Section 1 No person shall be elected to the office of the President more than twice, and no person who has held the office of President, or acted as President, for more than two years of a term to which some other person was elected President shall be elected to the office of President more than once. But this Article shall not apply to any person holding the office of President when this Article was proposed by the Congress, and shall not prevent any person who may be holding the office of President, or acting as President, during the term within which this Article becomes operative from holding the office of President or acting as President during the remainder of such term.[87]

Section 2 This article shall be inoperative unless it shall have been ratified as an amendment to the Constitution by the legislatures of three fourths of the several States within seven years from the date of its submission to the States by the Congress.

Amendment 23   [March 29, 1961]

Section 1 The District constituting the seat of Government of the United States shall appoint in such manner as the Congress may direct:

---

[85] Provisions like this are a means of keeping the books clear of unratified amendments. The Equal Rights Amendment proposed in the 1970s had such a provision, although the time limit for ratification was extended by Congress (to no avail—the second deadline passed without the votes needed for ratification). See Amendment 27.

[86] The repeal of Prohibition was the only amendment submitted to conventions in each state for ratification. Elected officials are naturally (and reasonably) wary of passionately debated issues that involve a large bipolar split. To side with either faction is to lose. It is far wiser to ignore such issues, if possible—and to pass them along to someone else, if not.

[87] Some historians see Amendment 22 as a posthumous slap at Franklin Roosevelt, the only president to break the two-term tradition established by Washington (who was ready to retire anyway). Would a single six-year term be better, allowing presidents to make their mark but eliminating shortsighted first-term policymaking aimed mostly at ensuring reelection? There are valid arguments on both sides of this question, but don't expect much tinkering in this area.

A number of electors of President and Vice President equal to the whole number of Senators and Representatives in Congress to which the District would be entitled if it were a State, but in no event more than the least populous State; they shall be in addition to those appointed by the States, but they shall be considered, for the purposes of the election of President and Vice President, to be electors appointed by a State; and they shall meet in the District and perform such duties as provided by the twelfth article of amendment.[88]

Section 2 The Congress shall have power to enforce this article by appropriate legislation.

Amendment 24 [January 23, 1964]

Section 1 The rights of citizens of the United States to vote in any primary or other election for President or Vice President, for electors for President or Vice President, or for Senator or Representative in Congress, shall not be denied or abridged by the United States or any state by reason of failure to pay any poll tax or other tax.[89]

Section 2 The Congress shall have power to enforce this article by appropriate legislation.

Amendment 25 [February 10, 1967]

Section 1 In case of the removal of the President from office or of his death or resignation, the Vice President shall become President.

Section 2 Whenever there is a vacancy in the office of the Vice President, the President shall nominate a Vice President who shall take office upon confirmation by a majority vote of both Houses of Congress.[90]

Section 3 Whenever the President transmits to the President pro tempore of the Senate and the Speaker of the House of Representatives his written declaration that he is unable to discharge the powers and duties of his office, and until he transmits to them a written declaration to the contrary, such powers and duties shall be discharged by the Vice President as Acting President.[91]

Section 4 Whenever the Vice President and a majority of either the principal officers of the executive departments or of such other body as Congress may by law provide, transmit to the President pro

---

[88] It was odd that before this amendment, residents of the capital, the one city absolutely obsessed with the operation of federal government, were unable to vote in presidential elections. Should the District of Columbia have voting representation in Congress as though it were a state?

[89] Strictly speaking, a poll tax is a "capitation" or head tax—a tax levied on every individual *as* an individual. In the South, however, the poll tax was one of several means to deny blacks access to voting polls. This amendment, along with the Civil Rights Act of 1964 and the Voting Rights Act of 1965, radically transformed electoral politics in the South. (See Chapters 5 and 6.)

[90] This is the only presidential appointment that must be approved by *both* houses of Congress. The nation's two top offices thus become self-regenerating, as evidenced by President Gerald Ford and his vice-president, Nelson Rockefeller. President Nixon chose Ford to be vice-president when Spiro Agnew resigned; Ford then became president when Nixon resigned, and he chose Rockefeller to be vice-president.

[91] Section 3 was used formally only once, when Ronald Reagan underwent surgery.

tempore of the Senate and the Speaker of the House of Representatives their written declaration that the President is unable to discharge the power and duties of his office, the Vice President shall immediately assume the powers and duties of the office as Acting President.

Thereafter, when the President transmits to the President pro tempore of the Senate and the Speaker of the House of Representatives his written declaration that no inability exists, he shall resume the powers and duties of his office unless the Vice President and a majority of either the principal officers of the executive department[s] or of such other body as Congress may by law provide, transmit within four days to the President pro tempore of the Senate and the Speaker of the House of Representatives their written declaration that the President is unable to discharge the powers and duties of his office. Thereupon Congress shall decide the issue, assembling within forty-eight hours for that purpose if not in session. If the Congress, within twenty-one days after receipt of the latter written declaration, or, if Congress is not in session, within twenty-one days after Congress is required to assemble, determines by two-thirds vote of both Houses that the President is unable to discharge the powers and duties of his office, the Vice President shall continue to discharge the same as Acting President; otherwise, the President shall resume the powers and duties of his office.[92]

Amendment 26 [June 30, 1971]

Section 1 The right of citizens of the United States, who are eighteen years of age or older, to vote shall not be denied or abridged by the United States or by any state on account of age.[93]

Section 2 The Congress shall have power to enforce this article by appropriate legislation.

Amendment 27 [May 7, 1992]

No law, varying the compensation for the services of the senators and representatives shall take effect, until an election of representatives shall have intervened.[94]

---

[92] The provisions in Section 4 regarding a president's disability are untested and fraught with potential difficulties. What if the vice-president and the required number of cabinet officials perceive a disability to exist but the president refuses to agree? Can Congress make a dispassionate, nonpartisan determination of a sitting president's ability to resume power? The dramatic possibilities are infinite.

[93] When does a child become an adult? The age of majority has many legal definitions. Before this amendment, eighteen-year-olds could be drafted but could not vote in many states; even after it, in most states they could vote but could not buy alcohol. In several states, persons too young to vote, be drafted, or buy a drink can be executed for a capital crime.

[94] Originally proposed by James Madison in 1789, this amendment became part of the Constitution two centuries later when Michigan became the 38th state to ratify it. A Senate resolution passed shortly thereafter recognized the amendment's validity but declared that four other amendments submitted to the states without time limits were dead.

APPENDIX C

U.S. PRESIDENTIAL ELECTIONS

Candidates (Party)	Popular Vote (Percent)	Electoral Vote	Candidates (Party)	Popular Vote (Percent)	Electoral Vote
1789			**1808**		
George Washington		69	James Madison (D-R)		122
John Adams		34	Charles C. Pinckney (F)		47
Others		35	George Clinton (I-R)		6
1792			**1812**		
George Washington		132	James Madison (D-R)		122
John Adams		77	DeWitt Clinton (F)		89
George Clinton		50	**1816**		
Others		5	James Monroe (D-R)		183
1796			Rufus King (F)		34
John Adams (F)		71	**1820**		
Thomas Jefferson (D-R)		68	James Monroe (D-R)		231
Thomas Pinckney (F)		59	John Quincy Adams (I-R)		1
Aaron Burr (D-R)		30	**1824**		
Others		48	John Quincy Adams[†]		
1800			(D-R)	30.5	84
Thomas Jefferson[†] (D-R)		73	Andrew Jackson (D-R)	43.1	99
Aaron Burr (D-R)		73	Henry Clay (D-R)	13.2	37
John Adams (F)		65	William H. Crawford		
Charles C. Pinckney		64	(D-R)	13.1	41
1804			**1828**		
Thomas Jefferson (D-R)		162	Andrew Jackson (D)	56.0	178
Charles C. Pinckney (F)		14	John Quincy Adams (N-R)	44.0	83

C-1

Candidates (Party)	Popular Vote (Percent)	Electoral Vote
1832		
Andrew Jackson (D)	55.0	219
Henry Clay (N-R)	42.4	49
William Wirt (A-M)		7
John Floyd (N-R)	2.6	11
1836		
Martin Van Buren (D)	50.9	170
William H. Harrison (W)	36.7	73
Hugh L. White (W)	9.7	26
Daniel Webster (W)	2.7	14
1840		
William H. Harrison* (W) (John Tyler, 1841)	53.1	234
Martin Van Buren (D)	46.9	60
1844		
James K. Polk (D)	49.6	170
Henry Clay (W)	48.1	105
James G. Birney (L)	2.3	
1848		
Zachary Taylor* (W) (Millard Fillmore, 1850)	47.4	163
Lewis Cass (D)	42.5	127
Martin Van Buren (F-S)	10.1	
1852		
Franklin Pierce (D)	50.9	254
Winfield Scott (W)	44.1	42
1856		
James Buchanan (D)	45.4	174
John C. Fremont (R)	33.0	114
Millard Fillmore (A)	21.6	8
1860		
Abraham Lincoln (R)	39.8	180
Stephen A. Douglas (D)	29.5	12
John C. Breckinridge (D)	18.1	72
John Bell (C-U)	12.6	39
1864		
Abraham Lincoln* (R) (Andrew Johnson, 1865)	55.0	212
George B. McClellan (D)	45.0	21
1868		
Ulysses S. Grant (R)	52.7	214
Horatio Seymour (D)	47.3	80
1872		
Ulysses S. Grant (R)	55.6	286
Horace Greeley (D)	43.9	66
1876		
Rutherford B. Hayes (R)	48.0	185
Samuel J. Tilden (D)	51.0	184
1880		
James A. Garfield* (R) (Chester A. Arthur, 1881)	48.3	214
Winfield S. Hancock (D)	48.2	155
James B. Weaver (G-L)	1.8	
1884		
Grover Cleveland (D)	48.5	219
James G. Blaine (R)	48.2	182
Benjamin F. Butler (G-L)	1.8	
1888		
Benjamin Harrison (R)	47.8	233
Grover Cleveland (D)	48.6	168
1892		
Grover Cleveland (D)	46.0	277
Benjamin Harrison (R)	43.0	145
James R. Weaver (PE)	8.5	22
1896		
William McKinley (R)	50.8	271
William J. Bryan (D; PO)	46.7	176
1900		
William McKinley* (R) (Theodore Roosevelt, 1901)	51.7	292
William J. Bryan (D; PO)	45.5	155
1904		
Theodore Roosevelt (R)	56.4	336
Alton B. Parker (D)	37.6	140
Eugene V. Debs (S)	3.0	

U.S. PRESIDENTIAL ELECTIONS

Candidates (Party)	Popular Vote (Percent)	Electoral Vote
1908		
William H. Taft (R)	51.6	321
William J. Bryan (D)	43.1	162
Eugene V. Debs (S)	6.0	
1912		
Woodrow Wilson (D)	41.8	435
Theodore Roosevelt (PR)	27.4	88
William H. Taft (R)	23.2	8
Eugene V. Debs (S)	6.0	
1916		
Woodrow Wilson (D)	49.3	277
Charles E. Hughes (R)	46.1	254
1920		
Warren G. Harding* (R)	61.0	404
(Calvin Coolidge, 1923)		
James M. Cox (D)	34.6	127
Eugene V. Debs (S)	3.5	
1924		
Calvin Coolidge (R)	54.1	382
John W. Davis (D)	28.8	136
Robert M. LaFollette (PR)	16.6	13
1928		
Herbert C. Hoover (R)	58.2	444
Alfred E. Smith (D)	40.8	87
1932		
Franklin D. Roosevelt (D)	57.3	472
Herbert C. Hoover (R)	39.6	59
Norman Thomas (S)	2.2	
1936		
Franklin D. Roosevelt (D)	60.7	523
Alfred M. Landon (R)	36.4	8
William Lemke (U)	1.9	
1940		
Franklin D. Roosevelt (D)	54.7	449
Wendell L. Wilkie (R)	44.8	82

Candidates (Party)	Popular Vote (Percent)	Electoral Vote
1944		
Franklin D. Roosevelt* (D)	52.8	432
(Harry S. Truman, 1945)		
Thomas E. Dewey (R)	44.5	99
1948		
Harry S. Truman (D)	49.5	303
Thomas E. Dewey (R)	45.1	189
J. Strom Thurmond (S-R)	2.4	39
Henry A. Wallace (PR)	2.4	
1952		
Dwight D. Eisenhower (R)	55.2	442
Adlai E. Stevenson (D)	44.5	89
1956		
Dwight D. Eisenhower (R)	57.4	457
Adlai E. Stevenson (D)	42.0	73
1960		
John F. Kennedy* (D)	49.9	303
(Lyndon B. Johnson, 1963)		
Richard M. Nixon (R)	49.6	219
1964		
Lyndon B. Johnson (D)	61.1	486
Barry M. Goldwater (R)	38.5	52
1968		
Richard M. Nixon (R)	43.4	301
Hubert H. Humphrey (D)	42.7	191
George C. Wallace (A-I)	13.5	46
1972		
Richard M. Nixon¶ (R)	60.6	520
(Gerald R. Ford, 1974)		
George S. McGovern (D)	37.5	17
1976		
Jimmy Carter (D)	50.6	297
Gerald R. Ford (R)	48.4	240

Candidates (Party)	Popular Vote (Percent)	Electoral Vote	Candidates (Party)	Popular Vote (Percent)	Electoral Vote
1980			**1988**		
Ronald Reagan (R)	51.0	489	George Bush (R)	53.4	426
Jimmy Carter (D)	42.3	49	Michael Dukakis (D)	45.6	111
John Anderson (I)	6.6	0	**1992**		
1984			Bill Clinton (D)	43	370
Ronald Reagan (R)	58.8	525	George Bush (R)	38	168
Walter Mondale (D)	40.6	13	Ross Perot (I)	19	0

PARTY ABBREVIATIONS: **A** = American; **A-I** = American Independent; **A-M** = Anti-Masonic; **C-U** = Constitutional Union; **D** = Democratic; **D-R** = Democratic-Republican; **F** = Federalist; **F-S** = Free Soil; **G-L** = Greenback-Labor; **I** = Independent; **I-R** = Independent-Republican; **L** = Liberty; **N-R** = National-Republican; **PE** = People's; **PO** = Populist; **PR** = Progressive; **R** = Republican; **S** = Socialist; **S-R** = States' Rights; **U** = Union; **W** = Whig.

[†]Elected by the House of Representatives.
[*]Died in office.
[¶]Resigned.

APPENDIX D

GLOSSARY

acid rain A highly acidic form of precipitation, caused by the combustion of fossil fuels, that can kill aquatic life and vegetation and may introduce dangerous pollutants into drinking water.

acquired immune deficiency syndrome (AIDS) Disease induced by HIV that leaves the body vulnerable to a variety of opportunistic diseases. Transmitted by intimate sexual contact or exchange of blood.

advocacy advertising Corporate advertising in the form of well-reasoned essays in prominent news media, designed to build a favorable corporate image and boost public support for the corporation, its products, and goals.

affirmative action The attempt to remedy past discrimination by favoring minorities or women in hiring in certain federal or federally funded programs.

agenda setting Phase of policy process during which a particular situation or problem is identified as appropriate for public action.

Aid to Families with Dependent Children (AFDC) Welfare program begun in the 1930s to provide assistance to mothers raising children by themselves; program most commonly thought of as "welfare."

alienation The sense of being an outsider, leading to feelings of powerlessness, futility, or meaninglessness.

amendment Addition to the U.S. Constitution; must be proposed by Congress and then ratified by at least three-quarters of the states.

amicus curiae brief A "friend of the court" brief, filed in a case by an interested group not party to the litigation.

Amnesty International Human rights organization, example of an effective Non-Governmental Organization (NGO) in international affairs.

antifederalists At the 1787 Constitutional Convention, opponents of the new Constitution, primarily citizens of rural and poorer areas.

appellate hearing Granted by appellate court following a trial—ordinarily determines questions of law, accepting facts as determined by trial court.

Articles of Confederation The first written constitution, ratified by the thirteen original states shortly before the end of the American Revolution (1781); established a weak national government and left strong powers to the states.

basic rights Fundamental claims that are believed to inhere in individuals as individuals and that government and society should honor, such as the rights to equal protection and free expression.

bicameral Composed of two houses or legislative chambers; system adopted for the U.S. Congress and most state governments.

Bill of Rights The first ten amendments to the U.S. Constitution, which supporters of the document

D-1

(Federalists) agreed to add in response to criticisms and to ensure the protection of various rights and liberties.

biodiversity Concerned with the fullest range of genetic material in lifeforms on earth.

blanket primary Election in which voters can choose to vote in more than one party's primary for different offices—for example, the Democratic primary for senator and the Republican primary for governor.

block grant Gives the funded agency greater discretion in spending grant funds; part of an effort to return control to state and local governments.

Boland Amendment Prohibited United States from funding Contra rebels in Nicaragua; illegally violated by Iran-Contra scheme.

Brown v. Board of Education of Topeka The 1954 U.S. Supreme Court ruling that segregated schools were unconstitutional.

bureaucracy The complex, hierarchically arranged organization composed of small subdivisions with specialized functions that carries out the day-to-day work of government.

cabinet The heads of the major federal administrative departments, plus any others specially designated by the president.

cabinet departments The sections of the federal executive branch represented in the cabinet that comprise the bulk of the federal bureaucracy and employ the majority of federal workers.

capitalism Economic system characterized by private ownership of most wealth and based on full freedom to buy and sell, accumulate wealth, and conduct business without government interference.

capital punishment The death penalty; can only be used for crimes which result in death; cannot be used against persons insane or under sixteen at the time of the crime.

cash transfers Method of disbursing benefits from welfare state programs, such as cash payments for social security or various types of public assistance to the poor.

categorical grant Contains narrow restrictions on spending; provides greater control for funding agency.

Central Intelligence Agency (CIA) Chief intelligence-gathering agency of the U.S. government; also engages in covert action.

checks and balances The political ideal embodied in the separation of powers, whereby each branch of government serves as a limit or check on the powers of the others.

chlorofluorocarbons (CFCs) Ingredients in many industrial products and processes; implicated in the depletion of the ozone layer of the atmosphere.

civic religion Confluence of religion and patriotism; secular political ties held with religious fervor.

civil cases Disputes between two parties (plaintiff and defendant), refereed by courts; includes tort, contract, family law. Distinguished from criminal cases.

circuit courts *See* U.S. courts of appeals.

civil disobedience A public act committed to arouse the conscience of society by a person fully willing to accept the punishment for that action prescribed by law.

Civil Rights Act of 1964 Legislation passed by Congress prohibiting segregation in public accommodations and discrimination in hiring based on race, religion, color, sex, or national origin.

civil service system A method of filling government posts based on "merit" as determined through competitive examinations overseen by the Civil Service Commission; contrast with the spoils system (q.v.).

Clean Air Act of 1963 Legislation establishing national air quality standards; amendments added in 1970 strengthened the act considerably.

clear and present danger An interpretation of the conflict between free speech and public order elaborated by Justice Oliver Wendell Holmes in the 1920s. The doctrine argues that only speech presenting a "clear and present danger" can be limited, as when someone shouts "fire" in a crowded theater.

clientele groups Interest groups that are directly affected by bureaucratic agencies; for example, labor unions are clientele groups of the Labor Department.

closed primary Election in which only voters registered in a particular party may vote in that party's primary election.

Cold War Global rivalry between the United States and the Soviet Union between the late 1940s and 1991 that divided the world into communist and Western spheres of influence.

Common Cause General-purpose public-interest lobby formed in 1970 that frequently focuses on procedural issues in Congress and supports public campaign financing and reform of the laws pertaining to lobbying disclosure.

common law Legal tradition in which experience is the life of the law. Uses past decisions (precedents) to decide present cases (the doctrine of *stare decisis*).

communism Assumes the ultimate disappearance of private property, economic classes, and coercive government. Distinct from socialism, which only assumes the public ownership of the major means of production.

comparable worth The concept that men and women should be paid according to equitable pay standards instead of unequal standards based on gender discrimination.

concurrent powers Powers exercised by both national and state governments, for example, the power to tax.

Connecticut Compromise Compromise of the Constitutional Convention of 1787 making Congress bicameral: In the Senate each state would have two representatives, and in the House of Representatives representation would be proportional to population.

conservatives People whose political philosophy stresses the virtues of individualism, unfettered economic activity, and minimal government involvement except in matters of defense.

containment Term coined in 1947 by George Kennan to describe the doctrine of containing the expansionist thrust of Soviet power until the Soviets learned to accommodate themselves to global realities.

contract bureaucracy A private firm hired by the government to perform the work of government, for example, a defense contractor who builds military hardware.

controlled capitalism Economic policy characterized by limited and specific government intervention in the regulation of the economy.

convergence theories Posit that capitalist and socialist economies eventually resemble one another in mixed economies.

cooperative federalism Marked by federal funding for programs administered by state and local governments, for example Aid to Families with Dependent Children.

criminal cases Court cases in which a prosecutor accuses the defendant of violating the criminal code. Distinguished from civil cases.

critical election In which a major realignment of electoral forces takes place resulting in a new, stable pattern of partisan support.

crossover voting Voting for a candidate of the opposing party in the primary, especially a weak candidate, in order to advance the electoral chances of a different candidate.

cross-sectional study In which a "snapshot" is taken of the characteristics of different age cohorts at a single time. Distinguished from a longitudinal study.

de facto segregation Racial segregation that results from housing patterns or other non-official actions. Distinguished from de jure segregation.

Defense Department The agency of the U.S. government that coordinates the country's military services to carry out the administration's defense policy.

deferred issues Public issues that are likely to return in one form or another if they are not originally dealt with satisfactorily.

de jure segregation Racial segregation which results from official, race-conscious policies. Outlawed by *Brown* v. *Board of Education* (1954).

delegated powers Powers that the U.S. Constitution specifically assigns to the jurisdiction of the national government.

democracy A system of government based on majority rule that provides protections for individual rights and liberties and strives to achieve a significant degree of equality among its citizens.

democrat A supporter of the concept of democracy. Distinguished from Democrat, a supporter of the Democratic Party in the United States.

Democratic party U.S. political party dominant since the 1828 election of Andrew Jackson as president.

Democratic-Republicans Political party that emerged in the 1820s from a split within the Republican party. A coalition of small farmers, small property owners, and local political leaders in the southern and mid-Atlantic states, it came to dominate American politics and was renamed the Democratic party.

demographics Characteristics of human populations, including age, ethnic identity, gender.

depression A severe contraction of the economy with extremely high unemployment. The Great Depression in the United States began in the late 1920s and lasted for a decade.

deregulation The drive to eliminate many existing government regulations and to reduce the power of regulatory agencies.

détente A phase of improved U.S.-Soviet relations in the early 1970s associated mainly with the Nixon administration.

deviating election "Normal" patterns of partisan support are temporarily disrupted. Distinguished from a critical election and a maintaining election.

diplomatic recognition The reception of official representatives from another sovereign state; the highest level of recognition.

direct-mail marketing Targeted solicitation mailing, often based on extremely accurate data about socioeconomic status and consumption patterns. Potentially undermines political parties as it provides candidates access to contributors directly.

direct socialization The process whereby children are deliberately taught specific political views, values, and behaviors.

disparate impact test Concentrates on results rather than procedures in determining the presence of discrimination.

displaced issues Public issues that flare up and then fade from public view, to be replaced by other issues or fragments of the original issues.

diverted issues Public issues that are handled by calling for a reevaluation of the problems involved.

Dred Scott v. Sanford The 1857 Supreme Court case that undid the Missouri Compromise, allowing the extension of slavery into U.S. territories. The Fourteenth Amendment (q.v.) overturned the *Dred Scott* decision.

dual federalism Exemplified in Taney Court decisions prior to the Civil War, which emphasized two distinct sets of functions assigned to the national government and the states.

due process clause Found in the Fifth and Fourteenth Amendments. Requires fair, nonarbitrary, just treatment of individuals by the government. Protects life, liberty, and property interests.

due process of law Procedural legal guarantees against the arbitrary use of government power, including guarantees of life, liberty, and property for citizens acting within the laws.

Earth Summit The United Nations Conference on Environment and Development, held in Rio de Janeiro in June, 1992.

effluent The polluted water released by cities and industries. Amendments to the federal Water Pollution Control Act passed in 1972 were designed to control the disposal of effluent by establishing schedules and standards.

egalitarian democracy Rule by the people based on a redistribution of wealth, equalization of educational opportunities, and enforcement of laws protecting individuals from exploitation.

elastic clause "Necessary and proper" clause found in Article I, Section 8 of the Constitution. The basis for implied powers belonging to the federal government.

electoral college Electors from the fifty states who formally elect the president and vice-president. Each state's electors are equal to its number of senators and representatives in Congress.

elitism Argues that control of society and government should be limited to a small number of influential persons of similar background, lifestyle, and political outlook.

employee stock ownership plans (ESOPs) A company's stock is held exclusively or primarily by the employees. An example of a hybrid economic form not capitalist or socialist.

enabling act An act of Congress allowing the citizens of a territory to draft a state constitution as part of the procedure for admission to the Union as a state.

energy independence National self-sufficiency in energy use. The United States currently depends heavily upon imported oil.

enumerated powers Those powers delegated to the national government that are spelled out explicitly in the Constitution. Distinguished from the delegated powers, which are implied.

environmental impact statement A federally mandated report spelling out specific environmental effects; must be prepared whenever proposals for legislation or other federal actions may significantly affect the quality of the environment.

Environmental Protection Agency (EPA) Body created in 1970 as a federal agency to coordinate national policy for issues affecting the environment.

equal protection of the laws The constitutional guarantee that no individual or group can be denied rights and privileges that are granted to others.

equal protection clause Found in the Fourteenth Amendment, assuring persons treatment as equals though not necessarily equal treatment under the law.

establishment clause Portion of the First Amendment to the U.S. Constitution commanding that Congress make no law "respecting an establishment of religion."

executive agreement An arrangement between a president and a foreign nation that, unlike a treaty, is not subject to Senate approval.

Executive Office of the President The complex of auxiliary services, including staff support, research, and high-level consultative bodies, that provide the president with assistance.

extraordinary politics The politics of protest and mass involvement.

Fairness Doctrine Rule originally established by the Federal Communications Commission to require broadcasters to provide "equal time" for opposing viewpoints; abolished in 1987 after President Reagan vetoed congressional attempts to make it law.

federal district courts Lowest level of the federal court system, which uses both grand and petit juries (q.v.) and from which appeals may be made to courts at the next federal level.

Federalist Papers Essays written by James Madison and Alexander Hamilton in 1787 and 1788 stressing the need for a strong central government and defending the new U.S. Constitution.

Federalists Supporters of the Constitution at the Constitutional Convention of 1787.

Federal Reserve System Independent regulatory agency that controls the U.S. money supply; functions essentially as the central bank of the United States.

federal system Form of government characterized by a constitutional division of power between national and local levels.

filibuster Senate tradition by which a vote on pending legislation may be delayed or killed by a senator's engaging in unlimited speechmaking. A filibuster may be terminated only by a vote of cloture.

First Amendment The amendment to the U.S. Constitution that provides for freedoms of speech, assembly, and the press; the right to petition for the redress of grievances; the protection of religious freedom; and the separation of church and state.

fiscal policies Government policies that involve the deliberate manipulation of elements of the national budget to change the direction of the economy.

focus group A small group of carefully selected individuals who are asked to discuss their responses to a campaign ad or issue. Used to more effectively "market" a candidate.

food stamp program Welfare program designed to give recipients greater purchasing power in the supermarket by making available coupons that have greater redemption value than their cost.

fossil fuels Nonrenewable energy sources created from organic matter.

Fourteenth Amendment Amendment to the U.S. Constitution ratified in 1868 that extended citizenship to the former slaves and provided the basis for a unitary national civil rights policy.

Freedom of Information Act Congressional act originally passed in 1966 and amended in 1974 entitling citizens access to government information, including some classified documents.

free enterprise Economic system that proposes that supply and demand be allowed to regulate the marketplace without government interference.

free exercise clause Part of the First Amendment to the U.S. Constitution commanding that Congress make no law "prohibiting the free exercise" of religion.

full faith and credit Constitutional provision that each state accept as valid the legal proceedings and records of every other state.

Gini Index Named for Italian economist Corrado Gini. The most commonly used measure of income inequality, with perfect equality at 0 and perfect inequality at 1.

global warming Projected gradual increase in atmospheric temperatures caused by burning of fossil fuels, other industrial processes.

Gramm-Rudman-Hillings A 1985 congressional antideficit law (named for its Senate sponsors) that set 1993 as a target for a balanced budget and specified interim deficit reductions for each year. The enforcement of automatic spending cuts was ruled unconstitutional by the Supreme Court for violating the separation of powers.

grandfather clause Part of Jim Crow laws that allowed whites to vote while excluding similarly situated blacks.

grand jury Body of jurors who determine if there is enough evidence to warrant a trial by a petit jury in a specific case.

Great Society The term applied to a collection of welfare-state programs instituted during the 1960s by the Johnson administration.

greenhouse effect The accumulation of energy-absorbing gases in the atmosphere. Results in global warming.

Green Party Environmentally active political organization that began in Germany in the 1970s. Counterparts exist in other industrialized democracies, including the United States.

gross national product The value of all goods and services produced by a nation.

habeus corpus Found in Article I, Section 9 of the Constitution, this legal writ allows a court to review the circumstances of a person's official detention.

Harrison Narcotic Act of 1914 The earliest major piece of federal legislation limiting access to certain drugs in the United States.

health maintenance organization (HMO) Provides comprehensive health services for a fixed fee, thus encouraging cost-savings, including emphasizing prevention over treatment.

human immunodeficiency virus (HIV) The virus that is believed to cause AIDS.

ideology A highly structured system of ideas applied to political and social issues in a coherent manner.

imagemaking The careful shaping of a candidate's public image for electoral advantage. Potential negative events are subjected to "spin control" (putting the candidate in positive light).

impeachment Legal procedure that empowers Congress to remove the president from office through trial by the U.S. Senate.

implementation Phase of policy process where statutes, rules, and policy statements are put into practice. Nearly always involves additional policy choices by implementers.

implied powers Powers not specifically enumerated in the Constitution that are useful to Congress in carrying out its delegated powers.

incremental politics Policymaking in steps or increments, which describes much of the day-to-day business of government.

incumbent The person currently holding a particular political office.

independent agencies Government bodies not subject to direct executive oversight, designed to insulate policymaking from partisan influence.

indirect representation Specific policy choices made by representatives at one or more removes from ordinary citizens.

indirect socialization The acquisition of attitudes and behavior patterns through emulation rather than deliberate teaching.

industrial policy Government coordination and often subsidy of research, development, manufacturing, and marketing decisions across the industrial sector of the economy, epitomized by the Ministry of International Trade and Industry (MITI) in Japan.

inherent powers Powers integral to national sovereignty, such as the power to wage war.

initiative Mechanism by which citizens, through petition, can present a measure directly to voters, thus circumventing the legislature.

in-kind transfers Components of welfare state programs that supply a specific kind of help as opposed to cash, for example, food stamps, or Medicaid benefits.

interelection stage Elected officials' time in office between elections.

interest group Nongovernmental organization unified by common goals or attitudes that organizes and lobbies in order to influence policy formulation and implementation.

interest group liberalism Pattern of decision making described by Theodore Lowi in which each participant in a political controversy receives something and therefore has some impact on the decision-making process.

intergovernmental organizations Voluntary organizations of sovereign states, such as the North Atlantic Treaty Organization (NATO) and the United Nations. Distinguished from Non-Governmental Organizations like Amnesty International or multinational corporations.

intergovernmental relations (IGR) Concept to replace federalism. Emphasizes absence of clear hierarchy, presence of a variety of players (not just state and federal officials), and the importance of policy considerations over cold legalisms.

iron triangle Policy-controlling subsystem composed of players in legislature, executive agencies, and targeted private sector. Congressional armed services committees, Pentagon officials, and defense contractors are an example.

Joint Chiefs of Staff (JCS) Committee made up of the heads of each of the armed services, with a head appointed by the president, that oversees military policy matters and reports to Congress and the president.

Judicial Conference of the United States Administrative body overseeing federal courts. Chaired by Chief Justice of the United States, with representation from Courts of Appeals and District Courts.

judicial council Administrative body overseeing courts within each federal circuit.

judicial review Power of the federal courts to review the acts of federal and state legislatures as well as the actions of executive agencies to determine if they conform to the provisions of the U.S. Constitution.

Keynesian economics Economic practices based on the theories of John Maynard Keynes, who argued that governments could use tax policy and government expenditures, including deficit spending, to stimulate economic recovery and growth.

Ku Klux Klan Extremist racist organization that is antiblack, anti-Semitic, anti-immigrant. Flowered in the South following the Civil War. Still active.

laissez-faire Economic policy that favors nonintervention by government in a nation's economy.

laissez-faire capitalism Economic policy in which government allows businesses to operate relatively free of regulation.

LAPS test Court-formulated test for obscenity. Does material lack serious literary, artistic, political, and scientific value? *Miller* v. *California* (1973).

layer-cake federalism When national government and state governments have clearly separate responsibilities. Distinguished from marble-cake federalism.

legitimation Phase of policy process involving formal actions—legislating, rule-making, or issuing a policy statement—that mark a chosen policy as official.

***Lemon* test** Court-formulated test to determine legitimate state involvement in religion without violating the establishment clause. Does activity have a secular purpose, does it neither advance nor inhibit religion, and does it avoid excessive entanglement with religion? *Lemon* v. *Kurtzman* (1971).

libel Legally proscribed speech that maliciously, falsely, and intentionally damages reputation.

liberal democracy Form of government in which majority rule is combined with respect for civil liberties and protection of individual rights.

liberalism Political philosophy in which social and political values are based on a belief in government by consent of the governed and in which rights and liberties are guaranteed to all persons.

liberation theology A strain of contemporary Catholic theology popular in Central America that emphasizes the revolutionary teachings of Jesus. Not officially sanctioned.

libertarianism Political theory that argues for least government.

line-item veto Allows an executive to veto one part of a bill without sacrificing the rest. Many governors have this power; the president does not.

longitudinal study Done over time to measure change in a single set of subjects. Distinguished from a cross-sectional study.

macroeconomics Study of system-wide economic phenomena—for example the relationship of the money supply to inflation.

macropolitics The big picture, populated by all the major political actors (for example, the president, Congress) and more frequently covered by the media. Distinguished from political subsystems.

maintaining election Normal pattern of partisan electoral support is maintained. Distinguished from a critical election and a deviating election.

majoritarian democracy Rule by the people based on preferences of more than 50 percent of voters.

majority leader Chief floor leader for a party in the House of Representatives or the Senate, charged with mobilizing party support during roll-call votes.

majority rule Decision making by more than 50 percent of the voters.

mandatory testing Medical testing mandated by law; an issue in the 1980s with regard to testing individuals for drug use and for AIDS.

marble-cake federalism Term coined by Morton Grodzins to describe the selective intervention of the federal government in most topical areas originally left to the states. No clear distinctions between the subjects handled by the federal government and those handled by the states.

Marbury v. Madison The 1803 U.S. Supreme Court case in which the Court set forth for the first time its power to declare acts of Congress unconstitutional.

markup Fine-tuning legislation in committee or subcommittee.

maximalist view of democracy The opinion that democracy encompasses more than free elections, which are a necessary but not sufficient condition for democratic life.

McCulloch v. Maryland The 1819 U.S. Supreme Court decision that upheld the federal government's right to create a national bank and thus legitimized the concept of implied powers (q.v.) and the supremacy of the national government.

means-tested When eligibility and/or the cost of participation is tied to income level.

Medicaid A state-option component of welfare state programs that provides medical assistance to the needy.

Medicare A component of welfare state programs that provides partial payments for medical care to everyone eligible for social security and all classified as disabled.

"Medigap" insurance Private insurance to cover the difference between the actual cost of medical services and what Medicare pays.

mercantilism Economic philosophy developed in the seventeenth century that advocated strong protectionist measures that would strengthen the nation's economy and lead to a favorable balance of trade.

microeconomics Study of economic phenomena from the standpoint of an individual player in the economic system—for example, the feasibility of starting a new airline in an unregulated environment.

Miller v. California Court case that formulated LAPS obscenity test; uses "contemporary community standards" rather than a national definition of obscenity.

minimalist view of democracy The opinion that democracy is the best way of avoiding the greater evils inherent in other political forms.

minority leader Leader of the minority party in either house of Congress.

Miranda v. Arizona The 1963 U.S. Supreme Court case dictating guidelines to be followed by police in the interrogation of suspects.

mixed economies Economic systems in which private ownership of the means of production is predominant, although government maintains a substantial role; characteristic of most Western democracies.

monetary policy Government regulation of the economy by controlling the money supply. Ordinarily controlled by the Federal Reserve Board. Distinguished from fiscal policy.

multinational development banks (MDBs) Large international financial organizations designed to encourage development and global economic stability and growth. The World Bank and the International Monetary Fund are examples.

multinational corporation (MNC) Business enterprise large enough to operate beyond the boundaries of any sovereign government. Attempts to regulate MNCs easily frustrated by porosity of national borders, ease of accounting transfers of profit and loss.

national committee Coordinating group at the top levels of the Democratic and Republican parties that attempts to establish basic party policy and plan national party activity.

national convention Replaced the caucus to choose national party candidates. Nowadays described as a "four day video press release" because of lack of substantive decision-making.

National Endowment for the Arts (NEA) Created in 1970 to be the primary agency for federal funding of arts projects. Dispenses money to state arts councils and to artists directly.

National Security Council (NSC) Body created by the National Security Act of 1947 to advise the president and coordinate domestic, diplomatic, and military policies in matters of national security.

natural rights Essential human guarantees, such as freedom, that a government cannot curtail or eliminate arbitrarily and still remain just.

New Deal President Franklin D. Roosevelt's administrative and legislative program of the 1930s that introduced government regulations in the economic sphere and welfare programs in the social sector.

New Jersey Plan Proposal at the Constitutional Convention of 1787 to limit each state to one representative in a unicameral legislature.

new judicial federalism Using state constitutions to extend protection for civil rights beyond what the Constitution dictates, as interpreted by the Supreme Court.

Non-Governmental Organizations (NGOs) International actors who are not national governments or Intergovernmental organizations.

Occupational Safety and Health Administration (OSHA) Federal agency created in 1970 to protect health and safety of American workers.

Office of Management and Budget (OMB) Largest component in the Executive Office of the President, charged with preparation of the federal budget; plays a significant role in shaping and overseeing governmental policymaking and in choosing its priorities.

oligarchy Rule by a small group.

omnibus bill Mega-legislation, hundreds or thousands of pages long, incorporating several major policy enactments. Used in part to discourage presidential vetoes.

open primary Election in which voters are free to vote in any party primary regardless of party registration.

opinions Legal explanations of a judicial decision handed down by judges.

ozone depletion Reduction of high layer of atmosphere that offers protection against dangerous radiation from outer space. Blamed on CFCs and other products of industrialization.

parliamentary democracy Form of government in which the legislature (parliament) is the supreme governing body and from which the executive leadership (cabinet) is drawn.

party caucus Small group of party regulars. Now largely superseded by direct primaries.

patronage The power to appoint specific people or groups to government jobs.

peaceful coexistence Expression coined in the 1950s by Soviet Premier Nikita Khrushchev to describe the type of relationship he preferred with the United States, which did not, however, preclude continued competition between the two countries.

Pentagon Papers Classified government documents on U.S. involvement in Vietnam leaked to and published by the *New York Times* in 1971;

subject of an intense legal battle in which the U.S. Supreme Court upheld the newspaper's right to publish the documents.

petit jury Body of jurors called to decide a disputed matter or determine a person's guilt or innocence in a trial court.

plea bargain Guilty plea on part of a defendant in exchange for reduction in charges. Without this common agreement struck between prosecution and defense, courts would be hopelessly overcrowded.

Plessy* v. *Ferguson The 1896 U.S. Supreme Court decision that "separate but equal" treatment of the races was legitimate under the Constitution; established a legal basis for segregation until overturned in 1954.

pluralism Power, widely diffused and fluid, is exercised primarily through group influence. No single group dominates policy.

pocket veto The president's ability to veto a piece of legislation by failing to sign it within ten days after the adjournment of Congress.

police powers Government's responsibility to protect the health, safety, welfare, and morals of citizens.

policy evaluation Measures policy outcomes against policy goals and objectives. Values effectiveness and efficiency.

policy formulation Phase of policy process when possible responses to perceived problem are spelled out and evaluated. One or more action steps are chosen.

political action committee (PAC) Organization formed to channel funds to selected candidates and to work for particular political goals.

political culture A society's attitudes toward the processes and institutions of politics.

political economy The complex interrelations between politics and economics and the study of their mutual effects.

political efficacy Belief that participation in politics can be effective, usually accompanied by a willingness to participate.

political machine Coterie of party professionals who get out the vote and provide services to constituents in return for steady support in elections.

political party Group of people organized on the basis of common political objectives who seek to gain political power.

political question doctrine Supreme Court's assertion that certain questions are "political" and need to be addressed exclusively by the political branches of government (the legislature and the executive). Protects the Court from damaging confrontations.

political socialization Processes whereby an individual acquires the political attitudes and behavior common to a particular culture.

political subsystems Small policy arenas in which a discrete group of actors control a narrow range of policy. Distinguished from macropolitics.

populist Term applied to a number of political movements in U.S. history that have arisen to defend the interests of the common citizen against institutions perceived as too big and oppressive.

Populist party Political party that arose in the South and West in the 1880s that campaigned for many socialist-sounding measures and for increased unionization.

pork barrel projects Special-interest bills advanced in Congress by a legislator for the benefit of his or her home district or state.

president pro tempore The presiding officer of the U.S. Senate; an honorific title usually bestowed on the senior majority-party senator, who serves as president of the Senate in the absence of the vice-president, the constitutionally mandated presiding officer.

primary election Political contest in which opponents vie for nomination as a party's designated candidate in a general election.

prior restraint Injunction prohibiting publication. American courts avoid prior restraint except under extreme circumstances.

privatization The effort to transfer a wide variety of public assets and programs to the private sector in an attempt to reduce government's role and enhance private enterprise; especially popular during the Reagan years.

Progressives Political movement early in this century. Strove to eliminate partisan influence in politics through nonpartisan elections, expert boards, and commissions.

progressive taxes Tax rate that increases as the income base increases. An income tax with higher rates for wealthier people is progressive. Distinguished from regressive and proportional taxes.

propaganda Information designed to manipulate popular perceptions of government, political actors, actions, or principles.

proportional (flat rate) tax Tax rate that stays the same as income base increases. Distinguished from progressive and regressive taxes.

proportional representation System under which each party is awarded seats in the legislature in more or less direct proportion to the percentage of the popular votes it receives in an election.

prosecutor The representative of the interests of the state in criminal legal proceedings brought against a defendant.

protectionism Barriers to trade to protect domestic manufacturers from foreign competition.

public assistance programs Components of welfare state programs in which need is the main basis for eligibility.

public-interest group Organization that seeks to advance causes that will benefit society as a whole and will not necessarily materially benefit the organization or its activists.

public opinion The patterns of attitudes of citizens on various subjects.

rally events Crises or other events that cause a rally-around-the-flag increase in popular support for the government (especially presidents).

Ralph Nader Consumer activist whose efforts championed the consumer movement and have spawned public-interest groups focused on consumer issues, the environment, health, science, regulatory reform, and energy.

randomness Statistical concept, necessary in claiming a small sample as representative of a larger universe.

realigning election Critical election that creates a new stable pattern of partisan support.

reapportionment Alteration of the pattern of representation among different electoral districts in accordance with changes in population in those areas over time.

recall Mechanism used to remove officials from office by a vote of ordinary citizens.

recession Economic downturn, less severe than depression. Lengthy recession gripped the United States from 1990 through 1992.

referendum Procedure by which citizens can vote on a piece of legislation directly.

regressive taxes Tax rate decreases as the base increases. When wealthier individuals pay a smaller proportion of taxes. Sales tax is generally regressive because people with lower incomes spend a larger percentage of their income in consumption. Distinguished from proportional or progressive tax.

regulatory commission Agency that regulates certain kinds of activities, particularly in the economic sphere, and can perform quasi-judicial functions (bringing charges, holding hearings, and imposing penalties for violations of rules).

renewable energy Alternative energy sources including solar, wind, and geothermal energy.

republican Favors elite control with democratic responsiveness. Favored by Founding Fathers.

Republican party Political party formed in the 1850s primarily to oppose the further extension of slavery; formed from a coalition of northern industrialists, merchants, workers, farmers, and freed slaves.

reserved powers Powers defined by the Tenth Amendment to the Constitution as "not delegated to the United States by the Constitution, nor prohibited by it to the States respectively, or to the people."

resource allocation Phase of policy process when resources are identified and committed to achieve targeted solution.

response (to policy) The feedback loop in the policy process, when implemented policy creates new demands, desires.

revenue sharing Programs under which a portion of federal revenues is disbursed among the states.

rider A special section added to a piece of legislation, often having little to do with the main content of that legislation.

Roth* v. *United States The 1957 U.S. Supreme Court ruling that rejected a previous ruling deeming as obscene any *part* of a book or other material that might "deprave and corrupt those whose minds are open to such immoral influences." It substituted the concept of the *whole* work's effect on the "average person."

rule of four U.S. Supreme Court practice of hearing a case if four of the Court's nine justices vote to hear it.

satyagraha Gandhi's term for "truth-force." The essence of a nonviolent mass campaign.

select committee Congressional committee established for limited time for special purpose. Also known as special committee. Usually does not have legislative authority, but may study, investigate, and make recommendations.

Senior Executive Service (SES) Established under Carter administration to increase responsiveness of Civil Service. Managers at the top of the Civil Service system trade job security for greater pay, status.

seniority rule The convention of having the longest-serving majority-party member of a congressional committee named as its chairperson. Party caucuses now sometimes pass over the senior member and install a junior person as chair.

separation of powers The distribution of governmental authority among the legislative, executive, and judicial branches to prevent the dominance of one branch.

sequestration Across-the-board budget cuts triggered by failure to meet Gramm-Rudman-Hillings deficit reduction targets. Harsh medicine intended to assure compliance, defeated by legislative sleight of hand.

services Programs provided as part of welfare state programs, such as education and job training.

set-asides Proportion of contracts or contract funds reserved for minority contractors. Limited to "narrow tailoring" by *Richmond* v. *Croson* (1989).

Seven Years' War Conflict from 1756 to 1763 between Great Britain and France for control of Canada and Spain for Florida, won by the British; known in the colonies as the French and Indian War.

Shays's Rebellion Uprising in 1786 by farmers, led by Daniel Shays, to protest mortgage foreclosures in western Massachusetts.

single-issue group A well-organized and intensely active special-interest group that focuses exclusively on one issue or set of issues.

single-member district A political area in which the person gaining the most votes in an election represents that district.

sit-in Mass action protest tactic epitomized by the Greensboro sit-ins in 1960. African-Americans filled seats at lunch counters where they were refused service, blocking business as usual.

social classes Distinct groups, differentiated by occupation or income, that usually have different lifestyles and may clash politically.

social insurance programs Components of welfare state programs in which past contributions are related to the benefits received (for example, social security).

socialism Political philosophy advocating the deliberate creation of greater economic equality, public ownership of major means of production, and considerable economic planning by government.

socialist Person who favors collective and government ownership of the means of production over individual or private ownership.

social rights Claims based on government's responsibility to use its powers to improve the quality of life. Examples are pure food and drug legislation, right to collective bargaining.

social security A self-supporting component of the U.S. welfare state that encompasses old-age and survivors' insurance and disability insurance programs.

solar power Energy drawn directly from the sun's radiation, as in photovoltaic cells for creating electricity, solar collectors to heat water. Distinguished from geothermal, fossil fuel, and nuclear energy.

sound bite Term used for short, pithy quotation used to characterize a candidate in a few seconds and create an image. Encouraged by broadcast media. Hostile to complex ideas, subtle differences.

sovereignty Claim by government to be able to make its own decisions independently. In federal system sovereignty theoretically divided between national government and states or provinces.

Speaker of the House Presiding officer of the U.S. House of Representatives, chosen by the members of the majority party.

spillover effects Unintended side effects that are not included in a policymaker's original calculations.

spoils system Process by which elected officials reward friends and supporters with government jobs.

spot ad Political advertising on television, usually of short duration; usually candidate-oriented, rather than addressing issues or party loyalty.

stagflation Term coined to describe a combination of high inflation and high unemployment.

Stamp Act British taxation legislation intending to make colonies pay for their own protection. Inflamed revolutionary sentiment.

standing committee Permanent congressional committee with defined (though often broad) jurisdiction.

standing to sue Court-recognized ability to bring case to court. Requires direct, personal stake in a threatened, legally protected interest.

stare decisis Heart of the common law tradition. "Let the decision stand." (Latin) Uses precedent to decide current case.

State Department Executive agency of the U.S. government responsible for foreign policy; maintains foreign service officers in several hundred posts in this country and overseas.

superdelegate Party regulars given delegate status to national convention outside of primary process. Meant to redress balance between "amateurs" and "party-pros."

Superfund Funding mechanism established by Congress in the 1970s to assist state and local governments in cleaning up hazardous toxic waste dump sites.

Supplemental Security Income (SSI) Program created as part of the welfare state in 1974 to provide added assistance to the aged, the blind, and the disabled; pays benefits on the basis of need and is federally funded with state supplements.

supply-side economics The central economic theory of the first Reagan administration, which holds that tax cuts will raise government revenues through increased production and thereby reduce rather than increase the budget deficits.

symbolic politics Nonsubstantive steps taken to reassure public that action is being taken. Can have real consequences, however.

tax expenditure Provision in tax code that reduces normal tax liability for a particular group or function. Provides specific economic benefits that do not appear as line items on budget. Example: the deductibility of mortgage interest on homes.

tax expenditure items Components of welfare state programs in which benefits for particular activities are derived through reductions in tax liability.

Tax Reform Act of 1986 Changes in the tax code designed to simplify it and make it more equitable; lowered the highest tax rates and reduced the number of tax brackets.

term limits Legal provisions that limit the number of times officeholders can be re-elected. Common in executive offices, now increasingly applied to legislative offices.

third parties Any organized political party other than the two main parties. Important source of innovation, seldom gain electoral success.

third-party government System in which government functions are carried out by state and local governments and by organizations in the private sector through contracts with the government.

trade deficit Excess imports over exports.

transfer payments Money paid to individuals by governments through social programs.

treatment as equals The attempt by government to treat all people as equals.

Treaty of Paris September 3, 1783. Ended the Revolutionary War.

tyranny of the majority The belief that political equality might lead to "mob rule."

unicameral Composed of only one house or legislative chamber.

unitary government Sovereignty is exercised by a single central government. Subordinate divisions carry out local functions. Distinguished from federal system of government.

unitary system Form of government in which the national government's authority is more or less uniformly enforced throughout the country.

United Nations Most prominent intergovernmental organization since its founding in 1945. Major operating units include Security Council, General Assembly, and Secretariat. Satellite organizations include World Health Organization (WHO), UN Children's Fund (UNICEF), and UN Educational, Scientific, and Cultural Organization.

United States Information Agency (USIA) Government organization in charge of overt propaganda for the United States.

unit rule Apportions representation on the basis of political divisions regardless of population. Traditionally resulted in over-representation of rural interests. Prohibited by one-person-one-vote rulings of Warren Court. *Reynolds* v. *Sims* (1964).

U.S. courts of appeals Intermediate-level federal courts with no original jurisdiction; consider cases that originated at a lower-level federal court.

U.S. Supreme Court Highest court in the U.S. federal system and in the nation.

victimless crime Illegal action in which there is no obvious victim (for example, prostitution). Real victims may be third parties.

Virginia Plan Plan submitted at the Constitutional Convention of 1787 for a bicameral legislature based on proportional representation.

Voice of America Government propaganda agency, broadcasts news and information radio in forty-two languages.

voucher systems Governnment policy that allows subsidies to follow students to schools of family choice. Some restrict choice to public schools, others include private schools.

War Powers Resolution Legislation passed in 1973 over the veto of President Nixon that requires the president to consult with Congress before sending U.S. troops into combat.

wealth The monetary value of what an individual or household owns, adjusted for indebtedness.

welfare state A set of social policies including pensions, unemployment insurance, health care coverage, and other benefits in which society accepts responsibility for the collective welfare of individuals.

Whig party Political party formed in 1828 from a fraction of the Republican party and remnants of the Federalists, which primarily appealed to New Englanders, especially those with business interests.

whip Subleader of either political party in the U.S. House of Representatives who notifies members of pending business, polls them on their voting intentions, and works to make sure they are present to vote on key issues.

White House Office Within the Executive Office of the President. Includes president's closest aides and advisors.

white primaries Racially exclusive primary election used in the one-party South to bar African-Americans from electoral politics. Prohibited by the Supreme Court in *Nixon* v. *Condon* (1932).

windfall profits Extraordinary corporate gains resulting from external factors, not company performance. Example: money made from high price of scarce oil during OPEC oil embargo in 1970s. Carter administration sponsored windfall profits tax.

INDEX

Abolitionists, 339
Abortion, 181–185, 632
   antiabortion lobby, 419–420
   antiabortion protests, 453–454
   challenges to *Roe* decision, 182–183
   public opinion on, 297–298
   status of states on, 184
Abrams, Jacob, 166
Abrams v. *United States*, 166
Absolute mobility, 251
Acheson, Dean, 36
Acid rain, 792–793
Adams, John, 30, 228, 324, 397, 539
Adolescent Family Life Act, 182
Advocacy advertising, of interest groups, 427
Affirmative action, 203–205
   Bakke case, 203–205
   purpose of, 203
   women, 217–218
AFL-CIO, 412
Age, and voter participation, 314
Agenda setting, in policymaking, 619–620, 632–634
Agnew, Spiro, 535, 548
Aid for International Development, 775
AIDS
   activism for, 625, 628

AIDS (*cont.*)
   development of medication for, 624
   policy aspects, 621–628
      cross-cultural view, 626–627
      governmental levels in, 622–623
      group influence, 625, 628
      resource allocation, 623–624
      response to public policy, 624–625
   public opinion on, 298
   testing as civil liberties issue, 739
Aid to Families with Dependent Children, 124, 135, 137, 141, 678, 681, 686–688
   criticisms of program, 687
   typical payment, 687
   welfare-to-work provisions, 687–688
Air bags, 566
Airline industry, deregulation of, 581, 650
Air pollution, 787, 789–794
   acid rain, 792–793
   dilemmas in solutions to, 793–794
   and global warming, 790–792
   legislation, 789–790
   and ozone depletion, 793

Alaska, 128
Alcohol
   legal drinking age, 147–148, 734
   as legal drug, 734
Alexander, Herbert, 375
Alien and Sedition Acts, 169, 228
Alienation, 21–22, 24, 292–293
   alienation index, 22
   components of, 293
   periods of, 292–293
   political, 21, 24
   and social class, 293
Altruism, of United States, 73–74
Amalgamated Food Employees Local 590 v. *Logan Valley Plaza, Inc.*, 171
Amendment process, 106–109
   proposal of amendment, 107–109
   ratification of amendment, 109
American colonies
   defiance against British authority, 87–89
   economy of, 642–643
   imperial authority, impact of, 86–87
   independence of, 93–94
   political environment of, 86
   Revolutionary War, 89–92
   socioeconomic climate of, 85
American Independent party, 339

INDEX

American Israel Public Affairs Committee, 423
American party, 339
American Revolution. *See* Revolutionary War
Americans with Disabilities Act of 1990, 223
American Voter, The, 287
Amicus curiae brief, 431
Amnesty International, 759, 760
Annapolis Convention, 95
Anthony, Susan B., 39
Antiabortion
  lobby, 419-420
  protests, 453-454
Antidemocratic attitudes, 19-20, 64
Antifederalists, 106, 161-162
Anti-Masonic party, 339
Antitrust laws, 132
Appellate courts, 592-593
Arizona v. *Mauro*, 180
Armstrong, William, 499
Army Corps of Engineers, 786
Art, public support of, 715
Arthur, Chester A., 574
Articles of Confederation, 83, 94-95, 96, 519
  limitations of, 94-95, 111
Arts, 719-721
  federal funding for, 720-721
  public support of, 719-721
Assassinations, in American history, 70, 72-73, 547
Atomic Energy Commission, 565
Attitudes
  public, 273-274
  See also Public opinion

Baker, James, 777
Bakke case, 203-205, 210
Balanced Budget and Emergency Deficit Control Act, 511-512
Barron v. *Baltimore*, 134, 163
Basic rights, and democracy, 9
Bay of Pigs, 636, 762
Beard, Charles, 111
Begin, Menachem, 753
Benenson, Peter, 759
Bentsen, Lloyd, 361
Bernstein, Carl, 542
Bicameral government, 96, 478
Biden, Joe, 388
Big Green, 42, 43, 45
Bill of Rights, 105, 106, 109, 125, 134, 161-163
  Amendments of, 162

Bill of Rights (*cont.*)
  and Fourteenth Amendment, 164-165
  See also Civil liberties
Black Americans
  all-black schools, 737-738
  and civil rights, 186-187
    affirmative action, 203-205
    quotas, 207
    school desegregation, 197-203
    separate but equal doctrine, 31-32, 197
    set-asides, 205-207
  as Democrats, 336
  economic progress of, 211-215
  public opinion on, 289-290, 298-299
  synthesis school of race relations, views of, 214-215
  voting rights for, 184-188
  See also Slavery
Black, Hugo, 164, 181
Blackmun, Harry, 221, 598
Blanket primary, 366
Block grants, 136
Bob Jones University v. *United States*, 176
Boland Amendment, 543-544
Bona fide occupational qualification, 217
Bond, Julian, 229
Booth, John Wilkes, 72
Bork, Robert, 477-478, 598
Bosnia-Herzegovina, 752, 755
Boston Tea Party, 88
Brady Bill, 420
Brady, James, 420
Brady, Sara, 420
Brandeis, Louis, 167, 545, 597
Breast implants, 567
Bremer, Arthur, 72
Brennan, William, 180, 207, 218, 609
Brown, Henry, 33
Brown, Jerry, 356, 362, 370
Brown v. *Board of Education of Topeka*, 198-199, 589, 605
Bryan, William Jennings, 334
Buchanan, Pat, 300, 356, 362
Budget
  alteration, methods of, 652-656
  and Congress, 476, 510-513
  federal deficit, 648, 664-665
  reconciliation process, 511
Budget Enforcement Act, 512
Bull Moose party, 335, 339

Bureaucracy
  cabinet departments, 563
  career track of, 561
  contract bureaucracies, 561
  criticisms of
    rules and regulations, 577
    size of bureaucracy, 575-577
    unresponsiveness issue, 573-575
  cross-cultural view, 568
  and democracy, 559, 571
  expertise of, 569-570
  historical view of, 560-561, 573-574
  independent agencies of, 563-564
  meaning of, 557-558
  and political process, 565-571
  public opinion of, 571
  reforms
    deregulation, 580-581
    merit-based pay raises, 574-575
    privatization, 576-577
    Senior Executive Service, 574, 575
    third-party government, 575-576
  regulatory commissions, 564-565
  specialization of agencies, 562
  Weber's conception of, 558-559
  women and minorities in, 561
Bureau of Intelligence, 748
Bureau of Reclamation, 786
Burger, Warren, 176, 179, 608, 716
Burnham, Walter Dean, 461
Bush, Barbara, 535
Bush, George, 171, 210, 215, 279, 296, 300, 323, 324, 356, 361, 362, 367, 369, 383, 506-507, 539, 545-547, 581, 659, 670, 774, 804-805
Bush, Neil, 403
Business organizations, 410-411
  and foreign policy, 749
  influence seeking of, 411-412
  types of, 411
  See also Corporations
Business Roundtable, 411
Busing, school desegregation, 200-202

Cabinet, 531-533
  challenges to President from, 531-533
  departments of, 531
  historical view, 563

INDEX

Cabinet (cont.)
  proposals for reshaping of, 532–533
  subcabinet, 533
Calhoun, John C., 130
Calloway, Enoch, 194
Campaigns. *See* Political campaigns
Campbell, Ben Nighthorse, 493
Camp David Peace Accords, 753
Canadian health-care system, 697, 698–699
Capitalism, 239–240
  controlled capitalism, 644–647
  criticisms of, 239–240
  and development of democracy, 7
  elements of, 239
  laissez-faire capitalism, 239, 643–644
Capital punishment. *See* Death penalty
Carter, Jimmy, 294–295, 309, 336, 340, 347, 356, 367, 374, 388, 394, 396, 508, 521, 538, 574–575, 746, 753, 763, 766, 773
Carter, Rosalyn, 534, 535
Cash transfers, meaning of, 681
Castro, Fidel, 28, 636, 765
Catastrophic Health Care Law, 694
Categorical grants, 136
Caucuses, influence of, 497–498
Centers for Disease Control, 695
  and AIDS crisis, 621
Central Intelligence Agency, 563–564, 750–751
  functions of, 748, 750
  future of, 750, 751
  types of covert activities, 750–751
Cermak, Anton, 72
Certificates of need, 697
Challenger, 570
Chambers, Whittaker, 36
Chaplinsky v. *New Hampshire*, 171
Checks and balances, 478
  process of, 99–102
  unwritten forms of, 101
Chief justice, 595
Child nutrition program, 701
Child pornography, 717, 719
Chinese Exclusion Act, 66
Chlorofluorocarbons, and ozone depletion, 793
Church-state separation, freedom of religion, aspects of, 174–178
Churchill, Winston, 12
Cigarettes, as legal drug, 734

Circuit courts, 595
Citizen-government relationship, 25–27
  and conflict, 27
  trust aspect, 25–27
City of Richmond v. *Croson*, 206–207
Civil Aeronautics Board, 581, 650
Civil cases, 588
Civil disobedience, 450–456
  antiabortion protests, 453–454
  civil war protests, 451–452
  and Gandhi, 455
  historical view, 450–451
  and law, 454
  Vietnam protests, 452–453
Civil liberties
  abortion issue, 181–185
  AIDS testing as issue, 739
  Bill of Rights, 161–163
  and federalism, 163–165
  freedom of press, 172–174
  freedom of religion, 174–178
  freedom of speech, 165–172
  rights of accused, 178–181
  right to vote, 185–188
Civil religion, 76
Civil rights
  Bill of Rights, 105
  and black Americans
    affirmative action, 203–205
    quotas, 207
    school desegregation, 197–203
    separate but equal doctrine, 31–32, 197
    set-asides, 205–207
  as Constitutional right, 195–196
  demonstrations, 442, 451–452
  disparate impact test, 207, 210
  gay rights, 218–221
  government repression of, 228–231
  group rights, 208
  public opinion on, 298–299
  rights of disabled, 222–224
  treatment as equals concept, 196–197
  and women
    affirmative action, 217–218
    gender discrimination legislation, 215–217
    protective discrimination, 217
Civil Rights Act of 1871, 453
Civil Rights Act of 1964, 141, 199, 204, 207, 317
  Title IX, 216
  Title VII, 216

Civil Rights Act of 1991, 539
Civil Rights Bill of 1990, 210
Civil Rights Bill of 1991, 207, 210
Civil Rights Restoration Act of 1988, 217, 525
Civil Service Commission, 574, 575
Civil service system, 574
Civil War, 53, 61, 104, 119
  and black Americans, 30–31, 34, 186
  impact on federalism, 130–131
Clandestine operations, forms of, 756
Clayton Act of 1914, 226
Clean Air Acts, 141, 631, 789–790, 793, 804
Clean Water Acts, 795, 796
Clear and present danger test, 167, 170
Cleveland, Grover, 38
Clientele groups, 571
Clinton, Bill, 309, 323, 324, 346, 356, 362, 363, 377, 395, 534, 670, 696, 777
Clinton, Hillary, 535
Closed primary, 366
Cluster sampling, 284
Coal, 810–811
Coelho, Tony, 405, 499
Cold War, 76, 761–764
  end of, 361, 413, 629, 758, 776–777
  history of, 761–764
  post–Cold War foreign policy, 765–772
  and United States as superpower, 745–746
Coleman, Roger, 181
Collazo, Oscar, 72
Collective bargaining, 226, 228
Colonies. *See* American colonies
Colorado v. *Spring*, 180
Commerce Act, 411
Commerce clause, 132–133
Committee on Committees, 484
Committee on Political Education, 412
Committees of Congress. *See* Congress, committees of
Committee to Defend Reproductive Rights v. *Myers*, 593
Common Cause, 382, 407, 415, 415–416
Common law, 588
Common Sense (Paine), 88
Commonwealth, 128

INDEX

Communism, 28
　and Cold War, 761–763
　elements of, 245n
　end in Soviet Union, 764
Community-based corrections, 727
Competitiveness Council, 581, 790, 805
Comprehensive Employment and Training Act, 576, 690
Conable, Barber B. Jr., 794
Concurrent powers, 124
Congress
　as bicameral legislature, 478
　and budget, 510–513
　　Gramm-Rudman-Hollings Act, 511–512
　　reforms to budget system, 510–511, 512–513
　and checks and balances, 478
　committees of, 483–488
　　committee assignments, 484, 487
　　fragmented responsibilities of, 486, 487–488
　　select committees, 483, 485
　　standing committees, 483, 484, 485
　　subcommittees, 487
　functions of
　　budget creation, 476
　　consent on presidential appointments, 477–478
　　investigative role, 477
　　lawmaking, 476
　　ombudsman function, 477
　　oversight function, 476
　　public policy forum, 475–476
　hierarchy of, 479–492
　lawmaking, 488–492
　leadership of, 481–483
　and lobbying, 427–428
　members of. *See* Congressional members
　and President, 503–510, 536–539
　　dealing with resistant Congress, 538–539
　　liaison staffers, job of, 537
　　patronage issue, 537–538
　　secrecy issue, 505–506
　　type of relationship, 503–505
　　veto power, 539
　　War Powers Resolution, 507–510
　reforms, 501–503
　representation, nature of, 474
　See also House of Representatives; Senate

Congressional Budget and Impoundment Control Act, 510–511
Congressional Budget Office, 511
Congressional Human Rights Foundation, 498
Congressional members
　ethics of, 499–501
　influences to
　　caucuses, 497–498
　　ideology, 495–497
　　interest groups, 498–499
　　political party, 495
　personal characteristics of, 493–494
Connecticut Compromise, 96–97
Conrail, 576
Conscientious objectors, rights of, 178
Consciousness-raising, and protest, 456
Conservatism, as political label, 294–296
Conservative liberals, views of, 61–62
Conservative socialism, 245
Consociational democracy, 29
Constitution
　amendment process, 106–109
　Bill of Rights, 105, 106
　division of power, 97–102
　elastic clause, 105
　importance of, 110–112
　indirect representation concept, 102
　national government, nature of, 96–97, 104–105
　supremacy clause, 104
Constitutional Convention, 83–84, 95–105
　participation at, 95
　proposals of
　　amendment process, 106–109
　　indirect representation, 102
　　limitation of power, 97–98, 124–125
　　national government, 96–97
　ratification of Constitution, 106
　unresolved issues of, 102, 104–106
Consumer Product Safety Commission, 417, 580
Containment, 762
Continental Congress, 93, 95
Contract bureaucracies, 561
Contras, 77, 295, 300, 538
Coonerty, Neal, 714

Cooperative federalism, 135
Corporations, 255–257
　and environmental issues, 803
　influence on political economy, 256, 257
　public opinion on, 299
　See also Business organizations
Corps of Engineers, 561, 562
Council of Economic Advisers, 531
Council on Environmental Quality, 531
Court of appeals, 593
Courts
　decision-making process, 600–601
　　basis of decisions, 591–592
　expansion of legal system, 611–612
　federal court system, 593–595
　flow of litigation, 599–600
　functions of, 588–591
　influences of, 589
　state court systems, 592–593
　types of legal cases, 588
Courts of appeals, 595
Cranston, Alan, 404, 405
Crime
　against property and persons, 724
　and drugs, 731–734
　and liberty, 722, 724
　victimless crime, 724
Crime rates, 728–731
　factors in interpretation of, 729
　victimization trends, 729–730
Criminal cases, 588
Criminal justice system, 591
　death penalty, 727–728
　law enforcement, 725–726
　plea bargaining, 592
　prisons, 726–727
Critical election, 306n
Cross-sectional studies, 274
Crotty, William, 315
Crucible, The (Miller), 36
Cuba, 636, 762, 765
Cuellar, Javier Perez de, 758
Cutback politics, 502–503
Czolgosz, Leon, 72

Danforth, John, 776
Darman, Richard, 530
Death penalty, 727–728
　public opinion on, 299, 728
Deaver, Michael, 405
Declaration of Independence, 55, 84, 89, 186, 194
Declaration of Sentiments, 38
DeConcini, Dennis, 404, 405, 502

Decrementalism, 136
De facto segregation, 200, 201, 202
Defense Department, 563
   and foreign policy, 748
Defense Intelligence Agency, 748
Defense spending
   defense budget, 260-261
   and end of Cold War, 413, 629
   and interest group activity, 413-415
   methods of continuing spending, 629
Deferred issues, 633-634
Deinstitutionalization, 223
   and homelessness, 704-705
De jure segregation, 200, 201
Delegated powers, 98, 122
Delegate theory, 474
Democracy
   basic elements of, 10
   and bureaucracy, 559, 571
   consociational democracy, 29
   criticisms of, 27-28, 30, 32
   democratic reforms, 37-45
   egalitarian democracy, 9-10
   and extraordinary politics, 444, 448-449
   future view of, 817-818
   ideal democracy, 11-12
   liberal democracy, 7-9
   majoritarian democracy, 6-7
   maximalist view of, 13-14
   minimalist view of, 12-13
   and political culture, 52-53
   power distribution in, 14-19
   problems related to
      citizen-government problems, 25-27
      failure to exercise rights, 19-24
      restrictions of democracy, 30-37
      unequal power distribution, 16-19
   and public opinion, 286-291
   and social control, 714
Democratic Leadership Council, 357
Democratic-Republicans, 332
Democrats
   characteristics of, 306, 336
   creation of national committee, 343
   historical view, 332, 335-336
   as liberals, 296
   nationalization of, 343
   New Deal Democrats, 306-308
   party reforms, 345-347
Demographics, meaning of, 66

Dennis et al v. *United States*, 36, 168
Department of Agriculture, 561-562, 563, 700
Department of Commerce, 563
Department of Defense, 561, 563
Department of Education, 563
Department of Energy, 563
Department of Health and Human Services, 561, 563
Department of Health, Education and Welfare, 199
Department of Housing and Urban Development, 563
Department of Labor, 563
Department of the Interior, 563
Department of Transportation, 563
Department of Veterans Affairs, 563
Depression, nature of, 644
   See also Great Depression
Deregulation, 580-581
   examples of, 581
   meaning of, 136, 580
   proponents of, 650-651
Detente, 763
Devalle, Eric Arturo, 766
Deviating election, 306n
Devolution, 136
Dewitt, Benjamin, 40
Dinkins, David N., 146
Diplomacy, 752-753
   diplomatic recognition, 752
   examples of, 752-753
Direct-mail marketing, lobbying, 427
Disability income program, 683
Disabled
   economic progress of, 224
   equal rights for, 222-224
   legislation related to, 222-223
Discrimination
   forms of, 68
   against immigrant groups, 65, 68-69
   remedies for. *See* Civil Rights
   segregation of black Americans, 30-34
Disparate impact test, 207, 210
Displaced issues, 633
District, 128
District courts, 595
District of Columbia, 128
Diverted issues, 634
Division of power, 97-102, 122-124
   checks and balances, 99-102
   national and state governments, 98-99, 104

Division of power (*cont.*)
   nature of, 99-100
   powers of federal government, 122-124
   powers of the states, 122-124
Dixiecrats, 336, 339, 343
Dixon, Julian, 499
Dole, Bob, 367, 768
Dole, Elizabeth, 566
Domestic partnership benefits, 219
Domestic Policy Council, 532
Douglas, Stephen A., 392-393
Douglas, William O., 164
Dred Scott v. *Sanford*, 133, 607
Drinking age, federal regulation of, 147-148, 734
Drugs, 731-734
   drug-related crime, 732
   legal aspects, historical view, 731-732
   legal drugs, 734
   legalization issue, 733-734
   rise in federal convictions, 729-730
   social costs of use, 734
Drug testing, 738-739
   mandatory testing, 738
   opponents of, 739
Dual citizenship, 118-119
Dual federalism, 133, 139, 606-607
Due process, meaning of, 9, 125, 163
Dukakis, Michael, 296, 369
Duke, David, 64, 362
Durenburger, Dave, 499
Durham, Christine, 593
Durkheim, Emile, 722
Dworkin, Andrea, 718

Eagleton, Thomas, 535
Earth Day, 787
Earth Summit, 783-784, 801, 805, 807
   achievements of, 784
Eastern Europe, 449, 629
Economic aid. *See* Foreign aid
Economic competition, global, 772-773
Economic Interpretation of the Constitution, An (Beard), 111-112
Economic issues, public opinion on, 299-300
Economic Policy Council, 532
Economic power, and democracy, 17-18

INDEX

Economic theory
  controlled capitalism, 644–647
  Keynesian economics, 646
  laissez-faire capitalism, 643–644
  mercantilism, 642–643
  See also Political economy
Economy
  countercyclical policy, 652
  depression, 644
  federal deficit, 648, 664–665
  and Federal Reserve Board, 658–659
  fiscal policy, 652–656
  historical view
    colonial period, 642–643
    early twentieth century, 644
    and Great Depression, 644–647
    historical view, post-World War II, 647–649
    nineteenth century, 643–644
  and industrial decline, 665–671
  inflation, 648
  microeconomic policy, 650–651
  monetary policy, 656–659
  recession, 644, 664
  stagflation, 644
  supply-side economics, 659–662
  and tax system, 662–664
Edgewood v. *Kirby*, 736
Education, 735–740
  for disabled children, 222–223
  equitable school funding, 735–737
  issues related to values, 737–740
Educational level
  and public sentiment, 304–305
  and voter participation, 314
Education for All Handicapped Children Act of 1975, 222–223
Edwards v. *California*, 128
Egalitarian democracy, 9–10
Eighteenth Amendment, 109, 732
Eighth Amendment, 162
Eisenhower, Dwight D., 391, 413, 521, 547, 746
Elastic clause, 105
Elections
  electoral patterns
    of recent past, 308–310
    types of, 306n
  interelection stage, 366
  and media, 387–398
  political campaigns, 364–372
  primary election, 365–366
  proportional representation, 327
  See also Presidential elections

Electoral college, 373–374
  function of, 102
  operation of, 373–374
  reform proposals, 374
Elitism, and power, 14
Ellsberg, Daniel, 173
El Salvador, 300, 508–509, 765
Embargo, purpose of, 755
Emergency Food Assistance Program, 701
Employee stock ownership plans, 247
Enabling act, 128
Endangered Species Act, 800–801
Endara, Guillermo, 766
Energy, 805–813
  alternative sources, 806–807, 811
  fossil fuels, 806, 810
  nuclear power, 811
  political issues, 809, 812–813
  rate of U.S. use, 807–808
  renewable sources, 807
Engels, Friedrich, 241
Engel v. *Vitale*, 175
Enumerated powers, 122, 123
Environment
  activism for, 802–803
  agencies/legislation related to, 787, 789–790, 793, 795–796, 797–802
  air pollution, 789–794
  Bush administration activities, 804–805
  and corporations, 803
  cross-cultural view, 798–799
  energy consumption, 805–813
  history of concern with, 786–787
  priorities for environmental issues, 787–788
  public opinion on, 299–300
  Reagan administration activities, 797, 803
  toxic chemicals, 797–802
  water pollution, 794–797
Environmental Defense Fund, 422
Environmental impact statement, 787
Environmental interest groups, 420, 422
  funding for, 422
  growth of, 420
  types of, 420, 422
Environmental Policy Institute, 422
Environmental Protection Agency, 431, 562, 563, 580, 787
Equal Employment Opportunity Commission, 580

Equality
  concept of, 195, 203
  cross-cultural view, 58–59
  meaning of, 60
  treatment as equals concept, 196–197
  See also Civil rights
Equal Pay Act of 1963, 215
Equal protection, 195–196, 736
  meaning of, 9, 163–164
Equal Rights Amendment, 109, 151
Espionage Act of 1917, 166
Establishment clause, 174, 176–177
Estonia, 757
Ethics, and congressional members, 499–501
Ethics in Government Act, 499
Ethics law, 434–435
Ethnic groups, and foreign policy, 749
Evans, Richard, 730
Exclusionary rule, 179, 610
Executive agreement, 524
Executive Office, 529–531
  National Security Council, 530–531
  Office of Management and Budget, 529–530
  White House Office, 529
Expansionism, foreign policy, 760–761
Extraordinary politics, 442–449
  basis of, 442
  and democracy, 444, 448–449
  government response to, 447–449
  nature of, 442–444
  reasons for, 444–446
  See also Protest

Fairness Doctrine, 389
Falwell, Jerry, 174, 621
Family, and political socialization, 278
Family Assistance Program, 708
Family Support Act, 687
Federal Aviation Administration, 581
Federal budget deficit, 648, 664–665
  and Keynesian economics, 652
  proposed solutions to, 664
  size of, 664
Federal Communications Commission, 564–565, 580, 581, 650
Federal court system, 593–595
  judicial review, 601–602
  noncompliance, overcoming, 605

Federal court system (*cont.*)
  overrule of decisions, 604
  restraints on power, 602, 604
  types of courts, 593–595
  See also Supreme Court
Federal Deposit Insurance
    Corporation, 564
Federal Election Campaign Act,
    378, 379
Federal Election Commission, 379
Federal Flag Protection Act of 1989,
    171
Federal government
  formation of. *See* Constitution;
    Constitutional Convention
  powers of
    expansion of powers, 122–123
    types of powers, 122–124
Federal Housing Administration,
    701–702
Federalism
  basis of
    division of powers, 122–124
    interstate obligations, 125, 128
    limitations on government,
      124–125
  and civil liberties, 163–165
  cooperative federalism, 135
  dual federalism, 133, 139
  duality of system, 118–119
  German system, 126–127
  influences on
    Civil War, 130–131
    Great Depression, 132
    industrial expansion, 131–132
  as intergovernmental relations,
    142–143
  layer cake federalism, 139
  marble cake federalism, 139
  new federalism
    Great Society, 135
    New Deal, 135
    Reagan strategy, 136–137
    revenue sharing programs,
      135–136, 138
  pros and cons of, 152
  relationship to states functioning,
    138–143
  and Supreme Court, 132–134
    cases in evolution of federalism,
      132–134
  tensions related to
    interstate tensions, 144, 146
    regional rivalries, 143–144
Federalist Papers, 93, 106
  Federalist No. 10, 408
  Federalist No. 51, 99

Federalist Papers (*cont.*)
  Federalist No. 78, 604
  nature of, 98–99
Federalists, 106, 332
Federal Flag Protection Act, 633
Federal Regulation of Lobbying Act,
    432–433
Federal Reserve System
  manipulation of economy,
    658–659
  member banks, 656
  and monetary policy, 656,
    658–659
  political influences to, 659
Federal Trade Commission, 565,
    581, 650
Feminism
  on obscenity, 718–719
  women's suffrage movement,
    37–39
  See also Women
Fetal tissue research, 696
Fifteenth Amendment, 30, 163, 186
Fifth Amendment, 162, 178,
    195, 739
Fighting words, First Amendment
    rights, 170–171
Filibuster, 491, 501
Fillilove v. *Klutznick*, 206
Finney, Joan, 453
First Amendment, 162, 164, 740
First Continental Congress, 88
First lady, role of, 533, 534–535
Fiscal policy, 652–656
  purpose of, 652
  spending policies, 653
  tax system, 653–656
Flag desecration, 170, 171, 633
Foley, Tom, 461
Food and Drug Administration, 224,
    417, 567
  workings of, 578–579
Food, Drug and Cosmetic Act of
    1938, 225
Food, Drug and Insecticide
    Administration, 225
Food Security Act, 700
Food stamps program, 678, 681,
    700–701
  purposes of, 700
Ford, Gerald, 72, 73, 295, 394, 508,
    548, 746
Foreign aid, 754, 774–776
  cross-cultural view, 776
  foreign aid agencies, 775
Foreign policy
  clandestine operations in, 756

Foreign policy (*cont.*)
  and Congress, 510
  diplomacy in, 752–753
  economic aspects of, 754–756,
    772–773
  and executive branch, 746–748
  expansionism, 760–761
  foreign aid, 774–776
  future view, 776–777
  historical view, 75–76
    Cold War, 761–764
    nineteenth century, 760–761
    post-Cold War, 765–772
    World Wars I and II, 761
  and human rights, 773–774
  and interest groups, 749
  and intergovernmental
    organizations, 758, 759–760
  internationalism, 300, 777–778
  interventionism, 300
  isolationism, 300, 760, 777
  military intervention, 756–757
  and multinational corporations,
    760
  and nongovernmental
    organizations, 758, 760
  and political elites, 748
  propaganda, use of, 754
  and public opinion, 300, 749,
    752
  and United Nations, 758–759
Foreman, Carol Tucker, 417
Fossil fuels, 806, 807, 810
Fourteenth Amendment, 30, 33, 39,
    125, 133, 134, 163, 168, 186,
    194, 195, 607
Fourth Amendment, 162, 739
Frankfurter, Felix, 177
Franklin, Benjamin, 95, 96
Fraser, Donald, 345
Freedom of Information Act, 384
Freedom of press, 172–174
  and libel suits, 173–174
  and prior restraint, 173
  threats to, 173–174
Freedom of religion, 174–178
  establishment clause, 174, 176
  free exercise clause, 174,
    177–178
  Lemon test, 176–177
Freedom of speech, 165–172
  advocacy of overthrow of
    government, 168–170
  clear and present danger test,
    167, 170
  current trends related to, 170
  free speech, nature of, 165–166

INDEX

Freedom of speech (*cont.*)
   limits on political speech, 166–168
   symbolic speech, 170–171
Free enterprise, meaning of, 61
Free exercise clause, 174, 177–178
Free trade zones, 669, 773
French Revolution, 92
Friends of the Earth, 422
Fromme, Lynette, 72
Full faith and credit provision, nature of, 125, 127
Fulton, Robert, 132
Fungicide and Rodenticide Act, 801

Gaines, Lloyd, 197
Galbraith, John Kenneth, 570
Gandhi, Mahatma, nonviolent protest of, 451, 455
Garfield, James, 72, 547, 574
Garner, Nance, 533
Gas, natural, 810
Gay rights, 218–221
   domestic partnership benefits, 219
   job benefits for homosexuals, 219–220
   military and homosexuals, 219
   movement for, 218
   privacy rights, 221
   public opinion on, 298
Gedulig v. *Aiello*, 217
Gender
   and public sentiment, 305
   and voter participation, 314
Gender discrimination
   and affirmative action, 217–218
   in military, 216
Gender gap, 305
General Agreement on Tariffs and Trade, 760
Gephardt, Richard, 361, 367
Gibbons v. *Ogden*, 132–133
Gideon v. *Wainwright*, 178
Gini index, 251n, 264
Ginsburg, Douglas, 478, 598
Gitlow, Benjamin, 167
Gitlow v. *New York*, 163–164, 167, 168
Glasnost, 764
Glenn, John, 404, 405
Global protection against limited strikes, 415, 629
Global warming, 790–792
Goldwater, Barry, 296, 301
Gooding v. *Wilson*, 171
Gore, Al, 369, 534, 535, 805

Government programs, oversight by Congress, 476
Government spending, 259–262
   defense budget, 260–261
   historical rise in expenditures, 259
   liberal and conservative views, 259–260
   social welfare spending, 261–262
   transfer payments, 261–262, 264
Gramm-Rudman-Hollings Act, 511–512
Grandfather clause, 187
Grand jury, 592
Granville, George, 88
Grass-roots movements, 56
Gray, Edwin, 404
Great Depression, 41, 143, 227, 243, 306, 529, 629
   events leading to, 644–646
   impact on federalism, 132
   and New Deal, 62, 646–647
   remedies to, 646–647
   and rise of Democrats, 306, 335–336
Great Society, 124, 510, 637, 689
   evaluation of, 680–681, 706
   as expansion of welfare state, 679–681
   as new federalism, 135
Greece (ancient), 450
   democracy in, 6
Greenhouse effect, 790–792
Green Party, German, 328–329
Green v. *School Board of New Kent County*, 199
Gregg v. *Georgia*, 610
Grenada, invasion of, 509, 752, 756
Griggs v. *Duke Power Co.*, 207
Grimke sisters, 37–38
Gross national product, size of, 247
Group rights, 208
Grove City College v. *Bell*, 216, 525
Guam, 128
Guest worker program, 67
Guiteau, Charles, 72
Gulf of Tonkin Resolution, 507
   and Congress, 540–541, 542
Gun control, 421
Gun lobby, 420

Habeas corpus, 180–181
Hague, 758
Haldeman, H.R., 528
Hamilton, Alexander, 95, 98, 122, 130, 332, 573, 604
Hamilton, Lee, 423

Hammer v. *Dagenhart*, 134
Hardwick, Michael, 220–221
Harkin, Tom, 62, 368
Harlan, John Marshall, 33, 194
Harrison Narcotic Act, 731
Harrison, William Henry, 332–333, 391, 547
Harris v. *McRae*, 182
Hart, Gary, 369, 388
Hawaii, 128
   health-care system, 150
Head Start, 124, 223, 680
Health and safety, 224–225
   legislation related to, 225, 555
   safety inspection procedures, 556–557
Health care
   crisis in, 692
   cross-cultural view, 698–699
   Hawaiian health-care system, 150
   Medicaid, 695
   Medicare, 693–694
   nursing home care, 695
   obstacles to reform, 692–693, 697
   private and public system, 691–692
   reform proposals, 696–700
Health-care insurance
   Canadian-style plan, 697
   to gay partners, 219–220
   insurance market reform, 697
   pay or play type, 697
Health maintenance organizations, 697
Hearst, William Randolph, 387
Hegemony, 248
Heilbroner, Robert, 664
Helms, Jesse, 61, 721
Helsinki Watch, 760
Hicklin v. *Regina*, 716
Hill, Anita, 299, 476, 729
Hinckley, John, 72
Hiss, Alger, 35–36
Ho Chi Minh, 73
Holmes, Oliver Wendell, 167
Homelessness
   causes of, 704–705
   federal support for homeless, 706
Homeownership Opportunities for People Everywhere, 704
Home rule, 124, 128
Hoover, J. Edgar, 230
House Committee on Standards of Official Conduct, 499
House of Representatives, 101, 308
   compared to Senate, 479
   and constituents, 477

House of Representatives (*cont.*)
  majority and minority leaders, 482
  Speaker of the House, 481–482
  term limits, 460–461
House Rules Committee, 491, 501
House Un-American Activities Committee, 36
House Ways and Means Committee, 502
Housing programs, federal, 701–704
Hughes, Charles Evans, 173
Human immunodeficiency virus (HIV), 622
  See also AIDS
Humanism, 55–56
Human rights, and foreign policy, 773–774
Human rights organizations, types of, 760
Humphrey, Hubert, 345, 367
Humphrey-Hawkins bill, 708
Huntington, Samuel, 30
Hussein, Saddam, 545, 755, 768–770, 774
Hustler Magazine v. *Falwell*, 174, 610

Iacocca, Lee, 566
Ideal democracy, 11–12
Ideology, 325
  ideological awareness, cross-cultural view, 331
  meaning of, 293
  and voting in Congress, 495–497
Ignorance, as threat to democracy, 24
Illinois v. *Perkins*, 180
Imagemaking, political, 389–393
Immigration
  discrimination against ethnic groups, 65, 68–69
  policy, historical view, 66–67
Immigration Act of 1965, 66
Immigration Act of 1990, 67
Immigration and Naturalization Service, 67
Immigration Reform and Control Act of 1986, 66–67
Impeachment, 520, 547
  power of, 100
Imperial presidency, 541
Implementation phase, of policymaking, 620, 636
Implied powers, 105, 122
Income distribution, 249–253
  cross-cultural view, 252, 253
  inequality of, 250–251

Income distribution (*cont.*)
  and mobility, 251, 253
  and social class, 249
Incremental politics, 630
Incumbent, 365–366
Independent agencies, 563–564
Indirect representation, nature of, 102
Individualism, meaning of, 60
Industrial expansion, impact on federalism, 131–132
Industrial Workers of the World, 229
Industry
  decline in U.S., 665–669
  industrial policy, 670–671
  proposals for revival of, 669–671
Inflation
  of 1970s, 648
  nature of, 648
  remedies for, 648
Initiatives
  advantages/disadvantages of, 40–41
  examples of, 42, 43
  function of, 40
In-kind transfers, meaning of, 681
Insurance market reform, 697
Intelligence agencies, 748
  See also Central Intelligence Agency
Intelligence committees, Congressional, 505–506
Interelection stage, 366
Interest group liberalism, and power, 15
Interest groups
  and bureaucracy, 571
  business organizations, 410–411
  defense lobby, 414–415
  and foreign policy, 749
  functions of, 407
  labor organizations, 412–413
  lobbying, operation of, 423–433
  as political subsystems, 409–410
  power of, 18
  problems of, 407–409
  public interest groups, 415–417
  public interest versus personal interests, 434–435
  single-issue groups, 418–423
    antiabortion lobby, 419–420
    environmental groups, 420, 422
    gun lobby, 420
    pro-Israel interests, 422–423
  See also Lobbying
Interest rates, control of, 658, 659

Intergovernmental lobbying, 430–431
Intergovernmental organizations, 758, 759–760
  types of, 758–759
Intergovernmental relations, 142–143
International Development Agency, 775
Internationalism, 300, 308, 777–778
  meaning of, 300
Interstate Commerce Commission, 571, 577, 581, 644
Interventionism, 308
  meaning of, 300
In vitro fertilization, 419
Iran, hostages in, 508
Iran-Contra affair, 384, 476, 506, 531, 766
  events of, 543–545
Iron triangle, 414
Isaac Walton League, 422
Isolationism, 300, 760, 777
  meaning of, 300
Israel, pro-Israel interest groups, 422–423

Jackson, Andrew, 332, 539, 574, 644
Jackson, Jesse, 348, 369, 376–377
Jackson, Robert H., 178
Japanese detention camps, 69, 448
Jay, John, 98, 111
Jefferson, Thomas, 55, 73, 89, 103, 105, 106, 122, 186, 332, 397, 539
Jim Crow laws, 607
Job Corps, 690
Job Corps Training Centers, 690
Job Opportunities and Basic Skills, 687
Job programs, federal, 689–690
Job Training Partnership Act, 690
John Paul II, Pope, 77
Johnson, Andrew, 525, 547
Johnson, Hiram, 40
Johnson, Lyndon, 73, 124, 135, 187, 199, 229, 265, 345, 369, 507, 539, 541, 653, 679–681
Johnson, Paul, 217
Joint Chiefs of Staff, role of, 748
Joyce, Diane, 217–218
Judicial Conference of the United States, 595
Judicial council, 595
Judicial review, 431, 588, 601–602
  cross-cultural view, 603

INDEX

Judicial review (cont.)
 historical view, 601–602
 meaning of, 588
Judiciary Act of 1789, 602
Jungle, The (Sinclair), 224–225
Justice Department, 199, 563, 567

Kahan, Mark, 650
Keating, Charles H., 404
Kelly, Patrick, 27, 453
Kelsey, Frances O., 578
Kemp, Jack, 704
Kennedy, Anthony M., 478, 598, 602
Kennedy, Edward, 62, 294
Kennedy, John F., 65, 72, 73, 187, 393, 442, 530, 539, 547, 636, 746
Kennedy, Robert, 70, 72, 345, 530
Kent State tragedy, 27, 448
Kerner Commission report, 212
Kessler, David, 578
Keynesian economics, 646, 652
 versus supply-side economics, 659, 660
Keynes, John Maynard, 646
Khrushchev, Nikita, 762
King, Martin Luther, Jr., 70, 187, 229, 442, 451
 civil rights demonstrations, 442, 451–452
 FBI harassment of, 230
 letter from Birmingham jail, 462–466
King, Rodney, 71
Kirkpatrick, Jean, 449
Kissinger, Henry, 530–531
Know-Nothing party, 339
Koop, C. Everett, 625
Korean War, 34, 524
Kramer, Larry, 625
Kraus, Bill, 625
Krim, Matilde, 625
Ku Klux Klan, 34, 62, 64, 441, 444
 historical view, 446–447

Labels, political, 294–296
Labor organizations, 412–413
 and foreign policy, 749
Labor unions, 412–413
 development of, 412
 influence seeking of, 412
 lobbying of, 412–413
La Follette, Robert, 339
Laissez-faire capitalism, 239, 643–644
Landsat, 576

Law, sources of, 600
Law enforcement system, 725–726
Lawmaking, 476, 488–492
 amendment process, 106–109
 Congressional committee consideration, 488, 491
 Congressional floor debate, 491
 Congressional votes on, 491
 filibuster, 491, 501
 implementation of law, 492
 origination of law, 488
 presidential consideration, 492
 proposal of legislation, 107–109, 488
 riders to law, 488, 490
 veto of law, 492
Lawyers Committee for Human Rights, 760
Layer cake federalism, 139
League of Nations, 746, 758, 761
Lebanon, withdrawal of troops, 509
Legislative Reorganization Act, 432, 483
Legitimation, in policymaking, 620
Lemon socialism, 257
Lemon test, 176–177
Lemon v. *Kurtzman*, 176–177
Lend Lease, 524
Levison, Stanley D., 230
Libel, meaning of, 173
Libel suits, and freedom of press, 173–174
Liberal democracy, 7–9
Liberalism, 54–78
 conservative liberals, 61–62
 eighteenth-century views, 56–57, 60
 failures of
  ethnic intolerance, 65–69
  foreign policy, 75–76
  religion/morality in politics, 76–78
  violence in American society, 69–71
 foundations of, 54–56
 New Deal liberalism, 62–63
 as political label, 294–296
 strength of, 61, 63
 values of, 60
Liberation theology, 77–78
Libertarianism, 64–65
 views of, 64–65
Liberty, meaning of, 60
Liberty Tree, 88
Libya, 756
Limits on government, meaning of, 60

Lincoln, Abraham, 130, 391, 392–393, 452, 525, 539, 547
Line-item veto, 539
Livingston, Robert, 132
Lobbying, 423–433
 advocacy advertising, 426
 by labor unions, 412
 concerns about, 432
 in Congress, 427–428
 direct-mail marketing, 427
 influence on courts, 431
 insider strategies, 425–426
 intergovernmental lobbying, 430–431
 outsider strategies, 426–427
 power, influencing factors, 423–425
 and president, 428–430
 regulation of, 432–433
 spending of lobbys, 431–432
 See also Interest groups
Local politics, 340, 342
 influence of, 340, 342
 political machine, 340
Lochner v. *New York*, 134
Locke, John, 56
Logrolling, 748
Longitudinal studies, 274
Lowi, Theodore, 15
Loyalty program, Truman, 35–36
Lukens, Buz, 499

MacArthur, Douglas, 110
McCain, John, 404
McCarthy, Eugene, 345
McCarthyism, 34–37, 229
 development of, 34–36
McCarthy, Joseph, 34, 387
McCulloch v. *Maryland*, 104, 105, 122, 133, 602
McGeady, Paul, 717
McGovern-Fraser Commission, 345
McGovern, George, 345, 347, 367, 535
McKinley, William, 72, 334, 547
Macroeconomics
 fiscal policy, 652–656
 monetary policy, 656, 658–659
Macropolitics, 409
Madison, James, 84, 93, 95, 98, 99, 101–102, 105, 112, 324, 332, 407–408
Magnet schools, 202
Maher v. *Roe*, 593
Maine v. *Moulton*, 180
Maintaining election, 306n
Majoritarian democracy, 6–7, 93

INDEX

Majority leader, 482
Majority rule, 272–273
   in ancient Greece, 6
   and elections, 8
Majority whip, 482
Malcolm X, 70, 187
Managed health care, 697
Manifest destiny, 75
Manufacturing, decline in U.S., 665–669
Mapplethorpe, Robert, 717, 718, 721
Marble cake federalism, 139
Marbury v. *Madison*, 602
Marcos, Ferdinand, 774
Market socialism, 247
Markup of bill, 491
Marshall, George C., 34
Marshall, John, 104, 132–133, 602, 606
Marshall, Thurgood, 180
Martin v. *Hunter's Lessee*, 104
Marx, Karl, 241
Maximalist view of democracy, 13–14
Mayaguez, 508
Means-testing, 678
Meat Inspection Act of 1906, 225
Media
   and campaigns. *See* Presidential campaigns, and media
   and elections, 387–398
   gathering of news by, 384–387
   importance of, 389
   influence on political agenda, 387
   and Persian Gulf War, 385, 386
   and presidency, 383–384, 386
   watchdog role, 383–384
Medicaid, 136, 141, 681, 695
   nature of, 695
   and nursing home care, 695
Medicare, 124, 141, 693–694
   changes to system, 694
   and Medigap insurance, 694
   workings of, 693–694
Meese, Edwin, 179, 405
Meiklejohn, Alexander, 166
Memphis Fire Department v. *Stotts*, 206
Mercantilism, 642–643
Merit System Protectors Board, 575
Metro Broadcasting v. *Federal Communications Commission*, 207
Michael M. v. *Superior Court of Sonoma County*, 196, 217
Michel, Robert, 18

Microeconomics, 650–651
Midler v. *Young & Rubicam*, 587, 590
Mikulski, Barbara, 502
Military
   and conscientious objection, 178
   gender discrimination, 216
   homosexuals in, 219
   See also Defense spending
Military-industrial complex, 413
Miller, Arthur, 36
Miller, Samuel F., 177
Miller v. *California*, 716–717
Millikan v. *Bradley*, 202, 610
Mill, John Stuart, 722, 724
Minersville School District v. *Gobitis*, 177
Minimalist view, of democracy, 12–13
Minorities
   in bureaucracy, 561
   See also specific groups
Minority business enterprise, 206, 207
Minority leader, 482
Miranda rules, 179–180
Miranda v. *Arizona*, 179
Missouri Compromise, 607
Missouri ex rel. Gaines v. *Canada*, 197
Mixed economies, 241–245
   characteristics of, 244
   development of, 241–244
Mobility
   absolute mobility, 251
   relative mobility, 251, 253
   social mobility, 251
   structural mobility, 251
Monarchy, 7
Mondale, Walter, 367, 369, 370
Monetary policy, 656–659
   Federal Reserve System, 656, 658–659
Monroe Doctrine, 760, 765
Monroe, James, 760
Montreal Protocol, 793
Moore, Sara Jane, 72
Moral Majority, 621
Mothers Against Drunk Drivers (MADD), 148
Motor Vehicle Safety Act, 416
Moynihan, Daniel Patrick, 707
Multilateral development banks, 775
Multinational corporations, and foreign policy, 760
Murray, Charles, 706
MX missile, 415, 538

Nader, Ralph, 45, 415–417
Nation, meaning of, 120
National Aeronautics and Space Administration (NASA), 563, 570
National Association for the Advancement of Colored People (NAACP), 186–187, 197, 215, 406
National Audubon Society, 420
National Cancer Institute, and AIDS crisis, 622, 624
National committee, 344
   creation of, 343
National conventions
   function of, 372
   presidential election, 343
National Endowment for the Arts, 720–721
National Environmental Policy Act, 787
National Institutes of Health, 695
National Labor Relations Board, 228
National Medal of Arts, 721
National Minimum Drinking Age Act, 734
National parks, 786
National Parks and Conservation Association, 422
National Rifle Association, 420, 421
National Right to Life Convention, 419
National Security Act, 530
National Security Agency, 748
National Security Council, 531
   and foreign policy, 747
   role of, 530–531
National Socialist Party v. *Skokie*, 171
National Space Council, 531
National Voter Registration Bill, 312–313
National Wildlife Federation, 422
Nation-state, meaning of, 120
Native Americans, 760, 761
   treatment of, 75
Naturalization Act, 169
Natural Resources Defense Council, 422
Natural rights of individuals, 56
Nazi party, 19–20
Near, Jay, 173
Near v. *Minnesota*, 173
Negative advertising, presidential campaigns, 370–371, 396–398
Neocapitalism, 245

INDEX

Neutrality Act of 1940, 524
New Deal, 62, 105
   and courts, 589
   as expansion of welfare state, 679
   impact on federalism, 132
   as new federalism, 135
   rational for, 646–647
New Deal coalition, 306–310
   break up of, 308, 353
   characteristics of, 306
   formation of, 306, 334–336
New Deal liberalism, 62–63
New Federalism program, 136–138
New Jersey Plan, 96
New judicial federalism, 593
New York Times v. *Sullivan*, 174
New York v. *Harris*, 180
Nicaragua, 300, 476, 538, 543, 765
Ninth Amendment, 162, 181
Nixon, Richard, 36–37, 135, 179, 201, 222, 229, 336, 367, 378–379, 393, 507, 525, 538, 539, 541, 542–543, 547, 732, 746, 753
Nofziger, Lyn, 405
Nongovernmental organizations, 758, 760
   types of, 260
Noriega, Manuel, 766–767, 774
Norris-LaGuardia Act of 1932, 227–228
North Atlantic Treaty Organization, 34, 759
North, Oliver, 476, 506, 544–545
Northwest Ordinance of 1787, 129
Novello, Antonia, 734
Nuclear disarmament, 777
Nuclear power, as energy source, 811
Nursing home care, Medicaid, 695
Nutrition programs, federal, 700–701

Oberstar, James, 144
Obscenity, 715–719
   court cases related to, 716
   criminal aspects, 717
   feminist view, 718–719
   and recordings, 717, 718
Occupational Safety and Health Act, 555
Occupational Safety and Health Administration, 217, 431, 577, 580, 636
O'Connor, Sandra Day, 206, 598, 611

Office of Management and Budget, 511, 531
   role of, 529–530
Office of National Drug Control Policy, 531
Office of Personnel Management, 575
Office of Policy Development, 531
Office of the U.S. Trade Representative, 531
Office of the Vice President, 531
Oil, 810
   consumption of, 807–808
   oil shortage, 634
   windfall tax issue, 809
Oil Producing and Exporting Countries (OPEC), 758, 808
Oligarchy, 18–19
Omnibus bills, 539
Open Door policy, 761
Open primary, 366
Open society, meaning of, 60
Operation Desert Shield, events of, 545–547, 768–769
Operation Desert Storm, 507, 509, 545–546
   See also Persian Gulf War
Operation Just Cause, 767
Operation Rescue, 419, 453
Opinions, court, 593
Oregon system, 41
Ornstein, Norman, 535
Ortega, Daniel, 510
Ortleb, Chuck, 625
Oswald, Lee Harvey, 72
Oxfam, 775
Ozone depletion, 793

Paine, Tom, 88
Panama, invasion of, 752, 765–768
Panama Canal Zone, 128, 130, 765–766
Panetta, Leon, 471–472
Parliament, British, 480–481
Parliamentary democracy, 503
Parochialism, 93
Parochial schools, federal aid issue, 176
Partisanship, and voter participation, 314
Party caucus, 343
Paterson, William, 96
Patriot missiles, 629
Patronage
   meaning of, 574
   and President, 537–538
Pay or play insurance plans, 697

Peace Corps, 73
Peaceful coexistence, 762
Peace lobby, 415
Pearl Harbor, 761
Pentagon Papers, 170, 384–385, 610
People's party, 339
Perestroika, 764
Perot, Ross, 309–310, 323, 324, 338, 356, 362–363, 377, 388, 395, 670
Persian Gulf War, 43, 71, 300, 317, 356, 361, 629, 752, 758
   and CIA, 750
   and Congress, 506–507, 509
   events of, 545–547, 768–770
   and media, 385, 386
   Operation Desert Shield, 545–547, 768–769
Pesticides, 801–802
Peters, Charles, 566–567
Petit jury, 592
Planned Parenthood of Missouri v. *Danforth*, 183
Plato, 15–16
Plea bargain, 592
Plessy v. *Ferguson*, 31–32, 33, 194, 197, 607
Pluralism, and power, 14–15
Pocket veto, 492
Police brutality, 71
Police powers, 123
   of federal government, 123–124
Policymaking
   boundaries of, 637
   incremental politics, 630
   and lobbyists, 433–434
   and public opinion, 316–317
   states, role in, 124, 148–151
   symbolic politics, 633
   See also Public policy
Political action committees (PACs), 379–380, 381, 382
   functions of, 379–380
Political campaigns, 364–372
   financing of, 374–383
   nonpresidential campaigns, 365–366
   presidential. *See* Presidential campaigns
   purposes of, 364–365
Political consultants, job of, 372, 389–391
Political culture
   cohesiveness in, 53
   and democracy, 52–53
   liberalism, 54–78
   meaning of, 52

INDEX   I-13

Political economy
　capitalism, 239–240
　mixed economies, 241–245
　socialism, 241, 246–248
　use of term, 238
Political economy of United States
　and corporations, 255–257
　decline of economic power, 248
　and government spending, 259–262
　income distribution, 249–253
　poverty, 257–259
　and taxation, 260
　wealth distribution, 253–255
Political efficacy, 291–293
　meaning of, 291–292
　public opinion on, 292
Political elites, and foreign policy, 748
Political knowledge, 287–288
　degrees of, 287
Political participation
　volunteerism, 316
　voting, 310–316
Political parties
　characteristics of, 325–326
　cross-cultural view, 327, 328–330
　decline of, 349, 352–353
　functions of, 326–327
　Great Britain, 341
　historical view
　　Democratic-Republicans, 332
　　Democrats, 332, 335–336
　　Federalists, 332
　　Populist party, 334
　　Republicans, 333, 335–337
　　third parties, 338–340
　　Whig party, 332
　local parties, 340, 342
　multiparty system, 327, 328
　national parties, 343–344
　post-New Deal, 336–337
　realignment of, 353–354
　reforms
　　Democratic reforms, 345–347
　　effects of reforms, 347–348
　　proposed reforms, 352–353
　　Republican reforms, 347
　responsibilities of, 354–356
　similarities and differences related to, 348–349, 350–351
　state parties, 342–343
　two-party system, 327–330
　voters opinions about, 352
Political Parties (Michel), 18
Political process
　and bureaucracy, 565–571
　in ideal democracy, 10–12

Political question doctrine, 602
Political socialization, 273–281
　and adolescence, 277–278
　and childhood, 274–278
　college influences, 279–281
　direct and indirect socialization, 274
　family influences, 278
　meaning of, 273
　research methods, 274
　school influences, 278–279
Political subsystems, 409–410
　typology of, 410
Politics, and religion, 76–78
Polling, 284–286
　accuracy factors, 284–285
　and national elections, 313–314
Polygamy, prohibition of, 177
Populist movements, 56
Populist party, 334, 339
Pork barrel projects, 505
Poverty, 257–259
　definitions of, 257
　distribution of, 258–259
　global, 774–776
Powell, Lewis, Jr., 203, 204, 736
Power
　in democracy, 14–19
　　distribution of power, 14–16
　　unequal distribution, 16–19
　economic power, 17
　and elitism, 14
　and interest group liberalism, 15
　and interest groups, 18
　oligarchy, 18–19
　and pluralism, 14–15
　republican position, 15–16
Prerogative government, 523
Presidency
　Cabinet, 531–533
　Executive Office, 529–531
　models for
　　hierarchical model, 528
　　open model, 528
　power of, 523–526
　　expansion of power, 523–525, 526–527
　　misuse of power, examples of, 540–547
　　prerogative government, 523
　presidential succession, 547
President
　and federal bureaucracy, 536
　and foreign policy, 746–747
　and lobbying, 428–430
　personal characteristics of, 528
　public expectations of, 526

President (*cont.*)
　relationship to Congress. *See* Congress, and President
　spouse of, 534–535
　unique position of, 520–521, 523
　and vice-president, 533–536
President pro tempore, 483, 488
Presidential appointments, Congressional consent, 477–478
Presidential campaigns, 366–372
　consultants, use of, 372, 389–391
　evaluation of candidates, criteria for, 370–371
　and expectations, 369
　financing of, 368, 370, 374–382
　　and democracy, 375–376, 381
　　election costs, 374–375
　　financing and victory of candidate, 368, 376–378
　　legislative party campaign committees, 378
　　political action committees (PACs), 379–380, 381, 382
　　reform efforts, 378–382
　and media
　　imagemaking role, 389–393
　　impact on election outcome, 388–389
　and issue-oriented candidates, 396
　negative advertising, 370–371, 396–398
　presidential debates, 393–395
　popular consent models, 373
　preconvention activity, 366–368
　time to enter race, 370
Presidential debates
　Lincoln-Douglas debates, 392–393
　and media, 393–394
　1992 election, 395
Presidential elections
　candidate selection, 371–372
　electoral college, 373–374
　national conventions, 343, 372
　1992 election, 361–363
　presidential campaigns, 366–372
　presidential debates in, 393–395
　See also Presidential campaigns
President's Council on Environmental Quality, 787, 803
Primary election, 365–366
　blanket primary, 366
　closed and open primaries, 366
Prior restraint, 173

INDEX

Prisons, 726–727
  rise in populations of, 726
  versus community-based corrections, 727
Private schools, voucher systems, 202
Privatization, 576–577
  criticism of, 577
  scope of, 576–577
Progressive era, 644
Progressive party, 339, 340
  reforms of, 40
Progressive taxes, 654
Prohibition, 109
Propaganda
  definition of, 754
  as foreign policy tool, 754
Property rights, 724
Proportional representation, 327
Proportional taxes, 654
Proposition 13, 43, 45
Proposition 128, 42
Proprietary colonies, 86
Protectionism, nature of, 669
Protest
  antiabortion protests, 453–454
  changing politics through, 460–461
  civil disobedience, 450–456
  civil rights demonstrations, 442, 451–452
  contexts for, 458–459
  forms of, 443–444
  limitations of, 459
  motivations for, 444–446
  retaliatory methods from established interest, 459
  sit-ins, 441–442
  steps in
    consciousness-raising, 456
    motivating others, 456–458
  student activism, 279–281
  Vietnam protests, 452–453
  violent protest, 444–445
  See also Extraordinary politics
Proxmire, William, 570
Public assistance. *See* Welfare state
Public attitudes
  diffuse support, 273
  specific support, 273–274
Public housing, 702
Public interest groups, 415–417
  Common Cause, 415–416
  purpose of, 415
  successes of, 416, 417
Public opinion, 281–293
  alienation of public, 292–293

Public opinion (*cont.*)
  and democracy, 286–291
  and foreign policy, 300, 749, 752
  meaning of, 281
  measures of, 284–286
    polling, 284–286
    surveys, 284
  on political efficacy, 291–293
  on political parties, 352
  and policymaking, 316–317
  and political knowledge, 287–288
  support for intolerance, 289–291
Public policy
  AIDS crises, example of, 621–628
  competing agendas, management of, 632
  definition of issues in, 629–632
  definitions of, 620
  evaluation of, 620, 636–637
  implementation of, 620, 636
  issues, categories of, 633–634
  phases of process, 619–621
  proposals, development of, 634–635
  and shifts in government agenda, 629–631
  and spillover effects, 630–631
  See also Policymaking
Public sentiment, 293–305
  and educational level, 304–305
  future view, 301–302
  and gender, 305
  liberalism and conservatism, 294–297
  on economic issues, 299–300
  on foreign policy, 300
  on social issues, 297–299
  and social class, 304
Public Works Employment Act, 205–206
Puerto Rico, as commonwealth, 128
Pure Food and Drug Act, 225

Qaddafi, Muammar al, 756
Quakers, 93
Quayle, Dan, 535, 581, 790, 805
Quotas
  foreign goods, 754
  job, 207

Race, and voter participation, 314
Radical Republicans, 186
Radice, Anne-Imelda, 721
Rally events, 302–303
Randolph, Edmund, 84, 460
Randomness, of surveys, 284
Rather, Dan, 384

Reagan Doctrine, 300
Reagan, Nancy, 534–535
Reaganomics. *See* Supply-side economics
Reagan, Ronald, 45, 61, 72, 130, 136–137, 182, 294, 314, 369, 383–384, 538, 539, 580, 746, 803
Realignment, political parties, 353–354
Reapportionment, 143, 147, 195
Recall, function of, 40
Recession, and 1992 election, 362, 363
Reconciliation process, budget, 511
Reconstruction, 525
Red Scare, McCarthyism, 34–37, 229
Reed, Thomas, 327
Referendum, 8, 40–41
  advantages/disadvantages of, 40–41
  function of, 40
  in Switzerland, 44
Reforms
  budgetary, 510–511, 512–513
  campaign financing, 378–382
  Congressional, 501–503
  political parties, 345–348, 352–353
  social security, 686
Refugee Act of 1980, 66
Regan, Donald, 385
Regents of the University of California v. Bakke, 203–205
Regressive taxes, 654
Regulation
  historical view, 644
  propositions about, 572
  types of, 577–578
Regulatory commissions, 564–565
  functions of, 564–565
Rehabilitation Act of 1973, 222
Rehnquist, William, 180, 196–197, 208, 431, 610
Relative deprivation, meaning of, 445
Relative mobility, 251, 253
Religion
  and American colonies, 86
  civil religion, 76
  in political life, 76–78
  political party preference by, 306, 307
Religious institutions, tax-exemption issue, 176

INDEX I-15

Rent supplement programs, 702–703
Repression, of civil rights by government, 228–231
Republic, The (Plato), 15
Republicanism, view of power, 15–16
Republicans, 338
   characteristics of, 306, 308
   as conservatives, 296
   and Great Depression, 306
   historical view, 335–337
   history of, 333
   nationalization of, 343–344
   party reforms, 347
   realignment of, 353–354
Research
   AIDS, 623–624
   federal spending trends, 667
   health research projects, 695–696
Reserve powers, 98, 122, 123
Resource allocation, in policymaking, 620
Response phase, of policymaking, 620
Revenue sharing programs, as new federalism, 135–136
Revolutionary War, 89–92
   American militia, characteristics of, 90, 91
   disadvantages to British, 90
   impact of, 91
   international factors, 90–91
   as protest movement, 443
Reynolds v. *Sims*, 147
Reynolds v. *United States*, 177
Richmond Newspapers v. *Virginia*, 173
Riders, to amendment, 488, 490
Riegle, Donald W., Jr., 404, 405
Rights of the accused, 178–181
   due process rights, 178
   exclusionary rule, 179
   habeas corpus, 180–181
   Miranda rules, 179–180
   right to counsel, 178
Robertson, Pat, 348, 369
Rockefeller, Nelson, 548
Roe v. *Wade*, 181–182, 183, 185, 419, 604
Roman Catholic Church, 77
Roosevelt, Eleanor, 534
Roosevelt, Franklin D., 18, 35, 62, 65, 72, 124, 132, 135, 205, 306, 335, 520, 524, 529, 539, 547, 589, 646, 693, 746

Roosevelt, Theodore, 72, 131, 323, 339, 391, 420, 786
Rosenberg, Ethel and Julius, 36
Roth v. *United States*, 716
Rousseau, Jean-Jacques, 12
Ruckelshaus, William, 803
Rudman, Warren, 500
Rule of four, 595
Rule of law, meaning of, 60
Rust v. *Sullivan*, 183, 298

Sabato, Larry, 396–397
Sadat, Anwar, 753
Safe Drinking Water Act, 795, 796
SALT II, 746
Samoa, 128
San Antonio Independent School District v. *Rodriguez*, 736
Sanders, Bernie, 64
SANE, 415
Sanford, Terry, 405
Saturday Press, 173
Satyagraha, 455
Savage, Gus, 499
Save the Children Fund, 775
Savings and loan scandal, 403–404
Schench v. *United States*, 166, 167
Schenck, Charles T., 166
School desegregation, 197–203
   Brown case, 198–199, 589
   busing, 200–202
   de facto segregation, 200, 201, 202
   de jure segregation, 200, 201
   enforcement of law, 199
   and magnet schools, 202
   versus intentional minority segregation, 737–738
   and voucher systems, 202
Schools
   magnet schools, 202
   and political socialization, 278–281
   school prayer issue, 175–176, 737
   voucher systems, 202
Second Amendment, 162
Second Continental Congress, 88, 89
Securities and Exchange Commission, 581
Security Council, 758
Sedition Act of 1798, 166, 169
Sedition Act of 1918, 166
Segregation, 30–34
   intentional minority segregation, 737–738
   methods of, 32
   Plessy v. *Ferguson*, 31–32, 33

Segregation (*cont.*)
   separate but equal concept, 31–32, 197
   See also School desegregation
Select committees, 483, 485
Selective Service system, 563
Senate, 101, 308
   compared to House of Representatives, 479
   leadership of, 482–483
   President pro tempore, 483
Senate Judiciary Committee, 597
Senate Select Committee on Ethics, 499, 500
Seneca Falls, feminist convention, 38, 39
Senior Executive Service, 574, 575
Seniority rule, 487
Separate but equal, 31–32, 197, 607
Separation of powers, 99, 503, 521
   See also Division of power
Set-asides, 205–207
   cases related to, 206–207
   purpose of, 205–206
Seventeenth Amendment, 102, 108, 478
Seventh Amendment, 162
Seven Years' War, 86–87, 90
Sex education, 737
Shays, Daniel, 95
Shays's Rebellion, 95
Shelton v. *Tucker*, 170
Sherman Antitrust Act, 411, 644
Shumer, Charles, 471–472
Sierra Club, 420, 422
Sinclair, Upton, 224–225
Single-issue groups, 418–423
Single-member districts, 327
Sirhan, Sirhan, 72
Sirica, John, 542
Sit-ins, 441–442
Sixth Amendment, 162, 178
Skinner v. *Oklahoma*, 219
Slaughterhouse Cases, 133, 134, 163, 164
Slavery
   abolition of, 30, 186
   abolition of slave trade, 93, 104
   development of slavery system, 186
   and framers of Constitution, 103, 104
   Jefferson's view, 103
Small Business Administration, 563
Smith Act, 168–170
Social class
   and income, 249

INDEX

Social class (cont.)
  and political alienation, 293
  and public sentiment, 304
  and voter participation, 314
Social control
  and arts, 719–721
  and democracy, 714
  obscenity issue, 715–719
Socialism, 241, 246–248
  criticisms of, 241, 246
  elements of, 241
  market socialism, 247
Social issues, public opinion on, 297–299
Socialist parties, and United States, 63–64
Social mobility, 251
Social rights
  health and safety, 224–225
  workers' rights, 226–228
Social security, 678, 681, 683, 686
  payments, calculation of, 683, 686
  reforms, 686
  strains on system, 686
  types of programs, 683
Social Security Act of 1935, 693
Social welfare programs
  conflicts related to, 264
  government spending, 261–262
  and income redistribution, 262, 264
  management of, 576
  types of, 141
Sodomy, homosexual right, 221
Solar power, 806–807
Somalia, 772
Sondheim, Stephen, 721
Sons of Liberty, 88
Souter, David, 598
Sovereignty powers, 98
Soviet Union
  and Cold War, 761–764
  end of Communism, 764
  Soviet coup, 157–160, 449
Spanish-American War, 75–76
Speaker of the House, 481–482, 488
Speedy Trial Act, 612
Spillover effects, 630–631
Split-ticket balloting, 334
Spoils system, 574
Spot ads, 392
Stagflation, nature of, 644
Stamp Act, 87–88
Standing committees, 483, 484, 485
Stanton, Edwin, 525
Stare decisis, 591
State, meaning of, 120, 757

State and Local Assistance Act of 1972, 136
State court system, 592–593
  judges, selection of, 597
  and new judicial federalism, 593
  types of courts, 592, 594
State Department, and foreign policy, 747
State politics, 342–343
  influence of, 342–343
  state committees, 342
States
  and Constitution
    admission to statehood, 128, 130
    due process, 125
    full faith and credit provision, 125, 128
    powers of state, 98, 104, 118–119, 122–124
  federal intervention
    reapportionment of legislative districts, 147
    regulation of drinking age, 147–148
  fiscal strains on, 145
  functioning within federal system, 138–143
  global view, 757
  importance in policy making, 124, 148–151
  unitary governments of, 124
States Rights Democratic party, 339
Statlee, Stuart M., 417
Stegner, Wallace, 721
Stevenson, Adlai, 391
Stewart B. McKinney Homeless Assistance Act, 706
Stockdale, James, 395
Stockman, David, 530
Stock market, 1929 crash, 645
Strategic Defense Initiative, 415, 629
Strategic Oil Reserve, 808, 812
Structural mobility, 251
Student Nonviolent Coordinating Committee, 229
Subcommittees, Congressional, 487, 491
Sun Belt, 143
Sununu, John, 528
Superdelegates, 346
Superfund, 141, 797–800
Super Tuesday, 369, 372
Supplemental Security Income (SSI), 690–691
Supply-side economics, 659–662
  evaluation of, 661–662

Supply-side economics (cont.)
  nature of, 660
  Reagan's economic goals, 659–660
  versus Keynesian economics, 659, 660
Supremacy clause, 104
Supreme Court, 100
  chief justice, 595
  and federalism, example cases, 132–134
  individual rights decisions, 607–611
  judges, selection of, 595–598
  judicial review, 431
  lobbyists influence on, 431
  nomination process, 477–478
  as policy review court, 600
  power distribution decisions, 606–607
  rule of four, 595
  self-restraint rules, 602, 604
  Warren court, 607–611
  See also Federal court system
Surveys
  public opinion, 284
  randomness of, 284
Swann v. *Charlotte-Macklenburg Board of Education*, 200–201
Sweatt v. *Painter*, 197
Symbolic politics, 633
Symbolic speech, First Amendment rights, 170–171

Taft-Hartley Act, 228, 524
Taft, William Howard, 324
Taney, Roger, 132, 606
Tariffs, 754
Taxation, 260
  business versus personal, 657
  cross-cultural view, 655–656
  policy issues, 653
  progressive taxes, 654
  proportional taxes, 654
  redistribution of income, 262, 264
  regressive taxes, 654
  sources of tax revenues, 655–656
  tax burden, nature of, 260
  tax equity issue, 662, 663–664
  tax reform, 653, 662–663
Tax expenditures
  largest items for, 684
  meaning of, 662, 684–685
Tax Reform Act of 1986, 653, 662–663, 703
  evaluation of, 663

INDEX I-17

Taylor, Zachary, 73, 333
Tennessee Valley Authority (TVA), 242–243, 564
Tenth Amendment, 123, 162
Tenure of Office Act, 525
Term limits, for state legislators, 460–461
Territories, of United States, 128, 130
Texas v. *Johnson*, 171, 610
Third Amendment, 162
Third parties, historical view, 338–340
Third-party government, 575–576
Third World, 802
  poverty of, 774–775
Thirteenth Amendment, 30, 163, 186
Thomas, Clarence, 215, 299, 475–476, 477, 598, 729
Thoreau, Henry David, 450–451
Thornburgh v. *American College of Obstetricians and Gynecologists*, 183
Three-fifths compromise, 104
Thurber, James A., 410
Thurmond, Strom, 336, 339, 343
Thurow, Lester, 572
Tinker v. *Des Moines Independent Community School District*, 171
Tocqueville, Alex de, 406, 612, 785
Torresola, Griselio, 72
Townshend duties, 88
Toxic chemicals, 797–802
  cost of cleanup, 797, 802
  pesticides, 801–802
  Superfund and cleanup, 797–800
Trade, global, 754, 773–774
Trade deficits, 248
Transfer payments, 261–262, 264
Treatment as equals concept, 196–197
Treaty of Paris, 91
Truman, Harry, 35, 72, 343, 524, 768
Trustee theory, 474
Tsongas, Paul, 362
Twenty-first Amendment, 109
Twenty-second Amendment, 547
Twenty-third Amendment, 128
Twenty-fifth Amendment, 547, 548
Tyler, John, 391, 547
Tyranny of the majority, meaning of, 60

Underemployment, 691
Unemployment, 665

Unemployment compensation, 691
Unicameral government, 96, 478
Unions
  collective bargaining, 226, 228
  development of, 226–228
Unitary system
  nature of, 121–122
  of states, 124
United Nations, 300, 758–759
  operation of, 758–759
United Nations Educational, Scientific and Cultural Organization, 758
United States Information Agency, 754
United States Postal Service, 564
United States v. *Eichman*, 172
United States v. *O'Brien*, 171
United States v. *Paradise*, 206
United States v. *Seeger*, 178
Universal manhood suffrage, 185

Values, and education, 737–740
Van Buren, Martin, 332
Verba, Sidney, 58
Veterans Administration, 702
Veto of law, 99
  Congressional reaction to, 539
  line-item veto, 539
  pocket veto, 492
Vice-president, 533–536
  role of, 534
Victimless crime, 724
Vietnam War, 229, 280, 308, 653
  and presidential war-making powers, 507, 541–542
  protests, 452–453
  rationale for, 762
Vietnam War Memorial, 720
Vigilantism, 70
Vinson, Fred M., 168, 607
Violence, in American society, 69–71, 74
Virginia Plan, 84, 96, 460
Virgin Islands, 128
Voice of America, 754
Volcker, Paul, 661
Volpe, John, 565
Volunteerism, 316
Voter participation
  and alienation, 21, 24
  cross-cultural view, 23
Voting, 310–316
  barriers to, 310, 312–314
  nonvoters, characteristics of, 315
  and registering, 311, 312

Voting (*cont.*)
  voting habits, influencing factors, 314–315
Voting reforms
  initiative, 40
  recall, 40
  referendum, 40
Voting rights, 185–188
  black Americans, 163, 184–188
  women, 39
Voting Rights Act of 1965, 187–188
Voucher systems, 202

Wagner Act, 228
Wallace, George, 70, 72, 339
Wallace v. *Jaffree*, 176
Walz v. *Tax Commissioner of the City of New York*, 176
Wards Cove Packing Co. v. *Antonio*, 207, 210
Ware, Edmund Asa, 193
Ware School, 193–194
War on Poverty, 265, 679–681, 690
War Powers Resolution, 507–510, 539, 546, 602, 756
  nature of, 508–509
  necessity for, 508–509, 542
Warren Commission, 73
Warren, Earl, 73, 147, 178, 431, 593, 598
  Warren court, 607–611
Warsaw Pact, 759
Warsaw Treaty Organization, 759
Washington, George, 72, 90, 324, 332, 523–524, 573
Washington Post, 384, 542
Watergate, 173, 309, 379, 384, 525, 528, 548
  events of, 542–543
Water pollution, 787–788, 794–797
  legislation, 795–796
Watson v. *Jones*, 177
Wealth, personal qualities related to, 259
Wealth distribution, 253–255
  consequences of inequality, 255
  inequality of, 254
Weber, Max, 558–559
Webster, Daniel, 130–131
Webster v. *Reproductive Health Services*, 183
Welfare state
  Aid to Families with Dependent Children, 686–688
  cross-cultural view, 682, 688–689
  evaluation of, 706–708
  expansion of, 679–681

INDEX

Welfare state (cont.)
  food stamp program, 700–701
  health research projects, 695–696
  homeless, support for, 706
  housing programs, 701–704
  job programs, 689–690
  and means-testing, 678
  Medicaid, 695
  Medicare, 693–694
  nursing home care, 695
  nutrition programs, 701
  rationale for, 678–679
  scope of, 677–678
  social security, 681, 683, 686
  Supplemental Security Income (SSI), 690–691
  tax expenditures for income security, 691
  unemployment compensation, 691
  See also Social welfare programs
Welsh v. *United States*, 178
West Virginia State Board of Education v. *Barnette*, 177
Whig party, 332–333, 338
Whip, majority, 482
White, Byron, 180, 206
White flight, 201
White House Office, role of, 529
White primaries, 187
Wilderness Society, 422
Wilson, Pete, 404
Wilson, Woodrow, 39, 131, 167, 324, 334–335, 483, 520, 597, 746, 761
Windfall profits, 809
Wirth, Tim, 501
Women
  in bureaucracy, 561
  gender discrimination
    affirmative action, 217–218
    legislation related to, 215–217
    protective discrimination, 217
  gender gap, 305
  and political advertising, 390–391
  and pornography, 718–719
  public opinions of, 305
  violence against, 74
Women, Infants and Children (WIC) program, 701
Women's suffrage, 37–40
  events of movement, 37–39
  right to vote, 39
Woodward, Bob, 542
Workers' rights, 226–228
  collective bargaining, 226, 228
  legislation related to, 227–228
Work Incentive Program, 690
Works Progress Administration, 720
World Bank, 775
World Health Organization, 758
World War I, 761
World War II, 761
Wright, Jim, 405, 499, 510
Wright, Richard, 193
Wygant v. *Jackson Board of Education*, 206

Yanayev, Gennady, 764
Yates v. *United States*, 170
Yellow-dog contracts, 227–228
Yeltsin, Boris, 237, 449, 764
Yugoslavia, 771–772

Zangara, Giuseppe, 72